Garage Sale & Flea Market ANNUAL

NINTH EDITION

CASHING IN ON
TODAY'S LUCRATIVE
COLLECTIBLES MARKET

cb
COLLECTOR BOOKS
A Division of Schroeder Publishing Co., Inc.

CURRENT VALUES ON: **TODAY'S COLLECTIBLES**
TOMORROW'S ANTIQUES

The current values in this book should be used only as a guide. They are not intended to set prices, which vary from one section of the country to another. Auction prices as well as dealer prices vary greatly and are affected by condition as well as demand. Neither the editors nor the publisher assumes responsibility for any losses that might be incurred as a result of consulting this guide.

Front cover: McCoy Lily bookends, 5½" x 5", 1948, green with decorated lily, $125.00 – 150.00; Gerber doll, premium, Sun Rubber, 1955, $140.00 (photo courtesy Joan Stryker Grumbaugh); Coca-Cola cardboard sign, 29" x 50", 1940, $675.00; Brayton Laguna Red Fox, 14", $175.00; Brush covered wagon cookie jar, $575.00; Iris and Herringbone butter dish, iridescent, $45.00.

Page 1: Abingdon vase, Laurel, blue, #442, 6", from $40.00 to $50.00; Bauer Pottery Gloss Pastel Kitchenware teapot, yellow, in-mold mark, eight-cup, from $150.00 to $200.00 (photo courtesy Jack Chipman); Chintz china bell, English Summertime, 4¼", $70.00 (photo courtesy Dorothy Malone Anthony); Boyds Bearstones, 1997, Ted and Teddy, 1E/2223, $125.00.

Cover design by Beth Summers
Book design by Terri Hunter and Beth Ray

Editorial Staff

Editors
Sharon and Bob Huxford

Research and Editorial Assistants
Michael Drollinger, Nancy Drollinger, Donna Newnum, Loretta Suiters

Searching For A Publisher?

We are always looking for people knowledgeable within their fields. If you feel that there is a real need for a book on your collectible subject and have a large comprehensive collection, contact Collector Books.

COLLECTOR BOOKS
P.O. Box 3009
Paducah, Kentucky 42002-3009
www.collectorbooks.com

Copyright © 2001 by Schroeder Publishing Co.

A Word From the Editor

By the time my schedule calls for me to sit down and write a word of introduction for the next edition of our *Garage Sale and Flea Market Annual,* summer is winding down in the Midwest, garage sale shopping has become mighty thin, and it's time to assess our purchases in terms of pricing them for resale. Garage sales are basically akin to kissing frogs — sometimes you go to several before one really pays off. When you're moving through week after week of rummaging, there are many times you're glad to be outside and getting some fresh air and exercise, but as far as finding 'goodies,' it just isn't happening. To paraphrase the fishermen's creed, though, 'A bad day of rummaging is better than a good day of working,' and I still love going because you never know what the next sale will produce. The summer has been interesting, though, and in looking over our list of purchases, there is a good variety of collectible items that will sell well at the local flea market we 'do' every fall here in west central Indiana (and, yes, several exceptionally nice items for eBay). One of our better weekends produced a partial service for eight of Blue Garland ($50.00), half a dozen Joe Camel match tins (25¢ each), a couple of really rare Marshall Studio (a defunct local pottery) hippopotamuses ($3.00 each), two great pieces of Guardian Service cookware ($65.00), fifteen pieces of Iroquois Russel Wright dinnerware ($3.50), some Garfield stuff, and a few M&J collectibles. What fun! A few weeks later, we hit pay dirt again: a Pfaltzgraff cheese and cracker set ($3.00), a piece of Roseville Futura (50¢, can you believe it!), a vintage record album signed by everyone in the band *except* Laurence Welk (50¢), a peach lustre punch set ($2.00), a Hagen-Renaker horse (25¢), a great anodized aluminum cake safe ($3.00), two beautiful pieces of Royal Haeger ($5.00 for both), some Depression glass, a Wedgwood bone china cup plate ($1.00), and a Precious Moments figurine (25¢). You needn't be a rocket scientist to find items like these, all it takes is the right sale and a trained eye.

If ever there was a good time for you to think of getting into the antiques and collectibles market, it is now. Buying and selling via Internet auctions has increased tenfold over last year's volume. Good merchandise always finds a ready market. This is a golden opportunity for you to add substantially to your income or at least to finance your own collections, which as we all know can sometimes require a goodly amount of money.

Garage sale buying and Internet selling complement each other perfectly. Earlier this summer, we decided to get our feet wet and plunge into online selling. In just three months, working a few hours off and on during weekday evenings and some of our spare time over the weekends, our sales amounted to $8,000.00. Even if after our original investments and selling fees we actually netted more like $5,000.00 — it was time well spent. Like thousands of others, we succumbed to the promise of a quick sale and in many cases better prices than we would even dream of asking at the flea market.

For example, one of our best buys this spring was a cast iron #12 Erie skillet with a low dome Griswold lid that we brought home for $10.00. They had seen very little use, and we were thrilled when the skillet brought $65.00 and the lid $265.00 via the Internet. A wonderful old pattern glass compote brought $175.00, the stopper for a pink Depression glass Mayfair water bottle brought $135.00 (our price was 50¢), and a miniature bottle of Arpege perfume still in the original box that I bought for a quarter sold for $26.00. A 50¢ tablecloth with a California map in pristine condition brought $35.00, a Royal Lace sauce dish ($3.00) went for $65.00, and my Skookum doll sold for $175.00 (it cost me $15.00). This is just a sampling — assorted items we've learned to watch for, just as you can, simply by studying a book such as this one. We know of many people who are supplementing their income substantially in this manner.

Internet buying and selling does have a downside. We've learned that it's not going to set the pace in the antiques and collectibles marketplace, it's only going to serve to confuse it. No way can it be relied upon to establish values. As for online auctions, they're very inconsistent! Depending on who's bidding, how affluent he is and how badly he wants it for his collection, prices for the same item may fluctuate wildly. The Kay Finch puppy that sold for $500.00 one week will sell for $800.00 a month or so later. My gray Fiesta gravy boat that wouldn't meet reserve one week will make book price when put back in the running the following week. The relatively common but still basically desirable collectible will often languish unnoticed, barely bringing half of 'book price' — in some cases no bid at all, while hard-to-find and unusual items sometimes sell for twice the established value, sometimes even more. As for the online malls, there are no bargains there. Since Internet antique dealers know they have a worldwide marketplace to draw buyers from, they'll just sit back and wait for that one who will gladly pay their asking price. If you've been shopping online you already know these things.

So the dust is settling a little now, and the direction of last year's whirlwind market seems a bit more predictable. We are beginning to understand that even though it has been forever altered and revamped, structure is still a necessary factor in its existence. For the person who wants to be a successful collector or dealer, having an understanding of the marketplace is not an option. Knowing what any given item went for on eBay last week is not enough. Whether you regard it as a hobby or a serious money-making opportunity, you must become knowledgeable to succeed. Use this book to make it work for you. It will serve as a tool to educate you toward becoming a wise garage sale and flea market shopper.

As usual, this year's edition touches on several new categories. If you're into garage sale shopping, you know that competition is fierce. You'll have a definite advantage over the average shopper if you'll first take the time to become familiar with new areas of activity. The key is knowledge. We'll suggest references for in-depth study, all written by today's leading experts. We're going to zero in on items from the 1940s on, since that's where the market's activity is strongest today. We'll list clubs and newsletters related to many specific areas; we recommend all of them very highly. There is much knowledge to be gleaned by networking through clubs with collectors whose interests are similar to yours. Trade papers are listed as well; they contain a wealth of timely information. If you're not already subscribing, see about getting sample copies.

An exclusive feature of this book is the section called Special Interests. It contains the addresses of authors, collectors, and dealers sorted by specific collectible categories. Not only are these people potential buyers, but under most circumstances, they'll be willing to help you with questions that remain after you've made an honest attempt at your own research. Just remember if you do write one of our people,

you will have to include an SASE if you want a response. And if you call, please consider the differences in time zones. But first, please, read the text. Then go to your library; you should be able to find most of the books we reference. Check them out for study — they're all wonderful.

If you'd like to collect some nice pieces to decorate your home or if you're interested in becoming a dealer but find there's no room in the budget for extra spending, we'll show you how to realize a profit from holding your own garage sale. And we'll give you some timely pointers on how to set up at your first flea market.

Remember that our prices in no way reflect what you will be paying at garage sales. Our values are well established and generally accepted by seasoned collectors and authorities; they have been checked over before publication by people well versed in their particular fields.

How to Hold Your Own Garage Sale

Just as we promised we would, here are our suggestions for holding your own garage sale. If you're toying with the idea of getting involved in the business of buying and selling antiques and collectibles but find yourself short of any extra cash to back your venture, this is the way we always recommend you get started. Everyone has items they no longer use; get rid of them! Use them to your advantage. Here's how.

Get Organized. Gather up your merchandise. Though there's not a lot of money in selling clothing, this is the perfect time to unload things you're not using. Kids' clothing does best, since it's usually outgrown before it's worn out, and there's lots of budget-minded parents who realize this and think it makes good sense to invest as little as possible in their own children's wardrobes. Everything should of course be clean and relatively unwrinkled to sell at all, and try to get the better items on hangers. Leave no stone unturned. Clean out the attic, the basement, the garage — then your parent's attic, basement, and garage. If you're really into it, bake cookies, make some crafts. Divide your house plants; pot the starts in attractive little containers — ladies love 'em. Discarded and outgrown toys sell well. Framed prints and silk flower arrangements you no longer use, recipe books and paperbacks, tapes, records, and that kitchen appliance that's more trouble to store than it's worth can be turned into cash to get you off and running!

After you've gathered up your merchandise, you'll need to price it. Realistically, clothing will bring at the most about 15% to 25% of what you had to pay for it, if it's still in excellent, ready-to-wear shape and basically still in style. There's tons of used clothing out there, and no one is going to buy much of anything with buttons missing or otherwise showing signs of wear. If you have good brand-name clothing that has been worn very little, you would probably do better by taking it to a resale or consignment shop. They normally price things at about one-third of retail, with their cut being 30% of that. Not much difference money-wise, but the garage-sale shopper that passes up that $150.00 suit you're asking $25.00 for will probably give $50.00 for it at the consignment shop, simply because like department stores, many have dressing rooms with mirrors so you can try things on and check them for fit before you buy. Even at $25.00, the suit is no bargain if you can't use it when you get it home.

Remember that garage-sale buyers expect to find low prices. Depending on how long you plan on staying open, you'll have one day, possibly two to move everything. If you start out too high, you'll probably be stuck with a lot of left-over merchandise, most of which you've already decided is worthless to you. The majority of your better buyers will hit early on; make prices attractive to them and you'll do all right. If you come up with some 'low-end' collectibles — fast-food toys, character glasses, played-with action figures, etc. — don't expect to get much out of them at a garage sale. Your competition down the block may underprice you. But if you have a few things you think have good resale potential, offer them at about half of 'book' price. If they don't sell at your garage sale, take them to a flea market or a consignment shop. You'll probably find they sell better on that level, since people expect to find prices higher there than at garage sales.

You can use pressure-sensitive labels or masking tape for price tags on many items. But *please* do not use either of these on things where damage is likely to occur when they are removed. For instance, (as one reader pointed out) on boxes containing toys, board games, puzzles, etc.; on record labels or album covers; or on ceramics or glass with gold trim or unfired, painted decoration. Unless a friend or a neighbor is going in on the sale with you, price tags won't have to be removed; the profit will all be yours. Of course, you'll have to keep tabs if others are involved. You can use a sheet of paper divided into columns, one for each of you, and write the amount of each sale down under the appropriate person's name, or remove the tags and restick them on a piece of poster board, one for each seller. I've even seen people use straight pins to attach small squares of paper which they remove and separate into plastic butter tubs. When several go together to have a sale, the extra help is nice, but don't let things get out of hand. Your sale can get *too* big. Things become too congested, and it's hard to display so much to good advantage.

Advertise. Place your ad in your local paper or on your town's cable TV information channel. It's important to make your ad interesting and upbeat. Though most sales usually start early on Friday or Saturday mornings, some people are now holding their sales in the early evening, and they seem to be having good crowds. This gives people with day jobs an opportunity to attend. You *might* want to hold your sale for two days, but you'll do 90% of your selling during the first two or three hours, and a two-day sale can really drag on. Make signs — smaller ones for street corners near your home to help direct passers-by, and a large one for your yard. You might even want to make another saying 'Clothing ½-Price after 12:00.' (It'll cut way down on leftovers that you'll otherwise have to dispose of yourself.) Be sure that you use a wide-tipped felt marker and print in letters big enough that the signs can be read from the street. Put the smaller signs up a few days in advance unless you're expecting rain. (If you are, you might want to include a rain date in your advertising unless your sale will be held under roof.) Make sure you have a lot of boxes and bags and plenty of change. If you price your items in increments of 25¢, you won't need anything but a few rolls of quarters, maybe ten or fifteen ones, and a few five-dollar bills. Then on the day of the sale, put the large sign up in a prominent place out front with some balloons to attract the crowd. Take a deep breath, brace yourself, and raise the garage door!

What to Do With What's Left. After the sale, pack up any good collectibles that didn't sell. Think about that consignment shop or setting up at a flea market. (We'll talk about that later on.) Sort out the better items of clothing for Goodwill or a similar charity, unless your city has someone who will take your leftovers and sell them on consignment. This is a fairly new concept, but some of the larger cities have such 'bargain centers.'

Learning to Become a Successful Bargain Hunter

Let me assure you, anyone who takes the time to become an informed, experienced bargain hunter will be successful. There is enough good merchandise out there to make it well worthwhile, at all levels. Once you learn what to look for, what has good resale potential, and what price these items will probably bring for you, you'll be equipped and ready for any hunting trip. You'll be the one to find treasures. They are out there!

Garage sales are absolutely wonderful for finding bargains. But you'll have to get up early! Even non-collectors can spot quality merchandise, and at those low garage sale prices (low unless of course held by an owner who's done his homework) those items will be the first to move.

In order for you to be a successful garage sale shopper, you have to learn how to get yourself organized. It's important to conserve your time. The sales you hit during the first early-morning hour will prove to be the best nine times out of ten, so you must have a plan before you ever leave home. Plot your course. Your local paper will have a section on garage sale ads, and local cable TV channels may also carry garage sale advertising. Most people hold their sales on the weekend, but some may start earlier in the week, so be sure to turn to the 'garage sales' ads daily. Write them down and try to organize them by areas — northwest, northeast, etc. At first, you'll probably need your city map, but you'll be surprised at how quickly the streets will become familiar to you. Upper middle-class neighborhoods generally have the best sales and the best merchandise, so concentrate on those areas, though sales in older areas may offer older items. (Here's where you have to interpret those sale ads.) When you've decided where you want to start, go early! If the ad says 8:00, be there at 7:00. This may seem rude and pushy, but if you can bring yourself to do it, it will pay off. And chances are when you get there an hour early, you'll not be their first customer. If they're obviously not ready for business, just politely inquire if you may look. If you're charming and their nerves aren't completely frayed from trying to get things ready, chances are they won't mind.

Competition can be fierce during those important early-morning hours. Learn to scan the tables quickly, then move to the area that looks the most promising. Don't be afraid to ask for a better price if you feel it's too high, but most people have already priced garage sale merchandise so that it will sell. Keep a notebook to jot down items you didn't buy the first time around but think you might be interested in if the price were reduced later on. After going through dozens of sales (I've done as many as thirty or so in one morning), you won't remember where you saw what! Often by noon, at least by mid-afternoon, veteran garage sale buyers are finished with their rounds and attendance becomes very thin. Owners are usually much more receptive to the idea of lowering their prices, so it may pay you to make a second pass. In fact some people find it advantageous to go to the better sales on the last day as well as the first. They'll make an offer for everything that's left, and since most of the time the owner is about ready to *pay* someone to take it at that point, they can usually name their price. Although most of the collectibles will normally be gone at this point, there are nearly always some useable household items and several pieces of good, serviceable clothing left. The household items will sell at flea markets or consignment shops, and if there are worthwhile clothing items, take them to a resale boutique. They'll either charge the 30% commission fee or buy the items outright for about half of the amount they feel they can ask, a new practice some resale shops are beginning to follow. Because they want only clothing that is in style, in season, and like new, their prices may be a little higher than others shops, so half of that asking price is a good deal.

Tag sales are common in the larger cities. They are normally held in lieu of an auction, when estates are being dispersed, or when families are moving. Sometimes only a few buyers are admitted at one time, and as one leaves another is allowed to take his place. So just as is true with garage sales, the early bird gets the goodies. Really serious shoppers begin to arrive as much as an hour or two before the scheduled opening time. I know of one who will spend the night in his van and camp on the 'doorstep' if he thinks the sale is especially promising. And he can tell you fantastic success stories! But since it's customary to have tag sale items appraised before values are set, be prepared to pay higher prices. That's not to say, though, that you won't find bargains here. If you think an item is overpriced, leave a bid. Just don't forget to follow through on it, since if it doesn't sell at their asking price, they may end up holding it for you. It's a good idea to check back on the last day of the sale. Often the prices on unsold items may have been drastically reduced.

Auctions can go either way. Depending on the crowd and what items are for sale, you can sometimes spend all day and never be able to buy anything anywhere near 'book' price. On the other hand, there are often 'sleepers' that can be bought cheaply enough to resell at a good profit. Toys, dolls, Hummels, Royal Doultons, banks, cut glass, and other 'high-profile' collectibles usually go high, but white ironstone, dinnerware sets from the '20s through the '50s, silverplated hollow ware, books, records, and linens, for instance, often pass relatively unnoticed by the majority of the buyers.

If there is a consignment auction house in your area, check it out. These are usually operated by local auctioneers, and the sales they hold in-house often involve low-income estates. You won't find something every time, so try to investigate the merchandise ahead of schedule to see if it's going to be worth your time to attend. Competition is probably less at one of these than in any of the other types of sales we've mentioned, and wonderful buys have been made from time to time.

Flea markets are often wonderful places to find bargains. I don't like the small ones — not that I don't find anything there, but I've learned to move through them so fast (to get ahead of the crowd), I don't get my 'fix'; I just leave wanting more. If you've never been to a large flea market, you don't know what you're missing. Even if you're not a born-again collector, I guarantee you will love it. And they're excellent places to study the market. You'll be able to see where the buying activity is; you can check and compare prices, talk with dealers and collectors, and do hands-on inspections. I've found that if I first study a particular subject by reading a book or a magazine article, this type of exposure to that collectible really 'locks in' what I have learned.

Because there are many types of flea market dealers, there are plenty of bargains. The casual, once-in-a-while dealer may not always keep up with changing market values. Some of them simply price their items by what they themselves had to pay for it. Just as being early at garage sales is important, here it's a must. If you've ever been in line waiting for a flea market to open, you know that cars are often backed up for several blocks, and people will be standing in line waiting to be admitted hours before the gate opens. Browsers? Window shoppers? Not likely. Competition! So if you're going to have a chance at all, you'd better be in line yourself. Take a partner and split up on the first pass so that you can cover the grounds more quickly. It's a common sight to see the serious buyers conversing with their partners via walkie-talkies, and if you like to discuss possible purchases with each other before you actually buy, this is a good way to do it.

Learn to bargain with dealers. Their prices are usually negotiable, and most will come down by 10% to 20%. Be polite and fair, and you can expect the same treatment in return. Unpriced items are harder to deal for. I have no problem offering to give $8.00 if an item is marked $10.00, but it's difficult for me to have to ask the price and then make a counter offer. So I'll just say 'This isn't marked. Will you take...?' I'm not an aggressive barterer, so this works for me.

There are so many reproductions on the flea market level (and at malls and co-ops), that you need to be suspicious of anything that looks too new! Some fields of collecting have been especially hard hit. Whenever a collectible becomes so much in demand that prices are high, reproductions are bound to make an appearance. For instance, Black Americana, Nippon, Roseville, banks, toys of all types, teddy bears, lamps, glassware, doorstops, cookie jars, prints, advertising items, and many other fields have been especially vulnerable. Learn to check for telltale signs — paint that is too bright, joints that don't fit, variations in sizes or colors, creases in paper that you can see but not feel, and so on. Remember that zip codes have been used only since 1963, and this can sometimes help you date an item in question. Check glassware for areas of wavy irregularities often seen in new glass. A publication we would highly recommend to you is called *Antique and Collector Reproduction News*, a monthly report of 'Fakes, Frauds, and Facts.' To subscribe, call 1-800-227-5531. You can find them on the Web at repronews.com. Rates are very reasonable compared to the money you may save by learning to recognize reproductions.

Antique malls and co-ops should be visited on a regular basis. Many mall dealers restock day after day, and traffic and buying competition is usually fierce. As a rule, you won't often find great bargains here; what you do save on is time. And if time is what you're short of, you'll be able to see a lot of good merchandise under one roof, on display by people who've already done the leg work and invested *their* time, hence the higher prices. But there are always underpriced items as well, and if you've taken the time to do your homework, you'll be able to spot them right away.

Unless the dealer who rents the booth happens to be there, though, mall and co-op prices are usually firm. But often times they'll run sales — '20% off everything in booth #101.' If you have a dealer's license, and you really should get one, most will give you a courtesy 10% discount on items over $10.00, unless you want to pay with a credit card.

Antique shows are exciting to visit, but obviously if a dealer is paying several hundred dollars to set up for a three-day show, he's going to be asking top price to offset expenses. So even though bargains will be few, the merchandise is usually superior, and you may be able to find that special item you've been looking for.

Mail order buying is not only very easy, but most of the time economical as well. Many people will place an ad in 'For Sale' sections of tradepapers. Some will describe and price their merchandise in their ad, while others offer lists of items they have in exchange for a SASE (stamped, self-addressed envelope). You're out no gas or food expenses, their overhead is minimal so their prices are usually very reasonable, so it works out great for both buyer and seller. I've made a lot of good buys this way, and I've always been fairly and honestly dealt with. You may want to send a money order or cashier's check to save time, otherwise (especially on transactions involving larger sums of money) the seller might want to wait until your personal check clears.

Goodwill stores and re-sale shops are usually listed in the telephone book. When you travel, it will pay you to check them out. If there's one in your area, visit it often. You never know what may turn up there.

Internet shopping is really catching on. There are set-price antique malls and online auctions. The great thing is the fact that there will be a higher concentration of your specific collectible interest available to you at the click of a mouse than you will ever find under one roof anywhere else. It's collectibles heaven. I've been able to buy items I didn't even know existed right from my own swivel chair. I haven't found things to be any more expensive than they would be from the other sources we've mentioned; in fact, I feel that some of my purchases have been real bargains. In every collecting category, there will always be those extremely rare and desirable pieces where the sky is the limit, and when such an item comes up for bid, I've seen some astronomical prices realized, but this has always been true, well before online shopping.

What's Hot on Today's Market

It isn't any secret that the market has undergone a total metamorphosis over the past couple of years. The Internet has changed its structure completely. Reproductions have taken a grim toll. Though rare items in any field may sell for astronomical prices, overall, the values of many collectibles have softened. Not because of a lack of interest — in fact, the number of collectors has increased, so has the number of dealers. But the venue has changed as well. It would be impossible to say what percentage of sales for antiques and collectibles can be accredited to Internet auctions, but whatever the number, it has been more than enough to exert a very strong influence. Many factors are at play here — these in particular: merchandise that you once had to search for on foot you now search for with a click of your mouse; instead of covering one antique show, one sale, one flea market at a time, you now cover the entire country — in minutes. So where once you were lucky to find one good piece of Jade-ite, you now have access to several. In other words, we have ready and easy access to a monumental supply of merchandise in thousands of categories. On eBay alone: 8,500 Hot Wheels; 2,300 pieces of Homer Laughlin China; 6,000 Coca-Cola items; 3,500 GI Joe collectibles; and 1,500 fishing lures. Secondly, when it comes to the final price, it is set by you, the buyer. If the reserve is higher than you want to pay, in most cases, you will have another opportunity to buy very soon and at your price. Where the established, traditional dealer would wait for a buyer willing to pay their asking price, the Internet auction shopper waits for a seller willing to take his offer. Many Internet sellers are weekend shoppers simply looking for a quick turnover. They know how the game works and don't expect to get 'book price.'

What has all this to do with reporting 'What's Hot' to you? It has dealers bewildered. When I asked my contacts around the country, I learned very little, but what I did learn was that few of them had the quick answers they normally do. ('Whatever it is, evidently I don't have any.' 'When you find out, let me know' — typical replies.) Is all gloom and doom? Not at all. At some point the supply will even out with the demand and the market will stabilize. Prices that had become over inflated over past years were due for an adjustment. Had that not happened, the number of new collectors wouldn't have increased as it has, and to keep the market healthy and active, new collectors are vital.

Toys. Good toys are consistently 'hot.' Hot Wheels remain good sellers, as do lunchboxes. Star Wars is lagging behind compared to previous years. TV show/character memorabilia is hot. GI Joe remains strong; so do vintage Barbie dolls. (Some of the newer Barbie dolls have cooled down because collectors are finding themselves overwhelmed with an overabundance of dolls who vary only in the color of their hair.) Fisher-Price toys are good, so are action figures — especially Amigos, Matt Mason, and Captain Action. Interest is especially high on the early wrestling figures. Slot cars continue to be a good investment. Transformers and Micronauts are popular. The Beanie Baby market is flailing but still has a devoted following, and high-end prices though down are still amazing.

Pottery and Porcelain. As always, good American pottery is a solid investment. Roseville seems to have been virtually unscathed by all the Chinese reproductions that have flooded the market for the past several years, and prices continue to climb. Rookwood will always be solid. Dealers report an increased interest in Hull Pottery. Good McCoy continues to be 'hot,' and Royal Haeger generates enthusiasm from an ever-increasing circle of its own devotees. California studio potters have been on top for several years and continue to be today, among them Kay Finch, Florence Ceramics, Brayton Laguna, and many others whose output may not have been quite as extensive: Brad Keeler, Will-George, Dorothy Kindell, Cleminson, Max Weil, Hedi Schoop, Sascha Brastoff, Howard Pierce, and Matthew Adams, for instance. Each possess diverse characteristics of their own that endear them to collectors. Don't overlook Red Wing, Camark, Cowan, Muncie, Van Briggle, Shawnee, and Abingdon. Aside from the vases and pots obviously made for the florist trade, any piece of marked American pottery (and unmarked, if you can identify its maker) is worth picking up at garage sale prices.

In dinnerware, the prime focus right now is on designer lines from the '50s — Hall by Zeisel, Homer Laughlin by Schreckengost, Russel Wright, Franciscan Starburst, and many others in that mid-century high-style genre. Restaurant china is attracting a lot of attention, and there are two volumes of in-depth information available on the subject. Good pieces of vintage Fiesta are still strong, and besides the old colors, watch for items in lilac — they're often as desirable as the old line. Pick up Pfaltzgraff when you can get nice serving and accessory pieces, especially in America, Gourmet, and Village. Several lines of Johnson Brothers dinnerware have become very collectible. Chintz patterns are very desirable, Lipper's Blue Danube is starting to draw a lot of attention, so is Blue Garland by Johann Haviland. Spode's Christmas Tree pattern sells well. Lefton's Holly lines are always good, and the Moss Rose pattern, also made in Japan, has emerged as a very popular collectible line, and it's fairly plentiful right now.

Glassware. Gene Florence's Fire-King and Kitchen Glassware books have helped promote the on-going popularity of Jade-ite, just as his Elegant Glassware book has promoted the sales of quality glassware. Dealers tell us that Fostoria, Heisey, and Cambridge sales are brisk and that Paden City has picked up this year. Colored glass, especially red, sells well for them. Crackle glass is well worth looking for, and you'll sometimes be able to pick up some nice Fenton items well underpriced — never pass them by. Westmoreland's mid-century carnival glass, milk glass, and giftware items are appreciating at a very nice pace. There's absolutely no interest in generic stemware, no matter how lovely, so don't be tempted to buy it up, unless you plan to use it yourself.

Jewelry. Good costume jewelry by well known designers continues to sell for amazing sums, but Marcia (Sparkles) Brown's new book on unsigned jewelry has caused collectors to take a second look at what Sparkles calls the 'orphans.' ('Learn to judge quality,' she urges collectors.) The Bakelite market is still strong, and any nice piece has excellent sales potential, though the average price may be somewhat lower than last year, due to the influence of Internet auctions and 'week-end dealers.'

Furniture. Good pine furniture is strong, especially in the east and south. Arts and Crafts style furniture is considered very trendy now; watch for pieces still in their original finish. Signed examples can be very pricey. Fifties Modern pieces such as the boomerang tables and the cube chairs are very good; chairs made of molded fiberglass or with a leather sling seat or an aluminum or wire-work frame typify this genre. Heywood-Wakefield furniture has a devoted following. And don't overlook the clocks and lighting fixtures from that era; good examples by noted designers often sell for several hundred dollars each.

Other Collectibles. Garfield, Snoopy, M&M collectibles, and Campbells Kids items sell steadily. Elvis memorabilia is hot, so are KISS collectibles and other items relating to the birth and maturing of rock 'n roll.

Sixties memorabilia is hot as well, especially kitchenware — anodized aluminum, Kromex canister sets, and pyrex bowls with assorted fired-on decorations, for instance. Smiley faces are enjoying a burst of retro enthusiasm, and there is an active market for the original issues. Posters, books, Peter Max art, pin-back buttons, and various types of other memorabilia having to do with the social activism of the hippie and beatnik movements find ready buyers.

How to Evaluate Your Holdings

When viewed in its entirety, granted, the antiques and collectibles market can be overwhelming. But in each line of glassware, any type of pottery or toys, or any other field I could mention, there are examples that are more desirable than others, and these are the ones you need to be able to recognize. If you're a novice, it will probably be best at first to choose a few areas that you find most interesting and learn just what particular examples or types of items are most in demand within that field. Concentrate on the top 25%. This is where you'll do 75% of your business. Do your homework. Quality sells. Obviously no one can be an expert in everything, but gradually you can begin to broaden your knowledge. As an added feature of our guide, information on clubs and newsletters, always a wonderful source of up-to-date information on any subject, is contained in each category when available. (Advisor's names are listed as well. We highly recommend that you exhaust all other resources before you contact them with your inquiries. Their role is simply to check over our data before we go to press to make sure it is as accurate as we and they can possibly make it for you; they do not agree to answer readers' questions, though some may. If you do write, you must send them an SASE. If you call, please take the time zones into consideration. Some of our advisors are professionals and may charge an appraisal fee, so be sure to ask. Please, do *not* be offended if they do not respond to your contacts, they are under no obligation to do so.)

There are many fields other than those we've already mentioned that are strong and have been for a long time. It's impossible to list them all. But we've left very little out of this book; at least we've tried to represent each category to some extent and where at all possible to refer you to a source of further information. It's up to you to read, observe the market, and become acquainted with it to the point that you feel confident enough to become a part of today's antiques and collectibles industry.

The thousands of current values found in this book will increase your awareness of today's wonderful world of buying, selling, and collecting antiques and collectibles. Use it to educate yourself to the point that you'll be the one with the foresight to know what and how to buy as well as where and how to turn those sleepers into cold, hard cash.

In addition to this one, there are several other very fine price guides on the market. One of the best is *Schroeder's Antiques Price Guide*; another is *The Flea Market Trader*. Both are published by Collector Books. *The Antique Trader Antiques and Collectibles Price Guide, Warman's Antiques and Their Prices,* and *Kovel's Antiques and Collectibles Price List* are others. You may want to invest in a copy of each. Where you decide to sell will have a direct bearing on how you price your merchandise, and nothing will affect an item's worth more than condition.

If you're not familiar with using a price guide, here's a few tips that may help you. When convenient and reasonable, antiques will be sorted by manufacturer. This is especially true of pottery and most glassware. If you don't find the item you're looking for under the manufacturer, look under a broader heading, for instance, cat collectibles, napkin dolls, cookie jars, etc. And don't forget to use the index. Most guides of this type have very comprehensive indexes — a real boon to the novice collector. If you don't find the exact item you're trying to price, look for something similar. For instance, if it's a McCoy rabbit planter you're researching, go through the McCoy section and see what price range other animal planters are in. Or if you have a frame-tray puzzle with Snow White and the Seven Dwarfs, see what other Disney frame-trays are priced at. Just be careful not to compare apples to oranges. You can judge the value of a 7" Roseville Magnolia vase that's not listed; just look at the price given for one a little larger or smaller and adjust it up or down. Pricing collectibles is certainly not a science; the bottom line is simply where the buyer and the seller finally agree to do business. Circumstances dictate sale price, and we can only make suggestions, which we base on current sales, market observations, and the expert opinions of our advisors.

Once you've found 'book' price, decide how much less you can take for it. 'Book' price represents a high average retail. A collectible will often change hands many times, and obviously it will not always be sold at book price. How quickly do you want to realize a profit? Will you be patient enough to hold out for top dollar, or would you rather price your merchandise lower so it will turn over more quickly? Just as there are both types of dealers, there are two types of collectors. Many are bargain hunters. They shop around — do the legwork themselves. On the other hand, there are those who are willing to pay whatever the asking price is to avoid spending precious time searching out pieces they especially want, but they represent the minority. You'll often see tradepaper ads listing good merchandise (from that top 25% we mentioned before) at prices well above book value. This is a good example of a dealer who knows that his merchandise is good enough to entice the buyer who is able to pay a little more and doesn't mind waiting for him (or her) to come along, and that's his prerogative.

Don't neglect to access the condition of the item you want to sell. This is especially important in online and mail-order selling. Most people, especially inexperienced buyers and sellers, have a tendency to overlook some flaws and to overrate merchandise. Mint condition means that an item is complete and undamaged — in effect, just as it looked the day it was made. Glassware, china, and pottery may often be found in mint condition, though signs of wear will downgrade anything. Remember that when a buyer doesn't have the option of seeing for himself, your written description is all he has to go by. Save yourself the hassle of costly and time-consuming returns by making sure the condition of your merchandise is accurately and completely described. Unless a toy is still in its original box and has never been played with, you seldom see a toy in mint condition. Paper collectibles are almost never found without deterioration or damage. Most price guides will list values that apply to glass and ceramics that are mint (unless another condition is specifically indicated within some descriptions). Other items are usually evaluated on the assumption that they are in the best as-found condition common to that area of collecting, for instance magazines are simply never found in mint condition. Grade your merchandise as though you were the buyer, not the seller. You'll be building a reputation that will go a long way toward contributing to your success. If it's glassware or pottery you're assessing, an item in less than excellent condition will be mighty hard to sell at any price. Just as a guideline (a basis to begin your evaluation, though other things will factor in), use a scale of one to five with good being a one, excellent being a three, and mint being a five. As an example, a beer tray worth $250.00 in mint condition would then be worth $150.00 if excellent and $50.00 if only good. Remember, the first rule of buying (for resale or investment) is 'Don't put your money in damaged goods.' And the second rule should be be, 'If you do sell damaged items, indicate 'as is' on the price tag, and don't price the item as though it were mint.' The Golden Rule applies just as well to us as antique dealers as it does to any other interaction. Some shops and co-ops have poor lighting, and damage can be easily missed by a perspective buyer — your honesty will be greatly appreciated. If you include identification on your tags as well, be sure it's accurate. If you're not positive, say so. Better yet, let the buyer decide.

Deciding Where to Best Sell Your Merchandise

Personal Transactions are just one of many options. Overhead and expenses will vary with each and must be factored into your final pricing. If you have some especially nice items and can contact a collector willing to pay top dollar, that's obviously the best of the lot. Or you may decide to sell to a dealer who may be willing to pay you only half of book. Either way, your expenses won't amount to much more than a little gas or a phone call.

Internet Auctions may be your preferred venue. Look at Completed Auctions for sales results of similar items to decide. Factor in the cost of photography (sales of items with no photograph suffer), image hosting, and listing fees. Remember that the cost of boxes and bubble wrap must also be considered, not to mention the time spent actually listing the item, answering e-mail questions, contacting the buyer with the winning bid, leaving feedback, etc.

Internet selling works. In fact, I know some dealers who have quit doing shows and simply work out of their home. No more unpacking, travel expenses, or inconvenience of any kind to endure. You may sell through a set-price online mall or an auction. If you choose the auction (eBay is the most widely used right now), you can put a 'reserve' on everything you sell, a safeguard that protects the seller and prevents an item from going at an unreasonably low figure should there be few bidders.

Classified Ads are another way to get a good price for your more valuable merchandise without investing much money or time. Place a 'For Sale' ad or run a mail bid in one of the collector magazines or newsletters, several of which are listed in the back of this book. Many people have had excellent results this way. One of the best to reach collectors in general is *The Antique Trader Weekly* (P.O. Box 1050, Dubuque, Iowa 52004). It covers virtually every type of antique and collectible and has a large circulation. If you have glassware, china, or pottery from the Depression era, you should have good results through *The Depression Glass Daze* (Box 57, Otisville, Michigan 48463). If you have several items and the cost of listing them all is prohibitive, simply place an ad saying (for instance) 'Several pieces of Royal Copley (or whatever) for sale, send SASE for list.' Be sure to give your correct address and phone number.

When you're making out your list or talking with a prospective buyer by phone, try to draw a picture with words. Describe any damage in full; it's much better than having a disgruntled customer to deal with later, and you'll be on your way to establishing yourself as a reputable dealer. Sometimes it's wise to send out photographs. Seeing the item exactly as it is will often help the prospective buyer make up his or her mind. Send an SASE along and ask that your photos be returned to you, so that you can send them out again, if need be. A less expensive alternative is to have your item photocopied. This works great for many smaller items, not just flat shapes but things with some dimension as well. It's wonderful for hard-to-describe dinnerware patterns or for showing their trademarks.

If you've made that 'buy of a lifetime' or an item you've hung onto for a few years has turned out to be a scarce, highly sought collectible, you have two good options: eBay and mail bids. Either way, you should be able to get top dollar for your prize.

If you do a mail bid, this is how you'll want your ad to read. 'Mail Bid. Popeye cookie jar by American Bisque, slight wear (or mint — briefly indicate condition), closing 6/31/95, right to refuse' (standard self-protection clause meaning you will refuse ridiculously low bids), and give your phone number. Don't commit the sale to any bidder until after the closing date, since some may wait until the last minute to try to place the winning bid.

Be sure to let your buyer know what form of payment you prefer. Some dealers will not ship merchandise until personal checks have cleared. This delay may make the buyer a bit unhappy. So you may want to request a money order or a cashier's check.

Be very careful about how you pack your merchandise for shipment. Breakables need to be well protected. There are several things you can use. Plastic bubble wrap is excellent, or scraps of foam rubber such as carpet padding (check with a carpet-laying service or confiscate some from family and friends who're getting new carpet installed). I've received items wrapped in pieces of egg-crate type mattress pads. (Watch for these at garage sales!) If there is a computer business near you, check their dumpsters for discarded foam wrapping and other protective packaging. It's best not to let newspaper come in direct contact with your merchandise, since the newsprint may stain certain surfaces. After you've wrapped them well, you'll need boxes. Find smaller boxes (one or several, whatever best fits your needs) that you can fit into a larger one with several inches of space between them. First pack your well-wrapped items snugly into the smaller box, using crushed newspaper to keep them from shifting. Place it into the larger box, using more crushed paper underneath and along the sides, so that it will not move during transit. Remember, if it arrives broken, it's still your merchandise, even though you have received payment. You may want to insure the shipment; check with your carrier. Some have automatic insurance up to a specified amount.

After you've mailed your box, it's good to follow it up with a phone call or an e-mail after a few days. Make sure it arrived in good condition and that your customer is pleased with the merchandise. Most people who sell by mail or the Internet allow a 10-day return privilege, providing their original price tag is still intact. For this purpose, you can simply initial a gummed label or use one of those pre-printed return address labels that most of us have around the house.

For very large or heavy items such as furniture or slot machines, ask your buyer for his preferred method of shipment. If the distance involved is not too great, he may even want to pick it up himself.

Flea Market Selling can either be a lot of fun, or it can turn out to be one of the worst experiences of your life. Obviously you will have to deal with whatever weather conditions prevail, so be sure to listen to weather reports so that you can dress accordingly. You'll see some inventive shelters you might want to copy. Even a simple patio umbrella will offer respite from the blazing sun or a sudden downpour. I've recently been seeing stands catering just to the needs of the flea market dealer — how's that for being enterprising! Not only do they carry specific items the dealers might want, but they've even had framework and tarpaulins, and they'll erect shelters right on the spot!

Be sure to have plastic table covering in case of rain and some large clips to hold it down if there's much wind. The type of clip you'll need depends on how your table is made, so be sure to try them out before you actually get caught in a storm. Glass can blow over, paper items can be ruined, and very quickly your career as a flea market dealer may be cut short for lack of merchandise!

Price your things, allowing yourself a little bargaining room. Unless you want to collect tax separately on each sale (for this you'd need a lot of small change), mentally calculate the amount and add this on as well. Sell the item 'tax included.' Everybody does.

Take snacks, drinks, paper bags, plenty of change, and somebody who can relieve you occasionally. Collectors are some of the nicest people around. I guarantee that you'll enjoy this chance to meet and talk them, and often you can make valuable contacts that may help you locate items you're especially looking for yourself.

Auction Houses are listed in the back of this book. If you have an item you feel might be worth selling at auction, be sure to contact one of them. Many have appraisal services; some are free while others charge a fee, dependent on number of items and time spent. We suggest you first make a telephone inquiry before you send in a formal request.

In Summation

Being the type of personality that God put on this earth with the distinct charge to 'seek out, collect and adhere to all things that are good and beautiful and preserve them for future generations,' I have tried to fulfill my destiny and have loved every minute doing it. I was blessed with a husband who enjoyed it just as much as I have. We've met wonderful people and found it to be not only pleasurable but profitable as well.

Anyone willing to take the time to research, attend shows, and study the market can become a successful collector and/or dealer, and there's never been a more exciting time to begin the hunt for today's collectibles, tomorrow's antiques. Good hunting!

Abbreviations

dia — diameter
ea — each
EX — excellent
G — good condition
gal — gallon
L — long, length
lg — large
M — mint condition
med — medium
MIB — mint in (original) box
MIP — mint in package
MOC — mint on card
NM — near mint

NMIB — near mint in box
NRFB — never removed from box
oz — ounce
pc — piece
pr — pair
pt — pint
qt — quart
sm — small
VG — very good
W — wide
w/ — with
(+) — has been reproduced

Abingdon

You may find smaller pieces of Abingdon around, but it's not common to find many larger items. This company operated in Abingdon, Illinois, from 1934 until 1950, making not only nice vases and figural pieces but some kitchen items as well. Their cookie jars are very well done and popular with collectors. They sometimes used floral decals and gold to decorate their wares, and a highly decorated item is worth a minimum of 25% more than the same shape with no decoration. Some of their glazes also add extra value. If you find a piece in black, bronze, or red, you can add 25% to those as well. Note that if you talk by phone about Abingdon to a collector, be sure to mention the mold number on the base.

For more information we recommend *Abingdon Pottery Artware, 1934 – 50, Stepchild of the Great Depression,* by Joe Paradis (Schiffer).

See also Cookie Jars.

Advisor: Louise Dumont (See Directory, Abingdon)

Club: Abingdon Pottery Collectors Club
Elaine Westover, Membership and Treasurer
210 Knox Hwy. 5, Abingdon, IL 61410; 309-462-3267

Ashtray, Daisy, #386, 4½" $20.00
Ashtray, donkey, #510, 5½" $50.00
Bookends, cactus, #370, 6", pr $70.00
Bookends, colt, #363, 5¾", pr $85.00
Bookends, Fern Leaf, #428, 5½", pr, from $40 to $45.00
Bowl, aster, oval, #450, 11½" L $55.00
Bowl, leaf, beige, #408, 6½" $50.00
Bowl, Panel, #460, 8" $25.00
Bowl, pineapple, #700D, 14¾" L, from $75 to...........$80.00
Bowl, Regency, green, #536, 7x9x5" $40.00
Bowl, Shell, #610, 9" $25.00
Cache pot, #558, 4¾", from $20 to..............................$25.00
Candle holders, star, #714, 4¼", pr $30.00
Compote, footed, pink, #568, 6" dia $24.00
Creamer & sugar bowl, Daisy, #681/#682, pr, from $40
    to $45.00

Figurine, Dutch boy, holding planter, #469, 8", from $25.00 to $30.00.

Figurine, Fruit Girl, #3904, 10".....................................$85.00
Figurine, goose, black, #571, 5", from $25 to.............$30.00
Figurine, gull, #562, 5", from $20 to............................$25.00
Figurine, peacock, #416, 7"...$50.00
Lamp base, Swirl, #252, 20½".....................................$100.00
Planter, donkey, #669, 7½", from $20 to $25.00
Planter, puppy w/decor, #652, 6¾", from $20 to........$25.00
Planter, w/bow, #120, blue...$20.00
Plate, Apple Blossom, #415, 11", from $35 to $45.00
Salt & pepper shakers, Daisy, range size, pr, from $15 to .$22.00
String holder, mouse, #712D, 8", from $75 to $135.00
Vase, Barre, #522, 9", from $30 to $35.00
Vase, fan, white, #484, 8" $35.00
Vase, Hackney, #659, 8½", from $25 to $30.00
Vase, Laurel, #600, 12"..$60.00

**Vase, Laurel, blue, #442, 6",
from $20.00 to $25.00.**

Vase, morning glory, #392, 5½", from $25 to..............$35.00
Vase, star, #463, 7", from $15 to $18.00
Vase, Swirl, #513, 9", from $15 to................................$25.00
Vase, tulip, #654, 6½", from $10 to $20.00
Vase, Varre, #522, 9", from $20 to $35.00
Vase, Volute, white, #412, 15½", from $75 to...........$125.00
Wall pocket, apron, #699, 6", from $40 to...................$50.00
Wall pocket, book form, #676D, 6½", from $30 to.....$48.00
Wall pocket, cherub bracket, #587, 7½", from $50 to..$65.00
Wall pocket, Triad, #640, 5½", from $35 to.................$40.00
Water jug, #113, 7½"...$90.00
Window box, #476, 10½", from $20 to.........................$25.00

Adams, Matthew

During the 1950s, while still in the employ of Sascha Brastoff, Matthew Adams developed the Alaska line which he later produced in his own studio. Though it is uncertain where it was that he relocated, it is assumed his studio was in Alaska, since some of these pieces have been found bearing a 'Made in Alaska' label. The line features seals, bears, glaciers, and mountains, all indigenous to the Alaska landscape.

Ashtray, walrus on green & white, 4½x5" **$28.00**
Bowl, moose, 3¾x7" **$35.00**
Box, seal on white, 2¼x6½x5½".................................**$50.00**
Cigarette jar, w/lid, 9" **$65.00**
Cigarette lighter...**$48.00**

Covered dish, bear on yellow, $150.00; Vase, polar bear on blue, $75.00; Vase, polar bear on green, $55.00.
(Photo courtesy Pat and Kris Secor)

Creamer, polar bear on blue, #181b............................**$35.00**
Mug, 3 igloos on dark brown, 4" **$22.00**
Vase, Eskimo, shouldered, 10"....................................**$65.00**
Vase, seal on gray & white w/gold mountains, 6"......**$35.00**

Advertising Character Collectibles

The advertising field holds a special fascination for many of today's collectors. It's vast and varied, so its appeal is universal; but the characters of the ad world are its stars right now. Nearly every fast-food restaurant and manufacturer of a consumer product has a character logo. Keep your eyes open on your garage sale outings; it's not at all uncommon to find the cloth and plush dolls, plastic banks and mugs, bendies, etc., such as we've listed here. There are several books on the market that are geared specifically toward these types of collectibles. Among them are *Advertising Character Collectibles* by Warren Dotz; *Zany Characters of the Ad World* by Mary Jane Lamphier; and *Cereal Box Bonanza, The 1950s,* by Scott Bruce. All are published by Collector Books. Others you'll enjoy reading are *Collectible Aunt Jemima* by Jean Williams Turner (Schiffer); *Cereal Boxes and Prizes, The 1960s* (Flake World Publishing) by Scott Bruce; and *Hake's Guide to Advertising Collectibles* by Ted Hake (Wallace-Homestead). *Schroeder's Collectible Toys, Antique to Modern,* is another source. (It is also published by Collector Books.)

See also Advertising Watches; Breweriana; Bubble Bath Containers; Cereal Boxes and Premiums; Character Clocks and Watches; Character and Promotional Drinking Glasses; Coca-Cola Collectibles; Fast-Food Collectibles; Novelty Radios; Novelty Telephones; Pez Candy Containers; Pin-Back Buttons; Salt and Pepper Shakers; Soda Pop Memorabilia.

Newsletter: *FLAKE, The Breakfast Nostalgia Magazine*
P.O. Box 481
Cambridge, MA 02140; 617-492-5004

Aunt Jemima

One of the most widely recognized ad characters of them all, Aunt Jemima has decorated bags and boxes of pancake flour for more than ninety years. In fact, the original milling company carried her name, but by 1926 it had become part of the Quaker Oats Company. She and Uncle Mose were produced in plastic by the F&F Mold and Die Works in the 1950s, and the salt and pepper shakers, syrup pitchers, cookie jars, etc., they made are perhaps the most sought-after of the hundreds of items available today. (Watch for reproductions.) Age is a big worth-assessing factor for memorabilia such as we've listed below, of course, but so is condition. Watch for very chipped or worn paint on the F&F products, and avoid buying soiled cloth dolls.

Advisor: Judy Posner (See Directory, Advertising)

Banner, Here Today!, Aunt Jemima...Serving Her Famous Pancakes, cloth, red, yellow, and white, 34x58", EX, $500.00.

Clipboard, New Aunt Jemima Butter Lite, yellow w/5 images of Aunt Jemima down side, for grocery store use, unused, M..**$75.00**
Cookbook, Pancakes Unlimited, 31 full-color pages w/pancake shaker offer on back, 1958, 6¼x4½", EX **$45.00**
Cookie jar, plastic Aunt Jemima figure, F&F Mold & Die Co, NM...**$450.00**
Creamer, Uncle Mose, F&F Mold & Die Co, EX..........**$80.00**
Doll, Breakfast Bear, blue plush, in chef's hat, apron & bandana, Aunt Jemima premium, 13", M..................**$175.00**

Dolls, stuffed oilcloth, 1940s – 50: Uncle Moses, 12", EX, $95.00; Aunt Jemima, 11", EX, $95.00.

Hat, paper, Aunt Jemima Breakfast Club/Eat a Better Breakfast..., red & black lettering & head image on white, 1953, EX+.................................**$50.00**

Junior Chef Pancake Set, Argo Industries, 1949, EX.**$150.00**

Magazine ad, Pancakes in 10 Shakes, illustrated steps featuring Ozzie & Harriet, 1958, 14x10½", EX...............**$20.00**

Magazine ad, 4-Flour Flavor of Aunt Jemima Pancakes, Southern scene above illustration of pancake on spatula, 1959, EX............**$20.00**

Measuring cup, beige plastic ¼-cup size w/Aunt Jemima embossed on handle, 1980s, EX...............................**$40.00**

Pancake mold, aluminum w/center handle & 4 animal shapes, Aunt Jemima embossed on surface, 8½" dia, EX...**$150.00**

Poster, Delicious! Let's Have Aunt Jemima's Often!/Aunt Jemima Buckwheats, cartoon image of family breakfast, 20", EX..**$165.00**

Pot holder, red graphics on white, 1970s, M...............**$35.00**

Recipe book, Cake Mix Miracles, 1950s, EX................**$35.00**

Recipe box, hard red plastic w/Aunt Jemima in red bandana w/white polka-dots, EX...................................**$225.00**

Salt & pepper shakers, Aunt Jemima & Uncle Mose, F&F Mold & Die Co, 3½", NM, pr................................**$45.00**

Salt & pepper shakers, Aunt Jemima & Uncle Mose, F&F Mold & Die Co, 5", pr.................................**$65.00**

Sign, cardboard stand-up, Aunt Jemima Pancake Flour/Self-Rising & Ready Mix..., diecut image in center, 20x13", VG+...**$375.00**

Spatula, Hurray! It's Aunt Jemima Day! lettered on plastic handle, EX...**$45.00**

Syrup pitcher, Aunt Jemima figural, F&F Mold & Die Co, 5½", EX...**$70.00**

Table card, cardboard cutout, Folks...It's a Treat To Eat Out Often...Bring the Whole Family..., 1953, 3x4¾", EX..**$55.00**

Tin, shows products on multicolor nostalgic background, Quaker limited edition, dated 1983, 6x5x5", EX ..**$25.00**

Big Boy and Friends

Bob's Big Boy, home of the nationally famous Big Boy, the original double-deck hamburger, was founded by Robert C. 'Bob' Wian in Glendale, California, in 1938. He'd just graduated from high school, and he had a dream. With the $300.00 realized from the sale of the car he so treasured, he bought a run-down building and enough basic equipment to open his business. Through much hard work and ingenuity, Bob turned his little restaurant into a multimillion-dollar empire. Not only does he have the double-deck two-patty burger to his credit, but car hops and drive-in restaurants were his creation as well.

With business beginning to flourish, Bob felt he needed a symbol — something that people would recognize. One day in walked a chubby lad of six, his sagging trousers held up by reluctant suspenders. Bob took one look at him and named him Big Boy, and that was it! It was a natural name for his double-deck hamburger — descriptive, catchy, and easy to remember. An artist worked out the drawings, and Bob's Pantry was renamed Bob's Big Boy.

The enterprise grew fast, and Bob added location after location. In 1969 when he sold out to the Marriott Corporation, he had 185 restaurants in California, with franchises such as Elias Big Boy, Frisch's Big Boy, and Shoney's Big Boy in other states. The Big Boy burger and logo was recognized by virtually every man, woman, and child in America, and Bob retired knowing he had made a significant contribution to millions of people everywhere.

Since Big Boy has been in business for over sixty years, you'll find many items and numerous variations. Some, such as the large statues, china, and some menus, have been reproduced. If you're in doubt, consult an experienced collector for help. Many items of jewelry, clothing, and kids' promotions were put out over the years, too numerous to itemize separately. Values range from $5.00 up to $1,000.00.

Advisor: Steve Soelberg (See Directory, Advertising)

Ashtray, square glass dish w/Frisch's logo & America's Favorite Hamburger in round center, 3½", EX.....**$20.00**

Ashtray, white ceramic w/full-figure Bob standing on side, average paint wear, 4x3¾"...................................**$110.00**

Ashtray, white w/figure on edge, 1950s, M...............**$350.00**

Bank, figure holding hamburger, ceramic **$500.00**

Bank, figure w/ or w/out hamburger, vinyl, M, ea.....**$25.00**

Bank, figure wearing red & white checked overalls, plastic, 1973, 9"...**$20.00**

Box, lunch/pencil; red plastic.....................................**$25.00**

Comic book, Adventures of Big Boy, #1 ....**$250.00**

Comic book, Adventures of Big Boy, #2-#5, ea........**$150.00**

Comic book, Adventures of Big Boy, #6-#10, ea......**$100.00**

Comic book, Adventures of Big Boy, #11-#100, ea **$50.00**

Comic book, Adventures of Big Boy, #101-#250, ea ..**$20.00**

Counter display, papier-mache figure w/hamburger, 1960s...**$500.00**

Cup, coffee; robin-egg blue w/Bob serving burger graphics, maroon inside, Walker China, 3"...........................**$50.00**

Decal, Big Boy for President, M.....................................**$5.00**

Doll, Dakin, complete w/hamburger & shoes...........**$150.00**

Figure, Bob on yellow surfboard w/blue wave underneath, PVC, 1990, 3"......$10.00

Food bag, Frisch's Big Boy Burger, 1950s, M......$25.00

Gameboard, mint and complete with game pieces, $200.00. (Photo courtesy Steve Soelberg)

Handbook, employee, 1956......$100.00

Key chain, flat silver-tone figure, M......$25.00

Kite, paper w/Big Boy logo......$500.00

Lighter, Bob's in red circle on 1 side, Big Boy logo on other side, Wellington Junior, dated 5-20-55, 1¼x2"....$100.00

Matchbook, Bob's logo & Big Boy w/hamburger on front w/Bob's Seasoning Salt on back, gold background, unused, EX......$20.00

Matchbook, lists Bob's California locations, red, tan & white on brown, lettering on each match, EX+......$20.00

Menu, Bob's original #1 location......$350.00

Mug, Big Boy China, Canoga Park drive-in......$25.00

Nodder, papier-mache figure, 1965......$800.00

Ornament, Happy Holidays......$20.00

Pen, Parker, MIB......$20.00

Pennant, felt, Big Boy Club, 1950s, 2 versions, ea.....$50.00

Plate, dinner; Elias Brothers, $50.00. (Photo courtesy Steve Soelberg)

Playing cards, red, unopened, M......$40.00

Store display, PVC w/4 figures......$100.00

Transistor radio, soda pop can shape, w/logo, working, M......$1,000.00

Tumbler, tall w/turquoise logo, 1956......$75.00

Watch, Windert, man's gold quartz, MIB......$150.00

Yo-yo, wood, blue or red, 1956......$50.00

Campbell Kids

The introduction of the world's first canned soup was announced in 1897. Later improvements in the manufacturing process created an evolutionary condensed soup. The Campbell's® Soup Company is now the primary beneficiary of this early entrepreneurial achievement. Easily identified by their red and white advertising, the company has been built on a tradition of skillful product marketing through five generations of consumers. Now a household name for all ages, Campbell's Soups have grown to dominate 80% of the canned soup market.

The first Campbell's licensed advertising products were character collectibles offered in 1910 — composition dolls with heads made from a combination of glue and sawdust. They were made by the E.I. Horsman Company and sold for $1.00 each. They were the result of a gifted illustrator, their creator, Grace Drayton, who in 1904 gave life to the chubby-faced cherub 'Campbell's Kids.'

In 1994 the Campbell's Soup Kids celebrated their ninetieth birthday. They have been revised a number of times to maintain a likeness to modern-day children. Over the years hundreds of licensees have been commissioned to produce collectibles and novelty items with the Campbell's logo in a red and white theme.

Licensed advertising reached a peak from 1954 through 1956 with thirty-four licensed manufacturers. Unusual items included baby carriages, toy vacuums, games, and apparel. Many of the more valuable Campbell's advertising collectibles were made during this period. In 1956 a Campbell's Kid doll was produced from latex rubber. Called 'Magic Skin,' it proved to be the most popular mail-in premium ever produced. Campbell's received more than 560,000 requests for this special girl chef doll.

For more information, we recommend *Campbell's Soup Collectibles, A Price and Identification Guide*, by David and Micki Young (Krause Publications). The book may be ordered through The Soup Collector Club.

Advisors: David and Micki Young (See Directory, Advertising)

Club: The Soup Collector Club
414 Country Lane Ct.
Wauconda, IL 60084
fax/phone: 847-487-4917
e-mail: dyoung@soupcollector.com

Website: www.soupcollector.com or Club site: clubs.yahoo.com/clubs/campbellssoupcollectorclub

Bank, chicken noodle soup can, Kids graphics w/poem on side, 4¾x3½" dia $20.00
Bank, pail w/lid, metal w/plastic handle, 6 different Campbell Kids graphics, Shackman, 1980, 2½", M..................$35.00
Bell, white frosted glass w/picture of 2 kids sitting on bridge fishing, Fenton Glass, 1984, 6½" $41.00
Clock, 2 Kids holding wooden spoons in pot (clock in center), w/sm plastic shelf & oven mitts, 1987, 9x13" $25.00
Coin purse, red w/girl's face, chain for handle, 2⅜x3" .$24.00
Coloring book, A Story of Soup, shows Kids in prehistoric dress, 1977, EX...$26.00
Comic book, Captain America & The Campbell Kids, promotional, Marvel, 1980, M...$24.00
Container, plastic soap dispenser w/plastic pump on top, MSR Imports, 1991, 4x3¼", MIP..............................$8.00
Cookie jar, ceramic, white w/Campbell Kids graphics, Westwood, 1991, MIB...$35.00
Cup, ceramic, Campbell Kids graphics, Westwood, M..$5.00
Cup, ceramic, M'm! M'm! Good!, M..............................$5.00
Cup, ceramic, Salute America, Campbell Kids as Uncle Sam & Liberty, 1986, M $21.00
Cup, plastic, M'm! M'm Good!, Campbell Kids graphics, w/lid, microwaveable, 1992, M.............................$5.00
Cup, plastic, molded Campbell Kid head, yellow hair, 1976, NM $12.00
Decal, Boy chef w/spoon raised in front of barbecue, Meyercord, 1954, 5x6x5", M..$8.00
Dish, Campbell Kid scene, Buffalo Pottery, 7½" dia ..$45.00
Doll, Campbell girl, rubber & vinyl w/cloth outfit, Ideal, 1955, 8", EX, minimum value $125.00
Doll, porcelain doll in pirate clothes, comes in lg soup can box, Home Shopper, 1995, 10", EX.....................$79.00
Doll kit, Boy & Girl Scottish Dolls, Douglas Co, 1979, ea...$35.00
Dolls, Campbell Boy & Girl, vinyl, 1970s, 9", set of 2, MIB $125.00
Dolls, Colonial boy & girl (Paul Revere & Betsy Ross replicas), 1976 premiums, 10", M, ea from $45 to.......$65.00

Dolls, vinyl boy and girl, ca 1972 (soup-label premium), unmarked, 10", from $30.00 to $45.00 each. (Photo courtesy Cindy Sabulis)

Elf Book, Rand McNally, *The Campbell Kids at Home,* **1954, 8x6½", M, $48.00.** (Photo courtesy Dave and Micki Young)

Figurine, Soup's On, girl w/bowl of soup, Campbell Kids Historical Series, ca 1983, 4" $40.00
Game, The Campbell Kids Shopping Game, Parker Bros, 1955, scarce, NMIB $65.00
Kaleidoscope, replica of alphabet vegetable soup can, 1981, 4¾x2½" dia $40.00
Ornament, Christmas; Warm & Hearty Wishes, Kid atop soup can, Enesco, 1993, MIB $20.00
Paperweight, etched glass, 1978, M $45.00
Plate, Chicken Noodle Soup, 2 Kids & teddy bear sitting at table, trimmed in 23k gold, Danbury Mint, 1994, 8" $35.00
Play-Kit, w/yo-yo, top, paddle ball & trick book, Duncan, 1963, MIP..$40.00
Puzzle, jigsaw; All Aboard, Jaymar Mfg, 28 pcs, 1986, VG $25.00
Salt & pepper shakers, ceramic, Campbell Kid as dancing chefs on sides, Westwood, 1991, MIB, pr.............$10.00
Salt & pepper shakers, figural, plastic, w/stoppers, F&F Plastic, ca 1955, 4¼", EXIB $40.00
Scarf, gold w/brown border, Campbell's in red around border , Kids sitting on mushrooms, 25x25"..............$30.00
Sled, Souper Slider, roll-up vinyl w/logo & Kid graphics, mail-in offer, Canada, 1986 ....$10.00
Tea set, Chilton, 1993, child size, MIB (Kid graphics) ..$20.00
Tureen, soup; brown w/4 Kids in white around pot, w/lid, 6" $55.00
Wristwatch, digital, red face w/silver band, 1986, M (in collector's tin)...$30.00

Cap'n Crunch

Cap'n Crunch was the creation of Jay Ward, whom you will no doubt remember was also the creator of the Rocky and Bullwinkle show. The Cap'n hails from the '60s and was one of the first heroes of the presweetened cereal crowd. Jean LaFoote was the villain always scheming to steal the Cap'n's cereal.

Advisor: Scott Bruce (See Directory, Advertising)

Bank, figural, painted plastic, 1973, VG $65.00
Bank, Treasure Chest, blue plastic, 1984, NM $10.00
Beanie, Tiger Shark Meanie, in original printed bag, M, from
 $16 to..$20.00
Big Slick Gyro Car, blue plastic, 1972, MIP $15.00
Binoculars, blue plastic, 1972, MIP $15.00
Boson whistle, blue & white w/Cap'n & Sea Dog, ca 1965,
 EX $10.00
Cap'n Crunch Cruiser, plastic, 1987, EX......................$10.00
Cap'n Rescue Kit, paper, 1986, MIP $10.00
Coloring book, Whitman, 1968, VG $20.00
Comic book, Center of the Earth, 1987, 8-page, EX...$10.00

Doll, Cap'n Crunch, plush, Quaker Oats Company, 1990, 18", $20.00.

Figure, Cap'n Crunch, blue plastic, 1986, 1½", VG.....$10.00
Figure, Cap'n Crunch, vinyl, 1970s, EX, from $40 to..$50.00
Figure, Smog Master, silver plastic robot, 1986, 1½", NM ..$15.00
Figure, Soggie, nearly clear plastic, 1986, 1½", EX.....$10.00
Frisbee, blue plastic w/Cap'n in center, MIP, 1970s, EX.....$50.00
Hand puppet, Cap'n, Dave, or Sea Dog, vinyl, 9", M, ea...$35.00
Handkerchief, white w/4 colorful scenes, EX, 8x8"....$50.00
Kaleidoscope, cardboard, 1965-65, 7", EX $35.00
Mempership kit, Quaker Oats, 1965, M (EX mailer), from
 $200 to..$300.00
Puzzle, 8 figures, wooden, Fisher-Price, 8½x12" $38.00
Ring, plastic figure, NM..$300.00
Treasure chest, tan w/Cap'n Crunch & skull & crossbones, 5
 gold coins, shovel, lock & treasure map inside, EX..$75.00
Tumbler, Ship Shape, plastic, 1963, 6", NM................$25.00
Wiggle figures, 3 different, 1969, EX, ea......................$50.00

Charlie Tuna

Poor Charlie, never quite good enough for the Star-Kist folks to can, though he yearns for them to catch him; but since the early 1970s he's done a terrific job working for them as the company logo. A dapper blue-fin tuna in sunglasses and a beret, he's appeared in magazines, done TV commercials, modeled for items as diverse as lamps and banks, but still they deny him his dream. 'Sorry, Charlie.'

Alarm clock, image of Charlie & Sorry Charlie sign on round
 face, 2 bells, footed, 1969, 4" dia, M....................$65.00
Bank, ceramic, 1988, 10", from $50 to $65.00
Bathroom scale, painted metal, 1970s, NM, from $65 to ..$75.00
Bracelet, embossed figure on gold-tone disk, M.........$10.00
Camera, figural, light blue & white, red mouth & hat, wrist
 strap, 1971 premium, EX......................................$60.00
Clock, wall; Charlie w/fish friend, quartz, 8½" dia $36.00
Doll, 2-tone blue w/pink hat & glass, vinyl, marked Star-Kist
 Foods, 7"..$65.00
Figure, vinyl Charlie, arms up (rare version), 1973, 7½", (M
 $125), MIB..$200.00
Figure, vinyl Charlie, blue w/Star-Kist on pink hat, 1973, 7",
 EX, from $50 to..$60.00
Figurine, printed cloth, vinyl bill on hat, pull string to talk,
 Mattel, 1969, 15"..$30.00
Key ring, raised design on gold-tone disk, M $10.00
Lamp, painted plaster figure of Charlie, EX $75.00
Mug, plastic Thermo Serve, It's Not About Nothin', It's Poetry!
 says Charlie to little fish, 1977, from $5 to $7.00
Patch, Charlie embroidered on green background w/yellow coral & orange starfish, Sorry Charlie sign, 1975,
 3", NM..$12.00
Pendant, Charlie on anchor, M $10.00
Telephone, figural, eyes lights up when phone rings, 1987
 premium $50.00

Telephone, plastic, Star-Kist Foods Inc., 1987, 10", $50.00.

Tumbler, Tell 'em Charlie Sent You, shows Charlie & girl
 tuna, 3½" $6.50

Watch, employee giveaway, shows Charlie w/fishhook & says Sorry Charlie, 1971, EX $60.00

Colonel Sanders

There's nothing fictional about the Colonel — he was a very real guy, who built an empire on the strength of his fried chicken recipe with 'eleven herbs and spices.' In the 1930s, the Colonel operated a small cafe in Corbin, Kentucky. As the years went by, he developed a chain of restaurants which he sold in the mid-'60s. But even after the sale, the new company continued to use the image of the handsome southern gentlemen as their logo. The Colonel died in 1980.

Advertisement, Colonel with cane, two-sided metal with pipe in center to mount on base, 55½", VG, $375.00.

Bank, figural, plastic, dated 1977, 7½"..........................$12.50
Bank, plastic figure, holding a bucket of chicken, no base, 1970s, 8", NM, from $20 to $30.00
Bank, plastic figure, red w/black tie, marked Marquardt Corp, 1972, 10"...$27.50
Bank, plastic figure standing on round base holding cane, Run Starling Plastics LTD, 1965, 13", NM, from $30 to $40.00
Bank, plastic figure w/arm around restaurant building & holding bucket of chicken, white w/red & black trim, 6", EX $125.00
Coin, Visit the Colonel at Mardi Gras, M.....................$10.00
Coloring book, Favorite Chicken Stories, 1960s, EX...$25.00
Cookie jar, glass painted as fried chicken bucket, from $275 to...$325.00
Hand puppet, white w/Colonel in white suit, plastic, 1960s, EX..$20.00

Lamp shade, glass, painted as fried chicken bucket, unmarked, from $275 to $325.00
Mask, multicolored plastic, 1960s, M...........................$38.00
Nodder, bisque, marked, Charlsprod Japan, 1960s, 7½", M, from $100 to...$125.00
Nodder, papier-mache, Tops Enterprises, c 1967, 7½", MIB...$150.00
Pin, Colonel's head, metal, EX......................................$6.50
Playset, Let's Play at Kentucky Fried Chicken, Child Guidance, 1970s, EX (EX box) $140.00
Poker chip, plastic, w/portrait, 1960s, M $17.50
Postcard, Colonel's original motel on linen, EX............$8.00
Print block, Kentucky Fried Chicken smiling face, metal mounted on hardwood, 1960s, 2⅜x1½", EX..........$9.50
Record album, Christmas Day w/Colonel Sanders, LP, RCA, 1968, EX...$25.00
Salt & pepper shakers, Colonel & Mrs Harland Sanders (busts), marked Marquardt Corp, 1972, 3½", pr, from $85 to...$95.00
Salt & pepper shakers, figural, salt w/white base, pepper w/black base, plastic, Starling Plastics Ltd, 1965, 4¼", pr...$35.00
Tie tac, gold-tone molded head w/diamond chip, M.$65.00
Wind-up toy figure, walks w/moving arms & nodding head, 3¼", NM..$15.00

Elsie the Cow and Family

She's the most widely recognized cow in the world; everyone knows Elsie, Borden's mascot. Since the mid-1930s, she's been seen on booklets and posters; modeled for mugs, creamers, dolls, etc.; and appeared on TV, in magazines, and at grocery stores to promote their products. Her husband is Elmer (who once sold Elmer's Glue for the same company), and her twins are best known as Beulah and Beauregard, though they've been renamed in recent years (now they're Bea and Beaumister). Elsie was retired in the 1960s, but due to public demand was soon reinstated to her rightful position and continues today to promote the company's dairy products.

Advisor: Lee Garmon (See Directory, Advertising)

Bank, Beauregard, red plastic figure, Irwin, 1950s, 5", EX $65.00
Butter mold, Elsie or Beulah, ea, M............................$28.00
Clock, round w/glass lens, metal frame, decal of Elsie in daisy in center, Borden's Milk & Ice Cream Sold Here, 21", VG $150.00
Comic book, Free w/Your Purchase of a Bottle of Elmer's Glue, shows Elsie & Elmer demonstrating uses for glue, 1950s, EX...$75.00
Cookie cutter, blue plastic w/embossed image of Elsie's head in daisy, 2¼" dia, EX..$48.00
Creamer, ceramic, Elsie's head w/polka-dot bow at neck, 1940s, 5", EX+ $85.00
Creamer & sugar bowl, molded plastic heads, marked TBC The Borden Co, Made in USA, 3½", from $45 to.$55.00

Creamer, Elsie figural, ceramic, $135.00. (Photo courtesy Lee Garmon)

Doll, Elsie, plush body w/rubber head & felt hooves, cloth ribbon around neck, moos when shaken, 1950s, 14", EX...**$125.00**
Drinking glass, painted image of Elsie, Elmer & Beauregard in 1776 garb, red, white & blue, M.....................**$22.00**
Figure, Elsie, PVC, 1993, 3½", M, from $10 to **$20.00**
Game, Elsie the Cow, Junior Edition, complete, EXIB .**$125.00**
Hand puppet, Elsie's baby, vinyl w/cloth body, EX ...**$75.00**
Lamp, Elsie holding Beauregard, 10" **$250.00**
Milk bottle topper, diecut litho w/Elmer's head in wreath above Season's Greetings From Borden's &... Your Milkman, M **$35.00**
Mug, Beulah portrait, gold trim, 1940s **$65.00**
Postcard, Elsie the Cow & Her Brand New Twins, color, 1957, EX...**$9.00**
Push-button puppet, Elsie, wood, EX.........................**$125.00**
Salt & pepper shakers, ceramic half-figures of Elsie & Elmer in chef hats, names in script on aprons, 4", VG, pr **$90.00**
Sign, embossed self-framed tin, Elsie's head in yellow daisy on white ground, 17½" square, NM+..................**$275.00**
Sign, light-up w/metal case, Borden's Ice Cream & Elsie's head in yellow daisy on white & blue ground, 9x27x4", EX+ **$220.00**
Sign, neon, diecut porcelain Elsie head on wooden stand-up platform, yellow & white tubing, VG **$1,700.00**
Sign, tin keyhole shape, Borden's Ice Cream, Elsie in daisy on white/blue background w/dealer name, 2-sided, 56x51", VG **$675.00**

Sugar bowl, Elmer figural, hat forms lid, ceramic, $100.00. (Photo courtesy Lee Garmon)

Thermometer, white w/Elsie's face in center, 12" dia.**$48.50**
Tie clip, multicolor enameled Elsie in daisy, M **$40.00**

Gerber Baby

Since the late 1920s, the Gerber company has used the smiling face of a baby to promote their line of prepared strained baby food. Several dolls and rubber squeeze toys have been made over the years. Even if you're a novice collector, they'll be easy to spot. Some of the earlier dolls hold a can of product in their hand. Look for the Gerber mark on later dolls. For further information see *A Collector's Guide to the Gerber Baby* by Joan Stryker Grubaugh, Ed.D.

Advisor: Joan Stryker Grubaugh (See Directory, Advertising)

Bells, Swiss; hangs on infant's crib, plastic w/metal bells inside, 1950s, MIB (sealed) **$20.00**
Book, The Story of an Idea, 1953 ....**$45.00**
Booklet, Bringing Up Baby, 1972...............................**$5.00**
Cap, golfer's, 1990 ....**$9.00**
Car sun visor, w/portrait & name................................**$15.00**
Doll, I'm a Gerber Kid, rag type w/yarn hair, dress or play clothes, Atlanta Novelty, 1981-84, 11½", ea..........**$20.00**
Doll, Pajama baby, w/matching pillow, toy & spoon, Atlanta Novelty, 1979-85, 17", MIB................................**$100.00**
Doll, Potty Time Baby, all original, Toy Biz, 1994, 15"...**$25.00**
Doll, premium, w/diaper & bib, Arrow Rubber & Plastic Co, 1965, MIB, from $55 to...**$65.00**
Dolls, boy & girl, squeak vinyl, Atlanta Novelty, 1985, 8", EX, ea **$20.00**
Duffle Bag, Gerber Life Insurance Co, 1990...............**$10.00**
Frisbee, Safety Comes in Cans..., lettering around image, blue & white, EX **$8.00**

Gift box with handle, cardboard, spoon attached to side, three baby tumblers inside, ca 1990, 7¼" long, $25.00. (Photo courtesy Joan Stryker Grubaugh)

Jar opener, rubber circle marked Safety Pays................**$2.00**
Picture, Gerber Baby, signed by Ann Turner Cook, 1978..**$20.00**
Playing cards, baby's face, double deck, 1990s, MIB ...**$9.00**

Playing cards, features Sun Rubber Gerber doll, complete, 1955, NMIB..**$45.00**

Print, copy of portrait drawing by Dorothy Hope Smith, recent (still being made today), 10x7⅞", $10.00. (Photo courtesy Joan Stryker Grubaugh)

Doll, Little Sprout, plush with felt hat and clothes, 1970s, from $20.00 to $30.00.
(Photo courtesy Lil West)

Spoon, Gerber baby on handle, marked Winthrop Silver Plate-Gerber, 4¼"..**$30.00**

Spoon, Oneida Stainless, 1972-1996, 5½"..........................**$8.00**

Tumbler, embossed plastic, 1971....................................**$3.00**

Green Giant

The Jolly Green Giant has been a well-known ad fixture since the 1950s (some research indicates an earlier date); he was originally devised to represent a strain of European peas much larger than the average-size peas Americans had been accustomed to. At any rate, when Minnesota Valley Canning changed its name to Green Giant, he was their obvious choice. Rather a terse individual himself, by 1974 he was joined by Little Green Sprout, with the lively eyes and more talkative personality.

In addition to a variety of toys and other memorabilia already on the market, in 1988 Benjamin Medwin put out a line of Little Green Sprout items. These are listed below.

Advisor: Lil West (See Directory, Advertising)

Bank, Little Sprout, composition, plays Valley of the Green Giant, 8½"..**$50.00**

Brush holder, Little Sprout, w/4 brushes, Benjamin Medwin, MIB...**$40.00**

Clock, Little Sprout holding round dial on front of base, w/talking alarm, 1986, 10½", EX...........................**$25.00**

Cookie jar, Little Sprout, Benjamin Medwin, 1990-92, MIB...**$65.00**

Dinnerware set, w/plate, cup, knife & fork, 1991, MIB...**$10.00**

Doll, Green Giant, cloth, 1966, 16", M (in original mailer), from $25 to...**$35.00**

Doll, Green Giant, vinyl, ca 1975, 9", EX..................**$85.00**

Doll, Little Sprout, stuffed cloth, 1974, 10½", NM.......**$15.00**

Doll, Little Sprout, talker, MIP..................................**$55.00**

Doll, Little Sprout, vinyl, 1970s-90s, 6½", EX, from $10 to..**$20.00**

Fabric, Green Giant & Little Sprout, heavy material, 48x45"...**$20.00**

Farm Factory, w/Little Sprout finger puppet & all accessories, MIB...**$20.00**

Flashlight, Little Sprout, MIB....................................**$45.00**

Jump rope, Little Sprout, MIB....................................**$20.00**

Kite, plastic, mail-in premium, late 1960s, 42x48", unused, M...**$30.00**

Lamp, Little Sprout holding balloons, Touch-on, 1985-86, 14½", M, from $35 to..**$45.00**

Lapel pin, Green Giant..**$7.00**

Magnet, Little Sprout, Benjamin Medwin, 1988, 2-pc, MIB...**$10.00**

Napkin holder, Little Sprout, Benjamin Medwin, MIB...**$10.00**

Planter, Little Sprout, Benjamin Medwin, 1988, MIB...**$35.00**

Puzzle, Green Giant, Planting Time in the Valley, 1000 pcs in can, 1981, EX...**$15.00**

Puzzle, Little Sprout, Sprout's Bedtime, 40 pcs in can, 1981...**$15.00**

Record, Green Giant 20th Birthday, 78 rpm, red wax, 7", VG...**$10.00**

Salt & pepper shakers, Little Sprout, Benjamin Medwin, 1990-92, MIB, pr...**$25.00**

Scouring pad holder w/pad, Little Sprout, Benjamin Medwin, 1988, MIP...**$15.00**

Spoon rest, Little Sprout, Benjamin Medwin, 1988, MIB...**$30.00**

Toy truck, Nylint, Green Giant Corn tractor-trailer, 21", VG...**$55.00**

Toy truck, Tonka, Green Giant Peas stake truck, 1953, EX..**$300.00**

Toy truck, Tonka, Green Giant tractor-trailer, 1951, M, from $150 to...**$200.00**

Wastebasket, metal, 1970s, $45.00. (Photo courtesy Lil West)

Silk tie, $25.00.
(Photo courtesy C.J. Russell and Pamela E. Apkarian-Russell)

Joe Camel

Joe Camel, the ultimate 'cool character,' was only on the scene for a few years as a comic character. The all-around Renaissance beast, he dated beautiful women, drove fast motorcycles and cars, lazed on the beach, played pool, hung around with his pals (the Hard Pack), and dressed formally for dinner and the theatre. He was 'done in' by the anti-cigarette lobby because he smoked. Now reduced to a real camel, his comic strip human persona is avidly collected by both women and men, most of whom don't smoke. Prices have been steadily rising as more and more people come to appreciate him as the great icon he is.

Advisor: C.J. Russell and Pamela E. Apkarian-Russell (See Directory, Halloween)

Ashtray, Smokin' Joe's Racing, white ceramic dish w/3 rests, 5" dia, M $33.00
Ashtray, Tell 'em Joe Sent You lettered on white center of triangular clear glass dish w/3 rests, M $10.00
Auto shade, colorful logo...$15.00
Cap, blue tie-dyed nylon baseball style w/embossed image on front, NM..$10.00
Card game, 48 cards, 6 dice, score pad & pencil, M..$35.00
Cigarette pack, Joe at piano..$8.00
Clock, Camel Lights, Joe as pool player $35.00
Clock, plastic Joe standing by round clock, battery-op, 1992, 20x23", NM..$90.00
Coaster set, square, MIB..$10.00
Counter mat, Joe in various activites in triangular reserves, EX...$10.00
Dartboard, arched top, Joe holding dart on 2-part front (opens), unused, 27x20", M.................................$250.00
Drink holder, Camel Joe figure.....................................$20.00
Duffle bag, 14x9x10½"...$28.00
Ice bucket, w/4 tumblers, 1992, M...............................$30.00
Mug, black w/Camel car, Joe & Hard Pack, 9¼" $15.00
Paperweight, glass, Hard Pack, 4⅓x2¾x¾", M..........$15.00
Shower curtain...$75.00

Standee, cardboard, Joe in leather jacket w/Camel cash booklet, life-size...$125.00
T-shirt, Beach Club, MIB..$10.00
Thermometer, Joe holding pack, diecut, 18½", EX.....$50.00
Tin, Smokin' Joe's Racing, w/sealed pack of book matches, inserts & catalogs, RJRC, 1994, M.........................$10.00
Tumbler, Joe's Place, MIB...$40.00
Wristwatch, Camel Journey, Joe on motorcycle revolves on face $100.00

M & M Candy Men

Toppers for M&M packaging first appeared about 1988; since then other M&M items have been introduced that portray the clever antics of these colorful characters. Toppers have been issued for seasonal holidays as well as Olympic events.

Advisors: Bill and Pat Poe (See Directory, Fast-Food Collectibles)

Banner, beach scene, plastic, 1995, 26x30" $12.00
Banner, Christmas scene w/train, Holiday Express, plastic, 1996, 26x30" $12.00
Bean bag toys, M&M shape, red, green, blue or yellow, 6", ea $10.00
Bean bag toys, peanut shape, golfer or witch, 6", ea $20.00
Book, Plain & Peanut & the Missing Christmas Present, 1993, NM..$6.00
Calculator, yellow w/different color M&M keys, MIB $20.00
Coin holder, set of 6 containers full of mini M&Ms, 1996, per set...$10.00
Cookie cutter, M&M shape, standing w/arms up, red plastic, 3" $4.00

Container, green, 1996, $10.00; Long-bed truck with ten boxes of mini candies, $15.00; Coin holder that held mini candies, came in six colors, Easter, 1997, $6.00. (Photo courtesy Bill and Pat Poe)

Dispenser, spaceship shape w/M symbol, press button to dispense candy, battery-op, red, yellow or blue, MOC, ea **$8.00**

Dispenser, 1991, M&M shape, brown, sm **$10.00**

Dispenser, 1991, M&M shape, holding bouquet of flowers, yellow, sm **$5.00**

Dispenser, 1991, M&M shape, red, lg **$15.00**

Dispenser, 1991, peanut shape, brown, sm **$10.00**

Dispenser, 1991, peanut shape, orange, green or yellow, sm, ea...**$5.00**

Dispenser, 1992, peanut shape, red, lg.......................**$20.00**

Dispenser, 1995, M&M Fun Machine, shaped like a gumball machine **$12.00**

Dispenser, 1995, peanut shape, football player, yellow, lg **$20.00**

Dispenser, 1995, peanut shape, yellow, lg **$30.00**

Dispenser, 1997, peanut shape, basketball player **$15.00**

Doll, M&M shape, plush, red, 12" **$15.00**

Doll, M&M shape, plush, 8"...**$12.00**

Dolls, M&M shape, plush, 4½" **$10.00**

Easy Bake Set, w/M&M stencil & spoon, MIB **$12.00**

Figure, M&M shape, bendable arms & legs, red, 5½" ..**$20.00**

Figure, peanut shape, bendable arms & legs, blue or yellow, 7", ea...**$20.00**

Magnet, red M&M shape or yellow peanut shape, plush, 2", ea...**$8.00**

Message board, magnet school bus shape, characters on top & hood of bus, M **$100.00**

Tin, Christmas 1992, dark green w/winter scene........**$12.00**

Tin, Christmas 1996, Taking a Break at the Diner, rectangular **$15.00**

Tin, 1988, blue w/stars & M&M's, sm **$10.00**

Tin, 1990, 50th Birthday, lg..**$15.00**

Topper, Christmas, M&M shape, several variations w/Santa hats, square base, ea **$10.00**

Topper, 1989, M&M shape, on ice skates wearing red Santa hat, green, round base **$3.50**

Topper, 1992, M&M shape, going down chimney w/bag of toys, green, round base...**$3.50**

Topper, 1992, peanut shape, w/bow & arrow, brown, heart w/arrow on round base **$7.00**

Topper, 1994, peanut shape, w/paint brush & chick in egg, turquoise, pink, lavender or lime green, round base, ea **$4.00**

Topper, 1995, M&M shape, postman holding pink valentine, red, round base...**$4.00**

Topper, 1995, M&M shape, w/Easter, bouquet & watering can, green, turquoise or lavender, round base, ea.**$4.00**

Topper, 1997, peanut shape, bag of toys on shoulder, green, round base...**$3.50**

Utensil holder, 1 in chef's hat holding rolling pin, 3 others hold spoon or wisk, Mars, 1996, NM **$5.00**

Wristwatch, M&M skate boarder as second hand, in plastic case w/cardboard sleeve, 1994............................**$50.00**

Wristwatch, M&M's on face, in padded sleeve, 1993..**$45.00**

Michelin Man (Bibendum or Mr. Bib)

Perhaps one of the oldest character logos around today, Mr. Bib actually originated in the late 1800s, inspired by a stack of tires that one of the company founders thought suggested the figure of a man. Over the years his image has changed considerably, but the Michelin Tire Man continues today to represent his company in many countries around the world.

Ashtray, ceramic, Mr Bib seated on rim, single rest ...**$55.00**

Ashtray, molded cream plastic Mr Bib on black base, 1940s, 6x3¾" dia, from $75 to...**$90.00**

Clock, white plastic over metal back with multicolor accents, Mr. Bib running, Michelin X, 14x16", EX, $135.00.

Costume, nylon & metal w/yellow sash, EX **$900.00**

Cuff links, gold-tone w/white Mr Bib on blue ground, ⅞" dia, pr...**$50.00**

Cup, plastic, Mr Bib on side, EX **$5.00**

Desk ornament/pen holder, ceramic Mr Bib figure, made for 100-year birthday, rare **$50.00**

Dice game, white plastic container w/3-D Mr Bib holds 8 dice w/black letters & blue Mr Bib figures, 3½x2½", M **$85.00**

Doll, rubber, Mr Bib standing holding baby & wearing blue bib w/Michelin in embossed lettering, 7"..........**$125.00**

Figure, ceramic, Mr Bib w/hands at waist, green glaze, 1950s, made in Holland, 12½" **$500.00**

Figure, plastic Mr Bib, adjusts to fit on top of truck cab, 1970s-80s, 18", EX...$140.00
Figure, plastic Mr Bib, 12", NM, from $50 to..............$75.00
Figure, plastic Mr Bib on motorcycle, EX.................$110.00
Key chain, 1½" figure of Mr Bib running, EX............$15.00
Nodder, attaches to dashboard, 2 styles, ea $18.00
Playing cards, Mr Bib courts, wide non-standard, VG ...$18.00
Puzzle, Mr Bib on motorcycle, put together to form figure, MIP...$55.00
Ramp walker, wind-up, MIB...$25.00

Sign, Michelin, Mr. Bib rolling tire, porcelain, 31½x27", NM, $300.00.

Standee, diecut cardboard figure wearing banner w/hand up as if to say Stop & other hand pointing, easel backed, 72", EX..$90.00
Watch fob, Mr Bib on front, Earth Moving Tires, 1½x1¾", EX..$20.00
Yo-yo, Mr Bib in black outline on white, EX..............$10.00

Mr. Peanut

The trademark character for the Planters Peanuts Company, Mr. Peanut, has been around since 1916. His appearance has changed a little from the original version, becoming more stylized in 1961. Today he's still a common sight on Planters' advertising and product containers.

Mr. Peanut has been modeled as banks, salt and pepper shakers, whistles, and many other novelty items. His image has decorated T-shirts, beach towels, playing cards, sports equipment, etc.

Today Mr. Peanut has his own 'fan club,' Peanut Pals, the collector's organization for those who especially enjoy the Planters Peanuts area of advertising.

Advisors: Judith and Robert Walthall (See Directory, Advertising)

Club: Peanut Pals
Judith Walthall, Founder
P.O. Box 4465, Huntsville, AL 35815; 256-881-9198. Website: www.peanutpals.org. Dues: Primary member, $20 per year; Associate member (16 years old and over), $10 per year; under 16 years old, $3 per year. Annual directory and convention news sent to members. For membership, write to PO Box 652, St. Clairsville, OH 43950. Sample newsletter: $2.

Apron, Gold Measure, blue, 1991, M $6.00
Ashtray, diecast figure in center of gold-wash dish, 50th anniversary, 1906-1956, Diecasters Co, 5x6", MIB w/booklet...$130.00
Bank, clear plastic figure, 1950s-70s, EX, from $90 to ..$125.00
Baseball, image of Mr Peanut, EX $5.00
Beach ball, blue & yellow w/image of Mr Peanut in blue, 1970s, 13½" dia, EX..$10.00
Belt, engraved image of Mr Peanut on gold-tone buckle, Nabisco Dinah Shore Invitational golf tournament, 1984, MIB $40.00
Bracelet, 6 plastic charms on brass-colored chain, 1941, VG $35.00
Container, painted papier-mache composition Mr Peanut figure against lg peanut, 12½x3" dia, VG..............$500.00
Cook booklet, Planter's Oil, 1948, EX........................$25.00

Cookie cutter, painted plastic, premium for buying Planter's Baking Nuts, no handle, 1990, 4¼", $4.00. (Photo courtesy Rosemary Henry)

Costume, Mr Peanut, cloth body w/molded plastic mask, 2-pc, 1970s, NMIB...$75.00
Dish set, child's, Melmac, 3 pcs, 1970s, MIB..............$20.00
Doll, jointed wood figure w/yellow body, black arms, legs, shoes & blue hat, 1930s, 9", EX $200.00
Doll, stuffed cloth, Chase Bag Co, 1967, 21", EX........$40.00
Doll, stuffed cloth, Chase Bag Co, 1970, 18", NM.......$25.00
Mug, tan plastic Mr Peanut head, M $10.00
Nodder, papier-mache, Lego, MIB $150.00
Paint book, American Presidents, 1960s, 32 pages, NM .$22.00
Poster, paper, Planters Mr Peanut Sale/Stock Up Now & Save!, Mr Peanut & girl w/sign, blue, 1950s, 15x36", EX..$100.00

Punchboard, cardboard, features different assortments, unused, 1940s, 8" square, EX.................................$85.00

Puppet, Mr Peanut figure, rubber, tan w/black hat & monocle, 1942, 6", EX.................................$750.00

Radio backpack, Munch 'N Go, 1991, EX, from $35 to ..$40.00

Salt & pepper shakers, green plastic figures, 1950s, 3¼", NMIB (w/mailer).................................$25.00

Salt & pepper shakers, pink plastic figures, 1960s, 3", MIP (marked planters in corner).................................$30.00

Salt and pepper shakers, red plastic Mr. Peanut figurals, 1950s, 3", $15.00 for the pair.

Standee, cardboard Mr Peanut figure, 12", M..............$10.00

Tankard, metal pewter type, Wilton, 1983, 4¾", M $10.00

Thermometer for deep fryer, Planters Peanut Oil, aluminum w/Mr Peanut in chef's hat & apron, MIB............$275.00

Tote bag, lg white, black & yellow image of Mr Peanut above Planters Peanuts lettered on blue cloth, 1980s, 18x12", M.................................$10.00

Toy train set, battery-op, 1988, MIB..........................$50.00

Wind-up figure, green plastic, 1950s-60s, 8½", NM ..$375.00

Old Crow

Old Crow collectors have learned to date this character by the cut of his vest and the tilt of his head along with other characteristics of his stance and attire. Advertising Kentucky whiskey, he appears as an elegant gent in his tuxedo and top hat.

Advisor: Geneva Addy (See Directory, Dolls)

Ashtray, black glass, 1¼x3½", EX $30.00

Bottle, bright red vest, gold cane, American, 12½" $75.00

Bottle, light red vest, yellow cane, Royal Doulton, 12½" ..$125.00

Bottle topper, ceramic figure, sm $35.00

Bottle topper, plastic figure..$35.00

Figure, brass w/We Pour It brass plaque on black base, 13", EX.................................$75.00

Figure, chalkware, no cane or glasses, 14"..................$45.00

Figure, composition, paint flaking, 9" $95.00

Figure, 5" crow in brass birdcage.................................$65.00

Glass, bourbon; crow & lettering in black on clear, 5"..$12.50

Glass, clear w/crow stem, Libbey.................................$35.00

Glass, Manhattan; Old Crow & figure in black on clear, 4¾".................................$15.00

Jigger, plastic...$18.00

Key chain, figural Old Crow...$10.00

Lamp, plastic lantern w/brass paint, Advertising Novelty Co, 13½".................................$75.00

Lamp, porcelain, red vest w/gold buttons, 1960s, 14", from $175 to.................................$195.00

Pitcher, glass w/metal ring & handle, 5".....................$25.00

Playing cards, Two Crows You See Good Luck to Thee, 2 decks, 1967, EX.................................$40.00

Roly-poly, plastic, leaded rocker, 9" $95.00

Stand for bottle, 3 crows: 9", 7" & 5", on 9" plastic base ..$95.00

Stand for bottle, 9" crow in birdcage (on side)...........$75.00

Standee, cardboard, 8"...$30.00

Stir stick, black plastic figure, Perfection Plastics, 1950s, 6½".................................$10.00

Thermometer, Taste the Greatness of Historic Old Crow, red, white & black, 13½", EX.................................$200.00

Display, composition crow in formal attire, much paint flaking, 30", G-, $400.00.

Poppin' Fresh (Pillsbury Doughboy) and Family

Who could be more lovable than the chubby blue-eyed Doughboy with the infectious giggle introduced by the Pillsbury Company in 1965. Wearing nothing but a neck scarf and a chef's hat, he single-handedly promoted the company's famous biscuits in a tube until about 1969. It was then that the company changed his name to 'Poppin' Fresh' and soon after presented him with a sweet-faced, bonnet-attired mate named Poppie. Before long, they had created a whole family for him. Many premiums such as dolls, salt and pepper shakers, and cookie jars have been produced over the years. In 1988 the Benjamin Medwin Co. made several items for Pillsbury; all of these white ceramic Doughboy items are listed below. Also offered in 1988, the Poppin' Fresh Line featured the plump little fellow holding a plate of cookies; trim colors were mauve pink and blue. The Funfetti line was produced in 1992, again featuring Poppin' Fresh, this time alongside a cupcake topped with Funfetti icing (at that time a fairly new Pillsbury product), and again the producer was Benjamin Medwin.

Advisor: Lil West (See Directory, Advertising)

Club: The Lovin' Connection
2343 10000 Rd.
Oswego, KS 67356; 316-795-2842

Bank, Poppin' Fresh, ceramic, 1980s mail-in premium, M **$35.00**
Beanie, Poppin' Fresh, 2 different styles, M, ea from $10 ....**$20.00**
Bowl, bread; Doughboy White Ceramic Line, embossed image, Benjamin Medwin, 1988, 16", rare, MIB, from $150 to **$200.00**
Bowls, mixing; Doughboy White Ceramic Line, embossed image, Benjamin Medwin/Portugal, 1988, scarce, set of 3, MIB **$75.00**

Canister, glass, clamp-on lid, from $18.00 to $25.00.

Canisters, Doughboy White Ceramic Line, embossed image, Benjamin Medwin, 1988, very scarce, set of 4, MIB, from $95 to..**$135.00**
Canisters, glass, marked Goodies w/image of Poppin' Fresh, glass or wooden knob, Anchor Hocking (unmarked), 1991, ea **$25.00**

Canisters, Poppin' Fresh Line, metal, mauve & blue on white, Benjamin Medwin, 1988, set of 4 ....**$100.00**
Cookie jar, Doughboy White Line, Benjamin Medwin, 1988, MIB **$50.00**
Cookie jar, Funfetti Line, Benjamin Medwin, 1991 .....**$50.00**
Cookie jar, Poppin' Fresh figure, ceramic, Cookies embossed across chest, 1973, 11", EX...............................**$75.00**
Creamer & sugar bowl w/spoon, Doughboy White Ceramic Line, 1988, MIB **$35.00**
Doll, Poppin' Fresh, stuffed cloth, pull-string talker, Mattel, 16", NM...**$100.00**
Doll, Poppin' Fresh, stuffed cloth, 1970s, 14", VG......**$15.00**
Doll, Poppin' Fresh, stuffed cloth, 1972, 11", EX, from $15 to **$20.00**
Doll, Poppin' Fresh, stuffed plush, 1982, M, from $40 to **$50.00**
Figure, Grandmommer, vinyl, 1974, 5", M, from $75 to....**$95.00**
Figure, Grandpopper, vinyl, 1974, 5¼", M, from $75 to...**$95.00**
Figure, Poppie Fresh, vinyl, 1972, 6", NM **$15.00**
Figure, Poppin' Fresh, cold-cast porcelain, set of 4 in various poses, 5", MIB **$60.00**
Figure, Poppin' Fresh, vinyl, 1971, 7", NM **$15.00**
Figure, Poppin' Fresh & Poppie, vinyl, on stands as a set, M, pr, from $35 to **$40.00**
Finger puppet, Biscuit (cat) or Flapjack (dog), vinyl, 1974, ea...**$35.00**
Finger puppet, Bun Bun (girl), Popper (boy), Poppie Fresh or Poppin' Fresh, vinyl, 1974, ea....................**$25.00**
Finger puppets, Poppin' Fresh & Pals, set of 3, rare, MIB...**$235.00**
Gumball machine, Poppin' Fresh, w/5 lbs of gum, MIB .**$300.00**
Jell-O mold, Doughboy White Ceramic Line, Benjamin Medwin/Portugal, 1988, MIB **$35.00**
Key chain, Poppin' Fresh figure, soft vinyl, MOC.........**$6.00**
Lotion/soap dispenser, Doughboy White Ceramic Line, embossed image, Benjamin Medwin, 1988, MIB..**$20.00**
Mug, ceramic, features Poppin' Fresh, 1985, 5", VG...**$15.00**
Mug, plastic Doughboy figure, 1979, 4½", from $10 to..**$15.00**
Mug, Poppin' Fresh Line, 1988 ....**$10.00**
Napkin holder, Doughboy White Ceramic Line, Benjamin Medwin, 1988, MIB..**$20.00**
Napkin holder, Funfetti Line, Benjamin Medwin, 1992, MIB..**$12.00**
Plant holder, Doughboy White Ceramic Line, Benjamin Medwin, 1988, MIB..**$25.00**
Playhouse, vinyl, w/4 finger puppets (Poppin' Fresh, Poppie, Popper & Bun Bun), 1974, rare, complete, from $250 to..**$300.00**
Pop-up can, Poppin' Fresh, blue version, EX **$300.00**
Pop-up can, Poppin' Fresh, orange version, M.........**$200.00**
Potpourri burner, Doughboy White Ceramic Line, Benjamin Medwin, 1988, rare, 3-pc, M **$50.00**
Salt & pepper shakers, ceramic, Poppin' Fresh, white w/blue details painted over glaze, 1969, 3½", EX, pr.......**$22.00**
Salt & pepper shakers, Funfetti Line, Poppin' Fresh & cupcake, 1992, MIB, pr **$20.00**
Salt & pepper shakers, plastic, Poppin' & Poppie Fresh, white w/blue details, dated 1974, 3½x4", pr **$25.00**

Salt & pepper shakers, range size, Doughboy White Ceramic Line, Benjamin Medwin, 1988, MIB, pr.................**$20.00**

Scouring pad holder w/pad, Dougboy White Ceramic Line, Benjamin Medwin, 1988, M **$20.00**

Soap dish, Poppie, Doughboy White Ceramic Line, Benjamin Medwin, 1988, M **$20.00**

Spoon holder, Funfetti Line, Benjamin Medwin, recent issue but dated 1988, MIB **$15.00**

Spoon rest, Doughboy White Ceramic Line, Poppin' & Poppie, Benjamin Medwin recent issue but dated 1988, MIB **$15.00**

Timer, plastic, digital, 1992, M....................................**$10.00**

Tool holder (no tools), Funfetti Line, Benjamin Medwin, 1992, 8", $12.00.

Tool holder w/tools, Doughboy White Ceramic Line, Benjamin Medwin, 1988..**$20.00**

Tool holder w/tools, Funfetti Line, Benjamin Medwin, 1992, MIB **$20.00**

Towel holder, Poppie, Doughboy White Ceramic Line, Benjamin Medwin, 1988, M **$25.00**

Towel holder, Poppin' Fresh, Doughboy White Ceramic Line, Benjamin Medwin, 1988, M **$25.00**

Towels, Poppin' Fresh Line, Cannon, 1988, 4-pc set, MIP **$30.00**

Trivet, Poppin' Fresh Line, 1988, M............................**$25.00**

Reddy Kilowatt

Reddy was developed during the late 1920s and became very well known during the '50s. His job was to promote electric power companies all over the United States, which he did with aplomb! Reddy memorabilia is highly collectible today, with the small-head plastic figures sometimes selling for $200.00 or more. On Reddy's 65th birthday (1992), a special 'one-time-only' line of commemoratives was issued. This line consisted of approximately thirty different items issued in crystal, gold, pewter, silver, etc. All items were limited editions and quite costly. Because of high collector demand, new merchandise is flooding the market. Watch for items such as a round mirror, a small hand-held game with movable squares, a ring-toss game, etc., marked 'Made in China.'

Advisor: Lee Garmon (See Directory, Advertising)

Ashtray, red pyro on clear glass, 3½" square, $18.00. (Photo courtesy Lee Garmon)

Charm, brass Reddy figure, on original card w/poem, c 1954, USA **$25.00**

Coaster, printed cardboard, 3½", from $5 to **$8.00**

Coloring book, PA Electric Co (PENELEC), 1960s, 14x10½", G...**$20.00**

Cookie cutter, red plastic Reddy head, 3"...................**$10.00**

Figure, hard rubber, 1930s, 3".......................................**$8.00**

Figure, lg head, red & white plastic on black outlet switchplate base, MCMLXI, 6", minimum value........**$150.00**

Figure, sm head, hands & feet, red & white plastic, on base (harder to find than lg-head version), 6", EX.....**$200.00**

Light switch, plastic glow-in-the-dark Reddy, MCMLXI, EX **$125.00**

Lighter, made in Japan for Price Associates, 2x1¼", EX (in original box)..**$40.00**

Measuring glass, shows Reddy holding logo above phrase, red on clear glass, 1930s, 4¾" **$42.00**

Napkins, set of 8, 1970, MIP..**$32.00**

Night light, Panelescent Sylvania, 3" dia, from $35 to ..**$40.00**

Note paper holder, 1" Reddy on 3x5" holder, Autopoint, EX **$25.00**

Plate, Syracuse China, 1950s, 7" **$85.00**

Playing cards, double deck, dated 1951, MIB.............**$45.00**

Postcard, 1¢, Reddy in cowboy hat, M **$8.00**

Recipe booklet, Take It Easy Recipes for Modern Homemakers, NM **$12.00**

Sign, diecut hardboard figure, red & white, 10x9", VG .**$115.00**

Sign, porcelain, No Tresspassing/company name lettered above Reddy Kilowatt, red & black on white, 11x16", M **$260.00**

Slide-tile puzzle, white w/red & blue graphics, reproduction, 3x3½" $10.00

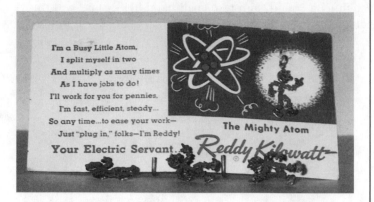

Pendant on original card, $35.00; Left to right (bottom): Stick pin: $18.00; Earrings, $25.00 for the pair.
(Photo courtesy Lee Garmon)

Smokey Bear

The year 1994 marked the 50th anniversary of Smokey Bear, the fire-prevention spokesbear for the State Foresters, Ad Council, and US Forest Service. After ruling out other mascots (including Bambi), by 1944 it had been decided that a bear was best suited for the job, and Smokey was born. When a little cub was rescued from a fire in a New Mexico national forest in 1950, Smokey's role intensified. Over the years his appearance has evolved from one a little more menacing to the lovable bear we know today.

The original act to protect the Smokey Bear image was enacted in 1974. The character name in the 'Smokey Bear Act' is Smokey Bear. Until the early 1960s, when his name appeared on items such as sheet music and Little Golden Books, it was 'Smokey *the* Bear.' Generally, from that time on, he became known as simply Smokey Bear.

Advisor: Glen Brady (See Directory, Advertising)

Ashtray, litho tin pail w/color image & Smokey Says Use Your Ashtray, clips on to chair or pole, 1960s, 4", unused, M..$50.00
Ashtray, metal bucket shape, Smokey Says Use Your Ashtray, for car use, from $20 to $25.00
Ashtray, Smokey standing w/shovel over campfire on cupped base, Norcrest, 3¾", MIB, $100 to.........$125.00
Bank, ceramic, white w/gold details, EX....................$60.00
Bank, ceramic figure, US Pat Off A-478, Norcrest, from $275 to..$300.00
Baseball cards, Smokey Bear's Fire Prevention Team, players Larry Sheets, Harold Baines & Jim Gartner, set of 3, 1987, M...$18.00
Bell, ceramic, Prevent Forest Fires on Smokey's sign, EX..$65.00
Belt buckle, cast metal, 2½x1¾"..................................$18.00
Blotter, I Will Be Careful, 1955, unused, EX.................$8.00
Bookmark, paper, Smokey & 8" ruler, dated 1961........$8.00

Candy jar, ceramic, unmarked Norcrest, from $400.00 to $425.00.
(Photo courtesy Fred and Joyce Roerig)

Coloring book, Whitman #1987, 1969, Smokey & friends on cover, unused, M $45.00
Doll, inflatable vinyl, MIP $245.00
Doll, 50th Anniversary, 12", MIB $30.00
Figurine, ceramic, holding remnants of burned tree, marked A-19, M $55.00
Game, Smokey Bear Put Out the Fires Pinball, Gordy, MOC .$15.00
Handkerchief, picnic scenes, 8", EX.............................$25.00
Magic slate, Watkins-Strathmore, 1969, EX $85.00
Plate, Smokey & friends in center, Melmac, 7", NM ...$25.00
Scarf, cotton, 12x12", EX..$20.00
Sign, cardboard, Flick Your Bick Carefully in My Woods, late 1970s, NM...$25.00
Spoon, plastic w/figural handle, M $12.50

Snap!, Crackle!, and Pop!

Rice Krispies, the talking cereal, was first marketed by Kellogg's in 1928. Capitalizing on the sounds the cereal made in milk, the company chose elves named 'Snap,' 'Crackle,' and 'Pop' as their logos a few years later. The first of the Rice Krispie dolls were introduced in 1948. These were 12" tall, printed on fabric for the consumer to sew and stuff. The same dolls in a 16" size were offered in 1954. Premiums and memorabilia of many types followed over the years; all are very collectible.

Advisor: Scott Bruce (See Directory, Advertising)

Binoculars, paper & plastic, 1980s, MIP......................$10.00
Canteen, yellow, white & red plastic, 1973, NM.........$25.00
Dolls, Snap!, Crackle!, or Pop!, stuffed cloth bodies w/vinyl heads, Rushton, 18", EX, ea $30.00
Dolls, Snap! Crackle! & Pop!, images stamped on cloth, uncut, set of 3, 1948, NM+..................................$160.00

Dolls, Crackle!, mint in box, $55.00; Pop! and Snap!, no box, $25.00 each. (Photo courtesy June Moon)

Hand puppets, cloth bodies w/soft plastic heads, felt hands, set of 3, 1950s, 8½", VG+..$75.00
Key chain, metal, paper & plastic, 1980s, EX.............$10.00
Parade drum, shows Snap!, Crackle!, Pop! & Toucan Sam, 4x9" dia, EX...$5.00
Ring, soft rubber face makes different expressions w/spinning dial, brass band, 1950s, EX $175.00
Salt & pepper shakers, ceramic Snap! & Pop! figures, Japan, 1950s, 2½", EX, pr...$85.00
Squeeze toy, plastic, 1978, EX....................................$35.00
Sticker, glow-in-the-dark paper, 1971, M $10.00

Tony the Tiger

Kellogg's introduced Tony the Tiger in 1953, and since then he's appeared on every box of their Frosted Flakes. In his deep, rich voice, he's convinced us all that they are indeed 'Gr-r-r-reat'!

Advisor: Scott Bruce (See Directory, Advertising)

Bank, plastic figure in orange, white & black, 1968, 9¼", EX...$50.00
Book, Coloring Fun, w/4 crayons, 1989, MIP $3.00
Design maker, Kooky Doodle, 1984, MIP....................$10.00
Doll, Bean Bag Bunch, w/tag, Kellogg's, MIP..............$9.00
Doll, plush, mail-in premium, 1997, 8" $8.00
Doll, squeeze vinyl, Product People, 1970s, 9", NM+..$100.00
Doll, stuffed cloth, 1973, 14", EX...............................$40.00
Duffle bag, cream, picture on front & back, drawstring closure, 17", EX...$10.00
Hat, plush w/paper tiger face & plush tail, mail-in premium, 1970s, child size, EX...$28.00
License plate for bicycle, orange plastic, 1973, 3x5", EX+...$12.00
Pen, Tony's Secret Message, 1980s, M..........................$3.00
Place mat, vinyl, characters on both sides, 1981, EX..$10.00

Plastic container, Kellogg Co., 1968, EX, from $75.00 to $95.00. (Photo courtesy Fred and Joyce Roerig)

Poster, Meet Tony on Tour, paper, 1989, 14x18", NM...$5.00
Radio, plastic figure w/name on base, Kellogg's premium, 1980, 7", NMIB $40.00
Valentine cards, set of 30, 1986, MIB $10.00

Miscellaneous

AC Spark Plugs, doll, AC man w/1 arm extended & other hand on hip, white & green w/AC on chest, green hat, 6", EXIB $160.00
AC Spark Plugs, doll, Sparky the Horse, inflatable vinyl w/logo, Ideal, 1960s, 25x15" L, EX.....................$100.00
Alka-Seltzer, bank, Speedy figure, vinyl, 5½", EX, minimum value $200.00
Alka-Seltzer, doll, Speedy, vinyl, 1960, 8", EX, from $500 to $700.00
Bazooka Bubble Gum, doll, Bazooka Joe, stuffed cloth, 1973, EX...$20.00

Blue Bonnet, bank, Blue Bonnet Sue, 1989, Nabisco, 8", from $30.00 to $35.00. (Photo courtesy Beverly and Jim Mangus)

Bosco Chocolate, doll, Bosco the Clown, vinyl, NM ..$45.00
Buster Brown Shoes, doll, Buster Brown, stuffed cloth, 1974, 14", NM...$40.00

Buster Brown Shoes, kite, 1940s, NM **$40.00**

Butterfinger Candy Bar, doll, Butterfinger Bear, stuffed plush, 1987, 15", M..**$22.50**

Cheer Detergent, doll, Cheer Girl, plastic w/cloth clothes, Proctor & Gamble, 1960, 10", NM **$20.00**

Cheetos, doll Chester Cheetah, stuffed plush, 18", EX...**$20.00**

Chiquita Bananas, salt & pepper shakers, ceramic, unmarked, 3", pr **$10.00**

Chucky Cheese Pizza, bank, vinyl Chucky Cheese figure, 7", EX..**$10.00**

Crayola Crayons, doll, Crayola Bear, stuffed plush, various colors, Graphics International, 1986, 6", NM, ea ..**$10.00**

Dairy Queen, salt & pepper shakers, ceramic figures of the Dairy Queen girls, 1960s, 4", EX, pr **$150.00**

Del Monte, bank, Big Top Bonanza Clown, plastic, 1985, 7", M, from $10 to **$15.00**

Del Monte, doll, Country Yumkin, Fruits or Veggies, stuffed plush, 1980s, 8" & 11", M, ea from $10 to............**$15.00**

Del Monte, doll, Shoo Shoo Scarecrow, 1983, stuffed plush, NM **$15.00**

Del Monte, lunch bag, features Del Monte Chipmunks, heavy nylon, 1992, unused, NM **$8.00**

Dow Brands, bank, Scrubbing Bubble, mail-in premium, 4¾", from $20.00 to $22.00. (Photo courtesy Beverly and Jim Mangus)

Energizer Batteries, doll, Energizer Bunny, plush, battery-operated, 24", M..**$45.00**

Energizer Batteries, squeeze light, Energizer Bunny figure, MIP (sealed) **$8.00**

Fisk Tires, bank, Fisk Tire Boy, plaster, all-white yawning figure standing w/tire & holding a candle, 1970s, 8½", NM **$130.00**

Florida Oranges, bank, Orange Bird, vinyl, 1974, MIP ..**$40.00**

Frito-Lay, eraser, Frito Bandito figural pencil topper, 1960s, 1½", M **$20.00**

Hamburger Helper, doll, Helping Hand, plush glove-like figure w/facial features on palm, 14", M...................**$10.00**

Hawaiian Punch, yo-yo, plastic butterfly shape w/image of Punchy, Imperial Toy, 1996, MIB **$6.00**

Icee, bank, Icee bear w/drink in front of him, rubber, 7", EX..**$30.00**

Icee, ring, Icee Bear, EX..**$15.00**

Jell-O, puppet, Mr Wiggle, red vinyl, 1966, M **$150.00**

Jif Peanut Butter, periscope, features Jifaroo the kangaroo, yellow cardboard, 1950s, 20", EX.......................**$25.00**

Jordache, doll, Jeans Man, Mego, 12", MIB **$30.00**

Keebler, cap, cotton baseball type w/Ernie the Keebler Elf embroidered on front, NM **$7.00**

Keebler, napkin holder, Ernie the Keebler Elf, from $10.00 to $15.00. (Photo courtesy Fred and Joyce Roerig)

Kodak, doll, Colorkins, stuffed, ca 1990, 8" to 10", ea..**$20.00**

Kool Cigarettes, salt & pepper shakers, plastic Willie & Millie penguins w/embossed names, 1950s, VG (VG box), pr..**$65.00**

Lee Jeans, doll, Buddy Lee as train engineer in Lee overalls, blue shirt & blue & white striped hat marked Lee, 13", EX **$180.00**

Little Caesar's, doll, Pizza Pizza Man, plush, holding pizza slice, 1990, EX...**$5.00**

Little Caesar's, picnic jug, lg w/image of Pizza Pizza man & Coke emblems, 1991, EX...**$5.00**

Meow Mix, figure, vinyl cat, EX **$35.00**

Mott's Apple Juice, doll, Apple of My Eye Bear, stuffed plush, 1988, M **$15.00**

Mr Goodbar, pillow, shaped like candy bar, 4x6", NM...**$8.00**

Mr Softee, license plate from ice cream truck, embossed color litho on metal w/logo & Mr Softee image, 1960s, 4x12", EX+ **$65.00**

Nestle Chocolate, doll, Chocolate Man, stuffed cloth, Chase Bag Co, 1970, 15", EX **$20.00**

Nestle Quik, doll, Quik Bunny, plush, 1980s mail-in, M...**$25.00**

Oscar Mayer, bank, Wienermobile, plastic, 1988, 10", M...**$25.00**

Ralston Purina, figure, Magic Pup, plastic w/painted features, cloth ears, w/ring that moves Pup's mouth, 1951, 3", NM...**$100.00**

Reese's, doll, Reese's Bear, in Reese's T-shirt, 1989, NM+..**$10.00**

Sambo's Restaurant, Family Funbook/Fun, Games & Puzzles/Featuring JT & the Tiger Kids, 1978, EX.**$32.00**

Sinclair Oil, soap, Dino the Dinosaur figure, MIB **$10.00**

Sprite, doll, Lucky Lymon, vinyl talker, 1990s, 7½", M ..**$25.00**

Sunbeam Bread, doll, Little Miss Sunbeam, vinyl w/rooted hair, cotton dress w/white apron, Eegee, 1959, 17", NM...**$50.00**

Swiss Miss Chocolate, doll, Swiss Miss, stuffed cloth w/vinyl face & yellow yarn hair, EX, minimum value.......**$25.00**

Tastee Freeze, doll, Miss Tastee Freeze, hard plastic, 1950s, 7", NM...**$20.00**

Tropicana Orange Juice, doll, Tropic-Ana, stuffed cloth, 1977, 17", NM...**$35.00**

Tupperware, doll, stuffs into satin Tupperware bowl, 13", M...**$25.00**

Tyson Chicken, doll, Chicken Quick, stuffed cloth, 13", VG...**$15.00**

Vlasic Pickles, doll, Stork, fluffy white fur w/glasses & bow tie, Trudy Toys, 1989, 22", NM **$30.00**

Advertising Tins

In her book *Modern Collectible Tins* (Collector Books), Linda McPherson declares these colorful, very attractive tin containers an official new area of collecting. There are so many of these 'new' tins around, though (she warns), that you'll probably want to narrow your choices down to either a specific type of product or company to avoid being inundated with them! She says the best of the lot are usually those offered as mail-in premiums and suggests we avoid buying tins with paper labels and plastic lids. Besides the esthetics factor, condition and age also help determine price. The values suggested below represent what you might pay in an antique store for tins in mint condition. But what makes this sort of collecting so much fun is that you'll find them much cheaper at garage sales, Goodwill Stores, and flea markets.

Advisor: Linda McPherson (See Directory, Advertising)

Newsletter: *Tinfax*
Jeannie Tucker
205 Broiley Woods Dr.
Woodstock, GA 30189
Subscription: $25 for 4 issues

American Licorice Co Stick Licorice, tall box w/hinged lid, yellow, black & white graphics, 7", from $6 to....**$10.00**

Andes Mints, octagonal box, Christmas graphics, 1994, 6x5", from $5 to...**$8.00**

Armour's Pork Tenderloins, round canister, yellow & blue, 6", from $20 to......................................**$25.00**

Bassett's Allsorts Liquorice, tall box w/canted corners, multi-colored graphics on dark blue background, 7", from $5 to...**$8.00**

Black Forest Gummy Bears, round canister w/bear & forest graphics, 1990, 6", from $8 to...............**$12.00**

Burma Shave Mug, Brush & Soap Set, tall box, red w/product graphics, 5¾", from $8 to **$12.00**

Cadbury's Roses Chocolates, heart shape, pink roses & white lettering on bright blue background, 9x10", from $10 to..**$14.00**

Charles Chips, round canister, red w/round drawing of girl's head, 1990, 9½", from $18 to **$22.00**

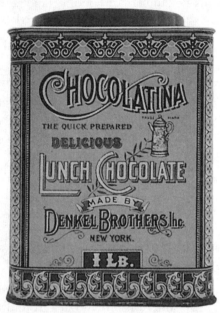

Chocolatina by Denkel Brothers Inc., Lunch Chocolate, 5¾x4x4", from $10.00 to $14.00. (Photo courtesy Linda McPherson)

Chupa Chups Fruit Lollipops, paint can shape w/bail handle, fruit on white w/blue & white borders, 7¾", from $14 to **$18.00**

Chupa Chups Ice Cream Flavored Lollipops, milk can shape, no bail handle, 6¼", from $10 to **$12.00**

Churchill's Cream Toffee, round carousel shape w/pointed lid, embossed carousel figures on sides, 5½", from $10 to...**$14.00**

Crayola, box, red 1992 Holiday Tin w/boy & girl coloring under Christmas tree, 3x6x6", from $10 to **$12.00**

Eight O'Clock Coffee, tall can, red w/product graphics, white coffee grinder lettered Ground To Order, 7", from $15 to **$20.00**

Empire Sewing Thread, spool shape w/thread & needle graphics, logo on top, blue, green, or red, 5¾", from $20 to...**$25.00**

Famous Amos Home Style Cookies, flat round, name above Black man in tropical shirt & hat, 3½x8" dia, from $10 to...**$14.00**

Four Star Kitchen Pretzels, round canister w/red, white & blue diamond graphics, 10", from $10 to **$14.00**

Fralinger's Original Salt Water Taffy, flat round, girl in swim cap surrounded by ocean waves, 3½x5½", from $6 to...**$10.00**

Hershey's Chocolate, football shape w/Superbowl XXIX paper label, Wilson & Official NFL logos, 1993, 3x5x7", from $10 to..**$12.00**

Hershey's Chocolate Dipped Pretzels, flat round, red w/Max the Moose graphics, 1993, 3x8" dia, from $10 to...**$14.00**

Hershey's Cocoa, round canister w/child in cocoa bean on white, gold lettering & trim, Cheinco, 7¼", from $15 to.............................**$20.00**

Hershey's Fun Tin/Snack Size Bar Assortment, tall round, candybar & confetti graphics on pink, 1991, 8¼", from $6 to.............................**$8.00**

Iams Eukanuba Cat Food, octagonal box, painter's image of cats by window w/lake scene beyond, 1997, 11¾", from $7 to.............................**$10.00**

Iams Nutritional Sample Pak, flat box, image of 3 cats, 2¾x6x6", from $5 to.............................**$7.00**

Jelly Belly, jelly bean shape, yellow & red graphics on white, 2¼x3½x6", from $6 to.............................**$8.00**

Kellogg's Froot Loops, tall box, Toucan Sam & bowl of cereal on red-orange background, 1984, 6½", from $14 to.............................**$18.00**

Kit Kat, candy bar shape, 1995, 2¼x5¼x9¼", from $12 to.**$14.00**

Levi & Strauss & Co Belt, flat round, w/early jeans logo, 2½x5½" dia, from $6 to.............................**$8.00**

Life Savers, round canister w/package graphics, 10¼", from $10 to.............................**$12.00**

Lucky Charms, tall box, leprechaun performing magic on bowl of Lucky Charms on red background, 5¼", from $4 to.............................**$7.00**

M&M's Cookies, flat round, 3 M&M's characters w/cookies & candy on brown background, 4¼x10" dia, from $12 to.............................**$16.00**

M&M's Peanut Chocolate Candies, round canister w/Vote '88 & July 4th graphics, 6", from $6 to.............................**$10.00**

Maltesers, oblong box w/hinged lid, white name & candy graphics on red w/gold trim, 2x4x11" L, from $8 to.............................**$12.00**

Maxwell House High Grade Coffee, round canister w/picture of building, blue w/trim top & bottom, 7½", minimum value.............................**$35.00**

Maxwell House Slow Roasted Coffee, tall box, dark blue w/1892 graphics, 1992, 6¾", from $10 to.............................**$14.00**

Mickey & Pals Adhesive Bandages, box w/flip tip, white w/Dr Mickey & Donald Duck bandaging Goofy, 4", from $3 to.............................**$5.00**

Milky Way Snack Bars, round canister, green w/white stars on blue panel, gold trim, 32-oz, 6", from $6 to ...**$10.00**

Morton's Free Running Salt, round canister, white lettering on blue, white lid, 5", from $4 to.............................**$7.00**

Nestle Goobers, box w/canted corners, blue w/white name on diagonal band, graphics top & bottom, 2x6x8", from $12 to.............................**$14.00**

Nestle Semi-Sweet Toll House Morsels, round canister, yellow w/package graphics, Cheinco, 7½", from $15 to.............................**$20.00**

Oreo Cookies, cookie shape w/blue paper label, 1992, 2x10" dia, from $12 to.............................**$16.00**

Post Grape-Nuts, flat box, 1925 breakfast graphics on yellow background, 3½x8x6¼", from $14 to.............................**$18.00**

Quaker Corn Meal, round canister, yellow w/graphics, red lid, The Best in Every Way, Cheinco, 7½", from $18 to.............................**$22.00**

Ritz Crackers, tall box, Limited Edition, red, 1986, 8¾", from $12 to.............................**$16.00**

Rose Brand Sugar, round canister, rose graphics & red name on white, green lid, 5¼", from $5 to.............................**$8.00**

Schwan's Ice Cream, round canister, white w/brown & yellow logo & graphics, 10¼", from $18 to.............................**$22.00**

Sun-Maid Oatmeal Raisin Cookies, box w/rounded corners, red w/raised logo & cookie graphics, 4x6x8", from $10 to.............................**$14.00**

Wessex Cake Co, oblong box w/delivery truck graphics, 7x7½x13½", from $25 to.............................**$30.00**

Whitman's Sampler, box w/rounded corners, hinged lid, yellow w/sampler graphics, 2x6x8½", from $20 to.............................**$25.00**

Woolco Creamy Mints, flat round, red w/name in diamond, yellow trim, 2x4¼x2¾", from $20 to.............................**$25.00**

Zesta Saltines, Keebler, 8x4½x4½", from $14.00 to $18.00. (Photo courtesy Linda McPherson)

Advertising Watches

The concept of the advertising watch is strictly twentieth century. Some were produced through the 1960s, but it wasn't until the early 1970s that watches were increasingly used for advertising. Now, many themes, subjects, and types are available. Collectible ad watches include mechanical/battery-operated pocket watches; mechanical/battery-operated wristwatches; digital/analog (with hands) watches; dress/sports watches; company logo/character watches; corporate/in-house watches; catalog/store retail watches; and giveaway/premium watches.

Condition, originality, cleanliness, scarcity, completeness, cross-collectibility, and buyer demand all affect value. The more recently issued the watch, the better its condition must be. Original mint packaging (including any paperwork) can triple value. Look for original watch offers and order forms on old packaging and magazines; they are desirable for documentation and are collectible in their own right. Look through 'parts boxes'; an old, nonworking ad pocket or wristwatch, even without a strap, may have value. A higher degree of wear is acceptable on an older watch.

A popular character/event will add value. Currently, demand is good for some '70s characters such as Mr. Peanut and Charlie the Tuna, the '80s – '90s M&M watches, and the '90s Pillsbury Doughboy. Demand for a watch that features a forgotten or less popular character may be limited, even if it is an older one, and value could be affected.

Great numbers of watches exist for Coca-Cola, Pepsi, various automobiles, Camel, and other tobacco products. These are usually of most interest to collectors who specialize in those fields. A 'reverse attitude' may exist — the more watches produced for a theme or character, the less desirable it is to the typical ad watch collector.

Copyright dates can lead to confusion about the age of a watch. The date may refer to the publishing date of the character or logo, not the year the watch was made. Date watches by style and features. Generally analog watches are more collectible than digital. A watch need not be working; most are not of high quality. Examine watches displayed in glass cases at outdoor shows for signs of moisture buildup and sun fading. Remove dead batteries only if you can do so without damaging the watch or packaging.

Common watches that currently have little value are the 1984 Ronald McDonald House — Coca-Cola carded watches, the 1995 Kodak Lion King, Life Cereals Mask and Where's Waldo watches, and all the Burger King, McDonald's, and Taco Bell watches for various movies.

Advisor: Sharon Iranpour (See Directory, Advertising Watches)

Newsletter: The Premium Watch Watch©
Sharon Iranpour, Editor
24 San Rafael Dr.
Rochester, NY 14618-3702; 716-381-9467 or fax: 716-383-9248; e-mail: watcher1@rochester.rr.com

Uncle Sam Kodak Election Watches, 1972 and 1988. One of three (Uncle Sam, Republican Party elephant, Democratic Party donkey) issued for both election years. Watches from 1972 were mechanical with red, white, and blue nylon straps; the offer was published in *Life*. Three film proofs of purchase and $4.95 were required for each. In 1988, each battery-operated watch was free with six film proofs of purchase. 1972 value: $25.00 MIB; 1988 value: $10.00 for mint.
(Photo courtesy Sharon Iranpour)

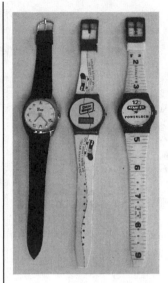

Logo watches: 1970s mechanical La Choy Foods with Chinese numbers, VG, $20.00; 1994 Oscar Mayer digital with famous jingle on the strap, M, $12.00; mid-1980s Stanley Powerlock tape measure watch, M, $45.00. (Photo courtesy Sharon Iranpour)

1976 Ritz Cracker and Tony the Tiger. Though often listed as scarce and valuable, these turn up regularly mint in the box and rarely sell for more than $200.00 each. (Photo courtesy Sharon Iranpour)

Mint-in-the-box examples: the Westinghouse Refrigerator pocket watch celebrates electrical efficiency (mint, value $75.00 each). Both a wristwatch and a pocket watch exist for the 1982 World's Fair (mint, $25.00 each). An original box in excellent condition can triple the value of a watch. (Photo courtesy Sharon Iranpour)

Pre-1970s

Many mechanical pocket and wristwatches are known; most appeal to 'masculine' interests and professions such as automobiles and related products. As early as the 1920s, Chevrolet gave wristwatches to top-performing salesmen; the watch case was in the shape of a car radiator front. Many commemorative watches were issued for special events like world's fairs.

Buster Brown Pocket Watch, 1928, EX **$175.00**

Buster Brown Pocket Watch, 1960s, VG.....................$75.00

Chevrolet Salesman's Award Wristwatch, 1927, EX...$400.00

FS Fertilizer Pocket Watch, G $35.00

Mr Peanut Wristwatch, yellow face, 1966, VG............$50.00

Mr Peanut Wristwatch, yellow face w/date window, 1967, VG...$50.00

NY World's Fair Ingraham Pocket Watch, 1939, VG.$500.00

Red Goose Shoes Wristwatch, 1960s, G.......................$130.00

Reddy Kilowatt Pocket Watch, 1930s, VG $250.00

Rexall Ingersoll Pocket Watch, 1908, EX $150.00

Shell Oil Girard-Perregaux Pocket Watch, 1940s, VG $350.00

St Louis World's Fair Ingersoll Pocket Watch, 1904, EX..$200.00

Toppie Elephant, 1950s, G...$100.00

Twinkie the Brown Shoe Elf, 1920s, G.......................$100.00

The 1970s

The most common were mechanicals with a heavy metal case, often marked Swiss Made. Some had wide straps with snaps or straps with holes. Mechanical digital watches and revolving disks appeared. As a general rule, special packaging had not been created. Wristwatches from the '70s are appearing at Internet auction sites and at shows in greater frequency due to growing interest. They are generally valued from $75.00 to $300.00 in very good to mint condition. Watches listed in this section are all mechanical wristwatches.

Big Boy, watch hands are arms, 1970, EX...................$75.00

Buster Brown, red costume, 1970s, VG $75.00

Charlie the Tuna, faces left, 1971, VG $50.00

Charlie the Tuna, faces right, 1973, VG $50.00

Count Chocula, Booberry & Frankenberry, Layfayette Watch Company, MIB $300.00

Ernie Keebler, 1970s, G..$50.00

Goodyear Tires, revolving disk, 1970s, G...................$50.00

Goofy Grape, 1976, G...$200.00

Mr Peanut, blue face, mechanical, digital, 1975, EX...$50.00

Punchy, mechanical, digital, red strap, 1970s, VG $50.00

Raid Bug Spray, revolving disk, 1970s, EX................$150.00

Ritz Cracker, 1971, MIB..$200.00

Ronald McDonald, 1970s, MIB $50.00

Scrubbing Bubbles, 1970s, VG.....................................$50.00

The 1980s

Digital and analog battery-operated watches became the norm; mechanicals all but disappeared early in the decade. Watches became slim and lightweight with plastic commonly used for both the case and the strap. Electronic hands (visible only when the battery is good), clam shell and pop-up digital watches appeared; revolving disks were frequently used. Toward the end of the decade, printing on straps began. Specially designed packaging became more commonplace. Hanger cards added design to otherwise plain digital watches. These are most desirable in excellent, unopened

condition. Watches from the 1980s are generally valued from $10.00 to $50.00 in mint condition. Watches listed in this section are battery operated unless noted otherwise.

Bart Simpson, by Butterfingers Candy, M...................$20.00

Brach's Peppermint, 1980s, MIB.................................$15.00

Campbell Kids, mechanical windup, 4 different, 1982, MIB (w/slip cover), ea..$75.00

Captain Midnight, by Ovaltine, 1988, M $40.00

Charlie the Tuna, 25th Anniversary, 1986, MIB..........$25.00

Cherry 7UP, 1980s, M $15.00

Kellogg's Atlantis Do & Learn Set, 1983, MIB $25.00

Kraft Cheese & Macaroni Club, 1980s, M $10.00

M&Ms, various, 1980s, M $25.00

Max Headroom, by Coca-Cola, 1987, man's/lady's, M...$10.00

Swiss Miss, mechanical windup, 1981, EX..................$50.00

Welch's Grape Juice, 1989, M $20.00

The 1990s

Case and strap design became innovative. New features were holograms on the watch face, revolving subdials, 'talking' features, water watches (liquid within case/straps), stopwatches and timers, game watches, giga pets, and clip-on clocks. Classic and retro styling became popular. Very well designed packaging including special boxes and printed tins became more common as did printed plastic straps. Clear printed resin straps (Swatch type) and diecut rubber straps emerged. Companies created their own retail catalogs and websites to sell logo merchandise. Licensing agreements produced many tie-ins with movies, TV, and sports events. Most plastic watches currently sell in the $5.00 to $15.00 range; there is little market for the most common. Quality, hard-to-find gold- and silver-tone watches rarely sell beyond $25.00 at the present.

Campbell Kids Vegetable Soup Watch, 1994, M..........$50.00

Dunkin Donuts, 1999, M..$10.00

Eggo Waffles Eggosaurus, 1990, M..............................$15.00

Kool Aid Hologram, 1991, M.......................................$15.00

Kraft Superbowl XXX, watch in goal post box, 1996, MIB $20.00

Mars Snicker's Anniversary, 1990, M $35.00

Mr Magoo, by Nutrasweet, 1995, M $30.00

Oreo Cookie Watch, 1998, M..$50.00

Pillsbury Doughboy Talking Watch, 1996, M $15.00

Quaker Chewy Granola Bars Wildlife Hologram Watch, 1993, M $5.00

The 2000s

At the turn of the twenty-first century, millennium ad watches were eagerly sought by collectors; it is unlikely any more will be made. Fewer premiums are being offered new on specially marked packages or on store forms. More offers and retail watches are appearing on Internet websites.

Online auction sites, primarily eBay, make it easier to find older watches, newer regional pieces, and corporate in-house watches from special projects or events.

Airline Memorabilia

Even before the Wright brothers' historic flight prior to the turn of the century, people have been fascinated with flying. What better way to enjoy the evolution and history of this amazing transportation industry than to collect its memorabilia. Today just about any item ever used or made for a commercial (non-military) airline is collectible, especially dishes, glasswares, silver serving pieces and flatware, wings and badges worn by the crew, playing cards, and junior wings given to passengers. Advertising items such as timetables and large travel agency plane models are also widely collected. The earlier, the better! Anything prewar is good; items from before the 1930s are rare and often very valuable.

See also Restaurant China.

Advisor: Dick Wallin (See Directory, Airline)

Book, Your Future As a Airline Stewardess, paperback, 1961, 158 pages, 4x7", EX **$35.00**
Desk model, Fairchild F-27 Friendship, chromed cast metal, on cast teardrop stand, 18" L, 22" wingspan, EX.......**$385.00**
Garmet bag, Braniff Airline, Dallas Cowboys helmet logo, black w/white letters, 1970s, 40x22", EX **$35.00**
Label, Cuban Airlines, red, white & blue graphics w/airplane, 1930s, 1¾x5", VG..**$40.00**

Napkins, Eastern Airlines, The Great Silver Fleet, two different for $15.00 each. (Photo courtesy Dick Wallin)

Pin, 10-year service, Boeing, 10k gold w/red stone, early screw-type back, EX..**$35.00**
Plate, collector; Pan American, made by Bauscher, 6 different designs, EX, ea, from $45 to.................................**$65.00**
Playing cards, China Southern, blue, M (sealed) **$65.00**
Playing cards, Mohawk Airlines, 20th Anniversary, 1945-65, complete, VG+ (in case) **$30.00**
Postcard, NC-4 flying boat, ca 1919, unused, EX........**$37.50**
Schedule, Official Airline Guide Worldwide Airline, fares & info, October 1952, missing back cover o/w VG.**$70.00**
Silverware, American Airlines Flagship, w/DC-3 nose on handle, VG, ea pc..**$25.00**

Akro Agate

Everybody remembers the 'Aggie' marbles from their childhood; this is the company that made them. They operated in West Virginia from 1914 until 1951, and in addition to their famous marbles they made children's dishes as well as many types of novelties — flowerpots, powder jars with scottie dogs on top, candlesticks, and ashtrays, for instance — in many colors and patterns. Though some of their glassware was made in solid colors, their most popular products were made of the same swirled colors as their marbles. Nearly everything they produced is marked with their logo: a crow flying through the letter 'A' holding an Aggie in its beak and one in each claw. Some children's dishes may be marked 'JP,' and the novelty items may instead carry one of these trademarks: 'JV Co, Inc,' 'Braun & Corwin,' 'NYC Vogue Merc Co USA,' 'Hamilton Match Co,' and 'Mexicali Pickwick Cosmetic Corp.'

In the children's dinnerware listings below, you'll notice that color is an important worth-assessing factor. As a general rule, an item in green or white opaque is worth only about one-third as much when compared to the same item in any other opaque color. Marbleized pieces are about three times higher than solid opaques, and of the marbleized colors, blue is the most valuable. It's followed closely by red, with green about 25% under red. Lemonade and oxblood is a good color combination, and it's generally three times higher, item for item, than the transparent colors of green or topaz.

For further study we recommend *The Collector's Encyclopedia of Children's Dishes* by Margaret and Kenn Whitmyer.

Club: Akro Agate Collectors Club
Roger Hardy
10 Bailey St., Clarksburg, WV 26301-2524; 304-624-4523

Chiquita, cup, baked-on colors, 1½"............................**$6.00**
Chiquita, teapot, baked-on colors, w/lid, 3"...............**$22.00**
Chiquita, 16-pc set, opaque green, MIB **$60.00**
Concentric Rib, cup, opaque colors other than green or white, 1¼" **$8.00**
Concentric Rib, saucer, opaque colors other than green or white, 2¾" **$2.50**

Concentric Rib, teapot and lid, green and white opaque, 3⅜", $14.00. (Photo courtesy Margaret and Kenn Whitmyer)

Concentric Rib, teapot, opaque colors other than green or white, w/lid, 3⅜" **$18.00**
Concentric Rib, 10-pc set, opaque green or white, MIB ..**$55.00**
Concentric Ring, lg, creamer, any opaque color, 1⅜" ...**$16.00**
Concentric Ring, lg, plate, solid opaque colors, 4¼" **$7.00**
Concentric Ring, lg, 21-pc set, solid opaque colors, MIB..**$350.00**
Concentric Ring, sm, cup, transparent colbalt, 1¼" **$30.00**
Concentric Ring, sm, saucer, any opaque color, 2¾"....**$3.50**

Interior Panel, American Maid Tea Set, marbleized green and white, 21-piece set, MIB, $550.00.

Interior Panel, lg, cereal bowl, lemonade & oxblood, 3⅜"..**$45.00**
Interior Panel, lg, cup, transparent green, 1⅜"..............**$9.00**
Interior Panel, lg, plate, marbleized green & white, 4¼"..**$18.00**
Interior Panel, lg, 21-pc set, pink & green lustre, MIB ..**$320.00**
Interior Panel, sm, cup, azure blue or yellow, 1¼" **$30.00**
Interior Panel, sm, plate, azure blue or yellow, 3¾" ..**$10.00**
Interior Panel, sm, sugar bowl, transparent green, topaz or green lustre, 1¼"..**$20.00**

Interior Panel, sm, 8-pc set, marebleized red & white, MIB **$150.00**
Interior Panel, sm, 16-pc set, pink lustre, MIB..........**$180.00**
Miss America, creamer, white w/decal, 1¼"...............**$65.00**
Miss America, plate, orange & white, 4½".................**$45.00**
Miss America, sugar bowl, white, w/lid, 2" **$80.00**
Miss America, 17-pc set, forest green, MIB **$700.00**
Octagonal, lg, creamer, beige or pumpkin, closed handle, 1½"..**$15.00**
Octagonal, lg, plate, green or white, 4¼".....................**$4.00**
Octagonal, lg, teapot, pink, yellow or other opaque colors, closed handles, 3⅝"......................................**$20.00**
Octagonal, sm, cup, lime green, 1¼"..........................**$27.00**
Octagonal, sm, tumbler, pumpkin or yellow, 2" **$20.00**
Raised Daisy, cup, blue, 1¼"....................................**$100.00**
Raised Daisy, teapot, yellow, 2⅜"..............................**$45.00**
Stacked Disc, lg, pitcher, green or white, 2⅞"............**$18.00**
Stacked Disc, lg, 21-pc set, solid opaque colors, MIB..**$370.00**
Stacked Disc, sm, creamer, opaque colors other than green or white, 1¼"..**$16.00**
Stacked Disc, sm, teapot, opaque green or white, w/lid, 3⅜"..**$15.00**
Stacked Disc & Interior Panel, lg, 21-pc set, any opaque color, MIB..**$425.00**
Stacked Disc & Interior Panel, sm, creamer, marbleized blue, 1¼"..**$45.00**
Stacked Disc & Interior Panel, sm, cup, pumpkin, 1¼"..**$16.00**
Stacked Disc & Interior Panel, sm, plate, transparent green, 3¼"..**$9.00**
Stacked Disc & Interior Panel, sm, saucer, marbleized blue, 2¾"..**$14.00**
Stacked Disc & Interior Panel, sm, tumbler, transparent green, 2" **$20.00**
Stacked Disc & Interior Panel, sm, 7-pc water set, transparent green, MIB..**$100.00**
Stippled Band, lg, cup, transparent azure, 1½"..........**$25.00**
Stippled Band, lg, saucer, transparent azure, 3¼".......**$12.00**
Stippled Band, lg, sugar bowl, transparent green, w/lid, 1⅞"..**$27.00**
Stippled Band, lg, 17-pc set, transparent green, MIB..**$160.00**
Stippled Band, sm, cup, transparent amber, 1¼" **$8.00**
Stippled Band, sm, sugar bowl, transparent green, 1¼" ..**$35.00**
Stippled Band, sm, 7-pc set, transparent green, MIB..**$70.00**

Aluminum

The aluminum items which have become today's collectibles range from early brite-cut giftware and old kitchen wares to furniture and hammered aluminum cooking pans. But the most collectible, right now, at least, is the giftware of the 1930s through the 1950s.

There were probably several hundred makers of aluminum accessories and giftware with each developing their preferred method of manufacturing. Some pieces were cast; other products were hammered with patterns created by either an intaglio method or repoussé. Machine embossing was utilized by some makers; many used faux hammering, and lightweight items were often decorated with pressed designs.

As early as the 1940s, collectors began to seek out aluminum, sometimes to add to the few pieces received as wedding gifts. By the late 1970s and early 1980s, aluminum giftware was found in abundance at almost any flea market, and prices of $1.00 or less were normal. As more shoppers became enthralled with the appearance of this lustrous metal and its patterns, prices began to rise and have not yet peaked for the products of some companies. A few highly prized pieces have brought prices of four or five hundred dollars and occasionally even more.

One of the first to manufacture this type of ware was Wendell August Forge, when during the late 1920s they expanded their line of decorative wrought iron and began to use aluminum, at first making small items as gifts for their customers. Very soon they were involved in a growing industry estimated at one point to be comprised of several hundred companies, among them Arthur Armour, the Continental Silver Company, Everlast, Buenilum, Rodney Kent, and Palmer-Smith. Few of the many original companies survived the WWII scarcity of aluminum.

During the '60s, anodized (colored) aluminum became very popular. It's being bought up today by the younger generations who are attracted to its neon colors and clean lines. Watch for items with strong color and little if any sign of wear — very important factors to consider when assessing value. Because it was prone to scratching and denting, mint condition examples are few and far between.

Prices differ greatly from one region to another, sometimes without regard to quality or condition, so be sure to examine each item carefully before you buy. There are two good books on the subject: *Hammered Aluminum, Hand Wrought Collectibles,* by Dannie Woodard; and *Collectible Aluminum, An Identification and Value Guide,* by Everett Grist (Collector Books).

See also Kitchen.

Basket, signed Rodney Kent, #429, $15.00.

Ashtray, Arthur Armour, water lilies & pads in center w/fluted rim, 6" square **$20.00**

Ashtray, Everlast, hammered w/hunting dog superimposed over shotgun w/2 flying geese on bowl, 3 extended rests, 6" dia **$25.00**

Basket, Buenilum, smooth polished oval dish w/serrated edge, split wire handle connects w/twist, 9"........**$15.00**

Basket, Everlast, flower-&-leaf band inside shallow fluted bowl w/serrated rim, single handle splits at ends, 9" dia **$10.00**

Basket, Farber & Shlevin, daisy pattern on deeply fluted bowl w/twisted handle, 13" **$27.00**

Bowl, Continental, mum spray in center w/lg flat pinched & serrated rim, applied leaf-shaped handles, 1x7" dia **$20.00**

Bowl, Rodney Kent, tulip design in deep center on hammered background, serrated rim, 11" dia **$18.00**

Bowl, Wendell August Forge, pine cone pattern in shallow dish w/ruffled rim, 7½" dia................................**$25.00**

Bowl, Wrought Farberware, morning glory pattern around rim w/hammered center, fancy looped handles, 13¼" dia **$15.00**

Box, Wendell August Forge, apple blossom pattern on lid w/tube handle, blue ceramic bottom, 4x5x2" **$90.00**

Bread tray, Rodney Kent, tulip pattern on oval tray w/fancy scalloped rim, applied tulip-&-ribbon handles, 8x13" **$25.00**

Buffet server, Rodney Kent, oblong hammered tray w/applied flower-&-ribbon trim at ends, round glass insert, 10"..**$18.00**

Cake basket, Canterbury Arts, rose spray in center on slightly hammered plate w/twisted handle, 12" dia......**$30.00**

Candle holder, Bruce Fox, cast oak leaf form w/acorn holder, 10"..**$35.00**

Candleabrum, Buenilum, 3 cups rest on twisted triple-loop collum w/flared arms attached to round base, 13½"....**$45.00**

Candlesticks, Everlast, hammered design on base w/upturned scalloped rim, fluted bobeche, 3x4" dia, pr............**$20.00**

Candy dish, Wendell August Forge, apple blossoms on smoked finish, dome lid w/hammered ball knob, 7" dia **$40.00**

Candy dish, Wrought Farberware, flower-&-leaf pattern, black knob on lid, Cambridge glass dish w/handles, 5½" square **$25.00**

Casserole, Everlast, hammered bowl w/band of stylized leaves & plumes incised on knobbed lid, 9¼" dia............**$12.00**

Casserole, Rodney Kent, hammered bowl & overlapping lid w/serrated edge, tulip-&-ribbon finial, 6x8" dia ...**$10.00**

Chocolate pot, Continental, mum pattern w/beaded bottom, hinged lid w/petal finial, handle w/applied flower trim, 10" **$85.00**

Cigarette box, 63 (Town), pine cones in center of hammered hinged lid, 2x3½x5½" **$75.00**

Coaster set, Continental, allover mum pattern w/fluted rim, 12-pc set in holder w/applied leaves on handle, 4" dia **$30.00**

Compote, Cromwell, flower & fruit pattern in 3 sections in shallow round dish w/serrated edge, pedestal base, 6"..**$10.00**

Creamer & sugar bowl, Rodney Kent, hammered w/fluted rims, fancy crisscross ribbon handles, w/oblong tray **$20.00**

Gravy boat, Buenilum, highly polished w/beaded rim, wire loop handle w/bead on tapered end, attached underplate, 6"..**$20.00**

Ice bucket, Canterbury Arts, hammered pattern on double-walled vessel w/angled handles, smooth lid w/knob, 8"...**$45.00**

Lazy Susan, Cromwell, fruit-&-flower pattern shows through 3-part glass dish in center, pattern on hammered rim, 15" dia **$18.00**

Meat platter, Everlast, stylized tree in center oval well w/grape leaves on 4 corners of rectangular rim, handled..**$45.00**

Mint dish, Wendell August Forge, dogwood pattern on plate w/notched rim, 3-part glass insert, 12" dia **$45.00**

Pie plate holder, Everlast, buttercup-&-leaf pattern incised in flat rim w/beaded handles, 9½" **$16.00**

Pitcher, Continental, wild roses on hammered background, serrated rim & base, sm spout w/ice lip, ear-shaped handle, 8"...**$35.00**

Pitcher, Everlast, bamboo pattern on double-walled vessel w/ice lip, bamboo-styled handle, 2-qt **$37.00**

Pitcher, Mirro, smooth polished contoured vessel w/wide handle tapering at both ends, 10" **$12.00**

Plate, Arthur Armour, dogwood-&-butterfly pattern w/fluted rim, 10" dia...**$45.00**

Plate, Wendell August Forge, dogwood pattern w/notched turned-up rim, 10" dia **$25.00**

Relish tray, Arthur Armour, repeated flying geese pattern on 4-part oblong tray w/upturned serrated rim, handled, 6x16" **$75.00**

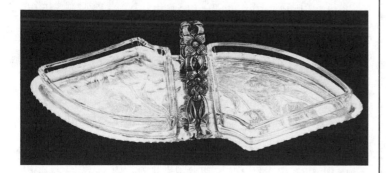

Relish, glass inserts, tulips motif, Rodney Kent, $18.00.

Sandwich tray, Everlast, band of hawthorn & fruit on rectangular tray w/upturned serrated rim, open handles, 9x14" **$16.00**

Sandwich tray, Everlast, spray of primroses & buttercups deeply carved on square tray w/comma-like design on rim, 12"x12" **$22.00**

Sandwich tray, Lehman, dogs & trees in roundel, hammered background, fluted rim, rounded corners, 12" square **$20.00**

Sandwich tray, Wendell August Forge, bittersweet pattern on hammered rectangle w/upturned notched rim, no handles, 8x11" **$25.00**

Serving tray, Arthur Armour, schooner & clouds in repousse on hammered background, long rolled handles, 9x13½" .**$50.00**

Serving tray, Canterbury Arts, band of berries, leaves & flowers on hammered oval w/fluted upturned rim, handled, 17x22" **$65.00**

Serving tray, Keystone Ware, allover flower & vines on rectangle w/2 upturned sides, slightly twisted handles, 10x15" **$15.00**

Silent butler, NS Co, bird-on-branch design on lid w/fluted & scalloped rim, patterned open wire handle, 6" dia..**$15.00**

Snack set, unmarked, flying ducks & cattails on rectangular self-handled serving tray, 9x12", w/2 snack trays, ea 4x6" **$16.00**

Snack tray, Wendell August Forge, Amish scene on hammered background, beveled patterned rim, 5x10".............**$65.00**

Tidbit tray, Everlast, dogwood pattern on round plate w/upturned fluted rim, hammered handle in center, 6" dia **$8.00**

Tiered tray, Everlast, bamboo pattern on 2 round tiers w/serrated rims, bamboo-styled handle **$18.00**

Vase, Arthur Armour, dogwood-&-butterfly pattern on cylinder w/rolled hammered base, 12" **$85.00**

Wastebasket, Wendell August Forge, bittersweet pattern on hammered background, creased rim...................**$150.00**

Anodized (Colored)

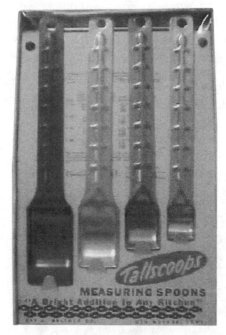

Measuring spoon set, Tallscoops, MIB, from $25.00 to $30.00. (Photo courtesy Pam and Bill Lange)

Ashtrays, crown-like shape, cigarettes held in notches, Parkit Safe, 3x1", set of 4, MIB......................................**$24.00**

Bowl, 6", Bascal, set of 8, EX **$26.00**

Cake salver, hot pink w/black handle on cover, Regal, 13" plate, EX **$30.00**

Candle holders, leaf-&-grape embossed pattern in bowl-like bottom, Kraft, 4½", EX, pr **$20.00**

Coasters, set of 8, M **$25.00**

Coffee maker, blue w/ivory Bakelite handles, West Bend FlavO-Matic, complete & working, EX.................**$25.00**

Creamer & sugar bowl on tray, gold w/black Bakelite handles, Neocraft, EX **$40.00**

Cups, 4½", in black rack, 16x8", w/white handles & rubber ball feet, Anohue, EX+ **$25.00**

Cups, 5½", M, set of 6...**$30.00**

Dessert bowls, w/glass inserts, 3½", set of 8, NM **$50.00**

Ice bucket, red apple shape, 7", NM.....................**$25.00**

Measuring scoops, ½-cup, ⅓-cup, & ¼-cup, NM, set of 3 ....**$20.00**

Napkin rings, narrow, set of 8, MIB.......................**$28.00**

Napkin rings, wide, in orginal plastic box, set of 4, M..**$50.00**

Pitcher, gold, w/ice lip, no mark, NM....................**$28.00**

Pitcher, green, w/8 5" tumblers, Colorcraft, Indpls Ind, NM **$60.00**

Popcorn set, 11" bowl & 4 5" individuals, M **$30.00**

Refrigerator boxes, 5¼x4⅜", set of 4, NM, from $40 to..**$50.00**

Rolling pin, w/stand, EX **$30.00**

Salad set, Bascal, lg bowl & 8 footed individuals, EX+ .**$50.00**

Shot glasses, 1¾", 6 in metal holder w/handle, Germany, MIB, from $25 to..**$35.00**

Shot glasses, 6 on tray, NM...................................**$30.00**

Soda/seltzer bottle, bright blue, Soda King, 11½", MIB..**$65.00**

Spoons, iced tea; 8", NM, set of 6 ....**$25.00**

Straw/stirrer, set of 12, M, from $25 to **$30.00**

Teapot, gold w/red plastic knob on lid, rattan-wrapped handle, Japan, 6½", EX.................................**$35.00**

Tree ornaments, Christmas bells, 2x2", set of 5 ....**$18.00**

Tree ornaments, twisted icicles, 15 in box, NM **$25.00**

Tumblers, 5", set of 6, M.......................................**$25.00**

Tumblers, 5", set of 8 in chrome carrying rack, Perma Hues, M **$45.00**

Tumblers, 5", w/matching 9" straws, set of 6, NM......**$45.00**

Tumblers, 5½", horizontal embossed rings, West Bend, set of 8, M **$35.00**

Angels

Angels, Birthday

Not at all hard to find and still reasonably priced, birthday angels are fun to assemble into 12-month sets, and since there are many different series to look for, collecting them can be challenging as well as enjoyable. Generally speaking, angels are priced by the following factors: 1) company — look for Lefton, Napco, Norcrest, and Enesco marks or labels (unmarked or unknown sets are of less value); 2) application of flowers, bows, gold trim, etc. (the more detail, the more valuable); 3) use of rhinestones, which will also increase the price; 4) age; and 5) quality of the workmanship involved, detail, and accuracy of painting.

#1194, angel of the month series, white hair, 5", ea, from $18 to...**$20.00**

#1294, angel of the month, white hair, 5", ea, from $18 to...**$20.00**

#1300, boy angels, wearing suit, white hair, 6", ea, from $22 to...**$25.00**

#1600 Pal Angel, month series of both boy & girl, 4", ea, from $10 to...**$15.00**

Arnart, Kewpies, in choir robes, w/rhinestones, 4½", ea, from $12 to...**$15.00**

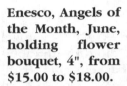

Enesco, Angels of the Month, June, holding flower bouquet, 4", from $15.00 to $18.00.

Enesco, angels on round base w/flower of the month, gold trim, ca, from $15 to...**$18.00**

High Mountain Quality, colored hair, 7", ea, from $30 to..**$32.00**

Kelvin, C-230, holding flower of the month, 4½", ea, from $15 to...**$20.00**

Kelvin, C-250, holding flower of the month, 4½", ea, from $15 to...**$20.00**

Lefton, #0489, holding basket of flowers, 4", ea, from $25 to...**$30.00**

Lefton, #0556, boy of the month, 5½", ea, from $25 to..**$30.00**

Lefton, #0574, day of the week series (like #8281 but not as ornate), ea, from $25 to **$28.00**

Lefton, #0627, day of the week series, 3½", ea, from $28 to...**$32.00**

Lefton, #0985, flower of the month, 5", ea, from $28 to..**$32.00**

Lefton, #130, Kewpie, 4½", ea, from $35 to **$40.00**

Lefton, #1323, angel of the month, bisque, ea, from $18 to..**$22.00**

Lefton, #1411, angel of the month, 4", ea, from $28 to ..**$32.00**

Lefton, #1987, angel of the month, ea, from $30 to ...**$35.00**

Lefton, #2600, birthstone on skirt, 3¼", ea, from $25 to..**$30.00**

Lefton, #3332, bisque, w/basket of flowers, 4", ea, from $25 to...**$30.00**

Lefton, #5146, birthstone in skirt, 4½", ea, from $22 to..**$28.00**

Lefton, #6224, applied flower/birthstone on skirt, 4½", ea, from $18 to...**$25.00**

Lefton, #6883, square frame, day of the week & months, 3¼x4", ea, from $28 to **$32.00**

Lefton, #6949, day of the week series in oval frame, 5", ea, from $28 to...**$32.00**

Lefton, #6985, musical, sm, ea, from $40 to................**$45.00**

Lefton, #8281, day of the week series, applied roses, ea, from $30 to...**$35.00**

Lefton, AR-1987, w/ponytail, 4", ea, from $18 to........**$22.00**

Lefton, 1987J, w/rhinestones, 4½", ea, from $25 to....**$30.00**

Napco, A1360-1372, angel of the month, ea, from $20 to...**$25.00**

Napco, A1917-1929, boy angel of the month, ea, from $20 to...**$25.00**

Napco, A1920, boy angel of the month with rabbit and basket, gold trim, 1956, 4¾", from $20.00 to $25.00.

Napco, A4307, angel of the month, sm, ea, from $22 to ...**$25.00**

Napco, C1361-1373, angel of the month, ea, from $20 to..**$25.00**

Napco, C1921-1933, boy angel of the month, ea, from $20 to **$25.00**

Napco, S1291, day of the week 'Belle,' ea, from $22 to..**$25.00**

Napco, S1307, bell of the month, ea, from $22 to......**$25.00**

Napco, S1361-1372, angel of the month, ea, from $20 to..**$25.00**

Napco, S1392, oval frame angel of the month, ea, from $25 to..**$30.00**

Napco, S401-413, angel of the month, ea, from $20 to ..**$25.00**

Napco, S429, day of the week angel (also available as planters), ea, from $25 to......................................**$30.00**

Norcrest, F-120, angel of the month, 4½", ea, from $18 to...**$22.00**

Norcrest, F-15, angel of the month, on round base w/raised pattern on dress, 4", ea, from $18 to **$22.00**

Norcrest, F-167, bell of the month, 2¾", ea, from $8 to ..**$12.00**

Norcrest, F-210, day of the week angel, 4½", ea, from $18 to...**$22.00**

Norcrest, F-23, day of the week angel, 4½", ea, from $18 to...**$22.00**

Norcrest, F-340, angel of the month, 5", ea, from $20 to...**$25.00**

Norcrest, F-535, angel of the month, 4½", ea, from $20 to...**$25.00**

Relco, 4¼", ea, from $15 to **$18.00**

Relco, 6", ea, from $18 to **$22.00**

SR, angel of the month, w/birthstone & 'trait' of the month (i.e. April - innocence), ea, from $20 to **$25.00**

TMJ, angel of the month, w/flower, ea, from $20 to..**$25.00**

Ucagco, white hair, 5¾", from $12 to **$15.00**

Wales, wearing long white gloves, white hair, Made in Japan, 6⅜", ea, from $25 to...**$28.00**

Angels, Zodiac

These china figurines were made and imported by the same companies as the birthday angels. Not as many companies made the Zodiac series, though, which makes them harder to find. Because they're older and were apparently never as popular as the month pieces, they were not made or distributed as long as the birthday angels. Examples tend to be more individualized due to each sign having a specific characteristic associated with it.

Japan, wearing pastel dress w/applied pink rose on head, standing on cloud base w/stars, 4½", ea, from $15 to...**$20.00**

Japan, wearing pastel dress w/rhinestones on gold stars, applied pink rose on head, 4", ea, from $20 to...**$25.00**

Josef, holds tablet w/sign written & shown in gold, 1960-1962, ea, from $30 to...**$40.00**

Josef, no wings, sign written in cursive on dress, 4", ea, from $30 to...**$40.00**

Lefton, K8650, applied flowers & gold stars, 4" when standing (1946-1953), ea, from $40 to **$45.00**

Napco, A2646, wearing gold crown, applied 'coconut' gold trim on dress hem, 5", ea, from $25 to.................**$30.00**

Napco, S1259, 'Your lucky star guardian angel' planter series, 4", ea, from $30 to..**$35.00**

Napco, S980, 'Your lucky star guardian angel,' 4", ea, from $22 to...**$28.00**

Semco, gold wings, applied roses & pleated ruffle on front edge of dress, 5", ea, from $20 to **$25.00**

Ashtrays

Ashtrays, especially for cigarettes, did not become widely used in the United States much before the turn of the century. The first examples were simply receptacles made to hold ashes for pipes, cigars, and cigarettes. Later, rests were incorporated into the design. Ashtrays were made in a variety of materials. Some were purely functional, while others advertised or entertained, and some stopped just short of being works of art. They were made to accommodate smokers in homes, businesses, or wherever they might be. Today their prices range from a few dollars to hundreds. Since they are comparatively new in the collectibles field, values are still fluctuating. For further information see *Collector's Guide to Ashtrays, Second Edition, Identification and Values,* by Nancy Wanvig.

See also specific glass companies and potteries; Japan Ceramics; Disney; Tire Ashtrays; World's Fairs.

Advisor: Nancy Wanvig (See Directory, Ashtrays)

Advertising, Ball, clear glass, canning jars, 3 rests, 3½" L...**$15.00**

Advertising, Bell Telephone, ceramic, phone figural, Call by numbers (vs Letters), It's twice as fast!, 1940s, 4⅝" L **$35.00**

Advertising, Blue Cross Plan, milk glass, 25th Anniversary, 1938-1963, 5⅛" L....................................**$10.00**

Advertising, Camel, cobalt glass, half circle, name in yellow, palm trees in green, 5 rests, 7¾" L.............**$35.00**

Advertising, Courvoisier Cognac, French, cream & green ceramic, Napoleon silhouettes on rise, 5⅞" dia ...**$17.00**

Advertising, Dairy Queen, clear glass, white name on red, 3⅜" L..**$11.00**

Advertising, Henckels, ceramic, German kitchen knives, picture of stylized men in center, 5¾" dia.................**$15.00**

Advertising, Hennessy Cognac, French, ashtray by Limoges, cream ceramic, 4" dia.................................**$9.00**

Advertising, Holland American Lines, ceramic, cruise ship, name in gold around rim, 4¼" dia.......................**$24.00**

Advertising, Johnny Walker Red, Scotch, red plastic, bump in center to knock off ashes, 3¾" dia.....................**$6.00**

Advertising, Monarch Ranges, brass, 2 circles w/pictures, Golden Jubilee 1896-1946, 4⅞" dia. **$31.00**

Advertising, Pabst Blue Ribbon, aluminum, blue finish, embossed logo, Good Old-Time Flavor, 4⅛" dia...**$11.00**

Advertising, Pepsi-Cola, stamped steel, gold, Say Pepsi Please, 2 inside rests, 5⅞" L....................................**$21.00**

Advertising, Piels, aluminum, Be Convinced! Try Piels Real Draft, 3 rests, 3½" dia.................................**$5.00**

Advertising, Pizza Hut, clear glass, stylized logo-impressed center, 5" dia **$7.00**

Advertising, Playboy Club, white glass, sm black bunny head in center, 1960s, 4" square **$12.00**

Advertising, Pyrex, clear glass, old, Ovenware-Flameware, Corning Glass Works, NY, 3⅞" L............**$15.00**

Advertising, Seagram's VO, whiskey, cobalt ceramic, 2 rests, letters in gold, 5" square **$9.00**

Advertising, Stroh's, Stroh Light, white ceramic, Official Beers of 1982 World's Fair, Knoxville, TN, 7⅞" L...........**$14.00**

Advertising, TraveLodge, smoky glass, decal w/bear mascot, Highway Hotels, 3½" square **$12.00**

Advertising, Tuborg, Danish beer, Imported Tuborg Beer, milk glass, crown logo, 5¼" L **$12.00**

Advertising, Winston, clear glass w/red decal, Nothin' But Taste - NO BULL, 4½" dia...................**$10.00**

Advertising, Wise Potato Chips, painted metal, Wholesale Delivery, salesman's sample, 6⅞" L.......................**$16.00**

Art Deco, bird figural on back, ceramic, match box holder, holes in head for matches, 2 cigarette rests, 4⅝"...**$38.00**

Art Deco, smoker set, brass, black bowl, plunger to sweep ashes, match holder, 2 cigarette rests, 1925, 3½" ...**$58.00**

Art glass, Murano glass clown sitting, top hat, 2 blue hands (cigarette rests), lap is big colorful bowl, 5¼" L.....**$90.00**

Art Nouveau, Kalk, crossed arrows (German factory), hand-painted orange ceramic, brass cigarette rest & edge, 5½" L **$45.00**

Art Nouveau, Pickard, china, hand-painted, mark #5 (1905-12), artist signed, raised cigarette rest, 4½" L.....**$160.00**

Arts & Crafts, Heintz, sterling on bronze rim, Pat Aug 1912, round w/2 extended rests, 6¾" L.......................**$215.00**

Casino, Caesar's Palace, clear glass, blue band around rim w/Roman scenes, 3⅝" dia................................**$5.00**

Casino, Harrah's, clear glass, red center, Reno & Lake Tahoe, 3½" square....................................**$8.00**

Cloisonne, bowl w/3 rests on incurvate rim, white w/floral design, blue interior, brass trim, China, 3¼" dia ..**$20.00**

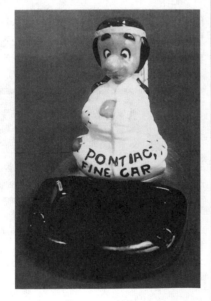

Advertising, Pontiac, Indian leaning against tree, ceramic, two rests, 5¾" high, EX, $110.00. (Photo courtesy Nancy Wanvig)

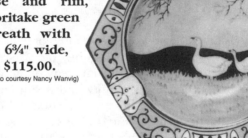

Decorative, hexagon with swan scene, black moriage on rise and rim, Noritake green wreath with M, 6¾" wide, M, $115.00.
(Photo courtesy Nancy Wanvig)

Majolica, figural trombone player, cigar holder, match holder & striker behind, 2 rests, 6½" **$300.00**

Novelty, cat's head, Reg No, plunger type, white ceramic, chrome top, makes cat sound when plunger moves up, 4⅝" L..**$50.00**

Novelty, nodder, girl in Austrian dress, metal head nods, souvenir Wein Germany, Made in Austria, 5⅛" **$70.00**

Advertising, Prudential Insurance, ceramic, raised letters, scene of rock logo, match pack holder, 6⅜" dia ...**$35.00**

Novelty, nodder, lady on lounge chair, pink clothes, red shoes, cigarette rest on side, leg & fan nod, 6" L **$95.00**

Novelty, nodder, man, ceramic, head nods, Yes Dear, Yes Dear written in center, Japan, 4" L **$48.00**

Novelty, smoker, clown head on book, bee between eyes, cigarette rest in mouth, Japan, 4⅛x4⅛" **$57.00**

Novelty, smoker, conductor, Holt Howard, bisque, rest hat feet, holes at ears & music score, 10¾"..............**$130.00**

Novelty, smoker, patchwork dog head, cigarette rest in mouth, holes in nose, Japan, 4½" L......................**$30.50**

Novelty, smoker, skull, teeth are rests, holes in eyes, Poor Old Fred - He Smoked in Bed, Japan, 5⅝" L.......**$35.00**

Sports, U Minnesota Football Mascot, chalkware, figural of gopher, MN-10,000 Lakes, MN, 6⅜" **$85.00**

Sports, Winston Cup, plastic (like rubber) tire, glass insert, stock car racing, Series-25th Anniversary, 2" **$28.00**

Victorian, man crossing pond, ceramic, place for matches & striker, log-form cigar or cigarette rest, 5" **$150.00**

Victorian, stacked seashells w/ornate brass cigar cutter, 1 rest, cutter is screwed to bottom shell, 5½" **$95.00**

Novelty, lion-head smoker, teeth and rest in mouth, holes in nose, Japan, 3⅝", EX, $45.00. (Photo courtesy Nancy Wanvig)

Autographs

'Philography' is an extremely popular hobby, one that is very diversified. Autographs of sports figures, movie stars, entertainers, and politicians from our lifetime may bring several hundred dollars, depending on rarity and application, while John Adams' simple signature on a document from 1800, for instance, might bring thousands. A signature on a card or cut from a letter or document is the least valuable type of autograph. A handwritten letter is generally the most valuable, since in addition to the signature you get the message as well. Depending upon what it reveals about the personality who penned it, content can be very important and can make a major difference in value.

Many times a polite request accompanied by an SASE to a famous person will result in receipt of a signed photo or a short handwritten note that might in several years be worth a tidy sum!

Obviously as new collectors enter the field, the law of supply and demand will drive the prices for autographs upward, especially when the personality is deceased. There are forgeries around, so before you decide to invest in expensive autographs, get to know your dealers.

Over the years many celebrities in all fields have periodically employed secretaries to sign their letters and photos. They have also sent out photos with preprinted or rubber stamped signatures as time doesn't always permit them to personally respond to fan mail. With today's advanced printing, even many long-time collectors have been fooled with a mechanically produced signature.

Advisors: Don and Anne Kier (See Directory, Autographs)

Newspaper: Autograph Times
2303 N 44th St., #225, Phoenix, AZ 85008; 602-947-3112
fax: 602-947-8363

Aaron, Hank; signed batting helmet **$120.00**

Allen, Woody; signed color photo, 8x10"+matt...........**$25.00**

Anderson, Loni; signed color photo, in swimsuit, 8x10"..**$18.00**

Anderson, Lynn; signed & inscribed black & white glossy photo, 8x10"..**$15.00**

Andrews, Dana; signed letter, concerning Ox-Bow Incident, 5 lines, 1982 ....**$15.00**

Avalon, Frankie; signed & inscribed black & white glossy photo, 8x10"...**$18.50**

Banderas, Antonio; signed color photo, 8x10"+matt...**$35.00**

Bennett, Tony; signed color photo, 8x10"+matt..........**$35.00**

Bird, Larry; signed golf ball **$25.00**

Bisset, Jacqueline; signed color photo, 8x10".............**$18.00**

Boone, Debby; signed & inscribed black & white glossy photo, shown singing, 8x10" **$15.00**

Borgnine, Ernest; signed 8-line note on bottom of letter to him **$10.00**

Bridges, Jeff; signed color photo, 8x10"+matt **$22.00**

Bronson, Charles; signed color photo, 8x10" **$25.00**

Clark, Roy; signed color photo, 8x10" **$14.00**

Clemente, Roberto; signed check, $500.00.

Cogan, Kevin; signed & inscribed color photo, 6½x4½" ..**$15.00**

Crawford, Cindy; signed color photo, sexy pose, 8x10"+matt..**$40.00**

Cronkite, Walter; signed black & white photo, 8x10". **$20.00**

Dalton, Timothy; signed color photo, 8x10"+matt **$35.00**

Dangerfield, Rodney; signed color photo, 8x10" **$25.00**

Denver, Bob; signed & inscribed black & white photo, 8x10" **$20.00**

Derek, Bo; signed black & white photo, in swimsuit, 8x10" **$18.00**

Douglas, Kirk; signed photo, half bust, 3½x5½" **$22.00**

Dreyfus, Richard; signed black & white photo, candid pose, 8x10" **$15.00**

Drury, James; signed & inscribed black & white glossy photo, as Virginian, 8x10", mounted on board **$20.00**

Duvall, Robert; signed black & white photo, 8x10"....**$25.00**

Falk, Peter; signed black & white photo, candid close-up, cigar stub in mouth, 8x10" **$15.00**

Fawcett, Farah; signed color photo, 8x10"+matt **$40.00**

Fields, Sally; signed color photo, 8x10" **$25.00**

Ford, Gerald; signed color photo, 8x10"....................**$40.00**

Franklin, Aretha; signed color photo, 8x10"+matt.......**$40.00**

Garner, James; signed black & white photo, 5½x3½" ..**$18.50**

Grant, Amy; signed color photo, 8x10".......................**$16.00**

Hall, Jerry; signed photo, scanty attire, 8x10" **$25.00**

Heston, Charlton; signed color photo, 5x7" **$22.00**

Irving, Amy; signed & inscribed black & white printed photo, candid pose, 10x14"....................................**$10.00**

Jackson, Alan; signed & inscribed black & white photo, 8x10" **$20.00**

Jones, Jennifer; signed black & white photo, sexy pose, ca 1958, 3½x5½" **$187.50**

Lancaster, Burt; signed color photo, 8x10"+matt **$95.00**

Lane, Nathan; signed color photo, 8x10".....................**$25.00**

Lee, Brenda; signed & inscribed color photo, 8x10" ..**$15.00**

Letterman, David; signed black and white 8x10" photo, $20.00.

Lords, Traci; signed color photo, 8x10"+matt **$35.00**

Mantle, Mickey; signed baseball cap..........................**$225.00**

McEntire, Reba; signed color photo, 8x10"+matt **$40.00**

McGillis, Kelly; signed color photo, 8x10"..................**$20.00**

McMillen, Tom; signed color basketball card, forward for Hawks..**$17.50**

Milano, Alyssa; signed color photo, 8x10"+matt **$35.00**

Nicholson, Jack; signed color photo, 8x10"+matt **$55.00**

Paltrow, Gwyneth; signed color photo, 8x10"+matt ...**$35.00**

Parton, Dolly; signed color photo, 8x10"....................**$28.00**

Quayle, Dan; signed color photo, 8x10"....................**$35.00**

Quinn, Anthony; signed color photo, 8x10"...............**$32.00**

Reeve, Christopher; signed color photo, 8x10"+matt..**$50.00**

Reynolds, Debbie; signed color photo, 8x10" **$22.00**

Roberts, Julia; signed color photo, 8x10"+matt **$65.00**

Ryan, Meg; signed color photo, 8x10"+matt...............**$55.00**

Schiffer, Claudia; signed color photo, sexy pose, 8x10"+matt..**$35.00**

Selleck, Tom; signed color photo, 8x10"+matt...........**$20.00**

Simon, Carly; signed color photo, 8x10"+matt **$30.00**

Slater, Christian; signed color photo, 8x10"+matt........**$30.00**

Spector, Ronnie (from the Ronettes); framed with record *Be My Baby*, $50.00.

Stallone, Sylvestor; signed color photo, 8x10"+matt ...**$75.00**

Stanwyck, Barbara; signed black & white photo, from Night Walker, 1964, 8x10"...**$68.50**

Starr, Blaze; signed black & white photo, 8x10" **$22.00**

Taylor, Rod; signed & inscribed black & white photo, half-bust pose, 8x10"..**$18.50**

Thompson, Emma; signed color photo, 8x10"+matt...**$30.00**

Walters, Barbara; signed color photo, 8x10"................**$25.00**

Watson, Tom; signed black & white photo, 8x10"......**$25.00**

West, Adam; signed color photo as Batman, 8x10"+matt..**$30.00**

Williams, Andy; signed & inscribed black & white photo, 8x10" **$18.50**

Winfrey, Oprah; signed color photo, 8x10"+matt........**$55.00**

Yokam, Dwight; signed color photo, 8x10"+matt **$30.00**

Zadora, Pia; signed color photo, 8x10"......................**$14.00**

Automobilia

Automobilia remains a specialized field, attracting antique collectors and old car buffs alike. It is a field that encompasses auto-related advertising and accessories like hood ornaments, gear shift and steering wheel knobs, sales brochures, and catalogs. Memorabilia from the high-performance, sporty automobiles of the sixties is very popular with baby boomers. Unusual items have been setting auction records as the market for automobilia heats up. Note: Badges vary according to gold content — 10k or sterling silver examples are higher than average. Dealership booklets (Ford, Chevy, etc.) generally run about $2.00 to $3.00 per page, and because many reproductions are available, very few owner's manuals sell for more than $10.00.

See also License Plates; Tire Ashtrays.

Advisor: Leonard Needham (See Directory, Automobilia)

Air gauge, Peerless Automobiles, logo on green dial, metal case, w/leather pouch, US Gauge Co, 2x3¼", EX+...$150.00

Badge, plant employee's; Studebaker, brass, $35.00. (Photo courtesy Jim and Nancy Schaut)

Bank, Ford, shaggy dog figure w/Ford collar, Florence Ceramics, 1960s, 8", EX...$45.00
Banner, 1954 Studebaker (block print)/World's Finest Performing V-8 (script) on purple silk w/gold fringe, 28x40", VG...$80.00
Booklet, The Gentle Art of Motoring, Cadillac, 1948, 12 pages, EX...$12.00
Brochure, Buick, 1955, 20 pages, VG $30.00
Brochure, Edsel, 1958, G $12.00
Brochure, Lincoln Quick Facts, 1950, 12 pages, VG...$12.00
Bulb kit, Cadillac — LaSalle Motor Cars Part No 42677, litho tin container complete w/contents, 2½x3½x1¾", EX..$135.00
Calendar, Nash, 1951, complete, EX $10.00
Catalog, Chevrolet Showroom, 1946, 29 pages, 9x11¼", VG...$275.00
Catalog, Ford Truck (Series 100-600) Chassis & Accessories, 1956 & 1957, 532 pages, G $20.00
Clock, GMC Trucks Sales/Service, neon, octagonal tin frame w/glass lens, white, orange & blue w/yellow center, VG...$800.00
Clock, Official AAA Station, round metal frame w/plastic lens, numbers around oval logo, light-up, 15" dia, VG...$60.00

Clock, Pontiac, plastic and metal, lights up, 19¼x14½x5", EX+, $300.00. (Photo courtesy Autopia Advertising Auctions)

Display rack, Ford Color Patch, Cover That Scratch With..., Factory-Matched Colors, 3 stepped shelves w/marquee, 19", G...$100.00

Fan, Chevrolet, It's Wise to Choose a Six, Let a Ride Decide, 11½x8", $90.00 each. (Photo courtesy Dunbar Gallery)

Gearshift knob, glass w/brown & tan swirls, 2" dia, EX..$50.00
Grille badge, Farmers Mutual Automobile Ins Co/Madison Wis, painted aluminum w/touring car & countryside, 3x4", NM+...$300.00
Hood ornament, Ford Mustang, sleek chrome horse figure, 5¾" NMIB (box reads Crowning Touch of Beauty!) $175.00
Hood ornament, Mack Jr Truck Bulldog, chrome-plated, early, EX...$75.00
Key case, Olds/Renault, brown leather, 1960s, logo, EX..$5.00
Key chain, '66 Olds Super Salesman, EX....................$15.00
License plate attachment, St Louis Cardinals, diecut embossed tin bird w/bat, 6½x4", EX+ $200.00
Lighter, Dodge, From Pickups to Diesel Power below yellow image of truck, cloisonne inlay on chrome, 2½x2", VG $30.00

Lighter, Downtown Ford Sales w/1950s-60s emblem, Zippo type, EX.................................**$20.00**

Lock & keys, Ford in script on brass padlock & 2 keys, 3x2x1", VG.................................**$70.00**

Magazine, Nash Airflyte, 1951, VG **$6.00**

Magazine, The Continental, 1965, VG.................................**$5.00**

Manual, owner's; Buick, 1949, EX.................................**$30.00**

Manual, owner's; Cadillac, 1962, EX.................................**$24.00**

Manual, owner's; Corvette, 1965, EX.................................**$90.00**

Manual, owner's; Dodge, 1954, VG.................................**$30.00**

Manual, owner's; Ford Mustang, 1967, EX.................................**$30.00**

Manual, owner's; Hudson, 1948, includes wiring & lubrication charts, EX.................................**$30.00**

Manual, owner's; Kaiser, 1947, VG.................................**$40.00**

Manual, owner's; Lincoln Continental, 1968, EX.........**$20.00**

Manual, owner's; Pontiac GTO/LeMans, 1972, EX......**$20.00**

Manual, owner's; 1957 Corvette, EX **$180.00**

Manual, service; Buick Chassis, 1957, 464 pages, EX.**$40.00**

Manual, service; Chevrolet Steering Gear, 1949, EX ...**$15.00**

Manual, service; Chevy Vega, 1972, EX **$12.00**

Manual, shop; Ford Truck, 1965, 64 pages, VG.........**$12.00**

Motometer, Boyce, VG **$60.00**

Mug, Chevrolet Truck Sales Award, shows 1847 Stakebed, 1961, EX **$115.00**

Oil can, Studebaker Special Motor Oil, 1-qt, waxed cardboard, yellow & blue, Studebaker Parts & Service Division, VG+.................................**$100.00**

Pamphlet, Buick, 1967, VG **$6.00**

Pamphlet, Chevrolet Custom Feature Accessories, 1966, NM.................................**$8.00**

Paper clip, Packard, brass w/radiator logo in center, flower decor on outer edges, 3¼x2½", EX+ **$330.00**

Paperweight, Chevrolet, metal bow-tie logo w/name on base, 2x3½x1½", EX.................................**$80.00**

Paperweight, GM Golden Milestones 1980-1958, Forward From Fifty, oval brass token imbedded in Lucite cube, EX.................................**$45.00**

Pin, Cadillac Craftsman, gold w/logo, 1947, EX.........**$35.00**

Playing cards, Cadillac emblem, double deck in plastic box, EX.................................**$10.00**

Postcard, Buick Roadmaster, 1955, G.................................**$7.00**

Postcard, Chevrolet, 1955, General Motor's 50 Millionth Car, NM.................................**$9.00**

Postcard, GMC, 1964, colorful image of blue truck & lg red barn in country setting, EX **$6.00**

Postcard, Kaiser-Darrin, 1953, lady standing admiring car, NM.................................**$20.00**

Postcard, Nash Airflyte, 1950, couple by car in front of lg house, NM **$8.00**

Poster, Chevrolet Impala Convertible, 1958, side-view image w/driver & beach scene beyond, framed, 19x32", EX **$100.00**

Poster, We Airline Check When We Chevy Tune/For Top-Flight Performance, mechanic working on 1960s Chevy, 44x17", EX.................................**$100.00**

Radiator cap ornament, woman's head (windblown hair), frosted glass, Corning, 4¾, NM+.................................**$250.00**

Radiator ornament, Super-Chief, Indian head w/red face, silver headdress w/multicolored trim, dated 1950, 4½", NMIB.................................**$125.00**

Ruler, Ford script on plastic, 8-cylinder cars on back, EX **$35.00**

Sign, Bus Station, black silhouette of passengers boarding bus on round 2-sided porcelain sign on pedestal base, 86", VG.................................**$275.00**

Sign, hardboard, Studebaker Authorized Service/Parts, diecut emblem, 2-sided, 9x13", VG+ **$85.00**

Sign, metal, FoMoCo Genuine Ford Parts, metal, red & white, 2-sided, 14x18", EX.................................**$60.00**

Sign, neon, Pontiac, red tubing forming Indian logo, 6, 8 & name in block letters on black glass, 27x38", VG..**$220.00**

Sign, paper on cardboard, Franklin Car/None Better/Younger Auto Co..., 12x18", G-.................................**$65.00**

Sign, porcelain, Marrow Trucking, diecut radiator shape, red, white, gray & black, 16x24", EX+.................................**$190.00**

Sign, Volkswagen Genuine Parts, blue and white on porcelain, 41x28", NM, $700.00. (Photo courtesy Autopia Advertising Auctions)

Tape measure, DeSoto Six, Product of Crysler, 1½", EX..**$50.00**

Thermometer, plastic lollipop, Chevrolet, red & white bow-tie logo, blue advertising on bottom panel, 6½", NM.................................**$150.00**

TV tray, Ford, metal w/folding stand, black w/names of Ford cars & dated in gold, Ford logo in center, 29", EX ..**$15.00**

Wrench, Cadillac #3933, open ended, ⅝" & ¹¹⁄₁₆", 6" L, G **$60.00**

Yardstick/cane, Studebaker-Packard Spring Driveway, May 1957, 1" square at lg end, M.................................**$25.00**

Autumn Leaf Dinnerware

A familiar dinnerware pattern to just about all of us, Autumn Leaf was designed by Hall China for the Jewel Tea Company who offered it to their customers as premiums. In fact, some people erroneously refer to the pattern as 'Jewel

Tea.' First made in 1933, it continued in production until 1978. Pieces with this date in the backstamp are from the overstock that was in the company's warehouse when production was suspended. There are matching tumblers and stemware all made by the Libbey Glass Company, and a set of enameled cookware that came out in 1979. You'll find blankets, tablecloths, metal canisters, clocks, playing cards, and many other items designed around the Autumn Leaf pattern. All are collectible.

Since 1984 the Hall company has been making special items for the National Autumn Leaf Collectors Club. These pieces are designated as such by the 'Club' marking that is accompanied by the date of issue. Limited edition items (also by Hall) are being sold by China Specialties, a company in Ohio; but once you become familiar with the old pieces, these are easy to identify, since the molds have been redesigned or were not previously used for Autumn Leaf production.

For further study, we recommend *The Collector's Encyclopedia of Hall China* by Margaret and Kenn Whitmyer. For information on company products, see Jewel Tea.

Advisor: Gwynneth M. Harrison (See Directory, Autumn Leaf)

Club: National Autumn Leaf Collectors' Club
Gwynneth Harrison
P.O. Box 1, Mira Loma, CA 91752-0001; 909-685-5434
e-mail: morgan99@pe.net

Newsletter: Autumn Leaf
Bill Swanson, Editor
807 Roaring Springs Dr.
Allen, TX 75002-2112; 972-727-5527
e-mail: bescome@home.com

Apron, oilcloth...**$700.00**
Baker, cake; Heatflow clear glass, Mary Dunbar, 1½-qt.**$65.00**
Baker, French; 2-pt, 1966-76, from $150 to **$175.00**
Baker, individual, oval (Fort Pitt 12-oz), 1966-76, from $200 to...**$225.00**
Baker, souffle; 4⅛"...**$12.00**
Bean pot, 1-handle...**$1,000.00**
Blanket, Vellux, Autumn Leaf, full-size.....................**$175.00**
Blanket, Vellux, blue, king-size.............................**$250.00**
Blanket, Vellux, blue, twin, 1979-??, from $140 to **$150.00**
Book, Autumn Leaf Story, from $40 to **$50.00**
Bottle, Jim Beam, broken seal, from $100 to **$110.00**
Bottle, Jim Beam, unbroken seal.............................**$120.00**
Bowl, fruit; 1936-76, 5½", from $3 to.......................**$6.00**
Bowl, mixing; 1933-76, 3-pc set, from $15 to **$20.00**
Bowl, Royal Glasbake, milk white, 4-pc set.............**$225.00**
Bowl, soup; flat, 8½"..**$20.00**
Bowl, vegetable; divided, oval, 1957-76, 10½", from $80 to **$125.00**
Bowl, vegetable; oval, Melmac, from $40 to **$50.00**
Bowl, vegetable; oval, w/lid, 1940-76, 10", from $50 to ..**$75.00**
Bowl lids, plastic, 7-pc set in pouch........................**$100.00**
Box, oatmeal; from $50 to **$100.00**

Butter dish, regular, 1959-60, 1-lb, from $350 to **$500.00**
Butter dish, smooth square top, ¼-lb......................**$1,200.00**
Butter dish, wing lid, ¼-lb....................................**$1,800.00**
Cake baker, heatflow clear glass, Mary Dunbar, 1½-qt, from $40 to...**$65.00**

Cake plate, on metal stand, 1958 – 69, $225.00.

Cake plate, 1937-76, from $20 to **$28.00**
Cake plate, 1958-69, on metal stand........................**$225.00**
Cake safe, side motif, 1950-53, from $35 to **$45.00**
Cake server, Harker, from $300 to **$500.00**
Calendar, 1920s-1930s, from $40 to.........................**$70.00**
Calendar, 1940s & newer, from $30 to......................**$50.00**
Candle holder, Christmas, club pc, 1994 ....**$125.00**
Candlestick, metal, Douglas, pr, from $70 to **$100.00**
Candy dish, metal base, from $450 to **$550.00**
Canister set, copper top, 4-pc, from $500 to............**$800.00**
Canister set, metal, 3-pc, from $200 to **$300.00**
Case, Jewel salesman's **$300.00**
Casserole, Heatflow clear glass, oval, w/lid, Mary Dunbar, 2-qt..**$125.00**
Casserole, Royal Glasbake, milk white, round, w/lid.**$90.00**
Casserole, Tootsie, round, w/lid, 2-qt, from $30 to **$45.00**
Clock, electric, 1956-69, from $400 to.....................**$550.00**
Clock, salesman's award **$400.00**
Coaster, metal, 3⅛"...**$8.00**
Coffee dispenser, 1941, from $200 to **$400.00**
Coffeepot, electric percolator, all china, from $300 to **$350.00**
Coffeepot, Jewels Best, 30-cup, from $500 to...........**$600.00**
Coffeepot, Rayed, 1937-49, 9-cup, from $30 to..........**$45.00**
Coffeepot, Rayed, 1937-76, 8-cup, from $30 to..........**$45.00**
Condiment set, 1938-39, 3-pc, from $80 to **$100.00**
Cookbook, 1984, club issue....................................**$45.00**
Cookbook, 1988, club issue....................................**$30.00**
Cooker, waterless, metal, Mary Dunbar, from $50 to .**$75.00**
Cookie jar, Big Ear, Zeisel.....................................**$275.00**
Cookie jar, Tootsie, Rayed, 1936-39, from $250 to ...**$300.00**
Cookware, 'new metal,' 7-pc set, from $400 to **$650.00**
Creamer & sugar bowl, Melmac, from $30 to **$40.00**
Creamer & sugar bowl, Rayed, 1930s style, 1934-40, from $60 to..**$80.00**

Cup, coffee; Jewel's Best, from $20 to........................**$30.00**
Cup, custard; Radiance, 1936-76, from $6 to..............**$10.00**
Cup, tea; regular, Ruffled-D **$6.00**
Dripper, metal, coffeepot, from $20 to **$25.00**
Flatware, silverplate, serving pc, ea, from $90 to **$100.00**
Flatware, silverplate, 1958-59, ea pc, from $30 to.......**$35.00**
Flatware, stainless steel, serving pc, ea, from $50 to..**$60.00**
Flatware, stainless steel, 1960-68, ea pc, from $25 to.**$30.00**
Fondue set, complete, 1980-??, from $150 to.............**$200.00**
Fork, pickle; Jewel Tea, from $40 to...........................**$75.00**
Glass, iced tea; frosted, 5½" **$20.00**
Goblet, gold & frost on clear, Libbey, footed, 6½-oz.**$65.00**
Goblet, gold & frost on clear, Libbey, footed, 10-oz ..**$65.00**
Gravy boat, w/underplate (pickle dish), 1942-76, from $40
   to...**$55.00**
Hot pad, metal back, round, 7¼" **$20.00**
Loaf pan, Mary Dunbar, from $40 to...........................**$65.00**
Meat chopper, jewel on handle, from $300 to **$450.00**
Mug, conic, 1966-76, from $50 to...............................**$65.00**
Napkin, muslin, 16", from $30 to **$50.00**
Pitcher/ball jug, #3, 1938-76, from $35 to...................**$40.00**
Place mats, set of 8, from $150 to.............................**$325.00**
Plate, dinner; Melmac, 10", from $15 to.....................**$20.00**
Plate, salad; Melmac, 7", from $12 to.........................**$20.00**
Plate, 1938-76, 6", from $5 to.....................................**$8.00**
Plate, 1938-76, 7¼", from $5 to **$10.00**
Plate, 1938-76, 8", from $12 to...................................**$18.00**
Plate, 1938-76, 10", from $12 to.................................**$18.00**
Platter, Melmac, oval, 14" **$50.00**
Platter, oval, 1938-76, 11½", from $20 to.....................**$28.00**
Platter, oval, 1938-76, 13½", from $20 to.....................**$28.00**
Playing cards, double deck, 1943-46, from $150 to..**$200.00**
Playing cards, single deck, 75th anniversary **$50.00**
Punch bowl & 12 cups, club pc, 1993, from $300 to ...**$350.00**
Range set, salt & pepper shakers & grease jar w/lid, 1936-76,
   from $50 to...**$60.00**
Refrigerator set, metal w/plastic lids, 3-pc...............**$275.00**

Saucepan, w/warmer base, Douglas...........................**$500.00**
Saucepan, wood handle, w/lid, 1½-qt.........................**$150.00**
Saucer, regular, Ruffled-D, 1936-76, from $1 to............**$3.00**
Scales, Jewel, Imperial or American, from $150 to...**$200.00**
Shelf liner, paper, 108" roll..**$50.00**
Shelf liner, plastic, 1956-57, from $125 to..................**$130.00**
Shoe polish, white, from $40 to **$55.00**
Skillet, metal, porcelain, 9½" **$125.00**
Skillet, top stoveware glass, Mary Dunbar.................**$175.00**
Stack set, 1951-76, 4-pc, from $100 to.......................**$125.00**
Sugar packet holder, Christmas, club pc, 1990 ....**$125.00**
Sweeper, Little Jewel **$175.00**
Syrup pitcher, club pc, 1995, from $55 to **$95.00**
Tablecloth, plastic, 54x54"..**$150.00**
Tea towel, 1956-57, 16x33", from $50 to **$60.00**
Teacup, regular, Ruffled-D, 1936-76, from $4 to **$6.00**
Teakettle, scale logo, from $300 to **$500.00**
Teapot, Aladdin, 1942-76, from $50 to.......................**$70.00**

Teapot, Birdcage, club piece, 1995, $145.00.

Teapot, Donut, club pc, 1993, from $300 to **$350.00**
Teapot, long spout, Rayed, 1935, from $50 to **$70.00**
Teapot, Newport, 1933, from $175 to **$200.00**
Teapot, Newport, 1978..**$200.00**
Teapot, Solo, club pc, 1991, from $75 to **$100.00**
Thermos, picnic jug, 1941-??, from $325 to **$375.00**
Tidbit tray, 3-tier, 1954-69, from $80 to **$100.00**
Tin, fruitcake; tan or white, from $7 to **$10.00**
Tin container, Cocoa, from $40 to...............................**$70.00**
Tin container, Coffee, paper labels **$100.00**
Tin container, Fruitcake, tan or white........................**$10.00**
Toy circus train, from $900 to **$1,200.00**
Toy truck, Jewel, green, from $350 to **$425.00**
Toy truck, Jewel semi-trailer, brown, from $1,000 to..**$1,600.00**
Trash can, red, metal..**$400.00**
Tray, coffee service; oval, 1934-??, 18¾", from $75 to **$100.00**
Tray, metal, oval, from $75 to **$100.00**

Salt and pepper shakers, Casper, from $20.00 to $30.00 for the pair; Range shakers, $30.00 for the pair.

Tray, wood & glass, from $100 to.............................**$130.00**
Tumbler, Brockway, 1975-76, 9-oz, from $30 to.........**$45.00**
Tumbler, Brockway, 1975-76, 13-oz, from $30 to......**$45.00**
Tumbler, iced tea; Libbey, frosted, 1940-49, 5½", from $15 to...**$20.00**
Tumbler, juice; Libbey, frosted, 1950-53, 3¾", from $25 to...**$32.00**
Utility jug, Rayed, 1937-76, from $20 to.....................**$25.00**
Vase, bud; club pc, 1994...**$40.00**
Vase, bud; sm or regular w/decal, 1940, from $175 to..**$225.00**
Vase, Edgewater, club pc, 1987.................................**$350.00**
Waffle iron, Manning-Bowman......................................**$95.00**
Warmer, oval, 1955-60, from $150 to.........................**$200.00**
Warmer, round, 1956-60, from $125 to.....................**$160.00**

Barbie Doll and Her Friends

Barbie was first introduced in 1959, and soon Mattel found themselves producing not only dolls but tiny garments, fashion accessories, houses, cars, horses, books, and games as well. Today's Barbie collectors want them all. Though the early Barbie dolls are very hard to find, there are many of her successors still around. The trend today is toward Barbie exclusives — Holiday Barbie dolls and Bob Mackies are all very 'hot' items. So are special-event Barbie dolls.

When buying the older dolls, you'll need to do a lot of studying and comparisons to learn to distinguish one Barbie from another, but this is the key to making sound buys and good investments. Remember, though, collectors are sticklers concerning condition; compared to a doll mint in box, they'll often give an additional 20% if that box has never been opened (or as collectors say 'never removed from box,' indicated in our lines by 'NRFB')! As a general rule, a mint-in-the-box doll is worth from 50% to 100% more than one mint, no box. The same doll, played with and in only good condition, is worth half as much (or less than that). If you want a good source for study, refer to one of these fine books: *A Decade of Barbie Dolls and Collectibles, 1981 – 1991,* by Beth Summers; *The Wonder of Barbie* and *The World of Barbie Dolls* by Paris and Susan Manos; *The Collector's Encyclopedia of Barbie Dolls and Collectibles* by Sibyl DeWein and Joan Ashabraner; *Barbie Doll Fashion, Vol I* and *Vol II,* by Sarah Sink Eames; *Barbie Exclusives, Books I* and *II,* by Margo Rand; *The Barbie Doll Boom, 1986 – 1995,* and *Collector's Encyclopedia of Barbie Doll Exclusives and More* by J. Michael Augustyniak; *The Barbie Doll Years, 4th Edition,* by Patrick C. Olds; *The Story of Barbie* by Kitturah Westenhouser; *Barbie, The First 30 Years, 1959 Through 1989,* by Stefanie Deutsch; *Collector's Guide to Barbie Doll Paper Dolls* by Lorraine Mieszala; and *Schroeder's Collectible Toys, Antique to Modern.* (All are published by Collector Books.)

Dolls

Allan, 1964, painted red hair, original outfit, straight legs, MIB...**$125.00**

Barbie, #1, 1958-59, brunette hair, MIB................**$10,000.00**
Barbie, #2, blond or brunette hair, MIB, ea, from $8,500 to..**$9,500.00**
Barbie, #3, 1960, blond hair, original swimsuit, NM.**$950.00**
Barbie, #4, 1960, blond or brunette hair, original swimsuit, M, ea, from $450 to...**$500.00**
Barbie, #5, 1961, blond hair, MIB............................**$650.00**
Barbie, #6, blond hair, original swimsuit, EX...........**$250.00**
Barbie, American Girl, 1964, platinum cheek-length hair, original swimsuit, NM...**$650.00**
Barbie, Angel Face, 1982, NRFB..............................**$40.00**
Barbie, Astronaut, 1986, NRFB...............................**$100.00**
Barbie, Beach Blast, 1989, NRFB.............................**$25.00**
Barbie, Beautiful Bride, 1976, NRFB.......................**$250.00**
Barbie, Birthday Party, 1992, NRFB..........................**$35.00**
Barbie, Bubble-Cut, 1961, blond or brunette hair, original swimsuits, NM, ea..**$200.00**
Barbie, Butterfly Princess (Black), 1994, NRFB..........**$25.00**
Barbie, Calvin Klein, 1996, Bloomindales, NRFB.......**$65.00**
Barbie, Chinese, 1993, Dolls of the World, NRFB.......**$50.00**
Barbie, Cinderella, 1997, Children's Collector Series, NRFB...**$55.00**
Barbie, City Sophisticate, 1994, Service Merchandise, NRFB...**$95.00**
Barbie, Dance Sensation, 1984, NRFB......................**$50.00**
Barbie, Day-to-Night, 1985, NRFB............................**$35.00**
Barbie, Dream Bride, 1991, NRFB............................**$50.00**
Barbie, Earring Magic, 1992, NRFB..........................**$25.00**
Barbie, Evening Sparkle, 1991, Home Shopping Club, NRFB...**$200.00**
Barbie, Fashion Queen, 1963, complete, MIB (no liner)...**$400.00**
Barbie, Frills & Fantasy, 1988, Wal-Mart, NRFB...........**$65.00**
Barbie, Gap, 1996, NRFB..**$75.00**
Barbie, Golden, 1990, Bob Mackie, MIB...................**$825.00**
Barbie, Grownin' Pretty Hair, 1971, NRFB................**$250.00**
Barbie, Happy Birthday, 1990, NRFB.........................**$35.00**
Barbie, Holiday, 1988, NRFB, minimum value.......**$1,000.00**
Barbie, Holiday, 1989, NRFB..................................**$250.00**
Barbie, Holiday, 1990, NRFB..................................**$250.00**
Barbie, Holiday, 1991, NRFB..................................**$250.00**
Barbie, Holiday, 1992, NRFB..................................**$150.00**
Barbie, Holiday, 1993, NRFB..................................**$200.00**
Barbie, Holiday, 1994, NRFB..................................**$175.00**
Barbie, Holiday, 1995, NRFB....................................**$75.00**
Barbie, Holiday, 1996, NRFB....................................**$50.00**
Barbie, Holiday, 1997, NRFB....................................**$35.00**
Barbie, Holiday Hostess, 1993, NRFB........................**$45.00**
Barbie, Icelandic, 1987, Dolls of the World, NRFB...**$125.00**
Barbie, Jewel Essence, 1996, Bob Mackie, NRFB.....**$150.00**
Barbie, Jewel Splendor, 1995, FAO Schwarz, NRFB.**$350.00**
Barbie, Kissing, 1979, w/bangs, NRFB.......................**$50.00**
Barbie, Living, 1970, blond hair, NRFB....................**$225.00**
Barbie, Magic Curl, 1982, NRFB...............................**$50.00**
Barbie, Moon Goddess, 1996, Bob Mackie, NRFB....**$175.00**
Barbie, My Fair Lady (Flower Seller), 1995, Hollywood Legends Series, NRFB...**$70.00**

Barbie, Newport, 1973, NRFB......................................$175.00
Barbie, Nutcracker, 1992, Ballet Series, NRFB...........$250.00
Barbie, Oreo Fun, 1997, NRFB $25.00
Barbie, Party Sensation, 1990, NRFB...........................$55.00

Barbie, Peruvian, 1985, Dolls of the World, NRFB, $85.00.
(Photo courtesy Beth Summers)

Barbie, Pink Ice, 1996, Toys R Us, NRFB $175.00
Barbie, Pretty Changes, 1980, NRFB $50.00
Barbie, Queen of Hearts, 1994, Bob Mackie, NRFB .$325.00
Barbie, Rappin' Rockin', 1991, NRFB $40.00
Barbie, Ribbons & Roses, 1995, Sears Exclusive, NRFB..$75.00
Barbie, Southern Belle, 1994, Great Eras, NRFB $125.00
Barbie, Sun Valley, 1973, NRFB.................................$100.00
Barbie, Super Dance, 1982, NRFB...............................$50.00
Barbie, Super Talk (Black), 1995, NRFB $25.00
Barbie, Sweet 16, 1973, NRFB $100.00

Barbie, Swirl Ponytail, 1964, brunette, NRFB, minimum value, $1,000.00 (M, from $400.00 to $500.00). (Photo courtesy Paris and Susan Manos)

Barbie, Teen Talk, 1991, NRFB....................................$75.00
Barbie, Thailand, 1998, Dolls of the World, NRFB......$25.00
Barbie, Twist 'N Turn, 1966, blond hair, MIB $600.00
Barbie, UNICEF (Black),1989, NRFB $35.00
Barbie, Vacation Sensation, 1986, Toys R Us, NRFB..$55.00
Barbie, Wedding Fantasy (Black), 1989, NRFB............$35.00
Barbie, 1982, Dolls of the World, NRFB $165.00
Brad, Talking, 1971, MIB $250.00
Casey, 1967, blond or brunette hair, MIB, ea............$450.00
Chris, 1967, blond hair, original outfit, NM $125.00
Christie, Malibu, 1973, MIB...$50.00
Christie, Twist 'N Turn, 1968, red hair, original outfit, NM $250.00
Francie, Growin' Pretty Hair, 1970, original outfit, NM..$150.00
Jamie, New & Wonderful Walking, blond hair, original outfit, EX $225.00
Kelly, Quick Curl, 1972, NRFB $175.00
Ken, Busy Talking, 1972, original outfit, VG $85.00
Ken, Doctor, 1987, MIB..$35.00
Ken, Earring Magic, 1993, MIB $45.00
Ken, Jewel Secrets, 1986, NRFB....................................$65.00

Ken, Mod Hair, 1972, MIB, $100.00.
(Photo courtesy Stephanie Deutsch)

Ken, Rhett Butler, 1994, Hollywood Legends Series, NRFB $75.00
Ken, Roller Skating, 1981, MIB...................................$50.00
Ken, Sun Valley, 1973, NRFB......................................$125.00
Ken, Walk Lively, 1972, MIB.......................................$150.00
Midge, All Stars, 1990, MIB $40.00
Midge, California Dream, 1988, MIB $50.00
PJ, Dream Date, 1983, MIB $50.00
PJ, Sweet Roses, 1983, NRFB $65.00
Ricky, 1965, original outfit & shoes, NM $75.00
Skipper, Dramatic New Living, 1970, original swimsuit, NM $50.00

Skipper, Pose 'N Play, 1973, MIP $125.00
Skipper, Sunset Malibu, 1971-74, NRFB $75.00
Skipper, Twist 'N Turn, 1970-71, NRFB $300.00
Skooter, 1963, brunette hair, original swimsuit & bows, MIB $175.00
Skooter, 1965, blond hair, bendable legs, MIB..........$225.00
Steffie, Walk Lively, 1968, original outfit & scarf, NM..$175.00
Teresa, Baywatch, 1994, NRFB $35.00
Teresa, Lights & Lace, 1990, NRFB.............................$30.00
Tutti, 1974, blond hair, original outfit, EX $60.00
Whitney, Style Magic, 1988, NRFB $65.00

Skipper, blond or red hair, bendable legs, 1965, MIB, from $350.00 to $400.00.

Accessories

Case, Golden Dream Barbie, vinyl with velcro closure, 1980, NM, $10.00. (Photo courtesy Beth Summers)

Case, Barbie, Bubble-Cut Barbie wearing Solo in the Spotlight on pink vinyl, 1963, rare, NM, from $75 to.................$85.00

Case, Barbie, Sophisticated Lady on black, blue or red vinyl, 1963, NM, ea, from $30 to $40.00
Case, Barbie & Francie, Barbie wearing Pretty & Wild & Francie wearing Smart Switch, 1965, NM $125.00
Case, Barbie & Ken, Barbie wearing Party Date & Ken wearing Saturday Night Date on black vinyl, 1963, EX.........$65.00
Case, Barbie & Midge, Barbie wearing Movie Date & Midge wearing Sorority Meeting w/Ken & Allan at side on blue, 1963, EX...$35.00
Case, Golden Dream Barbie, 1980, vinyl, EX.............$10.00
Case, Tuttie & Todd House, vinyl, NM $50.00
Furniture, Barbie & the Rockers Dance Cafe, 1987, MIB $50.00
Furniture, Barbie Dance Club Dancetime Shop, 1989, MIB $50.00
Furniture, Barbie Dream Bath & Beauty Center, 1984, MIB $25.00
Furniture, Barbie Dream Buffet, 1985, complete, MIB..$25.00
Furniture, Barbie Dream Glow Bed, 1986, MIB..........$25.00
Furniture, Barbie Fold 'N Fun House, 1994, M $50.00
Furniture, Go-Together TV Set, 1964, NM $6.00
Furniture, Pink Sparkles Armoire, 1990, NRFB............$25.00
Furniture, Pink Sparkles Fun Phone Center, 1990, NRFB $25.00
Furniture, Starlight Bed, 1990, complete, MIB..............$30.00
Furniture, Suzy Goose Vanity, 1963, complete, EX.....$35.00
Furniture, Sweet Roses Accents, 1988, NRFB $35.00
Furniture, Sweet Roses Refrigerator, 1987, NRFB........$25.00
Outfit, Baby Doll Pinks, #3403, complete, M $45.00
Outfit, Barbie, A Little Luxury, #4810, Fashion Fantasy, 1984, MIB $35.00
Outfit, Barbie, Anti-Freezers, #1464, 1970, MIB $150.00
Outfit, Barbie, Beautiful Bride, #1698, complete, M .$900.00
Outfit, Barbie, Bermuda Holiday, #1810, 1968, MIB.$300.00
Outfit, Barbie, Busy Gal, #981, complete, NM $195.00
Outfit, Barbie, Flower Wower, #1453, 1970, MIB........$75.00
Outfit, Barbie, Garden Wedding, #1658, complete, M ..$300.00
Outfit, Barbie, Holiday Dance, #1639, complete, EX..$300.00

Outfit, Barbie, Wedding of the Year, #5743, 1982, NRFB, $20.00. (Photo courtesy Beth Summers)

Outfit, Barbie, Ruffles 'N Swirls, #1783, complete, NM+ ..**$55.00**
Outfit, Barbie, Silken Flame, #977, complete, NM+ **$75.00**
Outfit, Barbie, Spot Star, #3353, complete, NM **$25.00**
Outfit, Barbie, Sweater Girl, #976, complete, EX **$55.00**
Outfit, Francie, Checker Chums, #3287, 1972, MIB ..**$150.00**
Outfit, Francie, Concert in the Park, #1256, complete,
    NM+ **$85.00**
Outfit, Francie, Gold Rush, #1222, complete, M **$85.00**
Outfit, Francie, Ice Blue, #1274, complete, M **$80.00**
Outfit, Francie, Nighty Brights Fashion Pak, 1970, MIP ..**$85.00**
Outfit, Francie, Polka-Dots & Rainbows, #1255, MOC...**$75.00**
Outfit, Francie, Side Kick, #1273, complete, M **$85.00**
Outfit, Francie, Zig-Zag Zoom, #3445, 1971, MIB.....**$100.00**
Outfit, Ken, College Student, #1416, 1965, MIB........**$550.00**
Outfit, Ken, Country Clubbin', #1400, NRFB.............**$175.00**

Outfit, Ken, Fountain Boy, #1407, 1964, NRFB, $150.00. (Photo courtesy Stephanie Deutsch)

Outfit, Ken, Midnight Blues, #1719, NRFB **$175.00**
Outfit, Ken, Night Scene, #1496, 1971, MIB **$100.00**
Outfit, Ken, Special Date, #1401, complete, NM+.......**$85.00**
Outfit, Ken, Wide Awake Stripes, #3378, 1972, MIB...**$60.00**
Outfit, Skipper, All Over Felt, #3476, NRFB **$150.00**
Outfit, Skipper, Chill Chasers, #1926, 1966, complete,
    NM+ **$55.00**
Outfit, Skipper, Eeny Meeny Midi, #1974, complete,
    EX **$50.00**
Outfit, Skipper, Fun Time, #1920, complete, NM........**$75.00**
Outfit, Skipper, Jazzy Jamys, #1967, 1969, complete, M .**$50.00**
Outfit, Skipper, Outdoor Casuals, #1915, 1965, MIB...**$85.00**
Outfit, Skipper, Red Sensation, #1901, NRFB **$165.00**
Outfit, Skipper, Silk 'N Fancy, #1902, complete, NM..**$50.00**
Outfit, Skipper, Sunny Pastels, #1910, complete, M....**$50.00**
Outfit, Skipper, Toe Twinklers Fashion Pak, 1970, MIP.**$65.00**
Outfit, Skipper, What's New at the Zoo, #1925, complete,
    EX **$55.00**
Outfit, Tutti, Pinky PJs, #3616, NRFB **$150.00**
Outfit, Tuttie, Plantin' Posies, #3609, 1967, complete, M...**$65.00**
Playset, Barbie Country Living House, 1973-77, complete,
    EX...**$75.00**
Playset, Barbie Dream Cottage, 1983, complete, M **$65.00**

Playset, Barbie Fold 'N Fun House, 1994, M...............**$50.00**
Playset, Barbie Lively Living House, 1970, MIB........**$200.00**
Playset, Barbie 6 o'Clock News Station, 1984, NRFB..**$50.00**
Playset, California Dream Barbie Hot Dog Stand, 1988,
    NRFB..**$50.00**
Playset, Olympic Village, 1975, MIB **$60.00**
Playset, Tutti & Chris Sleep & Play House, 1967, complete,
    M **$150.00**
Vehicle, Barbie & Skipper's Speedboat, Sears Exclusive, 1964,
    MIB **$300.00**
Vehicle, Cap'n Barbie Sun Cruiser, 1994, M.................**$20.00**
Vehicle, Skipper's Travelin' Trailer Deluxe Set, 1983, MIB.**$50.00**
Vehicle, Snowmobile, Montgomery Ward, 1972, MIB.**$65.00**
Vehicle, Sunsailer, 1975, NRFB **$55.00**
Vehicle, Western Fun Motorhome, 1989, MIB **$50.00**
Vehicle, 1957 Chevy Belair, 2nd edition, 1990, pink,
    MIB..**$125.00**

Gift Sets

Barbie Denim 'n Ruffles High Stepper Western Gift Set, 1995, NRFB, $100.00. (Photo courtesy J. Michael Augustyniak)

All American Barbie & Star Stepper, 1991, MIB **$65.00**
Barbie & Friends, 1983, NRFB **$55.00**
Barbie & Ken Campin' Out, 1983, NRFB...................**$100.00**
Barbie Loves Elvis, 1996, NRFB..................................**$75.00**
Birthday Fun Kelly, 1996, Toys R Us, MIB **$40.00**
Dance Magic Barbie & Ken, 1990, NRFB....................**$50.00**
Gap Barbie & Kelly, 1997, NRFB.................................**$50.00**
Holiday Sisters Barbie, Kelly & Stacey, 1998, NRFB ...**$50.00**
Loving You Barbie, 1984, NRFB **$65.00**
Rollerblade Barbie Snack & Surf Set, 1992, MIB **$75.00**
Western Stampin' Barbie, 1993, complete, MIB...........**$50.00**

Miscellaneous

Barbie Cologne, 1986, M..**$15.00**
Barbie Dream Cosmetic Set, 1985, complete, M **$20.00**
Barbie Magic Plastic Molding Machine, 1994, M........**$25.00**
Barbie Slumber Set, 1985, complete, M **$25.00**
Beanbag chair, hot pink w/colorful image of Barbie,
    Lewco/Mattel, 1990, NM................................**$15.00**

Bicycle accessory kit, Barbie, 1995, M $20.00
Binder, Skipper in Masquerade, blue or yellow vinyl, 1965, rare, M, minimum value..$250.00
Booklet, World of Barbie Fashion, 1968, M................$10.00
Box, Barbie as Truly Scrumptious, 1968, EX...............$65.00
Box, Midge, 1962, EX...$75.00
Calendar, Hallmark, 1996, M..$5.00
Clock radio, Barbie in 1962 convertible, 1996, M.....$100.00
Comb & mirror set, Superstar Barbie, 1977, NRFB $15.00
Hula Hoop, Barbie, 1991, EX $10.00
Kite, Roller Skating Barbie, 1988, plastic, MIP $15.00
Magazine, Barbie Bazaar, October 1988, M.................$50.00

Mattel-a-Phone, Barbie, M, minimum value $100.00.
(Photo courtesy Paris and Susan Manos)

Nurse Bag, Skipper, red vinyl, complete, minimum value $300.00.

Music box, Enchanted Evening Barbie, 1997, M.........$30.00
Video game, Barbie Super Model, Sega, 1993, M $35.00

Barware

From the decade of the '90s, the cocktail shaker has emerged as a hot new collectible. These micro skyscrapers are now being saved for the enjoyment of future generations, much like the 1930s buildings saved from destruction by landmarks preservation committees of today.

Cocktail shakers — the words just conjure up visions of glamour and elegance. Seven hard shakes over your right shoulder and you can travel back in time, back to the glamor of Hollywood movie sets with Fred Astaire and Ginger Rogers and luxurious hotel lounges with gleaming chrome; back to the world of F. Scott Fitzgerald and *The Great Gatsby*; or watch *The Thin Man* movie showing William Powell instruct a bartender on the proper way to shake a martini — the reveries are endless.

An original American art form, cocktail shakers reflect the changing nature of various styles of art, design, and architecture of the era between WWI and WWII. We see the graceful lines of Art Nouveau in the early '20s being replaced by the rage for jagged geometric modern design. The geometric cubism of Picasso that influenced so many designers of the '20s was replaced with the craze for streamline design of '30s. Cocktail shakers of the early '30s were taking the shape of the new deity of American architecture, the skyscraper, thus giving the appearance of movement and speed in a slow economy.

Cocktail shakers served to penetrate the gloom of depression, ready to propel us into the future of prosperity like some Buck Rogers rocket ship — both perfect symbols of generative power, of our perpetration into better times ahead.

Cocktail shakers and architecture took on the aerodynamically sleek industrial design of the automobile and airship. It was as Norman Bel Geddes said: 'a quest for speed.' All sharp edges and corners were rounded off. This trend was the theme of the day, as even the sharp notes of jazz turned into swing.

Cocktail shakers have all the classic qualifications of a premium collectible. They are easily found at auctions, antique and secondhand shops, flea markets, and sales. They can be had in all price ranges. They require little study to identify one manufacturer or period from another, and lastly they are not easily reproduced.

The sleek streamline cocktail shakers of modern design are valued by collectors of today. Those made by Revere, Chase, and Manning Bowman have taken the lead in this race. Also commanding high prices are those shakers of unusual design such as penguins, zeppelins, dumbbells, bowling pins, town crier bells, airplanes, even ladies' legs. They're all out there, waiting to be found, waiting to be recalled to life, to hear the clank of ice cubes, and to again become the symbol of elegance.

For more information we recommend *Vintage Bar Ware, An Identification and Value Guide*, by Stephen Visakay (Collector Books).

Advisor: Steve Visakay (See Directory, Barware)

Bar set, bowling ball opens to assortment of shot glasses & sm cylindrical chrome decanter, 1940s-50s, 13x8½" dia $65.00

Bar towel, black cloth w/red & white cocktail shakers, red bow ties & red hands w/white cuffs, 1950s **$25.00**

Bar towel, white cloth w/Black waiter in red, white & blue uniform holding w/tray aloft, 1940s.....................**$35.00**

Cocktail cup, chrome stem w/amber glass insert, Farber Bros, 1940s-60s, 4¼".....................................**$12.00**

Cocktail glass, ceramic, girl's torso, painted-on 2-pc bathing suit, 1950s...**$10.00**

Cocktail glass, glass w/Artist Models decal, nude obscured by palette which becomes invisible when filled, 1940s, 4¾"..**$12.00**

Cocktail glass, plastic, clear top w/colored coiled stem on black base, 1950s.......................................**$7.00**

Cocktail mixer, glass, cylindrical w/etched vertical lines, w/stirrer, silver cap & strainer, handled, Hawks, 1940s, 16"...**$250.00**

Cocktail mixer, novelty, red container w/train or airplane on chrome lid, battery-operated, Japan, 1950s-60s, 9", ea **$35.00**

Cocktail picks, plastic bowling pins atop chrome picks in chrome holder w/black plastic bowling ball handle, 1940s, 4" **$25.00**

Cocktail shaker, aluminum, mum design on hammered background, w/spout & screw cap, Continental Hand Wrought, 12"..**$45.00**

Cocktail shaker, aluminum, vertically ribbed cylinder w/Ezee Pour top, Emson Products, 1947, 12½"................**$65.00**

Cocktail shaker, chrome, cylindrical w/alternate polished & hammered bands, orange Catalin trim, Krome Kraft, 1940s, 13" **$55.00**

Cocktail shaker, chrome, Manhattan-style party size, Revere, 1939-41, 13" **$450.00**

Cocktail shaker, glass, horizontally ribbed cylinder w/chrome top, Imperial Glass, 1955, 14" **$55.00**

Cocktail shaker, glass, painted marsh scene w/duck in flight, silver-plated top & cobalt footed bottom, 1925-29, 9¼" **$110.00**

Cocktail shaker, glass, rooster motif engraved & cut, silver-plated top w/cork stoppers, ca 1928, 9½"............**$65.00**

Cocktail shaker, glass, roosters in military garb in red, white & blue pyro on cylinder w/chrome lid, 1942, 9½" **$50.00**

Cocktail shaker, hammered nickel plate w//black handle, 3-pc w/juicer, Bernard Rice's Sons, 13¾" **$75.00**

Cocktail shaker, metal, contoured w/morning glory motif on mottled reddish brown background, w/lid, Occupied Japan, 12" **$95.00**

Cocktail shaker set, aluminum, 11¼" blue anodized cylinder w/chrome top & 12" round tray, 1950s **$75.00**

Cocktail shaker set, chrome, Park set w/Zephyr shaker, 4 cups w/Catalin bases, round tray, Revere, 1937-41.......**$300.00**

Cocktail shaker set, chrome, pitcher w/polished & hammered bands, black compo handle, 6 stemmed cups, 1940s-60s **$100.00**

Cocktail shaker set, glass, shaker, ice bowl & 6 footed glasses, frosted w/sterling bands & rims, 1930s-40s **$75.00**

Decanter, novelty donkey carrying shot glasses & barrel, press down on right ear to fill cup, painted tin, 1940s, 9"..**$75.00**

Ice bucket, aluminum medieval helmet form, Hong Kong, 16"..**$20.00**

Ice bucket, glass, frosted pattern w/4 colored painted bands, wire handle, w/tongs, open................................**$35.00**

Ice bucket, glass, green Georgian pattern w/wire handle, open...**$40.00**

Ice bucket, glass bowl in handled aluminum holder w/cut-out leaves & acorns, w/ice tongs, Continental Silverlook...**$55.00**

Cocktail shaker, three chrome balls under a wooden handle, four bells on top ball, ca 1935, 14x5", $250.00. (Photo courtesy Stephen Visakay)

Ice bucket, Hex Optic, green glass with reamer top, Jeannette, from $40.00 to $45.00. (Photo courtesy Gene Florence)

Cocktail shaker, glass, footed conical shape w/chrome top, Alessi by Matteo Thun, 1987, 11½".............**$120.00**

Martini Spike (Vermouth Dispenser), plastic & metal, resembles mouth thermometer, in box, 6½" L...............**$30.00**

Napkins, linen, 4 tuxedoed gents, 2 cocktail glasses & shaker on checked ground, orange, brown & white, set of 8...**$75.00**

Shot glass, ceramic, girl's torso, painted-on 2-pc bathing suit, 1950s **$6.00**

Soda syphon, Globe Master, green enameled metal & plastic ball shape, England, 1950s, 10½" **$45.00**

Swizzle sticks, plastic playing cards hanging from glass cane-shaped sticks, set of 8 in box, 1940s, 6½"............**$18.00**

Tray, aluminum, anchor, rope & sea gull pattern w/hammered background, turned-up rim, rod handles, Everlast, 9x15" **$30.00**

Tray, aluminum, hunt scene w/dog & split-rail fence, turned-up rim, self-handled, Wendell August Forge, 9x17".......**$90.00**

Tray, metal, bubbly cocktail glass & stars in gold on red & black enamel background, 1940s-50s, 17½x14½" ..**$20.00**

Bauer Pottery

Undoubtedly the most easily recognized product of the Bauer Pottery Company who operated from 1909 until 1962 in Los Angeles, California, was their colorful 'Ring' dinnerware (made from 1932 until sometime in the early '60s). They made other lines of dinnerware that are collectible as well, although by no means as easily found. Bauer also made a line of Gardenware vases and flowerpots for the florist trade.

In the lines of Ring and Plain ware, pricing depends to some extent on color. Use the low end of our range of values for light brown, Chinese yellow, orange-red, jade green, red-brown, olive green, light blue, turquoise, and gray; the high-end colors are delph blue, ivory, dusky burgundy, cobalt, chartreuse, papaya, and burgundy. Black is 50% higher than the high end; to evaluate white, double the high side. An in-depth study of colors and values may be found in *The Collector's Encyclopedia of California Pottery, Second Edition,* and *Collector's Encyclopedia of Bauer Pottery,* both by Jack Chipman.

Gloss Pastel Kitchenware teapot, yellow, in-mold mark, eight-cup, from $150.00 to $200.00. (Photo courtesy Jack Chipman)

Brusche Al Fresco, plate, dinner; lime, 11½" **$12.00**

Cal-Art, bowl, matt green, swirl, 8" **$40.00**

Cal-Art, vase, matt pink, 10" **$85.00**

Gloss Pastel Kitchenware, custard cup, pink.................**$8.00**

Gloss Pastel Kitchenware, pitcher, ivory, 1-qt **$35.00**

La Linda, plate, dinner; green, 9" **$15.00**

La Linda, saucer, matt yellow.......................................**$6.00**

Monterey Moderne, cup & saucer, black, minimum value .**$45.00**

Monterey Moderne, plate, dinner; turquoise/olive green, 9½"...**$20.00**

Plain ware, bowl, salad; blue, 10½", from $85 to.....**$125.00**

Plain ware, butter plate, black, 4½", minimum value..**$135.00**

Plain ware, coffee server, wood handle, w/lid, from $65 to.**$95.00**

Plain ware, creamer, midget, red, from $45 to...........**$65.00**

Plain ware, lamp base, green, 4½", from $300 to.....**$450.00**

Plain ware, pitcher, 12", from $350 to **$525.00**

Plain ware, pudding dish, orange, #6, 10¼", from $80 to.**$120.00**

Ring, bottle, water; w/lid, from $275 to **$400.00**

Ring, bowl, batter; 2-qt, from $85 to.........................**$125.00**

Ring, bowl, berry; 4", from $20 to..............................**$30.00**

Ring, bowl, fruit; 5", from $25 to................................**$35.00**

Ring, bowl, mixing; #18, from $45 to **$65.00**

Ring, bowl, punch; 14", from $350 to........................**$525.00**

Ring, bowl, salad; low, 9", from $60 to **$90.00**

Ring, bowl, vegetable; oval, 8", from $85 to **$125.00**

Ring, candle holder, 2½", from $45 to **$65.00**

Ring, coffeepot, drip; from $300 to...........................**$400.00**

Ring, cookie jar, from $400 to **$600.00**

Ring, creamer, from $20 to **$30.00**

Ring, gravy bowl, from $100 to..................................**$150.00**

Ring, mustard jar, w/notched lid, from $250 to **$375.00**

Ring, nappy, #9, from $65 to **$95.00**

Ring, pitcher, 3-qt, from $125 to **$175.00**

Ring, plate, bread & butter; 5", from $30 to................**$45.00**

Ring, plate, dinner; 10½", from $65 to........................**$95.00**

Ring, plate, salad; 7½", from $30 to............................**$45.00**

Ring, platter, oval, 9", from $30 to **$45.00**

Ring, relish plate, divided, from $85 to **$125.00**

Ring, saucer, AD; from $60 to......................................**$90.00**

Ring, spice jar, #1, from $100 to................................**$150.00**

Ring, tumbler, w/handle, 3-oz, from $75 to **$100.00**

Beanie Babies

Who can account for this latest flash in collecting that some liken to the rush for Cabbage Patch dolls we saw many years ago! The appeal of these stuffed creatures is disarming to both children and adults, and excited collectors are eager to scoop up each new-found treasure. There is much to be learned about Beanie Babies. For instance, there are different tag styles, these indicate date of issue:

#1, Swing tag: single heart-shaped tag (Photos courtesy Amy Hopper)

#2, Swing tag: heart-shaped; folded, with information inside; narrow letters (Photos courtesy Amy Hopper)

#3, Swing tag: heart-shaped; folded, with information inside; wider letters (Photos courtesy Amy Hopper)

#4, Swing tag: heart-shaped; folded, with information inside; wider lettering with no gold outline around the 'ty'; yellow star on front; first tag to include a poem and birth date (Photos courtesy Amy Hopper)

#5, Swing tag: heart-shaped; folded, with information inside; different font on front and inside; birth month spelled out, no style numbers, website listed (Photos courtesy Amy Hopper)

#6, Swing tag: features holographic star with '2000' across star; inside: Ty, Inc., Ty Canada, Ty Europe, and Ty Japan; birthdate, website address, and poem in smaller font than #5; new safety precaution on back, smaller font, and UPC (Photos courtesy Amy Hopper)

Prices given are for toys with swing tags in mint or near-mint condition. For current Beanies with a #1, #2, or #3 tag, add $30.00 to $50.00 to the prices suggested below.

Advisor: Amy Hopper (See Directory, Beanie Babies)

Current

Ariel, #4288, fundraising bear for the Elizabeth Glaser Pediatric AIDS Foundation, from $10 to **$15.00**
Aruba, #4314, angelfish, from $7 to **$15.00**
Aurora, #4271, polar bear, from $7 to.......................**$10.00**
Bananas, #4316, orangutan, from $7 to **$15.00**
Buckingham, #4603, British bear, UK exclusive, from $90 to...**$120.00**
Bushy, #4285, lion, from $7 to **$10.00**
Buzzy, #4308, buzzard, from $7 to............................**$10.00**
Cashew, #4292, brown bear, from $7 to....................**$15.00**
Cheezer, #4301, mouse, from $7 to...........................**$10.00**
China, #4315, panda, from $7 to **$10.00**
Chinook, #4604, bear, Ty Canada exclusive, from $75 to **$95.00**
Cinders, #4295, black bear, from $7 to **$10.00**
Fetcher, #4298, chocolate lab, from $7 to.................**$10.00**
Glow, #4283, lightning bug, from $7 to.....................**$10.00**
Grace, #4274, praying bunny, from $7 to..................**$10.00**
Halo II, #4269, angel bear, from $7 to.......................**$15.00**
Howl, #4310, wolf, from $7 to....................................**$10.00**
Huggy, #4306, tan bear, from $10 to.........................**$20.00**
India, #4291, tiger, from $7 to **$15.00**

Lefty 2000, #4290, red, white, and blue donkey, USA exclusive, from $7.00 to $15.00; Righty 2000, #4289, red, white, and blue elephant, USA exclusive, from $7.00 to $15.00. (Photo courtesy Amy Hopper)

Lurkey, #4309, turkey, from $7 to **$10.00**
Niles, #4284, camel, from $7 to **$10.00**
Oats, #4305, horse, from $7 to **$10.00**
Peekaboo, #4303, turtle, from $7 to...........................**$10.00**
Pellet, #4313, hamster, from $7 to.............................**$10.00**
Prince, #4312, bullfrog, from $7 to............................**$10.00**
Rufus, #4280, dog, from $7 to **$10.00**
Runner, #4304, mustelidae, from $7 to **$10.00**

Sarge, #4277, German shepherd, from $7 to...............**$10.00**

Slayer, #4307, frilled dragon, from $7 to....................**$10.00**

Sneaky, #4278, leopard, from $7 to **$10.00**

Sniffer, #4299, beagle, from $7 to............................**$10.00**

Speckles, brown bear, e-Beanie exclusively through the Internet & Ty Trade on the official Ty website, from $15 to **$25.00**

Swampy, #4273, alligator, from $7 to........................**$10.00**

Swoop, #4268, pterodactyl, from $7 to **$10.00**

Tricks, #4311, dog, from $7 to.................................**$10.00**

Trumpet, #4276, elephant, from $7 to.......................**$10.00**

USA, #4287, American bear, USA exclusive, from $7 to.**$15.00**

Whiskers, #4317, dog, from $7 to **$10.00**

Wiggly, #4275, octopus, from $7 to...........................**$10.00**

Zodiac, Ox, #4319, Dog, #4326, Dragon, #4322, Goat, #4329, Horse, #4324, Monkey, #4328, Pig, #4327, Rabbit, #4321, Rat, #4318, Rooster, #4325, Snake, #4323, or Tiger, #4320, ea from $10 to..**$15.00**

Retired

#1 Bear, red w/#1 on chest, issued only to Ty sales reps, 253 made, minimum value **$5,700.00**

Ally, #4032, alligator **$45.00**

Almond, #4246, bear, from $5 to...............................**$10.00**

Amber, #4243, gold tabby cat, from $5 to **$10.00**

Ants, #4195, anteater, from $5 to..............................**$10.00**

Baldy, #4074, eagle, from $10 to...............................**$20.00**

Batty, #4035, pink bat, from $5 to.............................**$10.00**

Batty, #4035, tie-dyed bat, from $5 to........................**$15.00**

BB, #4253, birthday bear, from $10 to **$20.00**

Beak, #4211, kiwi bird, from $5 to.............................**$10.00**

Bernie, #4109, St Bernard, from $5 to **$10.00**

Bessie, #4009, brown cow **$45.00**

Blackie, #4011, bear, from $10 to..............................**$20.00**

Blizzard, #4163, white tiger, from $10 to **$20.00**

Bones, #4001, brown dog **$20.00**

Bongo, #4067, 1st issue, brown monkey.....................**$45.00**

Bongo, #4067, 2nd issue, brown monkey w/tan tail, from $10 to **$15.00**

Britannia, #4601, British bear, Ty UK exclusive, minimum value **$75.00**

Bronty, #4085, brontosaurus, minimum value...........**$550.00**

Brownie, #4010, bear, w/swing tag, minimum value..**$2,500.00**

Bruno, #4183, terrier, from $5 to..............................**$10.00**

Bubbles, #4078, yellow & black fish, minimum value....**$75.00**

Bucky, #4016, beaver, from $15 to.............................**$25.00**

Bumble, #4045, bee, minimum value **$300.00**

Butch, #4227, bull terrier, from $5 to............................**$10.00**

Canyon, #4212, cougar, from $5 to **$10.00**

Caw, #4071, crow, from $300 to **$400.00**

Cheeks, #4250, baboon, from $5 to **$10.00**

Chilly, #4012, polar bear, minimum value..............**$1,000.00**

Chip, #4121, calico cat, from $5 to............................**$10.00**

Chipper, #4259, chipmunk, from $5 to **$10.00**

Chocolate, #4015, moose, from $5 to **$15.00**

Chops, #4019, lamb, minimum value.........................**$75.00**

Claude, #4083, tie-dyed crab, from $5 to...................**$15.00**

Clubby, blue bear, BBOC exclusive, from $20 to **$25.00**

Clubby II, purple bear, BBOC exclusive, from $10 to.**$20.00**

Clubby III, from $10 to **$20.00**

Congo, #4160, gorilla, from $5 to..............................**$15.00**

Coral, #4079, tie-dyed fish, minimum value **$75.00**

Crunch, #4130, shark, from $5 to **$10.00**

Cubbie, #4010, brown bear, from $15 to.....................**$30.00**

Curly, #4052, brown bear, from $10 to.......................**$20.00**

Daisy, #4006, black & white cow, from $5 to **$15.00**

Derby, #4008, 1st issue, horse w/fine yarn mane & tail, minimum value **$1,500.00**

Derby, #4008, 2nd issue, horse w/coarse mane & tail, from $10 to **$20.00**

Derby, #4008, 3rd issue, horse w/white star on forehead, from $5 to **$15.00**

Derby, #4008, 4th issue, horse w/white star on forehead, fur mane & tail, from $5 to **$15.00**

Digger, #4027, 1st issue, orange crab, minimum value.**$350.00**

Digger, #4027, 2nd issue, red crab, minimum value...**$65.00**

Doby, #4110, doberman, from $5 to **$15.00**

Doodle, #4171, tie-dyed rooster, from $15 to.............**$25.00**

Dotty, #4100, dalmatian, from $5 to..........................**$15.00**

Early, #4190, robin, from $5 to..................................**$15.00**

Ears, #4018, brown rabbit, from $10 ....**$20.00**

Echo, #4180, dolphin, from $10 to **$15.00**

Eggbert, #4232, baby chick, from $5 to......................**$10.00**

Erin, #4186, green bear, from $10 to..........................**$20.00**

Eucalyptus, #4240, koala, from $5 to **$10.00**

Ewey, #4219, lamb, from $5 to..................................**$15.00**

Fetch, #4189, golden retriever, from $10 to................**$20.00**

Flash, #4021, dolphin, minimum value.......................**$60.00**

Fleece, #4125, white lamb w/cream face, from $5 to.**$15.00**

Fleecie, #4279, cream lamb w/purple neck ribbon, from $5 to **$10.00**

Flip, #4012, white cat, from $15 to............................**$30.00**

Flitter, #4255, pastel butterfly, from $5 to **$15.00**

Floppity, #4118, lilac bunny, from $10 to...................**$20.00**

Flutter, #4043, tie-dyed butterfly, minimum value **$400.00**

Fortune, #4196, panda bear, from $5 to **$15.00**

Freckles, #4066, leopard, from $5 to..........................**$15.00**

Frigid, #4270, king penguin, from $7 to.....................**$10.00**

Fuzz, #4237, bear, from $10 to **$20.00**

Garcia, #4051, tie-dyed bear, minimum value **$85.00**

Germania, #4236, German bear, Ty UK exclusive **$70.00**

Gigi, #4191, poodle, from $5 to **$15.00**

Glory, #4188, American bear w/stars, from $15 to **$25.00**

Goatee, #4235, mountain goat, from $5 to **$10.00**

Gobbles, #4034, turkey, from $5 to............................**$15.00**

Goldie, #4023, goldfish, from $20 to..........................**$35.00**

Goochy, #4230, jellyfish, from $5 to **$15.00**

Gracie, #4126, swan, from $10 to..............................**$20.00**

Groovy, #4256, bear, from $10 to..............................**$20.00**

Grunt, #4092, red razorback pig, minimum value **$80.00**

Halo, #4208, angel bear, from $10 to.........................**$20.00**

Happy, #4061, 1st issue, gray hippo, minimum value..**$375.00**

Happy, #4061, 2nd issue, lavender hippo, from $10 to.**$20.00**
Hippie, #4218, tie-dyed bunny, from $10 to **$20.00**
Hippity, #4119, mint green bunny, from $10 to.........**$20.00**
Hissy, #4185, snake, from $5 to **$10.00**

Holiday Teddy (1997), #4200, from $20.00 to $30.00. (Photo courtesy Amy Hopper)

Holiday Teddy (1998), #4204, from $20 to.................**$35.00**
Holiday Teddy (1999), #4257, from $10 to.................**$20.00**
Holiday Teddy (2000), #4332, from $10 to.................**$25.00**
Honks, #4258, goose, from $5 to **$10.00**

Hope, #4213, praying bear, from $5.00 to $15.00. (Photo courtesy Amy Hopper)

Hoot, #4073, owl, from $20 to......................................**$30.00**
Hoppity, #4117, pink bunny, from $10 to **$20.00**
Humphrey, #4060, camel, minimum value................**$900.00**
Iggy, #4038, all issues, iguana, from $5 to **$15.00**
Inch, #4044, worm w/felt antenna, from $70 to **$90.00**
Inch, #4044, worm w/yarn antenna, from $10 to **$20.00**
Inky, #4028, 1st issue, tan octopus w/no mouth, minimum value **$400.00**

Inky, #4028, 2nd issue, tan octopus w/mouth, minimum value **$350.00**
Inky, #4028, 3rd issue, pink octopus, from $10 to **$20.00**
Jabber, #4197, parrot, from $5 to.................................**$10.00**
Jake, #4199, mallard duck, from $5 to.........................**$10.00**
Jolly, #4082, walrus, from $5 to...................................**$15.00**
Kicks, #4229, soccer bear, from $10 to **$20.00**
Kiwi, #4070, toucan, minimum value..........................**$80.00**
Knuckles, #4247, pig, from $5 to **$10.00**
Kuku, #4192, cockatoo, from $5 to **$10.00**
Lefty, #4057, blue-gray donkey w/American flag, minimum value **$175.00**
Legs, #4020, frog, from $10 to **$20.00**
Libearty, #4057, white bear w/American flag, minimum value **$250.00**
Lips, #4254, fish, from $5 to **$15.00**
Lizzy, #4033, 1st issue, tie-dyed lizard, minimum value..**$400.00**
Lizzy, #4033, 2nd issue, blue lizard, from $15 to........**$25.00**
Loosy, #4206, Canada goose, from $5 to......................**$10.00**
Lucky, #4040, 1st issue, ladybug w/7 felt spots, minimum value **$125.00**
Lucky, #4040, 2nd issue, ladybug w/21 printed spots, minimum value **$300.00**
Lucky, #4040, 3rd issue, ladybug w/11 spots, from $10 to.**$20.00**
Luke, #4214, lab puppy, from $5 to............................**$10.00**
Mac, #4225, cardinal, from $5 to **$15.00**
Magic, #4088, dragon, from $20 to..............................**$35.00**
Manny, #4081, manatee, minimum value **$90.00**
Maple, #4600, bear, Ty Canada exclusive, minimum value..**$55.00**
Mel, #4162, koala, from $5 to.......................................**$10.00**
Millennium, #4226, bear, from $10 to **$20.00**
Mooch, #4224, spider monkey, from $5 to...................**$10.00**
Morrie, #4282, eel, from $7 to **$10.00**
Mystic, #4007, 1st issue, unicorn w/soft fine mane & tail, minimum value **$185.00**
Mystic, #4007, 2nd issue, unicorn w/coarse yarn mane & brown horn, from $15 to **$25.00**
Mystic, #4007, 3rd issue, unicorn w/iridescent horn, from $5 to...**$15.00**
Mystic, #4007, 4th issue, unicron w/iridescent horn, rainbow fur mane & tail, from $5 to **$15.00**
Nana, #4067, 1st issue of Bongo the monkey, minimum value **$2,400.00**
Nanook, #4104, husky dog, from $5 to **$15.00**
Neon, #4239, tie-dyed sea horse, from $5 to **$10.00**
Nibbler, #4216, cream rabbit, from $5 to....................**$15.00**
Nibbly, #4217, brown rabbit, from $5 to **$15.00**
Nip, #4003, 1st issue, gold cat w/white tummy, minimum value **$300.00**
Nip, #4003, 2nd issue, all gold cat, minimum value.**$400.00**
Nip, #4003, 3rd issue, gold cat w/white paws, from $10 to.**$25.00**
Nipponia, #4605, bear, Ty Japan exclusive, from $300 to **$400.00**
Nuts, #4114, squirrel, from $5 to **$15.00**
Osito, #4244, Mexican bear, sold in US, from $10 to .**$20.00**
Patti, #4025, 1st issue, maroon platypus, minimum value **$375.00**

Patti, #4025, 2nd issue, purple platypus, from $10 to....**$20.00**

Paul, #4248, walrus, from $5 to.....................................**$15.00**

Peace, #4053, tie-dyed bear w/embroidered Peace sign, from $10 to...**$25.00**

Peanut, #4062, light blue elephant, from $5 to...........**$15.00**

Peanut, #4062, royal blue elephant (manufacturing mistake), minimum value...**$2,500.00**

Pecan, #4251, gold bear, from $5 to **$10.00**

Peking, #4013, panda bear, minimum value **$900.00**

Periwinkle, blue bear, e-Beanie sold at retail stores, from $10 to..**$30.00**

Pinchers, #4026, lobster, from $10 to...........................**$20.00**

Pinky, #4072, flamingo, from $5 to **$10.00**

Pouch, #4161, kangaroo, from $5 to **$10.00**

Pounce, #4122, brown cat, from $5 to.........................**$10.00**

Prance, #4123, gray striped cat, $5 to **$10.00**

Prickles, #4220, hedgehog, from $5 to.........................**$10.00**

Princess, #4300, purple bear, commemorating Diana, Princess of Wales, PVC pellets, from $35 to.........**$45.00**

Princess, #4300, purple bear, commemorating Diana, Princess of Wales, PE pellets, from $10 to...........**$20.00**

Puffer, #4181, puffin, from $5 to **$10.00**

Pugsly, #4106, pug dog, from $5 to **$15.00**

Pumkin', #4205, pumpkin, from $10 to **$20.00**

Punchers, #4026, 1st issue of Pinchers the lobster, minimum value...**$2,325.00**

Quackers, #4024, 1st issue, duck w/no wings, minimum value..**$900.00**

Quackers, #4024, 2nd issue, duck w/wings, from $10 to.**$20.00**

Radar, #4091, black bat, minimum value.....................**$75.00**

Rainbow, #4037, chameleon, 4 versions, ea from $5 to ..**$15.00**

Rex, #4086, tyrannosaurus, minimum value.............**$400.00**

Righty, #4085, gray elephant w/American flag, minimum value...**$175.00**

Ringo, #4014, raccoon, from $10 to **$20.00**

Roam, #4209, buffalo, from $5 to................................**$10.00**

Roary, #4069, lion, from $5 to.....................................**$15.00**

Rocket, #4202, bluejay, from $5 ....**$10.00**

Rover, #4101, red dog, from $10 to..............................**$25.00**

Roxie, #4334, reindeer, from $7 to..............................**$15.00**

Sakura, #4602, Japanese bear, Japan exclusive, minimum value...**$120.00**

Sammy, #4215, tie-dyed bear, from $5 to **$15.00**

Santa, #4203, from $20 to...**$30.00**

Scaly, #4263, lizard, from $5 to **$10.00**

Scat, #4231, cat, from $5 to..**$10.00**

Schweetheart, #4252, orangutan, from $5 to **$10.00**

Scorch, #4210, dragon, from $5 to **$15.00**

Scottie, #4102, Scottish terrier, from $10 to **$20.00**

Scurry, #4281, beetle, from $7 to..................................**$10.00**

Seamore, #4029, white seal, minimum value **$75.00**

Seaweed, #4080, brown otter, from $10 to..................**$20.00**

Sheets, #4620, ghost, from $5 to **$15.00**

Signature Bear (1999), #4228, from $10 to **$20.00**

Signature Bear (2000), #4266, from $20 to **$40.00**

Silver, #4242, gray tabby cat, from $5 to **$10.00**

Slippery, #4222, gray seal, from $5 to..........................**$15.00**

Scoop, #4107, pelican, from $5.00 to $15.00. Teenie Beanie Baby, 1998, from $3.00 to $5.00. (Photo courtesy Amy Hopper)

Slither, #4031, snake, minimum value, $800.00.
(Photo courtesy Amy Hopper)

Slowpoke, #4261, sloth, from $5 to.............................**$10.00**

Sly, #4115, 1st issue, all brown fox, minimum value..**$90.00**

Sly, #4115, 2nd issue, brown fox w/white belly, from $10 to..**$20.00**

Smoochy, #4039, frog, from $5 to **$10.00**

Snip, #4120, Siamese cat, from $5 to **$15.00**

Snort, #4002, red bull w/cream feet, from $10 to.......**$20.00**

Snowball, #4201, snowman, from $20 to.....................**$30.00**

Snowgirl, #4333, snowwoman, from $7 to **$15.00**

Spangle, #4245, American bear w/blue face, from $20 to...**$30.00**

Spangle, #4245, American bear w/pink face, from $10 to...**$20.00**

Spangle, #4245, American bear w/white face, from $10 to...**$20.00**

Sparky, #4100, dalmatian, minimum value **$65.00**

Speedy, #4030, turtle, from $15 to **$25.00**

Spike, #4060, rhinoceros, from $5 to **$15.00**

Spinner, #4036, spider, from $5 to **$10.00**

Splash, #4022, whale, minimum value **$60.00**

Spooky, #4090, ghost w/orange neck ribbon.............$30.00
Springy, #4272, lavender bunny, from $5 to $15.00
Spunky, #4184, cocker spaniel, from $5 to $15.00

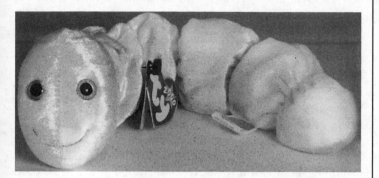

Squirmy, #4302, green worm, from $7.00 to $10.00.
(Photo courtesy Amy Hopper)

Squealer, #4005, pig, from $10 to $25.00
Steg, #4087, stegosaurus, minimum value $385.00
Stilts, #4221, stork, from $5 to $10.00
Sting, #4007, tie-dyed stingray, minimum value.........$60.00
Stinger, #4193, scorpion, from $5 to $10.00
Stinky, #4017, skunk, from $5 to $20.00
Stretch, #4182, ostrich, from $5 to $10.00
Stripes, #4065, 1st issue, gold tiger w/thin stripes, minimum value $225.00
Stripes, #4065, 2nd issue, caramel tiger w/wide stripes, from $10 to...$20.00
Strut, #4171, rooster, from $10 to $20.00
Sunny, yellow-orange bear, e-Beanie sold at retail stores, from $10 to...$30.00
Swirly, #4249, snail, from $5 to $15.00
Tabasco, #4002, bull w/red feet, minimum value.......$75.00
Tank, #4031, 1st issue, armadillo w/7 lines & no shell, minimum value $145.00
Tank, #4031, 2nd issue, armadillo w/9 lines & no shell, minimum value $195.00
Tank, #4031, 3rd issue, armadillo w/shell, minimum value...$80.00
Teddy, #4050, brown bear, new face, from $80 to....$125.00
Teddy, #4050, brown bear, old face, minimum value.....$975.00
Teddy, #4051, teal bear, new face, minimum value.....$1,000.00
Teddy, #4051, teal bear, old face, minimum value ...$825.00
Teddy, #4052, cranberry bear, new face, minimum value...$850.00
Teddy, #4052, cranberry bear, old face, minimum value...$825.00
Teddy, #4055, violet bear, new face, minimum value..$850.00
Teddy, #4055, violet bear, old face, minimum value ..$825.00
Teddy, #4056, magenta bear, new face, minimum value...$850.00
Teddy, #4056, magenta bear, old face, minimum value $825.00
Teddy, #4057, jade bear, new face, minimum value..$850.00

Teddy, #4057, jade bear, old face, minimum value ..$825.00
The Beginning, #4267, white bear w/silver stars, from $10 to.$25.00
The End, #4265, black bear, from $10 to.....................$20.00
Tiny, #4234, chihuahua, from $5 to $15.00
Tiptoe, #4241, mouse, from $5 to $10.00
Tracker, #4198, basset hound, from $5 to....................$15.00
Trap, #4042, mouse, minimum value........................$600.00
Tuffy, #4108, terrier, from $5 to.................................$15.00
Tusk, #4076, walrus, minimum value..........................$75.00
Twigs, #4068, giraffe, from $10 to..............................$20.00
Ty Billionaire Bear (1998), brown, new face, dollar sign on chest, issued only to Ty employees, minimum value $1,250.00
Ty Billionaire 2 Bear (1999), purple, BB on chest, issued only to Ty employees, minimum value...................$2,400.00
Ty Billionaire 3 Bear, from $2,500 to....................$4,500.00
Ty Employee Christmas Bear (1997), violet, new face, minimum value $1,900.00
Ty 2K Bear, #4262, from $10 to..................................$20.00
Valentina, #4233, fuchsia bear w/white heart, from $10 to $20.00
Valentino, #4058, white bear w/red heart, from $15 to ..$25.00
Velvet, #4064, panther, from $15 to $25.00
Waddle, #4075, penguin, from $10 to...........................$20.00
Wallace, #4264, green bear, from $10 to $20.00
Waves, #4084, whale, from $10 to..............................$15.00
Web, #4041, black spider, minimum value...............$600.00
Weenie, #4013, Daschund, from $10 to $20.00
Whisper, #4187, deer, from $5 to $10.00
Wise, #4194, 1998 graduation owl, from $10 to.........$15.00
Wiser, #4238, 1999 graduation owl, from $5 to..........$10.00
Wisest, #4286, 2000 graduation owl, from $7 to........$10.00
Wrinkles, #4103, bulldog, from $5 to $10.00
Zero, #4207, penguin w/Christmas cap, from $10 to..$20.00
Ziggy, #4063, zebra, from $10 to................................$20.00
Zip, #4004, 1st issue, black cat w/white tummy, minimum value...$300.00
Zip, #4004, 2nd issue, all black cat, minimum value..$585.00
Zip, #4004, 3rd issue, black cat w/white paws, from $10 to.$20.00
2000 Signature Bear, #4266, from $20 to $40.00

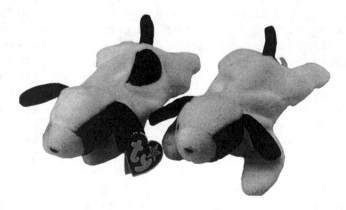

Spot, #4000, 1st issue, dog with no spot on back, minimum value, $850.00; 2nd issue, dog with black spot on back, $40.00. (Photo courtesy Amy Hopper)

Beanie Buddies

This line is of special interest to Beanie Babies collectors, since these animals are larger versions of the Beanie Babies. Like Beanie Babies, Beanie Buddies are periodically retired, and the listings will indicate this. Again, production of these animals is ongoing, so these listings may not include all of those produced during the year 2000. The next edition of *Garage Sale and Flea Market Annual* will reflect any new products.

Amber, #9341, cat, retired, from $10 to **$15.00**
Batty, #9378, bat, from $15 to **$40.00**
Batty, #9379, black bat, from $40 to **$55.00**
Beak, #9301, kiwi, retired, from $15 to **$25.00**
Bones, #9377, dog, from $10 to **$20.00**
Bongo, #9312, monkey, retired, from $10 to..............**$15.00**
Britannia, #9301, bear, UK exclusive, retired, from $110 to ..**$125.00**
Bronty, #9353, brontosaurus, retired, from $10 to **$20.00**
Bubbles, #9323, fish, retired, from $10 to **$15.00**
Bushy, #9382, lion, from $10 to **$15.00**
Chilly, #9317, bear, retired, from $10 to **$20.00**
Chip, #9318, calico cat, retired, from $10 to...............**$15.00**
Chocolate, #9349, moose, retired, from $10 to **$20.00**
Clubby, bear, Beanies Babies Official Club Gold member exclusive (mail-order only), retired, from $20 to .**$30.00**
Clubby II, bear, Beanie Babies Official Club Platinum member exclusive (mail-order only), retired, from $10 to ...**$25.00**
Clubby III, bear, retired, from $20 to...........................**$25.00**
Congo, #9361, gorilla, retired, from $10 to..................**$20.00**
Coral, #9381, tie-dyed fish, from $10 to......................**$15.00**
Digger, #9351, orange crab, retired, from $10 to **$15.00**
Digger, #9351, tie-dyed crab, retired, from $35 to **$45.00**
Dotty, #9364, dalmatian, retired, from $10 to..............**$15.00**
Employee Bear, #9373, from $10 to **$30.00**
Erin, #9309, Irish bear, retired, from $15 to................**$25.00**
Eucalyptus, #9363, koala bear, retired, from $10 to....**$20.00**
Fetch, #9338, golden retriever, retired, from $10 to....**$15.00**
Flip, #9359, white cat, from $10 to..............................**$20.00**
Flippity, #9358, bunny, retired, from $10 to.................**$20.00**
Flitter, #9384, butterfly, from $10 to............................**$15.00**
Fuzz, #9040, lg bear, retired, from $35 to....................**$40.00**
Fuzz, #9328, bear, retired, from $10 to **$20.00**
Germania, #9063, bear, retired, German exclusive, from $110 to..**$125.00**
Gobbles, #9333, turkey, retired, from $10 to...............**$20.00**
Goochy, #9362, jellyfish, retired, from $10 to **$15.00**
Groovy, #9345, tie-dyed bear, retired, from $10 to.....**$20.00**
Halo, #9337, angel bear, retired, from $10 to..............**$20.00**
Halo II, #9386, angel bear, from $10 to......................**$25.00**
Happy, #9375, lavender hippo, from $10 to **$15.00**
Hippie, #9038, x-lg bunny, retired, from $60 to **$70.00**
Hippie, #9039, lg bunny, retired, from $35 to.............**$45.00**
Hippie, #9357, bunny, retired, from $10 to **$20.00**
Hippity, #9324, mint green bunny, retired, from $10 to....**$15.00**
Hope, #9327, praying bear, retired, from $10 to.........**$15.00**
Humphrey, #9307, camel, retired, from $10 to **$20.00**
Inch, #9331, worm, retired, from $10 to......................**$15.00**

Jabber, #9326, parrot, retired, from $10 to...................**$15.00**
Jake, #9304, mallard duck, retired, from $10 to.........**$15.00**
Kicks, #9343, soccer bear, retired, from $15 to...........**$25.00**
Lefty, #9370, gray donkey, USA exclusive, retired, from $15 to..**$25.00**
Libearty, #9371, bear, lg, USA exclusive, from $35 to.**$50.00**
Libearty, #9371, bear, x-lg, USA exclusive, from $65 to.**$85.00**
Libearty, #9371, bear USA exclusive, from $15 to.......**$25.00**
Lips, #9355, fish, from $10 to **$15.00**
Lizzy, #9366, tie-dyed lizard, retired, from $10 to.......**$15.00**
Lucky, #9354, ladybug, retired, from $10 to................**$15.00**
Maple, #9600, bear, Ty Canada exclusive, retired, from $70 to.**$90.00**
Millennium, #9325, bear, retired, from $15 to **$25.00**
Nanook, #9350, Husky, retired, from $10 to **$15.00**
Osito, #9344, Mexican bear, retired, from $10 to........**$20.00**
Patti, #9320, platypus, retired, from $15 to.................**$20.00**
Peace, #9035, jumbo bear, from $130 to **$155.00**
Peace, #9036, x-lg, from $60 to.................................**$90.00**
Peace, #9037, lg bear, retired, from $35 to................**$50.00**
Peace, #9335, bear, retired, from $15 to.....................**$20.00**
Peanut, #9300, royal blue elephant, retired, from $10 to..**$20.00**
Peking, #9310, panda, retired, from $10 to.................**$20.00**
Pinky, #9316, flamingo, retired, from $10 to...............**$15.00**
Pouch, #9380, kangaroo, from $10 to..........................**$15.00**
Princess, #9329, bear, retired, from $15 to.................**$20.00**
Pumkin', #9332, pumpkin, retired, from $10 to **$20.00**
Quackers, #9302, duck w/no wings, retired, from $190 to...**$230.00**
Quackers, #9302, duck w/wings, retired, from $10 to..**$15.00**
Rainbow, #9367, chameleon, from $10 to **$15.00**
Rex, tyrannosaurus, retired, from $15 to......................**$20.00**
Righty, #9369, gray elephant, USA exclusive, retired, from $15 to..**$25.00**
Roam, #9378, buffalo, from $10 to...............................**$15.00**
Rover, #9305, dog, retired, from $15 to **$20.00**
Santa, #9385, retired, from $15 to **$30.00**
Schweetheart, #9330, jumbo orangutan, retired, from $125 to.**$150.00**
Schweetheart, #9330, lg orangutan, retired, from $35 to .**$45.00**
Schweetheart, #9330, x-lg orangutan, retired, from $60 to.**$80.00**
Schweetheart, #9330, orangutan, retired, from $10 to ..**$15.00**
Scorch, #9365, dragon, retired, from $10 to **$20.00**
Signature Bear (2000), #9348, retired, from $20 to **$30.00**
Silver, #9340, cat, retired, from $10 to **$15.00**
Slither, #9339, snake, retired, from $10 to **$15.00**
Smoochy, #9315, frog, retired, from $10 to **$15.00**
Sneaky, #9376, leopard, from $10 to............................**$15.00**
Snort, #9311, bull, retired, from $10 to........................**$15.00**
Snowboy, #9342, retired, from $15 to..........................**$25.00**
Spangle, #9336, bear, retired, from $10 to **$20.00**
Speedy, #9352, turtle, retired, from $10 to **$15.00**
Spinner, #9334, spider, retired, from $10 to **$15.00**
Squealer, #9313, pig, retired, from $10 to...................**$15.00**
Steg, #9383, stegosaurus, retired, from $15 to............**$20.00**
Stretch, #9303, ostrich, retired, from $10 to................**$15.00**
Teddy, #9372, old face teddy, teal, from $10 to...........**$20.00**
Teddy, #9306, cranberry bear, retired, from $15 to.....**$30.00**
Tracker, #9319, basset hound, retired, from $10 to.....**$15.00**
Twigs, #9308, giraffe, retired, from $90 to **$140.00**

Ty 2K, #9346, bear, retired, from $20 to......................**$30.00**
Valentino, #9347, bear, retired, from $10 to **$20.00**
Waddle, #9314, penguin, retired, from $10 to............**$15.00**
Wallace, #9387, from $15 to.......................................**$20.00**
Weenie, #9356, dachshund, retired, from $10 to.........**$15.00**
White Tiger, #9374, white tiger, from $10 to...............**$15.00**
Zip, #9360, cat, from $10 to...**$15.00**

McDonald's® Happy Meal Teenie Beanie Babies

The Teenie Beanie Babies debuted in April 1997 at McDonald's restaurants across the country. The result was the most successful Happy Meal promotion in the history of McDonald's. The toys were quickly snatched up by collectors, causing the promotion to last only one week instead of the planned five-week period. To date there have been four Teenie Beanie promotions, one annually in 1997, 1998, 1999, and 2000, and a special set, the American Trio, offered in November 2000.

1997, Chocolate (moose), Patti (platypus), or Pinky (flamingo), ea from $12 to..**$15.00**
1997, Chops (lamb), from $10 to **$12.00**
1997, Goldie (goldfish), Seamore (seal), Snort (bull), or Speedy (turtle), ea from $10 to..............................**$12.00**
1997, Lizz (lizard) or Quacks (duck), ea from $8 to...**$10.00**
1998, Bones (dog), Peanut (elephant), or Waddle (penguin), ea from $3 to...**$6.00**
1998, Bongo (monkey) or Doby (doberman), ea from $8 to.**$10.00**
1998, Happy (hippo), Inch (worm), Mel (koala), Pinchers (lobster), or Scoop (pelican), ea from $3 to...........**$5.00**
1998, Twigs (giraffe) or Zip (cat), ea from $6 to **$8.00**
1999, Ants (anteater), Freckles (leopard), Smoochy (frog), Spunky (cocker spaniel), from $2 to......................**$4.00**
1999, Claude (crab), Rocket (bluejay), Iggy (iguana), Strut (rooster), ea from $2 to...**$4.00**
1999, Nuts (squirrel), Stretchy (ostrich), Nook (husky), Chip (cat), ea from $2 to..**$4.00**
2000, At the Zoo: Tusk (walrus), Blizz (tiger), Schweetheart (orangutan), Spike (rhinoceros), ea from $2 to......**$4.00**
2000, Garden Bunch: Spinner (spider), Bumble (bee), Flitter (butterfly), Lucky (ladybug), ea from $2 to **$4.00**
2000, Under the Sea: Coral (fish), Sting (stingray), Goochy (jellyfish), Neon (sea horse), ea from $2 to...........**$4.00**

International Bears and Superstars

These were offered at McDonald's as separate purchases, specially packaged for collectors, and not included in Happy Meals.

1999, Britannia, British bear, from $4 to **$6.00**
1999, Erin, Irish bear, from $4 to..................................**$6.00**
1999, Glory, American bear, from $4 to........................**$6.00**
1999, Maple, Canadian bear, from $4 to **$6.00**
2000, Bronty, Rex or Steg, dinosaurs, ea from $3 to **$6.00**
2000, Bushy (lion), Springy (bunny), 'Mystery' items, ea from $2 to..**$5.00**

2000, Chilly (polar bear), Humphrey (camel), Peanut (royal blue elephant), The End (bear), ea from $3 to......**$6.00**
2000, Germania (German bear), Osito (Mexican bear), Spangle (American bear), ea from $4 to.................**$6.00**
2000, Election/American Trio, Lefty (blue-gray donkey), or Righty, (gray elephant), ea from $3 to....................**$6.00**
2000, Election/American Trio, Libearty (bear), from $3 to.**$7.00**
2000, Millennium, bear, offered only 6/13/2000, benefit for Ronald McDonald House Charities, from $5 to....**$10.00**

Beatles Collectibles

Possibly triggered by John Lennon's death in 1980, Beatles fans (recognizing that their dreams of the band ever reuniting were gone along with him) began to collect vintage memorabilia of all types. Recently some of the original Beatles material has sold at auction with high-dollar results. Handwritten song lyrics, Lennon's autographed high school textbook, and even the legal agreement that was drafted at the time the group disbanded are among the one-of-a-kind multi-thousand dollar sales recorded.

Unless you plan on attending sales of this caliber, you'll be more apt to find the commercially produced memorabilia that literally flooded the market during the '60s and beyond when the Fab Four from Liverpool made their unprecedented impact on the entertainment world. A word about their 45 rpm records: they sold in such mass quantities that unless the record is a 'promotional' (made to send to radio stations or for jukebox distribution), they have very little value. Once a record has lost much of its original gloss due to wear and handling, becomes scratched, or has writing on the label, its value is minimal. Even in near-mint condition, $4.00 to $6.00 is plenty to pay for a 45 rpm (much less if it's worn), unless the original picture sleeve is present. (An exception is the white-labeled Swan recording of 'She Loves You/I'll Get You'.) A Beatles' picture sleeve is usually valued at $30.00 to $40.00, except for the rare 'Can't Buy Me Love,' which is worth ten times that amount. (Beware of reproductions!) Albums of any top recording star or group from the '50s and '60s are becoming very collectible, and the Beatles' are among the most popular. Just be very critical of condition! An album must be in at least excellent condition to bring a decent price.

For more information we recommend *The Beatles, Second Edition*, by Barbara Crawford, Hollis Lamon, and Michael Stern (Collector Books).

See also Celebrity Dolls; Magazines; Movie Posters; Records; Sheet Music.

Advisor: Bojo/Bob Gottuso (See Directory, Character and Personality Collectibles)

Newsletter: Beatlefan
P.O. Box 33515, Decatur, GA 30033;
Send SASE for information

Badge, cardboard w/black & white group photo & I've Got My Movie Ticket Have You?, 3¾" dia, EX **$35.00**

Bracelet, black & white group photo disk on brass mounting, Yeh, Yeh, Yeh embossed on back, 1" dia, EX......**$70.00**

Cake topper, 3-D head shots w/facsimile signatures & band name on plastic panel w/rounded corners, 1964, 4½" L, EX **$130.00**

Coin holder, red rubber squeeze type, 2x3", VG+......**$75.00**

Cuff links, brass w/embossed faces, EX (on black & white Official Cuff Links card) **$200.00**

Cup, plastic, colored photos of each Beatle on sides, Buritte, 1964 (watch for similar reproduction), $80.00. (Photo courtesy Joe Hilton and Greg Moore)

Dolls, w/metal stands, Applause, 1987, 22", set of 4, MIP..**$390.00**

Fan club booklet, black & white photo on cover, 20 pages, 1970, EX..**$30.00**

Fan club picture cube, cardboard cube w/Apple logo on top, M (EX mailer)..**$75.00**

Figures, 'Hey Jude,' lead w/cardboard backdrop, EX **$100.00**

Figures, cartoon style, resin, 6", set of 4, EX............**$125.00**

Figures, cartoon style, resin, 12", set of 4, EX...........**$225.00**

Flasher button, flashes from group standing & The Beatles to 4 headshots w/names, Vari-vue, 2½" dia, ea........**$30.00**

Guitar, New Sound, complete w/red & clear nylon strings, original metal pegs, no sticker at top, VG+........**$530.00**

Gumball charms, black plastic record shape w/face of ea Beatle on 1 side & record label on reverse, set of 4, ¾", EX..**$25.00**

Gumball sticker, gold & black w/faces & names, w/clear plastic capsule, 1x3", EX **$25.00**

Headband, Love the Beatles, Betterwear USA, MIP....**$60.00**

Hummer, cardboard tube w/color head shots, names & musical notes, plastic tips, 11x¾" dia, VG+ **$175.00**

Key chain, flashes from photo to lettering, Hong Kong, 1960s, NM..**$70.00**

Magazine, Beatles on Broadway, Whitman, 1964, EX...**$18.00**

Magazine, Official Yellow Submarine, 49 pages, VG..**$45.00**

Mobile, Yellow Submarine, pop-out cardboard figures, Sunshine Art Studios, 9¼x14¼", EX....................**$180.00**

Necklace, brass locket w/The Beatles in raised letters, black & white photo inside, gold-tone chain, 1¼" dia, EX.**$160.00**

Necklace, oval silver-tone metal pendant w/black & white group photo under plastic dome, w/original chain, EX **$100.00**

Nesting dolls, hand-painted wood 5-pc set w/John being the largest (6½") to the Union Jack as the smallest, NM **$75.00**

Notebook (paper), group photo in doorway, Westab, 11x8½", unused, EX **$90.00**

Pen, various colors w/The Beatles & names in silver, VG+..**$90.00**

Pencil case, tan vinyl w/black & white group photo, names & The Beatles printed on front, EX **$220.00**

Pennant, I Love the Beatles, white & yellow on red felt, 29", EX **$230.00**

Pillow, waist-length group pose, VG **$160.00**

Pin, plastic guitar shape w/rubber-band strings w/faces & names, Beatles or Beatles Pin Up at top, 5½", EX, ea..........**$190.00**

Postcards, set of 6 w/1 ea of cartoon-style group member, Yellow Submarine & Sgt Pepper, 10x14", EX **$100.00**

Poster Put-Ons, poster w/over 60 rub-ons, Craftmaster, 21x15", unused, EX box **$220.00**

Record carrier, 45 rpm records, blue w/black handles, color group picture on front, Seagull, VG+..................**$370.00**

Ring, brass w/black & white round photo framed w/scalloped edge, adjustable band, VG+ **$70.00**

Rub-Ons, Yellow Submarine, Wheat Honeys or Rice Honeys cereal premium, 3½x2½" sheet, unused, ea.........**$50.00**

Scarf, triangular w/black photos & names in allover design on red cloth w/black vinyl tie string, EX..............**$90.00**

Thimbles, plastic, various colors w/individual black & white photos & names, set of 4, newer, EX....................**$15.00**

Tie tacs, pewter faces, set of 4, M (VG+ color card w/wallet photo at top)..**$80.00**

Tote bag, vinyl, photographed faces w/cartoon bodies, Wako Plastics/Japan, 14x13", EX..................................**$180.00**

Tray, multicolor with musical notes and star border, Great Britain, 13" square, VG, $50.00. (Beware of repros.) (Photo courtesy Bob Gottuso)

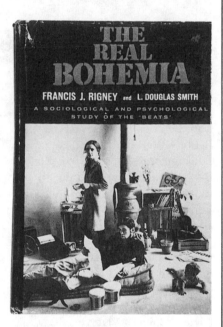

Wallet, white vinyl w/color group photo, Fun in Florida on reverse, brass edge trim w/snap closure & attached chain, EX $425.00

Beatnik Collectibles

The 'Beats,' later called 'Beatniks,' consisted of artists, writers, and others disillusioned with Establishment mores and values. The Beatniks were non-comformists, Bohemian free-thinkers who energetically expressed their disdain for society from 1950 to 1962. From a collector's point of view, the most highly regarded Beat authors are Allen Ginsberg, Lawrence Ferlinghetti, and Jack Kerouac. Books, records, posters, pamphlets, leaflets, and other items associated with them are very desirable. Although in their day they were characterized by the media as a 'Maynard G. Krebs' (of Dobie Gillis TV fame), today the contributions they made to American literature and the continuation of Bohemianism are recognized for their importance and significance in American culture.

Values are for examples in excellent to near-mint condition.

Advisor: Richard Synchef (See Directory, Beatnik and Hippie Collectibles)

Book, *The Real Bohemia*, Francis Rigney and Douglas Smith, NY, Basic Books, 1961, 'A Sociological and Psychological Study of the 'Beats',' $125.00. (Photo courtesy Richard Synchef)

Book, Adept, The; Michael McClure, NY: Delacorte Press, 1971, McClure's 2nd novel $120.00
Book, Beat Generation & The Angry Young Men, The; Feldman/Gartenberg eds, NY: Citadel Press, 1959, early anthology...............$150.00
Book, Satori in Paris, Jack Kerouac, NY: Grove Press, 1966, Beats 'most important' author $250.00
Book, Tales of Beatnik Glory, Ed Sanders, NY: Stonehill Pub Co, 1975, by founder of Peace Eye Bookstore & the Fugs $100.00

Book, Third Mind, The; William Burroughs & Brion Gysin, NY: Viking, 1978...............$175.00
Booklet, Beat Talk, Tulsa, OK: Studio Press, 1960, 30 pages, Beat 'glossary'...............$75.00
Booklet, Poisoned Wheat, Michael McClure, privately printed, San Francisco, 1965, rare, early anti-war poetry...$200.00

Booklet, *Poor Richard's Guide to Non-Tourist San Francisco*, Unicorn Publishing Co., 1958, $150.00. (Photo courtesy Richard Synchef)

Booklet, Roosevelt After Inauguration, William Burroughs (covers by Allen Ginsberg), NY: F — Y — Press, 1963, very scarce early collaboration by Ginsberg & Burroughs $550.00
Booklet, The Dead Star, William Burroughs, The Nova Broadcast Press, San Francisco, 1969, unusual format...........$225.00
Folder, The Beat Generation, MGM movie promotional tie-in, 1959, w/Mamie Van Doren, Ray Danton, others, 4 pages, rare...............$250.00
Magazine, City Lights #2, San Francisco, City Lights Books, 1952, very early Lawrence Ferlinghetti publication $300.00

Magazine, *City Lights*, #3, Spring 1953, San Francisco: City Lights, very early Ferlinghetti publication, $125.00. (Photo courtesy Richard Synchef)

Magazine, Fruitcup, San Francisco, Beach Books Texts & Documents, 1969, very comprehensive anthology, only issue..**$110.00**

Magazine, Playboy, The Beat Issue, July, 1959, Ginsberg, Kerouac, Corso, other Beat writers **$90.00**

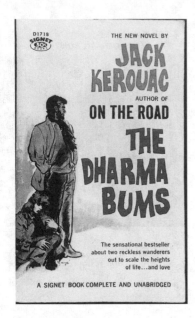

Paperback book, *Dharma Bums*, Jack Kerouac (author), NY, Avon, 1960, 1st printing, $75.00.
(Photo courtesy Richard Synchef)

Paperback, Wholly Communion, London, Lorimar Films, 1965, Ferlinghetti, others, movie tie-in..................**$80.00**

Paperback, Starting From San Francisco, Lawrence Ferlinghetti, Norfolk CT: New Directions, 1961, 33⅓ rpm records attached..**$220.00**

Periodical, Evergreen Review #2, 'The San Francisco Scene,' NY: Grove Press, 1959, gave Beat writers national exposure **$125.00**

Poster, The Beard, Michael McClure's award-winning play, premier, March 31, 1965, rare **$600.00**

Record, Ferlinghetti, Fantasy Records, #7014, monaural LP, 1961, Ferlinghetti reading some of his most famous poems **$175.00**

Record, Kadish, Allen Ginsberg, monaural LP, Atlantic Verbum Series #4011, 1965, Ginsberg reads entire classic poem..**$225.00**

Record, Lenny Bruce — American, monaural LP, Fantasy Records #7011, red vinyl, 1961..............................**$200.00**

Record, Poetry for the Beat Generation, Jack Kerouac, monaural LP, Hanover Records, 1959, Kerouac reads, Steve Allen at piano, absolutely classic **$575.00**

Beatrix Potter

Since 1902 when *The Tale of Peter Rabbit* was published by Fredrick Warne & Company, generations have enjoyed the adventures of Beatrix Potter's characters. Beswick issued ten characters in 1947 that included Peter Rabbit, Benjamin Bunny, Squirrel Nutkin, Jemima Puddleduck, Timmy Tiptoes, Tom Kitten, Mrs Tittlemouse, Mrs. Tiggywinkle, Little Pig Robinson, and Samuel Whiskers. The line grew until it included figures from other stories. Duchess (P1355) was issued in 1955 with two feet that were easily broken. Later issues featured the Duchess on a base and holding a pie. This was the first figure to be discontinued in 1967. Color variations on pieces indicate issue dates as do the different backstamps that were used. Backstamps have changed several times since the first figures were issued. There are three basic styles: Beswick brown, Beswick gold, and Royal Albert — with many variations on each of these. Unless stated otherwise, figures listed here are Beswick brown.

Advisor: Nicki Budin (See Directory, Beatrix Potter)

Mittens and Moppet, 1989, 3¾", $250.00.
(Photo courtesy Marbena Fyke)

And This Little Pig Had None, B6...............................**$55.00**
Apply Dappley, bottle out **$95.00**
Aunt Petitoes, B3 ....**$55.00**
Babbity Bumble, B6...**$250.00**
Benjamin Ate Lettuce Leaf, B6a.................................**$50.00**
Benjamin Bunny, ears out, 3B..................................**$195.00**
Benjamin Bunny, 3B..**$55.00**
Benjamin Bunny Bank, 3C..**$55.00**
Benjamin Bunny/Peter Rabbit, B3............................**$125.00**
Cecily Parsley, 3B **$95.00**
Chippy Hackee, B3..**$85.00**
Cottontail, B6 ....**$45.00**
Cottontail, 3B **$45.00**
Cousin Ribby, B6 ....**$50.00**
Diggory Diggory Delvet, 3B **$75.00**
Fierce Bad Rabbit, B3 ....**$50.00**
Flopsy, Mopsy, Cottontail, B3....................................**$65.00**
Foxy, reading, B6..**$95.00**
Foxy Whiskered Gentleman, 3B..................................**$75.00**
Ginger, B3 ....**$600.00**
Goody & Timmy Tiptoes, B6.....................................**$225.00**
Goody Tiptoes, B3...**$60.00**
Hunca Munca, C3 ....**$65.00**
Hunca Munca, 3B..**$65.00**
Hunca Munca Spills Beads, B6..................................**$125.00**
Jemima & Ducklings, B10a **$60.00**

Jemima Puddleduck, B3	**$55.00**
Jemima Puddleduck, gold, sm, B10	**$50.00**
Jemima Puddleduck/Nest, B6	**$45.00**
John Joiner, B6	**$55.00**
Johnny Townmouse, B3	**$55.00**
Johnny Townmouse/Bag, B6	**$325.00**
Lady Mouse, B3	**$65.00**
Lady Mouse Made Curtsey, B6	**$75.00**
Little Pig Robinson, B3	**$55.00**
Little Pig Robinson, B6	**$45.00**
Miss Dormouse, B6	**$85.00**
Miss Moppet, 3B	**$55.00**
Mr Alderman Ptolemy, B3	**$95.00**
Mr Benjamin Bunny, lilac, 3B	**$60.00**
Mr Benjamin Bunny/Peter Rabbit, B3	**$75.00**
Mr Benjamin Bunny/Peter Rabbit, B6	**$75.00**
Mr Jackson, B3	**$55.00**
Mr Jackson, B6	**$65.00**
Mr Jackson, 3A	**$75.00**
Mr Jeremy Fisher, C3	**$70.00**
Mr Jeremy Fisher, digging, B4	**$195.00**
Mr McGregor, arm down, B6	**$75.00**
Mrs Flopsy Bunny, B3	**$65.00**
Mrs Rabbit, cooking, B6	**$75.00**
Mrs Rabbit, 3B	**$60.00**
Mrs Rabbit w/Bunnies, 3B	**$85.00**
Mrs Tiggy Winkle, B3	**$55.00**
Mrs Tiggy Winkle Washing, Beswick/Ware, 8A	**$200.00**
Mrs Tittlemouse, 3B	**$45.00**
Mrs Tittlemouse, 3C	**$45.00**
Old Mr Bouncer, B6	**$55.00**
Old Mr Bouncer, C3	**$60.00**
Old Mr Brown, B3	**$60.00**
Old Mr Pricklepin	**$175.00**
Old Woman in Shoe, B3	**$45.00**
Old Woman in Shoe, knitting, B6	**$55.00**
Peter & the Red Hand, B6	**$65.00**
Peter Ate a Radish, B6	**$65.00**
Peter in Gooseberry Net, 6B	**$75.00**
Peter Rabbit, B3	**$55.00**
Peter Rabbit, 1st version, 3B	**$95.00**
Peter w/Daffodils, B6	**$50.00**
Pickles, 3A	**$450.00**
Pigling Band, B3	**$50.00**
Pigwig, B3	**$550.00**
Poorly Peter Rabbit, B3	**$75.00**
Poorly Peter Rabbit, B6	**$65.00**
Ribby & the Patty Pan, B6	**$55.00**
Sally Henny Penny, B3	**$75.00**
Simpkin, B3	**$650.00**
Sir Isaac Newton, 3B	**$450.00**
Squirrel Nutkin, red/brown, B3	**$95.00**
Susan, 3B	**$200.00**
Tabitha Twitchit/Miss Moppet, B3	**$150.00**
Tabitha Twitchit/Miss Moppet, B6	**$150.00**
Tailor of Gloucester, B3	**$55.00**
Thomasina Tittlemouse, B3	**$110.00**

Timmy Tiptoes, B2-B3	**$150.00**
Timmy Willie, B3	**$45.00**
Timmy Willie, B6	**$65.00**
Timmy Willie, sleeping, C3	**$175.00**
Tom Kitten, B4	**$75.00**
Tom Kitten, 1st version, 3B	**$85.00**
Tom Kitten in Rockery, 10A	**$45.00**
Tom Kitten w/Butterfly, 3C	**$325.00**
Tom Thumb, B6	**$55.00**
Tom Thumb, 3C	**$85.00**

Tabitha Twitchett, 1961, $50.00; Ribby, 1951, $65.00. (Photo courtesy Marbena Fyko)

Beer Cans

In January of 1935 the Continental Can Co. approached a New Jersey brewery with the novel idea of selling beer in cans. After years of research, Continental had perfected a plastic coating for the inside of the can which prevented the beer from contacting and adversely reacting to metal. Consumers liked the idea, and throw-away beer cans soon replaced returnable bottles as the most popular container in which to purchase beer.

The first beer can was a steel flat top which actually bore a picture of the newly invented 'can opener' and instructions on how to use it. Because most breweries were not equipped to fill a flat can, a 'cone top' was invented to facilitate passage through the bottle filler. By the 1950s the cone top was obsolete. Ten years later, can companies introduced a 'tab top' can which made the can opener unnecessary. Aluminum cans and cans ranging in size from six-ounce to one-gallon were popularized during the 1960s.

Beer can collecting reached its heyday during the 1970s. Thousands of collectors bought, drank, and saved cans throughout America. Unfortunately, the number of collectors receded, creating a huge supply of cans with minimal demand. There are many valuable beer cans today — however, they pre-date 1970. A post-1970 can worth more than a few dollars is rare.

Values are based on cans in conditions as stated. A can with flaws — rust, fading, or scratches — may still have value; however, it is generally much less than its excellent condition counterpart.

Advisor: Dan Andrews (See Directory, Beer Cans and Breweriana)

Newsletter: Beer Cans and Brewery Collectibles
Beer Can Collectors of America
747 Merus Ct., Fenton, MO 63026-2092
fax/phone: 314-343-6486; e-mail: bcca@bcca.com; http://www.bcca.com; Subscription: $30 per year for US residents; includes 6 issues and right to attend national CANvention®

Cone tops: Carling's Black Label Beer, Brewing Corporation, Cleveland OH, NM, $45.00; Fitzgerald's Carry-Y-Own Ale (j-spout), Troy NY, G, $90.00; Standard Sparkling Ale (j-spout), Rochester NY, $90.00; Gold Crest 51 (high profile), Tennessee Brewing, Memphis TN, G, $90.00.

Cone top, American Beer, American Brewing/Baltimore, 1940s, VG $70.00

Cone top, Berghoff 1887 Beer, Berghoff Brewing/Fort Wayne, 1940s, VG...................................$35.00

Cone top, Beverwyck Famous Beer, Beverwyck Brewing/Albany, 1930s, EX+ $110.00

Cone top, Buckeye Sparkling Dry Beer, Buckeye Brewing/Toledo, 1950s, EX+ $145.00

Cone top, Burger Premium Quality, Burger Brewing/Cincinnati, 1950s, VG+.....................$78.00

Cone top, Carling's Ale, Brewing Corp of America/Cleveland, 1940s, EX...$85.00

Cone top, E&B Special Beer, E&B Brewing/Detroit, 1940s, EX+ $40.00

Cone top, Falstaff Beer, Falstaff Brewing/Omaha, 1950s, G+ $15.00

Cone top, Goetz Country Club Beer, Goetz Brewing/St Joseph, 1950s, EX+ $40.00

Cone top, Iron City Beer Select Quality, Pittsburgh Brewing/Pittsburgh, 1950s, EX+.....................$60.00

Cone top, Kuebler Pilsner Beer, Kuebler Brewing/Easton, 1930s, G+ $100.00

Cone top, Maier Select Beer, Maier Brewing/Los Angeles, 1940s, VG $50.00

Cone top, Oertels '92 Lager Beer, Oertels Brewing/Louisville, 1950s, VG $40.00

Cone top, Peerless Beer, Lacrosse Brewing/Lacrosse, 1950s, EX+ $120.00

Cone top, Schlitz, Schlitz Brewing/Milwaukee, 1940s, EX ..$50.00

Cone top, Weber Waukesha Beer, W Waukesha Brewing/Waukesha, 1950s, NM+ $210.00

Crowntainer, Altes Lager Beer, Tivoli Brewing/Detroit, 1940s, VG $40.00

Crowntainer, Brucks Jubilee Beer, Bruckman Brewing/Cincinnati, 1940s, EX....................................$95.00

Crowntainer, Ebling Premium Beer, Ebling Brewing/New York, 1940s, EX....................................$45.00

Crowntainer, Fehr's X/L, Fehr Brewing/Louisville, 1940s, G+ $15.00

Crowntainer, Fitzgerald's Burgomaster Beer, Fitzgerald Bros/Troy, enameled, 1940s, EX+.....................$60.00

Crowntainer, Fitzgerald's Lager Beer, Fitzgerald's Brewing/Troy, 1940s, EX.....................................$45.00

Crowntainer, Gluek's Beer, Gluek Brewing/Minneapolis, 1940s, EX+..$35.00

Crowntainer, Grossvater Beer, Renner Brewing/Youngstown, 1940s, EX....................................$50.00

Crowntainer, Hanley's Peerless Ale, Hanley Brewing/Providence, 1940s, VG $55.00

Crowntainer, Neuweiler's Pilsener Beer, Neuweiler Brewing/Allentown, 1940s, EX+..............................$30.00

Crowntainer, Old Reading Beer, Old Reading Brewing/Reading, enameled, 1950s, M $100.00

Crowntainer, Old Shay Beer, Fort Pitt Brewing/Jeannette, 1940s, G+ $70.00

Crowntainer, Yoerg's Cave Aged Beer, Yoerg's Brewing/St Paul, 1950s, EX+ $200.00

Flat top, Balboa Export Beer, Southern Brewing/Los Angeles, 1940s, VG $65.00

Flat top, Ballantine Light Lager Beer, Ballantine Brewing/Newark, 1950s, VG+ $8.00

Flat top, Banner Extra Dry Premium Beer, Burkhardt Brewing/Akron, 1950s, EX+ $20.00

Flat top, Budweiser Lager Beer, Anheuser-Busch/St Louis, 1950s, EX...$20.00

Flat top, Bull Dog Ale, Grace Bros/Santa Rosa, 1950s, EX+ $20.00

Flat top, Drewrys Ale, Drewrys LTD/South Bend, Mountie & horse on copper, 1940s, VG $40.00

Flat top, Krueger Cream Ale, Krueger Brewing/Newark, 1950s, VG $50.00

Flat top, Neuweiler Cream Ale, Neuweiler Brewing/Allentown, 1950s, NM.......................................$75.00

Flat top, Old German Brand Beer, Lebanon Valley/Lebanon, 1950s, NM+..$40.00

Flat top, Ruppert Knickerbocker Beer, Ruppert Brewing/New York, 1940s, EX....................................$40.00

Flat top, Senate 250 Beer, Heurichs Brewing/Washington, 1950s, EX+ $70.00

Flat top, Senator's Club Premium Beer, Columbia Brewing/
Shenandoah, 1960s, EX+ **$75.00**
Flat top, Steinbeck Lager Beer, Grace Bros Brewing/Santa
Rosa, 1950s, EX..**$20.00**
Flat top, Stroz Gold Crest Beer, Stroz Brewing/Omaha, 1940s,
EX+ **$300.00**
Flat top, Tam O'Shanter Ale (Dry Hopped), American
Brewing/Rochester, gray version, 1930s, NM **$150.00**
Flat top, Topper Light Dry Ale, Rochester Brewing/Rochester,
yellow version, rolled, 1950s, G+ **$60.00**
Flat top, Topper Light Dry Beer, Rochester Brewing/
Rochester, 1950s, VG+...**$30.00**
Flat top, University Club Stout Malt Liquor, Miller Brewing/
Milwaukee, 1950s, NM **$30.00**
Pull tab, Bonanza Premium Beer, Old Dutch Brewing/
Allentown, 1970s, NM...**$10.00**
Pull tab, Fauerbach Beer, Fauerbach Brewing/Madison,
1960s, VG+ **$20.00**
Pull tab, Gibbons Season's Best, Lion Inc/Wilkes-Barre,
1960s, EX+...**$100.00**
Pull tab, Hudson House Beer, Maier Brewing/Los Angeles,
1960s, NM+...**$15.00**
Pull tab, Jax Draft Beer, Jackson Brewing/New Orleans,
1960s, EX+...**$15.00**
Pull tab, Orbit Premium Beer, Orbit Brewing/Miami, 1960s,
NM+ **$10.00**
Pull tab, Ox-Bow Beer, Walter Brewing/Pueblo, 1970s,
EX+..**$25.00**
Pull tab, Schlitz Genuine Draught Beer, Schlitz
Brewing/Milwaukee, 1970s, NM **$10.00**
Pull tab, Schmidt's Ale, Schmidt's Brewing/Philadelphia,
1960s, NM..**$15.00**
Pull tab, Steinbrau Genuine Draft, Maier Brewing/Los
Angeles, 1960s, NM **$25.00**
Pull tab, Waldbaums Premium Lager Beer, Eastern Brewing/
Hammonton, 1970s, EX+...**$10.00**

Bellair, Marc

A native of Ohio and a former designer for the Libbey
Glass Company, Marc Bellaire relocated in California in the
1950s and became one of many mid-century artisans from
that state whose work has grown increasingly popular with
collectors over the last decade. At one time, he was
employed by Sascha Brastoff. Bellaire is best known for his
Mardi Gras line, which was decorated with slim dancers in
spattered and striped colors of black, blue, pink, and white.
He did many other lines as well, among them Balinese,
Beachcomber, Friendly Island, Cave Painting, Hawaiian, and
Jungle Dancer.

Ashtray, Mardi Gras, 3 figures, 8 slots, 14¾".............**$225.00**
Ashtray, white shoe w/native figure across toe, 6".....**$70.00**
Bowl, Jungle Dancer, 11½x5½"................................**$150.00**
Bowl, man sitting on branch of tree playing flute on lime
green, 7½" **$90.00**

Box, African figure on lid, 6"............................**$95.00**
Dish, Mardi Gras, B46-S, w/lid, 8x5¾" **$165.00**
Figurine, bull, 9" **$345.00**

**Figurine, long-neck bird, 17",
$315.00.** (Photo courtesy
Pat and Kris Secor)

Plate, Jamaican, multicolor w/metallic brush strokes allover,
7¼"..**$85.00**
Plate, Jamaican beachcomber w/netting, gold trim, black
spray on rim, 9¼" **$100.00**
Platter, stylized bird w/foliage, 15½" **$150.00**
Platter, underwater design in sea-green colors, 16"..**$100.00**
Switch plate cover, dancer on blue, B-26, 4¾x3".....**$150.00**

Bells

Bell collectors claim that bells rank second only to the
wheel as being useful to mankind. Down through the ages
bells have awakened people in the morning, called them to
meals and prayers, and readied them to retire at night. We
have heard them called rising bells, Angelus Bells (for
deaths), noon bells, Town Crier bells (for important
announcements), and curfew bells. Souvenir bells are often
the first type collected, with interest spreading to other con-
temporaries, then on to old, more valuable bells. As far as
limited edition bells are concerned, the fewer made per bell,
the better. (For example a bell made in an edition of 25,000
will not appreciate as much as one from an edition of 5,000.)

For further information we recommend *World of Bells
#5, Bell Tidings, Lure of Bells, Collectible Bells, More Bell Lore,
Bells Now and Long Ago,* and *Legendary Bells,* all by Dorothy
Malone Anthony.

Advisor: Dorothy Malone Anthony (See Directory, Bells)

Newsletter: The Bell Tower
The American Bell Association
P.O. Box 19443, Indianapolis, IN 46219

Brass, carved & etched decor, 7½x5"..........................$15.00

Brass, cow finial, Jersey written below, Peerage, Birmingham, England, 4" $30.00

Brass, Dutch girl figural w/parasol & basket, England, 1940s-'50s, 3¾x2" $22.50

Brass, Dutch lady (knitting) handle, 3¼"....................$42.50

Brass, elephant figural, trunk forms handle, ca 1950, 4"..$16.50

Brass, lady figural, detailed floral attire, silvered, 5"...$78.00

Brass, man figural w/pointed hat, 5¾x3¼" $16.00

Brass, monkey figural, 2⅞x2" $25.00

Brass, owl figural handle, unmarked, 5"....................$28.00

Brass, Revolutionary soldier handle, 4½x2½" $27.50

Brass, schoolhouse type, #7 on wooden handle, 9½x5¼" $50.00

Brass, Southern lady figural, skirt forms bell, unmarked, 3½x3" $25.00

Brass, Tinker Bell figural, old, 3".............................$20.00

China, Boy Meets His Dog, Norman Rockwell, Gorham, 1979, 9" $20.00

China, English Rose, gold trim, Limoges, 5½"............$17.50

China, gold Christmas figures on white, Pickard, 1980, MIB...$140.00

China, Orchard Gold, Aynsley, 3½x2½" $27.50

China, Silent Night, Christmas 1979, Pickard, MIB....$140.00

Chintz china, English Summertime, 4¼", $70.00. (Photo courtesy Dorothy Malone Anthony)

Fenton, Temple Bell, 6¾", $35.00. (Photo courtesy Dorothy Malone Anthony)

Glass, amber opalescent, Liberty Bell Centennial 1776-1976, 4¼" dia $15.00

Glass, cranberry etched to clear, Bohemia sticker, 5¾x3⅜" $20.00

Glass, crystal, cut bird decor, glass ball & chain clapper, 8x3½" $12.50

Glass, crystal, cut diamond decor, 4" $18.00

Glass, crystal, Thumbprint, Viking, 5½x3½".............$22.50

Glass, pink slag, Inverted Strawberry, 6-sided handle, 6¼x3½" $15.00

Glass, ruby, paneled pattern, Viking label, 5½".........$27.50

Glass, ruby, 1979 Christmas, Avon, 7x3½" $15.00

Porcelain, Blue Willow, unmarked, 5¼x3" $27.50

Porcelain, Christmas, 3 figures ea side, Lladro, 1987, 3x3" $75.00

Porcelain, hand-painted mountain reserve on white, eagle finial, 6x5" wingspan $30.00

Red Riding Hood, sterling handle, chrome bell, 4½", $30.00. (Photo courtesy Dorothy Malone Anthony)

Silver, cherub handle, unmarked, 3" $15.00

Silver, embossed decor, Continental, 3½x2½"............$50.00

Silver, Queen Victoria figural, marked SAL w/lion, PF & shield, 2¾" $100.00

Silver, 3 Little Pigs, Disney, New England Collector's Society, 3¼" $12.50

Black Americana

There are many avenues one might pursue in the broad field of Black Americana and many reasons that might entice one to become a collector. For the more serious, there are documents such as bills of sale for slaves, broadsides, and other historical artifacts. But by and far, most collectors enjoy attractive advertising pieces, novelties and kitchenware items, toys and dolls, and Black celebrity memorabilia.

It's estimated that there are at least 50,000 collectors around the country today that specialize in this field. There are large auctions devoted entirely to the sale of Black Americana. The items they feature may be as common as a homemade pot holder or a magazine or as rare as a Lux Dixie Boy clock or a Mammy cookie jar that might go for several thousand dollars. In fact, many of the cookie jars have become so valuable that they're being reproduced; so are salt and pepper shakers, so beware.

For further study, we recommend *Black Collectibles Sold in America* by P.J. Gibbs.

See also Advertising, Aunt Jemima; Condiment Sets; Cookie Jars; Postcards; Salt and Pepper Shakers; Sheet Music; String Holders.

Advisor: Judy Posner (See Directory, Black Americana)

Apron, cotton-backed PVC w/Robertson's Marmalade advertising featuring Golly, Golly It's Good!, 1970s, 30x20", EX **$165.00**

Art plate, Tobacco Field (from Bits of the Old South series), Vernon Kilns, 1940, EX..**$55.00**

Ashtray, Dinah's Pancake & Chicken House, red graphics on clear glass, 1940s, 4¼" dia, EX **$55.00**

Birthday card, Ah Wishes Yo' De Best Birthday That You Ever Had!, girl chef presenting cake to boy w/dog, 1940s, M..**$18.00**

Book, Jazz Man, Mary Hays Weik, Atheneum, 1967, 3rd printing woodcuts by Ann Grifalconi, hardcover w/dust jacket, EX **$40.00**

Book, Little Alexander, Besse Schiff, Wartburg Press, 1955, hardcover, 30 pages, EX.......................................**$100.00**

Book, Little Black Sambo, Bannerman, 1948, hardcover, 20 multicolor pages w/4 multi-action mechanical pages, scarce, NM..**$200.00**

Book, Little Brown Koko Has Fun, 1945, 1st edition, hardcover w/dust jacket, 96 pages, EX **$65.00**

Book, *Nicodemus Helps Uncle Sam*, Inez Hogan author, 1943, from $60.00 to $95.00. (Photo courtesy P.J. Gibbs)

Book, Picture Story Book, Salter, 1943, cloth-like w/multicolored image of Sambo under umbrella & friends on cover, M...**$70.00**

Book, Steppin & Family, Hope Newell, 1942 Special Edition, illustrated by Anne Merriman Peck, hardbound, EX...**$50.00**

Book, Tag-Along Tooloo/1947 Children's Book, hardcover, 79 pages, EX **$65.00**

Book, The Little Professor of Piney Woods, Beth Day, 1955, 1st edition, hardcover w/dust jacket, 192 pages, NM **$60.00**

Book, The New Edition of the Encyclopedia of Jazz, Leonard Feather, 1962, hardcover w/dust jacket, 562 pages, EX...**$45.00**

Booklet, Quiz/Do You Know The Traffic Signs?, image of golliwog policeman, Robertson's Golden Shred premium, 1970s, EX **$38.00**

Bottle, Luzianne Mammy Instant Coffee, glass w/multicolored label, red & white tin lid, dated 1953, 4½", unused, M..**$125.00**

Canister, litho tin w/Uncle Ben's Converted Rice Advertising, 40th anniversary limited edition, 1943-1983, 7½", EX...**$35.00**

Cigarette box, wooden w/roll top that exposes fellow jumping up w/cigarette, 1940s, EX...............................**$125.00**

Coloring book, Little Black Sambo & Peter Rabbit, 1941, unused, EX, from $50 to **$60.00**

Coloring book, Little Brown Koko, illustrated by Dorothy Wadstaff, 1941, 22 pages, unused, EX.................**$95.00**

Cookbook, Cooking in High Cotton Vol V, Bettye N Starr, Cookbook Publishers, 1976, reprint, 184 pages, spiral-bound, EX **$40.00**

Cookbook, The Savannah Cook Book, Harriet Ross Colquitt, 1960 edition, introduction by Ogden Nash, sprial-bound, EX...**$40.00**

Crate, Mammy eating orange on label, wood & cardboard, Leesburg FL, 1940s, 11x18x11", EX **$135.00**

Dart board, litho tin w/multicolored Sambo graphic, Wyandotte, 1940s, 14x23", EX **$145.00**

Dinner bell, ceramic figural girl in white gown w/pink & gold trim kneeling in prayer, 1940s, EX...............**$55.00**

Doll, Beloved Belindy, stockinet face & torso w/stuffed cotton arms & legs, felt features, dressed, 1950s, 14", EX...**$75.00**

Doll, Kewpie, celluloid w/silver & gold top hat, Occupied Japan, 8", NM..**$75.00**

Doll, My Lovely Topsee, molded plastic w/dark skin tone & side-glance goggle eyes, unclothed, pigtails, 1940s, 5", MIP...**$60.00**

Doll, tiger, soft sculpture w/orange & black stripes, white plush trim, green eyes, Sambo's Restaurant premium, 6½"..**$35.00**

Fight program, Joe Louis vs Jersey Joe Walcott, June 23, 1943, EX **$175.00**

Figure, Dancing Sambo, multicolored cardboard mechanical figure dances by hidden working string, 1940s-50s, 12", MIP...**$80.00**

Figure, red cap porter, painted cast metal w/dark skin tone wearing gray uniform & carrying suitcases, 1940s, 3", EX..**$40.00**

Figure, trumpet player, brown-skinned w/red lips & hat, green-trimmed outfit, marked Occupied Japan, 2¾", EX..**$40.00**

Fire crackers, Dixie Boy brand w/full-color ethnic label, 1950s, MIP (unopened) **$38.00**

Game, Little Black Sambo, Cadaco Ellis, 1945, EXIB..**$175.00**

Game, Skillets & Cakes, Milton Bradley, 1946, complete, EXIB, from $150 to **$200.00**

Marionette, Jambo the Jiver, jointed wood w/cloth clothes, fiber hair, Talent Products, 1948, 14", VG..........**$175.00**

Menu, Sambo's Restaurants souvenir, 4-panel foldout w/glossy full-color finish, 1967, 6¾x4" (folded), EX..............**$45.00**

Music book, Count Basie's Piano Styles, w/15 solos from Basie's recordings, sepia & pink cover, 32 pages, 12x9", EX..**$35.00**

Noisemaker, man in dancing pose, litho tin, 1940s, EX.**$45.00**

Notepad holder, Mammy w/plastic torso, skirt forms pad, 1940s, 8½", EX **$85.00**

Paint booklet, Golly's Magic Painting Book, w/coupon for golliwog brooches & figures, 8 pages, 1970s, unused, M **$38.00**

Paperweight, cast-iron jockey figure w/brass ring, black skin, in white pants & shirt, red vest & hat, 1940s, 3½", EX..**$85.00**

Photo folder, Memories of Club Plantation souvenir, shows cotton bale & banjo player on cover, 1940s, EX..**$40.00**

Pin, bust form of black-skinned woman in rhinestone choker & shawl balancing gold-tone urn on head, 1940s, 2", EX..**$30.00**

Pin, carved wood image of brown-skinned soldier in khaki uniform w/yellow tie, painted features, 1940s, 4", EX **$85.00**

Plate, ceramic, blue on white w/image of cake bordered by scenes & 1903-1953 Hough Bakeries Inc advertising, 10", EX..**$75.00**

Poster, Before We Read series for schoolroom depicting children at play w/dolls, alphabet on back, 1940s, 27x20", M..**$125.00**

Poster, grocer ad w/Amos & Andy in chef's hats promoting specials, Campbell's Soup can at bottom, 1930s, 20x14", EX+ **$150.00**

Puppets, Life-Like Family, hand-painted rubber, set of 5 w/father, mother & 3 kids, Childcraft, 1940s, NMIB **$30.00**

Recipe cards, Southern Recipe Notes, brown-skinned Mammy serving cake on box cover, dated 1954, 9x5½" box, EX..**$75.00**

Record, Tales of Uncle Remus, 78 rmp, 3-record set, Capitol, 1947, EX (EX cover) **$85.00**

Roly-poly, clown, papier-mache, dark brown face w/red features, white outfit w/red trim, 5", EX.................**$420.00**

Roly-poly, golliwog boy, composition, dark brown movable head w/goggle eyes, green outfit w/red trim, 5", EX........**$420.00**

Salt & pepper shakers, jazz singer (brown-skinned female) & saxophone player (white-skinned male), ceramic, 1980s, M, pr **$45.00**

Salt & pepper shakers, Mammy & waiter, chalkware, very dark skin tone, red & black detail, 1940s, 3", EX, pr **$85.00**

Scorekeeping card, Hit the Jack w/Robertson's, golliwog graphics in black & red on white, 1970s, 4½x5", unused, EX..**$22.00**

Shade pull, hard plastic Mammy figure w/black skin tone, polka-dot dress w/white apron, 2½", EX..............**$35.00**

Shopping bag, cotton-backed PVC, w/Robertson's Marmalade advertising featuring Golly, Golly It's Good, 1970s, 20x14", EX **$165.00**

Tablecloth, New York City souvenir depicting Black band, city map & points of interest, multicolored, 1940s, 47x47", EX **$125.00**

Teapot, ceramic Mammy figure w/rare matt glaze, Gone w/the Wind 50th anniversary commemorative, 1988, M..**$175.00**

Thermos, Sambo's Restaurant, plastic, orange cup & handle, Aladdin, 1970s, 10½", EX **$70.00**

Tumbler, frosted glass w/Old Plantations advertising & image titled Garden View, 1940s, 6½", M......................**$25.00**

Wall pocket, chef sitting on old-fashioned stove, ceramic, 1940s, 5", EX **$125.00**

Black Cats

Kitchenware, bookends, vases, and many other items designed as black cats were made in Japan during the 1950s and exported to the United States where they were sold by various distributors who often specified certain characteristics they wanted in their own line of cats. Common to all these lines were the red clay used in their production and the medium used in their decoration — their features were applied over the glaze with 'cold (unfired) paint.' The most collectible is a line marked (or labeled) Shafford. Shafford cats are plump and pleasant looking. They have green eyes with black pupils; white eyeliner, eyelashes, and whiskers; and red bow ties. The same design with yellow eyes was marketed by Royal, and another fairly easy-to-find 'breed' is

Poster, lady holding sleepy child, Emory, 1967, 22x17", from $75.00 to $125.00.

a line by Wales with yellow eyes and gold whiskers. You'll find various other labels as well. Some collectors buy only Shafford, while others like them all.

When you evaluate your black cats, be critical of their paint. Even though no chips or cracks are present, if half of the paint is missing, you have a half-price item. Remember this when using the following values which are given for cats with near-mint to mint paint.

Advisor: Doug Dezso (See Directory, Candy Containers)

Ashtray, flat face, Shafford, hard-to-find size, 3¾"......**$45.00**
Ashtray, flat face, Shafford, 4¾" **$18.00**
Ashtray, head shape, not Shafford, several variations, ea from $12 to...**$15.00**
Ashtray, head shape w/open mouth, Shafford, 3" **$22.00**

Bank, seated cat with coin slot in top of head, Shafford, from $225.00 to $275.00.

Bank, upright cat, Shafford-like features, marked Tommy, 2-part, from $150 to..**$175.00**
Cigarette lighter, Shafford, 5½"...................................**$175.00**
Cigarette lighter, sm cat stands on book by table lamp .**$65.00**
Condiment set, upright cats, yellow eyes, 2 bottles & pr of matching shakers in wireware stand, row arrangement **$95.00**
Condiment set, 2 joined heads, J & M bows w/spoons (intact), Shafford, 4"...**$95.00**
Condiment set, 2 joined heads yellow eyes (not Shafford) **$65.00**
Cookie jar, cat's head, fierce expression, yellow eyes, brown-black glaze, heavy red clay, lg, rare **$250.00**
Cookie jar, lg head cat, Shafford, from $80 to **$100.00**
Creamer & sugar bowl, cat-head lids are salt & pepper shakers, yellow eyes variation, 5⅜" **$50.00**
Creamer & sugar bowl, Shafford **$45.00**
Cruet, slender form, gold collar & tie, tail handle **$12.00**
Cruet, upright cat w/yellow eyes, open mouth, paw spout **$30.00**

Cruets, oil & vinegar; cojoined cats, Royal Sealy, 1-pc (or similar examples w/heavier yellow-eyed cats), 7¼"..**$40.00**
Cruets, upright cats, she w/V eyes for vinegar, he w/O eyes for oil, Shafford, pr, from $60 to **$75.00**
Decanter, long cat w/red fish in his mouth as stopper...**$60.00**
Decanter, upright cat holds bottle w/cork stopper, Shafford...**$50.00**
Decanter set, upright cat, yellow eyes, +6 plain wines .**$35.00**
Decanter set, upright cat, yellow eyes, +6 wines w/cat faces **$50.00**
Demitasse pot, tail handle, bow finial, Shafford, 7½"..**$165.00**
Desk caddy, pen forms tail, spring body holds letters, 6½"..**$8.00**
Egg cup, cat face on bowl, pedestal foot, Shafford, from $95 to..**$125.00**
Grease jar, sm cat head, Shafford, scarce, from $95 to ..**$110.00**
Ice bucket, cylindrical w/embossed yellow-eyed cat face, 2 sizes, ea **$75.00**
Measuring cups, 4 sizes on wooden wall-mount rack w/painted cat face, Shafford, rare, from $350 to...............**$400.00**
Mug, Shafford, cat handle w/head above rim, standard, 3½"...**$55.00**
Mug, Shafford, cat handle w/head below rim, scarce, 3½"...**$95.00**
Mug, Shafford, scarce, 4", from $70 to........................**$80.00**
Paperweight, cat's head on stepped chrome base, open mouth, yellow eyes, rare...**$75.00**
Pincushion, cushion on cat's back, tongue measure ..**$25.00**
Pitcher, milk; seated upright cat, ear forms spout, tail handle, Shafford, 6" or 6½", ea................................**$150.00**
Pitcher, squatting cat, pour through mouth, Shafford, rare, 5", 14½" circumference...**$90.00**
Pitcher, squatting cat, pour through mouth, Shafford, scarce, 4½", 13" circumference...**$75.00**
Pitcher, squatting cat, pour through mouth, Shafford, very rare, 5½", 17" circumference..............................**$250.00**
Planter, cat & kitten in a hat, Shafford-like paint........**$30.00**
Planter, cat sits on knitted boot w/gold drawstring, Shafford-like paint, Elvin, 4¼x4½" **$30.00**
Planter, upright cat, Shafford-like paint, Napco label, 6" ..**$20.00**
Pot holder caddy, 'teapot' cat, 3 hooks, Shafford, from $170 to..**$195.00**
Salad set, spoon & fork, funnel, 1-pc oil & vinegar cruet & salt & pepper shakers on wooden wall-mount rack, Royal Sealy..**$200.00**
Salt & pepper shakers, long crouching cat, shaker in ea end, Shafford, 10"...**$165.00**
Salt & pepper shakers, range size; upright cats, Shafford, scarce, 5" **$65.00**
Salt & pepper shakers, round-bodied 'teapot' cat, Shafford, pr, from $125 to...**$140.00**
Salt & pepper shakers, seated, blue eyes, Enesco label, 5¾", pr...**$15.00**
Salt & pepper shakers, upright cats, Shafford, 3¾" (watch for slightly smaller set as well), pr **$25.00**
Spice set, triangle, 3 rounded tiers of shakers, 8 in all, in wooden wall-mount triangular rack, very rare...**$450.00**

Spice set, 4 upright cat shakers hook onto bottom of wire-ware cat-face rack, Shafford, rare.........................**$450.00**

Spice set, 6 square shakers in wooden frame, Shafford...**$175.00**

Spice set, 6 square shakers in wooden frame, yellow eyes .**$125.00**

Stacking tea set, mamma pot with kitty creamer and sugar bowl, yellow eyes, $80.00.

Stacking tea set, 3 cats w/red collar, w/gold ball, yellow eyes, 3-pc **$80.00**

Sugar bowl/planter, sitting cat, red bow w/gold bell, Shafford-like paint, Elvin, 4" **$25.00**

Teapot, bulbous body, head lid, green eyes, lg, Shafford, 7" **$75.00**

Teapot, bulbous body, head lid, green eyes, Shafford, med size, from $40 to **$45.00**

Teapot, bulbous body, head lid, green eyes, Shafford, sm, 4 - 4½" **$30.00**

Teapot, cat face w/double spout, Shafford, scarce, 5", from $200 to **$250.00**

Teapot, cat's face, yellow hat, blue & white eyes, pink ears, lg, from $40 to **$50.00**

Teapot, crouching cat, paw up to right ear is spout, green jeweled eyes, 8½" L..**$80.00**

Teapot, panther-like appearance, gold eyes, sm.........**$20.00**

Teapot, upright, slender cat (not ball-shaped), lift-off head, Shafford, rare, 8"....................................**$250.00**

Teapot, upright cat w/paw spout, yellow eyes & red bow, Wales, 8¼"..**$60.00**

Teapot, yellow eyes, 1-cup...**$30.00**

Teapot, yellow-eyed cat face embossed on front of standard bulbous teapot shape, wire bale **$60.00**

Thermometer, cat w/yellow eyes stands w/paw on round thermometer face..**$30.00**

Toothpick holder, cat on vase atop book, Occupied Japan **$12.00**

Tray, flat face, wicker handle, Shafford, rare, lg.......**$185.00**

Utensil (fork, spoon or strainer), wood handle, Shafford, scarce, ea...**$125.00**

Utensil rack, flat-backed cat w/3 slots for utensils, cat only...**$125.00**

Wall pocket, flat-backed 'teapot' cat, Shafford **$125.00**

Wine, embossed cat's face, green eyes, Shafford, sm.**$75.00**

Blair Dinnerware

American dinnerware has been a popular field of collecting for several years, and the uniquely styled lines of Blair Ceramics are very appealing, though not often seen except in the Midwest (and it's there that prices are the strongest). Blair was located in Ozark, Missouri, manufacturing dinnerware only from the mid-'40s until the early '50s. Gay Plaid, recognized by its squared-off shapes and brush-stroke design (in lime, brown, and dark green on white), is the pattern you'll find most often. Several other lines were made as well. You'll be able to recognize all of them easily enough, since most pieces (except for the smaller items) are marked.

Bowl, fruit/cereal; Gay Plaid, 6½" square, from $8.00 to $10.00.

Bowl, onion soup; Gay Plaid, w/lid, rope handle......**$20.00**

Bowl, Rick-Rack...**$12.00**

Casserole, Gay Plaid, rope handles.............................**$37.00**

Creamer, Bamboo, rope handle....................................**$17.00**

Creamer, Gay Plaid, rope handle **$16.00**

Cup, Autumn Leaf, rope handle **$10.00**

Cup & saucer, Gay Plaid, closed handle....................**$17.00**

Cup & saucer, Gay Plaid, rope handle........................**$12.00**

Nut dish, Autumn Leaf..**$8.00**

Plate, Bamboo, 8" square **$8.00**

Plate, dinner; Bamboo, square **$14.00**

Plate, dinner; Gay Plaid..**$14.00**

Plate, serving; Yellow Plaid, divided **$30.00**

Salt & pepper shakers, Gay Plaid, pr.........................**$14.00**

Sugar bowl, Bamboo, w/lid, rope handle **$17.00**

Tumbler, Gay Plaid...**$14.00**

Blue Danube

A modern-day interpretation of the early Meissen Blue Onion pattern, Blue Danube is an extensive line of quality dinnerware that has been produced in Japan since the early

1950s and distributed by Lipper International of Wallingford, Connecticut. It is said that the original design was inspired by a pattern created during the Yuan Dynasty (1260 – 1368) in China. This variation is attributed to the German artist Kandleva. The flowers depicted in this blue-on-white dinnerware represent the ancient Chinese symbols of good fortune and happiness. The original design, with some variations, made its way to Eastern Europe where it has been produced for about two hundred years. It is regarded today as one of the world's most famous patterns.

At least one hundred twenty-five items have at one time or another been made available by the Lipper company, making it the most complete line of dinnerware now available in the United States. Collectors tend to pay higher prices for items with the earlier banner mark (1951 to 1976), and reticulated (openweave) pieces bring a premium. Unusual serving or decorative items generally command high prices as well. The more common items that are still being produced usually sell for less than retail on the secondary market.

The banner logo includes the words 'Reg US Pat Off' along with the pattern name. In 1976 the logo was redesigned and the pattern name within a rectangular box with an 'R' in circle to the right of it was adopted. Very similar lines of dinnerware have been produced by other companies, but these two marks are the indication of genuine Lipper Blue Danube. Among the copycats you may encounter are Mascot and Vienna Woods — there are probably others.

Advisor: Lori Simnionie (See the Directory under Blue Danube)

Baker, oval, 10", from $50 to **$55.00**
Bell, 6" **$25.00**
Biscuit jar, 9", from $50 to...**$60.00**
Bone dish/side salad; crescent shape, banner mark, 9", from
    $18 to **$22.00**
Bowl, cereal; banner mark, 6" **$12.00**
Bowl, cream soup; w/lid, from $30 to............................**$35.00**
Bowl, dessert; 5½", from $8 to.......................................**$10.00**
Bowl, divided vegetable; 11x7½" **$50.00**
Bowl, lattice edge, 9", from $50 to.................................**$60.00**
Bowl, low pedestal skirted base, shaped rim, banner mark,
    2x9x12", from $70 to **$80.00**
Bowl, soup; 8½" **$15.00**
Bowl, vegetable; oval, 10" L, from $30 to.....................**$40.00**
Bowl, vegetable; 3¼x10", from $45 to **$50.00**
Bowl, vegetable; 9", from $35 to **$40.00**
Bowl, wedding; w/lid, footed, square, 8½x5", from $55
    to **$65.00**
Box, white lacquer ware, gold label w/rectangular logo,
    2¼x4½" **$30.00**
Butter dish, round, 8½" **$85.00**
Butter dish, stick type, ¼-lb, from $25 to.....................**$35.00**
Cache pot, w/handles, 8x8" **$45.00**
Cake pedestal, lattice edge, rectangular mark, 5x10" .**$75.00**
Cake pedestal, 4x10" **$55.00**

Cake server & knife, from $25 to **$30.00**
Candlesticks, 6½", pr, from $40 to **$50.00**
Candy dish, w/lid, from $50 to..**$60.00**
Casserole, individual; banner mark, 6" across handles ..**$35.00**
Casserole, 5½x10½" (across handles) **$65.00**
Chamber stick, Old Fashioned, 4x6" dia........................**$25.00**
Cheese board, wooden, w/6" dia tile & glass dome, from $25
    to **$35.00**
Chop plate, 12" dia **$40.00**
Coasters, set of 4, from $25 to.......................................**$35.00**
Coffee mug, 3⅛", set of 4, from $55 to **$60.00**
Coffeepot, embossed applied spout, ornate handle, 7½",
    from $60 to..**$70.00**
Condiment bowl, 2½" deep, w/saucer, 6¾" **$25.00**
Creamer, bulbous, 3½" **$16.00**
Creamer, ovoid, 3½" **$15.00**
Creamer & sugar bowl, 'y' handles, bulbous, 4¾", 3½", from
    $35 to **$40.00**
Cup & saucer, 'y' handle, from $8 to **$10.00**
Cup & saucer, angle handle, scalloped rims, from $7 to ..**$9.00**
Cup & saucer, demitasse **$10.00**
Cup & saucer, farmer's; 4x5" (across handle), from
    $15 to **$20.00**
Cup & saucer, Irish coffee; cylindrical cup, from $12
    to **$16.00**
Cutting board, 14x9½", +stainless steel knife.............**$30.00**
Dish, leaf shape, 5¾x4"...**$20.00**

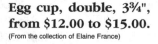

Egg cup, double, 3¾", from $12.00 to $15.00.
(From the collection of Elaine France)

Ginger jar, 5", from $35 to **$40.00**
Goblet, clear glass w/Blue Danube design, 7¼", set of
    12 ....**$60.00**
Gravy boat, double spout, w/undertray, 3½x6", from
    $35 to **$40.00**
Gravy boat, 6⅜x9¾", from $65 to **$75.00**
Hurricane lamp, glass mushroom globe **$75.00**
Ice cream scoop, cutting blade, no mark **$50.00**
Inkstand, 2 lidded inserts, shaped base, banner mark, 9"
    L...**$300.00**

Napkin holders, set of 4, from $30 to.........................$35.00
Napkins, Sunnyweave, set of 4, from $25 to..............$30.00
Pitcher, bulbous w/flared spout, fancy handle, 5¼", from $25
  to $30.00

Pitcher, bulbous with flared spout, fancy handle, 6¼", $40.00.
(From the collection of Elaine France)

Pitcher, milk; 'y' handle, 5¼", from $25 to $30.00
Plate, bread & butter; 6¾"...$6.00
Plate, devilled eggs, from $80 to $90.00
Plate, lattice rim, 8"...$15.00
Plate, triangular, 9¾" L..$50.00
Plate, 8¼", from $8 to $11.00
Plate, 10¼", from $10 to...$15.00
Platter, 12x8½", from $35 to $45.00
Platter, 14x10", from $60 to..$65.00
Salt & pepper shakers, dome top w/bud finial, bulbous bot-
  tom, 5", pr $40.00
Salt & pepper shakers, 5 holes in salt, 3 in pepper, 5", pr..$25.00
Salt box, wooden lid, 4¾x4¾" $55.00
Snack plate & cup $25.00
Soup ladle, from $35 to..$45.00
Soup tureen, w/lid, from $135 to...............................$150.00
Spooner, 4¾x4"...$50.00
Sugar bowl, ovoid, w/lid, 5", from $20 to $25.00
Tablecloth, 50x70", +4 napkins....................................$95.00
Tazza, attached pedestal foot, banner mark, 4½x15", from
  $85 to..$95.00
Tea tile/trivet, 6", from $18 to.....................................$25.00
Teakettle, enamel, wood handle, w/fold-down metal sides,
  9x9½"..$25.00
Teapot, 'y' handle, 6½", from $50 to.............................$60.00
Temple jar, 10½"...$60.00
Tidbit tray, 2-tier $35.00
Tidbit tray, 3-tier $40.00
Tray, fluted shell shape w/rolled end, sm $45.00
Undertray, for soup tureen $45.00
Vase, scalloped rim w/embossed decor, round foot, wide
  body, no mark, 6"...$20.00

Blue Garland

During the 1960s and 1970s, this dinnerware was offered as premiums through grocery stores. Its ornate handles, platinum trim, and the scalloped rims on the flat items and the bases of the hollow ware pieces when combined with the 'Haviland' backstamp suggested to most supermarket shoppers that they were getting high quality dinnerware for very little. And indeed the line was of good quality, but the company that produced it had no connection at all to the famous Haviland company of Limoges, France, who produced fine china there for almost one hundred years. The mark is Johann Haviland, taken from the name of the founding company that later became Philip Rosenthal and Co. This was a German manufacturer who produced chinaware for export to the United States from the mid-1930s until well into the 1980s. Today's dinnerware collectors find the delicate wreath-like blue flowers and the lovely shapes very appealing.

Bell, from $50 to...$60.00
Beverage server (teapot/coffeepot, w/lid, 11", from $60
  to $70.00
Bowl, fruit; 5⅛", from $4.50 to......................................$6.00
Bowl, oval, 10¾"...$65.00
Bowl, soup; 7⅝", from $9 to $12.00
Bowl, vegetable; 8½", from $25 to................................$35.00
Butter dish, ¼-lb, from $45 to $55.00
Butter pat..$10.00
Candlesticks, 3½x4", pr, from $75 to $85.00
Casserole/tureen, w/lid, 12", from $45 to $55.00
Chamberstick, metal candle cup & handle, 6" dia $75.00
Coaster/butter pat, 3¾" dia, from $10 to $12.00
Creamer, from $15 to..$18.00
Cup & saucer, flat, from $5 to $8.00
Cup & saucer, footed, from $10 to...............................$12.00
Gravy boat, w/attached underplate, from $35 to........$45.00

Gravy boat with undertray, from $35.00 to $45.00.

Plate, bread & butter; 6¼", from $3 to...........................$4.00
Plate, dinner; 10", from $8 to.......................................$10.00

Plate, salad; 7¾", from $7 to	**$9.00**
Platter, 13", from $22 to	**$28.00**
Platter, 14½", from $30 to	**$40.00**
Platter, 15½", from $35 to	**$45.00**
Salt & pepper shakers, 4¼", pr, from $35 to	**$40.00**
Sugar bowl, w/lid, from $18 to	**$22.00**
Teakettle, porcelain w/stainless steel lid	**$25.00**
Tidbit tray, 1-tier	**$45.00**
Tidbit tray, 3-tier	**$90.00**

Blue Ridge Dinnerware

Blue Ridge has long been popular with collectors, and prices are already well established, but that's not to say there aren't a few good buys left around. There are! It was made by a company called Southern Potteries, who operated in Erwin, Tennessee, from sometime in the latter '30s until the mid-'50s. They made many hundreds of patterns, all hand decorated. Some collectors prefer to match up patterns, while others like to mix them together for a more eclectic table setting.

One of the patterns most popular with collectors (and one of the most costly) is called French Peasant. It's very much like Quimper with simple depictions of a little peasant man with his staff and a lady. But they also made many lovely floral patterns, and it's around these where most of the buying and selling activity is centered. You'll find roosters, plaids, and simple textured designs, and in addition to the dinnerware, some vases and novelty items as well.

Very few pieces of dinnerware are marked except for the 'china' or porcelain pieces which usually are. Watch for a similar type of ware often confused with Blue Ridge that is sometimes (though not always) marked Italy.

The values suggested below are for the better patterns. To evaluate the French Peasant line, double these figures; for the simple plaids and textures, deduct 25% to 50%, depending on their appeal.

If you'd like to learn more, we recommend *The Collector's Encyclopedia of Blue Ridge Dinnerware, Identification and Values,* by Betty and Bill Newbound.

Advisors: Bill and Betty Newbound (See Directory, Dinnerware)

Newsletter: National Blue Ridge Newsletter
Norma Lilly
144 Highland Dr., Blountsville, TN 37617

Ashtray, advertising, round	**$70.00**
Baking dish, divided, 8x13"	**$30.00**
Basket, aluminum edge, 7"	**$25.00**
Batter jug, w/lid	**$90.00**
Bonbon, flat shell, Pixie	**$125.00**
Bowl, cereal/soup; 6"	**$25.00**
Bowl, divided, 9"	**$30.00**
Bowl, mixing; med	**$25.00**

Bowl, mixing; sm	**$20.00**
Bowl, vegetable; round, 8"	**$25.00**
Butter dish, Woodcrest	**$65.00**
Cake lifter	**$35.00**

Cake tray, Verna, Maple Leaf Shape, china, $70.00.

Celery, Skyline	**$45.00**
Character jug, china	**$700.00**
Child's feeding dish	**$150.00**
Child's mug	**$100.00**
Child's plate	**$125.00**
Chocolate pot	**$275.00**

Coffeepot, Ovoid Shape, from $150.00 to $160.00.

Creamer, Fifties shape	**$15.00**
Creamer, pedestal foot	**$65.00**
Cup & saucer, demitasse; china	**$50.00**
Cup & saucer, Holiday	**$65.00**
Custard cup	**$18.00**
Egg cup, double	**$30.00**
Egg cup, Premium	**$50.00**

Lamp, china...$250.00
Pitcher, Abbey, china.............................$180.00
Pitcher, Jane...$135.00
Pitcher, Sculptured Fruit, black handle, 7½" $95.00
Plate, aluminum edge, 12"......................$45.00
Plate, divided, heavy..............................$35.00

Plate, French Peasant, 9½", $50.00.

Plate, 6"..$8.00
Plate, 9¼", from $22 to $25.00
Plate, 10½" $30.00
Plate, 11½" $50.00
Platter, regular pattern..............................$40.00
Relish, heart shape, sm.............................$90.00
Relish, loop handle, china $85.00
Relish, T-handle $75.00
Salad spoon...$50.00
Salt & pepper shakers, Blossom Top, pr $65.00
Salt & pepper shakers, chickens, pr...........$150.00
Salt & pepper shakers, Good Housekeeping, pr $90.00
Salt & pepper shakers, Mallard, pr............$350.00
Salt & pepper shakers, Skyline, pr $25.00
Sconce $90.00
Sherbet...$25.00
Snack tray, Martha $175.00
Sugar bowl, Colonial, eared, open.............$30.00
Sugar bowl, Woodcrest, w/lid....................$30.00
Syrup jug, w/lid...$95.00
Teapot, Charm House $300.00
Teapot, Chevron handle............................$170.00
Teapot, Colonial.......................................$135.00
Teapot, Mini Ball $200.00
Teapot, Piecrust $130.00
Teapot, Snub Nose $190.00
Tidbit tray, 2-tier $30.00
Tidbit tray, 3-tier $45.00
Tile, round or square, 3"...........................$45.00
Toast, French Peasant, w/lid.....................$300.00

Tumbler, juice; glass $15.00
Vase, boot, 8" $110.00
Vase, bud..$175.00
Vase, handled, 7½"...................................$100.00
Vase, ruffled top, 9½"...............................$135.00
Vase, tapered..$110.00

Blue Willow Dinnerware

Blue Willow dinnerware has been made since the 1700s, first by English potters, then Japanese, and finally American companies as well. Tinware, glassware, even paper 'go-withs' have been produced over the years — some fairly recently, due to on-going demand. It was originally copied from the early blue and white wares made in Nanking and Canton in China. Once in awhile you'll see some pieces in black, pink, red, or even multicolor.

Obviously the most expensive will be the early English wares, easily identified by their backstamps. You'll be most likely to find pieces made by Royal or Homer Laughlin, and even though comparatively recent, they're still collectible, and their prices are very affordable.

For further study we recommend *Blue Willow Identification and Value Guide* by Mary Frank Gaston.

See also Homer Laughlin; Royal China.

Advisor: Mary Frank Gaston (See Directory, Dinnerware)

Newsletter: American Willow Report
Lisa Kay Henze, Editor
P.O. Box 900, Oakridge, OR 97463. Bimonthly newsletter, subscription: $15 per year, out of country add $5 per year

Newsletter: The Willow Word
Mary Berndt, Publisher
P.O. Box 13382, Arlington, TX 76094; Send SASE for information about subscriptions and the International Willow Collector's Convention

Bowl, vegetable; rectangular, w/lid, unmarked, 10½x6", from $120 to..$150.00
Bowls, stacking set of 4, w/lid, Made in Japan (Moriyama), 9", from $325 to $375.00
Butter dish, rectangular, ¼-lb, Japan, 6" L, from $60 to..$75.00
Butter warmer, unmarked Japan, from $75 to...........$100.00
Candelabrum, brass & ceramic, 3-light, w/matching side dishes, Shenango China mark, from $225 to......$250.00
Canister set, Flour, Sugar, Coffee, Tea, graduated sizes, barrel shaped, Japan, set of 4, from $350 to.................$450.00
Canister set, Flour, Sugar, Coffee, Tea, square tins, ranging from 7" to 4½", unmarked, set of 4, from $120 to..........$140.00
Carafe & warmer, Japan, 10" overall, from $225 to ..$275.00
Clock, tin, Smith's, Made in Great Britain, from $150 to..$165.00
Coffeepot, graniteware, unmarked, 6½", from $90 to...$110.00
Coffeepot, Japan, 7", from $100 to...........................$120.00
Compote, Shenango China, 3x6", from $50 to $60.00

Cookie jar, willow reserve on white pitcher form, McCoy, 9", from $40 to................**$50.00**
Creamer, hotel ware, Shenango China, 2½", from $30 to................**$35.00**
Creamer, Shenango................**$22.00**
Cup & saucer, demitasse; Japan, 2½", 4½", from $14 to..**$18.00**
Cup & saucer, Johnson Bros................**$12.50**
Cup & saucer, Pictorial border pattern, Noritake mark, 3", from $40 to................**$50.00**
Cup & saucer, USA, stacking................**$6.00**
Egg cup, double, unmarked Japan, 3¾", from $15 to ..**$20.00**
Egg cup, single, Japan, 1½-2", from $25 to................**$35.00**

Farmer's cup and saucer, Take Ye a Cuppe..., Buffalo, 3¼x5¾", 7⅝", $67.50.

Gravy boat, Shenango China, 6", from $45 to............**$55.00**
Ladle, Traditional center pattern, unmarked, 8", from $140 to................**$165.00**
Mug, farmer's; heavy & lg, Japan, 4", from $35 to......**$40.00**
Mug, inside decal, Japan................**$20.00**
Mug, unmarked Japan, 3½", from $10 to **$15.00**
Pitcher, iced tea; ice lip, Japan, tall................**$115.00**

Plate, American Limoges, Made in USA, 9½", from $18.00 to $20.00.
(Photo courtesy Mary Frank Gaston)

Plate, grill; Occupied Japan, 10½"................**$30.00**
Plate, grill; Traditional center & border patterns, Made in Japan, 10½", from $20 to **$25.00**
Plate, grill; Turner center pattern, Scroll & Flower border, Shenango China, 10", from $20 to................**$25.00**
Plate, Made in Japan, 8¾"................**$14.00**

Plate, pie; unglazed base for baking, Made in Japan (Moriyama) mark, 10", from $70 to................**$80.00**
Platter, Aldine China/Occupied Japan, 12"................**$55.00**
Salt & pepper shakers, barrel forms, Japan, pr................**$20.00**
Snack hound, 5 sections, Japan mark, from $65 to **$75.00**
Spoon rack, open planter pocket on right side, unmarked Japan, 8", complete, from $120 to................**$140.00**
Spoon rest, double style, Japan, 9", from $40 to........**$50.00**
Teapot, musical type, unmarked Japan, from $130 to ..**$150.00**
Tray, Reversed Traditional pattern, unmarked, ca 1950s, 19" dia, from $35 to................**$45.00**

Bookends

You'll find bookends in various types of material and designs. The more inventive their modeling, the higher the price. Also consider the material. Cast-iron examples, especially if in original polychrome paint, are bringing very high prices right now. Brass and copper are good as well, though elements of design may override the factor of materials altogether. If they are signed by the designer or marked by the manufacturer, you can double the price. Those with a decidedly Art Deco appearance are often good sellers. The consistent volume of common to moderately uncommon bookends that are selling online has given the impression that some are more easily available than once thought. Hence, some examples have not accrued in value. See *Collector's Guide to Bookends* by Louis Kuritzky (Collector Books) for more information.

Advisor: Louis Kuritzky (See Directory, Bookends)

Club:
Bookend Collector Club
Louis Kuritzky
4510 NW 175h Pl.
Gainesville, FL 32605; 352-377-3193
Quarterly full-color newsletter: $25 per year

Buccaneer, Conn Foundry, cast iron, 1930, 7¼", $125.00 for the pair. (Photo courtesy Louis Kuritzky)

American Legion, embossed military scene, bronze, ca 1939, 8", pr **$115.00**
Baby Shoes, gray metal, Pat 1940, 5½", pr **$60.00**
Bronco Rider, gray metal, Dodge, 1947, 5", pr............**$75.00**
Catwalk, embossed lion, aluminum, ca 1970, 3½", pr..**$25.00**
Cellists, painted chalk figure on polished stone base, JB Hirsch, ca 1940, pr **$135.00**
Deco Bust, gray metal, Abbot Schy 47, 1947, 7¼", pr...**$150.00**
Dogwood, gray metal, PM Craftsman, ca 1965, 5¼", pr..**$40.00**

Winged woman with Comedy and Tragedy masks, JB #1529, gray metal, 5", $250.00 for the pair. (Photo courtesy Louis Kuritzky)

Eve, Verona Factory, cast iron, 6¾", $175.00 for the pair. (Photo courtesy Louis Kuritzky)

Goldfish, Rookwood pottery, 1992, 4½", pr................**$85.00**
Harlequin Pair, painted boy & girl w/empty Chianti bottles behind, ca 1985, 11½", pr......................................**$65.00**
Heraldic Eagle, Syroco wood, ca 1935, 6", pr.............**$30.00**
Indiana Pigeon, Indiana Glass, ca 1940, 5½", pr **$75.00**
Lady Godiva, Haley Glass, ca 1940, 6", pr **$135.00**
Lincoln's Cabin, embossed scene, cast iron, Judd, 1925, 3¾", pr...**$50.00**
Patriotic Eagle, painted chalk, ca 1970, 5", pr.............**$20.00**
Pink Lady, painted chalk figure on polished stone base, JB Hirsch, 1943, 5½", pr..**$125.00**
Pirate Booty, relief scene, cast iron, Hubley, ca 1925, 4¾", pr **$65.00**
Ram, on rocky base, gray metal, SCC, 1974, 7", pr **$35.00**
Roundup, cowboys beside fence, gray metal, Phil Goodan, ca 1945, 6", pr...**$165.00**
Ruling Couple, seated Egyptian man & woman, Bellini Italy, ca 1980, 7", pr...**$85.00**
Sailfish, gray metal, PM Craftsman, ca 1965, 8", pr.....**$65.00**
Setters, on point, cast iron, Littco, ca 1925, 5", pr **$115.00**
Siam Couple, couple in relief, cast iron, ca 1926, 4¾", pr...**$50.00**
Three Musketeers, gray metal, Jennings Brothers shopmark, ca 1930, 5¾", pr...**$275.00**
Washington Crossing the Delaware, bronze finish on gray metal, K&O, ca 1932, 6¾", pr..............................**$125.00**
Ye Old Inn, Syroco Wood, company tag, ca 1940, 6¼", pr..**$35.00**

Books

Books have always fueled the mind's imagination. Before television lured us out of the library into the TV room, everyone enjoyed reading the latest novels. Western, horror, and science fiction themes are still popular to this day —especially those by such authors as Louis L'Amour, Steven King, and Ray Bradbury, to name but a few. Edgar Rice Burrough's Tarzan series and Frank L. Baum's Wizard of Oz books are regarded as classics among today's collectors. A first edition of a popular author's first book (especially if it's signed) is avidly sought after, so is a book that 'ties in' with a movie or television program.

Dick and Jane readers are fast becoming collectible. If you went to first grade sometime during the 1930s until the mid-1970s, you probably read about their adventures. These books were used all over the United States and in military base schools over the entire world. They were published here as well as in Canada, the Philippine Islands, Australia, and New Zealand; there were special editions for the Roman Catholic parochial schools and the Seventh Day Adventists', and even today they're in use in some Mennonite and Amish schools.

On the whole, ex-library copies and book club issues (unless they are limited editions) have very low resale values.

Besides the references in the subcategory narratives that follow, for further study we also recommend *Huxford's Old Book Value Guide* (Collector Books); *Collector's Guide to Children's Books, 1850 to 1950, Vols I, II,* and *III* by Diane McClure Jones and Rosemary Jones; and *Whitman Juvenile Books* by David and Virginia Brown. All are published by Collector Books.

Magazine: AB Bookman's Weekly
P.O. Box AB, Clifton, NJ 07015; 201-772-0020 or fax: 201-772-9281. Sample copies: $10.

Big Little Books

The Whitman Publishing Company started it all in 1933 when they published a book whose format was entirely different than any other's. It was very small, easily held in a child's hand, but over an inch in thickness. There was a cartoon-like drawing on the right-hand page, and the text was printed on the left. The idea was so well accepted that very soon other publishers — Saalfield, Van Wiseman, Lynn, World Syndicate, and Goldsmith — cashed in on the idea as well. The first Big Little Book hero was Dick Tracy, but soon every radio cowboy, cartoon character, lawman, and space explorer was immortalized in his own adventure series.

When it became apparent that the pre-teen of the '50s preferred the comic-book format, Big Little Books were finally phased out; but many were saved in boxes and stored in attics, so there's still a wonderful supply of them around. You need to watch condition carefully when you're buying or selling. For further information we recommend *Big Little Books, A Collector's Reference and Value Guide,* by Larry Jacobs (Collector Books).

Newsletter: Big Little Times
Big Little Book Collectors Club of America
Larry Lowery
P.O. Box 1242, Danville, CA 94526; 415-837-2086

Green Hornet Strikes, **Whitman #1453, 1940, VG, $85.00.**

Andy Panda in the City of Ice, Whitman #1441, NM .**$40.00**
Bambi's Children, Whitman #1497, NM **$70.00**
Blondie & Bouncing Baby Dumpling, Whitman #1476, NM...**$40.00**
Buck Jones in the Roaring West, Whitman #1174, VG .**$25.00**
Bugs Bunny in Risky Business, Whitman #1440, VG..**$35.00**
Captain Midnight & Sheik Joman Khan, Whitman #1402, EX..**$60.00**
Chester Gump Finds the Hidden Treasure, Whitman #766, EX **$50.00**
Dick Tracy & the Racketcer Gang, Whitman #1112, EX ..**$55.00**
Dick Tracy Solves the Penfield Mystery, Whitman #1137, VG **$55.00**
Donald Duck Gets Fed Up, Whitman #1462, EX **$50.00**

Flash Gordon & the Red Sword Invaders, Whitman #1479, NM **$85.00**
G-Man Breaking the Gambling Ring, Whtiman #1493, 1938, NM **$50.00**
G-Man Vs the Fifth Column, Whitman #1470, VG **$35.00**
Gene Autry & the Hawk of the Hills, Whitman #1493, NM **$50.00**
Green Hornet Cracks Down, Whitman #1480, NM...**$135.00**
In the Name of the Law, Whitman #1124, VG **$25.00**
Jungle Jim & the Vampire Woman, Whitman #1139, NM..**$75.00**
Little Annie Roonie & the Orphan House, Whitman #1117, VG...**$30.00**
Little Orphan Annie & the Mysterious Shoemaker, Whitman #1449, NM **$50.00**
Lone Ranger & the Red Renegades, Whitman #1489, EX **$50.00**
Mickey Mouse & the Magic Lamp, Whitman #1429, NM ..**$70.00**
Mutt & Jeff, Whitman #1113, NM **$75.00**
Perry Winkle & the Rinkeydinks Get a Horse, Whitman #1487, NM **$45.00**
Popeye & Castor Oyl the Detective, Whitman #1497, EX **$50.00**
Roy Rogers & the Deadly Treasure, Whitman #1437, VG **$40.00**
Smilin' Jack & the Escape From Death Rock, Whitman #1445, NM **$50.00**
Tailspin Tommy in the Famous Pay-Roll Mystery, Whitman #747, NM **$75.00**
Tillie the Toiler & the Wild Man of Desert Island, Whitman #1442, NM **$50.00**
Uncle Don's Strange Adventures, Whitman #1114, VG...**$30.00**

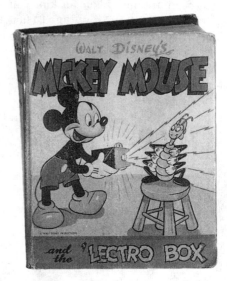

Walt Disney's *Mickey Mouse and the 'Lectro Box,* **Whitman, 1946, EX, $40.00.**

Children's Miscellaneous Books

Ali & the Ghost Tiger, Elaine Masters, green hardcover, 1st edition, Westminster Press, 1970, 154 pages, EX..**$15.00**
Alice in Wonderland, Elf/Rand McNally, 1951, EX......**$25.00**
Animals' Merry Christmas, Kathryn Jackson, Golden Press, pop-up tree, 1950, VG **$125.00**

Are All the Giants Dead?, Mary Norton, hardcover, 1st American Edition, Harcourt Brace, 1975, EX........**$15.00**

Baby Bunny, Wonder Book #545, 1952, EX.............**$12.00**

Back to the Slaughterhouse, Ronald Searle, 1st edition, oversize hardcover, MacDonald, 1951, 96 pages, EX..**$20.00**

Bambi, Whitman Tell-a-Tale #2548, 1972, EX................**$4.00**

Below the Root, Zilpha Keatley Snyder, Alton Raible illustrations, 1st edition, hardcover, Atheneum, 1975, EX...**$20.00**

Bumble, Magdalen Eldon, illustrated by author, oversize hardcover, Collins, 1950, 46 pages, EX.................**$20.00**

Captain's Daughter, Elizabeth Coatsworth, hardcover, 1st edition, Macmillan, 1950, 198 pages, w/dust jacket, EX.........**$25.00**

Casper & Wendy, Wonder Book #805, 1963, EX.........**$10.00**

Castaway Christmas, Margaret J Baker, R Kenendy black & white illustrations, Farrar, 1967, EX......................**$20.00**

Cinderella, 1 pop-up, Simon & Schuster, 1950, VG **$55.00**

Circus Alphabet, Whitman Tell-a-Tale #2531, 1974, EX..**$5.00**

Clarion the Kildeer, Helen Ross Russell, John Hamberger illustrations, 1st edition, hardcover, Hawthorn, 1970, EX..**$10.00**

Country School, Jerrold Beim, hardcover, 1st edition, Morrow, 1955, EX...**$10.00**

Crown Fire, Eloise Jarvis McGraw, hardcover, Coward-McCann, 1951, 254 pages, w/dust jacket, EX.......**$30.00**

Dino & the Mouse Who Had Hiccups, 4 pop-ups, 8 pages, 1974, EX..**$25.00**

Do Tigers Ever Bite Kings?, Barbara Wersba, 1st edition, hardcover, Atheneum, 1966, w/dust jacket, EX....**$40.00**

Dwarf on Black Mountain, Bill Knott, Ben Smith illustrations, hardcover, Steck-Vaughn, 1967, w/dust jacket, EX .**$20.00**

Elephant's Child, Rudyard Kipling, Kampman illustrations, 1st hardcover, Folett, 1969, EX **$20.00**

Figgs & Phantoms, Ellen Raskin, yellow hardcover, 1st edition, Dutton, 1974, w/dust jacket, EX **$30.00**

First Book of Prehistoric Animals, Alice Dickinson, Helene Carter illustrations, hardcover, Franklin Watts, 1954, EX **$10.00**

Freaky Friday, Mary Rodgers, hardcover, 1st edition, Harper & Row, 1972, EX...**$10.00**

Funny Friends in Mother Goose Land, Whitman Tell-a-Tale #2415-6, 1978, VG..**$6.00**

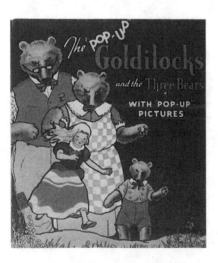

Goldilocks and the Three Bears, **Blue Ribbon, 1934, with three pop-ups, NM, $200.00.**

(Photo courtesy Larry Jacobs)

Giant John, Arnold Lobel, illustrations by author, 1st edition, oversize hardcover, Harper, 1964, EX **$15.00**

Girl Who Was a Cowboy, Phyllis Krasilovsky, blue pictorial hardcover w/red spine, 1st edition, Garden City, 1965, EX..**$10.00**

Good Morning Miss Dove, Frances Gray Paton, black & white illustrations, hardcover, Dodd Mead, 1954, EX.......**$10.00**

Grandfather Whiskers, MD; Nellie M Leonard, 1st edition, hardcover, Crowell, 1953, EX..................................**$20.00**

Grandpa, Barbara Borack, Ben Shector illustrations, hardcover picture book, Harper, 1967, EX.......................**$10.00**

Grandpa's Police Friends, Whitman Tell-a-Tale #2544, 1967, EX..**$6.00**

Grin & Giggle Book, Robert Pierce, 1st edition, oversize pictorial hardcover, Golden Press, 1972, EX..............**$35.00**

Henry in Lollipop Land, Wonder Book #664, 1953, EX..**$25.00**

Holiday at the Dew Drop Inn, Eve Garnett, hardcover, Vanguard, 1962, w/dust jacket, EX........................**$10.00**

Hong Kong Phooey & the Fortune Cookie Caper, Jean Lewis, hardcover, Rand McNally, 1975, EX **$10.00**

Hopalong Cassidy Lends a Helping Hand, Bonnie Books, 2 pop-ups, 1950, EX **$75.00**

Impatient Crusader, Florence Kelly's Life Story; Josephine Goldmark, 1st edition, University of Illinois, 1953, EX...**$20.00**

Jump-Rope Rhymes, Roger D Abrahams, U of Texas Press, 1st edition, hardcover, 1969, 228 pages, w/dust jacket, EX...**$30.00**

Katy's First Day, Whitman Tell-a-Tale #2403, 1972, EX..**$8.00**

Ken Follows the Chuck Wagon, Basil Miller, hardcover, Zondervan, 1950, EX **$10.00**

Kildee House, Rutherford G Montgomery, Barbara Cooney illustrations, Doubleday, 1949, 209 pages, EX......**$10.00**

Koko's Circus, Hank Hart, Animated Book Co, 1942, VG .**$55.00**

Laughing Dragon, Kenneth Mahood, 1st edition, oversize hardcover, Scribner, 1970, EX **$10.00**

Let's Be Enemies, Janice May Udry, Maurice Sendak illustrations, later editon, hardcover, Harper, EX...........**$15.00**

Lighthouse Keeper's Son, Nan Chauncy, VG Ambrus illustrations, 1st edition, hardcover, Oxford, 1969, EX....**$15.00**

Lion that Flew, James Reeves, Ardizzone illustrations, Chatto & Windus, 1974, w/dust jacket, EX......................**$40.00**

Little Mermaid, Hans Christian Anderson, Frascino illustrations, hardcover, Harper 1971 edition, EX...........**$10.00**

Little Princess, George MacDonald, William Pene du Bois illustrations, oversize hardcover, Crowel, 1962, EX.........**$20.00**

Look Through My Window, Jean Little, hardcover, 1st edition, Harper & Row, w/dust jacket, EX **$45.00**

My Little Book of Trains, Mattel giveaway, Whitman Tell-a-Tale #2421, 1978, EX **$10.00**

Nonsense Alphabet, Wonder Book #725, 1959, EX **$12.00**

Old Bones the Wonder Horse, Mildred M Pace, Wesley Dennis illustrations, hardcover, 1st edition, McGraw-Hill, 1955, EX..**$10.00**

Peppermint Pig, Nina Bawden, A Pendle illustrations, hardcover, 1st edition, Victor Gollancz, 1975, 160 pages, EX..**$20.00**

Pioneers: A Badger Book, Robin King, pictorial hardcover, Whitman, 1959, 92 pages, EX................................**$15.00**

Pippin's Journal or Rosemary Is for Remembrance, Rohon O'Grady, 1st American edition, Macmillan, 1962, 230 pages, EX..**$15.00**

Raggedy Andy's Treasure Hunt, Whitman Tell-a-Tale #2420, 1973, VG...**$8.00**

Raggedy Ann's Merriest Christmas, Wonder Book, 1952, NM...**$15.00**

Rainbow Round-A-Bout, 2 pop-ups & 2 revolving pictures, 10 pages, 1992, EX...**$15.00**

Resident Witch, Marian Place, pictorial hardcover, Washburn, 1970, EX...**$15.00**

Sea Fever, KM Peyton, hardcover, 1st edition, World, 1963, w/dust jacket, EX..**$15.00**

Secret of Gold, Madeleine Raillon, hardcover, 1st American edition, Harcourt Brace, 1965, EX.........................**$10.00**

Something Old, Something New; Susan Rinehart, Arnold Lobel illustrations, hardcover, 1st edition, Harper, 1961, EX...**$20.00**

Story of Florence Nightingale, Margaret Leighton, hardcover, Grosset, Signature Books edition, 1952, EX.........**$10.00**

Summerfield Farm, Mary Martin Black, oversize hardcover, 1st edition, Viking, 1951, 143 pages, w/dust jacket, EX...**$35.00**

Ten Brave Men, Sonia Daugherty, James Daugherty illustrations, Lippincott, 1951, EX **$15.00**

Three Bears, Whitman Tell-a-Tale #2592, 1968, EX **$5.00**

Three Young Kings, George Sumner Albee, oversize hardcover picture book, Keats illustrations, Watts, 1956, EX **$10.00**

Treasure in the Sun, Adeline Atwood, 1st edition, Houghton Mifflin, hardcover, 1954, EX............................**$15.00**

Troll Music, Anita Lobel, Harper, Weekly Reader edition, w/dust jacket, 1966, EX.................................**$10.00**

Unfriendly Book, Charlotte Zolotow, Dubois illustrations, 1st edition, Harper & Row, 1975, EX.................**$15.00**

Walter the Lazy Mouse, Marjorie Flack, Cyndy Szekeres illustrations, oversize hardcover, Doubleday, 1963, EX **$30.00**

Way of the Condor, Nathan Kravetz, WT Mars illustrations, hardcover, 1st edition, Crown, 1970, w/dust jacket, EX **$35.00**

What Did You Do When You Were a Kid?, Fred Sturner & Adolph Seltzer, hardcover, Weathervane, 1973, w/dust jacket, EX...**$15.00**

What I Want To Be When I Grow Up, Carol Burnett, Sheldon Secunda photos, 1st edition, Simon & Schuster, 1975, EX...**$10.00**

Wonderful Ice Cream Cart, Alice Rogers Hager, 1st edition, hardcover, Macmillan, 1955, w/dust jacket, EX....**$20.00**

Juvenile Series Books

Adventures of Dr Dolittle, pop-ups, Random House, ca 1960s, EX...**$40.00**

All About Dinosaurs, RC Andrews, hardcover, pictorial boards, Random House, 1953, EX....................**$10.00**

Babar's Fair, Jean de Brunhoff, oversize hardcover, Random House, EX...**$15.00**

Back of Beyond, George Franklin, American Heritage Series, Aladdin Books, 1952, EX.....................................**$10.00**

Bears' Almanac (Berenstain Bears), Stan & Jan Berenstain, Random House, 1970s, EX.................................**$150.00**

Beverly Gray College Mystery Series, Clair Blank, ca 1930 – 50, Grosset & Dunlap, 21 in the series, $10.00 each. (Photo courtesy Diane McClure Jones and Rosemary Jones)

Big Red, Jim Kjelgaard, Shannon Stirnweis illustrations, Holiday House Book Club Edition, EX.................**$10.00**

Billy Bunter, Frank Richards, Charles Skilton editions, from 1947-1952, EX, ea **$15.00**

Black Beauty, Whitman, hardcover, 1955, EX.............**$10.00**

Black Treasure (Sandy Steele), Roger Barlow, hardcover, Simon & Schuster, EX...**$10.00**

Borrowers Afield, Mary Norton, Beth & Joe Krush illustrations, 1st edition, Harcourt, 1955, EX....................**$10.00**

Child's Garden of Verses, Rand McNally Junior Elf Book, 1960s, EX...**$5.00**

Clue of the Screeching Owl (Hardy Boys), Franklin W Dixon, Grosset & Dunlap, 1962, EX.................................**$15.00**

Desmond's First Case, Herbert Best, hardcover, Viking, 1961, EX...**$10.00**

Five Little Peppers, hardcover, Whitman, 1955, EX **$10.00**

Five on a Hike Together, Enid Blyton, hardcover, Hodder & Stoughton, 1950, EX...**$10.00**

Hidden Valley of Oz, Rachel Cosgrove, 1st edition, blue hardcover w/paste-on picture, Reilly & Lee, 1951, 313 pages, EX **$150.00**

Janet Lennon at Camp Calamity, hardcover, Whitman, 1962, EX...**$20.00**

Koko of the Airways, Basil William Miller, hardcover, Zondervan, 1948, EX...**$10.00**

Lyle Finds His Mother, Bernard Waber, illustrated by author, hardcover, Houghton Mifflin, 1974, EX.................**$15.00**

Mike Mars Around the Moon, Donald Wolheim, Albert Orbaan illustrations, hardcover, Doubleday, 1964, EX........**$15.00**

Mystery of the Iron Box (Ken Holt), Bruce Campbell, hardcover, Grosset & Dunlap, 1952, EX.....................**$10.00**

Mystery on the Mississippi (Trixie Beldon), Kathryn Kenny, illustrated hardcover, Whitman, 1970, EX $10.00

Paddington Takes to TV, Michael Bond, Ivor Wood illustrations, 1st American Edition, 1974, w/dust jacket, EX $45.00

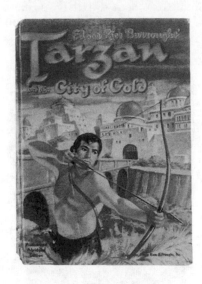

Tarzan and the City of Gold, Whitman #2307:49, Edgar Rice Burroughs, Authorized Edition, 1954, VG, $15.00.
(Photo courtesy David and Virginia Brown)

Little Golden Books

Everyone has had a few of these books in their lifetime; some we've read to our own children so many times that we still know them word for word, and today they're appearing in antique malls and shops everywhere. The first were printed in 1942. These are recognizable by their blue paper spines (later ones had gold foil). Until the early 1970s, they were numbered consecutively; after that they were unnumbered.

First editions of the titles having a 25¢ or 29¢ cover price can be identified by either a notation on the first or second pages, or a letter on the bottom right corner of the last page (A for 1, B for 2, etc.). If these are absent, you probably have a first edition.

Condition is extremely important. To qualify as mint, these books must look just as good as they looked the day they were purchased. Naturally, having been used by children, many show signs of wear. If your book is only lightly soiled, the cover has no tears or scrapes, the inside pages have only small creases or folded corners, and the spine is still strong, it will be worth about half as much as one in mint condition. A missing cover makes it worthless. Additional damage would of course lessen the value even more.

A series number containing an 'A' refers to an activity book, while a 'D' number identifies a Disney story.

For more information we recommend *Collecting Little Golden Books* by Steve Santi (who provided us with our narrative material).

Advisor: Ilene Kayne (See Directory, Books)

Activity book, 1955-63, hardcover, paper doll book w/paper dolls, EX **$35.00**
Activity book, 1955-63, hardcover, stamps, complete, EX..**$15.00**

Activity book, 1955-63, hardcover, wheel book w/wheel, EX **$10.00**
Band-Aid book, 1950-79, Helen Gaspard or Kathryn Jackson, Malvern illustrations, w/out band-aid insert, EX ..**$10.00**
Eager Reader Series, 1974-75, boxed set of 8, EX.......**$35.00**
General titles, later editions w/nonfiction titles, EX, ea ..**$5.00**
General titles, later editions w/popular comic strip characters, EX, ea **$8.00**
General titles, 1950s first editions, antique gold foil spine w/leaves & flower pattern, hardcover, ea............**$15.00**
General titles, 1960s 1st editions, antique gold foil spine w/leaves & flower pattern, hardcover, ea............**$12.00**
General titles, 1969-75, gold foil spine, w/animal pattern, hardcover 1st editions, ea **$8.00**
General titles, 1969-75, gold foil spine, w/animal pattern, hardcover later printings, ea **$4.00**
Giant Little Golden Book, 1957-59, Disney titles, EX, ea ..**$20.00**
Giant Little Golden Book, 1957-59, individual titles, ea **$10.00**
Jig-Saw Puzzle Book, 1949-50, various authors & illustrators, w/intact puzzle, EX..**$45.00**
Jig-Saw Puzzle Book, 1949-50, various authors & illustrators, w/out puzzle, ea **$10.00**
Popular illustrators Garth Williams & Eloise Wilkin, later editons, ea **$10.00**
Popular illustrators Garth Williams & Eloise Wilkin, 1st editions, ea **$20.00**

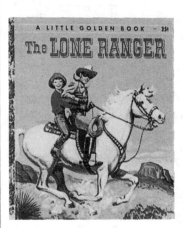

The Lone Ranger, #263, A edition, EX, $25.00.

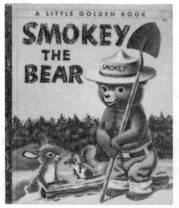

Smokey the Bear, #224, A edition, EX, $20.00.

Movie and TV Tie-Ins

Batman vs the Joker, softcover, Signet, 1st edition, 1966, M **$25.00**

Beaver & Wally, Beverly Cleary, paperback, Berkeley, 1961...$10.00

Beverly Hillbillies, Saga of Wildcat Creek, Doris Schroeder, Whitman #1572, 1963, EX......................................$15.00

Beverly Hillbillies Live It Up, softcover, Avon, 1965, NM, from $15 to...$20.00

Bewitched, The Opposite Uncle, Whitman #1572, 1970, EX...$20.00

Brady Bunch in Adventure on the High Seas, softcover, Tiger Beat, 1973, NM..$12.00

Chitty-Chitty Bang-Bang, softcover, 1968, EX.................$5.00

Dr Kildare Assigned to Trouble, Whitman #1547, 1963, EX...$12.00

Dragnet Case Stories, Whitman #1527, 1957, EX........$20.00

F Troup, The Great Indian Uprising, Whitman #1544, 1967, EX...$18.00

Family Affair, Buffy Finds a Star, Whitman #1567, 1970, EX...$15.00

Flipper, The Mystery of the Black Schooner, Whitman #2324, 1966, EX..$12.00

Fury & the Lone Pine Mystery, Whitman #1537, 1957, EX...$25.00

Garrison's Gorillas & the Fear Formula, Whitman #1548, 1968, EX...$15.00

Gene Autry & the Big Valley Grab, Whitman #2302:49, 1954, EX...$25.00

Gilligan's Island, Whitman #1566, 1966, EX................$18.00

Gunsmoke, Showdown on Front Street, Whitman #1529, 1969, EX...$15.00

Have Gun, Will Travel, Whitman #1568, 1959, EX.....$25.00

Hawaii Five-0, The Octopus Caper, Whitman #1553, 1971, EX...$12.00

High Chaparral, The Apache Way, Whitman #1591, 1969, EX...$15.00

I Spy, Message From Moscow, Whitman #1542, 1966, EX...$25.00

Ironside, Picture Frame Frame-Up, Whitman #1521, 1969, EX...$10.00

John Payne & the Menace at Hawk's Nest, Whitman #2385, 1943, EX...$22.00

Land of the Giants, softcover, Pyramid, 1968, EX.......$15.00

Lassie, Lost in the Snow, Steve Frazee, illustrated hardcover, Whitman, 1969, EX..$10.00

Lassie, Treasure Hunter, Whitman #1552, 1960, EX....$14.00

Leave It to Beaver, Cole Fannin, Whitman, 1962, EX.$20.00

Leave It to Beaver, Whitman #1526, 1962, EX.............$30.00

Lennon Sisters, The Secret of Holiday Island, Whitman #1544, 1960, EX...$10.00

Maverick, Whitman #1566, 1959, EX..........................$20.00

Mod Squad, Assignment: The Hideout, Whitman #1517, 1970, EX...$20.00

Munsters, The Last Resort, Whitman #1567, 1966, EX..$25.00

Nanny & the Professor, softcover, Lancer, 1970, VG.....$8.00

Patty Duke & the Adventure of the Chinese Junk, hardcover, Whitman, 1966, NM..$12.00

Patty Duke & the Adventures of the Chinese Junk, Whitman #2334, 1966, EX...$16.00

Real McCoys, black & white illustrations, pictorial hardcover, 1960, EX...$15.00

Real McCoys & the Danger at the Ranch, Cole Fannin, hardcover, Whitman, 1961, EX................................$20.00

Rin Tin Tin & the Ghost Wagon Train, hardcover, Whitman, 1958, EX...$18.00

Roy Rogers & the Enchanted Canyon, Whitman #1502:49, 1954, EX...$25.00

Walt Disney, The Swiss Family Robinson, Whitman #1625, 1960, EX...$8.00

Walt Disney's Annette, black & white illustrations, pictorial hardcover, Whitman, ca 1960, EX.........................$15.00

Walt Disney's the Gnome-Mobile, Whitman #1577, 1967, EX...$12.00

Missadventures of Merlin Jones, #1521, Mary Carey, published by Whitman, 210 pages, $10.00.
(Photo courtesy David and Virginia Brown)

Bottle Openers

A figural bottle opener is one where the cap lifter is an actual feature of the subject being portrayed — for instance, the bill of a pelican or the mouth of a four-eyed man. Most are made of painted cast iron or aluminum; others were chrome or brass plated. Some of the major bottle-opener producers were Wilton, John Wright, L&L, and Gadzik. They have been reproduced, so beware of any examples with 'new' paint. Condition of the paint is an important consideration when it comes to evaluating a vintage opener.

For more information, read *Figural Bottle Openers, Identification Guide,* by the Figural Bottle Opener Collectors. Number codes in our descriptions correspond with their book.

Advisor: Charlie Reynolds (See Directory, Bottle Openers)

Club: Figural Bottle Opener Collectors
Linda Fitzsimmons
9697 Gwynn Park Dr., Ellicott City, MD 21043; 301-465-9296

Newsletter: Just for Openers
John Stanley
3712 Sunningdale Way, Durham, NC 27707-5684; 919-419-1546.
Quarterly newsletter covers all types of bottle openers and corkscrews

Alligator, F-138, bronze 5"...**$20.00**
Alligator, F-139, white metal **$25.00**
Amish boy, F-31, cast iron, 4x2".....................**$275.00**
Bear head, F-426, cast iron, 3¾"....................**$130.00**
Beer drinker, F-406, cast iron, Iron Art **$40.00**
Billy goat, F-74a, aluminum, 2¾x1⅞" **$15.00**
Canadian Goose, F-105e, brass-plated cast iron, Norlin, 2⅛x3¾"..**$30.00**
Cat, F-95, brass, 2¼x3" **$40.00**
Cowboy w/guitar, F-27a, aluminum **$15.00**
Dolphin, F-152, chrome, Italy, 6½" **$110.00**
Donkey, F-60a, aluminum, 3½x3¼"..............**$15.00**
Donkey, F-61, cast iron.....................................**$50.00**
Elephant, F-46, cast iron..............................**$35.00**
Fish, F-164, abalone...**$35.00**
Fisherman, F-30b, brass, EX original paint, Riverside, 4x2½" **$30.00**
Foundryman, F-29, aluminum...................**$16.50**
Goat, F-71, cast iron, tall................................**$70.00**
Lamppost Drunk, F-1, cast iron, 4⅛" **$15.00**
Lamppost Drunk, F-1, mounted on ashtray..............**$20.00**
Lobster, F-168, cast iron, red & black paint................**$32.00**
Monkey, F-89, cast iron, black & white paint, 2⅝" ..**$210.00**
Monkey, F-89b, aluminum, 2⅝" **$15.00**
Negro, F-402, cast iron, wall mount....................**$75.00**
Nude, F-177, brass **$55.00**
Palm Tree Drunk, F-20, multicolored paint, plain stand..**$65.00**

Parrot (large) on perch, F-109, painted cast iron, 5¼", NM, $65.00.

Parrot, F-108, cast iron **$50.00**
Pretzel, F-232, cast iron....................................**$45.00**
Sea gull, F-123, cast iron **$60.00**
Sea horse, F-140, brass, Canada **$30.00**
Shovel, F-221, brass **$20.00**
Skunk, F-92d, aluminum, NM original paint, 2⅛x2⅞" ..**$60.00**
Squirrel, F-93, brass, 2⅝" **$15.00**
Street Walker, F-5, aluminum, 4½", NM.....................**$165.00**
Trout, F-159, cast iron **$120.00**
4-Eyed lady, F-407, cast iron, wall mount, EX..........**$130.00**
4-Eyed man, F-413, cast iron, wall mount, EX............**$60.00**

Boyd Crystal Art Glass

After the Degenhart glass studio closed (see the Degenhart section for information), it was bought out by the Boyd family, who added many of their own designs to the molds they acquired from the Degenharts and other defunct glasshouses. They are located in Cambridge, Ohio, and the glass they've been pressing in the more than 350 colors they've developed since they opened in 1978 is marked with their 'B in diamond' logo. All the work is done by hand, and each piece is made in a selected color in limited amounts — a production run lasts only about twelve weeks or less. Items in satin glass or an exceptional slag are especially collectible, so are those with hand-painted details, commanding as much as 30% more.

Note: An 'R' in the following lines indicates an item that has been retired.

Advisor: Joyce Pringle (See Directory, Boyd)

Airplane, Nile Green......................................**$13.50**
Angel, Cobalt...**$22.00**
Angel, Millennium Slag...................................**$17.00**
Artie the Penguin, Mint Julip **$10.00**
Artie the Penguin, Vanilla Coral......................**$15.00**
Bow Slipper, Alexandrite.................................**$28.50**
Bow Slipper, Harvest Gold...............................**$8.50**
Bunny on Nest, Peridot....................................**$29.00**
Bunny on Nest, Sunkist Carnival.....................**$10.00**
Candy the small Carousel Horse, Bernard Boyd Black...**$15.00**
Candy the small Carousel Horse, Maverick Blue **$12.00**
Cat Slipper, Avocado...**$9.50**
Cat Slipper, Ritz Blue..**$31.00**
Cat Slipper, Touch of Pink **$55.00**
Chick Salt, Caramel..**$15.00**
Chick Salt, Classic Black Slag...........................**$22.00**
Chick Salt, Copper Glo.....................................**$12.00**
Chick Salt, Marshmallow **$8.00**
Chick Salt, Mountain Haze................................**$12.00**
Chick Salt, Robin Egg Blue **$40.00**
JB Scotty, Confetti...**$280.00**
JB Scotty, Daffodil...**$30.00**
JB Scotty, Mulberry...**$110.00**
JB Scotty, Sunburst...**$22.00**
Jeremy the Frog, Green Bouquet **$15.00**
Jeremy the Frog, Tangy Lime.............................**$8.00**
Joey the Horse, Cashmire Pink.........................**$42.00**
Joey the Horse, December Swirl **$72.00**
Joey the Horse, Heatherbloom..........................**$65.00**
Joey the Horse, Impatient **$25.00**
Joey the Horse, Rubina **$70.00**
Joey the Horse, September Swirl.......................**$90.00**
Pooch the Dog, Oh Fudge.................................**$16.00**
Pooch the Dog, Wintergreen Slag **$45.00**
Sammy the Squirrel, Cardinal Red....................**$27.00**

Sammy Squirrel, Chasmine Pink, $22.50.

Sammy the Squirrel, Teal $16.00
Taffy the large Carousel Horse, Capri Blue $20.00
Taffy the large Carousel Horse, Cobalt $30.00
Turkey Salt, Crystal Carnival $10.00
Zack the Elephant, Autumn Splendor $60.00
Zack the Elephant, Ebony...$55.00
Zack the Elephant, Peacock Blue Swirl $20.00

Boyds Bears and Friends

The cold-cast sculptures designed by Gary M. Lowenthal such as we've listed here have become very dear to the heart of many collectors who enthusiastically pursue his Bearstones, Folkstones, and Dollstones lines, particularly first editions (1 Es). Counterfeits do exist. Be sure to watch for the signature bear paw print on Bearstones, the star on Folkstones, and the shoe imprints on the Dollstones. To learn more about the entire line of Boyd's Collectibles, we recommend this Internet price guide: *Rosie's Secondary Market Price Guide to Boyds Bears & Friends,* http://www.RosieWells.com.

Bearstones, 1993, Christian, 1E/2012 ....$110.00
Bearstones, 1993, Grenville & Neville, 2009 (version 1).$125.00
Bearstones, 1994, Arthur, 1E/2003.............................$100.00
Bearstones, 1994, Bailey's Birthday, 2E/2-14.............$130.00
Bearstones, 1994, Daphne, 3E/2226............................$30.00
Bearstones, 1995, Bailey, 2E/2260...............................$59.00
Bearstones, 1995, Elf Bear w/list, 1E/2252 ....$600.00
Bearstones, 1996, Bailey & Emily, 2E/2018 ....$90.00
Bearstones, 1997, Chelsea Kainada, 1E/22851 (BC)....$60.00
Bearstones, 1997, Wilson, 2E/2007..............................$398.00
Dollstones, 1995, Betsy w/Edmund, 1E/3503..............$50.00
Dollstones, 1995, Victoria w/Samantha, 3E/3502 ....$38.00
Dollstones, 1996, Anne, 1E/3599 ....$45.00
Dollstones, 1996, Michelle w/Daisy, 1E/3511..............$55.00
Dollstones, 1996, Patricia w/Molly, 2E/3501................$48.00
Dollstones, 1996, Rebecca w/Elliot, 1E/3509...............$58.00
Dollstones, 1997, Caitlin w/Emma & Edmund, 1E/3525.$57.00

Folkstones, 1994, Nikki w/candle, 2E/2801.................$50.00
Folkstones, 1994, Santa's Challenge, 2E/3002..............$67.00
Folkstones, 1994, Santa's Flight Plan, 2E/3000 ....$72.00
Folkstones, 1995, Beatrice, 1E/2836............................$42.00
Folkstones, 1996, Fixit, 1E/3600 ....$39.00
Folkstones, 1996, Robin, 1E/2816.................................$41.00
Folkstones, 1997, Yukon & Nanuk, 1E/27800 ....$50.00

Bearstones, 1997, Ted and Teddy, 1E/2223, $125.00.

Brastoff, Sascha

Who could have predicted when Sascha Brastoff joined the Army's Air Force in 1942 that he was to become a well-known artist! It was during his service with the Air Force that he became interested in costume and scenery design, performing, creating Christmas displays and murals, and drawing war bond posters.

After Sascha's stint in the Armed Forces, he decided to follow his dream of producing ceramics and in 1947 opened a small operation in West Los Angeles, California. Just six years later along with Nelson Rockefeller and several other businessmen with extensive knowledge of mass-production techniques, he built a pottery on Olympic Boulevard in Los Angeles.

Brastoff designed all the products while supervising approximately 150 people. His talents were so great they enabled him to move with ease from one decade to another and successfully change motifs, mediums, and designs as warranted. Unusual and varying materials were used over the years. He created a Western line that was popular in the 1940s and early 1950s. Just before the poodle craze hit the nation in the 1950s, he had the foresight to introduce his poodle line. The same was true for smoking accessories, and he designed elegant, hand-painted dinnerware as well. He was not modest when it came to his creations. He knew he was talented and was willing to try any new endeavor which was usually a huge success.

Items with the Sascha Brastoff full signature are always popular, and generally they command the highest prices. He modeled obelisks; one with a lid and a full signature would be regarded as a highly desirable example of his work. Though values for his dinnerware are generally lower than for his other productions, it has its own following. The Merbaby design is always high on collectors' lists. An unusual piece was found last year — a figural horse salt shaker, solid white with assorted stars. More than likely it was made as part of a set, possibly the Star Steed pattern. It was marked 'Sascha' under the glaze between the front legs.

The 1940 Clay Club pieces were signed either with a full signature or 'Sascha.' In 1947 Sascha hired a large group of artists to hand decorate his designs, and 'Sascha B' became the standard mark. Following the opening of his studio in 1953, a chanticleer, the name Sascha Brastoff, the copyright symbol, and a hand-written style number (all in gold) were used on the bottom, with 'Sascha B.' on the front or topside of the item. (Be careful not to confuse this mark with a full signature, California, U.S.A.). Costume designs at 20th Century Fox (1946 – 47) were signed 'Sascha'; war bonds and posters also carried the signature 'Sascha' and 'Pvt.' or 'Sgt. Brastoff.'

After Brastoff left his company in 1962, the mark became a 'R' in a circle (registered trademark symbol) with a style number, all handwritten. The chanticleer may also accompany this mark. Brastoff died on February 4, 1993. For additional information consult *The Collector's Encyclopedia of Sascha Brastoff* by Steve Conti, A. DeWayne Bethany, and Bill Seay. Another source of information is *The Collector's Encyclopedia of California Pottery* (Second Edition) by Jack Chipman. Both are available from Collector Books.

Advisor: Susan Cox (See Directory, California Pottery)

Ashtray, Abstract, hooded, #H1, 3".................................**$45.00**
Ashtray, bright green raised decor on mossy green, triangular, 7¾"...**$35.00**
Ashtray, Minos, hooded, 6"..**$120.00**
Ashtray, Rooftops, oblong, 3 rests, 14" L.....................**$85.00**
Bowl, enamel on copper, amber floral on green, #110AC, 10"..**$45.00**
Bowl, enamel on metal, autumn leaves on orange, free-form, 8½x6½"...**$30.00**
Bowl, enamel on metal, gold geometric on cobalt, 8", NM **$45.00**
Bowl, green & mustard band w/black & gold designs, 3-footed, irregular shape, 9" L..**$32.00**
Bowl, Misty Blue, free-form, #F40, 10" **$60.00**
Bowl, Oriental-style decor, free-form, 7¼x5½"...........**$24.00**
Bowl, Rooftops, 5½x6¾"...**$50.00**
Bowl, slightly carved abstract design, footed, full signature on underside, 10"...**$375.00**
Bowl, Star Steed, handles, 2⅛x7⅛"................................**$45.00**
Bowl, Star Steed, 3-legged, 9½x8½"............................**$135.00**
Bowl, Star Steed on blue, 2⅞x9x6⅞"............................**$35.00**
Bowl, vegetable; Surf Ballet, 2 compartments, pink, gold & white, 1950s, 2½x13¾"...**$45.00**
Box, Persian, #071, 10" **$175.00**
Box, Rooftops, #023, 5" dia **$80.00**
Box, Star Steed on gray, 7x4½" **$50.00**
Cachepot, Early Fish, 4" **$95.00**

Candle holder, resin, honey amber, grapes & leaves, paper label **$25.00**
Charger, enamel on metal, grapes w/gold curlicues, gold sticker, 17¾" **$90.00**
Charger, Surf Ballet, pink & cream w/gold, 14¼".......**$45.00**
Coffee set, Surf Ballet, silver on pink, 3-pc.............**$125.00**
Compote, enamel on copper, amber floral on green, 2x8"...**$35.00**
Creamer & sugar bowl, Surf Ballet, 1960s **$35.00**
Figure, cherub on whale holding shell, gold & black, 13½x10x6"...**$95.00**
Figure, Knight, gold plated, unsigned, 14"............**$1,400.00**
Figure, Percheron horse, antique crackle glaze, #S12, obscured signature, 13½"................................**$1,200.00**
Figure, polar bear, resin, honey amber, 4x7" **$295.00**
Humidor, pipe shape, lid bottom is ashtray.............**$350.00**
Obelisk, dark background w/leaves, w/lid, full signature, 21"...**$875.00**
Pitcher, Art Deco-style geometric bands on white, 7½"..**$35.00**
Pitcher, floral medallion on brown, bulbous, ca 1968, 10¾" **$60.00**
Planter, Star Steed, scalloped rim, 4¼x4½" **$35.00**
Plate, chop; Jewel Bird, #052, 15" **$150.00**
Plate, Flower Bouquet, first edition of Best of Sascha Series, 1979, 10"...**$30.00**
Plate, gold dragon-like decor on white, 9"..................**$40.00**
Plate, gold geometric linear decor on green, 10½" **$60.00**
Plate, gold metallic rings w/brown & blue swirls, full signature, 10¼"...**$250.00**
Plate, pie; stylized Amish rooster, full signature on front, early, 11½"..**$600.00**
Plate, slip-decorated flowers arranged in bowl, gold detail, signed & dated underside, 12"...........................**$900.00**

Plate, teal, maroon, and gold leaves, 12", $100.00; Vase, 5", $95.00.

Platter, pink & gold Deco-style swirls, 1950s, 14x10½" **$50.00**
Salt & pepper shakers, Star Steed horse shape, 3¼", pr...**$225.00**

Smoke set, mosaic, 3½" lighter & 6½x5" ashtray........**$50.00**
Switch plate, horse's head, shiny brass finish, molded signature, 10" **$100.00**
Tray, enamel on copper, gold geometric decor, 8".....**$55.00**
Tray, muted leaves on white matt, 8" **$110.00**
Tray, 5 stylized birds, 17¾" square **$115.00**
Vase, abstract decor in brown tones on white, shaped rim, 5¾x3¼"..**$30.00**
Vase, abstract female form, white on black, 5½"........**$60.00**
Vase, dark green w/leaves, straight-sided, 7"...........**$185.00**

Vase, grapes, amber resin cylinder, 10", $80.00.

Vase, gold geometric linear decor on green, 9½x7"...**$75.00**
Vase, Rooftops, #F20, 5¼"...**$55.00**
Vase, stylized tulip-like flower on brown, 5¾x3" **$35.00**
Vase, Tiki, resin, blue, 10¼x4" **$250.00**
Watercolor, wartime ruins in Bremen Germany, signed '45 Brastoff **$450.00**

Brayton Laguna

This company's products have proven to be highly collectible for those who appreciate their well-made, diversified items, some bordering on the whimsical. Durlin Brayton founded Brayton Laguna Pottery in 1927. The marriage between Durlin and Ellen (Webb) Webster Grieve a few years later created a partnership that brought together two talented people with vision and knowledge so broad that they were able to create many unique lines. At the height of Brayton's business success, the company employed over 125 workers and 20 designers.

Durlin's personally created items command a high price. Such items are hand turned, and those that were made from 1927 to 1930 are often incised 'Laguna Pottery' in Durlin's handwriting. These include cups, saucers, plates of assorted sizes, ashtrays, etc., glazed in eggplant, lettuce green, purple, and deep blue as well as other colors. Brayton Laguna's children's series (created by Lietta J. Dodd) has always been favored among collectors.

However, many lines such as Calasia (artware), Blackamoors, sculpture, and the Hillbilly line are picking up large followings of their own. The sculptures, Indian, and Peruvian pieces including voodoo figures, matadors, and drummers, among others, were designed by Carol Safholm. Andy Anderson created the Hillbilly series, most notably the highly successful shotgun wedding group. He also created the calf, bull, and cow set which was done in several glazes. While the purple set has been the most popular, they are relatively common and often a hard-sell today. But when the three-piece set is found in an elusive glaze, it is even more valuable than the wedding group. Webton Ware is a good line for those who want inexpensive pottery and a Brayton Laguna mark. These pieces depict farmland and country-type themes such as farmers planting, women cooking, etc. Some items — wall pockets, for instance — may be found with only a flower motif; wall hangings of women and men are popular, yet hard to find in this or any of Brayton's lines. Predominantly, the background of Webton Ware is white, and it's decorated with various pastel glazes including yellow, green, pink, and blue.

More than ten marks plus a paper label were used during Brayton's history. On items too small for a full mark, designers would simply incise their initials. Webb Brayton died in 1948, and Durlin died just three years later. Struggling with and finally succumbing to the effect of the influx of foreign pottery on the American market, Brayton Laguna finally closed in 1968.

For further study, read *The Collector's Encyclopedia of California Pottery* (Second Edition) by Jack Chipman (Collector Books).

Advisor: Susan Cox (See Directory, California Pottery)

Cookie jar, Christina, Swedish maid, ca 1941, 11" **$355.00**
Cookie jar, Honeycomb w/birds, 7¼"........................**$185.00**
Figurine, Bedtime, Victorian couple in nightclothes, ca 1943, 8¾"..**$175.00**
Figurine, Black baby w/white diaper, 4¼" **$85.00**
Figurine, Black dice player, on hands & knees, 5½x3½" ...**$85.00**
Figurine, Blackamoor holding cornucopia, jewels & gold slippers, 10"..**$150.00**
Figurine, Blackamoors, pastel jewels, gold bracelets & trim, 14", pr..**$210.00**
Figurine, bull, purple, 7x11½" **$130.00**
Figurine, cow, purple, 5½x9" **$200.00**
Figurine, drummer band member, dark skin tones, lg smile, 5¼"..**$90.00**
Figurine, Dutch boy & girl, blue clothes, 8", 6½", pr ..**$140.00**
Figurine, East Indian man in turban, hand extended, 12½" **$135.00**
Figurine, Figaro, 1 paw raised, Walt Disney's Pinocchio, 4½x3½" **$125.00**
Figurine, Francis, 8" **$75.00**
Figurine, jazz singer, pianist & piano, 3 pc set **$400.00**
Figurine, lady w/2 Russian Wolfhounds, ca 1943, 11" ..**$135.00**
Figurine, Mexican lady w/baskets, 8" **$115.00**

Figurine, Oriental couple w/baby riding piggyback, 7½", pr...**$155.00**

Figurine, owl, crackle face & brown body, #41-19 & #41-18, 7x5", 5x3", pr...**$40.00**

Figurine, Red Fox Babies, H-56/H-57, small, $65.00 for the pair. (Photo courtesy Lee Garmon)

Figurine, Sally, 7"...**$35.00**

Figurine, seals, aqua, #T-12/#T-13, 11" L, pr.............**$200.00**

Figurine, stylized bird, black w/twisted effect, 9½"..**$160.00**

Figurine, stylized duck, orange w/black around eyes & beak, 6x5½"..**$50.00**

Figurine, Zizi & Fifi, cats, maroon & green, pr.........**$500.00**

Flower holder, Mandy, Black girl w/open basket, 9" .**$75.00**

Pitcher, cityscape with drunk at lamppost, marked B2, $50.00.

Planter, Black lady kneels w/lg pot, ornate headdress, 8x8x10" **$65.00**

Planter, bonnet w/lg bow, flowered brim, 4½"...........**$55.00**

Planter, girl holds basket w/bird perched on it, 6½"..**$40.00**

Planter, vendor man w/cart, greens & browns, 11x9" ..**$60.00**

Plate, Oriental warrior, multicolored w/blue border, 10½"..**$500.00**

Salt & pepper shakers, Black peasants, K-26, 5½", pr ..**$24.00**

Salt & pepper shakers, clowns standing, 6½", pr **$80.00**

Salt & pepper shakers, Mammy & Chef, holding spoons, white aprons, 5½", pr...**$75.00**

Salt & pepper shakers, Peruvian couple, browns & white, pr...**$22.00**

Toothbrush holder, Gingham Dog **$22.00**

Vase, old peasant woman figural, 12", EX.................**$65.00**

Vase, sea horse figural, white w/turquoise trim, pocket on back trimmed in rose, 8½" **$150.00**

Breweriana

Breweriana refers to items produced by breweries which are intended for immediate use and discard, such as beer cans and bottles, as well as countless items designed for long-term use while promoting a particular brand. Desirable collectibles include metal, cardboard, and neon signs; serving trays; glassware; tap handles; mirrors; coasters; and other paper goods.

Breweriana is generally divided into two broad categories: pre- and postprohibition. Preprohibition breweries were numerous and distributed advertising trays, calendars, etched glassware, and other items. Because American breweries were founded by European brewmasters, preprohibition advertising often depicted themes from that region. Brewery scenes, pretty women, and children were also common.

Competition was intense among the breweries that survived prohibition. The introduction of canned beer in 1935, the postwar technology boom, and the advent of television in the late 1940s produced countless new ways to advertise beer. Moving signs, can openers, enameled glasses, and neon are prolific examples of postprohibition breweriana.

A better understanding of the development of the product as well as advertising practices of companies helps in evaluating the variety of breweriana items that may be found. For example, 'chalks' are figural advertising pieces which were made for display in taverns or wherever beer was sold. Popular in the 1940s and 1950s, they were painted and glazed to resemble carnival prizes. Breweries realized in addition to food shopping, women generally assumed the role of cook — what better way to persuade women to buy a particular beer than a cookbook? Before the advent of the bottle cap in the early 1900s, beer bottles were sealed with a porcelain stopper or cork. Opening a corked bottle required a corkscrew which often had a brewery logo.

Prior to the advent of refrigeration, beer was often served at room temperature. A mug or glass was often half warm beer and half foam. A 1" by 8" flat piece of plastic was used to scrape foam from the glass. These foam scrapers came in various colors and bore the logo of the beer on tap.

Before prohibition, beer logos were applied to glassware by etching the glass with acid. These etched glasses often had ornate designs that included a replica of the actual brewery or a bust of the brewery's founder. After prohibition, enameling became popular and glasses were generally 'painted' with less ornate designs. Mugs featuring beer advertising date back to the 1800s in America; preprohibition versions were generally made of pottery or glass. Ceramic mugs became popular after prohibition and remain widely produced today.

Tap handles are a prominent way to advertise a particular brand wherever tap beer is sold. Unlike today's ornate handles, 'ball knobs' were prominent prior to the 1960s. They were about the size of a billiard ball with a flat face that featured a colorful beer logo.

The books we recommend for this area of collecting are *World of Beer Memorabilia* by Herb and Helen Haydock, and *Vintage Bar Ware* by Stephen Visakay. (Both are published by Collector Books.)

See also Bar Ware; Beer Cans.

Advisor: Dan Andrews (See Directory, Breweriana)

Club: Beer Can Collectors of America
747 Merus Ct., Fenton, MO 63026
Annual dues: $27; although the club's roots are in beer can collecting, this organization offers a bimonthly breweriana magazine featuring many regional events and sponsors an annual convention; http://www.bcca.com

Clock, Mitchell's Premium Beer, electric, glass face, new clockworks, 15" dia, EX, **$220.00.**

Ashtray, Adolph Coors, white ceramic dish w/mountain logo on raised center, products embossed on rim, 4 rests, EX .**$35.00**

Ashtray, Schell's Beer, milk glass dish w/red lettering on flat round rim, 2 rests, 1950s, 5" dia, EX **$5.00**

Bank, Fitger's Beer/Natural Brewed, wood-look chalkware keg form w/4 black bands & embossed lettering, 1950s, 8", VG **$40.00**

Banner, Alaskan Brewing Co/Award Winning Beers From Juneau Alaska, vinyl, w/graphics, 2x6", NM+.......**$10.00**

Book, The Beer Book, by Will Anderson, 1973, NM+..**$25.00**

Bottle holder, Miller High Life Beer/The Champagne of Bottle Beer, cardboard, holds 2 1-qt bottles, 1940s, VG+.**$20.00**

Bottle opener, Fox Head 400 Beer, wood & metal bottle shape, 1950s, VG+ **$15.00**

Bridge set, Anheuser-Busch, score pad & 2 decks of cards in leather-type Amity folding case, 1973 sales convention, VG+..**$20.00**

Clock, Budweiser, mantel-type clock atop see-through base showing 12-team Clydesdale wagon w/driver, 16x17", NM **$60.00**

Clock, Narragansett Lager Beer/Since 1880, wood-look plastic light-up w/spindled rail atop, Roman numerals, 1970s, 21", VG+..**$30.00**

Clock, Pabst Blue Ribbon, square w/What'll You Have? on pediment w/chain hanger, light-up, EX.............**$100.00**

Clock, Time Out for Dawson's Ale & Beer, reverse-painted logo & numbers on glass lens, metal frame, 1940s, 16x16", EX+...**$200.00**

Coaster, Busch, red & green logo, pressed paper, 3x3½", NM..**$5.00**

Display, Anheuser-Busch chalkware A-&-Eagle logo, multi-colored, 1960s, 23x22", EX+.............................**$50.00**

Display, Blatz, 3-D pot-metal figures of a baseball umpire calling runner safe as catcher catches ball, EX ..**$175.00**

Display, Bud Man, painted cast-aluminum figure in red, white & blue, 1970s, 12x8", EX **$40.00**

Display, Duke, ceramic bucket w/3 frosty bottles in simulated ice, Ask for a Frosty..., 1950s, NM **$80.00**

Display, Falls City Beer/Here's Good Luck to You!, cast-metal swordfish atop oval sign on base, 1948, EX+ **$250.00**

Display, Grain Belt Beer, chalkware dog head, brown, 9", NM+ **$50.00**

Display, Pabst, man in early touring car on cobbled street & lg bottle against brick wall, plastic, 1960s, 16x17", NM **$80.00**

Display, Pabst, pot-metal boxing figure in ring w/bottle & sign reading On Tap, VG+.............................**$100.00**

Display, Pabst, train engine & bottle, Old Time Beer Flavor on base, plastic, 1960s, NM **$100.00**

Display, Schlitz, gold-tone plastic statue of classical woman holding up globe, light-up, 1960s, 45", EX+.......**$100.00**

Door push, Pabst Blue Ribbon Beer, painted metal, 2x9", VG **$40.00**

Drinking glass, Goebel 22 Beer, footed, red-painted label, 1940s, 5¼", M...**$15.00**

Drinking glass, Golden Glow Beer, flat bottom, brown- & red-painted label, 1940s, 5", NM....................**$20.00**

Foam scraper, Budweiser, red plastic w/gold A-&-Eagle logos flanking name, 1940s, EX..........................**$8.00**

Foam scraper, Geo Walter's 'Adler Brau' Appleton Beer, red on white, rounded ends, 1950s, VG+ **$45.00**

Foam scraper holder, Piels Beer embossed on side of chalkware army tank, 1944, 4½x9x4½", VG **$200.00**

Foam scraper holder, Piels Light Beer, metal & composition w/Burt & Harry toasting at bar, 1950s, 9", EX+....**$40.00**

Lamp, Schlitz, stained-glass hanger shaped like a carousel top w/name on every 4th panel, 14" dia, EX.......**$30.00**

Malted milk container, Pabst, metal w/2-sided advertising, EX **$60.00**

Menu board, Pennsylvania Dutch Old German Beer, tin blackboard w/bottle & glass, A Real Treat, 27x16", G **$40.00**

Miniature bottles, West Virginia Special, 1950s, EX+, pr **$40.00**

Motion lamp, Miller High Life bottle shape in ice bucket, plastic, working, EX...**$40.00**

Mug, Hamm's, clear glass w/Hamm's bear & name, M ..**$15.00**

Mug, Oldenberg Brewery, red and black on clear glass, 5¼", $12.00.

Patch, Ballantine Beer, ovoid, 7x7", EX+ **$5.00**

Plate, World Famous Budweiser Clydsdales, decal on white porcelain, gold-trimmed, 1970s, 11" dia, NM+ **$10.00**

Salt & pepper shakers, Coors, wooden barrels w/Coors in script, EX **$25.00**

Sign, back bar light-up, Budweiser/King of Beer/For Those Who Know, reverse-painted glass trapezoid shape on gold base, VG+ **$75.00**

Sign, cardboard, Duquesne/There's Only One.../Registered Premium, snowman serving lady, self-framed, 1950s, 17x23", NM **$45.00**

Sign, cardboard, Kingsbury, Wall-Eyed Pike, 3-D fish mounted on wood-look plaque, 12x24", EX **$30.00**

Sign, cardboard, Walter's Beer/It's Lighter, pheasant in flight, birch bark self-frame, 1950s, 18x23", NM+ **$40.00**

Sign, cardboard standup, Fort Pitt Beer/The Better Beer for Experienced Tastes, diecut hand-held cone-top can, EX.**$100.00**

Sign, cardboard standup, Stroz Beer/Refreshed With..., image of 3 cowboys on horses, space for bottle or can, VG+.......................**$150.00**

Sign, cardboard standup; Coors, shows the 3 Stooges playing football, Get Coors Equipped, 1988, 39x25", NM.**$25.00**

Sign, composition, Schlitz, No Bitterness, Just the Kiss of Hops w/bottle & hops images on woodgrain, 17x11", EX **$40.00**

Sign, hanger, Piels Light Beer, 3-D foil-covered Piels lettering & elf hold full glass, 1940s, 4x12", EX **$30.00**

Sign, light-up, Budweiser Beer, logo & name on wood-look emblem w/gold-tone frame, chain hanger, 1950s, 16x26", VG+.......................**$80.00**

Sign, neon; Budweiser, Anheuser-Busch/St. Louis/Beer lettered on aluminum frame, blue tubing, 9x28", NM, $315.00.

Sign, neon, Iroquois Ale-Beer, window style, 1950s, 13x20", no transformer o/w M.........................**$140.00**

Sign, plastic, Iron City Beer/Premium Quality — Real Beer, molded bar scene w/bartender & 3 patrons, 1950s, 9x15", NM.........................**$30.00**

Sign, porcelain, curved, Rahr's Elk's Head Beer of Oshkosh/Rahr Brewing Co..., white on red w/white border, EX+.........................**$200.00**

Sign, register light-up, Rommer's White Label in Bottles, reverse-painted glass atop metal base & backing, 1940s, EX+ **$115.00**

Sign, reverse-painted glass, Coors Golden Beer, black against gold foil ground, metal backing, 13½" dia, EX+ ..**$1,000.00**

Sign, reverse-painted glass, Pabst Quality Since 1844, lettering around B-&-hops logo in center, 1980s, 16" dia, NM+ **$20.00**

Sign, tin, Schlitz Malt Liquor, The Bull lettered above image of a bull crashing through brick wall, 34x23", EX.....**$20.00**

Sign, tin hanger, Sterling, We Serve Sterling Super-Bru above bottle image on vertical pennant shape, 19x9", VG+....**$100.00**

Sign, Vitrolite, curved, Walter Beer/Eau Claire Wis, w/logo, framed, 23x16", EX+.........................**$300.00**

Stein, Anheuser-Busch, Budweiser Girl, Italy, 1973, 1-litre.........................**$200.00**

Stein, Anheuser-Busch, Dolphins, Marine Conservation Series, dolphin finial, 6½", EX.........................**$40.00**

Stein, Anheuser-Busch, 10 Years Safe Service, 1978, 9"........**$100.00**

Stein, Anheuser-Busch, 20 Years Safe Service, 1984, 13½" ..**$100.00**

Stein, Anheuser-Busch, 30 Years Safe Service, 1994, 12½".........................**$100.00**

Stein, Anheuser-Busch Bevo Fox, ceramic figural, CS-160, EXIB.........................**$85.00**

Stein, Anheuser-Busch/Albert Stahl, Budweiser Frog, figural, 9½", EX.........................**$150.00**

Stein, Anheuser-Busch/Ceramarte, LA Olympic Committee, 1980, 10", EX.........................**$90.00**

Stein, Anheuser-Busch/Ceramarte, A-&-Eagle logo, CSL2, w/lid, 1975, 9¾", EX.........................**$100.00**

Stein, Anheuser-Busch/Ceramarte, American Homestead, Holiday Series, retired 1996, 7", EX.........................**$50.00**

Stein, Anheuser-Busch/Ceramarte, Bavarian house, ½-litre.........................**$200.00**

Stein, Anheuser-Busch/Ceramarte, Bud Man, hollow head, ½-litre **$250.00**

Stein, Anheuser-Busch/Ceramarte, Busch, CS-44, 1980, EX.........................**$100.00**

Stein, Anheuser-Busch/Ceramarte, Busch Gardens, blue & gray, 6½", EX **$75.00**

Stein, Anheuser-Busch/Ceramarte, Centennial Olympic Games, 1996, 5¾", EX.........................**$25.00**

Stein, Anheuser-Busch/Ceramarte, Christmas, Holiday Series, signed by artist, w/lid, 1997, 8¼", EX.................**$70.00**

Stein, Anheuser-Busch/Ceramarte, Clydesdale team in relief w/A-&-Eagle logo, pounded pewter lid, CSL29, 1976, EX.........................**$100.00**

Stein, Anheuser-Busch/Ceramarte, Declaration of Independence, 1976, 7⅝", EX **$100.00**

Stein, Anheuser-Busch/ Gertz, CS77, 'horseshoe' frames Clydesdale eight-horse hitch, 1987, $40.00.

Tap knob, Bavarian Old Style, enamel in chrome ball, EX **$80.00**

Tap knob, DuBois/Budweiser Beer, rectangular w/blue lettering on yellow plastic, 1950s, EX **$75.00**

Tap knob, E&B Ale, yellow plastic w/red, white & blue porcelain inserts w/gold trim, 1950s, EX+ **$40.00**

Tap knobs: Royal Bru, NM, $135.00; Carnegie Cream Ale, EX, $155.00; Anteek Beer, NM, $155.00.

Thermometer, Kaier's Beer/The Thirst Satisfier, metal dial type w/glass lens, 1960s, 10" dia.........................**$45.00**

Thermometer, Premium Highlander Beer, round w/logo on red & black plaid ground, temperature gauge in sm window, EX..**$150.00**

Thermometer, Walters Pueblo Colorado, round ship's wheel design, EX **$45.00**

Tip tray, Hamm's Beer, shows the Hamm's bear, 1981, NM..**$10.00**

Tray, Hamm's Preferred Stock Beer, red ribbon logo on cream & blue, deep gold-trimmed rim, 1960s, 13" dia, EX+ **$30.00**

Tray, Hanley's Peerless Ale, black & white bulldog image lying on name on black, red pie-plate rim, 1940s, 12" dia, NM+ **$75.00**

Tray, Narragansett Lagers/Ale, Gangway for Gansett, Dr Seuss drawing of Indian on roller skates, deep rim, 12" dia, VG+ **$40.00**

Tray, Old Dutch Lager Beer Ale & Porter, captain's image & red lettering on white, red deep rim, 1940s, 12" dia, NM+ **$60.00**

Tray, Schmidt's Beer/Quarts*Pints*Draught, lady pouring from bottle, red, white & black, pie-pan rim, 1940s, 12" dia, VG...**$65.00**

Tumbler, Bud Light's Spuds MacKenzie, thermo plastic, 6¼", EX **$5.00**

Whistle, Michelob, sterling silver, back engraved Good Luck From Michelob, Reed & Barton, EX.....................**$75.00**

Breyer Horses

Breyer horses have been popular children's playthings since they were introduced in 1952, and you'll see several at any large flea market. Garage sales are good sources as well. The earlier horses had a glossy finish, but after 1968 a matt finish came into use. You'll find smaller domestic animals too. They are evaluated by condition, rarity, and desirability; some of the better examples may be worth a minimum of $150.00. Our values are for average condition; examples in mint condition are worth from 10% to 15% more.

For more information and listings, see *Schroeder's Collectible Toys, Antique to Modern;* and *Breyer Animal Collector's Guide, Second Edition,* by Felicia Browell. (Both are published by Collector Books.)

Action Appaloosa Foal, 1989-93, Traditional scale......**$20.00**

Adios Famous Standardbred, 1969-80, Traditional scale ..**$40.00**

American Indian Pony, 1988-91, Traditional scale **$35.00**

Andalusian Foal (Hanoverian Family), matt bay, 1992-93, Classic scale..**$15.00**

Andalusian Mare (Sears Classic Andalusian Family), alabaster, 1984, Classic scale.......................................**$20.00**

Appaloosa Foal (JC Penney Breyer Collector's Family Set), matt bay peppercorn, 1986, Traditional scale.......**$25.00**

Appaloosa Stallion (Horses International), alabaster & sorrel w/black blanket & red roan, 1989, Traditional scale..**$60.00**

Arabian Foal, matt black, 1973-82, Classic scale **$25.00**

Arabian Mare (Bedouin Family Gift Set), 1995-96, Classic scale..**$10.00**

Arabian Stallion, matt bay, 1984-88, Little Bits scale...**$11.00**

Belgian, chestnut w/red & yellow ribbon, 1965-80, Traditional scale..**$100.00**

Black Beauty, 1980-83, Classic scale **$15.00**

Black Stallion (Black Stallion Returns Set), 1983-93, Classic scale..**$15.00**

Bucking Bronco, matt bay, 1967-70, Classic scale **$100.00**

Cantering Welsh Pony, matt bay w/yellow ribbon, 1971-73, Traditional scale..**$100.00**

Cantering Welsh Pony (Small World), matt liver chestnut w/green ribbons, 1988, Traditional scale............**$100.00**

Clydesdale Foal, light bay, 1990-91, Traditional scale..**$25.00**

Clydesdale (Circus Extravaganza), matt bay, 1994-95, Little Bits scale..**$9.00**

Duchess (Black Beauty Family Set), matt bay, Classic scale **$15.00**

Family Arabian Foal, glossy charcoal, 1961-67, Traditional scale **$25.00**

Family Arabian Foal (JC Penney), light chestnut, 1983, Traditional scale **$40.00**

Family Arabian Stallion, glossy alabaster, 1959-66, Traditional scale **$30.00**

Family Arabian Stallion, woodgrain, 1963-67, Traditional scale **$100.00**

Friesian (Action Drafters Set), dark bay, 1994-96, Traditional scale **$20.00**

Grazing Foal Bows, black, 1964-70, Traditional scale.**$50.00**

Grazing Mare Buttons, palomino, 1964-81, Traditional scale **$40.00**

Halla Famous Jumper, matt bay, 1977-85, Traditional scale **$60.00**

Jet Run (Sears US Olympic Team), matt chestnut, 1987, Classic **$30.00**

Jet Run (US Equestrian Team Gift Set), matt bay, 1980-83, Classic scale **$15.00**

Johar (Eagle & Pow Wow Set), black pinto, 1995, Classic scale **$35.00**

Kelso, 1975 – 90, dark bay, $20.00.
(Photo courtesy Carol Karbowiak Gilbert)

Kelso (Fine Horse Family), matt roan, 1994-96, Classic scale **$15.00**

Lady Roxana (King of the Wind Set), matt alabaster, 1990-93, Classic scale **$15.00**

Lipizzan Stallion, matt alabaster, 1975-80, Classic scale ..**$40.00**

Man O' War, matt red chestnut, 1975-90, Classic scale ...**$25.00**

Mego (Breyerfest Dinner Model), 1995, signed, Traditional scale **$100.00**

Merrylegs (Black Beauty Family), dapple gray, 1980-83, Classic scale **$15.00**

Might Mingo (Pony for Keeps Set), light dapple gray, 1990-91, Classic scale **$15.00**

Might Mingo (US Esquestrian Team Set), dapple gray, 1980-91, Classic scale **$15.00**

Morgan, woodgrain, 1963-85, Traditional scale.........**$750.00**

Morganglanz, 1980-87, Traditional scale **$60.00**

Mustang Foal (Trakehner Family), matt bay, 1992-94, Classic scale **$12.00**

Mustang Stallion (Pony for Keeps Set), chestnut w/gray legs, 1990-91, Classic scale..**$15.00**

Old Timer, matt alabaster, 1966-76, Traditional scale .**$50.00**

Polo Pony, matt bay, 1976-82, Classic scale **$60.00**

Proud Arabian Mare, red chestnut, 1991-92, Traditional scale **$40.00**

Quarter Horse Foal, palomino, 1975-82, Classic scale ..**$20.00**

Quarter Horse Gelding, glossy bay, 1959-66, Traditional scale **$150.00**

Quarter Horse Stallion, matt buckskin, 1984-88, Little Bits scale **$11.00**

Quarter Horse Stallion (Breyer Parade of Breeds), matt leopard appaloosa, 1988, Little Bits scale **$12.00**

Racehorse, woodgrain, 1958-66..............................**$250.00**

Rearing Stallion, matt bay, 1965-80, Classic scale **$30.00**

Roy Belgian Drafter, matt sorrel, 1989-90, Traditional scale **$45.00**

Ruffian, matt bay, 1977-90, Classic scale.....................**$35.00**

Running Foal, chestnut pinto, 1991-93, Traditional scale **$20.00**

Secretariat (Racehorse Set), glossy chestnut, 1990, Traditional scale **$45.00**

Silky Sullivan, matt brown, 1975-90, Classic scale **$25.00**

Terrang, buckskin, 1995, Classic scale **$15.00**

Tobe Rocky Mountain Horse, 1995-96........................**$20.00**

Trakehner, semi-gloss & matt bay, 1979-84, Traditional scale **$30.00**

Western Pony, dark brown, 1955-57, Traditional scale ..**$150.00**

Lying Foal, 1969 – 84, black blanket appaloosa, $30.00.

Other Accessories

Balking Mule, matt bay chestnut, 1968-73................**$150.00**
Bison...**$50.00**
Boxer, 1954-73 ....**$30.00**

Brahma Bull, 1958-93 ....**$50.00**
Calf **$30.00**
Donkey, w/red baskets, 1958-60 ....**$75.00**
Donkey, 1958-74 ....**$25.00**
Mother Bear, brown face, 1967-73 ....**$35.00**
Siamese Kitten, 1966-71 ....**$100.00**
St Bernard, semi-gloss/matt 2-tone, 1972-81...............**$40.00**

British Royal Commemoratives

While seasoned collectors may prefer the older pieces using circa 1840 (Queen Victoria's reign) as their starting point, even present-day souvenirs make a good inexpensive beginning collection. Ceramic items, glassware, metalware, and paper goods have been issued on the occasion of weddings, royal tours, birthdays, christenings, and many other celebrations. Food tins are fairly easy to find, and range in price from about $30.00 to around $75.00 for those made since the 1950s.

We've all seen that items related to Princess Diana have appreciated rapidly since her untimely and tragic demise, and in fact collections are being built exclusively from memorabilia marketed both before and after her death. For more information, we recommend *British Royal Commemoratives* by Audrey Zeder.

Advisor: Audrey Zeder (See Directory, British Royalty Commemoratives)

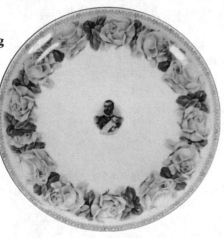

Charger, King George V portrait, floral border, Bavaria, 12½", $75.00.

Beaker, Charles/Diana wedding, footed base, black w/24k portrait & decor, Prinknash **$55.00**
Book, Royal Souvenirs, by Geoffrey Warren, hardback, 1977..**$45.00**
Bookmark, Charles/Diana wedding, white leather w/gold portrait & decor **$25.00**
Bookmark, Elizabeth II coronation, multicolor portrait & decor on woven silk..**$25.00**
Bookmark, Prince Edward wedding, white leather w/gold decor, 9x1½" **$15.00**

Bottle, Elizabeth II jubilee, amethyst glass w/embossed portrait & decor **$45.00**
Bowl, Charles/Diana wedding, black & white portrait, multicolor heart decor, 5½x⅞"...............................**$35.00**
Bowl, George VI coronation, sepia portrait, multicolor design, gold rim, 2¾" **$35.00**
Calendar, Elizabeth II coronation, perpetual standup, multicolor portrait, 7x5" **$45.00**
Cigarette card album, 50 multicolor cards from Elizabeth I to Charles & Diana, PJ Tips.......................**$35.00**
Coin, Princess Diana, 1999 5-pound, special pack, Royal Mint **$30.00**
Doll, Elizabeth II, state robes, vinyl, Nisbit, ca 1950, 8½" ..**$150.00**
Doll, Princess Diana, multicolor cardboard doll w/magnetic dresses, 1997 ....**$20.00**
Ephemera, Charles & Diana wedding car bumper sticker, black portrait, multicolor decor **$10.00**
Ephemera, Elizabeth II 1977 jubilee paper plate, blue w/jubilee insignia..**$5.00**
Ephemera, Elizabeth II 1977 jubilee pub beer mat, cardboard, 4x4" **$6.00**
Horse brass, Charles/Diana wedding, embossed portrait & decor on brass **$35.00**
Illustrated London News Record No, Elizabeth II coronation, blue cover, gold decor, 14x11" **$75.00**
Jewelry, Princess Diana earrings, multicolor portrait, silvertone bezel..**$35.00**
Magazine, Daily Mail, Princess Diana memorial, 9-6-97...**$30.00**

Magazine, *Holiday*, November 1957, The Queen of England, Part I, $25.00.

Magazine, Observer, Elizabeth II 1983 visit to California, 3-13-83 ....**$30.00**
Magazine, Sphere, Princess Margaret wedding, 5-14-60...**$35.00**
Medallion, Princess Elizabeth 1947 wedding, pot metal, 1⅝"..**$50.00**
Miniature, Charles/Diana wedding plate, multicolor portrait in wedding clothes, 2¼"......................................**$35.00**
Miniature, photo album of 1982 royal family, 1¼x2" .**$35.00**
Mug, Charles/Diana wedding, black portrait in red heart frame, Crown Trent **$40.00**

Mug, Charles/Diana wedding, multicolor Coat of Arms, footed base, Woods & Son, 3".............................**$25.00**

Mug, Charles/Diana wedding, shaded blue portrait/decor, straight sides, Spode.............................**$75.00**

Mug, Elizabeth II coronation, dark green w/maize, embossed portrait & decor, 4½"..............................**$40.00**

Mug, Elizabeth II 1972 wedding anniversary, multicolor decor, footed, Aynsley.............................**$65.00**

Mug, George VI coronation, multicolor portrait & decor, Art Deco style, 3"..............................**$35.00**

Mug, Prince William 1997 confirmation, multicolor portrait & decor, limited edition 80 ....**$125.00**

Mug, Princess Beatrice 1988 birthday, white w/gold decor, Wedgwood, 3"..............................**$100.00**

Mug, Princess Diana memorial, multicolor portrait, rose decor, bone china, Nelson **$35.00**

Mug, Princess Diana 1995 Japan visit, multicolor portrait & decor, Chown, limited edition of 50 ....**$125.00**

Mug, Princess Diana 30th birthday, multicolor portrait & decor, limited edition of 5000, Aynsley..............**$150.00**

Newspaper, Di Badly Injured, News of the World, 8-31-97 .**$60.00**

Novelty, Charles/Diana wedding foil sticker, multicolor decor, 5½x5"..............................**$6.00**

Novelty, Charles/Diana wedding place mat, multicolor decor, vinyl, 11x8¼".............................**$5.00**

Novelty, Elizabeth II coronation pocketknife, multicolor decor, 5x2½".............................**$45.00**

Novelty, Elizabeth II jubilee soap dish, plastic, multicolor portrait & decor **$25.00**

Novelty, Princess Diana memorial tree ornament, glass sphere, multicolor portrait.............................**$15.00**

Photograph, Princess Diana 1987 at London gala, black & white, 6x8".............................**$50.00**

Pin-back button, Charles/Diana wedding, black & white portrait, red, white & blue rim, 1½" **$15.00**

Pin-back button, George VI 1949 New Zealand visit, multicolor decor, 1½".............................**$35.00**

Pitcher, Elizabeth II coronation, treacle w/embossed tan portrait & decor, 4".............................**$45.00**

Plaque, 5 royal women, Queen, Queen Mother, Princesses Diana & Anne, Sarah **$25.00**

Plate, Charles/Diana wedding, multicolor portrait, embossed design on rim, 9½".............................**$65.00**

Plate, Charles/Diana wedding, multicolor portrait & decor, sloping sides, 5".............................**$25.00**

Plate, Elizabeth II coronation, multicolor portrait w/enameling & gold decor, Coalport **$125.00**

Plate, Elizabeth II 1959 Canada visit, multicolor decor, Paragon, 10½".............................**$125.00**

Plate, Prince William's 1st birthday, multicolor scene of Diana holding William, gold rim, 5"..............................**$55.00**

Plate, Princess Diana memorial, multicolor portrait, rose decor, bone China, 6"..............................**$35.00**

Plate, Princess Diana 1987, 3 portraits, Royal Doulton, 10½".............................**$250.00**

Postcard, Prince Charles 1969 investiture, gold portrait, multicolor decor **$15.00**

Postcard, Princess Eugenie 1990 birthday, multicolor, Enterprise, limited edition **$15.00**

Postcard, Queen Mother 2000 Millennium Queen, multicolor portrait & family tree **$5.00**

Poster, Princess Diana 1998, Dresses for Humanity, multicolor, 21x34".............................**$45.00**

Pressed glass, Charles/Diana wedding plate, portrait & decor on lavender, 3½".............................**$30.00**

Pressed glass, Prince William 10th birthday plate, portrait, amber, 3½".............................**$35.00**

Print, Elizabeth II, multicolor portrait w/Corgi dogs, 11¾x8½".............................**$12.00**

Print, Princess Diana memorial, artist signed Heiner, 11x16".............................**$50.00**

Puzzle, Elizabeth II, multicolor collage coronation tins, 247-pc, 11x17".............................**$25.00**

Puzzle, Princess Diana memorial, The English Rose, 500-pc, MIB **$50.00**

Scrapbook, Charles/Diana wedding, silver w/blue decor, unused, 12x9½".............................**$45.00**

Spoon, Charles/Diana wedding, embossed overlapping portrait on silverplate.............................**$25.00**

Spoon, Diana, multicolor portrait w/tiara, silverplate, ca 1982.............................**$25.00**

Stamps, Princess Diana 21st birthday, stamp block/6 different stamps, Jamaica.............................**$30.00**

Teapot, Queen Mother's 90th birthday, multicolor portrait wearing yellow, bone china, 2-cup.............................**$75.00**

Textile, Princess Elizabeth 1951 Canada visit, multicolor portrait & decor, 31x31".............................**$90.00**

Thimble, Charles/Diana wedding, blue Prince of Wales feather design, Highland, MIB **$35.00**

Thimble, Prince Henry 1984 christening, Queen Mother & baby, multicolor decor, Fenton.............................**$35.00**

Tin, Charles/Diana wedding, multicolor portrait & decor on cream, 4¼x3x3".............................**$35.00**

Tin, Elizabeth II coronation, multicolor portrait, octagonal, 5¼x4¼x1¼" **$35.00**

Tin, George VI coronation, multicolor portrait & decor, octagonal, 5x4".............................**$40.00**

Toby mug, Princess Diana, hand painted by Tootle, Kevin Frances, limited edition 900.............................**$350.00**

Tray, Charles/Diana wedding, multicolor portrait/royal residences, 14x14" **$50.00**

Trinket box, Charles/Diana wedding, multicolor portrait & decor, heart-shaped lid, Poole **$60.00**

Trinket box, George VI Canada visit, footed, w/lid, Adams.............................**$75.00**

Brock of California

This was the trade name of the B.J. Brock Company, located in Lawndale, California. They operated from 1947 until 1980, and some of the dinnerware lines they produced have become desirable collectibles. One of the most common themes revolved around country living, farmhouses, barns, chickens, and cows. Patterns were Rooster, California Farmhouse, and California Rustic. Shapes echoed the same concept — there were skillets, milk cans, and flatirons fashioned into sugar bowls, creamers, and salt and pepper shakers. The company marketed a three-piece children's set as well. Also look for their '50s modern line called Manzanita, with pink and charcoal branches on platinum. With the interest in this style of dinnerware on the increase, this should be one to watch.

Bowl, farm scene, 2x8½" **$20.00**
Bowl, serving; Rooster, 1¼x11x7½" **$40.00**
Casserole, Farmhouse, handles, w/lid, 5¾x7" **$60.00**
Creamer (stick handled) & sugar bowl (w/lid), vining floral
    on white to yellow, green trim **$22.50**
Creamer & sugar bowl, windmill scene **$17.50**
Cup & saucer, vining floral on white to light yellow....**$10.00**
Devilled egg plate, Pennsylvania Dutch, 12-well, 13"...**$18.00**
Mug, Rooster **$28.00**
Pitcher, Forever Yours, 4"..**$25.00**
Plate, Forever Yours, couple on bench, w/hanger, 11" .**$24.00**
Plate, Forever Yours, 9" **$10.00**
Plate, girl & cow, 8⅞" **$18.00**
Plate, Rooster, barnyard scene, 6½", 4 for...................**$32.00**

Plate, Rooster, 10¾", $15.00.

Platter, donkeys in farm scene on white, 14" **$35.00**
Platter, farm scene, 13" dia..**$22.50**
Platter, Farmhouse, 14x9"...**$30.00**
Platter, Wildflower, pink on cream, 14" **$20.00**
Salt & pepper shakers, Forever Yours, pr....................**$24.00**
Saucepan, farm scenes on white, green handle..........**$60.00**

Bubble Bath Containers

There's no hotter area of collecting today than items from the '50s through the '70s that are reminiscent of kids' early TV shows and hit movies, and bubble bath containers fill the bill. Most of these were made in the 1960s. The Colgate-Palmolive Company produced the majority of them — they're the ones marked 'Soaky' — and these seem to be the most collectible.

Each character's name is right on the bottle. Other companies followed suit; Purex also made a line, so did Avon. Be sure to check for paint loss, and look carefully for cracks in the brittle plastic heads of the Soakies. Our values are for examples in excellent to near mint condition.

For more information, we recommend *Schroeder's Collectible Toys, Antique to Modern,* and *Collector's Guide to Bubble Bath Containers* by Greg Moore and Joe Pizzo. (Both are published by Collector Books.)

Advisors: Matt and Lisa Adams (See Directory, Bubble Bath Containers)

Alvin (Chipmunks), Colgate-Palmolive, w/puppet, neck tag
    & contents, M..**$50.00**
Alvin (Chipmunks), Soaky, Reckards, 6x6", M **$30.00**
Aristocats, Avon, 1971, NM **$8.00**
Atom Ant, Purex, 1965, rare, EX+ **$40.00**
Auggie Doggie, Purex, 1967, rare, EX+ **$45.00**
Baba Looey, Purex, 1960s, NM....................................**$35.00**
Bambi, Colgate-Palmolive, 1960s, NM........................**$25.00**
Bamm-Bamm, Purex, 1960s, NM..................................**$35.00**
Barney & Baby Bop, Kid Care, M **$8.00**
Barney Rubble, Milvern (Purex), 1960s, NM+ **$35.00**

Batman, TM & DC Comics, Tsumara, International, Inc. (made in Thailand), 10", $5.00 to $6.00 full.

Betty Bubbles, Lander, 1950s, several variations, NM, ea..**$35.00**
Big Bad World, Tubby Time, 1960s, rare, NM............**$40.00**
Blabber Mouse, Purex, 1960s, rare, NM....................**$125.00**
Bozo the Clown, Colgate-Palmolive, 1960s, NM **$30.00**
Breezly the Bear, 1960s, rare, NM.............................**$150.00**
Broom Hilda, Lander, 1977, rare, EX..........................**$30.00**
Bullwinkle, Colgate-Palmolive, 1964-66, several color varia-
    tions, NM+, ea..**$40.00**
Bullwinkle, Fuller Brush, 1970, rare, NM....................**$60.00**
Care Bears, AGC, 1984, several variations, NM, ea, from $5
    to **$10.00**
Casper the Friendly Ghost, Colgate-Palmolive, 1960s, EX+..**$30.00**
Cecil Sea Serpent, Purex, 1960s, M **$75.00**

Creature From the Black Lagoon, Colgate-Palmolive, 1963,
NM+ **$125.00**
Dino, Purex, 1960s, rare, NM+ **$85.00**
Droop-A-Long Coyote, Purex, 1960s, rare, EX+ **$35.00**
Elmo, Softsoap, 1992, NM, from $5 to **$10.00**
ET, Avon, 1983, wearing bathrobe, NM+ **$10.00**
Felix the Cat, Colgate-Palmolive, 1960s, EX+ **$30.00**
Flintstones Fun Bath, Roclar (Purex), 1970s, MIB
(sealed)...**$75.00**
Goofy, Colgate-Palmolive, 1960s, w/cap head, M.......**$25.00**
Hot Wheels Race Car, Cosrich, 1993, NM..................**$15.00**
Huckleberry Hound, Milvern, 1960s, 15", M..............**$40.00**
Humpty Dumpty, Avon, 1960s, NM, from $5 to **$10.00**
Jinx w/Pixie & Dixie, Purex, 1960s, NM.....................**$30.00**
Jurassic Park Dinosaur, Cosrich, 1992, NM, from $5 to ..**$10.00**
Little Mermaid, Kid Care, 1991, M **$5.00**
Little Orphan Annie, Lander, 1977, NM, from $25 to..**$30.00**
Lucy (Peanuts), Avon, 1970, MIB **$20.00**
Mighty Mouse, Lander, 1978, rare, VG+......................**$20.00**
Miss Piggy, Calgon, Treasure Island outfit, M................**$8.00**
Mr Magoo, Colgate-Palmolive, 1960s, EX+ **$25.00**
Paul McCartney, Soaky, 1965, EX...............................**$75.00**
Peter Potamous, Purex, 1960s, M **$25.00**
Pokey, Novelty Packaging, 1987, NM **$40.00**
Popeye, Colgate-Palmolive, 1977, rare, NM.................**$35.00**
Quick Draw McGraw, Purex, 1960s, several variations, NM,
ea **$30.00**

Ricochet Rabbit, Purex, 1960s, $50.00. (Photo courtesy Greg Moore and Joe Pizzo)

Schroeder (Peanuts), Avon, 1970, MIB.........................**$25.00**
Scooby Doo, Colgate-Palmolive, 1977, NM **$45.00**
Sketetor (Masters of the Universe), Ducair Bio, NM+.**$15.00**
Smokey the Bear, Colgate-Palmolive, 1960s, NM **$25.00**
Thumper, Colgate-Palmolive, 1960s, EX **$25.00**
Wally Gator, Purex, 1963, rare, M...............................**$50.00**
Yogi Bear, Purex, 1960s, several variations, NM, ea ...**$40.00**

Wendy, Colgate-Palmolive, NM, from $30.00 to $35.00.

Cake Toppers

In many ways, these diminutive couples reflect our culture — they actually capture miniature moments in time, and their style of dress reflects the many changes made in fashion down through the years. The earliest cake toppers (from before the turn of the twentieth century) were made of sugar and disintegrated rapidly. Next came bridal couples of carved wood, usually standing on plaster (gum paste) bases. When molded, this material could be made into lovely platforms and backdrops for the tiny figures. It was sometimes molded into columns with gazebo-style or lattice roofs under which the dainty couples stood hand in hand. Good luck horseshoes representing all the best wishes for the bridal couple were popular as well.

By the 1920s and 1930s, plaster bases were still in use, but a flower bower replaced the columns and horseshoes. These bowers were constructed of wire and trimmed with cloth flowers, often lilies of the valley. The bridal figures of this period were usually porcelain or chalkware, and the brides' gowns became sleek and elegant, reflecting the Art Deco trend in fashion. Gone was the bustle and the prim pose. The groom looked equally elegant in black tie and tails. The pair now often took on a 'high society' air.

Then in the mid-1930s appeared the exact opposite — kewpies. These child-like figures with their wide-eyed, innocent faces were popular cake toppers well into the 1940s.

During WWII, military toppers became popular. It was now the groom who drew the most attention. He was dashing and patriotic in an Armed Forced uniform, and all branches of the military were represented. To complement the theme, a 48-star American flag or a red, white, and blue ribbon was often suspended from the center of the bower.

After the war, the bridal couple and the base they stood on were made of plastic — the latest rage. As for flowers and trim, there seemed no limit. Cabbage roses, strings of pearls, and huge gatherings of white netting added the final trim to oversized backdrops of hearts, cupids, birds, and bells. In the new millennium, fine china or delicate porcelain have become the materials of choice.

Cake toppers are fragile. Look them over carefully before purchasing. Expect to find them in all stages of completeness and condition. Chips, dents, broken parts, crumbling bases, or soiled clothing all seriously devalue a piece. Those in questionable or poor condition (unless extremely rare) are basically worthless. Prices suggested in the following listings apply to cake toppers that are compete with base, bower (or other finishing top), flowers, trim and lace, or clothing if applicable. A collectible topper should reflect minimal wear and obvious care.

Advisor: Jeannie Greenfield (See Directory, Cake Toppers)

Military couple arm-in-arm on plaster (gum paste) base, cloth bower of flowers & leaves on wire, 48-star flag in center **$60.00**
1900s couple on plaster (gum paste) base, bower of cloth flowers w/painted plaster centers **$50.00**
1930s couple on raised & sculpted base, cupola roof & columns w/lilies-of-the-valley trim, heavy, 10".....**$75.00**
1930s porcelain kewpies (crepe-paper attire) embrace under bower of cloth flowers, plaster embossed/sculptured base, 3"..**$50.00**

1930s, pair of 4" porcelain kewpies on cardboard platform under wire and crepe-paper arch, crepe-paper tux, dress of satin ribbons with crepe-paper trim, $50.00.

(Photo courtesy Jeannie Greenfield)

1940s couple, 3 lg bells on sides as backdrop, ea w/cloth flowers w/green velvet leaves & silver paper in centers..**$40.00**
1940s couple holding hands stands before table w/wedding ring, bower of cloth flowers & bell, plaster & chalkware **$50.00**
1950s couple, heart-theme base, lg heart w/netting, flower center & upturned bell w/white glitter as backdrop, plastic **$20.00**

Calculators

It is difficult to picture the days when a basic four-function calculator cost hundreds of dollars, especially when today you get one free by simply filling out a credit application. Yet when they initially arrived on the market in 1971, the first of these electronic marvels cost from $300.00 to $400.00. All this for a calculator that could do no more than add, subtract, multiply, and divide.

Even at that price there was an uproar by consumers as calculating finally became convenient. No longer did you need to use a large mechanical monster adding machine or a slide rule with all of its complexity. You could even put away your pencil and paper for those tough numbers you couldn't 'do' in your head.

With prices initially so high and the profit potential so promising, several hundred companies jumped onto the calculator bandwagon. Some made their own; many purchased them from other (often overseas) manufacturers, just adding their own nameplate. Since the product was so new to the world, most of the calculators had some very different and interesting body styles.

Due to the competitive nature of all those new entries to the market, prices dropped quickly. A year and a half later, prices started to fall below $100.00 — a magic number that caused a boom in consumer demand. As even more calculators became available and electronics improved, prices continued to drop, eventually forcing many high-cost makers (who could not compete) out of business. By 1978 the number of major calculator companies could be counted on both hands. Fortunately calculators are still available at almost every garage sale or flea market for a mere pittance — usually 25¢ to $3.00.

For more information refer to *A Guide to HP Handheld Calculators and Computers* by Wlodek Mier-Jedrzejowicz, *Collector's Guide to Pocket Calculators* by Guy Ball and Bruce Flamm (both published by Wilson/Barnett), and *Personal Computers and Pocket Calculators* by Dr. Thomas Haddock.

Note: Due to limited line length, we have used these abbreviations: flr — fluorescent; fct — function.

Advisor: Guy D. Ball (See Directory, Calculators)

Club: International Association of Calculator Collectors 14561 Livingston St., Tustin, CA 92781-0345 fax/phone: 714-730-6140; e-mail: mrcalc@usa.net Membership includes subscription to newsletter *The International Calculator Collector*

Related Website: http://www.oldcalcs.com

Adler, #60, 4-fct, 6-digit green flr, 4-AA battery pack, Japan, 4x6"...**$45.00**
Bowmar, #901B, 4-fct, red LED, sealed battery, Klixon keypad, USA, 1971, 3x5"..**$60.00**
Brother, #408C, 4-fct, mini-tube, sealed battery, Japan, 1972, 4x6¾"...**$55.00**

Calcu-Pen, $150.00. (Photo courtesy Guy Ball)

Caltronic, #606, 4-fct, red LED, 9V battery, 6-digit display, 12-digit capability, 3¼x6" **$50.00**

Casio, #8U, 4-fct, green flr, 5-AA batteries, decimal slide switch, Japan, 1974, 4¾x7" **$15.00**

Citizen, #810R, 4-fct, memory, %, green flr, sealed battery, Japan, 3½x6" **$40.00**

Commodore, #774D, 4-fct, red LED, 9V battery, USA, 1973, 2½x5½" **$30.00**

Concept, #24, 4-fct, memory, square root, green flr, 2-AA sealed batteries, Japan, 3x5¾" **$40.00**

Craig, #4515, 4-fct, red LED, 4-AA batteries, tan plastic body w/burgundy metal face, Japan, 3¼x5" **$40.00**

Elektronika, #C3-15, science-fct, red LED, 4-AA batteries, unique magnitude fct, USSR, 1977, 3½x6¾" **$50.00**

General Instrument, #EZ-2000, 4-fct, red LED, sealed battery, Canada, 1973, 3x6½" **$50.00**

Hewlett-Packard, #21, science-fct, red LED, sealed battery, USA, 1975, 2¾x5" **$45.00**

JC Penney, #2300, 4-fct, square root, memory, flr, sealed battery, Japan, 3x6¼" **$45.00**

Kings Point, #PC-2, 4-fct, %, LED, 9V battery, Japan, 2¾x5½" **$55.00**

Litronix, #2230R, 4-fct, memory, %, square root, sign change, red LED, sealed battery, Malaysia, 1975 .... **$45.00**

Lloyd's, #650, science-fct, 12-digit flr display, 4-AA batteries, 43 input keys, Japan, 1970s, 3½x5½" **$70.00**

Mark VI, 4-fct, memory, %, flr, 4-AA batteries, Japan, 1973, 4½x6" **$50.00**

Melcor, #480, 4-fct, memory, %, red LED, 9V battery, USA, 1974, 3x6" **$50.00**

Monroe-Litton, #20, 4-fct, red LED, sealed battery, USA, 1973, 3½x6" **$65.00**

Novus, #835, 4-fct, memory, square root, %, red LED, 9V battery, Hong Kong, 2¾x5½" **$15.00**

Omron, #8SR, science-fct, green flr, 2-AA batteies, 2-tone case, F-fct key, Japan, 3x4½" **$50.00**

Prinztronic, Asset, 4-fct, flr, 4-AA batteries, 3x4" **$50.00**

Radio Shack, #EC-241, 4-fct, memory, %, flr, 9V batteries, 1977, 3x5½" **$35.00**

Rockwell, #24RD, 4-fct, memory, %, square root, sign change, flr, 4-AA batteries, Japan, 1975, 3x6" **$25.00**

Royal, Digital 5-T, 4-fct, green flr, 4-AA batteries, black case, Malaysia, 3½x6" **$45.00**

Sanyo, #ICC-810, 4-fct, flr, sealed battery, Japan, 3½x6" **$50.00**

Sharp, #EL-215, 4-fct, memory, %, square root, green flr, 2-AA batteries, Korea, 3¼x5¼" **$15.00**

Sinclair, Oxford 300, science-fct, purple LED, 9V battery, black case, England, ca 1975-76, 3x6¼" **$75.00**

Sperry Remington Rand, #823-GT, 4-fct, %, flr, 4-AA batteries, Japan, 3¾x6" **$40.00**

Summit, #SL-10, 4-fct, memory, %, red LED, sealed battery, slanted display case, USA, ca 1974, 2¾x4¾" **$50.00**

Texas Instruments, #SR-56, science-fct, red LED, sealed battery, USA, 1976, 3⅛x6" **$30.00**

Texas Instruments, #TI-5025, 4-fct, memory, %, flr, sealed battery, paper tape printer, USA, 1979, 3½x7" **$25.00**

Toshiba, #BC-0801B, 4-fct, green flr, sealed battery, Japan, 1971-72, 4x6½" **$65.00**

Unisonic, #738, aka Slide Rulette, 4-fct, memory, %, sign change, green flr, 4-AA batteries, Japan, 3½x5¼" .. **$20.00**

Unitrex, #800D, 4-fct, %, flr, 4-AA batteries, horizontal, Japan, 6½x6" **$25.00**

California Raisins

Since they starred in their first TV commercial in 1986, the California Raisins have attained stardom through movies, tapes, videos, and magazine ads. Today we see them everywhere on the secondary market — PVC figures, radios, banks, posters — and they're very collectible. The PVC figures were introduced in 1987. Originally there were four, all issued for retail sales — a singer, two conga dancers, and a saxophone player. Before the year was out, Hardee's, the fast-food chain, came out with the same characters, though on a slightly smaller scale. A fifth character, Blue Surfboard (horizontal), was created, and three 5½" Bendees with flat pancake-style bodies appeared.

In 1988 the ranks had grown to twenty-one: Blue Surfboard (vertical), Red Guitar, Lady Dancer, Blue/Green Sunglasses, Guy Winking, Candy Cane, Santa Raisin, Bass Player, Drummer, Tambourine Lady (there were two styles), Lady Valentine, Boy Singer, Girl Singer, Hip Guitar Player, Sax Player with Beret, and four Graduates (styled like the original four, but on yellow pedestals and wearing graduation caps). And Hardee's issued an additional six: Blue Guitar, Trumpet Player, Roller Skater, Skateboard, Boom Box, and Yellow Surfboard.

Still eight more characters came out in 1989: Male in Beach Chair, Green Trunks with Surfboard, Hula Skirt, Girl Sitting on Sand, Piano Player, AC, Mom, and Michael Raisin. They made two movies and thereafter were joined by their fruit and vegetable friends, Rudy Bagaman, Lick Broccoli, Banana White, Leonard Limabean, and Cecil Thyme. Hardee's added four more characters in 1991: Anita Break, Alotta Style, Buster, and Benny.

All Raisins are dated with these exceptions: those issued in 1989 (only the Beach Scene characters are dated, and they're actually dated 1988) and those issued by Hardee's in 1991.

For more information we recommend *Schroeder's Collectible Toys, Antique to Modern* (Collector Books).

Applause, Captain Toonz, w/blue boom box, yellow glasses & sneakers, Hardee's Second Promotion, 1988, sm, M **$3.00**

Applause, FF String, w/blue guitar & orange sneakers, Hardee's Second Promotion, 1988, sm, M **$3.00**

Applause, Michael Raisin (Jackson), w/silver microphone & studded belt, Special Edition, 1989, M..................$20.00

Applause, Rollin' Rollo, w/roller skates, yellow sneakers & hat marked H, Hardee's Second Promotion, 1988, sm, M..................$3.00

Applause, SB Stuntz, w/yellow skateboard & blue sneakers, Hardee's Second Promotion, 1988, sm, M $3.00

Applause, Trumpy Trunote, w/trumpet & blue sneakers, Hardee's Second Promotion, 1988, sm, M $3.00

Applause, Waves Weaver I, w/yellow surfboard connected to foot, Hardee's Second Promotion, 1988, sm, M $4.00

Applause, Waves Weaver II, w/yellow surfboard not connected to foot, Hardee's Second Promotion, 1988, sm, M..................$6.00

Applause-Claymation, Banana White, yellow dress, Meet the Raisins First Edition, 1989, M..................$20.00

Applause-Claymation, Lick Broccoli, green & black w/red & orange guitar, Meet the Raisins First Edition, 1989, M.$20.00

Applause-Claymation, Rudy Bagaman, with cigar, purple shirt, and sandals, Meet the Raisins 1st edition, 1989, M, $20.00.
(Photo courtesy Larry DeAngelo)

CALRAB, Blue Surfboard, board connected to foot, Unknown Production, 1988, M..................$35.00

CALRAB, Blue Surfboard, board in right hand, not connected to foot, Unknown Production, 1987, M..........$50.00

CALRAB, Guitar, red guitar, First Commercial Issue, 1988, M.$8.00

CALRAB, Hands, left hand points up, right hand points down, Post Raisin Bran Issue, 1987, M..................$4.00

CALRAB, Hands, pointing up w/thumbs on head, First Key Chains, 1987, M..................$5.00

CALRAB, Hands, pointing up w/thumbs on head, Hardee's First Promotion, 1987, sm, M..................$3.00

CALRAB, Microphone, right hand in fist w/microphone in left, Post Raisin Brand Issue, 1987, M..................$6.00

CALRAB, Microphone, right hand points up w/microphone in left, Hardee's First Promotion, 1987, sm, M.......$3.00

CALRAB, Microphone, right hand points up w/microphone in left, First Key Chains, 1987, M..................$7.00

CALRAB, Santa, red cap & green sneakers, Christmas Issue, 1988, M..................$9.00

CALRAB, Saxophone, gold sax, no hat, First Key Chains, 1987, M..................$5.00

CALRAB, Saxophone, gold sax, no hat, Hardee's First Promotion, 1987, sm, M..................$3.00

CALRAB, Saxophone, inside of sax painted red, Post Raisin Bran Issue, 1987, M..................$4.00

CALRAB, Singer, microphone in left hand not connected to face, First Commercial Issue, 1988, M..................$6.00

CALRAB, Sunglasses, holding candy cane, green glasses, red sneakers, Christmas Issue, 1988, M..................$9.00

CALRAB, Sunglasses, index finger touching face, First Key Chains, 1987, M..................$5.00

CALRAB, Sunglasses, index finger touching face, orange glasses, Hardee's First Promotion, 1987, M............$3.00

CALRAB, Sunglasses, right hand points up, left hand points down, orange glasses, Post Raisin Bran Issue, 1987, M..................$4.00

CALRAB, Sunglasses II, eyes not visible, aqua glasses & sneakers, First Commercial Issue, 1988, M $6.00

CALRAB, Sunglasses II, eyes visible, aqua glasses & sneakers, First Commercial Issue, 1988, M..................$25.00

CALRAB, Winky, in hitchhiking pose & winking, First Commercial Issue, 1988, M..................$6.00

CALRAB-Applause, AC, 'Gimme 5' pose, tall pompadour & red sneakers, Meet the Raisins Second Edition, 1989, M..................$150.00

CALRAB-Applause, Alotta Style, w/purple boom box, pink boots, Hardee's Fourth Promotion, 1991, sm, MIP...$12.00

CALRAB-Applause, Anita Break, shopping w/Hardee's bag, Hardee's Fourth Promotion, 1991, sm, M $12.00

CALRAB-Applause, Bass Player, w/gray slippers, Second Commercial Issue, 1988, M..................$8.00

CALRAB-Applause, Benny, w/bowling ball, orange sunglasses, Hardee's Fourth Promotion, 1991, sm, MIP $20.00

CALRAB-Applause, Boy in Beach Chair, orange glasses, brown base, Beach Theme Edition, 1988, M........$15.00

Calrab-Applause, Boy w/Surfboard, purple board, brown base, Beach Theme Edition, 1988, M..................$15.00

CALRAB-Applause, Cecil Thyme (Carrot), Meet the Raisins Second Promotion, 1989, M..................$175.00

CALRAB-Applause, Drummer, black hat w/yellow feather, Second Commercial Issue, 1988, M..................$8.00

CALRAB-Applause, Girl w/Boom Box, purple glasses, green shoes, brown base, Beach Theme Edition, 1988, M.$15.00

CALRAB-Applause, Girl w/Tambourine, green shoes & bracelet, Raisin Club Issue, 1988, M..................$12.00

CALRAB-Applause, Girl w/Tambourine (Ms Delicious), yellow shoes, Second Commercial Issue, 1988, M....$15.00

CALRAB-Applause, Hands, Graduate w/both hands pointing up & thumbs on head, Graduate Key Chains, 1988, M..................$85.00

CALRAB-Applause, Hip Band Guitarist (Hendrix), w/headband & yellow guitar, Third Commercial Issue, 1988, M..................$22.00

CALRAB-Applause, Hip Band Guitarist (Hendrix), w/headband & yellow guitar, Second Key Chains, 1988, sm, M..................$65.00

CALRAB-Applause, Hula Girl, yellow shoes & bracelet, green skirt, Beach Theme Edition, 1988, M **$15.00**

CALRAB-Applause, Leonard Limabean, purple suit, Meet the Raisins Second Promotion, 1989, M **$125.00**

CALRAB-Applause, Microphone (female), yellow shoes & bracelet, Third Commercial Edition, 1988, M..........**$9.00**

CALRAB-Applause, Microphone (female), yellow shoes & bracelet, Second Key Chains, 1988, sm, M **$45.00**

CALRAB-Applause, Microphone (male), left hand extended w/open palm, Third Commercial Issue, 1988, M ...**$9.00**

CALRAB-Applause, Microphone (male), left hand extended w/open palm, Second Key Chains, 1988, sm, M..**$45.00**

CALRAB-Applause, Mom, yellow hair, pink apron, Meet the Raisins Second Promotion, 1989, M **$125.00**

CALRAB-Applause, Piano, blue piano, red hair, green sneakers, Meet the Raisins First Edition, 1989, M **$35.00**

CALRAB-Applause, Saxophone, black beret, blue eyelids, Third Commercial Issue, 1988, M **$15.00**

CALRAB-Applause, Saxophone, Graduate w/gold sax, no hat, Graduate Key Chain, 1988, M **$85.00**

CALRAB-Applause, Singer (female), reddish purple shoes & bracelet, Second Commercial Issue, 1988, M........**$12.00**

CALRAB-Applause, Sunglasses, Graduate w/index finger touching face, orange glasses, Graduate Key Chains, 1988, M **$85.00**

CALRAB-Applause, Valentine, girl holding heart, Special Lover's Edition, 1988, $8.00. (Photo courtesy Larry DeAngelo)

CALRAB-Applause, Valentine, I'm Yours, boy holding heart, Special Lover's Issue, 1988, M.................................**$8.00**

CALRAB-Claymation, Sunglasses/Singer/Hands/Saxophone or Graduate on yellow base, Post Raisin Bran, 1988, ea, from $45 to...**$65.00**

Miscellaneous

Balloon, Congo line, 1987, M **$12.00**

Belt, lead singer w/mike on buckle, 1987, EX...........**$15.00**

Book, Birthday Boo Boo, 1988, EX.............................**$10.00**

Bubble Bath, Rockin' Raisin, 24-oz, M **$4.00**

Cap, 1988, EX..**$5.00**

Coloring Book, Sports Crazy, 1988, EX.........................**$5.00**

Costume, Collegeville, 1988, MIB **$10.00**

Game, California Raisin board game, MIB..................**$25.00**

Mugs, Christmas Issue, 1988, set of 4, MIB **$60.00**

Party invitations, M **$15.00**

Pin-back button, California Raisins on Ice, 1988-89 Ice Capades, Applause...**$8.00**

Postcard, Claymation/Will Vinton, 1988, M...................**$5.00**

Poster, California Raisin Band, 22x28", M **$8.00**

Sticker album, Diamond Publishing, 1988, M..............**$15.00**

Sunshield, Congo Line, 1988, EX................................**$10.00**

Video, Hip To Be Fit, M...**$18.00**

Wallet, yellow plastic, 1988, EX..................................**$20.00**

Wind-up toy, figure w/right hand up & orange glasses, 1987, MIB...**$8.00**

Wind-up toy, w/left hand up & right hand down, plastic, 1987, MIB..**$8.00**

Wristwatch, Official Fan Club, w/3 different bands, Nelsonic, 1987, MIB **$50.00**

Bank, cereal box with lid, plastic, EX, from $10.00 to $15.00.
(Photo courtesy June Moon)

Camark Pottery

Camark Pottery was manufactured in CAMden, ARKansas, from 1927 to the early 1960s. The pottery was founded by Samuel J. 'Jack' Carnes, a native of east-central Ohio familiar with Ohio's fame for pottery production. Camark's first wares were made from Arkansas clays shipped by Carnes to John B. Lessell in Ohio in early to mid-1926. Lessell was one of the associates responsible for early art pottery making. These wares consisted of Lessell's lustre and iridescent finishes based on similar ideas he pioneered at Weller and other potteries. The variations made for Camark included versions of Weller's Marengo, LaSa, and Lamar. These 1926 pieces were signed only with the 'Lessell' signature. When

Camark began operations in the spring of 1927, the company had many talented, experienced workers including Lessell's wife and step-daughter (Lessell himself died unexpectedly in December, 1926), the Sebaugh family, Frank Long, Alfred Tetzschner, and Boris Trifonoff. This group produced a wide range of art pottery finished in glazes of many types, including lustre and iridescent (signed LeCamark), Modernistic/Futuristic, crackles, and combination glaze effects such as drips. Art pottery manufacture continued until the early 1930s when emphasis changed to industrial cast-ware (molded wares) with single-color, primarily matt glazes.

In the 1940s Camark introduced its Hand Painted line by Ernst Lechner. This line included the popular Iris, Rose, and Tulip patterns. Concurrent with the Hand Painted Series (which was made until the early 1950s), Camark continued mass production of industrial castware — simple, sometimes nondescript pottery and novelty items with primarily glossy pastel glazes — until the early 1960s.

Some of Camark's designs and glazes are easily confused with those of other companies. For instance, Lessell decorated and signed a line in his lustre and iridescent finishes using porcelain (not pottery) blanks purchased from the Fraunfelter China Company. Camark produced a variety of combination glazes including the popular drip glazes (green over pink and green over mustard/brown) closely resembling Muncie's — but Muncie's clay is generally white while Camark used a cream-colored clay for its drip-glaze pieces. Muncie's are marked with a letter/number combination, and the bottoms are usually smeared with the base color. Camark's bottoms have a more uniform color application.

For more information, we recommend the *Collector's Guide to Camark Pottery* by David Edwin Gifford, Arkansas pottery historian and author of *Collector's Encyclopedia of Niloak Pottery*. (Both books are published by Collector Books.)

Advisor: Tony Freyaldenhoven (See Directory, Camark)

Artware

Ball jug, green & yellow mottled, unmarked, 5¼".......**$80.00**
Basket, Rose Green Overflow, unmarked, 6¾".........**$120.00**
Bowl, cream mottled, unmarked, 9½x4¾"................**$180.00**
Bowl, ivory, unmarked, 4½"...**$20.00**
Bowl, Orange Green Overflow, 1st block letter, 6¾"x1¾"..**$80.00**
Candlestick, frosted green, unmarked, 6"....................**$60.00**
Humidor, cigarette; blue & white stipple, 1st block letter, 5¾"...**$100.00**
Pitcher, waffle batter; gray & blue mottled, parrot handle, early circular mold mark #200, 6¼"....................**$120.00**
Sugar jar, Autumn, 1st block letter, 8".........................**$80.00**
Vase, Autumn, 1st block letter, 5½".............................**$60.00**
Vase, Black & White Overflow, 1st block letter, 6".....**$40.00**
Vase, burnt orange, 2nd Arkansas inventory sticker, S-39, F-79, 6"...**$60.00**
Vase, frosted green, 1st block letter, 5½"....................**$60.00**
Vase, gray & blue mottled, unmarked, 4¾".................**$80.00**
Vase, Pastel Blue Overflow, 1st block letter, 9"........**$140.00**

Vase, Rose Green Overflow, Deco, unmarked, 6"....**$100.00**
Vase, Royal Blue, brown Arkansas sticker, 7"..............**$25.00**

Vases: Rose with green overflow, unmarked, 4", from $40.00 to $60.00; Blue and white stipple, first block letter, 4½", from $40.00 to $60.00. (Photo courtesy David Gifford)

Hand-Painted Ware

Candlestick, Festoon of Roses, blue, unmarked, 5¼"..**$35.00**
Pitcher, Festoon of Roses, rose pink, unmarked, 6½"...**$60.00**
Planter, majolica, mold mark Camark #831K USA, 8¼".**$100.00**
Vase, Festoon of Roses, rose pink, unmarked, 8¾"....**$90.00**
Vase, lily; 2-tone overspray, mold mark #537, 3½".....**$40.00**
Vase, Morning Glory II, blue, mold mark #800-R USA, 14"...**$225.00**
Vase, 2-tone overspray, unmarked, 10¼"..................**$100.00**

Industrial Castware

TV lamp/fishbowl, polar bear, maroon, $125.00.

Basket, bird on handle, marked USA, Camark N-34, 8".**$35.00**
Figurine, horse, unmarked, 10x8"................................**$60.00**

Fishbowl holder, Wistful Cat, unmarked, 8½" **$30.00**
Planter, rooster, marked USA Camark #501, 9" **$30.00**
Vase, fan; marked USA Camark #288, 10" **$30.00**
Vase, flared top, 3-lobed bottom, marked USA #974, 6½" **$20.00**
Vase, marked USA #598, 10" **$25.00**
Wall hanging, climbing cat unmarked, 16" **$60.00**

Vase, fish form, orange and brown mottle, 8", from $200.00 to $250.00.

Cambridge Glassware

If you're looking for a 'safe' place to put your investment dollars, Cambridge glass is one of your better options. But as with any commodity, in order to make a good investment, knowledge of the product and its market is required. There are two books we would recommend for your study, *Colors in Cambridge Glass,* put out by the National Cambridge Collectors Club, and *The Collector's Encyclopedia of Elegant Glass* by Gene Florence.

The Cambridge Glass Company (located in Cambridge, Ohio) made fine quality glassware from just after the turn of the century until 1958. They made thousands of different items in hundreds of various patterns and colors. Values hinge on rarity of shape and color. Of the various marks they used, the 'C in triangle' is the most common. In addition to their tableware, they also produced flower frogs representing ladies and children and models of animals and birds that are very valuable today. To learn more about them, you'll want to read *Animals and Figural Flower Frogs of the Depression Era* by Lee Garmon and Dick Spencer (Collector Books).

Advisor: Debbie Maggard (See Directory, Elegant Glassware)

Newsletter: *The Cambridge Crystal Ball*
National Cambridge Collectors, Inc.
P.O. Box 416, Cambridge, OH 43725-0416. Dues: $17 for individual member and $3 for associate member of same household

Apple Blossom, crystal, bowl, nut; 4-footed, individual, 3" **$50.00**
Apple Blossom, crystal, candlestick, keyhole; 2-light .**$22.50**
Apple Blossom, crystal, plate, bread & butter; square..**$5.00**
Apple Blossom, crystal, tumbler, #3025, 4-oz.............**$12.00**
Apple Blossom, pink or green, bowl, fruit/oyster cocktail; #3025, 4½-oz...**$22.00**
Apple Blossom, pink or green, bowl, relish; 4-part, 12" ...**$65.00**
Apple Blossom, pink or green, stem, water; #3130, 8-oz.**$32.50**
Apple Blossom, pink or green, tumbler, #3400, footed, 9-oz..**$27.50**
Apple Blossom, yellow or amber, bowl, cereal; 6".....**$28.00**
Apple Blossom, yellow or amber, comport, tall, 7" **$60.00**
Apple Blossom, yellow or amber, stem, parfait; #1066..**$100.00**
Apple Blossom, yellow or amber, tumbler, #3130, footed, 10-oz **$25.00**
Candlelight, crystal, bowl, #3900/54, flared, 4-toed, 10" .**$60.00**
Candlelight, crystal, bowl, #3900/62, flared, 4-toed, 12" ..**$75.00**

Candlelight, crystal, cake plate, scalloped handles, #3900/35, 13½", $75.00.

Candlelight, crystal, candy jar, #3900/165, w/lid, round...**$125.00**
Candlelight, crystal, cup, #3900/17..............................**$30.00**
Candlelight, crystal, pitcher, #3400/141, Doulton......**$350.00**
Candlelight, crystal, relish tray, #3900/125, 3-part, 9".**$47.50**
Candlelight, crystal, stem, cocktail; #3111, 3-oz..........**$35.00**
Candlelight, crystal, stem, low sherbet; #3111, 7-oz..**$17.50**
Candlelight, crystal, tumbler, iced tea; #3776, 12-oz..**$30.00**
Caprice, blue or pink, bowl, relish; #124, 3-part, 8"..**$45.00**
Caprice, blue or pink, cake plate, #36, footed, 13" ..**$395.00**
Caprice, blue or pink, candlestick, double; #69, 7½", ea..**$525.00**
Caprice, blue or pink, plate, cabaret; #26, 11½".........**$70.00**
Caprice, blue or pink, tumbler, #188, flat, 2-oz...........**$65.00**
Caprice, blue or pink, tumbler, juice; #310, flat, 5-oz..**$75.00**
Caprice, blue or pink, vase, rose bowl; #235, footed, 6"...**$150.00**
Caprice, crystal, bonbon, #154, 2-handled, square, 6"..**$15.00**
Caprice, crystal, bowl, relish; #126, 4-part, oval, 12"..**$80.00**
Caprice, crystal, candlestick, keyhole; #647, 2-light, 5"..**$20.00**

Caprice, crystal, creamer, #41, lg................................$13.00

Caprice, crystal, pitcher, #183, ball shape, 80-oz......$110.00

Caprice, crystal, saucer, #17.....................................$2.50

Caprice, crystal, stem, cocktail; #3, 3½-oz.................$25.00

Caprice, crystal, tumbler, oyster cocktail; #301, blown, 4½-oz $17.50

Caprice, crystal, vase, #252, blown, 4½"...................$55.00

Chantilly, crystal, bowl, tab handle, 11"....................$35.00

Chantilly, crystal, candy box, footed, w/lid..............$145.00

Chantilly, crystal, lamp, hurricane; candlestick base.$120.00

Chantilly, crystal, plate, salad; crescent shape..........$125.00

Chantilly, crystal, stem, low sherbet; #3600, 7-oz.......$15.00

Chantilly, crystal, stem, water; #3625, 10-oz...............$25.00

Chantilly, crystal, stem, wine; #3779, 2½-oz..............$32.00

Chantilly, crystal, tumbler, juice; #3625, footed, 5-oz .$15.00

Chantilly, crystal, vase, flower; high footed, 6".........$30.00

Cleo, blue, bowl, soup; tab handle, 7½"...................$50.00

Cleo, blue, mayonnaise, footed................................$55.00

Cleo, blue, sugar bowl, footed................................$30.00

Cleo, pink, green, yellow or amber, basket, upturned sides, 2-handles, Decagon, 7"..$22.00

Cleo, pink, green, yellow or amber, bowl, finger; #3115, w/liner..$30.00

Cleo, pink, green, yellow or amber, stem, #3115, 9-oz ..$30.00

Cleo, pink, green, yellow or amber, tumbler, #3115, footed, 12-oz...$35.00

Decagon, pastel colors, bowl, cream soup; w/liner ...$20.00

Decagon, pastel colors, bowl, vegetable; round, 11"..$30.00

Decagon, pastel colors, ice tub................................$35.00

Decagon, pastel colors, plate, 2-handled, 7" $9.00

Decagon, pastel colors, stem, cocktail; 3½-oz $14.00

Decagon, pastel colors, tumbler, footed, 5-oz............$10.00

Decagon, red or blue, bowl, bonbon; 2-handled, 6¼"...$20.00

Decagon, red or blue, creamer, footed.......................$20.00

Decagon, red or blue, plate, service; 12½"...................$50.00

Decagon, red or blue, sugar bowl, scalloped edge $20.00

Diane, crystal, bowl, #3122....................................$25.00

Diane, crystal, bowl, flared, 4-footed, 10" $45.00

Diane, crystal, bowl, relish; 3-part, 6½".....................$25.00

Diane, crystal, cabinet flask..................................$265.00

Diane, crystal, decanter, footed, lg..........................$185.00

Diane, crystal, pitcher, ball shape $155.00

Diane, crystal, plate, service; 4-footed, 12"................$40.00

Diane, crystal, stem, oyster/cocktail; #3122, 4½-oz $16.00

Diane, crystal, tumbler, #3122, 2½-oz......................$30.00

Elaine, crystal, bonbon, 2-handled, footed, 6" $20.00

Elaine, crystal, bowl, ear handle, 4-footed, oval, 12"..$47.50

Elaine, crystal, bowl, pickle; 9½"............................$25.00

Elaine, crystal, cocktail icer, 2-pc $60.00

Elaine, crystal, decanter, footed, lg $195.00

Elaine, crystal, pitcher, Doulton.............................$300.00

Elaine, crystal, stem, claret; #1402, 5-oz $32.50

Elaine, crystal, stem, cocktail; #3121, 3-oz.................$24.00

Elaine, crystal, stem, water; #3121, 10-oz $25.00

Elaine, crystal, stem, wine; #3104, 3½-oz...............$100.00

Elaine, crystal, sugar bowl, individual........................$12.00

Figurine, Buddha, amber, 5½".................................$225.00

Figurine, frog, crystal satin.....................................$25.00

Figurine, heron, crystal, lg, 12"..............................$135.00

Figurine, swan, Carmen, 6½"..................................$225.00

Figurine, swan, crystal, #1 style, 10½".....................$180.00

Figurine, swan, emerald, 3" $40.00

Figurine, swan, milk glass, 6½"...............................$125.00

Flower frog, Bashful Charlotte, Dianthus, 6½"..........$150.00

Flower frog, Draped Lady, amber, 8½", $195.00.

Flower frog, Draped Lady, crystal frost, 13¼"..........$175.00

Flower frog, Draped Lady, green frost, 8½".............$125.00

Flower frog, Mandolin Lady, crystal.........................$250.00

Flower frog, Rose Lady, crystal satin, tall base, 9¾".$225.00

Flower frog, Two Kids, crystal, 9¼".........................$200.00

Flower holder, blue jay, crystal................................$135.00

Flower holder, turtle, ebony...................................$225.00

Gloria, crystal, bowl, cranberry; 3½"........................$25.00

Gloria, crystal, candlestick, 6"................................$20.00

Gloria, crystal, cup, 4-footed, square........................$25.00

Gloria, crystal, tumbler, juice; #3115, footed, 5-oz......$12.00

Gloria, green, pink or yellow, bowl, celery/relish; 5-part, 12"...$60.00

Gloria, green, pink or yellow, bowl, relish; 2-part, 2-handled, 8"...$32.00

Gloria, green, pink or yellow, plate, bread & butter; 6"..$9.00

Gloria, green, pink or yellow, stem, low sherbet; #3120, 6-oz $15.00

Gloria, green, pink or yellow, tumbler, #3130, footed, 5-oz $20.00

Imperial Hunt Scene, colors, cup..............................$55.00

Imperial Hunt Scene, colors, saucer...........................$15.00

Imperial Hunt Scene, colors, stem, water; #3085, 9-oz...$45.00

Imperial Hunt Scene, crystal, candlestick, keyhole; 2-light .$17.50

Imperial Hunt Scene, crystal, mayonnaise, w/liner.....$30.00

Imperial Hunt Scene, crystal, stem, #1402, 14-oz........$50.00

Imperial Hunt Scene, crystal, tumbler, #1402, flat, tall, 10-oz $25.00

Mt Vernon, amber or crystal, bitters bottle, #62, 2½-oz..$55.00

Mt Vernon, amber or crystal, bowl, #117, crimped, rolled edge, 12"..$32.50

Mt Vernon, amber or crystal, bowl, #135, oval, 11".....**$25.00**

Mt Vernon, amber or crystal, bowl, rose; #106, 6½"...**$18.00**

Mt Vernon, amber or crystal, cake plate, #150, footed, 10½"...**$35.00**

Mt Vernon, amber or crystal, pitcher, #90, 50-oz **$80.00**

Mt Vernon, amber or crystal, tray, celery; #79, 12".....**$20.00**

Mt Vernon, amber or crystal, tray, relish; #80, 2-part, 12"...**$30.00**

Mt Vernon, amber or crystal, tumbler, iced tea; #20, footed, 12-oz **$17.00**

Mt Vernon, amber or crystal, vase, #46, footed, 10" ...**$50.00**

Portia, crystal, bowl, celery/relish; tab handle, 3-part, 9"...**$35.00**

Portia, crystal, bowl, cranberry; 3½" **$30.00**

Portia, crystal, candlestick, 3-light, 6" **$45.00**

Portia, crystal, creamer, footed **$12.00**

Portia, crystal, plate, 2-handled, 6" **$15.00**

Portia, crystal, stem, claret; #3126, 4½-oz...................**$40.00**

Portia, crystal, stem, tall sherbet; #3124, 7-oz.............**$15.00**

Portia, crystal, stem, wine; #3121, 2½-oz.....................**$35.00**

Portia, crystal, sugar bowl, footed **$12.00**

Portia, crystal, tumbler, water; #3130, 10-oz................**$15.00**

Rosalie, amber, bowl, bouillon; 2-handled **$15.00**

Rosalie, amber, bowl, 2-handled, 10".........................**$30.00**

Rosalie, amber, plate, cheese & cracker; 11".............**$40.00**

Rosalie, amber, plate, salad; 7½" **$6.00**

Rosalie, amber, sugar shaker **$210.00**

Rosalie, blue, pink or green, bowl, bonbon; 2-handled, 5½"...**$20.00**

Rosalie, blue, pink or green, bowl, flanged, oval, 15"..**$95.00**

Rosalie, blue, pink or green, ice tub...........................**$75.00**

Rosalie, blue, pink or green, saucer.............................**$5.00**

Rose Point, crystal, ashtray, #3500/125, 3½" **$35.00**

Rose Point, crystal, basket, #3400/1182, 2-handled, 6" ...**$37.50**

Rose Point, crystal, bowl, #3500/49, handled, 5" **$35.00**

Rose Point, crystal, bowl, #3900/28, footed, tab handle, 11½"..**$80.00**

Rose Point, crystal, bowl, #3900/54, 4-tab footed, flared, 10" **$70.00**

Rose Point, crystal, bowl, #993, 4-footed, 12½" **$90.00**

Rose Point, crystal, bowl, cereal; #3500/11, 6"............**$95.00**

Rose Point, crystal, candelabrum, #1338, 3-light.........**$65.00**

Rose Point, crystal, candlestick, #3121, 7" **$75.00**

Rose Point, crystal, candlestick, keyhole; #3400/646, 1-light, 5" **$35.00**

Rose Point, crystal, coaster, #1628, 3½" **$55.00**

Rose Point, crystal, cup, punch; #488, 5-oz.................**$37.50**

Rose Point, crystal, mayonnaise, #147, 8-oz..............**$175.00**

Rose Point, crystal, pickle dish, #3400/59, 9" **$65.00**

Rose Point, crystal, pitcher, ball; #3400/38, 80-oz.....**$195.00**

Rose Point, crystal, plate, #1397, rolled edge, 13½" ...**$70.00**

Rose Point, crystal, plate, salad; #3900/22, 8" **$20.00**

Rose Point, crystal, stem, claret; #3121, 4½-oz............**$92.50**

Rose Point, crystal, stem, cocktail; #3104, 3½-oz......**$275.00**

Rose Point, crystal, stem, cordial; #7966, plain foot, 1-oz **$135.00**

Rose Point, crystal, sugar bowl, #3400/16, footed **$85.00**

Rose Point, crystal, tray, #3500/67, round, 12"..........**$175.00**

Rose Point, crystal, trivet...**$95.00**

Rose Point, crystal, tumbler, #3900/117, 5-oz.............**$50.00**

Rose Point, crystal, tumbler, water; #3121, low footed, 10-oz **$30.00**

Rose Point, crystal, vase, #274, slender, 10" **$55.00**

Rose Point, crystal, vase, keyhole; #1233, footed, 9½" ..**$85.00**

Valencia, crystal, ashtray, #3500/124, round, 3¼" **$10.00**

Valencia, crystal, bowl, finger; #1402/100, w/liner **$35.00**

Valencia, crystal, ice pail, #1402/52............................**$75.00**

Valencia, crystal, saucer, #3500/1................................**$3.00**

Valencia, crystal, stem, wine; #3500, 2½-oz **$32.00**

Valencia, crystal, tumbler, #3400/100, 13-oz **$25.00**

Wildflower, crystal, bonbon, #3400/1180, 2-handled, 5¼" .**$20.00**

Wildflower, crystal, bowl, #3900/54, 4-footed, flared, 10"..**$37.50**

Wildflower, crystal, butter dish, #3400/52, 5"............**$135.00**

Wildflower, crystal, cocktail icer, #968, 2-pc...............**$65.00**

Wildflower, crystal, plate, service; #3900/26, 4-footed, 12"...**$40.00**

Wildflower, crystal, stem, cocktail; #3121, 3-oz...........**$22.50**

Wildflower, crystal, tumbler, juice; #3121, 5-oz...........**$18.00**

Wildflower, crystal, vase, #1237, keyhole footed, 9"...**$75.00**

Rose Point, crystal, divided dish with center handle, 7½" diameter, $140.00.

Cameras

Camera collecting as an investment or hobby continues to grow in popularity, as evidenced by the interest shown in current publications and at numerous camera shows that emphasize both user and classic collectible types.

Buying at garage sales, flea markets, auctions, or estate sales are ways to add to collections, although it is rare to find an expensive classic camera offered through these outlets. However, buying at such sales to resell to dealers or collectors can be profitable if one is careful to buy quality items, not common cameras that sell for very little at best, especially when they show wear. A very old camera is not necessarily valuable, as value depends on availability and quality.

Knowing how to check out a camera or to judge quality will pay off when building a collection or when buying for resale.

Some very general guidelines follow, but for the serious buyer who intends to concentrate on cameras, there are several reference books that can be obtained. Most are rather expensive, but some provide good descriptions and/or price guidelines.

There are many distinct types of cameras to consider: large format (such as Graflex and large view cameras), medium format, early folding and box styles, 35mm single-lens-reflex (SLR), 35mm range finders, twin-lens-reflex (TLR), miniature or sub-miniature, novelty, and other types — including the more recent 'point-and-shoot' styles, Polaroids, and movie cameras. Though there is a growing interest in certain types, we would caution you against buying common Polaroids and movie cameras for resale, as there is very little market for them at this time. Most pre-1900 cameras will be found in large-format view camera or studio camera types. From the 1920s to the 1930s, folding and box-type cameras were produced, which today make good collector items. Most have fairly low values because they were made in vast numbers. Many of the more expensive classics were manufactured in the 1930 – 1955 period and include primarily the Rangefinder type of camera and those with the first built-in meters. The most prized of these are of German or Japanese manufacture, valued because of their innovative designs and great optics. The key to collecting these types of cameras is to find a mint-condition item or one still in the original box. In camera collecting, quality is the most important aspect.

This updated listing includes only a few of the various categories and models of cameras from the many thousands available and gives current average retail prices for working models with average wear. Note that cameras in mint condition or like new with their original boxes may be valued much higher, while very worn examples with defects (scratches, dents, torn covers, poor optics, nonworking meters or range finders, torn bellows, corroded battery compartments, etc.) would be valued far less. A dealer, when buying for resale, will pay only a percentage of these values, as he must consider his expenses for refurbishing, cleaning, etc., as well as sales expenses. Again, remember that quality is the key to value, and prices on some cameras vary widely according to condition.

Typical collector favorites are old Alpa, Canon, Contax, Nikon, Leica, Rolleiflex, some Zeiss-Ikon models, Exakta, and certain Voigtlander models. For information about these makes as well as models by other manufacturers, please consult the advisor.

Advisor: C.E. Cataldo (See Directory, Cameras)

Agfa, Billy, early 1930s	$15.00
Agfa, box type, 1930-50, from $10 to	$30.00
Agfa, Isolette	$20.00
Agfa, Karat-35, 1940	$35.00
Agfa, Optima, 1960s, from $20 to	$50.00
Agroflex, Seventy-five, TLR, 1949-58	$7.00

Aires, 35III, 1958	$35.00
Alpa, Standard, 1946-52, Swiss	$1,500.00
Ansco, Cadet	$5.00
Ansco, Folding, Nr 1 to Nr 10, ea, from $10 to	$40.00
Ansco, Memar, 1954-58	$20.00
Ansco, Memo, 1927 type	$100.00
Ansco, Speedex, Standard, 1950	$15.00
Ansco, Super Speedex, 3.5 lens, 1953-58	$175.00
Argus A2F, 1940	$20.00
Argus C4, 2.8 lens w/flash	$30.00
Argux C3, Black brick type, 1940-50	$10.00
Asahi Pentax, Original, 1957	$200.00
Asahiflex 1, 1st Japanese SLR	$500.00
Baldi, by Balda-Werk, 1930s	$30.00
Bell & Howell Dial-35	$50.00
Bell & Howell Foton, 1948	$1,200.00
Bolsey, B2	$20.00
Braun Paxette I, 1952	$30.00
Burke & James, Cub, 1914	$20.00
Canon A-1	$165.00
Canon AE-1	$90.00
Canon AE-1P	$150.00
Canon F-1	$225.00
Canon IIB, 1949-53	$250.00
Canon III	$275.00
Canon IV, 1950-52	$350.00
Canon J, 1939-44, from $4,500 to	$6,000.00
Canon L-1, 1956-57	$400.00
Canon P, 1958-61	$300.00

Canon Rangefinder IIF, ca 1954, $350.00.
(Photo courtesy C.E. Cataldo)

Canon S-II, Seiki-Kogaku, 1946-47, from $600 to	$800.00
Canon S-II, 1947-49	$375.00
Canon T-50	$85.00
Canon TL	$80.00
Canon TX	$60.00
Canon VT, 1956-57	$300.00
Canon 7, 1961-64	$450.00
Canonet QL17	$35.00
Ciroflex, TLR, 1940s	$30.00
Compass Camera, 1938, from $1,000 to	$1,300.00
Conley, 4x5 Folding Plate, 1905	$150.00

Contessa 35, 1950-55, from $100 to **$150.00**
Contex II or III, 1936..**$450.00**
Detrola Model D, Detroit Corp, 1938-40.....................**$20.00**
Eastman Folding Brownie Six-20.................................**$12.00**
Eastman Kodak Baby Brownie, Bakelite **$10.00**
Eastman Kodak Bantam, Art Deco, 1935-38...............**$35.00**
Eastman Kodak Box Brownie 2A **$7.00**
Eastman Kodak Box Hawkeye No 2A.............................**$8.00**
Eastman Kodak Hawkeye, plastic...................................**$8.00**
Eastman Kodak Medalist, 1941-48, from $140 to **$200.00**
Eastman Kodak No 1 Folding Pocket camera.............**$20.00**
Eastman Kodak No 3A Folding Pocket camera..........**$30.00**
Eastman Kodak Pony 135 ....**$10.00**
Eastman Kodak Retina II..**$65.00**
Eastman Kodak Retina IIa..**$90.00**
Eastman Kodak Retina IIIc, from $125 to.................**$180.00**
Eastman Kodak Retina IIIC, from $300 to.................**$550.00**
Eastman Kodak Retinette, various models, ea, from $20
    to...**$50.00**
Eastman Kodak Signet 35...**$20.00**
Eastman Kodak Signet 80...**$60.00**
Eastman Kodak 35, 1940-51...**$25.00**
Eastman Premo, many models exist, ea, from $30 to..**$200.00**
Eastman View Cameras, early 1900s, from $100 to ..**$200.00**
Edinex, by Wirgen **$30.00**
Exakta II, 1949-50..**$130.00**
Exakta VX, 1951...**$85.00**
FED 1, USSR, postwar **$75.00**
FED 1, USSR, prewar, from $100 to **$200.00**
Fujica AX-3..**$90.00**
Fujica AX-5..**$125.00**
Fujica ST-701..**$70.00**
Graflex Pacemaker Crown Graphic, various sizes, ea, from
    $80 to...**$150.00**
Graflexs Speed Graphic, various sizes, ea, from $100 to ..**$200.00**
Hasselblad 1000F, 1952-57, from $500 to **$700.00**
Herbert-George, Donald Duck, 1946 ....**$35.00**

**Kodak No. 2 Folding Pocket Brownie,
1904 – 07, $40.00.** (Photo courtesy C.E. Cataldo)

Konica Autoreflex TC, various models, ea, from $60 to ..**$90.00**
Konica FS-1 ....**$75.00**

Konica III Rangefinder, 1956-59 ....**$125.00**
Kowa H, 1963-67 ....**$35.00**
Leica II, 1963-67...**$450.00**
Leica IID, 1932-38, from $250 to **$400.00**
Leica IIIf, 1950-56, from $300 to **$500.00**
Leica M3, 1954-66, from $600 to **$1,100.00**
Mamiya-Sekor 500TL, 1966 ....**$25.00**
Mamiyaflex, TLR, 1951, from $125 to..........................**$150.00**
Mercury Model II, CX, 1945 ....**$35.00**
Minolta Autocord, TLR **$100.00**
Minolta HiMatitic Series, various models, ea, from $15
    to..**$30.00**
Minolta SR-7..**$50.00**
Minolta SRT-101..**$70.00**
Minolta SRT-202..**$90.00**
Minolta X-700...**$165.00**
Minolta XD-11, 1977...**$150.00**
Minolta XG-1, XG-7, XG-9, XG-A, ea, from $50 to.....**$80.00**
Minolta 35, early Rangefinder models, 1947-50, ea, from $300
    to...**$500.00**
Minolta-16, miniature, various models, ea, from $15 to..**$30.00**
Minox B, spy camera **$125.00**
Miranda Automex II, 1963...**$70.00**
Nikkormat (Nikon), various models, ea, from $80 to ...**$150.00**
Nikon EM **$70.00**

Nikon F, 35mm, 1971, $250.00. (Photo courtesy C.E. Cataldo)

Nikon F, various finders & meters, ea, from $150 to ..**$275.00**
Nikon FG...**$130.00**
Nikon FM **$175.00**
Nikon S Rangefinder, 1951-54, from $350 to.............**$700.00**
Nikon S2 Rangefinder, 1954-58, from $300 to...........**$500.00**
Nikon S3 Rangefinder, 1958-60, from $500 to.......**$1,200.00**
Olympus OM-1 ....**$120.00**
Olympus OM-10...**$65.00**
Olympus Pen EE, compact half-frame **$35.00**
Olympus Pen F, compact half-frame SLR, from $150 to .**$200.00**
Pax, M3, 1957..**$40.00**
Pentax K-1000...**$100.00**
Pentax ME **$75.00**
Pentax Spotmatic, many models, ea, from $50 to.....**$150.00**
Petri FT, FT-1000, FT-EE & simalar models, ea **$70.00**

Petri-7, 1961 ....$20.00
Plaubel-Makina II, 1933-39........................$200.00
Polariod, most models, ea, from $5 to...........$10.00
Polariod SX-70...$35.00
Polariod 110, 110A, 110B, ea, from $30 to $50.00
Polariod 180, 185, 190, 195, ea, from $100 to...........$250.00
Praktica FX, 1952-57 ....$40.00
Praktica Super TL...$50.00
Realist Stereo, 3.5 lens...............................$100.00
Regula, King, various models, fixed lens, ea...............$25.00
Regula, King, various models, interchangeable lens, ea ..$75.00
Ricoh Diacord 1, TLR, built-in meter, 1958...................$75.00
Ricoh KR-30...$90.00
Ricoh Singlex, 1965 ....$80.00
Rolei 35, miniature, Germany, 1966-70.....................$275.00
Rolleicord II, 1936-50, from $70 to..............$90.00
Rolleiflex Automat, 1937 model $125.00
Rolleiflex SL35M, 1978................................$100.00
Rolleiflex 3.5E $300.00
Samoca 35, 1950s.......................................$25.00
Seroco 4x5, Folding Plate, Sears, 1901, from $90 to.$135.00
Spartus Press Flash, 1939-50 ....$10.00
Taron 35, 1955 ....$25.00
Tessina, miniature, from $300 to $500.00
Tessina, miniature in colors, from $400 to $700.00
Topcon Super D, 1963-74 ....$125.00
Topcon Uni $40.00
Tower 45, Sears, w/Nikkor lens $200.00
Tower 50, Sears, w/Cassar lens $20.00
Univex-A, Univ Camera Co, 1933..................$25.00
Voigtlander Bessa, various folding models, 1931-49, ea, from $15 to..$35.00
Voigtlander Bessa, w/rangefinder, 1936.....................$140.00
Voigtlander Brilliant, TLR, metal body version, 1933..$40.00
Voigtlander Vitessa L, 1954, from $150 to.................$300.00

Voightlander Vitessa T, 1957, $200.00.
(Photo courtesy C.E. Cataldo)

Voigtlander Vito II, 1950................................$50.00
Yashica A, TLR $45.00

Yashica Electro-35, 1966..............................$25.00
Yashica FX-70..$70.00
Yashicamat 124G, TLR, from $150 to.....................$200.00
Zeiss Baldur Box Tengor, Frontar lens, 1935, from $35 to $50.00
Zeiss Ikon Juwell, 1927-39...........................$500.00
Zeiss IKon Nettar, folding Roll Film, various sizes, ea, from $20 to $35.00
Zeiss Ikon Super Ikonta B, 1937-56..........................$150.00
Zenit A, USSR...$35.00
Zorki, USSR, 1950-56 ....$50.00

Zorki - 4, USSR Rangefinder, 1956 – 73, $65.00.
(Photo courtesy C.E. Cataldo)

Candlewick Glassware

This is a beautifully simple, very diverse line of glassware made by the Imperial Glass Company of Bellaire, Ohio, from 1936 to 1982. (The factory closed in 1984.) From all explored written material found so far, it is known that Mr. Earl W. Newton brought back a piece of the French Cannonball pattern upon returning from a trip. The first Candlewick mold was derived using that piece of glass as a reference. As for the name Candlewick, it was introduced at a Wheeling, West Virginia, centennial celebration in August of 1936, appearing on a brochure promoting the crafting of 'Candlewick Quilts.'

Imperial did cuttings on Candewick; several major patterns are Floral, Valley Lily, Starlight, Princess, DuBarry, and Dots. Remember, these are *cuts* and should not be confused with etchings. (Cuts that were left unpolished were called Gray Cut — an example of this is the Dot cut.) The most popular Candlewick etching was Rose of Sharon (Wild Rose). All cutting was done on a wheel, while etching utilized etching paper and acid. Many collectors confuse these two processes. Imperial also used gold, silver, platinum, and hand painting to decorate Candlewick, and they made several items in colors.

With over 740 pieces in all, Imperial's Candlewick line was one of the leading tableware patterns in the country. Due to its popularity with collectors today, it is still number one and has the distinction of being the only single line of glassware ever to have had two books written about it, a national newsletter, and over fifteen collector clubs across the USA devoted to it exclusively.

There are reproductions on the market today — some are coming in from foreign countries. Look-alikes are often mistakenly labeled Candlewick, so if you're going to collect this pattern, you need to be well informed. Most collectors use the company mold numbers to help identify all the variations and sizes. The *Imperial Glass Encyclopedia, Vol. 1*, has a very good chapter on Candlewick. Also reference *Candlewick, The Jewel of Imperial*, by Mary Wetzel-Tomalka; and *Elegant Glassware of the Depression Era* by Gene Florence (Collector Books).

Advisor: Joan Cimini (See Directory, Imperial Glass)

Newsletter: *The Candlewick Collector* (Quarterly)
Virginia R. Scott, Editor
Subscriptions, $7.00 direct to
Connie Doll
17609 Falling Water Rd., Strongsville, OH 44136; 440-846-9610
e-mail: CWCollector@aol.com

Creamer and sugar bowl on tray, #400/29/30, $40.00.

Ashtray, eagle, #1776/1, 6½"	**$45.00**
Ashtray, heart, #400/174, 6½"	**$15.00**
Ashtray, round, #400/133, 5"	**$8.00**
Ashtray/jelly, round, #400/33, 4"	**$12.00**
Ashtray/sugar dip, individual, #400/64	**$10.00**
Basket, handled, #400/40/0, 6½"	**$40.00**
Bell, #400/179, 4"	**$90.00**
Bowl, belled, shallow, #400/104B, 14"	**$95.00**
Bowl, centerpiece; flared, #400/13B, 11"	**$70.00**
Bowl, finger; footed, no beads, #3400	**$30.00**
Bowl, fruit; #400/3F, 6"	**$12.00**
Bowl, handled, #400/113B, 12"	**$165.00**
Bowl, heart w/hand, #400/49H, 5"	**$20.00**
Bowl, nappy, 3-footed, #400/206, 4½"	**$70.00**
Bowl, relish; 2-part, oval, #400/268, 8"	**$20.00**
Bowl, round, 2-handled, #400/62B, 7"	**$18.00**
Bowl, square, #400/233, 7"	**$145.00**
Bowl, vegetable; round, #400/69B, 8½"	**$35.00**
Bowl, 3-footed, #400/183, 6"	**$70.00**
Bowl, 3-part, w/lid, #400/216, 10"	**$400.00**
Bowl, 3-toed, #400/205, 10"	**$150.00**
Bowl/compote, crimped, footed, #400/67C, 9"	**$155.00**
Butter dish, w/bead top, #400/161, ¼-lb	**$30.00**
Candle holder, flower, round, #400/40F, 6"	**$30.00**
Candle holder, mushroom, flat edge, #400/86	**$35.00**
Candle holder, 2-light, #400/100	**$20.00**
Candle holder, 3-toed, #400/207, 4½"	**$95.00**
Candy box, plain feet, w/lid, #400/140	**$315.00**
Candy box, w/lid, shallow, #400/259, 7"	**$120.00**
Coaster, 10 spokes, #400/78, 4"	**$8.00**
Compote, 1-bead stem, oval, #400/137	**$1,500.00**
Compote, 2-bead stem, #400/66B, 5½"	**$22.00**
Creamer, plain foot, beaded handle, #400/31	**$11.00**

Cup, punch; old style, #400/211, 5-oz	**$35.00**
Decanter, w/stopper, #400/163, 26-oz	**$390.00**
Fork & spoon set, #400/75	**$35.00**
Ice tub, 2-handled, #400/168, 7"	**$195.00**
Jar tower, 3-section, #400/655	**$500.00**
Ladle, mayonnaise; 2-bead handle, #400/135, 6¼"	**$14.00**
Mayonnaise set, plate, bowl w/spoon, #400/23, 3-pc	**$36.00**
Mustard jar, w/spoon, #400/156	**$48.00**
Oil, handled, bulbous bottom, #400/279, 6-oz	**$85.00**
Pitcher, Liliputian, beads on base, #400/19, 16-oz	**$300.00**
Pitcher, plain, #400/424, earlier, 80-oz	**$75.00**
Plate, oval, #400/124, 12½"	**$85.00**
Plate, salad; #400/3D, 7"	**$10.00**
Plate, salad; oval, #400/38, 9"	**$45.00**
Plate, torte; #400/17D, 14"	**$45.00**
Plate, triangular, #400/266, 7½"	**$325.00**
Plate, w/indent, #400/50, 8"	**$15.00**
Plate, 2-handled, #400/145D, 12"	**$30.00**
Plate, 2-handled, #400/62D, 8½"	**$14.00**
Plate, 2-handled, #400/72D, 10"	**$16.00**
Platter, oval, #400/124D, 13"	**$90.00**
Salt & pepper shakers, individual, #400/109, pr	**$18.00**
Salt dip, #400/61, 2"	**$12.00**
Sauce boat, oval w/plate, #400/169	**$135.00**
Stem, claret; #3400, 5-oz	**$45.00**
Stem, cocktail; #3400, 4-oz	**$15.00**
Stem, cocktail; #3800, 4-oz	**$25.00**
Stem, cordial; #400/190, 1-oz	**$90.00**
Stem, iced tea/hi-ball; #4000, 12-oz	**$25.00**
Stem, low sherbet; #3800	**$25.00**
Stem, sherbet; #400/190, 5-oz	**$14.00**
Stem, water goblet; #3800, 9-oz	**$40.00**
Sugar bowl, plain footed, beaded handle, #400/31	**$11.00**
Tray, fruit; center handled, #400/68F, 10½"	**$160.00**
Tray, handled, #400/113D, 14"	**$45.00**
Tray, upturned handles, #400/42E, 5½"	**$18.00**
Tumbler, #400/19, 10-oz	**$10.00**
Tumbler, cocktail; footed, #400/19, 3-oz	**$20.00**
Tumbler, footed, #3400, 9-oz	**$18.00**
Tumbler, old fashioned; #400/18, 7-oz	**$45.00**
Tumbler, 1-bead stem, #3800, 12-oz	**$30.00**
Vase, beaded top, #400/198, 6" dia	**$295.00**

Vase, bud; bead foot, #400/28C, 8½".............................$75.00
Vase, fan; beaded handled, #400/87F, 8" $35.00
Vase, footed, #400/193, 10"..$350.00
Vase, lily bowl, 4-toed, #400/74J, 7" $175.00

Vinegar cruet, #400/166, six-ounce, $85.00; Oil cruet, #400/164, four-ounce, $45.00; Oval tray, #400/29, 6½", from $20.00 to $25.00.

Candy Containers

Most of us can recall buying these glass toys as a child, since they were made well into the 1960s. We were fascinated by the variety of their shapes then, just as collectors are today. Looking back, it couldn't have been we were buying them for the candy, though perhaps as a child those tiny sugary balls flavored more with the coloring agent than anything else were enough to satisfy our 'sweet tooth.'

Glass candy containers have been around since our country's centennial celebration in 1876 when the first two, the Liberty Bell and the Independence Hall, were introduced. Since then they have been made in hundreds of styles, and some of them have become very expensive. The leading manufacturers were in the east — Westmoreland, Victory Glass, J.H. Millstein, Crosetti, L.E. Smith, Jack Stough, T.H. Stough, and West Bros. made perhaps 90% of them — and collectors report finding many in the Pennsylvania area. Most are clear, but you'll find them in various other colors as well.

If you're going to deal in candy containers, you'll need a book that will show you all the variations available. A very comprehensive book, *Collector's Guide to Candy Containers* by Douglas M. Dezso, J. Leon Poirier, and Rose D. Poirier, was released early in 1998. D&P numbers in our listings refer to that book. Published by Collector Books, it is a must for beginners as well as seasoned collectors. Other references are *The Compleat American Glass Candy Containers Handbook* by Eilkelberner and Agadjaninian (revised by Adele Bowden) and Jenny Long's *Album of Candy Containers, Vol. 1* and *Vol. 2,* published in 1978 – 83, now out of print.

Because of their popularity and considerable worth, many of the original containers have been reproduced. Beware of any questionable glassware that has a slick or oily touch. Among those that have been produced are Amber Pistol, Auto, Carpet Sweeper, Chicken on Nest, Display Case, Dog, Drum Mug, Fire Engine, Independence Hall, Jackie Coogan, Kewpie, Mail Box, Mantel Clock, Mule and Waterwagon, Peter Rabbit, Piano, Rabbit Pushing Wheelbarrow, Rocking Horse, Safe, Santa, Santa's Boot, Station Wagon, and Uncle Sam's Hat. Others are possible.

Our values are given for candy containers that are undamaged, in good original paint, and complete (with all original parts and closure). Repaired or repainted containers are worth much less.

See also Christmas; Easter; Halloween.

Advisor: Doug Dezso (See Directory, Candy Containers)

Club/Newsletter: *The Candy Gram*
Candy Container Collectors of America
Joyce L. Doyle
P.O. Box 426, North Reading, MA 01864-0426

Airplane, TMA 44, 4 windows ea side, knob on top to attach red cardboard wings, D&P #86, ca 1939, 4" L, from $120 to..**$145.00**
Apothecary Jar, 16-point sunburst in bottom of base, D&P #113, ca 1940, 5¼x2", from $120 to....................**$125.00**
Boat, Cruiser; #s 1-14 marked in circle in cockpit, JH Millstein Co, D&P #102, ca 1945, 1⅝x4¾", from $20 to.....**$40.00**
Bulldog w/Oblong Base, Push-in closure w/Contents... Stough Co Patented, Jeannette PA, D&P #17, ca 1945, 3¾", from $40 to..**$50.00**
Bus, Greyhound w/Luggage Rack, embossed greyhounds ea side, Victory Glass Co, D&P #151, 1930s, 1⅝x5x1½", from $275 to..**$325.00**
Candelabrum, nickel steel tops, 8 holes in top, marked Van Style...USA..., D&P #317, ca 1920, 1¾x2⅜" dia base, from $35 to...**$45.00**
Car, Coupe - Long Hood w/Tin Wheels; thick roof, no window on back, lanterns ea side, D&P #160, 3x5¼x2", from $150 to...**$175.00**
Car, Miniature Streamlined; open base, 3-section (center for candy), Victory Glass, D&P #173, ca 1945, 4⅝" L, from $20 to...**$30.00**
Charlie Chaplin by Curved Barrel, Geo Borgfeldt & Co NY..., D&P #195, ca 1915, from $85 to **$115.00**
Chick, Baby Standing; Victory Glass Co, D&P #7, ca 1922, 3⅜x2¼x1⅜" oblong base, unmarked, from $100 to...**$125.00**
Elephant, GOP; gray body w/many details, oblong base, Victory Glass Co, D&P #43, ca 1924, 2¾x3⅛", from $175 to..**$250.00**
Gun, Beaded Border Grip; horizontal ribs on chamber, 5 slanted lines on ea side, Patented, D&P #390, 4⅛", from $18 to...**$25.00**
Gun, Stough's 1939 Pat Pending; 5 slanted lines on firing chamber, red tin closure, D&P #400, ca 1939, 4⅛", from $18 to.**$25.00**

Horn, Musical Clarinet 55, silver tin screw cap mounted to red & white cardboard tube, D&P #451, ca 1950, from $25 to...**$35.00**

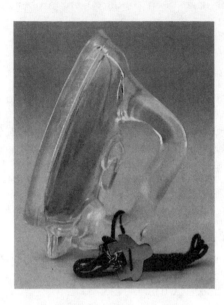

Iron, Electric, #305, 4½" L, from $50.00 to $60.00. (Photo courtesy Doug Dezso, J. Leon Poirier, and Rose D. Poirier)

Jack O'Lantern, Slant Eyes; wide vertical panels, screw cap, wire bail, D&P #265, from $175 to.......................**$225.00**

Lamp, Kerosene w/Swizzle Stick; screw-on chimney, gold-tone cap, Swizzle Stick candy candle holder, D&P #333, from $25 to..**$50.00**

Lamp, Metal Shade; 2⅛" dark blue metal shade held by white screw cap, D&P #335, 1970s, 3⅜x1¾", from $40 to .**$60.00**

Lantern, Pewter Top - Pewter Base, plastic shade, reflector & base, D&P #360, ca 1946, 4¼x5¼", from $25 to..**$35.00**

Little Doggie in the Window, whistle in hat, D&P #30, ca 1958, 3x1⅝x1¼", from $30 to................................**$50.00**

Mug, Eagle; embossed eagle front w/lacing surround, slotted tin push-in, D&P #431, ca 1909, 2½x2⅝", from $200 to..**$250.00**

Mug, Victory Glass Co; flat top loop handle w/curlicue at base, red metal screw-on shaker cap, D&P #434, 4", from $20 to..**$25.00**

Nurser, Plain; push-in disk under rubber nipple, TH Stough, D&P #123, 1954-57, 2⅝x1" dia, from $25 to **$35.00**

Passenger Airplane, tin screw-on nose cap, unpainted tin propeller, D&P #80, 5x5x4¾", from $400 to.......**$475.00**

Peter Rabbit, 3-leaf clover on right between legs, Jeannette PA...Millstein Co, D&P #60, 1948, 6¼", from $25 to **$30.00**

Rabbit w/Feet Together, Round Nose; tin screw-on closure, USA, D&P #67, 5¼x2⅛x2½", from $80 to..........**$100.00**

Santa w/Skis, red plastic w/green glued-on skis, open bag on back, Sears Roebuck, D&P #287, ca 1947, 4½", from $15 to..**$20.00**

Tank, Man in Turret; window on ea side; embossed treads, brown or olive driver's head, D&P #412, ca 1942, 4¼", from $50 to..**$60.00**

Telephone, Stough's Ringed Base; black wood receiver, screw cap w/bracket that holds receiver, D&P #247, 3⅝", from $35 to..**$45.00**

Telephone, Cog in Neck, #200, 4½", from $60.00 to $70.00. (Photo courtesy Doug Dezso, J. Leon Poirier, and Rose D. Poirier)

Top, Sm; solid point, 3 embossed rings, tin cap closure w/post, spring-loaded winder, D&P #443, ca 1929, 2⅜", from $100 to..**$125.00**

Village City Garage, red brick walls, white foundation, driver in doorway, D&P #136, 2⅞x2¾x1¾", from $125 to....**$150.00**

Cape Cod by Avon

You can't walk through any flea market or mall now without seeing a good supply of this lovely ruby red glassware. It was made by Wheaton Glass Co. and sold by Avon from the 1970s until it was discontinued in 1997, after a gradual phasing-out process that lasted for approximately two years. The small cruet and tall candlesticks, for instance, were filled originally with one or the other of their fragrances, the wine and water goblets were filled with scented candle wax, and the dessert bowl with guest soap. Many 'campaigns' featured accessory tableware items such as plates, cake stands, and a water pitcher. Though still plentiful, dealers tell us that interest in this glassware is on the increase, and we expect values to climb as supplies diminish.

Advisor: Debbie Coe (See Directory, Cape Cod)

Bell, Hostess; marked Christmas 1979, 6½".................**$22.50**

Bell, hostess; unmarked, 1979-80, 6½" **$17.50**

Bowl, dessert; 1978-90, 5"...**$14.50**

Bowl, rimmed soup; 1991, 7½" **$24.50**

Bowl, vegetable; marked Centennial Edition 1886-1986, 8¾"..**$39.50**

Bowl, vegetable; unmarked, 1986-90, 8¾" **$29.50**

Box, heart form, w/lid, 1989-90, 4" wide **$18.00**

Butter dish, w/lid, 1983-84, ¼-lb, 7" L.......................**$22.50**

Cake knife, red plastic handle, wedge-shaped blade, Regent Sheffield, 1981-84, 8" **$18.00**

Candlestick, 1975-80, 8¾", ea **$12.50**

Candlestick, 1983-84, 2½", ea **$9.75**

Candy dish, 1987-90, 3½x6" dia $19.50
Christmas ornament, 6-sided, marked Christmas 1990, 3¼" $10.00
Creamer, footed, 1981-84, 4"..$12.50
Cruet, oil; w/stopper, 1975-80, 5-oz...........................$12.50
Cup & saucer, 15th anniversary, marked 1975-1990 on cup, 7-oz..$24.50
Cup & saucer, 1990-93, 7-oz...$19.50
Decanter, w/stopper, 1977-80, 16-oz, 10½" $20.00
Goblet, champagne; 1991, 8-oz, 5¼" $14.50
Goblet, claret; 1992, 5-oz, 5¼".....................................$12.50
Goblet, water; 1976-90, 9-oz..$12.50
Mug, pedestal foot, 1982-84, 6-oz, 5".........................$12.50
Napkin ring, 1989-90, 1¾" dia $9.50
Pie plate, server, 1992-93, 10¾" dia $28.00
Pitcher, water; footed, 1984-85, 60-oz.........................$59.00
Plate, bread & butter; 1992-93, 5½" $9.50
Plate, cake; pedestal foot, 1991, 3½x10¾" dia $50.00
Plate, dessert; 1980-90, 7½"...$9.50
Plate, dinner; 1982-90, 11" $25.00
Platter, oval, 1986, 13"...$39.50
Relish, rectangular, 2-part, 1985-86, 9½"....................$19.50
Salt & pepper shakers, marked May 1978, ea $9.50
Salt & pepper shakers, unmarked, 1978-80, ea $6.00
Sauce boat, footed, 1988, 8" L $29.50
Sugar bowl, footed, 1980-83, 3½" $12.50
Tidbit tray, 2-tiered (7" & 10" dia), 1987, 9¾" $49.50
Tumbler, straight-sided, footed, 1988, 8-oz, 3½"..........$9.50
Tumbler, straight-sided, 1990, 12-oz, 5½"...................$12.50
Vase, footed, 1985, 8"..$24.00
Wine goblet, 1977-80, 3-oz, 4½".....................................$2.50

Candle holder, hurricane type with clear chimney, 1985, $42.00.

Cardinal China Company

This was the name of a distributing company who had their merchandise made to order and sold it through a chain of showrooms and outlet stores in several states from the late 1940s through the 1950s. (Although they made some of their own pottery early on, we have yet to find out just what they themselves produced.) They used their company name to mark cookie jars (some of which were made by the American Bisque Company), novelty wares and kitchen items, many of which you'll see as you make your flea market rounds. *The Collector's Encyclopedia of Cookie Jars* by Joyce and Fred Roerig (Collector Books) shows a page of their jars, and more can be seen in *American Bisque* by Mary Jane Giacomini (Schiffer).

See also Cookie Jars.

Cheese plate, w/mouse atop slab of cheese, 13x10"..$15.00
Dresser dish, Doxie-dog...$18.00
Egg dish, rooster in bright pastels, green painted scallops at rim, 2 sm & 1 lg well, 6" dia $18.00
Egg timer, windmill, 4½"...$45.00
Flower holder, turquoise on white, doughnut shape, 7" $8.00
Measuring spoon holder, cottage w/peaked roof, applied thermometer $15.00
Measuring spoon holder, flowerpot shape, plain (not basketweave) base $10.00
Measuring spoon holder, flowerpot shape w/basketweave base, w/spoons...$15.00

Measuring spoon holder, Measure Boy, $25.00.

Measuring spoon holder, windowsill planter shape w/plastic spoons as flowers $15.00
Ring holder, elephant figural, shamrocks, flat back w/hole for hanging...$15.00
Salt & pepper shakers, Chinese man & lady, green & yellow, pr..$22.00
Scissors holder, nest w/chicken figural $25.00
Shrimp boats, 4¾" L w/cardboard sail on wood pole, various colors, set of 4 ....$75.00
Spoon rest, double sunflower form.............................$10.00
String holder, nest w/chicken figural $30.00
Teabag holder, single 5-petal flower face...................$10.00

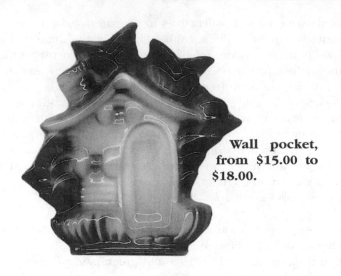

Wall pocket, from $15.00 to $18.00.

Carnival Chalkware

From about 1910 until sometime in the 1950s, winners of carnival games everywhere in the United States were awarded chalkware figures of Kewpie dolls, the Lone Ranger, Hula girls, comic characters, etc. The assortment was vast and varied. The earliest were made of plaster with a pink cast. They ranged in size from about 5" up to 16".

They were easily chipped, so when it came time for the carnival to pick up and move on, they had to be carefully wrapped and packed away, a time consuming, tedious chore. When stuffed animals became available, concessionists found that they could simply throw them into a box without fear of damage, and so ended an era.

Today the most valuable of these statues are those modeled after Disney characters, movie stars, and comic book heroes.

Chalkware figures are featured in *The Carnival Chalk Prize, Vols I* and *II,* and *A Price Guide to Chalkware/Plaster Carnival Prizes*, all written by Thomas G. Morris. Along with photos, descriptions, and values, Mr. Morris has also included a fascinating history of carnival life in America.

Advisor: Tom Morris (See Directory, Carnival Chalkware)

Army Sgt Bilco, bank, ca 1945-50, 12" **$75.00**
Bear, bank, marked Hunny Bear, Walt Disney Productions, 1940-50, 10½"...**$65.00**
Boy cook, apron & cook's hat, marked What's Cookin', JY Jenkins, ca 1949, 10"...**$70.00**
Boy tramp, holding a bag & stick, ca 1935-45, 11½" .**$45.00**
Bugs Bunny standing behind tree, marked What's Up Doc, ca 1940-50, 11½"..**$70.00**
Captain Marvel (figure identical to Superman), yellow & red, ca 1940-50, 14½"...**$135.00**
Cat & fishbowl, marked Universal Statuary, marked 1948, 11x4½" **$95.00**
Cow (comical), lg udder, marked Edw Botman, ca 1945-50, 6½"..**$45.00**

Donald Duck's nephew standing on drum w/coin in his hand, ca 1940-50, 10½" **$75.00**
Elephant, standing, flat back, ca 1940-50, 6½"...........**$25.00**
Ferdinand the Bull, sitting, ca 1940-50, 6½"...............**$45.00**
Girl w/lg sombrero, hands in jacket pockets, 1940-50, 14" **$85.00**
Hawk on perch, ca 1940-50, 8" **$35.00**
Henry (comic strip character), bald head, hands in pockets, ca 1940-50, 15"...**$95.00**
Horse, rearing, flat back, 1940-45, 6½"........................**$20.00**
Horse head, flat back, 1940-50, 6¾" **$25.00**
Hula girl, 1 hand behind head, add-on skirt, marked Danesi Co Toronto, 1948, 12" **$135.00**
Humpty Dumpty w/big smile sitting on fence, ca 1940-50, 11" **$45.00**
Jiminy Cricket (marked as such), Disney, ca 1940-50, 13½"...**$95.00**
Lamb/sheep, flat back, 1935-40, sm, up to 4" **$8.00**
Li'l Abner, standing w/1 hand behind back, ca 1935-45, 15½"..**$135.00**

Lone Ranger, bright paint, 16", $95.00.

Majorette holding baton, ca 1940-50, 15¼" **$55.00**
Miss America (as marked on front of base), 1940-50, 15¾" **$95.00**
Monkey sitting & scratching head, several variations, ca 1940-50, 12¼"..**$50.00**
Navy sailor at ease, ca 1935-45, 12¼".........................**$95.00**
Nude, reclining, may be marked Rosemead Statuary, ca 1940-50, 5½"...**$45.00**
Owl standing on stack of books, bank, ca 1945-50, 16"..**$65.00**
Pinocchio, standing w/hands in pockets, feather in hat, ca 1940-50, 11½"..**$120.00**
Porky Pig, standing, wearing sailor cap, ca 1940-50, 11"..**$65.00**
Rabbit, standing w/carrot, flat back, 1945-50, 5½" **$12.00**

Cat Collectibles

Cat collectibles continue to grow in popularity as cats continue to dominate the world of household pets. Cat memorabilia can be found in almost all categories, and this allows for collections to grow rapidly! Most cat lovers/collectors are attracted to all items and to all breeds, though some do specialize. Popular categories include Siamese, black cats, Kitty Cucumber, Kliban, cookie jars, teapots, books, plates, postcards, and Louis Wain.

Because cats are found throughout the field of collectibles and antiques, there is some 'crossover' competition among collectors. For example: Chessie, the C&O Railroad cat, is collected by railroad and advertising buffs; Felix the Cat, board games, puppets, and Steiff cats are sought by toy collectors. A Weller cat complements a Weller pottery collection just as a Royal Doulton Flambe cat fits into a Flambe porcelain collection.

Since about 1970 the array and quality of cat items have made the hobby explode. And, looking back, the first half of the twentieth century offered a somewhat limited selection of cats — there were those from the later Victorian era, Louis Wain cats, Felix the Cat, the postcard rage, and the kitchen-item black cats of the 1950s. But prior to 1890, cat items were few and far between, so a true antique cat (100-years old or more) is scarce, much sought after, and when found in mint condition, pricey. Examples of such early items would be original fine art, porcelains, and bronzes.

There are several 'cat' books available on today's market; if you want to see great photos representing various aspects of 'cat' collecting, you'll enjoy *Cat Collectibles* by Pauline Flick, *Antique Cats for Collectors* by Katharine Morrison McClinton, *American Cat-alogue* by Bruce Johnson, and *The Cat Made Me Buy It* and *The Black Cat Made Me Buy It*, both by Muncaster and Yanow.

See also Black Cats; Character Collectibles; Cookie Jars; Holt Howard; Lefton.

Advisor: Karen Shanks (See Directory, Cat Collectibles)

Newsletter: *Cat Talk*
Cat Collectors
Karen Shanks, President
PO Box 150784, Nashville, TN 37215
615-297-7403; www.catcollectors.com; email: musiccitykitty@yahoo.com
Subscription $20 per year US or $27 Canada.

Basket, wicker; cat woven in brown & tan, red button eyes, wooden ears, 7¼" $22.50
Bottle, Felina Fluffles, white cat w/blue skirt, holding fan, Avon, 1976, 5¼" $12.00
Bottle, perfume; blue w/embossed white kitten, metal, made in China $60.00
Candy dish, crystal, 9" $60.00

Figurine, black cat on overstuffed white w/floral chair, ceramic, Katz & Co, England, 5¼x5½" $25.00
Figurine, brass cat on 7" square marble base, 11" $150.00
Figurine, kitten in cream pitcher, licking 1 paw, pewter, marked 1983 Hudson Pewter USA, 1½" $24.00
Figurine, Siamese lying down, dark cream/black, Made in Japan label, 3¾" $10.00
Figurine, white cat in front of old-time radio, on oval base, coldcast porcelain, Border Fine Arts, 1987, 4¼" .. $65.00
Figurines, turquoise, long hair, ceramic, Made in China paper label, 6½", pr $38.00
Matchbox holder, metal w/cat atop, detailed, 2½x1½x3" $50.00
Pillow, orange tabby w/green background; reverse, gray tabby w/wine background, blue border w/white flowers, 16" square $12.50
Plaque, black cats w/colorful row of houses, pink background, 11¾x5½" $6.00

Plate, Playmates, Bradford Exchange, Velvet Paws Series, 1991, 9½", $35.00.
(Photo courtesy Marbena Fyke)

Salt & pepper shakers, royal blue w/pink & green floral detail & applied pink flowers at neck, 2½", pr $10.50
Tray, black w/long-haired white cat w/blue eyes, gold outlines, 12x18" $45.00

Character Cats

Cat in the Hat, bookends, cast iron, Midwest of Cannon Falls, MIB $55.00
Cat in the Hat, doll, plush, Mattel & Arcotoys, 1997, 39", NM $45.00
Cat in the Hat, jack-in-the-box, plays For He's a Jolly Good Fellow, Mattel, 1970, EX $105.00
Cat in the Hat, light shade, white glass w/painted scenes, 15" dia, NM $105.00
Cat in the Hat, model kit, Revell #Z-2000, 1959, NM (VG box) $285.00
Cat in the Hat, store banner, vinyl, 1995, 16x36", NM .. $80.00
Cat in the Hat, tea set, porcelain, Perjinkities Division of Midwest, 5-pc $55.00

Cat in the Hat, water globe, Whozit Friends Come To Visit, musical, 6½", MIB..................................**$50.00**

Cheshire Cat, bank, ceramic figure lying down w/lg toothy grin, muted gold glaze, unmarked, 4½x5¾", EX .**$85.00**

Chessie, cup & saucer, both white w/dark blue stripe, Chesapeake & Ohio Railway, Syracuse China....**$125.00**

Chessie, figurine, porcelain, limited edition for Silver Anniversary, 1988, 6x5"...............................**$85.00**

Chessie, plate, Sleep Like a Kitten, 50th Anniversary, 1983, 9"..**$110.00**

Chessie, pocketknife, 2-blade, Zippo, MIB..................**$55.00**

Chessie, valentine card, kitten sleeping in heart, red w/printed paper lace background, 9¼x7¼" **$85.00**

Felix the Cat, apron, full-body figure on gray background, Determined Products, 1990, adult size, EX..........**$30.00**

Felix the Cat, ashtray, on pedestal, black metal, Felix the Cat Productions, 1990, 20", EX....................**$60.00**

Felix the Cat, board game, Felix the Cat Game, Milton Bradley, 1960, G...**$35.00**

Felix the Cat, color & wipe-off book, 1958, EX..........**$32.00**

Felix the Cat, pencil box, American Pencil Company, 1935, EX...**$40.00**

Felix the Cat, Pep pin, shows Felix holding fish **$85.00**

Felix the Cat, salt & pepper shakers, ceramic, 1 black, 1 white, 4", MIB **$35.00**

Felix the Cat, Soaky, red w/blue lettering on chest, Colgate, ca 1960s, 11", M on original stand **$70.00**

Felix the Cat, watch, antique style w/black leather band, Fossil, 1993, EXIB **$50.00**

Figaro, book, figural, cloth, Dean's Rag Books, Great Britain, WDP, ca 1970s, 5½x7½", EX.......................**$35.00**

Figaro, planter, Figaro stands beside planter, stamped Made in Occupied Japan, 3½x3½", EX.......................**$50.00**

Figaro, plush figurine, Disney Classics, ca 1980s, 5", MIB...**$15.50**

Garfield, bank, bowling, Enesco, NM, from $35 to **$45.00**

Garfield, bank, sitting in green chair wearing Santa hat, Enesco, 1981, NM (VG box) **$45.00**

Garfield, bedding set, 2 pillow shams/1 full-size skirt/dust ruffle/1 top sheet, light blue w/Garfield on half moon, EX..**$45.00**

Garfield, bookends, Garfield on 1, Odie on the other, both sleeping, ceramic, Enesco, 1981, 4¼x4¼x5", pr ..**$45.00**

Garfield, Christmas Village Courthouse, bisque, Danbury Mint, 1990s, 9x9", MIB..................................**$40.00**

Garfield, figure, sitting, plush, Dakin, w/tag, 1981, 9½x10½", EX..**$6.00**

Garfield, figure dressed in sheep's clothes, w/bell & staff, Dakin, 1981, 10", M **$36.00**

Garfield, figurine, as Rodney Dangerfield, white base w/I Get No Respect in black letters, Enesco, 1981, 4½x3".**$50.00**

Garfield, figurine, Garfield & Arlene, Where Have You Been All My Life?, Enesco, 1980s, 4¼" **$60.00**

Garfield, figurine, Let the Honeymoon Begin, Enesco, 1980, M (VG box) **$40.00**

Garfield, figurine, pirate w/peg leg, sword, gold tooth & pirate hat, PVC, 1980s, 2½", EX............................**$36.00**

Garfield, figurine, The Mad Telemarketer, I Quit on base, holds phone w/ripped cord, Enesco, 1978, 3x4".**$36.00**

Garfield, figurine, wearing striped tie, To Dad...From a Chip Off the Old Block, Enesco, 1980s, 4"....................**$35.00**

Garfield, fishbowl (in belly), plastic, 18", M................**$45.00**

Garfield, lamp w/shade, figural bottom w/white shade w/Party Animal scenes, Prestigeline, 1980s, 14", NMIB **$50.00**

Garfield, music box, The Entertainer, plays piano w/Arlene on top, animated, Enesco, NM **$36.00**

Garfield, nodder, Wacky Wobbler, 7½", EXIB **$27.00**

Garfield, plate, Danbury Mint, Dear Diary Series, 1991, 8½", $35.00.

Garfield, plate, One Dog Open Sleigh, Danbury Mint, w/styrofoam container, EX..**$50.00**

Garfield, plate, sleeping in paper bag, Today I Look for a New Condo, Danbury Mint, w/23k gold decor, 1990, 8" **$60.00**

Garfield, plate, Winter Wonderland, Danbury Mint, w/styrofoam container, EX **$42.00**

Garfield, plush window sticker, 4 suction cups, 1 on ea arm & leg, Dakin, w/tag, 1981, 6½x7½" **$4.00**

Kitty Cucumber, carousel, 4 figures ride on horses, plays Carousel Waltz, Schmid, 1989, 5½x8¼", NMIB **$70.00**

Kitty Cucumber, Ferris wheel, animated, musical, 1991, MIB **$135.00**

Kitty Cucumber, figurine, bride & groom, Schmid, 3x4", EX **$38.00**

Kitty Cucumber, figurine, Kitty & Ellie at tea party, Schmid, MIB **$60.00**

Kitty Cucumber, figurine, Kitty as witch w/broom, 1995, MIB **$45.00**

Kitty Cucumber, figurine, Kitty gathering flowers, Schmid, MIB **$38.00**

Kitty Cucumber, figurine, Priscilla feeding ducks, Schmid, MIB **$32.00**

Kitty Cucumber, ornament, Maypole Dance................**$36.00**

Kliban, apron, mice & cheese printed on white, EX ..**$20.00**

Kliban, creamer, red bow on tail, Sigma Tastetester, 7x4¾", EX **$25.00**

Kliban, cup, graniteware w/cat on roller skates, red trim, signed B Kliban on bottom, 2¾", EX.....................$22.00
Kliban, doll, Cat in Hat, Knickerbocker, 1980s, 5".......$12.50
Kliban, jigsaw puzzle, 100-pc, 7x7", MIB.....................$10.00
Kliban, mug, Peace, Santa peeking in window, ceramic..$12.50
Kliban, paperweight, Aloha Cat, steel..........................$8.00
Kliban, pillow, stuffed figure, 22".............................$22.50
Kliban, pillow cases, wearing red sneakers, pr, EX....$30.00
Kliban, poster, Momcat, 1977, 24x18".......................$15.00
Kliban, rubber stamp, Butterfly Cats $15.00
Kliban, sheet, flannel, flat, twin size $25.00
Kliban, sheets (1 fitted/1 flat), full size, 2-pc set, M...$45.00
Kliban, T-shirt, Florida Yacht Cats, SS Feliner $35.00
Kliban, T-shirt, Sashimi, w/fish & chopsticks $20.00
Kliban, tumbler, plastic, 4½", EX...............................$29.00

Kliban, bank, wearing red sneakers, 1979, 6½", $85.00.
(Photo courtesy Marbena Fyke)

Cat-Tail Dinnerware

Cat-Tail was a dinnerware pattern popular during the late '20s until sometime in the '40s. So popular, in fact, that ovenware, glassware, tinware, even a kitchen table was made to coordinate with it. The dinnerware was made primarily by Universal Potteries of Cambridge, Ohio, though a catalog from Hall China circa 1927 shows a three-piece coffee service, and others may have produced it as well. It was sold for years by Sears Roebuck and Company, and some items bear a mark that includes their name.

The pattern is unmistakable: a cluster of red cattails (usually six, sometimes one or two) with black stems on creamy white. Shapes certainly vary; Universal used at least three of their standard mold designs, Camwood, Old Holland, Laurella, and possibly others. Some Cat-Tail pieces are marked Wheelock on the bottom. (Wheelock was a department store in Peoria, Illinois.)

If you're trying to decorate a '40s vintage kitchen, no other design could afford you more to work with. To see many of the pieces that are available and to learn more about the line, read *The Collector's Encyclopedia of American Dinnerware* by Jo Cunningham (Collector Books).

Advisors: Barbara and Ken Brooks (See Directory, Dinnerware)

Bowl, footed, 9½"...$20.00
Bowl, mixing; 8"...$23.00
Bowl, Old Holland shape, marked Wheelock, 6" $7.00
Bowl, soup; 8"...$15.00
Bowl, straight sides, 6¼"..$12.00
Bowl, 6¼"..$7.00
Butter dish, 1-lb..$50.00
Cake cover & tray, tinware $35.00
Cake plate, Mt Vernon..$25.00
Canister set, tin, 4-pc..$60.00
Casserole, w/lid..$30.00
Coffeepot, electric..$150.00
Coffeepot, 3-pc...$70.00
Cookie jar, from $100 to...$135.00
Cracker jar, barrel shape, from $75 to.........................$85.00
Creamer..$20.00
Cup & saucer, from $6 to...$10.00
Custard cup...$9.00
Gravy boat, from $18 to...$25.00
Jug, ball; ceramic-topped cork stopper.......................$37.50

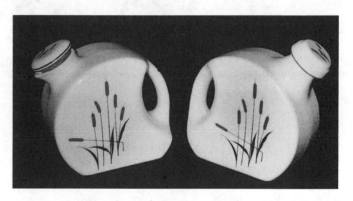

Jugs, canteen (note different style caps), $38.00 each. (Photo courtesy Barbara and Ken Brooks)

Jug, refrigerator; w/handle...$38.00
Jug, side handle, cork stopper....................................$38.00
Jug, 1-qt, 6"..$25.00
Match holder, tinware...$35.00
Pickle dish/gravy boat liner.......................................$20.00
Pie plate..$30.00
Pie server, hole in handle for hanging, marked Universal Potteries $25.00
Pitcher, glass w/ice lip, from $100 to..........................$125.00
Plate, chop..$35.00
Plate, dinner; Laurella shape, from $15 to...................$20.00
Plate, salad or dessert; round....................................$6.50
Plate, square, 7¼"..$7.00
Platter, oval, 11½", from $15 to $20.00
Platter, round, tab handle, 11"...................................$30.00
Salad set (fork, spoon & bowl), from $50 to................$60.00
Salt shaker, Salt or Pepper, glass, made by Tipp, lg, ea, from $25 to..$35.00

Saucer, from $3 to..$6.00
Saucer, Old Holland shape, marked Wheelock.............$6.00
Scales, metal...$37.00
Shaker set (salt, pepper, flour & sugar shakers), glass, on red
    metal tray, made by Tipp, from $60 to.................$65.00
Stack set, 3-pc w/lids, from $35 to.................................$40.00
Sugar bowl, w/lid, from $20 to $25.00
Tablecloth...$90.00
Teapot, 4-cup...$35.00
Tray, for batter set $75.00
Tumbler, juice; glass $30.00
Tumbler, marked Universal Potteries, scarce, from $65
    to $70.00
Tumbler, water; glass...$35.00
Waste can, step-on, tinware $35.00

Ice box set (covered bowls), 4", $12.00; 5", $18.50; and 6", $25.00. (Photo courtesy Barbara and Ken Brooks)

Catalin Napkin Rings

Plastic (Catalin) napkin rings topped with heads of cartoon characters, animals, and birds are very collectible, especially examples in red and orange; blue is also good, and other colors can be found as well.

Band, lathe turned, amber, red or green, 1¾"...............$8.00
Band, plain, amber, red or green, 2", ea........................$6.00
Band, plain, colors, 2", set of 6, MIB $40.00
Camel, inlaid eye rod $72.00
Chicken, no inlaid eyes...$35.00
Chicken, no inlaid eyes, amber w/green beak $50.00
Donald Duck, w/decal, from $65 to $80.00
Duck, no inlaid eyes $35.00
Elephant, ball on head...$35.00
Elephant, inlaid eye rod...$42.00
Elephant, no ball on head $35.00
Fish, no inlaid eyes...$30.00
Mickey Mouse, w/decal, from $70 to...........................$85.00
Rabbit, inlaid eye rod $42.00
Rabbit, no inlaid eyes...$35.00
Rocking horse, inlaid eye rod..$72.00
Schnauzer dog, no inlaid eyes...$30.00
Scottie dog, inlaid eye rod $50.00

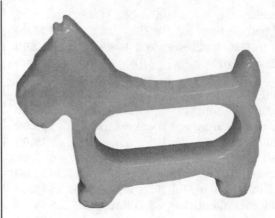

Scottie dog, no eye rod, $40.00. (Photo courtesy Candace Sten Davis and Patricia Baugh)

Ceramic Arts Studio

American-made figurines are very popular now, and these are certainly among the best. They have a distinctive look you'll soon learn to identify with confidence, even if you happen to pick up an unmarked piece. They were first designed in the '40s and sold well until the company closed in 1955. (After that, the new owner took the molds to Japan and produced them over there for a short time.) The company's principal designer was Betty Harrington, who modeled the figures and knicknacks that so many have grown to love. In addition to the company's marks (there were at least seven, possibly more), many of the later pieces she designed carry their assigned names on the bottom as well.

The company also produced a line of metal items to accessorize the figurines. These were designed by Liberace's stepmother, Zona, who was also Betty's personal friend and art director of the figurine line.

Though prices continue to climb, once in a while one of many unmarked bargains can be found, but first you must familiarize yourself with your subject!

Advisors: BA Wellman and John Canfield (See Directory, Ceramic Arts Studio)

Catalog Reprints: BA Wellman and John Canfield
P.O. Box 673, Westminster, MA 01473-1435
e-mail: bawellman@net1plus.com

Newsletter/Club: CAS Collectors Association
CAS Collector quarterly newsletter
P.O. Box 46
Madison, WI 53701; 608-241-9138
Newsletter $15; Annual membership, $15. Inventory record and price guide listing 800+ works, $12 postage paid

Ashtray, hippo, 5"...$200.00
Bank, Mr Blankety Blank, 4½" $100.00
Bell, Lillibelle, 6½"...$95.00
Blade bank, Tony the Barber $125.00

Bowl, Bonita, paisley shaped, 3¾" L $65.00
Candle holder, Bedtime boy, 4¾" $95.00
Candle holder, Hear No Evil, angel on cloud, 5"......$125.00
Candle holder, Triad girl, center, 5" $150.00
Figurine, Alice in Wonderland, kneeling, 4½"..........$200.00
Figurine, angel w/star, standing, 5½"......................$125.00
Figurine, Aphrodite, 7¾" $225.00
Figurine, Bali-Gong, crouched, 5½" $95.00
Figurine, birch-wood canoe, 8" L..............................$125.00
Figurine, Bird of Paradise, 3" $75.00
Figurine, black bear cub, 2¼"....................................$65.00
Figurine, Blythe & Pensive, 6½", 5", pr $200.00
Figurine, bunny baby, 2½" $40.00
Figurine, bunny mother running, 4½" $125.00
Figurine, Burmese woman, 4½" $125.00
Figurine, cat, Bright Eyes, looking forward, 3" $45.00
Figurine, cat, kitten sleeping, 1" $45.00
Figurine, cat mother, stylized, 4¼" $95.00
Figurine, child w/towel, 5" $120.00
Figurine, Cinderella, 6½" $75.00
Figurine, Colonial girl, 5" $65.00
Figurine, colt, Frisky..$85.00
Figurine, dachshund, standing, 3½", from $90 to.....$120.00
Figurine, devil imp, sitting, 3½" $150.00
Figurine, dog, Butch (Boxer), snuggle, 3" $95.00
Figurine, dog, Collie pup playing, 2¼"........................$45.00
Figurine, dog, Pekingese, 3" $90.00
Figurine, dog, Pomeranian, standing, 3" $80.00
Figurine, dog, Spaniel, sitting, 2¼" $65.00
Figurine, donkey, Dem, 4½" $125.00
Figurine, donkey mother, 3¼" $100.00
Figurine, duckling, 2¼" $75.00
Figurine, Dutch boy & girl, 4", pr $50.00
Figurine, Egyptian man & woman, rare, 9½", pr......$650.00
Figurine, elephant, Benny, 3½" $85.00
Figurine, elephant, Elsie, 5" $95.00
Figurine, elephant, Tembino, baby, 2½"....................$95.00
Figurine, ewe, 2" L $75.00
Figurine, fawn, 4¼" $50.00
Figurine, fish, straight tail, lg $80.00
Figurine, flute girl, 4½" $75.00
Figurine, fox, sneering at goose, 3¼" $95.00
Figurine, Gingham Dog, 2¾" $40.00
Figurine, girl praying, 3"..$50.00
Figurine, gremlin, standing, 4"..................................$250.00
Figurine, guitar man, on stool, scarce, 6½" $195.00
Figurine, harem girl, reclining, 6" L $85.00
Figurine, Isaac, 10" $125.00
Figurine, Japanese Kabuki man & woman, 8½", 6", pr .$600.00
Figurine, kangaroo mother, 4¾" $90.00
Figurine, lamb, plain, 3¾"..$65.00
Figurine, leopards, fighting, 3½", 6¼" L, pr, from $250 to..$300.00
Figurine, lion, 5½" L..$200.00
Figurine, Little Bo Peep, 5½" $35.00
Figurine, Little Miss Muffet #2, 4" $80.00
Figurine, Lover Boy, 4½"..$65.00
Figurine, Mr Skunky, 3" L $55.00

Figurines, Minnehaha and Hiawatha, from $265.00 to $295.00 for the pair.

Figurine, Peek-a-Boo pixie, 2½"..................................$65.00
Figurine, Petrov & Petruska, 5", 5¼", pr..................$100.00
Figurine, Pioneer Sam & Pioneer Suzie, 5½", 5", pr...$90.00
Figurine, pixie riding snail, 2¾" $65.00
Figurine, pixie sitting on bowl, 4½"..........................$125.00
Figurine, Praise angel, hand up, 6" $90.00
Figurine, rooster (fighting cock), 3¾" $75.00
Figurine, Sambo, 3½" $300.00
Figurine, Santa Claus, 2¼" $125.00
Figurine, Smi-Li & Mo-Pi, 5", pr, from $60 to.............$80.00
Figurine, Spring Sue, 5"..$85.00
Figurine, St George on Charger, 8½" $175.00
Figurine, Wee Eskimo boy & girl, 3¼", pr..................$35.00
Figurine, zebra, 5", from $165 to..............................$195.00
Figurine, Zulu man & woman, 5½", 7", pr..................$450.00
Head vase, African man, 8" $225.00
Head vase, Becky, 5¼" $165.00
Head vase, Lotus, 7¾"..$125.00
Head vase, Svea, 6" $175.00
Lamp, Manchu lantern holder, scarce $350.00
Metal accessory, arched window w/cross, 14"............$80.00
Metal accessory, corner web for spider, 4"................$95.00
Metal accessory, pyramid shelf, flat back $75.00
Miniature, Aladdin's lamp, 2" L................................$75.00
Miniature, pitcher, Diana Huntress, bisque, 3½".........$65.00
Miniature, teapot, Grapes, 2" $75.00
Miniature, teapot, swan form, open $50.00
Mug, Barber Shop Quartet, 3½" $150.00
Plaque, Blackamoor, 4¾" $295.00
Plaque, Comedy & Tragedy masks, 5", pr $165.00
Plaque, Hamlet & Ophelia, 8¼", pr $425.00
Plaque, Jack Be Nimble, 5"..$125.00
Plaque, sprite, tail up, 4½" $175.00
Plaque, Zor & Zorinda, 9", pr, ...$130.00
Salt & pepper shakers, bear mother & cub, brown, snuggle,
    pr..$90.00
Salt & pepper shakers, Calico Cat & Gingham Dog, pr..$125.00

Salt and pepper shakers, camels, $225.00 for the pair.

Salt & pepper shakers, dog & doghouse, snuggle, pr.....**$150.00**
Salt & pepper shakers, elf & mushroom, pr................**$65.00**
Salt & pepper shakers, fighting cocks, pr, from $70 to..**$80.00**
Salt & pepper shakers, horses' heads, pr....................**$65.00**
Salt & pepper shakers, mouse & cheese, 2½", pr, from $30
  to...**$40.00**
Salt & pepper shakers, Paul Bunyan & tree, pr........**$200.00**
Salt & pepper shakers, sea horse & coral, pr............**$145.00**
Salt & pepper shakers, Wee Chinese boy & girl, pr ...**$35.00**
Shelf sitter, banjo girl, 4" **$75.00**
Shelf sitter, canary, left (or right), 5" **$65.00**
Shelf sitter, cat, Mom, 4¾" **$100.00**
Shelf sitter, cat, Persian mother, 4¼"..........................**$50.00**
Shelf sitter, Chinese boy & girl, 3½", pr.....................**$40.00**
Shelf sitter, girl w/cat, 4¼"...**$65.00**
Shelf sitter, Greg & Grace, 7", 6½", pr **$190.00**
Shelf sitter, Maurice & Michelle, 7", pr, from $130 to ..**$165.00**
Vase, Flying Ducks, round, 2"....................................**$45.00**

Shelf sitters, Young Love Couple, $125.00 for the pair; Original bench, $18.00.

Cereal Boxes and Premiums

Yes, cereal boxes — your eyes aren't deceiving you. But think about it. Cereal boxes from even the '60s have to be extremely scarce. The ones that are bringing the big bucks today are those with a well-known character emblazoned across the front. Am I starting to make more sense to you? Good. Now, say the experts, is the time to look ahead into the future of your cereal box collection. They recommend going to your neighborhood supermarket to inspect the shelves in the cereal aisle today! Choose the ones with Batman, Quisp, Ninja Turtles, or some other cult phenomenon. Take them home and (unless you have mice) display them unopened, or empty them out and fold them up along the seam lines. If you want only the old boxes, you'll probably have to find an old long-abandoned grocery store or pay prices somewhere around those in our listings when one comes up for sale.

Store displays and advertising posters, in-box prizes or 'send-a-ways,' coupons with pictures of boxes, and shelf signs and cards are also part of this field of interest.

Our values are based on examples in mint condition. If you want to learn more about this field of collecting, we recommend *Toys of the Sixties* by Bill Bruegman; *Cereal Box Bonanza, The 1950s, ID and Values*, and *Cereal Boxes and Prizes, 1960s* , both by Scott Bruce.

See also Advertising Characters; Toys, Rings.

Advisor: Scott Bruce (See Directory, Advertising)

Newsletter: *FLAKE, The Breakfast Nostalgia Magazine*
P.O. Box 481
Cambridge, MA 02140; 617-492-5004

Boxes

Cheerios, General Mills, 1958, Annette doll and outfits on back, $300.00.
(Photo courtesy Scott Bruce)

All Stars, features Wizard of Oats w/Free Walking Finger
  Puppet on back, Kellogg, 1960, 9¾"..................**$150.00**
Alpha Bits, features Lovable Truly w/Fun 'n Games Postcard
  Magic cut-out game on back, Post, 1967, 8-oz, NM..**$225.00**
Cap'n Crunch, Free Comic Book Inside, Quaker, 1963,
  9½"...**$250.00**

Cheerios, Free on This Package/Lone Ranger Movie Ranch Wild West Town..., General Mills, 1957, 10¼" ...**$125.00**

Cocoa Krispies, features Coco the pink elephant w/USS Skate atomic submarine offer, Kellogg, 1960, 9½", VG .**$150.00**

Cocoa Krispies, head image of Snagglepus, Kellogg, 1963, M **$350.00**

Corn Crackos, Magic Monocle says It's Crunchy When You Crunch!!, Post, 1968, 8½" **$150.00**

Corn Flakes, Free! Yogi Bear Birthday Dell Comic, Kellogg, 1962, 11½"................**$500.00**

Corn Flakes, Huckleberry Hound's 'Win a Pair of Fords' contest, Kellogg, 1960, flat, NM................**$65.00**

Corn Flakes, Yogi Bear Birthday Party Comic, Kellogg, 1962, full, EX................**$480.00**

Country Corn Flakes, Get a Country Corn Flakes Scarecrow Costume..., General Mills, 1965, 11¼"................**$150.00**

Crispy Critters, Pink Elephant Toy, New! Compact Box, Post, 1965, 8"................**$200.00**

Crispy Critters, 5 License Plates Only 25¢, Post, 1968, 9½" **$300.00**

Froot Loops, features Toucan Sam w/Eldon Home Bowling Game offer, Kellogg, 1963, 9½"................**$350.00**

Frosted Flakes, shows Tony & Jr riding tricycle, Kellogg, 1955, 20"................**$150.00**

Frosty O's, Do-It-Yourself Indian Bead Set! 10¢ w/This Boxtop, shows Frosty Bear, General Mills, 1962, 9½"........**$200.00**

Frosty O's, Frosty Bear balancing cereal bowl on foot w/One Million Dollar Offer..., General Mills, 1960, 9½"...**$275.00**

Fruity Pebbles, Flintmobile, Kellogg, 1972, overwrap, NM **$100.00**

Honeycomb, Free Inside! 1969 Mercury, Post, 1968, 11" ..**$150.00**

Lucky Charms, Alphabet Cards on back, General Mills, 1967, 11"................**$150.00**

Maypo, features Marko Maypo w/shirt offer, Maltex, 1961, 7"................**$200.00**

OKs, Win Movin' Pictures of Huck an' Yogi Bear, shows Big Otis, Kellogg, 1960, 11½"................**$250.00**

Post Toasties, features Hopalong Cassidy offering Wild West Trading Cards in cereal box, w/wax overwrap, Post, 1951, 21"................**$750.00**

Raisin Bran, Free Inside! Looney Tunes Notch-Em Toy, Post/General Foods, 1956, 9½"................**$150.00**

Rice Honeys, Bambi Puppet Show Kit Inside This Package, Nabisco, 1967, 9½"................**$250.00**

Rice Krinkles, Bugs Bunny Magic Picture on Back Panel, features So-Hi w/bowl of cereal, Post, 1961, 9¾" ..**$125.00**

Rice Krispies, Free Inside!, Batman Ring, Kellogg, 1967, 10¼"................**$350.00**

Sugar Crisp, B-58 Jet Bomber Offer!, Post, 1958, 19½"..**$65.00**

Sugar Pops, Free Action Cut-outs, shows Pete shooting sugar into cereal bowl, Kellogg, 1959, 9½"................**$100.00**

Sugar Pops, New! Huck & Yogi Pin-Mates, shows Pete shooting sugar into cereal bowl, Kellogg, 1962, 8-oz.**$150.00**

Sugar Smacks, Quick Draw McGraw, Road Race game, Kellogg, 1964, flat, M................**$350.00**

Top 3, Free Football Trading Cards, shows boy cheerleader w/megaphone, Post, 1962, 10-oz **$15.00**

Trix, Free Tiddly-Winks Game Inside This Box, General Mills, 1967, 9½"................**$200.00**

Twinkles, Fun Time Package w/Scramble-Up Game, General Mills, 1964, 9½"................**$100.00**

Wheat Honeys, Free Inside! Bert the Chimney Sweep Pop-Up, Nabisco, 1964, 9½"................**$200.00**

Wheat Honeys, Free Inside! One of Six Jungle Pals From Walt Disney, Nabisco, 1967, 9½" **$175.00**

Wheaties, Get Bullwinkle's Electric Quiz Fun Game!, shows hurdler, General Mills, 1962, 9½"................**$200.00**

Premiums

Alpha-Bits, Free Offer, Doctor Dolittle Cartoon Kit, Post, 1967, 9½"................**$225.00**

Bank, Milton the Toaster, vinyl, Kellogg's Pop Tarts, 1970s, rare, MIB................**$165.00**

Beanie, Quaker Oats Quisp, MIB................**$400.00**

Booklet, Fun & Games, #2, #4, or #5, paper, Kellogg's Corny Snaps, 1978, M (original envelope), ea................**$20.00**

Bowl, Cherrios Kid & Sue, white Melmac, General Mills, 1969, VG................**$10.00**

Decoder, Apple Jacks, Dig 'em, Poppy, or Toucan Sam, plastic, M (assembled), ea................**$8.00**

Dick Dastardly's Mean Machine Wacky Racer, plastic, General Mills, 1969, 2¾x2", NM................**$45.00**

Doll, Cap'n Crunch, plush, 14", NM................**$75.00**

Doll, Count Chocula or Frankenberry, squeeze vinyl, General Mills, 1977, 8", NM, ea................**$125.00**

Doll, Dig 'Em, stuffed printed cloth, frontal view in ball cap & name on chest, 1973, 16", EX................**$22.00**

Doll, Dig 'Em, stuffed printed cloth, no hat, mouth open, looking up, Kellogg's written on arm, 11", VG **$15.00**

Doll, Kelly the Dog, stuffed printed cloth, black & white w/head cocked & looking up while licking chops, 8", EX **$25.00**

Doll, Trix Rabbit, plush, General Mills, 1980s, 20", EX ..**$50.00**

Post's Sugar Crisp, 1954, Roy Rogers paint set offer, EX, $200.00. (Photo courtesy Scott Bruce)

Eraser, Lucky the Leprechaun, General Mills Lucky Charms, 1969, 2", unused, M **$20.00**

Figurine, Quisp, ceramic, Quaker Oats, 5", NM........**$150.00**

Funscope, Toucan Sam, paper, Kellogg, 1982, M **$10.00**

Gyro Unicycle, plastic, Quaker Oats Quisp, 1970s, MIP **$75.00**

Iron-on transfer, Apple Jacks or Dig 'em, Kellogg, 1985, 6x8", M (in paper), ea......................................**$15.00**

Jungle Book Pals, 6 different plastic figures, Nabisco, 1967, 1½" to 3", ea **$15.00**

License plate, Ogg or Toucan Sam, blue plastic, Kellogg, 1973, 3x6", EX, ea...**$20.00**

Mask, Quick Draw McGraw, paper hood type, Kellogg, 1962, unassembled, MIP....................................**$45.00**

Mug, Dennis the Menace, molded head image in hat, Kellogg's Corn Flakes, 1962, 3½", NM **$20.00**

Mug, Yogi Bear, Kellogg's Corn Flakes, 1960, 3½", EX..**$20.00**

Mug (mini), Booberry, Count Chocula, or Frankenberry, plastic, General Mills, 1973, M, ea **$30.00**

Mug & bowl, Woody Woodpecker, embossed painted head image on mug w/log-shaped footed bowl, Kellogg, 1965, M/NM..**$40.00**

Page marker/paper clip, Dig 'em or Toucan Sam, plastic, Kellogg, 1979, NM, ea **$15.00**

Parade Drum, shows, Snap!, Crackle!, Pop! & Toucan Sam, Kellogg, 1983, 4x9" dia, EX...........................**$5.00**

Pencil topper/eraser, Booberry figure, General Mills, 1973, NM **$10.00**

Pencil topper/eraser, Count Chocula figure, General Mills, 1973, MIP...**$15.00**

Plate, Cheerios Kid & Bullwinkle, white Melmac, General Mills, 1969, VG.......................................**$15.00**

Record, The Banana Splits, 45 rpm, Kellogg, 1969, EX (w/sleeve)..**$35.00**

Ring, Batman, Kellogg's Rice Krispies, 1967.............**$15.00**

Ring, Quake, friendship, 1966, blue plastic, EX, $300.00.
(Photo courtesy Scott Bruce)

Safe Bike Booster, Toucan Sam or Sonny Sun, plastic, Kellogg, 1981, M, ea **$5.00**

Sugar Smacks, Free on Package Back! Jig-Jag Puzzle, Kellogg, 1966, 10"..**$175.00**

Tiddly Winks game, Trix Rabbit, red plastic, General Mills, late 1960s, EX..**$20.00**

Tumbler, Toucan Sam, Kellogg, 1977, VG **$20.00**

Character and Promotional Drinking Glasses

In any household, especially those with children, I would venture to say, you should find a few of these glasses. Put out by fast-food restaurant chains or by a company promoting a product, they have for years been commonplace. But now, instead of glass, the giveaways are nearly always plastic. If a glass is offered at all, you'll usually have to pay 99¢ for it.

Some are worth more than others. Among the common ones are Camp Snoopy, B.C. Ice Age, Garfield, McDonald's, Smurfs, and Coca-Cola. The better glasses are those with super heroes, characters from Star Trek and '30s movies such as 'Wizard of Oz,' sports personalities, and cartoon characters by Walter Lantz and Walt Disney. Some of these carry a copyright date, and that's all it is. It's not the date of manufacture.

Many collectors are having a good time looking for these glasses. If you want to learn more about them, we recommend *Tomart's Price Guide to Character and Promotional Drinking Glasses* by Carol Markowski, and *Collectible Drinking Glasses, Identification and Values*, by our advisors Mark Chase and Michael Kelly (Collector Books).

There are some terms used in the descriptions that may be confusing. 'Brockway' style refers to a thick, heavy glass that tapers in from top to bottom. 'Federal' style, on the other hand, is thinner, and the top and bottom diameters are the same.

Advisors: Mark Chase and Michael Kelly (See Directory, Character and Promotional Drinking Glasses)

Newsletter: *Collector Glass News*
P.O. Box 308
Slippery Rock, PA 16057; 724-946-2838; fax: 724-946-9012 or e-mail: cgn@glassnews.com; www.glassnews.com

Al Capp's Dog Patch Characters, 1975, flat bottom, Brockway, Daisy Mae, Li'l Abner, Mammy, Pappy, Sadie, ea, from $50 to..**$70.00**

Al Capp's Dog Patch Characters, 1975, flat bottom, Brockway, Joe Btptflk, from $60 to......................**$80.00**

Arby's, Bicentennial Cartoon Characters Series, 1976, 10 different, 5", ea, from $18 to **$25.00**

Arby's Actor Series, 1979, 6 different, smoke-colored w/black & white images, silver trim, numbered, ea, from $5 to..**$7.00**

Archies, Welch's, 1971 & 1973, many variations in ea series, ea, from $3 to..**$5.00**

Avon, Christmas Issues, 1969-72, 4 different, ea, from $2 to **$5.00**

Battlestar Galactica, Universal Studios, 1979, 4 different, ea, from $7 to...**$10.00**

BC Ice Age, Arby's, 1981, 6 different, ea, from $3 to ...**$5.00**

Beatles, Dairy Queen, group photo & signatures in white starburst, gold trim, Canadian, ea, from $95 to..**$125.00**

Burger Chef, Burger Chef & Jeff, Now We're Glassified!, from $15 to...**$25.00**

Burger Chef, Friendly Monster Series, 1977, 6 different, ea, from $20 to...**$35.00**

Burger King, Collector Series, 1979, 5 different, Burger King characters featuring Burger Thing, etc, ea, from $4 to...**$6.00**

Burger King, Have It Your Way 1776-1976 Series, 1976, 4 different, ea, from $4 to.....................................**$6.00**

Charles Dicken's A Christmas Carol, Subway, early 1980s, 4 different, ea, from $4 to.................................**$6.00**

Chipmunks, Hardee's (no logo on glass), 1985, Alvin, Simon, Theodore, Chipettes, ea from $2 to.......................**$4.00**

Cinderella, Disney/Libbey, 1950s-60s, set of 8.........**$120.00**

Currier & Ives, Arby's, 1975-76, 4 different, titled, ea, from $3 to...**$5.00**

Currier & Ives, Kraft Cheese, 1970s, Old Homestead in Winter, American Winter Scene, ea, from $1 to.....**$3.00**

Disney Characters, 1936, Clarabelle, Donald, F Bunny, Horace, Mickey, Minnie, Pluto, 4¼" or 4¾", ea, from $30 to..**$50.00**

Disney Characters, 1989 & 1990, frosted juice or water, 6 different face images in ea series, ea, from $5 to.......**$8.00**

Disney Collector Series, Burger King, 1994, multicolored images on clear plastic, 8 different, MIB, ea.........**$3.00**

Disney Film Classics, McDonald's/Coca-Cola/Canada, Cinderella, Fantasia, Peter Pan, Snow White & the Seven Dwarfs, ea...**$15.00**

Donald Duck, Donald Duck Cola, 1960s-70s, from $15 to...**$20.00**

Elsie the Cow, Borden, 1960, yellow daisy image, from $10 to...**$12.00**

ET, Pizza Hut, 1982, footed, 4 different, from $2 to.....**$4.00**

Flintstone Kids, Betty, Pizza Hut, Hanna-Barbera Productions, 1986, from $2.00 to $4.00.

Flintstones, Welch's, 1962 (6 different), 1963 (2 different), 1964 (6 different), ea, from $8 to.........................**$12.00**

Ghostbusters II, Sunoco/Canada, 1989, 6 different, ea, from $5 to...**$8.00**

Great Muppet Caper, McDonald's, 1981, 4 different, 6", ea..**$2.00**

Hanna-Barbera, Pepsi, 1977, Brockway, Dynomutt, Flintstones, Josie/Pussycats, Mumbly, Scooby, Yogi/Huck, ea, from $20 to.................................**$35.00**

Hanna-Barbera, 1960s, jam glasses w/Cindy Bear, Flintstones, Huck, Quick Draw, Yogi Bear, rare, ea, from $75 to.**$110.00**

Happy Days, Dr Pepper, 1977, Fonzie, Joanie, Potsie, Ralph, Richie, ea, from $8 to....................................**$12.00**

Happy Days, Dr Pepper/Pizza Hut, 1977, Fonzie or Richie, ea, from $10 to...**$15.00**

Happy Days, Dr Pepper/Pizza Hut, 1977, Joanie, Potsie, Ralph, ea, from $8 to...**$12.00**

Harvey Cartoon Characters, Pepsi, 1970s, action pose, Baby Huey, Casper, Hot Stuff, Wendy, ea, from $8 to..**$15.00**

Harvey Cartoon Characters, Pepsi, 1970s, static pose, Baby Huey, Casper, Hot Stuff, Wendy, ea, from $12 to.**$20.00**

Harvey Cartoon Characters, Pepsi, 1970s, static pose, Sad Sack, scarce, from $25 to.....................................**$35.00**

Honey, I Shrunk the Kids, McDonald's, 1989, plastic, 3 different, ea, from $1 to...**$2.00**

Howdy Doody, Welch's/Kagran, 1950s, 6 different, embossed bottom, ea, from $15 to......................................**$20.00**

Indiana Jones & the Temple of Doom, 7-Up (w/4 different sponsors), 1984, 4 different, from $8 to...............**$15.00**

Indiana Jones: The Last Crusade, white plastic, 4 different, ea, from $2 to...**$4.00**

Jewel Tea Jelly, Old Time Series, 1950s, 6 different, ea, from $2 to...**$4.00**

Jungle Book, Disney/Canada, 1966, 6 different, numbered, 5", ea, from $40 to..**$75.00**

Jungle Book, Disney/Canada, 1966, 6 different, numbered, 6½", ea, from $30 to...**$60.00**

Jungle Book, Disney/Pepsi, 1970s, Bagheera or Shere Kahn, unmarked, ea, from $60 to..................................**$90.00**

Keebler Soft Batch Cookies, 1984, 4 different, ea, from $7 to...**$10.00**

Kellogg's, 1977, Big Yella, Dig 'Em, Snap! Crackle! & Pop!, Tony, Tony Jr, Toucan Sam, ea, from $7 to.........**$10.00**

Leonardo TTV Action Series, Underdog, Pepsi, 5", from $8.00 to $15.00.

Leonardo TTV, Collector Series, Pepsi, Go-Go Gopher, Simon Bar Sinister, Sweet Polly, Underdog, 6", ea, from $15 to...**$25.00**

Mark Twain Country Series, Burger King, 1985, 4 different, from $8 to.....................................**$10.00**

Masters of the Universe, Mattel, 1983, Teela, He-Man, Skeletor, Man-At-Arms, ea, from $5 to.................**$10.00**

Masters of the Universe, Mattel, 1986, Battle Cat/He-Man, Man-at-Arms, Orko, Panthor/Skeletor, ea, from $3 to **$5.00**

McDonald's, McDonaldland Action Series, 1977, 6 different, ea..**$5.00**

McDonald's, McVote, 1986, 3 different, ea, from $4 to.**$6.00**

MGM Collector Series, Pepsi, 1975, Tom, Jerry, Barney, Droopy, Spike, Tuffy, ea, from $10 to **$15.00**

Mickey Mouse, Happy Birthday, Pepsi, 1978, Clarabelle & Horace, from $15 to **$20.00**

Mickey Mouse, Happy Birthday, Pepsi, 1978, Daisy & Donald, from $12 to **$15.00**

Mickey Mouse, Happy Birthday, 1978, Donald, Goofy, Mickey, Minnie, Pluto, Uncle Scrooge, ea, from $6 to **$10.00**

Mickey Mouse, Mickey's Christmas Carol, Coca-Cola, 1982, 3 different, ea **$10.00**

Norman Rockwell, Saturday Evening Post Series, Arby's, early 1980s, 6 different, numbered, ea, from $2 to............**$4.00**

Norman Rockwell, Saturday Evening Post Series, Country Time Lemonade, 4 different (w/ or w/o logo), ea, from $3 to...**$5.00**

Pac-Man, Arby's, from $2.00 to $4.00.

PAT Ward, Collector Series, Holly Farms Restaurants, 1975, Boris, Bullwinkle, Natasha, Rocky, ea, from $30 to **$50.00**

PAT Ward, Pepsi, late 1970s, action pose, Bullwinkle w/balloons, Dudley in Canoe, Rocky in circus, 5", ea, from $8 to...**$10.00**

Peanuts Characters, Camp Snoopy, McDonald's, 1983, white plastic w/Lucy or Snoopy, ea, from $5 to...............**$8.00**

Peanuts Characters, Kraft, 1988, Charlie Brown flying kite, Lucy on swing, Snoopy in pool, Snoopy on surfboard, ea **$2.00**

Pepsi, Historical Advertising Posters, 1979, 4 different, blue & white, ea, from $8 to.............................**$10.00**

Pocahontas, Burger King, 1995, 4 different, MIB, ea **$3.00**

Popeye, Kollect-A-Set, Coca-Cola, 1975, Popeye, from $7 to...**$10.00**

Popeye, Kollect-A-Set, Coca-Cola, 1975, 6 different, any except Popeye, ea, from $$5 to...........................**$7.00**

Popeye, Pals, Popeye's Famous Fried Chicken, 1979, 4 different, ea, from $10 to..........................**$20.00**

Rescuers, Pepsi, 1977, Brockway, Bernard, Bianca, Brutus & Nero, Evinrude, Orville, Penny, ea, from $8 to..**$15.00**

Rescuers, Pepsi, 1977, Brockway, Madame Medusa or Rufus, ea, from $25 to.......................................**$30.00**

Roger Rabbit, McDonald's, 1988, plastic, ea, from $1 to..**$3.00**

Smurf's, Hardee's, 1982 (8 different), 1983 (6 different), ea, from $1 to...**$3.00**

Snow White & the Seven Dwarfs, Libbey, 1937-38, verses on back, various colors, 8 different, ea, from $15 to...**$24.00**

Star Trek, Dr Pepper, 1976, 4 different, ea, from $20 to.**$25.00**

Star Trek, Dr Pepper, 1978, 4 different, ea, from $30 to..**$40.00**

Star Trek II: Search for Spock, Taco Bell, 1984, 4 different, ea, from $3 to...**$5.00**

Star Trek: The Motion Picture, Coca-Cola, 1980, 3 different, ea, from $10 to.......................................**$15.00**

Star Wars Trilogy: Empire Strikes Back, Burger King/Coca-Cola, 1980, 4 different, ea, from $7 to **$10.00**

Star Wars Trilogy: Return of the Jedi, Burger King/Coca-Cola, 1983, 4 different, ea, from $6 to **$8.00**

Star Wars Trilogy: Star Wars, Burger King/Coca-Cola, 1977, 4 different, ea, from $12 to **$15.00**

Super Heroes, Marvel, 1978, Federal, Spider-Woman, from $175 to...**$250.00**

Super Heroes, Marvel/7 Eleven, 1977, footed, Captain America, Fantastic Four, Howard the Duck, Thor, ea, from $20 to...**$35.00**

Super Heroes, Pepsi Super (Moon) Series/DC Comics, 1976, Green Lantern, Joker, Penguin, Riddler, ea, from $35 to **$50.00**

Super Heroes, Pepsi Super (Moon) Series/DC Comics or NPP, 1976, Batgirl, Batman, Robin, Shazam!, ea, from $10 to **$15.00**

Superman, NPP/M Pilanar & Son, 1964, 6 different, various colors, 4¼" or 5¾", ea, from $20 to.....................**$35.00**

Universal Monsters, Universal Studio, 1980, footed, Creature, Dracula, Frankenstein, Mummy, Mutant, Wolfman, ea, from $100 to...**$125.00**

Walter Lantz, Pepsi, 1970s, Space Mouse, from $150 to..**$250.00**

Walter Lantz, Pepsi, 1970s-80s, Woody Woodpecker/Knothead & Splinter, from $15 to.........................**$20.00**

Warner Bros, Arby's, 1988, Adventures Series, footed, Bugs Bunny, Daffy Duck, Porky, Sylvester & Tweety, ea, from $35 to...**$45.00**

Warner Bros, Pepsi, 1973, Brockway 12-oz, Bugs, Daffy, Road Runner, Sylvester, Tweety, ea, from $10 to **$15.00**

Warner Bros, Pepsi, 1979, Collector's Series, round bottom, Bugs/Daffy, Porky, Road Runner, Sylvester, Tweety, ea, from $7 to...**$10.00**

Warner Bros, Welch's, 1974, action poses, 8 different, phrases around top, ea, from $2 to...................................**$4.00**

Warner Bros, Welch's, 1976-77, 8 different, names around bottom, ea, from $5 to...**$7.00**

Wendy's, Clara Peller (Where's the Beef?) or Clara Peller (no phrase), ea, from $4 to...**$6.00**

Wild West Series, Coca-Cola, Buffalo Bill, Calamity Jane, ea, from $10 to...**$15.00**

Wizard of Oz, Coca-Cola/Krystal, 1989, 50th Anniversary Series, 6 different, ea, from $10 to **$15.00**

Wonderful World of Disney, Pepsi, 1980s, Alice, Bambi, Lady & the Tramp, Pinocchio, Snow White, 101 Dalmatians, ea..**$25.00**

Ziggy, 7-Up Collector Series, 4 different, ea, from $4 to...**$7.00**

Sylvester, Tweety, and bulldog, Warner Bros., Pepsi, 1976, from $5.00 to $10.00.

Character Banks

Since the invention of money there have been banks, and saving it has always been considered a virtue. What better way to entice children to save than to give them a bank styled after the likeness of one of their favorite characters! Always a popular collectible, mechanical and still banks have been made of nearly any conceivable material. Cast-iron and tin banks are often worth thousands of dollars. The ones listed here were made in the past fifty years or so, when ceramics and plastics were the materials of choice. Still, some of the higher-end examples can be quite pricey! (You can assume that all the banks we've listed here are ceramic, unless another type of material is mentioned in the description line.)

For more information see *Collector's Guide to Banks* by Jim and Beverly Mangus; several are shown in *The Collector's Encyclopedia of Cookie Jars* (there are three in the series) by Fred and Joyce Roerig. All of these books are published by Collector Books.

See also Advertising Character Collectibles; Cowboy Character Collectibles; Star Trek; Star Wars.

Advisor: Robin Stine (See Directory, Cleminson)

Andy Panda, cardboard, 1948, 6", EX **$30.00**

Andy Panda, name embossed on chest, painted composition, Crown Toy, 1939, 5", EX.....................................**$100.00**

Bambi, airbrushed ceramic, dairy ad on bottom, Leeds, 1940s, 7", EX **$100.00**

Big Bird, w/egg, composition, NM..............................**$20.00**

Bozo the Clown, plastic, 1972, NM.............................**$35.00**

Bugs Bunny, w/present, ceramic, Warner Bros, 1981, EX..**$50.00**

Bullwinkle, vinyl, Play Pal Plastics, 1973, 12", M........**$75.00**

Care Bears, Wish Bear on a Star, composition, NM....**$20.00**

Casper the Friendly Ghost, holding bag of money, ceramic, 1940s, 8", EX, from $200 to **$250.00**

Daffy Duck, leaning on tree trunk, painted metal, 6", EX **$135.00**

Donald Duck, Ucago, 1960s, MIB **$55.00**

Dr Dolittle, w/monkey & dog at feet, pink plastic w/blue trim, NM..**$50.00**

ET, standing on round green base, 6", EX...................**$30.00**

Flintstones, Barney & Bamm-Bamm, hard plastic, 13", M..**$75.00**

Flintstones, Fred, hard plastic, Homecraft, 14", M.......**$75.00**

Flipper, plastic, 1960s, 17½", NM **$45.00**

Goofy, head figure, Playpal Plastics, 1971, 12", NM ...**$30.00**

Huckleberry Hound, plastic, 1960, 10", EX.................**$35.00**

Humpty Dumpty, ceramic, unmarked Japan, 5", from $75.00 to $80.00.
(Photo courtesy Beverly and Jim Mangus)

Lambchop, plastic, Shari Lewis Enterprises, Made in China, 1993, from $10 to..**$12.00**

Li'l Abner, composition, Capp Enterprises, 1975, 7", M .**$100.00**

Linus the Lion-Hearted, plastic, Transogram, 1965, 10", EX...**$25.00**

Lion King, Mufasa & Simba, Made in China, from $30 to **$40.00**

Little Lulu, Play Pal Plastics, 7½", NM.........................**$50.00**

Marvin the Martian, Warner Bros, Made in China, 1994, M $24.00

Masters of the Universe, HG Toys Ltd, Made in Hong Kong, MIB, $12.00.

Miss Piggy, ceramic, Sigma, NM $50.00
Mr Sherman (Rocky & Bullwinkle), ceramic, PAT Ward, 1960, 6", VG $300.00
Pac-Man, EX $20.00
Peanuts, Linus as baseball catcher, 7", rare, NM $125.00
Peanuts, Lucy at desk, ceramic, NM $30.00
Peanuts, Snooy on rainbow, composition, NM $25.00
Peanuts, Woodstock, yellow plastic, 6", NM $35.00
Planet of the Apes, Dr Zaius, Play Pal Plastics, 1967, 10", NM $30.00
Planet of the Apes, General Urus, Play Pal Plastics, 1967, 18", M, from $35 to $40.00
Popeye, sitting w/spinach can, vinyl, Alan Jay, 1958, 8"...$75.00
Porky Pig, standing beside tree trunk, pot metal, 1940s, EX.$100.00
Raggedy Ann, seated w/hand to cheek, ceramic, musical, 6¾", EX...$40.00
Raggedy Ann & Andy, ceramic, musical, 4½", NM $20.00
Superman, compositon, Enesco, 1987, MIB $85.00
Teenage Mutant Ninja Turtles, plastic, Mirage Studios, 1990, M, from $8 to $10.00
Yogi Bear, plastic, 14", EX...$35.00
Ziggy, Tom Wilson Earthenware, from $35 to.............$50.00

Character Clocks and Watches

There is growing interest in the comic character clocks and watches produced from about 1930 into the 1950s and beyond. They're in rather short supply simply because they were made for children to wear (and play with). They were cheaply made with pin-lever movements, not worth an expensive repair job, and many were simply thrown away. The original packaging that today may be worth more than the watch itself was usually ripped apart by an excited child and promptly relegated to the wastebasket.

Condition is very important in assessing value. Unless a watch is in like-new condition, it is not mint. Rust, fading, scratching, or wear of any kind will sharply lessen its value, and the same is true of the box itself. Good, excellent, and mint watches can be evaluated on a scale of one to five, with excellent being a three, good a one, and mint a five. In other words, a watch worth $25.00 in good condition would be worth five times that amount if it were mint ($125.00). Beware of dealers who substitute a generic watch box for the original. Remember that these too were designed to appeal to children and (99% of the time) were printed with colorful graphics.

Some of these watches have been reproduced, so be on guard. For more information, we recommend *Comic Character Clocks and Watches* by Howard S. Brenner, and *Schroeder's Collectible Toys, Antique to Modern* (Collector Books).

See also Advertising and Promotional Wristwatches.

Advisor: Howard Brenner (See Directory, Character Clocks and Watches)

Clocks

Barbie Talking Alarm Clock, Barbie & Ken posing in front of clock face, pink plastic case, Quartz, 1983, M $20.00

Batman and Robin Talking Alarm Clock, Janex Corp., 1974, EX, $50.00. (Photo courtesy June Moon)

Buffy & Jody Alarm Clock, Buffy & Jody lettered on face, 1960s, M $125.00
Bugs Bunny Wall Clock, black plastic case w/image of Bugs holding carrot, electric, Seth Thomas, 1970, 10" dia, NM $85.00
David Cassidy Wall Clock, 1971, NM $100.00
Davy Crockett Animated Clock, log cabin w/image at right of clock, Haddon, 1950s, 4x12", EX, from $500 to.$800.00
Fred Flintstone Alarm Clock, full-figure image & Yabba Dabba Doo, arms keep time, yellow case w/red bells, 1973, M $65.00
Howdy Doody Alarm Clock, Howdy on bronco, Leadworks, 1988, 10", EX..$65.00

Howdy Doody Alarm Clock, Howdy's image on face, metal case, Western Clock, 1954, 5", EX.......................**$450.00**

Lone Ranger, Lone Ranger riding Silver on face, silver case, Bradley/Elgin, 1981, MIB, form $100 to..............**$125.00**

Maggie Simpson Alarm Clock, MIB, from $100 to....**$125.00**

Max Headroom Wall Clock, shaped like a wristwatch, NMIB **$65.00**

Mickey Mouse Alarm Clock, analog movement, double bell, Phinney-Walker, 4", EX...**$75.00**

Mickey Mouse Alarm Clock, image of Mickey running w/arms keeping time, round, Bayard, 1964, NM **$300.00**

Mickey Mouse Alarm Clock, Mickey's hands keep time, tan case, Ingersoll, 1940s, 5" dia, VG (box marked Luminous Hands) **$325.00**

Mork From Ork Talking Alarm Clock, plastic figure sits beside clock, Concept 2000, 1980, NM, from $40 to **$50.00**

Peanuts Alarm Clock, character faces as numbers, silver metal case, Japan, 1988, 3½" dia, MIB, from $45 to...........**$55.00**

Pluto Alarm Clock, image of Pluto in front of doghouse watching baby chicks, round, Bayard, 1964, NM............**$250.00**

Pluto Alarm Clock, plastic figure w/clock attached to his chest, clock hands shaped as dog bones, Allied, 8", EXIB..**$450.00**

Popeye Alarm Clock, litho tin w/color image on face, case & base, New Haven, 4", EX....................................**$850.00**

Raggedy Ann and Andy, wind-up alarm clock, metal with plastic face, Bobbs-Merril, West Germany, 1971, 5½", M, $95.00.

(Photo courtesy Kim Avery)

Roy Rogers & Trigger Alarm Clock, desert scene w/Roy on Trigger galloping & ticking off seconds, Ingraham, 4x4", NMIB..**$650.00**

Shmoo Pendulette Alarm Clock, figural w/dial in middle, Lux, 1950, 8", EXIB..**$275.00**

Snoopy & Charlie Brown Talking Alarm Clock, 2-D image of Snoopy & Charlie beside clock, plastic, Janex, 1974, MIB **$135.00**

Snoopy Alarm Clock, image of Snoopy w/tennis racket, black metal case, Equity, 1968, 5" dia, EX............**$30.00**

Snoopy Analog Clock, plush figure w/clock in stomach, Armitron, 1989, 9", MIB, from $25 to....................**$35.00**

Snow White & the Seven Dwarfs Alarm Clock, Snow White surrounded by dwarfs at ea number, Bayard, 1960, 4½" dia, NM...**$300.00**

Tweety Bird Talking Alarm Clock, battery-operated, Janex, 1978, EX...**$75.00**

Woody Woodpecker Pendulum Wall Clock, diecut Woody on horse, Columbia/Westclock, 1959, NMIB............**$500.00**

Pocket Watches

Buster Brown, 1960s, VG...**$75.00**

Captain Marvel, full-figure image, round chrome case, green plastic strap, Fawcett, 1948, EX.........................**$250.00**

Captain Marvel, full-figure image, round chrome case, green plastic strap, Fawcett, 1948, EXIB **$750.00**

Dane Dare, space scene w/spaceship & gun ticking off seconds, Ingersoll/Great Britian, 1950s, MIB...........**$800.00**

Lone Ranger & Silver, image on face, blue strap, silver chain, 1970, NM, from $75 to **$100.00**

Mary Marvel, full-figure image, round chrome case, red plastic strap, Fawcett, 1948, VG **$125.00**

Mickey Mouse, full-figure Mickey on face, plastic, Bradley, 1970s, 2" dia, EX..**$50.00**

Roy Rogers, lg image of Roy w/sm image of Roy on Trigger in background, w/stopwatch feature, Bradley, 1959, EX **$450.00**

Toy Story, Buzz Lightyear, limited edition of 7,500, Fossil, 1996, complete, M (M box & tin).......................**$125.00**

Toy Story, Woody, limited editon of 7,500, Fossil, 1996, complete, M (M box & tin).......................................**$125.00**

Wristwatches

Amazing Spider-Man, blue plastic band, Dabs, 1981, M (M box & slip case)...**$200.00**

Batman, Batman swinging from rope, leather band, Dabbs, 1977, MIB **$200.00**

Batman, limited edition, w/pin, Fossil, 1990, M (M tin box)...**$125.00**

Bionic Woman, image & lettering on face, vinyl band, MZ Berger, 1970s, NM, from $60 to **$80.00**

Buffy & Jody, image & names lettered on face, visible gears in back, various band colors, Sheffield, 1969, M......**$125.00**

Captain Marvel, Captain Marvel holding an airplane, vinyl band, Fawcett, 1948, EX....................................**$250.00**

Cinderella, Cinderella on face, w/plastic Cinderella figure, Timex, 1958, EXIB...**$150.00**

David Cassidy, photo image on face, 1970s, NM, from $150 to...**$200.00**

Davy Crockett, image of Davy holding rifle, green plastic case w/tooled brown leather band, WDP, 1955, NM **$135.00**

Dick Tracy, Tracy pointing gun on rectangular face, 1940s, VG...**$100.00**

Donald Duck, 50th Anniversary Registered Edition, battery-operated, complete w/paperwork, Bradley, 1950, MIB **$150.00**

Dr Seuss, Cat in the Hat, 1972, NM $250.00

Farrah Fawcett, photo image on face, vinyl band, 1970s, NM, from $100 to..$125.00

Flipper, glow-in-the-dark image of Flipper on face, ITF/MGM, M...$125.00

Fonz, photo image on face, vinyl band, Time Trends, 1976, MIB $75.00

Gene Autry, Gene w/6-shooter, round chrome case, black leather strap w/silver stitching, New Haven, 1951, EX, from $350 to..$400.00

Hardy Boys, 1970s, NM, from $50 to $75.00

Hopalong Cassidy, bust image on face, western motif on black band, complete w/saddle display, US Time, 1950, MIB $625.00

Josie & the Pussycats, complete w/3 bands, Bradley, 1971, MIB, from $300 to $350.00

Kaptain Kool & the Kongs, Kaptain Kool on face, 1977, from $75 to..$100.00

Mary Marvel, Mary in flying pose, Marvel Importing Corp, 1948, MIB, from $500 to $800.00

Mickey Mouse, Ingersoll, 1933, Mickey with large hands and seconds dial, chrome case and bracelet strap, MIB, $1,200.00. (Photo courtesy David Longest and Michael Stern)

Mickey Mouse, Mickey on rectangular face, vinyl band, Ingersoll/US Time, 1947, NM (EX box) $350.00

Minnie Mouse, Minnie's hands keep time, Bradley, 1970s, replaced band otherwise EX..................................$35.00

Mork From Ork, Mork waving, vinyl band, MZ Berger, 1979, M, from $60 to $80.00

Mr Magoo, Nutrasweet premium, 1995, M $30.00

New Zoo Review, features Charlie the Owl, black band, 1975, NM, from $40 to..$50.00

Partridge Family, family photo on face, 1970s, NM, from $150 to...$200.00

Roy Rogers, flasher image of Roy on Trigger waving hat, Many Happy Trails..., leather band, 1950s, EX...$200.00

Shaun Cassidy, cartoon image & Shaun Cassidy as Joe Dardy lettered on face, blue leather band, 1970s, NM....$75.00

Spider-Man, flip-top cover designed as Spider-Man's head, vinyl strap, Hope, 1990, MOC $25.00

Three Stooges, photo image, black band, Columbia Pictures, 1980, VG...$125.00

Welcome Back Kotter, flasher image of Barbarino on face, brown band, Pamco, 1976, MIP, from $75 to.....$100.00

Wonder Woman, Wonder Woman swinging on rope, hands keep time, blue band, Dabbs, 1977, EXIB $200.00

Character Collectibles

Any popular personality, whether factual or fictional, has been promoted through the retail market to some degree. Depending on the extent of their fame, we may be deluged with this merchandise for weeks, months, even years. It's no wonder, then, that the secondary market abounds with these items or that there is such wide-spread collector demand for them today. There are rarities in any field, but for the beginning collector, many nice items are readily available at prices most can afford. Disney characters, Western heroes, TV and movie personalities, super heroes, comic book characters, and sports greats are the most sought after.

For more information, we recommend *Character Toys and Collectibles* by David Longest; *Toys of the Sixties* and *Superhero Collectibles: A Pictorial Price Guide,* both by Bill Bruegman; *Collector's Guide to TV Memorabilia, 1960s and 1970s,* by Greg Davis and Bill Morgan; and *Howdy Doody* by Jack Koch. *Schroeder's Collectible Toys, Antique to Modern,* published by Collector Books contains an extensive listing of character collectibles with current market values.

See also Advertising Characters; Beatles Collectibles; Bubble Bath Containers; California Raisins; Character and Promotional Drinking Glasses; Character Watches; Coloring Books; Cookie Jars; Cowboy Character Collectibles; Disney Collectibles; Dolls, Celebrity; Elvis Presley Memorabilia; Movie Stars Posters; Paper Dolls; Pez Candy Containers; Pin-Back Buttons; Puzzles; Rock 'n Roll Memorabilia; Shirley Temple; Star Trek; Star Wars; Toys; Vandor.

Note: Our listings are often organized by the leading character with which they're associated (for example, Pokey is in the listings that begin Gumby) or the title of the production in which they appear. (Mr. T. is with A-Team listings.)

Club: Barbara Eden's Official Fan Club
P.O. Box 556
Sherman Oaks, CA 91403; 818-761-0267

Addams Family, hand puppet, Gomez, cloth & vinyl, Ideal, 1964, EX...$75.00

Adventure Boy, finger puppet, w/Skymobile, Remco, 1970, MIB $65.00

Alvin & the Chipmunks, Curtain Call Theater, Ideal, 1984, MIB, from $40 to..$50.00

Alvin & the Chipmunks, dolls, Alvin, Theodore or Simon, plush, Knickerbocker, 1963, 14", NM, ea.............$50.00

Alvin & the Chipmunks, harmonica, Plastic Inject Corp, 1959, 4", MOC $85.00

Archie, hand puppet, plastic & vinyl, 1973, EX $45.00

Archies, Jughead Ring Toss, 1987, MOC......................**$15.00**

Astro Boy, figure, ceramic, Japan, 1960s, 8", NM......**$200.00**

Astro Boy, slide-tile puzzle, Roalex, 1960s, MIB, from $100 to..**$125.00**

Baby Huey, bop bag, inflatable vinyl w/weighted bottom, Doughboy, 1966, 54", EX.......................................**$65.00**

Banana Splits, doll, any character, stuffed cloth, Hasbro, 1969, EX, ea..**$150.00**

Banana Splits, hand puppet, Bingo, plastic, 1968, EX..**$45.00**

Banana Splits, Stand-Up Rub-Ons, Hasbro, 1969, complete, NMIB, from $100 to.......................................**$150.00**

Barney Google, figure, Syroco, 1944, 4", EX.............**$65.00**

Batman, Activity Box, Whitman, 1966, complete, rare, NM.**$65.00**

Batman, Colorforms, 1966, complete, NMIB.............**$55.00**

Batman, doll, stuffed cloth w/molded plastic face, felt cape, 1966, 27", NM, from $100 to.............................**$200.00**

Batman, Fiddlesticks, Knickerbocker, 1979, complete, EXIB...**$45.00**

Batman, figure, Batman, rubber w/elastic string, Fun Things/NPPI, 1966, 5", NM (EX card).................**$125.00**

Batman, figure, Robin, rubber w/elastic string, Fun Things/NPPI, 1966, 5", NM (EX card)...................**$85.00**

Batman, Flying Batscout, figure in center of flying disk, Tarco, 1966, MOC..**$50.00**

Batman, Hot-Line Batphone, red plastic w/decals, Marx, 1966, 8", NMIB.......................................**$500.00**

Batman, make-up kit, Joker, 1989, MIP.....................**$15.00**

Batman, push-button puppet, Kohner, 1960s, NM....**$100.00**

Batman, skateboard, Batman & Joker w/Bat logo, Action Sports, 1989, 28", MIB......................................**$50.00**

Batman, slide-tile puzzle, red plastic, American Publishing Co, 1977, MOC......................................**$25.00**

Batman, Sparkle Paints, Kenner, 1966, complete, EXIB..**$75.00**

Batman, squirt gun, plastic head figure, Durham, 1974, EX..**$25.00**

Batman, Super-Gyro Batmobile, plastic, AHI/NPPI, 1973, 6", NMIB...**$125.00**

Batman, yo-yo, flasher seal, Duncan, early 1980s, MIP..**$30.00**

Batman & Robin, pinball machine, Marx, 1966, 22x10", EX..**$100.00**

Batman Returns, magic slate, Golden, 1992, MIB (sealed)..**$5.00**

Battlestar Galactica, ring, Lt Starbuck photo, MIB.......**$75.00**

Beany & Cecil, carrying case, red vinyl w/image of cast & Leakin' Lena, Bob Clampett, 1961, 9" dia, VG......**$50.00**

Beany & Cecil, pull toy, Leakin' Lena Pound 'N Pull, wooden boat shape, Pressman, 1961, 14", VG.............**$125.00**

Beany & Cecil, record player, Beany & Cecil & Their Pals, Bob Clampett, 1960s, rare, EX, from $200 to.....**$300.00**

Beatle Bailey, magic slate, Lowe, 1963, NM.............**$35.00**

Ben Casey, doctor kit, w/8 accessories, Transogram, 1960s, EX..**$35.00**

Ben Casey, paint-by-number set, Transogram, 1962, MIB (sealed)..**$125.00**

Betty Boop, Colorforms Big Dress-Up Set, 1970s, complete, MIB, from $35 to...**$45.00**

Betty Boop, doll, Ko-Ko the Clown, stuffed cloth w/rubber head, removable outfit, Presents, 1987, 12", NM..**$25.00**

Betty Boop, figure set, 5 hand-painted wooden figures that fit inside of ea other, Russia, 1980s, M................**$75.00**

Betty Boop & Bimbo, ashtray, porcelain figures on rim of fan-shaped blue & tan lustre dish, prewar Japan, 3", M.**$175.00**

Beverly Hillbillies, Colorforms Cartoon Kit, 1963, MIB, from $100 to...**$125.00**

Beverly Hillbillies, movie viewer, plastic, w/2 strips of film, Acme, 1964, MOC, from $50 to.............**$75.00**

Beverly Hillbillies, slide-tile puzzle, Roalex, 1963, 2x2", MOC..**$125.00**

Bewitched, broom, plastic w/head figure of Samantha in witch's hat, 36", MIP.......................................**$300.00**

Bionic Woman, Action Club Kit, complete w/sticker, membership card, photo & certificate, Kenner, 1975, M......**$65.00**

Blondie & Dagwood, figure, Dagwood, Syroco, Pillbury premium, 1944, 5", NM.......................................**$85.00**

Blondie & Dagwood, kazoo, tin sandwich shape, KFS, 1947, 6", NMIB...**$175.00**

Blondie & Dagwood, marionette, Dagwood, Hazelle's, 1950s, MIB..**$250.00**

Bozo the Clown, Colorforms Cartoon Kit, 1960, complete, EXIB..**$50.00**

Bozo the Clown, figure, bendable, Jesco, 1988, 6", MIP.**$6.00**

Bozo the Clown, Stitch-a-Story, Hasbro, 1967, MIB....**$50.00**

Brady Bunch, magic slate, Whitman, 1973, unused, NM, from $50 to...**$75.00**

Brady Bunch, tambourine, Larami, 1973, MIC............**$25.00**

Brady Bunch, tea set, plastic, Larami, 1973, MOC......**$25.00**

Buck Rogers, Official Utility Belt, plastic, Remco, 1979, complete, NMIB...**$55.00**

Bugs Bunny, Colorforms Cartoon Kit, 1958, complete, EXIB..**$75.00**

Bugs Bunny, doll, dressed as Davy Crockett, felt w/cloth clothes & coonskin cap, 1950s, EX....................**$325.00**

Bugs Bunny, jack-in-the-box, Mattel, 1962, from $50 to..**$75.00**

Bugs Bunny, lamp, Bugs seated in chair w/cheek resting in hand on square base w/name, Holiday Fair/Warner, 1970, 11", M...**$55.00**

Bugs Bunny, push-button puppet, Kohner, EX............**$20.00**

Bugs Bunny, sleeping bag, image of Bugs & various Looney Tunes characters, 1877, EX...............................**$25.00**

Bugs Bunny, vase, ceramic, Bugs figure leaning against tree trunk, Warner Bros, 1940s, 7", NM+.................**$60.00**

Bugs Bunny, yo-yo, plastic w/paper sticker seal, early 1990s, MIP..**$6.00**

Captain America, doll, stuffed cloth w/vinyl head, Super Baby series, Amsco, 1970s, 8", NM (VG box)......**$50.00**

Captain America, flashlight, plastic w/paper decal, Gordy International, 1980, 3½", MIP.............................**$30.00**

Captain America, hand puppet, plastic & rubber, Ideal, 1966, 11", NM..**$100.00**

Captain Kangaroo, Finger Paint Set, Hasbro, 1956, complete, EXIB..**$55.00**

Captain Kangaroo, party dress, cheesecloth w/colorful illustrations of various characters, 1966, EX.............**$15.00**

Captain Marvel, Flying Captain Marvel, uncut paper figure to assemble, Fawcett, 1944, unused, M (w/envelope).**$38.00**

Captain Marvel, Magic Flute, MOC............................$125.00

Care Bears, dolls, any character, Kenner, 1984, 3", MOC..$15.00

Casper the Friendly Ghost, doll, vinyl w/painted facial features & name across chest, Hungerford, 1960, 8", MIB...$50.00

Casper the Friendly Ghost, kite, Casper & Wendy, Saalfield, 1960, MIP...$20.00

Casper the Friendly Ghost, Stitch-a-Story, Hasbro, 1967, MOC (sealed) $50.00

Charlie McCarthy, doll, composition w/cloth clothes, Effanbee, 1940, 19", EX..$200.00

Charlie's Angels, AM Wrist Radio, Illco, 1977, MIB, from $250 to...$300.00

Charlie's Angels, Beauty Kit, plastic comb & mirror, any character, Fleetwood, 1977, MOC, ea.........................$15.00

CHiPs, Emergency Medical Kit, Empire, 1980, MIB $30.00

CHiPs, Wind 'N Watch Speedster, Buddy L, 1981, MOC..$35.00

Daisy Mae, Dogpatch USA, plaster figure, 1968, 8", $125.00.
(Photo courtesy June Moon)

Dennis the Menace, figure, plastic w/movable arms, 1954, 5", EX...$40.00

Dennis the Menace, phonograph, Hank Ketchum, 1960s, NM, from $100 to..$150.00

Deputy Dawg, badge, US Marshal, metal, Larami, 1973, MOC $12.00

Deputy Dawg, bop bag, inflatable vinyl w/weighted bottom, Doughboy, 1961, 54", NM.....................................$50.00

Dick Tracy, charm from gumball machine, any character, plastic head figure, EX, ea, from $20 to $25.00

Dick Tracy, doll, Dick Tracy, painted composition w/cloth clothes, movable mouth, 14½", EX $250.00

Dick Tracy, doll, Sparkle Plenty, rubber & plastic w/yarn hair, w/original tag, Ideal, 1947-50, NM, minimum value.$200.00

Dick Tracy, Fingerprint Lab, Parliament Toy, 1953, complete, EXIB...$135.00

Dick Tracy, hand puppet, Dick Tracy, cloth & vinyl, w/record, Ideal, 1961, 11", NMIB......................$125.00

Dick Tracy, Mini Color Televiewer, Larami, 1972, NMIP..$25.00

Dick Tracy, Sparkle Paints, Kenner, 1963, unused, complete, MIB $50.00

Dick Tracy, wallet, black vinyl, w/6 Crimestopper textbook cards, 1973, NM $20.00

Dinosaurs, doll, Baby Sinclair, stuffed talker w/plastic head, Hasbro, 1992, MIB......................................$50.00

Dr Dolittle, Animal Fist Faces, EXIB $40.00

Dr Dolittle, Mystery Chamber Magic Set, Remco, 1939, NMIB...$30.00

Dr Dolittle, projector, Ugly Mugly, w/slides from movie, Remco, NMIB $50.00

Dr Dolittle, Spelling & Counting Board, Bar-Zim, NMIP..$35.00

Dr Kildare, scrapbook, 1962, 14x11", unused, NM $65.00

Dr Seuss, jack-in-the-box, Cat in the Hat, Mattel, 1970, 5x5", EX..$65.00

Dr Seuss, See 'N Talking Storybook, Friends of Dr Seuss, Mattel, 1970, NM.......................................$200.00

Dr Shrinker, Dukes of Hazzard, Colorforms, 1981, NMIB..$30.00

Elvira, earrings, 1986, MOC......................................$35.00

ET, doll, plush, Showtime, 1982, 8", NM.......................$6.00

E.T., Night Light, chest glows, 1983, MIB, $35.00.

Family Affair, Fun Box, Whitman, 1970, complete, MIB ...$50.00

Family Affair, magic slate, Buffy & Jody, Watkins-Strathmore, 1970, NM, from $35 to...$45.00

Family Affair, tea set, Buffy, plastic, Chilton Toys, 46 pcs, M $75.00

Family Affair, wig, Buffy, brown or blond, Amsco, 1971, MIB, ea $100.00

Fantasy Island, Poster Art Set, Craft Master, 1978, MIP ..$40.00

Fearless Fly, kite, plastic w/full-color image, Roalex, 1967, MIP..$200.00

Felix the Cat, Pencil Coloring by Numbers, Hasbro, 1958, MIP..$50.00

Flash Gordon, compass, silver plastic w/yellow wristband, 1950s, MOC $75.00

Flintstones, bubble pipe, Bamm-Bamm, Transogram, 1963, MOC..$25.00

Flintstones, Cockamamies, 1961, complete, NMIB......**$35.00**

Flintstones, doll, Baby Pebbles, vinyl, w/bone in red hair, leopard-skin outfit, blanket, Ideal, 1960s, 14", EXIB **$55.00**

Flintstones, doll, Fred or Barney, plush & vinyl, Knickerbocker, 1960s, 12", NM, ea from $75 to..**$100.00**

Flintstones, finger puppet, Fred, Knickerbocker, M (VG card)...**$20.00**

Flintstones, Fuzzy Felt Playset, Standard Toyfraft, 1961, complete, EXIB **$75.00**

Flintstones, Play Fun Set, Whitman, 1965, complete, EXIB **$65.00**

Flintstones, push-button puppet, Dino, Kohner, 1960s, M **$65.00**

Flintstones, push-button puppet, Fred, Kohner, 1962, M **$75.00**

Flintstones, push-button puppet, Wilma, Kohner, 1960s, NM **$35.00**

Flintstones, squirt gun, Fred, plastic head figure, 1974, EX...**$25.00**

Flintstones, Stoneway Piano, Jaymar, 1961, 8x11", rare, EXIB **$200.00**

Flintstones, yo-yo, Fred, plastic w/molded head, 1970, NM **$12.00**

Flipper, Activity Box, Whitman, 1966, complete, MIB ..**$40.00**

Flipper, Plastic Stick-Ons, Standard Toykraft, 1965, complete, MIB **$40.00**

Flipper, ukelele, Mattel, 1968, MIP...........................**$100.00**

Flying Nun, chalkboard, Hasbro, 1967, 16x24", MIP ..**$75.00**

Flying Nun, Stitch-a-Story, Hasbro, 1967, complete, MIB...**$85.00**

Foghorn Leghorn, doll, stuffed plush, w/original tag, Warner Bros, recent, M, from $15 to **$20.00**

Foghorn Leghorn, hand puppet, plush, Warner Bros, 1970s, EX, from $20 to.................................**$30.00**

Full House, doll, Michelle, vinyl talker w/cloth clothes, Meritus, 1990, 15", MIB **$30.00**

Gilligan's Island, doll set, Gilligan, Skipper & Mary Ann, soft rubber, Playskool, 1977, M....................**$35.00**

Gilligan's Island, Gilligan's Floating Island, Playskool, 1977, complete, MIB, from $125 to **$150.00**

Green Hornet, Colorforms Cartoon Kit, 1965, complete, NMIB...**$100.00**

Green Hornet, hand puppet, plastic & vinyl, Ideal, 1966, 10", EX **$125.00**

Green Hornet, kite, Roalex, 1967, MIP **$200.00**

Green Hornet, Magic Rub-Off, Whitman, 1966, complete, EXIB...**$200.00**

Green Hornet, wrist radios, green plastic, Remco, 1966, 4", NMIB...**$200.00**

Gulliver's Travels, magic slate, Adventures of Gulliver, Watkins-Strathmore, 1969, no pencil, NM...........**$35.00**

Gumby, yo-yo, molded plastic, Spectra Star, NM..........**$5.00**

Gumby & Pokey, Lolly Pop-Up Puppet, 1967, unused, MIB...**$65.00**

Gumby & Pokey, Modeling Dough, Chemtoy, 1967, unused, MIB **$50.00**

Gumby, Astronaut Adventure Costume, Lakeside, 1965, #8123, MIP, from $12.00 to $15.00.

Happy Days, Bubb-A-Loons, Fonz, Imperial, 1981, MIP **$15.00**

Happy Days, Fonz Viewer, Larami, 1981, MOC..........**$20.00**

Happy Days, pinball machine, Coleco, 1976, MIB ...**$175.00**

Hardy Boys, Pocket Flix Cassette, Ideal, 1978, MIP....**$15.00**

Hardy Boys & Nancy Drew, Cartoonarama, 1978, MIB..**$60.00**

Harry & the Hendersons, doll, Harry, talker, Galoob, 24", MIB.**$80.00**

Heckle & Jeckle, magic slate, Lowe, 1952, NM...........**$25.00**

Herman & Katnip, Deep View Paint Set, Pressman, 1961, complete, NMIB...**$75.00**

Herman & Katnip, kite, Saalfield, 1960, MIP **$25.00**

Howdy Doody, Bee-Nee Kit, NMIB **$65.00**

Howdy Doody, boxing gloves, tan w/black image of Howdy, Parvey, 1950s, 6", NMIB.................................**$325.00**

Howdy Doody, Clock-A-Doodle, litho tin wind up, 1950s, NMIB...**$1,600.00**

Howdy Doody, doll, Howdy, cloth w/composition head, hands & feet, sleep eyes, Effanbee, 1947, 20", EX, minimum value **$400.00**

Howdy Doody, doll, Howdy, stuffed cloth, Applause, 1988, 18", EX...**$30.00**

Howdy Doody, doll, Princess, plastic w/cloth clothes, sleep eyes, Beehler, 7", NMIB **$225.00**

Howdy Doody, figure, Dilly Dally, jointed cardboard, unmarked, 12", rare, NM.................................**$50.00**

Howdy Doody, figure, Howdy, jointed cardboard, Snickers premium, 1950s, M (EX envelope)......................**$75.00**

Howdy Doody, flashlight, Circus Kee 'N Lite, semi-truck shape w/colorful image, pocket-size, MIB **$150.00**

Howdy Doody, football, brown w/black drawing of Howdy, white vinyl stitching, 1950s, 8", EX **$85.00**

Howdy Doody, hand puppet, Dilly Dally, cloth & rubber, 1950s, EX...**$75.00**

Howdy Doody, Magic Piano, Kagran, 15x10", EXIB...**$575.00**

Howdy Doody, marionette, Mr Bluster, Peter Puppet, 14", MIB...**$500.00**

Howdy Doody, night light, Howdy figure riding bull, ceramic, Leadworks, 1988, unused, M **$185.00**

Howdy Doody, raft, inflatable vinyl w/various character images, Ideal/Kagran, 9x9", MIP **$200.00**

Howdy Doody, Ranch House Tool Box, metal, Kagran, 1950s, EX..$200.00

Howdy Doody, Sand Forms, Ideal, 1952, MOC........$125.00

Howdy Doody, swim ring, inflatable vinyl, 1950s, 24" dia, EX $65.00

Howdy Doody, top, litho tin, LBZ/West Germany, NM..$125.00

Howdy Doody, ventriloquist doll, Howdy, Ideal, 1950s, 18", EX $200.00

Howdy Doody, Venus Paradise Coloring Set, Kagran, 1950s, complete, EXIB $200.00

HR Pufnstuf, doll, Pufnstuf or Witchiepoo, stuffed cloth, My Toy, 1973, 16", MIB, ea, from $300 to $400.00

HR Pufnstuf, tote bag, canvas w/image of Pufnstuf, Sid & Marty Krofft Productions Inc, 1976, 13x14", M..$125.00

HR Pufnstuf, umbrella, black, red, or blue, Sid & Marty Krofft Productions Inc, 1976, M, ea $125.00

Huckleberry Hound, Candy Factory gumball machine, litho tin & plastic, 1960, 11", EX......................$40.00

Huckleberry Hound, Colorforms Cartoon Kit, 1962, complete, NMIB $65.00

Huckleberry Hound, marionette, Pelham, 1960s, 9", scarce, NMIB..$450.00

Huckleberry Hound, TV Wiggle Blocks, plastic, set of 10 w/flasher images of Huck & friends, Kohner, 1962, NMIB..$135.00

Huckleberry Hound, Utility Belt, Remco, 1978, complete, NMIB..$25.00

I Dream of Jeannie, Dream Bottle, w/figure, Remco, 1976, MIB $175.00

I Dream of Jeannie, Magic Locket, 4-way mirror on chain, Harmony, 1975, MOC..............................$45.00

I Love Lucy, finger puppet, Little Ricky, vinyl w/cloth outfit & fleece blanket, Zany Toys, 1952, 8", NMIB, from $400 to...$500.00

Impossibles, magic slate, Watkins-Strathmore, EX $30.00

Incredible Hulk, Flip-It, Tillotson, 1977, MOC $50.00

Incredible Hulk, yo-yo, w/flasher seal, Duncan, early 1980s, NM $18.00

Indiana Jones & the Temple of Doom, sleeping bag, 1984, EX..$30.00

Inspector Gadget, Quick-Dry paint-by-number set, Avalon, 1983, MIB (sealed)......................................$20.00

James Bond, hand puppet, painted vinyl full-figure image w/Sean Connery likeness, Gilbert, 1965, 14", EX..$150.00

James Bond, 007 Electric Drawing Set, Lakeside, 1966, complete, EXIB, from $50 to $75.00

Jetsons, puffy magnets, George & Jane, 1970s, 4", EX, pr..$10.00

Jetsons, Slate & Chalk Set, 1960s, unused, MIB $100.00

Jonny Quest, paint-by-number set, Transogram, 1965, complete, EXIB, from $300 to $400.00

Josie & the Pussycats, Marvy Markers, Uchida of America, 1974, MIB $40.00

Josie & the Pussycats, Slick Ticker play watch, Larami, 1973, MOC, from $50 to..$75.00

Junior G-Men, Fingerprint Set, Hale-Ness Corp, early 1940s, complete, EX (G box) $150.00

Kaptain Kool & the Kongs, guitar, plastic, Emenee, 1977, 34", M $75.00

Kaptain Kool & the Kongs, phonograph, Vanity Fair, 1978, MIB $25.00

King Kong, Colorforms Panoramic Play Set, 1976, complete, EXIB..$25.00

Land of the Giants, Colorforms, 1968, complete, NMIB .$100.00

Land of the Lost, Direction Finder, Larami, 1975, MOC $30.00

Land of the Lost, Moon Spinners, Larami, 1975, MOC..$25.00

Lariat Sam, Colorforms Cartoon Kit, 1962, complete, EXIB..$35.00

Lassie, Trick Trainer, Mousely Inc, 1956, complete, NMIB..$175.00

Laurel (from Laurel and Hardy), plastic figure, 1972, 14", $65.00. (Photo courtesy June Moon)

Laurel & Hardy, dolls, Bend 'Em, Knickerbocker, 9", MIP (sealed), ea..$45.00

Laurel & Hardy, Pop-Up Our Hats figures, Coopex Plastics, 8", NM (EX box) $250.00

Laurel & Hardy, Stuff & Lace Dolls, Transogram, 1962, complete, MIB, ea..$30.00

Laverne & Shirley, paint-by-number set, Hasbro, 1981, MIB..$35.00

Laverne & Shirley, Pocket Flix Cassette, Ideal, 1978, MOC..$20.00

Li'l Abner, Picto-Puzzles, set of 6, Plas-Trix, MOC....$100.00

Little Audrey, doll, vinyl, unmarked, 13", EX $50.00

Little Audrey, kitchen set, Little Audrey Does the Dishes, 1960, complete, EXIB $75.00

Little House on the Prairie, tea set, 26 pcs, Ohio Art, 1980, MIB $100.00

Little Lulu, Cartoon-A-Kit, M Buell Kits Inc, 1948, complete, NM (EX box)..$200.00

Little Orphan Annie & Sandy, ashtray, Annie & Sandy on rim of fan-shaped white & tan lustre dish w/2 rests, 4x4", NM..$100.00

Little Red Riding Hood, tea set, litho tin, white w/red border, 11 pcs, Ohio Art, 1960s, NM, from $75 to..........**$100.00**

Looney Tunes, Toon-A-Vision, TV-style board w/knobs to create over 64,000 faces, 1950s, NM **$40.00**

Lover Boat, Poster Art Kit, Craft Master, 1978, MIP **$40.00**

Ludwig Von Drake, Needlepoint Set, Hasbro, 1961, complete, MIB (sealed)..**$35.00**

Magilla Gorilla, change purse, vinyl w/zipper closure, Estelle, 1960s, 3" dia, NMOC...............................**$35.00**

Magilla Gorilla, doll, stuffed plush body w/soft vinyl head, Ideal, 1960s, 18½", NM **$125.00**

Magilla Gorilla, Plastic Stick-Ons, Standard Toykraft, 1964, complete, EXIB....................................**$50.00**

Man From UNCLE, bop bag, vinyl, Dean/MGM, 1966, NMIP **$175.00**

Man From UNCLE, Foto Fantastiks Coloring Set, Faber, 1965, MIB **$165.00**

Marvel Super Heroes, Colorforms, 1983, complete, MIB ..**$20.00**

Marvel Super Heroes, Deluxe Sparkle Paints, Kenner, 1967, unused, MIB...**$150.00**

Marvel Super Heroes, finger puppets, Captain America, Hulk, Spider-Man, or Thor, vinyl, Imperial Toy, 1978, NM, ea **$15.00**

Miss Piggy, doll, stuffed fabric with vinyl head, rooted hair, removable dress, Fisher-Price, 1980, 14", $20.00.
(Photo courtesy Linda Baker)

Mighty Mouse, doll, rubber w/cloth cape, 1955, 10", EX...**$75.00**

Mighty Mouse, Presto-Paints, Kenner, 1963, complete, EXIB **$65.00**

Mork & Mindy, Colorforms Rub 'N Play, 1979, MIB...**$35.00**

Mork & Mindy, Colorforms Shrinky Dinks, 1979, MIB (sealed) **$25.00**

Mortimer Snerd, teeth, wax & plastic, Pilo Novelty, 1940s, unused, NM (in plastic bag w/illustrated card) **$65.00**

Mother Goose, magic slate set, Strathmore, 1945, complete, EXIB...**$35.00**

Mother Goose, Peepful Pals Playset, Whitman, complete, MIB **$50.00**

Mr Ed, hand puppet, pull-string talker, Mattel, 1962, MIB **$200.00**

Mr Magoo, doll, stuffed cloth w/rubber head, baseball uniform, 1967, 27", rare, NM......................**$150.00**

Mr Magoo, doll, stuffed cloth w/vinyl head, felt jacket w/knitted scarf, Ideal, 1964, 15", EX, minimum value...**$75.00**

Munsters, doll, baby Herman, vinyl w/cloth clothes, Ideal, 1965, NM **$65.00**

Muppets, stick puppets, any character, plastic, Fisher-Price, 1979, MOC, ea, from $5 to...........................**$10.00**

Nancy & Sluggo, dolls, stuffed vinyl w/cloth clothes, S&P Doll & Toy, 1954, 16", NM, ea, from $150 to.....**$200.00**

Nanny & the Professor, Colorforms Cartoon Kit, 1971, MIB...**$40.00**

New Zoo Revue, autograph doll, stuffed cloth, w/pen, 1970s, 11½", NM, from $25 to...........................**$30.00**

New Zoo Revue, Punch-O-Ball, Oak Rubber, 1973, MIP..**$35.00**

New Zoo Revue, Stamp Set, Imperial, 1973, MOC, from $30 to...**$40.00**

Our Gang, rowboat, plastic, Mego, 1975, 12½", MIB .**$40.00**

Peanuts, Deluxe Playset, 3 jointed dolls w/Lucy's psychiatrist's booth & stool, Determined #575, 1975, MIB, from $225 to...**$300.00**

Peanuts, doll, Charlie Brown, stuffed printed cloth pillow type, 1963, EX...**$40.00**

Peanuts, doll, Linus Thumb & Blanket, stuffed body w/soft plastic head & hands, Determined, 1983, 8", MIB .**$25.00**

Peanuts, doll, Snoopy, talker, World Wonder, 1986, MIB..**$100.00**

Peanuts, Drive-In Movie Theater, features Snoopy, Kenner, 1975, complete, MIB, from $150 to.....................**$200.00**

Peanuts, jam jar, Snoopy figure seated on domed lid, ceramic, M...**$55.00**

Peanuts, kaleidoscope, Snoopy Disco, Determined, 1979, EX...**$20.00**

Peanuts, megaphone, Charlie Brown, Chein, 1970, rare, EX **$45.00**

Peanuts, mug, Woodstock figure perched on handle of tree-trunk-type mug w/carved heart, ceramic, Teleflora, 1972, M **$35.00**

Peanuts, Peppermint Patty, stuffed printed cloth w/cloth shorts outfit, Ideal/Determined, 13½", MIB..........**$50.00**

Peanuts, purse, canvas w/image of Snoopy blowing bubbles, 9x8", M **$100.00**

Peanuts, skateboard, features Snoopy as Joe Camel, 1970s, NM **$100.00**

Peanuts, Stuff 'N Lace Dolls, Charlie Brown & Lucy or Linus & Snoopy, Standard Toykraft, 1961, NMIB, ea, from $150 to...**$170.00**

Peanuts, top, litho tin, Chein, 1969, MIB, from $75 to...**$75.00**

Pee Wee's Playhouse, clip-on figure, Pee Wee, scarce, NM...**$25.00**

Pee Wee's Playhouse, doll, Vance the Talking Pig, Matchbox, 1988, MIB **$55.00**

Phantom of the Opera, Rub-Ons Magic Picture Transfers, Hasbro, 1966, complete, NMIB...........................**$100.00**

Pink Panther, Cartoonarama, 1970, complete, EXIB ...**$60.00**

Pinky Lee, doll, Lose Your Head, squeeze rubber body w/pop-off head, 9", NM **$95.00**

Pinky Lee, xylophone, metal & plastic, Emenee, 1950s, EXIB **$75.00**

Pixie & Dixie, dolls, stuffed plush, Knickerbocker, 1960, 10", EX, pr...**$100.00**

Pixie & Dixie, Punch-O Punching Bag, inflatable vinyl w/weighted bottom, Kestral, 1959, 18", NMIB **$25.00**

Planet of the Apes, Mix 'N Mold Set, Burke, Dr Zaius, or Astronaut Virdon, rare, MIB, ea..........................**$100.00**

Planet of the Apes, squirt gun, Cornelius, plastic, AHI, 1970s, M...**$75.00**

Popeye, boxing gloves, red, Everlast, 1950s, MIP.......**$75.00**

Popeye, doll, Olive Oyl, stuffed cloth w/rubber head & composition feet, w/original heart-shaped tag, Effanbee, 16", EX **$325.00**

Popeye, doll, Popeye, stuffed cloth w/vinyl head & arms, Gund, 1957, 20", EX **$150.00**

Popeye, figure, Popeye, Syroco, 1944, 5", EX.............**$60.00**

Popeye, figure, Wimpy, Syroco, 1944, 4", EX.............**$60.00**

Popeye, gumball machine, bust figure w/pipe, Hasbro, 1968, VG **$50.00**

Popeye, harmonica, red, Plastic Injector Corp, 1958, 5", MIP **$45.00**

Popeye, pipe, wood & plastic, battery-operated, Micro-Lite/Putman, 1958, 5½x9", NM (on display card)....**$75.00**

Popeye, push-button puppet, Olive Oyl, Kohner, NM ..**$75.00**

Popeye, TV Eras-O-Board Set, Hasbro, 1958, complete, EXIB...**$75.00**

Porky Pig, jack-in-the-box, litho tin, Mattel, 1960s, NM **$100.00**

Quick Draw McGraw, doll, stuffed plush w/rubber head, felt gun w/holster & gun, Knickerbocker, 1962, 11", NM **$150.00**

Quick Draw McGraw, gloves, western-style cloth w/image, EX...**$25.00**

Raggedy Andy, vase, figure lying on stomach, ceramic, Bobbs-Merrill, 1976, EX...**$45.00**

Raggedy Ann, coin purse, vinyl figure w/zipper closure, Hallmark/Bobbs-Merrill, NM **$15.00**

Raggedy Ann, Colorforms Pop-Up Tea Party, complete, MIB...**$30.00**

Raggedy Ann, Colorforms Sew-Ons, 1976, MIB..........**$25.00**

Raggedy Ann, rug, round head image w/smiling face, blue, red & black features w/orange hair, 26" dia, EX..**$60.00**

Raggedy Ann, vase, seated figure w/legs spread & holding baby bottle, Replo #6565, 6", EX...**$45.00**

Raggedy Ann, Wipe-Off Slate, Pussy Willow Creations/Bobbs-Merrill, 1978, 7½", NM **$20.00**

Raggedy Ann & Andy, beach ball, Ideal, 1974, 20" dia, MIP **$30.00**

Raggedy Ann & Andy, child's cup, Johnny Gruelle art, Crooksville China, 1941, EX...**$65.00**

Raggedy Ann & Andy, child's feeding dish, Johnny Gruelle art, Crooksville China, 1941, 8¾" dia, EX.............**$85.00**

Raggedy Ann & Andy, Colorforms Pre-School Playset, 1980, MIB **$25.00**

Raggedy Ann & Andy, plate, Valentines Day 1978, ceramic, Schmid, MIB...**$50.00**

Raggedy Ann and Andy, Paste and Stick, Whitman, 1968, MIB, $30.00.

Raggedy Ann & Andy, Punch-O-Ball, Oak Rubber, 1972, 14" dia, MIP **$20.00**

Raggedy Ann & Andy, watering can, litho metal, Chein, 1973, 9", NM...**$35.00**

Ricochet Rabbit, pull toy, vinyl figure sitting on yellow plastic wagon, Ideal, 1964, EX...**$100.00**

Road Runner, yo-yo, molded plastic w/embossed seal, John Hart Toys Inc, 1974, MIP...**$40.00**

Rocky & Bullwinkle, Bullwinkle Electric Quiz, 1971, MOC (sealed) **$40.00**

Rocky & Bullwinkle, Bullwinkle's Kaleidoscope Puzzle, 1969, MOC...**$30.00**

Rocky & Bullwinkle, Rocky & His Friends Sewing Cards, Whitman, 1961, complete, NMIB...**$100.00**

Rootie Kazootie, magic set, 1950s, complete, NMIB.**$125.00**

Ruff & Reddy, Karbon Kopee Kit, Wonder Art, 1960, complete, EXIB **$75.00**

Scooby Doo, doll, stuffed plush, Sutton, 1970s, EX....**$40.00**

Scooby Doo, gumball machine, clear plastic head w/yellow base, Hasbro, 1968, EX **$25.00**

Sesame Street, doll, Big Bird, pull-string talker, Playskool, 1970s, 22", VG...**$25.00**

Sesame Street, figure set, PVC, set of 8, Applause, 1993, M **$20.00**

Sesame Street, key chain, any character, Fisher-Price, rare, MIB, ea...**$25.00**

Silly Sidney, crayon-by-number set, Transogram, 1965, complete, EXIB **$100.00**

Simpsons, doll, Bart, stuffed cloth w/vinyl head, arms & legs, Dandee, 16", MIB...**$15.00**

Simpsons, figure, any character w/5 interchangable balloons, PVC, Mattel, MOC, ea, from $20 to **$25.00**

Simpsons, Fun Dough Maker, MIB.............................**$30.00**

Simpsons, Rad Rollers, set of 6 marbles, Spectra Star, MOC **$15.00**

Simpsons, Sofa & Boob Tube, Mattel, MIB................**$65.00**

Six Million Dollar Man, CB Headset Radio Receiver, Kenner, 1977, MIB, from $40 to...**$50.00**

Six Million Dollar Man, Play-Doh Action Play Set, Kenner, 1979, complete, NMIB **$40.00**

Six Million Dollar Man, tattoos & stickers, Kenner, 1976, MOC..**$12.00**

Smurfs, Colorforms, complete, EXIB................**$35.00**

Smurfs, figure, Papa Smurf, ceramic, VG.................**$30.00**

Smurfs, sewing cards, MIB (sealed) **$25.00**

Smurfs, Smurf Village, ceramic, VG.........................**$35.00**

Space Angel, press kit, 1960s, complete, EX (EX folder) ..**$165.00**

Speedy Gonzales, hand puppet, vinyl, 1970s, EX.......**$15.00**

Spider-Man, Action Box, figure dances inside box, Fleetwood, 1978, MOC...**$50.00**

Spider-Man, Code Breaker, Gordy, 1980, MOC...........**$35.00**

Spider-Man, doll, stuffed talker, Mego, 1974, 28", M ..**$45.00**

Spider-Man, hand puppet, cloth & vinyl, Imperial, 1979, MIP...**$20.00**

Spider-Man, Power Shield, Funstuff, 1976, 13", MIP ...**$65.00**

Spider-Man, squirt gun, plastic head figure, 1974, EX .**$25.00**

Spider-Man, Web Maker, Chemtoys, 1977, MOC.......**$100.00**

Starsky & Hutch, AM Wrist Radio, Illco, 1977, MIB **$50.00**

Starsky & Hutch, Emergency Dashboard, Illco, 1977, MIB **$125.00**

Starsky & Hutch, Poster Put-Ons, Bi-Rite, 1976, MIP ..**$12.00**

Steve Canyon, Jet Helmet, Ideal, 1959, EXIB **$100.00**

Steve Canyon, school bag, yellow canvas w/color image, 1959, EX...**$75.00**

Superman, doll, Applause, 1988, 18", NM **$25.00**

Superman, doll, Ideal, 1939, jointed wood, red cloth cape, 12", EX, from $800.00 to $1,000.00.

Superman, Kid Paddlers, blue rubber swimming fins, Superswim Inc, 1956, NMIB **$100.00**

Superman, kite, Hi-Flier, 1984, MIP...........................**$30.00**

Superman, Muscle Building Set, Peter Puppet, 1954, complete, NMIB, from $40 to **$350.00**

Superman, playsuit, Ben Cooper/Superman Inc, 1940s-50s, complete, EXIB **$225.00**

Superman & Wonder Woman, Super-Sounds record player, white plastic, Dee-Jay, 1970s, EX **$75.00**

Sylvester the Cat, roly-poly, EX **$25.00**

Tarzan, Jungle Animals Set, Salco/Banner, 1966, complete & unused, NM (EX box) **$200.00**

Tarzan, Rub-Off Picture Set, Whitman, 1966, complete, VG (VG box) **$25.00**

Tarzan, Weebles Jungle Hut, Romper Room/ Hasbro, 1976, MIB, $85.00.
(Photo courtesy June Moon)

Tasmanian Devil, yo-yo, plastic, Magic Mountain souvenir, 1990s, NM..**$4.00**

Teenage Mutan Ninja Turtles, tote bag, repeated design, Mirage Studios, 1989, 14x8", NM **$20.00**

Teenage Mutant Ninja Turtles, water bopper, inflatable, 1990, 36", MIP **$25.00**

Tennessee Tuxedo, pencil-by-number set, Transogram, 1963, complete, EXIB **$100.00**

That Girl, wig case, 1960s, NM, from $75 to.............**$100.00**

Three Stooges, Colorforms Slap-Stick-On, 1959, scarce, MIB **$300.00**

Three Stooges, dolls, set of 3, Exclusive Premier/Target, 10"...**$100.00**

Three Stooges, flasher rings, any 3, EX, ea **$25.00**

Tom & Jerry, cups, ceramic, 3 different, ea w/interacting bomb scenes w/characters, Staffordshire/MGM, 1970, ea **$45.00**

Tom & Jerry, dolls, stuffed cloth, Georgene, 1949, 16" Tom & 7" Jerry, NM, pr...**$400.00**

Tom & Jerry, guitar, plastic, Mattel, 1960s, NM, from $100 to **$125.00**

Tom & Jerry, jack-in-the-box, Mattel, M, from $75 to ...**$100.00**

Top Cat, doll set, Top Cat & Benny the Ball & Spook, vinyl, Knickerbocker, 1960s, 8", EX.............................**$100.00**

Top Cat, viewer, plastic house shape w/look-through peep hole to see 8 action scenes, 3x2½", NMIB **$95.00**

Topo Gigio, hand puppet, American Character, 1960s, 12", MIB **$125.00**

Tweety Bird, charm, plastic figure, 1950s, ¾", NM.....**$15.00**

Underdog, harmonica, plastic w/figure at ea end, 1975, 8", NM **$25.00**

Underdog, iron-on transfers, set of 3 w/Underdog, Polly & Simon Barsinister, Vortex, 1960s, 8x10", unused, NM **$55.00**

Universal Monsters, sticker sheet, set of 8, 1960s, EX...**$50.00**

Welcome Back Kotter, bulletin board, Board King, 1976, M..$50.00

Welcome Back Kotter, Poster Art Kit, Board King, 1976, MIB..$45.00

Welcome Back Kotter, Sweat-hog Calculator, Remco, #650, 1976, MOC, $35.00.

Welcome Back Kotter, Sweathogs Cartoon Set, Toy Factory, 1977, MIB $40.00

Winky Dink, Paint Set, Pressman, 1950s, complete & unused, NMIB..$75.00

Winky Dink, Super Magic TV Kit, Winky Dink & You, Standard Toykraft, 1968, EXIB................................$85.00

Wizard of Oz, doll, Dorothy, jointed composition w/red checked rayon dress, 1939-40, 15½", M..........$1,500.00

Wizard of Oz, doll, Scarecrow, stuffed cloth w/painted mask face & yarn hair, Ideal, 1939, 17", NM............$1,000.00

Wizard of Oz, flasher ring, Cowardly Lion or Tin Woodsman, M, ea..$40.00

Wizard of Oz, purse, Wizard of Oz Ice Capades, vinyl w/zipper closure, 1950s, NM................................$75.00

Wizard of Oz, sunglasses, Scarecrow, yellow plastic, Multi-Kids/Lowes, 1989, MOC..........................$20.00

Wonder Woman, hand puppet, cloth & vinyl, Ideal, 1966, 11", MIP..$225.00

Wonder Woman, yo-yo, image on both sides, paper insert seal, Duncan, 1970s, NM..............................$15.00

Woody Woodpecker, jack-in-the-box, Mattel, M, from $100 to $150.00

Woody Woodpecker, Music Maker, litho metal, plays theme song, Mattel, 1963, NM..............................$65.00

Woody Woodpecker, Picture Dominoes, Saalfield, 1963, MIB (sealed)..$50.00

Woody Woodpecker, TV Coloring Pencil Set, Connecticut Pencil, 1958, complete, EXIB..........................$35.00

Woody Woodpecker, Woody Woodpecker's art gallery, Saalfield, 1962, complete, EXIB..........................$50.00

Yogi Bear, bubble pipe, red plastic figure, Transogram, 1963, MIP..$35.00

Yogi Bear, doll, Rick Ranger, stuffed cloth, Giaotelli, 10", rare, NM $65.00

Yogi Bear, Camera, 1960s, MIB, $65.00.
(Photo courtesy June Moon)

Yogi Bear, doll, stuffed cloth, Playtime, 1960s, 17", NM ..$50.00

Yogi Bear, doll, stuffed plush w/vinyl face, Knickerbocker, 1959, 10", EX..$75.00

Yogi Bear, Pay Fun Set, Whitman, 1964, complete, NMIB ..$50.00

Yogi Bear, push-button puppet, Yogi, Kohner, 1960s, M $65.00

Yogi Bear, Wipe-Off Coloring Cloth, Hanna-Barbera, 1960s, MIP, from $25 to $35.00

Cherished Teddies

First appearing on dealers' shelves in the spring of 1992, Cherished Teddies found instant collector appeal. They were designed by artist Priscilla Hillman and produced in the Orient for the Enesco company. Besides the figurines, the line includes waterballs, frames, plaques, and bells.

1991, Benji, HH6/481, M..$22.00

1991, Beth, #4HH9/290, 3½", M $25.00

1993, girl w/muff, ornament, #912832, MIB................$31.00

1993, Teddy & Roosevelt, #3H1/614, MIB..................$90.00

1994, girl teddy w/goose, spoon rest, 6½", MIB........$15.00

1995, Millie, Love Me Tender, #5I6/241, 3½", M.........$18.50

1996, Jessica, #155/438A, Special Artist Edition, MIB .$35.00

1997, Brett, dressed as Peter Pan w/Tinkerbear on shoulder, #302547, MIB..$21.50

1997, Christina, dressed as Cinderella, #302473, MIB $27.50

1997, Rex, #269999, MIB..$18.50

1997, Sweet 16 Birthday Bear, #466301, MIB $21.00

1998, American Teddy, ornament, #451010, 2¾", MIB ..$22.00

1998, Australian Teddy, ornament, #464120, 2¾", MIB .$14.00

1998, Cameron, Our Friendship Is Building w/Each New Adventure, Canadian Exclusive, MIB $30.00

1998, French Teddy, #450901, 2¾", MIB $16.00

1998, Humphrey, #8C9/507, MIB $25.00

1999, Chelsea & Daisy, Reunion Event pc, MIB..........$15.00

Christmas Collectibles

Christmas is nearly everybody's favorite holiday, and it's a season when we all seem to want to get back to time-honored traditions. The stuffing and fruit cakes are made like Grandma always made them, we go caroling and sing the old songs that were written two hundred years ago, and the same Santa that brought gifts to the children in a time long forgotten still comes to our house and yours every Christmas Eve.

So for reasons of nostalgia, there are thousands of collectors interested in Christmas memorabilia. Some early Santa figures are rare and may be very expensive, especially when dressed in a color other than red. Blown glass ornaments and Christmas tree bulbs were made in shapes of fruits and vegetables, houses, Disney characters, animals, and birds. There are Dresden ornaments and candy containers from Germany, some of which were made prior to the 1870s, that have been lovingly preserved and handed down from generation to generation. They were made of cardboard that sparkled with gold and silver trim.

Artificial trees made of feathers were produced as early as 1850 and as late as 1950. Some were white, others blue, though most were green, and some had red berries or clips to hold candles. There were little bottle-brush trees, trees with cellophane needles, and trees from the '60s made of aluminum.

Collectible Christmas items are not necessarily old, expensive, or hard to find. Things produced in your lifetime have value as well. To learn more about this field, we recommend *Christmas Ornaments, Lights, and Decorations, Vols I, II,* and *III,* by George Johnson (Collector Books).

Candy container, bell, pressed paper or papier-mache, foil cover w/applied Santa face, Japan, 1920-50s, 3", from $25 to **$30.00**
Candy container, boot, lady's high heeled; satin over cardboard, 1950s, 5½", from $30 to **$50.00**
Candy container, boot, red plastic, Merry Christmas, Rosbro, 1955, 4", from $5 to **$6.00**
Candy container, cornucopia, plain paper w/litho, sm, from $15 to **$25.00**

Candy containers, cornucopias by D. Blumchen & Co., new, various sizes, from $2.00 to $6.00 each.
(Photo courtesy George Johnson)

Candy container, egg shape, paper litho on pressed cardboard, 1½", from $10 to.......................................**$25.00**

Candy container, heart, red paper over cardboard w/angel print, separates at sides, 1¾-6", from $45 to **$90.00**
Candy container, pine cone, pressed paper w/ribbon, Western Germany US Zone, 1940s, from $25 to ..**$35.00**
Candy container, printed box, Santa on rectangular shape, Merry Christmas, Made in USA, 5¾", from $5 to .**$10.00**
Candy container, Santa in sled w/running deer, hard plastic, America, 1950s, 4" L **$25.00**
Candy container, Santa on skis, hard plastic, EX details, America, 1955, 3½", from $8 to **$10.00**
Candy container, Santa standing beside lg compo snowball, Made in West Germany, 3¾" **$25.00**

Candy containers: Santa boots, pressed paper covered with Venetian Dew and Dresden trim, 1930s – 50s, 6", from $20.00 to $30.00 each.
(Photo courtesy George Johnson)

Candy container, slipper, fabric over cardboard w/Dresden trim, 2¾-3¾", ea **$165.00**
Candy container, snowball, crushed glass over cardboard w/sm ribbon or holly sprig, 1980-90s, 2½-3¼", from $3 to **$4.00**

Decorations, styrofoam shapes, flat bells, trees, stars, and snowflakes, ca 1955, MIB, from $2.00 to $3.00.
(Photo courtesy George Johnson)

Light bulb, apple, painted milk glass, oval w/embossed leaves, base at top, Japan, 2½", from $10 to........**$15.00**

Light bulb, bear sitting, painted milk glass, Japan, 1950s, 2¾", from $75 to..**$85.00**

Light bulb, bird in birdhouse, multicolor on milk glass, base at top, Japan, 1935-50, 1½", from $15 to..............**$20.00**

Light bulb, bubble light, C-7 base, old, ea from $2 to....**$7.00**

Light bulb, cat w/ball, multicolor on milk glass, base at bottom, Japan, 2¼", from $70 to **$80.00**

Light bulb, children in shoe, painted milk glass, base at top, Japan, ca 1950, 2¼", from $70 to **$80.00**

Light bulb, clown w/mask, painted milk glass, Japan, 1950s, 3", from $25 to..**$35.00**

Light bulb, elephant on ball, multicolor on milk glass, base at top, Japan, 2¾", from $30 to **$40.00**

Light bulb, horn player, painted clear glass, embossed stripes on pants, 2¾", from $50 to **$60.00**

Light bulb, Indians on square, painted milk glass, Indian rider on ea side, Japan, 2¾", from $25 to **$35.00**

Light bulb, Mother Goose, painted milk glass, Paramount, Japan, 1955, from $15 to..**$25.00**

Light bulb, ocean liner, painted milk glass, 2 decks, portholes & anchor, Japan, ca 1950, 2¾", from $75 to **$100.00**

Light bulb, peacock w/feathered disk behind embossed bird, painted milk glass, Japan, 2¼", from $55 to.........**$65.00**

Light bulb, peacock w/wedge-shaped tail feathers, multicolor on milk glass, Japan, 2¼", from $40 to............**$50.00**

Light bulb, puffed-up cat, multicolor on milk glass, round shape w/embossed head & feet, Japan, 1½", from $55 to **$65.00**

Light bulb, Queen of Hearts, painted milk glass, Paramount, Japan, 2¾", from $25 to **$35.00**

Light bulb, rabbit sitting, painted milk glass, base at top, Japan, ca 1950, 2", from $25 to **$35.00**

Light bulb, raspberry, painted clear glass, bumpy pattern w/leaves at top, exhaust tip, 1½", from $20 to....**$30.00**

Light bulb, roly-poly boy, painted milk glass, dressed in vest, tie & hat, base at top, Japan, 2½", from $25 to ...**$35.00**

Light bulb, Santa Claus, painted clear glass, standard base at bottom, Japan, 4" or 7¼", from $100 to..............**$175.00**

Light bulb, Santa w/hump back & lg bag, painted milk glass, Japan, 4", from $15 to **$25.00**

Lights, Paramount Diamond Bright Set, Walt Disney, ca 1970, $14.00 to $18.00 each. (Photo courtesy George Johnson)

Lights: Stars on ball, ca 1950, 1¾", from $15.00 to $20.00; Rosebud, 2½", from $10.00 to $12.00; Ball with holly leaves, ca 1950, 1¾", from $10.00 to $12.00.
(Photo courtesy George Johnson)

Light bulb, squirrel eating nut, painted clear, US, mini, from $70 to..**$80.00**

Light-up Santa figure, painted molded plastic Santa standing w/ goodies in ea hand, hole for sm light, 1950s, 10", NM ...**$50.00**

Ornament, acorn, mold-blown, thick w/wide pike opening, Corning Glass, ca 1939, 2", from $5 to **$10.00**

Ornament, alligator, free-blown, standing, 1950s, scarce, from $70 to..**$80.00**

Ornament, American lantern, mold blown, 4 panels w/embossed stars in ea, 2¾", from $2 to **$4.00**

Ornament, angel on harp, mold-blown, flying onto the strings of harp, Germany, 1970, 3½", from $10 to.............**$15.00**

Ornament, apple, free-blown ball, often unsilvered, 1-2" dia, from $20 to..**$300.00**

Ornament, ball or sphere shape, free-blown, extremely common & ordinary, ¾-8" dia, from .01¢ to **$10.00**

Ornament, barrel w/rose, mold blown, embossed staves & 2 hoops, flower on side, Germany, 1½", from $15 to..**$25.00**

Ornament, bear in cone-shaped hat, paw to ear, mold-blown, 1950s, 4", from $35 to................................**$45.00**

Ornament, bell, free-blown, decal decor, common style, 1½-4", from $10 to..**$30.00**

Ornament, bell, honeycomb paper, America, 1920s-60s, 3-4", from $2 to..**$3.00**

Ornament, bell w/flowers, mold-blown, Germany, Czechoslovakia or Austria, 1½-2½", from $5 to...**$10.00**

Ornament, bird, glitter on cardboard, Japan, ca 1960, 3½", from $4 to..**$5.00**

Ornament, birdcage, tin, 3-D, round w/individual bars & base, sm cast bird inside, 1¾", from $40 to **$50.00**

Ornament, bulldog head, mold-blown, detailed fur, Germany, 1970s, 3", from $200 to......................**$225.00**

Ornament, carrot, mold-blown, long & slim w/embossed creases, silvering & orange paint, Germany, 3½-4", from $25 to...**$45.00**

Ornament, chalet, mold-blown, steep roof, 3 windows on front & back, no door, 1985, 2¾", from $15 to....**$25.00**

Ornament, clown on stump playing banjo, mold-blown, Germany, 1950s, 3¾-4¼", from $20 to **$30.00**

Ornament, duck, mold-blown, bumps on body, molded feathers, Germany, 1950s-70s, 2¾-3", ea from $25 to.....**$30.00**

Ornament, changing Santa face (front and back shown), ca 1950, from $18.00 to $20.00. (Photo courtesy George Johnson)

Ornament, dwarf w/pick, mold-blown, conical cap, Germany, 1980s, 2½", from $50 to **$75.00**

Ornament, elf head, mold-blown, made from old mold, Germany, 1970s, 3", from $15 to **$18.00**

Ornament, Father Christmas head, mold-blown, crushed glass trim, Germany, 1½-2½", from $45 to...........**$55.00**

Ornament, fish, mold-blown, embossed scales & fins, spun-glass tail, Japan, 1950s-90s, 2-3", from $15 to.......**$25.00**

Ornament, flowerpot, mold-blown, 5 embossed rings, wire-wrapped, holds fabric flower, 3½", from $25 to ..**$35.00**

Ornament, heart w/embossed indent of heart, mold-blown, 1¾", from $2 to **$5.00**

Ornament, heart w/embossed stars, mold-blown, Germany, 2", from $8 to **$12.00**

Ornament, icicle, free-blown, hollow funnel shape w/twists, 4-8", from $10 to **$15.00**

Ornament, icicle, solid glass, twisted & grooved, 2½", from $5 to..**$8.00**

Ornament, icicle, twisted metal, may be lacquered w/color, 5½", from .10 to ....**$.50**

Ornament, Indian smoking pipe, mold-blown, little detail, Germany, 1980s, 3½-4", from $20 to....................**$40.00**

Ornament, lighthouse, mold-blown, 6-sided w/windows, walkway at top, 1950s-60s, 3", from $35 to..........**$45.00**

Ornament, owl on leaf, mold-blown, flying position, Germany, 1970s, 3x2¼", from $75 to....................**$85.00**

Ornament, pear, free-blown, rounded bottom, few details, covered in crushed glass, 2-4", from $15 to **$30.00**

Ornament, rabbit, mold-blown, paws at chest, ears down, Germany, 1970s, 3¾", from $60 to.......................**$80.00**

Ornament, rose & daisy (double flower), mold-blown, 2" dia, from $20 to...**$30.00**

Ornament, rosette, foil in concentric circles, Germany, 2-3" dia, from $3 to **$5.00**

Ornament, Santa Claus, mold-blown, ¾-length, cap & hip coat, no legs or feet, Germany or Austria, 2-5½", from $20 to..**$65.00**

Ornament, Santa in airplane, mold-blown & scrap w/tinsel wire wings & propeller, Germany, 1950s-90s, from $20 to **$25.00**

Ornament, Santa w/bag & toys, mold-blown, sack over shoulder, feet end in square shape, 3-3¾", from $30 to.**$35.00**

Ornament, Santa w/basket, mold-blown, stern face, hooded cap, basket held at left side, 3", from $40 to........**$50.00**

Ornament, shoe w/ribbed toe, mold-blown, no bow, 1950s, 3", from $20 to **$30.00**

Ornament, snowflake, honeycomb paper, tightly pleated, 6½", from $25 to..**$30.00**

Ornament, snowflake, wire, 6-pointed, looped & bent silver wire, Germany, 2¾"...**$5.00**

Ornament, snowman, mold-blown, 3 sm balls tacked on ea other, white matt, USA, 3½", from $40 to.............**$50.00**

Ornament, string of beads, free-blown & mold-blown, faceted or fancy shapes, from $15 to....................**$30.00**

Ornament, table lamp, free-blown, pedestal attached to flattened base, Dresden trim, 1980s, 3-4", from $10 to.**$25.00**

Ornament, tomato, mold-blown, red paint, 2-2¾" dia, from $30 to...**$40.00**

Ornament, turkey embossed on oval, mold-blown, 2", from $15 to...**$25.00**

Ornament, umbrella (closed), free-blown, straight handle, no scrap trim or wire wrap, 4-7", from $15 to..........**$25.00**

Puppet, ventriloquist Santa w/moving eyes & mouth, diecut cardboard, Happi-Time Toy Town promo, Sears, 1948, 13", NM..**$30.00**

Cigarette Lighters

Collectors of tobacciana tell us that cigarette lighters are definitely hot! Look for novel designs (figurals, Deco styling, and so forth), unusual mechanisms (flint and fuel, flint and gas, battery, etc.), those made by companies now defunct, advertising lighters, and quality lighters made by Dunhill, Evans, Colibri, Zippo, and Ronson. For more information we recommend *Collector's Guide to Cigarette Lighters, Vols. I* and *II,* by James Flanagan (Collector Books).

Newsletter: *On the Lighter Side*
Judith Sanders
Route 3, 136 Circle Dr.
Quitman, TX 75783; 903-763-2795; SASE for information

Advertising, Fisk Tires, metal, black on silver, 2¼", EX, $65.00.

Advertising, Bosch spark plug, chromium & enameling, Bosch of Germany, ca 1975, 3¼x⅞" dia, from $15 to **$30.00**

Advertising, brass & enamel, General Electric Supply Co, Park Industries, late 1950s, 2¼x1½", from $10 to **$20.00**

Advertising, chromium & enamel, pocket size, My-lite, 1980s, 2¼x1½", from $5 to...**$15.00**

Advertising, chromium & enamel, tube-style, Redlite, late 1940s, 3x⅜" dia, from $20 to **$30.00**

Advertising, Lucky Strike, chromium & enamel, table size, Japan, late 1950s, 4⅜x3", from $20 to..................**$30.00**

Advertising, Marlboro Cigarettes promotional, brass, Zippo, ca 1991, 2¼x1½", M in gift box, from $15 to.......**$30.00**

Advertising, Venetian, chromium, slim, Zippo, ca 1992, 2¼x1¼", from $15 to...**$25.00**

Art Deco, chrome & Akro Agate smoke stand w/electric lighter, 2 ashtrays, covered cigarette receptacle, 1930s, 27"...**$150.00**

Art Deco, Electro-Match, black plastic w/gold trim, Korex Co, 1950s, 5¾x4½" dia, from $10 to **$25.00**

Art Deco, Spartan table lighter, chromium & enamel, Ronson, 1950s, 2⅜x3", from $10 to **$20.00**

Caricature, Bob Hope, 14k gold-plated rectangular style w/raised image of Hope on front, 1950s, 2", EX .**$50.00**

Decorative, brass & black plastic, ASR, early 1950s, 2¾x1⅞", from $10 to...**$20.00**

Decorative, brass & ceramic table lighter, Evans, late 1930s, 6½x3¼" dia, from $30 to **$50.00**

Decorative, Corinthian table lighter, urn shape, Zippo, ca 1960, 3⅞x2¼" dia, from $30 to **$50.00**

Decorative, crown shape, chromium w/gold trim, Prince, mid-1950s, 2⅝x2¼", from $25 to.........................**$35.00**

Decorative, egg shape, brass, Ronson, 2½x3", from $25 to **$40.00**

Decorative, green & white Wedgwood-style, Ronson, ca 1962, 2¾x2⅛", from $40 to...................................**$60.00**

Decorative, jockey figural, chromium, hinged cap conceals lighter, early 1950s, 8½x2⅞", from $150 to **$200.00**

Decorative, Juno, silverplated, Ronson, ca 1952, 6¼x2" dia at base, from $30 to...**$50.00**

Decorative, knight figural, chromium, light by pushing button helmet, Hamilton, late 1940s, 9½x2⅞", from $60 to .**$85.00**

Decorative, knight's helmet form, brass, lights by pushing down visor, mid-1950s, 5x4", from $10 to **$20.00**

Decorative, marble base w/gold-plated lighter, Alfred Dunhill, ca 1955, 2½x3¾", from $275 to **$325.00**

Decorative, Nordic, glass & chromium, Ronson, ca 1955, 3½x3⅜" dia, from $20 to **$30.00**

Decorative, rose form, chromium, lighter is under flower, mid-1960s, 2½x1⅝", from $20 to...........................**$30.00**

Decorative, Waterford crystal, butane, ca 1975, 3x3½", from $75 to..**$100.00**

Decorative, 3 gold-plated cherubs support lighter, ca 1935, 7x3⅛", from $25 to **$50.00**

Figural, dachshund, Imperial bronze, tail striker, Ronson, ca 1940, 4x9", from $150 to **$225.00**

Figural, donkey, brass, Japan, mid-1950s, 2x2½", from $15 to **$20.00**

Figural, elephant, chromium, strike type, Ronson, ca 1935, 5x3¾", from $50 to..**$175.00**

Figural, elephant, painted metal, Strikalite, late 1940s, 3x3½", from $25 to..**$35.00**

Figural, horse, painted ceramic, Japan, ca 1955, 5½x5½", from $15 to...**$25.00**

Figural, horse head, brass w/leather reins, lights when reins are pulled back, late 1940s, 4¾x3¾", from $50 to **$75.00**

Figural, Model-T Ford, brass, Made in Japan, mid-1950s, 3⅛x5", from $20.00 to $35.00. (Photo courtesy James Flanagan)

Figural, nude (chromium) stands in center of Bakelite ashtray, Harry Davis Molding Co, 1935, 5x6¾" dia, from $40 to..**$60.00**

Figural, nude w/basket on head, chromium, ca 1950, 6x2⅜", from $15 to...**$30.00**

Figural, penguin, gold & silverplate, ca 1960, 2x⅞" dia, from $40 to..**$70.00**

Figural, swan, chromium, Japan, early 1960s, 3x3¾", from $10 to..**$20.00**

Figural, wolf, brass, dressed as cowboy, w/striker, mid-1930s, 5½x2", from $250 to..**$350.00**

Lighter/case, brass & 2-toned enamel, early 1950s, 4½x3", from $30 to..**$50.00**

Lighter/case, chromium & burgundy enamel, Pal, Ronson, ca 1941, 4⅛x2", from $50 to.......................................**$80.00**

Lighter/case, chromium & leather, Lytacase, removable Adonis butane lighter by Ronson, late 1950s, 5x3¼", from $50 to...**$75.00**

Lighter/case, chromium & tortoise enamel, Sportcase, Ronson, ca 1936, 4⅛x2", from $50 to **$70.00**

Lighter/case, Mastercase, chromium w/black enameling, Ronson, ca 1933, 4¾x2½", from $25 to **$50.00**

Miniature, chromium, lift arm w/metal band, Made in Occupied Japan, ca 1948, 1⅝x1⅛", from $5 to....**$10.00**

Miniature, chromium w/leather bands, lift-arm, attached key chain, Made in Occupied Japan, 1948, ⅞x¾", from $20 to **$40.00**

Miniature, chromium w/painted scene, lift-arm, Made by Perky, ca 1950s, ⅞x¾", from $25 to **$40.00**

Novelty, brass & leather bellows, squeeze handles to operate lighter, mid-1690s, 2x7¼", from $20 to **$30.00**

Novelty, double-barrel shotgun form, chromium, butane, early 1980s, 3x20½", from $30 to **$50.00**

Novelty, gold-tone mechanical pencil w/lighter under cap, Albright in NY, mid-1950s, 5x½" dia, from $25 to .**$40.00**

Novelty, Gremlin, electric, Aircraft Novelty Co, mid-1930s, 4¼x4", from $75 to...**$100.00**

Novelty, lamp, brass w/painted shade, lights by pushing button base, 1950s, 3½x1¾", from $20 to.................**$35.00**
Novelty, lighter/flashlight, chromium & leather, Aurora, ca 1960, 2x2½", from $20 to....................................**$30.00**
Novelty, Model-T Ford car, ceramic, ca 1964, 3¼x4", from $10 to...**$20.00**
Novelty, motorcycle, chromium, butane, front wheels turns right to left, mid-1980s, 3½x6", from $35 to.........**$50.00**
Novelty, pistol, chromium w/black plastic grips, Japan, mid-1950s, 1½x2", from $15 to **$20.00**
Novelty, plastic butane canteen pocket lighter, Germany, late 1980s, 2¼x1⅜", from $15 to **$25.00**
Novelty, plastic butane ice skate, Germany, early 1990s, 2⅝x2½", from $15 to...**$25.00**
Novelty, plastic butane spark plug pocket lighter w/key chain, PLA, 1990s, 3x¾", from $5 to **$10.00**
Novelty, potbellied stove, brass, chimney comes off to reveal lighter, mid-1950s, 3¼", from $10 to **$20.00**
Novelty, telephone, electric, built-in clock & ashtrays on ea side, painted metal, late 1930s, 3½x1¼", $70 to..**$80.00**
Novelty, television, Swank, early 1960s, 2¾x3⅞", from $25 to...**$40.00**
Novelty, tennis ball w/3 rackets for base, chromium, ca mid-1960s, 6x3¼", from $20 to **$30.00**
Novelty, Thompson machine-gun form, chromium, butane, ca 1988, 3¾x11¼", from $35 to...........................**$60.00**
Novelty, 8-ball, plastic, mid-1960s, 3x2½", from $15 to..**$25.00**
Occupied Japan, car, chromium, button on left fender opens hood to reveal lighter, ca 1948, 1x3", from $75 to..**$100.00**
Occupied Japan, cowboy boot w/sunburst on front, silver-plated, ca 1950, 2⅞x2⅞", from $50 to **$70.00**
Occupied Japan, cowboy figural, silverplated, head hinged in back, ca 1948, 4x1¾", from $90 to.....................**$115.00**
Occupied Japan, gas pump, metal, squeeze nozzle to operate lighter, ca 1949, 3½x1¼", from $60 to **$80.00**
Occupied Japan, sewing machine w/plastic cigarette holder in base, lights by the needle, 3x4", from $150 to **$175.00**
Occupied Japan, ship, chromium w/red plastic detailing below lighter, ca 1950, 2x5", from $50 to **$70.00**
Pocket, brass & leather covered, lady's, Germany, mid-1950s, 1⅜x1½", from $25 to...**$40.00**
Pocket, brass w/ostrich-hide band, Elgin American, early 1950s, 1¾x1⅜", from $40 to **$60.00**
Pocket, chromium, lift-arm, leather band, Continental, ca late 1950s, 2⅛x1½", from $65 to **$90.00**
Pocket, chromium, lift-arm, Polo, England, ca 1932, 1¾x1½", from $75 to...**$100.00**
Pocket, chromium, musical wind-up, Prince, 1960s, 2⅛x1¾", from $25 to..**$45.00**
Pocket, chromium, striker type, Match King, late 1940s, 2⅝x1", from $15 to **$25.00**
Pocket, chromium & brass, enameled map of Texas, Continental, mid-1950s, 2x1⅝", from $30 to.........**$40.00**
Pocket, chromium pistol w/mother-of-pearl grips, Japan, early 1950s, 1½x2", from $25 to **$40.00**
Pocket, chromium w/watch in side, Eclydo Co, 1950s, 2½x1⅝", from $100 to..**$125.00**
Pocket, Director, chromium, Berkley, late 1940s, 1¾x2⅛", from $25 to...**$40.00**
Pocket, Flaminaire, chromium, butane, Parker, ca 1951, 2¾x1⅜", M in gift box, from $25 to.....................**$40.00**
Pocket, Gem, chromium finish w/rhinestones, Ronson, ca 1937, w/original gift box & cloth bag, from $75 to...........**$100.00**
Pocket, gold-plated & enamel w/bird on branch, butane, Colibri, mid-1970s, 2½x¾", from $30 to **$50.00**
Pocket, platinum-plated, Lektrolite, late 1930s, 1¾x1⅝", from $30 to...**$40.00**
Pocket, pouch style, Colibri, ca 1954, 2⅛x2", from $30 to **$45.00**
Pocket, silhouette of lady on chromium, Zippo, ca 1995, 2¼x1½", from $10 to **$20.00**
Pocket, Trickette, brass & rhinestones, Wisner, early 1950s, 1½x1¾", from $25 to **$40.00**
Table, airplane, chromium, lights by turning propeller, ca 1935, 3⅛x5¾x7¼", from $100 to........................**$125.00**
Table, brass & green marble, Evans, mid-1930s, 3⅝x3" dia, from $40 to **$60.00**
Table, brass & marble cube, mid-1950s, 3x2¼", from $20 to **$40.00**
Table, brass candlestick holder, lever on right side operates lighter at top of candle, 1920s, 5½x3½", $125 to...**$150.00**
Table, butane, gold-tone metal, Souvenir of World's Fair in New York, Monarch, ca 1961, 2¼x2¾", from $40 to **$60.00**
Table, chromium, lights when picked up, mid-1950s, 2⅜x3", from $20 to..**$30.00**
Table, Classic Jumbo, chromium & leather, lift-arm, Brevete (England), 1930s, 4⅜x3¼", from $140 to...........**$175.00**
Table, fur covered (resembles zebra), Evans, ca 1934, 3x1¾", from $35 to..**$50.00**
Table, Moderne, chromium, Zippo, ca 1966, 4⅛x2¼" dia at base, from $35 to **$50.00**
Table, painted brass replica lift-arm lighter, butane, ca 1988, 3⅛x2⅜", from $15 to...**$25.00**
Table, ship's wheel, chromium, Hamilton, late 1930s, 5⅛", from $60 to...**$80.00**
Table, Spirit of St Louis airplane, brass w/rubber tires, Swank, late 1940s, 1¾x5⅜x6⅝", from $80 to.................**$100.00**
Table, Statue of Liberty, batteries & butane, mid-1950s, 7½x3½", from $75 to..**$100.00**
Table, tankard, chromium, butane, early 1980s, 4¼x3", from $20 to...**$30.00**

Cleminson Pottery

One of the several small potteries that operated in California during the middle of the century, Cleminson was a family-operated enterprise that made kitchenware, decorative items, and novelties that are beginning to attract a considerable amount of interest. At the height of their productivity, they employed 150 workers, so as you make your rounds, you'll be very likely to see a piece or two offered for sale just about anywhere you go. Prices are not high; this may be a 'sleeper.'

They marked their ware fairly consistently with a circular ink stamp that contains the name 'Cleminson.' But even if you find an unmarked piece, with just a little experience you'll easily be able to recognize their very distinctive glaze colors. They're all strong, yet grayed-down, dusty tones. They made a line of bird-shaped tableware items that they marketed as 'Distlefink' and several plaques and wall pockets that are decorated with mottoes and Pennsylvania Dutch-type hearts and flowers.

In Jack Chipman's *The Collector's Encyclopedia of California Pottery, Second Edition,* you'll find a chapter devoted to Cleminson Pottery. Roerig's *The Collector's Encyclopedia of Cookie Jars* has additional information. (Both of these books are published by Collector Books.)

See also Clothes Sprinkler Bottles; Cookie Jars.

Advisor: Robin Stine (See Directory, California Pottery)

Bank, hope chest shape, white w/floral decoration, Here's Hoping, 3x4" **$25.00**
Bowl, Love Me on blue flowers & pink polka dots, heart shape, 2¾" **$15.00**
Cleanser shaker, Cleanser Kate, 6½" **$40.00**
Creamer, rooster, 5½" **$35.00**
Cup, clown face w/hat lid, from $60 to......................**$80.00**
Dish, clown w/balloons holding hoop for poodle, 7¾" dia **$45.00**
Hors d'ouvres set, 7 bowls (3 hearts, 3 bells, 1 circle), wooden lazy susan base, 16" dia..................................**$80.00**

Marmalade, flowerpot with strawberry finial, 4", from $25.00 to $30.00.

Napkin holder, pr of hands, white w/floral band at bottom, 2¼x5"..**$42.00**
Razor blade bank, man's face, 4" **$50.00**
Ring holder, bulldog, white & peach, from $35 to **$45.00**
Sock darner, represents little girl, soft blues................**$50.00**
String holder, heart shape, w/verse, 4½x5" **$45.00**
Sugar shaker, represents girl, 3⅛x6" **$30.00**
Wall plaque, apple decoration, 8¼" dia......................**$22.00**

Wall plaque, God Bless Our Mobile Home, white w/blue mobile home, 6¾" **$32.00**
Wall pocket, coffee grinder, w/verse, 5½x7"..............**$30.00**
Wall pocket, Dumbo the Elephant, 5x3½x2½", EX **$45.00**
Wall pocket, kettle form, w/verse, 7¼".......................**$30.00**
Wall pocket, Take Time for Tea, 7¾x6⅝" **$50.00**

Salt crock, wall mount, 5¾x6½", $65.00.

Clothes Sprinkler Bottles

With the invention of the iron, clothes were sprinkled with water, rolled up to distribute the dampness, and pressed. This created steam when ironing, which helped to remove wrinkles. The earliest bottles were made of hand-blown clear glass. Ceramic figurals were introduced in the 1920s; these had a metal sprinkler cap with a rubber cork. Later versions had a true cork with an aluminum cap. More recent examples contain a plastic cap. A 'wetter-downer' bottle had no cap but contained a hole in the top to distribute water to larger items such as sheets and tablecloths. These were filled through a large opening in the bottom and plugged with a cork. Some 'wetter-downers' are mistaken for shakers and vice versa. In the end, with the invention of more sophisticated irons that produced their own steam (and later had their own sprayers), the sprinkler bottle was relegated to the attic or, worse yet, the trash can.

The variety of subjects depicted by figural sprinkler bottles runs from cute animals to laundry helpers and people who did the ironing. Because of their whimsical nature, their scarcity and desirability as collectibles, we have seen a rapid rise in the cost of these bottles over the last couple of years.

See also Kitchen Prayer Ladies.

Advisor: Ellen Bercovici (See Directory, Clothes Sprinkler Bottles)

Cat, marble eyes, ceramic, American Bisque, from $350 to **$400.00**
Cat, variety of designs & colors, homemade ceramic, from $100 to..**$150.00**

Chinese man, handmade, from $50.00 to $150.00.
(Photo courtesy Ellen Bercovici)

Chinese man, Sprinkle Plenty, white, green & brown, holding iron, ceramic, from $175 to $225.00

Chinese man, Sprinkle Plenty, yellow & green, ceramic, Cardinal China Co, from $25 to............................$50.00

Chinese man, towel over arm, from $300 to.............$400.00

Chinese man, white & aqua, ceramic, Cleminson, from $40 to..$50.00

Chinese man, white & aqua w/paper shirt tag, ceramic, Cleminson, from $75 to..$100.00

Clothespin, face w/stenciled eyes & airbrushed cheeks & lips, from $200 to $250.00

Clothespin, hand decorated, ceramic, from $150 to .$200.00

Clothespin, red, yellow & green plastic, from $20 to.$40.00

Dearie Is Weary, ceramic, Enesco, from $350 to $500.00

Dutch boy, green & white ceramic, from $175 to $250.00

Dutch girl, white w/green & pink trim, wetter-downer, ceramic, from $175 to $250.00

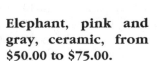

Elephant, pink and gray, ceramic, from $50.00 to $75.00.

Elephant, trunk forms handle, ceramic, American Bisque, from $400 to...$600.00

Elephant, white & pink w/shamrock on tummy, ceramic, from $100 to..$150.00

Emperor, variety of designs & colors, handmade ceramic, from $150 to..$200.00

Fireman, minimum value $1,000.00

Iron, blue flowers, ceramic, from $100 to $150.00

Iron, green ivy, ceramic, from $50 to $75.00

Iron, green plastic, from $35 to $55.00

Iron, lady ironing, ceramic, from $45 to.....................$75.00

Iron, man & woman farmer, ceramic, from $200 to .$275.00

Iron, souvenir of Aquarena Springs, San Marcos TX, ceramic, from $200 to..$300.00

Iron, souvenir of Florida, pink flamingo, ceramic, from $250 to...$325.00

Iron, souvenir of Wonder Cave, ceramic, from $250 to ..$300.00

Mammy, ceramic, possibly Pfaltzgraff, from $250 to ..$350.00

Mary Maid, all colors, plastic, Reliance, from $15 to ..$35.00

Mary Poppins, ceramic, Cleminson, from $250 to $350.00

Myrtle, ceramic, Pfaltzgraff, from $250 to $350.00

Peasant woman, w/laundry poem on label, from $200 to $300.00

Poodle, gray & pink or white, ceramic, from $200 to ..$300.00

Rooster, green, tan & red detailing over white, ceramic, from $125 to..$200.00

Clothing and Accessories

Watch a 'Golden Oldie' movie, and you can't help admiring the clothes — what style, what glamour, what fun! Due in part to the popularity of old movie classics and great new movies with retro themes, there's a growing fascination with the fabulous styes of the past — and there's no better way to step into the romance and glamour of those eras than with an exciting piece of vintage clothing!

'OOOhhh, it don't mean a thing, if it ain't got that S-W-I-N-G!' In 1935, Benny Goodman, 'King of Swing,' ushered in the swing era from Los Angeles's Polmar Ballroom. After playing two standard sets, he switched to swing, and the crowd went crazy! Swing's the 'in' thing in vintage clothing this year, and swing dance devotees are looking for the sassy styles of the late '30s through the mid-40s to wear clubbing. Swing era gals' clothing featured short full or pleated skirts, wide padded shoulders, and natural waistlines. Guys, check out those silk, wide ties that were worn with 'gangster-look' zoot suits!

Clothes of the 1940s though the 1970s are not as delicate as their Victorian and Edwardian counterparts; they're easier to find and much more affordable! Remember, the more indicative of its period, the more desirable the item. Look for pieces with glitz and glamour — also young, trendy pieces that were expensive to begin with. Look for designer pieces and designer look-alikes. Although famous designer labels are hard to find, you may be lucky enough to run across one! American designers like Adrian, Claire McMardell, Charles James, Mainboucher, Hattie Carnegie, Norell, Pauline Trigere, and Mollie Parnis came to the fore during World War II. The

'50s were the decade of Christian Dior; others included Balenciaga, Balmain, Chanel, Jacques Heim, Nina Ricci, Ann Fogarty, Oleg Cassini, and Adele Simpson. In the '60s and '70s, Mary Quant, Betsey Johnson, Givenchy, Yves St. Laurent, Oscar de la Renta, Galanos, Pierre Cardin, Rudi Gernreich, Paco Rabanne, Courreges, Arnold Scassi, Geoffrey Beene, Emilio Pucci, Zandra Rhodes, and Jessica McClintock (Gunne Sax) were some of the names that made fasion headlines.

Pucci, Lilli Ann of Calfornia, Eisenberg, and Adele Simpson designs contine to be especially sought after. Enid Colins imaginative bags are popular, but prices are lower than last year's. Look for lingerie — '30s and '40s lace/hook corsets, and '50s pointy 'bullet' bras (like the ones in the Old Maidenform Dream ads). For both men and women, '70s disco platform shoes (the wilder, the better); cowboy shirts and jackets, also fringed 'hippie' items. For men, look for bowling shirts, '50s 'Kramer' shirts, and '40s and '50s wild ties, especially those by Salvadore Dali.

Levi jeans and jackets made circa 1971 and before have a cult following, especially in Japan. Among the most sought-after denim Levi items are jeans with a capitol 'E' on a *red* tab or back pocket. The small 'e' jeans are also collectible; these were made during the late 1960s and until 1970 (with two rows of single stitching inside the back pocket). Worth watching for as well are the 'red line' styles of the '80s (these have double-stitched back pockets). Other characteristics to look for in vintage Levis are visible rivets inside the jeans and single pockets and silver-colored buttons on jackets with vertical pleats. From the same era, Lee, Wrangler, Bluebell, J.C. Penney, Oxhide, Big Yanks, James Dean, Doublewear, and Big Smith denims are collectible as well.

As with any collectible, condition is of the utmost importance. 'Deadstock' is a term that refers to a top-grade item that has never been worn or washed and still has its original tags. Number 1 grade must have no holes larger than a pinhole. A torn belt loop is permissible if no hole is created. There may be a few light stains and light fading. The crotch area must have no visible wear and the crotch seam must have no holes. And lastly, the item must not have been altered. Values in the listing here are for items in number 1 grade. There are also other grades for items that have more defects.

While some collectors buy with the intent of preserving their clothing and simply enjoy having it, many buy it to wear. If you do wear it, be very careful how you clean it. Fabrics may become fragile with age.

For more information, refer to *Vintage Hats and Bonnets, 1770 – 1970, Identifications and Values,* by Sue Langley; *Vintage Fashions for Women, the 1950s & '60s,* by Kristina Harris (Shiffer); *Clothing and Accessories From the '40s, '50s and '60s,* by Jan Lindenberger (Schiffer); *Vintage Denim* by David Little; *Shoes* by Linda O'Keefe; *Plastic Handbags* by Kate E. Dooner; *Fit To Be Tied, Vintage Ties of the '40s and Early '50s,* by Rod Dyer and Ron Spark; and *The Hawaiian Shirt* by H. Thomas Steele. For more information about denim clothing and vintage footwear see *How To Identify Vintage Apparel for Fun and Profit,* which is available from Flying Deuce Auction & Antiques (see Auction Houses).

Prices are a compilation of shows, shops, and Internet auctions. They are retail values and apply to items in excellent condition. Note: Extraordinary items bring extraordinary prices!

Unless noted, clothing in the following illustrations are from the collection of Sue Downing; photography by John Dowling, copyright 1999.

Advisors: Sue Langley, Clothing; Flying Deuce Auctions, Vintage Denim (See Directory, Clothing and Accessories)

Newsletter: *Costume Society of America*
55 Edgewater Dr., P.O. Box 73
Earleville, MD 21919
Phone: 410-275-1691 or fax: 410-275-8936;
www.costumesocietyamerica.com

Newsletter: *The Vintage Connection*
904 North 65 Street
Springfield, OR 97478-7021

1940s Women's Day Wear

Dress, Broadway motif print	**$145.00**
Dress, multicolor 'hands' printed on rayon	**$135.00**
Dress, orchids printed on rayon	**$60.00**
Dress, snails printed on rayon	**$65.00**
Halter top, green-checked printed cotton	**$20.00**
House dress, cotton print w/rickrack trim	**$24.00**
Playsuit, printed cotton, 1-pc, short legs	**$25.00**
Slacks, gray wool gabardine	**$45.00**
Suit, burgundy wool	**$145.00**
Suit, Lilli Ann, navy w/eyelet-trimmed jacket	**$250.00**
Suit, New Look, black wool, late '40s	**$110.00**
Suit, New Look, Eisenberg Original, gray gabardine	**$125.00**
Suit, New Look, gray rayon faille	**$62.00**
Suit, pink wool gabardine	**$115.00**
Suit blouse, white rayon	**$15.00**
Tennis shorts, cotton twill, pleated, wide legs	**$32.00**

1940s Women's Coats and Jackets

Coat, Pauline Trigere, wool tweed w/fitted waist	**$300.00**
Coat, red wool, fitted	**$65.00**
Coat, Swing style, beige wool	**$115.00**
Coat, Swing style, black velvet, ¾-length	**$80.00**
Jacket, black wool w/braid trim	**$75.00**
Jacket, tan wool, plain but nicely tailored	**$35.00**
Mink neckpiece w/head & tails	**$24.00**

1940s Women's Evening Wear

Cocktail dress, sequins, peplum, knee length	**$75.00**
Dinner dress, cotton floral, long w/bustle back	**$165.00**
Dinner gown, purple rayon crepe w/beaded neckline	**$200.00**
Evening coat w/hood, black rayon velvet, long	**$125.00**
Gown, black rayon crepe w/sequin trim, long	**$145.00**

1940s Women's Intimate Apparel/Lounge Wear

Bra, peach rayon satin, marked Miss America on label.**$6.00**
Corset, New Look, Waspy......................................**$25.00**
Corset, peach color, long, back-laced.........................**$20.00**
Dress & jacket, Hawaiian print, Made in Hawaii......**$125.00**
Lounging pajamas, Hawaiian print on rayon, wide legs..**$95.00**
Lounging robe, purple satin w/quilted & embroidered collar
    & cuffs **$130.00**
Nightie, rayon satin floral print.................................**$45.00**
Nightie, sheer black silk w/strategic decorations........**$75.00**
Panties, peach rayon, wide-leg step-ins......................**$10.00**
Panties, rayon satin, See No Evil print, glow-in-the-dark zip-
    per w/figural 3-monkeys pull **$55.00**
Robe, butterfly print on cotton seersucker, long.........**$55.00**
Slip, peach rayon satin **$8.00**

1940s Women's Accessories

Fedora, yellow Casablanca style..................................**$85.00**
Gloves, gauntlet style, brown cotton **$15.00**
Gloves, long evening mitts, jeweled black velvet.....**$125.00**
Hanky, cat w/rhinestone eyes, child's **$14.00**
Hat, black w/purple snood back, platter style.............**$45.00**
Hat, green felt petals, doll style..................................**$60.00**
Hat, red felt, wide brim...**$150.00**
Hat, straw toy style w/flowers & veil, sm..................**$35.00**
Hat, topper, black straw w/lg red 'wing' & back-tied
    veil...**$55.00**

Hat, velvet turban with knotted center front, Sears, 1940 – 41, from $35.00 to $55.00.
(Photo courtesy Sue Langley)

Hat, w/wimple (scarf across chin) **$115.00**
Purse, alligator bag, Cuba **$75.00**
Purse, clutch style, red plastic squares.......................**$30.00**
Purse, evening clutch style, pearls **$30.00**
Purse, fine floral needlepoint.....................................**$45.00**
Purse, rayon ribbed cord, plastic zipper ornament.....**$35.00**
Purse, Whiting & Davis, clutch style, silver w/rhinestone
    clasp...**$50.00**

Scarf, hats printed on silk **$15.00**
Shoes, alligator pumps, plain.....................................**$50.00**
Shoes, alligator sling-backs w/'Minnie ear' clips.........**$75.00**
Shoes, gold satin evening slippers **$35.00**
Shoes, platform style, green suede w/studs **$125.00**

1950s Women's Day Wear

Bathing suit, cotton plaid...**$25.00**
Bathing suit, gold lamè **$55.00**
Blouse, sleeveless, cotton..**$10.00**
Circle skirt, flocked floral trim & sequins **$45.00**
Circle skirt, masks printed on fabric **$35.00**
Cowboy shirt, cowboy on bucking bronco on back ..**$45.00**
Lounging dress, cotton w/printed Paris scenes...........**$35.00**
Sheath skirt, pink wool flannel...................................**$25.00**
Shirtwaist dress, pink cotton gingham **$45.00**
Suit, tweed w/mink collar...**$55.00**
Sundress, printed fabric w/hats, full skirt **$25.00**

1950s Women's Coats and Sweaters

Coat, Lilli Ann, pink wool, full skirt.........................**$275.00**
Coat, wool Pendleton plaid, ¾-length **$25.00**
Mexican jacket, red felt w/cowboy scene & laced edge .**$40.00**
Sweater, beaded cardigan style, from $35 to..............**$85.00**
Sweater, beige cashmere w/fur collar **$85.00**
Sweater set (shell & cardigan), purple orlon..............**$35.00**

1950s Women's Evening Wear

Ball gown, strapless, velvet & net w/sequin trim, long...**$300.00**
Coat, Swing style, navy silk faille, mid-calf length......**$55.00**
Cocktail dress, red velvet, bateau neckline, full skirt..**$125.00**
Cocktail dress, strapless, black lace, full skirt **$45.00**
Dress, rhinestone & pearl velvet top, taffeta circle skirt ..**$75.00**
Gown, chartreuse chiffon w/spaghetti straps............**$150.00**
Prom dress, strapless, red net w/white lace top.........**$25.00**
Suzy Wong Chinese dress, short & tight, from $35 to ..**$95.00**

1950s Women's Intimate Apparel/Lounge Wear

Net crinoline slip, $15.00.

Bra, Locket, strapless & boned, pointed 'Wonder Woman' look..**$15.00**
Bra, pointy 'bullet' style **$12.00**
Crinoline, hoop skirt..**$15.00**
Pajamas, baby doll, pink cotton print **$8.00**
Robe, aqua chenille, long **$40.00**

1950s Women's Accessories

Collar, detachable, gold jeweled, from India..............**$15.00**
Collar, detachable, white cotton pique **$6.00**
Gloves, white cotton, short, from $5 to **$10.00**
Hat, black felt w/red poinsettia trim, sm **$32.00**
Hat, green velvet w/strawberries, Emme label............**$22.00**
Hat, jeweled w/pearls & rhinestones, sm **$75.00**
Hat, mink, sm...**$22.00**
Hat, pink velvet w/ostrich feather trim, sm..................**$55.00**
Hat, profile style, red plaid cellophane straw **$28.00**
Hat, straw trimmed w/cherries, sm **$45.00**
Hat, wide brim, fine straw **$110.00**
Hat, wide brim, velvet-edged w/maribou.......................**$125.00**
Pop-it beads, plastic..**$5.00**
Purse, evening clutch style, velvet w/gold India embroidery **$35.00**
Purse, Lucite, gold & black, Dorset Rex 5th Ave **$130.00**
Purse, Lucite, gray marbleized.......................................**$85.00**
Purse, Lucite, red marbleized, Wilardy, rare.............**$700.00**
Purse, Lucite, shiny black, Rialto...................................**$250.00**
Purse, Lucite/hard plastic, from $25 to **$700.00**
Purse, velvet bag, jeweled & sequined poodle...........**$85.00**
Purse, whimsical: poodles, etc, from $45 to...............**$85.00**
Purse, wooden box style w/decoupage designs, from $35 to **$55.00**
Scarf/kerchief, floral print on silk................................**$15.00**
Scarf/kerchief, Moulin Rouge scene printed on silk ...**$75.00**
Shoes, black suede ballet-style flats **$22.00**
Shoes, Lucite Cinderella heels, from $25 to.................**$55.00**
Shoes, saddle style...**$20.00**
Shoes, stiletto heels...**$25.00**
Swimcap, decorated w/flowers.......................................**$22.00**

1960s – 70s Women's Day Wear and Coats

Blouse, Emilio Pucci, Saks 5th Ave, 1970s **$110.00**
Caftan, flamingo print, 1960s **$18.00**
Coat, acid green polka-dot polyester, 1960s................**$35.00**
Coat dress, Adele Simpson, faux leopard, 1960s **$125.00**
Coat dress, Galanos couture, black wool knit **$325.00**
Coat dress, yellow polka-dots, Twiggy label...............**$55.00**
Dress, Emilio Pucci, silk w/crystal bead tie, 1970s...**$225.00**
Dress, Emilio Pucci, silk w/matching sash, 1970s.....**$125.00**
Dress, Gunne Sax (Jessica McClintock), calico print, 1970s **$45.00**
Dress, paper, in original package, 1960s **$22.00**
Halter dress, pailsey print on tricot, long skirt...........**$25.00**
Jacket, Emilio Pucci, Saks 5th Ave, 1970s...................**$85.00**
Mini dress, Oleg Cassini, orange polyester, 1960s **$75.00**

Mini dress, paper, quilted metallic blue, 1960s **$45.00**

1960s – 70s Women's Evening Wear

Blouse, Emilio Pucci, Saks 5th Ave, 1970s **$110.00**
Coat, black, sequinned, long **$150.00**
Cocktail ensemble: short dress & coat, beaded **$125.00**
Cocktail mini dress, white w/allover beading............**$55.00**
Culotte dress, white polyester, long w/wide legs **$65.00**
Evening suit, Emilio Pucci, wool, 2-pc, 1970s..........**$125.00**
Mini dress, white crepe w/rhinestone zippers on neck & sleeves **$65.00**
Pants suit, bell-bottoms, satin Disco style, 1970s **$75.00**
Sheath dress, Ann Fogarty, brown velvet, long skirt..**$85.00**
Sheath dress & coat, white brocade w/poppies **$150.00**
Sheath gown, red satin, plain w/good tailoring, long skirt **$45.00**
Top, sequinned & beaded knit, sleeveless **$45.00**

1960s – 70s Women's Accessories

Go-go boots, green vinyl, 1960s...................................**$40.00**
Go-go boots, snakeskin late 1960s...............................**$85.00**
Hat, bubble toque, Jack McConnell, feathered, 1960s..**$125.00**
Hat, net whimsey, Sally Victor, w/hatbox...................**$24.00**
Hat, pillbox, red velvet w/gold India embroidery, 1960s..**$45.00**
Hat, toque, pink metallic brocade, 1960s **$12.00**
Purse, clear plastic over embroidered jeweled print...**$22.00**
Purse, Enid Collins, from $40 to................................**$75.00**

Hat, lampshade style, brown satin with faille bow, from $45.00 to $65.00. (Photo courtesy Sue Langley)

Purse, Hippie bag, long fringed suede, shoulder strap.**$12.00**
Purse, Judith Leiber, gold & rhinestones **$550.00**
Purse, Magazine..**$45.00**
Purse, silver faux leather w/plastic handles, lg...........**$12.00**
Shoes, Disco-style platforms, gunmetal multicolor, 1970s **$65.00**
Shoes, evening, square toes, silk w/gold & beaded lion head...**$55.00**

1940s – 70s Men's Wear

Bomber jacket, leather, souvenir, reversible **$500.00**

Bomber jacket, leather, souvenir, 1940s-60s, from $75 to **$500.00**

Bowling shirt, Pepsi, red, 1950s **$55.00**

Bowling shirt, teal blue, decorated, 1950s.................**$35.00**

Bowling shirt, 1950s, from $25 to **$75.00**

Cowboy shirt, royal flush yoke, 1950s **$42.00**

Hawaiian shirt, 100% cotton, made in Hawaii, $150.00.

(Photo courtesy/copyright John Dowling)

Hawaiian shirt, print by Frank MacIntosh, silk, Hookano label, from $600 to **$800.00**

Hawaiian shirt, rayon or cotton print, 1940s-50s, from $55 to...**$150.00**

Jacket, gabardine, zip front, 1950s, from $45 to **$400.00**

Leisure suit, polyester, bell-bottom pants, 1960s.........**$55.00**

Shirt, Disco style, photo scenes, 1970s, from $20 to ..**$55.00**

Shirt, Kramer style, pink gabardine w/black checks, 1950s **$45.00**

Shirt, photographic Disco style.....................................**$20.00**

Shoes, Disco platform style, brown leather-look vinyl....**$24.00**

Shoes, psychedelic Disco platform style, 3-color vinyl ...**$80.00**

Smoking jacket, blue corduroy w/rust satin trim, 1940s **$45.00**

Tie, hand-painted sailfish **$30.00**

Tie, Salvador Dali, Soaring Wall, EX **$250.00**

Vintage Denim

Bib overalls, Lee long L, house mark, 1930s, size M **$200.00**

Jacket, Big Mac work wear, triple-stitched, 1970s, never worn, size 40...**$125.00**

Jacket, Headlight, big buttons, 1940s, great color, size M/L..**$550.00**

Jacket, Hercules work wear, 1950s, excellent color, size M/L..**$350.00**

Jacket, Lee Stormrider 101-LJ, size 40, G **$85.00**

Jacket, Lee 91-J, loop tag, good color, 1950s, size 38..**$350.00**

Jacket, Levi, big E, indigo w/yellow seam thread stitching, size 42...**$25.00**

Jacket, Levi buckle back, exposed rivet, med-dark color, repaired, 34" waist...**$1,725.00**

Jacket, Levi Youth, 2nd edition, silver buttons, size 30..**$125.00**

Jacket, Lee Riders Brand, indigo denim, 1970s, $130.00.

Jacket, Levi 506, 1st edition, silver buckle, repaired, med **$350.00**

Jacket, Levi 506 XX, 2nd edition, good color, size M ..**$500.00**

Jacket, Levi 507 XX, good color, slight wear to cuffs, size med...**$350.00**

Jacket, Levi 507 XX, 2nd edition, med color, size M ..**$375.00**

Jacket, Levi 507 XX 2nd edition, med color, no patch, size 42/44...**$225.00**

Jacket, Osh Kosh B'gosh, Ideal zipper, size 44...........**$25.00**

Jacket, Penney's Foremost, 1-pocket, dark, size S **$75.00**

Jacket, Penney's Payday, triple-stitched, double-stitched collar, very dark, 1950s, size L...............................**$175.00**

Jeans, Lee, center tag, med color, 31" waist...............**$210.00**

Jeans, Levi buckle-backs, perfect patch, very dark, 1930s, 35" waist **$3,000.00**

Jeans, Levi sm e, single stitch, indigo, deadstock, 32" waist **$525.00**

Jeans, Levi 101, full red lines, red/black center patch, med-color, light soil, 32" waist..................................**$400.00**

Jeans, Levi 200 series, indigo, Scovill zipper, 32" waist .**$25.00**

Jeans, Lee Riders Full Cut Authentic Western, deadstock, $100.00.

Jeans, Levi 401 big E, A-patch, good color, repaired, 33" waist..**$375.00**
Jeans, Levi 501, red lines, #6 button, 25" waist...........**$25.00**
Jeans, Levi 501, red lines, dark blue, 33" waist.........**$120.00**
Jeans, Levi 501, single-stitched, med color, 34" waist ..**$125.00**
Jeans, Levi 501 big E, good color, 31"to 36" waist, from $400 to..**$525.00**
Jeans, Levi 501 big E, single-stitched red lines, #8 on top button, 30" waist **$175.00**
Jeans, Levi 501 big E, 2-color stitching, 34" waist.....**$300.00**
Jeans, Levi 501 big E S-patch, excellent color, 32" waist..**$600.00**
Jeans, Levi 501 sm e, indigo, 36" waist......................**$400.00**
Jeans, Levi 501 XX, dark, from 31" to 36" waist........**$500.00**
Jeans, Levi 501 XX, every garment guaranteed, med color, 32" waist..**$625.00**
Jeans, Levi 501 XX, every garment guaranteed, paper patch, good color, repaired, 33" waist...........................**$675.00**
Jeans, Levi 501 XX, every garment guaranteed, paper patch, 30" waist.................................**$1,100.00**
Jeans, Levi 501 XX, every garment guaranteed, very dark, 32" waist..**$925.00**
Jeans, Levi 501 XX, every garment guaranteed, very dark, 39" waist..**$400.00**
Jeans, Levi 501 XX, leather patch, excellent color, 37" waist **$975.00**
Jeans, Levi 501 XX, leather patch, good color, 31" waist ..**$800.00**
Jeans, Levi 501 XX, leather patch, 34" waist **$1,150.00**
Jeans, Levi 501 XX, 1-sided red tag, leather patch, excellent color, 31" waist.....................................**$900.00**
Jeans, Levi 501 XX WWII, donut button on top of fly, perfect leather patch, 35" waist...................................**$2,250.00**
Jeans, Levi 501 Z XX, excellent color, 32" waist, from $350 to.................................**$450.00**
Jeans, Levi 505 big E, full red lines, excellent color, 30" waist..**$350.00**
Jeans, Levi 505 big E, very dark, 34" waist...............**$225.00**
Jeans, Levi 505 sm e, indigo, 34" waist......................**$200.00**
Jeans, Levi 505 XX, good color, 35" waist **$550.00**
Jeans, Levi 517, single stitch, good color, 32" waist....**$55.00**
Jeans, Wrangler Blue Bell, white, 1960s, 34" waist...**$175.00**
Shirt, Coast Wide, chambray, union made, sanforized, size S all **$65.00**
Shirt, Levi Long Horn, excellent color, size M **$475.00**
Shirt, Sanforized, indigo w/painted buttons, Western style, dark indigo, size M..**$175.00**
Shirt, Sears Roebuck, 1950s, minor collar wear, size M ..**$160.00**

Jeans, Wrangler Blue Bell Brand, button fly, deadstock, $315.00.

Coca-Cola Collectibles

Coca-Cola was introduced to the public in 1886. Immediately an advertising campaign began that over the years and continuing to the present day has literally saturated our lives with a never-ending variety of items. Some of the earlier calendars and trays have been known to bring prices well into the four figures. Because of these heady prices and the extremely widespread collector demand for good Coke items, reproductions are everywhere, so beware! Some of the items that have been reproduced are pocket mirrors (from 1905, 1906, 1908 – 11, 1916, and 1920), trays (from 1899, 1910, 1913 – 14, 1917, 1920, 1923, 1926, 1934, and 1937), tip trays (from 1907, 1909, 1910, 1913 – 14, 1917, and 1920), knives, cartons, bottles, clocks, and trade cards. In recent years, these items have been produced and marketed: an 8" brass 'button,' a 27" brass bottle-shaped thermometer, cast-iron toys and bottle-shaped door pulls, Yes Girl posters, a 12" 'button' sign (with one round hole), a rectangular paperweight, a 1949-style cooler radio, and there are others. Look for a date line.

In addition to reproductions, 'fantasy' items have also been made, the difference being that a 'fantasy' never existed as an original. Don't be deceived. Belt buckles are 'fantasies.' So are glass doorknobs with an etched trademark, bottle-shaped knives, pocketknives (supposedly from the 1933 World's Fair), a metal letter opener stamped 'Coca-Cola 5¢,' a cardboard sign with the 1911 lady with fur (9" x 11"), and celluloid vanity pieces (a mirror, brush, etc.).

When the company celebrated its 100th anniversary in 1986, many 'centennial' items were issued. They all carry the '100th Anniversary' logo. Many of them are collectible in their own right, and some are already expensive.

If you'd really like to study this subject, we recommend these books: *Goldstein's Coca-Cola Collectibles* by Sheldon Goldstein; *Collector's Guide to Coca-Cola Items, Vols. I and II*, by Al Wilson; *Collectible Coca-Cola Toy Trucks* by Gael de Courtivron; *Petretti's Coca-Cola Collectibles Price Guide* by Allan Petretti; and *B.J. Summers' Guide to Coca-Cola, Vols. I and II.*

Advisor: Craig Stifter (See Directory, Soda Pop Collectibles)

Club: Coca-Cola Collectors Club International
P.O. Box 49166
Atlanta, GA 30359. Annual dues: $25

Ashtray, glass, red lettering on clear, square, EX........**$15.00**
Ashtray, metal w/molded cigarette holder, square, EX..**$20.00**
Ashtray, ruby glass, card suit shapes, 1950s, EX, set of 4 ....**$375.00**
Ashtray, tin, High in Energy, Low in Calories, 1950s, EX..**$20.00**
Bean bag, Enjoy Coca-Cola, dynamic wave, red, 1970s, VG **$25.00**

Blotter, Completely Refreshing, w/disc upper left, 1942, EX **$30.00**

Blotter, Over 60 Million a Day, bottle, 1960, lg, EX....**$12.00**

Book, Pause for Living, bound copy, red, 1960s, EX .**$12.00**

Booklet, Profitable Soda Fountain Operation, 1953, EX..**$65.00**

Bottle, St Louis Rams, NM...**$8.00**

Bottle, Tri-State Area Council, Boy Scouts of America, green, 1953, EX **$230.00**

Bottle, Wal-Mart Christmas, 1994, NM **$5.00**

Bottle, 1984 convention, Chicago IL, EX **$40.00**

Bottle, 1985 convention, Anaheim CA, 1958, EX **$40.00**

Bottle, Gold, 100th Anniversary, 1986, EX, $45.00. (Photo courtesy B.J. Summers)

Calendar, 1944, lady w/bottle, full pad, EX...............**$300.00**

Calendar, 1946, Sprite Boy on cover, 2 months & scene on ea page, EX..**$825.00**

Calendar, 1962, Enjoy That Refreshing New Feeling, boy & girl at dance, M...**$85.00**

Calendar, 1969, Things Go Better w/Coke, boy whispering to girl at table, full pad, G...........................**$45.00**

Carrier, aluminum, 6-pack w/separate compartments, Coca-Cola embossed on side, 1940-50s, EX...................**$95.00**

Carrier, aluminum w/red panel on side, 12-bottle, 1950s, EX...**$100.00**

Carrier, masonite, 6-pack, 1940s, EX...........................**$75.00**

Carton wrap, Holiday Hospitality, 1940s, M **$30.00**

Clock, electric, light-up base w/Coca-Cola, plastic w/fake pendulum, 1970s, G **$45.00**

Clock, electric, Swihart, 1950s, 8x6½" (unusual size), EX **$350.00**

Clock, light-up, aluminum case w/plastic case, red on white, Modern Clock Advertising Co, 1950s, 24" dia, VG **$350.00**

Clock, plastic, white background, electric, EX............**$85.00**

Coaster, aluminum, green, 1960s, EX............................**$4.00**

Coaster, metal, Juanita, 1984, EX.................................**$8.00**

Comic book, Refreshment Through the Ages, 1951, G .**$5.00**

Cooler, aluminum, 12-pack, 1950s, G **$85.00**

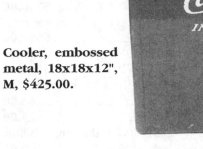

Cooler, embossed metal, 18x18x12", M, $425.00.

Cooler, stainless steel, Drink Coca-Cola on front in red, 6-pack, 1950s, EX.................................**$425.00**

Corkscrew, wall mounted, 1950s, EX..........................**$35.00**

Dart board, Drink Coca-Cola in center, 1950s, EX......**$85.00**

Door push, porcelain, Take Some Coca-Cola Home Today, white on red, 1950s, 34" L, NM......................**$525.00**

Fan, cardboard, Enjoy Coca-Cola, wooden handle, 1960s, EX..**$15.00**

Fan, cardboard fold-out, Coca-Cola Bottling Co, Bethlehem PA, 1950s, EX **$55.00**

Game, checkers, green & white pegs fit into yellow squares, 1970s, EX..**$65.00**

Game, ring toss, Santa at top of handle, VG..............**$25.00**

Glass, Drink Coca-Cola, bell shape, 1940s **$15.00**

Glass, Enjoy Coca-Cola, bell shape, 1970s...................**$5.00**

Ice pick, wooden handle, 1960s, EX............................**$10.00**

Lighter, can shape w/dynamic wave, M **$30.00**

Lighter, gold Sygnus stand-up, 1962, EX **$145.00**

Lighter, silver w/embossed bottle, flip-top, M............**$40.00**

Magazine, Pause for Living, single copy, 1960, EX.......**$8.00**

Magazine ad, National Geographic back cover, You Taste Its Quality, girl w/bottle, 1951, NM **$5.00**

Menu board, light-up design w/clock, 1960s, EX **$135.00**

Menu board, tin, arched top embossed w/fishtail design at top, NM **$375.00**

Napkin, Sprite Boy printed on white paper, 1950s, M **$15.00**

Opener, card suit, stainless steel in marked carrier sleeves, 1970s, EX..**$45.00**

Opener, Drink Coca-Cola, key shape w/bottle cap facsimile at top, 1920-50s, NM.............................**$35.00**

Opener, metal (referred to as bent metal), Drink Coca-Cola, wall mount, 1950, EX **$20.00**

Opener, Starr X, Drink Coca-Cola, 1940-80, EX **$25.00**

Place mats, Around the World, 1950s, EX, set of 4...**$20.00**

Pocketknife, stainless steel, 1 blade & nail file, 1950-60s, EX..**$30.00**

Pocketknife, truck shape, from seminar, 1972, EX......**$25.00**

Postcard, Bobby Allison & Coke, 1970s, NM..............**$12.00**

Postcard, 6 bottles w/wire-handled carton, 65th Anniversary, 1950s, EX.......................................**$15.00**

Poster, cardboard, Hospitality Coca-Cola, girl lights candle, bottle in foreground, 1950, 30x59", EX...............**$900.00**

Poster, cardboard, Play Refreshed, lady in cap fishing, 1950s, 20x36", VG.....................................**$350.00**

Poster, cardboard, Reece Tatum of Harlem Globetrotters w/basketball & bottle, 1952, 27x16", EX............**$700.00**

Poster, Home Refreshment, lady w/bottle, refrigerator door ajar, 1950s, 27x16", NM..............................**$550.00**

Radio, can shape w/dynamic wave, 1970s, EX..........**$45.00**

Radio, cooler form, lights up & plays, 1950s, EX.....**$900.00**

Schoolbook cover, Sprite Boy peeks from behind bottle on red, 1940-50s, EX...**$8.00**

Sheet music, It's the Real Thing, 1969, M....................**$25.00**

Sign, bottle hanger, Santa w/bottle, Twas the Night Before Christmas, fold-out story inside, 1950s, M..........**$200.00**

Sign, cardboard, couple on motor scooter, for side of truck, 1960s, 32x67", NM......................................**$225.00**

Sign, cardboard, Enjoy the Quality Taste, girl in swimsuit at beach, horizontal, 1956, 20x36", EX...................**$255.00**

Sign, cardboard, 6-pack diecut, 1954, 12", NM.........**$700.00**

Sign, cardboard bottle rack, Enjoy Coca-Cola, red & white, 1970s-80s, 18", EX...................................**$12.00**

Sign, celluloid, Coca-Cola in white on red, bottle in center, 1950s, 9" dia, EX...**$200.00**

Sign, light-up, Work Safely, plastic w/cardboard insert & paper cup on left of panel, 1950s, 15½" square, NM..**$725.00**

Sign, plastic, Be Really Refreshed..., curved barrel shape, 1960s, 17x8", EX..**$40.00**

Sign, porcelain, outdoor bottle, Drink Coca-Cola, 1950s, 16x4", G..**$475.00**

Sign, tin, Coca-Cola fishtail in center, bottle at right, red, green & white, 1960s, 56x32", NM.....................**$300.00**

Sign, tin, Drink Coca-Cola Enjoy the Refreshing New Feeling, self-framed, fishtail design, 1960x, 12x28", VG...**$200.00**

Sign, tin, 1950s, 28x19", NM, $550.00. (Photo courtesy Craig Stifter)

Thermometer, metal, Drink Coca-Cola in Bottles, Quality Refreshment, button at top, 1950s, EX................**$150.00**

Thermometer, metal, Enjoy Coca-Cola in white letters on red, round, EX...**$95.00**

Thermometer, metal & glass, Drink Coca-Cola Sign of Good Taste, Robertson, 1950s, 12" dia, EX..................**$150.00**

Thermometer, plastic, red & white, vertical scale, 1960s, 18x7", EX...**$35.00**

Toy truck, Buddy L #591-1350, steel, Japan, 1980s, 11", EX...**$100.00**

Toy truck, Corgi Jr, double-decker bus, 1974, 3", EX.**$20.00**

Toy truck, Durham Industries, van, 1970-80s, NM in original package **$30.00**

Toy truck, El Camino, giveaway at convention in OH, plastic, red & white, 1995, MIB..................................**$20.00**

Toy truck, pressed steel, yellow and red paint, 1940s, 18", EX, $525.00. (Photo courtesy Dunbar Gallery)

Toy truck, Renault, solid metal, red, 1970s, NM **$55.00**

Train set, Lionel, complete w/transformer, 1970s, EXIB..**$425.00**

Tray, 1940, Sailor Girl, 10½x13¼", NM.....................**$350.00**

Tray, 1942, Roadster, 10½x13¼", NM **$400.00**

Tray, 1955, Menu Girl, 10½x13¼", M, $65.00.

Tray, 1957, Birdhouse, 10½x13¼", NM.....................**$100.00**

Tray, 1957, Umbrella Girl, 10½x13¼", M..................**$375.00**

Tray, 1961, Pansy Garden, 10½x13¼", NM **$30.00**

Writing tablet, wildlife of the United States, 1970s, G ..**$5.00**

Coloring and Activity Books

Coloring and activity books representing familiar movie and TV stars of the 1950s and 1960s are fun to collect, though naturally unused examples are hard to find. Condition is very important, of course, so learn to judge their values accordingly. Unused books are worth as much as 50% to 75% more than one only partially colored.

Alice in Philcoland, Philco Corp/March of Dimes premium, 1949, unused, NM $45.00
Andy Panda Paint Book, Whitman, 1946, unused, EX..$40.00
Archies Coloring Book, Whitman, 1969, unused, M ...$40.00
Batman Sticker Book, Whitman, 1966, unused, EX $45.00
Beany & Cecil Coloring Book, Whitman, 1953, unused, EX...$45.00
Bedknobs & Broomsticks Coloring Book, 1971, few pages colored, EX..$15.00
Bette Davis Coloring Book, Merrill, 1942, unused, EX ...$65.00
Betty Grable Paint Book, Whitman, 1947, unused, EX...$55.00
Bob Hope Coloring Book, Saalfield, 1954, unused, EX $20.00
Bugs Bunny Coloring Book, Whitman, 1970, unused, M..$15.00

Bugs Bunny Porky Pig Paint Book, Whitman, 1946, unused, EX, $50.00.
(Photo courtesy David Longest)

Candid Camera Coloring Book, Lowe, 1963, few pages colored, EX...$25.00
Car 54 Where Are You? Coloring Book, Whitman, 1962, rare, few pages colored, NM $50.00
Chilly Willy Coloring Book, Saalfield, 1962, unused, NM......................................$35.00
Cinderella Coloring Book, Playmore, 1975, unused, M ..$15.00
Daffy Duck Coloring Book, Watkins-Strathmore, 1963, unused, M.....................................$35.00
Daniel Boone Coloring Book, Whitman, 1961, unused, EX......................................$25.00
David Cassidy Paint & Color Album, Artcraft, 1971, unused, NM $40.00

Dick Van Dyke Coloring Book, Saalfield, 1963, unused, EX..$40.00
Dinah Shore Paint Book, Whitman, 1943, unused, EX..$30.00
Ellsworth Elephant Coloring Book, Saalfield, 1962, unused, NM...$30.00
Felix the Cat Coloring Book, Saalfield, 1965, unused, M..$30.00
Figaro & Cleo Story Paint Book, Whitman, 1940, unused, NM...$75.00
Flipper Sticker Book, Whitman, 1966, unused, NM....$25.00
Flying Nun Coloring Book, Saalfield, 1968, unused, NM $35.00
Fritzi Ritz Coloring Book, Abbott, 1950s, few pages colored, EX..$30.00
Gene Autry Coloring Book, Whitman, 1949, unused, EX..$50.00
Gilligan's Island Coloring Book, Whitman, 1965, unused, NM...$50.00
Green Hornet Coloring Book, Whitman, 1966, unused, NM $75.00
Happy Days Coloring Book, Waldman, 1983, unused, NM $12.00
Heckle & Jeckle Coloring Book, Treasure, 1957, unused, EX...$15.00

Hopalong Cassidy Coloring Book, Whitman, Authorized Edition, 1951, NM, from $55.00 to $75.00.

Howdy Doody Follow the Dots, Whitman, 1955, unused, EX $30.00
Humpty Dumpty Coloring Book, Lowe, 1950s, unused, NM $15.00
I Love Lucy Coloring Book, Whitman, 1954, unused, NM $75.00
Incredible Hulk at the Circus Coloring Book, 1977, unused, M....................................$25.00
Jackie Gleason's TV Show Coloring Book, Abbott, 1956, unused, VG..$40.00
Josie & the Pussycats Coloring Book, Rand McNally, 1975, unused, NM.......................................$25.00
Lady & the Tramp Coloring Book, Whitman, 1955, unused, EX...$25.00
Land of the Lost Sticker Book, Whitman, 1975, unused, NM...$50.00

Little Orphan Annie's Coloring Book, 1943, unused, NM, $75.00.
(Photo courtesy David Longest)

Lone Ranger Coloring Book, Whitman, 1946, unused, EX..$85.00

Mighty Hercules Sticker Book, Lowe, 1963, unused, EX..$25.00

Millie the Lovable Monster Coloring Book, Saalfield, 1963, unused, EX $30.00

Miss America Coloring Book, 1990, unused, M $15.00

Munsters Sticker Book, Whitman, 1965, unused, M....$75.00

Nancy & Sluggo Coloring Book, Saalfield, 1950, unused, EX, from $50 to..$50.00

New Kids on the Block Coloring book, Golden, 1990, unused, NM $8.00

Old Yeller Coloring Book, Whitman, 1957, few pages colored, EX+..$20.00

Patience & Prudence Coloring Book, Lowe, 1957, unused, NM $45.00

Patty Duke Coloring Book, Whitman, 1966, unused, NM....$25.00

Pink Panther Coloring Book, Whitman, 1975, unused, EX ..$12.00

Porky Pig Coloring Book, Whitman, 1969, unused, M.$20.00

Rambo Coloring Book, 1979, unused, M.....................$15.00

Road Runner Paint & Coloring Book, Whitman, 1967, unused, VG $20.00

Roger Ramjet Coloring Book, Whitman, 1966, unused, NM..$50.00

Roy Rogers Paint Book, Whitman, 1944, unused, NM..$50.00

Shari Lewis & Her Pets Coloring Book, Saalfield, 1962, over-sized, unused, NM $40.00

Shirley Temple's Busy Book, Saalfield, 1959, unused, VG..$50.00

Skippy Coloring Book, Whitman, 1970, unused, EX ..$12.00

Smilin' Jack Coloring Book, Saalfield, 1946, unused, EX ..$30.00

Snooper & Blabber Coloring Book, Dell, 1960, few pages colored, rare, VG $25.00

Son of Flubber Coloring Book, Whitman, 1963, unused, EX..$15.00

Space Mouse Coloring Book, Saalfield, 1966, unused, M $25.00

Spider-Man Seeing Double Coloring Book, 1976, unused, EX..$15.00

Tammy & Her Family Coloring Book, Whitman, 1960s, unused, EX $20.00

Three Stooges Coloring Book, Lowe, 1959, unused, EX....$75.00

Thunderbirds Coloring Book, Whitman, 1968, unused, EX $30.00

Tinker Toy Paint Book, Whitman, 1939, unused, EX .$40.00

Tom & Jerry Coloring Book, Whitman, 1960s, unused, M $20.00

Tom Corbett, Saalfield, 1952, 15x11", VG+ $30.00

Tom Terrific Coloring Book, Treasure Books, 1957, unused, EX..$25.00

Underdog Coloring Book, Whitman, 1965, unused, VG ...$20.00

Voyage to the Bottom of the Sea Coloring Book, Whitman, 1965, few pages colored, EX $35.00

Wacky Witch Coloring Book, Whitman, 1971, unused, M ..$15.00

Welcome Back Kotter Sticker Book, Whitman, 1977, unused, NM $15.00

Winky Dink Coloring & Dot Book, Whitman, 1955, several pages colored, EX................................$25.00

Wonderbug Rock-A-Bye Buggy Coloring Book, 1978, unused, NM $20.00

Woody Woodpecker's Coloring Party Coloring Book, Saalfield, 1969, unused, NM................................$35.00

Yogi Bear Coloring Book, Charlton, 1971, unused, NM .$25.00

Zorro Coloring Book, Whitman, 1958, unused, VG....$30.00

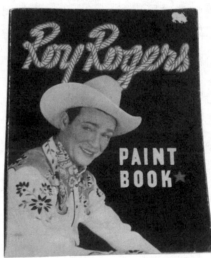

Roy Rogers Paint Book, Whitman, 1944, NM, $50.00. (Photo courtesy David Longest)

Comic Books

Though just about everyone can remember having stacks and stacks of comic books as a child, few of us ever saved them for more than a few months. At 10¢ a copy, new ones quickly replaced the old, well-read ones. We'd trade them with our friends, but very soon, out they went. If we didn't throw them away, Mother did. So even though they were printed in huge amounts, few survive, and today they're very desirable collectibles.

Factors that make a comic book valuable are condition (as with all paper collectibles, extremely important), content, and rarity, but not necessarily age. In fact, comics printed between 1950 and the late 1970s are most in demand by collectors who prefer those they had as children to the earlier comics. They look for issues where the hero is first introduced, and they insist on quality. Condition is first and foremost when it comes to assessing worth. Compared to a book in excellent condition, a mint issue might bring six to eight times more, while one in only good condition would be worth less than half the price. We've listed some of the more collectible (and expensive) comics, but many are worth very little. You'll really need to check your bookstore for a good reference book before you actively get involved in the comic book market.

Adventures of Bob Hope, Dell #30, VG **$25.00**
Adventures of Jerry Lewis, #21, G+..............................**$10.00**
Alvin & His Pals Merry Christmas, Dell, 1963, NM **$20.00**
Andy Griffith, Dell #1252, EX **$75.00**
Annie Oakley & Tagg, Dell #575, EX...........................**$30.00**
Atomic Mouse, #1, VG+ **$75.00**
Bambi's Children, Dell Four-Color #30, VG **$150.00**
Banana Splits, #3, VG+..**$10.00**

Bat Masterson, Dell Four Color #1013, 1959, VG, $15.00.
(Photo courtesy Bill Bruegman)

Beatles, Dell Giant #1, 1964, EX, from $75 to...........**$125.00**
Best of Donald Duck & Scrooge, Dell #2, 1967, EX...**$30.00**
Beverly Hillbillies, #7, VG+...**$18.00**
Bionic Woman, Charlton #1, 1977, NM.......................**$15.00**
Bonanza, Dell #210, 1962, EX **$125.00**
Brady Bunch, Dell #2, 1970, NM..................................**$50.00**
Brave & the Bold, Dell #43, EX+ **$225.00**
Bugs Bunny Christmas Funnies, Dell #7, NM.............**$50.00**
Bugs Bunny Halloween Parade, Dell Giant #1, EX ..**$100.00**
Calling All Kids, Dell #11, 1947, VG.............................**$6.00**
Captain Marvel Adventures, Dell #24, 1943, EX........**$175.00**
Captain Midnight, Fawcett #37, NM **$150.00**
Casper the Friendly Ghost, Dell #15, EX **$20.00**
Chilling Tales of Terror, Dell #4, 1970, NM **$8.00**
Chip 'n Dale, Dell Four-Color #581, VG.....................**$10.00**
Christmas w/Mother Goose, Dell #201, NM **$40.00**
Cisco Kid, Dell #17, VG **$20.00**

Daktari, #1, VG+...**$12.00**
Dale Evans Queen of the West, Dell #479, EX **$100.00**
Daniel Boone, Gold Key #10, 1967, EX.....................**$10.00**
Dennis the Menace, Dell #20, EX...............................**$15.00**
Donald Duck Beach Party, Dell Giant #1, EX............**$35.00**
Earth Man on Venus, Avon, 1951, EX **$325.00**
Elmer Fudd, Dell #689, NM **$25.00**
F-Troop, Dell #4, 1967, VG **$20.00**
Family Affair, Gold Key #1, 1970, NM.......................**$40.00**
Flash Gordon, Dell #5, 1967, EX **$10.00**
Flying Nun, Dell #4, 1967, NM **$30.00**
Gene Autry, Dell #51, VG **$20.00**
Gentle Ben, Dell #4, 1968, photo cover, EX..............**$10.00**
Get Smart, Dell #1, 1965, NM **$35.00**
Grandma Duck's Farm Friends, Dell #873, NM..........**$40.00**
Green Hornet, #1, VG **$40.00**
Gunsmoke, Dell Four-Color #844, EX **$45.00**
Happy Days, Gold Key #1, 1979, M............................**$15.00**

Hawkman, #1, DC Comics, NM, $500.00.
(Photo courtesy Bill Bruegman)

Hogan's Heroes, Dell #4, 1966, NM **$10.00**
Horse Soldiers, Dell, 1959, G+....................................**$20.00**
HR Pufnstuf, Gold Key #2, 1971, EX...........................**$40.00**
Huckleberry Hound, Dell #10, 1961, VG....................**$10.00**
Hunchback of Notre Dame, Dell #854, 1957, EX........**$40.00**
I Dream of Jeanie, Dell #1, 1966, NM, from $50 to....**$75.00**
I Love Lucy, Dell #25, 1959, NM **$35.00**
Incredible Hulk, Dell #198, EX **$15.00**
Iron Man, Dell #10, NM **$25.00**
Jesse James, Dell Four-Color #757, G+ **$15.00**
Jetsons, Gold Key #35, EX **$15.00**
John Carter of Mars, Gold Key #1, 1964, VG **$20.00**
Jungle Jim, Dell #12, 1949, G **$10.00**
Justice League of America, Dell #6, VG......................**$50.00**
Katzenjammer Kids, Dell #32, 1946, VG **$35.00**
Lady & the Tramp, Dell #1, 1955, VG..........................**$30.00**
Lassie, Dell #27, NM..**$15.00**
Legends of Daniel Boone, #3, G **$30.00**
Lil' Abner, Dell #61, 1947, NM....................................**$190.00**

Little Audrey TV Funtime, Harvey Giant #1, 1962, VG ...**$10.00**
Littlest Outlaw, Dell Four-Color #609, VG+ **$15.00**
Lone Ranger, March of Comics #310, photo cover, EX...**$45.00**
Lone Ranger Movie, Dell Giant, 1956, EX+ **$50.00**
Magilla Gorilla, Dell #8, 1966, EX **$15.00**
Man From UNCLE, #8, VG+ **$15.00**
Man in Space, Dell Four-Color #716, VG...................**$20.00**
Marvel Tales, Dell #121, 1954, VG **$35.00**
Mary Poppins, Gold Key, 1964, EX............................**$20.00**
MGM'S Mouse Musketeers, Dell #728, NM **$15.00**
Moby Dick, Dell #717, 1956, EX................................**$25.00**
Monkees, Dell #1, 1967, NM.....................................**$40.00**
Munsters, Dell #4, EX **$15.00**
My Favorite Martian, Dell #3, EX................................**$30.00**
Mystery in Space, Dell #12, NM................................**$175.00**
Nanny & the Professor, Dell #1, 1970, NM.................**$25.00**
Old Ironsides w/Johnny Tremin, Dell #874, 1957, EX..**$15.00**
Oswald the Rabbit, Dell #102, EX...............................**$30.00**
Outlaws of the West, Dell #15, VG+ **$15.00**
Partridge Family, Charlton #19, 1973, EX **$15.00**
Peter Pan, Dell #926, 1958, VG **$20.00**
Pixie & Dixie & Mr Jinx, Dell Four-Color #1196, 1961, EX..**$15.00**
Playful Little Audrey, Dell #1, EX................................**$110.00**
Popeye, Dell #8, 1959, EX **$15.00**
Raggedy Ann & Andy, Gold Key #2, 1972, NM **$25.00**
Red Ryder, Dell #69, 1949, NM................................**$35.00**
Restless Gun, Dell Four-Color #1146, VG...................**$25.00**
Rifleman, Dell #5, 1960, photo cover, EX....................**$35.00**
Rin-Tin-Tin & Rusty, Dell Four-Color #523, 1953, VG ..**$15.00**
Robin Hood, Dell #413, 1952, EX..............................**$30.00**
Rocky Lane, #5, VG...**$50.00**
Roy Rogers, #10, VG+ **$45.00**
Savage Tales, Dell #1, EX..**$50.00**
Sgt Fury, Dell #15, VG...**$12.00**

Shadow, DC #1, 1973, EX, $15.00.

Sheena, Queen of the Jungle, Dell #16, EX................**$35.00**
Six-Gun Heroes, Fawcett #15, 1952, EX.....................**$35.00**
Snagglepuss, Gold Key #2, 1964, VG.......................**$10.00**
Space Family Robinson, Dell #16, EX **$20.00**

Space Mouse, Dell Four-Color #132, 1960, VG **$15.00**
Spin & Marty, Dell #5, 1958, EX+..............................**$45.00**
Star Trek, Dell #3, 1967, EX+....................................**$135.00**
Steve Canyon, Dell #939, EX **$30.00**
Superboy, Dell #89, VG+ **$60.00**
Superman, Dell #25, 1941, VG **$225.00**
Superman's Girlfriend Lois Lane, Dell #13, NM **$100.00**
Tales From the Crypt, Dell #28, VG **$90.00**
Tales To Astonish, Dell #40, NM **$245.00**
Tarzan, Dell #27, 1951, EX.......................................**$35.00**

Tarzan, Dell #116, 1960, EX, from $7.00 to $10.00.

Tex Ritter, Fawcett #17, 1953, photo cover, EX...........**$30.00**
That Darn Cat, Gold Key, 1965, photo cover, EX.......**$20.00**
Tom & Jerry Back to School, Dell Giant #1, 1956, NM...**$125.00**
Tom Mix, Fawcett #2, VG **$110.00**
True FBI Adventures, True Comics #68, 1948, EX **$65.00**
Tweety & Sylvester, Dell #11, NM..............................**$20.00**
Voyage to the Bottom of the Sea, Gold Key #6, 1966, EX **$15.00**
Wacky Witch, Gold Key #7, 1972, NM.......................**$5.00**
Wild Wild West, Dell #2, 1966, EX.............................**$15.00**
Wyatt Earp, Dell #860, NM.......................................**$75.00**
X-Men, Marvel Comics, EX **$100.00**
Yogi Bear Jellystone Jollies, Gold Key #11, 1963, EX.**$15.00**
Zane Grey's Outlaw Trail, Dell Four-Color #511, 1954, EX..**$25.00**
101 Dalmatians, Dell Four-Color #1183, 1961, EX **$25.00**

Compacts and Purse Accessories

When 'liberated' women entered the work force after WWI, cosmetics, previously frowned upon, became more acceptable, and as as result the market was engulfed with compacts of all types and designs. Some went so far as to incorporate timepieces, cigarette compartments, coin holders, and money clips. All types of materials were used — mother-of-pearl, petit-point, cloisonne, celluloid, and leather among them. There were figural compacts, those with wonderful Art Deco designs, souvenir compacts, and some with advertising messages.

Carryalls were popular from the 1930s to the 1950s. They were made by compact manufacturers and were usually carried with evening wear. They contained compartments for powder, rouge and lipstick, often held a comb and mirror, and some were designed with a space for cigarettes and a lighter. Other features might have included a timepiece, a tissue holder, a place for coins or stamps, and some even had music boxes. In addition to compacts and carryalls, solid perfumes and lipstick cases are becoming popular collectibles as well.

For further study, we recommend *Vintage Ladies' Compacts, Vintage Vanity Bags and Purses,* and *Vintage and Contemporary Purse Accessories,* all by Roselyn Gerson; and *Collector's Encyclopedia of Compacts, Carryalls, and Face Powder Boxes, Volumes I* and *II,* by Laura Mueller.

Advisor: Roselyn Gerson (See Directory, Compacts)

Newsletter The Compacts Collector Chronicle
Powder Puff
P.O. Box 40
Lynbrook, NY 11563. Subscription: $25 (4 issues, USA or Canada) per year

Carryalls

DF Briggs, white metal, ballet duo silhouette on lid, detachable chain, lipstick & eyebrow crayon tubes, 3x2", from $125 to...**$150.00**
Evans, Basketweave, trimetal clutch, rose/silver/gold-tones, double access, 5½x3⅛", from $125 to.................**$150.00**
Evans, black satin pouch w/rhinestones, gold-tone vanity w/scenic lid, 2 hinged mirrors, 2½" dia case, 4½" overall...**$175.00**
Evans, Standard, gold-tone, single access, crossbar lid w/faux sapphires, complete accessories, 5½", from $125 to.......**$150.00**
Evans, Standard, silver-tone, double access, puff w/logo, comb, lipstick, coin holder & cigarette bar, 5½x3", from $150 to...**$175.00**
Evans, Standard, Sunburst silver-tone metal w/faux rhinestones, gold-tone interior, 5½x3⅛", from $75 to.**$100.00**
Evans, Sunburst, gold-tone metal, petite, no lighter, from $75 to...**$100.00**
Glamour, gold-tone metal w/mother-of-pearl & abalone shell checkered case, snake wrist chain, 4x3x1⅛", from $75 to...**$90.00**
La Mode, gold-tone cylinder, top lid w/shell decor, telescoping cigarette holder tube, 3½x1½" dia, from $225 to...**$250.00**
Terri, Lido, Bakelite vanity, beveled case, silk cord, Bakelite lipstick, hinged mirror, 3¼x2½", from $150 to...**$175.00**
Unmarked, Standard, gold-tone w/mother-of-pearl lid plaque & rhinestones, hinged mirror, 5¼", from $75 to...**$100.00**
Unmarked, Standard, gold-tone w/rhinestone crown, loose powder, pop-up lipstick, coin purse, comb & mirror, 5¼", from $65 to...**$75.00**
Unmarked, red padded leather on white metal, clutch style w/tasseled lipstick, spring releases, leather lined, 4¾"......**$175.00**

Volupte, Baton, brushed gold-tone metal, double access, fraternal crest, tasseled lipstick, 6⅞x2⅜", from $125 to..........**$150.00**
Volupte, gold-tone clutch, single access, tasseled lipstick, slip case, hinged mirror, 5¼x3", from $75 to............**$100.00**
Volupte, gold-tone metal w/faux gemstone notes, plays Blue Danube, 3 hinged interior compartments, 6x4¾x¾", from $250 to...**$300.00**
Volupte, gold-tone purse w/floral banding, black faille carrier, hinged mirrors, exterior lipstick access, 5¼"........**$200.00**

Volupte Oval Sophistacase, silver-embossed gilt lid, black faille carrying case, 1950s, shown open and closed, from $125.00 to $150.00.
(Photo courtesy Roselyn Gerson/Photographer Alvin Gerson)

Volupte, Super, gold-tone w/champleve Persian horses & tendrils, beveled mirror, 6x4¾", from $300 to....**$350.00**
Zell, gold-tone vanity, double access, woven basketry case, wrist chain, clip-on lipstick, loose powder, 3¼", from $50 to...**$75.00**
Zell, Round Towner, black & lurex damask, black moire interior, cigarette case clip, complete, 4x3¼", from $75 to......**$90.00**
Zell, Round Towner, gold-tone w/multicolored lurex damask, lid locket, affixed coin purse, gilt vinyl interior, 4"...**$65.00**

Compacts

Atomette, gold-tone suitcase w/tan leather covers, metal handle, 3x2⅛", from $80 to....................................**$120.00**
De Corday, Silver Queen, white golf ball shape, mirror & powder well inside, 2" dia, from $25 to...............**$50.00**
Elgin American, hammered gold-tone square w/rhinestone Christmas bell, red stone movable clapper, 2¾", from $60 to...**$100.00**
Elgin American, mother-of-pearl vanity, rouge compartment w/mother-of-pearl lid centered on compact lid, 2¾", from $60 to...**$100.00**
Elgin American, polished gold-tone w/5 red stones on lid, embossed scene, Queen for a Day, 3½x2¾", from $100 to...**$150.00**

Elgin American brushed gold-tone heart shape with cupid, hearts, and 'I Love You' in several languages, 3¼", from $60.00 to $100.00. (Photo courtesy Roselyn Gerson/Photographer Alvin Gerson)

Flato, gold-tone w/green pear-shaped stones, matching lipstick, w/powder well, puff & mirror, 2½x2⅛", from $150 to **$200.00**

France, souvenir of Paris, black enameling w/gold-tone Paris sites, 3½x2¾", from $125 to **$175.00**

Henriette, basket-shaped, black enamel w/gold-tone trim, metal interior, Pat #2138514, 2" dia, from $80 to .**$100.00**

Italy, textured gold-tone cat-face shape w/faux gemstone eyes, interior beveled framed mirror, 2¾x2", from $250 to **$350.00**

Kigu, gold-tone ball-shaped world globe, plastic interior, England, 1940s-50s, 1⅛" dia, from $150 to **$200.00**

Majestic, gold-tone egg shape, metal interior, 2x3", from $80 to..**$100.00**

Marbleized metal w/portrait transfer, mirror & powder well inside, 2¾" square, from $40 to **$60.00**

Miref, Mirador, gold-tone w/incised rings, slide-out lipstick, exterior mirrors, Paris, 2" dia, from $125 to **$175.00**

Princess, gold-tone purse-shaped compact with engraving, colored stones and raised enamel flowers, Czechoslovakia, 3½x3", from $150.00 to $200.00. (Photo courtesy Roselyn Gerson/Photographer Alvin Gerson)

Pygmalion, gold-tone ball shape w/engraved floral decor, plastic interior, 2⅛" dia, from $150 to.................**$200.00**

Richard Hudnut, Le Debut, 8-sided light blue vanity, 2 compartments separated by mirror, 2" dia, from $50 to .**$75.00**

Ritz, gold-tone souvenir (Hawaii), map of islands, side clip for lipstick, 3½x2½", from $60 to.....................**$100.00**

Schildkraut, gold-tone dial-a-date, 2 movable clock hands on dome, 3x2½", from $150 to **$175.00**

Telephone dial, green enameling w/engraved name on gold-tone cartouche, 3½", from $150 to...............**$200.00**

Unmarked, blue enameled suitcase w/gold-tone snap opening, 3¼x2¼", from $150 to **$175.00**

Vanity, red floral fabric & metal, black enamel & gold-tone at outer rim, 7x3¼" dia, from $100 to.....................**$150.00**

Volupte, brushed gold-tone w/red, white & blue enamel stripes & stones, 3x3", from $60 to **$80.00**

Volupte, gold-tone hand shape, white lace mitt decor on lid, 4½x2", from $200 to...**$250.00**

Volupte, white enameled lid w/red anchor & blue rope, 2½" dia, from $50 to **$70.00**

Zell, maroon hatbox w/gold-tone hardware anchor & USN emblem on lid, 3" dia, from $150 to....................**$175.00**

Lipsticks

Atomette, polished gold-tone w/rhinestone owl, 3 tiers of rhinestones below framed mirror on top, 2¼", from $50 to...**$70.00**

Coty, gold-tone tube w/green enamel bands, 2½", from $45 to..**$55.00**

Elizabeth Arden, gold-tone w/pearls & rhinestones at top, letter E repeated around lower rim, 2½", from $20 to **$30.00**

Florenza, brushed gold-tone tube w/green cabochon stones, 2", from $35 to...**$50.00**

Fuller Brush Co, brown marbleized tube w/yellow stones at top, 2¾", from $20 to..**$30.00**

Halston Fragrances Inc, gold-tone & silver-tone stylized heart shape tube, 2¾", from $35 to **$50.00**

Hazel Bishop, gold-tone, 3", from $25 to **$35.00**

Helena Rubinstein, Cracker Jack, black & gold stripe encircles tube, 2¾", from $30 to..................................**$40.00**

Helena Rubinstein, Stay Long, ribbed gold-tone tube w/amber-colored cabachon stone on top, 2⅜", from $10 to..**$15.00**

Lillie Dache, brushed gold-tone tube w/applied plastic figures on swing, 2½", from $45 to.........................**$55.00**

Lucien Lelong, rabbit fur-covered tube, 2¼", from $45 to.**$65.00**

Polly Bergen, brushed gold-tone & plum-colored enamel, turtle on top, 3", M in presentation box, from $10 to **$20.00**

Richard Hudnut, Du Barry gold-tone tube w/square Lucite base, faceted square rhinestone top, 2½", from $25 to...**$35.00**

Richard Hudnut, silver-tone octagon tube, 1⅞", from $10 to...**$15.00**

Salvador Dali, ribbed plastic silver-tone tube w/gold-tone lips, 3", 1997, MIB...**$15.00**

Schiaparelli, Schiap Atomic, shocking pink, white & silver plastic tube, 2¼", MIB, from $35 to **$50.00**

Tangee, white plastic w/red lettering & decor, 2", from $10 to...**$15.00**

Unmarked, black Bakelite w/rhinestones & gold beads, 2¼", from $40 to...**$60.00**

Unmarked, sterling tube w/faceted amethyst stone centered on lid, 2¼", from $100 to...............................**$125.00**

Weisner of Miami, pearls & Aurora Borealis rhinestones, 2¼", from $45 to...**$65.00**

Mirrors

Enameled, pink rose on blue, faux jade handle, decorative retainer, 5¾x2", from $15 to **$20.00**

Enameling, green marbleized, beveled mirror, Germany, 5¾x2¼", from $35 to.................................**$45.00**

Florenza, white & gold-tone w/applied leaves, red & green stones & 1 lg faux pearl, 4x1½", from $35 to **$50.00**

Gold-tone & black enamel, gold swirl in center, 4½x2½", from $15 to.................................**$25.00**

Gold-tone filigree w/pink cabochon stones, beaded retainer, 3¾x1½", from $30 to.................................**$40.00**

Gold-tone filigree w/twisted wire ring holder, green velvet center, scalloped retainer, 4x2⅞", from $50 to.....**$60.00**

Gold-tone plastic centered w/transfer scene on white plastic disk, 4½x2½", from $15 to.................................**$20.00**

Gold-tone set w/silver coin, scalloped retainer, Austria, 3¼x1⅝", from $35 to.................................**$55.00**

Gold-tone w/embossed decor & cabachon stones, faux jade handle, snap-closure carrying case, 4½x2", from $20 to.................................**$35.00**

Gold-tone w/green enameling & red flowers, 5½x2¼", from $35 to.................................**$50.00**

Gold-tone w/raised metal filigree design & turquoise stones, scalloped frame retainer, 4¼x1¾", from $20 to ...**$30.00**

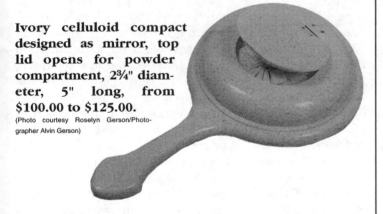

Ivory celluloid compact designed as mirror, top lid opens for powder compartment, 2¾" diameter, 5" long, from $100.00 to $125.00.
(Photo courtesy Roselyn Gerson/Photographer Alvin Gerson)

Limoges, white enamel w/courting scene, artist signed, colored stones in handle, 4x2½", from $25 to **$30.00**

Petit-point & gold-tone, wire retainer, mini, 3¾x1¼", from $20 to.................................**$30.00**

Silver-tone leaves in relief w/cabochon coral stones, framed retainer, 5x2½", from $25 to **$35.00**

Silver-tone w/cut-out flowers set w/rhinestones on mother-of-pearl disk, handle extends, folds against mirror, 3x2¾".................................**$40.00**

Silver-tone w/engraved decor, center lid w/portrait under glass dome, Denmark, 4½x2½", from $25 to **$35.00**

Solid Perfumes

Avon, gold-tone ring, set w/molded faux jade peacock, ⅞x1⅞", from $25 to.................................**$35.00**

Avon, gold-tone pendant, 1½x1⅛", from $15 to.........**$25.00**

Carolee, antique gold-tone walnut-shaped pendant, 1¼x1½", from $40 to.................................**$50.00**

Corday, brushed gold-tone purse pendant w/embossed foliage, 1½x1⅞", from $35 to **$45.00**

Corday, hammered gold-tone pendant framed by free-swing black plastic ring, 1¾x1¼", from $45 to...............**$55.00**

DuCaire, blue ceramic pendant w/painted tulips, silk neck cord, 1⅞x1¼", from $20 to **$30.00**

Estee Lauder, beige heart pendant w/gold cross-over stripes, black neck cord, Aliage fragrance, 1⅞x1⅞", $40 to.**$60.00**

Estee Lauder, cobalt enamel & gold-tone oblong pendant, suspended from mini oblong disk on chain, 1¾x1¼", from $45 to.................................**$55.00**

Estee Lauder, marbleized compositon compact pendant, Aliage fragrance, 1⅞", from $25 to.................................**$35.00**

Gold-tone & pewter-tone pendant w/bird & flower in relief on lid, scrolls on back, 1¼x1⅛", from $45 to **$55.00**

Gold-tone fish pendant, 2x1¼", from $45 to...............**$55.00**

Goldette, pewter-colored metal w/embossed profile of man's head, 1¾x1½", from $35 to **$45.00**

Harriet Hubbard Ayer, gold-tone bracelet w/mother-of-earl center & rhinestones, mirror, 1" dia, MIB, from $45 to **$55.00**

Helena Rubenstein (spelling variation in lid), stylized silver-tone shell pendant w/blue cabochon thumbpiece, from $25 to **$35.00**

Helena Rubinstein, gold-tone ring, set w/lg coral cabochon stone, ⅞x1⅞", from $15 to **$25.00**

Mary Chess, gold-tone oval pendant w/rhinestones, 1¾x1¼", from $75 to.................................**$90.00**

Max Factor, polished gold-tone elephant, red stone eyes, Hypnotique, 1¼x1½", from $45 to.................................**$55.00**

Max Factor, rabbit figural, silver-tone, Thailand, 1¼x1¼", from $40 to.................................**$50.00**

Revlon, gold-tone & green enamel, Moon Drops fragrance, 2⅛x2", from $35 to.................................**$45.00**

Revlon, gold-tone owl shape w/lg amethyst stone cabochon eyes, Intimate fragrance, 1½" dia, from $55 to.........**$65.00**

Revlon, Rajah's Elephant, gold-tone w/green enamel details, Moon Drops fragrance, 2¼x1½", from $75 to......**$95.00**

Unmarked, gold-tone basketweave pendant w/3 faceted red stones, from $30 to.................................**$40.00**

Viviane Woodward, Belle Fleure, gold-tone flower shape, 1" dia, from $35 to **$45.00**

Condiment Sets

Whimsical styling makes these sets a lot of fun to collect. Any species of animal, plant, or bird that ever existed and many that never did or ever will are represented, so an extensive collection is possible, and prices are still reasonable. These sets are usually comprised of a pair of salt and pepper shakers and a small mustard pot with spoon on a tray. Technically, the set must include a mustard pot to be considered a condiment set. Some never had a tray — but virtually all Japanese sets did. Others were figurals that were made in three parts. Though you'll find some with other backstamps, by and far the majority of these were made in Japan. (Ours are of generic Japanese origin unless a specific company is noted in our descriptions.) For more information, we recommend *Collector's Guide to Made in Japan Ceramics, Books I, II,* and *III,* by Carole Bess White; *Salt and Pepper Shakers, Vols I* through *IV,* by Helene Guarnaccia; and *Collectors Encyclopedia of Salt and Pepper Shakers, Figural and Novelty,* by Melva Davern. Note: Without the matching ceramic spoon, prices on condiment sets should be 25% to 40% less than values listed here. See also Black Americana.

Advisor: Carole Bess White (See Directory, Japan Ceramics)

Airplane figural, white opal lustre, Sarsaparilla Deco Designs NYCNY, Japan, 1981, 7½" L, from $20 to **$30.00**

Birds (3), multicolor lustre, on tray, Japan, 7¾" wide, from $125 to **$150.00**

Black & white cats (3) w/kitten (spoon) peeking from red ball of yarn (mustard), rug tray, ceramic, from $85 to **$90.00**

Bonzo type dogs (3) on tray, larger center dog (mustard) w/tongue spoon, lustreware, Japan, from $50 to... **$75.00**

Bonzo type dogs (3) on tray, white w/painted details, ceramic, Germany, from $60 to **$80.00**

Cottage figurals (3) on tray, shaped like teapot, creamer & sugar but really mustard & shakers, Japan, from $55 to **$65.00**

Cow w/2 heads, mustard in center of body, heads remove & serve as shakers, ceramic, Germany, 1930s, from $75 to **$90.00**

Dachshund figural, body is in 3 parts (2 shakers & mustard jar), 1960s, from $20 to **$22.00**

Deco floral, angular pieces (3) w/lustre glazes fit on tray, Japan, 6¼" wide, from $35 to **$45.00**

Deco-style exotic birds on white w/gray lustre, 3 pcs on tray, Japan, from $40 to **$50.00**

Dogs (2), lustreware, heads are shakers, body of larger dog is mustard, tongue is spoon, Japan, from $45 to . **$50.00**

Elephant w/Eastern man (mustard lid) on top, flower baskets on sides (shakers), ceramic, Japan, 1950s, from $100 to **$140.00**

Flower forms (3) w/butterfly finial on mustard, multicolored lustre, on tray, Japan, from $30 to **$50.00**

Kangaroos (adult w/2 smaller) w/boxing gloves, baby in pouch (mustard), boxing glove spoon, on tray, ceramic, from $60 to **$75.00**

Koala bears, 1 hangs from side of base, 2nd is lid for mustard, unmarked ceramic, from $45 to **$50.00**

Monkeys (3), See No Evil, Speak No Evil, Hear No Evil, on tray, ceramic, Japan, 1950, from $80 to **$120.00**

Penguins (4) on tray, multicolor, Japan, 7", from $35 to... **$50.00**

Pig (stacking 3-part body), blue clothes, ceramic, from $50 to **$65.00**

Rabbits (2) w/cabbage, on tray, ceramic, Japan, 1960s, from $65 to **$75.00**

Stacking duck figurals, Japan, 1930-50s, from $18 to . **$20.00**

Windmills (3 on tray), Japan, from $22 to **$25.00**

Cookbooks and Recipe Leaflets

Cookbook collecting is not new! Perhaps one of the finest books ever written on the subject goes back to just after the turn of the century when Elizabeth Robins Pennell published *My Cookery Books,* an edition limited to 330 copies; it had tipped-in photographs and was printed on luxurious, uncut paper. Mrs. Pennell, who spent much of her adult life travelling in Europe, wrote a weekly column on food and cooking for the *Pall Mall Gazette,* and as a result, reviewed many books on cookery. Her book was a compilation of titles from her extensive collection which was later donated to the Library of Congress. That this book was reprinted in 1983 is an indication that interest in cookbook collecting is strong and ongoing.

Books on food and beverages, if not bestsellers, are at the least generally popular. Cookbooks published by societies, lodges, churches, and similar organizations offer insight into regional food preferences and contain many recipes not found in other sources. Very early examples are unusually practical, often stressing religious observances and sometimes offering medical advise. Recipes were simple combinations of basic elements. Cookbooks and cooking guides of World Wars I and II stressed conservation of food. In sharp contrast are the more modern cookbooks often authored by doctors, dietitians, cooks, and domestic scientists, calling for more diversified materials and innovative combinations with exotic seasonings. Food manufacturers' cookbooks abound. By comparing early cookbooks to more recent publications, the fascinating evolution in cookery and food preparation is readily apparent.

Because this field is so large and varied, we recommend that you choose the field you find most interesting and specialize. Will you collect hardbound or softcover? Some collectors zero in on one particular food company's literature — for instance, Gold Medal Flour and Betty Crocker, the

Dwarf and toadstools, Crown Devon, from $90.00 to $110.00.

Pillsbury Flour Company's Pillsbury Bake-Offs, and Jell-O. Others look for more general publications on chocolate, spices and extracts, baking powers, or favored appliances. Fund-raising, regional, and political cookbooks are other types to consider.

Our advisor, Col. Bob Allen, has written *A Guide to Collecting Cookbooks* (Collector Books), a compilation of four large collections resulting in a much broader overview than is generally possible in a book of this type. It contains more than 300 color illustrations and in excess of 5,000 titles with current values.

Our suggested values are based on cookbooks in very good condition; remember to adjust prices up or down to evaluate examples in other conditions. For your convenience, our listings are grouped into categories representing various collecting areas.

Advisor: Bob Allen (See Directory, Cookbooks)

Club/Newsletter: *Cookbook Gossip*
Cookbook Collectors Club of America, Inc.
Bob and Jo Ellen Allen
P.O. Box 56
St. James, MO 65559-0056

Newsletter: *The Cookbook Collector's Exchange*
Sue Erwin
P.O. Box 32369
San Jose, CA 95152-2369

Pre-1900: Hardbound

American Cook Book, Mrs FL Gillette, c 1886, 1st edition **$250.00**
American Frugal Housewife, Mrs Lydia Child, c 1829, ca 1836, 20th edition **$110.00**
American Woman's Home, Catherine Beecher & Harriet Beecher Stowe, c 1869, 1st edition, 500 pages ..**$300.00**
Boston Cook Book, Mrs DA Lincoln (Mary J Lincoln), Roberts Brothers, Boston, c 1883, 1st edition **$125.00**
Boston Cooking-School Cook Book, Fannie M Farmer, Little, Brown & Co, c 1896, ca 1897, 2nd edition, 567 pages..**$350.00**
Centennial Cook Book, Ella Myers, Philadelphia......**$500.00**
Dixie Cook Book, AG Wilcox, Atlanta GA, c 1883, ca 1885, 688 pages..**$75.00**
Dr Chase's Recipes or Information for Everybody, c 1863, ca 1865, 25th edition **$125.00**
Experienced English Housekeeper Cook Book, Elizabeth Raffald, c 1769, 1st edition **$1,500.00**
Miss Leslie's New Receipts Cook Book, Eliza Leslie, 1850, 1851, 1854 ....**$200.00**
Mrs Hale's New Cook Book, Mrs Sarah J Hale, ca 1851..**$250.00**
New Cook Book & Marketing Guide, Maria Parloa, 1880, 1881, 1883 ....**$75.00**
Presidental Cook Book, Adapted From the White House Cook Book, Werner Company, 1895, 440 pages..**$75.00**

Waldorf Cook Book, 'Oscar' Maitre de Hotel, The Waldorf Hotel, NY, 1896....................................**$125.00**

Post-1900: Hardbound

Alice B Toklas Cook Book, Sir Francis Rose, illustrator, 1954, 296 pages..**$25.00**
Alice Foote MacDougall's Cook Book, 1935 ....**$25.00**
American Home All Purpose Cook Book, Virginia Jabeeb, 1960, 563 pages **$20.00**
Amy Vanderbilt's Complete Cook Book, illustrated by Andy Warhol, 1961, 811 pages **$20.00**
Better Homes & Garden Cook Book, Home Service Bureau, ring binder, c 1930, 1st printing............................**$95.00**
Betty Furness Westinghouse Cook Book, Julia Kiene, 1954, 496 pages..**$17.50**
Bible Cook Book, Marion Maeve O'Brien, Bethany Press, St Louis, 1958 ....**$17.50**
Butterick Cook Book, Butterick Publishing Company, NY, 1911 ....**$35.00**
Chez Maxim's Secrets & Recipes...Famous Restaurant in Paris, Countess of Toulouse Lautrec, 1962, 1st edition, 253 pages..**$25.00**

Come Into the Kitchen Cook Book, Mary and Vincent Price, first edition, 212 pages, $25.00.
(Photo courtesy Col. Bob Allen)

Country Kitchen, Della T Lutes, 1936, 259 pages **$25.00**
Cross Creek Cookery, Majorie Kinman Rawlings, c 1942, 1st edition, 254 pages..**$40.00**
Edgewater Beach Hotel Salad Book, Arnold Shircliffe, 1928 ....**$30.00**
Fashions in Foods in Beverly Hills, Beverly Hills Women's Club, foreword by Will Rogers, 1930, 2nd edition.**$45.00**
Fireside Cook Book, James A Beard, 1949, 322 pages ..**$25.00**
French Chef Cook Book, Julia Child, 1968.................**$30.00**
General Foods Cook Book, c 1932, 1st edition, 370 pages..**$35.00**
Gold Cook Book, Louis P DeGouy, 1947, 1948, 1,256 pages..**$35.00**

Good Housekeeping Everyday Cook Book, Isabel Gordon Curtis, Good Housekeeping Library #1, c 1903, 1st edition, 320 pages..**$60.00**

Graham Kerr Cook Book, The Galloping Gourmet, 1966, 1969 ....**$10.00**

Harvest of American Cooking, Mary Margaret McBride, regional histories and recipes, 1957, $25.00.
(Photo courtesy Col. Bob Allen)

Hobby Horse Cookery, Marjorie Hendricks, Watergate Inn Washington DC (site of Watergate scandal)..........**$17.50**

Hood Basic Cook Book, Majorie Heseltime, 1949 ......**$20.00**

House & Garden's Cook Book, Simon & Schuster, NY, 1958, 1st printing, 324 pages **$17.50**

Household Searchlight Cook Book, Ida Migiliero & others, Household Magazine, 1942, 1943, 1946................**$15.00**

How To Cook a Wolf, MFK Fisher, c 1944, 1st edition, 261 pages **$35.00**

International Cook Book, Alexander Fillippini, former Chef at Delmonicos of NY, c 1906, 1,059 pages **$35.00**

International Cook Book, MW Heywwod, World's Famous Chefs, Merchandiser's Inc, 1929, 1st edition, 383 pages **$30.00**

Jolly Times Cook Book, Marjorie Noble Osborn, Rand McNally & Co, Chicago, 1934, 1st edition **$25.00**

Joy of Cooking, Irma S Rombauer, Bobbs-Merrill Co, Indianapolis, 1936, 2nd edition **$75.00**

Kate Smith Company's Coming Cook Book, 1958......**$35.00**

Martha Washington Log Cabin Cook Book, Martha Washington Guild, Valley Forge, 1924 ....**$35.00**

Mastering the Art of French Cooking, Alfred A Knopf Publishers NY, 1961, 2nd printing, 716 pages......**$20.00**

Modern Priscilla Cook Book, Priscilla Publishing Co, 1924, 352 pages..**$35.00**

Mrs Apple Yard's Kitchen, Louise Andrews Kent, 1942..**$35.00**

New California Cook Book, Genevieve Callahan, 1946, 1955..**$27.50**

Out of Kentucky Kitchens, Marian Flexner, 1949........**$30.00**

Recipes of All Nations, Countess Morphy, 1945.........**$25.00**

Ruth Wakefield's Toll House Tried & True Recipes, c 1936, 1st edition..**$35.00**

Settlement Cook Book, Mrs Simon Kander, 1901, 1915, 1925, 14th printing..**$30.00**

Some Favorite Recipes of the Dutchess of Windsor, 1942 ....**$20.00**

Stillmeadow Cook Book, Gladys Tabor, 1947, 1st edition, 335 pages..**$45.00**

Streamline Cooking, Irma S Rombauer, Bobbs-Merrill Co Indianapolis, 1939, 1st edition, 239 pages **$50.00**

Taste of Texas, Jane Trahey, 1949 ....**$20.00**

Things...To Know About Cooking, Margaret Mitchell, Aluminum Cooking Utensil Co, aluminum-covered books, 1932, 80 pages...**$35.00**

Thomas Jefferson's Cook Book, Marie Kimball, Richmond VA, 1938..**$30.00**

Treasury of Great Recipes, Vincent & Mary Price, Doubleday, NY, 1965, 1st edition, 455 pages **$65.00**

What Cooks at Stillmeadow, Gladys Tabor, Philadelphia, 1958, 1st edition, 250 pages................................**$30.00**

When You Entertain - What To Do & How, Ida Bailey Allen, published by Coca-Cola Co, Atlanta GA, 1932, 124 pages..**$25.00**

Italian Regional Cooking, Ada Boni, printed in Italy, translated into English, 1969, 302 pages, $15.00. (Photo courtesy Col. Bob Allen)

White House Cookbook, Janet Halliday Ervin, Follett Publishing Co., c 1964, first printing, $20.00. (Photo courtesy Col. Bob Allen)

James Beard Cook Book, w/Isabel E Calvert, 1959, 1961, 456 pages..**$20.00**

White House Cook Book, Mrs FL Gillette & Hugo Zeimann, Saafield Publishing Co, c 1899, 1911 printing, 590 pages **$40.00**

Williamsburg Art of Cookery, Mrs Helen Bullock, 1942, 3rd edition...**$15.00**

Woman's Home Companion Cook Book, 1946..........**$20.00**

Wurlitzer Centennial Cook Book, 1856-1956, 3 generations of Farney & Wurlitzer family & friends recipes, 1956, 172 pages **$75.00**

200 Years of Charleston Cooking, Blanche S Rhett & Lettie Gay, 1934, 305 pages **$35.00**

Softcover (usually stapled)

A&P News, Ann Page, published weekly, Great Atlantic & Pacific Tea Co, December 2, 1929, 4 pages **$10.00**

Ad-ven-tur-ous Billy & Betty, Van Camps Products Co, Van Camp Canned Foods, 1923 ....**$20.00**

All About Eggs, Ida Bailey Allen, 1956, 15 pages **$8.00**

American Cooker Recipes Book, 1926.......................**$16.00**

American Way Cooking School Recipes, Joblin Globe & News Herald, 1941, 12 pages **$10.00**

Around the World Cook Book, Kalamazoo Stove & Furnace Co, 50th year..**$8.00**

Aunt Sammy's Radio Recipes, United States Dept of Agriculture, 1927, 142 pages **$16.00**

Ball Stem Pressure Cookers - Canners Cook Book, Ball Brothers Recipes **$25.00**

Be An Artist at the Gas Range - Successful Recipes, Mystery Chef, 1935, 96 pages **$14.00**

Big Boy Barbeque Book, Tested Recipe Institute, Inc, 1956, 1957...**$8.00**

Children's Party Book, Woman's World Magazine, 1929..**$16.00**

Duncan Hines Adventures in Good Cooking & the Art of Carving in the Home, 1960 ....**$3.00**

Encyclopedia of Cooking, Mary Margaret McBride, 1959 ..**$8.00**

Farm Journal's Country Cook Book, More Than a Thousand Recipes, Nell B Nichols, Food Editor, 1959, 420 pages **$8.00**

Favorite Recipes of the United Nations, foreword by Eleanor Roosevelt, 1956 ....**$8.00**

Fifty Two Sunday Dinners, Woman's World Magazine Co, 1924 ....**$16.00**

Gone With the Wind Cook Book, Movie Edition, 1940, 48 pages..**$35.00**

Gone With the Wind Cook Book, Pebeco Toothpaste & Tooth Powder, 1941, 48 pages.............................**$25.00**

Hollywood & Salad Bowl, Ann Page, A&P Grocery Stores, Movie Star's Recipes, ca 1930s.............................**$14.00**

Howdy Doody Cook Book, Welch Grape Juice, 1952..**$20.00**

Kate Smith's Favorite Recipes, General Foods Corp, Advertising Swans Down Cake Flour & Calumet Baking Powder, 1939...**$14.00**

Minnie Pearl Cooks, Special, author's edition, spiral, 1970.**$20.00**

Mrs Winslow's Domestic Recipes Book, 1877 ....**$30.00**

Nancy Pepper's Recipes, Electromaster Inc, 1947, 64 pages **$10.00**

New Orleans Cook Book, 1957.....................................**$10.00**

One Man's Family, 20th anniversary Souvenir, Mother Barbour's Favorite Recipes, Miles Laboratories, 1952, 48 pages..**$20.00**

Peter Pan Peanut Butter Cook Book, Derby Foods Inc, 1963, 26 pages..**$6.00**

Salad Bowl, Martha Adams, Best Foods Co, 1929.......**$14.00**

Victory Cook Book, Demetria Taylor, 1943, 32 pages ...**$10.00**

Woman's Day Cook Book of Favorite Recipes, 1963, 96 pages..**$6.00**

Wonderful World of Welch's, Welch Foods Inc, 1968...**$6.00**

Charity, Fund-Raising, and Regional

Amana Colony Recipes - Family Size Recipes...in the Amana Village for Over a Century, hardbound, 1948, 120 pages...**$25.00**

Children's Mission Cook Book, Children's Mission Inc, Canton OH, 1937 ....**$12.00**

From Kiwanis Kitchens, compiled by Delba Engelhardt, MO-ARK Division, softcover, 1985, 498 pages.............**$10.00**

I'd Rather Play Tennis Than Cook, Poppenberg & Parrish, for Pittsburg PA Smash Lannigan Home, softcover, 1970, 44 pages..**$6.00**

Lakes & Hills Cook Book, Christian Church, Branson MO, 1936, 80 pages **$12.00**

Nita Neighbor's Book of 100 Cooky Recipes, Gretchen Lamberton Winona MN, ca 1930s, 32 pages.........**$10.00**

Rotary Ann's Recipe Book, District 597, Fayette IA, 1964...**$6.00**

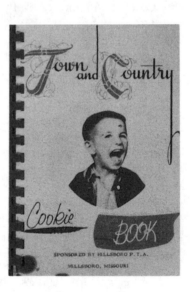

Town and Country Cookie Book, 1953, $8.00. (Photo courtesy Col. Bob Allen)

Win the War Cook Book, Reah Jeanette, Council of National Defense, MO Division, war work/relief, hardbound, 1918 ....**$30.00**

Political

Cook Book of the United Nations, softcover, 1964, 1965, 146 pages...**$6.00**

Favorite Recipes of Missouri, Family Edition, spiral, 1964, 192 pages..**$6.00**

Radio

Calling All Neighbors Cook Book, Centennial Edition, KSIS, MO, 1960, 102 pages **$6.00**

KTTR Hotline Cook Book, Rolla MO, softcover, 1968, 28 pages..**$6.00**

8 Years w/Your Neighbor Lady, Yankton-Sioux City, WNAX 570 on Your Dial, softcover, 1949, 72 pages........**$10.00**

Food Company Advertising Recipe Books

Art of Baking Bread, Yeast Foam, Northwest Yeast Co, softcover, ca 1930s, 25 pages....................................**$12.00**

Art of Cooking & Serving, 549 Tested Recipes, Proctor & Gamble Co, softcover, c 1937, 252 pages............**$12.00**

Art of Cooking w/Herbs & Spices, Milo Miloradoich, softcover, c 1950..**$8.00**

Aunt Jemima's Magical Recipes, Quaker Oats Co, c 1952, 26 pages..**$16.00**

Baker's Cocoanut Cut-Up Cakes, Franklin Baker Division, General Foods Corp, softcover, 1956, 28 pages.....**$8.00**

Betty Crocker Cook Book of All Purpose Baking, softcover, 1945..**$8.00**

Betty Crocker's $25,000 Recipe, hardcover spiral, 1933, 60 pages..**$20.00**

Betty Crocker's Picture Cook Book, hardcover 5-ring binder, 1st edition/printing, ca 1950 ....**$45.00**

Betty Crocker's Picture Cook Book, red cloth hardbound, 1st edition/printing, ca 1950 ....**$65.00**

Billy in Bunbury, Dr Price Baking Powder Factory, Royal Baking Powder Co, A Child's Fantasy, softcover, 1925, 20 pages..**$25.00**

Bread Basket, Fleischmann's Yeast, softcover, 1942, 40 pages..**$10.00**

Chiquita Banana's Recipe Book, United Fruit Co, softcover, c 1950, 18 pages..**$8.00**

Choice Recipes, Compliments of Baker's Chocolate & Breakfast Cocoa, softcover, 1916, 64 pages..........**$16.00**

Cox's New Simple Recipes - What To Do w/Gelatine, softcover, ca 1930s, 31 pages......................................**$12.00**

Dessert Lover's Handbook, Borden Co, softcover, 1969, 31 pages..**$6.00**

Diamond Cook Book, Compiled From Tested Recipes, Black chef on cover, Cream of Wheat Co, softcover, 1920.**$16.00**

Famous Recipes for Baker's Chocolate & Breakfast Cocoa, softcover, 1928, 64 pages **$14.00**

Gold Medal Flour Cook Book, Washburn Crosby Co, softcover, 1910, 74 pages **$20.00**

Healthful Cookery, Mary Dunbar, Jewel Tea Co, softcover, c 1929, 63 pages **$16.00**

Jack & Mary's Jell-O Recipe Book, Jack Benny & Mary Livingston, softcover, c 1937, 1st printing, 23 pages....................**$50.00**

Jell-O Polly Put the Kettle On We'll All Make Jell-O, Maxfield Parrish illustrated, softcover, 1924, 20 pages........**$75.00**

Joy of Jell-O, Story of Jell-O & Why It Grew, softcover, 1961, 1st edition, 95 pages..**$12.00**

Kingdom That Grew Out of a Little Boy's Garden, Dole Pineapple Co, 1927, 1928, 1929, 1930, 6th printing **$18.00**

Knox Gelatine Recipe Book, softcover, 1952, 39 pages...**$5.00**

Little Gingerbread Man, Ruth Plumly Thompson, Anonymously, 1923, 16 pages **$30.00**

Mazola Salad Bowl, Corn Products Refining Co, wooden salad bowl on cover, softcover, c 1938, 31 pages............**$12.00**

Nestles Semi-Sweet Chocolate Kitchen Recipes, softcover, 1959, 64 pages..**$8.00**

New & Easy Yeast Recipes, Breads, Cakes, etc, Red Star Yeast, 1974..**$5.00**

New Dr Price Cook Book for Use w/Dr Price's Baking Powder, softcover, 1921, 50 pages **$14.00**

Old Favorite Honey Recipes, American Honey Institute, softcover, 1945, 52 pages **$8.00**

Pillbury's 3rd Grand National Bake Off Prize Winning Recipes, softcover, 1953, 96 pages **$20.00**

Pillbury's 12th Grand National Bake Off 100 Recipes, softcover, 1961, 96 pages **$12.00**

Prudence Pevely's Pantry, Dedicated to Culinary Artists Pevely Dairy Co, softcover, 1939, 64 pages..........**$12.00**

Rawleigh's Good Health Guide Almanac Cook Book, softcover, 1946, 32 pages **$8.00**

'Round the Clock Recipes From Mary Alden, Quaker Oats & Mother Oats on cover, Quaker Oats Co, softcover, 1963, 48 pages..**$8.00**

Royal Recipe Parade, Royal Gelatine & Puddings, softcover, 1942, 48 pages **$10.00**

Rumford Fruit Cook Book, Rumford Baking Powder, softcover, 1927, 48 pages **$16.00**

Story of Chocolate & Cocoa, Hershey Chocolate Corp, softcover, 1936, 24 pages **$10.00**

Story of Crisco, Marion Harris Neil, Proctor & Gamble Co, hardcover, 1st edition, 1912, 231 pages................**$40.00**

Watkins Cook Book, Elaine Allen, JR Watkins Co, hardcover spiral, c 1945, 288 pages **$17.50**

75 Delicious Desserts, Mary Ellen Baker, Director, Home Economics Division, Nabisco, softcover, 1957, 28 pages..**$8.00**

Recipe Leaflets

Pastry Set, recipes by Marjorie Nobel Osborne, author of Jolly Time Cook Book, manufactured by Transogram Co. Inc., New York, c 1948, $3.00. (Photo courtesy Col. Bob Allen)

Heirloom Recipes, Kitchen-Tested Recipes, Betty Crocker, magazine recipe insert, ca 1965.................**$.50**

Jellies: How To Make Perfect Jellies w/Sure-Jell, printed both sides, 1939.................**$3.00**

Menu Magic w/Good Seasons Salad Dressing Mix, From General Foods Kitchens, 1960.................**$1.00**

Red Magic Recipes, How To Cook w/Heinz Ketchup, magazine recipe insert, ca 1960.................**$.50**

Tempting Banana Recipes, Chiquita Banana, 1953.......**$2.00**

25 Peachy Tricks, Cling Peaches Advisory Board, CA, ca 1955.................**$1.00**

Cookie Cutters

In recent years, cookie cutters have come into their own as worthy kitchen collectibles. Prices on many have risen astronomically, but a practiced eye can still sort out a good bargain. Advertising cutters and product premiums, especially in plastic, can still be found without too much effort. Aluminum cutters with painted wood handles are usually worth several dollars each, if in good condition. Red and green are the usual handle colors, but other colors are more highly prized by many. Hallmark plastic cookie cutters, especially those with painted backs, are always worth considering, if in good condition.

Be wary of modern tin cutters being sold for antique. Many present-day tinsmiths chemically antique their cutters, especially if done in a primitive style. These are often sold by others as 'very old.' Look closely because most tinsmiths today sign and date these cutters.

Molds, instead of cutting the cookie out, impressed a design into the dough. To learn more about both types (and many other old kitchenware gadgets as well), we recommend *300 Years of Kitchen Collectibles* by Linda Campbell Franklin and *Kitchen Antiques, 1790 to 1940*, by Kathryn McNerney. Also read *The Cookie Shaper's Bible* by Phyllis Wetherill and our advisor, Rosemary Henry.

Advisor: Rosemary Henry (See Directory, Cookie Cutters)

Newsletter: *Cookies*
Rosemary Henry
9610 Greenview Ln.
Manassas, VA 20109-3320
Subscription: $12.00 per year for 6 issues

Newsletter: *Cookie Crumbs*
Cookie Cutter Collectors Club
Ruth Capper
1167 Teal Rd. SW
Dellroy, OH 44620; 216-735-2839 or 202-966-0869

ABC set, Cooks Tools 2, 1¾", 1985, set of 26, MIB....**$25.00**
Angel, tin, flat back, 3½x4½" **$22.00**
Bear, running, tin, flat back, 8x5".................**$38.00**
Bear, tin, flat back, 5".................**$25.00**

Bird, tin, flat back, 5" **$48.00**
Blondie & Dagwood w/Daisy (dog), pup & girl, clear yellow plastic, Educational Products, KFS/HRM in crown, 5 for.................**$130.00**
Cat, copper, Martha (Stewart) by Mail, lg.................**$27.50**
Cat, tin, flat back, 3x3".................**$20.00**
Christmas tree, tin, flat back, strap handle, 6¼".........**$27.50**
Cross (religious), tin, 3¾x2¾" **$10.00**
Deer, running, tin w/flat back, handle, 2 round vent holes, 4x4¼".................**$60.00**
Democratic donkey, metal, MIB.................**$48.00**
Eagle, tin, flat back, handle, 3½x2¾".................**$12.00**
Elephant, tin, green painted wood handle, 3x3½" **$22.00**
Elephant, tin, red painted wood handle, 3x5½".........**$30.00**
Gingerbread man, clear (thick) plastic, diamond on tummy, 4½x3".................**$46.00**
Gingerbread man, plastic, Miller Cookie Cutter Company Enid OK, 4½x3¼" **$28.00**
Gingerbread man, tin, Germany, #10, 10¼".................**$25.00**
Girl scout, aluminum, Drip-O-Lator... on handle, 2½", EX.**$38.00**
GOP elephant, tin, giveaway from campaign in 1950s, 3", M.................**$28.00**
Halloween set, plastic, Hallmark, 1973, EX.................**$16.00**
Hansel, Gretel, witch, tree & gingerbread house, red plastic, Educational Products, 1947, 5-pc set.................**$110.00**
Heart, tin w/ruffled edge, 3x3".................**$30.00**
Heart, tin w/strap handle, rolled rim, 4".................**$40.00**
Heart (double, sm center heart leaves design), tin, 3¼x3½" **$33.00**
Heart in hand, tin, Hammersong Tinsmiths, B Cuckla, 5x3".................**$22.50**
Horse, tin, flat back, 5¼x4¼" **$45.00**
Horse, tin, strap handle, sm.................**$15.00**
Humpty Dumpty, older red plastic, HRM Co, 3½" **$18.00**
K shape, Kenmore advertising, Get More, Save More, blue plastic.................**$22.50**
Linus (Peanuts character), plastic, Hallmark.................**$12.50**
Lion, tin, flat back, 4x2".................**$16.00**

Loew's six-piece MGM cartoon set, Tom and Jerry and others, transparent red, 1956, $20.00 for the set.
(Photo courtesy Rosemary Henry)

Mickey Mouse, Disney, Tupperware............................**$10.00**
Mouse from Cinderella set, Walt Disney, red plastic, Loma
    Plastics, MOC **$50.00**
Mule, tin, flatback, 4½x2½" **$22.50**
Pig, tin, flat back, 2 lg vent holes, 3¾x2½".................**$38.00**
Pine tree, tin, strap handle, 3¾" **$28.00**
Rabbit, tin, Formay, 6"..**$40.00**
Rabbit, tin w/painted wood handle, marked A&J.......**$45.00**
Rooster, tin, flat back, 4" **$25.00**
Santa w/lg bag, tin, strapless, 7½x¾", EX **$120.00**
Scarecrow, painted plastic, Hallmark **$22.00**
Scooby Doo, yellow plastic, Hallmark, 1978, M in wrapper,
    from $18 to..**$22.00**
Snoopy astronaut, blue plastic, Hallmark, UFS Inc, 4½"..**$20.00**
Tinkerbelle, green-tone metal, Disneyland, 7¾" **$17.50**
Washington's axe, tin w/green painted wood handle...**$12.50**

Wear-Ever, five shapes on red plastic handle, $8.00.

Whale, tin, flat back, strap handle, 5".........................**$22.50**
4-leaf clover, tin, flat back, 3⅞"..................................**$27.50**

Cookie Jars

This is an area that for years saw an explosion of interest that resulted in some very high prices. Though the market has leveled off to a large extent, rare cookie jars sell for literally thousands of dollars. Even a common jar from a good manufacturer will fall into the $40.00 to $100.00 price range. At the top of the list are the Black-theme jars, then come the cartoon characters such as Popeye, Howdy Doody, or the Flintstones — in fact, any kind of a figural jar from an American pottery is collectible.

The American Bisque company was one of the largest producers of these jars from 1930 until the 1970s. Many of their jars have no marks at all; those that do are simply marked 'USA,' sometimes with a mold number. But their airbrushed colors are easy to spot, and collectors look for the molded-in wedge-shaped pads on their bases — these say 'American Bisque' to cookie jar buffs about as clearly as if they were marked.

The Brush Pottery (Ohio, 1946 – 71) made cookie jars that were decorated with the airbrush in many of the same colors used by American Bisque. These jars are strongly holding their values, and the rare ones continue to climb in price. McCoy was probably the leader in cookie-jar production. Even some of their very late jars bring high prices. Abingdon, Shawnee, and Red Wing all manufactured cookie jars, and there are a lot of wonderful jars by many other companies. Joyce and Fred Roerig's books *The Collector's Encyclopedia of Cookie Jars, Vols. I, II,* and *III,* cover them all beautifully, and you won't want to miss Ermagene Westfall's *An Illustrated Value Guide to Cookie Jars II,* another wonderful reference. All are published by Collector Books.

Warning! The marketplace abounds with reproductions these days. Roger Jensen of Rockwood, Tennessee, is making a line of cookie jars as well as planters, salt and pepper shakers, and many other items which for years he marked McCoy. Because the 'real' McCoys never registered their trademark, he was able to receive federal approval to begin using this mark in 1992. Though he added '#93' to some of his pieces, the vast majority of his wares are undated. He used old molds, and novice collectors are being fooled into buying the new for 'old' prices. Here are some of his reproductions that you should be aware of: McCoy Mammy, Mammy With Cauliflower, Clown Bust, Dalmatians, Indian Head, Touring Car, and Rocking Horse; Hull Little Red Riding Hood; Pearl China Mammy; and the Mosaic Tile Mammy. Within the past couple of years, though, one of the last owners of the McCoy Pottery Company was able to make a successful appeal to end what they regarded as the fradulent use of their mark (it seems that they at last had it registered), so some of the later Jensen reproductions have been marked 'Brush-McCoy' (though this mark was never used on an authentic cookie jar) and 'B.J. Hull.' Besides these forgeries, several Brush jars have been reproduced as well (see Roerig's books for more information), and there are others. Some reproductions are being made in Taiwan and China, however there are also jars being reproduced here in the states.

Cookie jars from California are getting their fair share of attention right now, and then some! We've included several from companies such as Brayton Laguna, Treasure Craft, Vallona Starr, and Twin Winton. Westfield's and Roerig's books have information on all of these. Advisor Mike Ellis is the author of *Collector's Guide to Don Winton Designs* (Collector Books); and another of our advisors, Bernice Stamper, has written *Vallona Starr Ceramics,* which we're sure you will enjoy.

Advisors: Susan Cox, Brayton, Laguna (See Directory, California Pottery); April Tvorak, Enesco (see Directory, Figural Ceramics); Pat and Ann Duncan, Holt Howard (See Directory, Holt Howard); Rick Spencer, Shawnee (See Directory, Shawnee); Mike Ellis, Twin Winton (See Directory, Twin Winton); Bernice Stamper, Vallona Star (See Directory, Vallona Star); Lois Wildman, Vandor (See Directory, Vandor).

Newsletter: *Cookie Jarrin' With Joyce*
R.R. 2, Box 504
Walterboro, SC 29488

A Little Company, Diva, from $100 to $150.00

A Little Company, Earth Goddess, from $140 to.......$175.00

A Little Company, Edmund on Vacation (Black man), from $130 to..$150.00

A Little Company, Gospel Singer, from $135 to.......$150.00

A Little Company, Pig, lg, from $175 to $200.00

A Little Company, Stella, from $165 to......................$180.00

Abingdon, Baby, Black, #561 ....$300.00

Abingdon, Choo Choo, #651 ....$150.00

Abingdon, Daisy Jar, marked Abingdon USA #677 .....$50.00

Abingdon, Fat Boy, marked Abingdon USA #495, 1941 ..$250.00

Abingdon, Hobby Horse, #602.................................$185.00

Abingdon, Humpty Dumpty, decorated, #663...........$250.00

Abingdon, Jack-in-the Box, marked Abingdon USA #611, 1947, from $275 to..$325.00

Abingdon, Little Girl Cooky Jar, marked Abingdon USA #693, from $60 to...$75.00

Abingdon, Little Miss Muffet, marked Abingdon USA #622, 1949 ....$205.00

Abingdon, Little Old Lady, black face, marked Abingdon USA #471, from $375 to...$400.00

Abingdon, Little Old Lady, brown trim, #471, from $300.00 to $325.00.
(Photo courtesy Fred and Joyce Roerig)

Abingdon, Little Old Lady, plaid apron, marked Abingdon USA #471, Dec B $300.00

Abingdon, Money Bag, marked Abingdon USA #588, 1947...$75.00

Abingdon, Mother Goose, marked Abingdon USA #695, from $295 to..$350.00

Abingdon, Pineapple, marked Abingdon USA #664, 1949.$95.00

Abingdon, Wigwam, marked Abingdon USA #665, 1949, from $250 to..$300.00

Abingdon, Windmill, marked Abingdon USA #678, 1949, from $200 to..$225.00

Advertising, Aramis Bear, from $65 to $85.00

Advertising, Avon Bear, sponged or spattered pattern, from $50 to...$65.00

Advertising, Barnum's Animal Crackers, Nabisco, carousel, from $30 to...$60.00

Advertising, Betty Crocker, red spoon logo & stripes on white jar...$90.00

Advertising, Blue Bonnet Sue, Benjamin & Medwin, from $60 to...$75.00

Advertising, Chips Ahoy! Jar, blue lettering w/red trim on white, unmarked..$45.00

Advertising, Eddie Bauer Bear, from $70 to $90.00

Advertising, Elsie the Cow, Pottery Guild, from $350 to..$425.00

Advertising, Katy the Korn Top Pig, Bartlow Bros Inc Korn Top, Haeger USA..$110.00

Advertising, Keebler, Magic Oven, from $25.00 to $35.00.
(Photo courtesy Fred and Joyce Roerig)

Advertising, Keebler Sandies Jar, red & white graphics w/elf on white $80.00

Advertising, Oreo Cookie, Think Big, from $50 to $75.00

Advertising, Oreo Panda Bear, Nabisco, from $30 to .$60.00

Advertising, Pillsbury Doughboy Funfetti, Benjamin & Medwin, from $55 to...$65.00

Advertising, Proctor & Gamble USA World Soccer Ball, from $45 to...$55.00

Advertising, Quaker Oats, Regal, from $100 to.........$125.00

Advertising, Snausages, talking dog, plastic, from $45 to...$65.00

American Bisque, Beehive, from $40 to $50.00

American Bisque, Boy Pig, airbrushed, unmarked $90.00

American Bisque, Carousel, from $100 to $125.00

American Bisque, Chef, standing, star on base, from $100 to..$135.00

American Bisque, Churn, #CJ-756, from $25 to...........$35.00

American Bisque, Davy Crockett (against forest), marked USA $750.00

American Bisque, Elephant, baby w/bib, from $150 to ..$200.00

American Bisque, French Poodle, #CJ751, from $100 to..$125.00

American Bisque, Girl, w/blackboard, from $325 to ..$355.00

American Bisque, Jack-in-the-Box, #CJ-753..............$150.00

American Bisque, Lamb, in overalls w/suspenders, from $60 to..$90.00

American Bisque, Magic Bunny, rabbit in hat, from $100 to **$125.00**

American Bisque, Owl, Collegiate, gold trim, from $125 to **$135.00**

American Bisque, Pennsylvania Dutch Girl or Boy, ea from $350 to **$385.00**

American Bisque, Recipe Jar, #CJ-563 .... **$110.00**

American Bisque, Rooster, several variations, ea from $75 to **$100.00**

American Bisque, Sadiron, from $100 to **$125.00**

American Bisque, Tortoise & Hare, w/flasher, from $525 to **$625.00**

American Bisque, Treasure Chest, #CJ-562 .... **$200.00**

American Bisque/Disney, Babes in Toyland, soldier standing guard at gate **$375.00**

American Bisque/Hanna-Barbera, Yogi Bear **$475.00**

Brayton Laguna, Grandma w/Wedding Band, from $500 to **$600.00**

Brayton Laguna, Mammy, yellow w/white apron, minimum value **$900.00**

Brayton Laguna, Matilda, from $435 to **$550.00**

Brayton Laguna, Swedish Maiden, from $475 to **$535.00**

Brush, Antique Touring Car, minimum value **$700.00**

Brush, Boy w/Balloons, minimum value **$800.00**

Brush, Cinderella Pumpkin, #W32, from $200 to **$275.00**

Brush, Circus Horse, gr **$950.00**

Brush, Clown, yellow pants **$250.00**

Brush, Cookie House, #W31 .... **$125.00**

Brush, Covered Wagon, dog finial, #W30, minimum value **$550.00**

Brush, Cow w/Cat on Back, brown, #W10 .... **$125.00**

Brush, Davy Crockett, no gold, marked USA **$300.00**

Brush, Dog & Basket **$250.00**

Brush, Donkey w/Cart, gray, ears down, #W33 .... **$400.00**

Brush, Elephant w/Ice Cream Cone **$500.00**

Brush, Fish, #W52 .... **$500.00**

Brush, Formal Pig, green hat & coat **$300.00**

Brush, Gas Lamp, #K1 .... **$75.00**

Brush, Granny, plain skirt, minimum value **$400.00**

Brush, Happy Bunny, white, #W25 .... **$225.00**

Brush, Hen on Basket, unmarked **$125.00**

Brush, Hillbilly Frog, minimum value **$4,500.00**

Brush, Hillbilly Frog, reissue (may or may not be marked Reissue by JD) **$150.00**

Brush, Hippo w/Monkey on Back, #W27, from $750 to ... **$850.00**

Brush, Humpty Dumpty, w/beany & bow tie **$275.00**

Brush, Little Angel **$800.00**

Brush, Little Boy Blue, #K24 Brush USA, lg **$800.00**

Brush, Little Girl, #017 .... **$550.00**

Brush, Little Red Riding Hood, gold trim, marked, lg, minimum value **$850.00**

Brush, Little Red Riding Hood, no gold, #K24 USA, sm. **$550.00**

Brush, Old Clock, #W10 .... **$165.00**

Brush, Old Shoe, #W23 .... **$125.00**

Brush, Peter, Peter Pumpkin Eater, #W24 .... **$300.00**

Brush, Peter Pan, gold trim, lg **$800.00**

Brush, Peter Pan, sm **$550.00**

Brush, Puppy Police **$585.00**

Brush, Sitting Pig, #W37, from $400 to **$450.00**

Brush, Smiling Bear, #W46 .... **$350.00**

Brush, Squirrel on Log, #W26 .... **$100.00**

Brush, Squirrel w/Top Hat, green coat **$250.00**

Brush, Stylized Owl **$350.00**

Brush, Stylized Siamese, #W41, from $400 to **$500.00**

Brush, Teddy Bear, feet together **$200.00**

Brush, Treasure Chest, #W28 .... **$150.00**

California Originals, Baseball Boy, from $60 to **$70.00**

California Originals, Bear w/Beehive on Stump, from $35 to **$45.00**

California Originals, Bulldog on top of Cookie Safe, from $85 to **$100.00**

California Originals, Christmas Tree, from $450 to ... **$525.00**

California Originals, Clown on Elephant, #896 .... **$45.00**

California Originals, Elf Schoolhouse, from $60 to ... **$75.00**

California Originals, Frog w/Bow Tie, #2645 .... **$45.00**

California Originals, Frosty the Snowman, from $250 to. **$300.00**

California Originals, Hippo, from $25 to **$50.00**

California Originals, Keystone Cop (Bobbie), from $100 to **$125.00**

California Originals, Man in Barrel, from $135 to **$165.00**

California Originals, Mushrooms on Stump, from $15 to.. **$25.00**

California Originals, Owl Sitting on Stump, from $50 to. **$60.00**

California Originals, Pelican, from $35 to **$65.00**

California Originals, Rabbit on Cookie Safe, from $65 to. **$85.00**

California Originals, Raggedy Ann or Raggedy Andy, ea from $100 to **$125.00**

California Originals, Rooster, from $35 to **$45.00**

California Originals, Sheriff on Cookie Safe, from $30 to. **$50.00**

California Originals, Squirrel on Stump, from $50 to. **$75.00**

California Originals, Train Engine, from $40 to **$60.00**

California Originals, Victrola, from $150 to **$250.00**

California Originals, Woody Woodpecker, antique finish, from $725 to **$865.00**

California Originals, Yellow Taxi **$175.00**

California Originals/DC Comics, Superman, brown, from $375 to **$425.00**

California Originals/DC Comics, Superman in Phone Booth, marked USA 846, 1978 .... **$600.00**

Brush, Humpty Dumpty, #W18, gold trim, from $400.00 to $500.00.
(Photo courtesy Fred and Joyce Roerig)

California Originals/DC Comics, Wonder Woman Cookie Bank, USA 847, 1878, 14" **$1,100.00**

California Originals/Disney, Donald Duck Leaning on Pumpkin, sepia wash on white, marked Walt Disney Productions 805 ....**$325.00**

California Originals/Disney, Ferdinand the Bull, from $100 to **$125.00**

California Originals/Disney, Tigger, #902 ....**$275.00**

California Originals/Disney, Winnie the Pooh, #900....**$200.00**

California Originals/Muppets Inc, Big Bird Chef, from $65 to.....................**$85.00**

California Originals/Muppets Inc, Ernie & Bert Fine Cookies, #977, scarce.....................**$425.00**

California Originals/Muppets Inc, Oscar the Grouch, from $75 to.....................**$100.00**

Cardinal, Cookie Kate, #301 ....**$125.00**

Cardinal, Cookie Safe, from $50 to **$75.00**

Cardinal, French Chef Head, from $100 to.............**$125.00**

Cardinal, Little Girl, from $100 to.....................**$125.00**

Cardinal, Pig Head, from $75 to.....................**$100.00**

Cardinal, Smart Cookie Head, from $110 to............**$135.00**

Certified International, Barney Rubble.....................**$55.00**

Certified International, Buddy Bear, from $20 to........**$25.00**

Certified International, Bugs Bunny Christmas, holding candy cane, from $85 to **$115.00**

Certified International, Chevy Corvette, from $50 to ..**$60.00**

Certified International, Dog on Jukebox, from $35 to ..**$40.00**

Certified International, Foghorn Leghorn, from $50 to .**$60.00**

Certified International, Fred Flintstone.....................**$55.00**

Certified International, Geranium, from $25 to **$35.00**

Certified International, Happy Hatters Funny Bunny, from $20 to.....................**$25.00**

Certified International, Marvin the Martian, from $55 to ..**$75.00**

Certified International, Raggedy Ann or Andy, ea from $50 to **$60.00**

Certified International, Tasmanian Devil w/NFL team colors, from $35 to.....................**$50.00**

Certified International, Tweety Bird **$50.00**

Certified International, Yosemite Sam, from $35 to **$45.00**

Clay Art, Baking Time, 1995, $35.00. (Photo courtesy Fred and Joyce Roerig)

Clay Art, Black Jazz Player, 1995.....................**$35.00**

Clay Art, Bloomin' Cat, from $50 to **$60.00**

Clay Art, Catfish, white or black, 1990.....................**$45.00**

Clay Art, Cookie Patrol (policeman), from $30 to.......**$35.00**

Clay Art, Cow in the Corn, from $40 to.....................**$50.00**

Clay Art, Dog Bone, 1991 ....**$45.00**

Clay Art, Humpty Dumpty, 1991 ....**$125.00**

Clay Art, James Dean, from $40 to.....................**$50.00**

Clay Art, Midnight Snack (fat couple hugging), from $60 to.....................**$70.00**

Clay Art, Ragtime Piano Player (Black man), from $40 to ..**$50.00**

Clay Art, Toaster, from $40 to.....................**$50.00**

Clay Art, Wizard of Oz, 1990.....................**$150.00**

Cleminson, Cookstove.....................**$175.00**

Cleminson, Pig.....................**$275.00**

Cleminson, Potbellied Stove, 9".....................**$225.00**

Danawares/Disney, Donald Duck Jar, w/hat finial, multicolor on white **$125.00**

Danawares/Disney, Winnie the Pooh Treehouse........**$95.00**

DeForest of California, Birdhouse, snow-capped, from $100 to.....................**$125.00**

DeForest of California, Chipmunk Holding Acorn, from $135 to.....................**$150.00**

DeForest of California, Clown, $145.00. (Photo courtesy Fred and Joyce Roerig)

DeForest of California, Cocky (Dandee Rooster)......**$350.00**

DeForest of California, Dachshund, from $135 to **$175.00**

DeForest of California, Elephant, from $45 to.............**$55.00**

DeForest of California, Girl w/Ponytail, from $1,000 to...**$1,100.00**

DeForest of California, Henny (Dandee Hen)...........**$225.00**

DeForest of California, Monkey w/Sailor Cap, from $150 to **$165.00**

DeForest of California, Nun, from $285 to **$350.00**

DeForest of California, Owl, #5537 ....**$35.00**

DeForest of California, Pig Head, from $125 to........**$150.00**

DeForest of California, Poodle, 1960 ....**$50.00**

DeForest of California, Puppy, #5515 ....**$55.00**

DeForest of California, Snappy Gingerbread Boy, from $125 to.....................**$175.00**

Department 56, Beehive.....................**$35.00**

Department 56, Cantaloupe, from $65 to **$80.00**

Department 56, Fishing Creel Basket.....................**$65.00**

Department 56, McNutt's Chicken Coupe Car, from $125 to **$150.00**
Department 56, Short Order Toaster **$60.00**
Department 56, Ugly Step Sisters, from $55 to...........**$85.00**
Department 56, Witch, from $150 to.........................**$200.00**
Doranne of California, Basket of Tomatoes, from $45 to..**$50.00**
Doranne of California, Butter Churn, from $35 to......**$40.00**
Doranne of California, Catsup Bottle, #CJ-68 ....**$40.00**
Doranne of California, Cow on Moon, #J-2..............**$375.00**
Doranne of California, Deer, from $100 to...............**$125.00**
Doranne of California, Doctor, #CJ-130 ....**$275.00**
Doranne of California, Dog w/Bow on head, from $60 to **$70.00**

Enesco, Bulldog, from $50.00 to $60.00. (Photo courtesy Fred and Joyce Roerig)

Doranne of California, Dragon, USA, $200.00. (Photo courtesy Joyce and Fred Roerig)

Enesco, Clown Head, #E-5835...................................**$150.00**
Enesco, Mickey Mouse Cookie Time Clock, from $400 to **$450.00**
Enesco, Old Woman in a Shoe, from $40 to..............**$50.00**
Enesco, Sweet Pickles Alligator, 1981, from $150 to...**$175.00**
Enesco, Three Little Pigs, from $40 to **$50.00**
Fitz & Floyd, Angel's Christmas.................................**$65.00**
Fitz & Floyd, Bunny Hollow, from $75 to.................**$100.00**
Fitz & Floyd, Busy Bunnies Tree, from $150 to........**$175.00**
Fitz & Floyd, Catarine the Great, from $165 to.........**$200.00**
Fitz & Floyd, Christmas Wreath Santa, from $150 to...**$190.00**
Fitz & Floyd, Clown, from $165 to............................**$175.00**
Fitz & Floyd, Cookie Factory, from $100 to **$125.00**
Fitz & Floyd, Dinosaur Holding Sack of Cookies, from $75 to..**$135.00**
Fitz & Floyd, Elephant, from $45 to...........................**$55.00**
Fitz & Floyd, Father Christmas Sleigh **$200.00**
Fitz & Floyd, Gooseberry Lane Truck, from $155 to ..**$175.00**
Fitz & Floyd, Hat Party Bear, from $125 to **$145.00**
Fitz & Floyd, Heidi Holstein **$90.00**
Fitz & Floyd, Herb Garden Rabbit.............................**$90.00**
Fitz & Floyd, Holiday Cat...**$130.00**
Fitz & Floyd, Kangaroo, from $100 to **$125.00**
Fitz & Floyd, Kittens of Knightsbridge, from $75 to ..**$100.00**
Fitz & Floyd, Kris Kringle Santa & Tree....................**$240.00**
Fitz & Floyd, Mayfair Bunny Rabbit, from $125 to ...**$150.00**
Fitz & Floyd, Mother Goose, from $150 to................**$200.00**
Fitz & Floyd, Mr Snowman, from $75 to **$100.00**
Fitz & Floyd, Old World Santa, from $125 to............**$165.00**
Fitz & Floyd, Peter the Great, from $65 to **$85.00**
Fitz & Floyd, Plaid Teddy Christmas Tree, from $125 to..**$150.00**
Fitz & Floyd, Prunella Pig, from $85 to **$110.00**
Fitz & Floyd, Queen of Hearts **$125.00**
Fitz & Floyd, Raccoon, from $75 to **$100.00**
Fitz & Floyd, Rose Terrace Rabbit.............................**$90.00**
Fitz & Floyd, Santa on Motorcycle, from $450 to **$550.00**
Fitz & Floyd, Santa's Magic Workshop, from $150 to ...**$185.00**
Fitz & Floyd, Scarecrow, from $85 to **$125.00**
Fitz & Floyd, Sheriff, from $295 to...........................**$325.00**
Fitz & Floyd, Strawberry Basket, from $60 to **$75.00**

Doranne of California, Eggplant, from $60 to **$70.00**
Doranne of California, Fire Hydrant, from $25 to.......**$50.00**
Doranne of California, Garbage Can, from $20 to......**$30.00**
Doranne of California, Hen, #CJ 100 ....**$45.00**
Doranne of California, Ice Cream Cone, from $30 to.**$40.00**
Doranne of California, Ice Cream Soda, from $40 to .**$45.00**
Doranne of California, Jeep, from $95 to **$125.00**
Doranne of California, Lunch Box, from $50 to..........**$60.00**
Doranne of California, Mailbox, from $50 to **$60.00**
Doranne of California, Monkey in Barrel, from $100 to **$125.00**
Doranne of California, Mother Goose, yellow or green, ea from $85 to...**$125.00**
Doranne of California, Owl Winking, from $35 to **$65.00**
Doranne of California, Peanut, #CJ 18.......................**$35.00**
Doranne of California, Rabbit in Hat, from $65 to **$85.00**
Doranne of California, Rocking Horse, from $165 to ...**$200.00**
Doranne of California, School Bus, #CJ-120..............**$175.00**
Doranne of California, Turtle, from $35 to..................**$45.00**
Doranne of California, Walrus, from $60 to................**$75.00**
Enesco, Bear Pull Toy, 1996 ....**$60.00**
Enesco, Betsy Ross, from $200 to **$235.00**

Fitz & Floyd, Victorian House, from $165 to.............**$200.00**
Flambro, Emmett Kelly Jr on Barrel, from $475 to ...**$700.00**
Fredericksburg Art Pottery, Cow on Moon, marked J 2 USA.....................**$250.00**
Fredericksburg Art Pottery, Dove, marked FAPCo USA..**$30.00**
Fredericksburg Art Pottery, Windmill, marked FAPCo ..**$50.00**
Goebel, Cat Head, from $125 to **$165.00**
Goebel, Owl, from $135 to.........................**$150.00**
Goebel, Parrot Head, wearing blue beanie **$80.00**

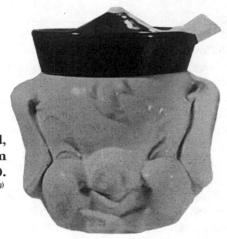

Goebel, Pig's Head, brown hat, from $100.00 to $125.00.
(Photo courtesy Fred and Joyce Roerig)

Hallmark, Christmas Bear, from $35 to **$60.00**
Hallmark, Santa, from $35 to **$50.00**
Happy Memories, Hopalong Cassidy, 15½" **$315.00**
Happy Memories, Hopalong Cassidy w/Topper, from $450 to....................**$500.00**
Happy Memories, James Dean, from $300 to **$350.00**
Happy Memories, Scarlett O'Hara, in green drapery dress, 14¾".................**$300.00**
Harry James, Barney Rubble, from $175 to...............**$200.00**
Harry James, Top Cat, from $200 to **$250.00**
Harry James/Turner Entertainment, Tom & Jerry, 7" .**$200.00**
Hearth & Home (H&HD), Bridesmaid, from $50 to ...**$75.00**
Hearth & Home (H&HD), Carousel Horse **$55.00**
Hearth & Home (H&HD), Cheetah **$55.00**
Hearth & Home (H&HD), Hippo **$40.00**
Hearth & Home (H&HD), Sundance Kid, from $50 to..**$100.00**
Hearth & Home (H&HD), Zebra, from $50 to **$60.00**
Hirsch, Basketball, from $100 to **$125.00**
Hirsch, Cookie Planet...**$85.00**
Hirsch, Covered Wagon, from $65 to **$85.00**
Hirsch, Gingerbread House..**$60.00**
Hirsch, Hen on Nest, from $60 to **$65.00**
Hirsch, Lot'sa Goodies! Chef.......................................**$275.00**
Hirsch, Monk, from $35 to...**$65.00**
Hirsch, Peck O' Cookies Rooster.................................**$225.00**
Hirsch, Pinocchio, from $475 to.................................**$535.00**
Hirsch, Treasure Chest, all brown, marked WH '58....**$70.00**
Holly Hobbie, cylindrical, from $85 to **$115.00**
Hull, Barefoot Boy, blue pants & red hat..................**$425.00**
Hull, Daisy, from $35 to..**$45.00**

Hull, Duck, from $40 to...**$50.00**
Hull, Little Red Riding Hood, closed basket, minimum value **$360.00**
Hull, Little Red Riding Hood, open basket, red shoes..**$850.00**
Hull, Little Red Riding Hood, poinsettia.................**$1,050.00**
Hull, Little Red Riding Hood, red spray w/gold bows, red shoes...**$950.00**
Hull, Little Red Riding Hood, white.........................**$200.00**
Japan, Alice's Adventures in Wonderland, house w/Alice's head coming out of roof & legs out front door, from $75 to **$95.00**
Japan, Cookie Time Clock w/Mouse Finial, blue w/multicolored trim...**$20.00**
Japan, Grandma, If All Else Fails Ask Grandma lettered on hat, orange **$20.00**
Japan, Hippo Fisherman **$35.00**
Japan, Horse Doctor..**$35.00**
Japan, Majorette Head, multicolored...........................**$25.00**
Japan, Pig Chef, white upper body w/multicolored accents, blue pants w/black belt **$30.00**
Japan, Professor Owl, w/scroll marked Cookies, brown..**$20.00**
Japan, Tom & Jerry Cookies, brown jar w/cookies embossed allover, Tom finial & Jerry on side w/colorful lettering...**$325.00**
Lefton, Bluebird, from $100 to **$125.00**

Lefton, Bossie, #6594, from $125.00 to $150.00. (Photo courtesy Loretta DeLozier)

Lefton, Cat Head, from $95 to **$125.00**
Lefton, Egg w/Bunny, from $65 to..............................**$85.00**
Lefton, Girl, #397, 8⅜" **$225.00**
Lefton, Lamb Head, from $150 to **$160.00**
Maddux of California, Bear Shopper, from $150 to..**$165.00**
Maddux of California, Beatrix Potter Rabbit.............**$100.00**
Maddux of California, Clown, very lg, from $325 to ..**$395.00**
Maddux of California, Queen, #2104, from $125 to .**$140.00**
Maddux of California, Raggedy Ann, #2108, from $250 to..**$300.00**
Maddux of California, Strawberry................................**$35.00**
Maddux of California, Walrus **$65.00**
McCoy, Animal Crackers Jar w/Clown Finial, marked USA, 1960, from $85 to **$100.00**

McCoy, Apple, airbrushed blush, 1950-64 ....**$50.00**
McCoy, Apple, 1967...**$60.00**
McCoy, Asparagus Bunch, unmarked, 1977-79 ....**$50.00**
McCoy, Astronauts, from $750 to **$850.00**
McCoy, Bananas, from $135 to...................................**$150.00**
McCoy, Barnum's Animals, from $350 to **$400.00**
McCoy, Barrel, Cookies sign on lid............................**$125.00**
McCoy, Basket of Potatoes..**$40.00**
McCoy, Bear, cookie in vest, no 'Cookies,' from $75 to .**$85.00**
McCoy, Bear, cookie in vest, w/'Cookies'....................**$85.00**
McCoy, Bear & Beehive, marked #143 USA **$45.00**
McCoy, Bear Hugging Cookie Barrel, marked #142 USA, 1978, from $75 to **$95.00**
McCoy, Betsy Baker, from $250 to **$300.00**
McCoy, Blue Willow Pitcher, #202 McCoy USA, 1973-75..**$50.00**
McCoy, Bobby Baker, #183, original **$65.00**
McCoy, Boy on Baseball, from $250 to **$300.00**
McCoy, Boy on Football, marked #222 McCoy USA, 1983, from $245 to...**$275.00**
McCoy, Burlap Bag, red bird on lid, from $50 to **$70.00**
McCoy, Burlap Cookie Sack, marked #207 McCoy USA, 1985..**$40.00**
McCoy, Caboose, from $200 to **$250.00**
McCoy, Cat on Coal Scuttle **$250.00**
McCoy, Chairman of the Board....................................**$550.00**
McCoy, Chilly Willy **$50.00**
McCoy, Chipmunk..**$125.00**
McCoy, Christmas Tree, minimum value **$800.00**
McCoy, Churn, 2 bands..**$35.00**
McCoy, Churn, 3 bands, wood-grain, unmarked, 1961...**$250.00**
McCoy, Circus Horse, black...**$250.00**
McCoy, Clown Bust **$75.00**
McCoy, Clyde Dog, from $200 to................................**$250.00**
McCoy, Coalby Cat, from $325 to **$375.00**
McCoy, Coca-Cola Can...**$100.00**
McCoy, Coffee Grinder...**$45.00**
McCoy, Coffee Mug **$45.00**
McCoy, Colonial Fireplace **$85.00**
McCoy, Concave Jar w/Lilies, black gloss, marked USA, mid-1930s **$40.00**
McCoy, Cookie Bank, 1961..**$165.00**
McCoy, Cookie Barrel w/Sign, brown wood-grain, marked #146 McCoy USA, 1969-72, from $35 to **$45.00**
McCoy, Cookie Bell, unmarked, 1953-66.....................**$50.00**
McCoy, Cookie Boy..**$225.00**
McCoy, Cookie Cabin..**$80.00**
McCoy, Cookie Jug, single loop, 2-tone green rope...**$35.00**
McCoy, Cookie Jug, w/cork stopper, brown & white..**$40.00**
McCoy, Cookie Log, squirrel finial, from $35 to **$45.00**
McCoy, Cookie Safe..**$65.00**
McCoy, Cookstove, black or white..............................**$35.00**
McCoy, Corn, row of standing ears, yellow or white, 1977 ....**$85.00**
McCoy, Corn, single ear, yellow.................................**$175.00**
McCoy, Cylinder, cobalt blue, marked USA #28..........**$40.00**
McCoy, Cylinder, Flower Panels, modern motif, yellow, marked, #254 McCoy USA, 1970-71.......................**$40.00**

McCoy, Cylinder, mustard w/green drip glaze, marked USA #28 ....**$45.00**
McCoy, Cylinder, w/red flowers.................................**$45.00**
McCoy, Cylinder w/Two Puppies, marked McCoy USA..**$200.00**
McCoy, Dalmatians in Rocking Chair, from $345 to.**$375.00**
McCoy, Dog in Doghouse w/Bird on Top, unmarked, 1983 ....**$250.00**
McCoy, Dog on Basketweave, from $75 to **$90.00**
McCoy, Duck on Basketweave, from $75 to **$90.00**
McCoy, Duck w/Leaf in Bill, yellow w/red bill, 1964, from $65 to **$85.00**
McCoy, Dutch Treat Barn..**$50.00**
McCoy, Eagle on Basket, from $35 to........................**$50.00**
McCoy, Early American Chest (Chiffoniere) **$85.00**
McCoy, Elephant w/Whole Trunk, unmarked, 1953.**$200.00**
McCoy, Engine, black...**$175.00**
McCoy, Forbidden Fruit, from $65 to..........................**$90.00**
McCoy, Fortune Cookies, marked McCoy USA, 1965-68.**$65.00**
McCoy, Freddie the Gleep, #189, original, minimum value **$500.00**
McCoy, Frontier Family Jar (Cookies), unmarked, 1964-71..**$55.00**
McCoy, Fruit in Bushel Basket, from $65 to..............**$80.00**
McCoy, Garbage Can, marked #350............................**$35.00**
McCoy, Gingerbread Boy on Ribbed Cylinder, marked USA, 1961...**$75.00**
McCoy, Grandfather Clock, black or brown...............**$90.00**
McCoy, Grandma w/Eyes Closed & Hands Folded, red & yellow w/white apron, marked, USA, 1972-73, from $90 to...**$120.00**
McCoy, Happy Face **$80.00**
McCoy, Hen on Basket, white......................................**$85.00**
McCoy, Hen on Nest, marked USA, 1958-59, from $85 to **$95.00**
McCoy, Hobnail (Ball-Shaped), unmarked, 1940 ......**$100.00**
McCoy, Hobnail (Heart-Shaped), unmarked, 1940, from $400 to...**$500.00**
McCoy, Hocus Rabbit **$45.00**
McCoy, Hot Air Balloon...**$40.00**
McCoy, Hound Dog, head down, 1977 ....**$35.00**
McCoy, Ice Cream Cone...**$45.00**
McCoy, Indian, majolica..**$400.00**
McCoy, Jack-O'-Lantern...**$600.00**
McCoy, Kangaroo, blue...**$300.00**
McCoy, Kettle, bronze, 1961 ....**$40.00**
McCoy, Kissing Penguins, from $100 to **$125.00**
McCoy, Kitten on Basketweave, from $75...................**$90.00**
McCoy, Kittens (2) on Low Basket, minimum value .**$600.00**
McCoy, Kittens on Ball of Yarn...................................**$85.00**
McCoy, Koala Bear **$85.00**
McCoy, Lamb on Basketweave, from $75 to **$90.00**
McCoy, Liberty Bell **$75.00**
McCoy, Little Clown **$75.00**
McCoy, Lunch Bucket, marked #377 USA **$35.00**
McCoy, Mac Dog **$95.00**
McCoy, Mammy, Cookies on base, white.................**$150.00**
McCoy, Milk Can, Spirit of '76....................................**$45.00**

McCoy, Milk Can w/Gingham Flowers, marked #333 USA **$40.00**

McCoy, Milk Can w/Liberty Bell, marked USA #154, from $75 to **$100.00**

McCoy, Mouse Head, w/'Mickey Mouse' ears, yellow, 1978 ....**$40.00**

McCoy, Mouse on Clock **$40.00**

McCoy, Mr & Mrs Owl, from $75 to **$90.00**

McCoy, Nursery, decal of Humpty Dumpty, from $70 to ..**$80.00**

McCoy, Oaken Bucket, from $25 to **$30.00**

McCoy, Panda Bear w/Swirl Cookie, marked #141 USA, 1978 ....**$200.00**

McCoy, Pear, 1952 ....**$85.00**

McCoy, Pears on Basketweave **$70.00**

McCoy, Penguin w/Cookie Sign on Chest, white w/black & red trim or solid white, marked McCoy, 1940-43, from $175 to **$200.00**

McCoy, Picnic Basket, from $65 to **$75.00**

McCoy, Pig, winking **$300.00**

McCoy, Pineapple, marked McCoy USA, 1956-57 ....**$80.00**

McCoy, Pineapple, Modern, from $75 to **$90.00**

McCoy, Popeye, cylinder **$200.00**

McCoy, Potbelly Stove, black......................................**$35.00**

McCoy, Puppy, w/sign **$60.00**

McCoy, Raggedy Ann **$110.00**

McCoy, Red Barn, cow in door, rare, minimum value ..**$350.00**

McCoy, Rooster, white, 1970-74...............................**$60.00**

McCoy, Sad Clown..**$85.00**

McCoy, Snoopy on Doghouse, marked United Features Syndicate, from $175 to......................................**$200.00**

McCoy, Snow Bear, from $65 to **$75.00**

McCoy, Soccer Ball, whistle finial, unmarked, 1978, minimum value..**$1,500.00**

McCoy, Strawberry, USA, 1971 – 1975, $45.00.
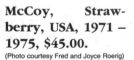
(Photo courtesy Fred and Joyce Roerig)

McCoy, Stump w/Frog, marked #216 McCoy USA, 1972.**$80.00**

McCoy, Stump w/Monkey, marked #253 McCoy USA (1970), from $50 to..**$60.00**

McCoy, Stump w/Rabbit, marked McCoy USA, 1971..**$50.00**

McCoy, Teapot (Cookies), metallic brown, marked McCoy USA, 1972 ....**$60.00**

McCoy, Tepee, slant top **$350.00**

McCoy, Timmy Tortoise **$45.00**

McCoy, Touring Car, from $85 to.............................**$100.00**

McCoy, Traffic Light...**$50.00**

McCoy, Tudor Cookie House **$125.00**

McCoy, Turkey, multicolored, marked McCoy USA, 1960..**$250.00**

McCoy, Uncle Sam's Hat, unmarked, 1973, from $650 to **$750.00**

McCoy, Upside Down Bear, panda **$50.00**

McCoy, WC Fields **$200.00**

McCoy, Windmill, from $85 to **$100.00**

McCoy, Wishing Well..**$40.00**

McCoy, Woodsy Owl, from $250 to **$300.00**

McCoy, Wren House, side lid **$175.00**

McCoy, Yosemite Sam, cylinder, from $150 to.........**$200.00**

McMe Productions, Cathy, 1994 ....**$150.00**

McMe Productions, Dale Evans, 1994 ....**$160.00**

McMe Productions, Roy Rogers Bust, 1994 ....**$160.00**

McMe Productions, Roy Rogers on Trigger, 1995 .....**$225.00**

Metlox, Apple, red w/brown & green stem **$65.00**

Metlox, Basset Hound, minimum value....................**$650.00**

Metlox, Beaver w/Bouquet of Daisies **$200.00**

Metlox, Brownie Scout Head, 9⅛", minimum value.**$750.00**

Metlox, Calf's Head, says Moo, from $300 to...........**$375.00**

Metlox, Clown, white w/black trim...........................**$200.00**

Metlox, Cookie Girl, color glazed..............................**$80.00**

Metlox, Daisy Topiary **$75.00**

Metlox, Dinosaur (Dina), blue, 1987........................**$150.00**

Metlox, Dinosaur (Mona), yellow, 1987...................**$175.00**

Metlox, Duck (Sir Francis Drake), white w/yellow bill & feet, green grass **$50.00**

Metlox, Fido, white or beige, Made in Poppytrail USA, $125.00. (Photo courtesy Fred and Joyce Roerig)

Metlox, Flamingo, minimum value............................**$750.00**

Metlox, Frog (Prince) w/Single Daisy, green w/white collar & yellow tie...**$250.00**

Metlox, Gingerbread, bisque, 3½-qt...........................**$125.00**
Metlox, Grapes, purple w/green leaf lid, from $200 to...**$250.00**
Metlox, Hippo (Bubbles) w/Water Lily on Back, yellow, minimum value **$350.00**
Metlox, Humpty Dumpty, seated w/feet **$275.00**
Metlox, Kangaroo w/Baby, minimum value...........**$1,000.00**
Metlox, Koala Bear **$125.00**
Metlox, Lamb w/Floral Collar **$325.00**
Metlox, Lion, yellow..**$175.00**
Metlox, Little Red Riding Hood, minimum value...**$1,250.00**
Metlox, Noah's Ark, color glazed **$175.00**
Metlox, Orange w/Blossom Finial **$65.00**
Metlox, Owls on Stump, bisque **$50.00**
Metlox, Panda Bear, no lollipop................................**$100.00**
Metlox, Parrot on Stump, green, minimum value **$350.00**

Metlox, Pear, green, Made in USA, $200.00. (Photo courtesy Fred and Joyce Roerig)

Metlox, Pineapple **$75.00**
Metlox, Pinocchio Head, 10¾" **$400.00**
Metlox, Pretzel Barrel **$125.00**
Metlox, Raccoon Cookie Bandit w/Apples, color glazed ..**$150.00**
Metlox, Rag Doll (Boy) **$200.00**
Metlox, Rag Doll (Girl)...**$175.00**
Metlox, Scottie Dog, black **$125.00**
Metlox, Spaceship w/Alien (Greetings Earth People), minimum value **$1,000.00**
Metlox, Strawberry, 9½" **$70.00**
Metlox, Teddy Bear w/Cookie, light tan in blue sweater .**$45.00**
North American Ceramics, Andretti Race Car, from $315 to.**$350.00**
North American Ceramics, Ford Victrola, from $200 to ..**$225.00**
North American Ceramics, Jingle Bear, from $150 to .**$175.00**
North American Ceramics, Moose, from $25 to **$35.00**
North American Ceramics, Porsche Convertible, from $125 to...**$150.00**
North American Ceramics, Train Engine, from $75 to ..**$110.00**
Omnibus, Alley Cat w/Bowling Ball **$40.00**
Omnibus, American Roadside Studebaker, from $45 to...**$65.00**
Omnibus, Around the World Santa, from $50 to........**$65.00**
Omnibus, Cabbage Patch Rabbit (rabbit on cabbage), from $25 to...**$35.00**

Omnibus, Chili Cow **$70.00**
Omnibus, Chunky the Snowman, from $35 to...........**$50.00**
Omnibus, Clover Hill Dairy Cow **$120.00**
Omnibus, Cookie Mailbox, from $40 to **$45.00**
Omnibus, Daisy Cow, from $50 to..............................**$75.00**
Omnibus, Easter Cottage Sweet Shop, from $45 to **$50.00**
Omnibus, French Country Hen **$65.00**
Omnibus, German Santa **$75.00**
Omnibus, Gingerbread House, from $40 to **$45.00**
Omnibus, Halloween Pumpkin, from $45 to...............**$50.00**
Omnibus, Hometown Tea Shop, from $25 to **$30.00**
Omnibus, Humpty Dumpty, from $100 to..................**$125.00**
Omnibus, Keystone Cop, from $40 to **$50.00**
Omnibus, Miss Kitty, from $50 to...............................**$65.00**
Omnibus, Noah's Ark Santa, from $45 to **$55.00**
Omnibus, Panda Bear, from $45 to **$50.00**
Omnibus, Rabbit on Cabbage.......................................**$60.00**
Omnibus, Safari Truck, from $45 to **$65.00**
Omnibus, Victorian Pig (pig couple), from $50 to......**$65.00**
Omnibus, Vintage Santa (Santa in sleigh), from $55 to ..**$75.00**
Omnibus, Yule Tree, from $95 to...............................**$115.00**

Purinton, Howdy Doody, unmarked, from $300.00 to $350.00.

Red Wing, Bob White, unmarked, from $100 to.......**$135.00**
Red Wing, Carousel, unmarked, from $900 to **$950.00**
Red Wing, Chef Pierre, blue, unmarked....................**$195.00**
Red Wing, Dutch Girl, yellow w/brown trim, marked, from $175 to...**$200.00**
Red Wing, Friar Tuck, green, marked........................**$300.00**
Red Wing, Happy the Children, verse on cylinder, from $100 to...**$150.00**
Red Wing, Jack Frost, short or tall, ea from $450 to...**$525.00**
Red Wing, King of Tarts, pink w/blue trim, marked ..**$1,000.00**
Red Wing, Monk, beige, from $75 to..........................**$100.00**
Red Wing, Monk, green, from $200 to **$275.00**
Red Wing, Pear, from $100 to **$125.00**
Red Wing, Peasant Design on Barrel Shape, brown w/painted-on colors..**$275.00**
Regal, Cat, from $400 to..**$450.00**

Regal, Clown w/Cookie, green collar, marked..........**$675.00**
Regal, Dutch Girl, from $650 to **$750.00**
Regal, Fisherman/Whaler, gold trim, unmarked.......**$650.00**
Regal, Goldilocks, marked **$375.00**
Regal, Little Miss Muffet, #705 ....**$385.00**
Regal, Majorette Head **$675.00**
Regal, Oriental Lady w/Baskets, unmarked..............**$600.00**
Regal, Poodle (Fi Fi), marked.............................**$650.00**
Regal, Toby Cookies, unmarked............................**$750.00**
Robinson-Ransbottom, Chef w/Bowl & Spoon, much gold
  trim, #411 ....**$225.00**
Robinson-Ransbottom, Hootie Owl, from $95 to......**$115.00**
Robinson-Ransbottom, Jocko the Monkey.................**$375.00**
Robinson-Ransbottom, Ol' King Cole, multicolored w/black
  pipe & mug...**$425.00**
Robinson-Ransbottom, Oscar the Doughboy, from $135
  to **$165.00**
Robinson-Ransbottom, Pig Sheriff, much gold trim,
  #363 ....**$175.00**
Robinson-Ransbottom, Tiger Cubs, from $85 to **$100.00**
Robinson-Ransbottom, Whale w/Hat, marked **$525.00**

Roman Ceramics, R2D2, marked Star Wars TM 1977 Twentieth Century-Fox Film Corporation, $165.00 to $175.00.

Shawnee, Cooky, white w/floral decals lg painted tulip &
  gold trim, marked USA.....................................**$300.00**
Shawnee, Cottage, marked USA #6........................**$1,350.00**
Shawnee, Drum Major, gold trim, marked USA 10, minimum
  value **$500.00**
Shawnee, Dutch Boy, marked Great Northern USA #1025 ..**$325.00**
Shawnee, Elephant (Jumbo), sitting upright, white w/yellow
  neck bow, marked USA #6..................................**$125.00**
Shawnee, Elephant (Lucky), sitting upright, decals & gold
  trim, marked USA **$825.00**
Shawnee, Fern Ware, yellow, marked USA **$85.00**
Shawnee, Fruit Basket, marked Shawnee 84.............**$225.00**
Shawnee, Happy, white w/floral decals, blue & gold trim,
  marked USA **$300.00**
Shawnee, Jack, cold-painted, marked USA...............**$125.00**
Shawnee, Jill, cold-painted, marked USA **$125.00**
Shawnee, Jug, blue, marked USA...........................**$95.00**

Shawnee, Little Chef Hexagon Jar, white w/multicolored &
  gold trim, marked USA....................................**$225.00**
Shawnee, Muggsy, decals & gold trim, marked Pat Muggsy
  USA **$875.00**
Shawnee, Muggsy, plain white w/blue trim, marked
  USA **$425.00**
Shawnee, Owl Winking, white w/trimmed face & neck,
  marked USA **$150.00**
Shawnee, Puss 'n Boots, decals & gold trim, marked Pat Puss
  'n Boots USA..**$625.00**
Shawnee, Sailor Boy, white w/cold-painted black trim,
  marked USA **$125.00**
Shawnee, Sailor Boy, yellow hair & gold neck tie, marked
  GOB & USA **$725.00**
Shawnee, Smiley the Pig, clover blossom, marked Pat Smiley
  USA **$500.00**
Shawnee, Smiley the Pig, white w/blue neck scarf, black
  hooves & buttons, marked USA **$300.00**
Shawnee, Winnie the Pig, brown coat w/green collar,
  marked USA #61 ....**$425.00**
Shawnee, Winnie the Pig, clover blossom, marked Winnie
  USA **$475.00**
Shawnee (New), Billy in Dad's Sheriff Uniform........**$175.00**
Shawnee (New), Farmer Pig................................**$175.00**
Shawnee (New), Sowly Pig.................................**$175.00**
Sierra Vista, Cottage, from $50 to **$65.00**
Sierra Vista, Dog on Drum, from $85 to..................**$100.00**
Sierra Vista, Elephant, blue w/white, black & yellow plaid
  vest...**$150.00**

Sierra Vista, House (Reversible), #51 California, $125.00.
(Photo courtesy Ermagene Westfall)

Sierra Vista, Owl, from $75 to **$100.00**
Sierra Vista, Rooster, brown matt stain **$50.00**
Sierra Vista, Spaceship, brown matt, unmarked........**$425.00**
Sierra Vista, Squirrel, from $100 to.......................**$135.00**
Sierra Vista, Train, happy face on front **$95.00**
Sigma, Agatha **$200.00**
Sigma, Beaver Fireman......................................**$275.00**
Sigma, Chef, from $125 to **$150.00**
Sigma, Circus Fat Lady **$200.00**
Sigma, Cubs Bear **$150.00**
Sigma, Duck w/Mixing Bowl, from $100 to..............**$125.00**
Sigma, Fat Cat, in pink dress w/red dots **$325.00**
Sigma, Fat Cat, in tuxedo, minimum value **$450.00**

Sigma, Kermit the Frog in TV $425.00
Sigma, Miss Piggy on Piano, from $235 to $265.00
Sigma, Panda Chef.. $95.00

Sigma, Peter Rabbit, $175.00.
(Photo courtesy Joyce and Fred Roerig)

Sigma, Santa w/Bag of Goodies $95.00
Sigma, Snowman $125.00
Sigma, Theodora Dog, from $125 to $135.00
Sigma, Wind in the Willows, 1981 .... $150.00
Treasure Craft, Auntie 'Em, from $65 to $75.00
Treasure Craft, Bart Simpson, from $35 to.................. $50.00
Treasure Craft, Baseball................................... $50.00
Treasure Craft, Bulldog Cafe, from $150 to $175.00
Treasure Craft, Cookie Balloon.......................... $40.00
Treasure Craft, Cookie Chef, from $55 to $75.00
Treasure Craft, Droopy Dog (I'm So Happy) $375.00

Treasure Craft, Grandma, marked, from $85.00 to $95.00. (Photo courtesy Fred and Joyce Roerig)

Treasure Craft, Grandpa Munster $275.00
Treasure Craft, Herman Munster $275.00
Treasure Craft, Hobby Horse, plaid............................ $55.00
Treasure Craft, Policeman Bear $40.00
Treasure Craft, Santa w/Glass Bowl, from $175 to ... $200.00

Treasure Craft/Disney, Aladdin Genie Seated Holding Magic Lamp $80.00
Treasure Craft/Disney, Buzz Lightyear, from $185 to.. $240.00
Treasure Craft/Disney, Donald Duck, seated w/arms folded $60.00
Treasure Craft/Disney, Goofy, seated Indian style...... $60.00
Treasure Craft/Disney, Simba (Lion King) $95.00
Treasure Craft/Henson, Fozzie Bear.......................... $50.00
Treasure Craft/Henson, Miss Piggy, seated in glamorous pose $50.00
Treasure Craft/Henson, Miss Piggy on Column Jar..... $75.00
Twin Winton, Bear in Fire Truck, from $85 to.......... $110.00
Twin Winton, Butler, from $300 to $350.00
Twin Winton, Church.. $500.00
Twin Winton, Cinderella's Pumpkin Coach, from $165 to .$200.00
Twin Winton, Cookie Catcher, from $100 to............ $125.00
Twin Winton, Cowboy Rabbit, Collector Series, fully painted.. $225.00
Twin Winton, Dutch Girl, Collector Series, fully painted ..$200.00
Twin Winton, Elf Bakery, from $75 to...................... $100.00
Twin Winton, Grandma's Cookie Barrel, from $80 to .$100.00
Twin Winton, Hobby Horse, Collector Series, fully painted $300.00
Twin Winton, Keystone Cop, from $85 to............... $100.00

Twin Winton, Lamb (For Good Little Lambs Only), Collector Series, fully painted, $175.00.
(Photo courtesy Fred and Joyce Roerig)

Twin Winton, Lion, from $65 to $85.00
Twin Winton, Noah's Ark, from $100 to.................... $125.00
Twin Winton, Pear w/Worm, wood stain w/painted detail, avocado green, pineapple yellow, orange or red, ea..$300.00
Twin Winton, Pirate Fox, Collector Series, fully painted, from $225 to... $250.00
Twin Winton, Pirate Fox, wood stain $75.00
Twin Winton, Police Bear, Collector Series, fully painted.$175.00
Twin Winton, Rabbit Gunfighter, from $75 to.......... $100.00
Twin Winton, Ranger Bear, Collector Series, fully painted.. $125.00
Twin Winton, Squirrel w/Cookie, from $40 to............ $50.00
USA Demand Marketing, Big Bird, Bert & Ernie, multicolored.. $45.00

USA Pottery By JD, Nancy (seated) **$200.00**
Vandor, Baseball **$55.00**
Vandor, Beethoven Piano.................................... **$65.00**
Vandor, Cowboy Mooranda, from $135 to **$185.00**
Vandor, Curious George on Rocketship...................... **$60.00**
Vandor, Fred & Pebbles Flintstone, from $325 to **$375.00**
Vandor, Frog Head, from $200 to............................. **$275.00**
Vandor, Honeymooners Bus, from $120 to **$150.00**
Vandor, Howdy Doody, head figure, from $350 to ..**$400.00**
Vandor, I Love Lucy Characters in Car, minimum value ..**$150.00**
Vandor, Mona Lisa **$55.00**
Vandor, Popeye, from $420 to........................... **$500.00**
Vandor, Radio, from $65 to.................................. **$100.00**
Vandor, Toaster **$125.00**
Viacom, Tommy Pickles (Rugrats)........................ **$40.00**
Wade, Brew Gaffer, 8⅜".................................... **$150.00**
Wade, Peasant Woman w/Tray of Cookies, 1991, 10½"...**$110.00**
Warner Bros, Batman, from $100 to........................ **$150.00**
Warner Bros, Bugs Bunny in Rabbit Hole, from $60 to..**$80.00**
Warner Bros, Daffy Duck as Baseball Player.............**$45.00**
Warner Bros, Foghorn Leghorn w/Dog & Henry Hawk, from
   $60 to.. **$80.00**
Warner Bros, Marvin the Martian w/Ray Gun, from $60 to .**$80.00**
Warner Bros, Pepe LePew on Coffee Cup (Caffe Pepe), from
   $65 to.. **$85.00**
Warner Bros, Pinky & the Brain, 1996, 12½" **$75.00**
Warner Bros, Porky Pig in TV, 1995, 10½"..................**$65.00**
Warner Bros, Superman Bust, from $75 to...............**$100.00**
Warner Bros, Tasmanian Devil as Santa, from $65 to..**$100.00**

Coors Rosebud Dinnerware

Golden, Colorado, was the site for both the Coors Brewing Company and the Coors Porcelain Company, each founded by the same man, Adolph Coors. The pottery's inception was in 1910, and in the early years they manufactured various ceramic products such as industrial needs, dinnerware, vases, and figurines; but their most famous line and the one we want to tell you about is 'Rosebud.'

The Rosebud 'Cook 'n Serve' line was introduced in 1934. It's very easy to spot, and after you've once seen a piece, you'll be able to recognize it instantly. It was made in solid colors — rose, blue, green, yellow, ivory, and orange. The rose bud and leaves are embossed and hand painted in contrasting colors. There are nearly fifty different pieces to collect, and bargains can still be found; but prices are accelerating, due to increased collector interest. For more information we recommend *Coors Rosebud Pottery* by Robert Schneider and *Collector's Encyclopedia of Colorado Pottery, Identification and Values,* by Carol and Jim Carlton.

Note: Yellow and white tends to craze and stain. Our prices are for pieces with minimal crazing and no staining. To evaluate pieces in blue, add 10% to the prices below; add 15% for items in ivory.

Advisor: Rick Spencer (See Directory, Regal China)

Newsletter: *Coors Pottery Newsletter*
Robert Schneider
3808 Carr Pl. N
Seattle, WA 98103-8126

Apple baker, w/lid... **$55.00**
Ashtray... **$175.00**
Baker, oval, deep, sm... **$25.00**
Baker, 9¼".. **$45.00**
Bean pot, lg.. **$68.00**
Bowl, mixing; 3-pt... **$45.00**
Bowl, pudding; 7-pt... **$75.00**
Cake knife... **$85.00**
Casserole, Dutch; sm... **$72.00**
Casserole, straight-sided, 8", w/lid......................... **$75.00**
Casserole, w/lid, 9½".. **$100.00**
Creamer, from $30 to... **$40.00**
Cup & saucer.. **$45.00**
Dish, fruit/sauce.. **$15.00**
Egg cup... **$50.00**

Honey pot, no spoon, with lid, from $150.00 to $175.00.

Loaf pan, from $40 to... **$50.00**
Plate, cake; 11"... **$45.00**
Plate, dinner; 8" **$25.00**
Plate, used under muffin cover, 6"............................ **$35.00**
Plate, 10".. **$40.00**
Plate, 7".. **$12.00**
Platter, 9x12", from $42 to..................................... **$48.00**
Ramekin, handled, 4¼" **$40.00**
Refrigerator set.. **$110.00**
Salt & pepper shakers, individual, pr....................... **$80.00**
Salt & pepper shakers, table, pr **$70.00**
Sugar bowl, w/lid.. **$40.00**
Sugar shaker... **$80.00**
Teapot, 6-cup, from $160 to **$185.00**
Tumbler, footed or w/handle, from $105 to..............**$130.00**

Coppercraft Guild

During the 1960s and 1970s, the Coppercraft Guild Company of Taunton, Massachusetts, produced a variety of copper and copper-tone items which were sold through the home party plan. Though copper items such as picture frames, flowerpots, teapots, candle holders, trays, etc., were their mainstay, they also made molded wall decorations such as mirror-image pairs of birds on branches and large floral-relief plaques that they finished in metallic copper-tone paint. Some of their pictures were a combination of the copper-tone composition molds mounted on a sheet copper background. When uncompromised by chemical damage or abuse, the finish they used on their copper items has proven remarkably enduring, and many of these pieces still look new today. Collectors are beginning to take notice.

Bowl, footed, plain, 4⅛x8¾" **$12.50**
Console set, footed bowl, 4½x7" and 2 4x3¾" candle holders, 3-pc...**$38.00**
Dish, embossed floral rim, 1½x11" **$15.00**
Flower bowl, 4-footed, 3⅞x9⅞" **$25.00**
Gravy boat, w/stand & candle warmer, 8½" L.............**$22.00**
Hurricane lamp, wood & copper, copper-trimmed glass globe, 9¾x4" **$20.00**
Mirror w/eagle finial, molded w/copper-tone finish, 21x14½"..**$35.00**
Mug, brass handle, sterling interior, 4 for....................**$12.50**
Pictures, farm scenes printed on burlap, molded frame w/copper-tone finish, 11x9", pr..............................**$15.00**
Plaques, birds on branches, facing pair, molded w/copper-tone finish, 1967, 14½" & 13½" L........................**$15.00**
Tray, scalloped rim, 12" L **$10.00**
Wall ornaments, mushrooms, 1 w/grasshopper, 2nd w/butterfly, molded w/copper-tone finish, pr...............**$15.00**
Wall shelf, 2-tier, embossed roses across top, molded w/copper-tone finish, 21x24"...................................**$15.00**

Corkscrews

When the corkscrew was actually developed remains uncertain (the first patent was issued in 1795), but it most likely evolved from the worm on a ramrod or cleaning rod used to draw wadding from a gun barrel. Inventors scurried to develop a better product, and as a result, thousands of variations have been made and marketed. This abundance and diversification invariably attracted collectors, whose ranks are burgeoning. Many of today's collectors concentrate their attention on one particular type — those with advertising, a specific patent, or figural pullers, for instance.

Our advisor has written a very informative book, *Bull's Pocket Guide to Corkscrews* (Schiffer), with hundreds and full-color illustrations and current values.

Advisor: Donald A. Bull (See Directory, Corkscrews)

Bull's head figural, brass plated, from $30 to..............**$40.00**
Can opener combination, Vaughan w/stamped price, from $5 to...**$10.00**
Cocktail spoon w/corkscrew attachment at handle w/advertising, bottle opener finial, from $10 to **$40.00**

Collapsible, Hollweg, common type, 3¼", from $75 to..**$85.00**
Double-lever, red body, modern, from $20 to............**$40.00**
Finger pull (2 or 3 fingers), w/cap lifter added, depending on marks, from $5 to **$50.00**
Folding, cap lifter & spiral worm, dark patina, from $100 to **$150.00**
Frame style, cheap imitation stag handle, from $3 to...**$4.00**
McDowell, Korkmaster, stainless steel, 1948, from $75 to..**$100.00**
Miniature, folding, simple spiral worm, from $25 to ..**$50.00**
Murphy, dark acorn T-handle, from $70 to...............**$100.00**
Needle style (air or gas is pumped manually into area between liquid & cork), from $1 to **$10.00**
Parrot figural, solid brass, web helix tail, 6¼", from $75 to **$100.00**
Peg & worm style w/button ends, faceted ends or ball ends, steel, brass, chrome, nickel or silver, ea from $75 to.........**$200.00**
Rockwell Clough Company advertising on wooden handle, from $10 to..**$50.00**

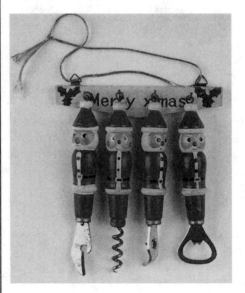

Santa Claus bar set including corkscrew, cap lifter, can opener, and can piercer, ca 1950s Christmas decoration, from $20.00 to $30.00.
(Photo courtesy Donald A. Bull)

Syroco, man in top hat, Old Codger (Codger, Topper), from $90 to...**$150.00**
Waiter's friend style w/single knife blade, advertising on side, from $15 to...**$25.00**
Walker, cast wire breaker & cap lifter on bell, Schlitz advertising on wooden handle, from $30 to **$50.00**
Williamson Power Corkscrew, self-pulling, w/cap remover, red, green or clear lacquered wood tube, from $20 to...**$30.00**
Williamson's Don't Swear corkscrew/bottle opener combination, colored Catalin sheath, from $25 to **$50.00**

Cottage Ware

Made by several companies, cottage ware is a line of ceramic table and kitchen accessories, each piece styled as a cozy cottage with a thatched roof. At least four English potteries made the ware, and you'll find pieces marked 'Japan' as well as 'Occupied Japan.' You'll also find pieces styled as windmills and water wheels. The pieces preferred by collectors are marked 'Price Brothers' and 'Occupied Japan.' They're compatible in coloring as well as in styling, and values run about the same. Items marked simply 'Japan' are worth considerably less.

Pitcher, embossed cottage on front, flower on handle, Price, very scarce, $135.00.

Bank, English, 5" L	**$85.00**
Bell, English (Price), rare, from $125 to	**$150.00**
Bowl, salad; English	**$65.00**
Butter dish, English	**$60.00**
Butter pat, embossed cottage, rectangular, Occupied Japan	**$17.50**
Chocolate pot, English	**$135.00**
Condiment set, 2 shakers & mustard on tray, Occupied Japan	**$45.00**
Condiment set, 2 shakers & mustard on 5" handled leaf tray	**$75.00**
Condiment set, 2 shakers & mustard pot on tray, row arrangement, 7¾"	**$45.00**
Condiment set, 3-part cottage on shaped tray w/applied bush, 4½"	**$75.00**
Cookie jar, lid w/dormer & chimney, 5½x4½x5", minimum value	**$125.00**
Cookie jar, pink, brown & green, square, Japan, 8½x5½"	**$65.00**
Cookie jar, rectangular w/wicker handle, English or Occupied Japan	**$85.00**
Cookie jar, windmill, wicker handle, English (Price), rare, 5", minimum value	**$135.00**
Cookie jar/canister, cylindrical, English, 8½x5"	**$125.00**
Cookie jar/canister, cylindrical, English, 8x3¾"	**$200.00**
Creamer, windmill, Occupied Japan, 2⅝"	**$25.00**
Creamer & sugar bowl, English, 2½x4½"	**$45.00**
Creamer & sugar bowl, w/lid, on tray, Occupied Japan	**$65.00**
Cup & saucer, English, 2½", 4½"	**$45.00**
Demitasse pot, English	**$100.00**
Dish w/cover, Occupied Japan, sm	**$35.00**
Egg cups, 4 on 6½" square tray, English	**$60.00**
Gravy boat & tray, English, rare, lg	**$250.00**
Grease jar, Occupied Japan	**$35.00**
Marmalade, English	**$40.00**
Mug, Price Bros	**$50.00**
Pin tray, English, 4" dia	**$20.00**
Pitcher, water; English	**$150.00**
Salt & pepper shakers, windmill, Occupied Japan, pr	**$20.00**
Sugar bowl, windmill, w/lid, Occupied Japan, 3⅞"	**$25.00**
Sugar box, for cubes, English, 5¾" L	**$45.00**
Tea set, child's, Japan, serves 4	**$150.00**
Teapot, English or Occupied Japan, 5"	**$45.00**
Teapot, English or Occupied Japan, 6½"	**$70.00**
Toast rack, English, from $65 to	**$75.00**
Tumbler, Occupied Japan, 3½"	**$10.00**

Cow Creamers

Cow creamers (and milk pitchers) have been around since before the nineteenth century, but, of course, those are rare. But by the early 1900s, they were becoming quite commonplace. In many of these older ones, the cow was standing on a platform (base) and very often had a lid. Not all cows on platforms are old, however, but it is a good indication of age. Examples from before WWII often were produced in England, Germany, and Japan.

Over the last fifty years there has been a slow revival of interest in these little cream dispensers, including the plastic Moo cows, made by Whirley Industries, U.S.A, that were used in cafes during the '50s. With the current popularity of anything cow-shaped, manufacturers have expanded the concept, and some creamers now are made with matching sugar bowls. If you want to collect only vintage examples, nowadays you'll have to check closely to make sure they're not new.

Advisor: Shirley Green (See Directory, Cow Creamers)

Delft-style blue windmill scene, incised Germany 6200, 3¾x5¾", from $75.00 to $85.00. (Photo courtesy Shirley Green)

Advertising, Dogpatch USA, white w/blue, Japan, 3½x4"	**$22.50**
Advertising, iridescent white, Worthing Parade, foreign, 4½x6"	**$28.00**
Advertising, Jell-O, multicolored, 5x6½"	**$175.00**

Arthur Wood, ironstone, w/sailboat on side, England, 5½x7"...$85.00

Borden Co, Elsie on side, mark on bottom, white w/gold trim, 5x7"...$55.00

Burleigh, lazy cow, blue & white, on base, 5x6½".....$60.00

C Cooke, w/suckling calf on platform, w/lid, 5x6½".$225.00

Calico, Burleigh, Staffordshire, England, ca 1975, 7" L, from $65 to.......................................$75.00

China, Blue Onion design, blue & white, sitting cow, 4x3½"...$20.00

Czech, marigold iridescent, reclining cow on base, 5½x7"..$55.00

Delft, blue & white w/windmill on side, bell, Holland, 4x6½"..$22.00

Goebel, full bee mark, brown & white, 4x6"..............$35.00

Holstein, black & white, K403 on bottom, 4½x8"......$48.00

Hummel, full bee mark, Germany, 1960s, 4x6", from $35 to..$45.00

Jackfield-type, red clay, w/lid, 19th century, on platform, 5½x7"..$175.00

Japan, Dabs paper sticker, common mold, comes in various colors and designs, 1950s – 60s, from $40.00 to $50.00. (Photo courtesy Shirley Green)

Japan, luster, creamer & sugar bowl, Texas longhorn, w/lid, 5x6½"...$125.00

Kenmar, pink w/bell, Japan, 5x6½"............................$30.00

Lefton, creamer & sugar bowl, tan w/white markings, 4x5½"..$42.00

McMaster, pottery, creamer & sugar bowl set, 4x6"....$37.00

Occupied Japan, green & tan, lg body, 6x5".............$65.00

Staffordshire, chintz, multicolored, w/lid, on platform, 5½x7"..$135.00

Staucht Frae the Coo, white w/gold, Germany, 6x5½"..$47.50

TG Green, reclining, tan, England, 4x6".....................$37.00

Unmarked, purple & white w/yellow horns, 3-pc set, 4x4½"..$17.50

Unmarked, white porcelain, for child's tea set, 1½x2" ..$15.00

Whirley, plastic, upright Moo Cow, 5x3"...................$15.00

Cowboy Character Collectibles

When we come across what is now termed cowboy character toys and memorabilia, it rekindles warm memories of childhood days for those of us who once 'rode the range' (often our backyards) with these gallant heroes. Today we can really appreciate them for the positive role models they were. They sat tall in the saddle; reminded us never to tell an un-truth; to respect 'women-folk' as well as our elders, animal life, our flag, our country, and our teachers; to eat all the cereal placed before us in order to build strong bodies; to worship God; and have (above all else) strong values that couldn't be compromised. They were Gene, Roy, and Tex, along with a couple of dozen other names, who rode beautiful steeds such as Champion, Trigger, and White Flash.

They rode into a final sunset on the silver screen only to return and ride into our homes via television in the 1950s. The next decade found us caught up in more western adventures such as Bonanza, Wagon Train, The Rifleman, and many others. These set the stage for a second wave of toys, games, and western outfits.

Annie Oakley was one of only a couple of cowgirls in the corral; Wild Bill Elliott used to drawl, 'I'm a peaceable man'; Ben Cartwright, Adam, Hoss, and Little Joe provided us with thrills and laughter. Some of the earliest collectibles are represented by Roy's and Gene's 1920s predecessors — Buck Jones, Hoot Gibson, Tom Mix, and Ken Maynard. There were so many others, all of whom were very real to us in the 1930s – '60s, just as their memories and values remain very real to us today.

Remember that few items of cowboy memorabilia have survived to the present in mint condition. When found, mint or near-mint items bring hefty prices, and they continue to escalate every year. Our values are for examples in good to very good condition.

For more information we recommend these books: *Roy Rogers, Singing Cowboy Stars, Silver Screen Cowboys, Hollywood Cowboy Heroes*, and *Western Comics: A Comprehensive Reference*, all by Robert W. Phillips. Other books include *Collector's Guide to Hopalong Cassidy Memorabilia* by Joseph J. Caro, *Collector's Reference & Value Guide to The Lone Ranger* by Lee Felbinger, *The W.F. Cody Buffalo Bill Collector's Guide* by James W. Wojtowicz, and *Roy Rogers and Dale Evans Toys and Memorabilia* by P. Allan Coyle.

See also Toys, Guns; Toys, Rings.

Advisor: Robert W. Phillips, Phillips Archives (See Directory, Character and Personality Collectibles)

Club/Newsletter: The Old Cowboy Picture Show
George F. Coan
PO Box 66
Camden, SC 29020; 803-432-9643

Club/Newsletter: Cowboy Collector
Joseph J. Caro, Publisher
P.O. Box 7486
Long Beach, CA 90807

Club/Newsletter: Hopalong Cassidy Fan Club International and *Hopalong Cassidy Newsletter*
Laura Bates, Editor
6310 Friendship Dr.
New Concord, OH 43762-9708; 614-826-4850

Newsletter: *Gene Autry Star Telegram*
Gene Autry Development Association
Chamber of Commerce
P.O. Box 158, Gene Autry, OK 73436

Newsletter: *The Lone Ranger Silver Bullet*
P.O. Box 553
Forks, WA 98331; 206-327-3726

Annie Oakley, doll, western clothing, 25", VG **$25.00**
Annie Oakley, notebook, photo image of Annie holding up guns, 1950s, 10x8", EX **$40.00**
Bat Masterson, holster set w/cane & vest, Carnell, 1958, no gun, NMIB...........**$225.00**
Bonanza, cup, litho tin, features Adam & the Ponderosa, 1960s, EX...........**$30.00**
Bonanza, Foto Fantastics Coloring Set, Eberhart Faber, 1965, complete, M (EX box) **$85.00**
Buffalo Bill, outfit, 3-pc, Leslie-Henry, 1954, NM (G box) **$75.00**
Cheyenne, cowboy gloves, fringed w/name & image of horse head, unused, M...........**$40.00**
Dale Evans, Colorforms Dress-Up Kit, EXIB **$75.00**
Dale Evans, outfit, w/skirt, vest, blouse & holster, Yankeeboy, EXIB...........**$300.00**
Daniel Boone, Fess Parker Super Slate, Whitman, 1964, NM...........**$50.00**
Daniel Boone, Woodland Whistle, Autolite, 1964, NMIB..**$100.00**
Davy Crockett, birthday card, diecut w/image of boy Davy greeting bear w/a smile, 1956, EX **$28.00**
Davy Crockett, cap, coonskin type w/rabbit fur tail & sides, plastic top w/image of Davy, 1950s, EX...........**$50.00**
Davy Crockett, Color TV Set, WDP, complete, NMOC .**$175.00**
Davy Crockett, doll, composition w/cloth clothes & coonskin cap, open/close eyes, Fortune Toy/WDP, 8", NMIB...........**$175.00**
Davy Crockett, doll, stuffed cloth w/hand-painted vinyl face, name on chest, unmarked, 1950s, 27", EX **$150.00**
Davy Crockett, lamp shade, pictures Davy w/rifle walking across creek w/cabin in distance, 1950s, 7", M..**$135.00**
Davy Crockett, magazine, The Real Life Story of Fess Parker/Walt Disney's Davy Crockett, 36 pages, Dell, 1955, VG...........**$30.00**
Davy Crockett, penknife, Imperial/WDP, 1950s, 4", NM...........**$35.00**
Davy Crockett, record, The Ballad of Davy Crockett, Peter Pan Peanut Butter premium, EX (w/unmailed envelope) **$25.00**
Davy Crockett, shirt, red flannel w/white images & signatures, Blue Bell/WDP, NM...........**$75.00**
Davy Crockett, soap bubbles, w/solution & wand, Chemical Sundries, 5", EX...........**$75.00**

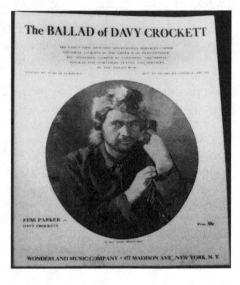

Davy Crockett, sheet music, 1954, EX, from $20.00 to $30.00.

Davy Crockett, song book, features 11 songs & photos from TV show, black & white photo cover of Fess Parker, 20 pages, EX+...........**$35.00**
Davy Crockett, teepee, tan canvas w/image & lettering, Walt Disney's Official Fess Parker..., 1950s, 70", EX...**$225.00**
Davy Crockett, toothbrush, plastic w/figural handle, DuPont/WDP, 1950s, NM (VG illustrated card)....**$50.00**
Davy Crockett, Wagon Train, horse-drawn coach w/3 units, plastic, Marx, 1950s, 14", NM (EX box) **$425.00**
Gene Autry, wallet, leather w/multicolored image of Gene on rearing Champion, ca 1950, NM (EX Always Your Pal box) **$125.00**
Gunsmoke, outfit, Matt Dillon, Kaynee, complete, EX (EX display box for 6 outfits)...........**$155.00**
Gunsmoke, outfit, Matt Dillon, Seneca, 1958, complete, EXIB **$125.00**
Hopalong Cassidy, bow tie, cloth w/western scenes, 1950, NMOC...........**$75.00**
Hopalong Cassidy, Coloring Outfit, Transogram, 1950, complete & unused, NMIB...........**$300.00**
Hopalong Cassidy, decal sheet, set of 4, 8x3" sheet, M..**$50.00**
Hopalong Cassidy, hand puppet, cloth w/vinyl head, 1950s, scace, NM **$200.00**
Hopalong Cassidy, horn, Bar 20 Ranch, plastic w/rubber honker at ea end, Perlin Products, 1950s, EX (VG box)...........**$250.00**
Hopalong Cassidy, mask, rubber, Traveler Trading Co, 8", NMIB...........**$225.00**
Hopalong Cassidy, photo album, brown leather w/embossed color image of Hoppy on Topper, original yellow cord, unused, EX...........**$150.00**
Hopalong Cassidy, sparkler, plastic bust figure w/metal plunger, 1950, 3", NM...........**$275.00**
Johnny Ringo, outfit, Yankeeboy, 1950s, complete, EXIB **$125.00**
Lone Ranger, badge, litho tin bust figure, 1960s, NM, from $45 to...........**$65.00**
Lone Ranger, bank, Lone Ranger on rearing Silver, plastic, 1958, NM, from $100 to **$135.00**

Lone Ranger, bank, vinyl boot shape w/cartoon artwork of Lone Ranger on Silver, British, 1960s, EX.............**$50.00**

Lone Ranger, compass, plastic wrist-type w/molded bust image & crossed guns, Peter Pan Peanut Butter, EX...**$130.00**

Lone Ranger, desk set, 1981, complete, NM, from $50 to..**$75.00**

Lone Ranger, doll, stuffed cloth w/composition face & rubber hands, sleep eyes, cloth clothes, Molly/TLR, 28", EXIB...**$375.00**

Lone Ranger, doll, Super Flex, Lakeside, 1967, 6", MOC....**$50.00**

Lone Ranger, doll, talker, stuffed cloth, Mego, 1972, 24", MIB **$100.00**

Lone Ranger, guitar, 1956, EX, from $150 to.............**$200.00**

Lone Ranger, hand puppet, cloth w/vinyl head, 1947, NMIB, from $175 to...**$200.00**

Lone Ranger, mask, watch & badge, 1960, MOC, from $45 to..**$65.00**

Lone Ranger, movie viewer (lg), Lone Ranger Rides Again, 1940, NMIB, from $200 to...................................**$250.00**

Lone Ranger, movie viewer (sm), Lone Ranger Rides Again, 1938-40, NMIB, from $150 to.............................**$200.00**

Lone Ranger, outfit, Yankeeboy, 1945-47, complete, NMIB, from $250 to...**$350.00**

Lone Ranger, party horn, litho tin, 1950, EX..............**$25.00**

Lone Ranger, phonograph, wood, Decca/TLR Inc, 5x12", VG..**$200.00**

Lone Ranger, scrapbook, 1940, EX.............................**$85.00**

Lone Ranger, squirt gun, plastic, 1974, EX **$25.00**

Lone Ranger, tattoos, set of 4 in folder, Fritos Potato Chips premium, 1959, scarce, M **$65.00**

Lone Ranger, toy wristwatch, plastic, 1980, MOC, from $75 to...**$100.00**

Lone Ranger & Tonto, sleeping bag, 1975, NM, from $75 to **$125.00**

Lone Ranger & Tonto, stamp set, Larami, 1981, MOC..**$25.00**

Maverick, TV Eras-O-Picture Book, Hasbro, 1959, complete, NM **$30.00**

Maverick, wallet & key case, black plastic w/color images of James Garner, photo ID on key case, Warner Bros, 1958, NM+ **$100.00**

Range Rider, chair, wooden folding type w/image on black fabric back, white fringe on bottom, 1956, 24", scarce, EX+ **$80.00**

Range Rider, tablet, color image & signature on cover, 1950s, 10x8", EX...**$10.00**

Red Ryder, Little Beaver Archery Set, Fred Harmon, 1950s, complete & unused, EX+ (EX+ card)...................**$100.00**

Rifleman, hat, red felt w/photo image of Chuck Conners on fabric label, Tex-Felt, 1958, NMIB **$75.00**

Rifleman, outfit, flannel & corduroy w/felt hat, Pla-Master, 1959, MIB **$250.00**

Rin-Tin-Tin, outfit w/gun & holster, Corporal Rusty, Iskin/Screen Gems, 1955, EXIB...........................**$225.00**

Roy Rogers, archery quiver, canvas & leather w/RR brand & signature, belt loop & leg string, 1950s, 16", EX..**$70.00**

Roy Rogers, bank, boot on horseshoe-shaped base, detailed metal w/copper lustre, 5", EX..............................**$75.00**

Roy Rogers, binoculars, black w/decal of Roy & Trigger, Herbert George, 1950s, NMIB...........................**$250.00**

Roy Rogers, binoculars, NM, $175.00.

Roy Rogers, book bag, brown vinyl w/shoulder strap, Roy & Trigger pictured on front, 1950s, VG **$65.00**

Roy Rogers, camera, plastic w/metal front plate, complete w/membership card, Herbert George, EXIB **$125.00**

Roy Rogers, Crayon Set, Standard Toykraft #940RR, 1950s, complete, VG (VG box) **$65.00**

Roy Rogers, fountain pen, name on side in script, EX..**$150.00**

Roy Rogers, guitar, red w/white image of Roy on Trigger, Range Rhythm, 1950s, EX **$185.00**

Roy Rogers, hand puppet, cloth w/rubber head, 1950s, VG **$100.00**

Roy Rogers, school bag, brown vinyl w/shoulder strap, sm middle pouch w/image of Roy on Trigger, 1950s, 14" L, EX **$100.00**

Roy Rogers, telescope, marked Roy Rogers & Trigger w/graphics of Roy on Trigger, 1950s, 14½", EX...**$80.00**

Roy Rogers, Trick Lasso, Knox-Reese, 1947, MIP (sealed).**$175.00**

Roy Rogers & Trigger, yo-yo, photo image, slimline shape w/view lens, All Western Plastics, 1950s, MIP......**$20.00**

Sky King, stamping kit, ink pad & rubber stamp w/name & address in litho tin box, 1953, 1¾x1¼", EX **$60.00**

Wild Bill Hickok, treasure map, complete w/Secret Treasure Guide, Kellogg's, 1950, NM (w/mailer)...............**$125.00**

Wild Bill Hickok & Jingles, Ranch Bunkhouse Kit, 1950s, complete, NM (NM pkg) **$65.00**

Wyatt Earp, outfit, Yankeeboy, 1950s, complete, VG (VG box) **$125.00**

Wyatt Earp, spur set, plastic, Selco, NMOC................**$50.00**

Wyatt Earp, tablet, Hugh O'Brian on cover, M...........**$25.00**

Wyatt Warp, guitar, 24", EX......................................**$120.00**

Zorro, charm bracelet, painted-gold metal w/photo, pistol & sword w/whip, WDP, 1950s, EX...........................**$50.00**

Zorro, cup, plastic boot shape w/Z handle, Zorro logo decal on side, WDP, 1950s, 6", EX+ **$40.00**

Zorro, gloves, black cotton knit w/canvas sleeve trim, red, white & black logo on ea, WDP, 1950s, EX+, pr.**$60.00**

Zorro, Magic Erasable Pictures, Transogram, 1950s, complete, EXIB...**$65.00**

Zorro, magic slate, Strathmore/WDP, 1955, EX...........**$50.00**

Zorro, wrist flashlight, black plastic w/red & green filters, nonworking, 1958, VG **$30.00**

Cracker Jack Toys

In 1869 Frederick Rueckheim left Hamburg, Germany, bound for Chicago, where he planned to work on a farm for his uncle. But farm life did not appeal to Mr. Rueckheim, and after the Chicago fire, he moved there and helped clear the debris. With another man whose popcorn and confectionary business had been destroyed in the fire, Mr. Rueckheim started a business with one molasses kettle and one hand popper. The following year, Mr. Rueckheim bought out his original partner and sent for his brother, Louis. The two brothers formed Rueckheim & Bro. and quickly prospered as they continued expanding their confectionary line to include new products. It was not until 1896 that the first lot of Cracker Jack was produced — and then only as an adjunct to their growing line. Cracker Jack was sold in bulk form until 1899 when H.G. Eckstein, an old friend, invented the wax-sealed package, which allowed them to ship it further and thus sell it more easily. Demand for Cracker Jack soared, and it quickly became the main product of the factory. Today millions of boxes are produced — each with a prize in every box.

The idea of prizes came along during the time of bulk packaging; it was devised as a method to stimulate sales. Later, as the wax-sealed package was introduced, a prize was given (more or less) with each package. Next, the prize was added into the package, but still not every package received a prize. It was not until the 1920s that 'a prize in every package' became a reality. Initially, the prizes were put in with the confection, but the company feared this might pose a problem, should it inadvertently be mistaken for the popcorn. To avoid this, the prize was put in a separate compartment and, finally, into its own protective wrapper. Hundreds of prizes have been used over the years, and it is still true today that there is 'a prize in every package.' Prizes have ranged from the practical girl's bracelet and pencils to tricks, games, disguises, and stick-anywhere patches. To learn more about the subject, you'll want to read *Cracker Jack Toys, The Complete Unofficial Guide for Collectors*, and *Cracker Jack, The Unauthorized Guide to Advertising Collectibles*, both by our advisor, Larry White.

Advisor: Larry White (See Directory, Cracker Jack)

Clicker-screamer, $40.00. (Photo courtesy Mary and Larry White)

Age Cards, paper, marked Printed in Germany **$19.50**
Alphabet pictogram, metal, w/letter & descriptive litho tin stand-up, set of 26, ea.............................**$32.00**

Arrow-back pin/pocket clip, metal Liberty Bell shape, marked Liberty **$87.50**
Baseball cards, Topps, Series I, set of 36, ea.................**$1.50**
Bike stickers, Z-1380, various colors, set of 10, ea **$4.50**
Blincode morse code semiphore card, marked Cracker Jack Co...**$9.00**
Book, Bonnie Birds, illus by Palmer Cox, Crack Jack box on back cover.......................................**$800.00**
Book, Children's Notes, paper......................................**$65.00**
Book, Cracker Jack Drawing Book, Dutch girl on cover **$105.00**
Book, Cracker Jack Puzzle Book, paper, dated 1917 inside **$125.00**
Book, Handy Andy, paper, Cracker Jack box on back, set of 16, ea **$75.00**
Book, Liddle Riddles, paper, several different, ea.........**$7.50**
Booklet, Twig & Sprig, Cracker Jack box on back **$75.00**
Brooch, on Famous Cracker Jack card, various types, ea.**$325.00**
Bubble pipe, ceramic w/dog face bowl, red, blue & pink **$9.50**
Charm, dirigible shape, metal w/celluloid insert **$95.00**
Charm, dog, camel, monkey, etc, white metal, ea........**$4.50**
Charm, eagle, bird, owl, Indian, etc, white metal, flat, ea...**$5.75**
Charm, tool, hammer, hatchet, chisel, etc, ea...............**$4.75**
Clicker, Dutch Boy, tin litho **$45.00**
Cracker Jack Ball Player, Joe Jackson, #103, 1914 ..**$12,000.00**
Cracker Jack Ball Player, others, 1914, set of 144, average price..**$50.00**
Cracker Jack Fortune Teller, plastic Jack & Bingo in envelope...**$135.00**
Endangered Species cards, #42, marked Cracker Jack-Borden, set of 20, ea **$3.50**
Eyeglasses, paper & celluloid, marked Cracker Jack Wherever You Look....................................**$87.00**
Figure, girl, earthenware **$40.00**
Figure, woman, wood & glass beads.............................**$50.00**
Finger Faces, clown, elephant or jester, paper, ea......**$36.00**
German village building, wood, unmarked or marked Germany, ea......................................**$27.50**
Hand Kinema, elephant & crab, paper, marked Japan..**$40.00**
Hand mirror, metal & glass, unmarked or marked Japan, doll size, ea......................................**$24.50**
Horse & wagon, japanned metal, marked USM(ail) ...**$40.00**
Indian headdress, paper, marked Me for Cracker Jack...**$250.00**
Iron-on patches, #1403, marked Cracker Jack - Borden, set of 35, ea **$5.50**
Jigsaw puzzle, various scenes, written in Japanese **$95.00**
Jigsaw puzzle, various scenes, 4 pcs plus front & back.**$10.00**
Kaleidoscope cards, #46, set of 15, ea **$3.75**
Lapel pin, Cracker Jack Junior Detective, metal.........**$35.00**
Magic slate, #1388, lift to erase, ea................................**$3.75**
Match shooter, gun, rifle, machine gun, etc, metal, marked Japan, ea......................................**$12.00**
Maze puzzle, Z-1376, basketball, skier, tic-tac-toe, etc, paper & plastic, ea......................................**$8.25**
Mirror, celluloid, glass & metal, round w/Cracker Jack box & logo, 4 different, ea.................................**$125.00**

Moving picture, Charlie Chaplin, paper, Cracker Jack box on back **$105.00**

Nits, plastic, marked R&L Australia, set of 20, ea **$4.50**

Note pads, #11, marked Cracker Jack - Borden, set of 20, ea **$4.50**

Palm puzzle, fox, pirate, cow, etc, paper & celluloid, marked Cracker Jack Co, ea **$80.00**

Palm puzzle, man smoking cigar, canary in cage, etc, paper & plastic, marked CJ Co, ea **$9.50**

Palm puzzle, old man, clown, crying baby, etc, paper & celluloid, marked Gee Cracker Is Good, ea **$87.00**

Paper doll, marked FW Rueckheim & Bro on back .**$127.00**

Pin-back button, Me for Cracker Jack w/Jack & Bingo .**$95.00**

Pin-back button, movie star, baseball or western themes, ea **$10.00**

Pin-back button, Victorian lady on celluloid front, red Cracker Jack insert **$87.50**

Postcard, Cracker Jack Bears, paper, set of 16, ea **$37.50**

Presidential coin, metal, marked Cracker Jack Co, set of 32, ea **$4.75**

Riddle book, paper, jester on front **$57.00**

Riddle cards, paper, postcard size, 20 per set, ea **$17.50**

Ring, 2 hearts, wagon wheel, badge, etc, white metal, ea **$9.50**

Rolling pin, wood, plain, doll size **$12.00**

Score counter, paper, made by JS Carroll **$250.00**

Serving tray, metal w/Cracker Jack box **$130.00**

Slide card, elf, eskimo, baker, etc, paper, marked Cracker Jack Co, ea **$87.00**

Snap-together circus wagon, gorilla, lion, etc, plastic, ea ...**$11.00**

Snap-together easel-back, 1827 US Buggy, Conestoga Wagon, etc, plastic, ea **$10.00**

Snap-together trophy, Champ Smiler, Best Dad, etc, plastic, ea **$9.50**

Spinner, 'blow-on-it,' Z-1379, marked Cracker Jack, set of 35, ea **$3.75**

Spoon rider, astronaut, cowboy, monkey, etc, plastic, ea ..**$7.50**

Stand-up, dolls of nations, Egypt, France, Holland, etc, plastic, set of 13, ea **$9.25**

Stand-up, milkman, cow, policeman, etc, plastic, ea **$3.50**

Stand-up, Officer, metal **$24.00**

State card, paper, flag of ea state on front, history on back, set of 55, ea **$12.50**

Stickers, Creatures of the Deep, set of 8, ea ....**$.50**

Super Hero cards, marked Cracker Jack, description in English & French, set of 20, ea **$2.75**

Tattoos, #81, marked Cracker Jack - Borden, set of 14, ea .**$2.50**

Tattoos, Z-1366, set of 9, ea **$1.25**

Top, embossed metal, marked Cracker Jack **$20.00**

Top, metal & wood, marked Always on Top **$44.00**

Top, metal w/ABC design **$30.00**

Walker, rabbit, man, police officer, dog, etc, unmarked, ea **$70.00**

Whistle, metal gun shape **$20.00**

Whistle, plastic w/2 tubes, marked CJ Co, various colors, ea **$5.50**

Whistle, Razz Zooka, paper, red & white **$37.50**

Crackle Glass

At the height of productivity from the 1930s through the 1970s, nearly five hundred companies created crackle glass. As pieces stayed in production for several years, dating an item may be difficult. Some colors, such as ruby red, amberina, cobalt, and cranberry, were more expensive to produce. Smoke gray was made for a short time, and because quantities are scarce, prices tend to be higher than on some of the other colors, amethyst, green, and amber included. Crackle glass is still being produced today by the Blenko Glass Company, and it is being imported from Taiwan and China as well. For further information on other glass companies and values we recommend *Crackle Glass, Identification and Value Guide, Book I* and *Book II*, by Stan and Arlene Weitman (Collector Books).

Advisors: Stan and Arlene Weitman (See Directory, Crackle Glass)

Basket, amberina w/clear handle, Pilgrim, 1949-69, 4¾", from $60 to **$75.00**

Basket, blue, thick blue handle, Kanawha, 1957-87, 3¾", from $40 to **$55.00**

Beaker, crystal with applied green leaves, Blenko, 1940s – 50s, 13", from $125.00 to $150.00.
(Photo courtesy Stan and Arlene Weitman)

Bottle, emerald green, long slim neck w/sloped shoulders, Label: Made in Spain, polished pontil, 11½", from $85 to **$100.00**

Bowl, crystal w/sea green stem & foot, Blenko, 1940s-50s, 8", from $75 to **$100.00**

Creamer & sugar bowl, amber, drop over handles, Bonita, 1931-53, 2¾", pr, from $75 to **$85.00**

Decanter, blue, pyramidal shape w/lg blue teardrop stopper, Rainbow, 1940s-60s, 7¾", from $85 to **$100.00**

Decanter, crystal, bulbous, ball stopper, Blenko, 1950s, 11½", from $100 to **$125.00**

Decanter, crystal w/applied cobalt medallion, cobalt teardrop stopper, Rainbow, 1940s-60s, 17", from $175 to...**$200.00**

Decanter, emerald green, pinched body, drop-over handle, Bischoff, 1950s, 9¾", from $85 to **$100.00**

Decanter, topaz, slim form w/ball stopper, Rainbow, 1953, 11", from $100 to **$125.00**

Hat, turquoise, 2 sides of rim turned down, Blenko, 1950s-60s, 3", from $45 to **$50.00**

Perfume atomizer, sea green, unknown maker, 3"+atomizer top, from $75 to..**$100.00**

Perfume bottle, pink, pyramidal w/embossed pink floral stopper, unknown maker, 4½", from $50 to.........**$75.00**

Perfume bottle, rose crystal, ball form w/ball stopper, unknown maker, 6¾", from $85 to **$100.00**

Pitcher, amberina, pulled-back handle, wide flared rim, unknown maker, 5", from $50 to **$60.00**

Pitcher, amberina, ruffled top, crystal ribbed drop-over handle, Pilgrim, 1949-69, 3½", from $45 to **$50.00**

Pitcher, amberina satin, waisted form, pulled-back handle, Kanawha, 1957-87, 6½", from $65 to **$75.00**

Pitcher, amethyst, bulbous body, drop-over handle, Pilgrim, 1949-69, 4½", from $55 to..............................**$65.00**

Pitcher, blue, drop-over handle, Rainbow, 1957-87, 3", from $35 to..**$40.00**

Pitcher, blue satin, bell-shaped body, pulled-back handle, Kanawha, 1957-87, 4½", from $50 to **$60.00**

Pitcher, emerald green, slim twisted shape w/flared foot, pulled-back handle, Bischoff, 1950s, 14", from $125 to **$150.00**

Pitcher, topaz, long neck, pulled-back handle, wide flared rim, Viking, 1944-60, 5¼", from $50 to.................**$55.00**

Pitcher, topaz, very slim, drop-over handle, Kanawha, 1957-87, 8", from $75 to..**$80.00**

Pitcher, vaseline yellow, cylindrical neck, ruffled rim, pulled-back crystal handle, Rainbow, 1940s-50s, 4", from $45 to **$50.00**

Shakers, olive green, slightly waisted slim forms, silver-tone metal tops, Kanawha, 1957-87, 6¾", pr, from $75 to **$100.00**

Swan dish, orange w/crystal head & neck, heart-shaped body, Kanawha, 1957-87, 6x7x5½", from $75 to **$100.00**

Vase, amethyst, flared neck, ruffled/scalloped rim, Birchoff, 1940-63, 7½", from $150 to................................**$175.00**

Vase, amethyst, stick neck, Hamon, 1940s-66, 9½", from $100 to..**$125.00**

Vase, amethyst, waisted form w/smooth rim, Blenko, 1960s, 4¾", from $60 to..**$85.00**

Vase, bud; vaseline, bulbous w/cylindrical neck, unknown maker, 6", from $50 to..**$75.00**

Vase, crystal w/sea green chain-like trim at neck, scalloped rim, Blenko, 1950s, 5¼", from $50 to **$75.00**

Vase, crystal w/sea green foot, flared rim, Blenko, 1940s-50s, 9", from $80 to..**$110.00**

Vase, deep yellow, pear-shaped w/3-ruffle top, Kanawha, 1957-87, 5¼", from $45 to......................................**$50.00**

Vase, green w/applied chain-like decor on cylindrical form, ruffled rim, Kanawha, 1957-87, 3½", from $45 to ..**$50.00**

Vase, olive green w/applied serpentine decor along long cylindrical neck, Pilgrim, 1949-69, 6¾", from $50 to **$75.00**

Vase, orange, waisted, ruffled top, Rainbow, 1940s-50s, 5", from $45 to..**$50.00**

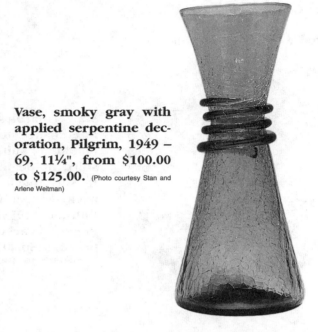

Vase, smoky gray with applied serpentine decoration, Pilgrim, 1949 – 69, 11¼", from $100.00 to $125.00. (Photo courtesy Stan and Arlene Weitman)

Vase, tangerine, waisted cylinder w/smooth rim, Blenko, 1960s, 12¼", from $110 to **$125.00**

Vase, teal, flared cylinder w/ruffled rim, Rainbow, 1940s-60s, 9", from $100 to **$125.00**

Vase, yellow-green, waisted, 3-scallop top, Jamestown, w/M original sticker (adds to value), 1959-68, 5", from $40 to..**$45.00**

Cuff Links

Cuff link collecting continues to be one of the fastest growing hobbies. Few collectibles are as affordable, available, and easy to store. Cuff links can often be found at garage sales, thrift shops, and flea markets for reasonable prices.

People collect cuff links for many reasons. Besides being a functional and interesting wearable, cuff links are educational. The design, shape, size, and materials used often relate to events, places, and products, and they typically reflect the period of their manufacture: examples are Art Deco, Victorian, Art Nouveau, Modern, etc. They offer the chance for the 'big find' which appeals to all collectors. Sometimes pairs purchased for small amounts turn out to be worth substantial sums.

Unless otherwise noted, the following listings apply to cuff links in excellent to mint condition.

Advisor: Gene Klompus (See Directory, Cuff Links)

Club: The National Cuff Link Society

Newsletter: *The Link*
Gene Klompus, President
P.O. Box 5700
Vernon Hills, IL 60010
Phone or fax: 847-816-0035; Dues $30 per year; write for free
booklet, *The Fun of Cuff Link Collecting.*
e-mail: Genek@cufflink.com

Related Website: www.cufflink.com

Six marbles interchange to match suit, shirt, or tie in these toggle-backed cuff links, ca 1953, Pierre Parke brand, $150.00.
(Photo courtesy Gene Klompus)

Abacus, retangular shape, sterling silver, toggle closure, ca 1960, ¾" L **$125.00**

Abalone, rectangular, in sterling silver surround, double-sided, ca 1940 ....**$95.00**

Apple shape, red enamel, 14k gold underlay, round lever closure, ca 1935, original apple crate-shape box, marked Royal...**$135.00**

Azure blue, round stones in base metal bezel, toggle closure, Anson brand, ca 1970..**$40.00**

Basketball shape, hoop pass-through closure, base metal, gold color, ca 1955 ....**$60.00**

Bon Ami scouring powder theme, can shape, gold plate, American toggle closure, backmarked Vox, ca 1949 ....**$175.00**

Car design, generic, oval, base metal, toggle closure, Pioneer brand, ca 1950...**$40.00**

Carpenter's square, L shape, sterling silver, lever closure, backmarked Prince & Patria, ca 1900.**$125.00**

Chevrolet logo, bow-tie shape, enamel over base metal, toggle closure, ca 1958..**$60.00**

Devils Head, faux ruby eyes, figural, classic shape, heavy patina on sterling silver, toggle closure, backmarked JT, ca 1940..**$95.00**

Dog (Cocker Spaniel), figural, head shape, wood, disk closure, ca 1895..**$110.00**

Donut, generic, round, pewter, toggle closure, backmarked Attleboro, ca 1950..**$55.00**

Dumpster, generic, detailed figural, base metal, brown, toggle closure, Hickok brand, ca 1955......................**$45.00**

Enamel, red & blue, round, sterling silver, double-sided w/chain connector, backmarked VL, ca 1905.....**$145.00**

Enamel, yellow, oval, base metal, toggle closure, ca 1949 .**$65.00**

Flag motif (American), round, base metal, dumbbell closure, backmark McKinley (name adds value), ca 1900 .**$255.00**

Giraffe, black & white stripes, vertical, silver alloy, lever closure, ca 1910 ....**$80.00**

Horse & jockey, black, red & white cold enamel, detailed figural, base metal, American toggle closure, marked Swank, ca 1960 ....**$55.00**

John F Kennedy Jr, figural bust, sterling silver, toggle closure, ca 1970, w/tie tack **$95.00**

Military, 101st Airborne crest w/eagle, base metal, black, red, yellow & white cold enamel, toggle closure, ca 1990 ....**$45.00**

Movie Projector, square faces, sterling silver, toggle closure, backmarked Silver & Elmo, ca 1955.....................**$60.00**

Separable 'Snapper' cuff links, ca 1923, square shape is unique (most were round), $75.00. (Photo courtesy Gene Klompus)

Vice-Presidential, Seal of VP Albert Gore autograph on underside, base metal, toggle closure, ca 1996..**$225.00**

World's Fair, New York, 1965, triangular, red & black enamel, toggle closure..**$90.00**

Accessories

Cuff links w/4 matching studs, mother-of-pearl, base metal bezels, ca 1933..**$125.00**

Tie bar, knife & fork figural, silver base metal, silver color, ca 1955 ....**$25.00**

Tie bar with Ronald Reagan facsimile autograph, Presidential seal, ca 1982, $55.00. (Photo courtesy Gene Klompus)

Tie tack, Fleur de Lis, red enamel, base metal, ca 1955 ....**$20.00**

Tie tack, Star of David, sterling silver, original box, ca 1950 ....**$25.00**

Cup and Saucer Sets

Lovely cups and saucers are often available at garage sales and flea markets, and prices are generally quite reasonable. If limited space is a consideration, you might enjoy starting a collection, since they're easy to display en masse on a shelf or one at a time as a romantic accent on a coffee table. English manufacturers have produced endless bone china cups and saucers that are more decorative than functional and just as many that are part of their dinnerware lines. American manufacturers were just about as prolific as were the Japanese. Collecting examples from many companies and countries is a wonderful way to study the various ceramic manufacturers. Our advisors have written *Collectible Cups and Saucers, Identification and Values, Books I* and *II* (Collector Books), with hundreds of color photos organized by six collectible categories: early years (1700 – 1875), cabinet cups, nineteenth and twentieth century dinnerware, English tablewares, miniatures, and mustache cups and saucers.

Advisors: Jim and Susan Harran (See Directory, Cups and Saucers)

Wedgwood, blue leafy band on white, waisted cup with loop handle, embossed Queen's Ware, 1950 to present, from $25.00 to $35.00. (Photo courtesy Jim and Susan Harran)

Bouillon, Chinese Green Bouquet pattern on white w/gold trim, Herend, 1950s-present, from $150 to **$200.00**
Coffee, leaf pattern on white w/gold trim, Rosenthal Studio Line, 1950s, w/dessert plate, from $50 to **$60.00**
Coffee, pink flowers & insects on white, fluted, tall, low ring handle, Lomonosov, 1930-50s, from $45 to..........**$60.00**
Coffee, Rochchild Bird pattern on white, scalloped rims, Osier border, Herend, 1950s-present, from $100 to **$125.00**
Demitasse, Blue Willow lithophane w/loop handle, straight-sided cup, unmarked Japan, 1930-50s, from $40 to..**$50.00**
Demitasse, Dunrobin, 16-rib cup w/loop handle, Royal Worcester, 1944-55, from $35 to **$45.00**
Demitasse, floral enameling low on white body, footed & 24-rib cup, Lenox, 1950s, from $40 to **$50.00**

Demitasse, floral transfer on white w/gold trim at rims & handle, Rorstrand, 1950-present, from $40 to.......**$50.00**
Demitasse, Husk pattern made for Williamsburg, creamware w/feathered loop handle, Wedgwood, 1950s, from $25 to...**$35.00**
Demitasse, medallions on turquoise band on white w/gold bands & angle handle, Hutschenreuther, 1925-41, from $40 to...**$55.00**
Demitasse, mixed pastel florals on white w/gold, 3-footed cup w/high goose-neck handle, Pirkenhammer, 1918-45, from $40 to...**$50.00**
Demitasse, Pansy on Dainty shape, Shelley, 1946-66, from $45 to...**$65.00**
Demitasse, parrot & flowers on white, straight-sided cup w/ring handle, Scammell China Co, 1926-54, from $40 to ...**$50.00**
Demitasse, strawberry-form cup (deep rose) w/green leaf-shaped saucer, Cemar, California, 1946-57, from $40 to...**$50.00**
Demitasse, turquoise, straight cup w/question-mark handle, Van Briggle, 1950s, from $60 to............................**$90.00**
Tea, Cairo, blue bird on branch pattern on white, scalloped, gold trim, Coalport, 1945-59, from $40 to **$50.00**
Tea, chintz on Royal Flute shape w/broken loop handle, James Kent Ltd, 1934-80, from $85 to.................**$100.00**
Tea, dainty purple flowers on white, kicked loop handle, Adderleys Ltd, 1962-present, from $30 to.............**$35.00**
Tea, flowers on coral, scalloped foot & handle on cup, Hutschenreuther, ca 1928-43, w/dessert plate, from $75 to...**$85.00**
Tea, forget-me-nots on white, partially ribbed footed cup, Paragon, 1957+, from $60 to................................**$75.00**
Tea, gold floral on ribbed melon-shape cup w/3 gold feet, Royal Sealy Japan, 1950+, from $35 to **$40.00**
Tea, hand-painted exotic flowers on maroon, scalloped, loop handle, Princess China, Occupied Japan, 1945-52, from $30 to...**$40.00**
Tea, Imari #1128, footed & slightly flared cup, Royal Crown Derby, ca 1971, from $80 to **$100.00**
Tea, multicolor cornflower band on white, pedestal cup w/coiled loop handle, Foley, 1945-63, from $35 to..**$45.00**
Tea, pink & white w/gold trim, scalloped edge, smooth rim to cup, Weimar, 1973-present, from $60 to...........**$70.00**
Tea, pink & white w/much gold, gold interior, Royal Doulton, ca 1902-56, sm, from $125 to...............**$175.00**
Tea, pink rose in black reserve on pale pink, scalloped & footed cup, Paragon, 1952-55, from $35 to **$45.00**
Tea, red & cream w/gold decor, ring handle, Alka-Kunst Alboth & Kaiser, Bavaria, 1927-53, w/sm plate, from $50 to...**$75.00**
Tea, rose transfer inside cup & saucer well, black bands w/gold stars form rim & decorate exterior, Lefton, 1949-55, from $40 to **$50.00**
Tea, scattered flowers on white, shallow footed cup w/angular handle, Rosenthal, 1949-54, from $50 to **$60.00**
Tea, scenic transfer on pale blue, footed, scalloped & leaf-molded cup w/ornate handle, Aynsley, 1950s, from $40 to...**$50.00**

Tea, swirled, scalloped & beaded top, swirled coral petals w/gold trim, Coalport, ca 1948-59, from $100 to ..**$125.00**

Tea, turquoise w/gold leafy design, corset-shaped cup w/loop handle, Aynsley, 1950s, from $35 to **$45.00**

Tea, Virginia Stock (chintz), flared cup w/D-shaped handle, Royal Standard, 1930-64, from $45 to **$65.00**

Czechoslovakian Glass and Ceramics

Established as a country in 1918, Czechoslovakia is rich in the natural resources needed for production of glassware as well as pottery. Over the years it has produced vast amounts of both. Anywhere you go, from flea markets to fine antique shops, you'll find several examples of their lovely pressed and cut glass scent bottles, Deco vases, lamps, kitchenware, tableware, and figurines.

More than thirty-five marks have been recorded; some are ink stamped, some etched, and some molded in. Paper labels have also been used. *Czechoslovakian Glass and Collectibles* by Diane and Dale Barta and Helen M. Rose, and *Made in Czechoslovakia* by Ruth Forsythe are two books we highly recommend for further study. (Both are published by Collector Books.)

Club: Czechoslovakian Collectors Guild International
P.O. Box 901395
Kansas City, MO 64190

Ceramics

Basket, black & white bands on yellow, black trim at rim & handle, 4¼", from $40 to **$45.00**

Basket, flower & vine design on white w/black handle & trim at base, 5", from $45 to **$5.00**

Basket, white pearlescent w/embossed braid decor, black trim along rim & handle, 4¼", from $35 to **$40.00**

Bowl, apple form, lid has leaf & stem, 6½", from $75 to **$80.00**

Box, bluebirds on branch on orange to white lid, orange to white base, w/lid, 1¾" dia, from $25 to **$30.00**

Candle holder/match holder/ashtray combination, lavender center, floral on purple, 6½x4½", from $45 to **$55.00**

Candlestick, white lustre w/3 dark blue bands, round top, square base, 4", from $30 to **$35.00**

Coaster, red w/single white flower in center, 3", set of 4...**$100.00**

Creamer, bright flowers in black oval on yellow, black handle & rim, Peasant Art Pottery, 3¼", from $60 to **$65.00**

Creamer, bright orange lower half & base, white above w/orange trim, white handle, bulbous, 3½", from $30 to **$35.00**

Creamer, bright red w/white handle, spout & rim, bulbous, 4", from $30 to **$35.00**

Creamer, cream lustre w/black angle handle, 2½", from $20 to **$25.00**

Creamer, dainty pink flowers on white w/gold trim along scaloped edge, 3¼", from $35 to..........................**$40.00**

Creamer, moose head w/open-mouth spout, antlers along rim, brown & cream shading to light blue-gray base, 3½", from $55 to **$60.00**

Cup & saucer, yellow-orange lustre w/blue-gray lustre inside, Victoria Crown China, 2¼", 5¼", from $15 to **$20.00**

Flower arranger, parakeet on stump, blue & rust w/black accents on dark stump, 5¼", from $40 to............**$45.00**

Flowerpot, multicolor floral on white (resembling chintz), gold at rim, Erphila, 4⅝", from $40 to **$50.00**

Mug, dark blue & gold design w/floral bouquets on white, gold rim & accents, 3⅝", from $35 to **$40.00**

Mug, rust, blue & white rectangles on white w/tan stripes, tan rim, top & handle, 3½", from $40 to **$45.00**

Nut bowl, flower shape, blue, green, white, and orange gloss, 6", from $15.00 to $20.00.
(Photo courtesy Dale and Diane Barta and Helen M. Rose)

Pitcher, bright flowers on yellow with black trim at rim & base, black curlique handle, flared top, 5¼", from $55 to **$60.00**

Pitcher, milk; mountain & river scenic, orange rim shades to beige, orange & beige handle, 6¼", from $500 to ..**$600.00**

Pitcher, milk; pink lustre over yellow-gold lustre divided by black line, black rim & handle, squat, 4⅝", from $40 to **$45.00**

Pitcher, multicolor fruit embossed on maroon ground, angle handle, 6½", from $70 to **$75.00**

Pitcher, orange flowers w/green vines on white, orange at rim, handle & base, w/lid, Erphila, 8¼", from $75 to **$85.00**

Pitcher, painted church scene w/green grass on body, orange top w/black trim, ornate handle, 7¾", from $70 to ..**$75.00**

Pitcher, ram figural, red & black on cream, horns form handle, Erphila, 8¼", from $165 to **$185.00**

Planter vase, multicolor fruit embossed on dark blue, black at rim, Erphila, 4⅝", from $25 to..........................**$30.00**

Sugar bowl, light orange shading to tan, petal style w/green rim, open, 2½", from $30 to **$35.00**

Sugar bowl, open shell design, white pearl lustre, ear-shaped handle, 4 raised feet, 2¼", from $50 to **$55.00**

Sugar bowl, pink & white variegated petal design w/green leaves at base, vine handle, china, 4", from $40 to .**$50.00**

Vase, beige, black & orange mottled lustre w/black stripe decor, ear-type handles, 9½", from $90 to............**$95.00**

Vase, beige w/red 'crackle' lines, black medallion on side & black ring at base, cut-out handles, 10", from $95 to **$105.00**

Vase, boy & girl cameo surrounded by flower garland on red-orange, black trim at rim & shoulder, 5¼", from $35 to **$40.00**

Vase, coaching scene w/horses on white, rust & green trim at top & bottom, cylindrical, 6¼", from $40 to **$45.00**

Vase, multicolor florals on dark brown with light green to tan top, angle handles, 7", from $50 to **$55.00**

Vase, orange w/orange, yellow & green flower garland in relief, fan shape, low handles, 5¼", from $30 to.**$35.00**

Vase, pearl gray lustre w/black rim & angle handles, waisted, 5½", from $25 to....................................**$30.00**

Vase, pink flowers & green leaves embossed on cream fan form w/stepped base, 4¼", from $25 to..............**$35.00**

Vase, white pearlescent body, orange rim & handles, 5¼", from $20 to..**$25.00**

Glassware

Atomizer, bright orange (cased) w/gold trim, 3", from $65 to **$75.00**

Ball vase, crystal w/intaglio floral decor, 5", from $75 to..**$80.00**

Basket, blue w/jet rim & clear applied handle, 6½", from $80 to...**$95.00**

Bowl, mottled autumn colors (cased), sm foot, incurvate rim, 4½", from $55 to **$60.00**

Box, dresser; crystal, amethyst base w/clear lid, 2¼" dia, from $50 to..**$55.00**

Candy basket, mottled autumn colors, ruffled rim, crystal thorn handle, 6½"...**$200.00**

Candy basket, red & yellow mottle w/crystal twisted thorn handle, 7" **$220.00**

Decanter, topaz tinted, carriage scene, Borokistol, 10¼"...**$140.00**

Honey pot, dark blue iridescent base & lid w/enamel design, 5", from $90 to **$95.00**

Perfume, cut, black transparent frost, matching stopper, 4⅞"...**$195.00**

Perfume bottle, clear cut base, prism-cut clear drop stopper, 4⅞", from $110 to...................................**$125.00**

Perfume bottle, cut, amber arch shape w/clear figure stopper, 5½" **$250.00**

Perfume bottle, cut crystal base, amethyst drop stopper w/intaglio cuttings, 6¾", from $170 to................**$180.00**

Perfume bottle, pressed, amber arch shape w/jewels, amber stopper, 3½" **$110.00**

Perfume bottle, pressed, Hobnail, cranberry opalescent, 5½"...**$85.00**

Pitcher, orange (cased) w/applied cobalt rim & handle, tri-corner top, 5", from $80 to **$85.00**

Shakers, ducks w/crystal bodies & porcelain heads, 2", pr, from $40 to...**$50.00**

Vase, black (cased) w/exotic bird enameling, silver rim & decor, 7¼", from $140 to **$145.00**

Vase, cobalt blue w/mottled colors (cased), twist design, shouldered, 4¾", from $70 to **$75.00**

Vase, maroon (cased) w/applied handles, 7", from $110 to **$125.00**

Vase, orange (cased) w/mottled colors on base, slim, 9", from $65 to...**$70.00**

Vase, orange (cased) w/ruffled top, applied flower decor, 7½", from $80 to...**$100.00**

Vase, pale blue crystal w/ridged design, 8", from $80 to..**$100.00**

Vase, red w/white & green mottle (cased), cobalt loop handles, 4⅝", from $95 to.......................................**$100.00**

Vase, variegated multicolor (cased) w/blue handles, 8⅜", from $90 to..**$100.00**

Vase, yellow (cased) w/cobalt serpentine decor, cobalt foot, 4¾", from $90 to...**$95.00**

Vase, yellow-orange (cased) w/applied jet rim, trumpet form, footed, 6¾", from $75 to..................................**$80.00**

Wine, bubbly green w/hand-painted decor, 4¼"........**$55.00**

Vase, cased, orange and yellow mottle, 8¼", from $45.00 to $50.00; Vase, cased, yellow and red streak, clear feet, 9¼", from $65.00 to $70.00. (Photo courtesy Dale and Diane Barta and Helen M. Rose)

Dakin

Dakin has been in the toy-making business since the 1950s and has made several lines of stuffed and vinyl dolls and animals. But the Dakins that collectors are most interested in today are the licensed characters and advertising figures made from 1968 through the 1970s. Originally there were seven Warner Brothers characters, each with a hard plastic body and a soft vinyl head, all under 10" tall. The line was very successful and eventually expanded to include more than fifty cartoon characters and several more that were advertising related. In addition to the figures, there are banks that were made in two sizes. Some Dakins are quite scarce and may sell for over $100.00 (a few even higher), though most will be in the $30.00 to $60.00 range. Dakin is now owned by Applause, Inc.

Condition is very important, and if you find one still in the original box, add about 50% to its value. Figures in the colorful 'Cartoon Theatre' boxes command higher prices than those that came in a clear plastic bag or package (MIP). More Dakins are listed in *Schroeder's Collectible Toys, Antique to Modern*, published by Collector Books.

Baby Puss, Hanna-Barbera, 1971, EX+ $100.00
Bambi, Disney, 1960s, MIP $35.00
Bamm-Bamm, Hanna-Barbera, w/club, 1970, EX $35.00
Barney Rubble, Hanna-Barbera, 1970, EX $40.00
Benji, 1978, cloth, VG..$10.00
Bozo the Clown, Larry Harmon, 1974, EX...................$35.00
Bugs Bunny, Warner Bros, 1971, MIP..........................$30.00
Bullwinkle, Jay Ward, 1976, MIB (TV Cartoon Theater Box) $60.00
Cool Cat, Warner Bros, w/beret, 1970, EX+ $30.00
Daffy Duck, Warner Bros, 1968, EX............................$30.00
Daffy Duck, Warner Bros, 1976, MIB (TV Cartoon box) $40.00
Deputy Dawg, Terrytoons, 1977, EX............................$50.00
Dino Dinosaur, Hanna-Barbera, 1970, EX $40.00
Donald Duck, Disney, 1960s, straight or bent legs, NMIB $30.00
Dream Pets, Bull Dog, cloth, EX $15.00
Dream Pets, Midnight Mouse, cloth, w/original tag, EX.$15.00
Dudley Do-Right, Jay Ward, 1976, MIB (TV Cartoon Theater box) $75.00
Dumbo, Disney, 1960s, cloth collar, MIB $25.00
Elmer Fudd, Warner Bros, 1968, hunting outfit w/rifle, EX $125.00
Elmer Fudd, Warner Bros, 1978, MIP (Fun Farm bag) .$75.00
Foghorn Leghorn, Warner Bros, 1970, EX+ $75.00
Fred Flintstone, Hanna-Barbera, 1970, EX...................$40.00

Goofy, Disney, cloth clothes, original tag, NM, $25.00.

Goofy Gram, Bull, I'm Mad About You, EX.................$25.00
Goofy Gram, Frog, Happy Birthday, EX.......................$25.00
Goofy Gram, Tiger, To a Great Guy, EX $25.00
Hoppy Hopperroo, Hanna-Barbera, 1971, EX+...........$75.00
Huey Duck, Disney, straight or bent legs, EX.............$30.00
Lion in Cage, bank, 1971, EX $25.00

Louie Duck, Disney, straight or bent legs, EX $30.00
Merlin the Mouse, Warner Bros, 1970, EX+.................$25.00
Minnie Mouse, Disney, 1960s, cloth clothes, EX.........$20.00
Olive Oyl, King Features, 1974, cloth clothes, MIP $50.00
Oliver Hardy, Larry Harmon, 1974, EX+......................$30.00
Pebbles Flintstone, Hanna-Barbera, 1970, EX............$35.00
Pink Panther, Mirisch-Freleng, 1971, EX+ $50.00
Pinocchio, Disney, 1960s, EX $20.00
Popeye, King Features, 1976, MIB (TV Cartoon Theater box) $50.00
Porky Pig, Warner Bros, 1976, MIB (TV Cartoon Theater box) $40.00
Ren & Stimpy, water squirters, Nickelodeon, 1993, EX ..$10.00
Road Runner, Warner Bros, 1976, MIB $45.00
Scooby Doo, Hanna-Barbera, 1980, EX $75.00
Scrappy Doo, Hanna-Barbera, 1982, EX+ $75.00
Snagglepus, 1971, EX...$100.00

Speedy Gonzalez, Warner Bros., M, $35.00.

Sylvester, Warner Bros, 1976, MIB (TV Cartoon box).$40.00
Tasmanian Devil, Warner Bros, 1978, rare, EX (EX Fun Farm bag)..$400.00
Top Banana, Warner Bros, NM....................................$25.00
Underdog, Jay Ward, 1976, MIB (TV Cartoon Theater box) $150.00
Yogi Bear, Hanna-Barbera, 1970, EX..........................$60.00
Yosemite Sam, Warner Bros, 1968, MIB......................$40.00

Advertising

Bay View Bank, 1976, EX+ $30.00
Bob's Big Boy, 1974, w/hamburger, EX+ $150.00
Buddie Bull, Buddig Meats, 1970s, cloth, EX.............$20.00
Diaperene Baby, Sterling Drug Co, 1980, EX.............$40.00
Freddie Fast Gas Attendant, 1976, M $100.00
Glamour Kitty, 1977, EX $200.00
Hobo Joe, bank, Hobo Joe's Restaurant, EX $60.00
Kernal Renk, American Seeds, 1970, rare, EX+........$300.00
Li'l Miss Just Rite, 1965, EX+....................................$75.00
Miss Liberty Bell, 1975, MIP......................................$75.00

Quasar Robot, bank, 1975, NM **$125.00**
Sambo's Boy, 1974, vinyl, EX+ **$75.00**
Sambo's Tiger, 1974, vinyl, EX+ **$125.00**
Smokey the Bear, 1976, M **$25.00**
St Bernard, Christian Bros Brandy, 1982, cloth, VG....**$20.00**
Woodsy Owl, 1974, MIP......................................**$60.00**

Decanters

The first company to make figural ceramic decanters was the James Beam Distilling Company. Until mid-1992 they produced hundreds of varieties in their own US-based china factory. They first issued their bottles in the mid-'50s, and over the course of the next twenty-five years, more than twenty other companies followed their example. Among the more prominent of these were Brooks, Hoffman, Lionstone, McCormick, Old Commonwealth, Ski Country, and Wild Turkey. In 1975, Beam introduced the 'Wheel Series,' cars, trains, and fire engines with wheels that actually revolved. The popularity of this series resulted in a heightened interest in decanter collecting.

There are various sizes. The smallest (called miniatures) hold two ounces, and there are some that hold a gallon! A full decanter is worth no more than an empty one, and the absence of the tax stamp doesn't lower its value either. Just be sure that all the labels are intact and that there are no cracks or chips. You might want to empty your decanters as a safety precaution (many collectors do) rather than risk the possibility of the inner glaze breaking down and allowing the contents to leak into the porous ceramic body.

All of the decanters we've listed are fifths unless we've specified 'miniature' within the description.

See also Elvis Presley Collectibles.

Advisor: Art and Judy Turner, Homestead Collectibles (See Directory, Decanters)

Newsletter: *Beam Around the World*
International Association of Jim Beam Bottle and Specialties Clubs
Shirley Sumbles, Executive Administrator
2015 Burlington Ave., Kewanee, IL 61443; 309-853-3370

Newsletter: *The Ski Country Collector*
1224 Washington Ave., Golden, CO 80401

Beam, Centennial Series, Civil War, North **$15.00**
Beam, Club Series, Fox, Red Distillery **$750.00**
Beam, Convention Series, #10 Norfolk Waterman, pewter...**$30.00**
Beam, Convention Series, #13 St Louis, stein..............**$50.00**
Beam, Convention Series, #17 Louisville **$45.00**
Beam, Convention Series, #21 Reno Cowboy Fox......**$65.00**
Beam, Convention Series, #9 Houston 1979...............**$25.00**
Beam, Executive Series, 1974 Twin Cherubs..............**$15.00**
Beam, Organization Series, Ducks Unlimited #1, Mallard, 1974 ....**$65.00**

Beam, Organization Series, Ducks Unlimited #6, Blue/Teal, 1980 ....**$50.00**
Beam, Organization Series, Ducks Unlimited #10, Mallard, 1984 ....**$95.00**
Beam, Organization Series, Ducks Unlimited #17, Tundra Swan, 1991 ....**$40.00**
Beam, Organization Series, Phi Sigma Kappa **$24.00**
Beam, People Series, Emmet Kelley........................**$35.00**
Beam, People Series, Mr Goodwrench **$70.00**
Beam, Regal China Series, Canadian Silo **$40.00**
Beam, Regal China Series, Tombstone......................**$14.00**

Beam, Sports Series, Bing Crosby National Pro-Am, $14.00.

Beam, Sports Series, Football Hall of Fame.................**$30.00**
Beam, Sports Series, Rocky Marciano **$40.00**
Beam, State Series, New Jersey, gray **$30.00**
Beam, Trophy Series, Catfish **$40.00**
Beam, Wheel Series, Ambulance.................................**$79.00**
Beam, Wheel Series, Cable Car **$60.00**
Beam, Wheel Series, Casey Jones' Train, caboose **$20.00**
Beam, Wheel Series, Casey Jones' Train, 5-pc set **$125.00**
Beam, Wheel Series, Duesenberg Convertible, light blue ..**$110.00**
Beam, Wheel Series, Ernie's Flower Cart.....................**$25.00**
Beam, Wheel Series, Ford Model A, Angelos Liquor..**$195.00**
Beam, Wheel Series, Jewel Tea **$75.00**
Beam, Wheel Series, Space Shuttle **$50.00**
Beam, Wheel Series, State Trooper, gray **$65.00**
Beam, Wheel Series, Tractor Trailer, orange...............**$65.00**
Beam, Wheel Series, Train (General), Flat Car...........**$80.00**
Beam, Wheel Series, Train (General), Wood Tender ...**$125.00**
Beam, Wheel Series, Train (Grant), Caboose, red.......**$75.00**
Beam, Wheel Series, Train (Grant), Locomotive **$90.00**
Beam, Wheel Series, Train (Turner), Box Car, yellow ...**$125.00**
Beam, Wheel Series, Train (Turner), Locomotive **$125.00**
Beam, Wheel Series, Train (Turner), Tank Car **$65.00**
Beam, Wheel Series, Train Bumper.............................**$15.00**
Beam, Wheel Series, Vendome Wagon **$35.00**
Beam, Wheel Series, Volkswagen, red or blue, ea **$75.00**
Beam, Wheel Series, 1903 Ford Model A, red............**$50.00**
Beam, Wheel Series, 1909 Thomas Flyer, blue...........**$65.00**
Beam, Wheel Series, 1913 Ford Model T, black.........**$55.00**

Beam, Wheel Series, 1917 Mack Fire Truck $125.00
Beam, Wheel Series, 1928 Ford Fire Chief $95.00
Beam, Wheel Series, 1929 Ford Phaeton $70.00
Beam, Wheel Series, 1929 Ford Police Car, blue $125.00
Beam, Wheel Series, 1929 Ford Woodie Wagon $75.00
Beam, Wheel Series, 1934 Ford Police Patrol Car, yellow..$195.00
Beam, Wheel Series, 1953 Chevrolet Corvette, white ...$175.00
Beam, Wheel Series, 1955 Chevrolet Corvette, red...$150.00
Beam, Wheel Series, 1956 Ford Thunderbird, black...$95.00
Beam, Wheel Series, 1956 Ford Thunderbird, green .$110.00
Beam, Wheel Series, 1957 Chevrolet, turquoise $70.00
Beam, Wheel Series, 1957 Chevrolet Convertible, PA, dark
    blue $80.00
Beam, Wheel Series, 1957 Chevrolet Convertible, red..$95.00
Beam, Wheel Series, 1957 Chevrolet Corvette, black .$70.00
Beam, Wheel Series, 1957 Chevrolet Corvette, green ..$175.00
Beam, Wheel Series, 1957 Chevrolet Corvette, red...$195.00
Beam, Wheel Series, 1959 Cadillac, white $250.00
Beam, Wheel Series, 1963 Chevrolet Corvette, green ..$350.00
Beam, Wheel Series, 1964 Ford Mustang, red...........$125.00
Beam, Wheel Series, 1968 Chevrolet Corvette, black .$895.00
Beam, Wheel Series, 1968 Chevrolet Corvette, maroon..$70.00
Beam, Wheel Series, 1968 Chevrolet Corvette, white ...$110.00
Beam, Wheel Series, 1969 Chevrolet Camaro Comvertible,
    orange $70.00
Beam, Wheel Series, 1969 Chevrolet Camaro Convertible, sil-
    ver $125.00
Beam, Wheel Series, 1970 Dodge Challenger, plum...$50.00
Beam, Wheel Series, 1970 Dodge Hot Rod, lime......$125.00
Beam, Wheel Series, 1974 Mercedes, green $45.00
Beam, Wheel Series, 1974 Mercedes, PA, sand beige.$50.00
Beam, Wheel Series, 1978 Chevrolet Corvette, Pace Car ..$250.00
Beam, Wheel Series, 1978 Chevrolet Corvette, yellow .$75.00
Beam, Wheel Series, 1984 Chevrolet Corvette, bronze ..$110.00
Beam, Wheel Series, 1984 Chevrolet Corvette, red.....$80.00
Beam, Wheel Series, 1986 Chevrolet Corvette, Pace Car, yel-
    low...$150.00
Brroks, American Legion, Houston, 1971 ....$31.00
Clem Harvey, Mount Hood..$17.00
Daviess County, American Legion, New Orleans, 1978..$19.00
Dickel, Powderhorn, qt size $15.00
Double Eagle, Series I, #1...$24.00
Ezra Brooks, Automobile & Transportation Series, Ontario
    Racer #10..$32.00
Ezra Brooks, Automobile & Transportation Series, 1931
    Duesenberg Phaeton, green..................................$28.00
Ezra Brooks, Clydesdale..$29.00
Ezra Brooks, Foremost Astonaut $19.00
Ezra Brooks, Lobster...$22.00
Ezra Brooks, New Hampshire State House..................$10.00
Ezra Brooks, Polish Legion $10.00
Ezra Brooks, Tennis Player $15.00
Famous First, Indy Racer #11.......................................$39.00
Garnier, Bouquet $20.00
Garnier, Partridge...$15.00
Garnier, Valley Quail, CA $19.00
Harvey's Bristol Cream, Coalport.................................$13.00

Hoffman, Dalmatian $29.00
Hoffman, Queen's Ranger, Drummer...........................$25.00
Jack Daniels, Belle of Lincoln......................................$29.00
Jack Daniels, Maxwell House $59.00
Kessler, Football Player $29.00
Kontinental, Gunsmith...$32.00
Kontinental, Stephen Foster $32.00
Lionstone, Betsy Ross $29.00
Lionstone, Cowboy $22.00
Lionstone, Gambler...$20.00
Lionstone, Squawman..$25.00
Lionstone Miniature, Tropical Birds Series, Macaw.....$25.00
Lionstone Miniature, Tropical Birds Series, Painted
    Bunting $24.00
Lord Calvert, Eider #4..$16.00
Lord Calvert, Wood Duck #2 ....$25.00
McCormick, Alexander Graham Bell.............................$25.00
McCormick, Bicentennial Series, John Hancock..........$19.00
McCormick, Bicentennial Series, Paul Revere.............$27.00
McCormick, Bicentennial Series, Thomas Jefferson $22.00

McCormick, Gunfighter Series, Black Bart, $35.00.

McCormick, JR Ewing..$49.00
Mike Wayne, Christmas Tree, green, music box $65.00
Old Bardstown, Foster Brooks $25.00
Old Bardstown, Surface Miner......................................$25.00
Old Commonwealth, Coal Miner Series, Standing w/Shovel
    #1, miniature $25.00
Old Commonwealth, Coal Miners Series, Coal Shooter
    #5 ....$29.00
Old Commonwealth, Firefighter Series, Fallen Comrade
    #4 ....$75.00
Old Commonwealth, Firefighter Series, Modern Hero
    #1 ....$69.00
Old Commonwealth, Firefighter Series, Nozzleman #2..$69.00
Old Crow, all chess pcs other than pawns, yellow or green,
    ea $19.00

Old Crow, Pawns, yellow or green, ea.........................$21.00
Old Fitzgerald, Irish Luck...$26.00
Old Fitzgerald, South Carolina Tricentennial.............$11.00
Old Mr Boston, Assyrian Convention, 1975................$21.00
Pacesetter, Ford Big Blue, miniature..........................$49.00
Pacesetter, Steiger 4-Wheel Drive.............................$195.00
Paramount, Ohio Governor James Rhodes.................$25.00
PM Specialists, Firemark, made to hang on wall also...$65.00
Sabra, Pilgrim Flask...$15.00
Ski Country, Animals, Brown Bear..............................$35.00
Ski Country, Animals, Fox on Log...............................$95.00
Ski Country, Animals, Raccoon...................................$46.00
Ski Country, Banded Waterfowl, Ducks Unlimited, Mallard, 1980 ....$75.00
Ski Country, Banded Waterfowl, Ducks Unlimited, Oldsquaw, miniature $35.00
Ski Country, Birds, Black Swan $45.00
Ski Country, Birds, Brown Pelican $55.00
Ski Country, Birds, Golden Pheasant $65.00
Ski Country, Birds, Peace Dove...................................$60.00
Ski Country, Birds, Whooping Crane, miniature $39.00
Ski Country, Christmas Series, Chickadees $69.00
Ski Country, Circus Series, Clown Bust.......................$65.00
Ski Country, Circus Series, Jenny Lind, yellow $132.00
Ski Country, Customer Specialties, Clyde $39.00
Ski Country, Customer Specialties, Ladies of Leadville, blue...$24.00
Ski Country, Customer Specialties, School of Mines Burro, miniatures $39.00
Ski Country, Domestic Animals, Labrador w/Pheasant.$79.00
Ski Country, Eagle Series, Harpy................................$129.00
Ski Country, Eagle Series, Majestic............................$229.00
Ski Country, Falcon Series, Peregrine, gallon size, 450 made $295.00
Ski Country, Falcon Series, Prairie, miniature.............$49.00
Ski Country, Fighting Gamecocks, miniature...............$45.00
Ski Country, Game Birds Series, Fighting Pheasants, ½-gallon size..$181.00
Ski Country, Game Birds Series, Prairie Chicken $59.00
Ski Country, Hawk Series, Red Shoulder....................$79.00
Ski Country, Horned & Antlered Series, Bighorned Ram, 1973 .$45.00
Ski Country, Horned & Antlered Series, Grand Slam Desert Bighorn, miniature......................................$40.00
Ski Country, Indian Ceremonial Dancers Series, Buffalo, miniature...$40.00
Ski Country, Indian Ceremonial Dancers Series, End of the Trail..$195.00
Ski Country, Owl Series, Great Gray Owl $75.00
Ski Country, Owl Series, Spectacled Owl, miniature ..$65.00
Ski Country, Waterfowl Series, Canadian Goose, 1973 ..$95.00
Ski Country, Waterfowl Series, Wood Duck, 1974 ....$149.00
Weller, Masterpiece..$23.00
Wild Turkey, Series I, #2..$149.00
Wild Turkey, Series II, #3, from $45 to......................$60.00
Wild Turkey, Series III, #4, Turkey & Eagle, from $70 to ..$90.00
Wild Turkey, Series III, #7, Turkey & Red Fox $95.00
Wild Turkey, Series III, #10, Turkey & Coyote $45.00

DeForest of California

This family-run company (operated by Jack and Margaret DeForest and sons) was located in California; from the early 1950s until 1970 they produce the type of novelty ceramic kitchenware and giftware items that state has become known for. A favored theme was their onion-head jars, bowls, ashtray, etc., all designed with various comical expressions. Some of their cookie jars were finished in a brown wood-tone glaze and were very similar to many produced by Twin Winton. (See also Cookie Jars.)

Onion-head spice jars, set of six in wireware frame, NM, $235.00 (at auction). (Photo courtesy Janice Wise)

Bowl, onion head, 11x13"...$30.00
Cheese container, Big Cheese, smiling face, 4x5".......$45.00
Cup & saucer, 99 More Years & It's Ours.....................$8.00
Figurine, egret, blue-green, 16¾" $38.00
Jam jar, face w/hat lid $25.00
Jar, Garlic, garlic head, 4¼x4½"..................................$25.00
Plaque, fish, gold trim, 9" L $22.00
Plate, onion head, 9"...$15.00
Plate, onion shape w/hand-painted face, 12½x10¾" .$28.00
Platter, brown pig, 1956, 13x13", from $30 to............$45.00
Tray, onion head, 5¾x6½"...$15.00

Degenhart

John and Elizabeth Degenhart owned and operated the Crystal Art Glass Factory in Cambridge, Ohio. From 1947 until John died in 1964, they produced some fine glassware. John was well known for his superior paperweights, but the glassware that collectors love today was made after '64, when Elizabeth restructured the company, creating many lovely moulds and scores of colors. She hired Zack Boyd, who had previously worked for Cambridge Glass, and between the two of them, they developed almost 150 unique and original color formulas.

Complying with provisions she had made before her death, close personal friends at Island Mould and Machine Company in Wheeling, West Virginia, took Elizabeth's moulds and removed the familiar 'D in a heart' trademark from them. She had requested that ten of her moulds be donated to the Degenhart Museum, where they remain today. Zack Boyd eventually bought the Degenhart factory and acquired the remaining moulds. He has added his own logo to them and is continuing to press glass very similar to Mrs. Degenhart's.

For more information, we recommend *Degenhart Glass and Paperweights* by Gene Florence, published by the Degenhart Paperweight and Glass Museum, Inc., Cambridge, Ohio.

Club: Friends of Degenhart
Degenhart Paperweight and Glass Museum
P.O. Box 186, Cambridge, OH 43725; Individual membership: $5 per year; membership includes newsletter, *Heartbeat*, a quarterly publication and free admission to the museum

Baby Shoe (Hobo Boot) Toothpick Holder, Nile Green..**$15.00**
Baby Shoe (Hobo Boot) Toothpick Holder, Pearl Gray...**$17.50**
Basket Toothpick Holder, Pink................................**$15.00**
Beaded Oval Toothpick Holder, Bloody Mary............**$40.00**
Bicentennial Bell, Custard....................................**$25.00**
Bicentennial Bell, Wonder Blue..............................**$12.00**
Bird Salt & Pepper, Baby Green, pr........................**$45.00**
Bird Salt & Pepper, Cobalt, pr..............................**$25.00**
Bird Salt & Pepper, Mint Green, pr........................**$50.00**
Bird Salt w/Cherry, Burnt Amber...........................**$20.00**
Bird Salt w/Cherry, Rubina..................................**$75.00**
Bird Toothpick Holder, Blue Slag............................**$35.00**
Bow Slipper, Champagne......................................**$15.00**
Bow Slipper, Milk Blue Slag..................................**$25.00**
Bow Slipper, Teal..**$15.00**
Bow Slipper, White w/Red Bow..............................**$30.00**
Buzz Saw Wine, Aqua..**$40.00**
Chick Covered Dish, Aqua, 2"...............................**$30.00**
Chick Covered Dish, Custard Slag, 2"......................**$35.00**
Chick Covered Dish, Jabe's Amber, 2".....................**$20.00**
Chick Covered Dish, Peach Blo, 2"..........................**$25.00**
Coaster, Sapphire..**$8.00**
Colonial Drape Toothpick Holder, Amber...................**$15.00**
Daisy & Button Creamer & Sugar, Opal White...........**$90.00**
Daisy & Button Creamer & Sugar, Pine Green............**$75.00**
Daisy & Button Salt, Amberina..............................**$15.00**
Daisy & Button Toothpick Holder, Dichromatic..........**$25.00**
Daisy & Button Wine, Amber................................**$20.00**
Daisy & Button Wine, Opal White...........................**$35.00**
Daisy & Button Wine, Vaseline..............................**$25.00**
Elephant Head Toothpick Holder, Amethyst...............**$25.00**
Elephant Head Toothpick Holder, Persimmon............**$25.00**
Elephant Head Toothpick Holder, Smoky Heather.....**$35.00**
Forget-Me-Not Toothpick Holder, Chad's Blue...........**$20.00**
Forget-Me-Not Toothpick Holder, Lavender Blue.......**$25.00**
Forget-Me-Not Toothpick Holder, Light Amethyst.......**$15.00**
Forget-Me-Not Toothpick Holder, Rubina..................**$125.00**
Forget-Me-Not Toothpick Holder, Sapphire...............**$15.00**
Gypsy Pot Toothpick Holder, Angel Blue...................**$20.00**
Gypsy Pot Toothpick Holder, Fawn.........................**$20.00**
Gypsy Pot Toothpick Holder, Golden Glo..................**$15.00**
Hand, Crystal..**$6.00**
Heart Jewel Box, Blue Jay...................................**$25.00**

Heart Toothpick Holder, Amber..............................**$15.00**
Heart Toothpick Holder, Cobalt..............................**$20.00**
Heart Toothpick Holder, Jade................................**$35.00**
Hen Covered Dish, Bluebell, 3"..............................**$45.00**
Hen Covered Dish, Caramel, Dark; 3".......................**$50.00**
Hen Covered Dish, Caramel, Dark; 5".......................**$100.00**
Hen Covered Dish, Persimmon, 5"...........................**$60.00**
High Boot, Forest Green......................................**$25.00**
Kat Slipper (Puss & Boots), Bloody Mary...................**$50.00**
Kat Slipper (Puss & Boots), Red.............................**$40.00**
Lamb Covered Dish, Bluebell, 5"............................**$65.00**
Lamb Covered Dish, Taffeta, 5".............................**$55.00**
Mini Pitcher, Angel Blue.....................................**$12.00**
Mini Pitcher, Elizabeth's Lime Ice..........................**$20.00**
Mini Pitcher, Red..**$25.00**
Mini Slipper w/out Sole, Caramel...........................**$45.00**
Mini Slipper w/Sole, Opalescent............................**$35.00**
Owl, Blue & White #3...**$75.00**
Owl, Caramel..**$75.00**
Owl, Dark Blue Fire...**$40.00**
Owl, Delft Blue..**$50.00**
Owl, End of Blizzard..**$50.00**
Owl, Ivorene..**$50.00**
Owl, Mint Green..**$35.00**

Owl, Misty Blue, $45.00.

Owl, Opal Variant...**$100.00**
Owl, Royal Violet...**$50.00**
Owl, Smoke...**$50.00**
Owl, Willow Blue...**$40.00**
Owl, Yellow Opal Dickie Bird................................**$200.00**
Pooch, Blue Gray...**$20.00**
Pooch, Buttercup Slag..**$35.00**
Pooch, Charcoal..**$20.00**
Pooch, Green Blue Marble....................................**$35.00**
Portrait Plate, Amethyst.....................................**$30.00**
Portrait Plate, Vaseline......................................**$40.00**
Pottie Salt, Fog...**$15.00**
Priscilla, Fawn..**$95.00**
Priscilla, Powder Blue..**$125.00**

Robin Covered Dish, Apple Green, 5" $65.00
Robin Covered Dish, Frosted Vaseline, rare, 5"..........$65.00
Seal of Ohio Cup Plate, Mint Green $12.00
Star & Dew Drop Salt, Custard $20.00
Star & Dew Drop Salt, Snow White $15.00
Stork & Peacock Child's Mug, Amethyst....................$20.00
Stork & Peacock Child's Mug, Blue Green $25.00
Stork & Peacock Child's Mug, Caramel......................$35.00
Stork & Peacock Child's Mug, Pink............................$20.00
Texas Boot, Chocolate...$25.00
Texas Boot, Milk White $15.00
Texas Creamer & Sugar, Milk White.........................$75.00
Tomahawk, Blue & White Slag....................................$75.00
Tomahawk, Blue Green $40.00
Turkey Covered Dish, Cambridge Pink, 5"..................$65.00
Turkey Covered Dish, Peach Blo, 5"...........................$50.00
Wildflower Candle Holder, Ruby.................................$40.00
Wildflower Candy Dish, Vaseline $25.00

deLee Art Pottery

Jimmie Lee Adair Kohl founded her company in 1937, and it continued to operate until 1958. She was the inspiration, artist, and owner of the company for the 21 years it was in business. The name deLee means 'of or by Lee' and is taken from the French language. She trained as an artist at the San Diego Art Institute and UCLA where she also earned an art education degree. She taught art and ceramics at Belmont High School in Los Angeles while getting her ceramic business started. On September 9, 1999, at the age of 93, Jimmie Lee died after having lived a long and wonderfully creative life.

The deLee line included children, adults, animals, birds, and specialty items such as cookie jars, banks, wall pockets, and several licensed Walter Lantz characters. Skunks were a favorite subject, and more of her pieces were modeled as skunks than any other single animal. Her figurines are distinctive in their design, charm, and excellent hand painting; when carefully studied, they can be easily recognized. Jimmie Lee modeled almost all the pieces — more than 350 in all.

The beautiful deLee colors were mixed by her and remained essentially the same for 20 years. The same figurine may be found painted in different colors and patterns. Figurines were sold wholesale only. Buyers could select from a catalog or visit the deLee booth in New York and Los Angeles Gift Marts. All figurines left the factory with name and logo stickers. The round Art Deco logo sticker is silver with the words 'deLee Art, California, Hand Decorated.' Many of the figures are incised 'deLee Art' on the bottom.

The factory was located in Los Angeles during its 21 years of production and in Cuernavaca, Mexico, for four years during WWII. Production continued until 1958, when Japanese copies of her figures caused sales to decline. For further study we recommend *deLee Art* by Joanne and Ralph Schaefer and John Humphries.

Advisors: Joanne and Ralph Schaefer (See Directory, deLee)

Figurine, Amigo, donkey w/ears pointed down, 5"....$60.00
Figurine, boy resting on his back w/hands under head, 4" $110.00
Figurine, boy sitting w/sailboat, 4"..............................$75.00
Figurine, Buddy, farmer boy, 7", from $45 to $60.00
Figurine, bunny, pink & white w/hand-painted floral decor, 5¼" $30.00
Figurine, Bunny Hug, 5½" $35.00
Figurine, Fritz, Dachshund, lying down w/eyes closed, 6" L $50.00
Figurine, Jimmy, boy dressed as aviator, 1940s..........$60.00
Figurine, Katrina, Dutch girl, 7".................................$30.00
Figurine, Kinky, lamb, standing, 5".............................$35.00
Figurine, Kitty, kitten playing w/ball, 4" $35.00
Figurine, Panchita, #89, 12"..$30.00

Figurine, Pat, girl holding skirt high, multicolor flower trim on white, 7", $30.00.

Figurine, peasant girl, 7" $25.00
Figurine, Precious, kneeling, 3½", from $120 to.......$155.00
Figurine, Rags, English Sheepdog, eyes obscured by hair, 4", from $75 to..$100.00
Figurine, Schnitz, Dachshund, standing w/open eyes, 6" L $60.00
Figurine, Siamese cat, standing tall w/tail wrapped around feet, 12" $125.00
Figurine, Siamese cat, 4" L $65.00
Figurine, Speedy, football player, 5" $125.00
Figurine, Squirt, skunk, 1940s, 5¼" L.........................$22.50
Figurine, Star, angel girl, 4"...$45.00
Figurine/flower frog, Miss Muffet, seated in wide hoop skirt w/spider & bowl, 5" $190.00
Figurine/planter, Audrey, 7"..$65.00
Figurine/planter, Hattie, 7½"......................................$45.00
Figurine/planter, Lou $55.00
Piggy bank, For My Mink Coat, 4½x6¾".................$130.00
Planter, Danny, blond tipping hat, blue, brown & white, 9" $32.00
Planter, skunk, wall hanging, 5x3½"............................$35.00
Shakers, skunk, silver label, 4", pr, from $100 to......$125.00

Depression Glass

Since the early '60s, this has been a very active area of collecting. Interest is still very strong, and although values have long been established, except for some of the rarer items, Depression glass is still relatively inexpensive. Some of the patterns and colors that were entirely avoided by the early wave of collectors are now becoming popular, and it's very easy to reassemble a nice table setting of one of these lines today.

Most of this glass was manufactured during the Depression years. It was inexpensive, mass-produced, and available in a wide assortment of colors. The same type of glassware was still being made to some extent during the '50s and '60s, and today the term 'Depression glass' has been expanded to include the later patterns as well.

Some things have been reproduced, and the slight variation in patterns and colors can be very difficult to detect. For instance, the Sharon butter dish has been reissued in original colors of pink and green (as well as others that were not original); and several pieces of Cherry Blossom, Madrid, Avocado, Mayfair, and Miss America have also been reproduced. Some pieces you'll see in 'antique' malls and flea markets today have been recently made in dark uncharacteristic 'carnival' colors, which, of course, are easy to spot.

For further study, Gene Florence has written several informative books on the subject, and we recommend them all: *The Pocket Guide to Depression Glass*, *The Collector's Encyclopedia of Depression Glass*, and *Very Rare Glassware of the Depression Years* (Collector Books).

Publication: *Depression Glass Daze*
Teri Steel, Editor/Publisher
Box 57, Otisville, MI 48463; 810-631-4593. The nation's marketplace for glass, china, and pottery

Adam, green, ashtray, 4½" $25.00
Adam, green, bowl, handle, 9" $27.50
Adam, green, bowl, w/lid, 9" $90.00
Adam, green, cup $25.00
Adam, green, plate, grill; 9" $25.00
Adam, pink, butter dish, w/lid $395.00
Adam, pink, candy jar, w/lid, 2½" $100.00
Adam, pink, tumbler, 4½" $40.00
Adam, pink or green, bowl, 7¾" $30.00
Adam, pink or green, plate, sherbet; 6" $11.00
Adam, pink or green, saucer, square, 6" $6.00
American Pioneer, crystal, pink or green, bowl, handle, 5" $20.00
American Pioneer, crystal, pink or green, coaster, 3½"...$35.00
American Pioneer, crystal, pink or green, cup $15.00
American Pioneer, crystal, pink or green, pilsner, 11-oz, 5¾" $150.00
American Pioneer, crystal or pink, candy jar, w/lid, 1½-lb...$100.00
American Pioneer, crystal or pink, plate, 6" $12.50

American Pioneer, crystal or pink, sugar bowl, 3½"...$20.00
American Pioneer, green, candlesticks, 6½", pr........$125.00
American Pioneer, green, creamer, 2¾".......................$20.00
American Pioneer, green, goblet, water; 8-oz, 6"........$57.50
American Pioneer, green, lamp, w/metal pole............$75.00
American Pioneer, green, saucer $5.00
American Pioneer, green, vase, round, 9" $235.00
American Pioneer, pink, plate, bread & butter.............$6.00
American Pioneer, pink, sugar bowl, open, footed $12.00
American Sweetheart, blue, bowl, console; 18".....$1,250.00
American Sweetheart, cremax, lamp shade..............$495.00
American Sweetheart, monax, bowl, soup; flat, 9½"..$90.00
American Sweetheart, monax, plate, salver; 12"........$22.00
American Sweetheart, pink, bowl, berry; flat, 3¾" $85.00
American Sweetheart, pink, pitcher, 80-oz, 8"..........$750.00
American Sweetheart, pink, tumbler, 9-oz, 4¼" $90.00
American Sweetheart, pink or monax, tidbit, 2-tier, 8" & 12" $60.00
American Sweetheart, red, plate, salver; 12" $185.00
American Sweetheart, smoke & other trims, sugar bowl, open, footed...$100.00

Anniversary, dinner plate, iridescent, 10", $6.00.

Aunt Polly, blue, bowl, berry; 4¾"..............................$18.00
Aunt Polly, blue, butter dish, w/lid...........................$225.00
Aunt Polly, blue, creamer $55.00
Aunt Polly, blue, plate, luncheon; 8" $20.00
Aunt Polly, blue, vase, footed, 6½"............................$55.00
Aunt Polly, green or iridescent, bowl, pickle; w/handles, oval, 7¼"...$15.00
Aunt Polly, green or iridescent, sherbet.....................$10.00
Aurora, cobalt or pink, bowl, deep, 4½"....................$60.00
Aurora, cobalt or pink, creamer, 4½".........................$25.00
Aurora, cobalt or pink, plate, 6½"..............................$12.50
Aurora, cobalt or pink, tumbler, 10-oz, 4¾"..............$27.50
Avocado, crystal, bowl, 2-handle, 5¼".......................$10.00
Avocado, crystal, tumbler..$35.00
Avocado, green, bowl, 3¼" deep, 9½" $175.00
Avocado, green, pitcher, 64-oz.................................$1,200.00
Avocado, green, sherbet..$65.00

Avocado, pink, bowl, salad; 7½".................................$45.00

Avocado, pink, cup, footed, 2 styles, ea......................$35.00

Avocado, pink, plate, luncheon; 8¼"..........................$17.00

Beaded Block, crystal, pink, green or amber, bowl, jelly; 2-handled, 5"...$20.00

Beaded Block, crystal, pink, green or amber, bowl, round, 6½"..$25.00

Beaded Block, crystal, pink, green or amber, candy jar, pear shaped..$295.00

Beaded Block, crystal, pink, green or amber, sugar bowl..$25.00

Beaded Block, ice blue, bowl, flared, round, 7¼"......$40.00

Beaded Block, milk white, plate, square, 7¾"...........$30.00

Beaded Block, red, bowl, handle, 5½"........................$32.00

Block Optic, green, bowl, salad; 7¼"........................$175.00

Block Optic, green, bowl, 1⅜x4¼"................................$9.00

Block Optic, green, butter dish, w/lid.........................$50.00

Block Optic, green, sherbet, 5½-oz, 3¼"......................$6.00

Block Optic, green, tumbler, 3"...................................$55.00

Block Optic, green, yellow or pink, sugar bowl, 3 styles, ea...$12.50

Block Optic, green or pink, comport, mayonnaise; 4" W..$90.00

Block Optic, green or pink, goblet, winc; 4½"...........$40.00

Block Optic, green or pink, plate, luncheon; 8"...........$7.00

Block Optic, green or yellow, plate, 12¾"..................$30.00

Block Optic, pink, bowl, console; rolled edge, 11¾".$75.00

Block Optic, pink, pitcher, bulbous, 54-oz, 7⅝".......$135.00

Block Optic, pink, tumbler, flat, 11-oz......................$18.00

Block Optic, yellow, candy jar, w/lid, 2¼".................$75.00

Block Optic, yellow, cup, 4 styles, ea..........................$8.00

Block Optic, yellow, goblet, thin, 9-oz, 7¼".............$40.00

Bowknot, green, bowl, cereal; 5½".............................$35.00

Bowknot, green, plate, salad; 7".................................$15.00

Bowknot, green, tumbler, 10-oz, 5"............................$25.00

Cameo, crystal or platinum, decanter, w/stopper, 10"..$225.00

Cameo, crystal or platinum, tumbler, water; 9-oz, 4"....$9.00

Cameo, green, bowl, cream soup; 4¾"........................$150.00

Cameo, green, candy jar, w/lid, low, 4".......................$90.00

Cameo, green, cookie jar, w/lid..................................$55.00

Cameo, green, creamer, 4¼".......................................$28.00

Cameo, green, ice bowl, 5½x3"..................................$185.00

Cameo, green, jam jar, w/lid......................................$185.00

Cameo, green, plate, grill; w/closed handles, 10½"....$75.00

Cameo, green, salt & pepper shakers, footed, pr.......$70.00

Cameo, green, vase, 8"..$40.00

Cameo, green or pink, goblet, wine; 3½".................$900.00

Cameo, pink, bowl, rimmed soup; 9".........................$135.00

Cameo, pink, cake plate, flat, 10½"...........................$175.00

Cameo, pink, cup, 2 styles, ea....................................$85.00

Cameo, pink, plate, dinner; 9½".................................$85.00

Cameo, yellow, bowl, console; 3-legs, 11"................$110.00

Cameo, yellow, plate, grill; 10½"..................................$8.00

Cameo, yellow, plate, sherbet; 6".................................$2.50

Cameo, yellow, saucer/sherbet plate, 6".......................$2.50

Cameo, yellow, tumbler, footed, 9-oz, 5"...................$17.50

Cherry Blossom, delphite, creamer............................$20.00

Cherry Blossom, delphite, sherbet.............................$16.00

Cherry Blossom, green, bowl, 2-handled, 9".............$75.00

Cherry Blossom, green, mug, 7-oz............................$200.00

Cherry Blossom, green or delphite, plate, sherbet; 6".$10.00

Cherry Blossom, pink, bowl, berry; 4¾"....................$20.00

Cherry Blossom, pink, tumbler, pattern at top, flat, 4-oz, 3½"..$22.00

Cherry Blossom, pink or green, pitcher, pattern at top, flat, 42-oz, 8"..$60.00

Cherry Blossom, pink or green, platter, divided, 13"..$70.00

Cherryberry, crystal or iridescent, bowl, berry; 4".........$6.50

Cherryberry, crystal or iridescent, comport, 5¾".........$18.00

Cherryberry, crystal or iridescent, plate, sherbet; 6".....$6.00

Cherryberry, pink or green, bowl, berry; deep, 7½"..$28.00

Cherryberry, pink or green, olive dish, handle, 5".....$22.00

Cherryberry, pink or green, sugar bowl, open, sm....$22.50

Chinex Classic, browntone or plain ivory, bowl, cereal; 5¾"...$5.50

Chinex Classic, browntone or plain ivory, butter dish, w/lid..$55.00

Chinex Classic, browntone or plain ivory, plate, sherbet; 6¼"...$2.50

Chinex Classic, browntone or plain ivory, saucer........$2.00

Chinex Classic, castle decorated, bowl, vegetable; 9" $40.00

Chinex Classic, castle decorated, cup.........................$15.00

Chinex Classic, castle decorated, plate, cake/sandwich; 11½"..$28.00

Chinex Classic, decal decorated, bowl, vegetable; 7"...$25.00

Chinex Classic, decal decorated, butter dish, w/lid....$75.00

Chinex Classic, decal decorated, plate, dinner; 9¾".....$8.50

Chinex Classic, decal decorated, sherbet, low footed...$11.00

Circle, green, bowl, 4½"..$8.00

Circle, green, bowl, 8"...$18.00

Circle, green, pitcher, 60-oz.......................................$75.00

Circle, green, sugar bowl, w/lid....................................$7.00

Circle, green, tumbler, tea; 10-oz, 5".........................$18.00

Circle, pink, creamer...$20.00

Circle, pink, plate, sherbet/saucer; 6"..........................$5.00

Circle, pink, saucer, w/cup ring....................................$3.00

Cloverleaf, black, cup..$20.00

Cloverleaf, green, bowl, salad; deep, 7"......................$55.00

Cloverleaf, green, salt & pepper shakers, pr..............$40.00

Cloverleaf, pink, green & yellow, bowl, dessert; 4"....$35.00

Cloverleaf, pink, plate, luncheon; 8"..........................$11.00

Cloverleaf, yellow, candy dish, w/lid........................$115.00

Cloverleaf, yellow, sherbet, footed, 3".......................$14.00

Cloverleaf, yellow or black, sugar bowl, w/lid, footed, 3⅝"..$20.00

Colonial, crystal, bowl, berry; lg, 9"..........................$25.00

Colonial, crystal, plate, sherbet; 6"..............................$3.00

Colonial, crystal, stem, water; 8½-oz, 5¾".................$25.00

Colonial, crystal, tumbler, footed, 10-oz, 5¼"...........$27.50

Colonial, green, stem, cocktail; 3-oz, 4".....................$25.00

Colonial, green, tumbler, lemonade; 15-oz.................$75.00

Colonial, pink, bowl, berry; 3¾".................................$52.50

Colonial, pink, butter dish, w/lid..............................$700.00

Colonial, pink, sherbet, 3"..$25.00

Colonial, pink, tumbler, juice; 5-oz, 3".......................$22.00

Colonial, pink or green, bowl, cream soup; 4½"........**$75.00**
Colonial, white, cup................**$8.00**
Colonial Block, crystal, bowl, 4"................**$4.00**
Colonial Block, crystal, creamer................**$6.00**
Colonial Block, pink or green, butter dish, w/lid.......**$45.00**
Colonial Block, pink or green, sherbet................**$6.00**
Colonial Block, white, sugar bowl, w/lid................**$10.00**
Colonial Fluted, green, bowl, berry; lg, 7½".............**$22.00**
Colonial Fluted, green, bowl, berry; 4"................**$11.00**
Colonial Fluted, green, plate, sherbet; 6"................**$3.00**
Colonial Fluted, green, sherbet................**$7.00**
Columbia, crystal, bowl, cereal; 5"................**$18.00**
Columbia, crystal, bowl, ruffled edge, 10½".............**$20.00**
Columbia, crystal, butter dish, w/lid................**$20.00**
Columbia, crystal, tumbler, water; 9-oz................**$30.00**
Columbia, pink, plate, bread & butter; 6"................**$15.00**
Columbia, pink, saucer................**$10.00**
Coronation, green, sherbet................**$75.00**
Coronation, pink, plate, luncheon; 8½"................**$4.50**
Coronation, pink or green, bowl, no handles, 8" **$175.00**
Coronation, pink or royal ruby, bowl, berry; handled,
    4¼"................**$7.00**
Coronation, royal ruby, bowl, nappy; handled, 6½" ..**$18.00**
Cremax, blue or decorated, creamer................**$10.00**
Cremax, blue or decorated, saucer, demitasse.............**$10.00**
Cremax, bowl, cereal; 5¾"................**$3.50**
Cremax, plate, dinner; 9¾"................**$4.50**
Cube, green, plate, luncheon; 8"................**$11.00**
Cube, pink, bowl, dessert; 4½"................**$6.50**
Cube, pink, butter dish, w/lid................**$70.00**
Cube, pink, creamer, 2⅝"................**$2.00**
Cube, pink, tumbler, 9-oz, 4"................**$72.50**
Diana, amber, bowl, console fruit; 11"................**$18.00**
Diana, amber, plate, 9½"................**$9.00**
Diana, crystal, ashtray, 3½"................**$2.50**
Diana, crystal, creamer, oval................**$8.00**
Diana, crystal, salt & pepper shakers, pr................**$30.00**
Diana, crystal or amber, sugar bowl, oval, open.........**$8.00**
Diana, pink, bowl, salad; 9"................**$22.00**
Diana, pink, plate, bread & butter; 6"................**$5.00**
Diana, pink, sherbet................**$12.00**
Dogwood, green, bowl, fruit; 10¼"................**$275.00**
Dogwood, green, cup, thin................**$40.00**
Dogwood, green, sherbet, low footed................**$115.00**
Dogwood, monax or cremax, plate, bread & butter; 6".......**$21.00**
Dogwood, monax or cremax, plate, cake; solid foot, 13"..**$195.00**
Dogwood, pink, bowl, cereal; 5½"................**$33.00**
Dogwood, pink, creamer, flat, thin, 2½"................**$20.00**
Dogwood, pink, plate, salver; 12"................**$35.00**
Dogwood, pink, tumbler, molded band................**$25.00**
Doric, delphite, bowl, berry; lg, 8¼"................**$135.00**
Doric, delphite, sherbet, footed................**$9.00**
Doric, green, bowl, cereal; 5½"................**$85.00**
Doric, green, bowl, vegetable; oval, 9"................**$45.00**
Doric, green, candy dish, 3-part................**$10.00**
Doric, green, plate, grill; 9"................**$25.00**
Doric, green, saucer................**$4.50**

Doric, green, tumbler, footed, 10-oz, 4"................**$90.00**
Doric, pink, butter dish, w/lid................**$70.00**
Doric, pink, cup................**$10.00**
Doric, pink, plate, sherbet; 6"................**$6.00**
Doric, pink, relish tray, 4x8"................**$22.00**
Doric, pink, tray, handled, 10"................**$18.00**
Doric, pink or green, bowl, berry; 4½"................**$11.00**
Doric & Pansy, green or teal, bowl, berry; 4½".........**$22.00**
Doric & Pansy, green or teal, butter dish, w/lid.......**$450.00**
Doric & Pansy, green or teal, plate, dinner; 9"..........**$38.00**
Doric & Pansy, green or teal, tray, handled, 10".......**$33.00**
Doric & Pansy, green or teal, tumbler, 10-oz, 4¼"...**$595.00**
Doric & Pansy, pink or crystal, bowl, handled, 9"......**$20.00**
Doric & Pansy, pink or crystal, cup................**$12.00**
Doric & Pansy, pink or crystal, saucer................**$4.00**
Floral, delphite, creamer, flat................**$77.50**
Floral, delphite, sherbet................**$85.00**
Floral, green, butter dish, w/lid................**$90.00**
Floral, green, plate, salad; 8"................**$16.00**
Floral, green, tray, for dresser set, oval, 9¼"...........**$195.00**
Floral, pink, bowl, berry; 4"................**$20.00**
Floral, pink, ice tub, oval, 3½"................**$850.00**
Floral, pink, tumbler, water; footed, 7-oz, 4¾"..........**$22.00**
Floral & Diamond Band, green, butter dish, w/lid...**$130.00**
Floral & Diamond Band, pink, bowl, berry; 4½"........**$10.00**
Floral & Diamond Band, pink, creamer, 4¾".............**$18.00**
Floral & Diamond Band, pink, tumbler, iced tea; 5" ..**$40.00**
Floral & Diamond Band, pink or green, plate, luncheon;
    8"................**$45.00**
Floral & Diamond Band, pink or green, tumbler, water; 4".**$25.00**
Florentine No 1, cobalt, creamer, ruffled................**$65.00**
Florentine No 1, cobalt, sugar bowl, ruffled.............**$60.00**
Florentine No 1, crystal or green, plate, dinner; 10"...**$18.00**
Florentine No 1, yellow or pink, bowl, cereal; 6".......**$30.00**
Florentine No 1, yellow or pink, butter dish, w/lid .**$160.00**
Florentine No 1, yellow or pink, saucer................**$4.00**
Florentine No 1, yellow or pink, tumbler, water; footed, 10-
    oz, 4¾"................**$24.00**
Florentine No 2, cobalt blue, comport, ruffled, 3½"...**$65.00**
Florentine No 2, crystal or green, bowl, berry; 4½"...**$14.00**
Florentine No 2, crystal or green, butter dish, w/lid ..**$110.00**
Florentine No 2, crystal or green, plate, sherbet; 6" **$4.00**
Florentine No 2, crystal or green, tumbler, juice; 5-oz,
    3⅜"................**$14.00**
Florentine No 2, pink, bowl, berry; lg, 8"................**$32.00**
Florentine No 2, pink, candy dish, w/lid................**$145.00**
Florentine No 2, pink, pitcher, 48-oz, 7½"................**$135.00**
Florentine No 2, yellow, ashtray/coaster, 5½"...........**$38.00**
Florentine No 2, yellow, bowl, 5½"................**$42.00**
Florentine No 2, yellow, plate, grill; 10¼"................**$18.00**
Florentine No 2, yellow, platter, oval, 11"................**$22.50**
Florentine No 2, yellow, salt & pepper shakers, pr....**$50.00**
Florentine No 2, yellow, tumbler, footed, 5-oz, 3¼" ..**$17.50**
Flower Garden w/Butterflies, amber or crystal, ashtray,
    w/match-pack holders................**$165.00**
Flower Garden w/Butterflies, amber or crystal, comport,
    7¼x8¼"................**$60.00**

Flower Garden w/Butterflies, amber or crystal, tumbler, 7½-oz **$175.00**

Flower Garden w/Butterflies, black, bowl, flying saucer shape, w/lid, 7¼" **$375.00**

Flower Garden w/Butterflies, black, cheese & cracker, footed, 5⅜x10" **$325.00**

Flower Garden w/Butterflies, blue or canary yellow, plate, 2 styles, 8", ea **$25.00**

Flower Garden w/Butterflies, blue or canary yellow, sandwich server, center handle **$110.00**

Flower Garden w/Butterflies, cologne bottle, w/stopper, 7½" **$350.00**

Flower Garden w/Butterflies, pink, green or blue-green, candy dish, w/lid, cone shape, 7½".....**$130.00**

Flower Garden w/Butterflies, pink, green or blue-green, comport, 4¾x10¼" **$65.00**

Flower Garden w/Butterflies, pink, green or blue-green, powder jar, flat, 3½" **$80.00**

Fortune, pink or crystal, bowl, berry; 4"....................**$8.00**

Fortune, pink or crystal, bowl, rolled edge, 5¼" **$18.00**

Fortune, pink or crystal, plate, sherbet; 6"..................**$5.00**

Fortune, pink or crystal, tumbler, juice; 5-oz, 3½"......**$10.00**

Fruits, green, tumbler, juice; 3½".............................**$60.00**

Fruits, green or pink, plate, luncheon; 8"..................**$10.00**

Fruits, pink, bowl, berry; 8"....................................**$45.00**

Fruits, pink, tumbler, combination of fruits, 4" **$22.00**

Georgian, green, bowl, berry; 4½"...........................**$10.00**

Georgian, green, butter dish, w/lid..........................**$85.00**

Georgian, green, creamer, footed, 3".......................**$12.00**

Georgian, green, plate, dinner; 9¼".........................**$25.00**

Georgian, green, saucer..**$3.00**

Georgian, green, tumbler, flat, 9-oz, 4"....................**$65.00**

Georgian, green, vegetable; oval, 9" **$62.00**

Hex Optic, pink or green, bowl, mixing; 7¼" **$12.00**

Hex Optic, pink or green, bowl, mixing; 9"................**$22.00**

Hex Optic, pink or green, bucket reamer **$55.00**

Hex Optic, pink or green, plate, luncheon; 8".............**$5.50**

Hex Optic, pink or green, salt & pepper shakers, pr.**$27.50**

Hex Optic, pink or green, tumbler, 9-oz, 3¾".............**$4.50**

Hobnail, crystal, goblet, water; 10-oz........................**$8.00**

Hobnail, crystal, tumbler, cordial; footed, 5-oz **$6.00**

Hobnail, crystal, tumbler, juice; 5-oz........................**$4.00**

Hobnail, crystal w/red trim, pitcher, 67-oz................**$30.00**

Hobnail, pink, cup...**$6.00**

Hobnail, pink, saucer/sherbet plate **$2.50**

Homespun, pink or crystal, bowl, berry; lg, 8¼".......**$24.00**

Homespun, pink or crystal, cup...............................**$11.00**

Homespun, pink or crystal, tumbler, no band, 9-oz, 4⅜"...**$22.00**

Indiana Custard, bowl, berry; lg, 1¾" deep, 9"..........**$35.00**

Indiana Custard, bowl, berry; 6½" **$27.00**

Indiana Custard, butter dish, w/lid...........................**$63.00**

Indiana Custard, creamer **$16.00**

Indiana Custard, plate, dinner; 9¾"..........................**$30.00**

Indiana Custard, plate, salad; 7½"............................**$18.00**

Iris, crystal, bowl, berry; beaded edge, 4½"...............**$45.00**

Iris, crystal, goblet, 8-oz, 5½"..................................**$26.00**

Iris, crystal or iridescent, creamer, footed..................**$12.00**

Iris, iridescent, bowl, soup; 7½"...............................**$60.00**

Iris, iridescent, vase, 9"...**$25.00**

Iris, transparent green or pink, bowl, salad; ruffled, 9½"..**$150.00**

Jubilee, pink, bowl, 3-footed, 5⅛x8" **$250.00**

Jubilee, pink, cup...**$40.00**

Jubilee, pink or yellow, vase, 13" **$350.00**

Jubilee, yellow, bowl, 3-footed, 13"........................**$225.00**

Jubilee, yellow, plate, sandwich; handled, 13½" **$50.00**

Jubilee, yellow, tumbler, juice; footed, 6-oz, 5" **$95.00**

Laced Edge, opalescent, basket bowl **$225.00**

Laced Edge, opalescent, bowl, oval, 11" **$150.00**

Laced Edge, opalescent, bowl, 5⅞"..........................**$37.50**

Laced Edge, opalescent, plate, salad; 8" **$35.00**

Laced Edge, opalescent, saucer................................**$15.00**

Lake Como, white w/blue scene, bowl, vegetable; 9¾"...**$55.00**

Lake Como, white w/blue scene, cup, St Denis **$30.00**

Lake Como, white w/blue scene, platter, 11".............**$75.00**

Lake Como, white w/blue scene, sugar bowl, footed ..**$32.50**

Laurel, blue, bowl, 3-legged, 10½"...........................**$70.00**

Laurel, ivory, bowl, soup; 7⅞"..................................**$35.00**

Laurel, ivory, creamer, short **$10.00**

Laurel, ivory, plate, grill; round or scalloped, 9⅛" **$15.00**

Laurel, ivory, sherbet/champagne, 5".......................**$50.00**

Laurel, white opalescent or green, bowl, berry; 4¾"..**$14.00**

Laurel, white opalescent or green, plate, sherbet; 6"..**$12.00**

Laurel, white opalescent or green, tumbler, flat, 9-oz, 4½"...**$60.00**

Lincoln Inn, blue or red, ashtray..............................**$17.50**

Lincoln Inn, blue or red, creamer **$22.50**

Lincoln Inn, blue or red, sherbet, cone shape, 4½" ...**$17.00**

Lincoln Inn, blue or red, tumbler, footed, 9-oz..........**$30.00**

Lincoln Inn, blue or red, vase, footed, 12"...............**$195.00**

Lincoln Inn, colors other than blue or red, bowl, crimped, 6"..**$8.50**

Lincoln Inn, colors other than blue or red, plate, 8"..**$10.00**

Lincoln Inn, colors other than blue or red, tumbler, footed, 5-oz..**$11.00**

Little Jewel, colors, bowl, 6½" **$15.00**

Little Jewel, colors, jelly, handled, 4½"......................**$12.00**

Little Jewel, crystal, bowl, honey; 5½" square............**$10.00**

Hobnail, pitcher, crystal, 67-ounce, $25.00; Decanter, crystal, with stopper, 32-ounce, $30.00; Luncheon plate, crystal with red trim, 8½", $5.00. (Photo courtesy Gene Florence)

Little Jewel, crystal, creamer **$8.00**
Little Jewel, crystal, pickle dish, 6½"........................**$12.50**
Lorain, crystal or green, bowl, cereal; 6" **$47.50**
Lorain, crystal or green, plate, sherbet, 5½"..............**$10.00**
Lorain, crystal or green, relish, 4-part, 8"..................**$20.00**
Lorain, crystal or green, sherbet, footed...................**$25.00**
Lorain, yellow, bowl, vegetable; oval, 9¾"................**$65.00**
Lorain, yellow, plate, luncheon; 8⅜" **$30.00**
Lorain, yellow, tumbler, footed, 9-oz, 4¾" **$35.00**
Madrid, amber, ashtray, 6" square............................**$225.00**
Madrid, amber, creamer, footed..............................**$7.00**
Madrid, amber, tumbler, 2 styles, 12-oz, 5½" **$22.00**
Madrid, amber or green, hot dish coaster, w/indent ..**$55.00**
Madrid, blue, bowl, vegetable; oval, 10" **$40.00**
Madrid, blue, platter, oval, 11½" **$24.00**
Madrid, green, bowl, salad; 8"................................**$17.50**
Madrid, green, sherbet, 2 styles, ea..........................**$12.00**
Madrid, pink, bowl, sauce; 5"..................................**$8.00**
Madrid, pink, plate, sherbet; 6"..............................**$3.50**
Manhattan, crystal, ashtray, 4" dia...........................**$12.00**
Manhattan, crystal, bowl, fruit; open handle, 9½" **$35.00**
Manhattan, crystal, plate, sandwich; 14" **$25.00**
Manhattan, crystal, relish tray, 4-part, 14"..................**$30.00**
Manhattan, crystal, vase, 8".....................................**$25.00**
Manhattan, pink, bowl, berry; handled, 5⅜"..............**$20.00**
Manhattan, pink, comport, 5¾".................................**$38.00**
Manhattan, pink, pitcher, tilted, 80-oz **$70.00**

Manhattan, pink, tumbler, 5¼", $22.00.

Mayfair (Federal), amber, bowl, sauce; 5" **$9.00**
Mayfair (Federal), amber, tumbler, 9-oz, 4½"..............**$30.00**
Mayfair (Federal), amber or green, plate, dinner; 9½"..**$14.00**
Mayfair (Federal), amber or green, platter, oval, 12" **$4.00**
Mayfair (Federal), crystal, bowl, cereal; 6"..................**$9.50**
Mayfair (Federal), crystal, plate, salad; 6¾"..................**$4.50**
Mayfair (Federal), green, creamer, footed...................**$16.00**
Mayfair (Open Rose), blue, bowl, vegetable; 10" **$80.00**
Mayfair (Open Rose), blue, bowl, vegetable; w/lid, 10"..**$150.00**
Mayfair (Open Rose), blue, pitcher, 37-oz, 6"...........**$165.00**
Mayfair (Open Rose), blue, tumbler, iced tea; 13½-oz, 5¼"..**$275.00**

Mayfair (Open Rose), crystal, platter, divided, open handles, oval, 12"..**$12.50**
Mayfair (Open Rose), green, candy dish, w/lid........**$595.00**
Mayfair (Open Rose), green, vase, sweet pea..........**$295.00**
Mayfair (Open Rose), green or yellow, butter dish, w/lid..**$1,300.00**
Mayfair (Open Rose), green or yellow, creamer, footed..**$225.00**
Mayfair (Open Rose), pink, bowl, cereal; 5½"............**$30.00**
Mayfair (Open Rose), pink, goblet, wine; 3-oz, 4½" ..**$110.00**
Mayfair (Open Rose), pink, sugar bowl, w/lid......**$1,535.00**
Mayfair (Open Rose), yellow, saucer w/cup ring.....**$150.00**
Miss America, crystal, bowl, cereal; 6¼"....................**$11.00**
MIss America, crystal, goblet, juice; 5-oz, 4¾" **$27.00**
Miss America, crystal, salt & pepper shakers, pr........**$33.00**
Miss America, green, cup..**$14.00**
Miss America, green, plate, 6¾" **$9.00**
Miss America, pink, bowl, fruit; straight sides, deep, 8¾"..**$80.00**
Miss America, pink, cake plate, footed, 12" **$60.00**
Miss America, pink, creamer, footed.........................**$22.00**
Miss America, pink, pitcher, 65-oz, 8".......................**$135.00**
Miss America, royal ruby, bowl, shallow, 11" **$900.00**
Moderntone, amethyst, cup, no handle **$15.00**
Moderntone, amethyst, custard................................**$15.00**
Moderntone, amethyst, sherbet **$12.00**
Moderntone, cobalt, ashtray, match holder in center, 7¾"..**$165.00**
Moderntone, cobalt, butter dish, w/metal lid...........**$100.00**
Moderntone, cobalt, plate, dinner; 8⅞" **$21.00**
Moderntone, cobalt, tumbler, 12-oz.........................**$125.00**
Moderntone, cobalt or amethyst, bowl, cereal; 6½" ..**$75.00**
Moondrops, blue or red, ashtray................................**$32.00**
Moondrops, blue or red, bowl, celery; boat shape, 11" .**$32.00**
Moondrops, blue or red, candlesticks, metal stem, 8½", pr..**$45.00**
Moondrops, blue or red, decanter, lg, 11¼" **$100.00**
Moondrops, blue or red, mayonnaise, 5¼" **$65.00**
Moondrops, blue or red, platter, oval, 12"..................**$45.00**
Moondrops, blue or red, vase, ruffled top, flat, 7¾" ..**$60.00**
Moondrops, colors other than blue or red, bowl, pickle; 7½"..**$20.00**
Moondrops, colors other than blue or red, butter dish, w/lid..**$275.00**
Moondrops, colors other than blue or red, creamer, miniature, 2¾"..**$11.00**
Moondrops, colors other than blue or red, goblet, 8-oz, 5¾"..**$20.00**
Moondrops, colors other than blue or red, pitcher, no ice lip, lg, 53-oz, 8⅛"..**$125.00**
Moondrops, colors other than blue or red, tumbler, juice; footed, 3-oz, 3¼" **$11.00**
Mt Pleasant, amethyst, black or cobalt, bowl, 2-handled, square or scalloped, 8"..**$35.00**
Mt Pleasant, amethyst, black or cobalt, cup **$14.00**
Mt Pleasant, amethyst, black or cobalt, plate, 2-handled, 8"..**$18.00**
Mt Pleasant, amethyst, black or cobalt, tumbler, footed ..**$25.00**
Mt Pleasant, pink or green, bowl, rose, 4" opening...**$18.00**
Mt Pleasant, pink or green, candlesticks, single, pr....**$20.00**

Mt Pleasant, pink or green, mayonnaise, 3-footed, 5½" ..**$18.00**

Mt Pleasant, pink or green, salt & pepper shakers, 2 styles, pr............**$24.00**

New Century, any color, tumbler, 5-oz, 3½" **$15.00**

New Century, green or crystal, ashtray/coaster, 5⅜" ..**$28.00**

New Century, green or crystal, goblet, wine; 2½-oz ..**$30.00**

New Century, green or crystal, plate, dinner; 10"......**$18.00**

New Century, green or crystal, plate, sherbet; 6".........**$5.00**

New Century, green or crystal, tumbler, footed, 5-oz, 4" ..**$20.00**

New Century, tumbler, green, footed, nine-ounce, 4⅞", $22.00.
(Photo courtesy Gene Florence)

New Century, green or crystal, tumbler, 5-oz, 3½"....**$15.00**

New Century, pink, cobalt or amethyst, cup.............**$20.00**

New Century, pink, cobalt or amethyst, pitcher, w/or w/out ice lip, 80-oz, 8"....................**$42.00**

New Century, pink, cobalt or amethyst, saucer **$7.50**

New Century, pink, cobalt or amethyst, tumbler, 10-oz, 5"....................**$33.00**

Newport, amethyst, cup **$10.00**

Newport, cobalt, bowl, berry; 4¾"...............**$22.00**

Newport, cobalt, plate, sandwich; 11¾" **$42.00**

Newport, cobalt, tumbler, 9-oz, 4½" **$42.00**

Newport, cobalt or amethyst, saucer.....................**$5.00**

No 610 Pyramid, crystal, bowl, berry; 4¾" **$11.00**

No 610 Pyramid, crystal, tumbler, footed, 11-oz **$75.00**

No 610 Pyramid, crystal or green, tumbler, footed, 11-oz..**$75.00**

No 610 Pyramid, green, pitcher..................**$225.00**

No 610 Pyramid, pink, creamer.....................**$35.00**

No 610 Pyramid, yellow, tray, for creamer & sugar bowl..**$55.00**

No 612 Horseshoe, green, bowl, berry; 4½" **$28.00**

No 612 Horseshoe, green, relish, footed, 3-part **$25.00**

No 612 Horseshoe, green or yellow, tumbler, footed, 9-oz **$30.00**

No 612 Horseshoe, yellow, bowl, vegetable; oval, 10½" ..**$33.00**

No 612 Horseshoe, yellow, plate, sherbet, 6"...............**$9.00**

No 616 Vernon, crystal, plate, luncheon; 8" **$6.00**

No 616 Vernon, crystal, tumbler, footed, 5".................**$15.00**

No 616 Vernon, green or yellow, creamer, footed......**$27.50**

No 616 Vernon, green or yellow, saucer **$4.00**

No 618 Pineapple & Floral, amber or red, comport, diamond shape..................................**$8.00**

No 618 Pineapple & Floral, amber or red, sugar bowl, diamond shape..................................**$10.00**

No 618 Pineapple & Floral, crystal, amber or red, plate, salad; 8⅜"..................................**$8.50**

No 618 Pineapple & Floral, crystal, ashtray, 4½" **$17.50**

No 618 Pineapple & Floral, crystal, plate, sandwich; 11½"..................................**$17.50**

Normandie, amber, bowl, berry; 5" **$9.00**

Normandie, amber, salt & pepper shakers, pr **$50.00**

Normandie, amber, tumbler, iced tea; 12-oz, 5"..........**$40.00**

Normandie, iridescent, plate, sherbet; 6" **$3.00**

Normandie, pink, creamer, footed **$14.00**

Normandie, pink, plate, dinner; 11".........................**$115.00**

Normandie, pink, sherbet...**$9.00**

Normandie, pink, tumbler, juice; 5-oz, 4" **$90.00**

Old Cafe, crystal or pink, bowl, berry; 3¾"....................**$9.00**

Old Cafe, crystal or pink, bowl, cereal; 5½" **$20.00**

Old Cafe, crystal or pink, cup **$10.00**

Old Cafe, crystal or pink, pitcher, 80-oz **$125.00**

Old Cafe, crystal or pink, tumbler, water; 4"............**$20.00**

Old Colony, frosted, cookie jar, w/lid.......................**$50.00**

Old Colony, pink, bowl, cereal; 6⅜" **$27.00**

Old Colony, pink, bowl, plain, 9½" **$28.00**

Old Colony, pink, butter dish, w/lid, 7¾".................**$67.50**

Old Colony, pink, plate, dinner; 10½"......................**$26.00**

Old Colony, pink, plate, solid lace, 13" **$85.00**

Old Colony, pink, sherbet; footed **$115.00**

Old English, pink, green or amber, candy dish, flat, w/lid **$50.00**

Old English, pink, green or amber, creamer **$17.50**

Old English, pink, green or amber, pitcher, w/lid....**$125.00**

Old English, pink, green or amber, sugar bowl, w/lid ...**$52.50**

Old English, pink, green or amber, vase, footed, 12".**$60.00**

Old Englixh, pink, green or amber, bowl, flat, 4".......**$20.00**

Orchid, crystal or green, creamer..............................**$50.00**

Orchid, red, black or blue, cake stand, square, 2" H .**$150.00**

Orchid, red, black or blue, vase, 8"..........................**$275.00**

Orchid, yellow, bowl, square, 4⅞"............................**$25.00**

Ovide, Art Deco, sugar bowl, open **$95.00**

Ovide, black, candy dish, w/lid **$45.00**

Ovide, decorated white, plate, dinner; 9" **$20.00**

Ovide, green, plate, sherbet; 6" **$2.50**

Oyster & Pearl, crystal or pink, bowl, fruit; deep, 10½" ..**$25.00**

Oyster & Pearl, crystal or pink, candle holders, 3½", pr.**$35.00**

Parrot, amber, butter dish, w/lid **$1,300.00**

Parrot, amber, platter, oblong, 11¼" **$75.00**

Parrot, green, bowl, berry; 5" **$28.00**

Parrot, green, hot plate, round, 5" **$995.00**

Parrot, green, plate, dinner; 9"...................................**$55.00**

Parrot, green or amber, saucer **$15.00**

Patrician, amber, crystal, pink or green, tumbler, 5-oz, 4"..**$33.00**

Patrician, amber, crystal or pink, plate, salad; 7½" **$15.00**

Patrician, amber or crystal, bowl, cream soup; 4¾" ...**$18.00**

Patrician, green, pitcher, molded handle, 75-oz, 8" **$145.00**

Patrician, pink, butter dish, w/lid..............................**$225.00**

Patrician, pink, salt & pepper shakers, pr **$90.00**
Patrick, pink, bowl, fruit; handled, 9" **$175.00**
Patrick, pink, goblet, juice; 6-oz, 4¾" **$80.00**
Patrick, pink, mayonnaise, 3-pc **$195.00**
Patrick, pink or yellow, candy dish, 3-footed, w/lid...**$175.00**
Patrick, yellow, saucer...**$12.00**
Peacock & Wild Rose, all colors, bowl, console; 14"..**$195.00**
Peacock & Wild Rose, all colors, bowl, flat, 8½"......**$125.00**
Peacock & Wild Rose, all colors, bowl, footed, 10½"..**$195.00**
Peacock & Wild Rose, all colors, cheese & cracker dish,
    set **$185.00**
Peacock & Wild Rose, all colors, ice tub, 6" **$195.00**
Peacock & Wild Rose, all colors, plate, 8"..................**$25.00**
Peacock & Wild Rose, all colors, saucer.....................**$15.00**
Peacock & Wild Rose, all colors, vase, 12" **$295.00**
Peacock Reverse, all colors, bowl, square, 4⅞".........**$42.00**
Peacock Reverse, all colors, cup **$90.00**
Peacock Reverse, all colors, plate, luncheon; 8½"......**$60.00**
Peacock Reverse, all colors, vase, 10".......................**$225.00**
Petalware, cremax, monax florette or fired-on decorations,
    plate, salver; 11"...**$25.00**
Petalware, crystal, bowl, cream soup; 4½" **$4.50**
Petalware, pink, creamer, footed **$8.00**
Petalware, pink, plate, sherbet; 6".............................**$2.50**
Petalware, red trim floral, sherbet, low foot, 4½".......**$38.00**
Petalware, red trim floral, tumbler, 12-oz, 4⅝" **$37.50**
Pillar Optic, amber, green or pink, pitcher, tilt; 80-oz...**$65.00**
Pillar Optic, amber, green or pink, tumbler, footed, 10-oz,
    5¼"...**$25.00**
Pillar Optic, crystal, mug, 12-oz.................................**$10.00**
Pillar Optic, crystal, tumbler, water; 9-oz...................**$2.50**
Primo, yellow or green, bowl, 4½" **$22.00**
Primo, yellow or green, coaster/ashtray **$8.00**
Primo, yellow or green, saucer....................................**$3.00**
Primo, yellow or green, tumbler, 9-oz, 5¾" **$30.00**
Princess, green, ashtray, 4½" **$75.00**
Princess, green, plate, sandwich; handle, 10¼" **$16.00**
Princess, green or pink, plate, sherbet; 5½"................**$10.00**
Princess, green or pink, sherbet, footed.....................**$25.00**
Princess, pink, bowl, hat shape, 9½".........................**$50.00**
Princess, topaz or apricot, butter dish, w/lid **$750.00**
Princess, topaz or apricot, tumbler, iced tea; 13-oz, 5¼"...**$33.00**
Queen Mary, crystal, ashtray, oval, 2x3¾"..................**$3.00**
Queen Mary, crystal, bowl, cereal; 6" **$6.00**
Queen Mary, crystal, coaster, 3½"..............................**$3.00**
Queen Mary, crystal, plate, salad; #438, 8¾".............**$5.50**
Queen Mary, pink, bowl, berry; 4½" **$6.00**
Queen Mary, pink, candy dish, w/lid, #490, 7¼" **$40.00**
Queen Mary, pink, creamer, footed **$50.00**
Queen Mary, pink, relish tray, 3-part, 12" **$18.00**
Radiance, amber, bowl, punch; 9" **$100.00**
Radiance, amber, decanter, handle, w/stopper **$100.00**
Radiance, ice blue or red, bowl, nut; 2-handle, 5" **$20.00**
Radiance, ice blue or red, comport, 5" **$30.00**
Radiance, ice blue or red, ladle, for punch bowl **$135.00**
Radiance, salt & pepper shakers, amber, pr................**$50.00**
Raindrops, green, bowl, cereal; 6" **$10.00**

Raindrops, green, salt & pepper shakers, pr............**$325.00**
Raindrops, green, tumbler, 5-oz, 3⅞"........................**$6.50**
Ribbon, black, salt & pepper shakers, pr **$45.00**
Ribbon, green, bowl, berry; 4" **$30.00**
Ribbon, green, tumbler, 10-oz, 6".............................**$33.00**
Ribbon, green or black, bowl, berry; 2 styles, lg, 8" ..**$35.00**
Ring, crystal, bowl, berry; 5" **$4.00**
Ring, crystal, pitcher, 80-oz, 8½"...............................**$22.00**
Ring, crystal, plate, sandwich; 11¼"...........................**$7.00**
Ring, crystal, vase, 8"..**$17.50**
Ring, decorated, decanter, w/stopper **$40.00**
Ring, decorated, tumbler, old fashioned; 8-oz, 4".......**$17.50**
Rock Crystal, colors other than red or crystal, bowl, salad;
    scalloped edge, 9"...**$50.00**
Rock Crystal, colors other than red or crystal, cake stand,
    footed, 2¾x11"..**$52.50**
Rock Crystal, crystal, bonbon, scalloped edge, 7½" ...**$22.00**
Rock Crystal, crystal, candelabra, 3-light, pr...............**$52.50**
Rock Crystal, crystal, ice dish, 3 styles, ea................**$40.00**
Rock Crystal, crystal, pitcher, scalloped edge, 1-qt...**$165.00**
Rock Crystal, crystal, plate, scalloped edge, 9" **$18.00**
Rock Crystal, crystal, stem, wine; 3-oz......................**$22.00**

Rock Crystal, pink, covered pitcher, large, $300.00.

Rock Crystal, red, bowl, (roll tray), 13" **$125.00**
Rock Crystal, red, cup, 7-oz.......................................**$70.00**
Rock Crystal, red, plate, plain or scalloped edge, 7½" ...**$21.00**
Rock Crystal, red, tumbler, whiskey; 2½-oz **$55.00**
Rose Cameo, green, bowl, cereal; 5" **$20.00**
Rose Cameo, green, plate, salad; 7" **$14.00**
Rose Cameo, green, tumbler, footed, 2 styles, 5"........**$25.00**
Rosemary, amber, bowl, berry; 5" **$6.00**
Rosemary, green, cup **$9.50**
Rosemary, green, sugar bowl, footed.........................**$12.50**
Rosemary, pink, platter, oval, 12"..............................**$32.00**
Roulette, crystal, bowl, fruit; 9"..................................**$9.50**
Roulette, crystal, tumbler, juice; 5-oz, 3¼"..................**$7.00**
Roulette, pink or green, plate, luncheon; 8½" **$7.00**
Roulette, pink or green, tumbler, footed, 10-oz, 5½" .**$32.00**
Round Robin, green, bowl, berry; 4" **$10.00**

Round Robin, green, sherbet **$9.00**	Starlight, crystal or white, creamer, oval **$8.00**
Round Robin, green or iridescent, plate, sherbet; 6" **$2.50**	Starlight, crystal or white, sherbet **$15.00**
Roxana, yellow, plate, 5½" **$10.00**	Starlight, pink, bowl, cereal; closed handles, 5½" **$12.00**
Roxana, yellow or white, bowl, 4½x2⅜" **$15.00**	Starlight, pink, plate, sandwich; 13" **$18.00**
Royal Lace, blue, cookie jar, w/lid **$375.00**	Strawberry, crystal or iridescent, bowl, 2x6¼" **$55.00**
Royal Lace, blue, tumbler, 9-oz, 4⅛" **$50.00**	Strawberry, crystal or iridescent, creamer, sm **$12.00**
Royal Lace, crystal, bowl, cream soup; 4¾" **$15.00**	Strawberry, crystal or iridescent, pickle dish, oval, 8¼"..**$9.00**
Royal Lace, crystal, pitcher, w/out ice lip, 64-oz, 8"...**$45.00**	Strawberry, pink or green, butter dish, w/lid...........**$195.00**
Royal Lace, green, candlesticks, straight edge, pr.......**$85.00**	Strawberry, pink or green, plate, salad; 7½" **$18.00**
Royal Lace, green, salt & pepper shakers, pr............**$130.00**	Strawberry, pink or green, tumbler, 8-oz, 3⅝" **$38.00**
Royal Lace, pink, bowl, ruffled edge, 3-legged, 10" ...**$95.00**	Sunburst, crystal, bowl, berry; 8½" **$18.00**
Royal Lace, pink, plate, luncheon; 8½" **$15.00**	Sunburst, crystal, relish, 2-part.................................**$12.00**
S Pattern, crystal, bowl, cereal; 5½" **$5.00**	Sunflower, green, saucer **$10.00**
S Pattern, crystal, plate, grill..............................**$6.50**	Sunflower, opaque, cup **$75.00**
S Pattern, crystal, tumbler, 10-oz, 4¾" **$8.00**	Sunflower, pink, ashtray, center design only, 5" **$9.00**
S Pattern, monax, plate, sherbet; 6" **$8.00**	Sunflower, pink or green, tumbler, footed, 8-oz, 4¾"...**$35.00**
S Pattern, yellow, amber or crystal w/trims, cup, thick or thin..**$4.50**	Swirl, delphite, candle holders, single branch, pr.....**$125.00**
S Pattern, yellow, amber or crystal w/trims, tumbler, 5-oz, 3½"..**$8.00**	Swirl, pink, bowl, salad; rimmed, 9" **$30.00**
Sandwich, amber or crystal, basket, 10" **$35.00**	Swirl, pink, plate, salad; 8" **$10.00**
Sandwich, amber or crystal, plate, luncheon; 8⅜".......**$4.75**	Swirl, pink, tumbler, 9-oz, 4" **$22.00**
Sandwich, pink or green, cruet, w/stopper, 6½-oz ..**$175.00**	Swirl, ultramarine, butter dish, w/lid **$305.00**
Sandwich, red, salt & pepper shakers, pr...................**$45.00**	Swirl, ultramarine, salt & pepper shakers, pr.............**$45.00**
Sandwich, teal blue, butter dish, w/domed lid **$155.00**	Tea Room, amber, creamer, footed, 4½" **$75.00**
Sharon, amber, bowl, berry; 5" **$8.50**	Tea Room, green, marmalade, w/notched lid **$195.00**
Sharon, amber, pitcher, no ice lip, 80-oz..................**$140.00**	Tea Room, green, tumbler, flat, 8-oz, 4¼" **$110.00**
Sharon, green, candy jar, w/lid **$160.00**	Tea Room, pink, plate, luncheon; 8¼" **$30.00**
Sharon, green, tumbler, thick, 9-oz, 4⅛" **$75.00**	Tea Room, pink, salt & pepper shakers, pr.................**$50.00**
Sharon, pink, bowl, fruit; 10½" **$45.00**	Tea Room, pink, tumbler, footed, 12-oz **$70.00**
Sharon, pink, salt & pepper shakers, pr **$55.00**	Tea Room, pink or green, bowl, finger **$60.00**
Ships, blue/white, cocktail shaker........................**$38.00**	Thistle, green, plate, luncheon; 8" **$22.00**
Ships, blue/white, saucer **$17.00**	Thistle, pink, bowl, fruit; lg, 10¼" **$395.00**
Ships, blue/white, tumbler, juice; 5-oz, 3¾"...............**$14.00**	Thistle, pink or green, saucer.................................**$10.00**
Sierra, green, cup...**$16.00**	Tulip, amethyst or blue, bowl, oval, oblong, 13¼" ..**$110.00**
Sierra, green, platter, oval, 11"...........................**$60.00**	Tulip, amethyst or blue, tumbler, juice; 2¾" **$28.00**
Sierra, pink, bowl, cereal; 5½" **$16.00**	Tulip, crystal or green, creamer................................**$20.00**
Sierra, pink, serving tray, 2-handle.......................**$20.00**	Tulip, crystal or green, plate, 6" **$9.00**
Spiral, green, bowl, berry; 4¾" **$5.00**	Twisted Optic, blue or canary yellow, bowl, cream soup; 4¾"..**$16.00**
Spiral, green, creamer, flat or footed...........................**$7.50**	Twisted Optic, blue or canary yellow, creamer..........**$12.50**
	Twisted Optic, blue or canary yellow, plate, salad; 7" .**$6.00**
	Twisted Optic, blue or canary yellow, vase, fan; 2-handle, 8"..**$85.00**
	Twisted Optic, pink, green or amber, candlesticks, 2 styles, 3", pr..**$25.00**

Spiral, green, ice tub, $30.00.

	Twisted Optic, pink, green or amber, sandwich server, open center handle **$20.00**
	US Swirl, green, tumbler, 12-oz, 4¾" **$14.00**
	US Swirl, pink, comport.................................**$20.00**
	US Swirl, pink, sherbet, 3¼" **$5.00**
	US Swirl, pink or green, bowl, oval, 2¾x8¼".............**$40.00**
	US Swirl, pink or green, butter dish, w/lid **$120.00**
	US Swirl, pink or green, plate, sherbet; 6⅛" **$2.50**
	Victory, amber, pink or green, bowl, cereal; 6½" **$14.00**
	Victory, amber, pink or green, goblet, 7-oz, 5"...........**$25.00**
Spiral, green, platter, 12" **$30.00**	Victory, amber, pink or green, saucer.............................**$4.00**
Spiral, green, saucer **$2.00**	Victory, black or blue, candlesticks, 3", pr.............**$125.00**
Spiral, green, tumbler, water; 9-oz, 5"....................**$7.50**	Victory, black or blue, plate, luncheon; 8" **$30.00**

Vitrock, white, bowl, berry; 4"..$5.00
Vitrock, white, plate, salad; 7¼".................................$2.50
Vitrock, white, platter, 11½" $33.00
Waterford, crsytal, lamp, spherical base, 4"................$26.00
Waterford, crystal, ashtray, 4"....................................$7.50
Waterford, crystal, plate, dinner; 9⅝".........................$11.00
Waterford, pink, butter dish, w/lid............................$220.00
Waterford, pink, saucer $6.00
Waterford, pink, tumbler, footed, 10-oz, 4⅞" $25.00
Windsor, crystal, bowl, berry; 4¾" $13.50
Windsor, crystal, candle holder, 1-handle...................$15.00
Windsor, crystal, plate, chop; 13".................................$14.00
Windsor, crystal, tumbler, footed, 4" $8.00
Windsor, green, bowl, vegetable; oval, 9½"...............$30.00
Windsor, green, plate, sherbet; 6"..................................$8.00
Windsor, green, tray, 1-handle, square, 4"..................$12.00
Windsor, pink, bowl, pointed edge, 8" $60.00
Windsor, pink, creamer $14.00
Windsor, pink, salt & pepper shakers, pr...................$40.00

Disney

The largest and most popular area in character collectibles is without doubt Disneyana. There are clubs, newsletters, and special shows that are centered around this hobby. Every aspect of the retail market has been thoroughly saturated with Disney-related merchandise over the years, and today collectors are able to find many good examples at garage sales and flea markets.

Disney memorabilia from the late '20s and '30s was marked either 'Walt E. Disney' or 'Walt Disney Enterprises.' After about 1940 the name was changed to 'Walt Disney Productions.' This mark was in use until 1984 when the 'Walt Disney Company' mark was introduced, and this last mark has remained in use up to the present time. Some of the earlier items have become very expensive, though many are still within the reach of the average collector.

During the '30s, Mickey Mouse, Donald Duck, Snow White and the Seven Dwarfs, and the Three Little Pigs (along with all their friends and cohorts) dominated the Disney scene. The last of the '30s characters was Pinocchio, and some 'purists' prefer to stop their collections with him.

The '40s and '50s brought many new characters with them — Alice in Wonderland, Bambi, Dumbo, Lady and the Tramp, and Peter Pan were some of the major personalities featured in Disney's films of this era.

Even today, thanks to the re-releases of many of the old movies and the popularity of Disney's vacation 'kingdoms,' toy stores and department stores alike are full of quality items with the potential of soon becoming collectibles.

If you'd like to learn more about this fascinating field, we recommend *Stern's Guide to Disney Collectibles, First* and *Second Series*, by Michael Stern; *The Collector's Encyclopedia of Disneyana* by Michael Stern and David Longest; *Character Toys and Collectibles* and *Toys, Antique and Collectible*, both by David Longest; and *Schroeder's Collectible Toys, Antique to*

Modern. All are published by Collector Books.

See also Character and Promotional Drinking Glasses; Character Banks; Character Watches; Cowboy Character Memorabilia; Dolls, Mattel; Games; Pin-Back Buttons; Puzzles; Salt and Pepper Shakers; Toys; Valentines.

Note: In the following listings, many of the characters have been sorted by the name of the feature film in which they appeared.

Advisor: Judy Posner (See Directory, Character and Personality Collectibles)

Aladdin, doll, Jasmine, Mattel, 1992, 8", MIB, $25.00.

Aladdin, doll, Prince Ali, Mattel, 1992, 8", MIB...........$25.00
Aladdin, pin, Genie holding lamp, cloisonne, 1993, M .$10.00
Aladdin, pin, Jasmine's tiger Raja, enamel, 1993, M......$8.00
Aladdin, Water Jewel Magic Gift Set, Mattel, 1994, MIB .$65.00
Alice in Wonderland, figure, United China & Glass/WDP,
    1970s, 5½", MIB...$35.00
Alice in Wonderland, marionette, Peter Puppet, 1952, EX .$175.00
Alice in Wonderland, paint set, Hasbro, 1969, M (sealed)....$50.00
Alice in Wonderland, phonograph, plastic w/metal spinner &
    tone arm, RCA-Victor, 1951, EX...........................$150.00
Alice in Wonderland, tea set, china, 11 pcs (including 2 lids),
    WDP, 1960s, MIB $150.00
Aristocats, rug, lg colorful image of characters, fringed on 2
    ends, 4x5 ft, EX..$375.00
Babes in Toyland, doll, Soldier, plush w/rubber head,
    Gundkins, 1961, 9½", scarce, NM.........................$40.00
Babes in Toyland, Jumping Jack Soldier, jointed wood figure
    w/pull-string actions, Jaymar, 1961, 9½", rare,
    NMIB...$100.00
Bambi, Christmas ornament, silver glass ball w/color image
    of Bambi, 1940s, 2½", VG......................................$12.00
Bambi, doll, Bambi, stuffed velvet, Character Novelty
    Co/WDP, 1940s, 12½", EX......................................$85.00
Bambi, figure, Bambi, ceramic, Shaw, 1940s, 8", M..$150.00
Bambi, figure, Bambi & Thumper, ceramic,
    Leonardi/England, 1940s, 9", EX $200.00

Bambi, figure, Bambi w/butterfly on tail, ceramic, Japan, 1970s, 5½", M..**$50.00**

Bambi, figure, Thumper & his girlfriend, ceramic, American Pottery, 1940s, NM, from $75 to.............................**$85.00**

Bambi, figure set, Bambi, Flower & Thumper, plastic, WDP, 1960s, 2" & 3", NM...**$40.00**

Bambi, mirror, full-color molded plastic frame w/Bambi, Thumper, Flower & Owl, 1960s, 20x24", NM.....**$250.00**

Bambi, planter, Bambi figure in front of log, ceramic, Leeds, 1940s, 5½", NM...**$35.00**

Bambi, planter, Bambi figure on lg green forested planter base, ceramic, Leeds, 1940s, 5", NM......................**$45.00**

Bambi, planter, Thumper figure next to pot, ceramic, Leeds, 1940s, 7", NM...**$35.00**

Black Hole, Colorforms, 1970s, complete, NMIB.......**$15.00**

Black Hole, sunglasses, plastic w/vari-vue style panel at top, WDP, 1979, MOC...**$15.00**

Cinderella, apron pattern, fold-up paper, features color-illustrated characters, JC Penney, 1950s, uncut, EX+..**$35.00**

Cinderella, doll, stuffed cloth w/yarn hair, WDP, 1950..**$300.00**

Cinderella, purse, green slipper w/zipper closure, 1970s, 5", MIP..**$25.00**

Disneyland, charm bracelet, Little Miss Disneyland w/charms of Mickey, Sleeping Beauty, Castle & Tinkerbell, 1950s, MIB **$35.00**

Disneyland, cup holder tray, tin, pictures 6 different attractions in bottom of ea cup section, 1970s, 11" dia, VG.....**$20.00**

Disneyland, guide book, Walt Disney's Disneyland — A Pictorial Souvenir & Guide, 1968, EX+ **$30.00**

Disneyland, guide book, Walt Disney's Guide to Disneyland, features Walt, Tinkerbell & castle, 1959, EX+.......**$60.00**

Disneyland, magazine (promotional), A Disneyland Holiday, Summer 1958, 30+ pages w/stories, illustrations & ads, EX+...**$30.00**

Disneyland, See 'N Say, Mattel, 1966, MIB.................**$75.00**

Disneyland, tray, litho tin, aerial image of early park, WDP, 1955, 12½x17", EX+..**$135.00**

Disneyland, woodburning set, 1955, complete, EXIB..**$125.00**

Donald Duck, Bean Bag Party Game, Parker/WDP, 1939, complete & unused, NM+ (EX+ box) **$175.00**

Donald Duck, bread wrapper, Debus, 16x17", complete, 1950s, EX...**$10.00**

Donald Duck, camera, plastic, Herbert George/WDP, 1950s, NM (worn box)..**$100.00**

Donald Duck, comic book, Donald Duck in Lost Lake, Wheaties giveaway, 1951, 7x3", NM....................**$15.00**

Donald Duck, doctor kit, WDP, 1940s, EXIB **$125.00**

Donald Duck, Funnee Movee Viewer, w/4 films, Irwin, 1960s, EX...**$40.00**

Donald Duck, paint set, Transogram, 1955, complete & unused, NMIB...**$125.00**

Donald Duck, planter, figural Donald holding up flower next to pot, ceramic, Leeds, 1940s, 6½", EX................**$45.00**

Donald Duck, planter, figural Donald w/hands on hips next to pot, Leeds, 1940s, 5", scarce, NM....................**$60.00**

Donald Duck, Skediddler, plastic figure w/movable arms & legs, Mattel, 1969, 5", NMIB.................................**$50.00**

Donald Duck, squirt gun, plastic head figure, 1974, EX..**$25.00**

Donald Duck, WWII booklet, What Is Propaganda?, lg image of Donald on cover, US War Dept/GI Roundtable Series, 1944, EX+ **$50.00**

Donald Duck, yo-yo, wood w/paper sticker seal, Hallmark, 1970s, MOC (card marked Disney Yo-Yo for Beginners) **$30.00**

Dumbo, doll, composition w/cloth ears, Cameo Doll, 1941, 8", EX..**$300.00**

Dumbo, hand puppet, cloth w/vinyl head, Gund, 1955, MIB...**$100.00**

Dumbo, wall pocket/shelf planter, Dumbo figure stuck in tree, ceramic, 1940s, 4", EX....................................**$40.00**

Ferdinand the Bull, doll, composition, Knickerbocker, 10", NM...**$575.00**

Goofy, Jumpkins figure, Kohner, 1960s, 5", MOC.......**$60.00**

Goofy, Talkin' Patter Pillow, 10 phrases, Mattel, 1969, MIB...**$125.00**

Hunchback of Notre Dame, doll, Quasimodo, Phoebus, Frollo, or Esmarelsa, vinyl, Applause, 1996, 9", MIB, ea **$12.00**

Jungle Book, doll, Baloo, stuffed velvet & felt, Japan, 1966, 6", NM...**$50.00**

Jungle Book, doll, Kaa or Vulture, stuffed cloth, 1967, M, ea **$40.00**

Lady & the Tramp, Colorforms Cartoon Kit, 1962, complete, NMIB...**$35.00**

Lady & the Tramp, doll, Tramp, stuffed cloth w/felt features & leather nose, w/original tag, 1960s, 6", NM......**$25.00**

Lady & the Tramp, figure, Peg, ceramic, Hagen-Renaker, 1950s, 2", M...**$165.00**

Lion King, Electronic Talking Bank, Think Way, MIB...**$40.00**

Little Mermaid, doll, Ariel, talker, Tyco, 1992, 18", MIB..**$50.00**

Little Mermaid, Talking Musical Sea Mirror, Ariel forms handle, push button for several phrases, 1995, MIB..**$20.00**

Mary Poppins, oil paint-by-number set, Hasbro, MIB (sealed) **$85.00**

Mary Poppins, plate, Sun Valley Melmac, 9½", unused, M **$30.00**

Mary Poppins, record album #3922, LP, w/storybook, EX...**$25.00**

Mary Poppins, Talking Telephone, battery-operated, w/records, Hasbro, NMIB **$200.00**

Mary Poppins, tea set, litho tin, 10 pcs, 1964, EX **$100.00**

Mickey, Donald & Pluto, switch plate, plastic w/color images, 1950s, MIP **$32.00**

Mickey, Donald & Tinkerbell shoe polish, Scuffy brand, 1960s, EX (EX box)..**$20.00**

Mickey, Minnie, Donald & Pluto, light shade (ceiling), milk glass disk w/multicolored images 1950s, 14", M....**$80.00**

Mickey Mouse, bookends/banks, painted cast-iron figures ea sitting against a book, WDP, 1960s, 5x4", pr......**$275.00**

Mickey Mouse, Candy Factory, Remco, 1973, NMIB ..**$75.00**

Mickey Mouse, doll, talker, stuffed cloth w/vinyl head, Horsman, 1978, MIB...**$55.00**

Mickey Mouse, gumball machine, head on red base, Hasbro, 1968, NM...**$50.00**

Mickey Mouse, lamp base, dancing figure, ceramic, 8", EX+..$40.00

Mickey Mouse, Magic Slate Blackboard, Strathmore, 1940s, complete, NM (EX box) $125.00

Mickey Mouse, music box, ceramic Mickey as magician w/50th birthday cake on round base, It's a Small World, Schmid, MIB..$75.00

Mickey Mouse, night light, TV shape w/image of Mickey reading to nephews at bedtime, multicolored plastic, 1950s, EX...$90.00

Mickey Mouse, pin, Disneyana banner on pie-eyed Mickey figure, cloisonne, 1980s, M $20.00

Mickey Mouse, pin, Mickey's Fire Dept, cloisonne, 1990s, M..$12.00

Mickey Mouse, planter, figural Mickey pushing cart on base, ceramic, D Brechner Co, 1960s, 5", EX+...............$65.00

Mickey Mouse, planter, figural w/Mickey holding flower next to ear, ceramic, 6½", EX...$35.00

Mickey Mouse, push-button puppet, wood w/plastic base, Kohner, 1948, 6½", NM $150.00

Mickey Mouse, talking telephone, battery-operated, plastic, Hasbro, 1964, complete, NMIB........................$200.00

Mickey Mouse, telephone, NN Hill Brass Co., marked Walt Disney, metal and wood with cardboard figure, 8", EX, $175.00. (Photo courtesy Michael Stern)

Mickey Mouse, yo-yo, plastic w/image of Mickey on unicycle, 1980s, MOC...$15.00

Mickey Mouse & Donald Duck, magic slate, 1951, EX..$25.00

Mickey Mouse Club, Acrobat Gym, Plastic Playthings/WDP, 1955, complete, MIB...$75.00

Mickey Mouse Club, Disneyball, inflatable vinyl, Kestral, 1950s-60s, NMIB...$30.00

Mickey Mouse Club, Fun Kit, Whitman, 1957, EXIB ..$75.00

Mickey Mouse Club, magic slate, Strathmore, 1950s, NM.$45.00

Mickey Mouse Club, marionette, Mouskeeter Girl, composition w/cloth clothes, EXIB $150.00

Mickey Mouse Club, typewriter, litho tin, T Cohn, 1950s, 7x10", EX..$75.00

Minnie Mouse, doll, Sun Rubber, 1950s, VG $65.00

Minnie Mouse, figure, Minnie w/golf clubs, bisque, 1970s, 4", NM $20.00

Mousketeers, television, tin litho with paper scroll, 1950s, VG, $150.00. (Photo courtesy David Longest and Michael Stern)

Nightmare Before Christmas, figure, Jack as Santa, Hasbro, 1993, MOC..$75.00

Nightmare Before Christmas, figure set, Lock, Shock & Barrel, w/3 masks, Hasbro, 1993, MIB $125.00

Nightmare Before Christmas, yo-yo, Barrel, plastic, Spectra Star, 1993, MOC $18.00

Peter Pan, bell, Tinkerbell, gold-tone metal figure atop bell, 1950s, 3", EX $60.00

Peter Pan, key chain, Tinkerbell, diecut plastic in fluorescent colors, 1970s, 3", NM..$15.00

Peter Pan, marionette, Peter Pan, Peter Puppet, 1953, 12", rare, EX+...$300.00

Peter Pan, pin, Peter Pan or Captain Hook figures in full color on gold-tone, 1950s, EX, ea $35.00

Pinocchio, clicker, Jiminy Cricket, yellow plastic head figure, 1950s, NM..$45.00

Pinocchio, Color Box, litho tin, Transogram/EDP, 1948, EX .$75.00

Pinocchio, doll, Pinocchio, jointed wood & composition w/felt hat, Ideal, 1940s, 11", NM (NM rare box).$550.00

Pinocchio, figure, Geppetto or Pinocchio, bisque, Multi-Products, 1940s, 2", NM, ea $100.00

Pinocchio, figure, Gideon or Honest John, bisque, Multi-Products, 1940s, 2", ea..$75.00

Pinocchio, figure, Jiminy Cricket, bisque, Multi-Products, 1940s, 5", NM...$100.00

Pinocchio, figure, Pinocchio, Fun-E-Flex, Ideal, 1940s, 5", rare, EX+...$200.00

Pinocchio, hand puppet, Pinocchio, cloth w/vinyl head, Knickerbocker, 1962, EX $30.00

Pinocchio, marionette, Pinocchio, Pelham, 1960s-70s, MIB...$135.00

Pluto, comic book, Pluto & the Mysterious Package, Wheaties giveaway, 1951, 7x3", NM.....................$15.00

Pluto, doll, Schuco, 1950s, 13", EX, minimum value .$350.00

Pluto, figure, ceramic, Brayton Laguna, 1940s, 6", M .$135.00

Pluto, Jingle Ball, vinyl w/image of Pluto & pups, Vangard, 1950s, EX...$30.00

Rocketeer, notebook, 4 different, Mead, ea...................$5.00

Rocketeer, wallet, Pyramid Handbag Co, M $40.00

Shaggy Dog, figures, 3 different w/driver, hitchhiker & wearing pajamas, ceramic, Enesco/WDE, 1960s, 5", ea.$75.00

Sleeping Beauty, Colorforms Dress Designer Kit, 1959, complete, MIB...$65.00

Sleeping Beauty, doll, w/Elise face, original pink satin gown, replaced crown, Madame Alexander, 1957, 16", EX..**$300.00**

Sleeping Beauty, figure, Flora the fairy, ceramic, Hagen-Renaker, 1950s, 2", NM **$150.00**

Sleeping Beauty, figure, Merryweather the fairy, ceramic, Hagen-Renaker, 1950s, 1¾", EX **$165.00**

Sleeping Beauty, mobile for crib, plastic figures w/metal attachment rod, Kenner, 1958, EXIB **$100.00**

Sleeping Beauty, paint-by-number set, Transogram, 1959, complete, MIB...**$100.00**

Sleeping Beauty, sewing set, Transogram, 1959, unused, scarce, EX **$65.00**

Snow White & the Seven Dwarfs, night light, Snow White figure on square base, plastic, 1950s, EX **$125.00**

Snow White & the Seven Dwarfs, planter, Snow White figure, ceramic, Leeds, 1940s, 6½", NM **$50.00**

Snow White & the Seven Dwarfs, print, glow-in-the-dark, Snow White, dwarf & forest friends by tree, framed, 1940s, M...**$48.00**

Snow White & the Seven Dwarfs, song book, Bourne Co, movie songs w/black & white illustrations, softcover, 1955, EX+ **$35.00**

Snow White & the Seven Dwarfs, top, litho tin, Chein, 1950s, EX...**$50.00**

Sword in the Stone, ring, pink or blue plastic, 1970s premium, NM, ea..**$15.00**

Three Little Pigs, tea set, white litho tin, 11 pcs, Ohio Art, NM, from $75 to **$100.00**

Three Little Pigs, top, lithographed metal, NM, minimum value $200.00.
(Photo courtesy Michael Stern)

Three Little Pigs & Big Bad Wolf, birthday card, White & Wyckoff Mfg Co, 1938, unused, NM **$60.00**

Toy Story, doll, Woody, talker, stuffed cloth w/vinyl head & hands, Think Way, NRFB **$50.00**

Toy Story, Dress-Up Set, Buzz Lightyear, Think Way, complete, MIB...**$40.00**

Various characters, frontier logs, w/instructions, Halsam, 1955, complete, NMIB..**$100.00**

Various characters, globe, 1950s, litho tin, M............**$225.00**

Various characters, kaleidoscope, litho cardboard, West Germany, 1970s-80s, EX **$35.00**

Various characters, Magic Erasable Pictures, Transogram, 1950s, unused, MIB..**$50.00**

Various characters, Model-Craft Character Molding & Coloring Set, WDP, 1950, unused, NM+ (EX+ box) **$200.00**

Various characters, Scramble 4 Faces, Halsam Products, 1950s, MIP **$50.00**

Various characters, top, tin w/on blue & white stripes, Chein, 1973, 6" dia, NM **$50.00**

Who Framed Roger Rabbit, doll, Roger Rabbit, talker, stuffed cloth, Playskool, 1988, MIB................................**$95.00**

Winnie the Pooh, Chatter Chum, Pooh, Mattel, 1978, MIB **$70.00**

Winnie the Pooh, doll, Piglet, stuffed cloth, Gund, 1960s, 12", NM **$50.00**

Winnie the Pooh, doll, Piglet, stuffed cloth, Sears, 1960s, 7", NM **$75.00**

Winnie the Pooh, figure, Eeyore seated in sorrowful pose w/head turned, ceramic, 1960s, EX......................**$55.00**

Winnie the Pooh, figure, Owl or Kanga, ceramic, Beswick of England, 1960s, 3¼", M, ea...................................**$50.00**

Winnie the Pooh, lamp base, Pooh seated in wagon pulled by Eeyore on flat round base, plastic, EX **$55.00**

Winnie the Pooh, squeak toy, Tigger, vinyl, Hollandhall, 1966, 7", NM...**$125.00**

Winnie the Pooh, Toon-A-Vision, Amsco, 1964, EX ...**$65.00**

Dog Collectibles

Dog lovers appreciate the many items, old and new, that are modeled after or decorated with their favorite breeds. They pursue, some avidly, all with dedication, specific items for a particular accumulation or a range of objects, from matchbook covers to bronzes.

Perhaps the Scottish terrier is one of the most highly sought-out breeds of dogs among collectors; at any rate, Scottie devotees are more organized than most. Both the Aberdeen and West Highland terriers were used commercially; often the two are found together in things such as magnets, Black & White Scotch Whiskey advertisements, jewelry, and playing cards, for instance. They became a favorite of the advertising world in the 1930s and 1940s, partly as a result of the public popularity of President Roosevelt's dog, Fala. For information on Scottish terriers see *A Treasury of Scottie Dog Collectibles, Identification and Values,* by Candace Sten Davis and Patricia Baugh (Collector Books).

Poodles were the breed of the 1950s, and today items from those years are cherished collectibles. Trendsetter teeny-boppers wore poodle skirts, and the 5-&-10¢ stores were full of pink poodle figurines with 'coleslaw' fur. For a look back at these years, we recommend *Poodle Collectibles of the '50s and '60s* by Elaine Butler (L-W Books).

Many of the earlier collectibles are especially prized, making them expensive and difficult to find. Prices listed here may vary as they are dependent on supply and demand, location, and dealer assessment.

Advisor: Elaine Butler, Poodles (See Directory, Poodle Collectibles)

Club: Heart of America Scottish Terrier Club
Ms. Nancy McGray
507 Kurzweil
Raymore, MD 64083

Newsletter: *Canine Collectibles Quarterly*
Patty Shedlow, Editor
736 N Western Ave., Ste. 314
Lake Forest, IL 60045; Subscription: $28 per year

Border Collie, book, Footrot Flats, softcover, published in New Zealand, 1987, 4½x7½", EX.........................$15.00
Bulldog, carnival cane, dog's head on wooden dowel rod, marked Japan, 33".................................$70.00
Bulldog, cigarette lighter w/striker on back, metal w/copper finish, Ronson, 4".................................$80.00
Bulldog, figurine, standing, well detailed, Ucagco, Japan, 7" long.................................$150.00
Bulldog, TV lamp, standing, Claes label, 13"...........$100.00
Cocker Spaniel, figurine, Bing & Grondahl, #2095, signed HR, 6½x9".................................$100.00
Cocker Spaniel, figurine, solid cast metal, 4½" L........$60.00
Cocker Spaniel, plate, 3 dogs playing in daisies, C Jagodits, Bradford Exchange, 1993, w/styrofoam package & papers, 8".................................$50.00
Cocker Spaniel, tumbler, w/3 painted-on dogs, 1940s, 5"..$40.00
Collie, creamer, figural, Occupied Japan, 4¼x5".........$40.00
Collie, figurine, black & white, Beswick England, 5x7"..$60.00
Collie, figurine, mother licking her pup, Lefton, 4½".$50.00
Pekingese, book, Puppies for Keeps, Dorothy Lathrop artwork sketches, 1943, ex-library, EX.....................$145.00
Pekingese, planter, lg eyes (frowning expression), brown glaze, 5½x8".................................$25.00
Pekingese, salt & pepper shakers, Goebel, 2½x3", pr......$165.00
Pekingese, salt & pepper shakers, 2¼x2½", pr...........$25.00
Poodle, apron, from Cut & Sew kit, from $4 to...........$6.00
Poodle, ashtray, mother & 5 pups at side of tray, from $8 to.................................$12.00
Poodle, bank, ceramic, Penny Saver on lid, For My Cadillac on base, dog tied to Eiffel Tower scene, unmarked, $15 to.................................$20.00
Poodle, brooch, gold-tone metal w/colored rhinestone eyes, from $8 to.................................$12.00
Poodle, casserole, Chi Chi, black on white, Glidden #167, from $30 to.................................$40.00
Poodle, cocktail napkin, embroidered decor, from $6 to...$8.00
Poodle, cup, head figural, ceramic, marked Italy, from $10 to.................................$15.00
Poodle, decanter, Garnier, w/corkscrew, from $15 to ..$20.00
Poodle, dish towel, dog in apron on white, no label, from $4 to.................................$6.00
Poodle, figurine, ceramic, turquoise w/coleslaw, 1950s, from $30 to.................................$35.00
Poodle, figurine, playing drums, ceramic, marked Patt 3807, from $10 to.................................$15.00
Poodle, figurine, sitting, rhinestones on body & eyes, paper label: Thames Hand Painted Japan, from $15 to..$20.00

Poodle, napkin ring, gold-tone metal w/red rhinestone eyes, unmarked, from $8 to.................................$10.00

Poodle, pin, rhinestones on silver-tone metal, unmarked, from $12.00 to $16.00. (Photo courtesy Elaine Butler)

Poodle, pincushion, enameled figural, marked Florenza, from $30 to.................................$35.00
Poodle, planter, pulling cart, ceramic, rhinestones & coleslaw, marked 1G2253, from $20 to $25.00
Poodle, plaque, painted ceramic, pink dogs on black, Hand painted by Helen DeTar California, pr, from $40 to..$50.00
Poodle, plaques, black-painted plaster, unmarked, pr, from $15 to.................................$20.00
Poodle, platter, ceramic, black & white egg shape, marked Holland, from $15 to.................................$20.00
Poodle, postcard, from $1 to.................................$2.00
Poodle, purse, sequined dog on wool, Graceline Master Purse, from $45 to.................................$50.00
Poodle, saucer, paper label marked Josef Originals, from $7 to.................................$10.00
Poodle, spice holder, mama w/pups, ceramic, black & red, from $20 to.................................$25.00
Poodle, swizzle stick, plastic, from $1 to...................$2.00
Poodle, tablecloth, poodles w/bones, no label, from $25 to.................................$30.00
Poodle, tea towel, hand embroidered, from $5 to........$7.00
Poodle, thermos, 2 poodles before Eiffel Tower, Aladdin, from $30 to.................................$35.00
Poodle, trash can, enamel on tin, Ransburg, from $20 to..$25.00
Poodle, tumblers, gold & black w/rhinestone collars on white frosted glass, 6 in black wire rack, from $50 to.....$60.00
Scottie, ashtray, etched crystal, ca 1940s, 4x2½", from $20 to.................................$35.00
Scottie, bank, metal, dog beside 8-ball, metal, 1950s, 4x3½x3½", from $80 to.................................$125.00
Scottie, bank, plastic, Reliable, ca 1950-60s, 7½", from $60 to.................................$80.00
Scottie, book rack, wooden dogs as ends of rack, dark stain, 6x6x10", from $20 to.................................$40.00
Scottie, bookends, composition, relief scene, brown paint, 1940s, 4½x5½", pr, from $30 to.................................$60.00

Scottie, bookends, flocked chalk figural, Made in Japan, 1950s, 5x4x4", pr, from $15 to **$20.00**

Scottie, bootscraper, cast-iron figural, 1970s, 5x10", from $40 to **$60.00**

Scottie, brooch, metal, 1950s, from $10 to **$20.00**

Scottie, doorstop, CI, head & tail up, 1940s, 9x3x8", from $150 to **$200.00**

Scottie, figurine, cold cast bronze, BOGART by ED, 1990s, 6", L, from $60 to **$70.00**

Scottie, figurine, flocked plastic, 1950s, 3½x3x1½", from $5 to **$10.00**

Scottie, figurine, head & tail up, pewter, 1950s, 1x2", from $10 to **$20.00**

Scottie, figurine, metal, Made in Japan, Canada souvenir sticker on side, 1940-50s, 4½x6x2", from $25 to ..**$50.00**

Scottie, frame, ceramic, 1980s, 4x5", from $5.00 to $15.00. (Photo courtesy Candace Sten Davis and Patricia Baugh)

Scottie, ice cream mold, metal, 2-pc, 1950s, 8x2x6", from $125 to **$150.00**

Scottie, mug, Lady & the Tramp, Disney, 1990s, from $6 to **$12.00**

Scottie, planter, ceramic, dog at mailbox, 1950s, 6x6x4", from $25 to **$35.00**

Scottie, planter, ceramic, floral on cream, painted pink bowl, Napco, Made in Japan, 1940s, 5½x7½x3", from $15 to **$20.00**

Scottie, salt & peppers shakers, plastic, red & black dogs on white, marked Richelain, 1940s, 3¼", pr, from $10 to **$15.00**

Scottie, stuffed toy, bear fur, 1950s, 14x7x9", from $75 to **$100.00**

Scottie, stuffed toy, mohair, Shuco, 10x4x8", from $180 to **$225.00**

Scottie, stuffed toy, plush, Heritage Collection, Ganz, 1990s, 12x8x12", from $25 to **$35.00**

Scottie, tape measure, metal & satin, Germany, 1940s, 1½x1", from $40 to...**$60.00**

Scottie, trinket box, porcelain, black dog on lid of red plaid box, 1990s, 2x2x2", from $10 to **$30.00**

Scottie, tumbler, red dog w/blue checks on clear, Hazel Atlas, 4½", from $8 to **$18.00**

Sheltie, postcard, real photo, ca 1918, lying on doorstop, EX...**$10.00**

Spaniel, bookends, brass-plated spelter, Frankart, 5½x7", pr..**$75.00**

Springer Spaniel, figurine, dark brown spots, Goebel, 1973, #7, 7x10"..**$100.00**

Springer Spaniel, planter, no manufacturer's mark, #953, 7½x6½"..**$30.00**

Welsh Collie, postcard, Salmon Series, EX.....................**$4.00**

Welsh Corgi, figurine, dark red w/white markings, Melba Ware, English, 6x8"..**$65.00**

Yorkie, figurine, molded plastic, Home Interiors, 6x8½" .**$35.00**

Yorkie, pendant necklace, enamel on copper disk, dog w/pink bow in hair on blue ground, 18" chain marked Germany **$10.00**

Yorkie, solid perfume, gold-tone w/black enamel eyes & pink bow, scent: Beautiful, Estee Lauder, MIB ..**$100.00**

Dollhouse Furniture

Some of the mass-produced dollhouse furniture you're apt to see on the market today was made by Renwal and Acme during the 1940s and Ideal in the 1960s. All three of these companies used hard plastic for their furniture lines and imprinted most pieces with their names. Strombecker furniture was made of wood, and although it was not marked, it has a certain recognizable style to it. Remember that if you're lucky enough to find it complete in the original box, you'll want to preserve the carton as well.

Advisor: Judith Mosholder (See Directory Dollhouse Furniture)

Acme, seesaw, red w/yellow handles **$10.00**

Acme, stroller, pink w/blue or white wheels, ea **$6.00**

Allied, chair, dining; red..**$2.00**

Allied, hutch, red **$4.00**

Best, bed, pink..**$5.00**

Blue Box, sink, bathroom; w/shelf unit.......................**$4.00**

Blue Box, table dressing; white w/pink........................**$4.00**

Donna Lee, chair, kitchen; white.................................**$5.00**

Donna Lee, sink, kitchen; white...................................**$6.00**

Endeavor, armoire, white w/red...................................**$5.00**

Endeavor, hutch, white w/red **$5.00**

Fisher-Price, bedroom set, #225, brass bed w/white dresser & mirror **$6.00**

Fisher-Price, fireplace, #270, MOC..............................**$3.00**

Fisher-Price, rocker, #273, MOC **$4.00**

Grand Rapids, chest of drawers, stained wood...........**$20.00**

Grand Rapids, dresser w/mirror, stained wood...........**$20.00**

Grand Rapids, rocker, stained wood...........................**$18.00**

Ideal, buffet, dark brown or marbleized maroon, ea .**$10.00**

Ideal, chair, dining room; marbleized maroon w/blue, red or yellow seat, ea **$10.00**

Ideal, end table/night stand, ivory w/blue **$8.00**

Ideal, highboy, marbleized maroon **$15.00**

Ideal, lamp, table; dark brown w/rose swirl shade **$20.00**
Ideal, shopping cart, white w/red basket...................**$40.00**
Ideal, table, dining; dark marbleized maroon **$20.00**
Ideal, table, picnic; white...**$20.00**
Ideal, tub, corner; blue w/yellow...............................**$18.00**
Ideal, vanity, ivory w/blue..**$18.00**
Ideal Petite Princess, boudoir chaise lounge, blue **$25.00**
Ideal Petite Princess, dressing table set, complete......**$28.00**
Ideal Petite Princess, Fantasy family............................**$75.00**
Ideal Petite Princess, Fantasy telephone set **$22.00**

Ideal Petite Princess, Grandfather Clock, missing folding screen, original box, $36.00.

Ideal Petite Princess, kitchen sink/dishwasher..........**$100.00**
Ideal Petite Princess, Little Princess bed, blue **$40.00**
Ideal Young Decorator, diaper pail, yellow w/blue....**$25.00**
Ideal Young Decorator, sink, bathroom; yellow w/blue ...**$40.00**
Irwin, pail, dark blue..**$6.00**
Irwin, tray, light blue...**$3.00**
Jaydon, bed, reddish brown swirl, w/spread **$18.00**
Jaydon, chair, living room; reddish brown swirl.........**$15.00**
Kilgore, bed, cast iron, green **$60.00**
Kilgore, chair, living room; cast iron, red **$45.00**
Kilgore, playground set, cast iron, blue, 3 pcs............**$75.00**
Kilgore, table, dressing; cast iron, green.....................**$60.00**
Marx, bedroom set, hard plastic, dark ivory, 8 pcs **$40.00**
Marx, chair, living room; hard plastic, red...................**$3.00**
Marx, chest of drawers, hard plastic, pink..................**$5.00**
Marx, crib w/molded bottle & rattle, hard plastic, green ...**$5.00**
Marx, hutch, soft plastic, brown **$3.00**
Marx, nightstand, hard plastic, yellow.........................**$5.00**
Marx, refrigerator, soft plastic, yellow **$3.00**
Marx, stove, soft plastic, yellow or ivory, ea **$3.00**
Marx, table, dining; hard plastic, dark maroon swirl **$3.00**
Marx, vanity, hard plastic, yellow..................................**$5.00**
Marx Little Hostess, chaise lounge, ivory w/pink **$10.00**
Marx Little Hostess, chest of drawers, block front, rust ...**$10.00**
Marx Little Hostess, table, tilt-top; black w/gold stenciling.**$10.00**
Mattel Littles, sink/icebox, MIB **$12.00**
Mattel Littles, sofa **$8.00**

Mattel Littles, stove, w/kettle & coffeepot, MIB **$15.00**
Plasco, buffet, brown, tan or marbleized reddish brown, ea..**$4.00**
Plasco, doll, baby; pink...**$25.00**
Plasco, dresser, tan w/yellow detail, 3 drawers **$15.00**
Plasco, nightstand, brown, tan or mauve, ea **$3.00**
Plasco, refrigerator, white w/blue base........................**$5.00**
Plasco, sofa, light blue w/brown base **$8.00**
Plasco, stove, no-base style, pink **$3.00**
Renwal, buffet, w/opening drawer, brown...................**$8.00**
Renwal, chair, club; blue w/brown base **$8.00**
Renwal, china closet, brown w/stenciling **$15.00**
Renwal, doll, brother; metal rivets **$30.00**
Renwal, doll, brother; plastic rivets..............................**$25.00**
Renwal, doll, mother; plastic rivets, pink **$25.00**
Renwal, doll, sister; metal rivets, yellow dress...........**$25.00**
Renwal, hamper, ivory..**$3.00**
Renwal, highboy, pink or blue......................................**$15.00**
Renwal, piano, marbleized brown **$30.00**
Renwal, scales, red..**$10.00**
Renwal, sofa, ivory w/brown base................................**$18.00**
Renwal, table, dining; brown, w/stenciling.................**$20.00**
Renwal, telephone, yellow w/red..................................**$22.00**
Strombecker, piano, baby grand; walnut **$20.00**
Strombecker, radio, floor; walnut w/etched detail......**$12.00**
Strombecker, sink, ivory or aqua, ea.............................**$8.00**
Strombecker, sofa, red..**$10.00**
Superior, chair, kitchen; olive green..............................**$3.00**
Superior, hutch, pink or red, ea **$5.00**
Superior, table, coffee; bright yellow **$8.00**
Superior, vanity w/mirror, blue.....................................**$5.00**
Tomy Smaller Homes, armoire **$10.00**
Tomy Smaller Homes, bentwood rocker **$8.00**
Tomy Smaller Homes, end table....................................**$8.00**
Tomy Smaller Homes, sofa, 3-pc...................................**$15.00**
Tootsietoy, bedroom set, girl's; complete, MIB.........**$125.00**
Tootsietoy, chair, living room; gold wicker-style w/cushion .**$18.00**
Tootsietoy, table, living room; gold **$20.00**
Wolverine, bed w/headboard **$12.00**
Wolverine, dresser w/mirror **$10.00**
Wolverine, playpen...**$8.00**

Tootsietoy, living room set, five-piece, NM, $65.00.

Dolls

Doll collecting is one of the most popular hobbies in the United States. Since many of the antique dolls are so expensive, modern dolls have come into their own and can be had at prices within the range of most budgets. Today's thrift-shop owners know the extent of 'doll mania,' though, so you'll seldom find a bargain there. But if you're willing to spend the time, garage sales can be a good source for your doll buying. Granted most will be in a 'well loved' condition, but as long as they're priced right, many can be re-dressed, rewigged, and cleaned up. Swap meets and flea markets may sometimes yield a good example or two, often at lower-than-book prices.

Modern dolls, those from 1935 to the present, are made of rubber, composition, magic skin, synthetic rubber, and many types of plastic. Most of these materials do not stand up well to age, so be objective when you buy, especially if you're buying with an eye to the future. Doll repair is an art best left to professionals, but if yours is only dirty, you can probably do it yourself. If you need to clean a composition doll, do it very carefully. Use only baby oil and follow up with a soft dry cloth to remove any residue. Most types of wigs can be shampooed with wig shampoo and lukewarm water. Be careful not to matt the hair as you shampoo, and follow up with hair conditioner or fabric softener. Comb gently and set while wet, using small soft rubber or metal curlers. Never use a curling iron or heated rollers.

In our listings, unless a condition is noted in the descriptions, values are for dolls in excellent condition.

For further study, we recommend these books: *Madame Alexander Dolls, 1965 – 1990,* by Pat Smith; *Doll Values, Antique to Modern, Third Edition,* and *Modern Collectible Dolls, Vols I, II, III,* and *IV,* by Patsy Moyer; *Black Dolls: 1820 – 1991* and *Black Dolls, Book II,* by Myla Perkins; *Chatty Cathy Dolls* by Kathy and Don Lewis; *Collector's Guide to Ideal Dolls* by Judith Izen; *Collector's Guide to Tammy* by Cindy Sabulis and Susan Weglewski; *Liddle Kiddles, An Identification Guide,* by Paris Langford (which includes other dolls as well); and *Collector's Encyclopedia of Vogue Dolls* by Judith Izen and Carol J. Stover. All these references are published by Collector Books.

See also Barbie and Friends; Shirley Temple; Toys (Action Figures and GI Joe); Trolls.

Magazine: *Doll Castle News*
37 Belvidere Ave., P.O. Box 247
Washington, NJ 07882
908-689-7042 or fax: 908-689-6320

Newsletter: Doll Collectors of America
30 Norwood Ave., Rockport, MA 01966-1730

Newsletter: *Doll Investment Newsletter*
P.O. Box 1982, Centerville, MA 02632

Newsletter: *Doll News*
United Federation of Doll Clubs
P.O. Box 14146, Parkville, MO 64152

Newsletter: *Modern Doll Club Journal*
Jeanne Niswonger
305 W Beacon Rd., Lakeland, FL 33803

Annalee

Barbara 'Annalee' Davis' was born in Concord, New Hampshire, on February, 11, 1915. She started dabbling at doll-making at an early age, often giving her creations to friends. She married Charles 'Chip' Thorndike in 1941 and moved to Meredith, New Hampshire, where they started a chicken farm and sold used auto parts. By the early 1950s, with the chicken farm failing, Annalee started crafting her dolls on the kitchen table to help make ends meet. She designed her dolls by looking into the mirror, drawing faces as she saw them, and making the clothes from scraps of material.

The dolls she developed are made of wool felt with 'hand-painted' features and flexible wire frameworks. The earlier dolls from the 1950s had a long white red-embroidered tag with no date. From 1959 to 1964, the tags stayed the same except there was a date in the upper right-hand corner. From 1965 to 1970, this same tag was folded in half and sewn into the seam of the doll. In 1970 a transition period began. The company changed its tag to a satiny white tag with a date preceded by a copyright symbol in the upper right-hand corner. In 1975 they made another change to a long white cotton strip with a copyright date. In 1982 the white tag was folded over, making it shorter. Many people mistake the copyright date as the date the doll was made — not so! It wasn't until 1986 that they finally began to date the tags with the year of manufacture, making it much easier for collectors to identify their dolls. Besides the red-lettered white Annalee tags, numerous others were used in the 1990s, but all reflect the year the doll was actually made.

For many years the company held a June auction on the premises; this practice has been discontinued. Annalee's signature can increase a doll's value by as much as $300.00, sometimes more, but at this time she is not signing *any* dolls. Only Chuck (her son) and Karen Thorndike are now signing them.

Remember, these dolls are made of wool felt. To protect them, store them with moth balls, and avoid exposing them to too much sunlight, since they will fade. Our advisor has been a collector for twenty years and a secondary market dealer since 1988. Most of these dolls have been in her collection at one time or another. She recommends 'If you like it, buy it, love it, treat it with care, and you'll have it to enjoy for many years to come.'

Our values are suggested for dolls in very good to excellent condition, not personally autographed by Annalee herself.

Advisor: Jane Holt (See Directory, Dolls)

Newsletter: *The Collector*
Annalee Doll Society
P.O. Box 1137, 50 Reservoir Rd., Meredith, NH 03253-1137;
1-800-433-6557

Mailman mouse (note flat face), 1970, 7", $250.00. (Photo courtesy Jane Holt)

Baby in pajamas, 1989, 18" **$40.00**

Boy on raft, holds pole w/white shirt tied to end, 1980 & 1981 only, 10" **$70.00**

Bunny, Easter Parade boy, white w/purple gingham vest, pink jacket, top hat, 1980, 30" **$95.00**

Bunny, Easter Parade lady, pink & white dress & bonnet w/eyelet trim, 1979, 29" **$95.00**

Bunny, Just in Time, multicolored vest w/gold watch & chain, 1998, 18", M **$50.00**

Bunny Artist, holds egg (felt) & paint brush, 1988, 18" ..**$75.00**

Bunny Artist, w/pink smock & blue beret, holds brush & pallette, 1993, 7" **$15.00**

Bunny girl, red hair, 1978, 21" **$95.00**

Bunny Sailor boy, 2000, 30" **$95.00**

Bunny w/carrot, 1985, 7" **$25.00**

Cabbage, smiling, 1995, 10½" dia **$25.00**

Caroller girl, 1974, 8" **$50.00**

Chick, fluffy yellow, 1991, 5" **$15.00**

Clown, red & white check shirt, plastic daisy on top of black hat, 1980, 18" **$125.00**

Clown, Society Doll, deflated balloon, 1990, 8½" **$40.00**

Clown, yellow hat & clothes, 1990, 30" **$75.00**

Colonial drummer boy, 1976, 18" **$95.00**

Colonial man w/apple, 1998, 10" **$60.00**

Cupid Kid in hanging heart, 1984, 7" **$95.00**

Dove, 1993, 10x8" **$25.00**

Duck in raincoat, carrying umbrella, 1985, 5" **$35.00**

Duck w/aviator hat & goggles, white scarf around neck, given out to pilots from Annalee while on her trips, 1983, 5" **$30.00**

Elephant, no hat, 1972, 8" **$150.00**

Elf, Christmas, green clothes, white pompom on hat, made many years to the present, 10" **$15.00**

Elf, green or pink clothes, 1961, 26", ea....................**$250.00**

Elf w/arm in sling, bandage on cheek, leg in cast, on crutch, 1971, 10" **$90.00**

Frog boy, purple & white checked rompers, 1980, 18"..**$75.00**

Ghost mouse, 1993, 7", NM **$25.00**

Gingerbread boy, dressed in red & green, 1994, 10" .**$35.00**

Indian maiden w/printed blanket, tan dress, 1991, 10"..**$50.00**

Jack Frost, holds snowflake, 1982, 10" **$50.00**

Leprechaun, dark green body, shamrock vest, 1977, 10"..**$55.00**

Leprechaun, Lucky, w/mushroom, 1997, 7" **$35.00**

Leprechaun w/pot of gold, 1993, 5" **$35.00**

Leprechaun w/sack, 1974, 10" **$75.00**

Monk, black robe, 1963, 10" **$150.00**

Monk w/skis & poles, brown robe, 1970, 10"...........**$165.00**

Mouse, Big Feather, Indian boy, 1997, 7" **$30.00**

Mouse, housewife, holds mop, hair in rollers, 1983, 7"..**$35.00**

Mouse, Maid Marian, 1990, 7" **$30.00**

Mouse, Oakey Dokey, 1997, 3" **$20.00**

Mouse, Pilgrim boy & girl, cranberry clothes, 1984, 12", pr..**$120.00**

Mouse, Pilgrim girl & boy, green plaid dress, 1991, 12", pr..**$80.00**

Mouse biker boy, red & white striped shirt, streamline bicycle, 1978, 7" **$30.00**

Mouse bride & groom, 1995, 3", pr........................**$35.00**

Mouse gardener, blue flowered dress & scarf, green gloves, 1992, 7" **$15.00**

Mouse girl holding felt heart, white body, 1999, 7"....**$25.00**

Mouse girl in tennis clothes, white dress w/pink collar, w/racket, 1975..**$30.00**

Mouse golfer boy or girl holding trophy & golf club, 1970s, ea **$25.00**

Mouse peeking from hole in Christmas stocking, 1992, 18½" overall **$20.00**

Mouse w/sled, green & white striped hat, 1991, 7"....**$20.00**

Mouse witch on broom (mobile), 1980, 7"................**$30.00**

Mouse witch w/trick-or-treat bag, 1986, 12".............**$50.00**

Mouse wizard, 1996, 3", M..................................**$25.00**

Mouse woodchopper w/axe & logs, 1980, 7" **$25.00**

Mrs Claus dressed in red, white & green, 1987, 18"...**$40.00**

Mrs Claus sitting in rocker reading Christmas book, 1997, 18" **$50.00**

Piccolo player, on green base, 1995, 5" **$35.00**

Pilgrim girl w/basket, blue, 1993, 10" **$40.00**

Pilgrim man w/basket, 1991, 10" **$40.00**

Polar bear fishing, 1989, 7", in glass dome.................**$50.00**

Reindeer, red nose, 1977, 36" **$100.00**

Reindeer w/saddlebags & gifts, red nose, 1970s, 18" .**$50.00**

Santa Claus carrying book of Good Boys & Girls, 1970s & 1980s, 18" **$65.00**

Santa in rocking chair soaking feet, 1991, 18" **$55.00**

Santa on skis, pack on his back, holds ski poles, 1979, 7".**$25.00**

Scarecrow, burlap hat, denim print overalls, 1976, 10"..**$75.00**

Skeleton Kid, w/trick-or-treat bag, 1988, 7"................**$35.00**

Skeleton Kid, 1996, 30" **$125.00**

Skunk girl w/flowers, 1982, 12" **$125.00**

Snowman, black hat w/green band & earmuffs, red scarf, green gloves, holds broom, 1992, 18" **$65.00**

Snowy Owl, green earmuffs, 1990, 10".........................**$35.00**
St Patrick's Day boy, shamrock shirt, on base, 1997, 7".**$25.00**
St Patrick's Day mouse, gray body, holds mug of beer, 1993,
    7"...**$25.00**
Sweetheart Kid, red dress, red velvet Santa's cap, w/1986
    Annalee Doll Society Pin, 7"...................**$100.00**
Teepee, 1994, 17"...**$45.00**
Thorny the Ghost, 1989, 18"...........................**$125.00**
Turkey, Tommy, brown w/orange feet, white collar, 1996,
    12"...**$135.00**
Unicorn, 1986, 10" **$50.00**
Valentine angel, 1997, 10" **$70.00**
Witch Kid, 1993, 30"..**$125.00**

Betsy McCall

The tiny 8" Betsy McCall doll was manufactured by the American Character Doll Company from 1957 through 1963. She was made from high-quality hard plastic with a bisque-like finish and hand-painted features. Betsy came in four hair colors — tosca, red, blond, and brunette. She had blue sleep eyes, molded lashes, a winsome smile, and a fully jointed body with bendable knees. On her back there is an identification circle which reads McCall Corp. The basic doll wore a sheer chemise, white taffeta panties, nylon socks, and Mary Jane-style shoes and could be purchased for $2.25.

There were two different materials used for tiny Betsy's hair. The first was a soft mohair sewn into fine mesh. Later the rubber skullcap was rooted with saran which was more suitable for washing and combing.

Betsy McCall had an extensive wardrobe with nearly one hundred outfits, each of which could be purchased separately. They were made from wonderful fabrics such as velvet, taffeta, felt, and even real mink. Each ensemble came with the appropriate footwear and was priced under $3.00. Since none of Betsy's clothing was tagged, it is often difficult to identify other than by its square snap closures (although these were used by other companies as well).

Betsy McCall is a highly collectible doll today but is still fairly easy to find at doll shows. The prices remain reasonable for this beautiful clothes horse and her many accessories. For further information we recommend *Betsy McCall, A Collector's Guide*, by Marci Van Ausdall.

Advisor: Marci Van Ausdall (See Directory, Dolls)

Newsletter: *Betsy's Fan Club*
Marci Van Ausdall
P.O. Box 946, Quincy, CA 95971-0946
e-mail: dreams707@aol.com; Subscription $16.00 per year or send $4 for sample copy

Doll, Ideal, all original, MIB **$225.00**
Doll, original outfit w/pink tissue & booklet, 8", MIB, mini-
    mum value **$225.00**
Doll, TV Time, #9153, all original, complete w/TV, M ..**$150.00**
Doll, Uneeda, all original, 11½", EX **$45.00**

Doll, w/trunk & wardrobe, 14", M............................**$500.00**
Everyday Calendar, Milton Bradley, EX in worn box .**$25.00**
Outfit, Birthday Party, MOC.....................................**$125.00**
Outfit, fur stole & muff, MIB **$225.00**
Outfit, Zoo Time, complete, VG...............................**$65.00**
Pattern, McCall's #2247, uncut **$25.00**

Dolls, American Character, Betsy McCall, all original, 29", M, $225.00; Sandy McCall, all original, 35", $500.00.
(Photo courtesy McMasters Doll Auctions)

Celebrity Dolls

Celebrity and character dolls have been widely collected for many years, but they've lately shown a significant increase in demand. Except for rarer examples, most of these dolls are still fairly easy to find at doll shows, toy auctions, and flea markets, and the majority are priced under $100.00. These are the dolls that bring back memories of childhood TV shows, popular songs, favorite movies, and familiar characters. Mego, Mattel, Remco, and Hasbro are among the largest manufacturers.

Condition is a very important worth-assessing factor, and if the doll is still in the original box, so much the better! Should the box be unopened (NRFB), the value is further enhanced. Using mint as a standard, add 50% for the same doll mint in the box and 75% if it has never been taken out. On the other hand, dolls in only good or poorer condition drop at a rapid pace.

See also Elvis Presley Memorabilia.

Advisor: Henri Yunes (See Directory, Dolls)

Al Lewis (Grandpa Munster), Remco, 1964, 6", MIB .**$200.00**
Alan Alda (Hawkeye Pierce), Woolworth, 1976, 8½",
    MOC **$30.00**
Andy Gibb, Ideal, 1979, 7½", NRFB............................**$50.00**
Angie Dickenson (Police Woman), Horsman, 1976, 9",
    MIB..**$60.00**
Annissa Jones (Buffy), Mattel, 1967, talker, 10", w/5" Mrs
    Beasley doll, MIB...**$450.00**

Audrey Hepburn (Breakfast at Tiffany's), Mattel, 1998, black or pink outfit, 11½", MIB **$85.00**

Barbara Eden (I Dream of Jeannie), Remco, 1972, 6½", MIB (sealed) **$100.00**

Beverly Hills 90210, Mattel, 1991, 5 different, 11½", MIB, ea **$65.00**

Boy George, LJN, 1984, 11½", scarce, MIB **$135.00**

Brooke Shields, LJN, 1982, 1st issue, 11½", NRFB......**$50.00**

Brooke Shields, LJN, 1983, 2nd issue, in swimsuit w/suntan body, 11½", rare, NRFB.................................**$95.00**

Captain & Tenille, Mego, 1970s, 12", MIB, ea **$60.00**

Carol Channing (Hello Dolly), Nasco Dolls, 1962, 11½", rare, MIB **$350.00**

Cher, Mego, 1976, 1st edition, pink dress, 12", MIB (sealed orange box)...**$70.00**

Cheryl Ladd (Kris), Hasbro, 1977, jumpsuit & scarf, 8½", MOC..**$40.00**

Cheryl Tiegs (Real Models), Matchbox, 1989, 11½", NRFB...**$55.00**

Clark Gable (Rhett Butler), World Dolls, 1980, 1st edition, 12", MIB (sealed) **$65.00**

Claudia Schiffer (Top Models Collection), Hasbro, 1995, 11½", rare, MIB **$100.00**

David Hasselhoff (Mitch), Toy Island, 1997, 12", NRFB..**$35.00**

Debbie Boone, Mattel, 1978, 11", MIB......................**$50.00**

Dennis Rodman (Bad As I Wanna Be), Street Players, 1995, 11½", MIB..**$55.00**

Desi Arnez (Ricky Ricardo), Applause, 1988, 17", MIB..**$50.00**

Diahann Carroll (Julia), Mattel, 1969, several different outfits, NRFB, ea, from $80 to.......................**$130.00**

Diana Ross (Supremes), Ideal, 1969, 19", MIB (sealed) ..**$150.00**

Dick Clark, Juro, 1958, 24", MIB **$250.00**

Dolly Parton, Eegee, 1980, 1st edition, red jumpsuit, 12", MIB (sealed) **$65.00**

Dolly Parton, Eegee, 1987, second issue, cowgirl outfit, 12", MIB, $50.00. (Photo courtesy June Moon)

Donna Douglas (Ellie Mae), 1964, jeans w/rope belt or yellow dress, MIB, ea.................................**$65.00**

Donnie & Marie Osmond, Mattel, 1976, gift set, 12", NRFB.**$125.00**

Dorothy Hamill, 1977, red olympic outfit w/medal, 11½", NRFB...**$75.00**

Dr J (Julias Erving), Shindana, Deluxe Set, 1977, w/outfits, 9½", MIB **$400.00**

Elizabeth Taylor (Butterfield 8 or Cat on a Hot Tin Roof), Tristar, 1982, 11½", MIB, ea **$125.00**

Farrah Fawcett (Jill), Hasbro, 1977, jumpsuit & scarf, 8½", MIB **$40.00**

Farrah Fawcett (Jill), Mego, 1981, lavender swimsuit, 12", rare, NRFB (photo on purple box)....................**$95.00**

Flip Wilson/Geraldine, Shindana, 1970, plush w/vinyl head, 2-sided, 16", MIB......................................**$65.00**

Flo-Jo, LJN, 1989, pink & blue athletic outfit w/bag, 11½", MIB **$85.00**

Fran Dresher (Nanny), Street Players, 1995, 3 different outfits, talker, 11½", MIB..............................**$55.00**

Fred Gwynne (Herman Munster), Presents, 1990, plush body w/vinyl head, 12", MIB.............................**$35.00**

Grace Kelly (The Swan or Mogambo), Tristar, 1982, 11½", MIB **$125.00**

Groucho Marks, Effanbee, 1983, 17", MIB.................**$90.00**

James Dean, DSI, 1994, Rebel Rouser outfit or City Streets outfit, 12", NRFB, ea....................................**$75.00**

Jimmy Walker (JJ from Good Times), Shindana, 1974, 15", MIB **$50.00**

Joe Namath, Mego, 1970, 11½", rare, MIB **$400.00**

John Travolta (On Stage...Superstar), Chemtoy, 1977, 12", MIB (sealed)..**$125.00**

John Wayne (Great Legends), Effanbee, 1981, Spirit of the West outfit, 17", MIB....................................**$125.00**

Judy Garland (Wizard of Oz), Multitoys, 1984, 50th Anniversary, rare, MIB.......................................**$100.00**

Julie Andrews (Mary Poppins), Horsman, 1964, 1st edition, 12", MIB..**$125.00**

Julie Andrews (Mary Poppins), Horsman, 1973, 2nd edition, 11", MIB..**$75.00**

Karen Mulder (Top Models Collection), Hasbro, 1995, 11½", rare, MIB...**$100.00**

Kate Jackson (Sabrina from Charlie's Angels), Hasbro, 1977, jumpsuit & scarf, 8½", MOC **$40.00**

KISS, Ace Frehley, Gene Simmons, Paul Stanley, or Peter Cris, Mego, 1978, 12", MIB (sealed), ea **$125.00**

Laverne & Shirley, Mego, 1977, 12", NRFB, pr..........**$125.00**

Lenny & Squiggy, Mego, 1977, 12", NRFB, pr...........**$200.00**

Macaully Caulkin (Home Alone), THQ Inc, 1989, screams, MIB **$25.00**

Madonna (Breathless Mahoney), Applause, 1990, black evening gown, 10", NRFB **$60.00**

Marie Osmond, Mattel, 1976, 11", MIB **$60.00**

Marilyn Monroe, DSI, 1993, issued in 6 different outfits, 11½", MIB (sealed), ea....................................**$60.00**

Marilyn Monroe, Tristar, 1982, issued in 8 different outfits, 11½", MIB (sealed) **$100.00**

MC Hammer, Mattel, 1991, gold outfit w/boom box, 11½", MIB **$85.00**

MC Hammer, Mattel, 1991, purple outfit, 11½", MIB..**$70.00**

Michael Jackson, LJN, 1984, issued in 4 different outfits, 11½", MIB (sealed), ea **$70.00**

Mr T, Galoob, 1983, 1st editon, bib overalls, 12", MIB ...**$60.00**

Mr T, Galoob, 1983, 2nd edition, vest & jeans, talker, 12", MIB **$75.00**

Naomi Campbell (Top Models Collection), Hasbro, 1995, 11½", rare, MIB...**$100.00**

New Kids on the Block (Hangin' Loose), 1990, 1st edition, 5 different dolls, 12", MIB, ea **$40.00**

New Kids on the Block (In Concert), 1990, 2nd edition, 5 different dolls, 12", MIB, ea..**$50.00**

Pam Dawber (Mork & Mindy), Mattel, 1979, 8½", MIB...**$50.00**

Pamela Anderson Lee (CJ from Baywatch), Toy Island, 1998, Deluxe Set, 11½", NRFB...**$35.00**

Parker Stevenson (Frank from the Hardy Boys), Kenner, 1978, 12", NRFB **$50.00**

Patty Duke (Patty Duke Show), Horsman, 1967, 12½", rare, NRFB...**$400.00**

Prince Charles, Goldberger, 1982, military wedding outfit, 12", NRFB **$250.00**

Princess Diana, Goldberger, 1982, silver dress, 11½", MIB (sealed)...**$350.00**

Princess Diana, Goldberger, 1982, wedding gown, 11½", MIB (sealed)...**$250.00**

Princess Diana, Peggy Nesbet/England, wedding gown, 1984, 8", M **$100.00**

Redd Fox, Shindana, 1977, cloth, talker, MIB.............**$45.00**

Rex Harrison (Dr Dolittle), Mattel, 1969, cloth body w/vinyl head, talker, 24", MIB **$130.00**

Richard Chamberlin (Dr Kildare), Bing Crosby Productions, 1962, rare, MIB **$450.00**

Robin Williams (Mork & Mindy), Mattel, 1979, w/space pak, 9", MIB **$45.00**

Roger Moore (James Bond in Moonraker), Mego, 1979, 12", MIB **$100.00**

Rosie O'Donnell, Mattel, 1998, 11½", NRFB...............**$50.00**

Sally Field (Flying Nun), Hasbro, 1967, 5", MIB.........**$80.00**

Selena, Arm Enterprises, 1996, 11½", MIB...................**$50.00**

Spice Girls (Girl Power), Galoob, 1997, 1st issue, 5 different, 11½", NRFB..**$95.00**

Susan Dey (Laurie Partridge), Remco, 1973, 16", rare, MIB **$250.00**

Suzanne Sommers (Chrissy from Three's Company), Mego, 1975, 12½", MIB..**$85.00**

Sylvester Stallone (Over the Top), Lewco Toys, 1986, 20", MIB (sealed) **$35.00**

Tatum O'Neal (International Velvet), Kenner, 1979, 11½", MIB **$85.00**

Three Stooges, Collins, 1982, set of 3, 13", MOC...**$140.00**

Vanilla Ice, THQ, 1991, issued in 3 different outfits, 12", MIB (sealed), ea...**$50.00**

Vanna White, Totsy Toys, 1990, limited edition, wedding dress, rare, MIB...**$125.00**

Vivian Leigh (Scarlett O'Hara), World Dolls, 1980, 1st issue, 12", NRFB...**$65.00**

Wayne Gretsky (The Great Gretsky/Le Magnifique), Mattel, 1987, 11½", MIB **$150.00**

Yvonne de Carlo (Lily Munster), Remco, 1964, MIB..**$150.00**

Chatty Cathy and Other Mattel Talkers

One of the largest manufacturers of modern dolls is the Mattel company, the famous maker of the Barbie doll. But besides Barbie, there are many other types of Mattel's dolls that have their own devotees, and we've tried to list a sampling of several of their more collectible lines.

Next to Barbie, the all-time favorite doll was Mattel's Chatty Cathy. She was first made in the 1960s, in blond and brunette variations, and much of her success can be attributed to that fact that she could talk! By pulling the string on her back, she could respond with eleven different phrases. The line was expanded and soon included Chatty Baby, Tiny Chatty Baby and Tiny Chatty Brother (the twins), Charmin' Chatty, and finally Singin' Chatty. They all sold successfully for five years, and although Mattel reintroduced the line in 1969 (smaller and with a restyled face), it was not well received. For more information we recommend *Chatty Cathy Dolls, An Identification & Value Guide,* by our advisors, Kathy and Don Lewis.

In 1960 Mattel introduced their first line of talking dolls. They decided to take the talking doll's success even further by introducing a new line — cartoon characters that the young TV viewers were already familiar with.

Below you will find a list of the more popular dolls and animals available. Most MIB (mint-in-box) toys found today are mute, but this should not detract from the listed price. If the doll still talks, you may consider adding a few more dollars to the price.

Advisors: Kathy and Don Lewis (See Directory, Dolls)

Animal Yacker, Crackers the talking plush parrot, 1964, 15½", MIB **$385.00**

Animal Yacker, Larry the talking plush lion, 1964, 15", EX **$85.00**

Baby Cheryl, 1965, MIB **$200.00**

Baby Drowsy, Black, 1968, 15", MIB **$175.00**

Baby Flip-Flop, JC Penney Exclusive, 1970, MIB........**$85.00**

Baby Sing-A-Song, 1969, 16½", MIB **$150.00**

Baby Small Talk, 1968, MIB..**$125.00**

Baby Tender Love, soft rubber, red gingham romper, EX ..**$45.00**

Baby Whisper, 1968, 17½", MIB.................................**$200.00**

Beany, cloth w/molded plastic shoes, plastic hat w/propeller, 1962, 17½", MIB **$250.00**

Beddie Bye Talk, Patter Pal, 1970, MIB **$80.00**

Black Chatty Baby, M...**$650.00**

Black Chatty Baby, w/pigtails, M...........................**$1,500.00**

Black Tiny Chatty Baby, M...**$650.00**

Bozo the Clown, blue & white polka-dot outfit, 1964, 18", MIB **$300.00**

Bugs Bunny, plush w/molded vinyl face & hands, 1962, MIB **$300.00**

Casper the Friendly Ghost, plastic face, plush cloth body, 1961, 15", EX...**$125.00**

Charmin' Chatty, auburn or blond hair, blue eyes, complete, MIB **$275.00**

Chatty Baby, brunette hair, red pinafore over white romper, original tag, MIB **$250.00**

Chatty Baby, early, brunette hair, brown eyes, M.....**$160.00**

Chatty Baby, open speaker, blond hair, blue eyes, M..**$250.00**

Chatty Baby, open speaker, brunette hair, brown eyes, M..**$375.00**

Chatty Cathy, brunette hair, brown eyes, M.............**$375.00**

Chatty Cathy, early, brunette hair, blue eyes, M **$85.00**

Chatty Cathy, later issue, brunette hair, brown eyes, M..**$850.00**

Chatty Cathy, later issue, open speaker, blond hair, blue eyes, M **$750.00**

Chatty Cathy, mid-year or transitional, brunette hair, brown eyes, M **$650.00**

Chatty Cathy, mid-year or transitional, open speaker, blond hair, blue eyes, M **$600.00**

Chatty Cathy, patent pending, brunette hair, blue eyes, M **$750.00**

Chatty Cathy, porcelain, 1980, MIB................**$750.00**

Chatty Cathy, reissue, blond hair, blue eyes, MIB **$80.00**

Cheerleader, several variations, 1970, MIB, ea **$75.00**

Chester O' Chimp, puppet, 1969, MIB......................**$185.00**

Dishonest John, hand puppet, 1963, EX...................**$150.00**

Drowsy, pink polka-dot outfit, 1965, EX **$50.00**

Drowsy Sleeper-Keeper, 1966, MIB..........................**$125.00**

Hi Dottie, Black, 1972, complete w/telephone, NM ...**$75.00**

Linus the Lionhearted, gold corduroy w/vinyl face, felt mane, 1966, 21", EX..**$125.00**

Mr Ed, hand puppet, 1965, 12", EX...........................**$150.00**

Nite-Nite, Patter Pillow, girl saying prayers, 1968, EX...**$55.00**

Patootie clown, happy face & sad face mask, yellow pointed hat, 1966, MIB **$350.00**

Porky Pig, pink twill w/striped jacket & blue bow, 1965, 17", EX **$175.00**

Pushmi-Pullyu, 2-headed llama, 1968, EX **$125.00**

Randi Reader, 1968, 19½", MIB **$175.00**

Scooba Doo, beatnik girl, long blond hair, compete, 1965, 23", EX **$100.00**

Shrinkin' Violette, cloth, purple skirt w/hot pink netting, yarn hair, 1964, 12", NM, minimum value **$100.00**

Singin' Chatty, blond hair, M **$250.00**

Somersalty, 1970, MIB **$200.00**

Story Book Small-Talk, Cinderella, 1969, EX...............**$55.00**

Storybook Small-Talk, Bo-Peep, 1969, MIB **$250.00**

Talking Baby First Step, blond rooted hair, w/roller skates, 1968, 18", MIB..**$225.00**

Tatters, yarn hair in low pigtails, patchwork clothes, 1965, MIB **$140.00**

Teachy Keen, 1966, MIB **$125.00**

Teachy Talk, 1970, MIB..**$50.00**

Timey Tell, MIB **$110.00**

Tiny Chatty Baby, blond hair, blue eyes, M..............**$250.00**

Tiny Chatty Baby, brunette hair, brown eyes, M **$300.00**

Tiny Chatty Twins, M, ea **$250.00**

Woody Woodpecker, corduroy w/medium-to-soft vinyl head, felt feathers on top of head, 1965, 18", MIB **$175.00**

Woody Woodpecker, hand puppet, 17", 1965, EX....**$125.00**

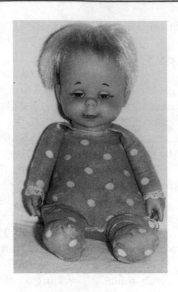

Baby Drowsy, played with, non-talking, 1965, $10.00 (MIB: $200.00).
(Photo courtesy Kathy and Don Lewis)

Dawn Dolls by Topper

Made by Deluxe Topper in the 1970s, this 6" fashion doll was part of a series sold as the Dawn Model Agency. They're becoming highly collectible, especially when mint in the box. They were issued already dressed in clothes of the highest style, or you could buy additional outfits, many complete with matching shoes and accessories.

Advisor: Dawn Diaz (See Directory, Dolls)

Dawn's Apartment, complete w/furniture **$50.00**

Doll, Dancing Angie, NRFB **$30.00**

Doll, Dancing Dale, NRFB **$50.00**

Doll, Dancing Dawn, NRFB **$30.00**

Doll, Dancing Gary, NRFB...**$40.00**

Doll, Dancing Glory, NRFB..**$30.00**

Doll, Dancing Jessica, NRFB......................................**$30.00**

Doll, Dancing Ron, NRFB **$40.00**

Doll, Dancing Van, NRFB...**$50.00**

Doll, Daphne, Dawn Model Agency, green & silver dress, NRFB..**$75.00**

Doll, Dawn Head to Toe, pink & silver dress, NRFB .**$90.00**

Doll, Dawn Majorette, NRFB.......................................**$75.00**

Doll, Denise, NRFB...**$75.00**

Doll, Dinah, NRFB..**$75.00**

Doll, Gary, NRFB **$30.00**

Doll, Jessica, NRFB **$30.00**

Doll, Kip Majorette, NRFB..**$45.00**

Doll, Longlocks, NRFB **$30.00**

Doll, Maureen, Dawn Model Agency, red & gold dress, NRFB.**$75.00**

Doll, Ron, NRFB **$30.00**

Outfit, Bell Bottom Flounce, #0717, NRFB **$25.00**

Holly Hobbie

In the late 1960s a young homemaker and mother, Holly Hobbie, approached the American Greeting Company with some charming country-styled drawings of children as proposed designs for greeting cards. Her concepts were well received by the company, and since that time thousands of Holly Holly items have been produced. Nearly all are marked HH, H. Hobbie, or Holly Hobbie.

Advisor: Donna Stultz (See Directory, Dolls)

Newsletter: *Holly Hobbie Collectors Gazette*
c/o Donna Stultz
1455 Otterdale Mill Rd.
Taneytown, MD 21787-3032; 410-775-2570
hhgazette@netscape.net
Subscription: $25 per year for 6 issues; includes free 50-word ad per issue, 'Free' sample issue available!

Doll, Grandma Holly, Knickerbocker, cloth, 24", MIB ..**$30.00**
Doll, Holly Hobbie, Heather, Amy or Carrie, Knickerbocker, cloth, 6", MIB, ea **$10.00**
Doll, Holly Hobbie, Heather, Amy or Carrie, Knickerbocker, cloth, 9", MIB, ea **$15.00**
Doll, Holly Hobbie, Heather, Amy or Carrie, Knickerbocker, cloth, 16", MIB **$25.00**
Doll, Holly Hobbie, Heather, Amy or Carrie, Knickerbocker, cloth, 27", MIB, ea **$35.00**
Doll, Holly Hobbie, Heather, Amy or Carrie, Knickerbocker, cloth, 33", MIB, ea **$45.00**
Doll, Holly Hobbie, 1988, scented, clear ornament around neck, 18", NRFB **$40.00**
Doll, Holly Hobbie Bicentennial, Knickerbocker, cloth, 12" **$30.00**
Doll, Holly Hobbie Day 'N Night, Knickerbocker, cloth, 14" **$20.00**
Doll, Holly Hobbie Dream Along, Holly, Carrie or Amy, Knickerbocker, cloth, 9", MIB, ea.........................**$15.00**
Doll, Holly Hobbie Dream Along, Holly, Carrie or Amy, Knickerbocker, cloth, 12", MIB, ea.......................**$20.00**
Doll, Holly Hobbie Talker, cloth, 4 sayings, 16", MIB ..**$30.00**
Doll, Little Girl Holly, Knickerbocker, cloth, 1980, 15", MIB **$30.00**
Doll, Robbie, Knickerbocker, cloth, 9", MIB................**$20.00**
Doll, Robbie, Knickerbocker, cloth, 16", MIB.............**$30.00**
Dollhouse, M...**$300.00**
Sewing machine, Durham, plastic & metal, battery-op, 1975, 5x9", EX **$40.00**
Sing-A-Long Electric Parlor Player, Vanity Fair, 1970s, complete w/booklet, scarce, NMIB **$45.00**

Ideal Dolls

The Ideal Toy Company made many popular dolls such as Shirley Temple, Betsy Wetsy, Miss Revlon, Toni, and Patti Playpal. Ideal's doll production was so enormous that since 1907 over 700 different dolls have been 'brought to life,' made from materials such as composition, latex rubber, hard plastic, and vinyl.

Since Ideal dolls were mass produced, most are still accessible and affordable. Collectors often find these dolls at garage sales and flea markets. However, some Ideal dolls are highly desirable and command high prices — into the thousands of dollars. These sought-after dolls include the Samantha doll, variations of the Shirley Temple doll, certain dolls in the Patti Playpal family, and some Captain Action dolls.

The listing given here is only a sampling of Ideal dolls made from 1907 to 1989. This listing reports current, realistic selling prices at doll shows and through mail order. Please remember these values are for dolls in excellent condition with original clothing.

For more information please refer to *Collector's Guide to Ideal Dolls: Identification and Values, Second Edition,* by Judith Izen (Collector Books).

See also Advertising Characters; Shirley Temple; and Dolls subcategories: Betsy McCall, Celebrity Dolls, and Tammy.

Club: Ideal Collectors Club
Judith Izen
P.O. Box 623, Lexington, MA 02173
Subscription: $20 per year for 4 issues; includes free wanted/for sale ads in each issue

Miss Revlon, 18", M with booklet and dress tag, $300.00.
(Photo courtesy McMasters Doll Auctions)

Baby Dreams, soft cloth w/vinyl head, 1975-76, 17", MIB, minimum value **$50.00**
Baby Kissy, 1962, 23", NRFB **$325.00**
Baby Whoopsie, 1978, 14", VG **$55.00**
Beauty Braider Velvet, 1973, EX.................................**$35.00**
Betsy Wetsy, 1937-38, original dress, EX (EX box)...**$300.00**
Bub-A-Dub Dolly, Black, 1979-80, 16", NRFB............**$50.00**
Clapping Baby, cloth & composition, original white dress, booties & lace bonnet, 15", EX, from $150 to....**$200.00**
Country Fashion Crissy, 1982-83, EX............................**$20.00**
Dina, purple playsuit, 1972-73, EX.............................**$50.00**
Goody Two Shoes, vinyl, original blue dress, 1965, 19", NMIB, minimum value **$125.00**
Kerry, 1971, green romper, EX **$55.00**

Little Betsy Wetsy, complete w/diaper & bottle (12 outfits sold separately), 1957, MIB, minimum value **$75.00**

Look Around Crissy, 1972, EX..................................**$40.00**

Look Around Velvet, Black, 1972, EX......................**$100.00**

Look Around Velvet, 1972, EX.................................**$35.00**

Magic Hair Crissy, 1977, EX....................................**$30.00**

Mia, 1971, turquoise romper, EX.............................**$50.00**

Movin' Groovin' Crissy, Black, 1971, EX **$100.00**

Movin' Groovin' Crissy, 1971, EX............................**$35.00**

Movin' Groovin' Velvet, 1971, EX............................**$35.00**

Newborn Thumbelina, vinyl w/foam-stuffed body, 1968-72, 9", MIB..**$85.00**

Patti Prays, stuffed cloth w/vinyl head & hands, 1957, NM **$75.00**

Patty Playpal, 1980s reissue, 36", MIB.....................**$375.00**

Swirla Curla Crissy, Black, 1973, EX **$100.00**

Swirla Curla Crissy, 1973, EX..................................**$35.00**

Swirly Daisies Velvet, 1974, EX...............................**$35.00**

Tara, Black, 1976, yellow gingham outfit, MIB **$85.00**

Thumbelina, cloth & vinyl, original blue & white knit outfit, 18", NMIB, from $150 to **$200.00**

Tiny Thumbelina, 1962-68, 14", MIB.......................**$185.00**

Twirly Beads Crissy, 1974, MIB **$65.00**

Velvet, 1970, 1st issue, purple dress, EX..................**$55.00**

Velvet, 1982 reissue, EX..**$30.00**

Jem

The glamorous life of Jem mesmerized little girls who watched her Saturday morning cartoons, and she was a natural as a fashion doll. Hasbro saw the potential in 1985 when they introduced the Jem line of 12" dolls representing her, the rock stars from Jem's musical group, the Holograms, and other members of the cast, including the only boy, Rio, Jem's road manager and Jerrica's boyfriend. Each doll was poseable, jointed at the waist, head, and wrists, so that they could be positioned at will with their musical instruments and other accessory items. Their clothing, their makeup, and their hairdos were wonderfully exotic, and their faces were beautifully modeled. The Jem line was discontinued in 1987 after being on the market for only two years.

Accessory, Jem Roadster, AM/FM radio in trunk, scarce, EX **$150.00**

Accessory, Jem Soundstage, Starlight House #14, EX, from $40 to...**$50.00**

Doll, Aja, 1st issue, from Holograms, M **$45.00**

Doll, Aja, 2nd issue, from Holograms, M..................**$90.00**

Doll, Ashley, Starlight Girl, no wrist or elbow joints, 11", M **$40.00**

Doll, Banee, Starlight Girl, no wrist or elbow joints, 11", M **$25.00**

Doll, Danse, from Holograms, NRFB **$60.00**

Doll, Danse, pink & blond hair, complete, 11", MIB..**$40.00**

Doll, Jem, Flash 'n Sizzle, NRFB..............................**$40.00**

Doll, Jem, Rock 'n Curl, M.......................................**$20.00**

Doll, Jem/Jerrica, Glitter 'n Gold, complete, 11", MIB ..**$50.00**

Doll, Jem/Jerrica, 1st issue, M...................................**$30.00**

Doll, Jetta, black hair w/silver streaks, complete, 11", MIB...**$40.00**

Doll, Kimber, 1st issue, from Holograms, M...............**$40.00**

Doll, Kimber, 2nd issue, from Holograms, M.............**$75.00**

Doll, Krissie, Starlight Girl, no wrist or elbow joints, 11", M **$35.00**

Doll, Pizzaz (Misfits), chartreuse hair, complete, 11", MIB ..**$40.00**

Doll, Raya, complete, 11", MIB.................................**$40.00**

Doll, Rio, Glitter 'n Gold, M **$25.00**

Doll, Rio, Glitter 'n Gold, pale vinyl, M....................**$125.00**

Doll, Rio, 1st issue, M..**$25.00**

Doll, Roxy, Misfit, 1st or 2nd issue, M, ea................**$50.00**

Doll, Shana, 1st issue, from Holograms, M................**$40.00**

Doll, Shana, 2nd issue, from Holograms, M...............**$225.00**

Doll, Stormer, Misfit, 2nd issue, M...........................**$60.00**

Doll, Video, complete, 11", MIB...............................**$40.00**

Glitter 'n Gold Roadster, M......................................**$150.00**

New Wave Waterbed, M..**$35.00**

Outfit, City Lights, MIP **$15.00**

Star Stage, M..**$30.00**

Clash, complete, MIB (box not shown), $40.00. (Photo courtesy Lee Garmon)

Liddle Kiddles

These tiny little dolls ranging from ¾" to 4" tall were made by Mattel from 1966 until 1979. They all had poseable bodies and rooted hair that could be restyled, and they came with accessories of many types. Some represented storybook characters, some were flowers in perfume bottles, some were made to be worn as jewelry, and there were even spacemen 'Kiddles.'

Serious collectors prefer examples that are still in their original packaging and will often pay a minimum of 30% (to as much as 100%) over the price of a doll in excellent condition with all her original accessories. A doll whose accessories are missing is worth from 65% to 70% less. For more information, we recommend *Liddle Kiddles* by Paris Langford and *Schroeder's Collectible Toys, Antique to Modern* (both published by Collector Books).

Advisor: Dawn Diaz (See Directory, Dolls)

Club: Liddle Kiddle Klub
Laura Miller
3639 Fourth Ave., La Crescenta, CA 91214

Apple Blossom Kologne, #3707, MIP...........................$60.00
Babe Biddle, #3505, complete, M...............................$50.00
Beach Buggy, #5003, NM..$50.00
Blue Funny Bunny, #3532, MIP...............................$100.00
Bunson Bernie, #3501, complete, M $75.00
Chitty-Chitty Bang-Bang Kiddles, #3597, MOC.........$250.00
Cinderiddle's Palace, #5068, plastic window version, M..$85.00
Dainty Deer, #3637, complete, M $45.00
Flower Charm Bracelet, #3747, MIP..........................$25.00
Flower Ring Kiddle, #3744, MIP $50.00
Freezy Sliddle, #3516, complete, M...........................$65.00
Gardenia Kologne, #3710, MIP $75.00
Greta Griddle, #3508, complete, M $85.00
Heart Pin Kiddle, #3741, MIP....................................$50.00
Heart Ring Kiddle, #3744, MIP $50.00
Honeysuckle Kologne, #3704, MIP.............................$60.00
Howard Biff Biddle, #3502, complete, M....................$75.00
Jewelry Kiddles Treasure Box, #3735 & #5166, M $40.00
Kiddle Komedy Theatre, #3592, EX $50.00
Kiddles Sweet Shoppe, #3807, NRFB.......................$200.00
Kleo Kila, #3729, complete, M...................................$50.00
Lady Crimson, #A3840, M in sealed package..............$85.00
Laffy Lemon, #3742, MIP..$85.00
Larky Locket, #3539, complete, EX $25.00
Liddle Biddle Peep, #3544, complete, M $125.00

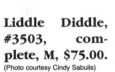

Liddle Diddle, #3503, complete, M, $75.00.
(Photo courtesy Cindy Sabulis)

Liddle Kiddles Kabin, #3591, EX $25.00
Liddle Kiddles Open House, #5167, MIB....................$40.00
Liddle Kiddles Talking Townhouse, #5154, MIB.........$75.00
Liddle Lion Zoolery, #3661, complete, M $200.00
Limey Lou Spoonfuls, #2815, MIP $25.00
Lola Locket, #3536, MIP $75.00

Lottie Locket, #3719, 1976 version, MIP.....................$25.00
Luana Locket, #3680, Gold Rush version, MIP $85.00
Luscious Lime, #3733, complete, M............................$55.00
Nappytime Baby, #3818, complete, M $75.00
Pink Funny Bunny, #3532, MIP................................$100.00
Rosebud Kologne, #3702, MIP...................................$60.00
Santa Kiddle, #3595, MIP $60.00
Sleep 'n Totsy Outfit, #LK5, MIP $25.00
Snap-Happy Living Room, #5173, NMIP.....................$20.00
Suki Skediddle, #3767, complete, M $25.00
Tiny Tiger, #3636, MIP $100.00
Vanilla Lilly, #2819, MIP $25.00

Littlechap Family

In 1964 Remco Industries created a family of four fashion dolls that represented an upper-middle class American family. The Littlechaps family consisted of the father, Dr. John Littlechap, his wife, Lisa, and their two children, teenage daughter Judy and pre-teen Libby. Interest in these dolls is on the rise as more and more collectors discover the exceptional quality of these fashion dolls and their clothing.

Advisor: Cindy Sabulis (See Directory, Dolls)

Carrying case, EX..$25.00
Doll, Doctor John, MIB $60.00
Doll, Judy, MIB $65.00
Doll, Libby, MIB..$45.00
Doll, Lisa, MIB $60.00
Family room, bedroom or Doctor John's office, EX, ea..$125.00
Outfit, Doctor John, complete, EX, from $15 to..........$30.00
Outfit, Doctor John, NRFB, from $30 to $50.00
Outfit, Judy, complete, EX, from $25 to $40.00
Outfit, Judy, NRFB, from $35 to $75.00
Outfit, Libby, complete, EX, from $25 to....................$35.00
Outfit, Libby, NRFB, from $35 to................................$50.00
Outfit, Lisa, complete, EX, from $20 to.......................$35.00
Outfit, Lisa, NRFB, from $35 to $75.00

Nancy Ann Storybook Dolls

This company was in business as early as 1936, producing painted bisque dolls with mohair wigs and painted eyes. Later they made hard plastic 8" Muffie and Miss Nancy Ann Style Show dolls. Debby (11") and Lori Ann (7½") had vinyl heads and hard plastic bodies. In the 1950s and 1960s, they produced a 10½" Miss Nancy Ann and Little Miss Nancy Ann, both vinyl high-heeled fashion-type dolls. For information we recommend *Modern Collectible Dolls* by Patsy Moyer.

Boy Blue, painted bisque, all original w/gold foil tag & brochure, 8", NM (NM blue-dot box), minimum value $35.00
Debut, Commencement Series, hard plastic, sleep eyes, all original w/gold wrist tag, 5", NM (NM box), minimum value $75.00

Lassie Fair, painted bisque, all original w/gold foil tag, 5", NM (NM fuchsia-dot box), minimum value **$50.00**

Lucy Locket, painted bisque, all original, 5", NM, minimum value **$275.00**

Miss Nancy Ann, vinyl, marked Nancy Ann on head, all original, 10½", NM, minimum value **$85.00**

Muffie, hard plastic, non-walker, several variations, 8", NM, ea, minimum value...**$175.00**

Muffie, hard plastic, walker, several variations, 8", NM, ea, minimum value **$150.00**

Muffie, vinyl, walker, several variations, 8", NM, ea, minimum value **$175.00**

New Moon, Operette Series, hard plastic, all original, w/tag, 5", NM, minimum value **$125.00**

Portuguese, painted bisque, jointed legs, all original w/wrist tag, 5", NM, minimum value **$325.00**

Thursday's Child Has Far To Go, painted bisque, all original w/silver tag, 5", NM (NM pink-dot box), minimum value ..**$75.00**

To Market To Market, painted bisque, all original w/silver tag, 5", NM (NM blue-dot box), minimum value .**$75.00**

Raggedy Ann and Andy

Raggedy Ann dolls have been made since the early part of the twentieth century, and over the years many companies have produced their own versions. They were created originally by Johnny Gruelle, and though these early dolls are practically nonexistent, they're easily identified by the mark, 'Patented Sept. 7, 1915.' P.F. Volland made them from 1920 to 1934; theirs were very similar in appearance to the originals. The Mollye Doll Outfitters were the first to print the now-familiar red heart on her chest, and they added a black outline around her nose. These dolls carry the handwritten inscription 'Raggedy Ann and Andy Doll/Manufactured by Mollye Doll Outfitters.' Georgene Averill made them ca 1938 to 1950, sewing their label into the seam of the dolls. Knickerbocker dolls (1963 to 1982) also carry a company label. The Applause Toy Company made these dolls for two years in the early 1980s, and they were finally taken over by Hasbro, the current producer, in 1983.

Our values are for dolls in mint condition, or nearly so. If your doll has been played with but is still in good condition with a few minor flaws (as most are), you'll need deduct about 75% from these prices. Refer to *The World of Raggedy Ann Collectibles* by Kim Avery, and *Doll Values, Antique to Modern,* by Patsy Moyer (Collector Books).

Advisor: Kim Avery

Applause, Raggedy Andy, Little Raggedys, Macmillan Inc, stuffed cloth w/yarn hair, 12", EX, from $25 to....**$30.00**

Applause, Raggedy Andy, stuffed cloth w/yarn hair, 25", EX, from $45 to...**$50.00**

Applause, Raggedy Ann & Andy sleeping bag dolls, stuffed cloth w/yarn hair, original tags, NM, ea, from $15 to **$20.00**

Applause, Raggedy Ann and Andy pair, 1986, 12", $28.00 to $32.00 each.
(Photo courtesy Kim Avery)

Applause, Raggedy Ann & Andy Sleepytime, stuffed cloth w/yarn hair, 17", EX, ea, from $30 to **$35.00**

Georgene Novelties Co, Raggedy Andy, stuffed cloth w/yarn hair, black outline nose, 1938-45, 19", EX, from $325 to .**$350.00**

Georgene Novelties Co, Raggedy Ann, stuffed cloth w/yarn hair, 1946-63, 19", EX **$100.00**

Georgene Novelties Co, Raggedy Ann & Andy, stuffed cloth w/yarn hair, late 1950s-1963, nude, 15", EX, ea...**$45.00**

Georgene Novelties Co, Raggedy Ann & Andy, stuffed cloth w/yarn hair, 1946-63, 19", EX, ea, from $95 to ..**$125.00**

Georgene Novelties Co, Raggedy Ann and Andy, stuffed cloth w/yarn hair, 1946-63, 15", EX, ea, from $80 to.......**$95.00**

Georgene Novelties Co, Raggedy Ann Awake/Asleep, cloth w/yarn hair, 1940-45, 12½", EX, from $275 to ...**$375.00**

Hallmark/Bobbs-Merrill Co, Raggedy Ann & Andy, stuffed cloth w/yarn hair, 1974, 6", EX, ea, from $20 to..**$25.00**

Ideal/Bobbs-Merrill, Raggedy Ann & Andy, inflatable vinyl, 1973, Ann: 21", Andy: 22", MIP, ea........................**$40.00**

Knickerbocker, Raggedy Andy, stuffed cloth w/yarn hair, Hong Kong, 40", w/original paper tag, NM, from $155 to .**$175.00**

Knickerbocker, Raggedy Ann, stuffed cloth w/yarn hair, original tag, 15", NM **$50.00**

Knickerbocker, Raggedy Ann, stuffed cloth w/yarn hair, plays Rock-A-Bye Baby, 15", NM **$40.00**

Knickerbocker, Raggedy Ann, stuffed cloth w/yarn hair, 31½", NMIB...**$125.00**

Knickerbocker, Raggedy Ann & Andy, cloth over wire w/yarn hair, 1960s, 9", EX, ea...............................**$25.00**

Knickerbocker, Raggedy Ann & Andy, stuffed cloth w/yarn hair, NY, mid-1960s, 15", EX, ea, from $35 to **$40.00**

Knickerbocker, Raggedy Ann & Andy, stuffed cloth w/yarn hair, Hong Kong, 15", EX, ea, from $30 to...........**$35.00**

Knickerbocker, Raggedy Ann & Andy, stuffed cloth w/yarn hair, early, Japan, 15", EX, ea, from $45 to...........**$55.00**

Knickerbocker, Raggedy Ann & Andy, stuffed cloth w/yarn hair, Malaysia, 15", EX, ea, from $25 to **$30.00**

Knickerbocker, Raggedy Ann & Andy, stuffed cloth w/yarn hair, Korea, 15", EX, ea, from $20 to **$25.00**

Knickerbocker, Raggedy Ann & Andy, stuffed cloth w/yarn hair, Taiwan, late 1970s to early '80s, 19", EX, ea, from $30 to...**$35.00**

Knickerbocker, Raggedy Ann & Andy, stuffed cloth w/yarn hair, sewn in China, 35", MIB, ea, from $145 to ..**$165.00**

Knickerbocker, Raggedy Ann & Andy Teach & Dress, stuffed cloth w/yarn hair, shiny shoes, Hong Kong, 20", EX, ea, from $50 to..**$55.00**

Playskool, Raggedy Ann & Andy, Christmas edition, 1990, 12", MIB..**$40.00**

Playskool, Raggedy Ann Christmas Doll, stuffed cloth w/yarn hair, 1988, MIB, from $35 to.................................**$40.00**

Strawberry Shortcake and Friends

Strawberry Shortcake came on the market with a bang around 1980. The line included everything to attract small girls — swimsuits, bed linens, blankets, anklets, underclothing, coats, shoes, sleeping bags, dolls and accessories, games, and many other delightful items. Strawberry Shortcake and her friends were short lived, lasting only until the mid-1980s.

Advisor: Geneva Addy (See Directory, Dolls)

Newsletter: *Berry-Bits*
Strawberry Shortcake Collector's Club
Peggy Jimenez
1409 72nd St., N Bergen, NJ 07047

Figure, Cherry Cuddler with Gooseberry, Strawberryland Miniatures, MIP, $15.00 to $20.00. (Photo courtesy Carolyn Berens)

Bike (motorized)..**$95.00**
Doll, Almond Tea, 6", MIB...............................**$25.00**
Doll, Apple Dumpling, 6", MIB **$25.00**
Doll, Apricot, 15", NM....................................**$35.00**
Doll, Berry Baby Orange Blossom, 6", MIB **$35.00**
Doll, Butter Cookie, 6", MIB............................**$25.00**
Doll, Lime Chiffon, 6", MIB.............................**$25.00**
Doll, Mint Tulip, 6", MIB.................................**$25.00**
Doll, Roller Skater...**$35.00**
Doll, Strawberry Shortcake, 12", NRFB **$45.00**
Doll, Strawberry Shortcake, 15", NM..........................**$35.00**

Dollhouse, M..**$150.00**
Dollhouse furniture, attic, 6-pc, rare, M......................**$140.00**
Dollhouse furniture, bathroom, 5-pc, rare, M **$65.00**
Dollhouse furniture, living room, 6-pc, rare, M **$85.00**
Figure, Merry Berry Worm, MIB **$35.00**
Figure, Mint Tulip w/March Mallard, PVC, MOC **$15.00**
Figure, Raspberry Tart w/bowl of cherries, MOC **$15.00**
Figure, Raspberry Tart w/rhubarb, PVC, 1", MOC **$15.00**
Figurine, Almond Tea w/Marza Panda, PVC, 1", MOC..**$15.00**
Figurine, Lemon Meringue w/Frapps, PVC, 1", MOC .**$15.00**
Figurine, Lime Chiffon w/balloons, PVC, 1", MOC **$15.00**
Storybook Play Case, M **$35.00**
Stroller, Coleco, 1981, M **$85.00**
Telephone, Strawberry Shortcake figure, battery-op, EX **$85.00**

Tammy and Friends

In 1962 the Ideal Novelty and Toy Company introduced their teenage Tammy doll. Slightly pudgy and not quite as sophisticated-looking as some of the teen fashion dolls on the market at the time, Tammy's innocent charm captivated consumers. Her extensive wardrobe and numerous accessories added to her popularity with children. Tammy had a car, a house, and her own catamaran. In addition, a large number of companies obtained licenses to issue products using the 'Tammy' name. Everything from paper dolls to nurses' kits were made with Tammy's image on them. Her success was not confined to the United States; she was also successful in Canada and several other European countries. See *Collector's Guide to Tammy, the Ideal Teen,* by Cindy Sabulis and Susan Weglewski (published by Collector Books) for more information.

Advisor: Cindy Sabulis (See Directory, Dolls)

Case, Tammy and Her Friends, green background, M, $30.00. (Photo courtesy Cindy Sabulis)

Accessory Pak, #9222-1, w/sleeveless blouse, necklace & hanger, NRFP..**$20.00**
Accessory Pak, #9244-5, w/sweater, scarf & hanger, NRFP **$25.00**

Accessory Pak, #9345-2, w/afternoon dress & shoes, NRFP **$25.00**

Case, Dodi, green background, EX **$30.00**

Case, Misty, pink & white background, EX **$25.00**

Case, Pepper, hatbox style, turquoise background, EX ..**$40.00**

Case, Pepper & Patti, Montgomery Ward's Exclusive, red background, EX **$50.00**

Case, Tammy Beau & Arrow, hatbox style, blue or red, EX, ea **$40.00**

Case, Tammy Model Miss, double trunk, red or black, EX, ea **$25.00**

Case, Tammy Traveler, red or green background, EX ..**$45.00**

Doll, Bud, MIB, minimum value **$600.00**

Doll, Dodi, MIB **$75.00**

Doll, Glamour Misty the Miss Clairol Doll, MIB.......**$150.00**

Doll, Grown Up Tammy, MIB **$75.00**

Doll, Misty, MIB **$100.00**

Doll, Patti, MIB **$200.00**

Doll, Pepper, 'carrot'-colored hair, MIB **$75.00**

Doll, Pepper, MIB **$65.00**

Doll, Pos'n Dodi, M (decorated box).......................**$150.00**

Doll, Pos'n Misty & Her Telephone Booth, MIB **$125.00**

Doll, Pos'n Pete, MIB **$125.00**

Doll, Pos'n Tammy, MIB **$100.00**

Doll, Pos'n Ted, MIB **$100.00**

Doll, Tammy, MIB **$75.00**

Doll, Tammy's Dad, MIB.......................................**$65.00**

Doll, Ted, MIB **$65.00**

Outfit, Dad & Ted, pajamas & slippers, #9456-5, MIB ..**$20.00**

Outfit, Pepper, Flower Girl, #9332-8, complete, M **$45.00**

Outfit, Tammy, Cheerleader, #9131-4 or #9931-7, complete, M, ea **$45.00**

Outfit, Tammy, Private Secretary, #9939-0, MIP **$75.00**

Pepper's Jukebox, M **$65.00**

Pepper's Treehouse, MIB **$150.00**

Tammy's Bubble Bath Set, NRFB **$75.00**

Tammy's Car, MIB...**$75.00**

Tressy

Tressy was American Character's answer to Barbie. This 11½" fashion doll was made from 1963 to 1967. Tressy had a unique feature — her hair 'grew' by pushing a button on her stomach. She and her little sister, Cricket, had numerous fashions and accessories.

Advisor: Cindy Sabulis (See Directory, Dolls)

Apartment, M **$150.00**

Beauty Salon, M...**$125.00**

Case, Cricket, M **$30.00**

Case, Tressy, M **$25.00**

Doll, Pre-Teen Tressy, M..**$75.00**

Doll, Tressy, MIB **$90.00**

Doll, Tressy in Miss America Character outfit, NM **$65.00**

Doll, Tressy w/Magic Makeup Face, M.......................**$25.00**

Doll Clothes Pattern, M **$10.00**

Gift Paks w/doll & clothing, NRFB, minimum value ..**$100.00**

Hair Accessory Paks, NRFB, ea.................................**$20.00**

Hair dryer, M **$40.00**

Hair or Cosmetic Accessory Kits, M, ea, minimum value .**$50.00**

Millinery, M **$150.00**

Outfits, MOC, ea ....!...**$30.00**

Outfits, NRFB, ea, minimum value **$65.00**

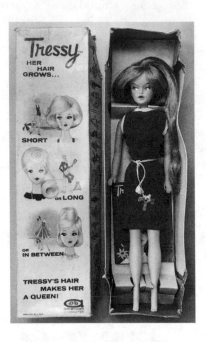

Doll, Tressy (with growing hair), MIB, $90.00. (Photo courtesy Cindy Sabulis)

Uneeda Doll Co., Inc.

The Uneeda Doll Company was located in New York City and began making composition dolls about 1917. Later a transition was made to plastics and vinyl. Listings here are for dolls that are mint in their original boxes.

Baby Dollikins, vinyl head, hard plastic jointed body w/jointed elbows, wrists & knees, 1960s, 21" **$45.00**

Baby Trix, hard plastic & vinyl, 1965, 19" **$30.00**

Bareskin Baby, hard plastic & vinyl, 1968, 12½" **$20.00**

Blabby, hard plastic & vinyl, 1962+, 14"......................**$28.00**

Coquette, Black, hard plastic & vinyl, 16" **$36.00**

Coquette, hard plastic & vinyl, 1963+, 16" **$28.00**

Dollikin, hard plastic & vinyl, multi-joints, 1960s, 20" .**$125.00**

Fairy Princess, hard plastic & vinyl, 1961, 32"...........**$110.00**

Freckles, ventriloquist doll, vinyl head, hands, rooted hair, cotton-stuffed cloth body, 1973, 30".....................**$70.00**

Freckles, vinyl head, rigid plastic body, marked 22 on head, 1960, 32" **$100.00**

Jennifer, hard plastic & vinyl, rooted side-parted hair, painted features, teen body, mod clothing, 1973, 18"..**$25.00**

Magic Meg, vinyl & plastic, rooted hair that grows, sleep eyes, 16" **$25.00**

Pir-thilla, vinyl, rooted hair, sleep eyes, blows up balloons, 1958, 12½"...**$12.00**

Pollyanna, vinyl & plastic, for Disney, 1960, 11" **$35.00**

Pollyanna, vinyl & plastic, for Disney, 1960, 31" **$150.00**

Purty, vinyl & plastic, painted features, long rooted hair, 1973, 11"..**$25.00**

Rita Hayworth as Carmen, composition, red mohair wig, unmarked, cardboard tag, 1948, 14".................**$565.00**

Serenade, vinyl & hard plastic w/rooted blond hair, blue sleep eyes, red & white dress, speaker in tummy, 1962, 21"..**$55.00**

Suzette, plastic & vinyl, 12"..**$65.00**

Tiny Teen, vinyl head, 6-pc hard plastic body, rooted hair, pierced ears, high-heels, 1957-59, 10½"............**$135.00**

Vogue Dolls, Inc.

Vogue Dolls Incorporated is one of America's most popular manufacturer of dolls. In the early 1920s through the mid-'40s, Vogue imported lovely dolls of bisque and composition, dressing them in the fashionable designs hand sewn by Vogue's founder, Jennie Graves. In the late '40s through the early '50s, they became famous for their wonderful hard plastic dolls, most notably the 8" Ginny doll. This adorable toddler doll skyrocketed into nationwide attention in the early '50s as lines of fans stretched around the block during store promotions, and Ginny dolls sold out regularly. A Far-Away-Lands Ginny was added in the late '50s, sold well through the '70s, and is still popular with collectors today. In fact, a modern-day version of Ginny is currently being sold by the Vogue Doll Company, Inc.

Many wonderful dolls followed through the years, including unique hard-plastic, vinyl, and soft-body dolls. These dolls include teenage dolls Jill, Jan, and Jeff; Ginnette, the 8" baby doll; Miss Ginny; and the famous vinyl and soft-bodied dolls by noted artist and designer E. Wilkin. It is not uncommon for these highly collectible dolls to turn up at garage sales and flea markets.

Over the years, Vogue developed the well-deserved reputation as 'The Fashion Leaders in Doll Society' based on their fine quality sewing and on the wide variety of outfits designed for their dolls to wear. These outfits included frilly dress-up doll clothes as well as action-oriented sports outfits. The company was among the first in the doll industry to develop the concept of marketing and selling separate outfits for their dolls, many of which were 'matching' for their special doll lines. The very early Vogue outfits are most sought after, and later outfits are highly collectible as well. It is wise for collectors to become aware of Vogue's unique styles, designs, and construction methods in order to 'spot' these authentic Vogue 'prizes' on collecting outings.

Values here are only a general guide. For further information we recommend *Collector's Guide to Vogue Dolls* by Judith Izen and Carol J. Stover (Collector Books).

Baby Dear, vinyl w/cloth body, ca 1960s, original, 16" ..**$165.00**

Brickette, vinyl, orange hair, freckles, green flirty sleep eys, rigid body & legs, swivel waist, 1960, played with, 22"....**$65.00**

Brikette, vinyl, rigid body & legs, ball-jointed twist & turn body, freckles, green sleep eyes, played with, 1960, 16"..**$15.00**

Ginnette, vinyl, open mouth, ca 1964, 8", MIB........**$200.00**

Ginny, hard plastic, molded lashes, walker, sleep eyes, aqua Bon Bon #80 dress, ca 1955, 8"........................**$225.00**

Ginny, hard plastic, painted lashes, poodle-cut wig, in pink poodle-cloth coat & hat, ca 1952, 8"...................**$400.00**

Ginny, hard plastic, strung, painted lashes, ca 1951, 8", with original box..**$400.00**

Ginny (as Wanda in Tiny Miss Series dress), hard plastic, painted lashes, missing hat, ca 1953, 8" **$200.00**

Ginny (Gym Kids Series), hard plastic walker, bent knees, molded lashes, ca 1956-57, 8" **$150.00**

Ginny (Kinder Crowd series), hard plastic, straight-leg walker, molded lashes, ca 1956, 8" **$200.00**

Ginny Nurse, hard plastic straight-leg walker, ca 1956, 8" **$325.00**

Ginny's Dream Cozy Bed, ca 1957..............................**$30.00**

Jeff, vinyl, blue sleep eyes, molded lashes, black painted hair, dressed as bridegroom, ca 1957-59, 11" **$75.00**

Jill, hard plastic, sleep eyes, earrings, in Record Hop yellow felt skirt w/black jersey top, ca 1958, 10½" **$175.00**

Kindergarten Series (Kay), hard plastic, strung, painted lashes, poodle cut-wig, blue organdy dress, ca 1952, 8" **$450.00**

Tiny Miss (Cheryl), hard plastic, strung, painted lashes, satin dress w/lace trim, replaced shoes, 8" **$400.00**

Toddles Dutch Boy and Girl, five-piece composition bodies, EX original clothes, 7", $300.00 for the pair. (Photo courtesy McMasters Doll Auctions)

Door Knockers

Though many of the door knockers you'll see on the market today are of the painted cast-iron variety (similar in design to doorstop figures), they're also found in brass and other metals. Most are modeled as people, animals, and birds; and baskets of flowers are common. All items listed are cast iron unless noted otherwise. Prices shown are suggested for examples without damage and in excellent original paint.

Advisor: Craig Dinner (See Directory, Door Knockers)

Buster Brown & Tige, cream shirt & pants, cream dog w/black spots, #200, 4¾x2" $635.00

Butterfly, black, green, yellow & pink, under pink rose, cream & purple backplate, 3½x2½"....................$225.00

Cardinal, red feathers w/black highlights on light brown branch, black & yellow berries, cream & green backplate, 5x3" $285.00

Cardinal, yellow & brown (female) on light brown branch, black & yellow berries, cream & green backplate, 5x3" $285.00

Castle, cream w/3 flags, blue sky, green trees, gold band, white oval backplate, 4x3" $265.00

Cottage, white w/peak & 2 chimneys, red roof, dark green trees behind cottage, cream oval backplate, 3½x2½" $535.00

Dancing Cupid, brown hair, white wings, 3 red roses, purple scarf on blue, cream oval backplate, Hubley #618, 3x4¼" $625.00

Dog, brown, at entrance to cream doghouse, pink dish in front of dog, dark brown backplate, 4x3" $865.00

Flower basket, deep basket w/blue bow, yellow & blue flowers w/2 pink roses, cream oval backplate, 4x3".....$65.00

Flower basket, yellow ribbon on white basket, pink & blue flowers w/green leaves, yellow & white backplate, 4x2½" $95.00

Flower basket, multi-color flowers on white backplate, 4x2", $85.00. (Photo courtesy Craig Dinner)

Ivy basket, light & dark green ivy in yellow basket, white backplate, 4½x2½" $135.00

Little girl facing/knocking on door, blue dress, brown hat w/black ribbon, black doll in left hand, rare, 3¾x2¾" $825.00

Morning Glory, purple-blue single flower w/1 bud, green leaves as backplate, 3x3" $325.00

Owl, yellow, light & dark brown & white feathers, black eyes & highlights on face, cream & green backplate, 4¾x3" $250.00

Parrot, faces right, on brown branch, multicolored feathers, green leaves, cream & green backplate, 4¾x2¾" ...$100.00

Peacock, blue, green, yellow & black feathers outstretched, black bird, white backplate, 3x3" $625.00

Rooster, holding branch, red comb & waddle, red, yellow & brown feathers, cream & green oval backplate, 4½x3" $235.00

Roses, pink & cream & green leaves, brown stems, cream oval backplate, signed Hubley #626, 3x4".........$345.00

Ship, gold waves & ship w/highlights, oval backplate w/blue waves, 4x2¾" $250.00

Snowy owl, mostly white feathers, black eyes & highlights on face, cream & green backplate, 4¾x3" $275.00

Spider on web, gray web w/black strings, orange, black & yellow spider, yellow, black & brown fly, 3½x1⅞"....$865.00

Woodpecker, red head w/black & white feathers, tree backplate, brown & green leaves w/pink flowers, 3¾x2½" $125.00

Victorian woman in profile (flesh tone), blond hair, yellow bonnet with blue ribbon and red roses, cream backplate, #613, 4x3", $425.00. (Photo courtesy Craig Dinner)

Doorstops

There are three important factors to consider when buying doorstops — rarity, desirability, and condition. Desirability is often a more important issue than rarity, especially if the doorstop is well designed and detailed. Subject matter often overlaps into other areas, and if they appeal to collectors of Black Americana and advertising, for instance, this tends to drive prices upward. Most doorstops are made of painted cast iron, and value is directly related to the condition of the paint. If there is little paint left or if the figure has been repainted or is rusty, unless the price has been significantly reduced, pass it by.

Be aware that Hubley, one of the largest doorstop manufacturers, sold many of their molds to the John Wright Company who makes them today. Watch for seams that do not fit properly, grainy texture, and too-bright paint. Watch for reproductions!

The doorstops we've listed here are all of the painted cast-iron variety unless another type of material is mentioned in the description. Values are suggested for original examples in near-mint condition and paint and should be sharply reduced if heavy wear is apparent. Recent auctions report even higher prices realized for examples in pristine condition. For further information, we recommend *Doorstops, Identification and Values*, by Jeanne Bertoia.

Club: Doorstop Collectors of America
Jeanie Bertoia
1881 Spring Rd.
Vineland, NJ 08361; 856-692-1881; Membership $20.00 per year, includes 2 *Doorstoppers* newsletters and convention. Send 2-stamp SASE for sample.

Apple Blossoms, in basket, Hubley, #329, 7⅝x5⅜", from $100 to...**$150.00**

Boston Terrier, black & white, facing right, full figure, Hubley, National Foundry & others, 10x10", from $65 to...**$100.00**

Cape Cod (house), Albany Foundry, 5¾x8¾", from $100 to...**$150.00**

Castle, on hill top w/winding road leading up, 8x5¼", from $275 to...**$350.00**

Cat, cleaning paw, Sculptured Metal Studios, 10¾x7½", from $400 to..**$475.00**

Cat, seated, tall slim form, full figure, Hubley, 10x3⅜", from $150 to...**$175.00**

Cocker Spaniel, full figure, Hubley, 6¾x11", from $225 to...**$275.00**

Crocodile, up on all 4s, mouth open, 5¾x11½", from $75 to...**$125.00**

Footmen (2 joined at shoulder on base), Hubley, #248, copyright Fish, 12⅛x8¼", minimum value.................**$750.00**

Fruits & Flowers, in basket, 13x7¼", from $200 to...**$275.00**

Giraffe, head up, Hubley, 12½x9", minimum value.**$750.00**

Gnome w/Shovel, 9½x4½", from $275 to.................**$325.00**

Golfer (sm), full figure, 6x3½", from $400 to...........**$475.00**

Grape Bowl, #20, 4⅛x7", from $100 to.....................**$150.00**

Halloween Cat, arched back, AM Greenblatt Studio #19 Copyright 1927, 9¼x6", from $175 to.................**$250.00**

Horse, standing proud, full figure, Hubley, 8½x8", from $125 to...**$200.00**

Humpty Dumpty, sitting on wall, full figure, #551, 4½x3½", from $300 to...**$350.00**

Lion, full figure, 7x8", from $100 to.........................**$175.00**

Malamute, 7¾x6¼", from $175 to.............................**$200.00**

Man w/Top Hat, full figure, 9⅜x3⅝", from $250 to.**$300.00**

Mary Quite Contrary, w/watering can, tool & flowers, #1292, 15x8", from $425 to...**$500.00**

Monkey, seated, full figure, 7x5", from $175 to........**$250.00**

Owl, on stump, 10x6", from $200 to.........................**$275.00**

Parrot, on perch, 7x3½", from $100 to......................**$150.00**

Pheasant, Hubley, #458, copyright Fred Everett, 8½x7½", from $250 to...**$300.00**

Pirate w/Chest, 9¼x6", from $200 to.......................**$275.00**

Policeman, dressed in blue, holds nightstick, Le Mur Lgt Co Pat, 7⅛x4", from $200 to....................................**$275.00**

Poppies & Cornflowers, Hubley, 3265, 7¼x6½", from $100 to...**$150.00**

Rooster, full figure, 15⅜x6⅛", from $275 to.............**$350.00**

Rooster, Spencer, 13¼x11", from $500 to.................**$575.00**

Rose Vase, Hubley, #441, 10½x8", from $100 to......**$175.00**

Colonial Woman, painted cast iron, Littco Products, 10", EX, $185.00.

Sealyham Terrier, painted cast iron, $880.00.

Deco Girl, holding skirt of dress wide, #1251, cJo, 9x7½", from $300 to...**$375.00**

Doberman Pinscher, full figure, Hubley, 8x8½", from $325 to...**$400.00**

Donald Duck, holds stop sign, copyright Walt Disney Productions 1971, 8⅜x5¼", from $200 to..........**$250.00**

Duck, head up, full figure, 11¼x7", from $175 to....**$225.00**

Dutch Girl, flower basket ea side, Hubley, #10, 9¼x5½", from $175 to...**$250.00**

Elephant, S117, 6½x8¼", from $150 to.....................**$225.00**

Elk, on rocky base, 11x10", from $125 to.................**$200.00**

Skier, lady holding skis in right arm, full figure, 12½x5", from $400 to...**$475.00**

Sophia Smith House, central chimney, 8¼x5½", from $250 to...**$300.00**

Spanish Girl, ruffled skirt, flowers at waist, w/fan & shawl, Hubley, #192, 9x5", from $175 to.....................**$250.00**

St Bernard, recumbent, full figure, Hubley, 3½x10½", from $325 to...**$375.00**

Sunbonnet Girl (lg), facing left, 9⅞x5½", from $400 to......**$450.00**

Terrier, running, wedge back, Spencer, Guilford, Conn, 4x7", from $175 to...**$225.00**

Totem Pole, 12x8½", from $100 to.............................**$150.00**

Tulips, in container w/lg blue bow, Hubley, 12¼x6⅞", from $225 to...**$300.00**

Turtle, full figure, 4¼x17", from $350 to **$400.00**

Whimsical Man, wood wedge, #1258, 7x3½", from $275 to..**$350.00**

Windmill, AA Richardson, 8x5⅝", from $125 to.......**$175.00**

Woman w/Hooped Dress, unmarked, 7x5¼", from $100 to..**$150.00**

Yawning Dog, full figure, 7x5", from $250 to **$325.00**

Duncan and Miller Glassware

Although the roots of the company can be traced back as far as 1865 when George Duncan went into business in Pittsburgh, Pennsylvania, the majority of the glassware that collectors are interested in was produced during the twentieth century. The firm became known as Duncan and Miller in 1900. They were bought out by the United States Glass Company who continued to produce many of the same designs through a separate operation which they called the Duncan and Miller Division.

In addition to crystal, they made some of their wares in a wide assortment of colors including ruby, milk glass, some opalescent glass, and a black opaque glass they called Ebony. Some of their pieces were decorated by cutting or etching. They also made a line of animals and bird figures. For information on these, see *Glass Animals of the Depression Era* by Lee Garmon and Dick Spencer (Collector Books).

Advisor: Roselle Schleifman (See Directory, Elegant Glass)

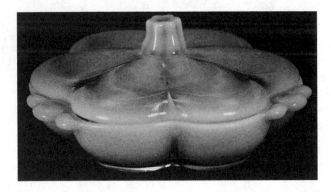

Canterbury, candy dish, Cape Cod Blue, three-part, three handles, with lid, $36.50.

Canterbury, ashtray, crystal, club shape, 3" **$7.00**

Canterbury, basket, crystal, 9¼x10x7¼" **$55.00**

Canterbury, bowl, crystal, crimped, 10½x5"................**$30.00**

Canterbury, bowl, crystal, flared, 8x2½"......................**$17.50**

Canterbury, bowl, crystal, 2-handled, round, 6x2"........**$9.50**

Canterbury, candle, crystal, 3½" **$12.50**

Canterbury, cigarette jar, crystal, w/lid, 4"..................**$20.00**

Canterbury, ice bucket/vase, crystal, 6" **$40.00**

Canterbury, pitcher, martini; crystal, 32-oz, 9¼" **$80.00**

Canterbury, plate, dinner; crystal, 11¼"......................**$27.50**

Canterbury, top hat, crystal, 3" **$18.00**

Canterbury, tumbler, juice; footed, 5-oz, 4¼"..............**$7.50**

Canterbury, vase, crystal, crimped, 4" **$17.50**

Canterbury, vase, crystal, flared, 12" **$85.00**

Caribbean, bowl, crystal, handled, 7"...........................**$25.00**

Caribbean, bowl, epergne; blue, flared edge, 9½" **$95.00**

Caribbean, cocktail shaker, blue, 33-oz, 9"................**$210.00**

Caribbean, ladle, punch; blue **$100.00**

Caribbean, plate, bread & butter; blue, 6¼"................**$10.00**

Caribbean, plate, crystal, 14"......................................**$35.00**

Caribbean, salt dip, blue, 2½" **$22.50**

Caribbean, stem, sherbet; crystal, footed, 4¼" **$8.00**

Caribbean, tray, blue, round, 12¾".............................**$55.00**

Caribbean, vase, crystal, footed, 10" **$50.00**

Figurine, donkey, cart & peon, crystal, 3-pc set, from $425 to..**$475.00**

Figurine, dove, crystal, head down, 11½" L, from $150 to **$175.00**

Figurine, duck, ashtray, crystal, 4", from $15 to..........**$20.00**

Figurine, duck, cigarette box, red, 6"..........................**$170.00**

Figurine, heron, crystal satin, 7", from $110 to **$120.00**

Figurine, swan, blue opal, W&F, spread wings, 10x12½", from $225 5o..**$245.00**

Figurine, swan, chartreuse, open back, 7", from $40 to .**$45.00**

Figurine, swan, milk glass w/red neck, 10½", from $400 to **$450.00**

Figurine, swordfish, crystal, from $225 to **$275.00**

Figurine, Sylvan, swan, yellow opal, 7½", from $140 to ..**$150.00**

Figurine, Tropical Fish, ashtray, pink opal, 3½" **$50.00**

First Love, bowl, crystal, #126, 10½x7x7"....................**$60.00**

First Love, bowl, rose; crystal, #115, 3x5"...................**$40.00**

First Love, candle, crystal, #115, low, 3".....................**$25.00**

First Love, comport, crystal, #111, 4¾x3½" **$27.50**

First Love, hat, crystal, #30, 4½"................................**$375.00**

First Love, nappy, crystal, #25, w/bottom star, 5x1" ...**$20.00**

First Love, pitcher, crystal, #5200 ....**$170.00**

First love, plate, crystal, #111, 13¼".............................**$60.00**

First Love, stem, cordial; crystal, #111 ....**$55.00**

First Love, tray, relish; #115, 11¾" **$45.00**

First Love, urn, crystal, #525, 5" **$37.50**

First love, vase, crystal, #506, footed, 10"..................**$115.00**

Sandwich, basket, crystal, w/loop handle, 11½" **$250.00**

Sandwich, bottle, oil; crystal, 5¾" **$35.00**

Sandwich, bowl, fruit; crystal, 3-part, 10" **$85.00**

Sandwich, cake stand, crystal, footed, plain stem, 13"..**$80.00**

Sandwich, candy box, crystal, w/lid, footed, 8½".......**$55.00**

Sandwich, comport, crystal, footed, 4½" **$20.00**

Sandwich, plate, dinner; crystal, 9½"...........................**$45.00**

Sandwich, relish, crystal, oval, 2-part, 7" **$20.00**

Sandwich, stem, cocktail; crystal, 3-oz, 4¼" **$15.00**

Sandwich, tumbler, water; crystal, footed, 9-oz, 4¾"..**$14.00**

Spiral Flutes, bowl, console; amber, pink or green, cupped, 12" **$30.00**

Spiral Flutes, bowl, nappy; amber, pink or green, 5" ...**$6.00**

Spiral Flutes, creamer, amber, pink or green, oval **$8.00**

Spiral Flutes, grapefruit, amber, pink or green, footed..**$20.00**

Spiral Flutes, pickle, amber, pink or green, 8⅝".........**$12.00**
Spiral Flutes, plate, luncheon; amber, pink or green, 8⅜"..**$4.00**
Spiral Flutes, saucer, amber, pink or green **$3.00**
Spiral Flutes, sugar bowl, amber, pink or green, oval..**$8.00**
SPiral Flutes, vase, amber, pink or green, 10½"..........**$37.00**
Tear Drop, bonbon, crystal, 4-handled, 6" **$12.00**
Tear Drop, bowl, salad; crystal, 9" **$27.50**
Tear Drop, cake salver, crystal, footed, 13" **$50.00**
Tear Drop, creamer, crystal, 6-oz.........................**$7.00**
Tear Drop, nut dish, crystal, 2-part, 6" **$10.00**
Tear Drop, plate, canape; crystal, 6" **$10.00**
Tear Drop, relish, crystal, 5-part, round, 12" **$30.00**
Tear Drop, shakers, crystal, 5", pr.......................**$25.00**
Tear Drop, stem, wine; crystal, 3-oz, 4¾"...............**$20.00**
Tear Drop, sweetmeat, crystal, center handle, 6½" **$35.00**
Tear Drop, tumbler, whiskey; crystal, footed, 2-oz, 2¼"..**$14.00**
Tear Drop, vase, crystal, footed, round, 9".................**$37.50**
Terrace, ashtray, crystal or amber, square, 3½"..........**$17.50**
Terrace, candy urn, cobalt or red, w/lid...................**$425.00**
Terrace, cup, crystal or amber...........................**$15.00**
Terrace, plate, cobalt or red, 7½"........................**$37.50**
Terrace, plate, sandwich; crystal or amber, handled, 11"..**$40.00**
Terrace, saucer, crystal or amber, demitasse................**$5.00**
Terrace, sugar bowl, cobalt or red, w/lid, 10-oz, 3".**$110.00**
Terrace, vase, crystal or amber, footed, 10"..............**$115.00**

Sandwich, cheese and cracker set, 3" compote, 13" plate, $75.00.

Easter Collectibles

The egg (a symbol of new life) and the bunny rabbit have long been part of Easter festivities; and since early in the twentieth century, Easter has been a full-blown commercial event. Postcards, candy containers, toys, and decorations have been made in infinite varieties. In the early 1900s many holiday items were made of papier-mache and composition and imported to this country from Germany. Rabbits were made of mohair, felt, and velveteen, often filled with straw, cotton, and cellulose.

Candy container, begging rabbit, pulp, US, 1940-50...**$55.00**
Candy container, dressed chick, cardboard w/spring neck, W Germany/US Zone, 1940-50..............................**$65.00**
Candy container, dressed rabbit, cardboard w/spring neck, W Germany/US Zone, 1940-50...........................**$75.00**
Candy container, egg, molded cardboard, W Germany, 1940-60, 3-8", from $25 to................................**$40.00**
Candy container, egg shape, children w/dog in highchair, chicks on floor, papier-mache w/litho, marked Germany, 2x3", EX..**$80.00**
Candy container, plain rabbit, cardboard w/spring neck, W Germany/US Zone, 1940-50.................................**$65.00**
Candy container, sitting rabbit, no basket, pulp, 1940-50 ....**$60.00**
Candy container, sitting rabbit, pulp, brown w/glass eyes, Burk Co, 1930 ....**$140.00**
Candy container, sitting rabbit next to lg basket, pulp, US, 1930-50 ....**$125.00**
Candy container, sitting rabbit w/basket on back, pulp, US, 1940-50 ....**$95.00**
Figure, chick pulling wagon w/rabbit, celluloid.........**$80.00**
Figure, dressed chick or duck, celluloid, 3-8", from $45 to..**$65.00**
Figure, dressed rabbit, celluloid, 3-8", from $65 to.....**$75.00**
Figure, rabbit, cotton batten w/paper ears, Japan, 1930-1950, 6"..**$85.00**
Figure, rabbit, cotton batten w/paper ears, Japan, 1930-50, 2-5", from $30 to **$45.00**
Figure, rabbit, plain, celluloid, 3-7", from $20 to........**$30.00**
Figurine, rabbit pushing or pulling cart, celluloid, sm to lg, from $60 to..**$95.00**

Toy, lithographed tin, offset wheels, early, 5½"x6", $125.00. (Photo courtesy Jon and Cindy Serensen)

Tin, Peter Rabbit Easter scenes, marked Tin Deco on bottom, 4½x2½", VG......................................**$155.00**
Toy, Magic Bunny, pump tail & balls in hat disappear then reappear in mouth, plastic, Irwin, 9½", EX (worn box) **$60.00**
Toy, wind-up; celluloid, Japan or Occupied Japan ..**$150.00**

Egg Cups

Egg cups were once commonplace kitchen articles that were often put to daily use. These small egg holders were commonly made in a variety of shapes from ceramics, glass, metals, minerals, treen, and plastic. They were used as early as ancient Rome and were very common on Victorian tables. Many were styled like whimsical animals or made in other shapes that would specifically appeal to children. Some were commemorative or sold as souvenirs. Still others were part of extensive china or silver services.

Recent trends in US dietary patterns have caused egg cups to follow butter pats and salt dishes into relative obscurity. Yet today in other parts of the world, especially Europe, many people still eat soft-boiled eggs as part of their daily ritual, so the larger china companies in those locations continue to produce egg cups.

Though many are inexpensive, some are very pricey. Sought-after categories (or cross-collectibles) include Art Deco, Art Pottery, Black Memorabilia, Chintz, Golliwogs, Majolica, Personalities, Pre-Victorian, Railroad, and Steamship. Single egg cups with pedestal bases are the most common, but shapes vary to include buckets, doubles, figurals, hoops, and sets of many types.

Pocillovists, as egg cup collectors are known, are increasing in numbers every day. For more extensive listings we recommend *Egg Cups: An Illustrated History and Price Guide,* by Brenda C. Blake (Antique Publications); and *Schroeder's Antiques Price Guide* (Collector Books).

Advisor: Brenda C. Blake (See Directory, Egg Cups)

Newsletter: *Egg Cup Collector's Corner*
Dr. Joan George, Editor
67 Stevens Ave., Old Bridge, NJ 08857; Subscription $20 per year for 4 issues; sample copies available at $5 each

Airplane, figural, yellow, Honiton, 1960s.....................**$22.00**
Arabia, red transfer, Made in Finland, square foot, 2" ..**$15.00**
Ba Ba Black Sheep, white w/decal, gold trim, unmarked, 2⅛"...**$15.00**
Bedale, Chintz pattern, goblet shape w/square base, Royal Winton **$80.00**
Betty Boop, lusterware hair, Made in Japan..............**$300.00**
Black cat, figural, sitting on orange lustre boot, marked Foreign..**$45.00**
Blue Willow, Made in Japan in blue ink stamp on bottom, 2⅜"...**$25.00**
Bluebird, figural, Lefton **$48.00**
Bristol, red, Crown Ducal, 1931, double.....................**$20.00**
Bunnykins, 2 scenes ea side, Royal Doulton, signed Barbara Vernon, 2"..**$150.00**
Cabbage leaf, green & white design w/butterfly, matching spoon, Made in China, ca 1900, 2¼" **$82.00**
Cardinal monk, red robe, Goebel **$175.00**
Chick, figural, cobalt glass w/handle, Westmoreland .**$14.00**

Chick figural, multicolor and black on white, Japan, 3", from $20.00 to $30.00. (Photo courtesy Carole Bess White)

Cornishware, alternating blue & white bands, TG Green, double, 4", from $30 to **$35.00**
Currier & Ives, red transfer, Across the Continent on inside, Homer Laughlin, 4½" **$35.00**
Doll face, Nippon, double, from $250 to **$385.00**
Donald Duck, riding motorcycle w/sidecar (cup), Walt Disney, Made in Japan, 3½" **$115.00**
Elephant, kneeling w/raised trunk, custard glass, 3½x2¾"...**$40.00**
Foghorn Leghorn, Acme Home Works, 1992, double..**$14.00**
Holly Hobbie, bucket style, 1978 ....**$13.00**
Howe's Caverns, blue logo & rim, goblet shape...........**$9.00**
Lion, figural, seated, brown pottery **$10.00**
Little Bo Peep, white w/decal, gold trim, unmarked, 2¼" ..**$22.00**
Mickey Mouse, silver & enamel, Chapman & Barden, ca 1950, 2"...**$125.00**
Ming, Lenox, double..**$45.00**
Mr Snowman, hat doubles as hat, Royal Doulton, 4¼"..**$95.00**
Paddington Bear, Wake Me For Breakfast, Paddington & Co Ltd, 1991, 2¾"...**$32.00**
Prince William, 1982 birthday, Coronet, goblet shape ..**$40.00**
Rabbit, brown, holding paint brush painting a blue cup, Goebel, 4"...**$60.00**
Sleepy, standing in front cup marked Sleepy, Walt Disney, 3"...**$160.00**
Snoopy in chef's hat, figural **$50.00**
Swee' Pea, single, Vandor, M......................................**$75.00**
Telletubbies, goblet shape, w/box & chocolate egg...**$10.00**
Train, locomotive shape, brown, O'Danaghue's **$18.00**
Union Castle Line, Edinburgh Castle, black geometric rim, 1930s..**$60.00**
Walking legs, figural, green shoes, Carlton Ware........**$40.00**

Egg Timers

Egg timers are comprised of a little glass tube (pinched in the center and filled with sand) attached to a figural base, usually between 3" and 5" in height. They're all the rage today among collectors. Most figural egg timers reached their heyday in the 1940s. However, Germany produced many beautiful and detailed timers much earlier. Japan followed suit by copying many German designs. Today, one may find timers from the United Kingdom as well as many foreign ports. The variety of subjects represented by these timers is endless. Included are scores of objects, animals, characters from fiction, and people in occupational or recreational activities. Timers have been made in many materials including bisque, china, ceramic, chalkware, cast iron, tin, brass, wood, and plastic.

Although they were originated to time a three-minute egg, some were also used to limit the duration spent on telephone calls as a cost-saving measure. Frequently a timer is designed to look like a telephone, or a phone is depicted on it.

Since the glass tubes were made of thin, fine glass, they were easily broken. You may recognize a timer masquerading as a figurine by the empty hole that once held the tube. Do not pass up a good timer just because the glass is missing. These can be easily replaced by purchasing a cheap egg timer with a glass tube at your local grocery story.

Listings are for timers in excellent to mint condition with their glass tubes attached.

Advisor: Ellen Bercovici (See Directory, Egg Timers)

Bear dressed as chef w/towel over arm, ceramic, Japan, 4"...**$65.00**
Bellhop, green, ceramic, Japan, 4½".....................**$60.00**
Bellhop on phone, ceramic, Japan, 3".................**$40.00**
Black chef sitting w/right hand raised holding timer, ceramic, many sizes & shadings, German, from $95 to **$120.00**
Black chef standing w/frying pan, chalkware, Japan...**$125.00**
Black chef standing w/lg fish, timer in fish's mouth, ceramic, Japan, 4¾"..................................**$125.00**
Bobby policeman, blue outfit, Japan **$95.00**
Boy skiing, ceramic, German, 3"...........................**$65.00**
Boy stands on head (plastic) which fills w/sand, ceramic, Cooley Lilley sticker, 3¾"........................**$50.00**
Boy w/black cap stands & holds black bird, ceramic, unmarked, 3½"...**$65.00**
Boy w/black cloak & cane, German, 3¾"...........**$65.00**
Boy w/red cap stands & holds different glass tubes in both hands, wooden, unmarked, 4½"...........**$35.00**
Bunny rabbit, floppy ears, timer in mouth, Japan **$75.00**
Cat, timer sits in his back, wooden.....................**$45.00**
Cat standing by base of grandfather clock, ceramic, German, 4¾"..**$65.00**
Cat w/ribbon at neck, ceramic, marked Germany......**$85.00**
Chef, combination music box, wooden, lg **$175.00**
Chef holding plate w/hole to hold timer which removes to change, ceramic, Japan, 3¾"...................**$50.00**
Chef in white on blue base holding spoon, ceramic, German, 4"...**$60.00**
Chef in yellow pants, white jacket, blue trim, holds platter of food, ceramic, Japan, 3½".........................**$50.00**
Chef standing in blue w/white apron, towel over right arm, timer in jug under left, ceramic, Japan, 4½".........**$50.00**

Chef winking, white clothes, timer in back, turn upside down to tip sand, ceramic, 4"............................**$50.00**
Chicken, wings hold tube, ceramic, German, 2¾"......**$50.00**
Chicken on nest, green plastic, England, 2½".............**$30.00**
Clown on phone, standing, yellow suit, ceramic, Japan, 3¾" **$65.00**
Clown sitting w/legs to side, timer in right hand, ceramic, German, 3¼"..**$85.00**
Colonial lady w/bonnet, variety of dresses & colors, ceramic, German, 3¾"...**$65.00**
Colonial man in knickers, ruffled shirt, waistcoat hides hat, ceramic, Japan, 4¾"..**$65.00**
Dutch boy kneeling, ceramic, Japan, 2½" **$40.00**
Dutch boy standing, ceramic, German, 3½"................**$65.00**
Dutch girl on phone, standing, blue & white, ceramic, Japan, 3¾"..**$50.00**
Dutch girl w/flowers, walking, chalkware, unmarked, 4½"...**$65.00**
Fisherman, fish wrapped around neck, timer in fish's mouth, German...**$95.00**
Geisha, ceramic, German, 4½" **$85.00**
Goebel, double, chefs, man & woman, ceramic, German, 4"...**$100.00**
Goebel, double, Mrs Pickwick, green, ceramic, German, 4"...**$150.00**
Goebel, double, rabbits, various color combinations, ceramic, German, 4½"..**$100.00**
Goebel, double, roosters, various color combination, ceramic, German, 4" **$100.00**
Goebel, lg owl w/holder on side..................................**$95.00**
Goebel, little girl w/chick on tip of her shoe **$95.00**
Goebel, single, chimney sweep, ceramic, German, 4¼"..**$70.00**
Goebel, single, Friar Tuck, ceramic, German, 4" **$70.00**
Golliwog, bisque, English, 4½" **$200.00**
Kitchen maid w/measuring spoons, ceramic, DAVAR, from $100 to..**$125.00**
Kitten w/ball of yarn, chalkware...................................**$50.00**
Leprechaun, shamrock on base, brass, Ireland, 3¼" ..**$40.00**
Lighthouse, blue, cream & orange lustre, ceramic, German, 4½"...**$85.00**
Mammy, tin, lithographed picture of her cooking, pot holder hooks, unmarked, 7¾"...**$150.00**
Mexican boy playing guitar, ceramic, German, 3½" ...**$65.00**
Mouse, white apron says 'Chef,' Josef Original...........**$50.00**
Mouse, yellow & green, chalkware, Josef Originals, Japan, 1970s, 3¼"...**$35.00**
Mrs Santa Claus, timer sits in bag next to her............**$75.00**
Newspaper boy, ceramic, Japan, 3¾"...........................**$85.00**
Parlor maid w/cat, ceramic, Japan, 4"..........................**$65.00**
Penguin, chalkware, England, 3¾".................................**$50.00**
Pixie, ceramic, Enesco, Japan, 5½" **$40.00**
Rabbit, holding carrot, timer in basket, Japan.............**$65.00**
Sailboat, lustreware, German **$95.00**
Sailor, blue, ceramic, German, 4" **$65.00**
Sailor w/sailboat, ceramic, German, 4" **$85.00**
Scotsman w/bagpipes, plastic, England, 4½" **$50.00**
Sea gull, ceramic w/lustre finish, German...................**$95.00**
Sultan, Japan, 3½"...**$75.00**

Telephone, black glaze on clay, Japan, 2"...................$35.00
Telephone, candlestick type on base w/cup for timer, wooden, Cornwall Wood Prod, So Paris ME..................$25.00
Veggie man or woman, bisque, Japan, 4½" $95.00
Welsh woman, ceramic, German, 4½" $85.00
Windmill w/dog on base, Japan, 3¾" $85.00

Santa Claus and present, ceramic, Sonsco/Japan, 5½", $75.00. (Photo courtesy Ellen Bercovici)

Elvis Presley Memorabilia

Since he burst upon the '50s scene wailing 'Heartbreak Hotel,' Elvis has been the undisputed 'King of Rock 'n Roll.' The fans that stood outside his dressing room for hours on end, screamed themselves hoarse as he sang, or simply danced until they dropped to his music are grown-up collectors today. Many of their children remember his comeback performances, and I'd venture to say that even their grandchildren know Elvis on a first-name basis.

There has never been a promotion in the realm of entertainment to equal the manufacture and sale of Elvis merchandise. By the latter part of 1956, there were already hundreds of items that appeared in every department store, drugstore, specialty shop, and music store in the country. There were bubble gum cards, pin-back buttons, handkerchiefs, dolls, guitars, billfolds, photograph albums, and scores of other items. You could even buy sideburns from a coin-operated machine. Look for the mark 'Elvis Presley Enterprises' (along with a 1956 or 1957 copyright date); you'll know you've found a gold mine. Items that carry the 'Boxcar' mark are from 1974 to 1977, when Elvis's legendary manager, Colonel Tom Parker, promoted another line of merchandise to augment their incomes during the declining years. Upon his death in 1977 and until 1981, the trademark became 'Boxcar Enterprises, Inc., Lic. by Factors ETC. Bear, DE.' The 'Elvis Presley Enterprises, Inc.' trademark reverted back to Graceland in 1982, which re-opened to the public in 1983.

Due to the very nature of his career, paper items are usually a large part of any 'Elvis' collection. He appeared on the cover of countless magazines. These along with ticket stubs, movie posters, lobby cards, and photographs of all types are sought after today, especially those from before the mid-'60s.

Though you sometime see Elvis 45s with $10.00 to $15.00 price tags, unless the record is in near mint to mint condition, this is just not realistic, since they sold in such volume. In fact, the picture sleeve itself (if it's in good condition) will be worth more than the record. The exceptions are, of course, the early Sun label records (he cut five in all) that collectors often pay in excess of $500.00 for. In fact, a near-mint copy of 'That's All Right' (his very first Sun recording) realized $2,800.00 at an auction held a couple of years ago! And some of the colored vinyls, promotional records, and EPs and LPs with covers and jackets in excellent condition are certainly worth researching further. For instance, though his *Moody Blue* album with the blue vinyl record can often be had for under $25.00 (depending on condition), if you find one of the rare ones with the black record you can figure on about ten times that amount! For a thorough listing of his records as well as the sleeves, refer to *Official Price Guide to Elvis Presley Records and Memorabilia* by Jerry Osborne.

For more general information and an emphasis on the early items, refer to *Elvis Collectibles* and *Best of Elvis Collectibles* by Rosalind Cranor, P.O. Box 859, Blacksburg, VA 24063 ($19.95+$1.75 postage each volume).

Special thanks to Art and Judy Turner, Homestead Collectibles (see Directory, Decanters) for providing information on decanters. See also Magazines; Movie Posters; Pin-back Buttons; Records.

Advisor: Lee Garmon (See Directory, Elvis Presley)

Bust, Clay Art, San Francisco, 1986, from $150.00 to $175.00. (Photo courtesy Lee Garmon)

Balloon toy, California Toytime, image of Elvis as boxer (Kid Galahad) on balloon w/cardboard feet, 4", EX....$75.00
Belt, white leather reproduction w/multicolor faux jewels, silver chains & buckles, EX................................$125.00

Bracelet, charm; Loving You, gold-tone metal, Elvis Presley Enterprises, 1956, 7", MOC......................$60.00

Bracelet, Loving You, Elvis Presley Enterprises, 1956, framed black & white photo, MOC (beware of repros), from $100 to......................$150.00

Card set, Golden Boys, A&BC Gum, 1958, 36 cards ..$80.00

Cigarette lighter, Artist of the Century, color portrait, Zippo, 2000, 4 in series, ea, from $25 to $30.00

Cigarette lighter, Zippo, 1980s, series of 6, ea, from $75 to $100.00

Concert pin, laughing portrait, 3⅜"......................$12.00

Decanter, McCormick, 1978, Elvis '77, plays Love Me Tender, 750 ml......................$125.00

Decanter, McCormick, 1978, Elvis Bust, no music box, 750 ml......................$75.00

Decanter, McCormick, 1979, Elvis '55, plays Loving You, 750 ml......................$125.00

Decanter, McCormick, 1979, Elvis '77 Mini, plays Love Me Tender, 50 ml......................$55.00

Decanter, McCormick, 1979, Elvis Gold, plays My Way, 750 ml......................$175.00

Decanter, McCormick, 1980, Elvis '55 Mini, plays Loving You, 50 ml......................$65.00

Decanter, McCormick, 1980, Elvis '68, plays Can't Help Falling in Love, 750 ml......................$125.00

Decanter, McCormick, 1980, Elvis Silver, plays How Great Thou Art, 750 ml......................$175.00

Decanter, McCormick, 1981, Aloha Elvis, plays Blue Hawaii, 750 ml......................$150.00

Decanter, McCormick, 1981, Elvis '68 Mini, plays Can't Help Falling in Love, 50 ml......................$55.00

Decanter, McCormick, 1981, Elvis Designer I White (Joy), plays Are You Lonesome Tonight, 750 ml..........$150.00

Decanter, McCormick, 1982, Aloha Elvis Mini, plays Blue Hawaii, 50 ml......................$175.00

Decanter, McCormick, 1982, Elvis Designer II White (Love), plays It's Now or Never, 750 ml......................$125.00

Decanter, McCormick, 1982, Elvis Karate, plays Don't Be Cruel, 750 ml......................$350.00

Decanter, McCormick, 1983, Elvis Designer III White (Reverence), plays Crying in the Chapel, 750 ml.$250.00

Decanter, McCormick, 1983, Elvis Gold Mini, plays My Way, 50 ml......................$125.00

Decanter, McCormick, 1983, Elvis Silver Mini, plays How Great Thou Art, 50 ml......................$95.00

Decanter, McCormick, 1983, Sgt Elvis, plays GI Blues, 750 ml......................$295.00

Decanter, McCormick, 1984, Elvis & Rising Sun, Plays Green, Green Grass of Home, 750 ml......................$495.00

Decanter, McCormick, 1984, Elvis Designer I Gold, plays Are You Lonesome Tonight, 750 ml......................$175.00

Decanter, McCormick, 1984, Elvis Designer II Gold, plays It's Now or Never, 750 ml......................$195.00

Decanter, McCormick, 1984, Elvis Karate Mini, plays Don't Be Cruel, 50 ml......................$125.00

Decanter, McCormick, 1984, Elvis on Stage, plays Can't Help Falling in Love, 50 ml (decanter only)......................$195.00

Decanter, McCormick, 1984, Elvis w/Stage, 50 ml (complete w/seperate stage designed to hold decanter) $450.00

Decanter, McCormick, 1984, Elvis 50th Anniversary, plays I Want You, I Need You, I Love You, 750 ml.......$495.00

Decanter, McCormick, 1984, Sgt Elvis Mini, plays GI Blues, 50 ml......................$95.00

Decanter, McCormick, 1985, Elvis Designer I White Mini, plays Are You Lonesome Tonight, 50 ml..........$125.00

Decanter, McCormick, 1985, Elvis Designer III Gold, plays Crying in the Chapel, 750 ml......................$250.00

Decanter, McCormick, 1985, Elvis Teddy Bear, plays Let Me Be Your Teddy Bear, 750 ml......................$695.00

Decanter, McCormick, 1986, Elvis & Gates of Graceland, plays Welcome to My World, 750 ml..................$150.00

Decanter, McCormick, 1986, Elvis & Rising Sun Mini, plays Green, Green Grass of Home, 50 ml..................$250.00

Decanter, McCormick, 1986, Elvis Designer I Gold Mini, plays Are You Lonesome Tonight, 50 ml..........$150.00

Decanter, McCormick, 1986, Elvis Designer I Silver Mini, Plays Are You Lonesome Tonight, 50 ml..........$135.00

Decanter, McCormick, 1986, Elvis Hound Dog, plays Hound Dog, 750 ml......................$695.00

Decanter, McCormick, 1986, Elvis Season's greetings, plays White Christmas, 375 ml......................$195.00

Decanter, McCormick, 1986, Elvis Teddy Bear Mini, plays Let Me Be Your Teddy Bear, 50 ml......................$295.00

Decanter, McCormick, 1986, Elvis 50th Anniversary Mini, plays I Want You, I Need You, I Love You, 50 ml $250.00

Decanter, McCormick, 1987, Elvis Memories, cassette player base, lighted top, extremely rare, 750 ml, from $1,000 to.$1,200.00

Doll, Celebrity Collection, World Doll, 1984, 21", MIB .$110.00

Doll, Comeback Special, black leather, Mattel, NRFB...$40.00

Doll, Comeback Special, Elvis Presley Enterprises, Hasbro, 1993, NRFB......................$38.00

Doll, Hound Dog, Smile Toy Co, stuffed plush w/Elvis lettered on white neck ribbon, NM......................$250.00

Doll, in Army uniform, w/badges, dog tag & duffle bag, Mattel, 12", MIB......................$45.00

Doll, in white jumpsuit, w/guitar, Eugene, 1984, 12", MIB.$52.00

Doll, Teen Idol, Hasbro, 1993, NRFB......................$42.50

Doll, 30th Anniversary of 1968 Television Special, 1st in series, NRFB......................$35.00

Figurine, Aloha From Hawaii, lights up, w/guitar, MIB.$40.00

Figurine, in white w/guitar, hands raised, Royal Orleans, 10", MIB......................$55.00

Flasher ring, 1957, EX, minimum value......................$100.00

Guitar, Lapin, 1984, MOC (sealed) $75.00

Key chain, flasher, full figure on yellow background, 2½x2", EX......................$20.00

Lamp, blue suede shoes, Elvis Presley Enterprises, 13x9¼x9¼", M......................$45.00

Menu, Sahara Tahoe Hotel, Elvis photo cover, 1974, 8½x11", M......................$60.00

Necklace, Love Me Tender, Elvis Presley Enterprises, 1956, from $175 to......................$225.00

Overnight case, Elvis Presley Enterprises, 1956, 6½x12x9", G $195.00

Paint-by-number set, Peerless Playthings, 1956, rare, complete, EX (EX box), minimum value **$3,000.00**

Painting on velvet, singing closeup w/mike, 18¾x22¾" in carved wood frame **$55.00**

Paperdoll Book Elvis, St Martin's Press, 1982, uncut, EX **$30.00**

Pen, Tickle Me, feather type, EX **$35.00**

Pennant, Birthplace Tupelo..., Elvis Presley Enterprises, 1962, M **$30.00**

Pin-back, full-color portrait on celluloid, Cioffi, Elvis Presley Enterprises, 1956, 3", EX **$55.00**

Pin-back button, Vari-Vue, flicker type, 1960s **$38.00**

Plate, Elvis at Gates of Graceland, Delphi, Bruce Emmett, 1988 limited edition **$45.00**

Pocketknife, guitar form, portrait & 1935-1977, 6" **$45.00**

Poster, Girl Happy, 1965, 41x27", EX+ **$110.00**

Poster, Trouble w/Girls, 1-sheet, 1969, EX **$52.00**

Ring, brass w/full-color image under clear bubble, 1956, EX **$200.00**

Scarf, concert give-away, silky, M **$40.00**

Sideburn sticker from gumball machine, 1590s, EX **$55.00**

Snow globe, blue suede shoes, porcelain musical base, Elvis Presley Enterprises, 5½", MIB **$30.00**

Song book, #1, 15 songs, 15 pictures, 1956, 35-page, EX ..**$52.50**

Tour photo, singing, down on 1 knee, full color, 8x10" **$25.00**

Ornament, Hallmark Keepsake, Elvis, gold, 1979, MIB, from $20.00 to $25.00.

Enesco

Enesco is a company that imports and distributes ceramic novelty items made in Japan. Some of their more popular lines are the Human Beans, Partners in Crime Christmas ornaments, Eggbert, Dutch Kids, and Mother in the Kitchen (also referred to as Kitchen Prayer Ladies, see also that category). Prices are climbing steadily. Several Enesco items are pictured in *The Collector's Encyclopedia of Cookie Jars, Volumes 1, 2,* and *3,* by Joyce and Fred Roerig (Collector Books).

Bell, Human Bean, 7 pictured on bell, 6" **$16.00**

Egg timer, windmill w/2 Dutch kids kissing, 4⅜", NMIB..**$68.00**

Figurine, Basil the Basset Hound, standing & begging...**$65.00**

Figurine, Dear God Kids, Dear God, Wait a Minute, Do You Have a Snowman in Heaven, 1983, 5" **$36.00**

Figurine, Dear God Kids, nurse, Let's Do Rounds Together, 1983, 4¾" **$40.00**

Figurine, Dear God Kids, The Most Wonderful Mom in the World, 1983, 4", MIB **$40.00**

Figurine, Dutch girl in pink dress, comes apart to form 4 measuring cups, EX **$46.00**

Figurine, Eggbert, the Dentist, 2x3", MIB **$20.00**

Figurine, Erin, Don't Worry Santa Won't Forget Us, Miss Martha's Collection, MIB **$75.00**

Figurine, Jeffrey, Bein' a Fireman Sure Is Hot & Thirsty Work, MIB **$95.00**

Figurine, Tis the Chocolate Season, little girl w/of tray chocolate goodies, Sisters & Best Friends Series, 5½" ...**$70.00**

Figurines, Dear God Kids, boy & girl stand in front of separate church windows w/verses on them, 1983, MIB, pr **$66.00**

Figurines, Saints Marching Band, 9-pc band, from 6" to 8½", MIB **$95.00**

Mug, coffee; Human Bean Loves Jelly Beans **$10.00**

Music box, Dear God Kids, couple getting married, 1984, 4¾", M **$60.00**

Music box, roller coaster, plays 6 tunes, MIB **$100.00**

Music box, sewing machine w/mice, 6", MIB **$90.00**

Music box, Sir Mickey to the Rescue, Mickey Mouse & Friends on carousel, lights up, 13" **$90.00**

Music box, typewriter w/mice, 1991, EX **$90.00**

Night light, Eggbert coming out of soccer ball, 1989, MIB **$365.00**

Night light, Wimbleduck, Eggbert coming out of tennis ball, 1989 ....**$290.00**

North Pole Station, 1987 ....**$80.00**

Ornament, Partners in Crime, dog & cat in Christmas stocking, 1994, 2½", MIB **$47.00**

Ornament, Partners in Crime, dog & cat in shopping bag, 1994, 2½" **$30.00**

Ornament, Partners in Crime, dog & cat in wreath, 1994 ..**$30.00**

Ornament, Santa Knitting Scarf, 1994, 2¼" **$25.00**

Snow dome, Eggbert in snow dome on top of golf ball .**$435.00**

Spoon holder, Mary Poppins, holds 2 spoons, musical, w/original string tag, 1964 ....**$175.00**

Toothbrush holder, Doc, Walt Disney's Snow White, stands beside barrel (holder), ca 1960, 4¼" **$65.00**

Eye Winker

Designed along the lines of an early pressed glass pattern by Dalzell, Gilmore and Leighton, Eye Winker was one of several attractive glassware assortments featured in the catalogs of L. G. Wright during the '60s and '70s. The line was extensive and made in several colors: amber, blue, green, crystal, and red. It was probably pressed by Fostoria, Fenton, and Westmoreland, since we know these are the companies that made Moon and Star for Wright, who was not a glass manufacturer but simply a distributing company. Red and green are the most desirable colors and are priced higher than the others we mentioned. The values given here are for red and green, deduct about 20% for examples in clear, amber, or light blue.

Though prices may have softened slightly due to Internet influence, this line is still very collectible, and as the increased supply made available through online auctions gradually diminishes, we expect values to return to the level they were several months ago.

Advisor: Sophia Talbert (See Directory, Eye Winker)

Ashtray, allover pattern, 4½" dia, from $20 to **$25.00**
Bowl, 4 toes, 2½x5", from $22 to.................................**$28.00**
Butter dish, allover pattern, 4½" dia lid, 6" base, from $50 to...**$65.00**
Candy dish, all over pattern, disk foot, w/lid, 5¼x5½" ..**$45.00**
Candy dish, oval, 4-toed, 5x3½".................................**$25.00**
Celery or relish, ruffled rim, oblong, 9½x5".......................**$40.00**
Compote, allover pattern except for plain flared rim, pat-terened lid, 10½x6"+finial **$70.00**
Compote, allover pattern except for plain flared rim & foot, patterned lid, 7x5", w/lid **$50.00**
Compote, allover pattern except for plain flared rim & foot, 7x7"...**$30.00**
Compote, jelly; patterned lid, plain foot & rim, 4¼x3½"..**$40.00**
Compote, ruffled rim, plain foot, 4-sided, 7x6"...........**$40.00**
Compote, ruffled rim, 4-sided, 6x10" **$50.00**
Creamer & sugar bowl, allover pattern, disk foot, sm, 3¼"..**$35.00**

Fairy lamp, allover pattern, disk foot, two-piece, from $50.00 to $60.00.
(From the collection of Sophia Talbert)

Goblet, plain rim & foot, 6¼"......................................**$25.00**
Marmalade, w/lid, 5¼x4"...**$45.00**
Pitcher, ruffled rim, plain foot, 1-qt, from $70 to........**$75.00**
Pitcher, 28-oz, 7¾", minimum value **$50.00**
Salt & pepper shakers, 4", pr...**$30.00**
Salt cellar, allover pattern, ruffled rim, 1¾"................**$10.00**
Sherbet, plain rim & foot, 4½".....................................**$20.00**
Toothpick holder, allover pattern, ruffled rim, 2¼" **$10.00**
Tumbler, 8-oz, from $30 to **$28.00**
Vase, ruffled rim, 3-sided, 3-toed, 7¾".........................**$50.00**
Vase, 3-footed, scalloped, 6" **$50.00**

Fast-Food Collectibles

Since the late 1970s, fast-food chains have been catering to their very young customers through their kiddie meals. The toys tucked in each box or bag have made a much longer-lasting impression on the kids than any meal could. Today it's not just kids but adults (sometimes entire families) who are clamoring for them. They're after not only the kiddie meal toys but also boxes, promotional signs used by the restaurant, the promotional items themselves (such as Christmas orna-ments you can buy for 99¢, collector plates, glass tumblers, or stuffed animals), or the 'under 3' (safe for children under 3) toys their toddler customers are given on request.

There have been three kinds of promotions: 1) national — every restaurant in the country offering the same item, 2) regional, and 3) test market. While, for instance, a test mar-ket box might be worth $20.00, a regional box might be $10.00, and a national, $1.00. Supply dictates price.

To be most valuable, a toy must be in the original pack-age, just as it was issued by the restaurant. Beware of deal-ers trying to 'repackage' toys in plain plastic bags. Most orig-inal bags were printed or contained an insert card. Vacuform containers were quickly discarded, dictating a premium price of $10.00 minimum. Toys without the original packaging are worth only about one-half to two-thirds as much as those mint in package, which are the values we give in our listings.

Toys representing popular Disney characters draw cross-collectors, so do Star Trek, My Little Pony, and Barbie doll toys. It's not always the early items that are the most col-lectible, because some of them may have been issued in such vast amounts that there is an oversupply of them today. At the same time, a toy only a year or so old that might have been quickly withdrawn due to a problem with its design will already be one the collector will pay a good price to get.

If you'd like to learn more about fast-food collectibles, we recommend *Tomart's Price Guide to Kid's Meal Collectibles* by Ken Clee; *The Illustrated Collector's Guide to McDonald's® Happy Meal® Boxes, Premiums and Promotions©, McDonald's® Happy Meal Toys in the USA, McDonald's® Happy Meal Toys Around the World,* and *Illustrated Collector's Guide to McDonald's® McCAPS,* all by Joyce and Terry Losonsky; *McDonald's® Collectibles* by Gary Henriques and Adre Duval; and *Schroeder's Collectible Toys, Antique to Modern* (Collector Books).

See also California Raisins.

Note: Unless noted otherwise, values are given for MIP items (when applicable).

Club: McDonald's© Collector Club
1153 S Lee St., PMB 200
Des Plaines, IL 60016-6503

Membership: $15 per year for individual or out of state, $7 for juniors, or $20 per family or international members; includes annual dated lapel pin, quarterly newsletter, and annual members directory; send LSASE for club information, chapter list, and publication list; http://www.mcdclub.com

Newsletter: *Sunshine Express* (monthly)
and club's Sunshine Chapter
Bill and Pat Poe founders and current officers
220 Dominica Circle E.
Niceville, FL 32578-4085
Club membership: as per above
850-897-4163; fax: 850-897-2606
e-mail: McPoes@aol.com

Newsletter: *Collecting Tips*
Meredith Williams
Box 633, Joplin, MO 64802. Send SASE for information.

Arby's, Babar's World Tour, finger puppets, 1990, ea...**$3.00**
Arby's, Babar's World Tour, storybooks, 1991, ea **$3.00**
Arby's, Looney Tunes Cars Tunes, 1989, ea **$3.00**
Arby's, Looney Tunes Characters, 1988, standing, ea ...**$5.00**
Arby's, Mr Men, 4 different, ea **$5.00**
Arby's, Yogi Bear Fun Squirters, 1994, ea **$4.00**
Burger King, Aladdin, 1992, ea..................................**$3.00**
Burger King, Archies, 1991, 4 different, ea...................**$4.00**
Burger King, Bone Age, 1989, 4 different, ea................**$5.00**
Burger King, Bonkers, 1993, 6 different, ea **$3.00**
Burger King, Captain Planet Flipover Star Cruisers, 1991, 4 different, ea **$2.00**
Burger King, Cool Stuff, 1995, 5 different, ea...............**$3.00**
Burger King, Glo Force, 1996, 5 different, ea................**$3.00**

Burger King, Glow-in-the-Dark Troll Patroll, 1993, four different, $3.00 each.

Burger King, Good Gobblin', 1989, 3 different, ea **$3.00**
Burger King, Goofy Max Adventures, 1995, any except yellow runaway car, ea **$3.00**
Burger King, Goofy Max Adventures, 1995, yellow runaway car **$4.00**
Burger King, It's Magic, 1992, 4 different, ea **$2.00**
Burger King, Lion King, 1994, 7 different, ea................**$3.00**

Burger King, Mini Record Breakers, 1989, 6 different, ea..**$2.00**
Burger King, Minnie Mouse, 1992 ....**$6.00**
Burger King, Pocahontas, 1995, 8 different, ea **$3.00**
Burger King, Spacebace Racers, 1989, 4 different, ea...**$3.00**
Burger King, Toy Story, 1995, Woody.........................**$8.00**
Burger King, Z-Bots w/Pogs, 1994, 5 different, ea........**$2.00**
Dairy Queen, Baby's Day Out Books, 1994, 4 different, ea..**$12.00**
Dairy Queen, Bobby's World, 1994, 4 different, ea **$5.00**
Dairy Queen, Space Shuttle, 6 different, ea..................**$3.00**
Dairy Queen, Tom & Jerry, 1993, 4 different, ea **$6.00**
Denny's, Adventure Seekers Activity Packet, 1993, ea..**$2.00**
Denny's, Flintstones Dino Racers, 1991, 3 different, ea.**$4.00**
Denny's, Jetson's Space Cards, 1992, 6 different, ea.....**$4.00**
Dominos Pizza, Avoid the Noid, 1988, 3 different, ea..**$5.00**
Dominos Pizza, Noid, 1989, bookmark.......................**$10.00**
Hardee's, Balto, 1995, 6 different, ea **$3.00**
Hardee's, Dinosaur in My Pocket, 1993, 4 different, ea.**$3.00**
Hardee's, Eek! the Cat, 1995, 6 different, ea.................**$3.00**
Hardee's, Flintstones First 30 Years, 4 different, ea.......**$3.00**
Hardee's, Halloween Hideaway, 1989, 4 different, ea..**$2.00**
Hardee's, Micro Super Soakers, 1994, 4 different, ea....**$3.00**
Hardee's, Nicktoons Cruisers, 1994, 8 different, ea.......**$3.00**
Hardee's, Shirt Tales, 1990, plush figures, 5 different, ea.**$5.00**
Hardee's, Speed Bunnies, 1994, 4 different, ea.............**$3.00**
Hardee's, Tune-A-Fish, 1994, 4 different, ea.................**$3.00**
Hardee's, X-Men, 1995, 6 different, ea **$3.00**
Long John Silver's, Fish Car, 1989, 3 different, ea........**$3.00**
Long John Silver's, I Love Dinosaurs, 1993, 4 different, ea **$4.00**
Long John Silver's, Once Upon a Forest, 1993, 2 different, ea **$4.00**
Long John Silver's, Water Blasters, 1990, 4 different, ea ..**$4.00**
McDonald's, Animaniacs, 1995, any except under age 3, ea...**$3.00**
McDonald's, Animaniacs, 1995, under age 3, ea...........**$5.00**
McDonald's, Babe, 1996, 7 different, ea **$3.00**
McDonald's, Bambi, 1988, 4 different, ea **$5.00**
McDonald's, Barbie/Hot Wheels, 1994, Barbie, any except Camp Teresa (variation) or under age 3, from $4 to.**$5.00**
McDonald's, Barbie/Hot Wheels, 1994, Camp Teresa...**$8.00**
McDonald's, Barnyard (Old McDonald's Farm), 1986, 6 different, ea...**$8.00**
McDonald's, Cabbage Patch Kids/Tonka Trucks, 1992, Cabbage Patch Kids, any except under age 3, ea..**$3.00**
McDonald's, Changables, 1987, 6 different, ea.............**$5.00**
McDonald's, Chip 'N Dale Rescue Rangers, 1989, 4 different, ea...**$4.00**
McDonald's, Circus Parade, 1991, ea...........................**$5.00**
McDonald's, Dinosaur Days, 1981, 6 different, ea **$2.00**
McDonald's, Ducktails, 1987, ea, from $5 to **$6.00**
McDonald's, Feeling Good, 1985, mirror, Birdie **$3.00**
McDonald's, Ghostbusters, 1987, pencil sharpener, ghost.**$3.00**
McDonald's, Halloween (What Am I Going To Be), 1995, any except under age 3, ea...**$3.00**
McDonald's, Halloween (What Am I Going To Be), 1995, under age 3, Grimace in pumpkin **$4.00**

McDonald's, Happy Birthday 15 Years, 1994, any except Tonka or Muppet Babies, ea, from $3 to **$5.00**

McDonald's, Happy Birthday 15 Years, 1994, Muppet Babies #11 train pc **$8.00**

McDonald's, Happy Birthday 15 Years, 1994, Tonka train pc, from $10 to.................................**$15.00**

McDonald's, Little Mermaid, 1989, 4 different, ea **$5.00**

McDonald's, Mac Tonight, 1988, any except under age 3, ea **$6.00**

McDonald's, Mac Tonight, 1988, under age 3, skateboard **$8.00**

McDonald's, Muppet Workshop, 1995, ea **$2.00**

McDonald's, New Archies, 1988, 6 different, M, ea **$6.00**

McDonald's, Oliver & Co, 1988, 4 different, M, ea **$2.00**

McDonald's, Power Rangers, 1995, any except under age 3, ea...**$3.00**

McDonald's, Power Rangers, 1995, under age 3 ....**$4.00**

McDonald's, Spider-Man, 1995, any except under age 3, ea...**$3.00**

McDonald's, Spider-Man, 1995, under age 3 ....**$4.00**

McDonald's, Turbo Macs, 1988, any except under age 3, ea **$4.00**

McDonald's, Turbo Macs, 1988, under age 3, Ronald in soft rubber car **$6.00**

McDonald's, Young Astronauts, 1992, any except under age 3, ea **$2.00**

McDonald's, Zoo Face, 1988, 4 different, ea **$4.00**

Pizza Hut, Air Garfield, kite, 1993 ....**$6.00**

Pizza Hut, Brain Thaws, 4 different, 1995, ea **$4.00**

Pizza Hut, Eureeka's Castle, 1990, hand puppets, 3 different, ea..**$5.00**

Pizza Hut, Marvel Comics, 4 different, 1994, ea...........**$4.00**

Pizza Hut, Mascot Misfits, 4 different, 1995, ea **$4.00**

Pizza Hut, Squirt Toons, 5 different, 1995, ea **$5.00**

Sonic, Airtoads, 6 different, ea.....................................**$4.00**

Sonic, All-Star Mini Baseballs, 1995, 5 different, ea **$4.00**

Sonic, Bone-A-Fide Friends, 1994, 4 different, ea **$3.00**

Sonic, Creepy Strawlers, 1995, 4 different, ea **$5.00**

Sonic, Squishers, 1995, 4 different, ea..........................**$5.00**

Sonic, Very Best Food, 1996, 4 different, ea.................**$4.00**

Subway, Battle Balls, 1995-95, 4 different, ea..............**$3.00**

Subway, Bump in the Night, 1995, 4 different, ea **$5.00**

Subway, Explore Space, 1994, 4 different, ea...............**$4.00**

Subway, Hurricanes, 1994, 4 different, ea **$4.00**

Subway, Tom & Jerry, 1995, 4 different, ea..................**$3.00**

Taco Bell, Congo, 1995, watches, 3 different, ea **$5.00**

Taco Bell, Happy Talk Sprites, Spark, Twinkle, or Romeo, 1983, plush, ea..**$6.00**

Taco Bell, Pebble & the Penguin, 1995, 3 different, ea ..**$5.00**

Wendy's, All Dogs Go To Heaven, 1989, 6 different, ea .**$2.00**

Wendy's, Animalinks, 1995, 6 different, ea **$2.00**

Wendy's, Ballsasaurus, 1992, 4 different, ea **$4.00**

Wendy's, Definitely Dinosaurs, 1988, 4 different, ea.....**$4.00**

Wendy's, Dino Games, 1993, 3 different, ea.................**$3.00**

Wendy's, Glo-Ahead, 1993, any except under age 3, ea .**$2.00**

Wendy's, Glo-Ahead, 1993, under age 3, finger puppet..**$3.00**

Wendy's, Wacky Windups, 1991, 5 different, ea............**$4.00**

Wendy's, Yogi Bear & Friends, 1990, 6 different, ea.....**$3.00**

White Castle, Bow Biters, 1989, Blue Meany................**$5.00**

White Castle, Castleburger Dudes, 1991, 4 different, ea ..**$6.00**

White Castle, Super Balls, 1994, 3 different, ea............**$5.00**

McDonald's, Flintstone Kids, 1988, $8.00 each.
(Photo courtesy Martin and Carolyn Berens)

Fenton Glass

Located in Williamstown, West Virginia, the Fenton company is still producing glassware just as they have since the early part of the century. Nearly all fine department stores and gift shops carry an extensive line of their beautiful products, many of which rival examples of finest antique glassware. The fact that even some of their fairly recent glassware has collectible value attests to its fine quality.

Over the years they have made many lovely colors in scores of lines, several of which are very extensive. Paper labels were used exclusively until 1970. Since then some pieces have been made with a stamped-in logo.

Numbers in the descriptions correspond with catalog numbers used by the company. Collectors use them as a means of identification as to shape and size. If you'd like to learn more about the subject, we recommend *Fenton Glass, The Second Twenty-Five Years,* and *Fenton Glass, The Third Twenty-Five Years,* by William Heacock; *Fenton Glass, The 1980s,* by James Measell; and *Fenton Art Glass, 1907 to 1939,* and *Fenton Art Glass Patterns, 1939 to 1980,* both by Margaret and Kenn Whitmyer.

Advisor: Ferill J. Rice (See Directory, Fenton Glass)

Club: Fenton Art Glass Collectors of America, Inc.
Newsletter: Butterfly Net
P.O. Box 384
Williamstown, WV 26187
Full membership $20 per year; $5 for each associate membership; children under 12 free

Club: Pacific Northwest Fenton Association
P.O. Box 881
Tillamook, OR 97141, 503-842-4815; Subscription: $20 per year; includes quarterly informational newsletter

Baskets

Black Rose, #7237, original sticker, 7" **$225.00**
Butterfly & Flowering Branch, Burmese, Connoisseur, 1985 .**$135.00**
Coin Dot, cranberry opalescent, 1947-64, 7" **$115.00**
Coralene, floral, #1135, signed Bill/Frank....................**$85.00**
Hobnail, blue opalescent, 1940-56, 4½" **$45.00**
Hobnail, cranberry opalescent, #3346, 8½" **$75.00**
Hobnail, cranberry opalescent, #3348, 10½" **$95.00**
Hobnail, cranberry opalescent, 1940-56, 4½" **$85.00**
Hobnail, cranberry opalescent, 1941-77, 7" **$95.00**
Hobnail, French opalescent, footed, handled, 6¼".....**$65.00**
Hobnail, green opalescent, 1940-43, 4½" **$75.00**
Hobnail, plum opalescent, #3837, 1969-70, 7" **$155.00**
Hobnail, topaz opalescent, #3834, 4½".......................**$65.00**
Iris on bone white, #7539, 1982, 7½" **$60.00**
Jamestown, silver, #7237, 7"..**$65.00**
Levay, #3837TO, med, 7" **$75.00**
Meadow Beauty, spiral rib, #1219, 1998, sm **$95.00**
Melon, blue overlay, #192, 10½" dia **$150.00**
Rose overlay, 1943-45, 5" dia......................................**$55.00**
Roses, Burmese, #7238, 7" **$185.00**
Silver turquoise, 7"..**$50.00**
Vasa Murrhina, Rose Mist, #6435, 7".........................**$90.00**

Bells

Barred Oval, Autumn Gold, #8369, 6" **$45.00**
Bird on Branch, Rosalene satin, #9667, hand-painted, J Wilshaw **$65.00**
Blue Rose/Blue Satin Medallion, #8267 ....**$45.00**
Butterfly & Flowering Branch, Burmese, Connoisseur, #9667, 1985 ....**$115.00**
Faberge, Rosalene, #8466RE..**$65.00**
Hobnail, plum opalescent, #3645, Levay, 1984 ....**$65.00**
Log Cabin on custard, #7667 ....**$65.00**
Nature's Christmas, #7466NC **$50.00**
New Born on custard, #7564 ....**$30.00**
Paisley, #6761RU...**$35.00**
Shell, Burmese, Connoisseur, 1986 ....**$125.00**
Snowman on opal satin, #7673SM, musical.................**$42.00**
Studebaker, #7668SU, limited edition of 5,000, 1986 ..**$85.00**

Carnival Glass

Note: Carnival glass items listed here were made after 1970.

Bowl, Butterfly & Berry, amethyst, #8428, heart shape, fantail interior, Special Room, 1990 ....**$75.00**
Chessie box, red, #9480, w/lid **$75.00**
Pitcher, plum, #6869, 1997..**$95.00**
Vase, Atlantis, crystal iridized, limited edition **$150.00**

Crests

Apple Blossom, vase, #7336, 4¼"................................**$40.00**
Black, bonbon, hdld, #7333...**$75.00**

Black, vase, fan; #7357 ....**$85.00**
Blue, comport, ftd, #7228..**$40.00**
Emerald, cake plate, #7215, 13" **$100.00**
Flame, cake plate, ftd, #7213, 13" **$140.00**
Flame, cake plate, ftd, #7213 ....**$135.00**
Flame, candle holders, #7474, pr **$125.00**
Gold, comport, low ftd, #7329....................................**$35.00**
Ivory, vase, 4" **$30.00**
Peach, candle holder, #7272, pr **$80.00**
Peach, epergne, #7200 ....**$150.00**

Peach, ewer, melon ribs, 9½", $62.50.

Peach, vase, #6059, 8½"...**$85.00**
Silver, basket, #7237, 7"...**$35.00**
Silver, bonbon, #7428, 8" **$12.00**
Silver, bottle, oil; #680 ....**$85.00**
Silver, bowl, #7223, 13" **$65.00**
Silver, bowl, #7224, 10" **$50.00**
Silver, bowl, dessert; shallow, #680............................**$22.50**
Silver, bowl, mayonnaise; #7203................................**$11.00**
Silver, bowl, shallow, #7316..**$46.00**
Silver, bowl, soup; #680, 5½" **$35.00**
Silver, candle holder, bulbous base, #1523, pr...........**$30.00**
Silver, candle holder, low, ruffled, #7271, pr.............**$25.00**
Silver, candlesticks, Yellow Roses, #7271, short, pr **$55.00**
Silver, comport, ftd, #7228 ....**$11.00**
Silver, creamer, ruffled top..**$50.00**
Silver, cup, threaded hdld, #7209 ....**$22.50**
Silver, epergne, 2-pc set, #7301 ....**$110.00**
Silver, plate, #680, 10" **$37.50**
Silver, plate, #680, 5½" **$6.00**
Silver, plate, #682, 12" **$35.00**
Silver, punch bowl, #7306..**$350.00**
Silver, punch cup, #7306 ....**$15.00**
Silver, relish, divided, #7334 ....**$32.50**
Silver, saucer, #7209..**$5.00**
Silver, shakers, #7406, pr...**$225.00**
Silver, sugar bowl, ruffled top **$45.00**

Silver, tidbit, 2-tier, #680..**$47.50**
Silver, tidbit, 3-tier, #680..**$47.50**
Silver, tumbler, ftd, #7342...**$57.50**
Silver, vase, #203, 4½"..**$12.50**
Silver, vase, #7450, 10"...**$115.00**
Silver, vase, #7453, 8"..**$25.00**
Silver, vase, #7454, 9"..**$47.50**
Silver, vase, double crimped, #7156, 6"....................**$19.00**
Silver, vase, fan topped, #7262, 12"........................**$110.00**
Silver, vase, fan; #36, 4½"..**$11.00**
Silver, vase, tulip; Beaded Melon, milk glass, 5".........**$30.00**
Silver, vase, Yellow Roses, crimped, 6"......................**$35.00**
Snow, vase, cranberry, crimped, 6"............................**$65.00**

Figurals and Novelties

Rabbit, amethyst iridescent, hollow, January 1971 – 72, 5½", $85.00.
(Photo courtesy Lee Garmon)

Alley cat, Burmese satin, #C5177, QVC 1996..............**$85.00**
Alley cat, Stiegel Green iridescent, #5177, QVC 1995.**$70.00**
Bear, Christmas Rose, sitting, #5151TS........................**$52.00**
Bear, Country Cranberry, #5151, blown, hollow.........**$55.00**
Bear, green & white slag iridized, #5151.....................**$55.00**
Bear, lt green iridized, Bailey, limited edition.............**$35.00**
Bear, opaque pale yellow, #5151.................................**$52.00**
Bear, sapphire blue opalescent, #5151, Gracious Touch..**$55.00**
Bear, Sea Mist Green, satin, #5151..............................**$45.00**
Bear, topaz opalescent, daydreaming, #5239................**$25.00**
Bear, topaz opalescent, reclining, #5233......................**$25.00**
Bear, topaz opalescent, sitting, #5151.........................**$25.00**
Bird, Happiness; custard w/holly, #5197CH.................**$50.00**
Bird, Happiness; lime sherbet, hand-painted green w/white floral, #5197..**$55.00**
Bird, Happiness; purple slag...**$45.00**
Bird, Happiness; Rosalene, #5197RE............................**$40.00**
Bird, Happiness; roses on custard, #5197, long tail....**$52.00**
Bird, Rosalene, #5163, sm...**$40.00**
Bunny, orange daisies on cameo satin, #5162.............**$50.00**
Bunny, Rosalene, #5162, light.......................................**$40.00**
Cat, Burmese, hand-painted floral, #C5165N, QVC 1995..**$75.00**
Cat, calico, black, yellow & white, #5165....................**$68.00**
Cat, strawberries on French opalescent, #5165............**$60.00**

Cat, tabby, gray stripe, #5165......................................**$58.00**
Cat, topaz opalescent, curious, #5243.........................**$25.00**
Cat, topaz opalescent, stylized, #5065.........................**$25.00**
Duckling, crystal w/hand-painted purple flowers & green leaves, #5169...**$65.00**
Duckling, roses on blue satin, #5169...........................**$40.00**
Duckling, strawberries on French opalescent, #5169..**$52.00**
Egg, Oriental, opal iridized, #5031WD, 1991, lg.........**$60.00**
Egg (on pedestal), Birth of a Saviour, #5146, limited edition...**$65.00**
Fawn, Magnolia & Berry, spruce green, #5160, 1996.**$50.00**
Fawn, Strawberries, white flowers on transparent green, #5160..**$55.00**
Horse, OSCAR, Rosalene, made for Heisey Collectors, 1990 souvenir, 4"..**$75.00**
Kitten, Natural Animals, #5119.....................................**$42.00**
Kitten, opaque shiny black, #5119................................**$60.00**
Kitten, topaz opalescent, stretching, #5119.................**$25.00**
Mouse, Pirate, #5148NIL, red/yellow clothing, eye patch..**$60.00**
Mouse, Rosalene, #5148, shiny.....................................**$55.00**
Mouse, topaz opalescent satin, #5148.........................**$45.00**
Mouse, white satin w/hand-painted pink roses, #5148..**$55.00**
Owl, Celeste Blue iridized, blown, lg...........................**$75.00**
Paperweight, Studebaker, #7698SU, limited edtion of 5,000, 1986..**$85.00**
Pig, True Blue Friends, blue & white slag, #5220, 1986..**$45.00**
Santa, #5299I2, limited editon of 3,750, 1997.............**$75.00**
Santa, #5299P7, 1997...**$50.00**
Swan, Rosalene, #5127RE, open....................................**$30.00**
Top hat, Coin Dot, cranberry opalescent, 1947-54......**$65.00**
Top hat, Ribbed Optic, blue opalescent, 1939, 3½"...**$60.00**
Unicorn, Burmese, hand-painted roses, #5253, QVC..**$78.00**
Whale, topaz opalescent, #5152....................................**$25.00**

Hobnail

Bottle, perfume; cranberry opalescent, 1948, scarce...**$110.00**
Bowl, cranberry opalescent, #389, triangular, 11".....**$130.00**
Cake plate, blue opalescent..**$85.00**
Candy jar, cranberry opalescent, #3883, w/lid..........**$220.00**
Candy jar, plum opalescent, #3887, footed...............**$200.00**
Cruet, vinegar; French opalescent.................................**$65.00**
Lighter, cigarette; white milk, #3692...........................**$28.00**
Mustard, blue opalescent, w/lid & paddle...................**$28.00**
Pitcher, plum opalescent, #3664, w/ice lip, 70-oz....**$260.00**
Pitcher, water; cranberry opalescent...........................**$250.00**
Salt & pepper shakers, blue opalescent, pedestal footed, 1940-43..**$50.00**
Salt & pepper shakers, French opalescent, flat, pr.....**$35.00**
Tumbler, cranberry opalescent, 1952-67, 20-oz...........**$37.50**
Vase, blue opalescent, crimped, 3"...............................**$28.00**
Vase, bud; plum opalescent, #3756, 8".......................**$45.00**
Vase, cranberry opalescent, #3853, 3".........................**$60.00**
Vase, cranberry opalescent, #3856, crimped, 5½".......**$35.00**
Vase, cranberry opalescent, #3859, 8".......................**$200.00**
vase, cranberry opalescent, crimped cup top, 4"........**$25.00**
Vase, cranberry opalescent, triangular top, 4"............**$25.00**

Vase, fan; blue opalescent, scalloped, footed, 6¼".....**$45.00**
Vase, French opalescent, triangular top, 4"...................**$9.00**
Vase, plum opalescent, #3758, med........................**$130.00**
Vase, plum opalescent, #3759, 1969-70, 18".............**$150.00**
Vase, topaz opalescent, crimped cup top, 4" **$20.00**

Vase, cranberry opalescent, #121, 10¾", $70.00.

Lamps

Fairy, Anticipation, #7300, 1983....................................**$55.00**
Fairy, Blue Burmese satinized, made for FAGCA, 1-pc...**$100.00**
Fairy, Burmese, plain, 1-pc..**$195.00**
Fairy, Christmas Morning, #7300, 1978 ....**$55.00**
Fairy, Dianthus, pink, blue & yellow on custard, #7300 ...**$60.00**
Fairy, Going Home, #7300, 1980.................................**$55.00**
Fairy, Hobnail, red carnival, 3-pc...............................**$65.00**
Fairy, holly on custard, 2-pc.......................................**$35.00**
Fairy, Nature's Christmas, #7300, 1979......................**$55.00**
Fairy, Owl, #5108RE **$55.00**
Fairy, Pekin Blue, #7500, 1980 ....**$85.00**
Fairy, red iridescent medallion, 3-pc...........................**$65.00**
Fairy, Roses on Burmese, 2-pc...................................**$65.00**
Fairy, Santa, milk glass..**$25.00**
Fairy, white holly on ruby **$35.00**
Gone-With-The-Wind, Poppy, sapphire blue iridized...**$200.00**
Hurricane, Dot Optic, cranberry opalescent, w/base...**$225.00**
Oil, red iridized puff, Levay, 1978...............................**$95.00**
Prayer, Madonna, crystal velvet, #5107, w/hardware..**$55.00**
Student, poppy pattern on marble base, honey amber over-
    lay **$80.00**
Student, Roses on Burmese **$575.00**
Student, Roses on Burmese, signed Louise Piper **$675.00**
Student, Shelly green roses, #9205............................**$165.00**

Miscellaneous

Amphora, Royal Purple, #2947, w/stand, 1955 ....**$260.00**
Ashtray, ball, #3648RV..**$38.00**
Bonbon, Butterfly, Rosalene, #8230 ....**$25.00**

Bonbon, Violets in the Snow, 6" **$28.00**
Bowl, Basketweave, Rosalene, #8222 ....**$30.00**
Bowl, Blue Burmese, #7660, McKee mold, Special Room,
    flared, 9½" dia..**$55.00**
Bowl, Carolina Dogwood, Rosalene, #8424.................**$45.00**
Bowl, Coin Dot, cranberry, 7" **$55.00**
Bowl, Coin Dot, cranberry opalescent, flared, 1947, 7" ...**$60.00**
Bowl, cranberry, #1728, crimped, lg **$125.00**
Bowl, Grape, Rosalene, #8457, 3-toed **$30.00**
Bowl, Hexagon Floral, Rosalene, #8226 ....**$65.00**
Bowl, planter; floral, Rosalene, #8226.........................**$60.00**
Bowl, rose; Dot Optic, ruby overlay, crimped, 1961, 4" ...**$40.00**
Bowl, rose; lavender opalescent iridized floral, limited edi-
    tion, 1989..**$45.00**
Bowl, rose; Louisa, green iridized, 1900s **$75.00**
Bowl, rose; Maple Leaf, Burmese.................................**$65.00**
Bowl, Violets in the Snow, flat, 10"..............................**$55.00**
Bowl, Water Lily, Rosalene, #8426, 3-toed...................**$50.00**
Candle holders, Water Lily, Rosalene, #8473, pr **$50.00**
Candy box, Baroque, custard, #9388 ....**$60.00**
Candy box, Bull's Eye, wisteria **$55.00**
Candy box, Chessie Cat, teal marigold iridized, #9480, 2-
    pc..**$95.00**
Candy box, Roses on custard, #7454 ....**$35.00**
Candy box, Spanish Lace, #3580 ....**$60.00**
Candy jar, Water Lily, custard satin, footed **$45.00**
Clock, hand-painted tulips, opalescent glass, #8691, styl-
    ized...**$65.00**
Comport, floral on Rosalene, #8422, footed.................**$50.00**
Compote, Blue Burmese, #8624, fluted, McKee mold, Special
    Room **$60.00**
Compote, Violets in the Snow, footed, #7429.............**$45.00**
Cuspidor, Cherry Wreath, Celeste Blue iridized opalescent,
    marked Crider #5, limited edition, sm **$125.00**
Cuspidor, Daisy & Button, marigold iridized, marked Crider,
    1981, sm...**$125.00**
Cuspidor, Frolicking Bears, aqua iridized opalescent, marked
    IGCA 1983 ....**$150.00**
Cuspidor, Grape & Cable, marigold iridized opalescent,
    lg...**$150.00**
Cuspidor, lady's; Persian Medallion, vaseline iridized, limited
    edition (Bailey) **$125.00**
Epergne, topaz opalescent, #7601, 1997, 5-pc, 13"...**$310.00**
Jar, Coin Dot, Rose Petal, blue opalescent, 1947 ......**$175.00**
Jar, temple; sunset cameo, #7488 ....**$65.00**
Jardiniere, Water Lily, custard satin, #8498 ....**$55.00**
Jug, Black Rose w/Roses, #2765, 1991, 6"................**$145.00**
Jug, melon; rose overlay, #192, bulbous, 8" **$65.00**
Perfume, Mary Gregory, cranberry, #2906, limited edition,
    #d, w/stopper..**$115.00**
Picture frame, blue frosted asters, #7596, oval...........**$50.00**
Pitcher, blue opalescent swirl, #1352, w/ice lip, 70-oz, +6
    barrel tumblers..**$350.00**
Pitcher, Burmese, #7461, plain **$110.00**
Pitcher, cranberry overlay, #1753, 70-oz, +5 tumblers ..**$275.00**
Pitcher, cream; Coin Dot, cranberry opalescent, 1947-56,
    4"..**$50.00**

Pitcher, Dot Optic, blue opalescent, sm **$55.00**	
Pitcher, lemonade; Burmese, child size, made for Doris Lechler, +6 cups.............................**$475.00**	
Pitcher, Maple Leaf, Burmese **$65.00**	
Planter/bowl, Water Lily, custard satin, 6-sided **$35.00**	
Plate, nativity, #9412FL, 8" **$65.00**	
Plate, Smoke & Cinders, #7618, Designer Series, 1984 ...**$85.00**	
Salt & pepper shakers, embossed rose, Burmese Satin, #9206, FAGCA, pr **$45.00**	
Tidbit, 2-tier, #7394SC..**$65.00**	
Tumblers, Coin Dot, cranberry, 1950-55, 7-oz, set of 6...**$175.00**	
Vanity set, Burmese, #F2905BG, limited edition **$295.00**	
Vase, Atlantis; peach opalescent iridized, made for MLT (Mike Taylor), limited edition.............................**$195.00**	
Vase, Blue Ridge, deep flare, 1939, 4½" **$75.00**	
Vase, bud; Holly on custard, #9056............................**$32.00**	
Vase, bud; Rosalene, #9056..**$30.00**	
Vase, Cactus, topaz opalescent, 1959, 5" **$45.00**	
Vase, Coin Dot, cranberry opalescent, double-crimped, 1947-48, 4½" **$50.00**	
Vase, Coin Dot, cranberry opalescent, 1959, 6" **$75.00**	
Vase, Coin Dot, French opalescent, double-crimped, 1947, 13"...**$95.00**	
Vase, Feather, Golden Flax, #1649, signed, 9"..........**$115.00**	
Vase, Fern, pale blue satin, pinched, #1720, 1952 ......**$70.00**	
Vase, hand; Colonial Blue, 1963 ....**$35.00**	
Vase, handkerchief; Lily of the Valley, topaz opalescent, #8450..**$55.00**	
Vase, Hanging Heart, turquoise, #8954, 4"..................**$55.00**	
Vase, hex; Asters on dark overlay, #1648, 9" **$110.00**	
Vase, Honeycomb, blue satin, #1721, pinched, 8½"...**$75.00**	
Vase, iris on bone white, oval, #7542, 1982 ....**$50.00**	
Vase, Lattice & Roses, Burmese, #CV163RB, round, sm.**$80.00**	
Vase, Log Cabin, #7257, 7½"..**$65.00**	
Vase, Melon Squat, rose overlay, #192, 5" **$45.00**	
Vase, Peacock Tail; amethyst iridized...........................**$75.00**	
Vase, Queen's Bird, Burmese, #3254, Connoisseur, 1996, 11"...**$250.00**	
Vase, ruby overlay, double-ring neck, 1958-62, 6"......**$45.00**	
Vase, Spiral, cranberry opalescent, #3161, 11"............**$90.00**	
Vase, Spiral, cranberry opalescent, cup-flared, 1939, 3½" dia **$85.00**	
Vase, Spiral, cranberry opalescent, double-ring neck, 1950s, 6"...**$85.00**	
Vase, Spiral, cranberry opalescent, flared, 8"..............**$75.00**	
Vase, Spiral, cranberry opalescent, ribbed, 1951-59, 5"...**$65.00**	
Vase, Spiral, cranberry opalescent, 1951-55, 5" **$95.00**	
Vase, swung; Grape & Cable, aqua opalescent iridized, 17" **$95.00**	
Vase, Thistle, rubena verde, #1561, 11" **$155.00**	
Vase, Tulip, apple green, #711, beaded, miniature, 4"...**$45.00**	
Vase, urn; Rib Optic, cranberry, #1552, 10½"..............**$95.00**	
Vase, Vasa Murrhina, Autumn Orange, 9½"..................**$75.00**	
Vase, Victorian Rose, #8805X3, 1993 Connoisseur #167/950..**$145.00**	

Fiesta

You still can find Fiesta, but it's hard to get a bargain. Since it was discontinued in 1973, it has literally exploded onto the collectibles scene, and even at today's prices, new collectors continue to join the ranks of the veterans.

Fiesta is a line of solid-color dinnerware made by the Homer Laughlin China Company of Newell, West Virginia. It was introduced in 1936 and was immediately accepted by the American public. The line was varied. There were more than fifty items offered, and the color assortment included red (orange-red), cobalt, light green, and yellow. Within a short time, ivory and turquoise were added. (All these are referred to as 'original colors.')

As tastes changed during the production years, old colors were retired and new ones added. The colors collectors refer to as '50s colors are dark green, rose, chartreuse, and gray, and today these are very desirable. Medium green was introduced in 1959 at a time when some of the old standard shapes were being discontinued. Today, medium green pieces are the most expensive. Most pieces are marked. Plates were ink stamped, and molded pieces usually had an indented mark.

In 1986 Homer Laughlin reintroduced Fiesta, but in colors different than the old line: white, black, cobalt, rose (bright pink), and apricot. Many of the pieces had been restyled, and the only problem collectors have had with the new colors is with the cobalt. But if you'll compare it with the old, you'll see that it is darker. Turquoise, periwinkle blue, yellow, and Seamist green were added next, and though the turquoise is close, it is a little greener than the original. Lilac and persimmon were later made for sale exclusively through Bloomingdale's department stores. Production was limited on lilac (not every item was made in it), and now that it's been discontinued, collectors are already clamoring for it, often paying several times the original price. Sapphire blue, a color approximating the old cobalt, was new a couple of years ago; it's also a Bloomingdale's exclusive, and the selection is limited. Probably another 'instant collectible' in the making! Then came chartreuse; it's a little more vivid than the chartreuse of the '50s. Gray was next, then Juniper (a rich teal), and the last color to be added was cinnabar (maroon).

Items that have not been restyled are being made from the original molds. This means that you may find pieces with the old mark in the new colors (since the mark is an integral part of the mold). When an item has been restyled, new molds had to be created, and these will have the new mark. So will any piece marked with the ink stamp. The new ink mark is a script 'FIESTA' (all letters upper case), while the old is 'Fiesta.' Compare a few, the difference is obvious. Just don't be fooled into thinking you've found a rare cobalt juice pitcher or individual sugar and creamer set, they just weren't made in the old line.

For further information, we recommend *The Collector's Encyclopedia of Fiesta, Ninth Edition,* by Sharon and Bob Huxford, and *Post86 Fiesta* by Richard Racheter (both from Collector Books).

Newsletter: *Fiesta Collector's Quarterly*
China Specialties, Inc.
Box 471, Valley City, OH 44280. $12 (4 issues) per year

Ashtray, '50s colors...$88.00
Ashtray, red, cobalt or ivory...$65.00
Ashtray, yellow, turquoise or light green....................$47.00
Bowl, covered onion soup; cobalt or ivory..............$725.00
Bowl, covered onion soup; red.................................$750.00
Bowl, covered onion soup; turquoise, minimum value ..$7,000.00
Bowl, covered onion soup; yellow or light green....$650.00
Bowl, cream soup; '50s colors....................................$75.00
Bowl, cream soup; med green, minimum value....$4,200.00
Bowl, cream soup; red, cobalt or ivory.......................$62.00
Bowl, cream soup; yellow, turquoise or light green ..$45.00
Bowl, dessert; 6", '50s colors $52.00
Bowl, dessert; 6", med green.....................................$600.00
Bowl, dessert; 6", red, cobalt or ivory $52.00
Bowl, dessert; 6", yellow, turquoise or light green.....$40.00
Bowl, footed salad; red, cobalt, ivory or turquoise ..$400.00
Bowl, footed salad; yellow or light green $340.00
Bowl, fruit; 4¾", '50s colors......................................$40.00
Bowl, fruit; 4¾", med green $525.00
Bowl, fruit; 4¾", red, cobalt or ivory.........................$35.00
Bowl, fruit; 4¾", yellow, turquoise or light green $28.00
Bowl, fruit; 5½", '50s colors......................................$40.00
Bowl, fruit; 5½", med green $75.00
Bowl, fruit; 5½", red, cobalt or ivory.........................$35.00
Bowl, fruit; 5½", yellow, turquoise or light green $28.00
Bowl, fruit; 11¾", red, cobalt, ivory or turquoise $340.00
Bowl, fruit; 11¾", yellow or light green $275.00
Bowl, individual salad; med green, 7½"....................$120.00
Bowl, individual salad; red, turquoise or yellow, 7½".$90.00
Bowl, nappy; 8½", '50s colors $65.00
Bowl, nappy; 8½", med green...................................$145.00
Bowl, nappy; 8½", red, cobalt, ivory or turquoise......$58.00
Bowl, nappy; 8½", yellow or light green....................$42.00
Bowl, nappy; 9½", red, cobalt, ivory, or turquoise.....$65.00
Bowl, nappy; 9½", yellow or light green....................$52.00
Bowl, Tom & Jerry; ivory w/gold letters $265.00
Bowl, unlisted salad; colors besides yellow, minimum
   value $1,200.00
Bowl, unlisted salad; yellow.....................................$110.00
Candle holders, bulb; red, cobalt, ivory or turquoise, pr..$140.00
Candle holders, bulb; yellow or light green, pr........$110.00
Candle holders, tripod; red, cobalt, ivory or turquoise,
   pr $650.00
Candle holders, tripod; yellow or light green, pr $485.00
Carafe, red, cobalt, ivory or turquoise......................$340.00
Carafe, yellow or light green $255.00
Casserole, French; standard colors other than yellow, mini-
   mum value $725.00
Casserole, French; yellow $300.00
Casserole, '50s colors $300.00
Casserole, med grcen, minimum value.....................$900.00
Casserole, red, cobalt or ivory..................................$225.00
Casserole, yellow, turquoise or light green...............$165.00

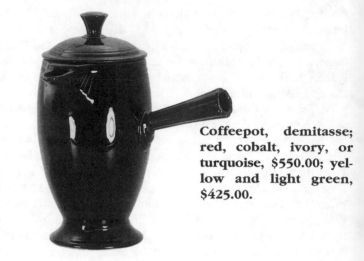

Coffeepot, demitasse; red, cobalt, ivory, or turquoise, $550.00; yellow and light green, $425.00.

Coffeepot, '50s colors...$350.00
Coffeepot, red, cobalt or ivory..................................$255.00
Coffeepot, yellow, turquoise or light green $195.00
Compote, sweets; red, cobalt, ivory or turquoise $100.00
Compote, sweets; yellow or light green $80.00
Compote, 12", red, cobalt, ivory or turquoise...........$200.00
Compote, 12", yellow or light green.........................$150.00
Creamer, regular; '50s colors.....................................$40.00
Creamer, regular; med green $90.00
Creamer, regular; red, cobalt or ivory.......................$35.00
Creamer, regular; yellow, turquoise or light green $22.00
Creamer, stick handled, red, cobalt, ivory or turquoise..$72.00
Creamer, stick handled, yellow or light green $48.00
Cup, demitasse; '50s colors......................................$375.00
Cup, demitasse; red, cobalt or ivory $80.00
Cup, demitasse; yellow, turquoise or light green........$68.00
Cup, see teacup
Egg cup, '50s colors $160.00
Egg cup, red, cobalt or ivory.....................................$72.00
Egg cup, yellow, turquoise or light green $60.00
Lid, for mixing bowl #1-#3, any color, minimum value ..$770.00
Lid, for mixing bowl #4, any color, minimum value...$1,000.00
Marmalade, red, cobalt, ivory or turquoise $325.00
Marmalade, yellow or light green $245.00
Mixing bowl #1, red, cobalt, ivory or turquoise $245.00
Mixing bowl #1, yellow or light green $180.00
Mixing bowl #2, red, cobalt, ivory or turquoise $130.00
Mixing bowl #2, yellow or light green $115.00
Mixing bowl #3, red, cobalt, ivory or turquoise $135.00
Mixing bowl #3, yellow or light green $125.00
Mixing bowl #4, red, cobalt, ivory or turquoise $160.00
Mixing bowl #4, yellow or light green $130.00
Mixing bowl #5, red, cobalt, ivory or turquoise $185.00
Mixing bowl #5, yellow or light green $160.00
Mixing bowl #6, red, cobalt, ivory or turquolse $275.00
Mixing bowl #6, yellow or light green $215.00
Mixing bowl #7, red, cobalt, ivory or turquoise $410.00
Mixing bowl #7, yellow or light green $350.00
Mug, Tom & Jerry; '50s colors.................................$100.00
Mug, Tom & Jerry; ivory w/gold letters....................$65.00

Mug, Tom & Jerry; red, cobalt or ivory $82.00

Mug, Tom & Jerry; yellow, turquoise or light green...$60.00

Mustard, red, cobalt, ivory or turquoise $265.00

Mustard, yellow or light green $210.00

Pitcher, disk juice; gray, minimum value................$3,000.00

Pitcher, disk juice; Harlequin yellow...........................$60.00

Pitcher, disk juice; red..$600.00

Pitcher, disk juice; yellow..$48.00

Pitcher, disk water; '50s colors $280.00

Pitcher, disk water; med green, minimum value ...$1,200.00

Pitcher, disk water; red, cobalt or ivory....................$170.00

Pitcher, disk water; yellow, turquoise or light green ..$125.00

Pitcher, ice; red, cobalt, ivory or turquoise $160.00

Pitcher, ice; yellow or light green $140.00

Pitcher, jug, 2-pt; '50s colors....................................$150.00

Pitcher, jug, 2-pt; red, cobalt or ivory......................$120.00

Pitcher, jug, 2-pt; yellow, turquoise or light green $88.00

Plate, cake; red, cobalt, ivory or turquoise, minimum
    value $1,000.00

Plate, cake; yellow or light green, minimum value ..$900.00

Plate, calendar; 1954 or 1955, 10" $45.00

Plate, calendar; 1955, 9"..$50.00

Plate, chop; 13", '50s colors......................................$100.00

Plate, chop; 13", med green.......................................$375.00

Plate, chop; 13", red, cobalt or ivory $60.00

Plate, chop; 13", yellow, turquoise or light green.......$42.00

Plate, chop; 15", '50s colors......................................$145.00

Plate, chop; 15", red, cobalt or ivory $80.00

Plate, chop; 15", yellow, turquoise or light green.......$50.00

Plate, compartment; 10½", '50s colors $75.00

Plate, compartment; 10½", red, cobalt or ivory...........$45.00

Plate, compartment; 10½", yellow, turquoise or light
    green $40.00

Plate, compartment; 12", red, cobalt or ivory.............$60.00

Plate, compartment; 12", yellow or light green..........$55.00

Plate, deep; '50s colors...$58.00

Plate, deep; med green $140.00

Plate, deep; red, cobalt or ivory $60.00

Plate, deep; yellow, turquoise or light green $38.00

Plate, 6", '50s colors...$9.00

Plate, 6", med green $20.00

Plate, 6", red, cobalt or ivory $7.00

Plate, 6", yellow, turquoise or light green $5.00

Plate, 7", '50s colors...$13.00

Plate, 7", med green $32.00

Plate, 7", red, cobalt or ivory $10.00

Plate, 7", yellow, turquoise or light green $9.00

Plate, 9", '50s colors...$22.00

Plate, 9", med green $45.00

Plate, 9", red, cobalt or ivory $18.00

Plate, 9", yellow, turquoise or light green $12.00

Plate, 10", '50s colors..$52.00

Plate, 10", med green $135.00

Plate, 10", red, cobalt or ivory $40.00

Plate, 10", yellow, turquoise or light green $32.00

Platter, '50s colors...$58.00

Platter, med green...$175.00

Platter, red, cobalt or ivory $45.00

Platter, yellow, turquoise or light green......................$35.00

Relish tray, gold decor, complete, minimum value...$250.00

Relish tray base, red, cobalt, ivory or turquoise $100.00

Relish tray base, yellow or light green $75.00

Relish tray center insert, red, cobalt, ivory or turquoise ..$60.00

Relish tray center insert, yellow or light green $50.00

Relish tray side insert, red, cobalt, ivory or turquoise ..$60.00

Relish tray side insert, yellow or light green...............$50.00

Salt & pepper shakers, '50s colors, pr.........................$45.00

Salt & pepper shakers, med green, pr........................$185.00

Salt & pepper shakers, red, cobalt or ivory, pr..........$30.00

Salt & pepper shakers, yellow, turquoise or light green,
    pr...$22.00

Sauce boat, '50s colors...$80.00

Sauce boat, med green..$180.00

Sauce boat, red, cobalt or ivory $85.00

Sauce boat, yellow, turquoise or light green..............$48.00

Saucer, demitasse; '50s colors...................................$100.00

Saucer, demitasse; red, cobalt or ivory $22.00

Saucer, demitasse; yellow, turquoise or light green....$18.00

Saucer, '50s colors..$6.00

Saucer, med green..$12.00

Saucer, original colors...$4.00

Saucer, red, cobalt or ivory...$5.00

Sugar bowl, w/lid, '50s colors, 3¼x3½".......................$75.00

Sugar bowl, w/lid, med green, 3¼x3½".......................$225.00

Sugar bowl, w/lid, red, cobalt or ivory, 3¼x3½"...........$58.00

Sugar bowl, w/lid, yellow, turquoise or light green,
    3¼x3½"..$48.00

Syrup, red, cobalt, ivory or turquoise $425.00

Syrup, yellow or light green.......................................$375.00

Teacup, '50s colors...$38.00

Teacup, med green..$60.00

Teacup, red, cobalt or ivory $35.00

Teacup, yellow, turquoise or light green.....................$25.00

Teapot, lg; red, cobalt, ivory or turquoise.................$225.00

Teapot, lg; yellow or light green................................$210.00

Teapot, med; '50s colors $325.00

Teapot, med; med green, minimum value $1,200.00

Teapot, med; red, cobalt or ivory $225.00

Teapot, med; yellow, turquoise or light green..........$165.00

Tray, utility; red, cobalt, ivory or turquoise................$42.00

Tray, utility; yellow or light green...............................$38.00

Tumbler, juice; chartreuse, Harlequin yellow or dark
    green..$600.00

Tumbler, juice; cobalt or ivory....................................$45.00

Tumbler, juice; red..$60.00

Tumbler, juice; rose..$65.00

Tumbler, juice; yellow, turquoise or light green.........$40.00

Tumbler, water; red, cobalt, ivory or turquoise $85.00

Tumbler, water; yellow or light green $65.00

Vase, bud; red, cobalt, ivory or turquoise $125.00

Vase, bud; yellow or light green $85.00

Vase, 8", red, cobalt, turquoise or ivory, minimum value .$700.00

Vase, 8", yellow or light green, minimum value $600.00

Vase, 10", red, cobalt, ivory or turquoise.................$950.00

Vase, 10", yellow or light green.................................$750.00
Vase, 12", red, cobalt, ivory or turquoise, minimum value.................................$1,300.00
Vase, 12", yellow or light green, mininum value...$1,100.00

Tray, figure-eight; turquoise or yellow, $400.00; cobalt, $100.00. Creamer, individual; red, $365.00; yellow, $80.00. Sugar bowl, individual; yellow, $125.00; turquoise, $365.00.

Kitchen Kraft

Bowl, mixing; 6", light green or yellow.......................$72.00
Bowl, mixing; 6", red or cobalt $78.00
Bowl, mixing; 8", light green or yellow.......................$85.00
Bowl, mixing; 8", red or cobalt $95.00
Bowl, mixing; 10", light green or yellow...................$115.00
Bowl, mixing; 10", red or cobalt $125.00
Cake plate, light green or yellow $55.00
Cake plate, red or cobalt...$65.00
Cake server, light green or yellow $145.00
Cake server, red or cobalt...$155.00
Casserole, individual; light green or yellow $150.00
Casserole, individual; red or cobalt..........................$160.00
Casserole, 7½", light green or yellow $85.00
Casserole, 7½", red or cobalt......................................$92.00
Casserole, 8½", light green or yellow $105.00
Casserole, 8½", red or cobalt....................................$115.00
Covered jar, lg; light green or yellow $320.00
Covered jar, lg; red or cobalt....................................$335.00
Covered jar, med; light green or yellow $290.00
Covered jar, med; red or cobalt.................................$300.00
Covered jar, sm; light green or yellow......................$290.00
Covered jar, sm; red or cobalt...................................$300.00
Covered jug, light green or yellow $280.00
Covered jug, red or cobalt...$290.00
Fork, light green or yellow $125.00
Fork, red or cobalt $135.00

Metal frame for platter...$26.00
Pie plate, spruce green $300.00
Pie plate, 9", light green or yellow.............................$45.00
Pie plate, 9", red or cobalt $48.00
Pie plate, 10", light green or yellow...........................$45.00
Pie plate, 10", red or cobalt $48.00
Platter, light green or yellow $70.00
Platter, red or cobalt...$75.00
Platter, spruce green...$350.00
Salt & pepper shakers, light green or yellow, pr......$100.00
Salt & pepper shakers, red or cobalt, pr $110.00
Spoon, light green or yellow.....................................$135.00
Spoon, red or cobalt $145.00
Stacking refrigerator lid, ivory $225.00
Stacking refrigerator lid, light green or yellow...........$75.00
Stacking refrigerator lid, red or cobalt $85.00
Stacking refrigerator unit, ivory $210.00
Stacking refrigerator unit, light green or yellow $48.00
Stacking refrigerator unit, red or cobalt......................$58.00

Finch, Kay

Wonderful ceramic figurines signed by sculptor-artist-decorator Kay Finch are among the many that were produced in California during the middle of the last century. She modeled her line of animals and birds with much expression and favored soft color combinations often with vibrant pastel accents. Some of her models were quite large, but generally they range in size from 12" down to a tiny 2". She made several animal 'family groups' and some human subjects as well. After her death a few years ago, prices for her work began to climb.

She used a variety of marks and labels, and though most pieces are marked, some of the smaller animals are not; but you should be able to recognize her work with ease, once you've seen a few marked pieces.

For more information, we recommend *Kay Finch Ceramics, Her Enchanted World,* by Mike Nickel and Cindy Horvath (Schiffer); *Collectible Kay Finch* by Richard Martinez, Devin Frick, and Jean Frick; and *The Collector's Encyclopedia of California Pottery, Second Edition,* by Jack Chipman (both by Collector Books). Please note: Prices below are for items decorated in multiple colors, not solid glazes.

Advisors: Mike Nickel and Cindy Horvath (See Directory, Kay Finch)

Cup, Kitten Face Toby, 3"...$100.00
Figurine, angel, #114a, #114b, or #114c, ea $50.00
Figurine, birds, Mr & Mrs, pastels, #454 & #455, 4½" & 3", pr $125.00
Figurine, cat, Ambrosia, #155, 10½", minimum value..$550.00
Figurine, cats, Hear/See/Do No Evil, #4734, #4835, #4836, 3-pc set...$495.00
Figurine, cats, Muff & Puff, pastels, #182 & #183, pr..$150.00
Figurine, choir boy, #210, 7½".....................................$95.00

Figurine, choir boy, kneeling, #211, 5½" $60.00
Figurine, dog, Dog Show Poodle, #5024, 5x4½" $550.00
Figurine, donkey, Long-Eared w/Basket, #4769, 4" ..$125.00
Figurine, ducks, Mama & Papa, #471 &#472, pr.......$500.00
Figurine, elephant, Peanuts, #191, 8½"....................$350.00
Figurine, fish, Guppy, #173, 2½".............................$125.00
Figurine, Goodey Couple, #122, 9½", pr..................$175.00
Figurine, Jezebel, #179, 6" $175.00
Figurine, lamb, standing, #109, 5½".........................$95.00
Figurine, owl, Hoot, #187, 8½" $150.00
Figurine, owl, Toot, #188, 5¾" $75.00
Figurine, owl, Tootsie, #189, 3¾" $35.00
Figurine, pheasant, #5300, 10"................................$295.00

Figurine, pig, Grumpy, 6¾x8", $295.00.

Figurine, rabbit, Bunny w/Jacket, #5005, 6" $175.00
Figurine, rabbit, Carrots, #473, 8¾"..........................$495.00
Figurine, squirrel family, Mama, Papa & Baby, #108a/108b/
   108c $125.00
Planter, Animal Blocks series, ea.................................$75.00

Fire-King

This is an area of collecting interest that you can enjoy without having to mortgage the home place. In fact, you'll be able to pick it up for a song, if you keep your eyes peeled at garage sales and swap meets.

Fire-King was a trade name of the Anchor Hocking Glass Company, located in Lancaster, Ohio. As its name indicates, this type of glassware is strong enough to stand up to high oven temperatures without breakage. From the early '40s until the mid-'70s, they produced kitchenware, dinnerware, and restaurant ware in a variety of colors. (We'll deal with Jade-ite, the most collectible of these colors later on in the book.) Blues are always popular with collectors, and Anchor Hocking made two, Turquoise Blue and Azurite (light sky blue). They also made pink, Forest Green, Ruby Red (popu-

lar in the Bubble pattern), gold-trimmed lines, and some with fired-on colors. During the late '60s they made Soreno in Avocado Green to tie in with home-decorating trends.

Bubble (made from the '30s through the '60s) was produced in just about every color Anchor Hocking ever made. You may also hear this pattern referred to as Provincial or Bullseye.

Alice was a mid-'40s to '50s line. It was made in Jade-ite and a white that was sometimes trimmed with blue or red. Cups and saucers were given away in boxes of Mother's Oats, but plates had to be purchased (so they're scarce today).

In the early '50s, they produced a 'laurel leaf' design in peach and 'Gray Laurel' lustres (the gray is scarce), followed later in the decade and into the '60s with several lines of white glass decorated with decals — Honeysuckle, Fleurette, Primrose, and Game Bird, to name only a few.

Anchor Hocking made ovenware in many the same colors and designs as their dinnerware. Their most extensive line (and one that is very popular today) was made in Sapphire Blue, clear glass with a blue tint, in a pattern called Philbe. Most pieces are still very reasonable, but some are already worth in excess of $50.00, so now is the time to start your collection. These are the antiques of the future! If you'd like to study more about Anchor Hocking and Fire-King, we recommend *Anchor Hocking's Fire-King & More* and *Collectible Glassware of the 40s, 50s, and 60s*, by Gene Florence. See also Jade-ite; Kitchen Collectibles.

Newsletter: *The '50s Flea!!!*
April and Larry Tvorak
P.O. Box 94
Warren Center, PA 18851; Subscription: $5 per year for 1 yearly postwar glass newsletter; includes free 30-word classified ad

Alice, cup & saucer, white $7.00
Alice, plate, white w/blue trim, 9½" $30.00
Alice, plate, white w/red trim, 9½" $50.00
Anniversary Rose, bowl, chili; rose decal on white, 5"..$12.00
Anniversary Rose, bowl, vegetable; rose decal on white,
   8¼"..$22.50
Anniversary Rose, cup & saucer, rose decal on white, 8-
   oz...$10.00
Anniversary Rose, snack tray, rose decal on white,
   11x6"...$8.00
Anniversary Rose, sugar bowl, rose decal on white,
   w/lid $15.00
Ashtray, Forest Green, set of 3: 3½", 4⅝", 5¾", from $20
   to..$22.50
Ashtray, Royal Ruby, 4 rests, 4¼" square, from $15 to..$18.00
Ashtray, Soreno, Cranberry Lustre, 6¼", from $18 to .$20.00
Blue Mosaic, cup & saucer, white, 5¾" $6.00
Blue Mosaic, plate, salad; decal on white, 7⅜".............$6.00
Blue Mosaic, soup plate, decal on white, 6⅝"...........$12.00
Bubble, bowl, berry; Royal Ruby, 8⅜" $20.00
Bubble, bowl, fruit; Forest Green, 4¼".........................$7.00
Bubble, candlesticks, Forest Green, pr $37.50

Bubble, pitcher, crystal iridescent, ice lip, 64-oz.........**$60.00**
Bubble, plate, dinner; Royal Ruby, 9⅜"........................**$24.00**
Bubble, plate, dinner; Sapphire Blue, 9⅜"....................**$7.00**
Bubble, stem, juice; Forest Green or Royal Ruby, 4-oz..**$10.00**
Bubble, stem, sherbet; Forest Green or Royal Ruby, 6-oz..**$9.00**
Bubble, tidbit, Royal Ruby, 2-tier.................................**$47.50**
Bubble, tumbler, lemonade; crystal iridescent, 16-oz.**$14.00**
Charm/Square, Azur-ite or white, bowl, dessert; 4¾"...**$6.00**
Charm/Square, bowl, salad; Ivory, 7⅜".......................**$23.00**
Charm/Square, bowl, soup; Forest Green, 6"..............**$18.00**
Charm/Square, creamer, Azur-ite or White..................**$12.00**
Charm/Square, plate, luncheon; Forest Green, 8⅜"......**$8.00**
Charm/Square, sugar bowl, Ivory..............................**$18.00**
Fishscale, bowl, dessert; shallow, 5½"........................**$10.00**
Fishscale, bowl, soup; Ivory, 7½"................................**$18.00**
Fishscale, cup & saucer, Ivory w/blue.........................**$25.00**
Fishscale, plate, salad; Ivory w/red, 7⅜"....................**$15.00**
Fleurette, bowl, soup; floral decal on white, 6⅝".......**$12.00**
Fleurette, cup, floral decal on white, 8-oz....................**$4.00**
Fleurette, plate, dinner; floral decal on white, 9⅛".......**$5.00**
Fleurette, sugar bowl, floral decal on white, w/lid.....**$10.00**
Forest Green, ashtray, 5¾" square...............................**$9.00**
Forest Green, cocktail shaker, 32-oz...........................**$22.00**
Forest green, punch bowl..**$22.50**
Forest Green, stem, cocktail; 4½-oz............................**$12.50**
Forest Green, stem, goblet; 9-oz...............................**$10.00**
Forest Green, tumbler, 7-oz..**$4.00**
Forest Green, vase, ivy ball, 4"......................................**$5.00**
Forget Me Not, bowl, dessert; floral decal on white, 4⅝"....**$8.00**
Forget Me Not, cup & saucer, floral decal on white, 8-oz..**$10.00**
Forget Me Not, plate, dinner; floral decal on white, 10"....**$14.00**
Forget Me Not, platter, floral decal on white, 9x12"...**$20.00**
Game Bird, ashtray, decal on white, 5¼"....................**$15.00**
Game Bird, plate, dinner; decal on white, 9⅛"............**$6.50**
Game Bird, tumbler, iced tea; decal on white, 11-oz.**$12.00**
Harvest, bowl, vegetable; decal on white, 8¼"...........**$15.00**
Harvest, plate, dinner; decal on white, 10"...................**$6.00**
Harvest, soup plate, decal on white, 6⅝".....................**$8.00**
Hobnail, goblet, tea; milk white, 13-oz.........................**$6.00**
Hobnail, vase, milk white, 9½"..................................**$10.00**
Honeysuckle, bowl, dessert; floral decal on white, 4⅝"..**$2.25**
Honeysuckle, plate, bread & butter; floral decal on white, 6¼"...**$15.00**
Honeysuckle, platter, floral decal on white, 9x12"......**$14.00**
Honeysuckle, tumbler, iced tea; floral decal on white, 12-oz...**$10.00**
Jane Ray, bowl, dessert; white, 4⅞"..........................**$10.00**
Jane Ray, bowl, vegetable; white, 8¼"......................**$25.00**
Jane Ray, cup & saucer, Ivory....................................**$22.00**
Jane Ray, cup & saucer, white...................................**$10.00**
Jane Ray, plate, dinner; Ivory, 9⅛"...........................**$22.50**
Laurel, bowl, dessert; Ivory or white, 4⅞"..................**$9.00**
Laurel, creamer, gray, ftd..**$5.00**
Laurel, plate, dinner; Ivory or white, 9⅛"..................**$14.00**
Laurel, plate, salad; Ivory or white, 7⅜"....................**$11.00**
Laurel, plate, serving; gray, 11"................................**$20.00**
Laurel, soup plate, gray, 7⅝"......................................**$16.00**
Laurel/Peach Lustre, bowl, dessert; 4⅞"........................**$4.00**
Laurel/Peach Lustre, bowl, vegetable; 8¼"..................**$10.00**

Laurel/Peach Lustre, creamer and sugar bowl, footed, $8.00 for the pair.

Laurel/Peach Lustre, cup & saucer, 8-oz........................**$4.50**
Laurel/Peach Lustre, plate, serving; 11"......................**$14.00**
Philbe, candy jar, crystal, low, w/lid, 4"..................**$215.00**
Philbe, cup, crystal..**$55.00**
Philbe, plate, luncheon; crystal, 8"..............................**$20.00**
Philbe, sugar bowl, crystal, footed, 3¼".....................**$70.00**
Primrose, bowl, Vintage, floral decal on white, footed, 10"...**$100.00**
Primrose, casserole, floral decal on white, knob lid, 1½-qt...**$12.00**
Primrose, gravy or sauce boat, floral decal on white...**$125.00**
Primrose, pan, utility baking; floral decal on white, 8x12½"...**$18.00**
Primrose, tumbler, floral decal on white, 11-oz..........**$25.00**
Royal Ruby, bowl, fruit; 4¼"..**$5.50**
Royal Ruby, goblet, ball stem.....................................**$11.00**
Royal Ruby, pitcher, upright, 3-qt..............................**$40.00**
Royal Ruby, punch cup, 5-oz...**$3.00**
Royal Ruby, tumbler, wine, footed, 2½-oz..................**$14.00**
Sheaves of Wheat, bowl, dessert; crystal, 4½"..............**$8.00**
Sheaves of Wheat, plate, dinner; crystal, 9"...............**$25.00**
Sheaves of Wheat, tumbler, juice; crystal, 6-oz...........**$15.00**
Soreno, ashtray, Avocado or milk white, 4¼"...............**$2.50**
Soreno, bowl, chip/salad; Aquamarine, 8½"................**$10.00**
Soreno, bowl, Lustre, Mardi-Gras or Aurora, 4-qt, 11⅜"...**$15.00**
Soreno, plate, serving; Avocado or milk white, 14"......**$6.00**
Soreno, sugar bowl, w/lid, Avocado or milk white......**$4.00**
Soreno, tumbler, iced tea; Honey Gold, 15-oz.............**$4.00**
Swirl, bowl, fruit/dessert; Azur-ite, 4⅞"........................**$7.00**
Swirl, bowl, vegetable; Ivory or white, 8¼"................**$20.00**
Swirl, cup & saucer, Azur-ite, 8-oz............................**$10.00**
Swirl, plate, dinner; Golden Anniversary, white w/gold trim, 9⅛"...**$7.50**
Swirl, platter, Sunrise, 12x9"......................................**$18.00**
Swirl, soup plate, Rose-ite, 7⅝"..................................**$75.00**
Swirl, sugar bowl, Ivory or white, flat, tab handles, w/lid..**$15.00**
Swirl, tumbler, iced tea; pink, 12-oz..........................**$10.00**
Three Bands, bowl, fruit/dessert; burgundy, 4⅞".......**$15.00**
Three Bands, cup & saucer, Ivory, 8-oz.....................**$15.00**

Three Bands, plate, dinner; burgundy, 9⅛" **$25.00**
Turquoise Blue, bowl, cereal (thin); 2x5" **$35.00**
Turquoise Blue, creamer & sugar bowl **$12.00**
Turquoise Blue, plate, w/cup indent, 9" **$6.00**
Turquoise Blue, plate, 7¼" **$12.00**
Vienna Lace, cup & saucer, white w/platinum trim (no decal) .**$8.00**
Vienna Lace, plate, dinner; lacy decal on white, 10" **$7.00**
Wheat, bowl, dessert; 4⅝" **$3.50**
Wheat, cake pan, decal on white, 8" square **$10.00**
Wheat, mug, decal on white **$15.00**
Wheat, plate, dinner; decal on white, 10" **$5.00**
Wheat, tumbler, tea; decal on clear, 11-oz **$8.00**

Fishbowl Ornaments

Prior to World War II, every dime store had its bowl of small goldfish. Nearby were stacks of goldfish bowls — small, medium, and large. Accompanying them were displays of ceramic ornaments for these bowls, many in the shape of Oriental pagodas or European-style castles. The fish died, the owners lost interest, and the glass containers along with their charming ornaments were either thrown out or relegated to the attic. In addition to pagodas and castles, other ornaments included bridges, lighthouses, colonnades, mermaids, and fish. Note that figurals such as mermaids are difficult to find.

Many fishbowl ornaments were produced in Japan between 1921 and 1941, and again after 1947. The older Japanese items often show clean, crisp mold designs with visible detail of the item's features. Others were made in Germany and some by potteries in the United States. Aquarium pieces made in America are not common. Those produced in recent years are usually of Chinese origin and are more crude, less colorful, and less detailed in appearance. In general, the more detail and more colorful, the older the piece. A few more examples are shown in *Collector's Guide to Made in Japan Ceramics* by Carole Bess White (Collector Books).

Advisor: Carole Bess White (See Directory, Japan Ceramics)

Bathing beauty on turtle, red, tan & green on white, 2½",
      from $20 to **$30.00**
Boy riding dolphin on wave, multicolored matt glazes, 3¾",
      from $20 to **$30.00**
Castle towers w/3 arches, tan lustre towers w/red arches on
      green & white rocks, 5¼" **$22.00**
Castle w/arch, multicolored, 2½" or 3½", ea **$20.00**
Colonade w/palm tree, green, blue & white, 3¾x4" ..**$20.00**
Coral w/deep sea diver, orange glossy glaze w/black image
      of diver, 3½" **$20.00**
Diver holding dagger, white suit & helmet, blue gloves,
      brown boots & black airpack, 4¾" **$22.00**
Doorway, stone entry w/open aqua wood-look door, 2" ..**$15.00**
Fish riding waves, 2 white fish on cobalt waves, 3½x3" **$22.00**
Lighthouse, orange, yellow & brown, 2x2½" **$16.00**
Lighthouse, tan, black, brown & green, 6½x4" **$26.00**

Mermaid on sea horse, white, green & orange glossy glazes,
      3¼", from $20 to **$30.00**
Mermaid on snail, 4", from $35 to **$45.00**
Mermaid on 2 seashells, multicolored matt glazes, 3½", from
      $30 to **$40.00**
Nude on starfish, bisque, 4½", from $40 to **$50.00**
Oriental building w/foundation archway, resembles Noah's
      Ark w/foundation & double stairway forming archway,
      2½" **$18.00**
Pagoda, triple roof, blue, green & maroon, 5½x3¼" ..**$20.00**
Sign on tree trunk, No Fishing, brown, black & white, 2½x4" .**$12.00**
Torii gate, multicolored glossy glazes, 3¾" **$22.00**

Castle, multicolored, black mark, 3¾", from $15.00 to $20.00; Castle, multicolored, unmarked, 4½", from $15.00 to $20.00. (Photo courtesy Carole Bess White)

Fisher-Price

Probably no other toy manufacture is as well known among kids of today as Fisher-Price. Since the 1930s they've produced wonderful toys made of wood covered with vividly lithographed paper. Plastic parts weren't used until 1949, and this can sometimes help you date your finds. These toys were made for play, so very few older examples have survived in condition good enough to attract collectors. Watch for missing parts and avoid those that are dirty. Edge wear and some paint dulling is normal and to be expected. Our values are for toys with minimum signs of such wear.

For more information we recommend *Fisher-Price Toys,* by Brad Cassity; *Modern Toys, American Toys, 1930 – 1980,* by Linda Baker; *Fisher-Price, A Historical, Rarity Value Guide,* by John J. Murray and Bruce R. Fox (Books Americana); and *Schroeder's Collectible Toys, Antique to Modern,* published by Collector Books.

Advisor: Brad Cassity (See Directory, Toys)

Club: Fisher-Price Collector's Club
Jeanne Kennedy
1442 N Ogden, Mesa, AZ 85205; Monthly newsletter with information and ads; send SASE for more information

Museum: Toy Town Museum
636 Girard Ave., PO Box 238, East Aurora, NY 14052;
Monday through Saturday, 10 – 4.

Action Bunny Cart, #502, 1949	$200.00
Adventure People Sea Explorer, #310, 1975-80	$25.00
Adventure People Sea Shark, #334, 1981-84	$25.00
Adventure People Sky Surfer, #375, 1978	$25.00
Band Wagon, #198, 1940-41	$350.00
Bob-Along Bear, #642, 1979-84	$10.00
Bulldozer, #311, 1976-77	$25.00
Bunny Racer, #474, 1942	$225.00
Busy Bunny Cart, #466, 1941-44	$75.00
Chick Cart, #407, 1950-53	$50.00
Chuggy Pop-Up, #616, 1955-56	$100.00
Cookie Pig, #476, 1966-70	$50.00
Donald Duck & Nephews, #479, 1941-42	$400.00
Donald Duck Drummer, #454, 1949-50	$300.00
Doughboy Donald, #744, 1942	$600.00
Ducky Cart, #51, 1950	$75.00
Ducky Daddles, #148, 1942	$225.00
Ducky Flip Flap, #715, 1964-65	$65.00
Dump Truckers Playset, #979, 1965-67	$75.00
Egg Truck, #749, 1947	$225.00
Fire Truck, #630, 1959-62	$50.00
Fuzzy Fido, #444, 1941-42	$225.00

Golden Gulch Express, #191, 1961, $100.00. (Photo courtesy Linda Baker)

Happy Hauler, #732, 1968-70	$35.00
Happy Hippo, #151, 1962-63	$85.00
Husky Construction Crew, #317, 1978-80	$30.00
Husky Farm Set, #331, 1981-83	$25.00
Husky Race Car Rig, #320, 1979-82	$30.00
Husky Roller Grader, #313, 1978-80	$20.00
Jingle Giraffe, #472, 1956	$225.00
Jolly Jalopy, #724, 1965	$15.00
Kitty Bell, #499, 1950-51	$125.00
Kriss Kricket, #678, 1955-57	$100.00
Lift & Load Railroad, #943, 1978-79	$50.00
Lift & Load Road Builders, #789, 1978-82	$20.00
Little Lamb, #684, 1964-65	$50.00
Little People Garage Squad, #679, 1984-90	$15.00

Molly Moo Cow, #132, 1972-78	$25.00
Mother Goose, #164, 1964-66	$35.00
Music Box Iron, #125, 1966, aqua w/yellow handle	$45.00
Picnic Basket, #677, 1975-79	$30.00
Play Family Camper, #994, 1973-76	$75.00
Play Family Nursery School, #929, 1978-79	$50.00
Play Family Station Fire Station, #928, 1980-82	$65.00
Play Family Western Town, #934, 1982-84	$65.00
Pony Chime, #758, 1948-50	$200.00
Pop-Up-Pal Chime Phone, #150, 1968-78	$40.00
Puffy Engine, #444, 1951-54	$85.00
Puppy Playhouse, #110, 1978-80	$10.00
Push Pullet, #194, 1971-72	$25.00
Queen Buzzy Bee, #314, 1956-58	$40.00
Rabbit Cart, #52, 1950	$75.00
Rock-A-Bye Bunny Cart, #788, 1940-41	$300.00
Roly Poly Chime Ball, #165, 1967-85	$5.00
Sports Car, #674, 1958-60	$85.00
Squeaky the Clown, #777, 1958-59	$250.00
Sunny Fish, #420, 1955	$225.00
Tailspin Tabby Pop-Up, #600, 1947	$250.00
Teddy Station Wagon, #480, 1942	$225.00
Teddy Tucker, #711, 1949-51	$225.00
Three Men in a Tub, #142, 1970-73, w/bell	$20.00
Three Men in a Tub, #142, 1974-75, w/flag	$10.00
Tiny Teddy, #634, 1955-57	$75.00
Tug-A-Bug, #628, 1975-77	$5.00
Walking Duck Cart, #305, 1957-64	$40.00
Woofy Wager, #447, 1947-48	$85.00
Ziggy Zilo, #737, 1958-59	$75.00

Fishing Lures

There have been literally thousands of lures made since the turn of the century. Some have bordered on the ridiculous, and some have turned out to be just as good as the manufacturers claimed. In lieu of buying outright from a dealer, try some of the older stores in your area — you just might turn up a good old lure. Go through any old tackle boxes that might be around, and when the water level is low, check out the river banks.

If you have to limit your collection, you might want to concentrate just on wooden lures, or you might decide to try to locate one of every lure made by a particular company. Whatever you decide, try to find examples with good original paint and hardware. Though many lures are still very reasonable, we have included some of the more expensive examples as well to give you an indication of the type you'll want to fully research if you think you've found a similar model. For such information, we recommend *Fishing Lure Collectibles, Second Edition,* by Dudley Murphy and Rick Edmisten; *The Fishing Lure Collector's Bible* by R.L. Streater with Rick Edmisten and Dudley Murphy; *19th Century Fishing Lures* by Arlan Carter; and *Collector's Guide to Creek Chub Lures & Collectibles* by Harold E Smith, M.D. All are published by Collector Books.

Advisor: Dave Hoover (See Directory, Fishing Lures)

Club: NFLCC Tackle Collectors
HC 3, Box 4012
Reeds Spring, MO 65737
Send SASE for more information about membership and their publications: *The National Fishing Lure Collector's Club Magazine* and *The NFLCC Gazette*.

Abbey & Imprie, Glowbody Minnow, luminous glass tube attached to spinning keels, EX in G- box.............**$80.00**

Arbogast, Sunfish Tin Liz, glass eyes, 1⅝", VG+.......**$190.00**

Chapman & Son, Pickerel, lg spinner w/3½" blade, hair & feather treble, VG **$75.00**

Creek Chub, Baby Chub Wiggler #200, natural chub scale finish, glass eyes, NM **$85.00**

Creek Chub, Baby Crawdad #400, natural crab finish, discontinued in 1964, 2¼", from $20 to **$30.00**

Creek Chub, Beetle, shiny black, NM........................**$165.00**

Creek Chub, Beetle, white & red finish, VG **$85.00**

Creek Chub, Bull Pup #F904, yellow scale finish, discontinued ca 1954, 1", from $40 to **$60.00**

Creek Chub, Fly Rod Pikie, pikie scale finish, double hook, 1¼", NM **$220.00**

Creek Chub, Husky Pike #2300, tiger-stripe finish on wood, discontinued ca 1978, 6", from $75 to **$80.00**

Creek Chub, Jointed Striper Pike #6839, tiger stripe finish, tack eyes, discontinued ca 1978, 6¼", from $60 to..........**$70.00**

Creek Chub, Pikie #700-P, plastic, brown trout finish, discontinued ca 1978, 4½", from $20 to **$30.00**

Creek Chub, Plunker #3224, Redwing Blackbird, black, red & yellow paint, discontinued ca 1978, 3", from $80 to.......**$90.00**

Creek Chub, Polly Wiggle, pollywog finish, black bead eyes, VG...**$140.00**

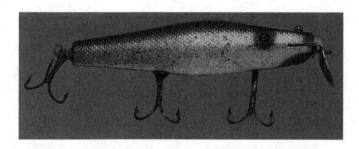

Creek Chub, Surfster #7300, three trebles, 1953, 6", from $20.00 to $30.00. (Photo courtesy Dudley Murphy and Rick Edmisten)

Creek Chub, Ultralight Jointed Pikie #9400-UL-P, pikie scale finish on wood, discontinued ca 1978, 1⅝", from $20 to **$25.00**

Creek Chub, Ultralight Nikie #9719-UL-P, frog finish, discontinued ca 1978, 1⅝", from $15 to **$25.00**

Creek Chub, Wiggler #100, Chub scale finish, VG **$40.00**

Heddon, Crab Wiggler #1800, green crackle back, glass eyes, L-rig hardware, EX..**$135.00**

Heddon, Crab Wiggler #1800, white w/red blended tail & eyes, U-shaped collar, L-rig hardware, VG **$95.00**

Heddon, Dowagiac Minno #00, red w/black, glass eyes, 4", VG..**$265.00**

Heddon, Dowagiac Minnow, frog finish, glass eyes, L-rig hardware, marked props, 5-hook, EX-................**$295.00**

Heddon, Fly Rod Flapfish, yellow finish, 1⅛", EX......**$15.00**

Heddon, Giant River Hunt #7510, pikie scale finish, glass eyes, Hared trailing treble, 3¼", VG **$330.00**

Heddon, Luny Frog #3500, VG.....................................**$85.00**

Heddon, Minnow #100, rainbow finish, brass cups & hardware, glass eyes, unmarked props, long gill marks, G...**$55.00**

Heddon, Salmon River Runt #8850, shiner scale w/lg red painted gills, teddy bear eyes, string rigged hooks, VG **$85.00**

Heddon, Sea Runt #610, red & white finish, painted eyes, surface hardware, 2⅝", EX.................................**$30.00**

Heddon, Sea Runt #610, red & yellow finish, glass eyes, surface hardware, 2⅝", VG **$110.00**

Heddon, Shrimpy-Spook, black & green w/red spots, toilet seat hardware, short production time, EX.........**$175.00**

Heddon, SOS Minnow #160, yellow perch finish, glass eyes, 2-pc hardware, 3½", EX **$100.00**

Heddon, Surface Bait #200, white, red & green spot finish, cup rigged hardware, 3-pin collar, 4¾", G **$165.00**

Heddon, Surface Minnow #300, green crackle back finish, glass eyes, marked props, cup hardware, 3⅝", VG **$165.00**

Heddon, Surface Minnow #300, green scale finish, belly & tail hooks, fat body, L-rig hardware, VG **$110.00**

Heddon, Torpedo, rainbow finish, glass eyes, L-rig hardware, 3½", VG **$40.00**

Jennings, Torpedo, silverplated hollow metal, wire shaft, blue glass bead at tail, feathered treble, 2⅞", VG **$350.00**

K&K, Animated Minnow, green & gold w/crosshatching on sides, lg glass eyes, tin tail, 3 double hooks, 4½", G **$135.00**

Keeling, Crab, black & yellow, EX..............................**$55.00**

Keeling, Surface Tom Wiggler, glass eyes, red head, white bait, 3¼", EX **$60.00**

Lure, Creek Chub, Pike, #2602, jointed, M (2PCCB)...**$55.00**

Moonlight Pickaroon, glass eyes, black back, red side, cream belly, 2 trebles, 4", VG **$95.00**

Pflueger, Globe, red & white finish, spring head, surface hardware, 2¾", EX in NM box..............................**$95.00**

Pflueger, Invincible Minnow, molded & painted hard rubber, black/green/red finish, 3 trebles, EX....................**$55.00**

Pflueger, Live Wire, silver side scale finish, red faceted glass eyes, 2 props, 3½", VG in G- box.......................**$130.00**

Pflueger, Neverfail Minnow, rainbow finish w/hand-painted gill marks, glass eyes, 3 hooks, VG+ **$110.00**

Pflueger, Razum Minow, rubber w/attached round keel at front, perch finish, 2", VG......................................**$30.00**

Pflueger, Soft Rubber Frog, loop-end weed guards over hooks, EX **$40.00**

Shakespeare, Egyptian Wobbler, black back, fancy tan scale finish w/black & yellow spots, EX in VG box ...**$250.00**

Shakespeare, Kazoo Trolling Minnow, reed body built on treble hook w/single hook at tail, 6½", EX **$85.00**

Shakespeare, Kingfish Wobbler, red & white finish, metal plate on back, EX in original box w/identifying card $85.00

Shakespeare, No-Grip Minnow, red & white finish, pressed eyes, marked rear prop, 4", VG..........$110.00

Shakespeare, Pad-Ler, red & white finish, Musky size, 3¾", VG..........$80.00

Shakespeare, Underwater Minnow #44, greenish blue back w/white belly (possible repainting), glass eyes (1 replaced), VG..........$110.00

Shakespeare, Wooden Minnow #42, fancy green scale finish, green crackle back, glass eyes, 3 trebles, 3¾", VG+ $110.00

South Bend, Panatella Minnow, green crackle back, hand-painted gill marks, 3 trebles, marked props, 4¼", VG $60.00

South Bend, Peach-Oreno, nickel finish, deep front hook cup, EX..........$55.00

South Bend, Vacuum, white w/red stripes, Howe's swivel hook hanger hardware, no eyes, 2⅜", VG $85.00

Winchester, Fluted Teardrop Spinner #9646, feathered treble, blue glass bead on shaft, red underside, EX......$110.00

Winchester, Spinner #9783, feathered treble, EX $100.00

Woods, Expert Minnow, traces of silver finish, yellow glass eyes, 3 hooks, 3", G-..........$195.00

Fitz & Floyd

If you've ever visited a Fitz & Floyd outlet store, you know why collectors find this company's products so exciting. Steven Spielberg has nothing on their designers when it comes to imagination. Much of their production is related to holidays, and they've especially outdone themselves with their Christmas lines. But there are wonderful themes taken from nature featuring foxes, deer, birds, or rabbits, and others that are outrageously and deliberately humorous. Not only is the concept outstanding, so is quality.

See also Cookie Jars.

Candle holders, iris flower forms, $28.00 pair.

Bath set, dinosaurs, vase & toothbrush holder, 1986, NM..$50.00

Bookends, raccoons, browns & grays, 1980, 5¼x6", pr $75.00

Bowl, serving; Coquille, white w/red shells, 1976, 9¼"......$65.00

Box, Queen of Hearts, stores playing cards, 1992, 2½x5x 6½".........$110.00

Candle holder, swan w/bent neck, tulips holds the candle, 6x5".........$25.00

Chip 'n dip, kangaroo mommy & baby, 10½x6" $85.00

Clock, White Rabbit w/pocket watch, Alice in Wonderland series, battery operated, 1992, 4½x4½" $100.00

Condiment dish, rooster, w/lid & spoon, 5"................$35.00

Creamer & sugar bowl, Queen Isabulla de Mastiff (sugar bowl), Royal Consort Purrdinand de Creme (creamer), 1990.........$40.00

Figurine, Gardening Gourmet Hen, stands atop mound of fresh vegetables, 13½", MIB $115.00

Figurine, mama bunny w/2 young ones on her back, 6x9".........$100.00

Figurine, Victorian dress bunny family w/balloons, 1995, 10".........$95.00

Mug, Cherub & Roses, pedestal foot, 5½", MIB..........$28.00

Pitcher, Gardener's Delight, vegetable motiff, MIB.....$35.00

Pitcher, Oceana Collection, shell shape w/seaweed handle, 10x11".........$80.00

Plate, Flamingo Road, 1978, 7½"..................$75.00

Platter, Rope & Holly, burgundy & gold, 2 handles, 1994, lg.........$85.00

Platter, Victorian Lace, white w/blue ribbons, violets & pink roses on handles, oval, 1994, 16x10"....................$70.00

Teapot, black w/multicolored Macaw parrot, tail feathers for handle, wing on lid, 7".........................$200.00

Teapot, fairy w/lavender flowers & green leaves, spout & handle wrapped w/vines, 1991, 42-oz, 7½" $155.00

Teapot, Paw de Deux, 1990, 32-oz, 9".......................$100.00

Teapot, rabbit w/tulips & daffodils, 22-oz, 8" $57.00

Tureen, Coq du Village Rooster, multicolored, 9½", MIB..$120.00

Florence Ceramics

During the '40s, Florence Ward began modeling tiny ceramic children as a hobby at her home in Pasadena, California. She was so happy with the results that she expanded, hired decorators, and moved into a larger building where for two decades she produced the lovely line of figurines, wall plaques, busts, etc., that have become so popular today. The 'Florence Collection' featured authentically detailed models of such couples as Louis XV and Madame Pompadour, Pinkie and Blue Boy, and Rhett and Scarlett. Nearly all of the Florence figures have names which are written on their bases.

Many figures are decorated with 22k gold and lace. Real lace was cut to fit, dipped in a liquid material called slip, and fired. During the firing it burned away, leaving only hardened ceramic lace trim. The amount of lace work that was used is one of the factors that needs to be considered when evaluating a 'Florence.' Size is another. Though most of the figures you'll find today are singles, a few were made as groups, and once in awhile you'll find a lady seated on a divan. The more complex, the more expensive.

There are Florence figurines that are very rare and unusual, i.e., Mark Anthony, Cleopatra, Story Hour, Grandmother and I, Carmen, Dear Ruth, Spring and Fall Reverie, Clocks, and many others. These may be found with a high price; however, there are bargains still to be had.

Our wide range of values reflects the amounts of detailing and lace work present. If you'd like to learn more about the subject, we recommend *The Collector's Encyclopedia of California Pottery, Second Edition,* by Jack Chipman; and *The Florence Collectibles, An Era of Elegance,* by Doug Foland.

Advisors: Doug Foland and Jerry Kline (See Directory, Florence Ceramics)

Club: Florence Ceramics of California Collectors Club
Jerry Kline
PO Box 937
Kodak, TN 37764
865-933-9060 or fax: 865-933-4492

Abigail, 8" **$185.00**
Adeline, blue or pink **$325.00**
Angel, 7¾" **$140.00**
Ann, yellow, 6" **$150.00**
Bea, 7¼" **$150.00**
Belle, 8" **$125.00**
Blossom girl, flower holder **$125.00**
Blueboy, 12" **$350.00**
Camille, lamp, from $300 to **$400.00**
Carol, lavender & white dress, 9" **$750.00**
Charles, 8¾" **$325.00**
Claudia, blue dress w/white trim & matching blue hat, 8½" **$250.00**
Claudia, 8¼" **$200.00**
David, 7½", from $125 to **$150.00**

Delia, 7¼", from $150.00 to $175.00.

Delia, lamp, from $200 to **$325.00**
Douglas, 8¼" **$175.00**

Ellen, 7" **$225.00**
Emily, flower holder, 8" **$60.00**
Fern, flower holder, from $150 to **$175.00**
Irene, 6" **$70.00**
Josephine, 9" **$350.00**
Karla, ballerina, 9¾" **$450.00**
Kay, flower holder, 7" **$60.00**
Lantern Boy, flower holder, 8¼" **$125.00**

Lavon, rare, 8½", $400.00.

Lillian, 7¼" **$150.00**
Louise, 7¼", from $80 to **$140.00**
Marie Antionette, 10½" **$375.00**
Matilda, 8½" **$175.00**
Patsy, flower holder, 6", from $50 to **$60.00**
Pinkie, 12" **$350.00**
Pompadour (bust).....................................**$350.00**
Rose Marie, pink lace dress, ringlets & gold bow in hair, 7" **$400.00**
Sally, flower holder, 4¾" **$40.00**
Sarah, 7½" **$130.00**
Shen, flower holder, bust, from $125 to ..**$145.00**
Shirley, hands away, 8" **$275.00**
Sue Ellen, 8¼" **$175.00**
Vivian, 10" **$395.00**
Wynkin & Blynkin, 5½", pr **$400.00**
Yulan, flower holder, bust, from $125 to .**$145.00**

Flower Frogs

Flower frogs reached their peak of popularity in the United States in the 1920s and 1930s. During that time nearly every pottery and glasshouse in the Unted States produced some type of flower frog. At the same time numbers of ceramic flower frogs were being imported from Germany and Japan. Dining tables and sideboards were adorned with flowers sparingly placed around dancing ladies, birds, and aquatic animals in shallow bowls.

In the 1930s garden clubs began holding competitions in cut flower arranging. The pottery and glass flower frogs proved inadequate for the task and a new wave of metal flower frogs entered the market. Some were simple mesh, hairpin, and needle holders; but many were fanciful creations of loops, spirals, and crimped wires.

German and Japanese imports ceased during World War II, and only a very few American pottery and glass companies continued to produce flower frogs into the 1940s and 1950s. Metal flower frog production followed a similar decline; particularly after the water soluble florist foam, Oasis, was invented in 1954.

Advisor: Bonnie Bull (See Directory, Flower Frogs)

Bird (swallow) on stump-like base, blue & pearl lustre, ceramic 6 holes, Made in Japan, 4½x4"...............**$28.00**

Bird on grassy base, orange w/yellow & black on wings, ceramic, 4x3"...**$22.50**

Bird on perch beside stump, pastel colors, ceramic, Made in Czechoslovakia, #31, 5½x3¼", NM.......................**$60.00**

Bird on stump, dark blue & brown, ceramic, Made in Japan, 9x4"..**$40.00**

Bird on stump, multicolor, ceramic, 3 holes, Made in Czechoslovakia, #18, sm...................................**$30.00**

Bird on stump, shades of green with red crest, Made in Japan, 7¼", $30.00.
(Photo courtesy Nada Sue Knauss)

Bird on stump, shiny multicolors, ceramic, 3 holes, Made in Japan, 4½"..**$36.00**

Bird sitting on oak tree stump w/acorn, yellow & brown, ceramic, 3 holes, Czechoslovakia, 5¼x3"..............**$36.00**

Butterfly on flower, multicolor, majolica-like pottery, 2x2½"...**$30.00**

Cherub w/cornucopia & basket, multicolor, ceramic, Made in Japan, 6⅝"..**$20.00**

Chrysanthemum w/pointed petals, lead, incised w/US Pat No 1916583 in circle, 1930s, 6" dia, EX......................**$53.00**

Deer, marked Loveland Colo, w/matching bowl, marked Loveland Pottery 137 & w/sticker: Loveland Art Pottery...Colo, NM...**$57.00**

Fish lying flat, shiny blue, pottery, 5 holes in back, 1½x3¾"...**$22.50**

Fish w/head & tail up (resting on its back), maroon & white, ceramic, Jamieson's Capistrano Calif, 6x5"...........**$18.00**

Frog, shiny white w/painted details, ceramic, 3x4"....**$45.00**

Frog on lily pad, ceramic, Dept 56 B St John, 3x6½".......**$30.00**

Giraffe neck & head, ceramic, Rosclane 603, 10", NM.**$49.00**

Green Jade-ite, 1½x3" dia...**$40.00**

Hedgehog, blue & white, ceramic, marked Delfts, 2¼".**$48.00**

Leaf w/holes on cage-type base, painted cast metal, Daisy Flower Holder...Calif Pat 6-29-16, 1½x5½x4½", EX...................**$46.00**

Loop holder, cast iron, marked JPO Patd, 1930s, 4½", VG.**$43.00**

Mermaid, seminude, white gloss, ceramic, Czechoslovakia, 1930s, 6⅞"..**$130.00**

Nude lady on rock, shiny white, ceramic, Japan, 7x5x4".**$28.00**

Nude lady w/flowers held to hip, flowers at base, white porcelain, #3770, 9"..**$180.00**

Nude lady w/hand to hair, white porcelain, Germany, #5911, 6¼"...**$110.00**

Nude seated, waves on base w/sea creature, white porcelain, Germany #4088, 4"..**$80.00**

Nude sitting on rock putting up her hair, ceramic, Haeger, 7x4¾"...**$50.00**

Nude woman (Deco style) w/panther, pottery, Germany, 6¾", NM..**$185.00**

Owl, brown w/white, ceramic, Made in Japan, 3¾"..**$18.00**

Parakeet, orange/yellow/brown, on circular brown base, pottery, 3 openings, unmarked Czechoslovakia, 4¼".**$40.00**

Parrot, blue & gold lustre, ceramic, Hand Painted Made in Japan mark, 5¼"...**$80.00**

Parrot, blue w/multicolor feathers, ceramic, Made in Japan, 6¾"..**$40.00**

Parrot, multicolor lustre, ceramic, 6 holes, Made in Japan, 2¾x1¾"...**$20.00**

Parrot, red-orange w/green & yellow, ceramic, 5 holes, unmarked, 4½"...**$27.50**

Parrot on bamboo-like shoots, multicolor lustre, ceramic, Japan, 3¼"...**$20.00**

Parrot on stump, multicolor & yellow, ceramic, 2 holes in stump, Made in Czechoslovakia, #11, 5¾"...........**$25.00**

Parrot perched on bamboo-like shoots, bright colors, ceramic, 7 holes, unmarked, 4x3½"................................**$32.00**

Rooster, multicolor, ceramic, 14 holes, unmarked, 10½".**$30.00**

Rose holder, double; lead, 1¾x4½x3", EX.................**$72.00**

Sailboat, green, pottery, Calienta, Made in California #72, 5"...**$30.00**

Scarf dancer, seminude, white gloss, ceramic, Germany, 7"..**$88.00**

Sea gull (in flight), crystal glass, 10 holes, Cambridge, 10"..**$40.00**

Sea horse, white matt, pottery, Red Wing #1048, 8¼x4½"...**$185.00**

Snowflake, cast iron, 12 sm holes, Japan, EX.............**$35.00**

Turtle, cast iron, insert removes, 3x6"........................**$60.00**

Umbrella, mauve/pale green, porcelain, 6 holes, #78, 8½"...**$20.00**

Water lilies, unmarked majolica, 1x5", pr.................**$36.00**

Wire spring coils (16) w/suction cup, Made in England, 6½" across, VG..**$51.50**

Woodpecker at side of stump, multicolor, ceramic, Czechoslovakia, 4¾", NM....................................$45.00
3-tiered, stackable holder, green pottery, Pat 2,496,758, 1950s, 2½" dia, 4½" dia, 6" dia............................$75.00

Fostoria

This was one of the major glassware producers of the twentieth century. They were located first in Fostoria, Ohio, but by the 1890s had moved to Moundsville, West Virginia. By the late '30s, they were recognized as the largest producers of handmade glass in the world. Their glassware is plentiful today and, considering its quality, not terribly expensive.

Though the company went out of business in the mid-'80s, the Lancaster Colony Company continues to use some of the old molds — herein is the problem. The ever-popular American and Coin glass patterns are currently in production, and even experts have trouble distinguishing the old from the new. Before you invest in either line, talk to dealers. Ask them to show you some of their old pieces. Most will be happy to help out a novice collector. Read *Elegant Glassware of the Depression Era* by Gene Florence; *Fostoria Glassware, 1887 – 1982,* by Frances Bones; *Fostoria, An Identification and Value Guide, Books I* and *II,* by Ann Kerr; and *Fostoria Stemware, Tableware, and Useful & Ornamental, The Crystal for America Series,* by Milbra Long and Emily Seate.

You'll be seeing a lot of inferior 'American' at flea markets and (sadly) antique malls. It's often priced as though it is American, but in fact it is not. It's been produced since the 1950s by Indiana Glass who calls it 'Whitehall.' Watch for pitchers with only two mold lines, they're everywhere. (Fostoria's had three.) Remember that Fostoria was handmade, so their pieces were fire polished. This means that if the piece you're examining has sharp, noticeable mold lines, be leery. There are other differences to watch for as well. Fostoria's footed pieces were designed with a 'toe,' while Whitehall feet have a squared peg-like appearance. The rays are sharper and narrower on the genuine Fostoria pieces, and the glass itself has more sparkle and life. And if it weren't complicated enough, the Home Interior Company sells 'American'-like vases, covered bowls, and a footed candy dish that were produced in a foreign country, but at least they've marked theirs.

Coin glass was originally produced in crystal, red, blue, emerald green, olive green, and amber. It's being reproduced today in crystal, green (darker than the original), blue (a lighter hue), and red. Though the green and blue are 'off' enough to be pretty obvious, the red is very close. Beware. Here are some (probably not all) of the items currently in production: bowl, 8" diameter; bowl, 9" oval; candlesticks, 4½"; candy jar with lid, 6¼"; creamer and sugar bowl; footed comport; wedding bowl, 8¼". Know your dealer!

Numbers included in our descriptions were company-assigned stock numbers that collectors use as a means to distinguish variations in stems and shapes.

Advisor: Debbie Maggard (See Directory, Elegant Glassware)

Newsletter/Club: *Facets of Fostoria*
Fostoria Glass Society of America
P.O. Box 826, Moundsville, WV 26041
Membership: $12.50 per year

American, crystal, ashtray, square, 2⅞"..........................$7.50
American, crystal, bonbon, 3-footed, 8".......................$17.50
American, crystal, bowl, centerpiece; 9½"..................$42.50
American, crystal, bowl, float; 11½"...........................$55.00
American, crystal, bowl, jelly; 4¼x4¼".......................$15.00
American, crystal, candlestick, 2-light, bell base, 6½"..$100.00
American, crystal, comport, jelly; 4½".........................$15.00
American, crystal, goblet, #2056, low foot, 9-oz, 4⅜"...$11.00
American, crystal, goblet, sherbet; #2056½, 4½-oz, 4½"..$10.00
American, crystal, hat, tall, 4"....................................$50.00
American, crystal, mug, Tom & Jerry; 5½-oz, 3¼"......$40.00
American, crystal, plate, salad; 8½"............................$12.00
American, crystal, salt, individual.................................$9.00
American, crystal, sugar shaker..................................$55.00
American, crystal, tray, relish; 4-part, 6½x9"..............$45.00
American, crystal, urn, square pedestal foot, 7½".......$35.00

American, crystal, vase, 9¾", $90.00.

Baroque, blue, bowl, relish; 3-part, 10"........................$30.00
Baroque, blue, saucer..$5.00
Baroque, crystal, bowl, square, 6"................................$8.00
Baroque, crystal, mayonnaise, w/liner, 5½"................$15.00
Baroque, yellow, candlestick, 2-light, 4½"..................$50.00
Baroque, yellow, tumbler, water; 9-oz, 4¼"................$25.00
Buttercup, crystal, candlestick, #2324, 4"....................$17.50
Buttercup, crystal, pitcher, #6011, 53-oz, 8⅞"...........$285.00
Buttercup, crystal, saucer, #2350..................................$5.00
Buttercup, crystal, vase, #6021, footed, 6"..................$95.00
Camellia, crystal, pitcher, 16-oz, 6⅛"..........................$85.00
Camellia, crystal, vase, #6021, footed, 6"....................$65.00
Century, crystal, bowl, snack; footed, 6¼"..................$14.00
Century, crystal, ice bucket...$65.00

Century, crystal, plate, luncheon; 8½" $12.50
Century, crystal, tray, muffin; handled, 9½" $30.00
Chintz, crystal, dinner bell $125.00
Chintz, crystal, pitcher, #5000, footed, 48-oz............$395.00
Chintz, crystal, plate, dinner; #2496, 9½" $55.00
Chintz, crystal, vase, #4108, 5"................................$95.00
Coin, amber, jelly, #1372/448.................................$17.50
Coin, amber or olive, ashtray, #1372/123, 5".............$17.50
Coin, amber or olive, ashtray, #1372/124, 10"............$30.00
Coin, blue, bowl, wedding; #1372/162, w/lid.............$90.00
Coin, blue, lamp, coach; #1372/320, oil, 13½".........$225.00
Coin, blue, vase, bud; #1372/799, 8"..........................$40.00
Coin, blue or ruby, candy jar, #1372/347, w/lid, 6⅜".$50.00
Coin, blue or ruby, creamer, #1372/680 ....$16.00
Coin, crystal, bowl, #1372/199, footed, 8½"...............$50.00
Coin, crystal, nappy, #1372/495, 4½"........................$22.00
Coin, crystal, tumbler, juice/old fashioned; #1372/81, 9-oz, 3⅝"..$30.00
Coin, crystal, vase, #1372/818, footed, 10" $45.00
Coin, crystal or olive, cigarette urn, #1372/381, footed, 3⅜"...$20.00
Coin, green, bowl, #1372/179, 8" $70.00
Coin, green, cruet, #1372/531, w/stopper, 7-oz $200.00

Coin, green, wedding bowl, with lid, 8¼", $135.00.

Coin, olive, stem, sherbet; #1372/7, 9-oz, 5¼" $45.00
Coin, ruby, candle holder, #1372/326, 8", pr.............$125.00
Coin, ruby, plate, #1372/550, 8" $40.00
Colony, crystal, bowl, finger; 4¾" $45.00
Colony, crystal, bowl, salad; 9¾" $37.50
Colony, crystal, lamp, electric..................................$165.00
Colony, crystal, plate, torte; 18"................................$95.00
Corsage, crystal, plate, #2337, 6½" $8.00
Corsage, crystal, plate, 8½" $12.50
Corsage, crystal, tumbler, water; #6014, footed, 9-oz, 5½"..$22.00
Fairfax, amber, bowl, soup; 7"...................................$17.00
Fairfax, amber, plate, chop; 13"..................................$14.00
Fairfax, green or topaz, creamer, footed.....................$10.00
Fairfax, green or topaz, tumbler, footed, 9-oz, 5¼"...$13.00
Fairfax, rose, blue or orchid, bonbon $12.50

Fairfax, rose, blue or orchid, pitcher, #5000.............$210.00
Heather, crystal, comport, 4⅜" $30.00
Heather, crystal, stem, cocktail; #6037, 4-oz, 5" $20.00
Heather, crystal, tray, utility; handled, 9⅛".................$45.00
Hermitage, amber, green or topaz, comport, #2449, 6"..$17.50
Hermitage, azure, pitcher, #2449, 1-pt......................$60.00
Hermitage, crystal, bowl, salad; #2449½, 6½" $6.00
Hermitage, crystal, vase, footed, 6" $22.00
Hermitage, wisteria, tray, relish; #2449, 3-part, 7¼" ...$50.00
Holly, crystal, bowl, baked apple; #2364...................$15.00
Holly, crystal, plate, cracker; #2364.........................$25.00
Holly, crystal, plate, dessert; #2337, 6".......................$5.00
Horizon, cinnamon, crystal or spruce, bowl, cereal; 5"..$12.00
Horizon, cinnamon, crystal or spruce, plate, sandwich; 11"...$15.00
Jamestown, amber or brown, butter dish, #2719/300, w/lid, ¼-lb...$24.00
Jamestown, amethyst, crystal or green, plate, torte; #2719/620, 2-part, 9⅛"..$42.50
Jamestown, blue, pink or ruby, tumbler, #2719/73, 9-oz, 4¼"..$25.00
June, crystal, bowl, baker; oval, 10"..........................$40.00
June, crystal, parfait, 5¼"...$35.00
June, pink or blue, candlestick, 3" $35.00
June, pink or blue, plate, grill; 10"..........................$110.00
June, yellow, goblet, cocktail; 3-oz, 5¼" $32.50
June, yellow, sweetmeat $20.00
Kashmir, blue, cup..$20.00
Kashmir, blue, stem, juice; footed, 5-oz....................$25.00
Kashmir, yellow or green, bowl, cereal; 6".................$30.00
Kashmir, yellow or green, plate, dinner; 10" $45.00
Kashmir, yellow or green, vase, 8"............................$90.00
Lido, crystal, candlestick, 4".....................................$20.00
Lido, crystal, stem, wine; #6017, 3-oz, 5½" $27.50
Mayflower, crystal, cup, #2560, footed......................$17.00
Mayflower, crystal, tumbler, juice; #6020, footed, 5-oz, 4⅞"...$17.50
Meadow Rose, crystal, bowl, handled, square, 4".......$11.00
Meadow Rose, crystal, plate, dinner; 9½"...................$45.00
Navarre, crystal, comport, #2496, 4¾" $35.00
Navarre, crystal, dinner bell......................................$60.00
Navarre, crystal, plate, luncheon; #2440, 8½" $22.00
Navarre, crystal, vase, #4108, 5" $100.00
New Garland, amber or topaz, bowl, fruit; 5"............$10.00
New Garland, amber or topaz, candlestick, 9½".........$30.00
New Garland, amber or topaz, lemon dish, 2-handled ..$15.00
New Garland, rose, platter, 12"..................................$45.00
New Garland, rose, salt & pepper shakers, footed, pr ..$100.00
New Garland, rose, tumbler, #4120, 5-oz $15.00
Romance, crystal, bowl, lily pond; #2364, 12"............$45.00
Romance, crystal, saucer, #2350.................................$5.00
Royal, amber or green, bowl, finger; #869, 4½" $20.00
Royal, amber or green, egg cup, #2350 ....$27.50
Royal, amber or green, vase, urn; #2324, footed $85.00
Seascape, opalescent, bowl, shallow, 8" $50.00
Seascape, opalescent, plate, buffet; 14" $65.00
Seville, amber, bowl, soup; #2350, 7¾" $20.00

Seville, amber, plate, dinner; #2350, sm, 9½"............**$12.00**
Seville, amber, stem, parfait; #870 ....**$30.00**
Seville, green, bowl, bouillon; #2350½, footed..........**$16.00**
Seville, green, creamer, #2350½, footed **$13.50**
Sun Ray, crystal, bonbon, 3-toed................................**$17.50**
Sun Ray, crystal, mustard, w/spoon & lid **$30.00**
Sun Ray, crystal, plate, 9½"......................................**$28.00**
Sun Ray, crystal, tumbler, juice; 5-oz, 4⅝"...............**$15.00**
Trojan, rose, candlestick, #2394, 2" **$22.00**
Trojan, rose, grapefruit, #5282½.............................**$60.00**
Trojan, rose, mayonnaise, #2375, w/liner **$60.00**
Trojan, topaz, bowl, baker; #2375, 9" **$65.00**
Trojan, topaz, plate, sauce; #2375 ....**$40.00**
Trojan, topaz, vase, #2369, 9".................................**$225.00**
Versailles, blue, mayonnaise, #2375, w/liner..............**$50.00**
Versailles, blue, plate, canape; #2375, 6" **$40.00**
Versailles, pink, green or yellow, salt & pepper shakers,
    #2375, footed, pr...**$95.00**
Versailles, pink or green, bowl, baker; #2375, 9"........**$55.00**
Versailles, pink or green, candy jar, #2331, 3-part, w/lid...**$155.00**
Vesper, amber, bowl, fruit; #2350, 5½" **$12.50**
Vesper, amber, plate, dinner; 10½".............................**$45.00**
Vesper, blue, bowl, baker; #2350, oval, 10½" **$125.00**
Vesper, blue, stem, water goblet; #5093 ....**$45.00**
Vesper, green, ashtray, #2350, 4".................................**$25.00**
Vesper, green, ice bucket, #2378 ....**$60.00**
Vesper, green, tumbler, #5100, footed, 9-oz **$16.00**

Royal, green, cologne/powder jar combination, $225.00.
(Photo courtesy Gene Florence)

Figurals and Novelties

Bird, candle holder, crystal, 1½"..................................**$20.00**
Cat, light blue, 3¾"...**$35.00**
Chanticleer, black, 10¾"...**$600.00**
Deer, blue, sitting or standing, ea **$55.00**
Duck w/3 ducklings, amber, set.....................................**$75.00**
Duckling, crystal, walking (+).......................................**$15.00**
Frog, blue, lemon or olive green, 1⅞", ea...................**$40.00**
Horse, bookend, crystal, 7¾", ea **$45.00**

Madonna, Silver Mist, w/base, original issue, 11¾" (+) ..**$80.00**
Owl, blue, lemon or olive green, 2¾", ea....................**$35.00**
Polar bear, topaz, 4⅝"..**$125.00**
Sea horse, bookend, crystal, 8", ea **$125.00**
Squirrel, amber, running or sitting, ea **$45.00**
St Francis, Silver Mist, original issue, 13½" (+) **$325.00**

Franciscan Dinnerware

Franciscan is a trade name of Gladding McBean, used on their dinnerware lines from the mid-'30s until it closed its Los Angeles-based plant in 1984. They were the first to market 'starter sets' (four-place settings), a practice that today is commonplace.

Two of their earliest lines were El Patio (simply styled, made in bright solid colors) and Coronado (with swirled borders and pastel glazes). In the late '30s, they made the first of many hand-painted dinnerware lines. Some of the best known are Apple, Desert Rose, and Ivy. From 1941 to 1977, 'Masterpiece' (true porcelain) china was produced in more than 170 patterns.

Many marks were used, most included the Franciscan name. An 'F' in a square with 'Made in U.S.A.' below it dates from 1938, and a double-line script 'F' was used in more recent years.

For further information, we recommend *The Collector's Encyclopedia of California Pottery, Second Edition,* by Jack Chipman.

Note: To evaluate maroon items in El Patio and Coronado, add 10% to 20% to suggested prices.

Advisors: Mick and Lorna Chase, Fiesta Plus (See Directory, Dinnerware)

Apple, ashtray, individual **$22.00**
Apple, bowl, divided vegetable..................................**$50.00**
Apple, bowl, mixing; sm...**$192.50**
Apple, bowl, rimmed soup **$30.00**
Apple, bowl, vegetable; 8"..**$35.00**
Apple, box, egg shape..**$215.00**
Apple, butter dish...**$50.00**
Apple, casserole, 1½-qt...**$145.00**
Apple, coffeepot...**$145.00**
Apple, creamer, regular...**$24.00**
Apple, cup & saucer, demitasse **$60.00**
Apple, jam jar..**$137.50**
Apple, mug, barrel, 12-oz **$55.00**
Apple, mug, 7-oz **$35.00**
Apple, pitcher, milk **$95.00**
Apple, plate, grill **$125.00**
Apple, plate, 6½" **$6.50**
Apple, plate, 9½" **$22.00**
Apple, salt & pepper shakers, apples, pr **$20.00**
Apple, sherbet...**$27.50**
Apple, soup ladle **$105.00**
Apple, teapot...**$165.00**
Apple, tile, square..**$50.00**

Coronado, bowl, casserole, w/lid, from $85 to.........**$125.00**
Coronado, bowl, cereal; from $15 to.........................**$20.00**
Coronado, bowl, rim soup; from $28 to....................**$32.00**
Coronado, butter dish, from $35 to...........................**$45.00**
Coronado, pitcher, 1½-qt, from $35 to **$60.00**
Coronado, plate, 7½", from $9 to..............................**$12.00**
Coronado, plate, 9½", from $15 to............................**$18.00**
Coronado, platter, oval, 15½", from $45 to **$60.00**
Coronado, teapot, from $65 to **$95.00**
Desert Rose, ashtray, square....................................**$295.00**
Desert Rose, bell, dinner..**$125.00**
Desert Rose, bowl, divided vegetable.......................**$45.00**
Desert Rose, bowl, fruit...**$8.00**
Desert Rose, bowl, mixing; med **$185.00**
Desert Rose, bowl, rimmed soup..............................**$28.00**
Desert Rose, bowl, vegetable; 9"..............................**$40.00**
Desert Rose, candle holders, pr **$145.00**
Desert Rose, cigarette box **$125.00**
Desert Rose, coffeepot, individual **$395.00**
Desert Rose, compote, lg **$75.00**
Desert Rose, cup & saucer, coffee............................**$85.00**
Desert Rose, cup & saucer, jumbo **$65.00**
Desert Rose, egg cup..**$35.00**
Desert Rose, gravy boat **$32.00**
Desert Rose, mug, cocoa; 10-oz **$135.00**
Desert Rose, pitcher, milk **$75.00**
Desert Rose, plate, chop; 14".....................................**$125.00**
Desert Rose, plate, coupe steak **$195.00**
Desert Rose, plate, 9½"...**$20.00**

Desert Rose, salt and pepper shakers, tall, $75.00; syrup pitcher, $75.00.

Desert Rose, soup ladle...**$95.00**
Desert Rose, soup tureen, flat bottom **$495.00**
Desert Rose, tile, in frame..**$75.00**
Desert Rose, tumbler, juice; 6-oz................................**$55.00**
El Patio, bowl, casserole; w/lid, from $85 to **$125.00**
El Patio, bowl, cream soup; w/underplate, from $40 to..**$50.00**
El Patio, bowl, salad; lg, from $35 to.........................**$50.00**
El Patio, butter dish, from $35 to **$45.00**

El Patio, cup & saucer, demitasse; from $28 to..........**$45.00**
El Patio, plate, individual crescent salad; from $25 to ..**$35.00**
El Patio, plate, 6½", from $6 to **$10.00**
El Patio, plate, 9½", from $15 to **$18.00**
El Patio, salt & pepper shakers, pr, from $20 to........**$30.00**
El Patio, teacup & saucer, from $12 to **$15.00**
Forget-Me-Not, bowl, vegetable................................**$45.00**
Forget-Me-Not, cup & saucer, coffee........................**$85.00**
Forget-Me-Not, plate, 6½" **$6.00**
Forget-Me-Not, salt & pepper shakers, pr.................**$35.00**
Ivy, ashtray, individual **$28.00**
Ivy, bowl, fruit..**$10.00**
Ivy, butter dish..**$65.00**
Ivy, creamer, regular...**$30.00**
Ivy, mug, barrel, 12-oz..**$70.00**
Ivy, plate, 10½"..**$25.00**
Ivy, sugar bowl, regular **$45.00**
Ivy, tumbler, 10-oz..**$45.00**
Meadow Rose, ashtray, oval **$125.00**
Meadow Rose, bowl, rimmed soup............................**$32.00**
Meadow Rose, box, heart shape **$165.00**
Meadow Rose, candy dish, oval................................**$295.00**
Meadow Rose, chop plate, 12"...................................**$75.00**
Meadow Rose, cup & saucer, demitasse....................**$55.00**
Meadow Rose, mug, barrel, 12-oz.............................**$50.00**
Meadow Rose, plate, 9½"...**$20.00**
Meadow Rose, sherbet **$25.00**
Meadow Rose, tile, square **$45.00**
Poppy, ashtray, individual..**$30.00**
Poppy, bowl, cereal...**$22.50**
Poppy, cup & saucer, coffee....................................**$127.50**
Poppy, plate, 8" **$18.00**
Poppy, salt & pepper shakers, pr.............................**$125.00**
Poppy, sugar bowl...**$48.00**
Starburst, ashtray, oval, lg...**$50.00**
Starburst, bowl, soup/cereal **$13.00**
Starburst, butter dish...**$45.00**
Starburst, creamer **$15.00**
Starburst, crescent salad **$40.00**
Starburst, cup & saucer **$25.00**
Starburst, gravy boat, w/attached undertray & ladle...**$40.00**
Starburst, lemon nappy/jam-jelly **$35.00**
Starburst, mug, sm..**$60.00**
Starburst, oil cruet...**$75.00**
Starburst, pepper mill...**$150.00**
Starburst, plate, dinner **$12.00**
Starburst, plate, 8"...**$8.00**
Starburst, salt & pepper shakers, sm, pr...................**$20.00**
Starburst, sugar bowl...**$25.00**

Frankoma

John Frank opened a studio pottery in Norman, Oklahoma, in 1933. The bowls, vases, coffee mugs, shakers, etc., he created bore the ink-stamped marks 'Frank Pottery' or 'Frank Potteries.' At this time, only a few hundred pieces were produced. Within a year, Mr. Frank had incorporated. Though not everything was marked, he continued to use these marks for two years. Items thus marked are not easy to find and command high prices. In 1935 the pot and leopard mark was introduced.

The Frank family moved to Sapulpa, Oklahoma, in 1938. In November of that year, a fire destroyed everything. The pot and leopard mark was never re-created, and today collectors avidly search for items with this mark. The rarest of all Frankoma marks is 'First Kiln Sapulpa 6-7-38,' which was applied to only about one hundred pieces fired on that date.

Grace Lee Frank worked beside her husband, creating many limited edition Madonna plates, Christmas cards, advertising items, birds, etc. She died in 1996.

Clay is important in determining when a piece was made. Ada clay, used until 1953, is creamy beige in color. In 1953 they changed over to a red brick shale from Sapulpa. Today most clay has a pinkish-red cast, though the pinkish cast is sometimes so muted that a novice might mistake it for Ada clay.

Rutile glazes were created early in the pottery's history; these give the ware a two-tone color treatment. However the US government closed the rutile mines in 1970, and Frank found it necessary to buy this material from Australia. The newer rutile produced different results, especially noticeable with their Woodland Moss glaze.

Upon John Frank's death in 1973, their daughter Joniece became president. Though the pottery burned again in 1983, the buildings were quickly rebuilt. Due to so many setbacks, however, the company found it necessary to file Chapter 11 in order to remain in control and stay in business. Mr. Richard Bernstein purchased Frankoma in 1991; it continues to operate.

Frank purchased Synar Ceramics of Muskogee, Oklahoma, in 1958; in late '50, the name was changed to Gracetone Pottery in honor of Grace Lee Frank. Until supplies were exhausted, they continued to produce Synar's white clay line in glazes such as 'Alligator, Woodpine, White Satin, Ebony, Wintergreen' and a black and white straw combination. At the Frankoma pottery, an 'F' was added to the stock number on items made at both locations. New glazes were Aqua, Pink Champagne, and Black, known as Gunmetal. Gracetone was sold in 1962 to Mr. Taylor, who had been a long-time family friend and manager of the pottery. Taylor continued operations until 1967. The only dinnerware pattern produced there was 'Orbit,' which is today hard to find. Other Gracetone pieces are becoming scarce as well.

If you'd like to learn more, we recommend *Frankoma Pottery, Value Guide and More,* by Susan Cox; and *Frankoma and Other Oklahoma Potteries* by Phyllis and Tom Bess.

Advisor: Susan Cox (See Directory, Frankoma)

Club/Newsletter: Frankoma Family Collectors Association
c/o Nancy Littrell
P.O. Box 32571, Oklahoma City, OK 73123-0771
Membership dues: $25; includes newsletter and annual convention

Ashtray, Tulsarama, Desert Gold, red clay, 1957, 7¾"..**$50.00**
Bookends, Irish Setter, Ada clay, Ivory, #430, 6½" ...**$225.00**
Bowl, Desert Gold, red clay, #214, 1950-74, 12".........**$30.00**
Canteen, Thunderbird, Prairie Green, leather thong, 6½"..**$65.00**
Catalog, 1950...**$35.00**
Christmas card, 1952...**$90.00**
Christmas card, 1967...**$70.00**
Christmas card, 1972...**$35.00**

Cigarette box, Prairie Green, $85.00. (Photo courtesy Susan Cox)

Jug, Iowa Sunshine, Prairie Green, Ada clay, 1950s, 6½"...**$60.00**
Lazy Susan, #94FC, 1947-63, 15".................................**$75.00**
Match cover, w/out matches, G- **$11.00**
Mug, Donkey, Carter/Mondale, 1977 ....**$45.00**
Mug, Elephant, Nixon-Ford, 1974................................**$250.00**
Mug, Elephant, 1973...**$50.00**
Pipe rest, #454, black, ca 1935-40 ....**$175.00**
Pitcher, Aztec, #551, Ada clay, mini **$55.00**
Pitcher, eagle, Dusty Rose, Ada clay **$35.00**
Pitcher, Widow Maker, Prairie Green, #T12, 1960-61..**$110.00**
Planter, basket shape, Mountain Haze, #188, 1989-91,
    4½"...**$20.00**
Plate, Conestoga Wagon, Pale Blue, 1971, 2,000 made .**$200.00**
Plate, dinner; Aztec, Desert Gold, #7FL, 10"................**$15.00**
Plate, Helen Keller..**$60.00**
Plate, Jesus the Carpenter, Teenager of the Bible.......**$40.00**
Plate, Symbols of Freedom, Bicentennial, 1976 ....**$40.00**
Plate, 50th Anniversary...**$30.00**
Postcards, of Frankoma family, factory, color.............**$18.00**
Salt & pepper shakers, barrel shape, Prairie Green, Ada Clay,
    #97H, 1950-61, 2¼", pr..**$25.00**
Sculpture, cat reclining, black gloss, Ada clay, #116,
    4½x9½" **$100.00**
Sculpture, Circus Horse, White Sand, #138, 4½".......**$195.00**
Sculpture, Gardener Girl, blue, #701, 5¾"................**$110.00**
Sculpture, Puma, seated, White Sand..........................**$75.00**
Sculpture, Swan, Ada clay, #168, 3" **$45.00**
Table bell, brown satin, #817, 1982-92, 6"..................**$25.00**
Teapot, Plainsman, 6-cup, #5T.....................................**$30.00**
Teapot, Wagon Wheel, Prairie Green, 2-cup, #94C.....**$40.00**
Toby mug, Uncle Sam, blue, #600, 1976......................**$25.00**
Trivet, Cherokee Alphabet, Flame **$6.50**

Trivet, Prairie Green, Cattle Brands, red clay $10.00
Vase, boot w/star, Ada clay.................................$30.00
Vase, bud; Flame, brown interior, 6¼"...................$50.00
Vase, collector; V-12, black & Terra Cotta, 1980, 13"..$65.00
Vase, collector; V-5, Flame w/black base, 1973, 13"...$85.00
Vase, cylinder, Praire Green, Ada clay, #28, 6" $45.00
Vase, Flying Goose, #60B, Ada clay, 1942-60, 6" $45.00
Vase, leaf handles, early glaze, #71, 1942, 10" $125.00
Vase, pillow; Red Bud, #63, 7" $45.00
Wall mask, Maiden, Ada clay, Prairie Green, #132, 4½"....$75.00
Wall pocket, Phoebe, #730, 1948-49, 7½" $100.00
Wall pocket, Wagon Wheel, Red Bud, #94Y, 7" $75.00

Freeman-McFarlan

This California-based company was the result of a union between Gerald McFarlin and Maynard Anthony Freemen, formed in the early 1950s and resulting in the production of a successful line of molded ceramic sculptures (predominately birds and animals, though human figures were also made) as well decorative items such as vases, flowerpots, bowls, etc. Anthony was the chief designer, and some of the items you find today bear his name. Glazes ranged from woodtones and solid colors to gold leaf, sometimes in combination. The most collectible of the Freeman-McFarlin figures were designed by Kay Finch, who sold some of her molds to the company in the early 1960s. The company produced these popular sculptures in their own glazes without Kay's trademark curlicues, making them easy for today's collectors to distinguish from her original work. This line was so successful that in the mid-'60s the company hired Kay herself, and until the late '70s, she designed numerous new and original animal models. Most were larger and more realistically detailed than the work she did in her own studio. She worked for the company until 1980. Her pieces are signed.

In addition to the signatures already mentioned, you may find pieces incised 'Jack White' or 'Hetrick,' both freelance designers affiliated with the company. Other marks include paper labels and an impressed mark 'F.McF, Calif USA,' often with a date.

Bowl, dark green flower form, pedestal foot, 6¼x10½"..$20.00
Candle holders, white, 3¾", pr.....................................$22.50
Candy bowl, pale green, curved handle, 1½x7¾"......$16.00
Figurine, comical cow, purple w/gold trim, 4x4" $28.00
Figurine, crouching siamese, 2-tone gray w/blue eyes, dated 1958, 12" L...$95.00
Figurine, duck, brown tones, bill close to chest, 5x5"..$35.00
Figurine, fox, gold-leaf finish, signed Anthony, #148, 9x6"...$115.00
Figurine, koala bear, gold, ca 1970s, 5x9" $65.00
Figurine, mare & colt, gold, #121, 10x10" $85.00
Figurine, owl, red, 6"..$22.50
Figurinc, reclining lion, brown tones, #811, 13x20", NM...$275.00
Figurine, turtle, gold-leaf finish, #162, 7½" L $35.00
Figurine, zebra, gold, signed Jack White #907, 10x11" ..$165.00

Leaf dish, gold, #766, 10½x4¼"....................................$20.00
Planter, mermaid, white, dated 1958, 8x7" $65.00
Plaque, butterfly, gold w/black eyes, signed Anthony, 12x6x3" $135.00
Vase, antique gold w/green inside, signed Anthony, #731, 8" $20.00
Vase, bud; tall thin conical shape, paper label, 10¾".$15.00

Figurine, cat pair, gold leaf, signed Anthony #133 Calif USA, 10½ x 11½", $125.00. (Photo courtesy Cathy Gelling)

Furniture

A piece of furniture can often be difficult to date, since many seventeenth- and eighteenth-century styles have been reproduced. Even a piece made early in the twentieth century now has enough age on it that it may be impossible for a novice to distinguish it from the antique. Sometimes cabinetmakers may have trouble identifying specific types of wood, since so much variation can occur within the same species; so although it is usually helpful to try to determine what kind of wood a piece has been made of, results are sometimes inconclusive. Construction methods are usually the best clues. Watch for evidence of twentieth-century tools — automatic routers, lathes, carvers, and spray guns.

For further information we recommend *Antique Oak Furniture* by Conover Hill; *Collector's Guide to Oak Furniture* by Jennifer George; *Heywood-Wakefield Modern Furniture* by Steven Rouland and Roger Rouland; *Collector's Encyclopedia of American Furniture, Vols I* and *II,* and *Furniture of the Depression Era*, all by Robert and Harriett Swedberg; and *American Oak Furniture* by Katherine McNerney. All are published by Collector Books.

Armchair, overstuffed type w/carved crest & hardwood frame, 1930s, 35x23", from $275 to $350.00
Armchair, selected hardwoods, 4 curved slats w/turned finials, turned arm posts, replaced rush seat, repairs, 41".$100.00
Armchair rocker, oak, single pressed-back, curved arms, turned details, 39"...$350.00

Armchair rocker, selected hardwoods, 4-slat ladder back, replaced woven splint seat, refinished, 39½".......**$85.00**

Armchair rocker, 6-spindle pressed back, spindle arm supports, cane seat, 37" **$235.00**

Bed, bunk; Conant-Bell, maple, simple styling, late 1940s, 81" L..**$300.00**

Bedroom set, Plymold Corporation, double bed (not shown), large and small chests, nightstand, postwar, four pieces in all, $800.00.

Bookcase, oak, 3 glass doors, beadwork detail at top, carved front legs (4), 62x60x13".......................**$1,495.00**

Cabinet, china; breakfront w/plain-cut veneer on sides, walnut burl veneer front facing, 1940s, 76x44x15"..**$895.00**

Cabinet, china; oak w/curved glass sides, central glass door, carved legs, 62x36x12"..**$800.00**

Cabinet, sewing; solid mahogany w/banding design at top, 1940s, 31x18x17"..**$225.00**

Chair, dining; Chippendale style, mahogany, reupholstered seats, 6 sides+2 arm **$2,850.00**

Chair, side; oak, 3-slat back w/simple pressed decor at top, shaped seat, 36"...**$110.00**

Chair, side; oak, 5-spindle back w/pressed crest, cane seat, 39", 6 for..**$900.00**

Chair, side; oak w/pressed back top slat, 4 spindles, saddle seat, 37", 4 for...**$750.00**

Chair, side; oak w/upholstered square in back & seat, middle 1930s, 36", set of 6..**$400.00**

Chair, side; Queen-Anne style, hardwood w/old dark finish, replaced rush seat, some age, 42", pr.................**$220.00**

Chair, side; selected hardwoods w/walnut stain, straight plank forms top of chair back, upholstered seat, 1940s, 30"...**$50.00**

Chair, side; solid oak w/vase splat back w/simple crest, upholstered seat, 37", set of 5 ....**$450.00**

Chest, cedar; waterfall w/satinwood, American & Oriental walnut veneers, mid-1930s, 22x46x19" **$340.00**

Chest of drawers, oak veneer sides, drawer fronts & solid oak top & frame, 2 short drawers over 3 long, 39x31x21"..**$350.00**

Chest of drawers, walnut veneer top, sides & 3 upper drawers, V-matched Oriental wood on bottom drawer, 1930s, 48x30" **$375.00**

Cupboard, kitchen; oak step-back, glass doors over 2 drawers over 2 flat-panel doors, 74x40x17"................**$950.00**

Cupboard, oak, 2 glass doors over 2 drawers over 2 flat-panel doors, straight-line (1 piece), bail handles, 79x38x14" **$825.00**

Dresser, oak, swing mirror attached, 2 short drawers over 2 long, casters, 70x42x22" **$285.00**

Dry sink, oak or ash, cut-out feet, paneled doors, 2 drawers, replaced hardware, refinished, 56x50x18" **$500.00**

Hutch, Early American maple, Conant-Bell, late 1940s, 75x52x20" **$1,250.00**

Stand, Country style, refinished curly maple, turned legs, 2 dovetailed drawers, 1-board top, 31x19" square **$1,200.00**

Stand, refinished cherry w/replaced 1-board curly maple top, turned legs, 29x19x20" **$150.00**

Stand, refinished walnut w/oak & walnut drawer fronts, turned legs, 2 drawers, repairs, 29x23x19"+2 11" leaves ...**$220.00**

Table, breakfast; oak, turned legs, 30x36x21"+2 10" drop leaves..**$225.00**

Table, dining; oak; paw feet w/center support, 30x42x42"..**$1,065.00**

Table, drop-leaf; Chippendale style, refinished mahogany, swing legs, 27x48x16"+2 16" leaves **$150.00**

Table, extension; plain-sliced oak veneer top & quarter-sawn oak veneer apron & base, 28x42" dia.................**$595.00**

Table, library (cut down to coffee table); quarter-sawn oak top, pillars, base & drawer, 22x42x26"...............**$425.00**

Table, occasional; plain-cut walnut veneer top & selected hardwood base, 1940s, 27x18x15" **$215.00**

Table, Pembroke, plain-cut mahogany veneer top & drop leaves, figured mahogany drawer front, 1940s, 27x15x22"+10" drops **$400.00**

Table, refinished curly maple, turned legs & feet, mortised stretchers & apron, 39x20x29" **$275.00**

Table, wine tasting; Chippendale style, mahogany w/old finish, tripod base w/turned column, dish-turned top, 23x14" dia..**$440.00**

Table desk, bleached mahogany top, sides & drawer, birch hardwood base, 1940s, 30x36x18" **$225.00**

Games

Games from the 1870s to the 1970s and beyond are fun to collect. Many of the earlier games are beautifully lithographed. Some of their boxes were designed by well-known artists and illustrators, and many times these old games are appreciated more for their artwork than for their entertainment value. Some represent a historical event or a specific era in the social development of our country. Characters from the early days of radio, television, and movies have been featured in hundreds of games designed for children and adults alike.

If you're going to collect games, be sure that they're reasonably clean, free of water damage, and complete. Most have playing instructions printed inside the lid or on a separate piece of paper that include an inventory list. Check the contents, and remember that the condition of the box is very important too.

If you'd like to learn more about games, we recommend *Toys, Antique and Collectible*, by David Longest; *Baby Boomer Games* by Rick Polizzi; *Schroeder's Collectible Toys, Antique to Modern* (all published by Collector Books) and *Board Games of the '50s, '60s & '70s* by Stephanie Lane.

Club: American Game Collectors Association
49 Brooks Ave., Lewiston, ME 04240

Newsletter: *Game Times*
Joe Angiolillo
4628 Barlow Dr., Bartlesville, OK 74006

Across the Continent, Parker Bros, 1952, NM (EX box), from $40 to...**$50.00**
Addams Family, Milton Bradley, 1973, NM (NM box). **$65.00**

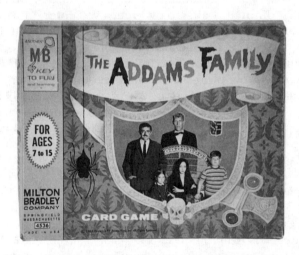

Addams Family Card Game, Milton Bradley, 1965, M (EX box), $30.00.

Advance to Boardwalk, Parker Bros, 1985, EXIB........**$20.00**
Amazing Spider-Man, Milton Bradley, 1967, EXIB....**$100.00**
Animal Twister, Milton Bradley, 1967, EXIB.................**$25.00**
Annie Oakley, Game Gems/T Cohn, 1965, EXIB........**$50.00**
Archie, Whitman, 1969, EXIB **$50.00**
Archie Bunker's Card Game, Milton Bradley, 1972, EXIB..**$15.00**
As the World Turns, Parker Bros, 1966, EXIB **$45.00**
Babes in Toyland, Parker Bros, 1961, EXIB **$50.00**
Balaroo, Milton Bradley, 1967, EXIB............................**$35.00**
Bash, Milton Bradley, 1965, EXIB................................**$25.00**
Batman Card Game, Whitman, 1966, NMIB **$50.00**
Batman Marble Game, 1966, rare, VG (VG box) **$45.00**
Battlestar Galactica, Parker Bros, 1978, MIB (sealed) .**$45.00**
Bewitched, Game Gems, 1965, rare, EXIB.................**$145.00**
Bop the Beetle, Ideal, 1962, MIB **$35.00**
Bugs Bunny Adventure, Milton Bradley, 1961, EXIB..**$40.00**
Camp Granada, Milton Bradley, 1965, EXIB................**$55.00**
Cannonball Run, Cadaco, 1981, EXIB **$20.00**

Captain Kangaroo's Tic Tagaroo, Milton Bradley, 1956, EXIB...**$35.00**
Casper Spooky Marble Maze, 1971, EXIB...................**$30.00**
Charlie's Angels Target Set, Placo, 1977, MIB **$50.00**
Cheyenne Target, Mettoy, 1962, EXIB........................**$225.00**
Columbo, Milton Bradley, 1973, EXIB **$20.00**
Crazy Clock, Ideal, 1964, NMIB..................................**$100.00**
Davy Crockett Indian Scouting, Whitman, NMIB, from $65 to **$85.00**
Detectives, Transogram, 1961, EXIB............................**$50.00**
Dick Tracy Electronic Target, 1961, NMIB..................**$100.00**
Dino the Dinosaur, Transogram, 1961, MIB **$75.00**
Dream House, Milton Bradley, 1968, rare, EXIB.......**$100.00**
Duran Duran, Milton Bradley, 1985, MIB **$85.00**
Espionage, Transogram, 1963, EXIB............................**$50.00**
Fangface, Parker Bros, 1979, EXIB..............................**$25.00**
FBI Crime Resistance, Milton Bradley, MIB **$85.00**
Flintstones Brake Ball, 1962, EXIB **$85.00**
Flying the Beam, Parker Bros, 1941, EXIB **$75.00**
Frankenstein Horror Target, Hasbro, 1965, EXIB......**$125.00**
Gabby Hayes Champion Shooting Target, Haecker Industries, 1950, EXIB..**$125.00**
Game of Charlie Brown & His Pals, 1959, EXIB.........**$60.00**
Game of Poor Jenny, All-Fair, 1972, EXIB **$150.00**
Get Smart Card Game, Ideal, 1966, unused, NMIB.....**$75.00**
Getaway Chase, DX, 1968, EXIB **$60.00**
Gidget, Standard Toykraft, 1965, NMIB **$125.00**
Green Acres, Standard Toykraft, 1965, MIB...............**$100.00**
Green Hornet Quick Switch, Milton Bradley, 1966, NMIB.**$300.00**
Groucho Marx TV Quiz, Pressman, 1950s, incomplete o/w VG (VG box)...**$75.00**
Groucho's You Bet Your Life, Lowell, 1955, rare, EXIB..**$100.00**
Happy Days, Parker Bros, 1976, EXIB **$20.00**
Hardy Boys Mystery Game: Secret of Thunder Mountain, Parker Bros, 1978, MIB (sealed) **$50.00**
Howdy Doody Dominos, Ed-U Cards, 1961, EXIB **$65.00**
Huckleberry Hound Western Game, Milton Bradley, 1958, NMIB...**$75.00**
Humpty Dumpty, Lowell, 1960, EXIB **$50.00**
Ironside, Ideal, 1967, EXIB **$100.00**
Jack & the Beanstalk, National Games, 1941, EXIB....**$40.00**
James Bond Message From M, Ideal, 1966, unused, MIB.**$350.00**
Jan Murray's Treasure Hunt, Gardner, 1959, EXIB......**$30.00**
Joe Palooka Boxing Game, Lowell, 1952, EXIB........**$150.00**
Journey to the Unknown, Remco, 1968, NMIB.........**$200.00**
Knight Rider, Parker Bros, 1983, EXIB **$30.00**
Knock Your Block Off, Hasbro, 1964, EXIB.................**$35.00**
Land of the Giants, Ideal, 1968, EXIB........................**$150.00**
Laugh-In's Squeeze Your Bippy, Hasbro, 1968, scarce, EXIB..**$60.00**
Laverne & Shirley, unused, MIB (sealed) **$25.00**
Legend of Jesse James, Milton Bradley, 1966, NMIB ..**$85.00**
Little Noddy's Taxi Game, Parker Bros, 1956, EXIB .**$100.00**
Lone Ranger Ring Toss, 1943, NMIB, from $350 to..**$450.00**
Lost in Space, Milton Bradley, 1965, EXIB **$75.00**
Love Boat World Cruise, Ungame, 1980, VG (VG box)..**$25.00**
Lucy Show, Transogram, 1962, EXIB **$250.00**

Mammoth Hunt, Cadaco, 1962, EXIB..........................$40.00
Man From UNCLE, Ideal, 1965, EXIB.........................$50.00
Mandrake the Magician, Transogram, 1966, NMIB ...$100.00
Mickey Mouse Club, Parker Bros, 1956, NMIB.........$100.00
Mighty Hercules, Hasbro, 1963, EXIB.......................$250.00
Muppet Game Show, Parker Bros, 1977, EXIB...........$20.00
Name That Tune, Milton Bradley, 1959, NMIB...........$50.00
Nancy Drew Mystery, Parker Bros, 1957, EXIB........$100.00
No Time for Sergeants, Ideal, 1964, EXIB $50.00
Off To See the Wizard, Milton Bradley, 1968, NMIB..$40.00
Operation Orbit, Transogram, 1962, EXIB.................$125.00
Perils of Pauline, Marx, 1964, EXIB...........................$65.00
Peter Rabbit, Gabriel, 1946, EXIB...............................$75.00

Petticoat Junction, Standard Toy Craft, EX (EX box), $100.00. (Photo courtesy John and Sheri Pavone)

Pie in Your Eye, Ideal, 1966, EXIB.............................$30.00
Pirate's Gold, All-Fair, 1946, EXIB $60.00
Raiders of the Lost Ark, Kenner, 1981, NMIB.............$25.00
Ranger Commandos, Parker Bros, 1944, EXIB...........$70.00
Road Runner, Milton Bradley, 1968, NMIB.................$50.00
Sea Hunt Under Water, Lowell, 1960, EXIB..............$100.00
Shotgun Slade, Milton Bradley, 1960, NMIB..............$75.00
Sleeping Beauty, Parker Bros, 1952, EXIB..................$50.00
Sleeping Beauty, Whitman, 1958, EXIB $40.00
Steve Canyon, Lowell, 1959, MIB................................$85.00
Straight Arrow, Selchow & Righter, 1950, EXIB $75.00
Super Heroes Bingo, Hasbro, 1978, MIB.....................$35.00
Superman Radio Quiz Master, 1948, EXIB...................$65.00
Terry & the Pirates Sunday Funnies, Ideal, 1972, MIB...$45.00
Think-A-Tron, Hasbro, 1961, EXIB..............................$75.00
Thunderbirds, Parker Bros, 1967, NMIB $85.00
Tom & Jerry, Transogram, 1965, NMIB......................$100.00
Treasure Island, Harett-Gilmar, 1955, EXIB $55.00
Uncle Wiggley, Milton Bradley, 1940s, NMIB..............$50.00
Uranium Rush, Gardner, 1950s, EXIB $100.00
Wally Gator, Transogram, EXIB $65.00
Walt Disney's Fantasyland, Parker Bros, 1950s, MIB ..$40.00
Welcome Back Kotter, Ideal, 1976, EXIB $20.00
Winnie the Pooh, Parker Bros, 1954, EXIB $40.00
Yacht Race, Parker Bros, 1961, VG (VG box)...........$100.00
Yankee Trader, Corey Games, 1941, VG (VG box).....$75.00
Zorro Beanbag-Darts, Gardner, 1965, EXIB................$65.00
77 Sunset Strip, Lowell, 1960, EXIB $60.00

Gas Station Collectibles

Items used and/or sold by gas stations are included in this very specialized area of advertising collectibles. Those with an interest in this field tend to specialize in memorabilia from a specific gas station like Texaco or Signal. This is a very regional market, with items from small companies that are no longer in business bringing the best prices. For instance, memorabilia decorated with Gulf's distinctive 'orange ball' logo may sell more readily in Pittsburgh than in Los Angeles. Gas station giveaways like plastic gas pump salt and pepper sets and license plate attachments are gaining in popularity with collectors. If you're interested in learning more about these types of collectibles, we recommend *Huxford's Collectible Advertising* by Sharon and Bob Huxford, and *Gas Station Memorabilia* by B.J. Summers and Wayne Priddy, both published by Collector Books.

See also Ashtrays; Automobilia.

Newsletter: *Petroleum Collectors Monthly*
Scott Benjamin and Wayne Henderson, Publishers
PO Box 556, LaGrange, OH 44050-0556; 440-355-6608. Subscription: $29.95 per year in US, Canada: $38.50; International: $65.95 (Samples: $5); website: www.pcmpublishing.com or www.oilcollectibles.com

Advisor: Scott Benjamin (See Directory Gas Station Collectibles)

Ashtray, Cities Service, chrome w/clear plastic dome-shaped logo in center, Park Industries, 8" dia, MIB..........$50.00
Badge, Station Manager, cloisonne Chevron emblem in red, white & blue inlay, 1½x1¼", NM.....................$230.00
Badge, Veedol emblem, red V w/gold wings, painted metal, 1x2½", NM..$100.00
Bank, Super Shell Gasoline logo & Saves on Stop-& Go Driving on black & white litho tin can w/slot in top, 3½", VG+...$70.00
Bank, Tanker System Saves, figural glass tank car w/round screw lid on top, 5¼" L, NM................................$75.00
Bank, Texaco, plastic fat attendant figure, green w/logos on chest & hat, black trim, 4⅞", EX+ $110.00
Bank, Texaco Fire Chief, cast metal gas pump w/paper decal, red, 5¾", EX..$275.00
Banner, Drain — Fill — Then Listen, Texaco Scottie dogs w/black & red lettering on white cloth, 36x80", EX................$190.00
Banner, Esso/World's First Choice, Happy the oil drip man saluting on black canvas background, white border, 83x36", VG $120.00
Banner, Get the Jump on Spring!/Complete Texaco Spring Changeover Now, frog graphics on white cloth, 1954, 33x84", NM+ $30.00
Booklet, Standard Oil Personalized Tourist Information, 1955, EX..$5.00
Brush, Socony Gasoline & Polarine Oil & Grease w/logos printed on wooden top, mohair bristles, 7", VG+.$40.00

Calendar, Texaco, 1952, round diecut cardboard star logo backing w/complete paper pad, 27x15", EX......**$325.00**

Calendar, Texaco Railroad Lubricants, 1966, pictures 94 different railroad insignias, 31½", EX+ **$160.00**

Clock, alarm; Texaco, round metal body w/cardboard face, glass lens, 5¼", NM **$300.00**

Clock, Ask For Bardahl..., black, red & green on round white lighted face w/metal case, electric, 12" dia, EX+ .**$200.00**

Clock, Mobil Oil horse w/numbers in red on reverse-painted glass, lighted background, metal case, electric, 15" dia, EX **$625.00**

Clothespin bag, gray cloth w/dealer Mobil Station advertising in red & blue, station premium, 10½x13", NM **$65.00**

Cookie tin, Gilmore, Christmas holly wreath around lion's head on lid, 10" dia, VG+ **$130.00**

Cup, Trop-Artic Auto Oil, litho tin, no handle, colorful landscape graphics w/open touring car, 2¾", EX+ ...**$190.00**

Decal, Standard, red, white & blue torch & oval logo w/name in black, 32x40", unused, M.................................**$20.00**

Display, Earl's Performance Products, rotors, mufflers & pipes make up 3-D man advertising various products, 54", EX **$200.00**

Display, Esso Handy Oil, 15x10" cardboard box w/diecut oil drop boy & 20 5½" yellow oil drop figures, EX **$350.00**

Display, Goodrich Silvertowns, 2-sided litho tin trapezoid-shaped tire holder in red, white on blue, 8x11x15", VG+ **$300.00**

First-aid kit, Pure Oil Co, blue metal case w/white advertising, wall-mount, partial contents, 10" square, EX+ **$30.00**

Flag, Texaco, round star logo sewn on bright green cloth, loops for rope on white strip, 48x75", EX..........**$500.00**

Globe, D-X Boron, glass lens w/plastic figural rocketship atop body, 3-pc, mid-1950s, 13½", from $800 to.......**$1,250.00**

Globe, Mobil Premium, red & blue on white, complete w/Capolite body, 13½" dia, NM..........................**$300.00**

Globe, Standard Oil crown, gold & white, 1-pc w/original ring mount & base, NM+ **$450.00**

Globe lens, Red Indian, red, white & black Indian head logo & lettering on white, complete, 13½" dia, EX, from $1500 to...**$2,000.00**

Grease tin, Polarine Cup Grease, litho tin, white w/gold lettering, slip lid, 12x12x12", VG+ **$50.00**

Gumball machine, early Texaco gas pump w/battery-operated plastic light-up globe, Olde Tyme Reproductions, 21", NM, from $75 to **$100.00**

Keyholder, Grizzly Gasoline, plastic & celluloid, blue logo on ivory-look cylinder, unused, 2½", EX+.................**$65.00**

Letter opener, Atlantic Refining Co, brass, shows early truck, 9", VG **$30.00**

Lighter, Husky, slimline pocket style, logo on red inlay, Peace/Japan, 2", NM **$85.00**

Lighter, Phillips 66, Zippo table-top w/logo & Award — New Customer Plan — 1957, NM **$100.00**

Lighter, Shell, table-top resembling a pocket style w/yellow logo on black inlay on both sides, 2½x3", NM....**$60.00**

Map, California, Wilshire Oil Co, 1962, G **$15.00**

Map rack, metal w/plastic fronts, free-standing pedestal, model MV4/serial 002173, 43x23x12", EX...........**$100.00**

Mechanical pencil, Richfield Products, w/perpetual calendar, 1940s eagle logo, 5", NM.......................................**$55.00**

Mug, Texaco, white ceramic w/thick round handle, Texaco green flag decal, green bands top & bottom, Wellsville China, NM **$190.00**

Notepad & pen, Cities Service, notepad in metal case w/lid & magnetic pen, 5x4", NM...................................**$50.00**

Oil bottles & carrier, Atlantic, 4 glass bottles w/embossed logo & metal tops in wire carrier, 16", EX..........**$250.00**

Oil can, Gargoyle Mobiloil, 1-qt, tin litho, red & black on white, Socony Vacuum Oil Co & winged horse logo below, EX..**$60.00**

Oil can, Gargoyle Mobiloil A Medium Body, 1-gal, litho tin, vertical, Gargoyle logo & black lettering on white, 10", VG **$35.00**

Oil can, Husky Mid-Continent Motor Oil, 1-qt, litho tin, 2 different Husky logos front & back on yellow, EX..**$425.00**

Oil can, Penn Bee Motor Oil, 1-qt, litho tin, bees & hive logo in black & white on yellow w/red trim, EX.......**$250.00**

Oil can, Phillips Trop-Artic Motor Oil, 1-qt, litho tin, igloo & palm tree graphics going from green to red, EX .**$650.00**

Oil can, Polarine Medium, ½-gal, rectangular, bare metal w/red & blue on white labels, handled, screw lid w/spout, NM+ **$135.00**

Oil can, Shell, ½-gal, logo embossed on copper can w/swing handle, VG **$100.00**

Oil can, Texaco Motor Oil F, ½-gal, rectangular w/handi-grip top, Clean Clear Golden logo on white label on green, NM **$325.00**

Oil can, Texaco 574 Motor Oil, 1-qt, logos on green, screw lid, 6½", EX+ **$60.00**

Oil can, Valvoline Oil Co, 1-gal, vertical, litho tin, dark green w/lettering, screw cap, 11½", VG........................**$300.00**

Oil display rack, Quaker State Motor Oil, 2-sided arched sign hanging from wire holder on metal rack, 50x22x16", VG+...**$170.00**

Oil display rack, Texaco Outboard Lubricants, wire, 3-tiered w/painted aluminum sign, dated 4-66, 45", EX+...**$550.00**

Pen & pencil set, Sunoco DX, sterling silver w/cloisonne logos, Parker, 1960s, EXIB **$65.00**

Pen holder, Standard, Service Station Cleanliness Award on ceramic base w/red, white & blue logo, 2-pc, EX+.............**$135.00**

Radiator cover, Shell Starts Quickly, diecut cardboard, Shell logo & red lettering on yellow, 2-sided, 12x19", EX...........**$40.00**

Salt and pepper shakers, Phillips 66, red plastic with paper decals, M, 2¾", $100.00 for the pair.

Sign, neon, Mobil, tubing outlining red molded plastic winged horse, 53" L, newer, EX+ **$725.00**

Sign, porcelain, Gargoyle Mobiloil CW for Gears, round w/neck clamp, black & red on white, 8¾x10¾", NM+ **$110.00**

Sign, porcelain, Marathon, runner on red & white bull's-eye disk w/Best in the Long Run on blue banner, 72" dia, EX **$1,200.00**

Sign, porcelain, No Admittance Except on Business (Shell Oil), rectangular, red on gold, 6x15", EX+ **$175.00**

Sign, porcelain, No Smoking (Texaco), single modern logo & black lettering on white, 4x23", NM+ **$150.00**

Sign, porcelain, Polarine Oil & Greases (For Motor Car & Motor Boat Lubrication), white on blue, 4½x19½", EX+ **$375.00**

Sign, reverse-painted glass, Let Us Check Your Oil For Safety, red & white, rounded corners, 7½x14½", NM+ ...**$30.00**

Sign, street, Goodrich Tires, tin pentagon shape on iron pedestal base, 48x28", VG **$500.00**

Sign, tin flange, Ask for Wolf's Head Motor Oil.., oval, white, red & black on red, white & green ground, 22x17", NM.**$200.00**

Sign, tin flange, Sinclair Oils, round, red lettering around green & white vertically striped center on white, 18", NM **$825.00**

Sign, wood, Atlas Spark Plugs/Trap That Gasoline Thief! Replace 'Ratty' Old Plugs w/.... on giant rat trap, 18½", EX...**$80.00**

Thermometer, plastic lollipop, Shell, sign w/dealer advertising on lower tab, 7", EX+ **$185.00**

Thermometer, porcelain, Kendall Motor Oils, red & black on white, black border, 27½x9¼", NM....................**$375.00**

Thermometer, porcelain, Prestone Anti-Freeze/You're Set Safe Sure, porcelain, gray, 36x9", EX..................**$160.00**

Gay Fad Glassware

What started out as a home-based 'one-woman' operation in the late 1930s within only a few years had grown into a substantial company requiring much larger facilities and a staff of decorators. The company, dubbed Gay Fad by her husband, was founded by Fran Taylor. Originally they decorated kitchenware items but later found instant success with the glassware they created, most of which utilized frosted backgrounds and multicolored designs such as tulips, state themes, Christmas motifs, etc. Some pieces were decorated with 22-karat gold and sterling silver. In addition to the frosted glass which collectors quickly learn to associate with this company, they also became famous for their 'bentware' — quirky cocktail glasses whose stems were actually bent.

Some of their more collectible lines are 'Beau Brummel' — martini glasses with straight or bent stems featuring a funny-faced drinker wearing a plaid bow tie; 'Gay Nineties' — various designs such as can-can girls and singing bartenders; '48 States' — maps with highlighted places of interest; 'Rich Man, Poor Man' (or Beggar Man, Thief, etc.); 'Bartender' (self-explanatory); 'Currier & Ives' — made to coordinate with the line by Royal China; 'Zombies' — extra tall and slim with various designs including roses, giraffes, and flamingos; and the sterling silver- and 22-karat gold-trimmed glassware.

Until you learn to spot it a mile away (which you soon will), look for an interlocking 'G' and 'F' or 'Gay Fad,' the latter mark indicating pieces from the late 1950s to the early 1960s. The glassware itself has the feel of satin and is of very good quality. It can be distinguished from other manufacturers' wares simply by checking the bottom — Gay Fad's are frosted; generally other manufacturers' are not. Hand-painted details are another good clue. (You may find similar glassware signed 'Briard'; this is not Gay Fad.) Listings below include Fire-King and Federal Glass pieces that were decorated by Gay Fad.

This Ohio-based company was sold in 1963 and closed altogether in 1965. Be careful of condition. If the frosting has darkened or the paint is worn or faded, it's best to wait for a better example.

Advisor: Donna S. McGrady (See the Directory, Gay Fad)

Cocktail shaker, The Last Hurdle (fox hunting scenes), 32-ounce, $35.00.
(Photo courtesy Donna McGrady)

Ashtray, Trout Flies, clear...**$6.00**

Batter bowl, Fruits, milk white, signed w/F (Federal Glass), handled...**$70.00**

Bent tray, Phoenix Bird, clear, signed Gay Fad, 13¾" dia .**$17.00**

Bent tray, Stylized Cats, clear, signed Gay Fad, 11½" dia...**$14.00**

Bent trays, classic design, paper label, 2 square trays in metal frame...**$22.00**

Beverage set, Colonial Homestead, frosted, 85-oz pitcher & 6 12-oz tumblers...**$60.00**

Beverage set, Magnolia, clear, 86-oz pitcher & 6 13-oz tumblers **$75.00**

Beverage set, Red Hibiscus, frosted, 86-oz ball pitcher & 6 13-oz round bottom tumblers **$80.00**

Bowl, chile; Fruits, 2¼x5" **$12.50**

Bowl, mixing; Poinsettia, red w/green leaves on Fire-King Ivory Swirl, 8"...**$45.00**

Bowl, splash-proof; Fruits, Fire-King, 4¼x6½"............**$55.00**

Bowls, nesting; Fruits, Fire-King, 6", 7½", 8¾", set of 3 .**$45.00**

Canister set, Red Rose, red lids, white interior, 3-pc ..**$55.00**

Casserole, Apple, open, oval, Fire-King Ivory, 1-qt..**$45.00**

Casserole, Apple, w/lid, Fire-King Ivory, 1-qt **$65.00**

Casserole, Fruits, divided, oval, Fire King, 11¾".........**$40.00**

Casserole, Fruits, w/lid, Fire-King, 1-qt.....................**$35.00**

Casserole, Peach Blossom, w/au gratin lid, Fire-King, 2-qt **$35.00**

Casserole, Rosemaling (tulips) on lid, clear, 2-qt, w/black wire rack..**$30.00**

Chip n' Dip, Horace the Horse w/cart, knife tail, 3 bowls, double old-fashion glass as head, signed Gay Fad.......**$60.00**

Cocktail set, Poodle, metal frame 'body' w/martini mixer, double old-fashion glass as head & 4 5-oz glasses, signed Gay Fad **$60.00**

Cocktail shaker, Ballerina Shoes, red metal screw-top lid, frosted, 32-oz, 7"..**$20.00**

Cocktail shaker, full-figure ballerina, frosted, 28-oz, 9"..**$35.00**

Cruet set, Oil & Vinegar, Cherry, clear.........................**$15.00**

Decanter set, Gay '90s, Scotch, Rye, Gin & Bourbon, frosted or white inside..**$80.00**

Goblet, Bow Pete, Hoffman Beer, 16-oz.....................**$15.00**

Ice tub, Gay '90s, frosted **$16.00**

Juice set, Tommy Tomato, frosted, 36-oz pitcher & 6 4-oz tumblers...**$45.00**

Loaf pan, Apple, Fire-King Ivory...................................**$35.00**

Luncheon set, Cattails, square plate, cup & saucer, tumbler, clear, 1 complete place setting, 4-pc.....................**$18.00**

Luncheon set, Fantasia Hawaiian Flower, 1 place setting (square plate, cup & saucer)...................................**$15.00**

Martini mixer, 'A Jug of Wine...,' w/glass stirring rod, clear, signed Gay Fad, 10⅝"..**$16.00**

Mix-A-Salad set, Ivy, 22-oz shaker w/plastic top, garlic press, measuring spoon, recipe book, MIB.....................**$70.00**

Mug, Fruits, stackable, Fire-King, 3"...........................**$15.00**

Mug, Notre Dame, frosted, 16-oz **$15.00**

Mug set, Here's How in a different language on ea mug, frosted, 12-pc **$72.00**

Pilsner set, Gay 90s, portraits: Mama, Papa, Victoria, Rupert, Aunt Aggie, Uncle Bertie, Gramps & Horace, frosted, 8-pc **$90.00**

Pitcher, Currier & Ives, blue & white, frosted, 86-oz ..**$60.00**

Pitcher, juice; Ada Orange, frosted, 36-oz **$30.00**

Pitcher, martini; cardinal & pine sprig, frosted, w/glass stirrer, 42-oz **$35.00**

Pitcher, Rosemaling (tulips), white inside, 32-oz **$28.00**

Plate, Fruits, lace edge, Hazel Atlas, 8½".....................**$17.50**

Punch set, turquoise veiling, bowl & 8 cups in metal frame..**$65.00**

Range set, Rooster, salt, pepper, sugar & flour shakers, frosted w/red metal lids, 8-oz, 4-pc **$40.00**

Refrigerator container, Distlefink on white, Fire-King, w/lid, 4x8"...**$50.00**

Salad set, Fruits, frosted, lg bowl, 2 cruets, salt & pepper shakers, 5-pc **$50.00**

Salad set, Outlined Fruits, lg bowl, 2 cruets, salt & pepper shakers, frosted, 5-pc..**$65.00**

Salt & pepper shakers, Fruits, 3½", pr, MIB **$50.00**

Salt & pepper shakers, Morning Glory, frosted w/red plastic tops, pr **$16.00**

Stem, bent cocktail, Beau Brummel, clear, signed Gay Fad, 3½-oz..**$14.00**

Stem, bent cocktail, Souvenir of My Bender, frosted, 3-oz..**$11.00**

Tea & toast, Magnolia, square plate w/cup indent & cup, clear **$11.00**

Tom & Jerry set, Christmas bells, milk white, marked GF, bowl & 6 cups..**$70.00**

Tumbler, Christmas Greetings From Gay Fad, frosted, 4-oz **$15.00**

Tumbler, Derby Winner Citation, frosted, 1948, 14-oz..**$50.00**

Tumbler, grouse, brown, aqua & gold on clear, signed Gay Fad, 10-oz...**$10.00**

Tumbler, Hors D'oeuvres, clear, 14-oz.......................**$10.00**

Tumbler, Kentucky state map (1 of 48), pink, yellow or lime, frosted, marked GF, 10-oz.....................................**$6.00**

Tumbler, Oregon state map on pink picket fence, clear, marked GF..**$6.00**

Tumbler, Pegasus, gold & pink on black, 12-oz **$10.00**

Tumbler, Say When, frosted, 4-oz **$5.00**

Tumbler, Zombie, flamingo, frosted, marked GF, 14-oz .**$18.00**

Tumbler, Zombie, giraffe, frosted, marked GF, 14-oz ...**$18.00**

Tumblers, angels preparing for Christmas, frosted, 12-oz, set of 8..**$72.00**

Tumblers, Dickens Christmas Carol characters, frosted, 12-oz, set of 8..**$65.00**

Tumblers, Famous Fighters (John L Sullivan & the others), frosted, 16-oz, set of 8...**$85.00**

Tumblers, French Poodle, clear, 17-oz, set of 8 in original box **$96.00**

Tumblers, Game Birds & Animals, clear, 12-oz, set of 8, MIB **$75.00**

Tumblers, Ohio Presidents, frosted, 12-oz, set of 8....**$60.00**

Tumblers, Rich Man, Poor Man (nursery rhyme), frosted, marked GF, 16-oz, set of 8..**$95.00**

Tumblers, Sports Cars, white interior, 12-oz, set of 8.**$45.00**

Vanity set, butterflies in meadow, pink inside, 5-pc...**$60.00**

Vase, Red Poppy, clear, footed, 10" **$22.00**

Waffle set, Blue Willow, 48-oz waffle batter jug & 11½-oz syrup jug, frosted, pr...**$95.00**

Waffle set, Little Black Sambo, frosted, 48-oz waffle batter jug, 11½-oz syrup jug..**$250.00**

Waffle set, Peach Blossoms, 48-oz waffle batter jug & 11½-oz syrup jug, frosted, pr...**$35.00**

Waffle set, Red Poppy, frosted, 48-oz waffle batter jug, 11½-oz syrup jug **$24.00**

Wine set, Grapes, decanter & 4 2½-oz stemmed wines, clear, 5-pc **$40.00**

Geisha Girl China

The late nineteenth century saw a rise in the popularity of Oriental wares in the US and Europe. Japan rose to meet the demands of this flourishing ceramics marketplace with a flurry of growth in potteries and decorating centers. These created items for export which would appeal to Western tastes and integrate into Western dining and decorating cultures, which were distinct from those of Japan. One example of the wares introduced into this marketplace was Geisha Girl porcelain.

Hundreds of different patterns and manufacturers' marks have been uncovered on Geisha Girl porcelain tea and dinnerware sets, dresser accessories, decorative items, etc., which were produced well into the twentieth century. They all share in common colorful decorations featuring kimono-clad ladies and children involved in everyday activities. These scenes are set against a backdrop of lush flora, distinctive Japanese architecture and majestic landscapes. Most Geisha Girl porcelain designs were laid on by means of a stencil, generally red or black. This appears as an outline on the ceramic body. Details are then completed by hand-painted washes in a myriad of colors. A minority of the wares were wholly hand painted.

Most Geisha Girl porcelain has a colorful border or edging with handles, finials, spouts, and feet similarly adorned. The most common border color is red which can range from orange to red-orange to a deep brick red. Among the earliest border colors were red, maroon, cobalt blue, light (apple) green, and Nile green. Pine green, blue-green, and turquoise made their appearance circa 1917, and a light cobalt or Delft blue appeared around 1920. Other colors (e.g. tan, yellow, brown, and gold) can also be found. Borders were often enhanced with gilded lace or floral decoration. The use of gold for this purpose diminished somewhat around 1910 to 1915 when some decorators used economic initiative (fewer firings required) to move the gold to just inside the border or replace the gold with white or yellow enamels. Wares with both border styles continued to be produced into the twentieth century. Exquisite examples with multicolor borders as well as ornate rims decorated with florals and geometrics can also be found.

Due to the number of different producers, the quality of Geisha ware ranges from crude to finely detailed. Geisha Girl porcelain was sold in sets and open stock in outlets ranging from the five-and-ten to fancy department stores. It was creatively used for store premiums, containers for store products, fair souvenirs, and resort memorabilia. The fineness of detailing, amount of gold highlights, border color, scarcity of form and, of course, condition all play a role in establishing the market value of a given item. Some patterns are scarcer than others, but most Geisha ware collectors seem not to focus on particular patterns.

The heyday of Geisha Girl porcelain was from 1910 through the 1930s. Production continued until the World War II era. During the 'Occupied' period, a small amount of wholly hand-painted examples were made, often with a black and gold border. The Oriental import stores and catalogs from the 1960s and 1970s featured some examples of Geisha Girl porcelain, many of which were produced in Hong Kong. These are recognized by the very white porcelain, sparse detail coloring, and lack of gold decoration. The 1990s have seen a resurgence of reproductions with a faux Nippon mark. These items are supposed to represent high quality Geisha ware, but in reality they are a blur of Geisha and Satsuma-style characteristics. They are too busy in design, too heavily enameled, and bear poor resemblance to items that rightfully carry Noritake's green M-in-Wreath Nippon mark. Once you've been introduced to a few of these reproductions, you'll be able to recognize them easily.

Note: Colors mentioned in the following listings refer to borders.

Advisor: Elyce Litts (See Directory, Geisha Girl China)

Ashtray, Temple A, heart form, red w/gold, M-in-Wreath mark..**$35.00**
Bowl, berry; River's Edge, green/orange/gold, 5".......**$28.00**
Bowl, dessert; Garden Bench H, cobalt w/black-outlined reserves...**$15.00**
Bowl, master berry; Fan A, cobalt/brick red/gold, scalloped..**$45.00**
Butter pat, Flower Gathering B, cobalt w/gold, round, 3"..**$8.00**
Chocolate pot, River's Edge, red w/gold, Kutani mark...**$95.00**
Cocoa pot, To the Teahouse, gold rim, Torii mark.....**$65.00**
Compote, Boat Festival, river scene, T in Cherry Blossom mark, 6" II..**$55.00**
Creamer, Long-Stemmed Peony, blue w/gold, slim, Made in Japan..**$15.00**
Creamer, Paper Carp, red-orange w/gold, Kutani mark...**$20.00**
Cup & saucer, AD; Basket B, 4 ladies, blue **$22.00**
Cup & saucer, AD; Flower Gathering D, red, Tashiro mark **$18.00**

Dresser tray, Blind Man's Bluff, cobalt blue ground, $85.00. (Photo courtesy Elyce Litts)

Egg cup, Cherry Blossom Ikebana, flowers in pot, cobalt.**$18.00**
Egg cup, double; Mother & Son A, blue-green...........**$20.00**
Jug, Battledore, apple green, fluted edge & base, ribbed, 5"..**$40.00**
Manicure jar, Parasol C: parasol, red Japan mark, 2¼" ..**$20.00**
Match holder, Garden Bench A, blue-green, hanging...**$35.00**

Mustard, Garden Bench C, cobalt w/gold, T in Cherry Blossom mark **$25.00**
Napkin ring, Temple, oval, #15A.............................**$30.00**
Plate, Battledore, red-orange, scalloped swirl, 6¼" **$15.00**
Plate, Visitor to the Court, blue w/gold, Japan mark, 7¼" **$22.00**
Plate, Writing A, scalloped cobalt w/gold lacing, Made in Japan, 7⅜" **$28.00**
Powder jar, Pug, brick red, 4¼" **$35.00**
Salt & pepper shakers, Bouncing Ball, blue-green, pr..**$22.00**
Tea strainer, Parasol/Lesson A, red, 2-pc.....................**$55.00**
Teacup, Garden Bench C, apple green w/gold, patterned interior **$4.00**
Teacup & saucer, Bicycle Race, red-orange w/gold ...**$30.00**
Teacup & saucer, Duck Watching B, blue-green w/white, marked...**$15.00**
Teacup & saucer, Peacock on Flowered Stone Roof, cobalt & gold...**$25.00**
Toothpick holder, Court Lady, 3 black-lined reserves, melon shape, cobalt border.......................................**$35.00**
Vase, Bamboo Trellis, red-orange, #14, 4½", pr..........**$30.00**

GI Joe

The first GI Joe was introduced by Hasbro in 1964. He was 12" tall, and you could buy him with blond, auburn, black, or brown hair in four basic variations: Action Sailor, Action Marine, Action Soldier, and Action Pilot. There was also a Black doll as well as representatives of many other nations. By 1967 GI Joe could talk, all the better to converse with the female nurse who was first issued that year. The Adventure Team series (1970 – 1976) included Black Adventurer, Talking Astronaut, Sea Adventurer, Talking Team Commander, Land Adventurer, and several variations. At this point, their hands were made of rubber, making it easier for them to grasp the many guns, tools, and other accessories that Hasbro had devised. Playsets, vehicles, and clothing completed the package, and there were kid-size items designed specifically for the kids themselves. The 12" dolls were discontinued by 1976.

Brought out by popular demand, Hasbro's 3¾" GI Joes hit the market in 1982. Needless to say, they were very well accepted. In fact, these smaller GI Joes are thought to be the most successful line of action figures ever made. Loose figures (those removed from the original packaging) are very common, and even if you can locate the accessories that they came out with, most are worth only about $3.00 to $10.00. It's the mint-in-package items that most interest collectors, and they pay a huge premium for the package. There's an extensive line of accessories that goes with the smaller line as well. Many more are listed in *Schroeder's Collectible Toys, Antique to Modern; Collector's Guide to Dolls in Uniform* by Joseph Bourgeois; and *Collectible Action Figures, Second Edition,* by Paris and Susan Manos, all published by Collector Books.

Note: A/M was used in the description lines as an abbreviation for Action Man.

12" Figures and Accessories

Accessory, Action Team Raft, orange or black, EX.....**$10.00**
Accessory, Adventure Team Fire Suit, silver, EX.........**$25.00**
Accessory, Air Cadet Hat, EX.................................**$17.00**
Accessory, Air Force Dress Jacket, MOC **$235.00**
Accessory, Army Poncho, gr, EX............................**$35.00**
Accessory, Australian Jacket, EX.............................**$45.00**
Accessory, Deep Sea Diver Gloves, EX, pr **$10.00**
Accessory, Dog Tag, VG......................................**$25.00**
Accessory, Green Beret Hat, EX+..........................**$60.00**
Accessory, Jeep Searchlight, EX.............................**$15.00**
Accessory, Life Ring, MOC...................................**$54.00**
Accessory, Military Police Trousers, brown, MOC **$70.00**
Accessory, Mountain & Artic Set, A/M, complete, MIB...**$55.00**
Accessory, Navy Basics, #7628, MOC.......................**$120.00**
Accessory, Scuba Tank, NM...................................**$25.00**
Accessory, Secret Mountain Post, complete, MIB **$125.00**
Accessory, Shore Patrol Jumper, w/full underarm zip, VG...**$39.00**
Accessory, Ski Patrol Boots, EX.............................**$15.00**
Accessory, Ski Patrol Skis & Poles, EX.....................**$60.00**
Accessory, USN Life Ring, w/rope, EX+ **$28.00**
Figure, Action Marine, complete, EX+ **$145.00**
Figure, Action Pilot, complete, MIB **$450.00**
Figure, Action Sailor, complete, MIB.......................**$450.00**
Figure, Action Soldier, complete, EX+.....................**$145.00**
Figure, Action Soldier, complete, NMIB....................**$355.00**
Figure, Adventure Team Adventurer, w/Kung Fu grip, complete, EX (EX box) **$285.00**
Figure, Adventure Team Man of Action, nude, EX.....**$65.00**
Figure, Adventure Team Talking Astronaut, complete, EX **$200.00**

Figure, Adventure Team Talking Commander, complete, NM (EX box), $275.00. (Photo courtesy Joseph Burgeois)

Figure, British Commando w/Chevrons, complete, VG ...**$385.00**
Figure, Deep Freeze, complete, NM **$285.00**
Figure, Deep Sea Diver, complete, MIB **$795.00**
Figure, German Soldier, #8100, complete, MIB **$1,750.00**

Figure, Green Beret, complete, EX $325.00
Figure, Home for the Holiday (African American), Wal-Mart, NRFB..$52.00
Figure, Japanese Imperial Soldier, complete, M........$699.00
Figure, LSO, complete, EX....................................$289.00
Figure, Marine, Toys-R-Us, NRFB $42.00
Figure, Marine Demolition, complete, NM $240.00
Figure, Navy Seal, FAO Schwarz, mail-order, rare, NRFB...$145.00
Figure, Ski Patrol, complete, EX............................$315.00
Figure, Space Ranger Patroller, A/M, complete, MIB..$95.00
Figure, Tank Commander, complete, EX...................$525.00
Figure, West Point Cadet, complete, EX...................$350.00
Vehicle, Adventure Team Helicopter, yellow, EXIB..$200.00
Vehicle, Fire Engine, A/M, MIP..............................$75.00
Vehicle, Motorcycle w/Sidecar, complete, MIB $425.00
Vehicle, Sea Wolf Submarine, EX (VG box) $265.00
Vehicle, Team Vehicle, yellow ATV, VG...................$55.00

3¾" Figures and Accessories

Accessory, Artic Blast, 1988, EX $12.00
Accessory, Battle Gear Accessory Pack #1, 1983, MIP..$16.00
Accessory, Battlefield Robot Tri-Blaster, 1988, NRFB..$30.00
Accessory, Cobra Condor Z25 Plane, 1988, MIB.........$80.00
Accessory, Cobra Overlord's Dictator Vehicle, w/Overlord figure, MIB..$25.00
Accessory, Cobra Wolf w/Ice Viper, 1985, NM...........$20.00
Accessory, Falcon Glider w/Grunt, complete, EX.....$100.00
Accessory, LCV Recon Sled, 1983, complete, EX $5.00
Accessory, Missile Launcher, 1983, EX.......................$5.00
Accessory, P-40 Warhawk w/Pilot Savage, 1995, MIP...$35.00
Accessory, Q Force Battle Gear, Action Force, MIP $5.00
Accessory, Shark w/Deep Six, complete, EX...............$25.00
Accessory, Whirlwind Twin Battle Gun, 1983, EX......$20.00
Figure, Ace, 1983, MIP $25.00
Figure, Annihilator, 1989, w/accessories, EX.............$10.00
Figure, Baroness, w/accessories, EX $30.00
Figure, Blizzard, 1988, w/accessories, EX..................$8.00
Figure, Chuckles, 1986, w/accessories, EX $8.00
Figure, Cobra Soldier, 1983, MIP $60.00
Figure, Crazylegs, 1986, MOC..................................$15.00
Figure, Dee-Jay, 1989, MOC....................................$14.00
Figure, Dojo, 1992, MOC...$10.00
Figure, Eels, 1992, MOC..$10.00
Figure, Footloose, 1985, MOC $30.00
Figure, Grunt, 1982-83, w/accessories, EX $20.00
Figure, Hawk, 1987, w/accessories, EX $15.00
Figure, Iron Grenadier, 1988, MOC...........................$18.00
Figure, Lady Jaye, 1985, MOC..................................$75.00
Figure, Lifeline, 1985, w/accessories, EX...................$10.00
Figure, Mainframe, 1986, w/accessories, EX...............$10.00
Figure, Metal-Hand, 1990, MOC $15.00
Figure, Night Force Outback, 1988, w/accessories, EX..$15.00
Figure, Ozone, 1993, MOC...$5.00
Figure, Ranger-Viper, 1990, MOC..............................$12.00
Figure, Recoil, 1989, MOC $15.00
Figure, Road Pig, 1988, MOC....................................$20.00

Figure, Scrap Iron, 1984, w/accessories, EX................$15.00
Figure, Shipwreck w/Parrot, 1985, MOC $70.00

Figure, Slip Stream, 1986, EX, from $6.00 to $8.00.

Figure, Slip Stream, 1987, w/accessories & ID card, EX..$10.00
Figure, Steeler, 1983, MOC.......................................$35.00
Figure, Street Fighter Blanka, 1993, MOC...................$10.00
Figure, Stretcher, 1990, MOC $15.00
Figure, Talking Battle Cobra Commander, 1991, MOC..$12.00
Figure, Tele-Viper, 1985, MOC..................................$42.00
Figure, Tiger Force Roadblock, 1998, w/accessories, EX..$10.00
Figure, Topside, 1990, MOC......................................$15.00
Figure, Tunnel Rat, 1987, MOC $25.00
Figure, Wild Bill, 1992, MOC....................................$10.00
Figure, Zandar, 1986, w/accessories, EX......................$8.00

Gilner

Gilner was a California company that operated in Culver City from the mid-1930s until 1957. They produced florist ware, figurines, and other types of decorative pottery. Their pixie line is very popular with today's collectors.

Figurine, birds, black w/gold speckles & trim, 15½", pr..$50.00
Figurine, pixie, 2¼x3¼" $45.00
Leaf dish, Black native w/metal loop earrings at side, 1952, 4x8"..$50.00
Leaf dish, pixie sits w/thoughtful expression at side, from $30 to..$40.00
Match holder/ashtray, pixie, 5½".............................$45.00
Pine cone dish, 12x12"...$22.00
Planter, angelfish w/reclining pixie, 5½x4" $90.00
Planter, pixie in green sitting on stump.....................$25.00
Planter, pixie lounging before treasure chest.............$60.00
Planter, pixie on log, 3½x6½" $12.50
Planter, pixie w/mushroom, 6x6" $22.00
Planter, train, #623, 5x8"...$80.00
Planter, 2 pixies & heart w/I Love U carved on stump, 3x5".$65.00

Planter, 2 red pixies on brim of hat $55.00
Salt & pepper shakers, pixie boy & girl, 3¼", pr........$32.00
Shelf sitter, pixie in red, 4"..$45.00
Vase, pixie sits on branch of green tree, 5"..................$20.00
Wall pocket, pixie on apple...$40.00
Wall pocket, pixie on bananas $40.00
Wall pocket, pixie on teacup, 4½x6½" $70.00

Wall pocket, pixie on green grapes, marked Gilner, California, 7¾", $50.00. (Photo description Freeda Perkins)

Glass Knives

Popular during the Depression years, glass knives were made in many of the same colors as the glass dinnerware of the era — pink, green, light blue, crystal, and more rarely, amber or white (originally called opal). Some were hand painted with flowers or fruit. The earliest boxes had poems printed on their tops explaining the knife's qualities in the pre-stainless steel days: 'No metal to tarnish when cutting your fruit, and so it is certain this glass knife will suit.' Eventually, a tissue flyer was packed with each knife, which elaborated even more on the knife's usefulness. 'It is keen as a razor, ideal for slicing tomatoes, oranges, lemons, grapefruit and especially constructed for separating the meaty parts of grapefruit from its rind...' Boxes add interest by helping identify distributors as well as commercial names of the knives.

When originally sold, the blades were ground to a sharp cutting edge, but due to everyday usage, the blades eventually became nicked. Collectors will accept reground, resharpened blades as long as the original shape has been maintained.

Documented US glass companies that made glass knives are the Akro Agate Co., Cameron Glass Corp., Houze Glass Corp., Imperial Glass Corp., Jeannette Glass Co., and Westmoreland Glass Co.

Internet final-bid auction prices indicate what a person is willing to pay to add a new or different piece to a personal collection and may not necessarily reflect any price guide values.

Advisor: Michele A. Rosewitz (See Directory, Glass Knives)

BK Co/ESP 12-14-20, crystal, hand-painted handle, 9" $35.00
BK Co/ESP 12-14-20, green, hand-painted handle, 9" .$60.00
Cryst-o-lite (3 Flowers), crystal, 8½" $10.00
Dur-X, 3-leaf, blue, 8½" or 9"...$45.00
Dur-X, 3-leaf, crystal, 8½" or 9"....................................$20.00
Dur-X, 3-leaf, green, 8½" or 9".......................................$45.00
Dur-X, 3-leaf, pink, 8½" or 9"...$45.00
Dur-X, 5-leaf, blue, 9"...$70.00
Dur-X, 5-leaf, crystal, 9"..$35.00
Dur-X, 5-leaf, green, 9"...$60.00
Dur-X, 5-leaf, pink, 9"...$55.00

Imperial Candewick, 8", $500.00. (Photo courtesy Michele A. Rosewitz)

Steel-ite, crystal, 8½"..$35.00
Steel-ite, green, 8½"..$75.00
Steel-ite, pink, 8½"...$70.00
Stonex, amber, 8½" $250.00
Stonex, crystal, 8½" $40.00
Stonex, green, 8½" $80.00
Stonex, opal, 8½" $350.00

Thumbguard, crystal with hand-painted handle, 9", $40.00. (Photo courtesy Michele A. Rosewitz)

Vitex (Star & Diamond), blue, 8½" or 9" $40.00
Vitex (Star & Diamond), crystal, 8½" or 9".................$20.00
Vitex (Star & Diamond), pink, 8½" or 9" $40.00

Golden Foliage

In 1935 Libbey Glass was purchased by Owens-Illinois but continued to operate under the Libbey Glass name. After World War II, the company turned to making tableware and still does today. Golden Foliage is just one of the many patterns made during the 1950s. It is a line of crystal glassware with a satin band that features a golden maple leaf as well as other varieties. The satin band is trimmed in gold, above and below. Since this gold seems to have easily worn off, be careful to find mint pieces for your collection. This pattern was made in silver as well.

Advisor: Debbie Coe (See Directory, Cape Cod)

Drink set, includes 6 jiggers & brass-finished caddy ..**$49.00**
Drink set, includes 8 tumblers (9-oz), ice tub & brass-finished caddy **$75.00**
Drink set, includes 8 tumblers (9-oz) & brass-finished caddy...**$48.00**
Goblet, cocktail; 4-oz...**$6.00**
Goblet, cordial; 1-oz..**$9.50**
Goblet, pilsner; 11-oz..**$9.50**
Goblet, sherbet; 6½-oz..**$4.50**
Goblet, water; 9-oz..**$6.50**
Ice tub, in metal 3-footed frame......................**$22.50**
Pitcher, 5¼", w/metal frame **$16.50**
Salad dressing set, includes 3 bowls (4") & brass-finished caddy **$19.50**
Tumbler, beverage; 12½-oz.................................**$9.50**
Tumbler, cooler; 14-oz...**$9.50**
Tumbler, juice; 6-oz...**$5.00**
Tumbler, old fashioned; 9-oz..............................**$6.00**
Tumbler, water; 10-oz..**$7.50**

Tumbler, jigger; two-ounce, $7.00 each.

Graniteware

Though it really wasn't as durable as its name suggests, there's still a lot of granite ware around today, though much of it is now in collections. You may even be able to find a bargain. The popularity of the 'country' look in home decorating and the exposure it's had in some of the leading decorating magazines has caused granite ware prices, especially on rare items, to soar in recent years.

It's made from a variety of metals coated with enameling of various colors, some solid, others swirled. It's color, form, and, of course, condition that dictates value. Swirls of cobalt and white, purple and white, green and white, and brown and white are unusual, but even solid gray items such as a hanging salt box or a chamberstick can be expensive, because pieces like those are rare. Decorated examples are uncommon — so are children's pieces and salesman's samples.

For further information, we recommend *The Collector's Encyclopedia of Granite Ware, Colors, Shapes, and Values,* by Helen Greguire (Collector Books).

Bowl, dough/salad; red & white lg swirl w/cobalt trim, lightweight, 1960s, NM **$65.00**

Bowl, mixing; yellow & white lg mottle w/black trim, lightweight, 1960s, NM **$65.00**
Bowl, mixing/salad; cobalt & white lg swirl w/black trim, white inside, lg, VG................................**$240.00**
Bowl, vegetable; red & white lg swirl (inside & out), black trim, oblong, 1950s, M **$165.00**
Butter dish, blue vining design on white, round, lg, VG ..**$275.00**
Canister, Sugar in dark blue letters on white, recessed strap handle, VG....................................**$95.00**
Coffee biggin, light blue shading to white, tall style, 4 pcs, complete, NM.......................................**$295.00**
Coffee biggin, solid yellow w/black trim, Bakelite knob on lid, 5 pcs, complete, NM **$395.00**
Coffee boiler, reddish brown & white med mottle, Cream City Garnet Ware...Milwaukee Wis, NM.............**$295.00**

Coffeepot, red and white large swirl with black trim, Bakelite knob, aluminum basket, ca 1950, 8½", M, $265.00. (Photo courtesy Helen Greguire)

Coffeepot, white w/green veining, med mottle, Elite, VG...**$145.00**
Creamer, blue & white lg mottle, blue strap handle, squatty, VG...**$395.00**
Creamer, blue veined chicken wire on white, squatty, VG...**$145.00**
Creamer, cream & green, squatty, NM **$85.00**
Cup & saucer, light blue & white lg mottle w/black trim, VG...**$135.00**
Custard cup, cobalt & white lg swirl w/black trim, white inside bowl, NM **$165.00**
Dipper, blue & white lg swirl w/black trim & handle, deep, rounded bottom, flat hooked handle, NM.........**$115.00**
Fruit jar filler, blue & white lg mottle, NM **$145.00**
Fry pan, red & white lg swirl w/black trim & handle, screwed-on handle, 1970s, sm, M **$125.00**
Grater, gray med mottle, curved shape, VG.............**$325.00**
Grater, gray med mottle, flat, Ideal, NM...................**$525.00**
Ladle, soup; cream w/green handle, M **$20.00**
Ladle, soup; gray med mottle, black turned wood handle, NM M..**$125.00**
Lady finger pan, gray mottle, Agate Nickel Steel Ware, L&G Mfg Co, M **$295.00**
Mold, fish form, solid white, lg, w/ring for hanging, NM...**$175.00**
Mold, fluted oval w/grapes imprints, white, ring for hanging, VG...**$135.00**
Mold, ribbed tube style, gray lg mottle, M **$95.00**

Muffin pan, blue & white lg swirl, white inside, 6-cup, NM .**$595.00**
Muffin pan, gray lg mottle, deep, 8-cup, NM..............**$75.00**
Muffin pan, light blue & white lg swirl allover, 8-cup, VG ...**$295.00**
Mug, blue & white fine mottle w/black trim, white inside, G **$55.00**
Mug, cobalt & white lg swirl, 2-cup, NM....................**$95.00**
Mug, gray med mottle, straight sides, NM..................**$25.00**
Pie plate, cobalt & white lg mottle, solid gray inside, NM..**$75.00**
Pie plate, cobalt & white lg swirl w/black trim, white inside, NM **$115.00**
Pipe plate, cobalt & white lg swirl w/black trim, white inside, deep dish type, VG.....................................**$85.00**
Pitcher, molasses; deep shaded violet, spun knob on lid, covered spout & thumb rest, NM........................**$265.00**
Pitcher, water; blue & white lg swirl w/black handle & trim, white inside, NM....................................**$225.00**
Pitcher, water; green shaded to cream w/black handle & trim, white inside, NM.................................**$325.00**
Plate, red & white lg swirl (inside & out), black trim, lightweight, 1960s, M...**$35.00**
Plate, yellow & white lg swirl (inside & out), black trim, lightweight, 1960s, 7¼", M...............................**$35.00**
Saucer, blue & white med mottle w/dark blue trim, VG ..**$35.00**
Scoop, spice; gray med mottle, pierced back, riveted strap handle & body, VG **$265.00**
Scoop, thumb; gray lg mottle, M................................**$195.00**
Skimmer, cobalt & white med mottle w/green veins, black handle, perforations in bowl, NM **$195.00**
Skimmer, white w/blue veins allover, perforated, NM..**$60.00**
Soup mug, cobalt & white lg swirl w/black trim, white inside, w/lid, lightweight, 1960s, M.......................**$75.00**
Spatula, gray lg mottle, top of spatula is tapered, NM...**$95.00**
Spoon, blue & white lg swirl, black handle, white inside bowl, VG **$125.00**
Spoon, mixing; blue & white lg mottle w/black handle, white inside bowl, VG **$65.00**
Syrup, gray & white lg mottle, NM **$215.00**
Syrup, white, nickel-over-brass lid & thumb rest, VG .**$195.00**
Teapot, blue & white fine mottle, 'Belle' shape, seamless, VG **$425.00**
Teapot, cobalt & white lg swirl, wooden handle, matching granite ribbed lid, M....................................**$525.00**
Teapot, gray med mottle, welded handle, lg gooseneck spout, M **$135.00**
Teapot, pink roses on white, brown trim, brass-plated thumb rest, NM **$175.00**
Teapot, red & white med swirl w/black trim, 1960s, M..**$125.00**
Teapot, white w/green veins, med swirl, Snow on the Mountain, Elite-Austria, VG............................**$225.00**
Teapot, white w/pewter trim, squatty, copper-trimmed bottom, M **$225.00**
Tray, gray med mottle, oval, NM................................**$165.00**
Tumbler, cobalt & white lg swirl w/black trim, white inside, VG **$450.00**
Utensil rack, light gray med mottle, holds 3 utensils, VG **$295.00**
Wash basin, gray lg mottle, w/eyelet, lg, VG............**$125.00**

Griswold Cast-Iron Cooking Ware

Late in the 1800s, the Griswold company introduced a line of cast-iron cooking ware that was eventually distributed on a large scale nationwide. Today's collectors appreciate the variety of skillets, cornstick pans, Dutch ovens, and griddles available to them, and many still enjoy using them to cook with.

Several marks have been used; most contain the Griswold name, though some were marked simply 'Erie.'

If you intend to use your cast iron, you can clean it safely by using any commercial oven cleaner. (Be sure to re-season it before you cook in it.) A badly pitted, rusty piece may leave you with no other recourse than to remove what rust you can with a wire brush, paint the surface black, and find an alternate use for it around the house. For instance, you might use a kettle to hold a large floor plant or some magazines. A small griddle or skillet would be attractive as part of a wall display in a country kitchen. It should be noted that prices are given for pieces in excellent condition. Items that are cracked, chipped, pitted, or warped are worth substantially less or nothing at all, depending on rarity.

Advisors: Grant Windsor (See Directory, Griswold)

Aebleskiver, #32, fully marked....................................**$35.00**
Ashtray, #770, square **$20.00**
Bowl, patty; #72...**$30.00**
Bowl, scotch; #3, slant/Erie trademark.......................**$45.00**
Bowl, Yankee; #3, Erie trademark **$65.00**
Bread stick pan, #22, fully marked **$25.00**
Cake mold, lamb, #866 ....**$100.00**
Cake mold, rabbit..**$275.00**
Cornstick pan, #273..**$20.00**
Dutch oven, #6, Tite-Top, w/top writing cover & trivet **$400.00**
Gas hot plate, #320, w/20" tall stand **$125.00**
Gem pan, #8, slant/EPU trademark............................**$200.00**
Griddle, #7, handle, block trademark **$35.00**
Griddle, #8, long, block trademark **$45.00**
Lemon squeezer, #2 Classic **$125.00**
Muffin pan, #10, pattern #949 w/cutouts....................**$30.00**
Muffin pan, #15, narrow band, fully marked **$250.00**
Muffin pan, #270, corn/wheat stick **$325.00**
Plett pan, #34, sm trademark **$20.00**
Popover pan, #18, wide handle, fully marked...........**$65.00**
Roaster, #5, oval, w/trivet & full writing cover **$400.00**
Sad iron, Griswold Erie, 5½-lb **$85.00**
Skillet, #0, early handle, block trademark **$75.00**
Skillet, #4, slant/Erie trademark................................**$100.00**
Skillet, #5, heat ring, slant/EPU trademark **$40.00**
Skillet, #6, Erie trademark **$100.00**
Skillet, #7, heat ring, block trademark **$50.00**
Skillet, #8, smooth bottom, block trademark..............**$25.00**
Skillet, #10, slant/EPU trademark **$100.00**
Skillet, #12, Griswold's Erie trademark **$225.00**
Skillet, #14, slant/EPU trademark **$800.00**

Skillet, breakfast; 5 in 1	**$150.00**
Skillet, snack; #42	**$30.00**
Skillet, utility; #768, square	**$45.00**
Skillet cover, #4 high dome, smooth	**$600.00**
Skillet cover, #8 high dome, raised letters	**$50.00**
Skillet cover, #12, low-top, writing	**$250.00**
Skillet griddle, #109, slant/EPU trademark	**$125.00**

Stick pan, #954, 11-stick, $25.00.

Trivet, #1739, lg coffeepot	**$100.00**
Trivet, #1740, star	**$35.00**
Trivet, #8, Dutch Oven	**$25.00**
Waffle iron, #11, square w/high bailed base	**$100.00**
Waffle iron, #8 American (#885 & #886), w/low side handle ring (#975)	**$45.00**

Guardian Ware

The Guardian Service Company was in business from 1935 until 1955. They produced a very successful line of hammered aluminum that's just as popular today as it ever was. (Before 1935 Century Metalcraft made similar ware under the name SilverSeal, you'll occasionally see examples of it as well.) Guardian Service was sold though the home party plan, and special hostess gifts were offered as incentives. Until 1940 metal lids were used, but during the war when the government restricted the supply of available aluminum, glass lids were introduced. The cookware was very versatile, and one of their selling points was top-of-the-stove baking and roasting — 'no need to light the oven.' Many items had more than one use. For instance, their large turkey roaster came with racks and could be used for canning as well. The kettle oven used for stove-top baking also came with canning racks. Their Economy Trio set featured three triangular roasters that fit together on a round tray, making it possible to cook three foods at once on only one burner; for even further fuel economy, the casserole tureen could be stacked on top of that. Projections on the sides of the pans accommodated two styles of handles, a standard detachable utility handle as well as black 'mouse ear' handles for serving.

The company's logo is a knight with crossed weapons, and if you find a piece with a trademark that includes the words 'Patent Pending,' you'll know you have one of the earlier pieces.

In 1955 National Presto purchased the company and tried to convince housewives that the new stainless steel pans were superior to their tried-and-true Guardian aluminum, but the ladies would have none of it. In 1980 Tad and Suzie Kohara bought the rights to the Guardian Service name as well as the original molds. The new company is based in California, and is presently producing eight of the original pieces, canning racks, pressure cooker parts, serving handles, and replacement glass lids. Quoting their literature: 'Due to the age of the GS glass molds, we are unable to provide perfect glass covers. The covers may appear to have cracks or breaks on the surface. They are not breaks but mold marks and should be as durable as the originals.' They go on to say: 'These glass covers are not oven proof.' These mold marks may be a good way to distinguish the old glass lids from the new, and collectors tell us that the original lids have a green hue to the glass. The new company has also reproduced three cookbooks, one that shows the line with the original metal covers. If you want to obtain replacements, see the Directory for Guardian Service Cookware.

Be sure to judge condition when evaluating Guardian Service. Wear, baked-on grease, scratches, and obvious signs of use devaluate its worth. Our prices range from pieces in average to exceptional condition. To be graded exceptional, the interior of the pan must have no pitting and the surface must be bright and clean. An item with a metal lid is worth approximately 25% more than the same piece with a glass lid.

Advisor: Dennis S. McAdams (See the Directory, Guardian Service Cookware)

Kettle oven, 8x12", with bail handle, glass lid, from $135.00 to $165.00. (Photo courtesy Marilyn Jewell, Revelry Antiques & Collectibles)

Ashtray, glass, w/knight & white stars logo, hostess gift, from $25 to	**$30.00**
Beverage urn (coffeepot), glass lid, no screen or dripper, common	**$20.00**
Beverage urn (coffeepot), glass lid, w/screen & dripper, 15"	**$50.00**
Can of cleaner, unopened	**$15.00**
Cookbook, Guardian Service or Pressure Cooker, from $20 to	**$35.00**
Cookbook, Silver Seal, 1936, 48-pg, EX	**$45.00**
Dome cooker, Tom Thumb; glass lid, w/handles, 3½x4⅞", from $25 to	**$35.00**

Dome cooker, 1-qt, glass lid, w/handles, 6¾" dia, from $25 to **$45.00**

Dome cooker, 2-qt, glass lid, w/handles, 4½x10½" dia, from $35 to **$50.00**

Dome cooker, 4-qt, glass lid, w/handles, 6½x10½" dia, from $35 to..**$55.00**

Fryer, breakfast; glass lid, 10", from $45 to **$60.00**

Fryer, chicken; glass lid, 12", from $75 to **$100.00**

Gravy boat, w/undertray, from $30 to **$50.00**

Griddle broiler, octagonal, w/handles, polished center, 16½" dia, from $20 to **$35.00**

Handle, clamp-on style, from $10 to............................**$15.00**

Handles, slip-on style, Bakelite, pr, from $20 to.........**$35.00**

Ice bucket, glass lid, liner & tongs, 9", from $50 to ...**$90.00**

Kettle oven, glass lid, bail handle, w/rack, 8x12" dia, from $135 to..**$165.00**

Omelet pan, hinged in center, black handle on each half, from $75 to...**$100.00**

Pot, triangular, glass lid, 7" to top of finial, 11" L, from $25 to **$45.00**

Pressure cooker, from $125 to.....................................**$165.00**

Roaster, glass lid, 4x15" L, from $85 to......................**$100.00**

Roaster, turkey; glass lid, no rack, 16½" L, from $100 to...**$135.00**

Roaster, turkey; glass lid, w/rack, 16½" L, from $125 to.**$165.00**

Service kit, w/3 cleaners, 1 brush, 1 cookbook, 1 clamp-on handle, pr of slip-on handles, steel wool, from $125 to **$150.00**

Tray, serving; hammered center, w/handles, 13" dia, from $20 to...**$30.00**

Tray/platter, w/handles, hammered surface, also used as roaster cover for stacking, 10x15" L, from $25 to............**$35.00**

Tumblers, glassware, stylized knight & shield in silver, & coasters w/embossed head of knight, 4 of each in metal rack **$80.00**

Tumblers & ashtray/coasters, glassware w/Guardian logo, white stars & gold trim, hostess gift, 6 of each, from $275 to...**$325.00**

Tureen, casserole; glass lid, from $65 to **$90.00**

Tureen, bottom; glass lid, from $40 to.........................**$65.00**

Tureen, top; glass lid, from $30 to **$45.00**

Gurley Candle Company

Gurley candles were cute little wax figures designed to celebrate holidays and special occasions. They are all marked Gurley on the bottom. They were made so well and had so much great detail that people decided to keep them year after year to decorate with instead of burning them. Woolworth's and other five-and-dime stores sold them from about 1940 until the 1970s. They're still plentiful today and inexpensive.

Tavern Novelty Candles were actually owned by Gurley. They were similar to the Gurley candles but not quite as detailed. All are marked Tavern on the bottom. Prices listed here are for unburned candles with no fading.

Advisor: Debbie Coe (See Directory, Cape Cod)

Christmas, angel, marked Gurley, 3" **$3.50**

Christmas, angel, marked Gurley, 5" **$8.50**

Christmas, baby angel on half moon, marked Gurley, 2½" **$10.00**

Christmas, Black caroler man w/red clothes, 3"............**$8.50**

Christmas, blue grotto w/star, angel & baby, 4½" **$10.00**

Christmas, caroler man w/red clothes, 7" **$8.50**

Christmas, caroler set: lamppost, girl & boy carolers w/song books, cello player, in package...........................**$35.00**

Christmas, choir boy or girl, 2¾", ea............................**$6.00**

Christmas, green candelabrum w/red candle, 5"...........**$7.50**

Christmas, grotto w/shepherd & sheep.......................**$14.50**

Christmas, lamppost, yellow cap & garland, 5½"..........**$6.00**

Christmas, reindeer, marked Tavern, 3½" **$2.50**

Christmas, Rudolph w/red nose, 3"...............................**$2.50**

Christmas, Santa, 6¼" **$12.00**

Christmas, Santa sitting on present on sled, 3" **$12.50**

Christmas, snowman running w/red hat, 3" **$8.50**

Christmas, snowman w/red pipe & green hat, 5" **$5.00**

Christmas, white church w/choir boy inside, 6" **$12.50**

Christmas, 3" deer standing in front of candle, 5"........**$6.50**

Easter, chick, pink or yellow, 3" **$5.00**

Easter, pink birdhouse w/yellow bird, 3" **$7.50**

Easter, pink egg w/bunny inside, 3" **$10.00**

Easter, pink egg w/squirrel inside, 3" **$12.00**

Easter, pink winking rabbit w/carrot, 3¼" **$3.50**

Easter, rabbit, pink or yellow, 3" **$5.00**

Easter, white lily w/blue lip & green candle, 3"............**$4.00**

Halloween, black cat (4") w/orange candlestick beside it ..**$18.00**

Halloween, black owl on orange stump, 3½" **$8.00**

Halloween, Frankenstein, later issue but harder to find, 6", MIB, $24.00.

Halloween, pumpkin w/black cat, 2½" **$8.00**

Halloween, pumpkin-face scarecrow, 5"........................**$8.50**

Halloween, skeleton, 8½" **$29.50**

Halloween, white ghost, 5"...**$18.00**

Halloween, witch, black, 8" **$18.50**

Halloween, witch w/black cape, 3½" $8.50

Halloween, 4" cut-out orange owl w/7½" black candle behind it $20.00

Other Holidays, birthday boy, marked Tavern, 3" $6.00

Other Holidays, bride & groom, 4½", ea....................$12.50

Other Holidays, Eskimo & igloo, marked Tavern, 2-pc..$10.00

Other Holidays, Western girl or boy, 3", ea..................$8.50

Thanksgiving, acorns & leaves, 3½"...........................$6.50

Thanksgiving, gold sailing ship, 7½".........................$10.00

Thanksgiving, Indian boy & girl, brown & green clothes, 5", pr..$30.00

Thanksgiving, Pilgrim girl or boy, 2½", ea $4.50

Thanksgiving, turkey, 2½"..$2.50

Thanksgiving, turkey, 5¾" $15.00

Hadley, M. A.

Since 1940, the M.A. Hadley Pottery (Louisville, Tennessee) has been producing handmade dinnerware and decorative items painted freehand in a folky style with barnyard animals, baskets, whales, and sailing ships in a soft pastel palette of predominately blues and greens. Each piece is signed by hand with the first two initials and last name of artist-turned-potter Mary Alice Hadley, who has personally created each design. Some items may carry an amusing message in the bottom — for instance, 'Please Fill Me' in a canister or 'The End' in a coffee cup! Examples of this ware are beginning to turn up on the secondary market, and it's being snapped up not only by collectors who have to 'have it all' but by those who enjoy adding a decorative touch to a country-style room with only a few pieces of this unique pottery.

Horses and pigs seem to be popular subject matter; unusual pieces and the older, heavier examples command the higher prices.

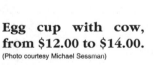
Egg cup with cow, from $12.00 to $14.00.
(Photo courtesy Michael Sessman)

Bank, penny; cow, 3x5x6½" $22.00

Bean pot, cow on 1 side, pig on other, w/lid, 6x9" ...$50.00

Bowl, cereal; cowboy twirling rope, 5" $22.00

Bowl, Our Dog, 2½ x7¾" $35.00

Butter dish, cow, w/dome lid, 4"x6⅜" dia $35.00

Canister set, flour, sugar, coffee & tea, flowers & scrollwork, EX $125.00

Casserole, cow & pig, 'The End' inside, w/lid, 5x10"..$55.00

Casserole, farm scene, pig & cow on lid, 5½ x8" $50.00

Casserole, whale & ship on lid, 'The End' inside, signed inside lid, 11" $60.00

Coffeepot, horse, w/lid, 8"...$165.00

Cookie jar, English cottage shape, Country pattern, 7½ x8" .$100.00

Creamer & sugar bowl, horse, ¼-pt..........................$35.00

Egg cup, horse, 4¼" $20.00

Egg cup, tall blue ship, double $22.00

Flowerpot, farmhouse, 5x5½"....................................$25.00

Gravy boat, cow, 3"...$48.00

Pie plate, horse, 1½" deep, 9" dia............................$45.00

Pitcher, character w/facial features, 6½" $27.00

Pitcher, cow, 'The End' inside, 7"...............................$45.00

Pitcher, house, w/lid, 6½"...$40.00

Plate, cake; 'Happy Anniversary,' 13" dia $55.00

Plate, clock, 7¾" $12.00

Plate, cowboy by campfire, 8" $22.00

Plate, dinner; house, 11" $20.00

Plate, dinner; wife, 11" $25.00

Plate, flag & firecrackers, 'Happy 4th of July,' 4"........$25.00

Plate, graduation; 'Congratulations,' 4"......................$25.00

Plate, luncheon; farmer, 9".......................................$20.00

Plate, luncheon; pig, 9"..$20.00

Platter, horse, oval, 11x7"..$50.00

Platter, horse, 1½" deep, oval, 14x9" $60.00

Razor blade holder, 'Razor Blades' on front, 4⅝" $28.00

Salt & pepper shakers, chicken shape, 5½", pr $35.00

Salt & pepper shakers, cow on salt, horse on pepper, 4⅜", pr $25.00

Shaker, cinnamon/sugar; 4½" $30.00

Tea tile, sheep, 6½"...$22.00

Hagen-Renaker

This California-based company has been in business since 1946, first in Monrovia, later in San Dimas. They're most famous for their models of animals and birds, some of which were miniatures, and some that were made on a larger scale. Many bear paper labels (if they're large enough to accommodate them), others were attached to squares of heavy paper printed with the name of the company. They also used an incised 'HR' and a stamped 'Hagen-Renaker.' In addition to the animals, they made replicas of characters from several popular Disney films under license from the Disney Studio.

Advisor: Gayle Roller (See Directory, Hagen-Renaker)

Newsletter: The Hagen-Renaker Collector's Club Newsletter c/o Jenny Palmer
3651 Polish Line Rd.
Cheboygan, MI 49721-9045

Figurine, Champ, satin matt glaze, from Pedigree Dogs line, no mark, 5", **$50.00.** (Photo courtesy Jack Chipman)

Figurine, An How (Siamese kitten), Monrovia, 4x3½"..**$30.00**

Figurine, bear papa, sitting, brown w/pinkish-beige ears & feet pads, yellow bow, Monrovia, 1949-50, 2x1¾"........**$30.00**

Figurine, Beau (Beagle dog), sitting male, Monrovia, 2½"..**$30.00**

Figurine, Beep (duckling), Monrovia, 2½ x2" **$20.00**

Figurine, Bingo (duckling), Monrovia, 2x2"................**$20.00**

Figurine, Bonnie (Collie), 1953......................................**$45.00**

Figurine, caterpillar family, mama w/4 babies, detailed faces, Monrovia, 1",½"...**$30.00**

Figurine, chicken family: rooster, hen & 2 chicks, 2", 1¼", ⅝"..**$20.00**

Figurine, Circus dog begging, 1955-56, 1½ x⅝"..........**$35.00**

Figurine, Country Mouse, yellow shawl w/patches, carries basket, very detailed, Monrovia, 3" **$20.00**

Figurine, Dash (Cocker Spaniel pup), 1959, 2½" **$55.00**

Figurine, Donald Duck, Disney, #5021, 1¾" **$140.00**

Figurine, donkey mama, walking, gray tones, 2"........**$20.00**

Figurine, Encore (Arabian horse), M Love, 5½"........**$160.00**

Figurine, Fez (horse), lying foal, Monrovia, 2¾x4¼" ...**$150.00**

Figurine, Forever Amber (horse), 5" **$135.00**

Figurine, frog playing piano, 2 pcs, frog, 1¼"; piano, 1⅜".....**$8.75**

Figurine, Harry (donkey foal), gray matt, 4" **$35.00**

Figurine, Jiggs (Boxer dog), w/ball, 2" **$40.00**

Figurine, Lippett (horse), Monrovia, 6¼x7¼"............**$160.00**

Figurine, Max (Boxer pup), 1¾".................................**$30.00**

Figurine, moose, cartoon-like figure, A-39, 2¼"..........**$20.00**

Figurine, Nobby (Bulldog pup), 2"..............................**$40.00**

Figurine, Pam & Bing (bulldogs), 1953, 2x3", pr **$72.50**

Figurine, parrot on branch, wings spread, recently discontinued, 4" **$18.00**

Figurine, Persian cat, papa, fluffy w/tail out, A-353, 1¾"..**$30.00**

Figurine, Quan Tiki (Siamese kitten), 3¾x2½" **$30.00**

Figurine, Roughneck (Morgan horse), B-550, 4½"......**$65.00**

Figurine, Sparkle (Persian cat), 6x2¼" **$30.00**

Figurine, zebra mama, A-173, 1983-86, 1½" **$20.00**

Shelf sitter, Alice in Wonderland, Disney, 3⅛"..........**$250.00**

Hall China Company

Hall China is still in production in East Liverpool, Ohio, where they have been located since around the turn of the century. They have produced literally hundreds of lines of kitchen and dinnerware items for both home and commercial use. Many of these have become very collectible.

They're especially famous for their teapots, some of which were shaped like automobiles, basketballs, doughnuts, etc. Each teapot was made in an assortment of colors, often trimmed in gold. Many were decaled to match their dinnerware lines. Some are quite rare, and collecting them all would be a real challenge.

During the 1950s, Eva Zeisel designed dinnerware shapes with a streamlined, ultra-modern look. Her lines, Classic and Century, were used with various decals as the basis for several of Hall's dinnerware patterns. She also designed kitchenware lines with the same modern styling. They were called Casual Living and Tri-Tone. All her designs are very popular with today's collectors, especially those with an interest in the movement referred to as '50s modern.'

Although some of the old kitchenware shapes and teapots are being produced today, you'll be able to tell them from the old pieces by the backstamp. To identify these new issues, Hall marks them with the shaped rectangular 'Hall' trademark they've used since the early 1970s.

For more information, we recommend *The Collector's Encyclopedia of Hall China* by Margaret and Kenn Whitmyer.

Newsletter: *Hall China Collector's Club Newsletter*
P.O. Box 360488, Cleveland, OH 44136

Acacia, bean pot, New England, #4 ....**$110.00**

Arizona, ashtray, Tomorrow's Classic............................**$6.00**

Arizona, bowl, celery; oval, Tomorrow's Classic.........**$15.00**

Arizona, casserole, Tomorrow's Classic, 2-qt..............**$35.00**

Arizona, jug, Tomorrow's Classic, 3-qt......................**$27.00**

Arizona, vinegar bottle, Tomorrow's Classic...............**$27.00**

Beauty, bowl, salad; 12"...**$40.00**

Beauty, marmite, w/lid..**$37.00**

Blue Blossom, canister, Radiance...............................**$190.00**

Blue Blossom, casserole, Sundial, #1 ....**$60.00**

Blue Blossom, jug, Five Band, 1½-pt............................**$60.00**

Blue Blossom, salt & pepper shakers, Five Band, pr .**$50.00**

Blue Bouquet, bean pot, New England, #4..............**$125.00**

Blue Bouquet, bowl, Thick Rim, 8½" **$30.00**

Blue Bouquet, cup, D-style...**$12.00**

Blue Bouquet, jug, Radiance **$80.00**

Blue Bouquet, plate, D-style, 9" **$14.00**

Blue Bouquet, soup tureen..**$290.00**

Blue Crocus, bowl, straight sided, 9" **$27.00**

Blue Crocus, salt & pepper shakers, handled, pr **$60.00**

Blue Floral, bowl, 7¾" **$14.00**

Blue Floral, bowl, 9"...**$18.00**

Blue Garden, butter dish, Zephyr, 1-lb.....................**$450.00**

Blue Garden, creamer, New York **$25.00**

Blue Garden, jug, ball; #4...**$90.00**

Blue Garden, teapot, Airflow......................................**$235.00**

Blue Garden, teapot, Philadelphia, 5-cup..................**$325.00**

Blue Willow, casserole, 5"...**$45.00**

Bouquet, ashtray, Tomorrow's Classic **$10.00**

Bouquet, bowl, vegetable; open, Tomorrow's Classic, 8¾" square **$21.00**

Bouquet, platter, Tomorrow's Classic, 17" **$35.00**

Buckingham, bowl, baker; open, Tomorrow's Classic, 11-oz **$16.00**

Buckingham, bowl, cereal; Tomorrow's Classic, 6".......**$9.00**

Buckingham, casserole, Tomorrow's Classic, 1¼-qt....**$35.00**

Buckingham, marmite, Tomorrow's Classic, w/lid......**$30.00**

Buckingham, vase, Tomorrow's Classic **$35.00**

Cactus, bowl, Five Band, 8¾"...**$27.00**

Cactus, jug, Five Band, 2-qt..**$60.00**

Cameo Rose, bowl, fruit; E-style, 5¼".............................**$6.50**

Cameo Rose, bowl, vegetable; round, E-style, 9"........**$22.00**

Cameo Rose, butter dish, E-style, ¼-lb.........................**$50.00**

Cameo Rose, gravy boat, E-style, w/underplate.........**$32.00**

Cameo Rose, plate, E-style, 6½"......................................**$4.00**

Cameo Rose, plate, E-style, 9¼".......................................**$9.00**

Cameo Rose, platter, oval, E-style, 11¼".....................**$16.00**

Cameo Rose, platter, oval, E-style, 13¼".....................**$18.00**

Caprice, bowl, cereal; Tomorrow's Classic, 6"..............**$7.00**

Caprice, candlestick, Tomorrow's Classic, 4½"...........**$22.00**

Caprice, Dinner plate, $6.50; Bowl, 9", $10.00; Cup and saucer, $8.00.

Caprice, platter, Tomorrow's Classic, 15" **$22.00**

Carrot/Golden Carrot, bowl, Radiance, 9" **$32.00**

Carrot/Golden Carrot, salt & pepper shakers, Five Band, pr **$22.00**

Christmas Tree & Holly, creamer, Irish coffee; E-style, 3-oz..**$22.00**

Christmas Tree & Holly, cup, E-style **$18.00**

Christmas Tree & Holly, tidbit, E-style, 2-tier **$55.00**

Clover (Pink), bowl, Thick Rim, 6" **$12.00**

Clover (Pink), jug, Medallion...**$60.00**

Clover/Golden Clover, casserole, round, #70, 10" **$55.00**

Clover/Golden Clover, teapot, Windshield................**$185.00**

Crocus, baker, French, fluted..**$22.00**

Crocus, bread box, metal...**$45.00**

Crocus, coffee dispenser, metal.....................................**$25.00**

Crocus, creamer, Medallion..**$16.00**

Crocus, leftover, rectangular **$55.00**

Crocus, plate, D-style, 6"...**$6.00**

Crocus, sugar bowl, Modern, w/lid...............................**$25.00**

Crocus, tidbit, D-style, 3-tier...**$60.00**

Eggshell, bean pot, Dot, New England, #3.................**$95.00**

Eggshell, casserole, Plaid or Swag, oval, 9¾"............**$50.00**

Eggshell, custard, Dot...**$9.00**

Eggshell, pretzel jar, Dot w/ivory body.....................**$110.00**

Fantasy, baker, rectangular...**$90.00**

Fantasy, bean pot, New England, #4 ....**$140.00**

Fantasy, bowl, fruit; Tomorrow's Classic, 5¾".............**$5.00**

Fantasy, creamer, morning set **$32.00**

Fantasy, creamer, Tomorrow's Classic...........................**$9.00**

Fantasy, jug, Donut **$195.00**

Fantasy, jug, Tomorrow's Classic, 1¼-qt.....................**$25.00**

Fantasy, sugar bowl, Tomorrow's Classic, w/lid **$16.00**

Fantasy, syrup, Sundial..**$150.00**

Fern, jug, Century **$18.00**

Fern, ladle, Century **$10.00**

Five Band, bowl, red or cobalt, 7¼"..............................**$18.00**

Five Band, casserole, colors other than red or cobalt, 8"..**$25.00**

Five Band, cookie jar, red or cobalt...............................**$85.00**

Flamingo, bowl, batter; Five Band **$95.00**

Flamingo teapot, Streamline **$310.00**

Flareware, bowl, Gold Lace, 6".......................................**$7.00**

Flareware, bowl, Radial, 8" **$7.00**

Flareware, casserole, Autumn Leaf, 3-pt **$10.00**

Flareware, cookie jar, Heather Rose.............................**$30.00**

Floral Lattice, cookie jar, Five Band **$150.00**

Floral Lattice, tea tile, round, 6" **$55.00**

French Flower, coffeepot, Washington.........................**$65.00**

French Flower, teapot, McCormick **$110.00**

Frost Flowers, ashtray, Tomorrow's Classic **$6.00**

Frost Flowers, egg cup, Tomorrow's Classic **$27.00**

Frost Flowers, gravy boat, Tomorrow's Classic **$27.00**

Frost Flowers, vase, Tomorrow's Classic......................**$30.00**

Game Bird, bowl, fruit; E-style, 5½".................................**$8.00**

Game Bird, bowl, Thick Rim, china, 8½" **$22.00**

Game Bird, cup, E-style **$14.00**

Game Bird, teapot, Windshield **$165.00**

Gold Label, bowl, salad; 9"..**$18.00**

Gold Label, teapot, Aladdin, Swag **$95.00**

Golden Glo, bowl, salad; 9¾"...**$14.00**

Golden Glo, mug, #343...**$12.00**

Harlequin, bowl, celery; oval, Tomorrow's Classic **$16.00**

Harlequin, jug, ball; #3, Tomorrow's Classic **$85.00**

Harlequin, plate, Tomorrow's Classic, 6" **$3.50**

Harlequin, vase, Tomorrow's Classic............................**$27.00**

Heather Rose, bowl, cereal; E-style, 6¼" **$6.00**

Heather Rose, bowl, Flare-shape, E-style, 8¾"............**$15.00**

Heather Rose, coffeepot, Washington, E-style, 30-oz..**$45.00**

Heather Rose, jug, Irish coffee; E-style **$16.00**

Heather Rose, plate, E-style, 10".....................................**$8.50**

Heather Rose, platter, oval, E-style, 15½" **$20.00**

Holiday, ashtray, Tomorrow's Classic...........................**$6.50**

Holiday, candlestick, Tomorrow's Classic, 8" **$30.00**

Holiday, plate, Tomorrow's Classic, 8"..........................**$5.00**

Holiday, vinegar bottle, Tomorrow's Classic $30.00
Homewood, bowl, fruit; D-style, 5½" $5.50
Homewood, bowl, Radiance, 9" $20.00
Homewood, salt & pepper shakers, handled, pr $36.00
Homewood, saucer, D-style $1.50
Lyric/Mulberry, ashtray, Tomorrow's Classic $8.00
Lyric/Mulberry, butter dish, Tomorrow's Classic $80.00
Lyric/Mulberry, egg cup, Tomorrow's Classic..............$25.00
Lyric/Mulberry, platter, Tomorrow's Classic, 15" $25.00
Meadow Flower, custard, Thick Rim...........................$16.00
Meadow Flower, jug, ball; #4 ....$110.00
Medallion, bowl, Lettuce, #3, 6" $9.00
Medallion, casserole, ivory.......................................$11.00
Medallion, jug, w/ice lip, colors other than Lettuce or ivory,
    5-pt..$35.00
Medallion, teapot, Lettuce, 64-oz.............................$90.00
Morning Glory, bowl, straight sides, 9" $25.00
Morning Glory, bowl, Thick Rim, 6" $13.00
Morning Glory, teapot, Aladdin................................$125.00
Mums, bowl, flat soup; D-style, 8½" $16.00
Mums, bowl, Radiance, 9"..$22.00
Mums, casserole, Radiance..$37.00
Mums, creamer, Art Deco...$20.00
Mums, custard, New York..$16.00
Mums, drip jar, Medallion, w/lid $27.00
Mums, gravy boat, D-style $27.00
Mums, pie baker..$32.00
Mums, plate, D-style, 8¼" $6.50
Mums, saucer, D-style..$2.50
Mums, sugar bowl, Medallion, w/lid...........................$22.00
Mums, teapot, Rutherford $180.00
No 488, bowl, Radiance, 6"..$14.00
No 488, bowl, round, D-style, 9¼" $37.50
No 488, cocette, handled $30.00
No 488, drip coffeepot, Radiance.............................$250.00
No 488, jug, ball; #3 ....$125.00
No 488, jug, Medallion $70.00
No 488, salt & pepper shakers, Teardrop, pr $36.00
No 488, saucer, D-style..$2.50
Orange Poppy, bowl, fruit; C-style, 5½" $7.00
Orange Poppy, bowl, Radiance, 6" $12.00
Orange Poppy, bowl, vegetable; C-style, round, 9¼"...$35.00
Orange Poppy, bread box, metal $50.00
Orange Poppy, cake plate $28.00
Orange Poppy, coffeepot, Great American..................$55.00
Orange Poppy, custard..$7.00
Orange Poppy, leftover, loop handle...........................$55.00
Orange Poppy, salt & pepper shakers, handled, pr ...$32.00
Orange Poppy, saucer, C-style....................................$3.00
Orange Poppy, teapot, Donut $350.00
Orange Poppy, wastebasket, metal.............................$50.00
Pastel Morning Glory, bowl, cereal; D-style, 6" $10.00
Pastel Morning Glory, cup, D-style $11.00
Pastel Morning Glory, cup, St Denis $35.00
Pastel Morning Glory, jug, ball; #3.............................$110.00
Pastel Morning Glory, jug, Donut $150.00
Pastel Morning Glory, saucer, D-style $2.50

Pastel Morning Glory, teapot, New York.................$160.00
Peach Blossom, bowl, cereal; Tomorrow's Classic, 6" ..$7.50
Peach Blossom, cup, Tomorrow's Classic.....................$7.00
Peach Blossom, gravy boat, Tomorrow's Classic $25.00
Peach Blossom, vase, Tomorrow's Classic..................$32.00
Pert, bean pot, Chinese Red, tab handles..................$60.00
Pert, creamer, Cadet..$9.00
Pert, jug, Cadet, 7½"..$13.00
Pinecone, ashtray, Tomorrow's Classic $6.00
Pinecone, bowl, fruit; E-style, 5¼"...............................$6.50
Pinecone, creamer, Tomorrow's Classic.....................$11.00
Pinecone, salt & pepper shakers, Tomorrow's Classic, pr..$20.00
Pinecone, saucer, E-style $1.50
Primrose, ashtray, E-style $10.00
Primrose, cake plate, E-style $15.00
Primrose, jug, Rayed, E-style $16.00
Primrose, sugar bowl, E-style, w/lid $14.00
Red Poppy, bowl, fruit; D-style, 5½"..............................$5.50
Red Poppy, bowl, Radiance, 7½" $16.00
Red Poppy, bowl, round, D-style, 9¼" $30.00
Red Poppy, cake safe, metal.......................................$35.00
Red Poppy, canister, glass, 1-gal $30.00
Red Poppy, creamer, Daniel $15.00
Red Poppy, jug, ball; #3...$60.00
Red Poppy, jug, milk/syrup; Daniel, 4" $47.00
Red Poppy, mixer cover, plastic $27.00
Red Poppy, pie baker...$35.00
Red Poppy, plate, D-style, 10".....................................$45.00

Red Poppy, salt and pepper shakers, handled, $34.00 for the pair.

Red Poppy, sugar bowl, Modern, w/lid.......................$25.00
Red Poppy, tablecloth, cotton $125.00
Ribbed, bowl, colors other than russet or red, 9½"....$10.00
Ribbed, bowl, salad; russet or red, 9" $18.00
Ribbed, ramekin, russet or red, 6-oz...........................$5.00
Ribbed, teapot, russet or red, Rutherford $210.00
Rose Parade, bowl, straight sides, 6"..........................$15.00
Rose Parade, casserole, tab handled $35.00
Rose Parade, drip jar, tab handled, w/lid $27.00
Rose Parade, teapot, Pert, 4-cup.................................$35.00
Rose White, bowl, Medallion, 8½"................................$22.00
Rose White, teapot, Pert, 6-cup $40.00
Royal Rose, bowl, straight sides, 6"..............................$16.00
Royal Rose, salt & pepper shakers, handled, pr $32.00
Rx, butter dish, ¼-lb..$55.00
Rx, saucer $3.00

Sear's Arlington, bowl, fruit; E-style, 5¼".............**$4.00**
Sear's Arlington, bowl, vegetable; E-style, w/lid.........**$28.00**
Sear's Arlington, plate, E-style, 7¼"................**$4.50**
Sear's Arlington, platter, oval, E-style, 11¼" **$14.00**
Sear's Arlington, saucer, E-style.................**$1.50**
Sear's Fairfax, bowl, cereal; E-style, 6¼".................**$6.00**
Sear's Fairfax, cup, E-style................**$5.00**
Sear's Fairfax, plate, E-style, 10" **$7.00**
Sear's Monticello, bowl, fruit; E-style, 5¼".................**$5.00**
Sear's Monticello, creamer, E-style................**$9.00**
Sear's Monticello, plate, E-style, 10"................**$7.00**
Sear's Monticello, saucer, E-style **$1.50**
Sear's Mount Vernon, bowl, oval, E-style, 9¼"...........**$16.00**
Sear's Mount Vernon, cup, E-style.................**$7.00**
Sear's Mount Vernon, plate, E-style, 10"................**$9.00**
Sear's Richmond/Brown-Eyed Susan, bowl, cereal; E-style, 6¼"................**$7.00**
Sear's Richmond/Brown-Eyed Susan, pickle dish, E-style, 9"................**$5.00**
Serenade, bowl, cereal; D-style, 6"................**$8.50**
Serenade, bowl, Radiance, 6" **$11.00**
Serenade, bowl, Radiance, 9"................**$16.00**
Serenade, creamer, Modern **$13.00**
Serenade, cup, D-style................**$9.00**
Serenade, plate, D-style, 9" **$8.00**
Serenade, pretzel jar................**$110.00**
Serenade, teapot, New York **$125.00**
Shaggy Tulip, custard, Radiance................**$13.00**
Shaggy Tulip, stack set, Radiance **$110.00**
Silhouette, baker, French; fluted................**$18.00**
Silhouette, bowl, flared 7¾"................**$35.00**
Silhouette, bowl, flat soup; D-style, 8½"................**$20.00**
Silhouette, bowl, fruit; D-style, 5½"................**$8.00**
Silhouette, bowl, Medallion, 8½"................**$22.00**
Silhouette, casserole, Medallion................**$40.00**
Silhouette, coffeepot, Medallion................**$110.00**
Silhouette, drip coffeepot, Kadota, all china **$250.00**
Silhouette, drip coffeepot, Medallion................**$300.00**
Silhouette, jug, #4, Medallion................**$30.00**
Silhouette, match safe................**$40.00**
Silhouette, mirror................**$75.00**
Silhouette, mug, beverage................**$45.00**
Silhouette, plate, D-style, 6"................**$6.50**
Silhouette, plate, D-style, 9"................**$18.00**
Silhouette, saucer, St Denis................**$10.00**
Silhouette, sugar bowl, Modern, w/lid................**$25.00**
Silhouette, tea tile, 6"................**$95.00**
Silhouette, waffle iron................**$150.00**
Spring, ashtray, Tomorrow's Classic................**$6.00**
Spring, butter dish, Tomorrow's Classic................**$80.00**
Spring, egg cup, Tomorrow's Classic................**$25.00**
Spring, gravy boat, Tomorrow's Classic................**$25.00**
Springtime, bowl, cereal; D-style, 6" **$8.00**
Springtime, cake plate................**$16.00**
Springtime, cup, D-style................**$7.50**
Springtime, custard **$7.00**
Springtime, jug, ball; #3................**$55.00**

Springtime, plate, D-style, 8¼" **$6.00**
Springtime, saucer, D-style................**$2.50**
Springtime, teapot, French................**$85.00**
Stonewall, bowl, Radiance, 6"................**$16.00**
Stonewall, casserole, Radiance **$32.00**
Stonewall, custard, Radiance................**$14.00**
Sundial, batter jug, red or cobaltr **$125.00**
Sundial, casserole, colors other than red or cobalt, #2, 5¼"................**$20.00**
Sundial, teapot, red or cobalt, 6-cup................**$125.00**
Sunglow, ashtray, Century................**$5.00**
Sunglow, jug, Century................**$18.00**
Sunglow, saucer, Century................**$1.50**
Tulip, bowl, fruit; D-style, 5½"................**$6.50**
Tulip, bowl, Radiance, 6"................**$11.00**
Tulip, bowl, Radiance, 9"................**$22.00**
Tulip, bowl, round, D-style, 9¼"................**$30.00**
Tulip, bowl, Thick Rim, 8½"................**$30.00**
Tulip, canisters, metal, 4-pc set................**$50.00**
Tulip, coffeepot, Perk................**$60.00**
Tulip, gravy boat, D-style................**$27.00**
Tulip, platter, oval, D-style, 13¼"................**$25.00**
Tulip, saucer, St Denis................**$9.00**
Wild Poppy, baker, oval................**$55.00**
Wild Poppy, coffeepot, Washington, 12-cup............**$225.00**
Wild Poppy, custard, Radiance................**$16.00**
Wild Poppy, teapot, New York, 8-cup................**$310.00**
Wildfire, bowl, cereal; D-style, 6"................**$11.00**
Wildfire, cake plate................**$30.00**
Wildfire, casserole, Thick Rim................**$30.00**
Wildfire, coffee dispenser, metal................**$22.00**
Wildfire, creamer, Pert................**$30.00**
Wildfire, cup, D-style................**$14.00**
Wildfire, egg cup................**$70.00**
Wildfire, plate, D-style, 9"................**$10.00**
Wildfire, salt & pepper shakers, handled, pr..............**$36.00**
Wildfire, saucer, D-style................**$2.50**
Yellow Rose, bowl, fruit; D-style, 5½"................**$5.50**
Yellow Rose, bowl, salad; 9"................**$16.00**
Yellow Rose, coffeepot, Dome................**$35.00**
Yellow Rose, cup, D-style................**$9.00**
Yellow Rose, custard................**$11.00**
Yellow Rose, platter, oval, D-style, 11¼"................**$16.00**
Yellow Rose, sugar bowl, Norse, w/lid................**$25.00**

Teapots

Airflow, red, 8-cup................**$165.00**
Albany, Gold Special (gold decals), 6-cup................**$60.00**
Automobile, red or cobalt, 6-cup................**$650.00**
Baltimore, red, 6-cup................**$200.00**
Bellvue, red, 6 or 10-cup................**$75.00**
Blue Blossom, Airflow................**$250.00**
Blue Willow, Boston, 4-cup................**$200.00**
Football, red or cobalt, 6-cup................**$650.00**
French, Gold Label (gold decal), 6-cup................**$37.00**
French, red, 12-cup................**$140.00**

Globe, red	$160.00
Hollywood, red, 6-cup	$110.00
Hook Cover, colors other than red, 6-cup	$30.00
Illinois, red, 6-cup	$300.00
Manhattan, colors other than red, 2-cup	$55.00
Melody, red, 6-cup	$245.00
Morning Glory, Aladdin	$125.00
Newport, decal decoration, 7-cup	$85.00
Parade, gold label, 6-cup	$30.00

Plume, pink with gold floral decoration, $70.00. (Photo courtesy Margaret and Kenn Whitmyer)

Rhythm, red, 6-cup	$175.00
Star, turquoise or cobalt, 6-cup	$35.00
Streamline, red, 6-cup	$130.00
Surfside, emerald or canary, 6-cup	$100.00
Windshield, maroon & gold, 6-cup	$45.00

Hallmark

Since the early 1970s when Hallmark first introduced their glass ball and yarn doll ornaments, many lines and themes have been developed to the delight of collectors. Many early ornaments are now valued at several times their original price. This is especially true of the first one issued in a particular series. For instance, Betsy Clark's first edition issued in 1973 has a value today of $125.00 (MIB).

If you'd like to learn more about them, we recommend *Hallmark Ornaments 2000* by Rosie Wells (www.rosie wells.com).

Our values are for ornaments that are mint and in their original boxes.

Advisor: The Baggage Car (See Directory, Hallmark)

Newsletter: The Baggage Car
3100 Justin Dr., Ste. B
Des Moines, IA 50322; 515-270-9080 or fax 515-223-1398
Includes show and company information along with current listing

A Child's Gift, QXM4234, miniature, 1996	$12.50
A Merry Flight, QXM4073, miniature, 1994	$12.50
Acorn Squirrel, QXM5682, miniature, 1989	$9.00
Acorn Wreath, QXM5686, miniature, 1990	$12.00
Air Express, QX5977, Keepsake, 1995	$17.50
Babies First Christmas, QXM514-5, miniature, 1993	$12.50
Baby-sitter, QX253-1, 1984	$14.00

Betsy Clark, QX133-1, 3rd edition, 1975	$75.00
Cherry Jubilee, QX4532, Keepsake, 1989	$19.50
Child's Fourth Christmas, QX466-1, Keepsake, 1992	$24.50
Christmas Cuckoo, clock QX4801, 1988	$40.00
Classic American Cars, QX527-5, Keepsake, 1993	$40.00
Cozy Kayak, QXM5551, miniature, 1992	$14.00
First Christmas Together, QX505-5, 1981	$25.00
From Our Home to Yours, QX2166, Keepsake, 1990	$19.50
Godparent, QX2417, Keepsake, 1995	$17.00
Grandpa, bear on sled, QX5851, Keepsake, 1996	$17.50
Here Comes Santa, Santa's Express, QX143-4, 2nd edition, MIB	$275.00
Holiday Puppy, QX412-7, 1983	$30.00
Ice Show, QX5946, Keepsake, 1994	$19.50
It's a Wonderful Life, QLX7237, Keepsake, 1991	$75.00
Jesus Loves Me, QX3147, cameo, Keepsake, 1991	$9.50
Jolly St Nick, QX4296, special edition, 1985	$75.00
Old World Gnome, QX4345, Keepsake, 1989	$29.50
Santa Gone Fishing, QX4794, 1988	$19.00
Santa's Roadster, QXM5665, miniature, 1989	$14.50
Space Shuttle, QLX7396, Keepsake, 1995	$50.00
Spoon Rider, QX5496, Keepsake, 1990	$9.75
St Louie Nick, QX453-9, 1987	$30.00
Sun & Fun Santa, QX492-2, 1985	$40.00
Terrific Teacher, QX5309, Keepsake, 1991	$14.50
The Eagle Has Landed, QLX7486, Keepsake, 1994	$50.00
Three Little Kittens, QMX5694, miniature, 1988	$18.50
Tin Soldier, QX483-6, 1982	$50.00
Unicorn, QX426-7, 1983	$55.00
Visions of Sugarplums, QXM402-2, miniature, 1993	$16.50
Wee Toymaker, QXM5967, miniature, 1991	$15.00
Winnie the Pooh, Eeyore, QX571-2, miniature, 1993	$19.50
Winter Suprise, penguins, QX4443, Keepsake, 1990	$19.50
Woodland Babies, QXM5444, 2nd edition, miniature, 1992	$15.00

Keepsake Ornament, Merry Olde Santa, 1990, first edition, MIB, from $60.00 to $65.00.

Halloween

Halloween is now the second biggest money-making holiday of the year, and more candy is sold at this time than for any other holiday. Folk artists are making new items to satisfy the demands of collectors and celebrators that can't get enough of the old items. Over one hundred years of celebrating this magical holiday has built a social history strata by strata, and wonderful and exciting finds can be made in all periods! From one dollar to thousands, there is something to excite collectors in every price range, with new collectibles being born every year. For further information we recommend *Collectible Halloween, More Halloween Collectibles, Halloween: Collectible Decorations & Games, Salem Witchcraft and Souvenirs,* and *Anthropomorphic Beings of Halloween* (all published by Schiffer); also see *Around Swanzey* (Arcadia). The author of these books is Pamela E. Apkarian-Russell (Halloween Queen), a freelancer who also writes an ephemera column for *Unravel the Gavel, Barrs Postcard News, Antiques Journal, Postcard Collector, Antique Trader, Journal of Antiques and Collectibles, Joy of Halloween,* and others.

Advisor: Pamela E. Apkarian-Russell (See Directory, Halloween)

Publisher of Newsletter: *Trick or Treat Trader*
P.O. Box 499, Winchester, NH 03470; 603-239-8875; e-mail: halloweenqueen@cheshire.net; website: http://adam.cheshire.net/~halloweenqueen/home.html; Subscription: $15 per year in USA ($20 foreign) for 4 quarterly issues

Bank, Schultz, Whitman Candy, modern, $14.00.
(Photo courtesy Pamela Apkarian-Russell)

Basket, thin wooden boards w/painted faces, West Germany, from 3½" to 5" tall, ea from $225 to **$275.00**
Bendee, pumpkin-faced man, Burger King premium.**$10.00**
Bolo ties, Nightmare Before Christmas, pewter, set of 6..**$300.00**
Booklet, ad promo; Weeny Witch, cb, features game suggestions, table decor, place cards, etc, Visking, 1951, unused, NM **$30.00**
Candle holder, jack-o'-lantern w/almond-shaped eyes, papier-mache, triangular smile, wire handle, 1950s, 6", EX+ **$65.00**
Candy container, ball shape w/smiling face, hat & feet, cardboard, West Germany..**$75.00**
Candy container, beet-headed clown, composition, Germany, 3½" **$200.00**
Candy container, devil-headed person w/vegetable body, composition, 6" **$300.00**

Candy container, hollow disk w/smiling face, pressed cardboard, string hanger **$150.00**
Candy container, jack-o'-lantern w/bug eyes, glass, original paint..**$95.00**
Candy container, pumpkin-face man, composition, 3½"...**$175.00**
Candy container, pumpkin-head policeman, glass ...**$800.00**
Cup, Nightmare Before Christams, plastic, from movie theater..**$55.00**
Decoration, bat w/movable wings, paper.....................**$6.00**
Decoration, jack-o'-lantern man, moving parts, printed paper..**$8.00**
Decoration, owl, cardboard w/fold-out paper wings .**$30.00**
Decoration, owl, paper w/tissue paper fold-out tummy, American..**$20.00**
Decoration, scarecrow, cardboard, w/accordion-pleated haystack, MIP **$30.00**
Diecut, devil w/pitch fork, heavily embossed cardboard, German, lg **$150.00**
Diecut, devil w/pitch fork, heavily embossed cardboard, German, med **$125.00**
Diecut, flying witch, heavily embossed cardboard, German **$145.00**
Diecut, owl & man in moon, embossed cardboard, German **$130.00**
Figurine, owl, pulp w/glass eyes (actually a bird decoy) .**$140.00**
Game, Witzi-Wits The Fortune Teller, Alderman Fairchild Co, 1928, VG+ (VG+ box) **$75.00**
Hat, orange felt w/printed black cat and jack-o'-lantern, conical..**$15.00**
Hat, owl front w/fold-around black & orange check band, paper & crepe paper **$20.00**
Horn, cardboard litho, wooden mouth bit **$65.00**
Lantern, black cat & owl, cardboard & tissue paper, simple dome-shaped top on ea of 4 panels **$65.00**
Lantern, folded/slotted cardboard litho, double sided..**$75.00**
Lantern, jack-o'-lantern, owl-like rings around eyes, pointed ears, pressed cardboard, German.......................**$500.00**
Lantern, jack-o'-lantern, pulp or egg-carton type, 1950s, from $50 to..**$125.00**
Lantern, jack-o'-lantern face, folding paper on wire frame, folds up, fragile..**$40.00**
Lantern, owl, cast iron, openwork forms feathers of body, original..**$85.00**
Lantern, owl, cast iron, openwork forms feathers of body, reproduction..**$15.00**
Lantern, pumpkin face, pressed cardboard w/paper insert, German..**$125.00**
Lantern, singing jack-o'-lantern, papier-mache, molded features, sizes vary, from $75 to..**$175.00**
Motionette dancing Snoopy, Charlie Brown & Lucy, all in Halloween costumes sitting in display boxes, set of 3 ....**$85.00**
Napkin, owl, black cats & smiling jack-o'-lantern printed on paper, M..**$1.00**
Noisemaker, drum type w/hanging bells, wood & paper..**$95.00**
Noisemaker, jack-o'-lantern, crepe paper-covered cardboard w/wire arms, cylindrical body, could be filled w/candy **$45.00**

Noisemaker, wooden ratchet w/pressed cardboard jack-o'-lantern head, Germany.............................**$175.00**

Nut cup, jack-o'-lantern, papier-mache......................**$20.00**

Plater, papier-mache, hand-painted owl & Luna Goddess on moon crescent in blue sky.............................**$95.00**

Postcard, pumpkin-face children & black cat, easel back..**$22.00**

Sheet music, Mr Ghost Goes to Town, American Academy of Music, 1936, NM **$30.00**

Snow globe, Trick or Treat, figures & jack-o'-lanterns, Hallmark **$14.00**

Squeeze toy, crying pumpkin, Made in Boston USA..**$45.00**

Toy, pumpkin-face man, hard plastic, push up from bottom to make dance **$35.00**

Yo-Yo, jack-o'-lantern, tin, modern..............................**$8.00**

Harker Pottery

Harker was one of the oldest potteries in the country. Their history can be traced back to the 1840s. In the '30s, a new plant was built in Chester, West Virginia, and the company began manufacturing kitchen and dinnerware lines, eventually employing as many as three hundred workers.

Several of these lines are popular with collectors today. One of the most easily recognized is Cameoware. It is usually found in pink or blue decorated with white silhouettes of flowers, though other designs were made as well. Colonial Lady, Red Apple, Amy, Mallow, and Pansy are some of their better-known lines that are fairly easy to find and reassemble into sets.

If you'd like to learn more about Harker, we recommend *The Collector's Encyclopedia of American Dinnerware* by Jo Cunningham, and *The Collector's Guide to Harker Pottery* by Neva Colbert, both published by Collector Books.

Cameo, plate, 8½", $7.50.

Amy, fork..**$45.00**
Amy, jug, Hi-rise.................................**$50.00**
Amy, rolling pin...................................**$100.00**
Amy, server **$27.00**
Amy, teapot..**$17.00**

Amy, teapot..**$40.00**
Basket, plate **$3.00**
Brim, plate, snack **$8.00**
Calico Tulip, baking dish, individual **$10.00**
Calico Tulip, creamer **$14.00**
Cameo Rose, bowl, salad; yellow.......**$35.00**
Cameo Rose, casserole, w/lid...............**$40.00**
Cameo Rose, rolling pin, pink w/white handles, from $130 to..**$150.00**
Cameo Rose, shaker, pink....................**$12.00**
Cameo Shellware, teapot......................**$35.00**
Cherry Blossom, platter, meat..............**$15.00**
Cottage, casserole, w/lid **$17.00**
Cottage, fork..**$30.00**
Deco-Dahlia, jug, utility; 6"...............**$22.00**
Deco-Dahlia, pie baker **$25.00**
Deco-Dahlia, server **$22.00**
English Countryside, jar, tall...............**$35.00**
Fruits, pitcher, Regal, 7".....................**$45.00**
Jessica, bowl, utility; lg.....................**$40.00**
Lisa, bowl, utility; Arches shape **$35.00**
Mallow, jar, lard; w/lid.......................**$25.00**
Mallow, jug, w/lid...............................**$25.00**
Mallow, plate, serving/utility..............**$27.00**
Mallow, plate, 8".................................**$14.00**
Pansy, bowl, 6" **$8.00**
Pansy, pepper shaker **$18.00**
Petit Point Rose I, pie baker...............**$27.00**
Petit Point Rose II, bowl, utility; 6x11½"...............**$40.00**
Petit Point Rose II, cake server............**$27.00**
Petit Point Rose II, casserole, w/lid, 8"..**$35.00**
Petit Point Rose II, custard, individual **$6.00**
Rose Spray, bowl, serving; 8" **$18.00**
Rose Spray, creamer **$16.00**
Rose Spray, plate, breakfast; square; 9" **$12.00**
Rose Spray, plate, dessert; round, 6"....**$8.00**
Rose Spray, plate, salad; 7" **$6.00**
Rosebud, pepper shaker **$12.00**
Ruffled Tulip, bowl, w/lid....................**$22.00**
Ruffled Tulip, tray, serving/utility, 11¾".........**$30.00**
White Rose, drippings jar.....................**$25.00**
White Rose, pie baker, Carv-Kraft **$25.00**
White Rose, teapot................................**$35.00**

Hartland Plastics, Inc.

The Hartland company was located in Hartland, Wisconsin, where during the '50s and '60s they made several lines of plastic figures: Western and Historic Horsemen, Miniature Western Series, and the Hartland Sport Series of Famous Baseball Stars. Football and bowling figures and religious statues were made as well. The plastic, virgin acetate, was very durable and the figures were hand painted with careful attention to detail. They're often marked.

Though prices have come down from their high of a few years ago, rare figures and horses are still in high demand.

Dealers using this guide should take these factors into consideration when pricing their items: values listed here are for the figure, horse (unless noted gunfighter), hat, guns, and all other accessories for that particular figure in near-mint condition with no rubs and all original parts. All parts were made exclusively for a special figure, so a hat is not just a hat — each one belongs to a specific figure! Many people do not realize this, and it is important for the collector to be knowledgeable. An excellent source of information is *Hartland Horses and Riders* by Gail Fitch.

In our listings for sports figures, mint to near-mint condition values are for figures that are white or near-white in color; excellent values are for those that are off-white or cream-colored. These values are representative of traditional retail prices asked by dealers; Internet values for Hartlands, as is so often the case nowadays, seem to be in a constant state of flux.

See also *Schroeder's Collectible Toys, Antique to Modern* (Collector Books).

Advisor: James Watson, Sports Figures (See Directory, Hartland)

Advisors: Judy and Kerry Irvin, Western Figures (See Directory, Hartland)

Sports Figures

Babe Ruth, NM/M, from $175 to	**$200.00**
Dick Groat, EX, from $800 to	**$1,000.00**
Dick Groat, NM/M, from $1,200 to	**$1,500.00**
Don Drysdale, EX, from $275 to	**$300.00**
Don Drysdale, NM/M, from $325 to	**$400.00**
Duke Snider, EX, from $300 to	**$325.00**
Duke Snider, M, from $500 to	**$600.00**
Eddie Mathews, NM/M, from $125 to	**$150.00**
Ernie Banks, EX, from $200 to	**$225.00**
Ernie Banks, NM/M, from $250 to	**$350.00**
Harmon Killebrew, NM/M, from $400 to	**$500.00**
Henry Aaron, EX, from $150 to	**$175.00**
Henry Aaron, NM/M, from $200 to	**$250.00**
Little Leaguer, 6", EX, from $100 to	**$125.00**
Little Leaguer, 6", NM/M, from $200 to	**$250.00**
Louie Aparacio, EX, from $200 to	**$225.00**
Louie Aparacio, NM/M, from $250 to	**$350.00**
Mickey Mantle, NM/M, from $250 to	**$350.00**
Minor Leaguer, 4", EX, from $50 to	**$75.00**
Minor Leaguer, 4", NM/M, from $100 to	**$125.00**
Nellie Fox, NM/M, from $200 to	**$250.00**
Rocky Colavito, NM/M, from $600 to	**$700.00**
Roger Maris, EX, from $300 to	**$350.00**
Roger Maris, NM/M, from $350 to	**$400.00**
Stan Musial, EX, from $150 to	**$175.00**
Stan Musial, NM/M, from $200 to	**$250.00**
Ted Williams, NM/M, from $225 to	**$300.00**
Warren Spahn, NM/M, from $150 to	**$175.00**
Willie Mays, EX, from $150 to	**$200.00**
Willie Mays, NM/M, from $225 to	**$250.00**

Yogi Berra, w/mask, EX, from $150 to	**$175.00**
Yogi Berra, w/mask, NM/M, from $175 to	**$250.00**
Yogi Berra, w/out mask, NM/M, from $150 to	**$175.00**

Horsemen and Gunfighters

Alkine Ike, NM	**$150.00**
Annie Oakley, NM	**$275.00**
Brave Eagle, NM	**$200.00**
Bret Maverick, w/gray horse, rare, NM	**$600.00**

Buffalo Bill, NM, $300.00.

Bullet, w/tag, NM	**$100.00**
Cactus Pete, NM	**$150.00**
Champ Cowgirl, NM	**$150.00**
Cheyenne, w/tag, NM	**$190.00**
Cochise, NM	**$150.00**
Commanche Kid, NM	**$150.00**
Dale Evans, green, NM	**$125.00**
Davy Crockett, NM	**$500.00**
General Custer, NMIB	**$250.00**
General George Washington, NMIB	**$175.00**
General Robert E Lee, NMIB	**$175.00**
Gil Favor, prancing, NM	**$650.00**
Gil Favor, semi-rearing, NM	**$550.00**
Jim Hardy, NMIB	**$300.00**
Jockey, NM	**$150.00**
Josh Randle, NM	**$650.00**
Lone Ranger, champ, black breast collar, NM	**$125.00**
Paladin, NMIB	**$350.00**
Rebel, NMIB	**$1,200.00**
Roy Rogers, walking, NMIB	**$300.00**
Seth Adams, NM	**$275.00**
Sgt Preston, reproduction flag, NM	**$650.00**
Tom Jeffords, NM	**$175.00**
Tonto, NM	**$150.00**
Wyatt Earp, w/tag, NMIB	**$250.00**

Head Vases

These are fun to collect, and prices are still reasonable. You've seen them at flea markets — heads of ladies, children, clowns, even some men and a religious figure now and then. A few look very much like famous people — there's a Jackie Onassis vase by Inarco that leaves no doubt as to who it's supposed to represent!

They were mainly imported from Japan, although a few were made by American companies and sold to florist shops to be filled with flower arrangements. So if there's an old flower shop in your neighborhood, you might start your search with their storerooms.

If you'd like to learn more about them, we recommend *Head Vases, Identification and Values*, by Kathleen Cole.

Newsletter: *Head Hunters Newsletter*
Maddy Gordon
P.O. Box 83H, Scarsdale, NY 10583, 914-472-0200
Subscription: $24 per year for 4 issues; also holds convention

Art Deco lady, Japan, #KKS230A, head looking up in wide-brimmed hat, allover white glaze, 5½" $30.00

Art Deco lady, USA #50N, long-necked head w/deep-set eyes & mouth, tam worn on side, allover green glaze, 7½" $50.00

Asian couple, Manchu & Lotus, white w/black hair, brows & eyes, he w/black beard, 7½" & 8", pr $250.00

Baby, unmarked, #S688B, eyes & mouth open, head framed w/pink ruffled hat, bow tied at neck, 5" $38.00

Baby, unmarked, lg eyes, open mouth, blue & white stocking hat & sweater, 5" $30.00

Baby, VCAGCO (paper label), head tilted, eyes open, blue bow atop head, yellow bodice w/blue bow & ruffled trim, 6" $50.00

Black lady, Relpo, #6673, eyes open looking up, black Afro hair, peach lips, shoulders w/thin straps, earrings, 6½" $200.00

Boy, unmarked, freckled face, plaid bodice w/real ribbon bow, 7" $45.00

Boy, unmarked, red polka-dots on white hat & bodice, gold-trimmed hat & neck bow, 7½" $45.00

Christmas girl, Napco, #CX2702, open hand to tilted head, open eyes, red, white & green decorated wide-brimmed hat, 6" $75.00

Christmas lady, Inarco, #E195, red poinsettia on white hat & white & black bodice, gold trim, pearl jewelry, 4½" .$65.00

Clown, Inarco, #E6730, white face w/black, red & orange features, red curly hair, blue & yellow hat & collar, 5½" $50.00

Clown, Napco, #IH-2243, hand w/finger pointing up, red polka-dots & nose, white ruffled collar w/heavy gold trim, 6¼" $50.00

Colonial lady, Inarco, #E1062, black-gloved hand w/gold-trimmed fan to cheek, blond banana curls, pearl earrings, 6" $60.00

Dutch lady, Inarco, #E1611, hand to chin, blond curls under white hat, black, yellow & white bodice, gold trim, 5½" $300.00

Geisha girl, unmarked, open fan to mouth, head decor w/tassel, gold eyelashes & trim, 4¾" $40.00

Girl, Inarco, #E3157, blond side-swept hair w/blue daisy, open eyes, pink boat-necked bodice, 5½" $45.00

Girl, Made in Japan, w/umbrella, looped pigtails w/bows, flat-brimmed hat, flower at center of striped bodice, 5" $75.00

Girl, unmarked, white headscarf w/stylized floral design, lg black protruding lashes, frosted hair, 5½" $40.00

Girl, unmarked, winking behind feathered fan, blond upswept hair, plumed hat w/sm brim, 6" $75.00

Girl with umbrella, unmarked, 4¼", $60.00.

Glamour girl, unmarked, head turned w/shoulder up to chin, allover white glaze w/gold features & trim, no hat, 6½" $23.00

Glowing Gertie, Napco, novelty type w/side-glance eyes, wide toothy smile, molded pearl necklace, low-cut bodice, 4" $30.00

Lady, Inarco, #E1756 (Lady Aileen), jeweled crown & pendant, head tilted, frosted hair w/ponytail, 1964, 5½" $75.00

Lady, Inarco, #E190/S, white-cuffed hand to chin, short blond hair, black hat & V-neck bodice, pearls, 1961, 4¾" $40.00

Lady, Inarco, #E2104, gloved hand to chin, head tilted, gold-trimmed rose in short hair, w/ or w/out pearl necklace, 7" $125.00

Lady, Inarco #E191/M/c, blond curls frame forehead under pink plumed hat, pink bodice w/white collar, pearls, 5½" $45.00

Lady, Japan, gloved hand to tilted face, long blond hair, flat-brimmed hat w/row of cut-out circles, molded pearls, 5" $45.00

Lady, Napco, #C3282A, hand w/bracelet & painted nails up to cheek, white feather hat w/gold trim, black bodice, 1958, 6" $50.00

Lady, Napco, #C4891A, hand w/black ruffled cuff & pearl bracelet to cheek, brown curls, black hat w/bow, 1961, 8½" $250.00

Lady, Napcoware, #C7498, eyes open, frosted hair, blue hat w/white bow, blue cowl collar w/pearls, 11" **$450.00**

Lady, Relpo, #A-1229, 2 white-gloved hands to tilted face, eyes open, rose-covered tall pillbox hat, 6½" **$65.00**

Lady, Robens, #501, head turned, yellow upswept hair w/braided crown, white flowered bodice w/gold trim, pearls, 6½" **$50.00**

Lady, Rubens, blond curls & ponytail at shoulder under straw hat w/lg gold-trimmed blue daisy, daisies around bodice, 6" **$70.00**

Madonna, Royal Windsor, praying, blue & white, 8" ..**$48.00**

Madonna, unmarked, arms crossed, blue & white w/gold trim, 5" **$23.00**

Praying boy, Inarco, #E978, 1962, 5" **$40.00**

Praying girl, Inarco, #E1579, 1964, 6" **$45.00**

Southern Belle, Acme Ware, pink bonnet w/lg blue bow tied at neck, 2 lg pink roses on pink bodice, gold trim, 6" ..**$50.00**

Teenage girl, Inarco, #E6211, eyes open, blond hair, yellow & white bodice w/high ruffled collar, pearl earring, 5" .**$55.00**

Teenage girl, Incarco, #E6211, eyes open, blond windswept hair, orange turtleneck sweater, 5" **$55.00**

Teenage girl, Lark, #JN-4113, eyes open, short blond hair w/ribbon bow, button bodice w/bow & lace trim, pearls, 7" **$150.00**

Teenage girl, Relpo, #2004, head turned, eyes open, blond hair w/bows in 2 strands, orange bodice, pearl earrings, 7" **$150.00**

Teenage girl, unmarked, side-glance eyes, blond flip, gold mod hat w/leapord spots, pink & white V-neck bodice, 5" **$55.00**

Uncle Sam, unmarked, allover light green glaze, 6½" ..**$30.00**

Young girl, unmarked, eyes open, long blond frosted hair w/green bow, green sleeveless bodice, pearl earrings, 7" **$300.00**

Young lady, Enesco, eyes open, hair parted in middle w/lg upswept curls, blue bows on sides, pearl earrings, 7½" **$250.00**

Young lady, Inarco, #E6210, head tilted, eyes open, blond hair w/side-swept ponytail, pale lips, pearl earrings, 6½" **$175.00**

Young lady, Parma (paper label), #A448, eyes open, full frosted curls, white ruffled collar w/gold trim, pearls, 7" **$200.00**

Young lady, Relpo, #K1175L, tilted head w/chin resting on clasped hands, brimmed pillbox w/plaid bow, pearls, 6½" **$75.00**

Young lady, Relpo, #1694L, gloved hand w/fingers spread, eyes open, short frosted hair w/tam, upturned collar, 7½" **$300.00**

Young lady, VCAGCO (paper label), head tilted, blond hair w/white scarf, square-cut bodice, peach airbrushing, 6" **$55.00**

Heisey Glass

From just before the turn of the century until 1957, the Heisey Glass Company of Newark, Ohio, was one of the largest, most successful manufacturers of quality tableware in the world. Though the market is well established, many pieces are still reasonably priced; and if you're drawn to the lovely patterns and colors that Heisey made, you're investment should be sound.

After 1901 much of their glassware was marked with their familiar trademark, the 'Diamond H' (an H in a diamond) or a paper label. Blown pieces are often marked on the stem instead of the bowl or foot.

Numbers in the listings are catalog reference numbers assigned by the company to indicate variations in shape or stem style. Collectors use them, especially when they buy and sell by mail, for the same purpose. Many catalog pages (showing these numbers) are contained in *The Collector's Encyclopedia of Heisey Glass* by Neila Bredehoft. This book and *Elegant Glassware of the Depression Era* by Gene Florence are both excellent references for further study. If you're especially interested in the many varieties of glass animals Heisey produced, you'll want to get *Glass Animals and Flower Frogs of the Depression Era* by Lee Garmon and Dick Spencer. All are published by Collector Books.

Newsletter: *The Heisey News*
Heisey Collectors of America
169 W Church St., Newark, OH 43055; 612-345-2932

Crystolite, crystal, ashtray, $150.00. (Photo courtesy Gene Florence)

Charter Oak, crystal, plate, salad; #1246, Acorn & Leaves, 6" **$5.00**

Charter Oak, Flamingo, bowl, finger; #3362...............**$17.50**

Charter Oak, Hawthorne, stem, cocktail; #3362, 3-oz...**$45.00**

Charter Oak, Marigold, tumbler, #3362, flat, 12-oz **$35.00**

Charter Oak, Moongleam, candlestick, #129, Tricorn, 3-light, 5" **$110.00**

Chintz, crystal, bowl, mint; footed, 6" **$20.00**

Chintz, crystal, platter, oval, 14" **$35.00**

Chintz, Sahara, comport, oval, 7" **$85.00**

Chintz, Sahara, stem, saucer champagne; #3389, 5-oz..**$25.00**

Crystolite, crystal, bonbon, 2-handled, 7½" **$15.00**

Crystolite, crystal, cigarette holder, footed...................**$35.00**

Crystolite, crystal, plate, shell shape, 7" **$32.00**

Crystolite, crystal, tray, celery; rectangular, 12" **$38.00**

Crystolite, crystal, vase, 12"...**$225.00**

Empress, Alexandrite, plate, 6" **$40.00**

Empress, cobalt, bowl, floral; dolphin foot, 11".........**$375.00**

Empress, Flamingo, vase, flared, 8" **$120.00**

Empress, Flamingo or Sahara, bowl, cream soup **$30.00**
Empress, Moongleam, bowl, nappy; 8" **$45.00**
Empress, Sahara, jug, footed, 3-pt...........................**$210.00**
Greek Key, crystal, bowl, almond; footed, 5" **$40.00**
Greek Key, crystal, bowl, banana split; flat, 9" **$45.00**
Greek Key, crystal, creamer.....................................**$50.00**
Greek Key, crystal, plate, 7" **$50.00**
Greek Key, crystal, straw jar, w/lid **$350.00**
Greek Key, crystal, tumbler, water; 5½-oz **$50.00**
Ipswich, crystal, bowl, floral; footed, 11" **$70.00**
Ipswich, crystal, candy jar, w/lid, ¼-lb.....................**$175.00**
Ipswich, green, tumbler, soda; footed, 8-oz **$85.00**
Ipswich, pink, creamer..**$70.00**
Ipswich, Sahara, pitcher, ½-gal...............................**$350.00**
Lariat, crystal, basket, footed, 8½" **$165.00**
Lariat, crystal, bowl, celery; handled, 10" **$35.00**

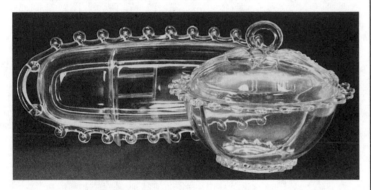

Lariat, crystal, candy dish, with lid, $55.00; Relish, $35.00.

Lariat, crystal, cup, punch **$8.00**
Lariat, crystal, plate, dinner; 10½" **$125.00**
Lariat, crystal, stem, wine; pressed, 3½-oz **$24.00**
Lariat, crystal, tumbler, juice; footed, 5-oz................**$22.00**
Lodestar, Dawn, bowl, 8"...**$65.00**
Lodestar, Dawn, plate, 14".......................................**$90.00**
Minuet, crystal, bowl, finger; #3309 ....**$50.00**
Minuet, crystal, bowl, sauce; footed, 7½" **$70.00**
Minuet, crystal, candlestick, #112, 1-light **$35.00**
Minuet, crystal, plate, salad; 7" **$18.00**
Minuet, crystal, saucer..**$10.00**
Minuet, crystal, vase, #5013, 5"................................**$50.00**
New Era, crystal, cup, after dinner...........................**$70.00**
New Era, crystal, stem, low sherbet; 6-oz...................**$15.00**
Octagon, crystal, bowl, #500, 6" **$14.00**
Octagon, crystal, plate, 14" **$22.00**
Octagon, Flamingo or Sahara, basket, #500, 5".........**$300.00**
Octagon, Flamingo or Sahara, tray, celery; 12" **$25.00**
Octagon, Hawthorne, ice tub, #500 ....**$115.00**
Octagon, Moongleam, creamer, hotel size..................**$35.00**
Old Colony, yellow, bowl, nappy; 4½" **$14.00**
Old Colony, yellow, creamer, individual **$40.00**
Old Colony, yellow, plate, 4½"..................................**$7.00**
Old Colony, yellow, stem, claret; #3390, 4-oz............**$30.00**
Old Colony, yellow, stem, cocktail; #3380, 3-oz.........**$25.00**

Old Colony, yellow, tumbler, bar; #3380, footed, 1-oz..**$45.00**
Old Sandwich, crystal, mug, beer; 12-oz....................**$35.00**
Old Sandwich, crystal, sundae dish, 6-oz...................**$18.00**
Old Sandwich, green, stem, wine; 2½-oz....................**$55.00**
Old Sandwich, pink, creamer, oval............................**$22.00**
Old Sandwich, yellow, bowl, popcorn; footed, cupped...**$75.00**
Orchid, crystal, bottle, French dressing; 8-oz............**$195.00**
Orchid, crystal, bowl, epergne; 9½".........................**$525.00**
Orchid, crystal, bowl, floral; Waverly, crimped, 13" ...**$95.00**
Orchid, crystal, comport, footed, oval, 7"..................**$145.00**
Orchid, crystal, pitcher, 73-oz..................................**$500.00**
Orchid, crystal, salt & pepper shakers, pr **$85.00**
Orchid, crystal, stem, sherbet; #5022 or #5025, 6-oz ..**$25.00**
Orchid, crystal, vase, bud; footed, square, 8" **$225.00**
Plantation, crystal, ashtray, 3½"...............................**$45.00**
Plantation, crystal, butter dish, oblong, w/lid, ¼-lb .**$110.00**
Plantation, crystal, cup, punch **$35.00**
Plantation, crystal, saucer..**$10.00**
Plantation, crystal, stem, fruit/oyster cocktail; 4-oz.....**$35.00**
Pleat & Panel, crystal, bowl, nappy; 4½".....................**$6.00**
Pleat & Panel, green, stem, 8-oz **$40.00**
Pleat & Panel, pink, pitcher, 3-pt **$140.00**
Provincial, crystal, bowl, gardenia; 13" **$40.00**
Provincial, crystal, tumbler, juice; footed, 5-oz...........**$14.00**
Provincial, Limelight Green, creamer, footed **$95.00**
Queen Ann, crystal, bowl, mint; dolphin foot, 6".......**$18.00**
Queen Ann, crystal, ice tub, w/metal handles **$60.00**
Queen Ann, crystal, plate, 7" **$8.00**
Queen Ann, crystal, vase, flared, 8" **$55.00**
Ridgeleigh, crystal, bottle, cologne; 4-oz **$130.00**
Ridgeleigh, crystal, bowl, floral; oblong, 13"...............**$70.00**
Ridgeleigh, crystal, bowl, nappy; square, 5"................**$25.00**
Ridgeleigh, crystal, cup, beverage **$12.00**
Ridgeleigh, crystal, plate, square, 7"..........................**$24.00**
Ridgeleigh, crystal, salt & pepper shakers, pr **$45.00**
Ridgeleigh, crystal, stem, sherbet; blown, 5-oz **$20.00**
Ridgeleigh, crystal, vase, 8".....................................**$75.00**
Rose, crystal, bowl, gardenia; Waverly, 10" **$75.00**
Rose, crystal, bowl, mint; footed, 5½" **$37.50**
Rose, crystal, creamer, Waverly, footed.....................**$35.00**
Rose, crystal, plate, sandwich; Waverly, 11" **$60.00**
Rose, crystal, tray, celery; Waverly, 12"......................**$65.00**
Rose, crystal, vase, violet; Waverly, footed, 3½".......**$110.00**
Saturn, crystal, bowl, baked apple **$20.00**
Saturn, crystal, bowl, salad; 11"................................**$40.00**
Saturn, crystal, oil bottle, 3-oz **$55.00**
Saturn, crystal, stem, 10-oz **$20.00**
Saturn, crystal, tumbler, 10-oz..................................**$20.00**
Saturn, Zircon or Limelight, bowl, whipped cream; 5"..**$150.00**
Saturn, Zircon or Limelight, candle block, 2-light.....**$350.00**
Saturn, Zircon or Limelight, stem, sherbet; 4½-oz **$70.00**
Stanhope, crystal, bowl, salad; 11"............................**$90.00**
Stanhope, crystal, plate, 7".......................................**$20.00**
Stanhope, crystal, stem, claret; #4083, 4-oz **$25.00**
Stanhope, crystal, vase, ball; 7".................................**$90.00**
Twist, crystal, bowl, nappy; 4" **$10.00**
Twist, green, cocktail shaker, metal lid **$400.00**

Twist, marigold, platter, 12" $75.00
Twist, pink, oil bottle, w/#78 stopper, 2½-oz $100.00
Twist, yellow, bowl, mint; 2-handled, 6" $20.00
Victorian, crystal, bowl, finger $25.00
Victorian, crystal, plate, 7" $20.00
Victorian, crystal, stem, oyster cocktail; 5-oz.............$20.00
Victorian, crystal, vase, 5½" $60.00
Waverly, crystal, bowl, gardenia; 13" $30.00
Waverly, crystal, bowl, salad; 7" $20.00
Waverly, crystal, candle holder, 3-light $70.00
Waverly, crystal, plate, luncheon; 8" $10.00
Waverly, crystal, salt & pepper shakers, pr $60.00
Waverly, crystal, tray, celery; 12" $20.00
Waverly, crystal, vase, footed, 7" $35.00
Yeoman, crystal, bowl, banana split; footed.................$7.00
Yeoman, crystal, tumbler, whiskey; 2½-oz $3.00
Yeoman, marigold, saucer...$10.00
Yeoman, pink, bowl, preserve; oval, 6"........................$12.00
Yeoman, pink, plate, bouillon underliner; 6" $13.00
Yeoman, yellow, cruet, oil; 2-oz...................................$80.00

Figurals and Novelties

Airedale, crystal...$650.00
Chick, crystal, head down or up, ea...........................$95.00
Colt, amber, kicking $650.00
Colt, cobalt, rearing...$1,500.00
Colt, crystal, standing...$100.00
Doe head, bookend, crystal, 6¼", ea.........................$850.00
Donkey, crystal $295.00
Duck, flower block, crystal $140.00
Elephant, amber, sm...$1,650.00
Elephant, crystal, sm...$225.00
Fish, bookend, crystal, ea $160.00
Fish, match holder, crystal, 3x2¾".............................$180.00
Gazelle, crystal, 10¾"..$1,200.00
Goose, crystal, wings down...$450.00
Hen, crystal, 4½" $350.00
Horse head, frosted, bookend, ea..............................$140.00
Kingfisher, Moongleam, flower block $250.00
Mallard, crystal, wings half $200.00
Piglet, crystal, standing..$100.00
Pouter pigeon, crystal, 7½" L $800.00
Ram head, stopper, crystal, 3½" $160.00
Rooster, crystal, 5½x5" $350.00
Rooster head, cocktail shaker, crystal, 1-qt.................$75.00

Scottie, crystal, H89, ca 1941 – 46, 3½", from $150.00 to $175.00. (Photo courtesy Candace Sten Davis and Patrica J. Baugh)

Sea horse, cocktail, crystal...$160.00
Sow, crystal, 3x4½" $800.00
Swan, crystal, master nut, #1503..................................$45.00
Tiger, paperweight, crystal, 2¾x8"...............................$900.00

Hippie Collectibles

The 'Hippies' perpetuated the 'Beatnik' genre of rebellious, free-thinking, Bohemian nonconformity during the decade of the 1960s. Young people created a 'counterculture' with their own style of clothing, attitudes, music, politics, and behavior. They created new forms of art, theatre, and political activism. The center of this movement was the Haight-Ashbury district of San Francisco. The youth culture culminated there in 1967 in the 'Summer of Love.' Woodstock, in August 1969, attracted at least 400,000 people. Political activism against the Viet Nam War was intense and widespread. Posters, books, records, handbills, and other items from that era are highly collectible because of their uniqueness to this time period.

Advisor: Richard Synchef (See Directory, Beatnik and Hippie Collectibles)

Admission ticket, Woodstock Music & Art Fair, Globe Ticket Co, Aug 1969, 1- or 3-day ticket $125.00
Book , Do It!, Jerry Rubin, NY: Simon & Schuster, 1970, Yippie (Youth International Party) founder's first book...$250.00
Book, Boo Hoo Bible, Art Kleps, San Cristobal, MN: Toad Books, 1971, by founder of Neo-American (psychedelic) Church $140.00
Book, Buried Alive, Biography of Janis Joplin, Myra Friedman, Wm Morrow Co, 1973, compassionate biography of rock star $90.00
Book, Electric Kool Aid Acid Test, Tom Wolfe, NY: Farrar, Straus & Giroux, 1968, best chronicle of beginning of Ken Kesey & the Merry Pranksters, important ...$700.00
Book, Garage Sale, Ken Kesey, NY: Viking, 1973, contributors include Allen Ginsberg, Paul Krassner, Neal Cassady, others..$225.00
Book, Guitar Army, John Sinclair, NY: Douglas, 1972, by founder of the White Panther Party $175.00
Book, Politics of Ecstacy, Timothy Leary, NY: Putnam, 1968, significant work by Harvard professor turned LSD guru...$250.00
Book, Woodstock Nation, Abbie Hoffman, NY: Random House, 1969, Yippie founder's classic.................$400.00
Bumper sticker, Lyndon's Bridge Is Falling Down, blue letters on orange, early 1968, anti-LBJ, 3½x15"...............$75.00
Bumper sticker, Pat Paulsen for President, Peter Geller Distributors, We Cannon Stand Pat, red, white & blue, 1968, 1x4" $80.00
Comic, underground, Arcade: Comic Review No 1, Spring 1975, Print Mint: SF, cover by Robert Crumb, edited by Art Spiegelman & Bill Griffith, scarce $160.00

Comic, underground, Feds 'N Heads, Austin TX: 1968, Gilbert Shelton, rare **$250.00**

Comic, underground, Mr Natural, San Francisco Comic Book Co, 1971, Robert Crumb issue **$200.00**

Comic, underground, Zap Comix #5, Apex Novelties, 1970, Crumb & many others, first printing (50¢ price)...**$150.00**

Figurine, hippie man making peace sign, 'High There,' American Greeting Corp, 1971, 6" **$65.00**

Handbill, Diggers/Communications Co, 1967, about 300 different w/info re: Summer of Love in Haight Ashbury, from $50 to **$450.00**

Handbill, Human Be-In, Gathering of the Tribes, Jan 14, 1967, Rick Griffin artist, 8½x11", seminal counterculture event **$500.00**

Handbill, Love Thy Neighbor, Jerry Barish Bail Bonds, Mouse, Bowen, Travis artists, 1967, 9x6", rare ...**$200.00**

Handbill, Milwaukee 14, June 9, 1969, Milwaukee 14 Defense Committee, 8½x11", rare **$200.00**

Handbill, Straight Theatre, San Francisco, artist unknown, 1967, promoting venue in Haight Ashbury **$100.00**

Handbill, Yippie! Youth International Party, 1968 Pre-Democratic Convention in Chicago, red, white, and blue, 8½x11", $600.00. (Photo courtesy Richard Synchef)

Jigsaw puzzle, Life, Peter Max artist, Schugall NY, 1970, 500 pcs, 7½x5½" **$125.00**

Magazine, Avant Garde, Ralph Ginsburg ed, Jan 1968, Premiere issue (only 12 issues published)..........**$175.00**

Magazine, Life, Mar 25, 1966, LSD cover story w/ photographs **$50.00**

Magazine, Look, July 15, 1969, How Hippies Raise Their Children **$40.00**

Magazine, Psychedelic Review #6, 1965, important early scholarly writing about hallucinogens **$160.00**

Magazine, Radical America, An SDS Journal of the History of American Radicalism, Nov-Dec 1967, Vol 1, No 3, rare **$125.00**

Magazine, Ramparts, Sept 1969, Eldridge Cleaver From Exile **$50.00**

Magazine, Realist, Paul Krassner ed, #90, May-June 1971, An Impolite Interview w/Ken Kesey **$80.00**

Magazine, Saturday Evening Post, Nov 2, 1968, Bob Dylan & the Pop Scene, Dylan on cover **$50.00**

Newspaper, Berkeley Barb, Vol 4, No 2, Jan 13, 1967, The Human Be-In issue **$80.00**

Newspaper, East Village Other, Special Woodstock Issue, Aug 1, 1969, w/map of Woodstock on front page **$250.00**

Newspaper, Peace & Freedom News, Vol 1, No 1, Mar 30, 1968, short-lived paper affiliated w/Black Panther party **$200.00**

Newspaper, Rising Up Angry, Vol 1, No 2, Aug 1969, from radical Chicago collective **$60.00**

Newspaper, San Francisco Oracle, No 1, Nov 20, 1966, 1st issue (only 12 published), newspaper of Haight Ashbury in 'Summer of Love,' important **$400.00**

Newspaper, SDS New Left Notes, Vol 4, No 24, July 8, 1969, Bring the War Home! issue **$125.00**

Newspaper, Sundance, White Panther Information Service, Ann Arbor MI, Vol 1, No 1, July 4, 1970, premiere issue of White Panther Party, very scarce **$300.00**

Newspaper, Yipster Times, Vol 1, No 5, Mar 1973, Youth International Party News Service, collectible......**$150.00**

Paperback, Acid Eaters, Rolf Kirby, NY: BB Sales, 1968, photos from actual movie, classic **$90.00**

Paperback, Electric Tibet, James Doukas, N Hollywood, Dominion, 1969, early study of psychedelic music scene in San Francisco **$100.00**

Paperback, Hippies, The; by correspondents of Time, Joe Brown ed, NY: Time, 1967, surprisingly objective book **$60.00**

Paperback, LSD: Problem-Solving Psychedelic, PG Strafford & BH Golightly, NY: Award Books, 1967, examination of LSD use..**$75.00**

Paperback, New Communes: Coming Together in America, Englewood Cliffs NJ, Prentice Hall Inc, 1971, communal history **$60.00**

Paperback, Revolution at Berkeley: Crisis in American Education, NY: Dell Pub Co, 1965, discusses Free Speech Movement **$60.00**

Paperback, Telling It Like It Was: Chicago, Riots, Arthur Miller, Allen Ginsberg, Abbie Hoffman, many others, NY: Signet, 1969, personal accounts of participants & observers of 1968 Democratic Convention activities..................**$75.00**

Paperback, 1001 Ways To Beat the Draft, Tuli Kupferberg & Robert Bachlow, Grove Press, 1967, great period piece **$70.00**

Pillow, Peter Max, inflatable plastic, ca 1969, 16x16", any of 8 different styles **$120.00**

Pinback button, Free Speech Movement, Berkeley CA, 1964, white letters on blue, 1", beginning of student protests **$200.00**

Pinback button, King Lyndon the First, w/Johnson's head crowned, white on red, ca 1968, 1½" **$50.00**

Poster, Human Be-In, A Gathering of the Tribes, Jan 14, 1967, artists Mouse, Kelley & Bowen, Bindweed Press, SF, absolute classic & important '60s poster.............**$800.00**

Poster, Invocation for Maitreya, Lenore Kandel, poster by Michael Bowen, photos by Gene Anthony, blue & white on purple, scarce **$150.00**

Poster, Pooh, A Coffee House, artist Morningstar, The Bindweed Press, SF, 1967, 20x14", for popular hang-out **$80.00**
Poster, Weed Patch, SF, black & red on peach paper, 1967, 20x13", advertisement for Haight Street 'head shop' **$150.00**
Poster, Zen Benefit, Gary Snyder Poetry, Mar 15, 1968, Fillmore Auditorium (SF), red & white on black, 20x13", benefit for Zen Mountain Center **$175.00**
Program, Woodstock Music & Art Fair, Aug 1969, 52 pages, 8½x11", rare **$800.00**
Record, Can You Pass the Acid Test?, Ken Kesey & The Merry Pranksters, Sound City Productions, 1966, very rare .**$550.00**
Record, Confrontation at Harvard, 1969, Buddah Records, 2-record set tells about takeover of part of school ..**$150.00**
Record, FSM's Sound & Songs of the Demonstration!, FSM-Records Dept, Berkeley CA, 1964, important documentation of first (1964) campus student protests ...**$175.00**
Record, Hey, Hey...LBJ! & Other Songs of the US antiwar movement, sung by Bill Frederick, Monterey Park CA, Crisis Records, 1967, protest songs **$75.00**
Record, LSD, Capital Records #2574, ca 1966, comments by Timothy Leary, Allen Ginsberg, Mrs Aldous Huxley, others **$200.00**
Record, Sound of Dissent, Mercury Records #61203, 1969, sounds of various speakers & antiwar demonstrations **$75.00**
Stickers, various peace signs, etc, Atomic Energy Group, 1967, ea **$10.00**

Record, *The Trip,* motion picture soundtrack, Sidewalk ST 5908, 1970, American International Pictures Tie-in, $200.00. (Photo courtesy Richard Synchef)

Holt Howard

Now's the time to pick up the kitchenware (cruets, salt and peppers, condiments, etc.), novelty banks, ashtrays, and planters marked Holt Howard. They're not only marked but dated as well; you'll find production dates from the 1950s through the 1970s. (Beware of unmarked copy-cat lines!) There's a wide variety of items and decorative themes; those you're most likely to find will be from the rooster (done in golden brown, yellow, and orange), white cat (called Kozy

Kitten), and Christmas lines. Not as easily found, the Pixies are by far the most collectible of all, and in general, Pixie prices continue to climb.

Internet auctions have affected this market with the 'more supply, less demand' principal (more exposure, therefore in some cases lower prices), but all in all, the market has remained sound. Only the very common pieces have suffered.

Advisors: Pat and Ann Duncan (See Directory, Holt Howard)

Christmas

Beverage set, smiling Santa face surrounded by white fur, top of ea pc is red w/white fur, 7" pitcher, +4 2½" shots **$75.00**
Butter pats, holly leaves & berries, 2¾", set of 4 ....**$32.00**
Cake stand, musical: Jingle Bells, white w/3-D holly leaves & berries **$85.00**
Candelabra, Santa trio, gift packages hold candles, 5x8" ..**$60.00**
Candle holder, double; 3 choir boys hold lg song book ..**$38.00**
Candle holder, Santa in cowboy hat riding stagecoach pulled by 4 reindeer jumping over NOEL, 9" L **$90.00**
Candle holders, angels, white w/'spaghetti' trim on robes, cuffs, & hoods, 1 w/bell, 1 w/package, 4", +snowflake hangers **$70.00**
Candle holders, camel figurals, 4", pr **$50.00**
Candle holders, children dressed as Wise Men, 3½", set of 3 ....**$55.00**
Candle holders, Santa in coach laden with Christmas gifts, wearing cowboy hat, 3x4", pr **$42.00**
Candle huggers, figural snowmen, Christmas tree hats, red scarfs, pr, from $30 to **$35.00**
Carousel, Santa holds metal spinner w/2 candles, spins from heat of flames **$50.00**
Christmas tree, bottle-brush style w/fruit, foil ornaments & bird decorations, 15" **$40.00**
Christmas tree, electric, 10" **$70.00**
Cookies/candy jar, roly-poly Santa figure, 3-pc, minimum value **$150.00**
Cups, Santa face w/snowflake eyes, stick handle is point of Santa's hat, set of 4 ....**$35.00**
Dish, Santa face, 7¼x5½" **$42.00**
Figurines, Santas shaped as letters: N, O, E, L, 3⅞", set of 4 ....**$65.00**
Head vase, girl w/drop earrings, holly head band, pearl necklace, 4" **$85.00**
Match holder, Santa w/bongo drum, 4½" **$30.00**
Place card holders/figurines, elves, 3", set of 4 ....**$55.00**
Planter, angel standing before square pot, 'spaghetti' trim on robe, cuffs & hood, 4¼x3¾x2¾" **$55.00**
Punch bowl, ladle & 8 cups, white w/holly sprig, paneled, 10-pc set **$65.00**
Salt & pepper shakers, angel figurals, 3½", pr **$22.00**
Salt & pepper shakers, Christmas trees w/Santa's face on ea, 'S' & 'P,' 4½', pr..**$25.00**
Salt & pepper shakers, Santa & his bag, Santa: 3", pr .**$35.00**
Salt & pepper shakers, Santa's head is salt, stacks on pepper body, from $30 to **$40.00**

Salt & pepper shakers, standing Santas, 5½", pr.........**$18.00**

Salt & pepper shakers, stylized deer, 1 buck & 1 doe, pr..**$30.00**

Salt & pepper shakers, 2 stacked gift boxes, 'Merry Xmas' on top, pr.................**$15.00**

Snack set, Santa waving on plate, red cup fits off-center well, 8½".................**$28.00**

Taper holder, elf in sleigh w/candy cane runners, 'spaghetti' trim at top of sleigh, 5" L.................**$28.00**

Tray, Santa, beard forms tray, 7¾", from $25 to.........**$30.00**

Votive candle holder, Santa, dated 1968, 3".................**$20.00**

Wall pocket, Santa face, 'Greetings' across crown-like hat band, gold trim.................**$175.00**

Kozy Kitten

Ashtray, cat on square plaid base, 4 corner rests, from $60 to.................**$75.00**

Bud vase, cat in plaid cap & neckerchief, from $75 to.**$100.00**

Butter dish, cats peeking out on side, ¼-lb, rare.....**$150.00**

Cookie jar, head form, from $40 to.................**$50.00**

Cottage cheese keeper, cat knob on lid.................**$100.00**

Creamer & sugar bowl, stackable.................**$195.00**

Letter holder, cat with coiled wire back, from $45.00 to $60.00.
(Photo courtesy Pat and Ann Duncan)

Memo finder, full-bodied cat, legs cradle note pad, from $100 to.................**$115.00**

Powdered cleanser shaker, full-bodied lady cat wearing apron, w/broom.................**$150.00**

Salt & pepper shakers, cat's head, pr.................**$30.00**

Salt & pepper shakers, head form, 1 in plaid cap, in wireware napkin holder frame, from $50 to.................**$75.00**

Salt & pepper shakers, tall cats, pr.................**$40.00**

Salt & pepper shakers, 4 individual cat heads, stacked on upright dowel, from $90 to.................**$120.00**

Sewing box, figural cat w/tape-measure tongue on lid..**$100.00**

Spice set, stacking; from $150 to.................**$175.00**

Spice shaker, cat head w/loop atop for hanging, 2½x3"..**$35.00**

String holder, head only, from $50 to.................**$65.00**

Sugar shaker, cat in apron carries sack w/word Pour, shaker holes in hat, side spout formed by sack, rare, from $120 to.................**$145.00**

Tape measure, cat on cushion.................**$85.00**

Wall pocket, cat's head, from $50 to.................**$65.00**

Pixie Ware

Candlesticks, pr, from $45 to.................**$55.00**

Cherries jar, flat head finial on lid, w/cherry pick or spoon.**$150.00**

Chili sauce, rare, minimum value.................**$350.00**

Cocktail cherries, from $175 to.................**$200.00**

Cocktail olives, winking green head finial on lid, from $120 to.................**$135.00**

Cocktail onions, onion-head finial, from $160 to......**$175.00**

Cruets, oil & vinegar, Sally & Sam, pr, minimum value ..**$250.00**

Decanter, Devil Brew, striped base, 10½", rare, minimum value.................**$275.00**

Decanter, Whiskey, w/winking head stopper, minimum value.................**$225.00**

Decanter, 300 Proof, flat-head stopper w/red rose, minimum value.................**$225.00**

Dish, flat-head handle w/crossed eyes & pickle nose, green stripes, minimum value.................**$100.00**

French dressing bottle, minimum value, from $160 to..**$175.00**

Honey, very rare, minimum value.................**$500.00**

Hors d'oeurve, head on body pierced for toothpicks, exaggerated tall hairdo, saucer base, from $225 to...**$250.00**

Instant coffee jar, brown-skinned blond head finial, hard to find, minimum value.................**$250.00**

Italian dressing bottle, from $160 to.................**$175.00**

Jam & jelly jar, flat-head finial on lid.................**$75.00**

Ketchup jar, orange tomato-like head finial on lid, from $75 to.................**$90.00**

Mayonnaise jar, winking head finial on lid, minimum value.................**$250.00**

Mustard jar, yellow head finial on lid, from $75 to....**$90.00**

Olive jar, winking green head finial on lid, from $100 to.................**$125.00**

Onion jar, flat onion-head finial on lid, 1958.................**$200.00**

Relish jar, green flat head on lid.................**$200.00**

Russian dressing bottle, from $165 to.................**$175.00**

Salt & pepper shakers, gourd form, pointed beak & 'eye' suggests bird-like appearance, stripes, no pixie, pr ..**$30.00**

Salt & pepper shakers, Salty & Peppy, attached flat head w/painted wood handle, pr.................**$125.00**

Salt & pepper shakers, squat w/wide angled shoulder, stripes, no pixie, pr.................**$25.00**

Spice set, stacking; from $135 to.................**$150.00**

Sugar bowl, Lil' Sugar w/spoon & pixie lid, +cream crock, pr, minimum value.................**$200.00**

Towel hook, flat head w/sm loop hanger, rare, minimum value.................**$200.00**

Ponytail Princess

Candle holder, girl shares figure-8 platform w/flower-head candle cup, from $50 to.................**$60.00**

Lipstick holder, from $50 to.................**$65.00**

Tray, double; 2 joined flower cups, girl between, from $50 to.**$65.00**

Salt and pepper shakers, $45.00 for the pair. (Photo courtesy Pat and Ann Duncan)

Rooster

Ashtray/teabag holders, set of 4, from $35 to **$40.00**
Bowl, cereal; 6" **$15.00**
Bud vase, figural rooster, from $25 to **$30.00**
Butter dish, embossed rooster, ¼-lb **$65.00**
Chocolate pot, tall & narrow w/flaring sides, embossed rooster on front **$70.00**
Cigarette holder, wooden w/painted-on rooster, wall mount, holds several packs **$150.00**
Coffeepot, electric...**$85.00**
Coffeepot, embossed rooster **$85.00**
Cookie jar, embossed rooster **$150.00**
Creamer & sugar bowl, embossed rooster, pr............**$50.00**
Cup & saucer, from $20 to....................................**$25.00**
Dish, figural rooster w/open-body receptacle.............**$25.00**
Egg cup, double; figural rooster.............................**$25.00**
Jam & jelly jar, embossed rooster...........................**$60.00**
Ketchup jar, embossed rooster **$50.00**
Mug, embossed rooster (3 sizes), ea from $10 to **$15.00**
Mustard jar, embossed rooster on front, w/lid **$50.00**
Napkin holder **$35.00**
Pincushion, 3¼x4", from $65 to **$75.00**
Pitcher, embossed rooster on front, cylindrical w/indents on side for gripping, no handle, tall, from $50 to.....**$60.00**
Pitcher, syrup; embossed rooster on front, tail handle, from $30 to...**$40.00**
Pitcher, water; flaring sides, tail handle, tall, from $50 to.**$60.00**
Plate, embossed rooster, 8½", from $20 to.................**$25.00**
Platter, embossed rooster, oval, from $28 to **$35.00**
Recipe box, wood w/painted-on rooster, from $75 to .**$100.00**
Salt & pepper shakers, figural rooster, tall, pr, from $25 to **$30.00**
Spoon rest, figural rooster, from $30 to **$20.00**
Tray, facing left..**$20.00**
Trivet, tile w/rooster in iron framework, from $40 to...**$50.00**

Miscellaneous

Ashtray, golfer figural, 5½" **$95.00**
Ashtray, hunter w/gun to shoulder, smoke holes in ears & mouth, 5"..**$35.00**

Ashtray, little old lady w/bottle of booze, skirt forms tray, exposes her feet...**$40.00**
Bank, Coin Kitty, bobbing head finial, from $100 to.**$135.00**
Bank, Dandy Lion, bobbing head, from $100 to **$135.00**
Bank, piggy, w/polka-dotted neck ribbon, 3x4".........**$40.00**
Bowl, watermelon, rind outside, pink inside w/seeds, 2¼x6".**$40.00**
Candle climbers, Honey Bunnies, w/bases, 4-pc set..**$50.00**
Candle holders, bride & groom, 4", pr **$50.00**
Candle holders w/bluebird huggers, birds: 1⅝" wide, pr...**$65.00**
Cherry jar, Cherries If You Please lettered on sign held by butler, minimum value **$250.00**
Cocktail shaker, bartender theme, +4 tumblers..........**$75.00**
Coffee mug, Nixon's face on currency.......................**$60.00**
Decanter, Vodka, man in Russian hat, from $50 to.....**$55.00**
Desk accessories, Cock A Doddle Do (birds), sharpener, pencil holder, set..**$60.00**
Desk set, pelican, compartment in bill, tape dispenser in tail .**$85.00**
Jam 'n Jelly jar, girl's head w/5-petal hat finial, from $60 to..**$70.00**
Ketchup jar, tomato-face finial w/leaf hair, 6" **$60.00**
Martini shaker, butler (Jeeves), 9" **$200.00**
Match holder, pink mouse w/cane, unmarked, 6" **$48.00**
Merry Cocktail Mice, hors d'oeuvre (hole in tail for toothpick), hangs on rim of glass tumbler, sct of 5, MIB **$135.00**
Mug, Nursery Rhymes, footed, verse printed in wide graphic band..**$25.00**
Mugs, Blue Willow, set of 4...................................**$45.00**
Mustard jar, hamburger-head finial, 5½" **$85.00**
Napkin ring, sm white, yellow & green bird atop white ring, dated 1958, 1" dia **$110.00**
Note pad holder, 3-D lady's hand **$45.00**
Onions jar, Onions If You Please lettered on sign held by butler (Jeeves), minimum value **$200.00**
Paper clip, painted square faces w/black back clip, rare, pr.**$50.00**
Pencil sharpener, whale figural, sharpener in mouth, 3¾" L.**$55.00**
Pitcher, blue forals on white, 1964-65, +4 mugs, 5-pc..**$75.00**
Planter, bull, white w/ring in nose.............................**$35.00**
Plate, Rake 'N Spade, MIB **$20.00**
Playing card holder, on base w/3-D bust of granny holding playing cards, from $45 to **$55.00**
Salt & pepper shaker, poodle & cat, 4½", 4", pr.........**$40.00**
Salt & pepper shakers, chick figural w/yellow topknot, beak & feet, original tag marked 'Lil Bo Peep, pr.........**$50.00**
Salt & pepper shakers, goose & golden egg, pr **$40.00**
Salt & pepper shakers, Moo Cow, working 'mooing' mechanism, 3¼", pr...**$42.50**
Salt & pepper shakers, New York Thruway souvenir, stylized girls w/wings marked Lil' Pepper & Lil' Salt, red & white, pr..**$25.00**
Salt & pepper shakers, Rock 'N Roll kids, heads on springs, pr...**$125.00**
Salt & pepper shakers, tiger, big smile, 3½", pr..........**$25.00**
Snack set, tomato cup & lettuce leaf plate, 1962........**$25.00**
Super scooper, Hot Stuff, red & white, w/lid, 6" **$50.00**
Tape dispenser, stylized poodle w/red neck band & pencil sharpener **$50.00**
Tray, butler (Jeeves), 4¾" wide...............................**$150.00**
Votive candle holder, pig, pastel, dated 1958, 5½".....**$45.00**

Homer Laughlin China Co.

Since well before the turn of the century, the Homer Laughlin China Company of Newell, West Virginia, has been turning out dinnerware and kitchenware lines in hundreds of styles and patterns. Most of their pieces are marked either 'HLC' or 'Homer Laughlin.' As styles changed over the years, they designed several basic dinnerware shapes that they used as a basis for literally hundreds of different patterns simply by applying various decals and glaze treatments. A few of their most popular lines are represented below. If you find pieces stamped with a name like Virginia Rose, Rhythm, or Nautilus, don't assume it to be the pattern name; it's the shape name. Virginia Rose, for instance, was decorated with many different decals.

For further information see *The Collector's Encyclopedia of Homer Laughlin Pottery* and *American Dinnerware, 1880s to 1920s*, both by Joanne Jasper (Collector Books); and *Homer Laughlin, A Giant Among Dishes*, by Jo Cunningham (Schiffer). *The Collector's Encyclopedia of Fiesta, Ninth Edition*, by Sharon and Bob Huxford has photographs and prices of several of the more collectible lines such as listed here. Also recommended is *Homer Laughlin China 1940's and 1950's* by Jo Cunningham (Schiffer).

See also Fiesta.

Advisor: Darlene Nossaman, See Directory, Dinnerware)

Club/Newsletter: Homer Laughlin China Collector's Association (HLCCA)
P.O. Box 26021
Crystal City, VA 22215-6021; Dues $25.00 single; $40.00 couple or family, includes *The Dish* magazine (a 16-page quarterly), free classifieds.

Century plate, 10", from $12.00 to $15.00; Marigold sugar bowl, from $12.00 to $15.00; Rhythm creamer, from $8.00 to $10.00; Colonial sauce boat, from $18.00 to $20.00.
(Photo courtesy Darlene Nossaman)

Century Shape (available in Wild Rose, Black Dahlia, Cal Rose, Gold Band, Briar Rose)

For lines with a Mexican decal, add 40% to 50% to these values.

Bowl, fruit; from $5 to.......................................**$7.00**

Bowl, serving; round, 9", from $15 to.....................**$18.00**
Bowl, soup; 7½", from $10 to **$12.00**
Casserole, w/lid, from $40 to................................**$45.00**
Creamer, from $8 to...**$10.00**
Plate, 7", from $5 to..**$7.00**
Plate, 9", from $10 to...**$12.00**
Platter, 11", from $14 to......................................**$16.00**
Platter, 13", from $16 to......................................**$18.00**
Sauce boat, from $15 to.......................................**$18.00**
Saucer, from $3 to...**$5.00**
Sugar bowl, w/lid, from $15 to **$18.00**
Teacup, from $6 to **$8.00**
Teapot, from $50 to **$60.00**

Colonial Shape (available in Arbutus, Colonial Violet, Holly and Berry, Pansy, Hampshire)

Bowl, fruit; 5", from $5 to....................................**$7.00**
Bowl, serving; round, 8", from $16 to.......................**$18.00**
Bowl, soup; 8", from $8 to....................................**$10.00**
Butter dish, w/lid, from $50 to...............................**$60.00**
Cake plate, 13", from $25 to..................................**$30.00**
Casserole, w/lid, 8", from $35 to.............................**$40.00**
Creamer, from $12 to..**$15.00**
Plate, 7", from $8 to..**$10.00**
Plate, 9", from $10 to...**$12.00**
Plate, 10", from $12 to..**$14.00**
Platter, 11", from $20 to......................................**$24.00**
Platter, 13", from $25 to......................................**$28.00**
Saucer, from $4 to...**$5.00**
Sugar bowl, w/lid, from $22 to **$24.00**
Teacup, from $8 to **$10.00**
Teapot, from $65 to **$75.00**

Marigold Shape (available in Pennsylvania Dutch, Ellen, Spring Garden, Silver Rose, Garden Path)

Bowl, fruit; 5½", from $4 to..................................**$5.00**
Bowl, serving; 9", from $12 to................................**$15.00**
Bowl, soup; 8", from $8 to....................................**$10.00**
Casserole, w/lid, from $30 to.................................**$35.00**
Creamer, from $10 to..**$15.00**
Plate, 7", from $6 to..**$8.00**
Plate, 9", from $8 to..**$10.00**
Plate, 10", from $10 to..**$12.00**
Platter, 10½", from $14 to **$16.00**
Platter, 13", from $16 to......................................**$18.00**
Sauce boat, from $14 to.......................................**$18.00**
Saucer, from $3 to...**$4.00**
Teacup, from $6 to **$8.00**

Rhythm Shape (available in Cinderella, Symphony, Sun Valley, Fifth Avenue, Sweet Pea)

Bowl, fruit; 5½", from $5 to..................................**$8.00**
Bowl, serving; round, 8½", from $13..........................**$15.00**
Bowl, soup; 8", from $10 to...................................**$12.00**

Casserole, w/lid, from $35 to..................................**$40.00**
Plate, 7", from $6 to...**$8.00**
Plate, 9", from $8 to..**$10.00**
Plate, 10", from $10 to.....................................**$12.00**
Platter, oval, 11½", from $14 to **$16.00**
Platter, oval, 13½", from $16 to **$18.00**
Sauce boat, from $14 to **$18.00**
Saucer, from $3 to...**$4.00**
Shakers, Swing shape, pr, from $16 to **$18.00**
Sugar bowl, w/lid, from $14 to **$16.00**
Teacup, from $6 to...**$8.00**
Teapot, from $40 to..**$45.00**

Theme Shape (available in Della Robbia, Stratford, Surrey, Heather Lane, Cameo)

Bowl, fruit;, from $5 to....................................**$7.00**
Bowl, serving; oval, 9", from $14 to.....................**$16.00**
Bowl, soup; 8", from $8 to................................**$10.00**
Casserole, w/lid, from $25 to.............................**$35.00**
Creamer, from $12 to..**$14.00**
Plate, 7", from $6 to...**$8.00**
Plate, 9", from $10 to.......................................**$12.00**
Plate, 10", from $12 to......................................**$14.00**
Platter, 11", from $16 to....................................**$18.00**
Platter, 13", from $18 to....................................**$20.00**
Sauce boat, from $15 to....................................**$18.00**
Saucer, from $5 to...**$7.00**
Sugar bowl, w/lid, from $14 to **$16.00**
Teacup, from $6 to...**$8.00**
Teapot, from $45 to..**$55.00**

Triumph Shape (available in Cynthia, Spring Rose, Linda, October Leaves, Woodland)

Bowl, fruit; 5½", from $2 to **$4.00**
Bowl, serving; round, 8½", from $10 to **$12.00**
Bowl, soup; 8½", from $8 to...............................**$10.00**
Casserole, w/lid, from $20 to.............................**$24.00**
Creamer, from $6 to..**$8.00**
Plate, 7", from $4 to...**$6.00**
Plate, 9", from $6 to...**$8.00**
Plate, 10", from $8 to.......................................**$10.00**
Platter, 11", from $10 to....................................**$12.00**
Platter, 13", from $12 to....................................**$14.00**
Sauce boat, from $8 to......................................**$10.00**
Sugar bowl, w/lid, from $8 to **$10.00**
Teacup, from $5 to...**$7.00**
Teapot, from $35 to..**$40.00**

Horton Ceramics

In 1949 Mr. Horace Horton and his wife, Gerry, began production of ceramics in Eastland, Texas. Mrs. Horton designed most all wares which were sold to florists, department stores, and gift shops. The line consisted of ashtrays, contemporary planters and vases, novelty items, western-designed dinnerware, casual outdoor food service pieces, and jardinieres. Numbers and letters found in listings given here refer to the mold numbers which appear on the bottom of each piece.

Advisor: Darlene Nossaman (See Directory, Horton Ceramics)

Ashtray, blue w/green fish inside, #KS120, sm **$9.00**
Ashtray, dark blue or turquoise, free-form, #212 ....**$8.00**
Ashtray, variety of colors, tubular, #126, 6x6½" **$10.00**
Baby bootie, pink or blue, #B4, 4" **$12.00**
Head vase, baby, pink or blue, #BH, 4" **$22.00**

Head vase, from $35.00 to $40.00.
(Photo courtesy Darlene Nossaman)

Honey jar, brown & yellow, 3".................................**$12.00**
Planter, black, green or mushroom color, ladle shape, #709, 6x3"..**$14.00**
Planter, green, burgundy or mustard, #512...................**$9.00**
Planter, green, mustard or pink, palm-frond shape, #922, 20"...**$22.00**
Planter, pink, green, blue or yellow, moon shape, #4612 .**$10.00**
Planter, turquoise & white or plum & white, cedar type, #36, 4x3x2½"...**$18.00**
Planter, white, pink, black or green, #5L, 5x5"...........**$12.00**
Planter, white, turquoise, black or plum, fluted in gold mesh base, #49W, 3½x4½" **$20.00**
Stein, brown & white, w/cow-head handle, 20-oz **$15.00**
Vase, contemporary, 2-tone gold, pink or black, #807, 4x7" **$12.00**
Vase, novelty; Mr & Mrs Snow people, white body, variety of colors, #C7..**$22.00**
Vase, textured in green & white or black & white, #C6, 5x6" **$18.00**
Vase, white blue, sand or coral, #G92, 5x9"...............**$14.00**
Vase, yellow, green, pink or white, #246, 4x6"...........**$12.00**

Hull

Hull has a look of its own. Many lines were made in soft, pastel matt glazes and modeled with flowers and ribbons, and as a result, they have a very feminine appeal.

The company operated in Crooksville (near Zanesville), Ohio, from just after the turn of the century until they closed in 1985. From the 1930s until the plant was destroyed by fire in 1950, they preferred the soft matt glazes so popular with today's collectors, though a few high gloss lines were made as well. When the plant was rebuilt, modern equipment was installed which they soon found did not lend itself to the duplication of the matt glazes, so they began to concentrate on the production of glossy wares, novelties, and figurines.

During the '40s and '50s, they produced a line of kitchenware items modeled after Little Red Riding Hood. Original pieces are expensive today and most are reproduced by persons other than Hull. (See also Little Red Riding Hood.)

Hull's Mirror Brown dinnerware line made from 1960 until they closed in 1985 was very successful for them and was made in large quantities. Its glossy brown glaze was enhanced with a band of ivory foam, and today's collectors are finding its rich colors and basic, strong shapes just as attractive now as they were back then. In addition to table service, there are novelty trays shaped like gingerbread men and fish, canisters and cookie jars, covered casseroles with ducks and hens as lids, vases, ashtrays, and mixing bowls. It's easy to find, and though you may have to pay 'near book' prices at co-ops and antique malls, bargains are out there. It may be marked Hull, Crooksville, O; HPCo; or Crestone.

If you'd like to learn more about this subject, we recommend *The Collector's Encyclopedia of Hull Pottery* and *Ultimate Encyclopedia of Hull Pottery*, both by Brenda Roberts; and *Collector's Guide to Hull Pottery, The Dinnerware Lines*, by Barbara Loveless Gick-Burke.

Advisor: Brenda Roberts (See Directory, Hull)

Basket, Tuscany, green and cream, 8¼", from $60.00 to $85.00.

Basket, Magnolia, floral on pink, matt, #10, 10½", from $350 to **$410.00**
Basket, Wildflower, floral on 2-toned body, pink handle, W-16, 10½", from $350 to **$410.00**

Candle holder, Bow-Knot, floral on blue to green, B-17, 4", from $130 to **$165.00**
Candle holder, double; Wildflower (Numbered Series), floral on pink, #69, 4", from $165 to **$195.00**
Candle holder, Open Rose, bird form, pink & yellow roses on pink, #177, 6½", from $155 to **$215.00**
Candle holder, Parchment & Pine, pine cones & scrolls decor, unmarked, 5" L, from $25 to................................**$35.00**
Candle holder, Water Lily, floral on pink to turquoise, L-22, 4½", from $60 to..**$75.00**
Candle holder, Wildflower, floral on pink to yellow, unmarked, from $50 to...**$65.00**
Candle holders, Serenade, birds on branch, Regency Blue w/Sunlight Yellow interior, S-16, 6½", pr, from $120 to **$160.00**
Cornucopia, Dogwood, floral on yellow to green, #522, 3¾", from $95 to...**$125.00**
Cornucopia, Water Lily, floral on pink to ivory, L-7, 6½", from $95 to...**$135.00**
Cornucopia, Woodland, floral on pink, W-2, 5½", from $75 to **$100.00**
Creamer, Blossom, Cinderella Kitchenware, #28, 4½", from $45 to..**$65.00**
Creamer, Ebb Tide, shell form, white w/green wash, E-15, 4", from $75 to...**$100.00**
Creamer, Magnolia, blue floral on ivory, H-21, 3¾", from $0 to **$55.00**
Flower bowl, Imperial, embossed leaf, 4½x5½", from $3 to **$5.00**
Flowerpot, Fiesta, scalloped & folded shape, shiny black, #40, 4¼", from $20 to................................**$30.00**
Flowerpot, Sunglow, floral on bright yellow, #97, 5½", from $30 to..**$40.00**
Flowerpot, Sunglow, floral on bright yellow, flared rim, #97, 5½", from $30 to..**$40.00**
Jardiniere & pedestal, Imperial, moss green & mahogany w/white flow, F-85, short, from $90 to...............**$120.00**
Leaf dish, Imperial, moss green & mahogany w/white flow, from $20 to...**$25.00**
Novelty, cat figurine, blue bow, painted details on white, unmarked, 7", from $275 to......................**$375.00**
Novelty, Corky Pig, bank, Mirror Brown, 5", from $50 to..**$75.00**
Novelty, flowerpot, embossed rings, flared rim, #95, 4½", from $15 to...**$20.00**
Novelty, leaf dish, deep rose to dark green, #85, 13", from $35 to..**$45.00**
Novelty, Old Spice shaving mug, 3", from $22 to.......**$30.00**
Novelty, parrot w/cart planter, pink, yellow & green, #60, 6x9½", from $45 to..**$65.00**
Novelty, pig planter, floral decor, opening in back, #60, 5", from $30 to...**$45.00**
Novelty, poodle planter, rose & green on white, #114, 8", from $45 to...**$65.00**
Novelty, rooster figurine, #951, 7", from $40 to..........**$65.00**
Novelty, Teddy bear planter, bittersweet, #811, 7", from $30 to **$45.00**

Pitcher, Bouquet, Cinderella Kitchenware, #22, 64-oz, from $175 to..**$230.00**

Pitcher, Floral, yellow daisy-like flowers on ivory, brown trim at rim, #46, 6", from $40 to..**$55.00**

Pitcher, Sunglow, floral on bright yellow, twisted rope trim at rim, #55, 7½", from $145 to....................................**$185.00**

Planter, Blossom Flight, floral on basketweave, stylized handle, 10½", from $95 to.................................**$125.00**

Planter, Imperial, twin swans, white, from $40 to......**$60.00**

Planter, Madonna, Imperial Flower Club pc, 7½x9", from $30 to...**$40.00**

Planter, Poppy, multicolor floral on blue to pink, handles, #602, 6½", from $220 to......................................**$270.00**

Planter, Regal, green to ivory, footed bowl shape, #301, 3½", from $10 to..**$15.00**

Planter, swan figural, Imperial, white, F-23, 8½" **$30.00**

Planter/candle holder, Continental/Tropicana, 4", from $25 to...**$35.00**

Salt & pepper shakers, Floral, yellow S & P letters on ivory, #44, 3½", pr, from $30 to.....................................**$40.00**

Sugar bowl, Magnolia, blue floral on ivory gloss, handles, w/lid, H-22, 3¾", from $40 to..............................**$60.00**

Sugar bowl, Rosella, white flowers w/green leaves on ivory, open, R-4, 5½", from $45 to...................................**$65.00**

Teapot, Magnolia, floral on pink, matt, #23, 6½", from $215 to...**$260.00**

Vase, double bud; Woodland, bright yellow to pink, W-15, 8½", from $95 to.......................................**$135.00**

Vase, Iris, floral on pink to blue, handles, #407, 4¾", from $90 to..**$125.00**

Vase, Iris, floral on yellow to pink, handles, #402, 7", from $160 to...**$200.00**

Vase, Magnolia, floral on pink, handles, #13, 4¾", from $40 to...**$60.00**

Vase, Mardi Grass, white, low handles, #215, 9", from $45 to **$65.00**

Vase, Mayfair, hand holding vase, light green, #83, 7¾" , from $50 to...**$70.00**

Vase, Open Rose, pink & yellow roses on pink, handles, #123, 6½", from $130 to......................................**$160.00**

Vase, Open Rose, pink & yellow roses on pink, low handles, #130, 4¾", from $75 to..**$105.00**

Vase, Rosella, white floral w/green leaves on coral, R-2, 5", from $70 to...**$95.00**

Vase, Rosella, white flowers w/green leaves on ivory, R-14, 8½", from $130 to......................................**$160.00**

Vase, Serenade, floral on yellow, S-1, 6½", from $50 to....**$70.00**

Vase, Thistle, floral on pink, angle handles, #52, 6½", from $130 to...**$150.00**

Vase, Water Lily, white flower on apricot to walnut, handles, L-2, 5½", from $45 to......................................**$65.00**

Vase, Wildflower, floral on pink to yellow, handles, W-1, 5½", from $45 to...**$65.00**

Vase, Wildflower, floral on yellow to pink, low handles, W-12, 9½", from $165 to......................................**$240.00**

Vase, Wildflower (Numbered Series), floral on pink, #78, 8½", from $290 to..**$360.00**

Vase, Woodland, floral on yellow to green, W-1, 5½", from $75 to...**$105.00**

Vase, Woodland, floral on yellow to green, W-16, 8½", from $225 to...**$275.00**

Wall pocket, Bow-Knot, cup & saucer shape, B-24, 6", from $265 to...**$310.00**

Wall pocket, Woodland, floral on shell form, ivory to pink, W-13, 7½", from $225 to......................................**$275.00**

Window box, Woodland, floral on pink, W-14, 10" L, from $160 to...**$210.00**

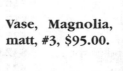

Vase, Magnolia, matt, #3, $95.00.

Dinnerware

Avocado, butter dish, 7¾", from $20 to......................**$25.00**

Avocado, creamer or jug, 8-oz....................................**$9.00**

Avocado, gravy boat w/tray.......................................**$80.00**

Avocado, plate, dinner; 10¼".......................................**$8.00**

Avocado, teapot, 5-cup **$25.00**

Centennial, bean pot, 7x9".......................................**$110.00**

Centennial, bowl, cereal; 5¾".....................................**$50.00**

Centennial, salt & pepper shakers, 3", pr **$60.00**

Country Belle, coffee cup, stemmed...........................**$10.00**

Country Belle, coffee cup saucer.................................**$7.00**

Country Belle, creamer & sugar bowl........................**$21.00**

Country Belle, plate, dessert **$9.00**

Country Belle, plate, salad **$8.00**

Country Belle, platter, oval **$25.00**

Country Belle, salt & pepper shakers, w/handles, pr.**$32.00**

Country Belle, souffle dish..**$29.00**

Country Squire, bean pot, 2-qt **$28.00**

Country Squire, bowl, mixing; 6¾" **$12.00**

Country Squire, bowl, spaghetti; 10¼".......................**$17.00**

Country Squire, plate, dinner; 10¼" **$9.00**

Country Squire, salt & pepper shakers, 3¾", pr.........**$16.00**

Crestone, bowl, custard; 6-oz, from $3 to....................**$5.00**

Crestone, bowl, fruit; 6" **$6.00**

Crestone, bowl, 6", from $4 to....................................**$6.00**

Crestone, casserole, w/lid, 32-oz................................**$25.00**

Crestone, gravy boat/syrup, 10-oz, from $30 to.........**$40.00**

Crestone, gravy boat & saucer, 10-oz..........................**$32.00**
Crestone, plate, dinner; 10¼" **$12.00**
Crestone, plate, 10¼", from $10 to.........................**$12.00**
Crestone, plate, 7½", from $4 to.............................**$6.00**
Crestone, platter, well-in-tree; 14x10".....................**$50.00**
Crestone, salt & pepper shakers, 3¾", pr, from $25 to..**$30.00**
Crestone, teapot, 5-cup, from $95 to **$145.00**
Gingerbread Man, child's bowl................................**$80.00**
Gingerbread Man, child's cup..................................**$80.00**
Gingerbread Man, coaster, brown or gray, 5x5" **$30.00**
Gingerbread Man, cookie jar, brown **$125.00**
Gingerbread Man, server, brown, 10x10" **$30.00**
Gingerbread Man, server, gray or sand, 10x10" **$50.00**
Gingerbread Train Engine......................................**$500.00**
Heartland, bowl, soup/salad; 12-oz.........................**$9.00**
Heartland, coffeepot...**$50.00**
Heartland, creamer **$15.00**
Heartland, pitcher, 36-oz.......................................**$40.00**
Heartland, plate, dinner **$12.00**
Heartland, platter, oval..**$25.00**
Heartland, salt & pepper shakers, handles, pr **$32.00**
Mirror Almond, ashtray, 8", from $20 to...................**$25.00**
Mirror Almond, baker, open, 13⅜", from $85 to.......**$115.00**
Mirror Almond, bean pot, 2-qt, from $30 to..............**$40.00**
Mirror Almond, bowl, 10¼", from $25 to **$30.00**
Mirror Almond, casserole, chicken figural lid, 2-pt, from $75
    to..**$100.00**
Mirror Almond, coffeepot, 8-cup, from $30 to **$40.00**
Mirror Almond, double server, 14½", from $140 to..**$165.00**
Mirror Almond, French casserole, open, 5¼", from $12
    to **$15.00**
Mirror Almond, mug, 9-oz, from $4 to.........................**$6.00**
Mirror Almond, plate, 6¼", from $3 to..........................**$4.00**
Mirror Almond, plate, 9⅜", from $8 to **$10.00**
Mirror Almond, salt & pepper shakers, 3¾", pr, from $14
    to...**$18.00**
Mirror Almond, snack set, from $20 to **$25.00**
Mirror Almond, steak plate, 11¾", from $20 to..........**$25.00**
Mirror Almond, teapot, from $20 to **$30.00**
Mirror Almond, tray, 11x12", from $110 to................**$155.00**
Mirror Brown, ashtray, 8", from $20 to **$25.00**
Mirror Brown, baker, open, 3-pt, from $15 to.............**$20.00**
Mirror Brown, bowl, divided vegetable; 10¾", from $20 to.**$30.00**
Mirror Brown, bowl, salad; 6½", from $16 to **$25.00**
Mirror Brown, bowl, 10¼", from $20 to **$30.00**
Mirror Brown, butter dish, ¼-lb, from $20 to **$25.00**
Mirror Brown, casserole, figural duck lid, 2-pt, from $75
    to **$100.00**
Mirror Brown, chip 'n dip, 11¼", from $45 to **$65.00**
Mirror Brown, coffeepot, 8-cup, from $30 to..............**$40.00**
Mirror Brown, cookie jar, 94-oz, from $30 to..............**$45.00**
Mirror Brown, cup & saucer, 6-oz, 5½", from $6 to **$9.00**
Mirror Brown, Dutch oven, 3-pt, from $30 to.............**$40.00**
Mirror Brown, French casserole, w/lid, 5¼", from $14
    to **$18.00**
Mirror Brown, gravy boat & saucer, 15-oz, 10¼", from $55
    to...**$75.00**

Mirror Brown, creamer and sugar bowl, $14.00 each; Teapot, $35.00.

Mirror Brown, jar, w/lid, 12-oz, from $12 to **$15.00**
Mirror Brown, jug, 1-qt, from $25 to.........................**$35.00**
Mirror Brown, jug, 5-pt, from $40 to **$60.00**
Mirror Brown, leaf chip 'n dip, 15", from $25 to **$35.00**
Mirror Brown, mug, 9-oz, from $4 to.........................**$6.00**
Mirror Brown, pie plate, 9¼", from $18 to..................**$24.00**
Mirror Brown, plate, 6½", from $3 to.........................**$4.00**
Mirror Brown, plate, 8½", from $6 to.........................**$8.00**
Mirror Brown, plate, 10¼", from $8 to **$10.00**
Mirror Brown, salt & pepper shakers, pr, from $14 to .**$18.00**
Mirror Brown, server, w/figural chicken lid, 13⅜", from $165
    to..**$225.00**
Mirror Brown, server, 10", from $12 to **$16.00**
Mirror Brown, snack set, from $20 to **$25.00**
Mirror Brown, steak plate, 11¾", from $20 to.............**$25.00**
Mirror Brown, steak plate, 14", from $20 to................**$25.00**
Mirror Brown, stein, 16-oz, from $8 to **$10.00**
Mirror Brown, toast 'n cereal, from $20 to **$25.00**
Mirror Brown, vase, bud; 9", from $16 to...................**$22.00**
Provincial, baking dish, 3-pt **$22.00**
Provincial, beer stein, 16-oz......................................**$22.00**
Provincial, bowl, mixing; 6¾"....................................**$20.00**
Provincial, coffee cup (mug), 9-oz **$9.00**
Provincial, plate, salad; 6½" **$11.00**
Provincial, salt & pepper shakers, w/corks, 3¾", pr....**$24.00**
Rainbow, bowl, mixing; 7"..**$12.00**
Rainbow, coffee cup, 6-oz **$6.00**
Rainbow, cup & saucer, 5-oz, 5½" dia, from $6 to.......**$9.00**
Rainbow, leaf tray, 12", from $35 to **$50.00**
Rainbow, mug, 9-oz, from $4 to.................................**$6.00**
Rainbow, pitcher, 7½", from $25 to **$35.00**
Rainbow, plate, luncheon; 8½"...................................**$9.00**
Rainbow, plate, 8½", from $6 to.................................**$8.00**
Rainbow, plate, 10¼", from $8 to...............................**$10.00**
Rainbow, soup 'n sandwich tray, 9¾", w/5" mug, from $20
    to..**$25.00**
Rainbow, tidbit tray, 10", from $30 to........................**$40.00**
Ridge, bowl, vegetable; gray or sand, 2½x7½"..........**$10.00**
Ridge, creamer, any color **$10.00**

Ridge, cup & saucer, any color	$10.00
Ridge, plate, dinner; gray or sand, 10¼"	$8.00
Ridge, steak plate, any color, 9½x12"	$11.00
Ring, coffee cup, brown	$7.00
Ring, coffeepot, brown	$50.00
Ring, custard cup, brown	$8.00
Ring, plate, dinner; brown	$12.00
Ring, platter, oval, brown	$18.00
Tangerine, bowl, soup/salad; 6½"	$7.00
Tangerine, jug, 2-pt.	$29.00
Tangerine, plate, salad; 6½"	$5.00
Tangerine, salt & pepper shakers, w/corks, 3¾", pr	$16.00
Tangerine, teapot, 5-cup	$30.00
Tangerine, water jug, 80-oz	$32.00

Imperial Glass

Organized in 1901 in Bellaire, Ohio, the Imperial Glass Company made carnival glass, stretch glass, a line called NuCut (made in imitation of cut glass), and a limited amount of art glass within the first decade of the century. In the mid-'30s, they designed one of their most famous patterns (and one of their most popular with today's collectors), Candlewick. Within a few years, milk glass had become their leading product.

During the '50s they reintroduced their NuCut line in crystal as well as colors, marketing it as 'Collector's Crystal.' In the late '50s they bought molds from both Heisey and Cambridge. Most of the glassware they reissued from these old molds was marked 'IG,' one letter superimposed over the other. When Imperial was bought by Lenox in 1973, an 'L' was added to the mark. The ALIG logo was added in 1981 when the company was purchased by Arthur Lorch. In 1982 the factory was sold to Robert Stahl of Minneapolis. Chapter 11 bankruptcy was filled in October that year. A plant resurgence continued production. Many Heisey by Imperial animals done in color were made at this time. A new mark, the NI for New Imperial, was used on a few items. In November of 1984 the plant closed forever and the assets were sold at liquidation. This was the end of the 'Big I.'

Numbers in the listings were assigned by the company and appeared on their catalog pages. They were used to indicate differences in shapes and stems, for instance. Collectors still use them.

For more information on Imperial we recommend *Imperial Glass* by Margaret and Douglas Archer; *Elegant Glassware of the Depression Era* by Gene Florence; *Imperial Carnival Glass* by Carl O. Burns; and *Imperial Glass Encyclopedia, Vol I, A – Cane, Vol II, Cane – M,* and *Volume III, M to Z,* edited by James Measell. To research Imperial's glass animals, refer to *Glass Animals of the Depression Years* by Lee Garmon and Dick Spencer.

See also Candlewick.

Note: To determine values for Cape Cod in colors, add 100% to prices suggested for crystal for Ritz Blue and Ruby; Amber, Antique Blue, Azalea, Evergreen, Verde, black, and milk glass are 50% higher than crystal.

Advisor: Joan Cimini (See Directory, Imperial)

Club: National Imperial Glass Collectors' Society, Inc. P.O. Box 534, Bellaire, OH 43906. Dues: $15 per year (+$3 for each additional member of household), quarterly newsletter: *Glasszette,* convention every June

Ashtray, Cape Cod, crystal, #160/150, double rest, 5½"	$22.00
Basket, Azure Blue Carnival, daisy	$75.00
Basket, Crocheted Crystal, 9"	$40.00
Bottle, cologne; Cape Cod, crystal, w/stopper, #1601	$60.00
Bottle, ketchup; Cape Cod, crystal, #160/237, 14-oz.	$210.00
Bowl, Beaded Block, opal, deep, 6" dia	$35.00
Bowl, Cape Cod, crystal, oval, crimped, #160/131C, 12"	$90.00
Bowl, console; Crocheted Crystal, 11"	$30.00
Bowl, cream soup; Diamond Quilted, pink or green, 4¾"	$10.00
Bowl, finger; Mt Vernon, crystal, 5"	$12.00
Bowl, fruit; Katy, blue opalescent, 4½"	$30.00
Bowl, fruit; Katy, blue or green w/opalescent edge, 4½"	$30.00
Bowl, lily; Beaded Block, green, 4½" dia	$18.00
Bowl, mint; Cape Cod, crystal, handled, #160/51F, 6"	$20.00
Bowl, Narcissus; Crocheted Crystal, 7"	$40.00
Bowl, Pansy, Helios carnival, scalloped edge, oval, #478, 9"	$70.00
Bowl, soup; Cape Cod, crystal, tab handled, #160/198, 5½"	$18.00
Bowl, spider; Cape Cod, crystal, handled, #160/180, 4½"	$26.00
Bowl, vegetable; Cape Cod, crystal, oval, #160/221, 10"	$70.00
Bowl, vegetable; Katy, green opalescent, 9"	$100.00
Butter dish, Cape Cod, crystal, handled, w/lid, #160/144, 5"	$42.00
Butter dish, Mt Vernon, crystal, 5"	$30.00

Cake plate, Crochet Crystal, footed, $40.00.

Candle holder, Cape Cod, crystal, saucer style, #160/175, 4½"	$20.00
Candle holder, Crocheted Crystal, double, 4½"	$15.00
Candle holder, Crocheted Crystal, single, 6" W	$20.00
Candy dish, blue satin, bee finial, marked LIG #825, 5x5"	$45.00

Candy jar, caramel slag, Louis XIV, 4-footed, #176, 6"..**$70.00**
Carafe, wine; Cape Cod, crystal, #160/185, 26-oz.....**$195.00**
Celery, Crocheted Crystal, oval, 10" **$25.00**
Cigarette lighter, black, footed, #1602 ....**$30.00**
Creamer, Beaded Block, green **$25.00**
Creamer, Cape Cod, crystal, footed, #160/31 ....**$15.00**
Creamer, caramel slag, flat, #666 ....**$35.00**
Creamer, Crocheted Crystal, footed **$20.00**
Creamer, Diamond Quilted, blue or black.................**$20.00**
Cup, Katy, blue opalescent....................................**$35.00**
Cup, Katy, blue or green w/opalescent edge.............**$35.00**
Cup, punch; Crocheted Crystal, open handle................**$7.50**
Egg cup, Cape Cod, crystal, #160/225 ....**$32.50**
Figurine, Asiatic pheasant, amber **$200.00**
Figurine, chick, milk glass, head down **$10.00**
Figurine, Clydesdale, Verde Green.........................**$150.00**
Figurine, colt, Horizon Blue, kicking **$35.00**
Figurine, cygnet, Horizon Blue..............................**$25.00**
Figurine, donkey, Meadow Green Carnival.................**$50.00**
Figurine, filly, Verde Green, head backwards **$110.00**
Figurine, flying mare, amber, NI mark, rare..........**$1,500.00**
Figurine, mallard, caramel slag, wings down............**$200.00**
Figurine, mallard, light blue stain, wings down.........**$35.00**
Figurine, piglet, amber, standing **$40.00**
Figurine, rooster, amber **$450.00**
Figurine, swan, purple slag, glossy, 8".....................**$95.00**
Figurine, wood duckling, floating, Sunshine Yellow satin .**$20.00**
Figurine/jar, owl, caramel slag, 6½"..........................**$65.00**
Figurine/paperweight, tiger, Jade Green slag, 8" L **$85.00**
Hors d'oeuvre dish, Crocheted Crystal, 4-part, 10½" dia...**$30.00**
Jar, peanut; Cape Cod, crystal, handled, w/lid, #160/210, 12-oz **$65.00**
Jug, Beaded Block, green, 5¼" **$110.00**
Ladle, mayonnaise; Cape Cod, crystal, 1 bead, #160/165...**$15.00**
Lamp, hurricane; Crocheted Crystal, 11" **$50.00**
Mayonnaise ladle, Crocheted Crystal.........................**$8.00**
Mug, Cape Cod, crystal, #160/188, 12-oz....................**$40.00**

Pitcher, Cape Cod, crystal, two-quart, $80.00.

Plate, Beaded Block, opal, 8¾" **$30.00**
Plate, bread & butter; Katy, green opalescent, 6½" **$18.00**

Plate, crescent salad; Cape Cod, crystal, #160/12, 8" ..**$50.00**
Plate, Crocheted Crystal, 9½"....................................**$12.50**
Plate, Crocheted Crystal, 17"......................................**$40.00**
Plate, dinner; Katy, green opalescent, 10" **$85.00**
Plate, mayonnaise; Crocheted Crystal, 7½"..................**$7.50**
Plate, Mt Vernon, crystal, round, 8"..........................**$10.00**
Plate, salad; Diamond Quilted, pink or green, 7" **$6.00**
Plate, torte; Cape Cod, crystal, #1608F, 13½" **$37.50**
Plate, windmill, caramel slag, #514, 10¾" **$140.00**
Relish, Cape Cod, crystal, oval, 3-part, #160/55, 9½" .**$35.00**
Relish, Crocheted Crystal, 3-part, 11½" **$25.00**
Salt & pepper shakers, Cape Cod, crystal, footed, #160/116, pr..**$25.00**
Spooner, Mt Vernon, crystal......................................**$22.00**
Stem, water goblet; Crocheted Crystal, 9-oz, 7⅛" **$14.00**
Stem, water; Cape Cod, crystal, #1602, 9-oz...............**$9.50**
Stem, wine; Crocheted Crystal, 4½-oz, 5½"................**$17.50**
Sugar bowl, Beaded Block, green **$25.00**
Sugar bowl, Cape Cod, crystal, footed, #160/31 ....**$15.00**
Sugar bowl, Crocheted Crystal, flat **$25.00**
Toothpick holder, Azure Blue, #505, marked IG **$18.50**
Tumbler, Grapes, milk glass, #1950/473, 9-oz.............**$13.50**
Tumbler, juice; Crocheted Crystal, footed, 6-oz, 6".....**$10.00**
Tumbler, Katy, blue opalescent, 9-oz.........................**$55.00**
Tumbler, water; Cape Cod, crystal, #160, 10-oz..........**$15.00**
Vase, Cape Cod, crystal, footed, #160/28, 8½"............**$42.50**
Vase, caramel slag, footed, #529, 10" **$170.00**
Vase, Crocheted Crystal, 8" **$35.00**
Vase, fan; Diamond Quilted, dolphin handles, blue or black **$75.00**
Vase, Tri-corn, caramel slag, #192, IG mark, 8½" **$160.00**

Indiana Glass

From 1972 until 1978, Indiana Glass Company produced a line of iridescent 'new carnival' glass, much of which was embossed with grape clusters and detailed leaves in a line they called Harvest. It was made in blue, gold, and lime, and was evidently a good seller for them, judging from the amount around today. They also produced a line of 'press cut' iridescent glass called Heritage, which they made in amethyst and Sunset (amberina). Collectors always seem to gravitate toward lustre-coated glassware, whether it's old or recently made, and there seems to be a significant amount of interest in this line.

There was also a series of four Bicentennial commemorative plates made in blue and gold carnival: American Eagle, Independence Hall, Liberty Bell, and Spirit of '76. They're valued at $12.00 for the gold and $15.00 for the blue, except for the American Eagle plate, which is worth from $12.00 to $15.00 regardless of color.

This glass is a little difficult to evaluate, since you see it in malls and at flea markets with such a wide range of 'asking' prices. On one hand, you'll have sellers who themselves are not exactly sure what it is they have but since it's 'carnival' assume it should be fairly pricey. On the other hand, you have those who've just 'cleaned house' and want to get rid of it. They may have bought it new themselves and know it's not very old and wasn't expensive to start with. There has been much of it for sale on Internet auctions; the surplus has driven prices downward, as is true with so many of the newer collectibles.

In addition to the iridescent glass lines, Indiana produced colored glass baskets, vases, etc., as well as a line called Ruby Band Diamond Point, a clear diamond-faceted pattern with a wide ruby-flashed rim band. We've listed some of the latter below; our values are for examples with the ruby-flashing in excellent condition.

Over the last ten years, the collectibles market has changed. Nowadays, some shows' criteria regarding the merchandise they allow to be displayed is 'if it's no longer available on the retail market, it's OK.' I suspect that this attitude will become more and more widespread. At any rate, this is one of the newest interests at the flea market/antique mall level, and if you can buy it right (and like its looks), now is the time!

See also King's Crown; Tiara.

Iridescent Amethyst Carnival Glass (Heritage)

Basket, footed, 9x5x7", from $30 to $35.00
Butter dish, 5x7½" dia, from $20 to $25.00

Candle holders, Harvest, embossed grapes, from $22.00 to $28.00 for the pair.

Center bowl, 4¾x8½", from $25 to $35.00
Goblet, 8-oz, from $14 to $18.00
Pitcher, 8¼", from $35 to $45.00
Punch set, 10" bowl & pedestal, 8 cups, & ladle, 11-pc ..$100.00
Swung vase, slender & footed w/irregular rim, 11x3" ..$25.00

Iridescent Blue Carnival Glass

Basket, Canterbury, waffled pattern, flared sides drawn in at handle, 11x8x12", from $35 to $45.00
Basket, Monticello, allover faceted embossed diamonds, square, 7x6", from $25 to $35.00
Butter dish, Harvest, embossed grapes, ¼-lb, 8" L, from $15 to $20.00
Candy box, Harvest, embossed grapes w/lace edge, w/lid, 6½", from $20 to $25.00

Candy box, Princess, diamond-point bands, pointed faceted finial, 6x6" dia, from $15 to $20.00
Canister/Candy jar, Harvest, embossed grapes, 7" $25.00
Canister/Cookie jar, Harvest, embossed grapes, 9" $40.00
Canister/Snack jar, Harvest, embossed grapes, 8" $30.00
Center bowl, Harvest, embossed grapes w/paneled sides, 4-footed, 4½x8½x12", common, from $15 to $20.00
Cooler (iced tea tumbler), Harvest, embossed grapes, 14-oz, set of 4, from $28 to $32.00
Creamer & sugar bowl on tray, Harvest, embossed grapes, 3-pc, from $20 to $25.00
Egg/Hors d'oeuvre tray, sectioned w/off-side holder for 8 eggs, 12¾" dia, from $20 to $25.00
Garland bowl (comport), paneled, 7½x8½" dia, from $20 to $25.00
Goblet, Harvest, embossed grapes, 9-oz, set of 4, from $25 to $30.00
Hen on nest, from $10 to...$15.00
Pitcher, Harvest, embossed grapes, 10½", common, from $30 to $40.00
Plate, Bicentennial; American Eagle, from $12 to $15.00
Plate, hostess; Canterbury, allover diamond facets, flared crimped rim, 10", from $20 to $25.00
Punch set, Princess, 26-pc, from $60 to $80.00
Tidbit, allover embossed diamond points, shallow w/flared sides, 6½", from $12 to $15.00
Wedding bowl (sm compote), Thumbprint, footed, 5x5", from $9 to...$12.00

Iridescent Gold Carnival Glass

Basket, Canterbury, waffle pattern, flaring sides drawn in at handle terminals, 9½x11x8½", from $30 to $40.00
Basket, Monticello, lg faceted allover diamonds, square, 7x6", from $20 to $25.00
Candy box, Harvest, embossed grapes, lace edge, footed, 6½x5¾", from $15 to...$20.00
Candy dish, Harvest, embossed grapes, lace edge, footed, 6½", from $15 to $20.00
Canister/Candy jar, Harvest, embossed grapes, 7", from $20 to $25.00
Canister/Cookie jar, Harvest, embossed grapes, 9", from $30 ....$35.00
Canister/Snack jar, Harvest, embossed grapes, 8", from $25 to ..$30.00
Center bowl, Harvest, oval w/embossed grapes & paneled sides, 4½x8½x12", from $15 to $20.00
Console set, wide naturalistic leaves form sides, 9" bowl w/pr 4½" bowl-type candle holders, 3-pc $30.00
Cooler (iced tea tumbler), Harvest, 14-oz, from $6 to ..$8.00
Egg relish plate, 11", from $15 to $20.00
Goblet, Harvest, embossed grapes, 9-oz, from $7 to....$9.00
Hen on nest, 5½", from $10 to $15.00
Pitcher, Harvest, embossed grapes, 10½", from $35 to ..$40.00
Plate, hostess; diamond embossing, shallow w/crimped & flared sides, 10", from $12 to $15.00
Punch set, Princess, 6-qt bowl w/12 cups, 12 hooks & ladle, 26-pc, from $60 to $80.00

Relish tray, Vintage, 6 sections, 9x12¾", from $15 to. **$18.00**

Salad set, Vintage, embossed fruit, apple-shaped rim w/applied stem, 13", w/fork & spoon, 3-pc, from $15 to **$20.00**

Wedding bowl (sm compote), 5x5", from $9 to.........**$12.00**

Wedding bowl, Harvest, embossed grapes, 8x8½", from $22.00 to $28.00.

Iridescent Lime Carnival Glass

Candy box, Harvest, embossed grapes w/lace edge, w/lid, 6½ **$15.00**

Canister/Candy jar, Harvest, embossed grapes, 7", from $20 to.........**$30.00**

Canister/Cookie jar, Harvest, embossed grapes, 9", from $30 to.........**$35.00**

Canister/Snack jar, Harvest, embossed grapes, 8", from $25 to..**$30.00**

Center bowl, Harvest, embossed grapes, paneled sides, 4-footed, 4½x8½x12", from $15 to **$20.00**

Compote, Harvest, embossed grapes, 7x6", from $15 to ..**$20.00**

Console set, Harvest, embossed grapes, 10" comport w/compote-shaped candle holders, 3-pc, from $30 to....**$40.00**

Cooler (iced tea tumbler), Harvest, embossed grapes, 14-oz, from $6 to.........**$8.00**

Creamer & sugar bowl on tray, Harvest, embossed grapes, 3-pc, from $18 to **$22.00**

Egg/Relish tray, 12¾", from $18 to **$22.00**

Goblet, Harvest, embossed grapes, 9-oz, from $7 to....**$9.00**

Hen on nest, from $10 to.........**$15.00**

Pitcher, Harvest, embossed grapes, 10½", from $28 to...**$35.00**

Plate, hostess; allover diamond points, flared crimped sides, 10", from $12 to **$15.00**

Punch set, Princess, 26-pc, from $60 to.........**$80.00**

Salad set, Vintage, embossed fruit, apple-shaped rim w/applied stem, 13", w/fork & spoon, 3-pc, from $20 to **$30.00**

Snack set, Harvest, embossed grapes, 4 cups & 4 plates, 8-pc, from $25 to **$35.00**

Iridescent Sunset (Amberina) Carnival Glass (Heritage)

Basket, footed, 9x5x7", from $40 to **$50.00**

Basket, squared, 9½x7½", from $50 to **$60.00**

Bowl, crimped, 3¾x10", from $40 to **$50.00**

Butter dish, 5x7½" dia, from $35 to **$40.00**

Cake stand, 7x14" dia, from $55 to **$60.00**

Center bowl, 4¾x8½", from $40 to **$45.00**

Creamer & sugar bowl **$40.00**

Dessert set, 8½" bowl, 12" plate, 2-pc, from $50 to ...**$65.00**

Goblet, 8-oz, from $12 to.........**$18.00**

Pitcher, 7¼", from $40 to **$55.00**

Pitcher, 8¼", from $50 to **$65.00**

Plate, rim w/4 lg & 4 sm opposing lobes, 2x14", from $35 to..**$45.00**

Punch set, 10" bowl, pedestal, 8 cups, & ladle, 11-pc..**$125.00**

Rose bowl, 6½x6½", from $20 to **$25.00**

Sauce set, 4½" bowl, 5½" plate, w/spoon, 3-pc, from $20 to **$25.00**

Swung vase, slender, footed, w/irregular rim, 11x3", from $25 to **$30.00**

Tumbler, 3½", from $10 to.........**$15.00**

Patterns

Canterbury, basket, waffle pattern, Lime, Sunset, or Horizon Blue, 5½x12", from $35 to **$50.00**

Monticello, basket, lg faceted diamonds overall, Lemon, Lime, Sunset, or Horizon Blue, square, 7x6", from $25 to .**$30.00**

Monticello, basket, lg faceted diamonds overall, Lemon, Lime, Sunset, or Horizon Blue, 8¾x10½", from $35 to ...**$40.00**

Monticello, candy box, lg faceted overall diamonds, w/lid, Lemon, Lime, Sunset, or Horizon Blue, 5¼x6", from $15 to **$20.00**

Ruby Band Diamond Point, butter dish, from $20 to .**$28.00**

Ruby Band Diamond Point, chip & dip set, 13" dia, from $18 to **$25.00**

Ruby Band Diamond Point, comport, 14½" dia, from $15 to **$20.00**

Ruby Band Diamond Point, cooler (iced tea tumbler), 15-oz, from $8 to.........**$10.00**

Ruby Band Diamond Point, creamer & sugar bowl, 4½", from $12 to **$15.00**

Ruby Band Diamond Point, creamer & sugar bowl, 4¾", on 6x9" tray, from $15 to.........**$22.00**

Ruby Band Diamond Point, goblet, 12-oz, from $9 to .**$12.00**

Ruby Band Diamond Point, On-the-Rocks, 9-oz, from $8 to **$10.00**

Ruby Band Diamond Point, pitcher, 8", from $15 to ..**$20.00**

Ruby Band Diamond Point, plate, hostess; 12", from $12 to **$18.00**

Ruby Band Diamond Point, relish tray, 3-part, 12" dia, from $15 to.........**$20.00**

Ruby Band Diamond Point, salt & pepper shakers, 4", pr, from $15 to.........**$20.00**

Indianapolis 500 Racing Collectibles

You don't have to be a Hoosier to know that unless the weather interfers, this famous 500-mile race is held in Indianapolis every Memorial day and has been since 1911.

Collectors of Indy memorabilia have a plethora of race-related items to draw from and can zero in on one area or many, enabling them to build extensive and interesting collections. Some of the special areas of interest they pursue are autographs, photographs, or other memorabilia related to the drivers; pit badges; race programs and yearbooks; books and magazines; decanters and souvenir tumblers; and model race cars.

Advisor: Eric Jungnickel (See Directory, Indy 500 Memorabilia)

Ashtray, winged wheel, 500 Mile Race Soovenir (sic) of Motor Speedway, china, Japan mark, plentiful production, 4", $15.00.

Ashtray, ceramic, round, 3 rests on straight rim, 74th/May 27, 1990, red & black on white, 4½" dia **$13.00**

Ashtray, dark glass w/race scene, car & IMS logo, 3½" dia **$15.00**

Ashtray, Indianapolis Motor Speedway '500,' white ceramic w/gold trim & winged wheel logo........................**$20.00**

Bank, metal, #32 Haroun's Marmon Wasp, '11 Indy Winner, stamped w/sponsoring bank, 7"...........................**$50.00**

Banner, black w/Eightieth Indianapolis 500 May 26, 1996 & Indy car on purple circle, 36x60"..........................**$15.00**

Banner, 1992, white w/colorful winged logo, 36x60", M...**$20.00**

Bell, white china, colorful Indy scene w/logo & checkered flags, inside label says Karol Western **$15.00**

Brick, from the track, WC Culver, Pat May 21, 1901 ..**$75.00**

Cigarette lighter, silver w/IMS logo on front, track scene, state on Indiana on back, Zippo **$25.00**

Coin, 1991 Diamond Anniversary, logo on front, track scene on back, 1 troy oz silver, silver-colored felt case, EX..**$26.00**

Decal, IMS/USAC logo, dated 1960 ....**$12.00**

Decal, water-dip style, shows IMS Main Gate & period car, 1960s...**$15.00**

Decanter, Al Unser's Johnny Lightning race car, blue w/gold, #2 ....**$75.00**

Decanter, black w/winged wheel logo on front, JW Dant, 1969 ....**$30.00**

Decanter, Mario Andretti, red #9 car, Old Mr Boston.**$50.00**

Decanter, Mark Donohue's Sunoco McLaren #66, bottled by Hoffman Distillery, w/original box **$95.00**

Decanter, May 30th 1970, yellow race car on front, winged wheel logo on back, Jim Beam, 1970 ....**$20.00**

Flag, black & white checks, Indianapolis Speedway, #1 car shown **$10.00**

Game, Auto Racing, Recreates Indy 500, official game of US Auto Club, Avalon Hill, 1979, EX **$35.00**

Game, Champion Spark Plugs Auto Race, premium, 1932, M **$75.00**

Glass, clear w/black letters, Golden Anniversary, 1961, list of winners from 1911-1961, EX...............................**$15.00**

Glasses, hi-ball; lists all winning drivers through 1969, set of 6, M (in original shipping box) **$55.00**

Hat, Coca-Cola & 75th Indy 500 in black & white, M .**$15.00**

Jacket, black nylon w/chest patch of silver Mustang, racing flags, 1979 Indy 500 Pace Car, EX.........................**$70.00**

Jacket, Snap-On, white w/red trim, 1988, Rick Mears, EX **$25.00**

Lighter, cigarette; silver w/Indy 500 logo, Zippo, EX .**$25.00**

Lunch box, Auto Race Magnetic Game Kit, w/thermos, playing pieces & spinner, 1967, M **$125.00**

Magazine, Sports Illustrated, June 5, 1978, Unser's 3rd cover, NM **$12.00**

Model, '64 Mustang Indy Pace Car, Monogram, 1995, complete..**$10.00**

Model, Kraco Special March 88C, AMT, 1989, MIB (sealed) **$25.00**

Pamphlet, Why I Became a Race Car Driver, by Wilbur Shaw, Firestone Tires, 1940...**$15.00**

Pass, Driver's Meeting, 1967, 5½x3½" **$55.00**

Pennant, Indianapolis Motor Speedway, May 30, 1938, blue w/colorful racing scene, 28½"..............................**$200.00**

Pennant, Souvenir of Indianapolis Speedway, red w/IMS logo, 500-mile race, crossed flags & race car on left, 1950s..**$75.00**

Pillow sham, Souvenir of Indianapolis Speedway, pink silk w/race scene **$30.00**

Pin, Firestone around top of tire, brass, Bastian Bros, 1952, EX **$150.00**

Pinball game, 500 Mile Speedway Game, pictures race scenes, w/spinner & bell, Wolverine Toy Co, 22", EX **$25.00**

Pit badge, 1950, bronze **$150.00**

Pit badge, 1952, bronze, Firestone Tire **$125.00**

Pit badge, 1956, silver, IMS Main Gate........................**$90.00**

Pit badge, 1958, EX **$75.00**

Pit badge, 1960, bronze, Champion Spark Plug..........**$50.00**

Pit badge, 1961, gold-colored metal, EX......................**$75.00**

Pit badge, 1963, bronze, EX..**$65.00**

Pit badge, 1965, Wing & Wheel, bronze, EX..............**$55.00**

Pit badge, 1969, bronze, salutes movie 'Winning'.......**$75.00**

Pit badge, 1971, EX **$50.00**

Pit badge, 1982, silver, Camero **$65.00**

Pit badge, 1989, bronze, STP **$50.00**

Pit badge, 1991, bronze, Dodge **$50.00**

Pitcher, clear glass w/Indy 500, etched, M **$38.00**

Plaque, 75 Years of Racing Legends, shows winners of previous races, EX...**$50.00**

Poster, Champion Spark Plug dealer's, pictures, Donohue, Parsons & others..**$20.00**

Program, 1925, scored..**$350.00**

Program, 1929, VG **$210.00**
Program, 1930, soiled, loose pages.........................**$200.00**
Program, 1937, EX **$150.00**
Program, 1939, VG **$75.00**
Program, 1940, M..**$100.00**
Program, 1953, w/line-up insert, 2-page centerfold w/pace car, NM **$40.00**
Program, 1955, NM...**$50.00**
Program, 1956, information, advertisements, photos, 95 pages, VG **$25.00**
Program, 1961, 50th Anniversary, M **$35.00**
Program, 1962, unused scoring chart insert, NM **$30.00**
Program, 1969, 8-page insert, EX **$25.00**
Program, 1977-80s, any, EX **$10.00**
Record, Great Moments From the Indy 500 (1911 to 1974), 33⅓ rpm, narrated by Sid Collins, M.............**$20.00**
Salt & pepper shakers, smoked glass w/wood handles, depicts IMS logo, IMS Main Gate, race car, 4½", pr............**$25.00**
Seat cushion, Indianapolis 500 Speedway, black & white checks w/1970s race car **$25.00**
Sign, Sterling Beer w/Al Unser's winning car, 1978, 18x9½", EX...**$30.00**
Ticket, 1929, w/rain check, shows race scene w/pagoda, NM..**$100.00**
Ticket, 1936, box seat, Speedway diagram on back, EX .**$65.00**
Ticket, 1946, 31st International Sweepstakes, VG.......**$40.00**
Ticket, 1955, w/rain check, shows previous year's winner AJ Foyt, M...**$30.00**
Ticket, 1955, 39th International Sweepstakes, shows 1964 winner, M **$45.00**
Ticket, 1973, shows previous year's winner R Mears .**$10.00**
Ticket, 1991, VIP Suite, unused...........................**$15.00**
Tie bar & cuff links, Parnelli Jones in helmet, gold-filled, 3-pc **$50.00**
Tray, Falstaff Beer, 1975, shows 3 Indy cars racing & lists all winners through 1974, EX...................**$45.00**
Tumbler, IMS logo, 1953 ....**$25.00**
Tumbler, IMS logo on front, winners listed on back, Tony Hulman facsimile signature, 1968.................**$20.00**
Yearbook, 1947, Floyd Clymer, features Mauri Rose...**$30.00**
Yearbook, 1961, Floyd Clymer, Foyt's 1st win **$50.00**
Yearbook, 1972, Carl Hugness, 1st annual Hugness...**$75.00**
Yearbook, 1982, Carl Hugness, Johncock cover..........**$30.00**

Italian Glass

Throughout the century, the island of Murano has been recognized a one of the major glass-making centers of the world. Companies including Venini, Barovier, Aureliano Toso, Barvini, Vistosi, AVEM, Cenedese, Cappellin, Seguso, and Archimede Seguso have produced very fine art glass, examples of which today often bring several thousand dollars on the secondary market — superior examples much more. Such items are rarely seen at the garage sale and flea market level, but what you will be seeing are the more generic glass clowns, birds, ashtrays, and animals, generally

referred to simply as Murano glass. Their values are determined by the techniques used in their making more than size alone. For instance, an items with gold inclusions, controlled bubbles, fused glass patches, or layers of colors is more desirable than one that has none of these elements, even though it may be larger. For more information concerning the specific companies mentioned above, see *Schroeder's Antiques Price Guide* (Collector Books).

Bell, pink frosted diamond pattern, original metallic Murano label, 5¾x4½" **$60.00**
Bowl, amethyst & gold, Murano, 3¼x8½x9"..............**$36.00**
Bowl, multicolor gold flecks in deep purple, irregular scallops, 1960s, 2½x19" **$60.00**
Compote, white w/gold fleckes, green grapes ea end w/clear gold-flecked leaf at ea handle, 7⅞x11½".............**$55.00**
Dish/tray, deep rose red w/scattered millifiori canes resembling seashells, 1½x10x9½" **$42.00**

Ewer, royal blue, cased, amber foot and rim, applied red cherries, 13", $95.00.

Figurine, cat, clear w/cobalt spots, white & black eyes, 1960s, 7x5½" **$45.00**
Figurine, clown w/hat & ball, 1950s, 8¾" **$65.00**
Figurine, dog w/head up, red, blue, black & brown, 9" .**$80.00**
Figurine, rooster, bright & vivid colors, air bubbles, w/Murano tag, 13x5x5" **$75.00**
Pear, clear & shadowed w/aquamarine blue & gold specks, applied leaf, Salviati, 6" **$35.00**
Vase, peach, amber, green & blue and clear, free-flowing shape, 12" **$65.00**

Jade-ite Glassware

For the past few years, Jade-ite has been one of the fastest-moving types of collectible glassware on the market. It was produced by several companies from the 1940s through 1965. Many of Anchor Hocking's Fire-King lines were available in the soft opaque green Jade-ite, and Jeannette Glass as well as McKee produced their own versions.

It was always very inexpensive glass, and it was made in abundance. Dinnerware for the home as well as restaurants and a vast array of kitchenware items literally flooded the country for many years. Though a few rare pieces have become fairly expensive, most are still reasonably priced, and there are still bargains to be had.

For more information we recommend *Anchor Hocking's Fire-King & More, Kitchen Glassware of the Depression Years,* and *Collectible Glassware of the 40s, 50s, and 60s,* all by Gene Florence.

Canister, round, with lid, 32-ounce, from $25.00 to $30.00.

Ashtray, Fire-King (unmarked), 4¼" square, from $28 to .**$30.00**
Baker, Ovenware, Fire-King, 2½x5", from $50 to **$60.00**
Bowl, batter; ¾" band at top, Fire-King, from $20 to.**$25.00**
Bowl, berry; Laurel, McKee, 9".......................................**$20.00**
Bowl, bulb; Fire-King, 6¼", from $18 to......................**$20.00**
Bowl, cereal; Restaurant Ware, flanged rim, Fire-King, 8-oz **$25.00**
Bowl, cereal; Shell, Fire-King, 6⅜"...............................**$30.00**
Bowl, cereal; 1700 Line, Fire-King, 5⅞".......................**$25.00**
Bowl, chile; Heinz Soups, 2-Minute Service advertising on side, from $30 to...**$35.00**
Bowl, custard; Ovenware, deep, ruffled top, Fire-King, from $40 to..**$50.00**
Bowl, dessert; Charm, Fire-King, 4¾".........................**$15.00**
Bowl, dessert; Jane Ray, Fire-King, 4⅞" **$10.00**
Bowl, dessert; Sheaves of Wheat, Fire-King, 4½" **$35.00**
Bowl, dessert; Shell, Fire-King, 4¾"............................**$14.00**
Bowl, dessert/custard; Philbe, Fire-King, 5-oz, from $45 to **$50.00**
Bowl, fruit; Restaurant Ware, Fire-King, 4¾".............**$12.00**
Bowl, mixing; Fire-King, 4¾", from $30 to..................**$35.00**
Bowl, mixing; floral decals, Fire-King, 8½", 3-qt, from $65 to **$75.00**
Bowl, mixing; Swirl, Fire-King, 6", from $10 to **$12.50**
Bowl, oatmeal; Jane Ray, Fire-King, 5⅞".....................**$24.00**
Bowl, salad; Charm, Fire-King, 7⅜"............................**$50.00**
Bowl, soup plate; Jane Ray, Fire-King, 7⅝" **$25.00**
Bowl, soup; Charm, Fire-King, 6"................................**$45.00**

Bowl, vegetable; Jane Ray, Fire-King, 8¼" **$24.00**
Bowl, vegetable; Shell, Fire-King, round, 8½" **$28.00**
Bowl, vegetable; Three Bands, Fire-King, 8¼"...........**$40.00**
Bowl, vegetable; 1700 Line, Fire-King, 8½"................**$30.00**
Casserole; French; Ovenware, w/lid, Fire-King, 5"+handle, from $125 to...**$200.00**
Comport, Fire-King, 6", from $40 to...........................**$45.00**
Creamer, Charm, Fire-King..**$20.00**
Creamer, Jane Ray, Fire-King **$9.00**
Creamer, Shell, footed, Fire-King................................**$25.00**
Cup, Charm, Fire-King..**$12.00**
Cup, demitasse; Jane Ray, Fire-King **$40.00**
Cup, demitasse; Restaurant Ware, Fire-King...............**$35.00**
Cup, Jane Ray, Fire-King...**$7.00**
Cup, Restaurant Ware, narrow rim, Fire-King.............**$10.00**
Cup, Restaurant Ware, straight sides, Fire-King, 6-oz ...**$9.00**
Cup, Shell, Fire-King, 8-oz **$10.00**
Cup, St Denis, 1700 Line, Fire-King, 9-oz....................**$12.00**
Cup, Swirl, Fire-King **$40.00**
Cup, Three Bands, Fire-King, 8-oz...............................**$50.00**
Cup & saucer, Alice, Fire-King......................................**$7.00**
Cup & saucer, demitasse; plain, Fire-King, from $50 to..**$70.00**
Cup & saucer, demitasse; souvenir of Jeanerette LA, Fire-King, from $60 to...**$65.00**
Egg cup, Fire-King, from $28 to **$32.00**
Flowerpot, smooth top, Fire-King, 3⅝", from $16 to..**$18.00**
Loaf pan, Ovenware, Fire-King, 5x9", from $30 to **$35.00**
Mug, coffee; Restaurant Ware, Fire King, 7-oz **$7.00**
Mug, Philbe, Fire-King, 8-oz, from $65 to **$75.00**
Pitcher, ball; plain, Fire-King, 80-oz, from $250 to ...**$300.00**
Pitcher, milk; Beaded & Bar, Fire-King, 20-oz, from $100 to **$125.00**
Pitcher, milk; plain, Fire-King, 20-oz, from $45 to......**$50.00**
Plate, Alice, Fire-King...**$25.00**
Plate, bread & butter; Restaurant Ware, Fire-King, 5½" ..**$12.00**
Plate, dinner; Charm, Firc-King, 9¼"..........................**$50.00**
Plate, dinner; Jane Ray, Fire-King, 9⅛".......................**$11.00**
Plate, dinner; Restaurant Ware, Fire-King, 9"..............**$24.00**
Plate, dinner; Sheaves of Wheat, Fire-King, 9"...........**$45.00**
Plate, dinner; Shell, Fire-King, 10"..............................**$28.00**
Plate, dinner; Swirl, Fire-King......................................**$80.00**
Plate, dinner; 1700 Line, 9⅛".......................................**$20.00**
Plate, grill; Laurel, McKee, 9⅛"...................................**$12.00**
Plate, luncheon; Charm, Fire-King, 8⅜".....................**$28.00**
Plate, luncheon; Restaurant Ware, Fire-King, 8" **$65.00**
Plate, Restaurant Ware, 5-compartment, Fire-King, 9⅝"..**$38.00**
Plate, salad; Charm, Fire-King, 6⅝".............................**$22.00**
Plate, salad; Jane Ray, Fire-King, 7¾" **$12.00**
Plate, salad; Laurel, McKee, 7½"..................................**$10.00**
Plate, salad; Shell, Fire-King, 7¼"................................**$25.00**
Plate, 3-compartment, Restaurant Ware, Fire-King, 9⅝"..**$17.00**
Platter, Charm, Fire-King, 11x8"..................................**$65.00**
Platter, Jane Ray, Fire-King, 12x9"...............................**$25.00**
Platter, oval, Restaurant Ware, Fire-King, 11½" **$26.00**
Platter, Shell, Fire-King, 13x9½" **$85.00**
Salt & pepper shakers, Fire-King, pr, from $40 to **$45.00**
Salt & pepper shakers, Laurel, McKee, pr **$60.00**

Saucer, Charm, Fire-King, 5⅜" **$3.00**
Saucer, Jane Ray, Fire-King **$2.00**
Saucer, Restaurant Ware, Fire-King, 6" **$4.00**
Saucer, Swirl, Fire-King **$20.00**
Sugar bowl, Charm, Fire-King...................................**$20.00**
Sugar bowl, Jane Ray, w/lid, Fire-King.......................**$29.00**
Sugar bowl, Shell, footed, open, Fire-King.................**$25.00**

Japan Ceramics

This category is narrowed down to the inexpensive novelty items produced in Japan from 1921 to 1941 and again from 1947 until the present. Though Japanese ceramics marked Nippon, Noritake, and Occupied Japan have long been collected, some of the newest fun-type collectibles on today's market are the figural ashtrays, pincushions, wall pockets, toothbrush holders, etc., that are marked 'Made in Japan' or simply 'Japan.' In her books called *Collector's Guide to Made in Japan Ceramics* (there are three in series), Carole Bess White explains the pitfalls you will encounter when you try to determine production dates. Collectors refer to anything produced before WWII as 'old' and anything made after 1952 as 'new.' Backstamps are inconsistent as to wording and color, and styles are eclectic. Generally, items with applied devices are old, and they are heavier and thicker. Often they were more colorful than the newer items, since fewer colors mean less expense to the manufacturer. Lustre glazes are usually indicative of older pieces, especially the deep solid colors. When lustre was used after the war, it was often mottled with contrasting hues and was usually thinner.

Imaginative styling and strong colors are what give these Japanese ceramics their charm, and they also are factors to consider when you make your purchases. You'll find all you need to know to be a wise shopper in the books we've recommended.

See also Blue Willow; Cat Collectibles; Condiment Sets; Flower Frogs; Geisha Girl; Holt Howard; Kreiss; Lamps; Lefton; Napkin Dolls; Occupied Japan Collectibles; Powder Boxes; Toothbrush Holders; Wall Pockets.

Advisor: Carole Bess White (See Directory, Japan Ceramics)

Newsletter *Made in Japan Info Letter*
Carole Bess White
P.O. Box 819
Portland, OR 97207; fax: 503-281-2817; send SASE for information; no appraisals given; e-mail: CBESSW@aol.com

Ashtray, falcon, Deco style, shiny maroon & green, 3¼", from $20 to **$30.00**
Ashtray, Good Old Days, well-dressed man sits beside barrel (cigarette holder), black mark, 3¾", from $26 to.**$55.00**
Ashtray, hand figural, shiny white, marked, 2¾", from $12 to...................................**$18.00**
Ashtrays, card suits, red, black & white shiny glazes, rectangular, 3¼", set of 4, from $30 to...................................**$40.00**

Bell, Chef figural, shiny white w/multicolor details, red mark, 3", from $18 to **$25.00**
Biscuit barrel, multicolored fruits in relief on yellow crackle, woven rattan handle, black mark, 5½", from $45 to..**$65.00**
Bookends, dog & books, shiny green, pre-WWII, black mark, 3¾", pr, from $22 to **$35.00**
Bookends, Hummel-like boy & girl reading, shiny multicolor, red mark, 5¾", pr, from $28 to **$38.00**
Butter dish, tomato on green base, black mark, 3¼", from $38 to...................................**$52.00**
Cache pot, bunny & cart, multicolor lustre, red mark, 3½", from $15 to...................................**$20.00**
Cache pot, lady sitting at side of fence, tan lustre w/multicolor figure, black mark, 4", from $12 to.............**$20.00**
Cache pot, 3 Art Deco girls, shiny black & white, black mark, 3½", from $18 to...................................**$28.00**
Cache pot/cigarette holder, calico monkey, multicolor on white, black mark, 3½", from $18 to **$28.00**
Cache pot/cigarette holder, pig figural, shiny multicolor, black mark, 2¾", from $18 to...................................**$22.00**
Candy dish, Deco-style geometric design, shiny multicolor, divided interior, w/lid, red mark, 4¼", from $40 to **$70.00**
Cigarette jar, calico clown dog, ashtray ruff, black mark, 6¼", from $35 to...................................**$55.00**
Cigarette jar/humidor, owl, yellow matt, red mark, 5", from $45 to...................................**$55.00**
Condiment set, Deco design in blue & multicolored lustres, 2 cruets+2 shakers+mayonnaise w/lid & spoon on tray, $80 to...................................**$125.00**
Condiment set, 3 red tomatoes on wide green tray, black mark, 6¼" L tray, from $22 to **$35.00**
Demitasse set, floral, tan & multicolor lustre, 8¾" pot+creamer & sugar bowl+4 cups & saucers, from $130 to **$155.00**
Figurine, calico dog, red mark, 4½", from $15 to.......**$20.00**
Figurine, cat w/ball, shiny multicolor, no mark, 2¼", from $10 to...................................**$15.00**
Figurine, clown, shiny multicolor, red mark, 4¾", from $12 to **$18.00**
Figurine, lady holding skirt, 1 arm up over head, shiny green dress, red mark, 7½", from $38 to.....................**$55.00**
Figurine, lady skier, multicolor matt, black mark, 7¾", from $48 to...................................**$58.00**
Flower basket, yellow & blue stripes, tan lustre foot, red mark, 7", from $46 to **$66.00**
Flower bowl, blue & orange lustre w/multicolored flowers, red mark, 6½", from $28 to **$52.00**
Flower holder, lady w/basket, shiny green & white, red mark, 7½", from $27 to **$37.00**
Hair receiver, roses w/cobalt trim, green mark, 2¼", from $50 to...................................**$60.00**
Incense burner, man w/hole in mouth for smoke, attached tray, blue/tan lustre, 3¼", $30 to **$40.00**
Incense burner, Oriental figure w/pot, shiny blue & green, 4½", from $18 to...................................**$25.00**
Inkwell, bird figural, blue & tan lustre, red mark, 5", from $38 to...................................**$52.00**

Liquor flask, All's Well That Ends Well, dog & flask, painted bisque, black mark, 4¼", from $52 to...................**$85.00**

Liquor flask, His Masters Breoth (sic), tan & orange lustre, black mark, 3¾", from $40 to.............................**$65.00**

Liquor flask, Life Preserver, bathing beauty & life preserver, painted bisque, black mark, 4¾", from $65 to...**$125.00**

Lunch box/canister, floral on yellow, 2-part stacking, pre-WWII, red mark, 6¼" W, from $26 to...................**$45.00**

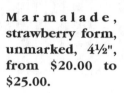

Marmalade, strawberry form, unmarked, 4½", from $20.00 to $25.00.

Mayonnaise, Art Deco floral, green, cream, yellow & orange lustre, pre-WWII mark, 3¼", from $35 to.............**$65.00**

Muffineer set, Art-Deco panels, tan lustre w/shiny green & yellow, black trim, red mark, 2 pcs, 5¾", from $50 to...**$80.00**

Muffineer set, Art-Deco triangular decor, shiny green, red & yellow, black trim, red mark, 7½", from $50 to...**$86.00**

Nodder, Scotsman, Chance It Girls (kilt lifts up), multicolored matt, black mark, 4", from $78 to..........................**$95.00**

Pincushion, calico dog w/lustre top hat, black mark, 3¼", from $26 to...**$36.00**

Pincushion, calico horse, multicolor on shiny white, black mark, 3½", from $18 to **$28.00**

Pincushion, dog, shiny orange, marked, 2½", from $13 to...**$22.00**

Pincushion, elephant, shiny white, post-1960, unmarked, 2¼", from 6 to..**$7.00**

Pincushion, girl w/lg basket, shiny multicolor, red mark, 3¼", from $19 to...**$29.00**

Pincushion, lion, Deco Style, tan lustre, red mark, 2½", from $13 to..**$24.00**

Pincushion, man w/accordion, tan lustre w/shiny multicolor, black mark, 3¾", from $19 to................................**$23.00**

Pincushion, ox & cart, blue & yellow lustres, black mark, 2½", from $16 to..**$23.00**

Pincushion, sailor boy, painted bisque, 3¼", from $23 to....**$33.00**

Pitcher, cow figural, shiny brown, label, 5¼", from $18 to ..**$22.00**

Pitcher, dog figural, shiny multicolor, Souvenir of Splitrock Lighthouse, green mark, 6½", from $48 to **$50.00**

Pitcher, horse figural, shiny multicolor, black mark, 4", from $19 to...**$28.00**

Pitcher, ships scene, lavender & tan lustre, white handle, black mark, 6", from $35 to **$50.00**

Powder jar, clown sits on lid, shiny multicolor & cream, black mark, 5½", from $35 to **$45.00**

Relish, tulips in pot on white w/green lustre, 2-part w/center handle, red mark, 7¾" L, from $22 to..................**$37.00**

Salt & pepper shakers, carrot form, orange w/green, 4¼" L, pr, from $10 to...**$15.00**

Shoe, shiny multicolor & cream, lady's high heel, black mark, 5", from $10 to **$15.00**

Tea set, cherry blossoms on white & gold lustre, 4½" pot+creamer & sugar bowl+6 cups & saucers+6 7¼" plates **$150.00**

Teapot, delicate swirling design, opal lustre w/silver trim, black mark, 5½", from $32 to..............................**$47.00**

Teapot, Pekingese dog figural, green matt, black mark, 6¾", from $136 to..**$152.00**

Teapot, tomato face, red-orange w/greenery at top, 5¾", w/matching set of 4 cups, from $68 to.................**$85.00**

Vase, Art Deco-style floral, blue & red w/multicolored lustre, gold upturned handles, red mark, 8½", from $45 to **$60.00**

Vase, Art Deco-style floral reserve, blue, cream & orange lustre, pre-WWII, red mark, 6¼", from $48 to **$60.00**

Vase, Art-deco band on shiny orange, shouldered, sm flared rim, blue mark, 6", from $46 to.............................**$52.00**

Vase, bud; Scottie dogs before vase, white & orange lustre, black mark, 4¼", from $8 to.................................**$15.00**

Vase, clown figural, green & white lustre w/multicolor dots, red mark, 3¼", from $18 to **$28.00**

Vase, enameled flowers on shiny brown, sm handles, yellow mark, 7½", from $18 to **$28.00**

Vase, multicolor dragons, shouldered, sm rim, 13", from $210 to...**$255.00**

Vase, multicolor florals on tan & blue lustre, shouldered, illegible mark, 9", from $60 to **$86.00**

Vase, Oriental lady stands beside vase, blue lustre w/multicolor figure, 6¼", from $25 to **$45.00**

Whisk broom, dog's head, shiny black & white, 3¾", from $25 to...**$40.00**

Jewel Tea Company

At the turn of the century, there was stiff competition among door-to-door tea-and-coffee companies, and most of them tried to snag the customer by doling out coupons that could eventually be traded in for premiums. But the thing that set the Jewel Tea people apart from the others was that their premiums were awarded to the customer first, then 'earned' through the purchases that followed. This set the tone of their business dealings which obviously contributed to their success, and very soon in addition to the basic products they started out with, the company entered the food-manufacturing field. They eventually became one of the country's largest retailers. Today their products, containers, premiums, and advertising ephemera are all very collectible.

Advisors: Bill and Judy Vroman (See Directory, Jewel Tea)

Baking Powder, Jewel, cylindrical tin w/script logo & white lettering, 1950s-60s, 1-lb, from $20 to **$30.00**

Cake decorator set, late 1940s, from $50 to **$65.00**

Candy, Jewel Mints, round green tin, 1920s, 1-lb, from $30 to **$40.00**

Candy, Jewel Tea Spiced Jelly Drops, orange box w/orange & white lettering, from $20 to **$30.00**

Cereal, Jewel Quick Oats, cylindrical box w/white & orange lettering, from $40 to..**$50.00**

Cocoa, Jewel or Jewel Tea, various boxes, ea, from $25 to **$45.00**

Coffee, Jewel Blend, orange & gold w/white lettering & logo, paper label **$40.00**

Coffee, Jewel Private Blend, brown w/white lettering, 1-lb, from $15 to..**$25.00**

Coffee, Jewel Special Blend, brown stripes on white, white & orange lettering on brown circle, 2-lb, from $15 to ..**$25.00**

Coffee, Royal Jewel, yellow w/brown & white, 1-lb, from $20 to **$35.00**

Coffee, West Coast, orange & brown w/white lettering, bell at top center, 1960s, 2-lb, from $25 to **$35.00**

Dishes, Melmac, 8 place settings, from $150 to........**$170.00**

Extract, Jewel Imitation Vanilla, brown box w/orange & white lettering, 1960s, 4-oz, from $20 to **$30.00**

Extract, Jewel Lemon, orange, blue & white, 1916-19, from $40 to..**$50.00**

Flour sifter, litho metal, EX **$485.00**

Garment bag, 1950s, MIP, from $25 to.......................**$30.00**

Laundry, Daintflakes, pink & blue box marked Soft Feathery Flakes of Pure Mild Soap, from $25 to **$30.00**

Laundry, Daybreak Laundry Set, from $15 to.............**$20.00**

Laundry, Grano Granulated Soap, blue & white box marked Made For General Cleaning, 2-lb, from $25 to.....**$30.00**

Laundry, Pure Gloss Starch, teal & white box, from $25 to **$30.00**

Malted milk mixer, Jewel-T, from $40 to **$50.00**

Mix, Jewel Sunbrite Mix, Mason jar w/paper label & metal screw lid, 1960s, 26-oz, from $15 to **$25.00**

Mix, Jewel Tea Coconut Dessert, round tan tin w/brown & white logo & lettering, 1930s, 14-oz, from $30 to.**$40.00**

Mix, Jewel Tea Devil's Food Cake Flour, 1920s, 10-oz, from $30 to..**$40.00**

Mix, Jewel Tea Prepared Tapioca, tall square orange & brown striped tin w/logo & brown lettering, 1930s, from $25 to..**$35.00**

Mixer, Mary Dunbar, electric w/stand, bowl & original hang tag, white...**$100.00**

Mixer, Mary Dunbar, hand-held style w/stand, 1940, from $40 to..**$50.00**

Napkins, paper w/printed pattern, box of 200 ....**$25.00**

Nuts, Jewel Mixed Nuts, round brown-striped tin w/orange & brown lettering, 1960s, 1-lb, from $15 to **$20.00**

Peanut Butter, Jewel Tea, glass jar w/paper label & screw lid, 1930s, 1-lb, from $30 to **$40.00**

Pickle fork, Jewel-T, from $20 to.................................**$25.00**

Razor blades, Jewel-T...**$5.00**

Salesman's award, Ephraim Coffee cup w/saucer, 1939, 1-qt (given to top 400 salesmen), from $175 to........**$350.00**

Scales, Jewel-T, from $45 to..**$55.00**

Sweeper, Jewel, gold lettering on black, 1930s-40s, from $80 to..**$100.00**

Sweeper, Jewel Little Bissell, from $40 to...................**$50.00**

Sweeper, Jewel Suction Sweeper, early 1900s, lg **$150.00**

Sweeper, Jewel Suction Sweeper, tan lettering on dark tan, 1930s-40s, from $60 to **$100.00**

Tea bags, Jewel Tea, box w/dragon logo, gold & brown, 1948 ....**$65.00**

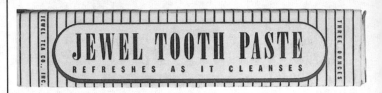

Toothpaste, Jewel Tooth Paste, MIB, from $15.00 to $20.00. (Photo courtesy Bill and Judy Vroman)

Jewelry

Today's costume jewelry collectors may range from nine to ninety and have tastes as varied as their ages, but one thing they all have in common is their love of these distinctive items of jewelry, some originally purchased at the corner five-&-dimes, others from department stores and boutiques.

Costume jewelry became popular, simply because it was easily affordable for all women. Today jewelry made before 1954 is considered to be 'antique,' while the term 'collectible' jewelry generally refers to those pieces made after that time. In 1954 costume jewelry was federally recognized as an American art form, and the copyright law was passed to protect the artists' designs. The copyright mark (c in a circle) found on the back of a piece identifies a post-1954 'collectible.'

Quality should always be the primary consideration when shopping for these treasures. Remember that pieces with colored rhinestones bring the higher prices. (Note: A 'rhinestone' is a clear, foil-backed, leaded glass crystal — unless it is a 'colored rhinestone' — while a 'stone' is not foiled.) A complete set (called a parure) increases in value by 20% over the total of its components. Check for a manufacturer's mark, since a signed piece is worth 20% more than one of comparable quality, but not signed. Some of the best designers are Miriam Haskell, Eisenberg, Trifari, Hollycraft, and Joseff.

Early plastic pieces (Lucite, Bakelite, and celluloid, for example) are very collectible. Some Lucite is used in combination with wood, and the figural designs are especially desirable.

There are several excellent reference books available if you'd like more information. Look for *Unsigned Beauties of Costume Jewelry* by our advisor, Marcia Brown. Lillian Baker has written several books: *Art Nouveau and Art Deco Jewelry; Twentienth Century Fashionable Plastic Jewelry; 50 Years of Collectible Fashion Jewelry;* and *100 Years of Collectible Jewelry.* Books by other authors include *Collectible Costume Jewelry* by Fred Rezazadeh; *Collector's Encyclopedia of Hairwork Jewelry* by C. Jeanenne Bell, G.G.; and video books *Hidden Treasures Series* by Christie Romero and Marcia Brown. All but the video are available through Collector Books.

Advisor: Marcia Brown (See Directory, Jewelry)

Club/Newsletter: *Vintage Fashion and Costume Jewelry Newsletter Club*
P.O. Box 265, Glen Oaks, NY 11004

Bracelet, Boucher, simulated coral stones & gold-tone metal, from $90 to......**$125.00**

Bracelet, Miriam Haskell, 3 strands of white opaque glass beads w/floral seed bead & rhinestone clasp, from $100 to......**$160.00**

Bracelet, unmarked, antique gold finish, 7 strands w/alternating snake skin chains & rows of gold chaton rhinestones......**$110.00**

Bracelet, unmarked, black Bakelite w/carved flowers & plain polished squares w/brass links, from $175 to....**$235.00**

Bracelet, unmarked, blue teal pearlized Lucite bangle, thin, from $25 to......**$85.00**

Bracelet, unmarked, encrusted seed beads among swirling gold fans & blue iridescent stones, hinged......**$125.00**

Bracelet, unmarked, hinged plastic bangle, black w/rhinestone inlay......**$50.00**

Bracelet, unmarked, multi-shaped lavender rhinestone cuff.**$75.00**

Bracelet, unmarked, pink rhinestones of various sizes, 2" W.**$95.00**

Bracelet, unmarked, red Lucite square links (7), 1950s, from $55 to......**$85.00**

Bracelet, unmarked, red translucent Bakelite bangle, faceted, from $125 to......**$195.00**

Bracelet, unmarked, yellow plastic flowers on chain.**$12.00**

Bracelet, unmarked, 2 pearl strands w/pearl & rhinestone decor......**$25.00**

Bracelet, Weiss, double line of rhinestones, from $85 to.**$115.00**

Bracelet & earrings, unmarked, brown & white plastic squares alternate, 3 pcs, from $45 to......**$65.00**

Bracelet & earrings, unmarked, lavender enamel leaves, iridiscent rhinestones in pear clusters, 3 pcs......**$68.00**

Bracelet & earrings, unmarked, purple cabochons in silver plating, 3 pcs......**$150.00**

Bracelete, unmarked, butterscotch Bakelite w/deeply carved floral decor, bangle, from $125 to......**$175.00**

Brooch, Beaucraft, silver musical note, sm, from $15 to .**$20.00**

Brooch, Boucher, gold-plated hedgehog w/Burmese ruby glass cabochon eyes, 1¾", from $150 to......**$205.00**

Brooch, Brooks, Christmas tree, multicolor stones on gold-tone tree, from $40 to......**$60.00**

Brooch, BSK, leaf form, autumn-tones enameled on metal, from $45 to......**$60.00**

Brooch, Czechoslovakia, spider w/2 purple rhinestones & 8 gold-plated legs......**$25.00**

Brooch, Gerry's, bird figural, enameling on gold-tone metal, sm, from $10 to......**$20.00**

Brooch, JJ, owl figural, jewel tummy, from $30 to **$45.00**

Brooch, KJL, black thermoset plastic & rhodium set w/rhinestones, 1960-90, from $85 to......**$125.00**

Brooch, Krementz, flower form w/cultured pearls, from $65 to......**$95.00**

Brooch, Star, white plastic & clear rhinestones in flower shape, from $20 to......**$27.50**

Brooch, unmarked, antiqued gold-plate butterfly w/glued-in lavender & plum foil-backed rhinestones, 1960s, 3½"......**$125.00**

Brooch, unmarked, Bakelite horse head w/glass eye & metal chain, from $195 to......**$245.00**

Brooch, unmarked, black navette rhinestones, gold plated......**$35.00**

Brooch, unmarked, Christmas tree w/multicolored navette rhinestones draped to form branches......**$75.00**

Brooch, unmarked, enameled firefly w/pavé body & wing tips......**$45.00**

Brooch, unmarked, feather shape w/white diamond & black chaton rhinestones......**$78.00**

Brooch, unmarked, flower spray w/citrine to topaz rhinestones......**$25.00**

Brooch, unmarked, gold-plated bow w/light & dark lavender rhinestones......**$58.00**

Brooch, unmarked, gold-plated lizard w/multicolored navettes......**$35.00**

Brooch, unmarked, lion's face lined in black & clear rhinestones, silver lengths of sm chain create mane..**$185.00**

Brooch, unmarked, pavé ribbon w/blue enameling & blue cabachon on knot......**$64.00**

Brooch, unmarked, pavé stork w/multicolored feathers...**$48.00**

Brooch, unmarked, pink, lavender & clear rhinestone flower w/gold-tone stem......**$48.00**

Brooch, unmarked, plastic circle bridged w/rhinestones..**$12.00**

Brooch, unmarked, red carved Bakelite flower, lg, from $175 to......**$225.00**

Brooch, unmarked, sterling silver fish w/reverse-carved Lucite side......**$225.00**

Brooch, unmarked, sterling vermeil flower w/lg emerald-cut topaz, 1940s......**$62.00**

Brooch, unmarked, yellow hydrangea blossom with clear rhinestone chatons, enameled leaf swedged to flower, $52.00.
(Photo courtesy Marcia Brown)

Brooch, unmarked, yellow enamel woodpecker perched on gold-tone bough **$48.00**

Brooch, unmarked, 5 rows of rhinestones in various shapes w/chaton center stone, 4½" **$135.00**

Brooch, Warner, white satin, frosted & clear rhinestones, lg, from $60 to **$90.00**

Brooch, Weisner, domed shape w/faceted clear rhinestones, from $45 to **$65.00**

Brooch, Weiss, faceted rhinestones of various shapes, lg, from $80 to **$120.00**

Brooch & earrings, Austrian, green cabochon flat backs & dark green chatons, 3 pcs **$48.00**

Brooch & earrings, Boucher, turquoise & rhinestones in knotted gold metal, 3 pcs, from $300 to **$400.00**

Brooch & earrings, Carnegie, flower form, enamel leaves & framed glass petals, 3 pcs, from $105 to **$160.00**

Brooch & earrings, DaneCraft, sterling vermeil & cultured pearls form grape clustre, 3 pcs, from $100 to ..**$150.00**

Brooch & earrings, Sarah Coventry, gold-plated filigree w/plastic oval cabachons, green rhinestones & faux pearls, 3 pcs **$120.00**

Brooch & earrings, Sherman, yellow topaz rhinestones in floral shape, 3 pcs, from $65 to **$95.00**

Brooch & earrings, silver-tone lacy leaf w/gray glued-in rhinestones, 1960s, from $65 to **$105.00**

Brooch & earrings, unmarked, aurora borealis chatons in 3 layers swedged to gold-plated flower petals, 3 pcs......**$45.00**

Brooch & earrings, unmarked, lg faceted Chinese red dentelle rimmed w/aurora borealis rhinestones, 3 pcs **$60.00**

Brooch & earrings, unmarked, milk white glass cabochons in feather design w/clear rhinestones, 3 pcs **$55.00**

Brooch & earrings, unmarked, ruby red & aurora borealis rhinestone star, prong-set, rhodium plated, 3 pcs, from $135 to **$175.00**

Brooch & earrings, unmarked, yellow & Chinese red rhinestones, sm veined gold leaves in circle, 3 pcs **$65.00**

Brooch & earrings, Van Dell, sterling vermeil & pink faceted rhinestones form flowers, 3 pcs, from $65 to.......**$95.00**

Brooch & earrings, Vogue, purple, green & blue iridescent rhinestones, 2" cushion brooch, 2" earrings, 3 pcs, $125 to **$160.00**

Brooch & earrings, Weiss, red stones form strawberries, sm green stones form leaves, 3 pcs, from $80 to **$100.00**

Brooch/pendant & earrings, Celebrity, green central stone in field of rhinestones, teardrop shape, 3 pcs, from $45 to **$75.00**

Clips, unmarked, baguette (3) rhinestones w/6 sm chaton guards, pr **$54.00**

Clips, unmarked, gold filigree w/emerald green chatons, pr .**$85.00**

Earrings, Coro, aurora borealis stones, pr, from $20 to ..**$30.00**

Earrings, Coro, lg aquamarine stones, pr, from $30 to .**$40.00**

Earrings, Eisenberg, Austrian crystal blue rhinestones w/clear chatons, 1950s, 1½", pr, from $175 to **$215.00**

Earrings, Emmons, white thermoset plastic in patented gold-tone, pr, from $15 to **$25.00**

Earrings, Hollycraft, multicolor stones on gold-tone flower form, pr, from $60 to **$80.00**

Earrings, Lisner, rhinestones on sm leaf shape, pr, from $15 to **$25.00**

Earrings, Miriam Haskell, white glass center bead surrounded by sm black & white beads, pr, from $60 to ..**$85.00**

Earrings, Newhouse, 3 colors of rhinestones, clip style, pr, from $30 to **$45.00**

Earrings, Regency, blue iridescent rhinestones, pr, from $90 to **$125.00**

Earrings, unmarked, aurora borealis rhinestone cluster, pr ..**$38.00**

Earrings, unmarked, black Bakelite crescent shape studded w/clear rhinestones, pr **$35.00**

Earrings, unmarked, black Bakelite egg shapes, lg, pr, from $50 to **$70.00**

Earrings, unmarked, black navettes surround clear chaton rhinestone w/clear square rhinestones filling in at points, pr **$52.00**

Earrings, unmarked, black plastic flowers w/rhinestone centers, pr **$18.00**

Earrings, unmarked, blue faceted pear-shaped glass stones capped w/rhinestones, pr **$45.00**

Earrings, unmarked, colored button type rimmed in clear rhinestones, pr, from $12 to **$18.00**

Earrings, unmarked, enameled floret w/individual sunburst rhinestone center, pr **$15.00**

Earrings, unmarked, green chaton surrounded by clear faux diamonds, pr **$12.00**

Earrings, unmarked, green Lucite buttons w/green rhinestones, 1950s, clip, pr, from $35 to **$45.00**

Earrings, unmarked, green rhinestone studs, pr..........**$28.00**

Earrings, unmarked, leaves of aurora borealis rhinestones, pr **$40.00**

Earrings, unmarked, molded plastic flowers w/rhinestone centers, screw-type, button style, 1960s, pr, from $10 to **$20.00**

Earrings, unmarked, orange baguettes & chatons wrap around brown cabochons, pr **$38.00**

Earrings, unmarked, peridot stud & chain w/golden lanterns, peridot chatons decorate seams of lanterns, pr ...**$55.00**

Earrings, unmarked, pink opaque cabachons w/pink chaton-cut rhinestones, prong set, 1¼", pr, from $45 to .**$60.00**

Earrings, unmarked, red plastic squares form petals, red cabachon center with clear rhinestones, $38.00; Gold-plated drops with plastic flowers and clear rhinestones, $18.00. (Photo courtesy Marcia Brown)

Earrings, unmarked, round Bakelite circle w/glued-in rhine-stones, pr **$50.00**

Earrings, unmarked, Sterling silver w/pink & green chatons & clear rhinestones, pr **$68.00**

Earrings, unmarked, strung 'pearl' loops w/rhinestone ron-dels & balls, pr **$50.00**

Earrings, Weiss, blue rhinestones, drop style, pr, from $35 to **$50.00**

Earrings, West Germany, peach-colored flower, pr.....**$30.00**

Necklace, bracelet, brooch & earrings, Kramer, black opaque glass stones, 5 pcs, from $185 to **$200.00**

Necklace, bracelet & earrings, Coro, faux turquoise nuggets & blue rhinestones, 4 pcs, from $95 to **$135.00**

Necklace, bracelet & earrings, Evans, pastel guilloche enam-el beads w/gold-plated metal spacers, 4 pcs, from $200 to **$250.00**

Necklace, Celebrity Gems, gold-tone base metal pendant w/black plastic oval cabochon, black dangles, 1970s, from $50 to **$80.00**

Necklace, Coro, leaf & grape clusters, gold-tone metal w/faux citrine rhinestones, 1950s, from $95 to ..**$120.00**

Necklace, Hobé, antiqued gold filigree metalwork cross w/garnets, from $175 to **$225.00**

Necklace, Hobé, multicolor pastel beads, 4-strand, from $55 to **$80.00**

Necklace, Kramer, antiqued gold plate w/prong-set lemon yellow rhinestones, unusual V shape, 1950s, from $250 to **$350.00**

Necklace, Monet, slide style, from $25 to **$40.00**

Necklace, Pam, iridescent stones & enamel leaves in floral motif, from $35 to **$50.00**

Necklace, Renoir, copper w/white enameled links, 1950s, from $125 to **$175.00**

Necklace, Trifari, faux sapphire flowers w/clear rhinestone spacers & flower centers, Trifanium plates, ¼" W, from $65 to **$90.00**

Necklace, Trifari, rose gold-plated choker w/prong-set clear diamond-cut rhinestones, front links: ¾" W, from $110 to **$175.00**

Necklace, unmarked, blood red hearts & faux pearls in links **$35.00**

Necklace, unmarked, cameo brooch in frame of faux pearls & black beads on gold-tone chain **$38.00**

Necklace, unmarked, gold & brown cabochons feather out from iridescent chaton rhinestone, brown rhinestones in chain **$30.00**

Necklace, unmarked, graduated iridescent same-color rhine-stones, dainty size..**$38.00**

Necklace, unmarked, pink glass faceted beads w/fuchsia beads & cranberry rhinestones, single strand.......**$35.00**

Necklace, unmarked, 2 strands of faux pearls w/baroque faux pearl clasp..**$28.00**

Necklace & bracelet, unmarked, clear, gold & topaz rhine-stones form links, 2 pcs **$55.00**

Necklace & earrings, Coro, metal leaves & various faceted stones of varied colors & shapes, 3 pcs, from $95 to **$140.00**

Necklace & earrings, Eisenberg, topaz & clear rhinestones, 3 pcs, from $150 to..**$190.00**

Necklace & earrings, Napier, pavé set heart pendant w/silver-metal base, matching earrings, 3 pcs, from $40 to..**$65.00**

Necklace & earrings, unmarked, aurora borealis stones of var-ious shapes in 1" wide semi-collar look, 3 pcs **$62.00**

Necklace & earrings, unmarked, blue plastic beads w/cen-ter drop of blue navette rhinestones, blue chatons chain **$30.00**

Necklace & earrings, unmarked, white glass cabochons among clear chaton rhinestones, 3 pcs.................**$40.00**

Ring, Avon, higher quality w/inset faux stone, from $10 to **$25.00**

Ring, Eisenberg Ice, yellow topaz teardrop-shaped stone, from $80 to...**$140.00**

Ring, Emmons, simulated pearls & turquoise, from $30 to.**$45.00**

Ring, Judy Lee, green & citrine rhinestones, from $45 to....**$65.00**

Ring, unmarked, blue chaton encircled w/clear rhine-stones..**$35.00**

Ring, unmarked, blue iridescent chatons fill dome **$54.00**

Ring, unmarked, diamond-shaped opalene cabochon w/row of purple chatons..**$42.00**

Ring, unmarked, gold-plated, twin diamond rhinestone navettes..**$20.00**

Ring, unmarked, gold-plated dome w/red rhinestones .**$28.00**

Ring, unmarked, gold-plated square filled w/opalene cha-tons **$38.00**

Ring, unmarked, gold-plated w/7 topaz rhinestones..**$38.00**

Ring, unmarked, lg blue faceted navette glass stone set like a diamond on gold-plated band..........................**$68.00**

Ring, unmarked, lg lavender center w/circle of clear rhine-stones..**$35.00**

Ring, unmarked, marcasite cabachon w/sm marcasites down ribs & around rim **$55.00**

Ring, unmarked, opalene clusters on gold-plated finish..**$45.00**

Ring, unmarked, red Bakelite w/carved daisy pattern, lg, from $175 to...**$235.00**

Ring, unmarked, red cabochon w/2 rows of hammered gold & 1 row of openwork, adjustable size.................**$15.00**

Ring, unmarked, rhodium finish w/clear rhinestones high-lighted w/emerald green rhinestones...................**$18.00**

Ring, unmarked, rhodium-plated w/clear rhinestones & ruby navettes..**$28.00**

Ring, unmarked, sm Christmas tree of green rhinestones w/red chaton on top & pot is clear rhinestones, adjusts to fit **$12.00**

Ring, unmarked, tiger-eye cabochon encircled w/clear rhine-stones..**$45.00**

Johnson Bros.

There is a definite renewal of interest in dinnerware col-lecting right now, and just about any antique shop or mall you visit will offer a few nice examples of the wares made by this Staffordshire company. They've been in business since well before the turn of the century and have targeted the American market to such an extent that during the 1960s and 1970s, as much as 70% of their dinnerware was sold to distributors in this country. They made many scenic patterns, some of which may already be familiar to you. Among them are Friendly Village, Historic America, and Old Britain Castles. They produced lovely floral patterns as well, and with the interest today's collectors have been demonstrating in Chintz, dealers tell me that Johnson Brothers' Rose Chintz and Chintz (Victorian) sell very well for them, especially the latter. In addition to their polychrome designs, they made several patterns in both blue and pink transferware.

Though some of their lines, Friendly Village, for instance, are still being produced, most are no longer as extensive as they once were, so the secondary market is being tapped to replace broken items that are not available anywhere else.

In addition to their company logo, much of their dinnerware is also stamped with the pattern name. Today they're a part of the Wedgwood group.

For more information on marks, patterns, and pricing, we recommend *Johnson Brothers Dinnerware Pattern Directory and Price Guide* by Mary J. Finegan.

Advisor: Mary J. Finegan (See Directory, Dinnerware)

Apple Harvest, coaster	**$8.00**
Apple Harvest, coffee mug, minimum value	**$18.00**
Apple Harvest, cup, tea	**$10.00**
Apple Harvest, plate, dinner	**$16.00**
Autumn's Delight, creamer	**$32.00**
Autumn's Delight, plate, luncheon	**$14.00**
Autumn's Delight, platter, sm	**$40.00**
Autumn's Delight, tureen, minimum value	**$200.00**
Barnyard King, plate, bread & butter	**$8.00**
Barnyard King, plate, buffet; 10½-11"	**$30.00**
Barnyard King, plate, salad; square or round	**$14.00**
Century of Progress, bowl, cereal/soup; square, round or lug, ea	**$12.00**
Century of Progress, bowl, fruit/berry	**$10.00**
Century of Progress, cup, tea	**$12.00**
Century of Progress, plate, buffet; 10½" to 11"	**$30.00**
Coaching Scenes, bowl, rimmed soup	**$15.00**
Coaching Scenes, bowl, vegetable; oval	**$35.00**
Coaching Scenes, coaster	**$9.00**
Coaching Scenes, coffee mug, minimum value	**$20.00**
Devonshire, bowl, fruit	**$9.00**
Devonshire, butter dish, w/lid	**$55.00**
Devonshire, creamer	**$32.00**
Devonshire, jug	**$50.00**
Dorchester, bowl, rimmed soup	**$16.00**
Dorchester, bowl, soup; square or round, 7"	**$14.00**
Dorchester, creamer	**$35.00**
Dorchester, sugar bowl, w/lid	**$48.00**
English Chippendale, bowl, fruit/berry	**$10.00**
English Chippendale, cup & saucer, jumbo	**$40.00**
English Chippendale, cup & saucer, demitasse	**$24.00**
English Chippendale, egg cup	**$20.00**

Fish, butter dish, w/lid	**$55.00**
Fish, plate, chop	**$55.00**
Fish, plate, salad; square or round	**$12.00**
Fish, salt & pepper shakers, pr	**$45.00**
Friendly Village, bowl, fruit/berry	**$8.00**
Friendly Village, bowl, vegetable; round	**$25.00**
Friendly Village, butter dish	**$50.00**
Friendly Village, coaster	**$8.00**
Friendly Village, coffee mug	**$18.00**
Friendly Village, creamer	**$30.00**
Friendly Village, cup & saucer, demitasse	**$20.00**
Friendly Village, egg cup	**$15.00**
Friendly Village, platter, sm (up to 12")	**$35.00**

Friendly Village, platter, 20½", $200.00.

Friendly Village, sauce boat	**$40.00**
Friendly Village, sugar bowl, w/lid	**$40.00**
Gamebirds, relish	**$22.00**
Gamebirds, saucer, tea	**$6.00**
Gamebirds, teapot, minimum value	**$95.00**
Harvest Fruit, platter, med, 12" to 14"	**$55.00**
Harvest Fruit, relish	**$25.00**
Harvest Fruit, sauce boat	**$48.00**
Hearts & Flowers, bowl, cereal/soup; square, round or lug, ea	**$11.00**
Hearts & Flowers, plate, dinner	**$18.00**
Hearts & Flowers, sugar bowl, w/lid	**$45.00**
His Majesty, coffee mug, minimum value	**$25.00**
Historic America, butter dish, w/lid	**$60.00**
Historic America, egg cup	**$20.00**
Historic America, plate, cake; minimum value	**$60.00**
Historic America, salt & pepper shakers, pr	**$48.00**
Indies, bowl, vegetable; round	**$30.00**
Indies, gravy boat	**$45.00**
Indies, pitcher	**$50.00**
Indies, platter, med, 12"-14"	**$50.00**
Merry Christmas, platter, turkey; 20½", minimum value	**$200.00**
Millstream, cup & saucer, jumbo	**$35.00**
Millstream, cup & saucer, demitasse	**$22.00**
Millstream, jug	**$50.00**
Millstream, tureen, minimum value	**$200.00**
Old Britain Castles, demitasse set	**$24.00**

Old Britain Castles, plate, dinner; minimum value **$20.00**
Old Britain Castles, plate, luncheon............................**$16.00**
Old Britain Castles, tureen, minimum value.............**$200.00**
Olde English Countryside, coaster................................**$9.00**
Olde English Countryside, coffeepot, minimum value...**$95.00**
Olde English Countryside, salt & pepper shakers, pr.**$45.00**
Olde English Countryside, saucer, tea..........................**$6.00**
Persian Tulip, cup, tea...**$12.00**
Persian Tulip, plate, dinner; minimum value **$20.00**
Persian Tulip, plate, salad; square or round................**$14.00**
Persian Tulip, saucer, tea **$7.00**
Rose Bouquet, bowl, soup; square or round, 7".........**$13.00**
Rose Bouquet, bowl, vegetable; round........................**$30.00**
Rose Bouquet, creamer **$32.00**
Rose Bouquet, sugar bowl, w/lid................................**$45.00**
Rose Chintz, bowl, fruit/berry **$10.00**
Rose Chintz, bowl, rimmed soup **$16.00**
Rose Chintz, sugar bowl, w/lid **$48.00**
Rose Chintz, tureen, minimum value **$200.00**
Strawberry Fair, bowl, vegetable; round.....................**$35.00**
Strawberry Fair, coffee mug, minimum value.............**$25.00**
Strawberry Fair, creamer...**$35.00**
Strawberry Fair, gravy boat **$48.00**
Strawberry Fair, platter, lg, 14" plus, minimum value .**$75.00**
Tally Ho, butter dish, w/lid..**$60.00**
Tally Ho, coaster **$10.00**
Tally Ho, salt & pepper shakers, pr **$48.00**
Tally Ho, teapot, minimum value...............................**$100.00**
Wild Turkeys, bowl, rimmed soup...............................**$16.00**
Wild Turkeys, creamer **$35.00**

Willow, teapot, minimum value, $80.00.

Winchester, plate, bread & butter..................................**$7.00**
Winchester, plate, buffet; 10½" to 11"..........................**$28.00**
Winchester, plate, salad; square or round **$12.00**
Winchester, saucer, tea **$6.00**

Josef Originals

Figurines of lovely ladies, charming girls, and whimsical animals marked Josef Originals were designed by Muriel Joseph George of Arcadia, California, from 1945 to 1985.

Until 1960, they were produced in California. But production costs were high, and copies of her work were being made in Japan. To remain competitive, she and her partner, George Good, found a company in Japan to build a factory and produce her designs to her satisfaction. Muriel retired in 1982; however, Mr. Good continued production of her work and made new designs of his staff's creation. The company was sold in late 1985, and the name is currently owned by Applause; a limited number of figurines bear this name. Those made during the ownership of Muriel are the most collectible. They can be recognized by these characteristics: the girls have a high-gloss finish, black eyes, and most are signed. Brown-eyed figures date from 1982 through 1985; Applause uses a red-brown eye. The animals were nearly always made with a matt finish and were marked with paper labels. Later animals have a flocked coat. Our advisors, Jim and Kaye Whitaker have three books which we recommend for further study: *Josef Originals, Charming Figurines; Josef Originals, A Second Look;* and *Josef Originals, Figurines of Muriel Joseph George* (currently available, no repeats of Books 1 and 2). All correspondence requires a self-addressed stamped envelope. Please note: All figurines have black eyes unless specified otherwise. As with so many collectibles, values have been impacted to a measurable extent since the advent of the Internet.

See also Birthday Angels.

Advisors: Jim and Kaye Whitaker (See Directory, Josef Originals)

Newsletter: *Josef Original Newsletter*
Jim and Kaye Whitaker
P.O. Box 475 Dept. GS
Lynnwood, WA 98046; Subscription (2 issues): $10 per year

A Warm Hello, Thinking of You Series, girl on phone, Japan, 5"..**$50.00**
Birthstone Dolls, January thru December, Japan, 3½", ea..**$25.00**
Boxer Dog, Champion Series, Japan, 5" **$22.00**
Buggy Bugs Series, various poses, wire antenna, Japan, 3½", ea **$15.00**
Bunny Hutch Series, Japan, 4"....................................**$15.00**
China, Poland, etc, Little International Series, Japan, 4", ea **$45.00**
Christmas music box, girl decorating tree, Japan, 7" ..**$65.00**
Doll of the Month, tilted head, California, 3¼"..........**$50.00**
Elephant, w/white tusks, Japan, 6¾" **$50.00**
Farmer's Daughter, girl w/hen & basket of eggs, Japan, 5" **$50.00**
First Love Series, Tony & Tina, Japan, 5", ea **$50.00**
Gray cat, wall plaque, California **$50.00**
Happy Anniversary music box, Japan, 7¼" **$70.00**
Happy Home w/Dove greeting Angel, Japan, 3¾".....**$45.00**
Hawaii, Small World Series, brown eyes, Japan, 4½" .**$40.00**
Hunter, beautiful standing horse, Japan, 6" **$25.00**
It's a Wonderful World Series, figurines, Japan, 3½", ea....**$35.00**
Italian Aristocrats, lady & escort, Japan, 7", ea...........**$90.00**

Jeanne, Colonial Days Series, Japan, 9" $135.00
Joseph's Children Johnny, w/marbles, California, 4¾" .$110.00
Kennel Club Series, Yorkshire, etc, Japan, 3" $18.00

Lara's Theme music box, 6", $70.00. (Photo courtesy Jim and Kaye Whitaker)

Love Letters From Love Story, Romance Series, Japan, 8" ..$125.00
Make Believe Series, Japan, 4½" $35.00
Mama Ballerina, California, 7" $85.00
Mary Ann & Mama, California, 4" & 7", pr $145.00
Mermaid Lipstick Holder, white w/beige trim, Japan, 4" .$85.00
Mice, Christmas, Japan, 2¾", ea $12.00
Miss Mary, Nursery Rhymes Series, Japan, 4" $45.00
Missy, girl in bonnet, several colors, California, 4" $45.00
Nanette, half doll w/jewels, several colors, California,
    5½" $65.00
New Hat from First Time, Japan, 4½" $40.00
Nurse, in yellow holding baby, Career Girl Series, Japan,
    5¾" $60.00
Parasol Girl Series, 3 in set, Japan, 6¾" $75.00
Pixie, Christmas Helper, painting toys, Japan, 4¾" $35.00
Pixies, green trimmed in red & gold, various poses, Japan, 2"
    to 3¼", ea $30.00
Poodle from Poodle & Siamese, Japan, 4¼" $30.00
Rose, girl w/flower hat, Flower Girl Series, Japan, 4¼" ...$40.00
Rose Garden Series, brown eyes, 6 different, Japan, 5¼",
    ea $65.00
Ruby, girl wearing crown w/ruby set in, Little Jewels Series,
    Japan, 3½" $35.00
Santa, w/kiss on forehead, Japan, 4¾" $60.00
Secret Pal, girl w/fan, various colors, California, 3½" .$40.00
Skunk, w/white hair tuft on head, Japan, 2½", ea $18.00
Sports Angels Series, angels playing various sports, Japan,
    2¾", ea $35.00
Tabby Cat, I Love My Cat, orange, on base, Japan, 3½" ...$15.00
Three Kings, set of 3, Japan, 8½" to 11" $70.00
Watusi Luau Series, hunter in pot, natives, etc, Japan, 5",
    ea $65.00
Wee Ching, Wee Ling, Chinese Children, boy w/dog, girl
    w/cat, California, widely copied $75.00

Wee Folks, various poses, Japan, 4½", ea $20.00
World's Greatest Series, bowler, boxer, etc, Japan, 4½", ea ..$25.00

Kaye of Hollywood

This was one of the smaller pottery studios that operated in California during the 1940s — interesting in that people tend to confuse the name with Kay Finch. Kay (Schueftan) worked for Schoop before striking out on her own; because her work was so similar to that of her former employer's, a successful lawsuit was brought against her, and it was at this point that the mark was changed from Kaye of Hollywood to Kim Ward.

Figurine, lady w/pink & blue hat, white muff, pink skirt,
    #3141, 11" $110.00
Flower holder, Chinaman, 12", from $50 to $60.00
Planter, girl figural, 9x5¼x3" $30.00
Wall pocket, head of girl w/flowers at temples, applied eye-
    lashes, #324, 5¾", NM $200.00

Keeler, Brad

California pottery is becoming quite popular among collectors, and Brad Keeler is one of the better known designers. After studying art for a time, he opened his own studio in 1939 where he created naturalistic studies of birds and animals. Sold through giftware stores, the figures were decorated by airbrushing with hand-painted details. Brad Keeler is remembered for his popular flamingo figures and his Chinese Modern Housewares. Keeler died of a heart attack in 1952, and the pottery closed soon thereafter. For more information, we recommend *The Collector's Encyclopedia of California Pottery, 2nd Edition,* by Jack Chipman.

Covered dish, lobster on head of lettuce, leaf base, #871, 7½"
    H $78.00
Figurine, bluejay, #19, 9½", from $65 to....................$75.00
Figurine, cockatoo, pink & gray, 10" $75.00
Figurine, flamingo, upright, 12", from $90 to............$125.00
Figurine, peacock hen, #715, 10½" $115.00
Figurine, peacock w/long flowing tail, #701, 16", from $130
    to..$145.00
Figurine, Siamese cat on red pillow, #944, 4½" $55.00
Figurine, spaniel, #750, 5½" L $38.00
Figurines, birds, #17 & #18, 6x4¾", 8x4", pr $95.00
Figurines, flamingos, wings up, #842 & #732, 6¾", pr..$200.00
Figurines, flamingos, 1 w/head up, 2nd w/head down, 10",
    7½", pr $230.00
Figurines, pheasants, #38A & #38B, 12" L, pr $165.00
Pitcher, fish figural, 11x6", NM $90.00
Platter, fish curled along rim, about to swallow fishing fly,
    #140, 11⅛" dia $90.00
Platter, lobster, #868, 9" $35.00
Vase, parrot beside stump, #412, 6" $55.00

Divided dish, Tomato ware, green leaves form sections, $65.00.

Kentucky Derby Glasses

Since the the late 1930s, every running of the Kentucky Derby has been commemorated with a special glass tumbler. Each year at Churchill Downs on Derby day you can buy them filled with mint juleps. In the early days this was the only place where these glasses could be purchased. Many collections were started when folks carried the glasses home from the track and then continued to add one for each successive year they attended the Derby.

The first glass appeared in 1938, but examples from then until 1945 are extremely scarce and are worth thousands — when they can be found. Because of this, many collectors begin with the 1945 glasses. There are three: the tall version, the short regular-size glass, and a jigger. Some years, for instance 1948, 1956, 1958, 1974, and 1986, have slightly different variations, so often there are more than one to collect. To date a glass, simply add one year to the last date on the winner's list found on the back.

Each year many companies put out commemorative Derby glasses. Collectors call them 'bar' glasses (as many bars sold their own versions filled with mint juleps). Because of this, collectors need to be educated as to what the official Kentucky Derby glass looks like.

These prices are for pristine, mint-condition glasses with no chips or flaws. All colors must be bright and show no signs of fading. Lettering must be perfect and intact, even the list of past winners on the back. If gold trim has been used, it must show no wear. If any of these problems exist, reduce our values by 50% to 75%, depending on the glass and the problem. Many more Kentucky Derby shot glasses, jiggers, cordials, boreals, and shooters in various colors and sizes were produced — too many to list here. But be aware that these may present themselves along the collecting trail.

Advisor: Betty L. Hornback (See Directory, Kentucky Derby and Horse Racing)

1940, aluminum	$800.00
1941-1944, plastic Beetleware, ea, from $2,500 to	$4,000.00
1945, jigger	$1,000.00
1945, regular	$1,400.00
1945, tall	$425.00

1946, clear frosted w/frosted bottom, L in circle	$100.00
1947, clear frosted, w/frosted bottom, L in circle	$100.00
1948, clear bottom	$200.00
1948, frosted bottom	$225.00
1949	$200.00
1950	$425.00
1951	$600.00
1952	$200.00
1953	$160.00
1954	$200.00
1955	$135.00
1956, 4 variations, ea, from $150 to	$275.00
1957, gold & black on front	$110.00
1958, Gold Bar	$175.00
1958, Iron Liege	$210.00
1959	$80.00
1960	$80.00
1961	$100.00
1962	$75.00
1963	$50.00
1964	$50.00
1965	$70.00
1966	$55.00
1967	$55.00
1968	$55.00
1969	$60.00
1970	$65.00
1971	$50.00
1972	$45.00
1973	$55.00
1974, Federal, regular or mistake, ea, from $125 to	$175.00
1974, mistake (Canonero in 1971 listing on back)	$18.00
1974, regular (Canonero II in 1971 listing on back)	$16.00
1975	$12.00
1976	$14.00
1976, plastic	$12.00
1977	$12.00
1978	$14.00
1979	$14.00
1980	$20.00
1981	$14.00
1982	$12.00
1983	$10.00
1984	$10.00
1985	$10.00
1986	$14.00
1986 ('85 copy)	$20.00
1987	$10.00
1988	$10.00
1989	$9.00
1990	$8.00
1991	$8.00
1992	$8.00
1993	$7.00
1994	$7.00
1995	$7.00
1996	$6.00

1997	$6.00
1998	$4.00
1999	$4.00
2000	$3.00
2001	$3.00

Bluegrass Stakes Glasses, Keeneland, Lexington, KY

1996	$15.00
1997	$13.00
1998	$12.00
1999-2000, ea	$10.00

Breeders Cup Glasses

1985, Aqueduct, not many produced	$300.00
1988, Churchill Downs	$40.00
1989, Gulfstream Park	$70.00
1990, Belmont Park	$45.00
1991, Churchill Downs	$15.00
1991, Churchill Downs, mistake	$50.00
1992, Gulfstream Park	$30.00
1993, Santa Anita	$35.00
1993, Santa Anita, 10th Running, gold	$40.00
1994, Churchill Downs	$10.00
1995, Belmont Park	$20.00
1996, Woodbine, Canada	$30.00
1997, Hollywood Park	$20.00
1998, Churchill Downs	$10.00
1999, Gulfstream Park	$7.00
2000, Churchill Downs	$7.00

Festival Glasses

1968	$95.00
1984	$20.00
1985-86, no glass made	
1987-88, ea	$16.00
1989-90, ea	$14.00
1991-92, ea	$12.00
1993, very few produced	$75.00
1994-95, ea	$10.00
1996-98, ea	$8.00
1999-2000, ea	$6.00

Jim Beam Stakes Glasses

1980, 6"	$350.00
1981, 7"	$300.00
1982	$275.00
1983	$65.00
1984	$45.00
1985	$25.00
1986	$25.00
1987-88, ea	$20.00
1988-90, ea	$15.00
1991-93, ea	$12.00

1994-95, ea	$12.00
1996-97, ea	$10.00
1998	$8.00
1999, sponsored by 'Gallery Furniture.com'	$9.00
2000, Spiral Stakes	$8.00

Shot Glasses

1987, 1½-oz, red or black, ea	$350.00
1987, 3-oz, black	$700.00
1987, 3-oz, red	$1,500.00
1988, 1½-oz	$40.00
1988, 3-oz	$60.00
1989, 1½-oz	$35.00
1989, 3-oz	$45.00
1990, 1½-oz	$35.00
1991, 1½-oz	$35.00
1991, 3-oz	$40.00
1992, 1½-oz	$20.00
1992, 3-oz	$25.00
1993, 1½-oz or 3-oz, ea	$15.00
1994, 1½-oz or 3-oz, ea	$14.00
1995, 1½-oz or 3-oz, ea	$14.00
1996, 1½-oz or 3-oz, ea	$13.00
1997, 1½-oz or 3-oz, ea	$12.00
1998, 1½-oz or 3-oz, ea	$10.00
1999, fluted whiskey, 1½-oz	$10.00
2000, fluted whiskey, 1½-oz	$8.00

WAMZ Radio KY Derby Bar Glass, Sponsored by Jim Beam

1991	$45.00
1992	$40.00
1993	$25.00
1994	$20.00
1995	$15.00
1996	$12.00
1997	$12.00
1998	$12.00
1999-2000	$10.00

Kindell, Dorothy

Yet another California artist that worked during the prolific years of the '40s and '50s, Dorothy Kindell produced a variety of household items and giftware, but today she is best known for her sensual nudes. One of her most popular lines consisted of mugs, a pitcher, salt and pepper shakers, a wall pocket, bowls, a creamer and sugar set, and champagne glasses, featuring a lady in various stages of undress, modeled as handles or stems (on the champagnes). In the set of six mugs, she progresses from wearing a glamorous strapless evening gown to ultimately climbing nude, head-first into the last mug. These are relatively common but always marketable. Except for the salt and pepper shakers, the other items from the nude line are scarce and rather pricey.

Champagne glasses, nude stems (there are six in the series), each from $225.00 to $275.00.
(Photo courtesy Jack Chipman)

Head vase, Asian, 5½x4", from $135 to **$160.00**
Head vase, island lady w/lg gold earrings, hair in updo, 5¼" **$80.00**
Mug, horse profile, twisted rope handle, 5x3" **$25.00**
Mug, nude handle, one of the series, 5¼" to 6", ea from $40 to **$50.00**
Pitcher, water; figural nude handle, from $350 to **$435.00**
Salt & pepper shakers, figural nude handles, pr.........**$50.00**

King's Crown, Thumbprint

Back in the late 1800s, this pattern was called Thumbprint. It was first made by the U.S. Glass Company and Tiffin, one of several companies who were a part of the US conglomerate, through the 1940s. U.S. Glass closed in the late '50s, but Tiffin reopened in 1963 and reissued it. Indiana Glass bought the molds, made some minor changes, and during the 1970s, they made this line as well. Confusing, to say the least! Gene Florence's *Collectible Glassware of the 40s, 50s, and 60s,* explains that originally the thumbprints were oval, but at some point Indiana changed theirs to circles. And Tiffin's tumblers were flared at the top, while Indiana's were straight. Our values are for the later issues of both companies, with the ruby flashing in excellent condition.

Ashtray, square, 5¼" **$25.00**
Bowl, crimped, 4½x11½"...**$125.00**
Bowl, flared, footed **$85.00**
Bowl, mayonnaise; divided, 5" **$65.00**
Bowl, 5¾"...**$20.00**
Cake salver, footed, 12½" **$75.00**
Candle holder, 2-light, 5½" **$95.00**
Candy box, flat, w/lid, 6" **$60.00**
Compote, flat, sm..**$25.00**
Cup **$8.00**
Lazy susan, w/ball-bearing spinner, 8½x24" **$295.00**
Pitcher..**$185.00**
Plate, mayonnaise liner; 7⅜"...**$12.00**
Plate, snack; w/indent, 9¾" **$15.00**

Plate, torte; 14½"...**$85.00**
Punch set, w/foot, 15-pc...**$850.00**
Relish, 5-part, 14"...**$110.00**
Saucer..**$8.00**
Stem, claret; 4-oz **$13.00**
Stem, water goblet; 9-oz **$12.00**
Sugar bowl **$25.00**
Tumbler, juice; 4½-oz...**$14.00**
Vase, bud; 12¼" **$90.00**

Kitchen Collectibles

If you've never paid much attention to old kitchen appliances, now is the time to do just that. Check in Grandma's basement — or your mother's kitchen cabinets, for that matter. As styles in home decorating changed, so did the styles of appliances. Some have wonderful Art Deco lines, while others border on the primitive. Most of those you'll find still work, and with a thorough cleaning you'll be able to restore them to their original 'like-new' appearance. Missing parts may be impossible to replace, but if it's just a cord that's gone, you can usually find what you need at any hardware store.

Even larger appliances are collectible and are often used to add the finishing touch to a period kitchen. Please note that prices listed here are for appliances that are free of rust, pitting, or dents and in excellent working condition.

During the nineteenth century, cast-iron apple peelers, cherry pitters, and food choppers were patented by the hundreds, and because they're practically indestructible, they're still around today. Unless parts are missing, they're still usable and most are very efficient at the task they were designed to perform.

A lot of good vintage kitchen glassware is still around and can generally be bought at reasonable prices. Pieces vary widely from custard cups and refrigerator dishes to canister sets and cookie jars. There are also several books available for further information and study. If this area of collecting interests you, you'll enjoy *300 Years of Kitchen Collectibles* by Linda Campbell, and *Kitchen Antiques, 1790 – 1940*, by Kathryn McNerney. Other books include *Kitchen Glassware of the Depression Years* and *Anchor Hocking's Fire-King & More* by Gene Florence; *Collector's Encyclopedia of Fry Glassware* by H.C. Fry Glass Society; *The '50s and '60s Kitchen, A Collector's Handbook and Price Guide*, by Jan Lindenberger; and *Fire-King Fever* and *Pyrex History and Price Guide*, both by April Tvorak.

See also Aluminum; Clothes Sprinkler Bottles; Fire-King; Glass Knives; Griswold; Kitchen Prayer Ladies; Porcelier; Reamers.

Advisor: Jim Barker, Appliances (See Directory, Appliances)

Appliances

Baby bottle warmer, Electestreem Baby Chef BB101, black Bakelite, 1947, 3¾x4", EX **$10.00**

Baby bottle warmer, Sunbeam, chrome bullet shape, plastic thermometer, black handles, 1940s, 12½"..............**$30.00**

Blender, Osterizer #10 Vitra Mix, chrome, beehive shape, EX..**$25.00**

Blender, Osterizer #235 Series, chrome, beehive shape, 4-cup, 14½", EX **$55.00**

Blender, Waring #1006, bar type w/timer, 2-speed, EX.**$40.00**

Blender, Waring DL-202, chrome, beehive shape, EX ..**$20.00**

Blender, Waring Imperial RL-6, chrome & glass, EX...**$35.00**

Can opener, Sunbeam, turquoise, electric, 1950s, 9", EX.**$32.00**

Can opener, Sunbeam #54-S1, yellow pedestal base, ca 1960s, EX...**$18.00**

Coffeepot, Presto, chrome, Deco style w/black base, EX..**$20.00**

Egg poacher, Sunbeam Model E, 6½x7" w/handles ...**$22.00**

Juicer, Acme Juicerator 5001, 17 lbs, EXIB **$75.00**

Juicer, Acme Model 7001, stainless steel blade, basket & strainer, ¼-hp motor, EX......................................**$90.00**

Juicer, Atlas, 1950s-60s, EX **$65.00**

Juicer, Champion G5-NG842S, white plastic housing, EX..**$120.00**

Juicer, Juiceman II, ½-hp motor, 120 volts, 14x10", NM...**$110.00**

Juicer, Osterizer #403, white enamel & chrome, 1950s, NM w/booklet..**$50.00**

Mixer, drink; Arnold, chrome w/white enamel base, 17", EX...**$55.00**

Mixer, Hamilton Beach, complete with Seville Yellow bowls, $200.00. (Photo courtesy Gene Florence)

Mixer, hand; Dormeyer Dormey 7500, 5-speed, EX ...**$15.00**

Mixer, hand; General Electric #10M47, pink, 3-speed, EX...**$35.00**

Mixer/blender, Knapp Monarch, EX.............................**$27.50**

Percolator, General Electric, chrome & brown Bakelite, squatty egg shape, 1950s, 9-cup, EX.....................**$20.00**

Percolator, Mary Proctor-Silex #01932, gold floral on glass body, ca 1967, 10-cup, NM...................................**$30.00**

Percolator, unmarked, red anodized aluminum, Deco style, 8-cup, electric, EX+...**$35.00**

Percolator, Vacuum, aluminum w/pyrex bottom, 12-cup, 1950s, NM..**$55.00**

Percolator, Westinghouse, floral on white, Deco style, 12", EX **$15.00**

Toaster, Challenge, drop sides, EX..............................**$22.00**

Toaster, Proctor Silex #20218, 2-slice, 1960s, EX........**$12.50**

Toaster, Sunbeam T-20B, chrome, Deco style, EX......**$40.00**

Toaster, Sunbeam T-35 Radiant Control, 1950s, EX **$40.00**

Toaster, Toastermaster, engraved floral on chrome, 2-slice, EX **$15.00**

Miscellaneous Gadgets and Glassware

Apple corer, White Mountain, Goodell Co, Antrim NJ, green painted cast iron, red wooden handle, 10x6", EX..**$26.00**

Apple parer, corer, slicer, LL Bean, White Mountain, M in worn box...**$18.00**

Batter set, crystal jug & syrup pitcher w/black lids & tray, Paden City, from $125 to **$150.00**

Bean slicer, Alexanderwerk Johnenschneider, cast iron, crank type, EX...**$18.00**

Bowl, Delphite (blue), horizontal ribs, Jeannette Glass Co, 5½", from $65 to..**$70.00**

Bowl, Dots, green on white opaque, scalloped edge, McKee, 9", from $22 to..**$25.00**

Bowl, mixing; green transparent, 9", from $22 to.......**$25.00**

Butter dish, amber, embossed ribs, rectangular, Federal Glass, 1-lb, from $30 to..**$35.00**

Canister, fired-on tulips on clear, lg, from $15 to **$20.00**

Canister, Tea, black letters on Seville Yellow, 48-oz, from $60 to..**$70.00**

Canister, Vitrock w/fruit decal, glass lid, Hocking, from $7 to..**$85.00**

Canisters, Century, spun aluminum, raised letters, copper-tone lids, set of 4, EX...**$15.00**

Casserole, Kold or Hot, green transparent Tufglas, w/lid, sm, from $15 ....**$18.00**

Chopper, Foley, red wooden T-handle, stainless steel blades, spring-loaded inner blade, 7½"..............................**$8.00**

Chopper, Hazel Atlas, glass jar, red wood handle, 11" ...**$12.00**

Chopper, Lorraine Metal Mfg Co, NY City NY, green depression glass w/metal lid & plunger, EX+..................**$45.00**

Chopper, wood handle w/single rocker blade............**$12.00**

Coffee dripolator, clear glass, 3-pc, sm, from $20 to ..**$25.00**

Condiment set, Emerald-Glo, Paden City, metal frame, w/spoon, from $40 to...**$50.00**

Cookie jar, Kromex, spun aluminum, black lid, EX....**$30.00**

Cookie jar, Kromex, spun aluminum, yellow lid, EX..**$40.00**

Cookie jar, Pewtertone, liberty bell shape, spun aluminum, 13", NM...**$18.00**

Crushed fruit/cookie jar, Paden City Party Line, pink, from $70 to...**$75.00**

Cup, soup; fired-on color, square sides, from $3 to **$4.00**

Egg beater, A&J High Speed, butterscotch Bakelite handles, stainless steel blades, EX..**$20.00**

Egg beater, clear glass base w/internal agitator, metal lid w/red wooden crank in top, EX...........................**$25.00**

Egg beater, Flint, Ekco, ca 1950s-60s, NM **$8.50**

Egg beater, Flint's Best, beaters marked stainless steel, 1950s-60s, EX..**$10.00**

Egg beater, Ladd #1, spring-shaped winding knob, curved tooth gears, 9¾"..**$10.00**

Egg beater, Maynard, manual rotary, EX......................**$8.00**

Egg beater, Turbine Egg Beater by the Cassady Fairbank Mfg Co, lt rust, 10" **$60.00**

Funnel, canning; Sanitary Fruit Jar Funnel, white ironstone, 4¾" **$20.00**

Funnel, cobalt glass, 8-oz, 6x5" **$20.00**

Funnel, Nesco 5 Articles in 1, tin w/red tin handle, 8¼"....**$20.00**

Funnel, vaseline glass, 4-oz **$15.00**

Garnishing set, Acme, dated 1935, MIB, $35.00. (Photo courtesy Fran Carter)

Grease jar, Kromex, spun aluminum, w/strainer, EX..**$15.00**

Grinder, Griswold #3, NMIB **$60.00**

Grinder, Lorraine Mfg, green painted cast iron, clamps on table, 7½", VG..**$25.00**

Grinder, Rollman #11, cast iron, 6¼", EX **$18.00**

Grinder, Universal #2, 3 cutters & 5 accessories **$20.00**

Grinder, Universal #3, Landers, Frary & Clark, NMIB.**$35.00**

Grinder, Winchester #32 in wood box **$60.00**

Ice bucket, frosted glass w/multicolor (4) stripes, metal handle & tongs, from $30 to **$35.00**

Ice bucket, Kromex, spun aluminum, NM..................**$20.00**

Ice bucket, Paden City Party Line, amber, from $30 to ..**$32.50**

Ice pick, cast iron, tulip-shaped end w/sm hook on side as opener **$20.00**

Ice pick, red painted wood handle, unmarked, 8", NM .**$12.00**

Jar wrench, Triumph, adjusts for 4 sizes, EX...............**$15.00**

Jar wrench, Wizard, hinged hairpin type....................**$10.00**

Lemon squeezer, Arcade #2, cast iron **$24.00**

Lemon squeezer, porcelain w/gold trim, #258 on bottom, 2½x4½" **$25.00**

Lemon squeezer, Squeezit, fish figural, 1950s-60s, M.**$10.00**

Lemon squeezer, Sunkist, steel, Made in USA, 9½" L.**$15.00**

Lemon squeezer, WMF Ritter Citro, hinged metal, 1950s, MIB...**$8.00**

Measuring cup, blue, 3-spout, Fire-King, from $25 to ..**$30.00**

Measuring cup, Cream Dove Brand Peanut Butter & Salad Dressing, from $20 to **$30.00**

Measuring cup, crystal, Jeannette, 1-cup, from $40 to ..**$45.00**

Measuring pitcher, custard, McKee, 4-cup, from $35 to..**$40.00**

Measuring pitcher, Diamond Check, red or black, McKee, 2-cup, from $35 to **$40.00**

Mug, Forest Green, Cambridge, from $40 to..............**$50.00**

Mug, root beer; green, from $30 to............................**$35.00**

Mug, Tally-Ho, red, Cambridge, from $28 to..............**$30.00**

Napkin holder, Fan Fold, Forest Green, from $135 to...**$150.00**

Napkin holder, white, Nar-O-Fold, from $50 to..........**$55.00**

Pan, egg poacher; copper w/brass handle, cooks 4, Germany, EX **$10.00**

Pan, egg poacher; Mirro, aluminum, 4-cup, Bakelite handle, 8" dia, NM..**$20.00**

Pan, egg poacher; Pyrex, 4 cups, rack & lid, all glass, 10" **$35.00**

Paper towel/waxed paper dispenser, Kromex, spun aluminum w/black plastic sides, EX............................**$22.00**

Pea huller/bean slicer, Vaughan's, cast metal, 2 blades, green handle, Deco style, 1930s, 11" **$15.00**

Pitcher, Chesterfield, amber glass, w/lid, from $90 to ..**$100.00**

Pitcher, water; Paden City Rena Line, green transparent w/embossed swirls, from $35 to..............................**$40.00**

Popcorn set, Mirro, spun aluminum, lg bowl & 4 servers, EX...**$20.00**

Potato masher, Bakelite handle, 1940s, 8¾" **$30.00**

Potato masher, twisted wire w/green wooden handle .**$12.00**

Potato masher, twisted wire w/wooden handle marked W Germany, 13" **$16.50**

Refrigerator bowl, Crisscross, pink, w/lid, Hazel Atlas, 4x4", from $25 to...**$30.00**

Refrigerator dish, Chalaine Blue, rectangular, 4x5", from $40 to **$50.00**

Refrigerator dish, cobalt, Hazel Atlas, 5¾" dia, from $50 to **$75.00**

Refrigerator dishes, Hex Optic, pink, Jeannette Glass, 3 pcs (2 bases, lid), from $55 to **$65.00**

Refrigerator jar, Hex Optic, green, 4½x5", from $22 to ..**$25.00**

Rolling pin, chrome w/red plastic handles, 1940s-50s, 15" **$15.00**

Rolling pin, clambroth w/wooden handles, from $100 to **$125.00**

Rolling pin, maple, 1-pc...**$20.00**

Rolling pin, maple w/moving handles, NM.................**$30.00**

Rolling pin, Roll-Rite, Good Housekeeping Institute, 14", NM..**$40.00**

Rolling pin, tight-grained wood w/red wooden handles..**$15.00**

Rolling pin, wood w/worn green painted handles.....**$10.00**

Salad fork & spoon, clear w/blue pointed handles, pr, from $50 to **$60.00**

Salt & pepper shakers, Delphite Blue, Jeannette, 8-oz, pr, from $45 to **$50.00**

Salt & pepper shakers, Kromex, spun aluminum, EX, pr...**$15.00**

Salt & pepper shakers, Roman Arch, fired-on colors, McKee, pr, from $16 to **$20.00**

Salt shaker, fired-on color w/colored metal top, various colors, ea, from $5 to **$6.00**

Sifter, Androck Hand-i-Sifter, painted tin, red wood handle **$22.50**

Sifter, Bromwell Radio, tin, 5¾x4½" **$24.00**

Sifter, green anodized aluminum, mechanical squeeze handle **$17.50**

Sifter, Hunter's Sifter...Made in USA, tin w/wooden knob, 6½"......**$20.00**

Sifter, tin w/painted flowers, red wood knob, NM **$24.00**

Skillet, Pyrex, clip-on handle, 6½"......**$35.00**

Soap dish, cobalt, Home Soap Company, from $22 to......**$25.00**

Spatula, heart shape, Bakelite handle......**$12.50**

Spatula, star design, red wooden handle......**$7.50**

Spice jars, spun aluminum w/black lids, set of 8 in aluminum rack, EX......**$30.00**

Sugar shaker, crystal, West Sanitary Automatic Sugar, from $20 to......**$25.00**

Syrup pitcher, Moongleam Green, Heisey, metal lid, from $70 to......**$75.00**

Syrup pitcher, Paden City #198, amber, 8-oz, from $45 to.....**$55.00**

Syrup pitcher, pink, Standard Glass, metal lid, from $50 to...**$55.00**

Timer, Lux, white plastic w/black ribbing, chrome-plated dial, 1950s, EX......**$15.00**

Timer, Mark Time Portable Time, 2-speed, metal & red enamel, MIB......**$20.00**

Timer, Mirro, Lux, aluminum, 4x4"......**$18.00**

Tumbler, Crisscross, crystal, Hazel Atlas, 9-oz, from $30 to......**$40.00**

Tumbler, West Bend, aluminum, wheat motif, 5 bands engraved around bottom, 10-oz, set of 6......**$6.00**

Water bottle, Forest Green, Duraglas, metal cap, from $20 to......**$25.00**

Water bottle, green transparent, embossed ribs, Hocking Glass, from $30 to......**$35.00**

Water bottle, green transparent, embossed ribs, shouldered form w/metal lid, 32-oz, from $25 to......**$35.00**

Water dispenser, custard, McKee, from $110 to......**$125.00**

Whip, cream/egg; Dunlap's Sanitary, green wood handles, EX......**$18.00**

Whip/mixer, Kwik-Whip, aluminum w/Bakelite top, jar style, 1950s, 8", EX......**$8.50**

Whip/separator, curled wire, black plastic handle......**$8.00**

Kitchen Prayer Ladies

The Enesco importing company of Elk Grove, Illinois, distributed a line of kitchen novelties during the 1960s that they originally called 'Mother in the Kitchen.' Today's collectors refer to them as 'Kitchen Prayer Ladies.' The line was fairly extensive — some pieces are common, others are very scarce. All are designed around the figure of 'Mother' who is wearing a long white apron inscribed with a prayer. She is more commonly found in a pink dress. Blue is harder to find and more valuable. Where we've given ranges, pink is represented by the lower end, blue by the higher. If you find her in a white dress with blue trim, add another 10% to 20%. For a complete listing and current values, you'll want to order *Prayer Lady Plus+* by April and Larry Tvorak. This line is pictured in *The Collector's Encyclopedia of Cookie Jars, Volume 1* and *2*, by Joyce and Fred Roerig (Collector Books).

Advisor: April Tvorak (See Directory, Kitchen Prayer Ladies)

Bank, Mother's Pin Money, from $175.00 to $250.00. (Photo courtesy Beverly and Jim Mangus)

Air freshener......**$150.00**

Bell, from $75 to......**$125.00**

Candle holders, pr......**$200.00**

Canister, pink, ea......**$300.00**

Canister set, pink, complete, from $1,200 to......**$1,500.00**

Cookie jar, blue......**$495.00**

Cookie jar, pink......**$395.00**

Crumb tray or brush, from $125 to......**$200.00**

Egg timer, from $100 to......**$135.00**

Instant coffee jar, spoon-holder loop on side......**$150.00**

Mug......**$125.00**

Napkin holder, pink, from $25 to......**$30.00**

Picture frame, minimum value......**$175.00**

Planter......**$75.00**

Plaque, full-figure......**$100.00**

Ring holder......**$50.00**

Salt & pepper shakers, pr, from $12 to......**$20.00**

Soap dish, from $35 to......**$50.00**

Spoon holder, upright......**$65.00**

Sprinkler bottle, blue, minimum value......**$600.00**

Sprinkler bottle, pink, minimum value......**$500.00**

String holder, from $135 to......**$145.00**

String holder, wall mount, from $135 to......**$145.00**

Sugar bowl, w/spoon......**$60.00**

Tea set, pot, sugar & creamer......**$300.00**

Toothpick holder, 4½", from $20 to......**$24.00**

Vase, bud; pink, from $100 to......**$125.00**

Kreiss & Co.

Collectors are hot on the trail of figural ceramics, and one of the newest areas of interest are those figurines, napkin dolls, planters, mugs, etc., imported from Japan during the 1950s by the Kreiss company, located in California. Though much of their early production was run of the mill, in the late 1950s, the company introduced unique new lines — all bizarre, off the wall, politically incorrect, and very irreverent — and today it's these items that are attracting so much attention. There are several lines. One is a totally zany group of caricatures called Psycho-Ceramics. There's a Beatnick series, Nudies, and Elegant Heirs (all of which are strange little creatures), as well as some that are very well done and tasteful. Several will be inset with with colored 'jewels.' Many are marked either with an ink stamp or an in-mold trademark (some are dated), so you'll need to start turning likely-looking items over to check for the Kreiss name.

There's a very helpful book now on the market, called *Kreiss Novelty Ceramics*, written by and available from our advisors, Michele and Mike King.

See also Napkin Ladies.

Advisors: Michele and Mike King (See Directory, Kreiss; Psycho Ceramics)

Beatniks

Figure, man dressed in Santa suit, It Was the Night Before Happysville, 6½", from $75 to **$100.00**
Figure, man in blue, Work? Man I Deny It's Existence, on base, 7", from $75 to **$100.00**

Figure, Picasso? Who's That Cat?, from $400.00 to $500.00. (Photo courtesy Michele and Mike King)

Figure, uppity man sits w/legs crossed, Dad, Whatever It Is, I'm Against It, 4¾" (5½" on base), from $75 to.**$100.00**

Christmas Psycho Ceramics

Figure, drunk w/lg red nose at green & white lamppost, Rudolf the Red Nosed Reindeer, from $100 to...**$150.00**
Figure, Santa in green, Mrs Santa Claus Left My Christmas Suit in the Cleaners, 4¾", from $125 to **$175.00**
Figure, Santa w/lg red nose, No More for You Rudolph, You're Driving!, 7", from $100 to........................**$125.00**
Figure, yellow w/lipstick marks, mistletoe branch on head, Who Cares What It Looks Like - I Get Results, 4½", from $125 to..**$175.00**
Figure, yellow w/tongue out, holly on head, recumbent, 2½x5¼", from $175 to...**$225.00**

Elegant Heirs

Figure, bald man w/1 hand to temple, other to stomach, 6¼", from $275 to...**$325.00**
Figure, blond lady w/blue coat & green bow in hair, I Never Go in for Fads, I Have My Own Ideas!, 4¼", from $100 to...**$150.00**
Figure, furrowed brow, eyes crossed, holds red valentine in front, 6¼", from $275 to..**$325.00**
Figure, hobo raising glass, Man of Distinction, Hell...It's All I Could Afford!, 6½", from $75 to **$100.00**
Figure, hobo w/safety pin through pants, It Takes All Kinds, 6½", from $100 to...**$125.00**
Figure, man in prison clothes w/ball & chain, On Vacation, 6¼", from $50 to..**$75.00**
Figure, old woman in bikini, Is That All You Crazy Men Ever Think About?, from $100 to **$125.00**
Mug, man w/dark hair, smiling, w/cigarette in hand, 4¼", from $100 to..**$150.00**

Moon Beings

Figure, orange-red to black long-necked creature w/fuzzy topknot, 4¾", from $250 to................................**$300.00**
Figure, yellow & black dog-like creature, 4½", from $250 to..**$300.00**

Psycho Ceramics

Ashtray, pensive maroon creature, I Have the Nervous Cigarette Habit, 4¾", from $150 to......................**$200.00**
Ashtray, woebegone green figure w/gun to head, The Doc Said To Quit Smoking or Else, 5", from $150 to **$200.00**
Egg cup, brown creature w/huge teeth & thick eyebrows, 2½", from $200 to..**$250.00**
Figure, angry purple creature w/pink plastic hair, What Happened to the Dress You Bought Last Year?, 5", from $400 to..**$450.00**
Figure, blue lg-eyed creature, Looking for Someone w/a Little Authority? I Have as Little as Anyone, 4¾", from $100 to **$150.00**
Figure, brown creature w/huge teeth & thick eyebrows, We Welcome Your Suggestions w/Enthusiasm!, 4¾", from $150 to..**$200.00**
Figure, strange multicolor creature, I Was Born This Way, What's Your Excuse?, 4¾", from $100 to **$150.00**
Figure, television screens for eyes, I Can Take TV or Leave It Alone, 4¼", from $150 to....................................**$200.00**
Figure, woebegone green figure w/gun to head, Nothing Seems To Work for Me Anymore!, 5", from $150 to **$200.00**
Mug, creature w/footprints allover, People Walk All Over Me, 4¾", from $150 to..**$200.00**
Mug, creature w/1 blue & 1 yellow side, black separation, The Doc Said Something About a Split Personality, from $125 to..**$175.00**
Mug, yellow figure w/stern expression, I'm the Brains of This Outfit, 5", from $100 to **$150.00**

Miscellaneous

Bank, yellow figure in red hat w/ax, In Case of Fire Lift Up Hat, under hat: Not Now Stupid! In Case of Fire, from $150 to **$200.00**

Bell, Daffy Bell, 3 stacking creatures, 4½", from $25 to ..**$75.00**

Figure, cave family, 2 adults, 4¾" & 2 children, 2½", each parent attached to child by chain, from $100 to **$150.00**

Figure, dinosaur, 5½", 2 cavemen, 2½", attached by chain, from $100 to.................**$150.00**

Figure, Good Time Charlie on elephant w/2nd smaller elephant on top, A Little Fun Don't Hurt No One, 5¾", from $100 to.................**$150.00**

Lamps

Aladdin Electric Lamps

Aladdin lamps have been made continually since 1908 by the Mantle Lamp Company of America, now Aladdin Mantle Lamp Company in Clarksville, Tennessee. Their famous kerosene lamps are highly collectible, and some are quite valuable. Many were relegated to the storage shelf or thrown away after electric lines came through the country. Today many people keep them on hand for emergency light.

Few know that Aladdin Industries, Inc. was one of the largest manufacturers of electric lamps from 1930 to 1956. They created new designs, colorful glass, and unique paper shades. These are not only collectible but are still used in many homes today. Many Aladdin lamps, kerosene as well as electric, can be found at garage sales, antique shops, and flea markets. You can learn more about them in the books *Aladdin Electric Lamps* and *Aladdin — The Magic Name in Lamps, Revised Edition,* written by J.W. Courter, who also periodically issues updated price guides for both kerosene and electric Aladdins.

Advisor: J.W. Courter (See Directory, Lamps)

Newsletter: *Mystic Lights of the Aladdin Knights*
J.W. Courter
3935 Kelley Rd., Kevil, KY 42053. Subscription: $25 (6 issues, postpaid 1st class) per year with current buy-sell-trade information. Send SASE for information about other publications.

Bed lamp, B-45, Whip-o-lite shade, NM, from $75 to ..**$100.00**

Bedroom lamp, ceramic, P-51, from $30 to.................**$40.00**

Boudoir lamp, New Series, Alacite, G-40, 1949, from $40 to **$50.00**

Bridge lamp, B-125, from $125 to **$175.00**

Floor lamp, Alacite ring, candle arms, #3998, from $250 to **$350.00**

Floor lamp, fluorescent 15" tubes (2), from $150 to...**$225.00**

Floor lamp, reflector, #3460, from $150 to **$200.00**

Floor lamp, Type A, #3349, from $150 to **$200.00**

Junior floor lamp, Colonial, amber or green bowl, C-130, EX, from $250 to.................**$300.00**

Pin-up lamp, cast white metal, plated, M-350, EX, from $60 to.................**$90.00**

Table lamp, Alacite, G-265, from $60 to.....................**$70.00**

Table lamp, Alacite, illuminated base, G-303, EX, from $50 to.................**$75.00**

Table lamp, brass metal, M-495, from $35 to **$45.00**

Table lamp, G-85, from $150 to **$200.00**

Table lamp, metal & moonstone, MM-70, from $200 to...**$250.00**

Table lamp, Opalique, G-181, from $150 to.............**$200.00**

Table lamp w/planter, ceramic, P-408, from $75 to..**$125.00**

Torchier floor lamp, #4598, EX, from $250 to..........**$300.00**

Boudoir lamp, G-24, Alacite, Cupid figural, with shade, EX, from $200.00 to $250.00. (Photo courtesy Bill and Treva Courter)

Aladdin Kerosene Mantle Lamps

Floor lamp, Model B, gold plated & oxidized bronze lacquer, B-426, from 1941-42/1946-51, EX, from $175 to ..**$225.00**

Floor lamp, Model B, satin gold, B-298, 1939-40, from $300 to.................**$350.00**

Hanging lamp, Model #12, tilt frame, w/parchment shade, VG, from $200 to.................**$250.00**

Hanging lamp, Model 23, brass w/glass shade, several types, ea, from $75 to **$150.00**

Shelf lamp, Model 23, Lincoln Drape, clear, 1975-82, complete w/burner, from $90 to **$100.00**

Table lamp, Model B, Tall Lincoln Drape, ruby crystal, B-77, EX (beware of reproductions), from $800 to ..**$1,000.00**

Table lamp, Model B, Treasure, chromium, B-136, NM, from $175 to.................**$225.00**

Table lamp, Model B, Victoria 1947, ceramic w/oil fill, worn gold bands, B-25, from $350 to.................**$450.00**

Table lamp, Model B, Washington Drape, bell stem, clear crystal, B-47, 1940-41, EX, from $175 to.............**$225.00**

Table lamp, Model 23, Short Lincoln Drape, amber, undated (made in 1974), from $75 to.................**$100.00**

Table lamp, Model 23, Short Lincoln Drape, cobalt, signed Aladdin 1998 in glass, complete, NM, from $70 to .**$90.00**

Wall bracket lamp, Model 23, aluminum font, w/correct burner, flame spreader & 2-part wall bracket but no shade, from $50 to..$75.00

Wall bracket lamp, Model 6, w/font, correct burner, flame spreader, 2-part bracket but no shade, from $150 to $200.00

Figural Lamps

Many of the figural lamps on the market today are from the 1930s, 1940s, and 1950s. You'll often see them modeled as matching pairs, made primarily for use in the boudoir or the nursery. They were sometimes made of glass, but most were ceramic, so unless another material is mentioned in our descriptions, assume that all our figural lamps are ceramic. Several examples are shown in *Collector's Guide to Made in Japan Ceramics, Books I, II,* and *III,* by Carole Bess White (Collector Books).

See also Occupied Japan.

Advisor: Dee Boston (See Directory, Lamps)

Bali girl, ceramic w/green glass finial, mark No 166-657 Pat Pend, 1940s, original shade, 28"..........................$115.00

Cherub, molded spelter, beside opal globe, ca 1950, 28"..$75.00

Child reading on grassy base, multicolor, ceramic, w/pink shade, 15"...$35.00

Collie dog beside tree, ceramic, red fiberglas shade w/black lacing, 1950s, 13" $110.00

Deco-style dancer, painted base metal, opaque shade, 1940s, table size..$50.00

Deco-style dancer stands before bulb w/in arch, painted plaster, 1950s, 13½x11½x4" $100.00

Draped nude peers into fire pit, plaster, red glass jewels at pit, 16", VG..$170.00

Girl holding flowers, 2 brown ponytails, flat straw hat, multicolor, ceramic, on brass base, missing shade, 25½" $150.00

Maidens (3) hold hands around lamp, brass or white metal, Accurate Casting A4181, Italy, 1940s, 21" $40.00

Mexican man sleeping, frosted figural w/flashed color, original white frosted glass shade, 13" $50.00

Spanish dancer in red, chalkware, 1950s, 19" to top of socket $25.00

Motion Lamps

Though some were made as early as 1920 and as late as the 1970s, motion lamps were most popular during the 1950s. Most are cylindrical with scenes such as waterfalls and forest fires and attain a sense of motion through the action of an inner cylinder that rotates with the heat of the bulb. Prices below are for lamps with original parts in good condition with no cracks, splits, dents, or holes. Any damage greatly decreases the value. As a rule of thumb, the oval lamps are worth a little more than their round counterparts. **Caution** — some lamps are being reproduced. (These are indicated in our listings with a +.) Currently in production are Antique Autos, Trains, Old Mill, Ships in a Storm, Fish, and three Psychedelic lamps. The color on the scenic lamps is much bluer, and they are in a plastic stand with a plastic top. There are quite a few small motion lamps in production that are not copies of the 1950s lamps. For further information we recommend *Collector's Guide to Motion Lamps* by Sam and Anna Samuelian (Collector Books), which contains full-page color photographs and useful information.

Advisors: Jim and Kaye Whitaker (See Directory, Lamps)

Annie lamp, Johnson Co, 1981, 11" $50.00

Antique Autos, Econolite, 1957, 11" + ...$125.00

Aquarium, glass bowl for fish, motion below in stand, 1931..$300.00

Bicycles, Econolite, 11" $150.00

Boy & Girl Scouts, Econolite, 10"................................$150.00

Christmas trees, green, blue, red, & white, paper, 1950s, 10" to 24", ea, from $75 to $110.00

Colonial Fountain Scene In Action, metal, 1930s, 10"..$200.00

Davy Crockett $200.00

Disneyland Express, Econolite, 1955, 11" $155.00

Elephant Lady Fortune Teller, chalk, S&S, 1930s, 12" ...$200.00

Elvgrin Pin-up Girls $300.00

Firefighters, LA Goodman, 1957, 11"........................$250.00

Fireplace, Econolite, 1958, 11".................................$150.00

Fish, Fresh Water, Econolite, 1950s, 11"...................$105.00

Fish, Salt Water, Econolite, 1950s, 11" + ...$110.00

Forest Fire, Econolite, 1955, 11"...............................$130.00

Forest Fire, Rotovue Jr, 1949, 10" $125.00

Forest Fire, Scene In Action, 1931, 10" $200.00

Fountain of Youth, Rotovue Jr, 1950, 10" $110.00

Indian Chief, Gritt Inc, 1920s, 11"............................$100.00

Indian Maiden, Gritt Inc, 1920s, 11".........................$100.00

Japanese Twilight, Scene In Action, 1931, 13" $185.00

Jet Planes, Econolite... $210.00

Merry Go Round, Rotovue Jr, 1949, 10"....................$100.00

Miss Liberty, Econolite, 1957, 11"............................$250.00

More Here Than Meets the Eye, Hawaiian Girl, paper front, 1952, 12"..$200.00

Niagara Falls, Econolite, 1955, 11"............................$95.00

Niagara Falls, Rotovue Jr, 1949, 10".........................$75.00

Niagara Falls, Scene In Action, 1931, 10" $150.00

Old Mill, Econolite, 1965, 11" +................................$110.00

Op Art Lamp, Visual Effects, 1970s, 13"....................$55.00

Oriental Fantasy, LA Goodman, 1957, 11"................$110.00

Oriental Scene, Econolite, 1959, 11" $165.00

Sailboats, LA Goodman, 1954, 14" $110.00

Sailing Ships, Econolite +...$150.00

Seattle World's Fair, Econolite...................................$175.00

Seven Up $75.00

Snow Scene, Church or Cabin, Econolite, 1957, 11".$150.00

Snow Scene, LA Goodman $95.00

The Bar Is Open, Visual Effects, OP Art, 1970s, 13".....$5.00

Totville Train, Econolite, 1948, 11"...........................$150.00

Trains, Econolite, 1956, 11" + ...$125.00

Tropical Fish, Econolite, 1954, 11" $95.00

Truck & Bus, Econolite, 1962, 11"............................$150.00
Venice Canal, Econolite, 1963, 11" $200.00
White Christmas, Econolite, flat front, 11" $190.00
Why You Should Never Drink the Water, paper front, 1946-
    49, 4 sizes, ca...$145.00

Steamboats, Econolite, 1957, 11", $130.00.

TV Lamps

By the 1950s, TV was commonplace in just about every home in the country but still fresh enough to have our undivided attention. Families gathered around the set and for the rest of the evening delighted in being entertained by Ed Sullivan or stumped by the $64,000 Question. Pottery producers catered to this scenario by producing TV lamps by the score, and with the popularity of anything from the '50s being what it is today, suddenly these lamps are making an appearance at flea markets and co-ops everywhere.

See also Maddux of California; Morton Potteries, Royal Haeger.

Ballerina, plastic w/fiberglas shade, from $100 to $125.00
Blue jays (2) among rocky base w/leaves & acorns, bright
    colors, bisque, from $65 to $75.00
Bulldogs (2), brown & black, ceramic, eyes light up, signed
    Williams Ceramics WH45 Claes, from $120 to ...$135.00
Coach w/horses & 3 figures on base, multicolor pastels,
    bisque, light in brass base, from $100 to............$110.00
Deer leaping among grasses, green, ceramic, from $55
    to $65.00
Doe & fawn in relief at front, planter behind, brown & gray,
    ceramic, from $75 to...$85.00
Duck, flying, planter, mallard-style painting, ceramic, 12",
    from $75 to..$90.00
Duck, flying, wooden base, brown w/blue seafoam-like trim,
    ceramic, from $82 to..$97.00
Gazelle, leaping, planter behind, green, ceramic, from $70 to .$90.00
Gondola w/windows that light up, gondolier at right, green,
    ceramic, from $85 to..$90.00

Horse, Deco style, white w/gold flecks, front legs appear to
    straddle planter, from $75 to.................................$95.00
Horse, leaping, by fence, white w/black mane & tail, ceram-
    ic, from $75 to...$85.00
Horse, rearing, shiny black, ceramic, w/planter behind, from
    $65 to...$80.00
Horse head, Deco, black w/black & white streaked mane,
    light inside, from $75 to...$95.00
Leopard on base, brown tones, plaster, 14", from $200 to..$250.00
Madonna, praying, white, ceramic, from $45 to $55.00
Oriental boy pulls figure in rickshaw, pagoda behind, white
    metal, from $75 to $100.00
Paddle boat w/planter in top, green w/gold trim, ceramic,
    from $70 to...$90.00
Panther, shiny black, pottery, planter openings in front, from
    $65 to...$75.00
Rooster, crowing, on fence, multicolor, ceramic, signed Lane,
    from $95 to...$100.00
Sailboat, white sails & brown hull, ceramic, brass footed
    base, marked Made in California #3500-5321855, from
    $60 to...$85.00
Sailing ship, ceramic w/metal sails, portholes light up, from
    $75 to...$80.00
Scotty dogs (2), black & white w/red details, pressed paper,
    from $75 to...$95.00
Swan, green, ceramic, holes in wings to emit light from
    behind, from $80 to..$95.00
Swordfish, chartreuse green w/gold, ceramic, from $75
    to $95.00

L.E. Smith

Originating just after the turn of the century, the L.E. Smith company continues to operate in Mt. Pleasant, Pennsylvania, at the present time. In the 1920s they introduced a line of black glass that they are famous for today. Some pieces were decorated with silver overlay or enameling. Using their own original molds, they made a line of bird and animal figures in crystal as well as in colors. The company is currently producing these figures, many in two sizes. They were one of the main producers of the popular Moon and Star pattern which has been featured in their catalogs since the 1960s in a variety of shapes and colors.

If you'd like to learn more about their bird and animal figures, *Glass Animals of the Depression Era* by Lee Garmon and Dick Spencer has a chapter devoted to those made by L.E. Smith. See also *A Collector's Guide to Modern American Slag Glass* by Ruth Grizel.

See also Eye Winker; Moon and Star.

Basket, Bird of Paradise, red, upright feathers form deeply
    scalloped rim, center handle, ca 1980, 13½".......$40.00
Basket, Cane & Daisy, ruby, center handle, 1997, 13"...$40.00
Basket, Dominion, ruby, diamond-pattern base, flaring pan-
    els w/rounded tops, 1997, 7" W...........................$25.00
Basket, Pineapple, ruby, 14½" W................................$40.00

Basket, ruby, prs of narrow leaves, embossed/textured, 1997, 5¾" W $25.00

Bookend, Goose Girl, ruby, 1979, 6" $35.00

Bookend, Goose Girl, ruby, 1979, 8" $45.00

Bookend, horse, Almond Nouveau slag, rearing, 8", ea, from $50 to $60.00

Bookend, horse, crystal, rearing, ea $55.00

Bookend, rooster, ruby, 1960, 9" $75.00

Bookend, thrush, ruby carnival, 1980, 9" $30.00

Bowl, berry; footed, robin blue, 4" $16.00

Bowl, console; black, #1022/4, 3-footed, ca 1930s, 6" ..$30.00

Bowl, console; black, 3-footed, ca 1930s, 9" $45.00

Bowl, Dolly, red carnival $38.00

Bowl, nappy, heart shape, Almond Nouveau slag, 6" ..$25.00

Bowl, turkey, dark blue, footed, oval, 7" $65.00

Bowl, Wigwam, flared $30.00

Box, piano shape, black, 1992, 6½" $45.00

Butter dish, Almond Nouveau slag, made in 1980, from $40.00 to $45.00.

Candle holder, #4041a, Almond Nouveau slag, 7½", ea $25.00

Candle holder, angel, kneeling, slag, ea $25.00

Candle holders, angel, kneeling, green, pr $26.00

Candlestick, wigwam, black, ca 1935, 3¼" $20.00

Candy dish, ruby, cone shape, paneled w/embossed designs, 1990, 2½" $12.00

Canoe, Daisy & Button, purple carnival $25.00

Covered dish, duck, black, 1992, 7" $45.00

Covered dish, hen on nest, #820a, Almond Nouveau slag, 6" $50.00

Covered dish, hen on nest, ruby, miniature, 1990, 3¼" L ...$15.00

Covered dish, rooster, standing, Almond Nouveau slag, 9", from $75 to $85.00

Covered dish, rooster, standing, white carnival $75.00

Cup & saucer, Do Si Do, black, ca 1930s $12.00

Cup & saucer, Mt Pleasant, black, ca 1930s $12.00

Dresser set, Colonial, cologne bottle & powder jar, purple $50.00

Egg plate, ruby, 1990, 10¾" $60.00

Figurine, bear, Almond Nouveau slag, #6654A, 4½" ...$45.00

Figurine, bear, baby, head turned or straight, crystal, 3", ea .$60.00

Figurine, bear, papa, crystal, 4x6½" $250.00

Figurine, bird, flying, Almond Nouveau slag, 9", from $45 to $50.00

Figurine, bird, head up or down, Almond Nouveau slag, 5", pr $65.00

Figurine, camel, recumbent, amber, 4½x6" $60.00

Figurine, camel, recumbent, cobalt, 4½x6" $65.00

Figurine, camel, recumbent, crystal, 4½x6" $45.00

Figurine, cock, fighting, blue, 9" $55.00

Figurine, elephant, crystal, 1¾" $12.00

Figurine, Goose Girl, amber, 5½" $35.00

Figurine, Goose Girl, crystal, original, 6" $25.00

Figurine, Goose Girl, ice green carnival, 5½" $60.00

Figurine, Goose Girl, red, 5½" $50.00

Figurine, horse, recumbent, amberina, 9" L $150.00

Figurine, horse, recumbent, blue, 9" L $115.00

Figurine, horse, recumbent, green, 9" L $100.00

Figurine, lamb, black, marked C in circle, ca 1930s, 2¼" L $18.00

Figurine, praying Madonna, crystal $35.00

Figurine, rabbit, crystal, miniature $10.00

Figurine, rooster, butterscotch slag, limited edition, #208 ...$85.00

Figurine, swan, Almond Nouveau slag, 5" $55.00

Figurine, swan, crystal lustre, limited edition, w/certificate, lg $55.00

Figurine, swan, ice pink carnival, 2" $15.00

Figurine, swan, milk glass w/decoration, 8½" $45.00

Figurine, swan, open back, #15a, Almond Nouveau slag, 4½" $20.00

Figurine, swan, open back, #650, Almond Nouveau slag, 9" $45.00

Figurine, thrush, blue frost $20.00

Figurine, unicorn, pink, miniature $20.00

Flowerpot, black, plain, ca 1930s, 3½" $12.00

Flowerpot & saucer, black, finely ribbed sides, ca 1930s, 5½" $35.00

Lamp, candle; black base w/frosted ribbed shade, 1992, 7½" $35.00

Lamp, fairy; turtle figural, green $25.00

Lamp, hurricane; black, low base w/clear chimey, 1992, 12" $35.00

Lamp, hurricane; black, low base w/clear chimey, 9" ...$30.00

Nappy, heart shape, #4630a, Almond Nouveau slag, 6" ..$25.00

Novelty, boot on pedestal, green or amber $12.00

Novelty, coal bucket, #125a, Almond Nouveau slag, 5" ..$25.00

Novelty, shoe skate, ice blue, limited edition, 4" $25.00

Novelty, slipper, Daisy & Button, Almond Nouveau slag, 6" $35.00

Novelty, slipper, Daisy & Button, amber $8.00

Novelty, slipper, Daisy & Button, purple carnival $25.00

Nut dish, Mt Pleasant, black, #505, 8" dia $25.00

Paperweight, hexagon shape, black, 1992, 3" $20.00

Paperweight, oval, black, 1992, 5" $20.00

Paperweight, star shape, black, 1992, 5" $23.00

Pitcher, water; Heritage, red carnival $40.00

Pitcher, water; Hobstar, ice green, w/6 tumblers $125.00

Pitcher, water; Tiara Eclipse, green $70.00

Plate, Abraham Lincoln, purple carnival, #706/1195, 9" ...$40.00

Plate, George Washington Bicentennial, black, 1932, 8" ..$85.00

Plate, Herald, Christmas 1972, purple carnival, lg $40.00

Plate, Jefferson Davis, 1972, purple carnival, lg $40.00

Plate, Mt Pleasant, black, ca 1930s, 8" $12.00

Plate, Robert E Lee, 1972, purple carnival, lg **$40.00**
Plate, Silver Dollar Eagle, 1972, purple carnival, lg **$40.00**
Sandwich tray, black, shield-shape open center handle, ca 1930s, 10" dia **$40.00**
Soap dish, swan, clear, 8½" **$22.50**
Sugar bowl, Homestead, pink **$8.00**
Table set, Mt Pleasant, black, creamer, open sugar, salt & pepper shakers & tray, ca 1930s, 5-pc **$170.00**
Toothpick holder, Daisy & Button, amberina **$12.50**
Tray, black, center open heart-shape handle, low gallery rim, ca 1930s, 6" dia **$15.00**
Tray, sandwich; Mt Pleasant, black, ca 1930s, 13½" dia **$85.00**
Tumbler, Bull's Eye, red carnival **$22.00**
Urn, black, 2-handled, footed, 8" **$20.00**
Vase, bud; #33a, Almond Nouveau slag, 6½" **$35.00**
Vase, corn, crystal lustre, very lg **$37.00**
Votive, owl's head, #668a, Almond Nouveau slag, 2" .**$25.00**

Lefton China

China, porcelain, and ceramic items with that now familiar mark, Lefton, have been around since the early 1940s and are highly sought after by collectors in the secondary marketplace today. The company was founded by Mr. George Zoltan Lefton, an immigrant from Hungary. In the 1930s he was a designer and manufacturer of sportswear, but eventually his hobby of collecting fine china and porcelain led him to initiate his own ceramic business. When the bombing of Pearl Harbor occurred on December 7, 1941, Mr. Lefton came to the aid of a Japanese-American friend and helped him protect his property from anti-Japanese groups. Later, Mr. Lefton was introduced to a Japanese factory owned by Kowa Koki KK. He contracted with them to produce ceramic items to his specifications, and until 1980 they made thousands of pieces that were marketed by the Lefton company, marked with the initials KW preceding the item number. Figurines and animals plus many of the whimsical pieces such as Bluebirds, Dainty Miss, Miss Priss, Cabbage Cutie, Elf Head, Mr. Toodles, and Dutch Girl are eagerly collected today. As with any antique or collectible, prices vary depending on location, condition, and availability. For the history of Lefton China, information about Lefton factories, marks, and other identification methods, we highly recommend the *Collector's Encyclopedia of Lefton China, Volumes I, II, III,* and *Lefton Price Guide* by our advisor Loretta DeLozier (Collector Books).

See also Birthday Angels; Cookie Jars.

Advisor: Loretta DeLozier (See Directory, Lefton)

Club: National Society of Lefton Collectors

Newsletter: *The Lefton Collector*
c/o Loretta DeLozier
PO Box 50201
Knoxville, TN 37950-0201
Dues: $25 per year (includes quarterly newsletter)

Ashtray, Miss Priss, blue cat, #1524 ....**$50.00**
Ashtray, White Holly, leaf shape, #6056, 7" **$20.00**
Bank, Green Holly, bell shape w/red bow atop, #158 ...**$35.00**
Bank, Love Nest, bluebird pr in birdhouse, #7485, 7" ..**$125.00**
Bank, Miss Priss, blue cat in flowered hat, #4916 ....**$400.00**
Bank, Root of All Evil, devil seated on money bag, #4923, 8" ..**$65.00**
Bell, ivory bisque w/applied pastel flowers, #783, 4¾" ..**$15.00**
Bird, cardinal, female, #1005, 5¼" **$35.00**
Bookends, dog heads on woodgrained planks, #7484, 4¾" **$45.00**
Bowl, Pink Clover, #2503, 6¼" **$15.00**
Bowl, swan shape, pink w/white lily of the valley, #195, 5½" **$50.00**
Bowl, white swan w/roses, #1388, 5¾" **$35.00**
Box, candy; White Italian Romance, piano shape, #655 ...**$30.00**
Box, Luscious Lilac, w/lid, round, #2963, 3¼" **$18.00**
Bust, Madonna, pink matt, #1720, 8" **$35.00**
Cake plate, Green Heritage, roses on light green, #719 ..**$40.00**
Candle holder, Italian Romance, beige, #805, 6" **$15.00**
Candy dish, Floral Mood, leaf shape, #4669, 5¾" **$25.00**
Canister set, Sweet Violets, #2875, 4-pc **$100.00**
Cheese dish, Bluebird Line, #437 ....**$300.00**
Cigarette set, French Rose, lighter, box & 4 trays, #3835 ....**$45.00**
Coffeepot, Brown Heritage Floral, #1866 ....**$175.00**
Coffeepot, Floral Chintz, #8033 ....**$150.00**
Colonial Village, Belle Union Saloon, #07482 ....**$75.00**
Colonial Village, Country Post Office, #07341 ....**$65.00**
Colonial Village, House of Blue Gables, #06337 ....**$70.00**
Colonial Village, Ryman Auditorium, #08010 ....**$65.00**
Cookie jar, Bluebird Line, #289 ....**$375.00**
Cookie jar, boy's head in chef's hat, #396, 8" **$300.00**
Cookie jar, Dainty Miss, lady's head, in yellow hat w/pink bow under her chin, #040 ....**$250.00**
Cookie jar, elf head, #3969, 8½" **$300.00**
Cookie jar, Mr Toodles, white long-haired dog w/blue ribbons, #3236 ....**$225.00**
Cookie jar, white w/daisies, #39 ....**$40.00**
Cookie jar, yellow bird, #291, 10½" **$50.00**
Creamer & sugar bowl w/lid, Floral Chintz, #8034 .....**$65.00**
Creamer & sugar bowl w/lid, Silver Wheat, #2154 .....**$25.00**
Cup & saucer, Blue Paisley, #2339 ....**$20.00**
Cup & saucer, floral on white, very ornate, #4256 .....**$35.00**
Cup & saucer, Four Seasons, #780 ....**$40.00**
Dish, Americana, 3-compartment, #937 ....**$50.00**
Dish, Green Holly, 3-compartment, #1351 ....**$35.00**
Egg cup, Violet Chintz, #664 ....**$35.00**
Figurine, angel w/flowers, wearing blue robe, glazed, #00780, 6½", facing pr **$15.00**
Figurine, angels sitting in flowers, #2724, 4", facing pr ...**$85.00**
Figurine, bay horse, #2211, 7" **$75.00**
Figurine, bluegill swimming in coral, naturalistic colors, #1072, 4½" **$40.00**
Figurine, boy & girl w/rabbits at feet, #7453, 6½", ea ...**$65.00**
Figurine, bride & groom, childlike, #941, 3½", pr **$65.00**
Figurine, cardinal on flowering limb, #7020, 7" **$65.00**
Figurine, cat w/hat & organ grinder, #7567, 4" **$18.00**

Figurine, clown, #02146, 6¼", $55.00. (Photo courtesy Loretta DeLozier)

Figurine, Cocker Spaniel, white w/brown markings, #00412, 4½" $22.50

Figurine, Colonial man (& lady), he w/basket, she holding flowers in her apron, #5151, 7½", pr $175.00

Figurine, Colonial man & woman, #8180, 10¼", pr..$250.00

Figurine, Growing Up Girls #8, Marika's Originals, #4662, 5½" $35.00

Figurine, heron, naturalistic, #1541, 6½"......................$40.00

Figurine, hunter, #609, 8" $55.00

Figurine, Indigo Bunting on flowering branch, #1706, 7" $110.00

Figurine, Kewpie sitting on leaf, #2992, 3½"..............$30.00

Figurine, Madelaine, in long blue gown, white ruffles down the front, holding closed parasol, #5745, 7½"....$175.00

Figurine, man & lady, period attire, on common base w/delicate flowers, #4050, 7" $200.00

Figurine, man holding boy in arms, #7778, 6½" $85.00

Figurine, man or woman feeding ducks & chickens, #7271, 7¾" $60.00

Figurine, nurse holding baby, #2739, 5½" $45.00

Figurine, old man & woman on bench, #4728, 4½"...$38.00

Figurine, old man sitting playing cards, #5087, 6½"...$65.00

Figurine, old man w/dog, #6885, 8"............................$65.00

Figurine, poodle, gray, #6659, 6"................................$40.00

Figurine, red squirrel w/acorns & leaves, #4492, 8" ..$90.00

Figurine, reindeer, lying down, green w/gold bell, long ears, #5218, 4½", facing pr..$35.00

Figurine, Rose Madonna bust, #835, 7".......................$65.00

Figurine, Ruffed Grouse, naturalistic, #2668, male & female, 5", pr..$75.00

Figurine, Russian Lady, in elegant white robe w/gold trim, #752, 11"..$200.00

Figurine, tabby cat, #6364, 4½".....................................$25.00

Figurine, Valentine girl, #033, 4"..................................$20.00

Figurine, Victorian lady w/umbrella, #1570, 6¼"......$145.00

Figurine, white rabbit, #880 ....$30.00

Figurine, Yellow Warbler on blossoming branch, #440, 6"...$40.00

Figurines, Spirit of '76 Soldiers, #2041, 3-pc set........$145.00

Frame, Heavenly Hobos, house shape w/bride & groom, #04638, 4¾" $35.00

Jam jar, fruit finial on basketweave base, #5108, 5½" $18.00

Jam jar, grape cluster, purple, #4852, 5" $30.00

Jam jar, Lilac Chintz, w/spoon & tray, #202 ....$40.00

Jam jar, Miss Priss, blue cat head, #1515 ....$75.00

Lamp, miniature; Green Holly, #4229, 5½" $45.00

Mug, Fruits of Italy, highly embossed allover fruit pattern, pale colors, #1211, 11" L $18.00

Mug, Miss Priss, blue cat head, #1503, 4" $75.00

Music box, Christmas angel on bell base, #637, 7".....$60.00

Music box, Santa & Snowman, plays Santa Claus Is Coming to Town, #10398, 6"...$45.00

Night light, mouse beside lg mushroom, #7920, 6" $28.00

Perfume set, Only a Rose, #385, 3-pc........................$110.00

Pitcher, Poinsettia, #4389, 6¼"....................................$85.00

Pitcher, water; To a Wild Rose, #2562 ....$125.00

Pitcher & bowl, Brown Heritage Fruit, #3289, sm $35.00

Pitcher & bowl, green daisy, #5777, 4¼"....................$22.00

Planter, ABC block, #2128, 4"......................................$12.00

Planter, beagle w/lg eyes before receptacle, #6974, 6"..$28.00

Planter, birdhouse, sign lettered Home Tweet Home, bird on perch, #50261, 5" $45.00

Planter, Santa on white reindeer, #1496, 6" $30.00

Planter, squirrel, green w/lg eyes, before white receptacle, #5766, 6½" $15.00

Salt & pepper, Mr & Mrs Claus in rocking chairs, #8139, pr $25.00

Salt & pepper shakers, Dark Green Heritage, single rose on bell shape, #30132, pr $25.00

Salt & pepper shakers, egg boy & girl, #7782, pr.......$15.00

Salt & pepper shakers, White Christmas, #825, pr $25.00

Sleigh, Green Holly, #2637, 10½"................................$55.00

Snack set, Rose Chintz, #637 ....$35.00

Tea set, Heavenly Rose, stacking, 3 pcs plus sugar bowl lid, #20596 ....$200.00

Teapot, Cardinal w/holly on white, #1655 ....$125.00

Teapot, Dainty Miss, girl's head, white hat w/red intersecting lines & blue flower finial, #321 ....$175.00

Teapot, elf's head, #3973 ....$185.00

Teapot, Heirloom Elegance, #5394.............................$160.00

Teapot, 25th Anniversary, musical, #1137....................$45.00

Tidbit tray, Festival, blue & green grapes on white w/gold trim, 2-tier, #2624 ....$45.00

Vase, Brown Heritage Fruit, #3117, 8¾" $75.00

Vase, ewer; boy or girl in relief, #154, 6" $55.00

Vase, head; lady w/ruby, #2251, 6"..............................$85.00

Vase, Only a Rose, white w/applied rose at waist, #420, 6" $45.00

Wall plaque, girl w/watering can, flowerpot (separate), #2630, 2 pcs $125.00

Wall plaque, mermaid, #4574, 6", pr $75.00

Wall pocket, girl w/basket, #50264, 7"......................$150.00

Wall pocket, Green Heritage, rose cluster on oval shape, #045, 6½" $45.00

Teapot, rose design, #2117, $55.00. (Photo courtesy Loretta DeLozier)

Letter Openers

If you're cramped for space but a true-blue collector at heart, here's a chance to get into a hobby where there's more than enough diversification to be both interesting and challenging, yet one that requires very little room for display. Whether you prefer the advertising letter openers or the more imaginative models with handles sculpted as a dimensional figure or incorporating a penknife or a cigarette lighter, for instance, you should be able to locate enough for a nice assortment. Materials are varied as well, ranging from silverplate to wood. For more information, we recommend *Collector's Guide to Letter Openers* by Everett Grist (Collector Books).

Advisor: Everett Grist (See Directory, Letter Openers)

Advertising, brass, Diversified Industries, Inc, Roseville, Mich, marked B&B, St Paul Minn **$22.00**
Advertising, brass, Ocean Accident & Guarantee Corporation **$25.00**
Advertising, gold plated, Holiday Inns of America **$6.00**
Advertising, plastic, Lincoln Center, New York **$3.00**
Advertising, white metal, Mobile Asphalt Co, Inc, Whistler, Alabama **$6.00**
Advertising, yellow plastic, Yellow Pages in black **$3.00**
Bakelite, orange & yellow marbleized, Peekskill NY . **$25.00**
Bone, cut-out totem in handle **$20.00**
Brass, anchor handle, spear-shaped blade, marked India . **$8.00**
Brass, dragon's head handle, erotic scene on blade ... **$35.00**
Brass, elephant handle **$10.00**
Brass, enameled bird & Peace on handle, marked Terra Sancta Guild 1968, Israel **$8.00**
Brass, Falstaff figural handle, engraved Falstaff on blade, Peerage, England mark **$15.00**
Brass, nude 3-D handle, Great Smoky Mountains **$18.00**
Brass, Revolutionary patriot on horse forms handle, marked England **$10.00**
Brass, smiling Chinese elder w/long beard (forming blade) **$15.00**
Butterscotch Bakelite handle w/hand-painted flowers, Ocean City, MD **$25.00**

Chrome, University of Tennessee, Knoxville **$6.00**
Combination bookmark, chrome color, Saratoga Springs NY **$15.00**
Combination bookmark, steel, Texas Centennial, Dallas .. **$6.00**
Combination cigarette lighter & ruler blade, fishing fly in body of lighter, Mardi Gras '67, Japan **$40.00**
Combination clippers & file in pewter & steel fish figural handle, shield at base of handle shows mule & word Missouri **$10.00**
Combination magnifier, red plastic w/brass shield, Annapolis, marked SP, made in USA **$6.00**
Combination magnifier & ruler, clear plastic w/red plastic sheath, Bausch & Lomb **$3.00**
Combination pen & magnifier, plastic & brass, Souvenir of Laguna Beach, FL on the Gulf of Mexico **$12.00**
Combination pen knife, plastic & steel, Great Smoky Mts, knife blade: Imperial USA **$10.00**
Combination pen knife (handle), celluloid & steel, Shakespeare's birthplace, Stratford-upon-Avon, Made in Germany **$25.00**
Combination ruler & knife, plastic, brass & steel, blade marked Stainless Steel, Florida souvenir, Japan.... **$10.00**
Copper, Arts & Crafts style, Roanoke Island, NC **$10.00**
Enamel & brass, overall flower decor, red tassel **$30.00**
French ivory, plain **$10.00**
Gold & black-colored pot metal, native girl's head figural handle **$25.00**
Gold plated, rifle w/attached bayonet form, Alabama Polytechnic Institution **$6.00**
Gold plated w/jeweled handle, plain slim metal blade .. **$8.00**
Gold-plated metal, eagle figural handle **$8.00**
Gold-tone metal, sword shape, Home of Franklin D Roosevelt, Hyde Park, NY **$6.00**
Leather handle w/black braided border, wood blade ... **$6.00**
Lucite, 3 US pennies in clear handle, paper label, Unique, Canada **$15.00**
Lucite handle w/reverse-carved & painted fish, Gulf Shores, Alabama **$15.00**
Mother of pearl, plain, sm **$15.00**
Nickel, fleur-de-lis handle, Italy **$6.00**
Pewter, dancing frog handle, Metzke 1979 .... **$12.00**
Plastic, bright blue, thunderbird handle **$3.00**
Plastic & steel, religious motto, M-Cor, USA **$3.00**
Plastic hollow handle w/seashells & white sand, Gulf Shores, Alabama Beach Sand **$18.00**
Plastic imitation stag handle, plain stainless blade, West Virginia souvenir **$4.00**
Plastic w/magnifying blade, clear & simple, w/leather sheath **$3.00**
Porcelain w/hand-painted roses, signed R Riddle **$45.00**
Resin, Hawaiian totem handle **$4.00**
Silverplated, bamboo-style handle **$10.00**
Silverplated floral handle, steel blade, International Silver **$5.00**
Stag handle, steel blade **$10.00**
Sterling, Pennsylvania State College, Hawks **$15.00**
Turquoise handle, brass blade, India **$15.00**

Walrus bone, carved polar bear at tip of handle **$45.00**

White metal, golf clubs & bag forms handle, Metzke 1985 ....**$15.00**

White metal, letter holder in handle, Mailway **$6.00**

Wood, dragon form w/abalone inlay..........................**$15.00**

Wood, hippo handle w/letter holder in mouth, plain blade **$15.00**

Wood, painted duck handle, copyright 1987 Dakin Inc, San Francisco, Product of China **$8.00**

Wood, sword shape, Souvenir of Union Station, St Louis, MO..**$10.00**

Wood handle, plain, stainless steel blade, from $3 to ..**$4.00**

Lucite, reverse-carved and filled rose, Bircraft, $30.00.
(Photo courtesy Everett Grist)

L.G. Wright

Until closing in mid-1990, the L.G. Wright Glass Company was located in New Martinsville, West Virginia. Mr. Wright started his business as a glass jobber and then began buying molds from defunct glass companies. He never made his own glass, instead many companies pressed his wares, among them Fenton, Imperial, Viking, and Westmoreland. Much of L.G. Wright's glass was reproductions of Colonial and Victorian glass and lamps. Many items were made from the original molds, but the designs of some were slightly changed. His company flourished in the 1960s and 1970s. For more information we recommend *The L.G. Wright Glass Company* by James Measell and W.C. 'Red' Roetteis (Glass Press).

Ashtray, Daisy & Button, ruby, 5½" **$12.00**

Basket, Daisy & Button, ruby, 7½".............................**$22.00**

Basket, English Hobnail, black, made from Westmoreland mold, marked WG, 1990s, 9" **$35.00**

Bell, Daisy & Button, ruby, 6½" **$35.00**

Bowl, Cherry, #7-16, slag glass, oval, 10", minimum value **$95.00**

Bowl, Cherry, #7-17, slag glass, oval, 5".....................**$45.00**

Bowl, Daisy & Button, amber, 5" **$15.00**

Bowl, sauce; Thistle, cobalt blue, 4½".........................**$12.50**

Bowl, sauce; Thistle, crystal, 4½" **$12.00**

Bowl, Stork & Rushes, black carnival, beaded band, 1995, 8½"..**$45.00**

Butter dish, Cherry, #7-2, slag glass **$80.00**

Candy dish, Paneled Grape, amber, footed, w/lid, 6½x4"...**$35.00**

Canoe, Daisy & Button, ruby, 4¼" **$20.00**

Compote, Palm Beach, apple green, ca 1930, 8½" **$95.00**

Compote, Wild Rose, green, 13"..................................**$25.00**

Covered dish, Atterbury duck, any color, unmarked, 11" ..**$70.00**

Covered dish, cat on nest, #80-2, cobalt blue slag, 5" ..**$75.00**

Covered dish, cat on nest, #80-2, purple or caramel slag.**$50.00**

Covered dish, cat on nest, #80-2, ruby slag, 5"...........**$95.00**

Covered dish, cow on nest, #80-3, cobalt blue slag, 5"..**$75.00**

Covered dish, cow on nest, #80-3, purple or caramel slag, 5" **$50.00**

Covered dish, cow on nest, #80-3, ruby slag, 5".........**$95.00**

Covered dish, duck on flange base, amethyst w/white head **$65.00**

Covered dish, duck on flange base, milk glass or opaque blue w/milk glass head **$50.00**

Covered dish, flatiron, amber, w/lid, 5x8½"...............**$50.00**

Covered dish, hen on nest, #70-8, amethyst w/white head or white w/amethyst head, 7½" **$65.00**

Covered dish, hen on nest, #70-8, purple or caramel slag glass, 8"...**$75.00**

Covered dish, hen on nest, #70-8, ruby slag, 8" **$295.00**

Covered dish, hen on nest, #80-7, cobalt blue slag, 5"..**$75.00**

Covered dish, hen on nest, #80-7, purple or caramel slag, 5" **$50.00**

Covered dish, hen on nest, #80-7, ruby slag, 5" **$95.00**

Covered dish, hen on nest, amberina, red or vaseline, #70-8, 8", ea..**$75.00**

Covered dish, horse on nest, #80-8, cobalt blue slag, 5" ..**$75.00**

Covered dish, horse on nest, #80-8, purple or caramel slag, 5" **$50.00**

Covered dish, horse on nest, #80-8, ruby slag, 5" **$95.00**

Covered dish, lamb on nest, #80-9, cobalt blue slag, 5"..**$90.00**

Covered dish, lamb on nest, #80-9, purple or caramel slag, 5" **$65.00**

Covered dish, lamb on nest, #80-9, ruby slag, 5" **$125.00**

Covered dish, owl's head on nest, #80-10, cobalt blue slag, 5" **$75.00**

Covered dish, owl's head on nest, #80-10, custard, 5" .**$50.00**

Covered dish, owl's head on nest, #80-10, purple or caramel slag, 5" **$50.00**

Covered dish, owl's head on nest, #80-10, ruby slag, 5"...**$95.00**

Covered dish, owl's nead on nest, #80-10, amber, 5".**$45.00**

Covered dish, rooster on nest, #80-12, cobalt blue slag, 5" **$75.00**

Covered dish, rooster on nest, #80-12, purple or caramel slag, 5" **$50.00**

Covered dish, rooster on nest, #80-12, ruby slag, 5" ..**$95.00**

Covered dish, swan on nest, #80-14, cobalt blue slag, 5" **$75.00**

Covered dish, swan on nest, #80-14, purple or caramel slag, 5" **$50.00**

Covered dish, swan on nest, #80-14, ruby slag, 5" **$95.00**

Covered dish, turkey on nest, #80-15, lilac mist, 5"....**$55.00**

Covered dish, turkey on nest, #80-15, cobalt blue slag, 5" **$75.00**

Covered dish, turkey on nest, #80-15, purple or caramel slag, 5" **$50.00**

Covered dish, turkey on nest, #80-15, ruby slag, 5" ...**$95.00**

Covered dish, turtle, 'Knobby Back,' amber, lg...........**$95.00**

Covered dish, turtle, 'Knobby Back', dark green, lg.**$135.00**

Covered dish, turtle on nest, #80-16, amber, 5".........**$20.00**

Covered dish, turkey, purple slag, large, minimum value, $700.00. (Photo courtesy Sharon Thorener)

Covered dish, turtle on nest, #80-16, cobalt blue slag, 5" ..**$75.00**
Covered dish, turtle on nest, #80-16, purple or caramel slag, 5" **$50.00**
Covered dish, turtle on nest, #80-16, ruby slag, 5" **$95.00**
Creamer, Cherry #7-4, slag glass................................**$60.00**
Dish, Daisy & Button, ruby, oval, 4-footed, ca 1950s, 5" L **$12.00**
Goblet, Cherry, #7-12, slag glass **$30.00**
Goblet, Daisy & Button, ice blue, 5", set of 6 ....**$75.00**
Goblet, Double Wedding Ring, ruby satin, 6¼" **$20.00**
Goblet, Paneled Grape, amber, 8-oz........................**$15.00**
Lamp, fairy; Diamond Point, 3-pc, 7"......................**$110.00**
Lamp, fairy; Thistle, crystal, 3-pc............................**$35.00**
Lamp, fairy; Wild Rose, green & crystal, ruffled base, 3-pc, 6" **$40.00**
Lamp, oil; Daisy & Button, ruby, 12" **$75.00**
Lamp base, Daisy & Fern, cranberry, bulbous inverted pear form, ornate metal base **$95.00**
Lamp shade, American Beauty, embossed roses, pink overlay, 1950s-60s, 6¾x10"..**$65.00**
Mustard jar, Ferdinand (bull's head), #77-46, purple slag .**$55.00**
Novelty, pump, #77-95, purple slag **$65.00**
Novelty, trough, #77-96, purple slag **$45.00**
Pitcher, Cherry, green, 5" **$32.00**
Pitcher, water; Cherry, #7-14, slag glass....................**$175.00**
Plate, Log Cabin, Crystal Mist, oval, limited edition, 1971, 9", from $40 to...**$50.00**
Plate, Paneled Grape, ruby, 7½", from $30 to............**$35.00**
Salt dip, Cherry, crystal, master, 1¾x3¼" **$30.00**
Salt dip, swan, crystal satin, 3¾" L **$12.00**
Slipper, Daisy & Button, black, ca 1980s, 2¼x5¼" **$20.00**
Sugar bowl, Cherry, #7-5, slag glass, minimum value...**$50.00**
Sugar bowl, Paneled Grape, amber, sm......................**$15.00**
Sugar bowl, Thistle, cobalt blue, 4½" **$26.00**
Toothpick, Daisy & Button slipper, ruby, 1950...........**$12.00**
Top hat, Daisy & Button, ruby, 2¼"............................**$15.00**
Tray, Daisy & Button, light blue, 3-part, 7½x4½".......**$25.00**
Tumbler, Cherry, #7-9, slag glass................................**$35.00**
Tumbler, iced tea; Cherry, #7-15, slag glass **$40.00**
Tumblers, Inverted Thumbprint, cranberry, ca 1970, set of 6, from $50 to...**$60.00**

Liberty Blue

'Take home a piece of American history!,' stated an ad from the 1970s for this dinnerware made in Staffordshire, England. Blue and white depictions of George Washington at Valley Forge, Paul Revere, Independence Hall — fourteen historic scenes in all — were offered on different place-setting pieces. The ad goes on to describe this 'unique…truly unusual…museum-quality…future family heirloom.'

For every five dollars spent on groceries you could purchase a basic piece (dinner plate, bread and butter plate, cup, saucer, or dessert dish) for fifty-nine cents on alternate weeks of the promotion. During the promotion, completer pieces could also be purchased. The soup tureen was the most expensive item, originally selling for $24.99. Nineteen completer pieces in all were offered along with a five-year open stock guarantee.

Beware of 18" and 20" platters. These are recent imports and not authentic Liberty Blue. For more information we recommend Jo Cunningham's book, *The Best of Collectible Dinnerware* (Schiffer).

Advisor: Gary Beegle (See Directory, Dinnerware)

Platter, 14", $95.00.

Bowl, cereal; 6½", from $12 to...................................**$15.00**
Bowl, flat soup; 8¾", from $20 to **$22.00**
Bowl, fruit; 5", from $6 to **$6.50**
Bowl, vegetable; oval, from $40 to **$45.00**
Bowl, vegetable; round, from $40 to **$45.00**
Butter dish, w/lid, ¼-lb...**$55.00**
Casserole, w/lid **$125.00**
Coaster...**$12.50**
Creamer, from $18 to..**$22.00**
Creamer & sugar bowl, w/lid, original box................**$80.00**
Cup & saucer, from $7 to...**$9.00**
Gravy boat, from $32 to..**$38.00**
Gravy boat liner, from $22 to **$30.00**
Mug, from $10 to **$12.00**
Pitcher, 7½"...**$125.00**

Plate, bread & butter; 6", from $4 to	**$4.50**
Plate, dinner; 10", from $6 to	**$8.00**
Plate, luncheon; scarce, 8¾"	**$24.00**
Plate, scarce, 7", from $9 to	**$12.00**
Platter, 12", from $35 to	**$45.00**
Salt & pepper shakers, pr, from $38 to	**$42.00**
Soup ladle, plain white, no decal, from $30 to	**$35.00**
Soup tureen, w/lid	**$425.00**
Sugar bowl, no lid	**$10.00**
Sugar bowl, w/lid	**$28.00**
Teapot, w/lid, from $95 to	**$145.00**

License Plates

Some of the early porcelain license plates are valued at more than $500.00. First-year plates are especially desirable. Steel plates with the aluminum 'state seal' attached range in value from $150.00 (for those from 1915 to 1920) down to $20.00 (for those from the early 1940s to 1950). Even some modern plates are desirable to collectors who like those with special graphics and messages.

Our values are given for examples in good or better condition, unless noted otherwise. For further information see *License Plate Values* distributed by L-W Book Sales.

Advisor: Richard Diehl (See Directory, License Plates)

Newsletter: *Automobile License Plate Collectors*
Gary Brent Kincade
P.O. Box 712, Weston, WV 26452; 304-842-3773

Magazine: *License Plate Collectors Hobby Magazine*
Drew Steitz, Editor
P.O. Box 222
East Texas, PA 18046; phone or fax: 610-791-7979; e-mail: PL8Seditor@aol.com or RVGZ60A@prodigy.com; Issued bimonthly; $18 per year (1st class, USA). Send $2 for sample copy.

1910, Massachusetts, porcelain	**$100.00**
1912, Connecticut, porcelain, truck	**$40.00**
1912, New Jersey, porcelain	**$100.00**
1913, New Hampshire, porcelain, triangular, Visitor	**$125.00**
1914, New Jersey	**$75.00**
1916, Maine, poor	**$10.50**
1916, Wyoming, porcelain	**$280.00**
1917, Massachusetts	**$25.00**
1917, Rhode Island, porcelain, touched up	**$80.00**
1918, Missouri, fair	**$15.50**
1918, Wyoming, repainted	**$80.00**
1919, Connecticut	**$10.50**
1919, Maryland, fair	**$15.00**
1920, New Jersey	**$20.00**
1924, Nevada, repainted	**$20.00**
1924, South Dakota	**$14.50**
1925, Arkansas, rebuilt/repainted, pr	**$50.00**
1925, Florida, repainted	**$60.00**

1925, Louisianna, repainted	**$80.00**
1926, New Mexico, repainted	**$30.00**
1927, California	**$20.00**

1929, Michigan, heavy painted metal, EX, $60.00 for the pair.

1929, New Jersey	**$18.50**
1930, Nevada, fair+	**$15.50**
1931, Connecticut	**$14.50**
1934, Nebraska	**$8.50**
1936, British Columbia, Canada	**$20.00**
1936, California, fair	**$8.50**
1936, Texas, fair	**$16.50**
1937, Massachusetts	**$11.50**
1938, Rhode Island	**$16.50**
1939, Minnesota	**$11.50**
1940, Illinois	**$9.50**
1940, Michigan	**$15.50**
1940, New Jersey	**$13.50**
1943, Pennsylvania, tab	**$10.00**
1944, Arkansas, fiberboard	**$50.00**
1947, Utah, some rust	**$14.50**
1948, Oregon	**$18.50**
1948, Pennsylvania	**$8.50**
1950, Virginia, pr	**$15.00**
1951, South Dakota	**$14.50**
1952, Minnesota	**$7.50**
1954, Kansas	**$6.50**
1954, Michigan	**$12.50**
1955, Wisconsin	**$12.50**
1956, California	**$15.50**
1958, Florida	**$8.50**
1958, Ohio	**$7.50**
1959, Rhode Island	**$9.50**
1960, Alaska	**$12.50**
1960, Tennessee	**$10.50**
1961, Hawaii, base undated	**$8.50**
1962, New York, pr	**$15.00**
1963, Washington DC	**$10.50**
1964, Utah	**$12.50**
1966, Alaska, totem pole	**$12.50**
1966, Wisconsin	**$4.50**
1968, Mississippi	**$6.50**
1968, South Carolina	**$5.50**

1970, Northwest Territories, Canada	**$55.00**
1971, Delaware	**$5.50**
1971, Iowa	**$4.00**
1972, Montana	**$5.00**
1975, North Carolina, First in Freedom	**$10.50**
1976, Alaska, bear	**$22.00**
1976, Oklahoma, Bicentennial	**$10.50**
1977, Oregon, Pacific Wonderland	**$25.00**
1978, West Virginia, blue border map	**$12.50**
1980, Nevada	**$6.50**
1984, Alabama	**$2.50**
1985, North Carolina, First in Flight	**$3.50**
1986, Louisianna	**$10.50**
1986, Louisianna, World's Fair	**$15.50**
1987, North Dakota, Teddy	**$9.50**
1987, Texas, Sesquicentennial	**$6.50**
1987 Iowa, sunflower	**$5.50**
1988, Washington	**$3.50**
1991, Florida, mantee	**$20.00**
1993, South Carolina, bird	**$7.50**
1994, Georgia, Olympics	**$20.00**
1996, Arizona, Environment	**$8.50**
1996, Nebraska, Chimney Rock	**$4.50**
1997, Oklahoma	**$7.50**
1998, Iowa, new type	**$7.50**
1998, Oregon, Trail	**$15.00**
1999, New Hampshire	**$7.50**

Little Red Riding Hood

This line of novelty cookie jars, canisters, mugs, teapots, and other kitchenware items was made by both Regal China and Hull. Today any piece is expensive. There are several variations of the cookie jars. The Regal jar with the open basket marked 'Little Red Riding Hood Pat. Design 135889' is worth about $350.00. The same with the closed basket goes for about $25.00 more. An unmarked Regal variation with a closed basket, full skirt, and no apron books at $600.00. The Hull jars are valued at about $350.00 unless they're heavily decorated with decals and gold trim, which can add as much as $250.00 to the basic value.

The complete line is covered in *The Collector's Encyclopedia of Cookie Jars* by Joyce and Fred Roerig (Collector Books), and again in *Little Red Riding Hood* by Mark E. Supnick.

Bank, wall hanging, from $1,200 to	**$1,500.00**
Butter dish, from $325 to	**$350.00**
Canister, cereal	**$1,375.00**
Canister, salt	**$1,100.00**
Canister, tea	**$700.00**
Canisters, coffee, sugar or flour, ea from $600 to	**$700.00**
Cookie jar, closed basket, minimum value	**$375.00**
Cookie jar, open basket, from $300	**$350.00**
Cookie jar, open basket, gold stars on apron, minimum value	**$675.00**

Cookie jar, open basket, red shoes	**$850.00**
Cookie jar, poinsettia	**$1,050.00**
Cookie jar, red spray w/gold bows, red shoes	**$950.00**
Cookie jar, red spray w/gold bows, red shoes, from $700 to	**$750.00**
Cookie jar, stars on apron, minimum value	**$675.00**
Cookie jar, white	**$200.00**
Creamer, top pour, no tab handle, from $400 to	**$425.00**
Creamer, top pour, tab handle, from $350 to	**$375.00**
Lamp, from $1,500 to	**$1,800.00**
Match holder, wall hanging, from $800 to	**$850.00**
Mustard jar, w/spoon	**$425.00**
Pitcher, 7"	**$350.00**
Pitcher, 8"	**$400.00**
Planter, hanging, from $475 to	**$500.00**
Shakers, Pat Design 135889, med size, pr, from $800 to	**$900.00**
Shakers, 3¼", pr, from $60 to	**$90.00**
Spice jar, from $650 to	**$750.00**
Sugar bowl, w/lid, from $300 to	**$425.00**
Teapot, from $325 to	**$375.00**
Wolf jar, red base, from $925	**$975.00**
Wolf jar, yellow base, from $750	**$800.00**

Bank, standing, from $650.00 to $750.00.
(Photo courtesy Pat Duncan)

Little Tikes

For more than twenty-five years, this company (a division of Rubbermaid) has produced an extensive line of toys and playtime equipment, all made of heavy-gauge plastic, sturdily built and able to stand up to the rowdiest children and the most inclement weather. As children usually outgrow these items well before they're worn out, you'll often see them at garage sales, priced at a fraction of their original cost. We've listed a few below, along with what we feel would be a high average for an example in excellent condition. Since there is no established secondary market pricing system, though, you can expect to see a wide range of asking prices.

Beauty Salon w/Swivel Chair, sink w/faucet, hose sprayer, peg board, mirror, attached side fold-out table, EX.........**$90.00**

Bike, 3-wheeler; pedal type, storage compartment on back, 29x19x20", EX **$32.00**

Boat, ratcheting throttle, steering wheel, shape allows rocking action, EX..................................**$30.00**

Bookshelf, 2 blue shelves w/white sides, EX.............**$42.00**

Cottage Toddler Bed, pink cottage w/blue roof, green shutters & white frame, EX........................**$110.00**

Country Kitchen, refrigerator, microwave, dishwasher, stove top, oven, sink, fold-out island, 58x21x43" **$75.00**

Easel, 1 side has chalkboard, other has pad of paper, removable tray ea side, folds, 43" **$28.00**

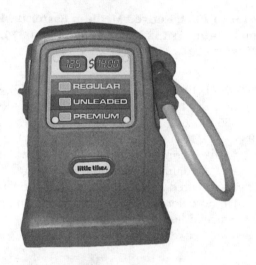

Gas Pump, child size, from $15.00 to $20.00.

Patio set, for Barbie Dollhouse, comes w/grill, table w/umbrella & 2 chairs, MIB..................**$45.00**

Race Car Toddler Bed, blue w/black & white wheels, crib size, EX................................**$95.00**

Road & Rail set, Tikes Peaks, comes w/car, boat, train, helicopter, & 4 toddle tots, complete w/52 pcs, EXIB.**$80.00**

Rocker/rider, motorcycle; red w/white front fender, blue removable base, 30x32"..................**$24.00**

Sandbox/pool, moat & castle, 46x9x29", EX **$40.00**

Slide, blue steps w/red slide, EX.....................**$35.00**

Step2 Double Seat Swing, tan & teal, safety bar, 10x17½x12", EX **$112.00**

Toy box, soccer ball shape, white & black, w/lid, 22x25", from $60 to.......................**$80.00**

Tractor & trailer/cart, green 3-wheeled tractor w/white & yellow 2-wheeled trailer, EX.................**$42.00**

Washer & dryer, w/fold-out ironing board & iron, 47x12¾x23", EX **$42.00**

Workbench, fold-out table, peg board, vise, phone & many tools, 40".............................**$90.00**

Lladro Porcelains

Lovely studies of children and animals in subtle colors are characteristic of the Lladro porcelains produced in Labernes Blanques, Spain. Their retired and limited editions are popular with today's collectors.

Aggressive Goose, #1288, 8¼", MIB **$300.00**
Barrow of Blossoms, #1419 ....**$485.00**
Birthday Party, #6314, MIB **$360.00**
Bless This Child, #5996, 9", MIB **$260.00**
Boy w/Goat, #4506, 11" **$210.00**

Bride and Groom, 1998, MIB, $110.00; M, $85.00.

Dainty Lady, #4934, 13¼" **$170.00**
Dancer, #5050, 12", MIB.....................**$160.00**
Fisher Boy, #4809, MIB......................**$110.00**
Flamenco Dancing Girl, #5390, 5½"...........**$210.00**
Food for Ducks, #4849, 6½x10" **$170.00**
Girl & New Lamb, #2223, 8½", MIB...........**$185.00**
Girl Graduate, 10½", MIB **$155.00**
Girl w/Doll, #5045, 11½" **$175.00**
Girl w/Flower, #4596, 6" **$150.00**
Girl w/Jugs, #4875, 12½" **$175.00**
Happy Anniversary, #6475, 12" **$255.00**
Hebrew Scholar, #6029G, 9¼", MIB...........**$150.00**
Kitty Confrontation, #1442, 3½" **$210.00**
Lady w/Shawl (holding umbrella, dog on leash), #4914, 16¼".....................................**$315.00**
Let's Make Up, #5555 ....**$185.00**
Litter of Love, signed Juan Vincente, #1441, 5", MIB..**$425.00**
Mirage (mermaid), #01415, 6x4½", MIB **$210.00**
My Buddy, Lladro Collector's Society, 1989, #7609, 8" .**$325.00**
My Pretty Yorkie, #6635, 7x6"..................**$290.00**
Nature's Song, #6310, MIB **$200.00**
Naughty Dog, #4982, 9" **$200.00**
New Playmates, #5456, 4¾" **$165.00**
New Shoes, #6487, 8", MIB...................**$120.00**
Pals Forever, Lladro Collector's Society 15th Anniversary, MIB **$280.00**
Perfect Performance (ballerina), #7641, 10", MIB **$265.00**
Peter Pan, signed Hugh Robinson, #07259, 1993, MIB...**$765.00**

Pick of the Litter, #7621, MIB **$260.00**
Playful Friends, #5609, 1988, MIB **$145.00**
Playful Piglets, #5228, 3x7½" **$160.00**
Playing Doctor, boy & teddy, 8", MIB **$160.00**
Sad Parting, #5583, 13x7½" **$175.00**
Sancho Panza, #1031, 11" **$395.00**
School Days, Lladro Collector's Society, #7604, 1988,
    MIB **$500.00**
Sea Fever, #5166, 9" **$265.00**
Sitting Pretty, #5699, MIB **$125.00**
Solace, mother consoles daughter, #15142, 10½" **$210.00**
Spring, #5217, 7½" **$195.00**
Spring Is Here, #5223, MIB **$150.00**
Spring Token, #05604, 8¾" **$160.00**
Stocking for Kitty, #6668 ....**$200.00**
Story Hour, #5786, 10x8½" **$290.00**
Summer Angel, #06148, 9¼", MIB **$135.00**
Summer on the Farm, #5285, 9½" **$265.00**
Summer Stroll, Lladro Collector's Society, #7611, 1991 ..**$185.00**
Waiting To Tee Off, #5301 ....**$185.00**
Wildflower, #5030, 11", MIB **$565.00**
Will You Marry Me?, #5447, 11½x10½", NM **$600.00**
Young Lady in Trouble, #34912, 10½" **$185.00**

Longaberger Baskets

In the early 1900s in the small Ohio town of Dresden, John Wendell ('J.W.') Longaberger developed a love for hand-woven baskets. In 1973 J.W. and his fifth child, Dave, began to teach others how to weave baskets. J.W. passed away during that year, but the quality and attention to detail found in his baskets were kept alive by Dave through the Longaberger Company®.

Each basket is hand-woven, using hardwood maple splints. Since 1978 each basket has been dated and signed by the weaver upon completion. In 1982 the practice of burning the Longaberger name and logo into the bottom of each basket began, guaranteeing its authenticity as a Longaberger Basket®.

New baskets can be obtained only through sales consulants, usually at a basket home party. Collector and speciality baskets are available only for a limited time throughout the year. For example, the 1992 Christmas Collection Basket was offered only from September through December 1992. After this, the basket was no longer available from Longaberger®. Once an item is discontinued or retired, it can only be obtained on the secondary market.

This information is from *The Seventh Edition Bentley Collection Guide*, published in June 1999. See the Directory for ordering information or call 1-800-837-4394.

Advisor: Jill S. Rindfuss (See Directory, Longaberger Baskets)

Baskets

Note: Values are for baskets only, unless accessories such as liners and protectors are mentioned in the description. Sizes may vary as much as one inch.

Prior to 1982, Retired Medium Easter Basket, one swinging handle, 5x13x8", from $66.00 to $75.00. (From the collection of Nancy McDaniels)

1979-93, Retired Mini Cradle™ (basket only), sm, rectangular, no color trim or weave, no handles, wood rockers, from $85 to **$120.00**
1983, JW Medium Market® (basket only), rectangular, blue weave & trim, 1 stationary handle, brass tag: Longaberger - JW Medium Market, from $1,346 to **$1,800.00**
1983-86, Retired Family Picnic™ (basket only), big, rectangular, no color trim or weave, 2 swinging handles, divided attached lid, from $326 to **$390.00**

1984, Christmas Collection Holly Basket, 2¼x15x8", from $325.00 to $475.00. (From the collection of Nancy McDaniels)

1986, Medium Chore™ (basket only), rectangular, no color weave or trim, 2 swinging handles, from $53 to .**$55.00**
1986-90, Hostess Collection Large Hamper™ (basket only), large, rectangular, no color weave or trim, attached woven lid, knob near front of lid, no handles, from $241 to **$305.00**
1987, Easter Signature Single Pie™ (basket only), square, red, blue & green weave, 1 stationary handle, all have Dave Longaberger's signature, from $233 to **$375.00**
1988, All-American Cake™ (basket only), square, red & blue weave & trim, 1 stationary handle, also came w/divider shelf, from $155 to **$225.00**

1988, Holiday Hostess Large Market™ (basket only), rectangular, red & green weave, red or green trim, 1 stationary handle, from $114 to..............................**$161.00**

1988-97, Heartland Medium Key™ (basket only), rectangular, Heartland Blue shoestring weave, 1 leather loop, metal bracket for hanging, Heartland burned-in logo on bottom, from $44 to...**$60.00**

1991, Holiday Hostess Tree-Trimming™ (basket only), tall, round opening, red & green weave, red & green trim, 1 swinging handle, from $150 to.........................**$200.00**

1992, Father's Day Paper™ (basket only), rectangular, higher in back, Dresden blue & burgundy trim, no handles, from $105 to...**$130.00**

1992, JW Cake® (basket only), square, blue accent weave & trim, 2 swinging handles, divider shelf, brass tag: Longaberger - JW Cake, w/box, from $167 to.**$290.00**

1992-96, Hostess Collection Mail™ (basket only), tall w/rectangular opening, no color weave, no handles, attached lid, metal hanger on back for mounting, ⅜" weaving, from $118 to..**$140.00**

1992-99, Booking/Promo Lavender™ (basket only), oval, no color trim or weave, 2 leather ears, ⅜" weave, from $32 to...**$53.00**

1993, All-Star Trio™ (w/liner & protector), rectangular, red & blue weave & trim, 2 leather ears, from $57 to ...**$95.00**

1993, Crisco® Baking™ (basket only), oval, red & blue weave & trim, 2 leather ears, burned-in Crisco® logo, from $105 to...**$120.00**

1993, Holiday Basket of Thanks™ (basket only), rectangular, natural w/red & green trim, 2 leather ears, brass tag: 1993 - Longaberger Holiday Basket of Thanks, from $72 to..**$115.00**

1993, Incentive Paint the Town™ (basket only), rectangular, green, blue & red shoestring weave, 1 stationary handle, from $100 to **$150.00**

1993, Shades of Autumn Harvest™ (basket only), rectangular, green, rust & deep blue weave w/rust trim, 1 swinging handle, from $101 to..**$130.00**

1994, Bee Basket™ (basket only), rectangular, rose pink & purple weave, 1 swinging handle, brass tag: Celebrate Your Success - 1994 - Bee Basket, from $167 to .**$270.00**

1994, Boo™ (basket only), rectangular, orange & black weave & trim, 1 swinging handle, from $93 to..............**$135.00**

1995, Horizon of Hope™ (basket only), rectangular, no color weave or trim, 1 stationary handle, American Cancer Society logo on bottom, from $75 to **$95.00**

1995, Mother's Day Basket of Love™ (basket only), round, pink weave & trim, 2 leather ears, from $74 to ...**$85.00**

1995, Pumpkin™ (basket only), round, orange & black trim, orange accent weave, 1 swinging handle, from $95 to **$150.00**

1995, Sweetheart Sweet Sentiments™ (basket only), square, red trim & shoestring accent weave, 1 swinging handle, from $67 to...**$85.00**

1995, Traditions Family™ (basket only), oval, green trim & accent weave, 1 swinging handle, brass tag, box, from $193 to..**$270.00**

1995-96, Collectors Club Charter Membership™ (basket only), tall w/rectangular opening, blue & green weave & trim, 2 swinging handles, commemorative brass tag, club logo on bottom, w/box, from $105 to.........................**$178.00**

1995-97, Woven Traditions Spring® (basket only), square, red, blue & green shoestring weave, 1 stationary handle, from $60 to..**$65.00**

1996, Employee Christmas Cracker™ (basket only), rectangular, red & green shoestring weave, no handles, from $80 to...**$100.00**

1997, Special Event Inaugural™ (basket only), round, blue trim, red & blue accent weave, 1 stationary handle, pewter tag: Longaberger - 1997 - Inaugural Basket, from $60 to...**$75.00**

1997, 20th Century - First Edition™ (basket only), rectangular, natural basket w/flag design, 1 swinging handle, brass tag marked as First Edition, box, from $75 to **$90.00**

1998, Collectors Club 25th Anniversary™ (basket only), rectangular, woven flag design, 2 swinging handles, pewter tag, from $194 to **$250.00**

1999, Lots of Luck™ (basket only), round, green chain link weave & trim, no tag, stationary handle, ⅜" weave, special burned-in logo, from $90 to **$130.00**

1999, May Series Daisy™ (basket only), round, blue weave & trim, 1 swinging handle, ⅜" weave, board bottom, from $60 to..**$80.00**

2000, Cheers™ (basket only), oval, stained, periwinkle & purple double rim, 1 stationary handle board bottom w/burned-in logo, commemorative silver tag, from $61 to..**$70.00**

Miscellaneous

1990, Father Christmas Cookie Mold™ - First Casting, brown pottery, inscription on back: Longaberger Pottery - First Casting - Christmas 1990, w/box, from $92 to...**$115.00**

1990-1991, Roseville Grandma Bonnie's Apple Pie Plate™, pottery, blue accents, embossing on bottom: Roseville, Ohio, box, from $54 to **$60.00**

1993, Commemorative Santa Pewter Ornaments™ (set of 4), gift box, from $60 to **$105.00**

Lu Ray Pastels

This was one of Taylor, Smith, and Taylor's most popular lines of dinnerware. It was made from the late 1930s until sometime in the early 1950s in five pastel colors: Windsor Blue, Persian Cream, Sharon Pink, Surf Green, and Chatham Gray.

If you'd like more information, we recommend *Collector's Guide to Lu Ray Pastels* by Kathy and Bill Meehan (Collector Books).

Baker, vegetable; gray, oval, 9½"	**$30.00**
Baker, vegetable; oval, 9½"	**$20.00**
Bowl, coupe soup; flat	**$15.00**
Bowl, coupe soup; gray, flat	**$25.00**
Bowl, fruit; gray, 5"	**$16.00**

Bowl, fruit; 5" $5.00
Bowl, lug soup; tab handled $20.00

Bowls, mixing; 5½", $125.00; 7", $125.00; 8¾", $100.00; 10¼", $150.00.

Butter dish, gray, w/lid $90.00
Butter dish, w/lid.......................................$50.00
Casserole, w/lid $125.00
Chocolate creamer, after dinner, individual...............$95.00
Chocolate pot, after dinner..............................$200.00
Coaster/nut dish...$65.00
Creamer, from $8 to......................................$10.00
Cup/bowl, cream soup.....................................$70.00
Egg cup, double..$24.00
Egg cup, double; gray....................................$30.00
Epergne, flower vase.....................................$110.00
Jug, water; footed.......................................$125.00
Nappy, vegetable; round, 8½" $20.00
Pitcher, fruit juice.....................................$200.00
Pitcher, water; yellow, flat bottom $95.00
Plate, gray, 9"..$20.00
Plate, 6"..$3.00
Plate, 7"..$12.00
Plate, 8"..$20.00
Plate, 9"..$10.00
Platter, 11½" $16.00
Platter, 13"...$19.00
Relish dish, 4-part......................................$95.00
Sauce/gravy boat $28.00
Sauce/gravy boat, w/fixed stand, any color but yellow...$35.00
Sauce/gravy boat, w/fixed stand, yellow..................$22.50
Saucer, after dinner; gray $10.00
Saucer, chocolate $30.00
Saucer, cream soup.......................................$28.00
Sugar bowl, after dinner; individual, w/lid..............$40.00
Sugar bowl, w/lid $15.00
Teapot, curved spout.....................................$125.00
Teapot, flat spout.......................................$160.00
Tumbler, fruit juice.....................................$50.00
Tumbler, water...$80.00
Vase, bud..$400.00

Lunch Boxes

Character lunch boxes made of metal have been very collectible for several years, but now even those made of plastic and vinyl are coming into their own.

The first lunch box of this type ever produced featured Hopalong Cassidy. Made by the Aladdin company, it was constructed of steel and decorated with decals. But the first fully lithographed steel lunch box and matching thermos bottle was made a few years later (in 1953) by American Thermos. Roy Rogers was its featured character.

Since then hundreds have been made, and just as is true in other areas of character-related collectibles, the more desirable lunch boxes are those with easily recognizable, well-known subjects — western heroes; TV, Disney, and cartoon characters; and famous entertainers like the Bee Gees and the Beatles.

Values hinge on condition. Learn to grade your lunch boxes carefully. A grade of 'excellent' for metal boxes means that you will notice only very minor defects and less than normal wear. Plastic boxes may have a few scratches and some minor wear on the sides, but the graphics must be completely undamaged. Vinyls must retain their original shape; brass parts may be tarnished, and the hinge may show signs of beginning splits. If the box you're trying to evaluate is in any worse condition than we've described, to be realistic, you must cut these prices drastically. Values are given for boxes without matching thermoses, unless one is mentioned in the line. If you'd like to learn more, we recommend *Collector's Guide to Lunch Boxes* by Carole Bess White and L. M. White and *Schroeder's Collectible Toys, Antique to Modern,* both by Collector Books.

Note: Watch for reproductions marked 'China.'

Metal

Addams Family, 1974, with thermos, EX, $100.00.

Adam-12, 1972, VG.......................................$50.00
Annie Oakley, 1955, w/thermos, EX.......................$300.00
Archies, 1969, VG+ $85.00
Atom Ant, 1966, G.......................................$60.00

Batman & Robin, 1966, G **$95.00**
Beatles, 1965, blue, VG **$375.00**
Bedknobs & Broomsticks, 1972, VG **$30.00**
Bee Gees, 1978, EX **$40.00**
Beverly Hillbillies, 1963, w/thermos, M **$500.00**
Bionic Woman, 1978, EX **$85.00**
Bonanza, 1963, green rim, EX **$150.00**
Bugaloos, Aladdin, 1971, NM **$100.00**
Cabbage Patch Kids, 1983, VG **$10.00**
Care Bear Cousins, 1985, w/thermos, M **$45.00**
Care Bears, 1983, blue rim, w/thermos, G **$20.00**
Cartoon Zoo, 1962, G.. **$80.00**
Chan Clan, 1973, w/thermos, EX **$100.00**
Charlie's Angels, 1978, w/thermos, M **$175.00**
Clash of the Titans, 1980, VG+ **$20.00**
Cracker Jack, 1979, VG **$20.00**
Davy Crockett/Kit Carson, 1955, VG **$225.00**
Dawn, M **$75.00**
Disney Express, 1979, w/thermos, M **$50.00**
Doctor Dolittle, 1967, w/thermos, EX **$100.00**
Evel Knievel, 1974, w/thermos, VG+ **$75.00**
Fall Guy, 1981, VG+ **$50.00**
Family Affair, 1969, w/thermos, EX **$135.00**
Fat Albert, EX **$50.00**
Fess Parker, 1964, VG **$150.00**
Flintstones, 1971, w/thermos, M............................. **$225.00**
Flying Nun, Aladdin, 1968, EX **$125.00**
Ghostland, 1977, VG **$30.00**
Gomer Pyle, 1966, VG **$100.00**
Gremlins, 1984, w/thermos, VG+ **$20.00**
Gunsmoke, 1959, w/thermos, VG+........................... **$250.00**
Hair Bear Bunch, 1971, EX **$85.00**
Hee-Haw, 1970, EX **$100.00**
Hogan's Heroes, 1966, dome top, EX **$300.00**
Howdy Doody, 1954, EX **$300.00**
HR Pufnstuf, Aladdin, 1971, EX **$75.00**
Incredible Hulk, 1978, EX **$30.00**
It's About Time, dome top, NM................................. **$400.00**
Jetsons, 1963, dome top, G+ **$350.00**
Jungle Book, 1966, VG+ **$100.00**
Kung Fu, 1974, EX **$50.00**
Little House on the Prairie, 1978, EX **$55.00**
Lone Ranger, 1954, EX **$400.00**
Luggage Plaid, 1955, EX **$65.00**
Major League Baseball, 1968, VG+............................ **$35.00**
Man From UNCLE, 1966, w/thermos, EX **$150.00**
Masters of the Universe, 1983, w/thermos, M **$50.00**
Partridge Family, 1971, EX... **$85.00**
Pebbles & Bamm-Bamm, 1971, EX **$80.00**
Pinocchio, 1971, VG **$60.00**
Popples, 1986, w/thermos, M **$75.00**
Racing Wheels, 1977, w/thermos, VG+...................... **$35.00**
Return of the Jedi, 1983, w/thermos, NM................. **$125.00**
Ronald McDonald Sheriff of Cactus Canyon, 1982,
   VG **$25.00**
Scooby Doo, 1973, yellow rim, w/thermos, M.......... **$175.00**
Six Million Dollar Man, 1978, w/thermos, EX **$70.00**

Sleeping Beauty, Canadian, 1960, EX, $700.00.
(Photo courtesy Mike's General Store)

Space: 1999, 1975, w/thermos, VG **$45.00**
Strawberry Shortcake, 1981, w/thermos, EX............... **$25.00**
Superfriends, 1976, w/thermos, EX **$50.00**
Tarzan, 1966, w/thermos, EX...................................... **$125.00**
Tom Corbett Space Cadet, 1954, EX **$250.00**
Traveler, 1962, red rim, VG **$45.00**
Underdog, 1974, w/thermos, EX............................ **$1,000.00**
Universal Plaid, 1959, EX **$65.00**
Walt Disney School Bus, 1960s, dome top, EX **$50.00**
Welcome Back Kotter, 1977, NM **$85.00**
Yankee Doodle, 1975, w/thermos, VG **$35.00**
Yogi Bear Memos, NM **$65.00**

Plastic

A-Team, 1985, red, w/thermos, EX **$25.00**
Alf, 1987, red, w/thermos, NM **$18.00**
Barbie, 1990, purple, w/thermos, EX **$6.00**
Batman, 1982, blue, VG **$5.00**
Benji, 1974, blue, VG **$15.00**
Cabbage Patch Kids, 1983, yellow, w/thermos, EX **$10.00**
Chip 'N Dale Rescue Rangers, light blue, NM............. **$10.00**
Dick Tracy, 1990, w/thermos, NM................................ **$10.00**
Disney School Bus, 1990, M (sealed)........................... **$35.00**
GI Joe, 1985, w/thermos, EX **$10.00**
Jem, 1986, purple, w/thermos, EX **$14.00**
Kermit the Frog, 1981, dome top, EX **$15.00**
Little Mermaid, EX **$5.00**
Mickey Mouse Head, 1988, w/thermos, M **$50.00**
Mork & Mindy, Thermos, 1978, w/thermos, EX.......... **$35.00**
Mr T, 1984, orange, w/thermos, EX **$30.00**
My Little Pony, 1989, blue, w/thermos, EX **$12.00**
Pink Panther, 1984, w/thermos, EX............................. **$20.00**
Pound Puppies, 1986, red, VG **$10.00**
Rugrats, 3-D, EX... **$10.00**
Snoopy, 1981, orange, dome top, w/thermos, EX...... **$35.00**
Superman, 1980, dome top, w/thermos, EX................ **$40.00**
Teenage Mutant Ninja Turtles, 1990, purple, w/thermos,
   M **$15.00**
Tiny Toon Adventures, 1990, purple, w/thermos, EX .**$10.00**
Voltron, 1984, blue, w/thermos, NM **$15.00**

Vinyl

Animaniacs, hot pink, EX..............................$15.00
Barbarino, Aladdin, 1977, brunch bag w/zipper closure,
    EX $75.00
Corsage, 1970, VG $50.00
Dawn, 1970, w/thermos, EX......................$175.00
Donnie & Marie, 1978, brunch bag, EX....................$125.00
Dr Seuss, rare, EX.................................$150.00
Go-Go Dancers, 1965-66, red, EX.............................$100.00
Liddle Kiddles, 1968, NM........................$150.00
New Zoo Revue, 1975, w/thermos, EX.....................$225.00
Pebbles & Bamm-Bamm, 1971, EX.........................$125.00
Pussycats, 1968, brunch bag, NM......................$250.00
Roy Rogers Saddlebag, 1960, EX........................$225.00
Sesame Street, 1981, yellow, w/thermos, M $75.00
Snoopy, 1977, brunch bag, w/thermos, EX...............$95.00
Soupy Sales, 1960s, blue w/red handle, EX.............$300.00
Space: 1999, 1974, G $20.00
Teenage Mutant Ninja Turtles, 1988, blue softee, EX ...$8.00
Wonder Woman, 1977, w/thermos, VG+ $150.00

Thermoses

Values are give for thermoses in excellent condition; all are made of metal unless noted otherwise.

Adam-12, 1972, plastic, EX...........................$25.00
Atom Ant, 1966, EX.................................$45.00
Banana Splits, 1969, EX............................$100.00
Barney & Baby Bop, plastic, EX......................$5.00
Bionic Woman, Aladdin, 1977, plastic, EX................$15.00
Buck Rogers in the 25th Century, EX $35.00
Bugaloos, Aladdin, 1971, plastic, EX.....................$25.00
Captain Kangaroo, plastic, EX $10.00
Charlie's Angels, 1977, plastic, EX.....................$15.00
CHiPs, 1977, plastic, NM $12.00
Davy Crockett, 1955, NM $75.00
Donny & Marie, 1976, plastic, NM $15.00
Family Affair, 1969, EX.............................$50.00
Flintstones, NM, from $35 to.......................$45.00
Green Hornet, 1967, EX............................$150.00
Guns of Will Sonnett, 1968, EX......................$75.00
Hopalong Cassidy, 1950, EX........................$75.00
It's a Small World, EX..............................$90.00
King Kong, 1977, plastic, NM $20.00
Little House on the Prairie, 1978, plastic, M..............$20.00
Man From UNCLE, 1966, EX........................$75.00
Marvel Super Heroes, 1976, plastic, VG....................$20.00
Mary Poppins, 1964, EX............................$45.00
Pac-Man, Aladdin, 1980, plastic, VG $12.00
Partridge Family, 1971, EX..........................$40.00
Pussycat, 1968, NM.................................$55.00
Scooby Doo, EX.....................................$25.00
Tarzan, 1966, M.....................................$50.00
Winnie the Pooh, 1976, plastic, M.......................$70.00
Woody Woodpecker, 1972, plastic, G $30.00

Maddux of California

Founded in Los Angeles in 1938, Maddux not only produced ceramics but imported and distributed them as well. They supplied chain stores nationwide with well-designed figural planters, TV lamps, novelty and giftware items, and during the mid-1960s their merchandise was listed in every major stamp catalog. Because of an increasing amount of foreign imports and an economic slowdown in our own country, the company was forced to sell out in 1976. Under the new management, manufacturing was abandoned, and the company was converted solely to distribution. Collectors have only recently discovered this line, and prices right now are affordable though increasing.

#0300, figurine, puppy, 6x5½"....................$15.00
#0515, planter, flamingo, pink, 10¼" $45.00
#0527, Chinese pheasant, 11½"......................$20.00
#0627, TV lamp, stallion, 13".......................$35.00
#0808, TV lamp, pearl-tone shell, 13"................$40.00
#0828, TV lamp, swan planter, white porcelain, 12½" .$40.00
#0841, TV lamp, head of Christ, 3-D planter...............$45.00

#858, TV lamp, horse, from $65.00.
(Photo courtesy Tom Santiso)

#0887, TV lamp, Persian Glory (horse head), 11½"....$50.00
#0894, TV lamp, Toro (bull) charging, walnut, 11½"..$40.00
#0924, stag standing, natural colors, 12½"..................$15.00
#0969, Early Birds, black matt, tangerine, 14½", pr $25.00
#0982, horse prancing $20.00
#2000, snack set, embossed grapes, cup & tray..........$25.00
#3006, TV lamp/planter, half-circle $25.00
#3095A, bowl, pedestal foot, 6 individual servers......$25.00
#3302, bank, cat, yellow $25.00
Bank, smiling pig, red or green, 12" L.......................$25.00
Cats, Deco style, black matt, 12½", facing pr..............$50.00
Cookie jar, Chipmunk on Stump, C Romanelli, from $130 to.$145.00
Cookie jar, Grapes, purple w/green leaves on white, #3112,
    10" $55.00
Cookie jar, Shopping Cat, from $135 to...................$155.00
Wall pocket, bird in metal holder (resembles cage),
    7x7"+cage $35.00

Magazines

There are a lot of magazines around today, but unless they're in fine condition (clean, no missing or clipped pages, and very little other damage); have interesting features (cover illustrations, good advertising, or special-interest stories); or deal with sports greats, famous entertainers, or world-renowned personalities, they're worth very little, no matter how old they are. Address labels on the fronts are acceptable, but if your magazine has one, follow these guidelines. Subtract 5% to 10% when the label is not intruding on the face of the cover. Deduct 20% if the label is on the face of an important cover and 30% to 40% if on the face of an important illustrator cover, thus ruining framing quality. If you find a magazine with no label, it will be worth about 25% more than one in about the same conditon but having a label. For further information see *The Masters Price & Identification Guide to Old Magazines* (5th edition now available); *Life Magazines, 1898 to 1994; Saturday Evening Post, 1899 – 1965;* and several other up-to-the-minute guides covering specific magazine titles, all by our advisor Denis C. Jackson.

See also TV Guides.

Advisors: Denis C. Jackson; Don Smith, Rare National Geographics (See Directory, Magazines)

Newsletter: *The Illustrator Collector's New* (Sample issue: $3.50; Subscription $18.00 per year in U.S.)
Denis C. Jackson, Editor
P.O. Box 1958
Sequim, WA 98382; Phone: 360-452-3810
www.olypen.com/ticn; e-mail: ticn@olypen.com

Agricultural Digest, 1934, November, Parrish cover, NM...**$60.00**
America, 1953, Jack Dempsey, EX.................................**$4.00**
American Hetritage, 1968, April, Mickey Mouse cover, VG..**$25.00**
American Legion, 1931, April, Ty Cobb article, NM ...**$12.00**
Art Photography, 1956, April, Sophia Loren cover, VG .**$10.00**
Avante Garde, 1969, #8, Picasso, NM...........................**$35.00**
Baseball Digest, 1951, April, Joe DiMaggio cover, VG...**$30.00**
Baseball Illustrated, 1975, Reggie Jackson cover, EX..**$15.00**
Better Homes & Gardens, 1935, September, EX **$23.00**
Cabaret Quarterly, 1956, #5, Jayne Mansfield, nude models, NM **$35.00**
Cad, 1965, June, VG **$20.00**
Classic Photography, 1956, Winter, VG.......................**$14.00**
Collier's, 1945, June, Harry Truman, EX.......................**$7.00**
Collier's, 1953, August, Brooklyn Dodgers, EX **$20.00**
Collier's, 1955, November, Bette Davis cover, EX.......**$20.00**
Confidential, 1952, December, Vol 1 #1, VG **$18.00**
Cosmopolitan, 1936, July, Crandall cover, EX **$12.00**
Cosmopolitan, 1952, November, Queen Elizabeth II cover, EX...**$20.00**
Cosmopolitan, 1955, October, Audrey Hepburn article, EX.**$11.00**
Country Song Roundup, 1957, August, Elvis cover, VG .**$15.00**
Cue, 1953, June 27, Marilyn Monroe cover, NM **$35.00**

Esquire, 1951, September, Marilyn Monroe gatefold, EX..**$125.00**
Esquire, 1960, November, Lenny Bruce article, EX.....**$10.00**
Evergreen, 1969, June, Bobby Kennedy cover, EX.....**$20.00**
Family Circle, 1942, October 16, Judy Garland cover, EX..**$20.00**
Family Circle, 1945, January 19, Shirley Temple cover, EX **$12.00**
Family Circle, 1946, April 26, Marilyn Monroe cover, EX **$350.00**
Family Circle, 1957, April, Debbie Reynolds cover, VG..**$3.00**
Famous Models, 1950, April-May, VG **$28.00**
Favorite Westerns, 1960, August, John Wayne cover, EX...**$8.00**
Fortune, 1948, railroad cover, EX...............................**$30.00**
Good Housekeeping, 1933, February, Jessie Wilcox Smith art cover, EX **$24.00**
Good Housekeeping, 1937, October, Pearl Buck, Petty art ads, EX...**$15.00**
Good Housekeeping, 1969, February, Paul Newman cover, VG **$7.00**
Gourmet, 1940s-50s, VG-EX, ea, from $3 to.................**$5.00**
Hustler, 1977, November, EX **$8.00**
Jack & Jill, 1961, May, Roy Rogers cover, EX.............**$10.00**
Ladies' Home Journal, 1933, December, choir singers on cover, NM **$15.00**
Ladies' Home Journal, 1934, January, reclining lady on cover, NM **$12.00**
Ladies' Home Journal, 1939, September, paper doll cutout .**$14.00**
Ladies' Home Journal, 1967, June, Twiggy cover, VG ..**$2.00**
Ladies' Home Journal, 1973, July, Marilyn Monroe article, EX...**$13.00**
Liberty, 1940, June 15, Going Fishing by Tomde, EX.**$15.00**
Liberty, 1947, August 2, Cary Grant cover, EX **$5.00**
Life, 1938, February 7, Gary Cooper, Fair....................**$20.00**
Life, 1939, May 1, Joe DiMaggio, Petty art, EX............**$75.00**
Life, 1940, September 2, Dionne Quintuplets cover, EX ...**$35.00**
Life, 1941, June 3, Statue of Liberty, EX........................**$9.00**
Life, 1942, November 16, NC Wyeth art for corn ad, EX..**$16.00**
Life, 1945, April, 16, Eisenhower, EX **$12.00**
Life, 1947, November 17, Howard Hughes, EX...........**$15.00**

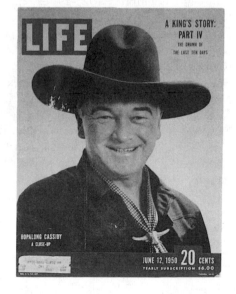

Life, 1950, June 12, Hopalong Cassidy cover, EX, from $45.00 to $50.00.

Life, 1951, June 7, Phyllis Kirk cover, EX........................$7.00
Life, 1951, September 3, Gina Lollobrigida cover, EX.$10.00
Life, 1952, November 13, Marilyn Monroe ad, other stars, EX......................................$20.00
Life, 1953, July 20, Senator John Kennedy cover, EX.$10.00
Life, 1959, April 20, Marilyn Monroe, Mickey Mantle ad, EX......................................$50.00
Life, 1960, February, 1, Dinah Shore cover & article, EX...$4.00
Life, 1963, September 6, Norman Rockwell ad, EX $17.00
Life, 1964, August 28, Beatles cover & article, EX $40.00
Life, 1964, May 22, Barbra Streisand, baseball, EX $30.00
Life, 1971, March 19, Ali/Frazier, EX $35.00
Life, 1972, September 8, Marilyn Monroe, EX............$19.00
Look, 1937, May, Vol 1 #5, Jean Harlow article $40.00
Look, 1946, October 15, Ted Williams cover, NM......$85.00
Look, 1950, December 5, Esther Williams cover, EX..$20.00
Look, 1952, September 9, Marilyn Monroe cover, EX.$55.00
Look, 1954, June 1, Jackie Gleason, EX........................$12.00
Look, 1958, April 29, Winston Churchill cover, EX.....$15.00
Look, 1958, June 24, Hugh O'Brien cover, EX............$12.00
Look, 1963, February 12, Grace Kelly cover, EX.........$25.00
Look, 1963, January 9, Beatles article, EX $28.00
Look, 1966, December 13, John Lennon cover, VG+ .$28.00
Look, 1967, February 6, John Kennedy, EX..................$6.00
Look, 1970, September, 8, Greta Garbo, EX..................$7.00
Mad Magazine, 1982, July, Greatest American Hero cover, NM...................................$5.00
McCall's, 1932, February, Zane Grey article, EX...........$8.00
McCall's, 1951, June, Greta Garbo cover & article, VG+ ...$10.00
McCall's, 1960, April, Marilyn Monroe, EX $19.00
McCall's, 1968, May, Raquel Welch, EX $5.00
Modern Photography, 1956, September, glamour issue, EX.$10.00
Modern Romance, 1941, June, VG $11.00
Movie Classic, 1936, October, Glenda Farrell cover, G ...$22.00
Movie Life, 1949, February, Alan Ladd cover, NM $15.00
Movie Mirror, 1975, May, Elvis & Linda's secret wedding ceremony, EX...............................$20.00
National Geographic, 1915-16, ea $15.00
National Geographic, 1917-24, ea.................................$9.00
National Geographic, 1925-29, ea.................................$8.00
National Geographic, 1930-45, ea.................................$7.00
National Geographic, 1946-55, ea.................................$6.00
National Geographic, 1956-57, ea.................................$5.50
National Geographic, 1968-89, ea.................................$4.50
National Geographic, 1990-present, ea $2.00
New Yorker, 1953, April 6, VG...................................$10.00
Newsweek, 1933, February 17, Vol 1 #1, EX..............$30.00
Newsweek, 1941, September 8, Hitler cover, VG $10.00
Newsweek, 1946, September 14, Ted Williams, EX....$75.00
Newsweek, 1957, July 1, Stan Musial, EX....................$25.00
Parade, 1959, August, Lassie, NM $25.00
Parade, 1962, June, Liz Taylor, NM $25.00
Peek, 1940, July, Betty Grable cover, VG $10.00
Photoplay, 1966, April, Peyton Place cast, NM.............$8.00
PIC, 1940, April 2, Lana Turner cover, EX...................$15.00
Pictorial Review, 1934, May, Dottie Darlings paper dolls, EX.......................................$18.00

Playboy, 1955, February, Jayne Mansfield, EX $150.00
Playboy, 1957, May, Julie Newmar..............................$22.00
Playboy, 1958, May, Tina Louise $24.00
Playboy, 1960, January, Stella Stevens $39.00
Playboy, 1964, July, Brigitte Bardot.............................$24.00
Playboy, 1971, July, Linda Evans.................................$15.00
Playboy, 1974, April, Jane Fonda $14.00
Playboy, 1983, February, Kim Basinger $12.00
Police Gazette, 1940, April, Carol Landis cover, EX......$7.00
Popular Science, 1937, November, EX..........................$8.00
Popular Song Hits, 1947, May, Betty Grable cover, VG..$9.00
Ramparts, 1965, November, John F Kennedy puzzle cover, NM.......................................$25.00
Reader's Digest, 1962, October, What It Was Like To Be Marilyn Monroe, EX......................$15.00
Redbook, 1936, June, Tunney & Louis, EX....................$8.00
Redbook, 1947, March, movie ads, EX $7.00
Redbook, 1953, March, Marilyn Monroe cover & article, EX......................................$57.00
Redbook, 1954, November, Grace Kelly cover, EX.....$15.00
Redbook, 1954, specialty issues range from $4 to $10 w/some up to...........................$50.00
Redbook, 1955, October, Jackie Gleason cover, EX......$6.00
Rolling Stone, 1967, November 9, #1, John Lennon (not 1986 repro), NM, from $175 to...........$200.00
Rolling Stone, 1968, April 27, #9, Beatles cover, NM..$100.00
Rolling Stone, 1968, August 10, #15, Mick Jagger, NM....$130.00
Rolling Stone, 1968, February 24, #6, Janis Joplin, EX+.$185.00
Rolling Stone, 1968, September 28, #18, The Who, EX.....$55.00
Rolling Stone, 1969, #37, Elvis Presley, EX.................$20.00
Rolling Stone, 1971, November 11, #95, Beach Boys, EX.......................................$16.00
Rolling Stone, 1974, March 14, #156, Bob Dylan, M...$20.00
Rolling Stone, 1974, November 7, #173, Evel Knievel, NM $18.00
Rolling Stone, 1975, #198, Bob Dylan, EX....................$8.00
Rolling Stone, 1981, January 22, John Lennon nude cover, VG $40.00
Rolling Stone, 1984, #415, Beatles, EX $7.00
Saturday Evening Post, 1943, December 25, Mead Schaeffer cover, EX $10.00
Saturday Evening Post, 1946, April 6, Norman Rockwell cover, Hawaii article, VG $65.00
Saturday Evening Post, 1953, March 28, Bing Crosby article, EX $12.00
Saturday Evening Post, 1957, April 20, Yogi Berra, EX...$40.00
Saturday Evening Post, 1959, September 24, Rockwell Family Tree cover, EX.........................$45.00
Screen Guide, 1951, March, Betty Grable, Roy Rogers, etc, NM $15.00
Screenland, 1946, February, Paulette Goddard, Ann Sothern, Roy Rogers, etc, EX+ $20.00
Silver Screen, 1958, June, Mitzi Gaynor, EX $12.00
Sport, 1974, Pete Rose, EX...$10.00
Sports Illustrated, 1956, April 23, Billy Martin cover, EX...$15.00
Sports Illustrated, 1962, July 2, Mickey Mantle, EX...$100.00
Sports Illustrated, 1964, Koufax cover, EX...................$32.00

Sports Illustrated, 1968, January 15, swimsuit issue, EX .**$38.00**
Sports Illustrated, 1980, February 4, Christie Brinkley, EX.**$40.00**
Sports Illustrated, 1982, August, 1982, EX **$49.00**
Sports Illustrated, 1988, March 21, Larry Bird, EX.......**$10.00**
Time, 1935, April 15, Dizzy Dean, EX **$65.00**
Time, 1938, Frank Capra cover, EX.............................**$28.00**
Time, 1941, October 10, Joe Louis, EX **$25.00**
Time, 1955, Oppenheimer, EX.....................................**$10.00**
Time, 1965, December 24, Gemini 7 article, VG...........**$5.00**
Time, 1971, March 8, Ali-Frazer cover, EX..................**$12.00**
True Confessions, 1938, February, Carole Lombard cover,
     Zoe Mozert art, EX..**$35.00**
True Crime, May, 1955, VG...**$5.00**
True Love, 1940, May, Joan Fontaine cover, VG.........**$15.00**
True Story, 1935, April, Zoe Mozert art cover, EX **$30.00**
True Story, 1938, September, Deanna Durbin cover, EX...**$26.00**
Tuff Stuff, 1990, July, Nolan Ryan cover, VG **$5.00**
TV Star Parade, 1960, November, Debbie Reynolds, EX...**$6.00**
Vogue, 1940, January, swimsuit cover, EX..................**$12.00**
Walt Disney Magazine, 1958, February, Annette Funicello
     article, NM **$15.00**
Who, 1941, April, Vol 1 #1, Winston Churchill, VG....**$20.00**

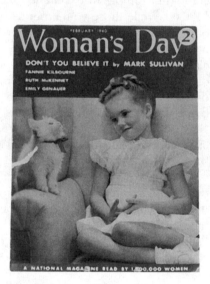

Woman's Day, 1940, February, girl and kitten on cover (note 2¢ price in corner), $3.00.

Woman's Home Companion, 1950, March, VG+...........**$3.00**
Woman's Home Companion, 1956, December, VG **$2.00**
Yachtsman's Magazine, 1942, May, EX........................**$20.00**

Pulp Magazines

As early as the turn of the century, pulp magazines were beginning to appear, but by the 1930s, their popularity had literally exploded. Called pulps because of the cheap wood-pulp paper they were printed on, crime and detective stories, westerns, adventure tales, and mysteries were the order of the day. Crime pulps sold for as little as 10¢; some of the westerns were 15¢. Plots were imaginative and spicy, if not downright risque. The top three publishers were Street and Smith, Popular, and the Thrilling Group. Some of the more familiar pulp-magazine authors were Agatha Christie,

Clarence E. Mulford, Erle Stanley Gardner, Ellery Queen, Edgar Rice Burroughs, Louis L'Amour, and Max Brand. Until the 1950s when slick-paper magazines signed their death warrant, they were published by the thousands. Because of the poor quality of their paper, many have not survived. Those that have are seldom rated better than very good. A near-mint to mint example will bring a premium price, since it is almost impossible to locate one so well preserved. Except for a few very rare editions, many are in the average price range suggested below — some much lower.

Advisor: J. Grant Thiessen (Pandora's Books Ltd.), Pulp Magazines (See Directory, Magazines)

Adventure, 1933, May 1, VG...............................**$15.00**
All-Story Love Stories, 1945, October, VG **$10.00**
Amazing Stories, 1930, October, G.............................**$20.00**
Amazing Stories, 1931, January, G+.........................**$25.00**
Amazing Stories, 1931, November, G.........................**$10.00**
Amazing Stories, 1932, March, G.............................**$10.00**
Amazing Stories, 1933, January, G **$10.00**
Amazing Stories, 1934, September, VG **$25.00**
Amazing Storics, 1941, December, VG.......................**$15.00**
Amazing Stories, 1943, February, VG+......................**$75.00**
Amazing Stories, 1947, June, G+.............................**$8.00**
Amazing Stories, 1948, September, G+.......................**$8.00**
Amazing Stories, 1953, January, VG **$8.00**
Amazing Stories, 1969, January, VG **$7.00**
Analog, 1973, April, Vol 92 #2, VG...........................**$2.50**
Analog, 1977, August, Vol 107 #8, VG **$3.00**
Argosy, 1933, July 1, G...**$8.00**
Argosy, 1935, May 4, G **$7.00**
Argosy, 1939, October 28, G.....................................**$6.00**
Asimov, 1980, July, Vol 4 #7, VG+ **$2.50**
Astonishing, 1942, March, VG+ **$35.00**
Astounding, 1940, May, VG+...................................**$40.00**
Avenger, 1940, November, VG/EX..............................**$50.00**
Avon Fantasy Reader, 1949, #9, G+..........................**$10.00**
Avon Fantasy Reader, 1950, #14, G **$7.00**
Avon Fantasy Reader, 1951, #17, G+.........................**$10.00**
Best Detective, 1937, January, G **$20.00**
Captain Future, 1941, Spring, VG+...........................**$35.00**
Captain Zero, 1950, March, VG **$40.00**
Cosmic Stories, 1941, July, VG.................................**$25.00**
Dime Mystery, 1935, May, VG.................................**$80.00**
Dime Mystery, 1941, May, VG **$30.00**
Doc Savage, 1935, January, G...................................**$60.00**
Doc Savage, 1940, October, VG **$50.00**
Enterprise Incidents, 1984, January, #13, VG.............**$9.00**
Exciting Football, 1946, Fall, VG **$8.00**
Famous Fantastic Mysteries, 1939, September-October, Vol 1
     #1, G **$10.00**
Famous Fantastic Mysteries, 1940, January, Vol 1 #4,
     Fair **$7.50**
Famous Fantastic Mysteries, 1942, June, Vol 4 #2, G+..**$12.00**
Famous Fantastic Mysteries, 1942, November, Vol 5 #1,
     G+..**$10.00**

Famous Fantastic Mysteries, 1947, February, Vol 8 #1, G+ $8.00

Famous Fantastic Mysteries, 1949, October, Vol 11 #1, G+ $7.00

Famous Fantastic Mysteries, 1951, December, Vol 13 #1, G+ $6.00

Famous Fantastic Mysteries, 1953, June, Vol 14 #4, G ..$5.00

Famous Spy Stories, 1940, May/June, VG $30.00

Fantastic Adventures, 1939, May, Vol 1 #1, VG $20.00

Fantastic Adventures, 1941, November, Vol 3 #9, G ...$10.00

Fantastic Adventures, 1947, Vol 9 #6, G $8.00

Fantastic Novels, 1940, July, Vol 1 #1, Poor $10.00

Fantastic Novels, 1941, January, Vol 1 #4, G $9.00

Fantastic Novels, 1948, May, Vol 2 #1, G $7.50

Fantastic Novels, 1950, March, Vol 3 #6, G+ $6.50

Fantasy & Science Fiction Magazine, 1950, Summer, Vol 1 #3, G+ $4.00

Fantasy & Science Fiction Magazine, 1970, July, Vol 39 #1, VG $9.50

Fighting Aces, 1943, July, G $30.00

Flying Aces, 1933, August, VG $20.00

Future, 1950, May-June, Vol 1 #1, G+ $10.00

Future, 1954, March, VG $8.00

G-Men, 1939, October, VG $25.00

Galaxy, 1950, October, Vol 1 #1, G+ $8.00

Giant Western, 1952, August, VG $7.00

Imagination, 1950, October, Vol 1 #1, G $6.00

Jungle Stories, 1942, Winter, G $30.00

Max Brand's Western, 1952, January, VG $10.00

Phantom Detective, 1946, November, VG $20.00

Planet Stories, 1947, Fall, VG+ $20.00

Popular Detective Magazine, 1934, January, G $25.00

Rio Kid, 1942, February, VG $15.00

Science Fiction Quarterly, 1940, #1, VG $30.00

Spider, 1939, June, VG $85.00

Startling Stories, 1948, November, VG $15.00

Super Science Stories, 1944, April, VG $25.00

Texas Rangers, 1948, October, VG $15.00

Thrilling Detective, 1940, August, G $15.00

Thrilling Wonder, 1941, October, VG $13.00

Thrilling Wonder, 1946, Summer, VG $10.00

Unknown Stories, November, VG+ $50.00

Weird Tales, 1934, September, VG $75.00

Wonder Stories, 1935, October, EX $23.00

Wonder Story Annual, 1952, VG $10.00

Marbles

There are three broad categories of collectible marbles, the antique variety, machine-made, and contemporary marbles. Under those broad divisions are many classifications. Everett Grist delves into all three categories in his book called *Big Book of Marbles* (Collector Books).

Sulfide marbles have figures (generally animals or birds) encased in the center. The glass is nearly always clear; a common example in excellent condition may run as low as $100.00, while those with an unusual subject or made of colored glass may go for more than $1,000.00. Many machine-made marbles are very reasonable, but if the colors are especially well placed and selected, good examples sell in excess of $50.00. Peltier comic character marbles often bring prices of $100.00 and up with Betty Boop, Moon Mullins, and Kayo being the rarest and most valuable. Watch for reproductions. New comic character marbles have the design printed on a large area of plain white glass with color swirled through the back and sides.

No matter where your interests lie, remember that condition is extremely important. From the nature of their use, mint-condition marbles are very rare and may be worth as much as three to five times more than one that is near mint. Chipped and cracked marbles may be worth half or less, and some will be worthless. Polishing detracts considerably.

Advisor: Everett Grist (See Directory, Marbles)

The Shadow, December 15, 1936, excellent graphics, VG+, $300.00.

(Photo courtesy George Bernier)

Shadow, 1937, December 1, VG $80.00

Short Stories, 1944, July 25, VG $13.00

Short Stories, 1948, March 25, VG $10.00

Corkscrews, limeade, ⅝", $15.00 each.
(Photo courtesy Everett Grist)

Agate, old, hand-made, ⅝" $25.00

Akro Agate Moonie, white opal $3.00

Bennington type, glazed clay, ⅝" $2.00

China, hand-painted leaf-like pattern on China-grade fired clay, ⅝" $45.00

Clay, common, ⅝" ....$.50

Comic character, Sandy $90.00

Comic character, Skeezix **$100.00**
Corkscrew, tricolor, ⅝" **$15.00**
Corkscrew, white opaque & translucent color, Akro Agate, ⅝" **$20.00**
Diaper Folds, black, orange & opaque swirls, ¾" **$125.00**
Divided Core, yellow & red w/red, white & blue outer ribbons, inner threads of alternating white & yellow, ⅝" **$45.00**
Lutz-type one, clear swirl, blue & white-bordered gold-color surface swirls, ⅝" **$125.00**
Mica flakes in transparent glass, colors vary, ⅝" **$25.00**
Peppermint swirl, opaque red, white & blue swirls, ⅝"...**$100.00**
Rocket, translucent, black & orange swirl, ¹¹⁄₁₆".......**$200.00**
Slag, amber w/orange lace, ¹¹⁄₁₆" **$60.00**
Slag, aqua, ¾" **$15.00**
Slag, green or purple, ¾", ea................................**$10.00**
Slag, red & white on crystal base, ⅝" **$30.00**
Slag, royal blue, ¹¹⁄₁₆" **$10.00**
Slag, yellow, ¾" **$80.00**
Sulfide, rabbit, 1¾" **$250.00**
Swirl, orange & yellow, ¾" **$25.00**
Transparent swirl, latticinio white core, blue & orange outer bands, ⅝" **$20.00**
Transparent swirl, latticinio yellow core, red & white outer bands, ⅝" **$25.00**

Max, Peter

Born in Germany in 1937, Peter Max came to the United States in 1953 where he later studied art in New York City. His work is colorful and his genre psychedelic. He is a prolific artist, best known for his designs from the '60s and '70s that typified the 'hippie' movement. In addition to his artwork, he has also designed housewares, clothing, toys, linens, etc. In the 1970s, commissioned by Iroquois China, he developed several lines of dinnerware in his own distinctive style. Today, many of those who were the youth of the hippie generation are active collectors of his work.

See also Hippie Collectibles.

Advisor: Richard Synchef (See Directory, Beatnik and Hippie Collectibles)

Ashtray, green & white checkerboard w/blue, red, black & yellow center surrounded by red & blue ring, white border, 6½" dia **$80.00**
Book, Meditations, drawings & quotes, McGraw-Hill, 1972, EX...**$85.00**
Book, Superposter Book, 16 pages +12x36" superposter, information & art, softcover, 1st edition, 1970, 11½x16" **$110.00**
Book, The Peter Max Book of Needlepoint, step-by-step instructions, co-author Regina Cohen, Pyramid Gift Edition, 1972 ....**$65.00**
Book, The Peter Max Land of the Blue, 15 double-page posters, Franklin Watts Inc, 1970, EX.................**$125.00**

Catalog, 1970 San Francisco Museum Show, pictures pcs displayed at show, 7x10", EX...............................**$105.00**
Clock, alarm; art work on clock face, General Electric, 5x3x2", VG **$70.00**
Coffee mug, white w/round design of woman & the word LOVE, Syracuse China, 1960s, 3¾x3".................**$85.00**
Fondue pot, lid has artwork, EX **$85.00**
Plate, butterfly design w/gold trim, Syracuse China, 1960s, 12"..**$115.00**
Poster, Our Gang, multicolored, signed, 1967, 24x36", NM...**$160.00**
Poster, 100 Clintons, designed for President's Dinner 1993, 27x36" **$55.00**
Poster, 2 people running through a giant peace sign accompanied by white doves, 1971, 16x11" **$57.50**
Print, multicolored design, done for Apple Computer Company, 1995, 10x8", matted to 14x11" **$50.00**
Puzzle, Carousel Mindflowers, Springbok, 1967, EXIB ..**$75.00**
Puzzle, Life magazine motif & Love art, 1970, 6¾x11", VG (original box) **$55.00**
Saucepan, blue w/red & yellow designs, enameled, 3x6" **$80.00**
Scarf, red, pink, blue & yellow design, Made in Japan, 15x70", EX **$60.00**
Scarf, red w/orange-haired lady, 26" square **$65.00**
Sticker, advertising Arizona Tea, Statue of Liberty head, multicolored, 11x13" **$15.00**
Tie, black w/joggers in blue & maroon pyramids, 100% silk, made in Italy, 1990 ....**$15.00**
Trivet, enamel design over metal, 6" dia **$80.00**

Book, New Age Organic Vegetarian Cookbook, by Peter Max and Ronwen Vathsala Proust, Pyramid Books, 1971, EX, $70.00.

McCoy Pottery

This is probably the best known of all American potteries, due to the wide variety of goods they produced from 1910 until the pottery finally closed only a few years ago.

They were located in Roseville, Ohio, the pottery center of the United States. They're most famous for their cookie jars, of which were made several hundred styles and variations. (For a listing of these, see the section entitled Cookie Jars.) McCoy is also well known for their figural planters, novelty kitchenware, and dinnerware.

They used a variety of marks over the years, but with little consistency, since it was a common practice to discontinue an item for awhile and then bring it out again decorated in a manner that would be in sync with current tastes. All of McCoy's marks were 'in the mold.' None were ink stamped, so very often the in-mold mark remained as it was when the mold was originally created. Most marks contain the McCoy name, though some of the early pieces were simply signed 'NM' for Nelson McCoy (Sanitary and Stoneware Company, the company's original title). Early stoneware pieces were sometimes impressed with a shield containing a number. If you have a piece with the Lancaster Colony Company mark (three curved lines — the left one beginning as a vertical and terminating as a horizontal, the other two formed as 'C's contained in the curve of the first), you'll know that your piece was made after the mid-'70s when McCoy was owned by that group. Today even these later pieces are becoming collectible.

If you'd like to learn more about this company, we recommend *The Collector's Encyclopedia of McCoy Pottery* and *The Collector's Encyclopedia of Brush-McCoy Pottery*, both by Sharon and Bob Huxford; and *McCoy Pottery, Collector's Reference & Value Guide, Vols 1 & 2*, by Bob and Margaret Hanson and Craig Nissen. All are published by Collector Books.

A note regarding cookie jars: beware of *new* cookie jars marked McCoy. It seems that the original McCoy pottery never registered their trademark, and for several years it was legally used by a small company in Rockwood, Tennessee. Not only did they use the original mark, but they reproduced some of the original jars as well. If you're not an experienced collector, you may have trouble distinguishing the new from the old. Some (but not all) are dated #93, the '#' one last attempt to fool the novice, but there are differences to watch for. The new ones are slightly smaller in size, and the finish is often flawed. He has also used the McCoy mark on jars never produced by the original company, such as Little Red Riding Hood and the Luzianne mammy. Only lately did it become known that the last owners of the McCoy pottery actually did register the trademark; so, having to drop McCoy, he has since worked his way through two other marks: Brush-McCoy and (currently) BJ Hull.

See Also Cookie Jars.

Advisors: Margaret and Bob Hanson

Newsletter: *NM Xpress*
Carol Seman, Editor
8934 Brecksville Rd., #406, Brecksville, OH 44141

Ashtray, I Should Have Danced All Night, image of pregnant lady in center of round white dish, marked McCoy, from $35 to...**$50.00**

Ashtray, Zane's Truce Commemoration, marked McCoy, from $50 to...**$60.00**

Bank, Lucky Penny Puppy, from $50 to.....................**$60.00**

Basket, pine cone decoration, standard glazes, marked McCoy, 1945, 6x8½", from $40 to **$50.00**

Basket, tulip blossoms & leaves form basket w/woven-look handle, 1954, 9x5½", from $90 to **$110.00**

Bookends, birds w/blossom branch, pastel colors, 1940s, 6", from $175 to...**$225.00**

Bookends, violin planters, white, turquoise or matt black, marked McCoy, 1959, 10", pr, from $100 to.......**$150.00**

Candle holder/planter, rectangular dish w/leaf-shaped holder, marked NM, 1940s, 2x8x6", rare, from $250 to **$300.00**

Candy dish, Golden Brocade Line, pedestal foot, 1970, 8", from $25 to..**$35.00**

Cat dish, Pussy Cat, Pussy Cat Where Have You Been embossed on side, marked McCoy, 1940s, 6½", from $70 to...**$100.00**

Centerpiece, Grecian design banded around incurvate rim of pedestal bowl, 10x10", from $30 to......................**$40.00**

Centerpiece, leaf form, unmarked, 1920s-30s, from $50 to **$70.00**

Centerpiece & candle holder set, Starburst line, marked MCP, 1972, 3 pcs, from $80 to **$100.00**

Coffee service, 48-oz pot w/4 18-oz mugs, repeated design w/steaming cups & medallions, 1965, set, from $100 to...**$120.00**

Creamer, pineapple design, Islander Collection Kitchenware, 1979, from $15 to..**$25.00**

Creamer & sugar bowl, leaves & berries relief, light blue matt, 1920s-30s, ea, from $40 to..........................**$50.00**

Flower bowl, Antique Rose Line, footed ball shape w/handles, pink on white w/gold trim, 6½x9½", from $40 to...**$50.00**

Flower bowl, Grecian design in gold band around incurvate rim, from $25 to..**$35.00**

Flower holder, Hands of Friendship (lady's hands holding floral bouquet), marked NM, late 1930s-early 1940s, from $60 to...**$150.00**

Flower holder, top hat w/embossed floral design, various colors, marked NM, 1940s, 4", from $25 to **$40.00**

Flowerpot w/attached underplate, repeated embossed vertical leaf design, unmarked, 1920s-30s, 6", from $50 to .**$90.00**

Grease jar, cabbage shape, green, 1954, 7", from $100 to **$125.00**

Hanging planter, bird, '70s style, 1976, from $30 to ...**$40.00**

Hanging planter, owl, Lancaster mark, 1976, from $35 to **$45.00**

Jardiniere, hobnail design on 4-footed square pot, solid pastel, marked USA, early 1940s, 5½", from $60 to ..**$80.00**

Jardiniere, swirl design w/pedestal foot, marked McCoy, 1962, 7", from $20 to...**$25.00**

Lamp, hyacinth shape w/leaves, marked McCoy, 1950, 8", from $400 to...**$500.00**

Lamp, wagon wheel, w/original shade, unmarked, 1954, 8", from $75 to...**$100.00**

Pitcher, ball form w/embossed hobnail design, solid pastel, unmarked, 1940s, 6", from $100 to **$150.00**

Pitcher, pig form, various colors, marked McCoy, 1940s, 5", very rare, from $500 to **$600.00**

Pitcher & bowl, ship motif, marked McCoy, 1973, 9½x11½", from $60 to...**$80.00**

Pitcher & bowl set, Flow Blue-type w/leaves, marked MCP, 1974, 14x11½", from $100 to **$150.00**

Planter, bird dog pointing, brown or white w/black speckles, marked McCoy, 1959, 7¾", from $125 to **$175.00**

Planter, coal bucket, black w/embossed gold eagle design, wire handle, marked McCoy, 1974, from $35 to ..**$45.00**

Planter, donkey (baby) w/head turned & nose up, various solid colors, unmarked, early 1940s, 7x7½", from $30 to **$40.00**

Planter, ducks in flight atop round leaf-formed dish, marked McCoy, 1955, 8½x10¾", from $125 to **$175.00**

Planter, frog w/separate umbrella, marked McCoy, 1954, from $125 to **$175.00**

Planter, geometric fanned line design, various solid colors, unmarked, 1940s, 3x5", from $35 to **$50.00**

Planter, lamb, gold trimmed, marked McCoy, 1954, 8½", from $95 to **$120.00**

Planter, lamb, white, black or gray, marked NM, early 1940s, 3x4½", from $50 to **$60.00**

Planter, log w/embossed axe & chain, gold trimmed, marked McCoy, 1954, 4x8½", from $80 to **$110.00**

Planter, panther, chartreuse, unmarked, 1950, from $40 to **$60.00**

Planter, panther, metallic gold, unmarked, 1950, from $70 to **$90.00**

Planter, pelican, multicolored floral decor on white w/gold trim, marked, NM, 1940s, 5¾x7¾", from $100 to...**$150.00**

Planter, plow boy on horse by watering trough, hand-decorated colors on white, marked McCoy, 1955, 8x7", from $250 to...**$350.00**

Planter, plow boy on horse by watering trough, standard brown glazes, marked McCoy, 1955, from $100 to...**$125.00**

Planter, poodle, pink on white, marked McCoy, 1956, 7½x7½", from $100 to...**$150.00**

Planter, rabbits (2) & stump, pink & blue, 1951, from $100 to...**$125.00**

Planter, rectangular pedestal, diagonal panels w/leaves, marked, McCoy, 1950s, 4½x9", from $20 to.........**$30.00**

Planter, rolling pin w/Blue Boy, green or yellow w/slight variations, 1952, 7½", from $60 to........................**$75.00**

Planter, scoop w/Mammy, marked McCoy, 1953, 7½", from $150 to...**$200.00**

Planter, spinning wheel w/cat & dog, green w/white dog, 1953, 7¼x7¼", from $30 to...................................**$40.00**

Planter, sprinkling can, pink rose on white w/gold trim, Antique Rose Line, marked McCoy, 1959, 7x6", from $50 to...**$60.00**

Planter, star shape (rectangular), various solid colors, marked NM, early 1940s, 5½x8", from $40 to....................**$60.00**

Planter, twin swans, green, 1953, 8½", from $50.00 to $60.00. (Photo courtesy Margaret and Bob Hansen and Craig Nissen)

Planter, turtle, green, 1970s, 5x8", from $20 to **$25.00**

Planter, turtle, light yellow (rare), 1970s, 5x8", from $35 to **$50.00**

Planter, wheelbarrow w/rooster, yellow & green, yellow & brown or white & black, marked McCoy, 1955, 7x10½", $100 to..**$125.00**

Planter, zebra, marked McCoy, 1956, 6½x8½", from $550 to..**$700.00**

Porch jar, floral design w/vertical ribbing at bottom, marked NM, 1940s, 11x9½", from $150 to.....................**$200.00**

Salt & pepper shakers, together form cabbage head, 1954, pr, from $75 to...**$100.00**

Spoon rest, spoon bowl shape w/various designs, marked McCoy #232, 1975, ea, from $15 to.....................**$25.00**

Strawberry jar, green gloss or white gloss, red clay, marked McCoy, 1975, 9", from $35 to **$40.00**

Sugar bowl, pineapple design, Islander Collection Kitchenware, 1979, from $20 to..........................**$25.00**

Tea pot, octagonal w/floral motif, bamboo handle, marked McCoy, 1970s, from $30 to **$40.00**

Teapot, cat form, black & white w/red neck bow, 1969 (beware of German look-alike), from $95 to **$150.00**

Teapot, leaves & berries motif, unmarked, 1920s-30s, from $75 to...**$100.00**

Vase, birds, leaves & berries embossed around bulbous middle w/long trumpet neck, marked McCoy, 1950, from $35 to...**$50.00**

Vase, brocade decor (white) on 4-sided pedestal w/leaf handles, marked McCoy, 1957, 6½", from $40 to **$50.00**

Vase, butterflies (embossed), V-cut top & bottom, w/handles, various pastel colors, marked USA, 10", from $150 to...**$225.00**

Vase, cornucopia (upright) w/embossed flowers at base, scalloped rim, unmarked, 1920s-30, 10", from $90 to.**$125.00**

Vase, fan w/leaves around base, marked McCoy, 1954, 14½", from $150 to...**$200.00**

Vase, heart shape w/roses, footed, various solid colors & finishes, unmarked, 1940s-50s, 6", from $50 to **$75.00**

Vase, hyacinth shape, pink, blue or lavender, marked McCoy, 1950, 8", from $100 to...**$125.00**

Vase, ivy decor w/angled twig handles, 1953, 9", from $100 to...**$150.00**

Vase, lily (wide), white w/various leaf colors & trim, 1956, 8½", from $350 to...**$400.00**

Vase, magnolia branch on slanted form, marked McCoy, 1953, 8½", from $150 to **$175.00**

Vase, pitcher form w/rose decal on white, gold trim, marked McCoy, 1959, 9", from $35 to **$40.00**

Vase, ribbed design (horizontal) on tall cylindrical neck w/low bulbous body, marked McCoy, 1960, 6¼", from $25 to **$30.00**

Vase, ribbed design (vertical) w/banded rim, various greens or white, marked McCoy, late 1950s, 14", from $75 to **$90.00**

Vase, swirl design w/pedestal foot, marked McCoy, 1962, 8", from $25 to **$35.00**

Vase, tulip (double) shape, various colors, marked McCoy, late 1940s, 8", from $85 to **$110.00**

Wall pocket, butterfly, marked NM, 7x6", from $250 to ..**$350.00**

Wall pocket, pear w/leaf branch, gold trimmed, unmarked, early 1950s, 7", from $155 to **$200.00**

Vase, blue matt, 14", from $250.00 to $300.00. (Photo courtesy Margaret and Bob Hansen and Craig Nissen)

Brown Drip Dinnerware

One of McCoy's dinnerware lines that was introduced in the 1960s is beginning to attract a following. It's a glossy brown stoneware-type pattern with frothy white decoration around the rims. Similar lines of brown stoneware were made by many other companies, Hull and Pfaltzgraff among them. McCoy simply called their line 'Brown Drip.'

Baker, oval, 9" **$1.00**
Baker, oval, 10½" **$10.00**
Baker, oval, 12½", from $18 to **$22.00**
Bean pot, individual, 12-oz **$4.00**
Bean pot, 1½-qt, from $15 to **$20.00**
Bean pot, 3-qt, from $25 to **$30.00**
Bowl, cereal; 6" **$6.00**
Bowl, lug soup; 12-oz **$8.00**
Bowl, lug soup; 18-oz **$10.00**
Bowl, spaghetti or salad; 12½" **$20.00**

Bowl, vegetable; divided **$12.00**
Bowl, vegetable; 9" **$12.00**
Butter dish, ¼-lb **$15.00**
Candle holders, pr, from $18 to **$22.00**
Canister, coffee **$45.00**
Casserole, 2-qt **$15.00**
Casserole, 3½ qt **$20.00**
Casserole, 3-qt, w/hen-on-nest lid, from $45 to **$50.00**
Corn tray, individual, from $15 to **$20.00**
Creamer **$5.00**
Cruet, oil & vinegar, ea, from $12 to **$15.00**
Cup, 8-oz **$5.00**
Custard cup, 6-oz **$4.00**
Gravy boat, from $12 to **$15.00**
Mug, pedestal base, 12-oz **$7.50**
Mug, 12-oz, from $6 to **$8.00**
Mug, 8-oz **$5.00**
Pie plate, 9", from $15 to **$18.00**
Pitcher, jug style, 32-oz **$20.00**
Plate, dinner; 10" **$10.00**
Plate, salad; 7" **$6.50**
Plate, soup & sandwich; w/lg cup ring **$10.00**
Platter, fish form, 18" **$32.00**
Platter, oval, 14", from $12 to **$18.00**
Salt & pepper shakers, pr, from $6 to **$9.00**
Saucer **$3.00**
Souffle dish, 2-qt **$9.50**
Teapot, 6-cup, from $18 to **$22.00**
Trivet, concentric circles, round **$12.00**

Melmac Dinnerware

The postwar era gave way to many new technologies in manufacturing. With the discovery that thermoplastics could be formed by the interaction of melamine and formaldehyde, Melmac was born. This colorful and decorative product found an eager market due to its style and affordability. Another attractive feature was its resistance to breakage. Who doesn't recall the sound it made as it bounced off the floor when you'd accidentally drop a piece.

Popularity began to wane: the dinnerware was found to fade with repeated washings, the edges could chip, and the surfaces could be scratched, stained, or burned. Melmac fell from favor in the late '60s and early '70s. At that time, it was restyled to imitate china that had become popular due to increased imports.

As always, demand and availability determine price. Our values are for items in mint condition only; pieces with scratches, chips, or stains have no value. Lines of similar value are grouped together. As there are many more manufacturers other than those listed, for a more thorough study of the subject we recommend *Melmac Dinnerware* by Gregory R. Zimmer and Alvin Daigle Jr.

See also Russel Wright.

Advisors: Gregory R. Zimmer and Alvin Daigle Jr. (See Directory, Melmac)

Internet Information: Melmac Dinnerware Discussion List: www.egroups.com; search for MelmacDinnerware

Aztec, Debonaire, Flite-Lane, Mar-Crest, Restraware, Rivieraware, Stetson, Westinghouse

Debonaire, Dinner plate, from $2.00 to $3.00; Cereal bowls, from $2.00 to $3.00 each. (Photo courtesy Gregory R. Zimmer and Alvin Daigle Jr.)

Bowl, serving; from $4 to	**$5.00**
Bowl, soup; from $3 to	**$4.00**
Butter dish, from $5 to	**$7.00**
Cup & saucer, from $2 to	**$3.00**
Gravy boat, from $5 to	**$6.00**
Plate, bread; from $1 to	**$2.00**
Plate, salad; from $2 to	**$3.00**
Salt & pepper shakers, from $4 to	**$5.00**
Sugar bowl, w/lid, from $3 to	**$4.00**
Tumbler, 10-oz, from $7 to	**$8.00**
Tumbler, 6-oz, from $6 to	**$7.00**

Boontoon, Branchell, Brookpark, Harmony House, Prolon, Watertown Lifetime Ware

Bowl, cereal; from $4 to	**$5.00**
Bowl, divided vegetable; from $8 to	**$10.00**
Bowl, fruit; from $3 to	**$4.00**
Bowl, serving; from $8 to	**$10.00**
Bowl, soup; w/lid, from $5 to	**$6.00**
Bread tray, from $8 to	**$10.00**
Casserole, w/lid, from $20 to	**$25.00**
Creamer, from $5 to	**$6.00**
Cup & saucer, from $3 to	**$4.00**
Gravy boat, from $6 to	**$8.00**
Jug, w/lid, from $20 to	**$25.00**
Plate, bread; from $2 to	**$3.00**
Plate, compartment; from $10 to	**$12.00**
Plate, dinner; from $4 to	**$5.00**
Plate, salad; from $4 to	**$5.00**
Platter, from $8 to	**$10.00**

Salad tongs, from $12 to	**$15.00**
Sugar bowl, from $6 to	**$8.00**
Tidbit tray, 2-tier, from $12 to	**$15.00**
Tidbit tray, 3-tier, from $15 to	**$18.00**
Tumbler, 10-oz, from $12 to	**$15.00**
Tumbler, 6-oz, from $10 to	**$12.00**

Fostoria, Lucent

Bowl, cereal; from $7 to	**$9.00**
Bowl, serving; from $15 to	**$18.00**
Butter dish, from $15 to	**$18.00**
Creamer, from $8 to	**$10.00**
Cup & saucer, from $8 to	**$12.00**
Plate, bread; from $3 to	**$4.00**
Plate, dinner; from $6 to	**$8.00**
Platter, from $12 to	**$15.00**
Relish tray, from $15 to	**$18.00**
Sugar bowl, w/lid, from $12 to	**$15.00**

Metlox Pottery

Founded in the late 1920s in Manhattan Beach, California, this company initially produced tile and commercial advertising signs. By the early '30s, their business in these areas had dwindled, and they began to concentrate their efforts on the manufacture of dinnerware, artware, and kitchenware. Carl Gibbs has authored *Collector's Encyclopedia of Metlox Potteries*, published by Collector Books, which we recommend for more information.

Carl Romanelli was the designer responsible for modeling many of the figural pieces they made during the late '30s and early '40s. These items are usually imprinted with his signature and are very collectible today. Coming on strong is their line of 'Poppets,' made from the mid-'60s through the mid-'70s. There were eighty-eight in all, whimsical, comical, sometimes grotesque. They represented characters ranging from the seven-piece Salvation Army Group to royalty, religious figures, policemen, and professionals. They came with a name tag, some had paper labels, others backstamps. If you question a piece whose label is missing, a good clue to look for is pierced facial features.

Poppytrail and Vernonware were the trade names for their dinnerware lines. Among their more popular patterns were California Ivy, California Provincial, Red Rooster, Homestead Provincial, and the later embossed patterns, Sculptured Grape, Sculptured Zinnia, and Sculptured Daisy.

Some of their lines can be confusing. There are two 'rooster' lines, Red Rooster (red, orange, and brown) and California Provincial (this one is in dark green and burgundy), and two 'homestead' lines, Colonial Homestead (red, orange, and brown like the Red Rooster line) and Homestead Provincial. Just remember the Provincial patterns are done in dark green and burgundy. See also Cookie Jars.

Advisor: Carl Gibbs, Jr. (See Directory, Metlox)

Dinnerware

#200 series/Poppy Trail, creamer, from $18 to............**$20.00**

#200 series/Poppy Trail, cup & saucer, demitasse; from $28 to............**$32.00**

#200 series/Poppy Trail, salt & pepper shakers, S&P shapes, pr, from $20 to......................**$24.00**

Antique Grape, butter dish, from $55 to....................**$60.00**

Antique Grape, platter, oval, 14¼", from $45 to.........**$50.00**

Blueberry Provincial, creamer, 6-oz, from $20 to........**$22.00**

Blueberry Provincial, pitcher, 2¼-qt, from $65 to.......**$70.00**

California Aztec, chop plate, from $80 to....................**$85.00**

California Aztec, cup & saucer.................................**$24.00**

California Aztec, platter, 13"....................................**$65.00**

California Geranium, gravy ladle..............................**$20.00**

California Geranium, plate, dinner............................**$12.00**

California Golden Blossom, bowl, soup......................**$18.00**

California Golden Blossom, celery dish.......................**$45.00**

California Ivy, coaster, 3¾"......................................**$20.00**

California Ivy, mug, 7-oz, from $25 to.......................**$28.00**

California Ivy, salt & pepper shakers, sm, pr.............**$28.00**

California Peach Blossom, bowl, lug soup; from $22 to...**$25.00**

California Peach Blossom, creamer............................**$28.00**

California Peach Blossom, tumbler............................**$28.00**

California Provincial, butter dish..............................**$95.00**

California Provincial, cup & saucer............................**$18.00**

California Provincial, egg cup...................................**$35.00**

California Provincial, sprinkling can, from $105 to...**$115.00**

California Provincial, vegetable bowl, 10", $65.00.

California Strawberry, bowl, soup; 6¾", from $14 to.**$15.00**

California Strawberry, creamer, 10-oz.........................**$22.00**

California Strawberry, salt & pepper shakers, pr........**$24.00**

Colonial Heritage, cup & saucer................................**$15.00**

Colonial Heritage, sugar bowl, w/lid.........................**$30.00**

Della Robbia, bowl, divided vegetable; 12⅛", from $50 to........................**$55.00**

Della Robbia, cup & saucer, from $13 to...................**$16.00**

Homestead Provincial, bowl, cereal; 7¼".....................**$20.00**

Homestead Provincial, plate, bread & butter; 6⅜".....**$12.00**

Homestead Provincial, plate, salad; 7½", from $14 to..**$16.00**

Homestead Provincial, sugar bowl, w/lid...................**$40.00**

La Mancha, baker, 10¾", from $35 to........................**$40.00**

La Mancha, mug, 10-oz, from $18 to.........................**$20.00**

La Mancha, teapot, 6-cup, from $85 to......................**$95.00**

Lotus, coffeepot, 6-cup, from $135 to........................**$145.00**

Lotus, sugar bowl, w/lid, 11-oz, from $35 to.............**$38.00**

Navajo, bowl, fruit; from $12 to...............................**$14.00**

Navajo, chop plate, 13"..**$65.00**

Navajo, salt & pepper shakers, pr.............................**$36.00**

Provincial Blue, coffeepot, 7-cup, from $130 to.......**$140.00**

Provincial Fruit, bowl, soup; 8½"..............................**$18.00**

Provincial Fruit, sugar bowl, w/lid...........................**$25.00**

Provincial Rose, mug, 8-oz, from $18 to....................**$20.00**

Provincial Rose, teapot..**$120.00**

Red Rooster, butter dish..**$75.00**

Red Rooster, flour canister, from $85 to....................**$95.00**

Red Rooster, plate, dinner; 10"................................**$16.00**

Sculptured Daisy, mug, 8-oz.....................................**$20.00**

Sculptured Daisy, salad fork & spoon set...................**$55.00**

Sculptured Daisy, tumbler, 11-oz..............................**$30.00**

Sculptured Grape, creamer, 10-oz.............................**$28.00**

Sculptured Grape, jam & jelly, 8⅛", from $55 to.......**$60.00**

Sculptured Zinnia, bowl, vegetable; 9½", from $35 to.**$40.00**

Sculptured Zinnia, plate, dinner; 10½".......................**$13.00**

Sculptured Zinnia, platter, oval, 12½".......................**$40.00**

Sculptured Zinnia, teapot, 6-cup...............................**$100.00**

Vineyard, coffeepot, 8-cup, from $85 to.....................**$95.00**

Vineyard, soup tureen, from $165 to.........................**$180.00**

Woodland Gold, bowl, divided vegetable; 9", from $40 to..**$45.00**

Woodland Gold, cup & saucer, from $12 to................**$14.00**

Yorkshire, plate, salad; from $10 to..........................**$12.00**

Yorkshire, tumbler, lg, from $20 to...........................**$25.00**

Poppets

Colleen, girl with coiled hair, 7¼", from $45.00 to $55.00.
(Photo courtesy Jeannie Fedock)

Arnie, golfer, 6½", from $35 to.................................**$45.00**

Conchita, Mexican girl, 8¾", from $50 to...................**$60.00**

Eliza, flower vendor, 5⅝", from $45 to.......................**$55.00**

Elliot, boy tennis player, w/4" bowl, from $35 to.......**$45.00**

Jenny, seated girl, 8¾", from $35 to.............................$45.00
Mike, boy w/pot, 5½", from $25 to $35.00
Monica, nun, 8", from $35 to.....................................$45.00
Nellie, girl w/bird, 8⅝", from $45 to.........................$55.00
Pamela, girl in gown, from $35 to.............................$45.00
Raymond, barrister, w/4" bowl, from $45 to $55.00
Schultz, tradesman/grocer, 8½", from $45 to.............$55.00
Zelda, choral lady #2, 7⅝", from $35 to $45.00

Miscellaneous

Alice in Wonderland, Disney, from $350 to $400.00
American Royal Horse, colt, standing, Nostalgia Line, 3x4",
    from $65 to...$70.00
Bear, standing, miniature, 6½", from $70 to..............$75.00
Burro, Nostalgia Line, from $55 to $60.00
Dinosaur, miniature, 4½", from $185 to....................$195.00
Dumbo (elephant), Disney, mini, 1¾", from $175 to...$200.00
Figaro (cat), standing, Disney, from $175 to.............$225.00
Fire wagon, Nostalgia Line, from $90 to...................$100.00
Flamingo, head down, miniature, 6¼", from $45 to...$50.00
Mickey Mouse, Disney, from $350 to $400.00
Old Mill ensemble, Nostalgia Line, 2-pc, from $200 to..$225.00
Santa, Nostalgia Line, from $85 to.............................$95.00
Squirrel, miniature, 2", from $30 to $35.00
Thumper (rabbit), Disney, lg, from $85 to $95.00

Milk Bottles

Between the turn of the century and the 1950s, milk was bought and sold in glass bottles. Until the '20s, the name and location of the dairy was embossed in the glass. After that it became commonplace to pyro-glaze (paint and fire) the lettering onto the surface. Farmers sometimes added a cow or some other graphic that represented the product or related to the name of the dairy.

Because so many of these glass bottles were destroyed when paper and plastic cartons became popular, they've become a scarce commodity, and today's collectors have begun to take notice of them. It's fun to see just how many you can find from your home state — or try getting one from every state in the union!

What makes for a good milk bottle? Collectors normally find the pyro-glaze decorations more desirable, since they're more visual. Bottles from dairies in their home state hold more interest for them, so naturally New Jersey bottles sell better there than they would in California, for instance. Green glass examples are unusual and often go for a premium; so do those with the embossed baby faces. (Watch for reproductions here!) Those with a 'Buy War Bonds' slogan or a patriot message are always popular, and cream-tops are good as well.

Some collectors enjoy adding 'go-alongs' to enhance their collections, so the paper pull tops, advertising items that feature dairy bottles, and those old cream-top spoons will also interest them. The spoons usually sell for about $6.00 to $10.00 each.

Advisor: John Shaw (See Directory, Milk Bottles)

Newsletter: *The Milk Route*
National Association of Milk Bottle Collectors, Inc.
Thomas Gallagher
4 Ox Bow Rd., Westport, CT 06880-2602; 203-454-1475

Newsletter: *Creamers*
Lloyd Bindscheattle
P.O. Box 11, Lake Villa, IL 60046-0011
Subscription: $5 for 4 issues

Blais Dairy Farm, Webster Rd, Kewiston ME, orange pyro,
    square qt..$15.00
Boy elf & Sparkle, blue pyro, amber square qt $10.00
Cloverdale, Mandan, Dickinson, Bismark ND, red & blue pyro
    sour cream or cottage cheese jar, 12-oz, EX...........$21.50

Cole Farm Dairy, Biddeford, ME, brown pyro, half pint, $9.00.

Columbia Dairies, SC, green pyro, squat round qt, EX+...$26.50
Dawn, orange pyro w/a black Store on 2 shoulders, from
    Athol & Orange, light wear, square qt...................$10.00
Dublin Coop Dairies, war slogan, round pint.............$18.00
Dyke's Dairy, Youngsville - Warren PA, red pyro, light wear,
    tall round qt $23.50
Elm Dairy, Le Roy NY, brown pyro, light wear, square
    qt $10.00
Ferland's Dairy, Mexico ME, ½-pt.................................$15.00
Freeman's Dairy, Best by Test on back, red pyro, dairy
    creamer..$12.50
Fulton Dairy, EK Rowlee, no city or state shown, brown
    pyro, round qt..$17.50
Furtado's Dairy, New Bedford MA, orange pyro, square ½-
    pt $10.00
J Waskewicz Dairy, Bungay Rd, Seymour CT, maroon pyro,
    tall round qt $15.00
Laurington Dairy, SC, orange pyro, squat round qt....$26.50
McAdams Dairy Products, JF McAdams & Bros Inc, orange
    pyro, tall round qt $35.00
Melrose Dairy, Ormond FL, blue pyro, light wear, tall round
    qt $20.00

New Mexico Collega, A&MA, red pyro front & back, light wear, squat round qt **$28.00**

North Chatham Dairy, NY, dairy building on back, red pyro, round qt...**$25.00**

Party Tonight.../You Never Outgrow..., green & orange pyro, square cream top, w/repro spoon.........**$32.00**

Pelton's Farm Dairy, Monticello NY, blue pyro, same front & back, round pt **$40.00**

Pet Dairy Products, red pyro, light wear, squat round qt **$15.00**

Plains, Ayrshire cows on front, red & green pyro, round pt..**$22.00**

Queensboro Farm Products, maroon pyro, wide-mouth sour cream jar.......................................**$15.00**

Romney Dairy, Romney WV, red pyro, square ½-pt ..**$15.50**

Sill's Farm Dairy, Greenport LI (Long Island), orange pyro, squat round qt...................................**$25.00**

Spencer Milk Co, Sidney NY, Gill, ¼-pt........................**$18.50**

St Charles Dairy, St Charles MO, red & green pyro, Christmas design (for eggnog), square qt **$12.50**

State of Maine Cheese Co & lighthouse scene, blue pyro, square qt...**$16.00**

Valley Farm, St Louis MO, orange pyro front & rear, square qt **$10.00**

Vermont Country, Christmas design (for eggnog), square qt **$17.50**

Waukon IA, red pyro, light wear, tall round qt...........**$26.00**

Wayside Farm Dairy, Janeczek's, green & orange pyro both sides, squat qt **$22.50**

Wheeler & Taylor, Keene NJ, black pyro, squat round qt ..**$17.50**

Zenda Farms, Clayton NY, orange pyro, tall round pint..**$12.00**

Miller Studios

Imported chalkware items began appearing in local variety stores in the early '50s. Cheerfully painted hot pad holders, thermometers, wall plaques, and many other items offered a lot of decorator appeal. While not all examples will be marked Miller Studios, good indications of that manufacturer are the holes on the back where stapled-on cardboard packaging has been torn away — thus leaving small holes. There should also be a looped wire hanger on the back, although a missing hanger does not seem to affect price. Copyright dates are often found on the sides. Miller Studios, located in New Philadelphia, Pennsylvania, is the only existing U.S.A. firm that makes hand-finished wall plaques yet today. Although they had over three hundred employees during the '60s and '70s, they presently have approximately seventy five.

Advisors: Paul and Heather August (See Directory, Miller Studios)

Angels, cherub's face, orange, 1954, pr, from $18 to .**$10.00**

Angels, 2 cherubs & oval mirror, gold, 1966, 3-pc set, from $16 to...**$20.00**

Animals, bear toothbrush holder, M17, tan & brown, 1954, from $16 to..**$18.00**

Animals, bunny toothbrush holder, yellow & black, from $30 to...**$32.00**

Animals, cat w/pencil holder, yellow & black, 1957, from $15 to...**$18.00**

Animals, elephant, pink & red, 1972, 4-pc set, from $18 to...**$24.00**

Animals, elephant toothbrush holder, M16, yellow w/faded polka dots, from $17 to............................**$20.00**

Animals, horse head, brown, 1951, from $12 to.........**$14.00**

Animals, pig, blue & white, sm, from $10 to **$12.00**

Animals, poodle lady in bathtub w/Bathometer plaques, 1973, from $8 to...**$12.00**

Animals, poodle plaques, black & white, round, 1947, pr, from $20 to...**$25.00**

Animals, poodle plaque, black and white, 1969, from $10.00 to $12.00.

Animals, poodle plaques, pink & blue, square, 1972, pr, from $12 to...**$15.00**

Animals, Scottie dog head, yellow & black, pr, from $8 to...**$10.00**

Birds, bluebird, blue & yellow, 1970, sm, pr, from $8 to...**$10.00**

Birds, cardinal, red, 1972, pr, from $8 to....................**$10.00**

Birds, crested cockatoos, M30, light blue-gray, 1957, pr, from $18 to...**$20.00**

Birds, flying pheasant, M36, red, 3-pc set, from $25 to ..**$30.00**

Birds, owl, white, 1978, 11", pr, from $8 to **$10.00**

Birds, swan, pink, oval, 1965, pr, from $8 to.............**$10.00**

Birds, swan plaques, pink, oval, 1965, pr, from $9 to ..**$12.00**

Birds, swan plaques, pink & white, round, 1958, pr, from $14 to...**$16.00**

Figures, Dutch boy & girl, yellow & red, 1953, pr, from $26 to...**$28.00**

Figures, Raggedy Ann & Andy, blue & orange, pr, from $28 to...**$32.00**

Fish, family, blue, 1950s, 9", 4-pc set, from $16 to.....**$20.00**

Fish, frolicking w/starfish, yellow, 1977, 4-pc set, from $13 to **$17.00**

Fish, gaping mouths, pr w/bubbles, pink, 7", 4-pc set, from $10 to..**$14.00**

Fish, male & female, black, 1954, pr, from $12 to......**$14.00**

Fish, male w/top hat & female w/umbrella, green, 1969, pr, from $10 to..**$12.00**

Fruit, bunch, brown & yellow, round, 1968, from $6 to...**$8.00**

Fruit, carrot bunch, orange & green, 1971, from $6 to.**$8.00**

Fruit, cherry plaque, pink, yellow & black, square, 1956, pr, from $18 to..**$20.00**

Fruit, grapes on wood, gold, 1964, from $10 to **$12.00**

Fruit, lg mushrooms, yellow & brown, 1977, pr, from $13 to...**$16.00**

Hot pad holder, cabbage head w/female face, green & yellow, 1959, from $14 to...............................**$16.00**

Hot pad holder, Campbell Soup Kid boy & girl, yellow, 1964, pr, from $24 to.......................................**$26.00**

Hot pad holder, peach w/funny face, yellow, 1972, pr, from $8 to..**$10.00**

Hot pad holder, sunflower, Let's Be Happy, yellow & green, 1972, pr, from $16 to.............................**$20.00**

Note pad, bird, Make a Note, yellow & red, 1954, from $17 to..**$20.00**

Note pad, fruit, Don't You Forget It, blue & red, 1968, from $10 to...**$15.00**

Note pad, owl w/pencil holder, red & yellow, 1970, from $12 to...**$15.00**

Thermometer, fruit bunch, multicolor, 1981, from $10 to..**$12.00**

Thermometer, mermaid, aqua & white, 1976, from $14 to..**$17.00**

Thermometer, potbelly stove, Weather Watcher, gold, 1965, from $8 to..**$11.00**

Thermometer, Sniffy Skunk, M55, black & yellow, from $28 to..**$30.00**

Model Kits

By far the majority of model kits were vehicular, and though worth collecting, especially when you can find them still mint in the box, the really big news are the figure kits. Most were made by Aurora during the 1960s. Especially hot are the movie monsters, though TV and comic strip character kits are popular with collectors too. As a rule of thumb, assembled kits are valued at about half as much as conservatively priced mint-in-box kits. The condition of the box is just as important as the contents, and top collectors will usually pay an additional 15% (sometimes even more) for a box that retains the factory plastic wrap still intact. For more information, we recommend *Aurora History and Price Guide* by Bill Bruegman (Cap'n Penny Productions), and *Classic Plastic Model Kits* by Rick Polizzi. *Schroeder's Toys, Antique to Modern,* contains prices and descriptions of hundreds of models by a variety of manufacturers. (The latter two books are published by Collector Books.)

Club: *International Figure Kit Club*

Magazine: *Kit Builders* Magazine
Gordy's
P.O. Box 201
Sharon Center, OH 44274-0201
216-239-1657 or fax: 216-239-2991

Magazine: *Model and Toy Collector Magazine*
137 Casterton Ave., Akron, OH 44303
216-836-0668 or fax: 216-869-8668

Adams, Chuck Wagon, 1958, MIB **$35.00**
Addar, Evel Knievel's Wheelie, 1974, MIB................**$125.00**
AEF, Aliens, Bishop, 1980, MIB **$35.00**
AEF, Aliens, Warrior Alien, 1980, MIB......................**$40.00**
Airfix, Corythosaurus, 1970, MIB (sealed) **$30.00**
Airfix, Skeleton, 1970, MIB **$20.00**
AMT, Flintstone's Family Sedan, 1974, MIB..............**$90.00**
AMT, Girl From UNCLE Car, 1967, MIB....................**$250.00**
AMT, Munster Koach, 1964, MIB..............................**$150.00**
AMT, My Mother the Car, 1965, MIB........................**$75.00**
AMT, Star Trek, Mr Spock, 1967, MIB......................**$150.00**
AMT/Ertl, A-Team Van, 1983, MIB............................**$30.00**
AMT/Ertl, Airwolf Helicopter, 1984, MIB (sealed).......**$25.00**
AMT/Ertl, Riptide, 1960 Corvette, 1984, MIB (sealed)...**$25.00**
Anubis, Jonny Quest, Turu the Terrible, 1992, MIB....**$60.00**
Aoshima, Back to the Future, Delorian, 1989, MIB **$40.00**
Arii, Southern Cross, ATAC-Bowie Emerson, MIB......**$25.00**
Aurora, Adventure Series, Spartacus, 1964, MIB **$275.00**
Aurora, Archie's Car, 1969, MIB................................**$85.00**
Aurora, Batman, 1964, MIB..**$225.00**
Aurora, Comic Scenes, Lone Ranger, 1974, MIB **$50.00**
Aurora, Customizing Monster Kit, MIB **$120.00**
Aurora, Dick Tracy Space Coupe, 1967, MIB...........**$100.00**
Aurora, Dracula, 1972, MIB (sealed)........................**$200.00**
Aurora, Famous Fighters, Confederate Raider, 1959, MIB ..**$375.00**
Aurora, Famous Fighters, Steve Canyon, 1958, MIB.**$175.00**
Aurora, Godzilla, 1969, glow-in-the-dark, MIB..........**$200.00**
Aurora, Godzilla, 1972, glow-in-the-dark, MIB..........**$150.00**
Aurora, Green Beret, 1966, MIB **$150.00**
Aurora, Incredible Hulk, 1966, MIB **$250.00**
Aurora, Lone Ranger, 1967, MIB **$250.00**
Aurora, Mad Dentist, 1972, MIB **$375.00**
Aurora, Mod Squad Station Wagon, 1969, MIB.........**$125.00**
Aurora, Monster Scenes, Gruesome Goodies, 1971, MIB...**$75.00**
Aurora, Monster Scenes, Pain Parlor, 1971, MIB **$140.00**
Aurora, Witch, 1972, glow-in-the-dark, MIB..............**$100.00**
Bachmann, Birds of the World, Meadowlark, 1950s, MIB..**$30.00**
Bachmann, Dogs of the World, Dalmatian, 1960s, MIB...**$30.00**
Bachmann, Fisher Boy, 1962, MIB **$80.00**
Bandai, Gundman, Mobile Suit Tallgeese, 1995, MIB.**$30.00**
Bandai, Thunderbird, 1984, MIB **$40.00**
Billiken, Frankenstein, 1988, vinyl, NRFB................**$100.00**
Billiken, Mummy, vinyl, MIB....................................**$220.00**
Billiken, Saucer Man, MIB..**$70.00**
Dark Horse, Mummy, 1995, MIB..............................**$150.00**
Dimensional Designs, Mad Doctor, 1992, NM (EX box)..**$75.00**

Eldon, Moon Survey, 1966, MIB $50.00
FX, Tales From the Darkside, Gargoyle, resin, 17", MIB .. $120.00
Hawk, Bobcat Roadster, 1962, MIB $30.00
Hawk, Cherokee Sports Roadster, 1962, MIB $30.00
Hawk, Explorer 18 Satellite, 1960, MIB $70.00
Hawk, Jupitor C/Explorer, 1966, MIB $50.00
Hawk, Silly Surfers, Woodie on a Surfari, 1964, MIB .. $100.00
Hawk, Weird-Ohs, Huey's Hut Rod, 1969, MIB $50.00
Horizon, Dracula, 1988, MIB $50.00
Horizon, Indiana Jones, Dr Jones, 1993, MIB $20.00
Horizon, Indiana Jones, Indiana, 1993, MIB $60.00
Horizon, Marvel Universe, Spider-Man, 1988, MIB $40.00
Horizon, Mummy, 1993, MIB $60.00
Imai, Armored Knights, Archduke II, 1984, MIB $10.00
Imai, Orguss, Cable, 1994, MIB $40.00
Imai, Orguss, Dr Doom, 1991, MIB $40.00
Imai, Orguss, Spider-Man, 1994, new pose, MIB $30.00
Imai, Orguss, Thor, 1993, MIB $50.00
ITC, Brontosaurus Skeleton, 1962, MIB $100.00
ITC, Bumble Bee, 1950s, MIB $65.00
Life-Like, Ankylosaurus, 1968, MIB $30.00
Life-Like, Cro-Magnon Man, 1973, MIB $40.00
Lindberg, Dimetrodon, 1979, MIB $20.00
Lindberg, Green Ghoul, 1965, MIB $50.00
Lindberg, Mad Maestro, 1965, MIB $225.00

MPC, Incredible Hulk, 1979, MIB $35.00
MPC, Pirates of the Caribbean, Dead Men Tell No Tales or Fate of the Mutineers, 1972, MIB, ea $55.00
MPC, Spider-Man, 1978, MIB (sealed) $60.00
MPC, Star Wars, Darth Vader TIE Fighter, 1978, MIB .. $35.00
MPC, Wacky Races Mean Machine, 1969, MIB $100.00
Palmer, African Tribal Mask, 1950, MIB $70.00
Palmer, Spirit of '76 Diorama, 1950s, MIB $100.00
Pyro, Indian Chief, 1960, MIB $60.00
Pyro, Rawhide Cowpuncher, 1958, MIB $60.00
Revell, '31 Ford Woody, 1964, MIB $85.00
Revell, Apollo Astronaut on Moon, 1970, MIB $100.00
Revell, Baja Humbug, 1971, MIB $85.00
Revell, Bonanza, Ben, Hoss & Little Joe, 1966, MIB . $160.00
Revell, Dune, Ornithopter, 1985, MIB (sealed) $60.00
Revell, Gemini Astronaut, 1967, MIB $55.00
Revell, Gemini Capsule, 1967, MIB $75.00
Revell, Sand Crawler, 1985, MIB (sealed) $50.00
Screamin', Air Assault Martian, 1995, MIB $50.00
Screamin', Star Wars, Boba Fett, 1994, MIB $50.00
Screamin', Suburban Commando, General Suitor Mutant, 1991, MIB $55.00
Takara, Crusher Joe, Hunter Diskhound, MIB $20.00
Toy Biz, Ghost Rider, 1996, MIB $30.00
Toy Biz, Wolverine, 1996, MIB (sealed) $30.00

Marx, White House, with eight Presidential figures, 1950s, MIB, $75.00.

Monogram, Bad Medicine, 1970s, MIB $60.00
Monogram, Baja Bandito or Beast, 1969-70, MIB, ea . $55.00
Monogram, Bathtub Buggy, 1960s, MIB $90.00
Monogram, Frankenstein, 1983, MIB $70.00
Monogram, Go Bots, Cy-Kill, 1984, MIB $40.00
Monogram, Mummy, 1983, MIB $25.00
Monogram, Snoopy on the Highwire, 1972, MIB $30.00
Monogram, Wolfman, 1983, MIB (sealed) $60.00
MPC, Alien, 1979, MIB $70.00
MPC, Bearcat, 1971, MIB $65.00
MPC, Beatles Yellow Submarine, 1968, MIB (sealed) .. $300.00
MPC, Digger Trike, 1970, MIB $45.00
MPC, Dukes of Hazzard, Daisy's Jeep, 1980, MIB $50.00
MPC, Fonz & His Bike, MIB $35.00

Modern Mechanical Banks

The most popular (and expensive) type of bank with today's collectors are the mechanicals, so called because of the antics they perfrom when a coin is deposited. Over three hundred models were produced between the Civil War period and the first World War. On some, arms wave, legs kick, or mouths open to swallow up the coin — amusing nonsense intended by the inventor to encourage and reward thriftiness. Some of these original banks have been known to sell for as much as $20,000.00 — well out of the price range most of us can afford! So many opt for some of the modern mechanicals that are available on the collectibles market, including Book of Knowledge and James D. Capron, which are reproductions marked to indicate that they are indeed replicas. But beware — unmarked modern reproductions are common.

Reynolds Toys have been producing banks from their own original designs since 1971; some of Mr. Reynolds' banks are in the White House and the Smithsonian.

Advisor: Dan Iiannotti (See Directory, Banks)

Artillery Bank, Book of Knowledge, NM $385.00
Bobby Riggs & Billy Jean King, John Wright, limited edition of 250, scarce, NM $1,275.00
Boy on Trapeze, Book of Knowledge, NM $525.00
Bozo, 25M, Reynolds, 1974, edition of 10 .... $950.00
Cat & Mouse, Book of Knowledge, M $375.00
Cat Boat, Richards/Utexiqual, NM $925.00
Clown on Globe, James Capron, M $925.00

Eagle & Eaglets, Book of Knowledge, M	**$450.00**
Elephant, John Wright, MIB	**$275.00**
Father Christmas, 10M, Reynolds, 1972, 1 made ea year at Christmas	**$850.00**
Frog (Two Frogs), James Capron, NM	**$625.00**
Gloomy Gus, 18M, Reynolds, 1974, edition of 10	**$2,800.00**
Humpty Dumpty, Book of Knowledge, M	**$350.00**
Indian Shooting Bear, Book of Knowledge, M	**$425.00**
Lion on Monkeys, James Capron, M	**$1,050.00**
Magician, Book of Knowledge, M	**$425.00**

Cruet	**$17.50**
Cup, E-2431	**$5.00**
Lamp, hurricane style, 9⅜"	**$25.00**
Pitcher, #82853, footed, 6"	**$15.00**
Pitcher, 6"	**$12.00**
Vase, E-3096, 7¾"	**$10.00**

Candle lantern, $15.00; Salt and pepper shakers, $12.00 for the pair.

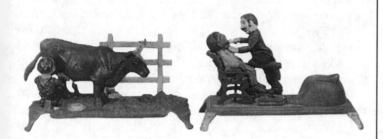

Milking Cow, Book of Knowledge, NM, $350.00; Dentist, Book of Knowledge, NM, $275.00.

Monkey, James Capron, NM	**$375.00**
Oregon Trail, 51M, Reynolds, 1993, edition of 50	**$800.00**
Owl (Turns Head), Book of Knowledge, M	**$300.00**
Paddy & the Pig, Book of Knowledge, M	**$385.00**
Professor Pug Frog, James Capron, M	**$1,025.00**
Race Course Runners, James Capron, EX	**$675.00**
Tammany Bank, Book of Knowledge, NMIB	**$400.00**
Train Man, 1M, Reynolds, 1971, edition of 30	**$350.00**
Trick Pony, Book of Knowledge, NM	**$375.00**
Trolley, 2M, Reynolds, 1971, edition of 30	**$450.00**
US & Spain, Book of Knowledge, M	**$375.00**
World's Fair, Book of Knowledge, bronze version, NM	**$450.00**

Mood Indigo by Inarco

This line of Japanese-made ceramics probably came out in the 1960s, and enough of it was produced that a considerable amount has reached the secondary market. Because of the interest today's collectors are exhibiting in items from the '60s and '70s, it's beginning to show up in malls and co-ops, and the displays are surprisingly attractive. The color of the glaze is an electric blue, and each piece is modeled as though it were built from stacks of various fruits. It was imported by Inarco (Cleveland, Ohio) and often bears that company's foil label.

Centerpiece, stacked-up fruit on ribbed incurvate base, 12x6"	**$15.00**
Coffee/teapot	**$15.00**
Cookie jar/canister, E-2374, 8"	**$15.00**
Creamer & sugar bowl, w/lid, from $10 to	**$12.50**

Moon and Star

Moon and Star (originally called Palace) was first produced in the 1880s by John Adams & Company of Pittsburgh. But because the glassware was so heavy to transport, it was made for only a few years. In the 1960s, Joseph Weishar of Wheeling, West Virginia, owner of Island Mould & Machine Company, reproduced some of the original molds and incorporated the pattern into approximately forty new and different items. Two of the largest distributors of this line were L.E. Smith of Mt. Pleasant, Pennsylvania, who pressed their own glass, and L.G. Wright of New Martinsville, West Virginia, who had theirs pressed by Fostoria and Fenton. Both companies carried a large and varied assortment of shapes and colors. Several other companies were involved in its manufacture as well, especially of the smaller items. All in all, there may be as many as one hundred different pieces, plenty to keep you involved and excited as you do your searching.

The glassware is already very collectible, even though it is still being made on a limited basis. Colors you'll see most often are amberina (yellow shading to orange-red), green, amber, crystal, light blue, and ruby. Pieces in ruby and light blue are most collectible and harder to find than the other colors, which seem to be abundant. Purple, pink, cobalt, amethyst, tan slag, and light green and blue opalescent were made, too, but on a lesser scale.

Current L.E. Smith catalogs contain a dozen or so pieces that are still available in crystal, pink, cobalt (lighter than the old shade), and these colors with an iridized finish. A new color was introduced in 1992, teal green, and the water set in sapphire blue opalescent was pressed in 1993 by Weishar

Enterprises. They are now producing limited editions in various colors and shapes, but they are marking their glassware 'Weishar,' to distinguish it from the old line. Cranberry Ice (light transparent pink) was introduced in 1994.

Our values are given for ruby and light blue. For amberina, green, and amber, deduct at least 30%. These colors are less in demand, and unless your prices are reasonable, you may find them harder to sell. Read *Mysteries of the Moon and Star* by George and Linda Breeze for more information.

Ashtray, allover pattern, moons form scallops along rim, 4 rests, 8" dia..**$25.00**

Ashtray, moons at rim, star in base, 6-sided, 5½".......**$18.00**

Ashtray, moons at rim, star in base, 6-sided, 8½".......**$25.00**

Banana boat, allover pattern, moons form scallops along rim, 9", from $28 to...**$32.00**

Banana boat, allover pattern, moons form scallops along rim, 12"...**$45.00**

Basket, allover pattern, moons form scallops along rim, footed, incurvate upright handles, 4", from $15 to.....**$22.00**

Basket, allover pattern, moons form scallops along rim, solid handle, 9", from $50 to...**$65.00**

Bell, pattern along sides, plain rim & handle, from $35 to **$45.00**

Bowl, allover pattern, footed, crimped rim, 7½", from $25 to **$35.00**

Butter dish, allover pattern, scalloped foot, patterned lid & finial, 6x5½" dia...**$45.00**

Butter dish, allover pattern, stars form scallops along rim of base, star finial, oval, ¼-lb, 8½"............................**$50.00**

Butter/cheese dish, patterned lid, plain base, 7" dia, from $50 to..**$65.00**

Cake plate, allover pattern, low collared base, 13" dia, from $50 to...**$60.00**

Cake salver, allover pattern w/scalloped rim, raised foot w/scalloped edge, 5x12" dia, from $50 to...........**$60.00**

Cake stand, allover pattern, plate removes from standard, 2-pc, 11" dia **$75.00**

Candle bowl, allover pattern, footed, 8", from $25 to .**$30.00**

Candle holder, allover pattern, bowl style w/ring handle, 2x5½", ea...**$18.00**

Candle holders, allover pattern, flared & scalloped foot, 6", pr, from $40 to...**$50.00**

Candle holders, allover pattern, flared base, 4½", pr, from $20 to..**$25.00**

Candle lamp, patterned shade, clear base, 2-pc, 7½", from $20 to..**$25.00**

Candy dish, allover pattern on base & lid, footed ball shape, 6"...**$25.00**

Canister, allover pattern, 1-lb or 2-lb, from $12 to......**$15.00**

Canister, allover pattern, 3½-lb or 5-lb, from $18 to ..**$22.00**

Chandelier, dome shape, 14" dia, w/font, amber, from $300 to...**$365.00**

Chandelier, ruffled dome shape w/allover pattern, amber, 10"...**$100.00**

Cheese dish, patterned base, clear plain lid, 9½", from $65 to...**$70.00**

Compote, allover pattern, footed, flared crimped rim, 5", from $15 to..**$22.00**

Compote, allover pattern, raised foot, patterned lid & finial, 7½x6", from $30 to..**$40.00**

Compote, allover pattern, raised foot on stem, patterned lid & finial, 10x8", from $50 to................................**$65.00**

Compote, allover pattern, raised foot on stem, patterned lid & finial, 12x8", from $60 to................................**$75.00**

Compote, allover pattern, scalloped foot on stem, patterned lid & finial, 8x4", from $35 to **$40.00**

Compote, allover pattern, scalloped rim, footed, 5½x8", from $28 to...**$35.00**

Compote, allover pattern, scalloped rim, footed, 5x6½", from $15 to...**$20.00**

Compote, allover pattern, scalloped rim, footed, 7x10", from $35 to...**$45.00**

Console bowl, allover pattern, scalloped rim, flared foot w/flat edge, 8"...**$25.00**

Creamer, allover pattern, raised foot w/scalloped edge, 5¾x3"...**$35.00**

Creamer & sugar bowl (open), disk foot, sm, from $25 to **$35.00**

Cruet, vinegar; 6¾", from $65 to **$75.00**

Decanter, bulbous w/allover pattern, plain neck, foot ring, original patterned stopper, 32-oz, 12", from $75 to........**$90.00**

Epergne, allover pattern, 1-lily, flared bowl, scalloped foot, minimum value **$95.00**

Epergne, allover pattern, 2-pc, 9", minimum value **$65.00**

Fairy lamp, cylindrical dome-top shade, 6", from $25 to **$35.00**

Goblet, water; plain rim & foot, 5¾", from $15 to **$22.00**

Goblet, wine; plain rim & foot, 4½", from $12 to.......**$15.00**

Jardiniere, allover pattern, patterned lid & finial, 9¾", minimum value..**$85.00**

Jardiniere/cracker jar, allover pattern, patterned lid & finial, 7¼", minimum value...**$65.00**

Jardiniere/tobacco jar, allover pattern, patterned lid & finial, 6", minimum value...**$45.00**

Jelly dish, allover pattern, patterned lid & finial, stemmed foot, 10½", from $55 to..**$65.00**

Jelly dish, patterned body w/plain flat rim & disk foot, patterned lid & finial, 6¾x3½"...............................**$35.00**

Lamp, miniature; amber..**$145.00**

Lamp, miniature; blue, from $185 to........................**$225.00**

Lamp, miniature; green **$185.00**

Lamp, miniature; milk glass.......................................**$245.00**

Lamp, miniature; red...**$235.00**

Lamp, oil or electric; allover pattern, all original, amber, from $175 to...**$200.00**

Lamp, oil or electric; allover pattern, all original, red or light blue, 24", minimum value....................................**$350.00**

Lamp, oil; allover pattern, all original, common, 12", from $75 to...**$100.00**

Lighter, allover patterned body, metal fittings, from $40 to..**$50.00**

Nappy, allover pattern, crimped rim, 2¾x6", from $12 to..**$18.00**

Pitcher, water; 7½", from $65.00 to $80.00; Tumbler, iced tea; 5", from $18.00 to $22.00.

Plate, patterned body & center, smooth rim, 8".........**$35.00**

Relish bowl, 6 lg scallops form allover pattern, 1½x8"...**$35.00**

Relish dish, allover pattern, 1 plain handle, 2x8" dia, from $35 to...**$40.00**

Relish tray, patterned moons form scalloped rim, star in base, rectangular, 8" **$35.00**

Salt & pepper shakers, allover pattern, metal tops, 4x2", pr, from $25 to...**$35.00**

Salt cellar, allover pattern, scalloped rim, sm flat foot..**$8.00**

Sherbet, patterned body & foot w/plain rim & stem, 4¼x3¾", from $25 to...**$28.00**

Soap dish, allover pattern, oval, 2x6" **$12.00**

Spooner, allover pattern, straight sides, scalloped rim, raised foot, 5¼x4", from $45 to **$50.00**

Sugar bowl, allover pattern, patterned lid & finial, sm flat foot, 5¼x4", from $35 to **$40.00**

Sugar bowl, allover pattern, straight sides, patterned lid & finial, scalloped foot, 8x4½", from $35 to.............**$40.00**

Sugar shaker, allover pattern, metal top, 4½x3½" **$50.00**

Syrup pitcher, allover pattern, metal lid, 4½x3½", from $65 to..**$75.00**

Toothpick holder, allover pattern, scalloped rim, sm flat foot...**$10.00**

Tumbler, juice; no pattern at rim, short pedestal foot, 4½", from $18 to..**$22.00**

Tumbler, juice; no pattern at rim or on disk foot, 5-oz, 3½", from $12 to..**$15.00**

Tumbler, no pattern at rim or on disk foot, 7-oz, 4¼", from $12 to...**$15.00**

Mortens Studios

During the 1940s, a Swedish sculptor by the name of Oscar Mortens left his native country and moved to the United States, settling in Arizona. Along with his partner, Gunnar Thelin, they founded the Mortens Studios, a firm that specialized in the manufacture of animal figurines. Though he preferred dogs of all breeds, horses, cats, and wild animals were made, too, but on a much smaller scale.

The material he used was a plaster-like composition molded over a wire framework for support and reinforcement. Crazing is common, and our values reflect pieces with a moderate amount, but be sure to check for more serious damage before you buy. Most pieces are marked with either an ink stamp or a paper label.

Airedale, standing, black & tan, #741, 5¾x4¾"...........**$95.00**

Basset Hound, standing, black & white w/tan, #878, 3¼x5¼"...**$95.00**

Boston Bull Terrier pup, black & white, round stamp, #838, 3½"...**$75.00**

Boxer, male, fawn, round & oval stickers, #780, 6½" ..**$100.00**

Boxer, sitting, 4½" **$70.00**

Chihauhau, round sticker, #777a, 5½", EX+ **$85.00**

Chinchilla Persian cat, cream, round & oval stickers, #912, 6" L **$100.00**

Cocker Spaniel, begging, red, #764, 5" **$75.00**

Cocker Spaniel pup, sitting, black, #820, 3¼"............**$65.00**

Collie, sitting, tan & cream, #791, 5¾"......................**$95.00**

Collie, wall plaque...**$195.00**

Dalmatian pup, sitting, #812, 3¼" **$65.00**

English Setter, wall plaque, #9507.............................**$160.00**

Fox Terrier, tan & cream, smooth coat, #772b, 5¼" ...**$75.00**

French Poodle, cream, French cut, #788, 3½x4".........**$95.00**

German Shepherd, standing, tan & black, #755, 6½" ..**$100.00**

Horse, black, running, #112e......................................**$100.00**

Horse, gray, #652, 4½x5" **$85.00**

Irish Setter pup, 3"..**$35.00**

Lion bookends, $125.00 for the pair.

Lion, recumbent, 4x6" **$135.00**

Lynx..**$175.00**

Pekingese, standing, red & tan, #740, 4½x3½".........**$100.00**

Persian cat, standing, gray & cream, #908...................**$95.00**

Scottie dog, sitting, hard to find, 4½".........................**$150.00**

Wire Hair Terrier, begging, #557, rare, 3"...................**$165.00**

Morton Pottery

Six different potteries operated in Morton, Illinois, during a period of ninety-nine years. The first pottery, established by six Rapp brothers who had immigrated from Germany in the mid-1870s, was named Morton Pottery Works. It was in operation from 1877 to 1915 when it was reorganized and renamed Morton Earthenware Company. Its operation, 1915 – 1917, was curtailed by World War I. Cliftwood Art Potteries, Inc. was the second pottery to be established. It operated from 1920 until 1940 when it was sold and renamed Midwest Potteries, Inc. In March 1944 the pottery burned and was never rebuilt. Morton Pottery Company was the longest running of Morton's potteries. It was in operation from 1922 until 1976. The last pottery to open was the American Art Potteries. It was in production from 1947 until 1961.

All of Morton's potteries were spin-offs from the original Rapp brothers. Second, third, and fourth generation Rapps followed the tradition of their ancestors to produce a wide variety of pottery. Rockingham and yellow ware to Art Deco, giftwares, and novelties were produced by Morton's potteries.

To learn more about these companies, we recommend *Morton's Potteries: 99 Years, Vol. II,* by Doris and Burdell Hall.

Advisors: Doris and Burdell Hall (See Directory, Morton Pottery)

Morton Pottery Works — Morten Earthenware Company, 1877 – 1917

Crock, sauerkraut, Rockingham, four-gallon with 10" diameter press, $200.00.
(Photo courtesy Doris and Burdell Hall)

Bowl, banded yellow ware, 4½"	**$30.00**
Cuspidor, Rockingham, 7"	**$50.00**
Jug, Dutch; brown Rockingham, 3-pt	**$75.00**
Miniature, pitcher, green, 1¾"	**$25.00**
Mug, yellow ware, banded, 1-pt	**$85.00**
Pitcher, multicolor (green/brown/yellow), #245, 6"	**$150.00**
Teapot, Rebecca, brown Rockingham, 5¼-pt	**$125.00**

Cliftwood Art Potteries, Inc., 1920 – 1940

Bookends, squirrel on log, brown chocolate drip, 5½x5½x3", pr	**$110.00**
Creamer, cow figural, brown chocolate drip, 6½x3½x1½"	**$85.00**
Dinnerware, sugar bowl, apple green, w/lid	**$25.00**
Figurine, Billiken doll, brown, 7½"	**$125.00**
Flower frog, Lorelei figural, green, 6½"	**$75.00**
Lamp, flattened bulb, blue-gray drip, #6, 16½"	**$75.00**
Miniature, lioness, yellow & brown, 6¾x3¼x1"	**$50.00**
Planter, heron, turquoise matt, 6"	**$24.00**
Stein, barrel shape, German motto on white, 4½"	**$30.00**
Vase, tree trunk form, green, 9"	**$70.00**

Midwest Potteries, Inc., 1940 – 1944

Creamer, cow figural, white w/14k gold decor, 5½x7x2"	**$15.00**
Figurine, cock, fighting, blue & brown, 6"	**$18.00**
Figurine, hen, white & gold, 3¾"	**$18.00**
Figurine, horse, rearing, brown drip, 10¾"	**$35.00**
Figurine, September Morn, nude female, 14k gold, 11½"	**$100.00**
Figurine, wild turkey, brown & tan spray, 12"	**$30.00**
Miniature, polar bear, white, 2"	**$12.00**
Planter, deer reclining, brown & white, 6½x5½"	**$18.00**
TV lamp, Siamese cats, brown & white, 13¼" adult & 8" kitten	**$75.00**

Morton Pottery Company, 1922 – 1976

Christmas item, Mrs Claus, planter/vase, 9½"	**$35.00**
Christmas item, Santa Claus, nut cup	**$12.00**
Easter item, bunny, planter, brown & pink, #430, 5"	**$14.00**
Easter item, chick on decorated egg planter, 4½x4"	**$12.00**
Figurine, Boston Terrier, black & white, 7"	**$40.00**
Flowerpot soaker, calla lily, yellow & green	**$15.00**
Head vase, 1940s style w/pillbox hat, white matt, #406	**$45.00**
Lamp, Davy Crockett, adult figure w/bear, green & brown	**$125.00**
Lamp, Easter bunny w/carrot, male	**$50.00**
Lamp, old woman shoe house	**$35.00**
Political giveaway, figurine, donkey, Kennedy, brown, 2"	**$35.00**
Spatterware, custard cup, green, brown & white, 5-oz	**$20.00**
Spatterware, pitcher, milk; brown, yellow & green, w/advertising, 4½"	**$75.00**
Thanksgiving item, turkey, figurine, white, mini, 2½"	**$15.00**
Thanksgiving item, turkey, planter, natural colors, #3335, lg	**$45.00**
Valentine item, heart vase, red, #428, 5¾"	**$12.00**
Wall plaque, fish, multicolor	**$18.00**
Wall plaque, rooster, natural colors	**$25.00**

American Art Potteries, 1947 – 1963

Candlestick, black, 3 cups, #140, 6x7½"	**$30.00**
Creamer, bird figural, tail handle, black & green spray	**$15.00**
Doll parts, 3" head & appendages, hand-painted natural colors	**$60.00**
Figurine, hog, Poland China, natural colors, 5½"	**$40.00**
Flower frog, bird on stump, #98, 8½"	**$20.00**

Planter, bluebird on bent branch, blue & cobalt spray, 7¼" **$18.00**

Planter, rabbit beside stump, brown, white, pink & green spray, 4¾" **$18.00**

TV lamp, birds on branch, planter base, mauve & blue spray, 11" **$30.00**

TV lamp, conch shell, mauve & gray, #131, 7¼" **$30.00**

Vase, ewer form, pink, gray & gold, 8½" **$24.00**

Vase/flower frog, inverted mushroom form, green & yellow spray, 4¾" **$18.00**

Wall pocket, apple w/3 leaves, red & gr **$18.00**

Wall pocket, dustpan, decor, #81, 8" **$25.00**

Moss Rose

Though the Moss Rose pattern has been produced by Staffordshire and American pottery companies alike since the mid-1800s, the line we're dealing with here was primarily made between the late 1950s into the 1970s by Japanese manufacturers. Even today you'll occasionally see a tea set or a small candy dish for sale in some of the chain stores. (The collectors who're already picking this line up refer to it as Moss Rose, but each importer had their own name for the line.) The pattern consists of a briar rose with dark green mossy leaves on stark white glaze. Very often it is trimmed in gold. In addition to dinnerware, many accessories and novelties were also made.

Refer to *Schroeder's Antiques Price Guide* (Collector Books) for information on the early Moss Rose pattern.

Advisor: Geneva Addy (See Directory, Imperial Porcelain)

Ashtrays, stacking; butterfly shape, from 4x6" to 2x3¾", set of 4 ....**$20.00**

Butter dish, w/lid, 2½x3½x7¼" **$45.00**

Creamer, footed, 4" **$13.00**

Cup, gold trim, footed, 2½x3½" **$12.00**

Dresser box, open handles, w/lid, oval, 5¾x3½" **$35.00**

Dresser box, ruffled edge, gold trim, w/lid, round, footed, 6¼x3½" **$35.00**

Flower frog, 5½x6" **$50.00**

Lamp, Aladdin; gold trim, 5¾" **$18.00**

Lamp, oil; frosted chimney, round base, 8" **$36.00**

Mustard jar, w/notched lid & spoon, marked Bond Ware, 4" **$40.00**

Salt & pepper shakers, pr **$18.00**

Smoking set, lighter, cigarette holder & 4 ashtrays, gold trim, EX **$40.00**

Sugar bowl, gold trim, w/lid, 4x5½" **$13.00**

Teacup & saucer, gold rim, marked Cresent China Japan **$10.50**

Teapot, gold trim, locking lid, electric, 6x6" **$30.00**

Teapot, musical, plays Tea For Two **$55.00**

Tidbit tray, 3-tier, gold trim, EX **$25.00**

Trinket box, gold trim, 3x4½x2½" **$20.00**

Vase, bud; 8" **$23.00**

Platter, Ucago, rare, 12", from $65.00 to $85.00.
(Photo courtesy Pam Kozak)

Motion Clocks (Electric)

Novelty clocks with some type of motion or animation were popular in spring-powered or wind-up form for hundreds of years. Today they bring thousands of dollars when sold. Electric-powered or motor-driven clocks first appeared in the late 1930s and were produced until quartz clocks became the standard, with the 1950s being the era during which they reached the height of their production.

Four companies led their field. They were Mastercrafters, United, Haddon, and Spartus in order of productivity. Mastercrafters was the earliest and longest-lived, making clocks from the late '40s until the late '80s. (They did, however, drop out of business several times during this long period.) United began making clocks in the early '50s and continued until the early '60s. Haddon followed in the same time frame, and Spartus was in production from the late '50s until the mid-'60s.

These clocks are well represented in the listings that follow; prices are for examples in excellent condition and working. With an average age of forty years, many now need repair. Dried-out grease and dirt easily cause movements and motions not to function. The other nemesis of many motion clocks is deterioration of the fiber gears. Originally intended to keep the clocks quiet, fiber gears have not held up like their metal counterparts. For fully restored clocks, add $50.00 to $75.00 to our values. (Full restoration includes complete cleaning of motor and movement, repair of same; cleaning and polishing face and bezel; cleaning and polishing case and repairing if necessary; and installing new line cord, plug, and light bulb if needed.) Brown is the most common case color for plastic clocks. Add 10% to 20% or more for cases in onyx (mint green) or any light shade. If any parts noted below are missing, value can drop one-third to one-half. We must stress that 'as is' clocks will not bring these prices. Deteriorated, non-working clocks may be worth less that half of these values.

Note. When original names are not known, names have been assigned.

Advisors: Sam and Anna Samuelian (See Directory, Motion Clocks)

Haddon

Based in Chicago, Illinois, Haddon produced an attractive line of clocks. They used composition cases that were hand painted, and sturdy Hansen movements and motions. This is the only clock line for which new replacement motors are still available.

Granny rocking (Home Sweet Home), Haddon, $125.00.
(Photo courtesy Sam and Anna Samuelian)

Rocking Horse (Rancho), composition, from $150 to...**$200.00**
Teeter Totter, children on seesaw, from $125 to......**$175.00**

Mastercrafters

Based in Chicago, Illinois, this company produced many of the most appealing and popular collectible motion clocks on today's market. Cases were made of plastic, with earlier examples being a sturdy urea plastic that imparted quality, depth, and shine to their finishes. Clock movements were relatively simple and often supplied by Sessions Clock Company, who also made many of their own clocks.

Airplane, Bakelite & chrome, from $175 to...............**$225.00**
Blacksmith, plastic, from $75 to **$100.00**
Carousel, plastic, carousel front, from $175 to..........**$225.00**
Church, w/bell ringer, plastic **$100.00**
Fireplace, plastic, from $60 to **$90.00**
Swinging Bird, plastic, w/cage front, from $125 to ..**$150.00**
Swinging Girl, plastic, from $100 to............................**$125.00**
Swinging Playmates, plastic, w/fence, from $100 to.**$125.00**
Waterfall, plastic...**$100.00**

Spartus

This company made clocks well into the '80s, but most later clocks were not animated. Cases were usually plastic, and most clocks featured animals.

Cat, w/flirty eyes, plastic, from $25 to **$40.00**
Panda Bear, plastic, eyes move, from $25 to **$40.00**

Water Wheel (L style), plastic, from $20 to **$30.00**
Waterfall & Wheel, plastic, from $50 to......................**$75.00**

United

Based in Brooklyn, New York, United made mostly cast-metal cases finished in gold or bronze. Their movements were somewhat more complex than Mastercrafters'. Some of their clocks contained musical movements, which while pleasing can be annoying when continuously run.

Ballerina, wooden, from $75 to...................................**$125.00**
Bobbing Chicks, metal case, various colors, from $35 to.**$50.00**
Bobbing Chicks, wooden house, green & red, from $40 to .**$60.00**
Cowboy w/Rope, metal, wooden base, from $100 to ...**$150.00**
Dancers, metal w/square glass dome, from $100 to.**$150.00**
Davy Crockett, metal, 10", rare...................................**$650.00**
Fireplace, metal, gold, from $50 to **$75.00**
Fireplace, w/man & woman, spinning wheel & moving fire, from $125 to..**$150.00**
Fishing Boy, metal, fishing pole & fish move, from $125 to..**$150.00**
Huck Finn, fishing pole & fish move, from $150 to.**$175.00**
Hula Girl & Drummer, wooden, from $200 to..........**$250.00**
Majorette w/Rotating Baton, from $75 to **$125.00**
Owl, metal on wooden base, eyes move, from $75 to...**$100.00**
Windmill, pink plastic case, minor cracks in plastic, from $75 to..**$100.00**

Miscellaneous

God Bless America, flag waves, from $75 to **$100.00**
Klocker Spaniel, from $50 to **$75.00**
Poodle, various colors, from $75 to **$100.00**

Motorcycle Collectibles

At some point in nearly everyone's life, they've experienced at least a brief love affair with a motorcycle. What could be more exhilarating than the open road — the wind in your hair, the sun on your back, and no thought for the cares of today or what tomorrow might bring. For some, the passion never diminished. For most of us, it's a fond memory. Regardless of which description best fits you personally, you will probably enjoy the old advertising and sales literature, books and magazines, posters, photographs, banners, etc., showing the old Harleys and Indians, and the club pins, dealership jewelry and clothing, and scores of other items of memorabilia such as collectors are now beginning to show considerable interest in. For more information and a lot of color photographs, we recommend *Motorcycle Collectibles With Values* by Leila Dunbar (Schiffer). See also License Plates.

Advisor: Bob 'Sprocket' Eckardt (See Directory, Motorcycles)

Banner, Harley Cycle Wear/Wrangler, denim, Harley logo above Cycle Wear, Built by Wrangler below, 1960s, 48x36", NM...**$600.00**

Belt buckle, 1955 Gypsy Tour, gold w/AMA enameled logo, EX **$175.00**

Book, Indian Riders' Instruction Book, 1937, 44 pages, illustrated cover, 7x5", EX, $125.00.

Book, Story of Harley-Davidson, 1960s, 56 pages, EX .**$35.00**

Bracelet, 1951 Gypsy Tour, metal ID type w/blue lettering & AMA logo, heavy chain band, NM **$110.00**

Brochure, Indian, America's Pioneer Motorcycle, 1942, NM **$200.00**

Brochure, Indian Motorcycles, 40th Anniversary, 1941, EX **$90.00**

Catalog, Harley-Davidson/1954 Accessory Catalog, blue & yellow, 37 pages, EX...**$120.00**

Catalog holder, Indian, metal ring binder, script lettering, red & black, VG **$180.00**

Clock, Harley-Davidson, octagonal light-up, logo in center, 1940s, 18x18", EX...**$2,700.00**

Clock, Indian Motorcycles, black numbers & red lettering on white, glass front w/metal frame, 18½" dia, NM .**$1,700.00**

Decal, for gas tank, sleek profile image of Indian head w/Indian scripted on headdress, Knickerbocker, NY, 12x4", EX **$40.00**

Dexterity game, Harley-Davidson/1941/Yours For More Fun With A..., shows couple on motorcycle, round, EX **$160.00**

Handbill, Harley-Davidson for 1940, EX......................**$65.00**

Hat, adult, Harley-Davidson, black cloth w/white visor & braid, embroidered orange, white & black wing emblem & name, EX **$90.00**

Hat, child's, Harley-Davidson, black cloth w/white visor & braid, embroidered white wing emblem w/blue wheel, VG..**$25.00**

Key chain, 1951 Gypsy Tour, gold-tone metal arrowhead shape w/AMA logo in center, blue inlay, 1½x1½", EX **$50.00**

Kidney belt, brown leather, older style, 6" at widest point, 40" L, VG...**$25.00**

Magazine, Custom Chopper, November, 1971, EX........**$5.00**

Money clip, AMA Award, dated 1961, MOC.................**$70.00**

Oil can, Harley-Davidson Genuine Motor Oil for Two Cycle Motors, 8-oz, black labels on orange can, 4", EX ..**$135.00**

Oil can, Oilzum Motorcycle Oil/Choice of Champions, 1-gal, white w/man on orange logo, EX.....................**$130.00**

Pin, AMA Gypsy Tour 1948, gold-tone motorcycle rider atop V-shaped shield w/bannered border, enameled center, 1½", NM...**$60.00**

Pin, Harley-Davidson, sterling, 2" wings, VG **$50.00**

Pin, Indian Motorcycles, silver-tone metal saddle tank shape w/Indian embossed on red inset, 1940s, 1", EX+ .**$170.00**

Postcard, 1941 Indian '45'/Featuring The New 'Double Action' Spring Frame, motorcycle in landscape, 3½x5½", NM **$40.00**

Poster, Goodyear Tires, Thrills/Spills!/Motorcycle Races, shows action bike w/rider & black arrow, 1950s, 15x9", NM **$700.00**

Shirt, Motormaids From Kansas Admire (on black), med blue, long sleeve, early 1960s, EX **$125.00**

Sign, glass, Harley-Davidson Sales/Service/Parts/Accessories, shield logo in center, lettered corners, 7x9", EX..**$1,200.00**

Sign, neon, Harley-Davidson Motor Cycles, tubing borders black-painted wood plaque w/embossed gold lettering, 30x40", NM...**$850.00**

Sign, porcelain, Harley-Davidson Genuine Oil, diecut oil can shape in black & orange, 11x8", rare, EX **$1,600.00**

Sign, porcelain, Mobiloil D/Recommended for All Motor Cycle Engines, w/Gargoyle logo & black rider silhouette, 9x11", EX...**$1,825.00**

Sign, tin, Harley-Davidson Cigarettes, smiling couple on motorcycle behind product name, 1984, 17x21", EX........**$60.00**

Sign, tin, Harley-Davidson Motor Cycles Sales/Service, Motorcycle Headquarters/address, trademark colors, 18x24", EX..**$600.00**

Stick pin, Indian Motorcycles, gold-tone metal w/round Indian head emblem on end, ½" dia, EX...........**$180.00**

String tie, Harley-Davidson, w/detailed metal motorcycle clasp, green, NM...**$185.00**

Tie clip, gold-tone motorcycle on wire bar, Gypsy Tour, 1949, ¾x1¼", EX+ **$65.00**

Visor, Harley-Davidson, leather w/stamped logo on bill, M **$30.00**

Watch fob, Indian Motorcycles, gold & black metal arrowhead form w/head image of Indian, 2", rare, EX...........**$100.00**

Windbreaker, Harley-Davidson, 1970s, EX **$50.00**

Wristwatch, Harley-Davidson, logo on rectangular face w/curved sides, black leather band, working, VG **$600.00**

Movie Posters and Lobby Cards

Although many sizes of movie posters were made and all are collectible, the preferred size today is still the one-sheet, 27" wide and 41" long. Movie-memorabilia collecting is as diverse as films themselves. Popular areas include specific films such as *Gone With the Wind, Wizard of Oz,* and others; specific stars — from the greats to character actors; directors such as Hitchcock, Ford, Spielberg, and others; specific film types such as B-Westerns, all-Black casts, sports related, Noir, '50s teen, '60s beach, musicals, crime, silent, radio characters, cartoons, and serials; specific characters such as Tarzan, Superman, Ellery Queen, Blondie, Ma and Pa Kettle, Whistler, and Nancy Drew; specific artists like Rockwell, Davis, Frazetta, Flagg, and others; specific art themes, for instance, policeman, firemen, horses, attorneys, doctors, or nurses (this list is endless). And some collectors just collect posters they like. In the past twenty years, movie memorabilia has steadily increased in value, and in the last few years the top price paid for a movie poster has reached $453,500.00. Movie memorabilia is a new field for collectors. In the past, only a few people knew where to find posters. Recently, auctions on the east and west coasts have created much publicity, attracting scores of new collectors. Many posters are still moderately priced, and the market is expanding, allowing even new collectors to see the value of their collections increase.

Advisors: Cleophas and Lou Ann Wooley, Movie Poster Service (See Directory, Movie Posters)

Adventures of Mark Twain, Fredric March as Mark Twain w/Alexis Smith, 3-sheet, 81x41", VG+ $45.00

Alias Jesse James, Bob Hope, 1959, ½-sheet, 28x22", VG..$25.00

An Affair To Remember, Cary Grant & Deborah Kerr, 1957, 1-sheet, linen-backed, 41x27", EX $500.00

Animal Farm, George Orwell animated film, 1955, insert, 36x14", NM+ $100.00

Apartment, Jack Lemmon & Shirley MacLaine, 1960, 1-sheet, 41x27", G $75.00

Around the World in 80 Days, David Niven, 1957, 1-sheet, 41x27", VG..$80.00

Baby Doll, Carroll Baker in baby bed sucking her thumb, 1956, 3-sheet, 81x41", VG+ $175.00

Bambi, 1966 reissue, style A, 1-sheet, 41x27", EX.......$30.00

Batman & Robin Part 2, 1966 remake, 1-sheet, 41x27", VG $75.00

Beau Brummell, Elizabeth Taylor, 1954, 1-sheet, 41x27", VG+ $50.00

Beneath the Planet of the Apes, James Franciscus, Charlton Heston, 1970, 1-sheet, 41x27", EX.........................$45.00

Between Heaven & Hell, Robert Wagner & Terry Moore, 1956, ½-sheet, 28x22", VG $35.00

Beyond the Valley of the Dolls, 1970, 1-sheet, 41x27", EX $125.00

Big Jack, Wallace Berry & Marjorie Main, 1949, lobby card set, 11x14" ea, EX $65.00

Billy the Kid in Santa Fe, Robert Steele, 1944, 3-sheet, 81x41", EX $100.00

Birdman of Alcatraz, Burt Lancaster, Saul Bass art, 1962, 1-sheet, 41x27", G+..$50.00

Birds Do It, Soupy Sales, 1966, 1-sheet, 41x27", EX...$45.00

Blazing Saddles, Mel Brooks, 1974, 1-sheet, 41x27", EX..$65.00

Boom, Elizabeth Taylor, 1968, 1-sheet, 41x27", NM....$35.00

Born To Be Bad, Joan Fontaine, 1950, 1-sheet, 41x27", G+ $85.00

Born Yesterday, Judy Holliday, William Holden & Brodrick Crawford, 1951, insert, 36x14", VG+ $75.00

Call of the South Seas, Allan Lane & Janet Martin, 1943, 1-sheet, 41x27", VG+ $50.00

Captain Eddie, Fred MacMurry as WWI ace Eddie Rickenback, 1945, insert, 36x14", VG+..................$50.00

Cat Girl, Barbara Shelley, 1957, ½-sheet, EX+ $75.00

Charade, Audery Hepburn & Cary Grant, stone litho, 1963, daybill, 30x13", NM $100.00

Come Dance With Me, Brigitte Bardot, 1960, 1-sheet, 41x27", EX..$50.00

Cosmic Man, Bruce Bennett & John Carradine, 1959, lobby card set, 11x14" ea, EX..$100.00

Cosmic Monsters, Forrest Tucker, 1958, set of 3 lobby cards, 11x14" ea, EX $75.00

Dangerous When Wet, Tom & Jerry, 1953, insert, 36x14", EX..$85.00

Desiree, Marlon Brando as Napoleon w/Jean Simmons & Merle Oberon, 1954, window card, 14x22", VG+ ..$50.00

Destination 60,000, Preston Foster & Coleen Gray, 1957, ½-sheet, 28x22", EX+ $40.00

Diary of a Madman, Vincent Price, 1963, 1-sheet, 41x27", VG..$40.00

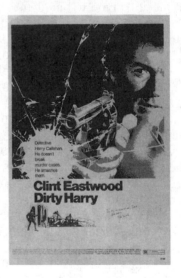

Dirty Harry, Warner, 1971, 41x27", NM, $155.00.

Don't Give Up the Ship, Jerry Lewis, 1959, ½-sheet, 28x22", VG $45.00

Door-to-Door Maniac, Johnny Cash, 1966, 1-sheet, 41x27", EX..$60.00

Dr No, Sean Connery, 1962, 1-sheet, 41x27", EX........$60.00

Easy Rider, Peter Fonda & Dennis Hopper, 1972, 1-sheet, 41x27", scarce, EX..$75.00

Escape From the Planet of the Apes, Roddy McDowall, 1971, 1-sheet, 41x27", EX+ $50.00

Face of Fu Manchu, Christopher Lee, 1965, 1-sheet, 41x27", NM $50.00

Fantastic Voyage, Raquel Welch, 1966, 3-sheet, 81x41", VG+..$75.00

Farmer's Daughter, Loretta Young & Joseph Cotton, 1947, ½-sheet, EX..$75.00

Feathered Spirit, Roland Winters as Charlie Chan, 1948, 1-sheet, 41x27", EX....................................$200.00

Fiddler on the Roof, 1972, 1-sheet, 41x27", EX...........$30.00

Follow That Dream, Elvis Presley, 1962, 60x40", EX....$190.00

Forbidden Planet, 1956, 36x14", NM, $1,200.00.

Forbidden Planet, 1972 remake, VG.........................$100.00

Fuller Brush Man, Red Skelton, 1948, 6-sheet, 81x81", VG+...$100.00

Gambling House, Victor Mature & Terry Moore, 1951, 1-sheet, 41x27", EX....................................$60.00

Giant, Elizabeth Taylor, Rock Hudson & James Dean, 1969, window card, 14x22", VG+...................................$175.00

Gigantis the Fire Monster, Japanese film, 1959, 1-sheet, 41x27", VG+..$200.00

Glenn Miller Story, Jimmy Stewart, 1954, window card, 14x22", VG..$65.00

Grand Theft Auto, Ron Howard, 1977, 1-sheet, 41x27", EX...$25.00

Green Hornet, Bruce Lee, 1974, 1-sheet, 41x27", EX..$60.00

Guess Who's Coming to Dinner?, Spencer Tracy, Kathrine Hepburn & Sidney Poitier, 1967, 1-sheet, 41x27", EX $30.00

Harvey, James Stewart, 1950, 1-sheet, 41x27", rare, EX ..$975.00

Hell on Wheels, Marty Robbins, 1967, 1-sheet, 41x27", EX+ $65.00

House on Haunted Hill, Vincent Price w/haunted house & skeleton, 1958, 1-sheet, linen-backed, 41x27", rare, EX...$850.00

How To Stuff a Wild Bikini, Annette Funicello & Mickey Rooney, 1965, 1-sheet, EX $75.00

I'll Be Yours, Deanna Durbin & Tom Drake, 1946, insert, 36x14", G+...$50.00

I'll Cry Tomorrow, Susan Hayward as singer Lillian Roth, 1955, lobby card set, 11x14" ea, VG+...................$75.00

Ice Station Zebra, Rock Hudson & Jim Brown, 1969, 1-sheet, 41x27", EX $25.00

If You Knew Susie, Eddie Cantor & Joan Davis, 1947, 3-sheet, 81x41", VG+..$100.00

In Like Flint, artwork by Bob Peak, 1967, 1-sheet, 41x27", VG+...$75.00

Invasion of the Animal People, John Carradine, 1962, 1-sheet, 41x27", VG.....................................$45.00

Iron Petticoat, Kathrine Hepburn & Bob Hope, 1956, insert, 36x14", EX $50.00

Kissin' Cousins, Elvis Presley, 1964, 3-sheet, 41x81", EX..$100.00

Lassie's Great Adventure, Jon Provost, 1963, 1-sheet, 41x27", VG...$25.00

Left Hand of God, Humphery Bogart & Gene Tierney, lobby card, 11x14", EX+..$25.00

Let's Make It Legal, Marilyn Monroe, 1951, lobby card, 11x14", EX+...$150.00

Lost in Alaska, Abbot & Costello, 1952, 1-sheet, 41x27", VG...$65.00

Love in the Afternoon, Audrey Hepburn & Gary Cooper, 1957, insert, 36x14", EX...................................$80.00

Mad Max, Mel Gibson, 1980, 1-sheet, EX...................$75.00

Malcom X, 1972, 1-sheet, 41x27", NM......................$50.00

Man w/the Golden Arm, Frank Sinatra & Eleanor Parker, artwork by Saul Bass, 1956, window card, 14x22", EX $75.00

Man With the Golden Gun, Roger Moore, 1974, 1-sheet, 41x27", VG...$50.00

Mary Poppins, Julie Andrews, style B, 1964, 1-sheet, 41x27", G+...$40.00

Mississippi Gambler, Kent Taylor, Frances Langford & Shemp Howard, 1942, 1-sheet, 41x27", VG...................$50.00

Modesty Blaze, artwork by Bob Peak, 1966, 1-sheet, 41x27", VG...$45.00

Never Say Goodbye, Errol Flynn & Eleanor Parker, 1946, 1-sheet, 41x27", VG $150.00

Night Stage to Galveston, Gene Autry, 1952, ½-sheet, 28x22", EX...$75.00

No Highway in the Sky, Marlene Dietrich & James Stewart, 1951, 1-sheet, 28x22", VG+ $75.00

Northern Pursuit, Errol Flynn, 1943, 1-sheet, 41x27", EX.$250.00

Painted Hills, Lassie portrait, 1951, 1-sheet, 41x27", VG+...$50.00

Pickup Alley, Anita Ekberg, 1957, 1-sheet, 41x27", EX ...$40.00

Range Beyond the Blue, Eddie Dean, 1947, 1-sheet, 41x27", EX...$60.00

Rocky, Sylvester Stallone, 1977, 1-sheet, 41x27", EX ..$45.00

Roman Holiday, Audrey Hepburn & Gregory Peck, 1962 reissue, 60x40", VG...$85.00

Sad Sack, Jerry Lewis, 1958, 1-sheet, 41x27", EX........$35.00

Sand Pebbles, Steve McQueen, 1967, 60x40", EX.....$175.00

Sandpiper, Elizabeth Taylor & Richard Burton, 1965, ½-sheet, 28x22", VG+ $65.00

She Creature, Marla English, 1956, 1-sheet, 41x27", NM ..$350.00

Slattery's Hurricane, Veronica Lake, Richard Widmark & Linda Darnell, 1949, ½-sheet, 28x22", VG+ $65.00

Some Like It Hot, Marilyn Monroe & Tony Curtis, 1958, lobby card, 11x14", EX....................................$75.00

Spirit of St Louis, Jimmy Stewart as Charles Lindburgh, 1957, 1-sheet, 41x27", VG+ $50.00

Spirits of the Dead, Brigitte Bardot, Jane & Peter Fonda, 1969, 1-sheet, 41x27", EX **$25.00**

St Valentines Day Massacre, 1967, set of 8 lobby cards, 11x14" ea, EX **$40.00**

Story of GI Joe, Burgess Meredith as Ernie Pyle, 1944, insert, 36x14", VG **$60.00**

Strait Jacket, Joan Crawford, 1964, 1-sheet, 41x27", Fair ..**$75.00**

Suddenly Last Summer, Elizabeth Taylor in white bathing suit, 1960, 3-sheet, 41x81", EX **$200.00**

The Burglar, Jane Mansfield, 1957, ½-sheet, 28x22", VG+ **$75.00**

The Enforcer, Clint Eastwood, 1977, 1-sheet, 41x27", G.**$20.00**

The Gauntlet, Clint Eastwood, fantasy artwork by Frank Frazetta, 1977, ½-sheet, 28x22", NM **$40.00**

Tokyo Rose, Lotus Long, 1946, 1-sheet, VG+ **$65.00**

Treat 'Em Rough, Eddie Albert, 1941, insert, 36x14", EX+ **$50.00**

Twist Around the Clock, Chubby Checker & others, 1961, lobby card set, 11x14" ea, EX **$130.00**

Untamed, Tyrone Power & Susan Hayward, 1955, ½-sheet, 28x22", EX **$50.00**

Valley of the Sun, Lucille Ball & James Craig, 1942, 1-sheet, linen-backed, 41x27", EX **$250.00**

Vanishing American, Scott Brady, 1955, 1-sheet, 41x27", EX **$60.00**

Young Bill Hickok, Roy Rogers & Gabby Hayes, 1940, 1-sheet, linen-backed, 41x27", EX **$600.00**

Napkin Dolls

Cocktail, luncheon, or dinner..., paper, cotton, or damask..., solid, patterned, or plaid — regardless of size, color, or material, there's always been a place for napkins. In the late 1940s and early 1950s, buffet-style meals were gaining popularity. One accessory common to many of these buffets is now one of today's hot collectibles — the napkin doll. While most of the ceramic and wooden examples found today date from this period, many homemade napkin dolls were produced in ceramic classes of the 1960s and 1970s.

For information on napkin dolls as well as egg timers, string holders, children's whistle cups, baby feeder dishes, razor blade banks, pie birds, laundry sprinkler bottles, and other unique collectibles from the same era, we recommend *Collectibles for the Kitchen, Bath and Beyond*; for ordering information see our advisor's listing in the Directory.

Advisor: Bobbie Zucker Bryson (See Directory, Napkin Dolls)

Betson's yellow Colonial lady, bell clapper, marked Hand Painted Japan, 8½", from $75 to...........................**$90.00**

California Originals, toothpick holder basket over head, foil label, 13¾", from $75 to...**$85.00**

California Originals, white Spanish dancer w/gold trim, splits in rear only, foil label, 13", from $110 to **$125.00**

Enesco, Genie at Your Service, holding lantern, paper label, 8", from $125 to..**$150.00**

Goebel, half doll on wire frame, marked Goebel, W Germany, ca 1957, 9", from $175 to **$195.00**

Holland Mold, Daisy, No 514, 7¼", from $75 to.........**$90.00**

Holland Mold, Rebecca No H-265, 10½", from $135 to.**$165.00**

Holland Mold, Rosie, No H-132, 10¼", from $55 to...**$65.00**

Holt Howard, pink Sunbonnet Miss, marked Holt Howard 1958, 5", from $95 to...**$125.00**

Japan, angel, pink, holding flowers, 5⅜", from $110 to..**$150.00**

Japan, lady in green w/pink umbrella, bell clapper, unmarked, 9", from $75 to **$90.00**

Japan, lady in pink dress w/blue shawl & yellow hat, 8½", from $60 to..**$75.00**

Japan, Santa, marked Chess, 1957, 6¾", from $95 to.**$115.00**

Kreiss & Co, blue lady w/candle holder behind hat, from $60 to..**$75.00**

Kreiss & Co, green lady holding fan, candle holder behind fan, marked, 8¾", from $70 to..............................**$90.00**

Kreiss & Co., yellow doll with gold trim holds muff, jewelled eyes, candle holder in hat, marked, 10", from $95.00 to $110.00.
(Photo courtesy Bobbie Zucker Bryson)

Kreiss & Co, yellow doll w/poodle, jeweled eyes, necklace & ring, candle holder behind hat, marked, 10¾", from $95 to..**$125.00**

Man (bartender), holding tray w/candle holder, 8¾", from $95 to..**$115.00**

Metal, silhouette of Deco woman, black & gold w/wire bottom, 8⅞", from $125 to **$150.00**

Miss Versatility Cocktail Girl, 13", from $65 to **$85.00**

Rooster, white w/red & black trim, slits in tail for napkins, w/egg salt & pepper shakers, from $35 to...........**$45.00**

Sevy Etta, wood w/marble base, marked USD Patent No 159,005, 11½", from $35 to **$45.00**

Swedish doll, wooden, marked Patent No 113861, 12", from $25 to...**$35.00**

Wooden Jamaican lady, movable arms, papel label: Ave 13 Nov 743, A Sinfonia, Tel 2350 Petropolis, 6", from $65 to..**$85.00**

Wooden pink & blue doll w/strawberry toothpick holder on head, 8", from $60 to..**$75.00**

Yamihaya Bros, lady holding yoke w/bucket salt & pepper shakers, hat conceals candle holder, from $100 to **$135.00**

New Martinsville

Located in a West Virginia town by the same name, the New Martinsville Glass Company was founded in 1901 and until it was purchased by Viking in 1944 produced quality tableware in various patterns and colors that collectors admire today. They also made a line of glass animals which Viking continued to produce until they closed in 1986. In 1987 the factory was bought by Mr. Kenneth Dalzell who reopened the company under the title Dalzell-Viking. He used the old molds to reissue his own line of animals, which he marked 'Dalzell' with an acid stamp. These are usually priced in the $50.00 to $60.00 range. Examples marked 'V' were made by Viking for another company, Mirror Images. They're valued at $15.00 to $35.00, with colors sometimes higher.

Advisor: Roselle Schleifman (See Directory, Elegant Glass)

Basket, Janice, cobalt or red, 9x6½" $155.00
Bonbon, Radiance, red or blue, 6" $30.00
Bookend, elephant figural, crystal, 5½", ea, from $75 to ...$90.00
Bowl, Janice, cobalt or red, flared rim, 12" $95.00
Bowl, Janice, flared, crystal, 11" $40.00
Bowl, Prelude, crystal, 3-footed, crimped, 9" $50.00
Candle holders, swan, ruby, pr $70.00
Candlestick, Janice, crystal, 2-light, 5x5" $40.00
Candlestick, Prelude, crystal, 4" $17.50
Candlesticks, Moondrops, cobalt or red, ruffled, 5", pr ..$45.00
Comport, Radiance, amber, 6" $24.00
Creamer, Janice, crystal, 6-oz $14.00
Creamer, Prelude, crystal $12.50
Creamer, Radiance, red or blue $25.00
Cruet, Radiance, cobalt or red, ind $75.00
Cup, Janice, red or blue $25.00
Figurine, bear baby, crystal, head turned or straight, 3"....$60.00
Figurine, bunny, crystal, head up, scarce, 1" $60.00
Figurine, hen, crystal, 5" $75.00
Figurine, horse, crystal, head up, 8" $95.00
Figurine, pig mama, crystal, from $300 to $300.00
Figurine, rooster w/crooked tail, crystal, 7½", from $75
    to $75.00
Figurine, seal baby w/ball, crystal, from $55 to $55.00
Figurine, wolfhound, crystal, 7" $95.00
Figurine, woodsman, crystal, square base, 7⅜" $135.00
Lamp base, German shepherd, pink $125.00
Mayonnaise, Janice, crystal, round $15.00
Mayonnaise, Prelude, crystal, 3-pc $35.00
Mayonnaise, Radiance, 3-pc set $40.00
Pitcher, Oscar, red $95.00
Plate, Janice, crystal, handles, 12" $35.00
Plate, Prelude, crystal, 11" $27.00
Plate, salad; Janice, red, 8" $20.00
Punch cup, Radiance, red or blue, flat $15.00
Relish, Prelude, crystal, 3-part, handles, 7" $15.00
Sherbet, Janice, crystal $12.00
Stem, cordial, Prelude, crystal, 1-oz $40.00
Stem, water; Prelude, crystal, 9-oz $25.00
Tumbler, Janice, red or blue $30.00
Tumbler, Moondrops, cobalt or red, 7-oz, 4⅜" $20.00
Tumbler, Radiance, amber, 9-oz $20.00
Vase, Janice, crystal, ball shape, 9" $55.00
Vase, Prelude, crystal, crimped, 10" $65.00
Whiskey, Moondrops, cobalt, 2-oz $20.00

Tumbler, Radiance, blue, nine-ounce, $30.00; Matching 64-ounce pitcher, $235.00. (Photo courtesy Gene Florence)

Nichols, Betty Lou

This California artist/potter is probably best known for her head vases, which display her talents and strict attention to detail to full advantage. Many of her ladies were dressed in stylish clothing and hats that were often decorated with applied lace, ruffles, and bows; the signature long eyelashes are apparent on nearly every model she made. Because these applications are delicate and susceptible to damage, mint-condition examples are rare and very valuable. Most of her head vases and figurines carry not only her name but the name of the subject as well.

Figurine, Anna, repairs, 11¼" $55.00
Figurine, Dick, Christmas angel, wide open bag, 6½"..$135.00
Head vase, Becky, 5⅝" $95.00
Head vase, Demi-Dorable, 3½", from $110 to $135.00
Head vase, Flora Belle, green, yellow & white plaid hat &
    dress w/ruffles, lg, EX $260.00
Head vase, Flora Belle, blond w/plaid bodice & trim on hat,
    lg, M $850.00
Head vase, Jill, sm repair, 4" $95.00
Head vase, Linda, blue w/white polka-dotted dress & hat,
    brown hair, 4½x5¾", M $275.00
Head vase, Michelle, celery green dress, blond hair, 6x5",
    NM $255.00
Head vase, Nellie, blue w/white polka dot dress w/cream
    ruffles, bl hat, 5", NM $180.00
Head vase, Nellie, green striped dress, 5", from $200 to ..$250.00
Head vase, praying nun, white habit, hands folded.$135.00

Head vase, Vicki, brunette dressed in ivory w/hand-painted roses, 8", M..................$625.00
Planter, fence, yellow & brown, 3½x9½", from $85 to ...$100.00
Planter, Olga, 7½x11¼", EX..................$40.00

Figurine/flower holder, Margot, 10½", NM, $150.00.

Novelty Radios

Novelty radios come in an unimaginable variety of shapes and sizes from advertising and product shapes to character forms, vehicles, and anything else the manufacturer might dream up. For information on these new, fun collectibles read *Collector's Guide to Novelty Radios* by Marty Bunis and Robert Breed, and *Schroeder's Collectible Toys, Antique to Modern* (Collector Books).

Ajax Laundry Detergent, product box style w/antenna, Hong Kong, 5x3½", from $50 to..................$75.00
Alka-Seltzer, can shape w/painted image of screw cap, Taiwan, 1971, from $50 to..................$75.00
Annie Sing-A-Long, LJN/Hong Kong, 8", from $35 to...$50.00
Bartender, ceramic bartender (actually a liquor bottle) standing behind bar, Gamble's Import Corp/Japan, from $75 to..................$100.00
Basketball, w/braided carrying strap, no markings, 3½" dia, from $25 to..................$35.00
Big Bird, molded 2-D head image w/red & white striped bow tie, 5", from $15 to..................$25.00
Big Foot, 2-D image w/name on belt, Sutton Associates/Hong Kong, 1974, 9", from $40 to......$60.00
Blinking Gorilla, holding soccer ball, plastic, 6½", from $15 to..................$25.00
Bullwinkle, figural, PAT/Hong Kong, 12", from $200 to..................$250.00
Cabbage Patch Kids, purse style w/loop strap, Original Appalachian Artworks/Playtime Products, 1983, 4½", from $20 to..................$35.00
Carriage Lamp, metal antique style w/cigarette lighter & thermometer, Japan, 9½", from $40 to..................$50.00

Disco Sound/Hi-Fi, w/dancing couple on disco floor, Hong Kong, 7x8", from $45 to..................$55.00
Electrical Wall Outlet, designed to fit standard duplex outlet, powered from AC lines, Japan, 6x5", from $40 to..$55.00
Flashlight w/Key Chain, round, Admiral, 3¾" dia, from $30 to..................$40.00
Guess Men?, black triangle w/red dial, headset, also a version for women, give-away w/purchase of perfume, from $35 to..................$45.00
Incredible Hulk, 2-D figure, Marvel/Amico, 1978, 7", from $50 to..................$75.00
King Kong, plush figure w/vinyl face, hands & feet, Amico Inc/Tiawan, 1986, 13", from $25 to..................$35.00
Kodak Ekaprint 100 Copier-Duplicator, Hong Kong, 3½x6", from $75 to..................$100.00
Kraft Macaroni & Cheese Dinner, product box shape, 1992, from $30 to..................$45.00
Marlboro Filter Cigarettes, shaped like cigarette pack, Japan, 13x9", from $75 to..................$100.00
Mickey Mouse Minizoo, 2-D lion shape w/image of Mickey as lion tamer, WDP, from $35 to..................$50.00

Mighty Mouse on Cheese, Vanity Fair/Via Com International, 1978, 5", M, $150.00. (Photo courtesy Marty Bunis and Robert F. Breed)

Orange Spot Carbonated Drink, orange can shape, from $25 to..................$35.00
Patches Rag Doll, cloth body, Heritage International, 16", from $35 to..................$45.00
Penguin, black & white plastic 3-D figure, moving wing up & down moves the controls, Hong Kong, 6½", from $60 to..................$70.00
Radiodiget Padlock, w/Radio Watch & head headset, plastic, 3x1", from $25 to..................$40.00
Santa Bear Lunchbox, Fun Designs, 1986, 9x8", from $35 to.$50.00
Simpsons, Up & At 'Em Man! (Bart on skateboard), 6½x8", EX, from $35 to..................$50.00
Snoopy Flashbeagle, 4" square, from $15 to..................$25.00
Spider-Man Wrist Radio, Marvel/Janex, 1976, 2½x10½", from $45 to..................$60.00
Steinweigh (sic) Grand Piano, wood, w/matching bench, Japan, 7", from $100 to..................$125.00
Telephone, princess style w/rotary dial, blue, ivory or pink plastic, Ross Electronic Corp/Japan, 3x7", from $50 to $75.00

Television Set, plastic w/simulated color image on screen, Hong Kong, 4x6", from $35 to **$50.00**
Tony's Pizza, cloth cooler bag w/AM-FM radio in lid, 7½x12", from $25 to...**$40.00**
V8 100% Vegetable Juice, can shape, from $35 to **$50.00**
10-4 Good Buddy! Teddy Bear, plush, Dakin, 1976, 18", from $25 to...**$35.00**

Novelty Telephones

Novelty telephones modeled after products or advertising items are popular with collectors — so are those that are character related. For further information we recommend *Schroeder's Collectible Toys, Antique to Modern* (Collector Books).

AC Spark Plug, EX...**$35.00**
Alvin, 1984, 15", M...**$60.00**

Bart Simpson, Columbia Tel-Com, 1990s, MIB, $35.00.

Batmobile (Batman Forever), MIB, from $35 to..........**$50.00**
Bugs Bunny, Warner Exclusive, MIB, from $60 to......**$70.00**
Cabbage Patch Girl, 1980s, EX, from $65 to................**$75.00**
Charlie Tuna, 1987, MIB, from $50 to..........................**$65.00**
Crest Sparkle, MIB, from $50 to **$75.00**
Darth Vader, 1983, MIB...**$200.00**
Ghostbusters, M **$100.00**
Keebler Elf, EX, from $60 to **$70.00**
Little Green Sprout, EX..**$75.00**
Little Orphan Annie & Sandy, Columbia Pictures, 1982, 11", EX **$100.00**
Mario Bros, 1980s, MIB **$50.00**
Mickey Mouse, Western Electric, 1976, EX.................**$175.00**
New Kids on the Block, Big Step Productions, 1990, MIB, from $20 to...**$30.00**
Oscar Mayer Wiener, EX **$65.00**
Raggedy Ann & Andy, Pay Phone, 1983, 7½", EX......**$40.00**

Snoopy & Woodstock, American Telephone Corp, 1976, touch-tone, EX **$100.00**
Snoopy as Joe Camel, 1980s, MIB................................**$55.00**
Spider-Man Climbing Down Chimney, NM, from $165 to .**$200.00**
Strawberry Shortcake, M **$55.00**
Superman, early version w/rotary dial, M **$500.00**
Winnie the Pooh, square base, M, from $225 to **$250.00**
Ziggy, 1989, MIB..**$75.00**

Occupied Japan Collectibles

Some items produced in Japan during the period from the end of WWII until the occupation ended in 1952 were marked Occupied Japan. No doubt much of the ware from this era was marked simply Japan, since obviously the 'Occupied' term caused considerable resentment among the Japanese people, and they were understandably reluctant to use the mark. So even though you may find identical items marked simply Japan or Made in Japan, only those with the more limited Occupied Japan mark are evaluated here.

Assume that the items described below are ceramic unless another material is mentioned. For more information, we recommend *The Collector's Encyclopedia of Occupied Japan* (there are five in the series) by Gene Florence. (All are published by Collector Books.)

Newsletter: *The Upside Down World of an O.J. Collector*
The Occupied Japan Club
c/o Florence Archambault
29 Freeborn St., Newport, RI 02840-1821. Published bimonthly. Information requires SASE.

Ashtray, antimony, fancy border, 2 rests, oval, 5x3".....**$5.00**
Ashtray, frog w/open mouth **$14.00**
Ashtray, hand figural, metal...**$10.00**
Ashtray, jasper, light blue, classical figures, 4x3" **$10.00**
Ashtray, metal, Statue of Liberty in center...................**$15.00**
Ashtray holder, elephant figural, high gloss brown, w/4 trays **$20.00**
Bowl, fruit decor on white, cut-out design along rim, 7"..**$15.00**
Bowl, lacquered wood, Karavan/Hand Turned, 4x11½" ..**$25.00**
Bowl, salad; wood, 10" **$25.00**
Bowl, soup; red roses w/black & gold, 7½" **$5.00**
Bowl, vegetable; apple decor, 8"..................................**$16.00**
Bust, cherub w/music scroll, black w/pink wings, Lamore, 4" **$35.00**
Bust, man in tricorn hat, lady w/pompadour, bisque, 5¾", pr..**$65.00**
Child's set, teapot, cup & saucer, & sugar bowl, tomato forms **$42.00**
Christmas item, nativity figures, 2½", 7-pc set............**$80.00**
Cigarette box, Oriental man carries box w/dragon finial, 6⅜"...**$27.00**
Clicker, metal, chicken figural, 1½"..............................**$8.00**
Cocktail shaker, lacquerware w/morning-glory vines on front, metal base, 11¼" **$60.00**

Creamer, lemon figural................................**$10.00**
Creamer & sugar bowl, floral sprays & blue lustre band..**$14.00**
Cup & saucer, black & white checkered border.........**$12.00**
Cup & saucer, crab apples on white w/gold trim.......**$12.50**
Cup & saucer, demitasse; flowers on white w/gold trim..**$12.50**
Cup & saucer, demitasse; Oriental house scene.........**$12.00**
Cup & saucer, flower on white shading to yellow, gold trim................................**$15.00**
Cup & saucer, red hearts & black trim......................**$10.00**
Cup & saucer, river scene w/gold trim, Aurger design....**$24.00**
Cup & saucer, yellow w/gold trim, floral interior, Jyoto..**$12.50**
Dinnerware set, apples or crab apples, serves 6+gravy+platter................................**$250.00**
Dinnerware set, dogwood on ivory w/gold trim, serves 8................................**$300.00**
Dinnerware set, Livonia (Dogwood), serves 12+casserole+platter................................**$450.00**
Dinnerware set, Livonia (Dogwood), serves 6+gravy boat+platter................................**$250.00**
Dinnerware set, Rochelle, Grace China, serves 4+serving pcs................................**$200.00**
Dinnerware set, simple pattern, serves 4...................**$225.00**
Dinnerware set, simple pattern, serves 8+platter+2 lg bowls................................**$350.00**
Dinnerware set, Wild Rose, Fuji China, serves 8+2 serving pcs................................**$300.00**
Doll, celluloid, baby in snowsuit................................**$45.00**
Figurine, American Indian chief, 5⅛"................**$16.00**
Figurine, angel lying on back holding bowl, 5½".......**$45.00**
Figurine, ballerina, gold net skirt, 4½"...............**$30.00**
Figurine, Black fiddler, 5"................................**$40.00**
Figurine, boy by fence, hat w/feather, multicolor clothes, bisque, 7⅝"................................**$55.00**
Figurine, boy playing accordion, multicolor, 5".........**$12.00**
Figurine, boy seated w/duck, multicolor, 4"...............**$11.00**
Figurine, cellist man & lady, Maruyama, 8¼"...........**$125.00**
Figurine, cherub on sea creature blowing shell horn, 3¾"................................**$30.00**
Figurine, Colonial man in blue coat & light blue vest, 7"................................**$35.00**
Figurine, Colonial man in ruffled shirt, striped pants, 4½"................................**$11.00**
Figurine, couple w/dog, man holds binoculars in raised hand, painted bisque, 10"................................**$100.00**
Figurine, Cupid on sled, bisque, 5"...............**$35.00**
Figurine, elephant, metal w/celluloid tusks, trunk up, 3x4¼"................................**$15.00**
Figurine, frog w/accordion, bisque, 4"...............**$20.00**
Figurine, girl on fence playing violin, multicolor, 4¼".**$7.00**
Figurine, girl w/song book, Ucagco China, 5¾".........**$30.00**
Figurine, hula girl, 4½"................................**$20.00**
Figurine, Hummel-type girl w/flower basket, multicolor, 6"................................**$25.00**
Figurine, lady w/flower basket, Delft Blue, 5"............**$20.00**
Figurine, lady w/tambourine, Delft Blue, 4¾"...........**$20.00**
Figurine, ladybug w/bat, black jacket, 2¼"................**$7.00**
Figurine, Oriental lady w/muff, 8"................................**$32.00**

Figurine, lady with fan, 9¾", from $40.00 to $45.00.

Figurine, Oriental musician seated w/flute, 4½".........**$12.00**
Figurine, peacock w/plume tail, multicolor, 5"..........**$18.00**
Figurine, Schnauzer dog, multicolor, 3¾"....................**$10.00**
Figurine, Spanish dancer, Delft Blue, 5⅜"................**$20.00**
Lamp base, courting couple, 6½", pr..........................**$75.00**
Lamp base, Mary & lamb, bisque.............................**$100.00**
Leaf dish, lacquered metal, hand-painted bamboo on red, Maruni, 6"................................**$12.00**
Lemon dish, hand-painted flowers w/gold trim, loop handle, 5¾"................................**$12.00**
Match safe, brown w/yellow, white & blue flower design, 6¼"................................**$38.00**
Mug, cannibal figure handle, 4¼"................................**$37.00**
Mug, tavern scene in relief, multicolor on cobalt, 6"..**$20.00**
Planter, bird beside house, 3"................................**$9.00**
Planter, boot, 6½"................................**$14.00**
Planter, boy & bird beside basket, red mark, 6¼x4¼"...**$75.00**
Planter, boy beside cactus, 4"................................**$8.00**
Planter, coolie boy beside stump, multicolor, 5½"......**$14.00**
Planter, Dutch girl holds wide basket planter, multicolor, 4½"................................**$10.00**
Planter, girl w/cart, 2⅝"................................**$8.00**
Planter, lady & shell, bisque, 5½x6½"........................**$75.00**
Planter, Santa figure, 6"................................**$35.00**
Plate, dinner; crab apples on white w/gold trim........**$20.00**
Plate, ivory band w/gold trim, Meito, 6½"...................**$8.00**
Platter, apple decor, 15"................................**$25.00**
Salt & pepper shakers, baseball players, comical appearance, pr................................**$30.00**
Salt & pepper shakers, bride & groom, pr.................**$25.00**
Salt & pepper shakers, chicks in basket, pr...............**$22.50**
Salt & pepper shakers, hen sitting, rooster standing, multicolor, 2¼", 3", pr................................**$15.00**
Shelf sitter, ballerina, net skirt, 5"................................**$30.00**
Teapot, aluminum, 9"................................**$35.00**
Tile, hand-painted maple leaves, 3⅜" square.............**$18.00**
Toby jug, balding man, graying hair, beard & mustache, 2¼".**$12.00**

Toby jug, Sairey Gamp, 4½x4" **$35.00**
Toby mug, General McArthur, 5" **$55.00**
Toby mug, man w/red beard, jeweled cap, 2½" **$15.00**
Toby mug, winking man, 4" **$25.00**
Tray, metal, leaf form, mk Economy, 5" **$6.00**
Tray, silverplate, Chicago souvenir, 5x3" **$5.00**
Umbrella, paper, 18" **$28.00**
Vase, amber glass, 2¾" **$20.00**
Vase, compositon, multicolor hunt scene, diapering handles, 5x7¼" **$12.00**
Vase, jasper, man w/grapes in basket, scrolled decor, 2¾" **$9.00**
Vase, lg applied rose on bulbous body, 4¼" **$17.00**
Vase, swan form, multicolor, 5" **$20.00**
Vase, Wedgwood type, 6⅛" **$30.00**
Wall plaque, cup & saucer, 3¼" **$8.00**
Wall plaque, duck in flight, 5" **$25.00**
Wall plaque, flying duck, 6½", EX..............................**$28.00**

Old MacDonald's Farm

This is a wonderful line of novelty kitchenware items fashioned as the family and the animals that live on Old MacDonald's Farm. It's been popular with collectors for quite some time, and prices are astronomical, though they seem to have stabilized, at least for now.

These things were made by the Regal China Company, who also made some of the Little Red Riding Hood items that are so collectible, as well as figural cookie jars, 'hugger' salt and pepper shakers, and decanters. The Roerigs devote a chapter to Regal in their book *The Collector's Encyclopedia of Cookie Jars* and, in fact, show the entire Old MacDonald's Farm line.

Advisor: Rick Spencer (See Directory, Regal China)

Spice set, six-piece, from $125.00 to $150.00 each.

Butter dish, cow's head.................................**$220.00**
Canister, flour, cereal or coffee, med, ea, from $225 to ..**$275.00**
Canister, pretzels, peanuts, popcorn, chips or tidbits, lg, ea, from $325 to.................................**$375.00**
Canister, salt, sugar or tea, med, ea, from $225 to ...**$275.00**
Canister, soap or cookies, lg, ea, from $350 to.........**$425.00**
Cookie jar, barn, from $295 to **$325.00**
Creamer, rooster, from $110 to **$125.00**

Grease jar, pig, from $200 to **$250.00**
Pitcher, milk; from $425 to **$450.00**
Salt & pepper shakers, boy & girl, pr **$80.00**
Salt & pepper shakers, churns, gold trim, pr **$95.00**
Salt & pepper shakers, feed sacks w/sheep, pr........**$195.00**
Sugar bowl, hen.................................**$135.00**
Teapot, duck's head, from $295 to.............................**$325.00**

Paper Dolls

One of the earliest producers of paper dolls was Raphael Tuck of England, who distributed many of their dolls in the United States in the late 1800s. Advertising companies used them to promote their products, and some were often included in the pages of leading ladies' magazines.

But over the years, the most common paper dolls have been those printed on the covers of a book containing their clothes on the inside pages. These were initiated during the 1920s and because they were inexpensive retained their popularity even during the Depression years. They peaked in the 1940s, but with the advent of television in the '50s, children began to loose interest. Be sure to check old boxes and trunks in your attic; you just may find some!

But what's really exciting right now are those from more recent years — celebrity dolls from television shows like 'The Brady Bunch' or 'The Waltons,' the skinny English model Twiggy, and movie stars like Rock Hudson and Debbie Reynolds. Our values are for paper dolls in mint, uncut, original condition. Just remember that cut sets (even if all original components are still there) are worth only about half as much. Damaged sets or those with missing pieces should be priced accordingly. Prices below are for uncut and original paper dolls in mint condition.

If you'd like to learn more about them, we recommend *Price Guide to Lowe & Whitman Paper Dolls* and *Price Guide to Saalfield and Merrill Paper Dolls* by Mary Young. Other references: *Schroeder's Collectible Toys, Antique to Modern;* and *Toys, Antique and Collectible,* by David Longest.

Advisor: Mary Young (See Directory, Paper Dolls)

Newsletter: *Paper Dolls News*
Ema Terry
P.O. Box 807
Vivian, LA 71082; Subscription: $12 per year for 4 issues; want lists, sale items, and trades listed

Annette in Hawaii, Whitman #1969, 1961...................**$60.00**
Annie Laurie, Lowe #1030, 1941.................................**$75.00**
Army & Navy Wedding Party, Saalfield #2446, 1943....**$125.00**
Baby Dolls, Saalfield #1954, 1941.................................**$35.00**
Betsy McCall, Whitman #1969, 1971 ....**$25.00**
Betty Grable, Merrill #2552, 1953 ....**$200.00**
Beverly Hillbillies, Whitman #1955, 1964....................**$85.00**
Blondie, Saalfield #4434, 1968 ....**$75.00**
Bob Cummings Fashion Models, Lowe #2407, 1957...**$75.00**

Bride Doll, Lowe #1043...**$55.00**
Carol Heiss, Whitman #1964, 1961 ....**$70.00**
Cinderella, Saalfield #2590, 1950 ....**$75.00**
Claudette Colbert, Saalfield #2451, 1943....................**$150.00**
Connie Francis, Whitman #1956, 1963 ....**$85.00**
Daisy Mae & Li'l Abner w/Mammy & Pappy, Saalfield #2360, 1941 ....**$125.00**
Darling Dolls, Saalfield #6169, 1964...........................**$30.00**
Debbie Reynolds, Whitman #1956, 1960 ....**$85.00**
Dinah Shore, Whitman #1963, 1958.............................**$75.00**
Dodie From My Three Sons, Saalfield #5115, 1971.....**$35.00**
Elizabeth, Lowe #2750, 1963.......................................**$30.00**
Fashion Previews, Lowe #1246, 1949...........................**$45.00**

Flying Nun, Saalfield #6069, 1969, MIB, from $50.00 to $60.00.
(Photo courtesy Greg Davis and Bill Morgan)

Giselle MacKenzie, Saalfield #4421, 1957 ....**$90.00**
Gloria's Make-Up, Lowe #2585, 1952...........................**$50.00**
Hayley Mills in Summer Magic, Whitman #1966, 1963 ..**$60.00**
Hedy Lamarr, Merrill #3482, 1942...............................**$250.00**
Hedy Lamarr, Saalfield #2600, 1951 ....**$125.00**
Jack or Jill, Lowe #9301 or #9302, 1963, ea................**$40.00**
Jane Russell, Saalfield #4328, 1955 ....**$95.00**
Janet Leigh, Lowe #2405, 1957 ....**$90.00**
Janet Lennon, Whitman #1964, 1958...........................**$60.00**
Joan Caulfield, Saalfield #2725, 1953 ....**$115.00**
Julia, Saalfield #4435, 1968...**$60.00**
Julie Andrews, Saalfield #4424, 1958...........................**$90.00**
June Allyson, Whitman #1956, 1955.............................**$90.00**
Kathy, Lowe #9986, 1962 ....**$60.00**
Kewpies, Saalfield #1332, 1963....................................**$60.00**
Kim Novak, Saalfield #4409, 1957 ....**$125.00**
Lace & Dress Puppy or Kitty, Lowe #8902 or #8903, ea...**$18.00**
Mod Matchmates, Whitman #1953, 1970.....................**$10.00**
Mopsy & Popsy, Lowe #2713, 1971 ....**$10.00**
Nurses Three, Whitman #1964, 1964............................**$40.00**
Oklahoma!, Whitman #1954, 1956................................**$125.00**
Ozzie & Harriet, Saalfield #4319, 1954........................**$125.00**
Paper Doll's Beauty Contest, Lowe #1026, 1941 ....**$95.00**
Petticoat Junction, Whitman #1954, 1964....................**$100.00**
Quintuplets, Saalfield #1352, 1964...............................**$60.00**

Raggedy Ann & Andy, Whitman #1962, 1974 ....**$18.00**
Rita Hayworth, Dancing Star, Merrill #3478, 1942.....**$300.00**
Robin Hood & Maid Marian, Saalfield #2748, 1956.....**$75.00**
Rosemary Clooney, Lowe #2569, 1956..........................**$125.00**
Sally Twinkletoes & Peggy Twirl, Saalfield #4415, 1966 ...**$16.00**
Seven & Seventeen, Merrill #3441, 1945.....................**$125.00**
Shirley Temple Play Kit, Saalfield #9859, 1958.............**$90.00**
Story Princess, Saalfield #2761, 1957..........................**$70.00**
Susan Dey as Laurie (Partridge Family), Saalfield #4218, 1972...**$45.00**
Toni Hair-Do Cut-out Colls, Lowe #1284, 1950...........**$75.00**
Trica (Nixon), Saalfield #4248, 1970............................**$45.00**
TV Tap Stars, Lowe #990, 1952 ....**$25.00**
Victory Volunteers, Merrill #3424, 1942......................**$125.00**
Walt Disney's Pinocchio, Whitman #935, 1939...........**$200.00**
Wishnik Cut-Outs, Whitman #1965, 1965 ....**$40.00**
Wonderful World of the Brothers Grim, Saalfield, #1336, 1962...**$40.00**

Pencil Sharpeners

The whittling process of sharpening pencils with pocketknives was replaced by mechanical means in the 1880s. By the turn of the century, many ingenious desk-type sharpeners had been developed. Small pencil sharpeners designed for the purse or pocket were produced in the 1890s. The typical design consisted of a small steel tube containing a cutting blade which could be adjusted by screws. Mass-produced novelty pencil sharpeners became popular in the late 1920s. The most detailed figurals were made in Germany. These German sharpeners that originally sold for less than a dollar are now considered highly collectible!

Disney and other character pencil sharpeners have been produced in Catalin, plastic, ceramic, and rubber. Novelty battery-operated pencil sharpeners can also be found. For over fifty years pencil sharpeners have been used as advertising giveaways — from Baker's Chocolates' and Coca-Cola's metal figurals to the plastic 'Marshmallow Man' distributed by McDonald's. As long as we have pencils, new pencil sharpeners will be produced, much to the delight of collectors.

Advisors: Phil Helley; Martha Hughes (See Directory, Pencil Sharpeners)

Bakelite, Bambi figural, WDP, 1¾x1"...........................**$95.00**
Bakelite, Dopey, figural, 1¾", VG.................................**$95.00**
Bakelite, Dumbo, WDP, figural, 1⅝", EX....................**$85.00**
Bakelite, elephant, figural, 1x1⅝"...............................**$45.00**
Bakelite, Hep Cats, round & fluted, 1½x½", EX.........**$65.00**
Bakelite, Jiminy Cricket, figural, WDP, 1939, 2", EX ...**$95.00**
Bakelite, Joe Carioka, WDP, 1¼"................................**$40.00**
Bakelite, Lampwick figural, 1⅝x1⅛"............................**$100.00**
Bakelite, Mickey Mouse in metal framed center, WDP, 1" square, EX...**$150.00**
Bakelite, Minnie Mouse, 1x¾" **$75.00**
Bakelite, Panchito, WDP, 1", EX..................................**$45.00**

Bakelite, photo of Spanky in metal ring, octagonal, 1¼x1¼" **$125.00**
Bakelite, Pluto, WDP, 1⅜" **$45.00**
Bakelite, Popeye, figural, King Features Syndicate, 1929, 1¾", EX...**$85.00**
Bakelite, Scottie Dog, Czechoslovokia, 1930s, 1½", EX .**$40.00**
Bakelite, Shmoo (L'il Abner), figural, 1950s, 2⅛".......**$65.00**
Bakelite, Timothy Mouse, WDP, 1¼x1¾", VG **$175.00**
Bakelite, Tower of Americas from the 1968 Hemisfair, Made in Japan, 1¼x3"...................................**$25.00**
Bakelite, US Army Tank, 2" **$60.00**
Bakelite, WWII fighter plane, 2¼x2¾" **$65.00**

Celluloid, elephant figural, from $45.00 to $75.00. (Photo courtesy Shirley Dunn)

Celluloid, Pinocchio, figural, marked Japan, 3".......**$100.00**
Ceramic, Quick Draw McGraw, 1960s, 2", EX...........**$35.00**
Metal, Black man face w/hat & bow tie, Made in Japan, 2" **$65.00**
Metal, Coco-Cola bottle, figural, 1¾" **$30.00**
Metal, cuckoo clock, diecast, Germany, 2"...............**$75.00**
Metal, Deco piano player, Germany, 1¾x1¾"............**$95.00**
Metal, dolphin, made in Miguel South Africa, 2⅜" **$45.00**
Metal, Eiffel Tower, Germany, 2x1x1"......................**$75.00**
Metal, Empire State Building, figural, 5" **$40.00**
Metal, English guard in guardhouse, Germany, 1½x1½" ..**$75.00**
Metal, frog sitting wearing crown, Germany, 1¼x1¼" .**$65.00**
Metal, George Washington bust, Germany, 1⅝x1¼" ..**$75.00**
Metal, Lifebouy Toilet Soap, 1x¾x½" **$95.00**
Metal, Mayflower sailing ship, Made in Japan, 2¼x2" ...**$35.00**
Metal, Mississippi warship, figural, in original box.....**$35.00**
Metal, rabbit sitting upright, Germany, 1¾x1½" **$65.00**
Metal, rifle, Japan, 3½" **$75.00**
Metal, soccer player on base, Germany, 1⅝x1¼".....**$110.00**
Metal, Surcouf Warship, figural, in original box..........**$35.00**
Metal, Thunderbird Convertible, removable plastic top, spare tire on rear, in original box..................**$35.00**
Metal, trumpet, Germany, 2⅛x⅝"........................**$60.00**
Metal, Uncle Sam, full-figure, walking, 2x1".................**$75.00**
Plastic, gun shape w/G-Man decal, 1¼x2" **$25.00**
Plastic, My Unico, cylindrical w/painted detail, Sanrio Co, 1984, 1¾"...**$25.00**
Plastic, Raggedy Andy, figural sitting on base w/Keep Sharp w/Raggedy Andy, electric, Janex, 1974, 6½" **$25.00**
Plastic, Unisphere, New York World's Fair, in original box..**$35.00**

Plastic, US Army tank, Keep 'em Rolling, 1⅞"...........**$40.00**
Plastic, Wiggle TV, girl w/hula hoop, ca 1960s, 2x2x1", EX...**$75.00**
Tin litho, Atlas holding up globe, Germany, 1⅝" dia globe, 2¾"...**$75.00**

Pennsbury Pottery

From the 1950s throughout the 1960s, this pottery was sold in gift stores and souvenir shops along the Pennsylvania Turnpike. It was produced in Morrisville, Pennsylvania, by Henry and Lee Below. Much of the ware was hand painted in multiple colors on caramel backgrounds, though some pieces were made in blue and white. Most of the time, themes centered around Amish people, barber shop singers, roosters, hex signs, and folksy mottos.

Much of the ware is marked, and if you're in the Pennsylvania/New Jersey area, you'll find a lot of it. It's fairly prevalent in the Midwest as well and can still sometimes be found at bargain prices.

Advisor: Shirley Graff (See Directory, Pennsbury)

Ashtray, Amish, 5"..**$25.00**
Ashtray, Pennsbury Inn, 8" **$45.00**
Bank, Hershey Kisses, 4"...................................**$20.00**
Bowl, Delft Toleware, 9"...................................**$40.00**
Bowl, Dutch Talk, 9".......................................**$90.00**
Bowl, pretzel; Red Barn, 12x8" **$150.00**

Bowl, Rooster, two-part, 9½x6¼", $50.00.

Candle holder, Holly, 5½"...................................**$45.00**
Candlesticks, hummingbirds, #117, 5", pr..................**$250.00**
Charger, St George Slaying the Dragon, 13½"...........**$225.00**
Coaster, Doylestown Trust Company, 1896-1958, 5"...**$25.00**
Coaster, Quartet, face of 1 of 4 men, 5", ea **$20.00**
Compote, Holly, 5" **$45.00**
Cookie jar, Harvest, w/lid, 8"..............................**$150.00**
Cup & saucer, Hex **$30.00**

Desk basket, Layfayette, 4" $60.00
Dispensers, oil & vinegar; Amish, 7", pr.................$150.00
Figurine, Blue Jay, #108, 10½" $400.00
Figurine, Chickadee, #111, 3½" $110.00
Figurine, Marsh Wren, #106, 6½" $120.00
Figurine, Nut Hatch, #110, 3½" $120.00
Figurine, rooster & hen, white leghorn, pr $450.00
Figurine, Wood Duck, #114, facing right, 10" $375.00
Mug, beverage; Red Barn, 5" $60.00
Mug, coffee; Eagle, 3¼" $25.00
Pie pan, Picking Apples, 9"...$85.00
Pie plate, Red Rooster, 9"...$55.00
Pitcher, Gay Ninety, 7¼" $125.00
Pitcher, Tulip, 4" $40.00
Plaque, Mercury Dime, 8" $65.00
Plaque, Picking Flowers, 6" $40.00
Plaque, Swallow the Insult, 5x7" $50.00
Plaque, The Bark, Charles W Morgan, 11x8" $110.00
Plaque, Walking to Homestead, 6" $40.00
Plate, Black Rooster, 10"...$35.00
Plate, Blue Dowery, 10" $35.00
Plate, Courting Buggy, 8" $85.00
Plate, Harvest, 11"...$90.00
Plate, Tree Tops, 1960-69, ea......................................$45.00
Plate, Two Birds Over Heart, 11" $85.00
Powder jar/casserole, Hex, w/lid, 6½"........................$65.00
Tile, Red Rooster, 6" square...$30.00
Tray, Colt 31 Caliber, 7½x5" $50.00
Tray, dresser; Tulip, pastel shades, 7½x4"..................$35.00
Tray, Horses, octagonal, 5x3" $30.00
Tray, relish; Tulip, 3-part, triangular, 14½x11½" $95.00

Pepsi-Cola

People have been enjoying Pepsi-Cola since before the turn of the century. Various logos have been registered over the years; the familiar oval was first used in the early 1940s. At about the same time, the two 'dots' between the words Pepsi and Cola became one, though more recent items may carry the double-dot logo as well, especially when they're designed to be reminiscent of the old ones. The bottle cap logo came along in 1943 and with variations was used through the early 1960s.

Though there are expensive rarities, most items are still reasonable, since collectors are just now beginning to discover how fascinating this line of advertising memorabilia can be. There are three books in the series called *Pepsi-Cola Collectibles*, written by Bill Vehling and Michael Hunt, which we highly recommend. Another good reference is *Introduction to Pepsi Collecting* by Bob Stoddard. For more information we recommend *Value Guide to Advertising Memorabilia* by B.J. Summers (Collector Books).

Note: In the descriptions that follow, P-C was used as an abbreviation for Pepsi-Cola; the double-dot logo is represented by the equal sign.

Advisor: Craig Stifter (See Directory, Pepsi-Cola)

Newsletter: *Pepsi-Cola Collectors Club Express*
Bob Stoddard, Editor
P.O. Box 817
Claremont, CA 91711; Send SASE for information.

Ashtray, ceramic, mini Pepsi bottle w/lamp shade in center of round dish, Bill's Novelties embossed on bottom, EX+ $275.00
Bottle carrier, cardboard, 6-pack, 12 Full Servings/P=C logo on horizontal stripes, 1950, VG $35.00
Bottle carrier, wood, 6-pack, dowel handle, 1940, EX..$100.00
Bottle carrier, wood, 6-pack, triangular ends stamped w/red Bottles, P=C logos on front & back, cut-out handle, EX+ $140.00
Bottle opener, metal triangular shape w/Drink Pepsi-Cola engraved on handle, 1950s, EX+ $20.00
Calendar, 1944, Our America, framed, 22x17", EX......$30.00
Calendar, 1947, complete, NM....................................$85.00

Clock, plastic, light-up, 1950s, VG, $175.00. (Photo courtesy Gary Metz)

Clock, rectangular light-up w/curved metal backdrop, even numbers, Say Pepsi Please, 1960s, 18x12", EX.....$80.00
Clock, round, Be Sociable/Have a Pepsi, sm bottle cap on yellow & white, glass front, metal frame, 1955, 15" dia, NM $875.00
Coaster, Ask for Pepsi=Cola/The Perfect Mixer, contour logo, 1940, 4¼" dia, EX+ $15.00
Dispenser, streamline style, Drink P=C Ice Cola Ice Cold, red, white & blue, NM, from $525 to $600.00
Dispenser, wooden barrel w/stainless steel interior, painted blue w/red stripes between metal bands, 2 taps, 30", EX $415.00
Display rack, wire, 3-tiered w/diecut bottle cap logo, 1940s, 42x22", VG $175.00
Door handle, tin, Enjoy P=C on top tab, Bigger/Better on bottom tab, red, white & blue, 1940s, EX $150.00
Door push bar, porcelain, Have a Pepsi flanked by bottle cap logos on yellow, 1950s, 3x32", EX....................$125.00
Game, Big League Baseball, 1950s-60s, EX..............$100.00
Lighter, slanted bottle cap on yellow, 2½", NM..........$85.00
Menu board, tin blackboard w/wood-look frame & red rope border, Drink P=C/Bigger-Better, 1940s, 30x20", NM+..$250.00

Menu board, tin blackboard w/yellow border, Have a Pepsi slogan & bottle cap logo above, 1950s, 30x20", NM+ .**$175.00**

Miniature six-pack, yellow-striped cardboard carrier w/6 swirl glass bottles w/caps, 2½", EX........................**$70.00**

Napkin holder, trapezoidal w/bottle cap logo on white center band, Drink on blue ends, 1940s, EX **$350.00**

Pocketknife, P-C 5¢ in blue on bone handle, 3", EX..**$60.00**

Radio, red, white & blue fountain dispenser shape w/leather strap, Say Pepsi Please, 1950s, EX+ **$375.00**

Sign, cardboard, self-framed, Certified Quality, lady lounging on floor w/Pepsi, bottle cap logo, 1940s, 22x28", EX+ .**$650.00**

Sign, cardboard stand-up/hanger, Say Mix Mine w/P=C for a Grand Rum Drink, red, white & blue, 1950s, 39x33", EX+ **$225.00**

Sign, celluloid stand-up/hanger, bottle cap shape, Drink P-C, 1950s, 9" dia, EX+..**$100.00**

Sign, glass on free-standing wooden base, bottle cap left of 20¢/10¢, yellow, 1950s-60s, 12x17", NM............**$200.00**

Sign, light-up, molded plastic Santa waving w/Pepsi bottle in toy bag, easel-back, 1960s, EX+ **$150.00**

Sign, masonite flange, P=C bottle-cap shape, 1940s, 12x13", G **$220.00**

Sign, paper, Ice Cold Pepsi...More Bounce to the Ounce, clown holding bottle cap, red, white & blue, 1940s, 28x20", EX..**$200.00**

Sign, porcelain, Drink (upper left), P=C cap in center, Iced lower right on yellow, rounded corners, 1950s, 12x29", NM+ **$500.00**

Sign, tin, Ice Cold Drinks on starry sky above stream, polar bear & bottle cap, 1960s-70s, 23x23", EX+ **$525.00**

Sign, tin bottle cap shape, P-C, 1950s, 20", NM+ **$375.00**

Syrup can, 1-gal, red, white & blue bands, P-C bottle caps on center bands, 1951, EX...**$65.00**

Tape measure, chrome Zippo lighter-type case w/gray plastic bottom, EX **$45.00**

Thermometer, dial type w/glass lens, metal frame, Drink P-C Ice-Cold, red, white & blue, 1951, 12" dia, NM+.........**$1,000.00**

Thermometer, tin, Any Weather's Pepsi Weather on card w/ribbon, bottle cap above, 1950s, 25x9", NM ..**$250.00**

Thermometer, tin, Say Pepsi Please/Pepsi (block letters) logo below, yellow, 1967, 28", EX **$75.00**

Toy truck, Marx, plastic flatbed w/wooden wheels, bottle cap decals on doors, EX+ **$75.00**

Tray, P=C bottle cap in center, round w/straight deep sides, 12" dia, EX..**$150.00**

Whistle, plastic double bottle shape, 3", EX................**$80.00**

Perfume Bottles

Here's an area of bottle collecting that has come into its own. Commercial bottles, as you can see from our listings, are very popular. Their values are based on several factors. For instance, when you assess a bottle, you'll need to note: is it sealed or full, does it have its original label, and is the original package or box present.

Figural bottles are interesting as well, especially the ceramic ones with tiny regal crowns as their stoppers.

Advisor: Monsen & Baer (See Directory, Perfume Bottles)

Club: International Perfume Bottle Association (IPBA)
Coleen Abbott, Membership Secretary
396 Croton Rd.
Wayne, PA 19087; Membership: $45 USA or $50 Canada

German porcelain, Dutch boy figural, metal crown stopper, 3", $85.00. (Photo courtesy Monsen and Baer Auctions)

Ann Klein II, clear w/black lid, ⅛-oz, MIB **$30.00**

Avon, Perfume Petite Mouse, frosted glass w/gold head & tail, ¼-oz, 1970, MIB **$17.50**

Babs, Forever Yours, clear heart w/brass ball cap & chain held by 2 metal hands under glass dome, gold label, 3".**$190.00**

Blue Waltz, cobalt heart shape w/label, full, 3", NM ..**$32.00**

Bourjois, Evening in Paris, cobalt w/silver label, full, 15-oz, M **$18.00**

Brajan, Matin Clair, clear Deco stacked squares & circle design, 2½", MIB **$100.00**

Charbert, Amber, clear w/molded rays around base, gold tag at neck, empty, 2½", in sm gold box....................**$25.00**

Christian Dior, Diorama, clear w/vertical ribs, gold metal cap, 2⅜", M in black pouch & pink satin-lined box..**$120.00**

Christian Dior, Miss Dior, clear urn shape w/molded ring 'handles,' some perfume remaining, 3¾", in white & gold box..**$132.00**

Christian Dior, Miss Dior, laydown w/ribbon at neck, 3½", MIB **$35.00**

Coty, A Suma, frosted w/buffed highlights, 1930s, 2¼"..**$40.00**

Coty, Emeraude, frosted bottle w/metal cap & base, emerald stone dangle at neck, 2½", MIB **$88.00**

Coty, L'Origan, frosted w/foil label, Lalique, 5½"+stopper..**$30.00**

D'Orsay, Fantastique, clear w/molded ribs (resembling piece of ice), gold label, 3", w/original black pouch.....**$66.00**

D'Orsay, Fantistique, clear elongated pyramid form w/sharply pointed stopper, gold label, ca 1952, 5½", NMIB...**$188.00**

D'Orsay, Intoxication, clear w/pleated sides, silver metal cap, near empty, 2¼", in original box **$65.00**

Dana, Voodoo, clear w/black cap, mounted on metal base, 2¾", 1950s, in diamond-shaped black & gold box **$110.00**

Darnee, Jasmin, clear square w/brown frosted glass stopper, gold label, 3x2¼", in original satin-lined box **$38.00**

Elizabeth Arden, My Love, clear w/frosted feather-shaped stopper, 3⅜", in gold foil box w/tassel & Lucite door **$360.00**

Estee Lauder, Knowing, solid perfume pineapple shape w/gold & green enameling, MIB **$85.00**

Estee Lauder, White Linen, unopened, .09 fluid oz, 1½x1", MIB **$20.00**

Estee Lauder, Youth Dew, gold metal container for solid perfume, 1½x2", M in fitted blue box **$40.00**

Evital, Eve, clear w/massive cross-shaped stopper, applied medallion on front, 3½", empty, in original box...**$145.00**

Hattie Carnegie, Carnegie Blue, clear shouldered bottle w/face stopper, half full, 2½", NMIB **$180.00**

Helena Rubenstein, Command Performance, clear triangular shape w/gold metal cap, 2", in gold box **$110.00**

Hilberts, Stolen Sweets, decanter shape w/gem-like stopper, sealed, 7" **$120.00**

Jackie Collins, black cat lid w/green rhinestone eyes, black bottle w/gold spots, 2-oz, 1994 ....**$22.50**

Jacques Fath, Fath's Love, clear w/molded pleats & gold label, nearly full, 2¾", in green box **$77.50**

Jean Patou, Moment Supreme, clear w/blown-out 'bubbles,' silver foil label, 2½"..**$32.50**

Jeanne Lanvin, black glass, glass dauber & rubber atomizer, gold spout, 3½x2½", NM **$60.00**

La Duchessa di Parma, Vera Violetta, frosted urn shape w/flame stopper, molded classical heads ea side, 5¼" **$90.00**

Lancome, Magie, clear square form w/indented square center, gold metallic labels, gold cap, 2¼", MIB........**$35.00**

Lancome, Magie, frosted wand shape w/molded stars, gold label, gold metal cap, unopened, 5", MIB **$80.00**

Laura Ashley No 1, concentrated cologne, spray bottle, 2-oz **$80.00**

Lubin, Ocean Bleu, clear w/molded ridges, gold label, gold cap, nearly full, 2⅛", in cream-colored box **$65.00**

Lucien Lelong, clear feather shape, round screw-on ball stopper, no labels, 2¼"..**$40.00**

Lucien Lelong, Sirocco travel set, 3 items: cologne, solid perfume & vial, in gold box w/celluloid cover, unused............**$22.50**

Mary Chess, Tapestry, cream perfume solid in shape of pocketwatch w/red stones & cameo in center, 2", w/gold box...**$110.00**

Mary Chess, White Lilac, clear knight chess-pc shaped bottle, white enamel label, 4⅜", MIB **$65.00**

Mary Dunhill, Flowers of Devonshire, ribbed ball w/silver label, full, sealed, 3", in floral box **$330.00**

Matchabelli, Beloved, enameled blue & gold crown-shape bottle & stopper, empty, 2¼", in original box....**$165.00**

Ralph Lauren, Tuxedo, square black bottle, near full, 4-oz **$70.00**

Revlon, Moon Drops, solid perfume in golden metal apple shape on gold chain, 1½", M in green flocked box .**$65.00**

Richard Hudnut, Deauville, clear w/scalloped sides, gold label on bottom, 2⅜", in teal silk bag (worn)......**$55.00**

Schiaparelli, So Sweet, clear rectangular bottle w/cube stopper, gold label on front, unopened, 3¾", MIB...**$155.00**

Schiaparelli, Soucis, cube stopper, black & gold label, 3", NM...**$48.00**

Waterford Crystal, Lismore, gold & green label, 5⅞"..**$72.50**

Waterford Crystal (Marquis), Sweet Memories, heart-shaped top, 4", M **$25.00**

Worth, Dans la Nuit, cobalt ball shape, matching stopper w/molded name & crescent moon, 1¾" **$65.00**

Worth, Je Reviens, light blue glass w/worn label, marked R Lalique, 3"..**$78.00**

Worth, Miss Worth, clear geometric diamond shape, ca 1977, 4½"..**$100.00**

Yardley, Freesia, clear w/4 molded protrusions at top, gold label, nearly full, 2½", w/floral box **$25.00**

Lucien Lelong, Tailspin, miniature, 2½", $20.00.
(Photo courtesy Monsen and Baer Auctions)

Pez Candy Dispensers

Though Pez candy has been around since the late 1920s, the dispensers that we all remember as children weren't introduced until the 1950s. Each had the head of a certain character — a Mexican, a doctor, Santa Claus, an animal, or perhaps a comic book hero. It's hard to determine the age of some of these, but if yours have tabs or 'feet' on the bottom so they can stand up, they were made in the last ten years. Though early on, collectors focused on this feature to evaluate their finds, now it's simply the character's head that's important to them. Some have variations in color and design, both of which can greatly affect value.

Condition is important; watch out for broken or missing parts. If a Pez is not in mint condition, most are worthless. Original packaging can add to the value, particularly if it is one that came out on a blister card. If the card has special graphics or information, this is especially true. Early figures were sometimes sold in boxes, but these are hard to find. Nowadays you'll see them offered 'mint in package,' sometimes at premium prices. But most intense Pez collectors say that those cellophane bags add very little if any to the value.

For more information, refer to *A Pictorial Guide to Plastic Candy Dispensers Featuring Pez* by David Welch; *Schroeder's Collectible Toys, Antique to Modern* (Collector Books); and *Collecting Toys #6* by Richard O'Brien.

Advisor: Richard Belyski (See Directory, Pez)

Newsletter: *Pez Collector's News*
Richard and Marianne Belyski, Editors
P.O. Box 124
Sea Cliff, NY 11579; 516-676-1183; www.peznews.com;
Subscription: $19 for 6 issues

Angel, no feet	$60.00
Baloo, w/feet	$20.00
Barney Bear, no feet	$40.00
Barney Bear, w/feet	$30.00
Batman, no feet	$15.00
Batman, no feet, w/cape	$100.00
Batman, w/feet, blue or black, ea, from $3 to	$5.00
Captain America, no feet	$100.00
Charlie Brown, w/feet, from $1 to	$3.00
Charlie Brown, w/feet & tongue	$20.00
Daffy Duck, no feet	$15.00
Dalmatian Pup, w/feet	$50.00

Donald Duck and Mickey Mouse, no feet, from $10.00 to $15.00.
(Photo courtesy Michael Stern)

Dumbo, w/feet, blue head	$25.00
Elephant, no feet, orange & blue, flat hat	$90.00
Foghorn Leghorn, w/feet	$95.00
Gorilla, no feet, black head	$100.00
Gyro Gearloose, w/feet	$6.00
Hulk, no feet, dark green	$60.00
Hulk, no feet, light green, remake	$3.00
Indian Maiden, no feet	$175.00

Jiminy Cricket, no feet	$200.00
Knight, no feet	$300.00
Lamb, no feet	$15.00
Lamb, w/feet, from $1 to	$3.00
Lion w/Crown, no feet	$100.00
Mexican, no feet	$250.00
Monkey Sailor, no feet, w/white cap	$50.00
Mowgli, w/feet	$15.00
Nurse, no feet, brown hair	$175.00
Octopus, no feet, black	$85.00
Papa Smurf, w/feet, red	$6.00
Peter Pez (A), no feet	$65.00
Peter Pez (B), w/feet, from $1 to	$3.00
Pink Panther, w/feet	$5.00
Policeman, no feet	$55.00
Pumpkin (A), no feet, from $10 to	$15.00
Raven, no feet, yellow beak	$60.00
Ringmaster, no feet	$300.00
Rudolph, no feet	$60.00
Scrooge McDuck (A), no feet	$35.00
Scrooge McDuck (B), w/feet	$6.00
Smurf, w/feet	$5.00
Smurfette, w/ft	$5.00
Snow White, no feet	$175.00
Snowman (A), no feet	$10.00
Space Trooper Robot, no feet, full body	$325.00
Sylvester (A), w/feet, cream or white whiskers, ea	$5.00
Teenage Mutant Ninja Turtles, w/feet, 8 variations, ea, from $1 to	$3.00
Tinkerbell, no feet	$275.00
Tyke, w/feet	$15.00
Uncle Sam, no feet	$250.00
Valentine Heart, from $1 to	$3.00
Winnie the Pooh, w/feet	$75.00
Witch, 3-pc, no feet	$10.00
Woodstock, w/feet, from $1 to	$3.00
Woodstock, w/feet, painted feathers	$15.00
Yappy Dog, no feet, orange or green, ea	$65.00
Yosemite Sam, w/feet, from $1 to	$3.00

Pfaltzgraff Pottery

Pfaltzgraff has operated in Pennsylvania since the early 1800s making redware at first, then stoneware crocks and jugs, yellow ware and spongeware in the '20s, artware and kitchenware in the '30s, and stoneware kitchen items through the hard years of the '40s. In 1950 they developed their first line of dinnerware, called Gourmet Royale (known in later years as simply Gourmet). It was a high-gloss line of solid color accented at the rims with a band of frothy white, similar to lines made later by McCoy, Hull, Harker, and many other companies. Although it also came in pink, it was the dark brown that became so popular. Today these brown stoneware lines have captured the interest of young collectors as well as the more seasoned, and they all contain more than enough unusual items to make the hunt a bit of a challenge and loads of fun.

The success of Gourmet was just the inspiration that was needed to initiate the production of the many dinnerware lines that have become the backbone of the Pfaltzgraff company.

A giftware line called Muggsy was designed in the late 1940s. It consisted of items such as comic character mugs, ashtrays, bottle stoppers, children's dishes, a pretzel jar, a cookie jar, etc. All of the characters were given names. It was very successful and continued in production until 1960. The older versions have protruding features, while the later ones were simply painted on.

Village, an almond-glazed line with a folksy, brown stenciled tulip decoration, is now discontinued. It's a varied line with many wonderful, useful pieces, and besides the dinnerware itself, the company catalogs carried illustrations of matching glassware, metal items, copper accessories, and linens. Of course, all Pfaltzgraff is of the highest quality, and all these factors add up to a new area of collecting in the making. Several dinnerware lines are featured in our listings. To calculate the values of Yorktowne, Heritage, and Folk Art items not listed below, use Village prices.

For further information, we recommend *Pfaltzgraff, America's Potter,* by David A. Walsh and Polly Stetler, published in conjunction with the Historical Society of York County, York, Pennsylvania.

Christmas Heritage, bowl, soup/cereal; #009, 5½", from $2 to **$3.50**
Christmas Heritage, cheese tray, #533, 10½x7½", from $5 to **$7.00**
Christmas Heritage, pedestal mug, #290, 10-oz.............**$4.50**
Christmas Heritage, plate, dinner; #004, 10", from $4 to ..**$5.50**
Gourmet Royale, ashtray, #AT32, skillet shape, 9", from #10 to **$15.00**
Gourmet Royale, ashtray, #321, 7¾", from $12 to **$15.00**
Gourmet Royale, ashtray, 12", from $15 to.................**$18.00**
Gourmet Royale, baker, #321, oval, 7½", from $18 to..**$20.00**
Gourmet Royale, baker, #323, 9½", from $20 to.........**$24.00**
Gourmet Royale, bean pot, #11-1, 1-qt, from $20 to..**$22.00**
Gourmet Royale, bean pot, #11-2, 2-qt, from $28 to..**$30.00**
Gourmet Royale, bean pot, #11-3, 3-qt.......................**$35.00**
Gourmet Royale, bean pot, #11-4, 4-qt.......................**$45.00**
Gourmet Royale, bean pot, #30, w/lip, lg, from $45 to..**$50.00**
Gourmet Royale, bean pot warming stand..................**$12.00**
Gourmet Royale, bowl, #241, oval, 7x10", from $15 to..**$18.00**
Gourmet Royale, bowl, cereal; #934SR, 5½" **$6.00**
Gourmet Royale, bowl, mixing; 6", from $8 to **$14.00**
Gourmet Royale, bowl, mixing; 8", from $12 to **$14.00**
Gourmet Royale, bowl, salad; tapered sides, 10", from $25 to **$28.00**
Gourmet Royale, bowl, soup; 2¼x7¼", from $6 to **$8.00**
Gourmet Royale, bowl, spaghetti; #319, shallow, 14", from $15 to **$20.00**
Gourmet Royale, bowl, vegetable; #341, divided, from $20 to **$24.00**
Gourmet Royale, butter dish, #394, ¼-lb stick type ...**$12.00**
Gourmet Royale, butter warmer, #301, stick handle, double spout, 9-oz, w/stand, from $18 to **$22.00**

Gourmet Royale, candle holders, tall, w/finger ring, 6", pr, from $25 to..**$35.00**
Gourmet Royale, canister set, 4-pc, from $60 to.........**$75.00**
Gourmet Royale, casserole, hen on nest, 2-qt, from $75 to **$95.00**
Gourmet Royale, casserole, individual, #399, stick handle, 12-oz, from $10 to **$12.00**
Gourmet Royale, casserole, stick handle, 1-qt, from $15 to.**$18.00**
Gourmet Royale, casserole, stick handle, 3-qt, from $25 to.**$30.00**
Gourmet Royale, casserole, stick handle, 4-qt, from $32 to.**$40.00**
Gourmet Royale, casserole-warming stand.................**$10.00**
Gourmet Royale, chafing dish, w/handles, lid & stand, 8x9", from $30 to..**$35.00**
Gourmet Royale, cheese shaker, bulbous, 5¾", from $18 to..**$22.00**

Gourmet Royale, chip 'n dip, two-piece set, with stand, #306, from $30.00 to $35.00.

Gourmet Royale, chip 'n dip, #311, molded in 1 pc, 12", from $22 to..**$30.00**
Gourmet Royale, coffee server, on metal & wood stand, 10¾", from $100 to..**$125.00**
Gourmet Royale, creamer, #382, from $5 to.................**$7.00**
Gourmet Royale, cruet, coffeepot shape, fill through spout, 5", from $20 to **$22.00**
Gourmet Royale, cup, from $2 to.................................**$3.00**
Gourmet Royale, cup & saucer, demitasse **$18.00**
Gourmet Royale, egg/relish tray, 15" L, from $22 to ..**$28.00**
Gourmet Royale, gravy boat, #426, 2-spout, lg, +underplate, from $14 to..**$16.00**
Gourmet Royale, gravy boat, w/stick handle, 2-spout, from $15 to..**$20.00**
Gourmet Royale, jug, #384, 32-oz, from $32 to **$36.00**
Gourmet Royale, jug, #386, ice lip, from $40 to **$48.00**
Gourmet Royale, ladle, sm, from $12 to.....................**$15.00**
Gourmet Royale, ladle, 3½" dia bowl w/11" handle, from 18 to..**$20.00**
Gourmet Royale, Lazy Susan, #220, 5-part, molded in 1 pc, 11", from $22 to **$28.00**
Gourmet Royale, Lazy Susan, #308, 3 sections w/center bowl, 14", from $32 to..**$36.00**

Gourmet Royale, mug, #391, 12-oz, from $6 to **$8.00**

Gourmet Royale, mug, #392, 16-oz, from $12 to.......**$14.00**

Gourmet Royale, pie plate, #7016, 9½", from $14 to .**$18.00**

Gourmet Royale, plate, dinner; #88R, from $3.50 to.....**$4.50**

Gourmet Royale, plate, egg; holds 12 halves, 7¾x12½", from $20 to **$22.00**

Gourmet Royale, plate, grill; #87, 3-section, 11", from $18 to..**$20.00**

Gourmet Royale, plate, salad; 6¾", from $3 to **$4.00**

Gourmet Royale, plate, steak; 12", from $15 to **$20.00**

Gourmet Royale, platter, #320, 14", from $20 to.........**$25.00**

Gourmet Royale, platter, #337, 16", from $25 to.........**$30.00**

Gourmet Royale, rarebit, #330, w/lug handles, oval, 11", from $15 to **$18.00**

Gourmet Royale, relish dish, #265, 5x10", from $15 to..**$17.00**

Gourmet Royale, roaster, #325, oval, 14", from $30 to ..**$35.00**

Gourmet Royale, roaster, #326, oval, 16", from $50 to ..**$60.00**

Gourmet Royale, salt & pepper shakers, #317/#318, 4½", pr, from $12 to **$14.00**

Gourmet Royale, salt & pepper shakers, bell shape, pr, from $25 to **$35.00**

Gourmet Royale, scoop, any size, from $15 to **$18.00**

Gourmet Royale, serving tray, round, 4-section, upright handle in center **$22.00**

Gourmet Royalc, shirred egg dish, #360, 6", from $10 to ..**$12.00**

Gourmet Royale, souffle dish, #393, 5-qt, +underplate, from $65 to **$70.00**

Gourmet Royale, sugar bowl, from $5 to **$7.00**

Gourmet Royale, teapot, #381, 6-cup, from $18 to.....**$22.00**

Gourmet Royale, tray, tidbit; 2-tier, from $15 to **$18.00**

Gourmet Royale, tray, 3-part, 15½" L, minimum value...**$35.00**

Heritage, butter dish, #002-028, from $6 to **$8.00**

Heritage, cake/serving plate, #002-529, 11¼" dia, from $9 to **$12.00**

Heritage, cup & saucer, #002-002, 9-oz...........................**$3.00**

Heritage, soup tureen, #002-160, 3½-qt, from $25 to.**$35.00**

Muggsy, ashtray **$125.00**

Muggsy, bottle stopper, head, ball shape **$85.00**

Muggsy, canape holder, Carrie, lift-off head pierced for toothpicks, from $125 to...**$150.00**

Muggsy, cigarette server...**$125.00**

Muggsy, clothes sprinkler bottle, Myrtle, Black, from $275 to **$375.00**

Muggsy, clothes sprinkler bottle, Myrtle, white, from $250 to **$350.00**

Muggsy, cookie jar, character face, minimum value.**$250.00**

Muggsy, mug, action figure (golfer, fisherman, etc), any, from $65 to **$85.00**

Muggsy, mug, Black action figure............................**$125.00**

Muggsy, mug, character face, ea, from $35 to **$38.00**

Muggsy, shot mug, character face, ea, from $40 to **$50.00**

Muggsy, tumbler **$60.00**

Muggsy, utility jar, Handy Harry, hat w/short bill as flat lid, from $175 to..**$200.00**

Planter, donkey, brown drip, common, 10", from $15 to...**$20.00**

Planter, elephant, brown drip, scarce, from $90 to ..**$100.00**

Village, baker, #236, rectangular, tab handles, 2-qt, from $12 to **$15.00**

Village, baker, #237, square, tab handles, 9", from $10 to **$14.00**

Village, baker, #24, oval, 10¼", from $8 to **$10.00**

Village, baker, #240, oval, 7¾", from $6 to...................**$8.00**

Village, bean pot, 2½-qt..**$35.00**

Village, beverage server, #490, from $24 to................**$28.00**

Village, bowl, batter; w/spout & handle, 8", from $35 to...**$42.00**

Village, bowl, fruit; #008, 5"..**$4.00**

Village, bowl, mixing; #453, 1-qt, 2-qt, & 3-qt, 3-pc set, from $50 to..**$60.00**

Village, bowl, rim soup; #012, 8½" **$6.00**

Village, bowl, serving; #010, 7", from $8 to **$12.00**

Village, bowl, soup/cereal; #009, 6" **$4.50**

Village, bowl, vegetable; #011, 8¾", from $12 to **$15.00**

Village, bread tray, 12", from $15 to **$18.00**

Village, butter dish, #028...**$8.00**

Village, canisters, #520, 4-pc set, from $50 to **$60.00**

Village, casserole, w/lid, #315, 2-qt, from $18 to........**$25.00**

Village, coffee mug, #89F, 10-oz, from $6 to................**$8.00**

Village, coffeepot, lighthouse shape, 48-oz, from $30 to ..**$35.00**

Village, cookie jar, #540, 3-qt, from $18 to.................**$25.00**

Village, creamer & sugar bowl, #020, from $9 to **$12.00**

Village, cup & saucer, #001 & #002...........................**$3.50**

Village, flowerpot, 4½", from $15 to **$20.00**

Village, gravy boat, #443, w/saucer, 16-oz, from $12 to...**$15.00**

Village, ice bucket, canister w/lid **$175.00**

Village, onion soup crock, #295, stick handle, sm, from $6 to **$8.00**

Village, pedestal mug, #90F, 10-oz **$4.50**

Village, pitcher, #416, 2-qt, from $20 to.....................**$25.00**

Village, plate, dinner; #004, 10¼", from $3 to..............**$4.50**

Village, platter, #016, 14", from $18 to........................**$22.00**

Village, quiche, 9", $20.00; measuring cups, from $6.00 to $8.00 each.

Village, soup tureen, #160, w/lid & ladle, 3½-qt, from $40 to **$45.00**

Village, spoon rest, #515, 9" L, from $6 to....................**$7.50**

Village, table light, #620, clear glass chimney on candle holder base, from $12 to **$14.00**

Pie Birds

Pie birds are hollow, china or ceramic kitchen utensils. They date to the 1800s in England, where they were known as pie vents or pie funnels. They are designed to support the upper crust and keep it flaky. They also serve as a steam vent to prevent spill over.

Most have arches on the base and they have one, and *only* one, vent hole on or near the top. There are many new pie birds on both the US and British markets. These are hand painted rather than airbrushed like the older ones.

The Pearl China Co. of East Liverpool, Ohio, first gave pie birds their 'wings.' Prior to the introduction in the late 1920s of an S-neck rooster shape, pie vents were non-figural. They resembled inverted funnels. Funnels which contain certain advertising are the most sought after.

The first bird-shaped pie vent produced in England was designed in 1933 by Clarice Cliff, a blackbird with an orange beak on a white base. The front of the base is imprinted with registry numbers. The bird later carried the name Newport Pottery; more recently it has been marked Midwinter Pottery.

Advisor: Linda Fields (See Directory, Pie Birds)

Newsletter: Pie Birds Unlimited
Patricia Donaldson, Editor
PO Box 192
Acworth, GA 30101-0192

Advertisemant, TG Green, on pie funnel, England, 1993 to present **$10.00**
Benny the Baker, all white, Far East Import, 4¾".....**$150.00**
Bird, cobalt, stoneware, New Hampshire pottery, new, 4¼" **$20.00**
Black chef, yellow, red & white attire, brown spoon, Taiwan, 4½" **$10.00**
Blackbird, 2-pc, marked Royal Worchester, England, 1960-mid-1980s **$75.00**
Blackbird on log, marked Artone Pottery England **$50.00**
Bluebird, black speckles, heavy pottery, US, 1950s....**$50.00**
Boy w/'Pie Boy' painted down leg, USA...................**$300.00**
Canary, yellow w/pink lips...**$40.00**
Crow dressed as chef, holds pie, marked SB, England, new...**$30.00**
Elephant on drum, marked CCC (Cardinal China), solid pink base..**$120.00**
Funnel, Pyrex glass..**$30.00**
Funnel, white, unmarked, England **$15.00**
Green Willow, decaled, new **$15.00**
Humpty Dumpty..**$50.00**
Morton 'patches' pie bird, USA.....................................**$30.00**
Pelican on stump, yellow bill & feet, England............**$52.50**
Rooster, multicolor, Cleminson **$45.00**
Royal Commemorative pie funnel, England **$35.00**
Snowman w/pie, dressed in hat, scarf & mittens, ceramic **$45.00**

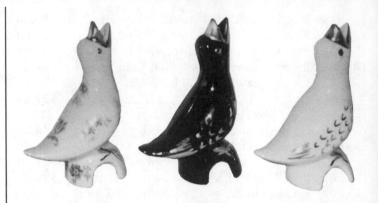

Songbirds trimmed in gold, Chic Pottery, Zanesville, Ohio, 1936 – 61, from $125.00 to $150.00. (Photo courtesy Linda Fields)

Witch, holding pie, w/painted bird flying out, marked SB **$40.00**

Pierce, Howard

Howard Pierce studied at the Chicago Art Institute, California's Pomona College and the University of Illinois. He married Ellen Van Voorhis of National City, California, who was also to become his business partner. Howard worked alongside William Manker for a short time, and today it is sometimes difficult tell one artist's work from the other's without first looking at the marks. This is especially true with some of their vases, nut cups, trays, and cups and saucers.

Howard was creative with his designs and selective with his materials. Since Howard worked at Douglas in Long Beach, California, during World War II, it is thought that pewter may have been one of the first mediums he worked with. The pewter lapel pins he created early on are considered very desirable by today's collectors and usually sell in the $200.00 to $300.00 range. He dabbled in polyurethane for only a short time as he found he was allergic to it. Today these polyurethane pieces — made nearly exclusively for his immediate family — are scarce and costly. They are extremly lightweight, usually figures of birds on bases. They were hand painted, and many of them have a powdery feel. Howard made a few pieces from aluminum and bronze. Bisque, cement, and porcelain (some with Mount St. Helen's ash) were also used for a limited number of items. (Be cautious not to confuse Howard's 'textured' items with the Mount St. Helen's ash pieces.) Howard's creativity extended itself to include paper as a workable medium as well, as he often made their own Christmas cards. His love for wildlife was constant throughout his career, and he found porcelain to be the best material to use for wildlife models.

Howard's earliest mark was probably 'Howard Pierce' in block letters. This was used on metalware (especially the lapel pins), but also can be found on a few very small ceramic animals. After the Pierces moved to Claremont, California, they used this mark: 'Claremont Calif. Howard Pierce,' usually with a stock number. A rubber stamp 'Howard Pierce

Porcelains' was used later. Eventually 'Porcelains' was omitted. Not all pieces are marked, especially when part of a two- or three-piece set. As a rule, only the largest item of the set is marked.

In 1992 due to Howard's poor health, he and Ellen destroyed all the molds they had ever created. Later, with his health somewhat improved, he was able to work a few hours a week, creating miniatures of some of his original models and designing new ones as well. These miniatures are marked simply 'Pierce.' Howard Pierce passed away in February 1994. For further information see *Collector's Encyclopedia of Howard Pierce Porcelain* by Darlene Hurst Dommel (Collector Books).

Advisor: Susan Cox (See Directory, California Pottery)

Bank, turtle, black high gloss w/green high gloss shell, 3x8" **$175.00**
Bowl, maroon w/gold interior, 4x8½" **$100.00**
Brooch, dog, pewter, 3¾" **$265.00**
Creamer & sugar bowl, orange to yellow gloss, 2½" .**$100.00**
Figurine, bison, white high gloss, 2½x3⅜" **$75.00**
Figurine, dolphin riding wave, brown to black matt w/orange highlights, 9½x6½" **$200.00**
Figurine, gazelle, Art Deco, brown & white, 11" **$185.00**
Figurine, gazelle, brown high gloss, #100P, 4x11¼".**$125.00**
Figurine, girl holding bird, experimental glaze, blue, green, 7¼" **$95.00**
Figurine, goose, gray high gloss, 6¼x7" **$25.00**
Figurine, hippopotamus, blue, 2½x6½" **$175.00**
Figurine, hippopotamus, dark green, 10" L................**$175.00**
Figurine, hummingbird, brown & white, 6" **$125.00**
Figurine, mother bear, standing on hind legs, 7"........**$75.00**
Figurine, native female, black & white matt, 2½x7¼" ...**$95.00**
Figurine, quail (2) in tree, 3¼x9" **$100.00**
Figurine, robin, black w/orange breast, 3½x4½"........**$75.00**
Figurines, hen & rooster, brown & white, #251P, 7½", 9¼", pr **$125.00**
Flower arranger, St Francis of Assisi w/birds, greenish brown to blue matt, unmarked, 6½x11½"....................**$225.00**

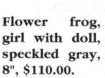

Flower frog, girl with doll, speckled gray, 8", $110.00.

Planter, pale blue w/white gazelles on dark blue, 2½x9¾"..**$175.00**
Vase, chartreuse gloss w/bisque standing fawn & tree, 11½" **$110.00**
Vase, deep green gloss w/matt white deer & bisque tree insert, 11½" **$125.00**
Vase, green gloss w/white bisque fish insert, 8".......**$140.00**
Whistle, sparrow, brown & white, 2¾" **$170.00**

Pin-Back Buttons

Literally hundreds of thousands of pin-back buttons are available; pick a category and have fun! Most fall into one of three fields — advertising, political, and personality related, but within these three broad areas are many more specialized groups. Just make sure you buy only those that are undamaged, are still bright and unfaded, and have well-centered designs and properly aligned printing. The older buttons (those from before the 1920s) may be made of celluloid with the paper backing printed with the name of a company or a product.

See also Political.

Advisor: Michael McQuillen (See Directory, Pin-Back Buttons)

Archie Club Member, face image, red, white & blue, 1960s, 1½", M (w/membership card, letter & envelope) ...**$75.00**
Basketball Dream Team, McDonald's, 1994, M **$5.00**
Bat Kids Fan Club, bust portrait on silver, 1966, 2½", NM..**$35.00**
Batman & Robin, I'm a Batman Crime Fighter, red, white & blue, 1⅜", EX **$20.00**
Batman & Robin, Join the Secret Society, color image of Batman & Robin, 1966, 3½", MIP **$25.00**
Beatles, black & white group photo w/names in red on white background, NM **$25.00**
Beatles, I Still Love the Beatles, red, white & blue, 3½", EX **$25.00**
Beauty & the Beast, heart shape, 1991 ....**$5.00**
Betty Boop, black on cream, Cabaret, Cinema, 1960s, 1½", VG..**$40.00**
Bugs Bunny, Six Flags Over Georgia, multicolored image of Bugs w/carrot, 1981, NM..**$6.00**
Cat in the Hat, Happy 30th Anniversary, black, white & orange, 1987, 2½", EX..**$25.00**
Cisco Kid, I Eat Cisco Kid's Butter-Nut Bread, white w/red lettering, 1950s, 1", VG......................................**$25.00**
Creepy Magazine Fan Club, monster in center, 1968, 2½", EX..**$25.00**
Darkwing Duck, multicolored, 1990s, 3", NM **$3.00**
Davy Crockett Indian Fighter, yellow & red image of Davy w/rifle on the frontier, 1950s, 1½", EX **$15.00**
Dick Tracy, Authorized Guide to Dick Tracy/50th Anniversary, 2¼", M **$25.00**
Disneyana Convention Center, flasher, 1994, 4", NM..**$10.00**
Dumbo D-X, red & gray on white, 1¼", NM **$35.00**

Effanbee Dolls, Finest & Best, bluebird above pink & blue lettering on yellow background, ¾", VG **$18.00**

Famous Monsters Club, Phantom of the Opera, 1974, 2½", EX...**$25.00**

Flash Gordon, image of Flash having sword fight w/Ming, 1974, 3", NM..**$20.00**

Gene Autry, photo on blue, purple or red backgrounds, 1950s, 1¼", EX, ea **$25.00**

Hank Aaron, Thanks Milwaukee, 1954-1976, full color w/black lettering, 2¼", EX **$15.00**

Hard Rock Cafe, Save the Planet We Recycle, M **$5.00**

Hopalong Cassidy Daily in Chicago Tribune, red background, 1¼", NM..**$45.00**

Ideal Fun & Games Day, green, blue, red & white, 4", EX..**$25.00**

Incredible Hulk, Official Member Super Hero Club, Button World, 1966, 3", NM..**$25.00**

Ink Spots/Decca Records, group photo on yellow background, 3½", NM..**$15.00**

Iron Man, Official Member Super Hero Club, Button World, 1966, 3 " dia, MIP **$50.00**

Jackie Gleason Fan Club, Awa-a-ay We Go!, image of Jackie in checked suit, 1½", EX.....................................**$35.00**

John Travolta for President, image of John wearing Uncle Sam top hat, Midland Records, 1976, 1⅜", EX.....**$20.00**

KISS, Madison Square Garden, WPLJ Radio, NYC, Dec, 1977, M **$18.00**

Lassie, I Voted for Lassie, 1950s, NM **$35.00**

Little Mermaid, purple lettering, Disney, 1980s, 3", NM..**$3.00**

Mad, What Me Worry? I'm Voting Mad — Alfred E Neuman for President, color image of Alfred, 1960s, 2½", NM...**$75.00**

Marvel Comics Convention '75, various characters surround lettering, red, yellow & white, 3", NM **$30.00**

Mickey Mouse's 60th Birthday, shows Mickey shaking hands w/Steamboat Willie, 1988, 3", NM..........................**$10.00**

Mork From Ork, full-color photo, Paramount, 1979, EX...**$8.00**

Spider-Man Official Member Super Hero Club, Button World, 1966, 3", MIP, $50.00. (Photo courtesy Bill Bruegman)

Official Member Superman Club, white w/multicolored image, 3½", NM **$22.00**

Oliver & Co, 1988, 3", M..**$5.00**

Peace, cartoon image of Garfield-type cat in Santa hat w/arm around mouse sitting atop piece of cheese, M.......**$4.00**

Peanuts, Snoopy Come Home, yellow, 1972, 6", M....**$15.00**

Peanuts, You're a Good Man Charlie Brown, Charlie Brown on pitcher's mound, orange background, 1½", VG **$12.00**

Pocahontas, features characters, Disney, 1995, rectangular, NM..**$4.00**

Pocahontas, Sing Along Songs video button, 1995, rectangular, NM **$8.00**

Popeye the Sailor, 1980s, 1¼", M **$5.00**

Rescuers Down Under, set of 4 showing faces of major characters, Disney, 1980s, 2⅛", NM **$10.00**

Rin-Tin-Tin, Every Kid Needs a Super Dog, black & white, 2¼", EX..**$5.00**

Roy Rogers, My Pal, black, red & white, 1950s, 1¾", EX..**$75.00**

Roy Rogers & Trigger, black & white photo on yellow, w/attached red & yellow ribbon, 1950s, 1¾", EX.**$50.00**

Santa's Visitor North Pole NY, green & red image of Santa, reindeer & house on white, NM............................**$2.00**

Scroogebusters Since 1969, stop symbol w/lettering superimposed over bust image of Scrooge, multicolored, M..**$3.00**

Sea World, Shamu & His Crew, multicolored image, NM..**$5.00**

Shmoo Club, black & white image on green metal, Sealtest premium, 1948, 1" dia, EX+.................................**$30.00**

Snow White & the Seven Dwarfs, set of 8 by Benay-Albee, 1975, 4", EX..**$60.00**

St Thomas Rodeo Homecoming October 18th 1940, cowboy on horse w/Whoa Johnny in rope lettering, blue & white, 2", NM **$25.00**

Tarzan, image on blue background, 1974, 3", NM......**$25.00**

Tom & Jerry, Stroehmann's Bread, red, white & black, 1⅛", EX..**$25.00**

Toy Story, Buzz Lightyear, theatre employee button, 3", rare, NM **$15.00**

Toy Story, video release, 1995, rectangular, NM **$10.00**

Trix Rabbit, Yes! Let the Rabbit Eat Trix, General Mills, 1976, EX..**$15.00**

Yogi Bear, School Police Parents, multicolor image of Yogi wearing DARE shirt, NM **$4.00**

Yogi Bear for President, red, white & blue, 1964, 3", EX **$35.00**

Kellogg's Pep Pins

Chances are if you're over fifty, you remember them — one in each box of PEP (Kellogg's wheat-flake cereal that was among the first to be vitamin fortified). There were eighty-six in all, each carrying the full-color image of a character from one of the popular cartoon strips of the day — Maggie and Jiggs, the Winkles, Dagwood and Blondie, Superman, Dick Tracy, and many others. Very few of these cartoons are still in print.

The pins were issued in five sets, the first in 1945, three in 1946, and the last in 1947. They were made in Connecticut by the Crown Bottle Cap Company, and they're marked PEP on the back. You could wear them on your cap, shirt, coat, or the official PEP pin beanie, a orange and white cloth cap made for just that purpose. The Superman pin — he was the only D.C. Comics Inc. character in the group — was included in each set.

Values are given for pins in near mint condition; prices should be sharply reduced when foxing or fading is present. Any unlisted pins are worth from $10.00 to $15.00.

Advisor: Doug Dezso (See Directory, Candy Containers)

Bo Plenty, NM	**$30.00**
Corky, NM	**$16.00**
Dagwood, NM	**$30.00**
Dick Tracy, NM	**$30.00**
Early Bird, NM	**$6.00**
Fat Stuff, NM	**$15.00**
Felix the Cat, NM	**$85.00**
Flash Gordon, NM	**$30.00**
Flat Top, NM	**$30.00**
Goofy, NM	**$10.00**
Gravel Girtie, NM	**$15.00**
Harold Teen, NM	**$15.00**
Inspector, NM	**$12.50**
Jiggs, NM	**$25.00**
Judy, NM	**$10.00**
Kayo, NM	**$20.00**
Little King, NM	**$15.00**
Little Moose, NM	**$15.00**
Maggie, NM	**$25.00**
Mama De Stross, NM	**$30.00**
Mama Katzenjammer, NM	**$25.00**
Mamie, NM	**$15.00**
Moon Mullins, NM	**$10.00**
Navy Patrol, NM	**$6.00**
Olive Oyle, NM	**$30.00**
Orphan Annie, NM	**$25.00**
Pat Patton, NM	**$10.00**
Perry Winkle, NM	**$15.00**

Phantom, NM, $80.00. (Photo court esy Doug Dezso)

Pop Jenks, NM	**$15.00**
Popeye, NM	**$30.00**
Rip Winkle, NM	**$20.00**
Skeezix, NM	**$15.00**
Superman, NM	**$45.00**
Toots, NM	**$15.00**
Uncle Walt, NM	**$20.00**
Uncle Willie, NM	**$12.50**

Winkles Twins, NM	**$90.00**
Winnie Winkle, NM	**$15.00**

Pinup Art

Some of the more well-known artists in this field are Vargas, Petty, DeVorss, Elvgren, Moran, Ballantyne, Armstrong, and Phillips, and some enthusiasts pick a favorite and concentrate their collections on only his work. From the mid-thirties until well into the fifties, pinup art was extremely popular. As the adage goes, 'Sex sells.' And well it did. You'll find calendars, playing cards, magazines, advertising, and merchandise of all types that depict these unrealistically perfect ladies. Though not all items will be signed, most of these artists have a distinctive, easily identifiable style that you'll soon be able to recognize.

Unless noted otherwise, values listed below are for items in at least near-mint condition.

Advisor: Denis Jackson (See Directory, Pinup Art)

Newsletter: *The Illustrator Collector's News*
Denis Jackson, Editor
P.O. Box 1958
Sequim, WA 98382; 360-452-3810
www.olypen.com/ticn
e-mail: ticn@olypen.com

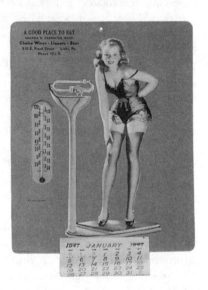

Calendar, 1947, illustrated by Elvgren, 12x8", EX, $135.00.
(Photo courtesy Dunbar Gallery)

Ad for Jergen's Face Powder, Vargas, black-haired girl on stomach holding medal, 1943, 11x9", M **$12.00**
Blotter, Elvgren, Anchors A-Wow, 1951, NM **$11.00**
Blotter, Elvgren, Drawing Attention, girl w/easel & brush, salesman's sample, 1950s, 4x9", NM **$10.00**
Blotter, Moran, Chief Attraction, Indian girl, 1944, NM ...**$12.00**
Blotter, Moran, When a Girl Says No, Brown & Bigelow, 1953, EX **$8.00**
Blotter, Mozert, leggy girl in short military-style garb w/great dane, Brown & Bigelow, 1940s, EX **$8.00**

Book, Playboy's Vargas Girls, Playboy Press, coyright 1972, paperback, NM......**$50.00**

Booklet, Pinups by Zoe Mozert, Brown & Bigelow, 11 pages, early 1940s, 4x5", EX......**$100.00**

Calendar, Armstrong, Brown & Bigelow, 1958, 21x14", EX......**$65.00**

Calendar, DeVross, 1959, 32x16", NM......**$60.00**

Calendar, Elvgren, Fascination, 1954, 17x10", NM (w/original envelope)......**$40.00**

Calendar, Esquire/Chiriaka, 1953, 9x11", EX......**$45.00**

Calendar, Esquire/Chiriaka, 1954, EX (w/original envelope)......**$50.00**

Calendar, Esquire/Moore, 1951, 11x8½", EX......**$40.00**

Calendar, Esquire/Petty, 1947, 12x9", EX+......**$50.00**

Calendar, Esquire/Petty, 1955, 11x8", EX......**$40.00**

Calendar, Esquire/Varga, 1944, 12x8½", EX......**$45.00**

Calendar, Moran, The Artist's Model, 1937, 23x11", metal strips both ends, NM......**$100.00**

Calendar, Moran, 1943, A Modern Eve, Brown & Bigelow, 32½x11¼", EX+......**$355.00**

Calendar, Moran, 1948, automotive advertising, 14x8", EX.**$40.00**

Calendar, Moran, 1949, The Maid of Baltimore, 40x16", EX+.**$50.00**

Calendar, Mozert, 1942, Texaco advertising, 19x10", EX.**$60.00**

Calendar, Nickel, JF; How's Your Morale, 1947, GMC advertising, 45x23", VG......**$145.00**

Calendar, Sinclair girl, 1940, service station advertising, metal strips both ends, NM......**$170.00**

Calendar, Wicks, Ren; Harold's Club, 1969, 26x20", NM...**$35.00**

Calendar, Zoe Mozert, Winners All, 1951, 23x11", NM......**$75.00**

Cartoon, Petty, I Suppose This Bum Check Is Your Idea of a Joke!, Esquire, EX......**$15.00**

Cartoon, Petty, Talk About Gratitude, Esquire, EX.....**$12.00**

Date book, Randall, 12 pages, 1952, 9½x16", EX......**$65.00**

Gatefold, Ludlow, Anita Ekberg in sheet, Esquire, NM...**$18.00**

Gatefold, Vargas, Curves Are Trumps, redhead in yellow swimsuit dropping cards, Esquire, July, 1941, EX......**$70.00**

Greeting card, MacPherson, fully dressed girl undresses as card unfolds, EX......**$14.00**

Magazine print, Vargas, blond in sheer white gown & silver heels, Esquire, 1940, 14x10", NM......**$14.00**

Memo pad, MacPherson, The MacPherson Sketches of 1948, 12 pages, NM......**$90.00**

Mutoscope card, Armstrong, On the Beam, brunette in low-cut costume w/straw hat tied around her neck, EX......**$12.00**

Mutoscope card, Mozert, A Run on Sugar, blond in black lingerie & stockings, M......**$10.00**

Mutoscope card, Mozert, blond in military garb being chased by unseen pursuer, 1940s, NM......**$10.00**

Playing cards, Armstrong, Remembrance, Brown & Bigelow, 1939, unused, M (VG box)......**$50.00**

Playing cards, Elvgren, American Beauties, different girl on ea card, Brown & Bigelow, 1950s, NMIB......**$100.00**

Playing cards, Vargas, Esquire, 1941, MIB (sealed).....**$65.00**

Poscard, Petty, linen, TWA, WWII era, NM......**$40.00**

Poster, Bird Busters III, girl in short open vest & skimpy shorts holding shotgun while seated on AA shells, 28x17", NM......**$45.00**

Poster, Bird Busters Offer You More, blond in white skin-tight bodysuit & glasses w/arms behind head on black, 28", NM......**$45.00**

Poster, Super Galena Motor Oil/First Choice for All Seasons, sexy girls on snow skis & water skis, 1950s, 34x58", NM......**$120.00**

Poster, The Petty Girl, blond in maroon teddy, 22x14", VG......**$50.00**

Print, Buell, All American Girl, 11x13", EX......**$18.00**

Print, DeVross, portrait of pretty redhead looking over her shoulder, NM......**$35.00**

Print, Elvgren, Ankles Away, sailor girl w/dress blowing in the wind, 1940s, 9½x7", NM......**$15.00**

Print, Elvgren, Barrel of Fun, girl on barrel w/guitar, 1968, 16x20", EX......**$40.00**

Print, Elvgren, Slip Off Shore, girl standing on rocky shore w/row boat & dog floating away, 1950s, 6x5", NM..**$10.00**

Print, Kohn, Living Art, reclining nude, 9½x7½", NM...**$12.50**

Print, Mozert, Anytime, girl in strapless white gown & flower, 1951, 11x23", EX......**$50.00**

Program, Ice Capades; Petty drum majorette on skates, 1943, EX......**$50.00**

Program, Petty, Ice Capades, I'm 21, redhead against blue background, 1961, EX......**$55.00**

Punchboard, 26 girls on stand-up base, used in bars, 1940s, NM......**$30.00**

Sign, paper litho, Kist Orange, smiling blond in black low-cut black dress w/bottle, signed Elvgren, 18x14", VG.**$210.00**

Sketch pad, The Butcher Takes the Best Cuts Home, 1954, 9x14", EX......**$100.00**

Playing Cards

Here is another collectible that is inexpensive, easy to display (especially single cards), and very diversified. Among the endless variations are backs that are printed with reproductions of famous paintings and pinup art, carry advertising of all types, and picture tourist attractions and world's fair scenes. Early decks are scarce, but those from the '40s on are usually more attractive anyway, so pick an area that interests you most and have fun! Though they're usually not dated, you may find some clues that will help you to determine an approximate date. Telephone numbers, zip codes, advertising slogans, and patriotic messages are always helpful.

Everett Grist has written an informative book, *Advertising Playing Cards* (published by Collector Books), which we highly recommend to anyone interested in playing cards with any type of advertising.

See also Pinup Art

Club/Newsletter: American Antique Deck Collectors
52 Plus Joker Club
Clear the Decks, quarterly publication
Larry Herold, Auctioneer
300 E. 34th St., Apt. 6E
New York, NY 10016; e-mail: herojr@banet.net

ACE Transportation Co, Brown & Bigelow, bridge size, 1950, MIB **$40.00**

Alice in Wonderland, Alice & White Rabbit backs, Western Publishing, 1950s, 52, no Joker, VG in worn box..**$20.00**

American Pipe, Brown & Bigelow, 52+2 Jokers, ca 1942, NMIB **$6.00**

Amtrak, Hoyle, 52+2 Jokers, 1987, NMIB **$10.00**

Baltimore & Ohio Railroad, scenic backs, 1953, VG-, no box **$25.00**

Bass Pro Shops, fishing lure backs, WW Concepts, double deck, 1986, NM in paper box **$25.00**

Beaux Belle, pocket size, 1950s, 2x2¾", MIB, sealed.**$12.50**

Bicycle #808, Emblem, blue backs, 52 (no Joker), VG ..**$25.00**

Bowl-Up, bowling cartoons, Stancraft, 1965, 52+2 Jokers, NMIB..**$15.00**

Bowlers Victory Legion, Western Publishing, ca 1945, 52+Joker, EXIB...**$22.00**

Butchart Gardens, Victoria BC, Japan souvenir deck, MIB **$3.00**

Canadian National, oval souvenir scenes, narrow, 52+Joker+score card, c 1935, VG in torn box **$25.00**

Canteen Capers, Western Playing Cards, narrow, 1940s, 52 (no Joker)+extra card, M, no box **$15.00**

Carling Black Label Beer, beer can-shaped cards, Remembrance, 1950s, MIB...............................**$15.00**

Cartoonists' Pack, Carta Mundi, 1980, 52+4 Jokers, NMIB ..**$50.00**

Charger sports team, 1969, M in celluloid wrapper **$6.00**

Circus Circus, US Playing Cards, 52+2 Jokers+extra card, NMIB..**$3.00**

Colonial Art Playing Cards, Morgan Press, nonstandard 3¼x4⅞", Block illustrations, 52+Joker+extra card, EXIB..**$22.00**

Dallas Cowboy Cheerleaders, color photos, 52+2 Jokers+title card, NMIB **$10.00**

Edward Waite Tarot, 1970s Dutch version, 78+blank-faced card, MIB...**$20.00**

General Electric Refrigerators, sphinx & refrigerator backs, narrow, 52, no Joker, NM, no box **$10.00**

Golden Nugget, US Playing Cards, 52+Joker+special Ace, ca 1972, EXIB...**$3.00**

Goldwater Campaign, nonstandard courts, 1964, MIB, sealed **$40.00**

Goldwater for President, AU H20 on backs, face on courts, 1966, MIB...**$50.00**

Greyhound, Service to All 84 States, narrow, 1950s, MIB, sealed **$35.00**

Heileman's Old Style, 1960s, MIB, sealed...................**$27.50**

Honeymoon in Vegas, Gemaco, 1993, M in celluloid wrapper...**$2.00**

Ireland, Irish Tourist Association, Dublin, oval photos, 52 selected views, 52+2 Jokers, 1950, EXIB...............**$15.00**

Mary Lee Candies, Brown & Bigelow, narrow, special Aces, 52+special Joker+fact card, NM in G box............**$16.50**

Museum of Modern Art, NY City, Takenobu Igarishi, Austria, double deck, 1993, MIB **$18.00**

Nesquik, Disney characters on repeated courts, Nestle, 52+Joker, NM, no box **$16.00**

New York World's Fair, unisphere backs, Stancraft, fair photo each card, 52+2 Jokers, gold edge, M in plastic box **$12.00**

Ohio State University, football field backs, MIB...........**$2.00**

Olympic Games, Los Angeles, US Playing Cards, 1984, MIB **$5.00**

Personalities Souvenir, 52 different photo backs, nonstandard 1⅝x2¼", cheap paper, EX.......................................**$12.50**

Politicards, political caricatures, 1971, M in celluloid wrapper...**$16.00**

Politicards, political caricatures on courts, Keith Nichols, Jimmy Carter on original box, 1980, MIB, sealed .**$10.00**

Pontiac Tempest, US Playing Cards, double deck, ca 1968, MIB **$14.00**

Pullman Bridge Playing Cards, red & gold backs, double logo on Joker, 52+Joker+score card, VG in G- box **$10.00**

Ripley's Believe It or Not, 52 cartoons, Stancraft, 1962, 52+2 Jokers, EXIB **$15.00**

Salvador Dali Poker, from Tarot Universal deck of 78, 1984, 52+2 Jokers+score card, MIB **$100.00**

Scenic views of Hong Kong China, ca 1970, M in cellophane wrapper **$6.00**

Scottie dog backs, United States Playing Card Company, ca 1932, from $10.00 to $20.00 per deck. (Photo courtesy Candace Sten Davis and Patricia J. Baum)

Smithsonian Institute, famous person backs, double deck, MIB **$10.00**

Snap-On Tools Western, M in worn box **$5.00**

Snoopy Playing Cards, Snoopy as sports fan backs, Hallmark, 52+2 Jokers, NMIB...**$10.00**

Souvenir of Seven Falls Colorado, Brown & Bigelow, 52+Joker, 1940-65, NMIB.......................................**$8.00**

Tee-Up, golf cartoons, Creative Playing Cards, 1962, 52+2 Jokers, NMIB..**$15.00**

Time Magazine Commemorative, retro style w/Hardy-type courts, Whitney style Aces, 52+Joker+fact card, MIB..............**$50.00**

Trip Trap, ea pip cards has different narcotic, courts & Aces carry warnings, Stancraft, 1970, NMIB **$40.00**

TWA Collector's Series, Douglas DC-9, US Playing Cards, 1966, M in celluloid wrapper...............................**$12.00**

Union Pacific, Zion National Park backs, 52 (no Joker), NMIB **$18.00**

USS General Randall Navy vessel Arrco, 52+extra card in worn paper slip box...**$6.00**

Vanity Fair, US magazine covers on 10s through Aces, 52+2 special Jokers, NMIB **$25.00**

Vargas Pin-Up, Esquire, 1941, 52+Joker+special card, NMIB **$45.00**

World Beauty Hong Kong, full-face picture of all nudes, 52+Joker, MIB...**$20.00**

250th Birthday of Detroit MI, double deck, Brown & Bigelow, 104+4 Jokers, 1951, M in VG box..........**$10.50**

Political Memorabilia

Political collecting is one of today's fastest-growing hobbies. Between campaign buttons, glassware, paper, and other items, collectors are scrambling to acquire these little pieces of history. Before the turn of the century and the advent of the modern political button, candidates produced ribbons, ferrotypes, stickpins, banners, and many household items to promote their cause. In 1896 the first celluloid (or cello) buttons were used. Cello refers to a process where a paper disc carrying a design is crimped under a piece of celluloid (now acetate) and fastened to a metal button back. In the 1920s the use of lithographed (or litho) buttons was introduced.

Campaigns of the 1930s through the 1990s have used both types of buttons. In today's media-hyped world, it is amazing that in addition to TV and radio commercials, candidates still use some of their funding to produce buttons. Bumper stickers, flyers, and novelty items also still abound. Reproductions are sometimes encountered by collectors. Practice and experience are the best tools in order to be aware.

One important factor to remember when pricing buttons is that condition is everything. Buttons with any cracks, stains, or other damage will only sell for a fraction of our suggested values. Listed below are some of the items one is likely to find when scrutinizing today's sales.

For more information about this hobby, we recommend you read Michael McQuillen's monthly column 'Political Parade' in *Antique Week* newspaper.

Advisor: Michael McQuillen (See Directory, Political)

Club: A.P.I.C. (American Political Items Collectors) of Indiana
Michael McQuillen
P.O. Box 50022
Indianapolis, IN 46250-0022
e-mail: mcquillen@politicalparade.com or website: www.politicalparade.com; National organization serving needs of political enthusiasts; send SASE for more information

Ashtray, Lyndon Johnson in gold on side of white ceramic cowboy hat, 6½" **$17.00**

Badge, Ike 1954 Indiana Republican State Convention, blue, white & gold, celluloid, 1½", EX **$55.00**

Badge, Johnson (Keating for US Senate), felt, stick-on type, 3", EX...**$25.00**

Badge, Republican National Convention Assistant Door Keeper, purple ribbon, 1960, EX **$50.00**

Badge, Republican National Convention Delegate at Large, blue & yellow ribbon, 1956, EX **$75.00**

Badge, John Kennedy multicolor portrait button above flasher of White House and Capitol, Inauguration information on purple ribbon, 1961, 7¼", EX, $20.00.

Badge, Truman 1949 Inaugural Souvenir, EX on original card...**$20.00**

Badge, Young Republican National Convention, black, white, red & gray celluloid, 1953, w/blue & gold ribbon, EX **$25.00**

Balloon, Wallace for President, unused, 1972 ....**$5.00**

Bottle stopper, Nelson Rockefeller, multicolor figural, 5", EX...**$90.00**

Bottle stoppers, John F Kennedy & Lyndon B Johnson, pr, MIB **$150.00**

Bumper sticker, Kennedy/Johnson jugate, orange & black, NM **$15.00**

Card, MacArthur for President, music on reverse, 1948, 6x8½", EX...**$35.00**

Charm bracelet, Win w/Stevenson, blue on gold w/red rose & green petals, EX...**$25.00**

Doll, Voo-Doo Reaganomics, cloth Reagon doll w/stickpins, 5", EX in original box...**$15.00**

Dollar token, Senator Goldwater, 1964 ....**$5.00**

Hat, LB Johnson, heavy paper, black & cream, folded, 3½" **$5.00**

Key case, Truman Inaugural, leather, It's a Fair Deal w/Harry, St Louis, EX+ **$65.00**

Letter opener/pen, JF Kennedy, Martin L King & RF Kennedy memorial, EX...**$20.00**

License plate, Hoover, black & cream, minor rust......**$30.00**

License plate, Reagan, red, white & blue, 1981, M.....**$10.00**

Lighter, George Bush as Rambo, 3¼", EX **$10.00**

Match book, Dwight D Eisenhower, white house embossed, multicolor, seal on reverse, EX............................**$20.00**

Medal, Ike 1953 Official Inaugural bust, bronze, M....**$35.00**

Mirror, Hoover/Curtis jugate, w/Iowa candidate, black & white, 2", EX **$275.00**

Mirror, JFK portrait, black & white oval, 2¾", EX.......**$25.00**

Pamphlet, Yale Students for McGovern, 1972, 17x11", EX..**$10.00**

Pen, I Swiped This From Harry S Truman, gray, blue, black & white, EX..**$50.00**

Pin-back, JFK Victory, 60 superimposed over V, black & silver, 1", EX..**$40.00**

Pin-back, LBJ for Ex-President, blue & white, 3", EX .**$15.00**

Pin-back, LSD Not LBJ, red on orange, 1¼", VG........**$15.00**

Pin-back, Make Love Not War, red, white & blue, ¾", VG+ .**$15.00**

Pin-back, McGovern/Eagleton, NM **$6.00**

Pin-back, Nixon/Agnew jugate, multicolor oval, Slovak, 1¼", EX...**$10.00**

Pin-back, Peace & Freedom Party, Cleaver/Mage jugate, black & white, 1968, 1½", EX..............................**$15.00**

Pin-back, Reagan Country 1984 Convention, California Delegation pin, multicolor on celluloid, 3", EX .**$100.00**

Pin-back, Register for Peace Indianapolis, blue & white, celluloid, 1970s, 1¼", VG...**$10.00**

Pin-back, Roosevelt for EX President, red, white, blue oval, 1⅝", EX..**$20.00**

Pin-back, Stop the Draft, white on green, celluloid, 1½", VG...**$15.00**

Pin-back, Truman Fights for Human Rights, blue & white, ⅞", EX **$175.00**

Pin-back, Truman for Ex-President, closed-back style, red, white & blue, 2¼", EX.....................................**$35.00**

Pin-back, Vietnam - America's Hungary?, white on blue, celluloid, 1½", VG...**$25.00**

Pin-back, Willkie, black & white litho w/suspended key, NM..**$24.00**

Pin-back, Win w/(JFK portrait), red, white & blue litho, ½", EX..**$45.00**

Plate, President & Mamie Eisenhower portraits, 12", NM..**$25.00**

Poster, Don't Cop Out - Vote!, Vote McDope in '72, Sheridan, Rip Off Press, 23x17½", VG **$45.00**

Poster, Expose - Confront GOP Convention, blue & yellow on red, 1972, 22x17", EX......................................**$35.00**

Poster, Kennedy (Robert) for President, portrait, 1968, 12x16", NM **$37.50**

Poster, Kennedy/Johnson jugate, Two Great Democrats, red, white, blue & black, 27x41", EX...........................**$250.00**

Poster, Ted Roberts holds peace symbol made of wire, tape, stick & board, black & white, 23½x15", NM **$40.00**

Pot holder, Kennedy for President, M..........................**$32.00**

Program, Eisenhower 1953 Inaugural, gold on blue, EX ..**$30.00**

Program, Truman 1949 Inauguration, many pictures, EX .**$40.00**

Ribbon, Truman Reception Committee, paper, EX **$40.00**

Ribbon badge, Citizens for Eisenhower, white on blue, EX...**$25.00**

Ribbon badge, Reagan 1981 Presidential Inaugural Ball Committee, red, white, blue & gold, EX................**$30.00**

Salt & pepper shakers, MacArthur cap & pipe, gold, brown, cream & green on ceramic, EX, pr......................**$55.00**

Sheet music, Hubert Humphrey March, EX.................**$15.00**

Sheet music, I Like Ike, Irving Berlin, red, white & blue, EX...**$25.00**

Stickpin, Ike embossed on side of elephant, NM on original card **$15.00**

Ticket, FDR/Wallace 1941 Inaugural, EX **$30.00**

Porcelier China

The Porcelier Manufacturing Company was founded in East Liverpool, Ohio, in 1926. They moved to Greensburg, Pennsylvania, in 1930, where they continued to operate until closing in 1954. They're best known for their extensive line of vitrified china kitchenware, but it should also be noted that they made innumerable lighting fixtures

The company used many different methods of marking their ware. Each mark included the name Porcelier, usually written in script. The mark can be an ink stamp in black, blue, brown, or green; engraved into the metal bottom plate (as on electrical pieces); on a paper label (as found on lighting fixtures); incised block letters; or raised block letters. With the exception of sugar bowls and creamers, most pieces are marked.

Our advisor for this category, Susan Grindberg, has written the *Collector's Guide to Porcelier China, Identification and Values* (Collector Books).

Advisor: Susan Grindberg (See Directory, Porcelier)

Ball jug, Beehive Crisscross **$90.00**

Batter pitcher, Barock-Colonial, ivory, red or blue, #2014..**$85.00**

Beverage cooler, high or low barrel, ea **$60.00**

Boiler, Beehive Floral Spray, 4-cup.............................**$35.00**

Bowl, spaghetti; Basketweave Wildflowers **$125.00**

Canister, Serv-All, coffee, salt, sugar or tea, platinum trim, ea **$80.00**

Casserole, Country Life, w/lid, 9½"..........................**$110.00**

Casserole, no decal, w/lid..**$30.00**

Creamer and sugar bowl, Tree Trunk, $30.00 each.
(Photo courtesy Susan Grindberg)

Creamer, Basketweave Wild Flowers **$12.00**

Creamer, Flower Pot..**$12.00**

Creamer, Silhouette, part of hostess set **$30.00**

Cup, US Department of Defense **$6.00**

Electric urn, Basketweave Wild flowers.....................**$130.00**

Lighting fixture, single ceiling, floral decor **$30.00**

Lighting fixture, triple ceiling w/Field Flowers decal .**$60.00**

Mug, Wildlife, pheasant, sailfish, hunting dog or horse head, gold trim, ea..**$40.00**

Percolator, Golden Wheat, electric, #120 ....$85.00
Percolator, Pink Flower w/platinum trim, electric.......$60.00
Percolator, Tulips, electric, #10.................................$140.00
Pitcher, Flight, disc form $100.00
Pitcher, Hearth, disc form $85.00
Pitcher, Ribbed Band, 2-cup $35.00
Pitcher, water; Field Flowers..$55.00
Pot, Basketweave Floral, w/decorated dripper, 6-cup ...$85.00
Pot, Basketweave Wildflowers, 6-cup $60.00
Pot, Colonial, Black-Eyed Susan, 6-cup $65.00
Pot, Colonial, no decor, 4-cup...$30.00
Pot, Dainty Rose, 4-cup...$45.00
Pot, Dutch Boy & Girl, gold trim, 8-cup.......................$75.00
Pot, Flight, 8-cup $50.00
Pot, Goldfinches, 4-cup $35.00
Pot, Rooster, 6-cup $125.00
Pot, Solid, tankard shape, no decal, 6-cup..................$30.00
Salt & pepper shakers, many designs & decals, pr, from $20
    to $35.00
Sandwich grill, Scalloped Wild Flowers, from $320 to...$350.00
Sugar bowl, American Beauty Rose, w/lid $18.00
Sugar bowl, Field Flowers w/platinum trim, w/lid $8.00

Teapot, Cameo Floral, six-cup, $90.00.
(Photo courtesy Susan Grindberg)

Teapot, Serv-All, platinum, gold or red & black trim, #3011 ....$55.00
Tray, wooden go-with for Silhouette Hostess Set, #2611 ..$80.00
Urn, Orange Poppy, electric......................................$130.00
Waffle iron, Scalloped Wildflowers, from $225 to $300.00
Wall sconce, Barock-Colonial $40.00

Powder Jars

Ceramics

With figural ceramics becoming increasingly popular, powder jars are desired collectibles. Found in various subjects and having great eye appeal, they make interesting collections. For more information we recommend *Collector's Guide to Made in Japan Ceramics* (there are three in series) by Carole Bess White (Collector Books).

Advisor: Carole Bess White (See Directory, Japan Ceramics)

Bamboo w/flower motif, black & white on orange, Japan, 3½" dia, from $15 to...$20.00
Colonial lady, blue hoop skirt, ¾-figure lid, Japan, 7", from $30 to $45.00

Colonial lady with rose in right hand, bouquet in other, Japan, 7", from $125.00 to $165.00. (Photo courtesy Carole Bess White)

Dog pr, white w/black ears etc, atop basketweave lid (w/fruit decal) & bowl, Japan, 4", from $25 to $45.00
Flapper, orange coat w/white trim, Japan, 4", from $70 to $85.00
Flowers in relief (red, blue & green) over entire dome lid, yellow bowl, Japan, 3¾" dia..................................$20.00
Garden scene, on white background w/blue border, solid blue jar w/gold trim, Noritake, 4¾" dia................$65.00
Heart shape, Oriental lady w/fan on heart shape in center of lid, Noritake, 3", from $300 to $400.00
Lady, half-figure in pink dress w/hands folded, floral decor on pink jar, Noritake, 5", from $295 to...............$355.00
Lady, hoop skirt as lid & bowl, gold & multicolored lustre glazes, Goldcastle, 4", from $65 to........................$85.00
Landscape, fall scene, earth tones, Noritake, green mark #27, 3½" dia $75.00
Oriental lady w/parasol in orange dress atop purple lustre scalloped lid & jar, Noritake, from $295 to $355.00
Pierrot, yellow costume w/multicolored trim, Goldcastle, 4¼", from $75 to..$100.00
Rabbit, ear cocked, on hexagonal lid & bowl, yellow w/multicolored trim, Japan, 5¼", from $45 to $65.00

Glassware

Glassware items such as powder jars, trays, lamps, vanity sets, towel bars, and soap dishes were produced in large quantities during the Depression era by many glasshouses who were simply trying to stay afloat. They used many of the same colors as they had in the making of their colored Depression glass dinnerware that has been so popular with collectors for more than thirty years.

Some of their most imaginative work went into designing powder jars. Subjects ranging from birds and animals to Deco nudes and Cinderella's coach can be found today, and this diversity coupled with the fact that many were made in several colors provides collectors with more than enough variations to keep them interested and challenged.

Advisor: Sharon Thoerner, Glass Powder Jars (See Directory, Powder Jars)

Annabella, pink transparent..**$175.00**
Annette w/2 dogs, crystal **$85.00**
Babs II, pink frost, 3-footed, sm version **$155.00**
Ballerina, pink frost...**$185.00**
Bassett hound, green frost...**$195.00**
Bassett hound, pink frost, from $145 to **$165.00**
Cameo, green frost..**$275.00**
Carrie, black, draped nude figural stem **$195.00**
Cinderella's Coach, pink frost w/black lid, rectangular body, sm footrest for coachman, lg **$195.00**
Cleopatra II, crystal, shallow base, deep lid, 4¾".......**$95.00**
Crinoline Girl, crystal, off-the-shoulder gown, flowers in right hand, embossed bows on skirt...........................**$40.00**
Crinoline Girl, pink frost, off-the-shoulder gown, flowers in right hand, embossed bows on skirt...................**$120.00**
Dancing Girl, blue transparent, feminine features, rope trim at top of base..**$480.00**
Dancing Girl, green frost, feminine features, rope trim at top of base...**$120.00**
Delilah II, green frost **$95.00**
Dolly Sisters, green frost **$225.00**
Elephant w/carousel base, green frost........................**$255.00**
Elephants battling, pink frost.......................................**$135.00**
Godiva, satin, nude seated on diamond-shaped base ..**$185.00**
Gretchen, green transparent **$195.00**
Horse & coach, pink frost, round **$350.00**
Jackie, Jade-ite **$275.00**
Joker, green transparent **$85.00**
Lillian III, crystal, stippled lid, w/hexagonal band......**$50.00**
Lillian VII, pink frost, cone-shaped base **$195.00**
Lovebirds, green frost **$75.00**
Martha Washington, crystal, Colonial lady between boy & girl **$100.00**
Martha Washington, green frost, Colonial lady between boy & girl..**$150.00**
Martha Washington, pink frost, Colonial lady between boy & girl...**$130.00**
Minstrel, crystal **$50.00**
Minstrel, crystal w/green paint **$85.00**
My Pet, 3 Scotties on lid, crystal.................................**$75.00**
My Pet, 3 Scotties on lid, pink transparent...............**$225.00**
Penguins, pink frost, dome top **$300.00**
Rapunzel, pink or green frost, ea...............................**$250.00**
Rin-Tin-Tin, green transparent...................................**$225.00**
Scottie, puff box, Akro Agate, blue............................**$140.00**
Scottie, puff box, Akro Agate, milk glass **$115.00**
Southern Belle, green frost **$195.00**

Sphinx, yellow frost..**$275.00**
Spike Bulldog, pink frost **$125.00**
Terrier, pink frost, sm base **$135.00**
Terrier, pink transparent, lg base, rare......................**$300.00**
Twins, green frost...**$150.00**
Vamp, pink frost, flapper's head forms finial **$120.00**
Victorian Lady, green frost...**$175.00**

Wendy, fully painted, $145.00. (Photo courtesy Sharon Thoerner)

Precious Moments

Precious Moments is a line consisting of figurines, picture frames, dolls, plates, and other items, all with inspirational messages. They were created by Samuel J. Butcher and are produced by Enesco Inc. in the Orient. You'll find these in almost every gift store in the country, and some of the earlier, discontinued figurines are becoming very collectible.

Baby's First Pet, #520705, Flower mark, 1988, suspended in 1994, 5¾", M **$70.00**
Bless Those Who Serve Their Country, #527289, 1991, 5½", MIB **$55.00**
Brotherly Love, #100544, Olive Branch mark, 1986, suspended 1989, 5", M **$85.00**
Cheers to the Leader, #104035, 1987, 5½", M..............**$45.00**
Clowns, girl w/balloon, #12238B, Dove mark, 1984, 4½", M **$25.00**
Congratulations Princess, #106208, Flower mark, 1986, M..**$30.00**
Dawn's Early Light, #PM-831, Cross mark, 1983 Special Edition, 4½", M, from $50 to **$60.00**
Don't Let the Holidays Get You Down, #522112, Bow & Arrow mark, 1988, retired 1993, 4¾", M.............**$95.00**
Dropping In for Christmas, E-2350, 1982, retired, M ..**$52.00**

Eggs Over Easy, #E-3118, Fish mark, 1979, retired 1983, 5½", M..**$75.00**

Faith Is a Victory, #521396, G Clef mark, 1992, retired 1993, MIB w/papers.......................................**$145.00**

Faith Takes the Plunge, #111153, Cedar Tree mark, 1987, 5¾", M...**$45.00**

Friend Is Someone Who Cares, #520632, Bow & Arrow mark, 1988, retired 1995, M...........................**$55.00**

God Bless America, #102938, 1986 Limited Edition, MIB...**$55.00**

God Bless the USA, #527654, Vessel mark, MIB.........**$35.00**

God Is Love Dear Valentine, #523518, retired, M.......**$38.00**

God Sent His Son, #E-0507, Cross mark, 1983, suspended 1987, 5", M...**$40.00**

God Sent You Just in Time, musical, #15504, 1989, retired 1989, 6½", M..**$95.00**

God Understands, E-1379B, 1978, suspended in 1984, Fish mark, 5", M, $85.00.

God's Speed, #E-3112, Fish mark, 1979, retired 1983, 5", M...**$35.00**

Here Is My Song, 2-pc, #12394, 1984, 5", 2", M.........**$35.00**

His Little Treasure, #PM931, 1993 Members only, 4", MIB w/insert..**$32.00**

Honk If You Love Jesus, 2-pc, #15490, Dove mark, 1985, M...**$30.00**

I Believe in Miracles, E-7156, 1983, M.....................**$70.00**

I Get a Bang Out of You, #12262, Olive Branch mark, retired 1997, 1st issue in the Clowns series, MIB.............**$65.00**

Isn't He Precious, #E-5379, Cross mark, 1984, 4¾", M.**$45.00**

Jesus Is the Light, E-1373-G, 1938, M......................**$45.00**

Jesus Is the Sweetest Name I Know, #523097, Bow & Arrow mark, 1988, suspended 1993, 5½", M **$35.00**

Let Love Reign, #E-9273, Fish mark, 1982, 5½", M.....**$65.00**

Lord Bless You & Keep You, #E-4720, 1980, 5¼", MIB ..**$120.00**

Lord Help Me Make the Grade, #106216, Cedar Tree mark, 1987, suspended 1990, 5½", M.............................**$45.00**

Lord Is the Best Gift of All, #110930, Cedar Tree mark, 5½", M...**$35.00**

Lord Keep Me on My Toes, #100129, Dove mark, 1985, retired 1985, 6", M..**$85.00**

Lord Will Carry You Through, #12467, Olive Branch mark, 1985, retired 1988, 6", M...................................**$85.00**

Love Is Kind, E-1379/A, 1983, retired, M...................**$60.00**

Love Rescued Me, #102393, Flower mark, 1985, 5½".**$35.00**

Loving You Dear Valentine, #PM873, Olive Branch mark, 1986, 5½", M..**$35.00**

Make a Joyful Noise, E-1374/G, 1983, M...................**$40.00**

Make Me a Blessing, #100102, Cedar Tree mark, 1986, retired 1990, 5½", M...**$75.00**

May Your Future Be Blessed, #525316, Butterfly mark, 1992, 6", M..**$35.00**

My Days Are Blue Without You, #520802, 1988, suspended 1991, 7", M...**$85.00**

Peace on Earth, E-2804, 1982, retired, M..................**$85.00**

Praise the Lord Anyhow, E-1374/b, 1982, M..............**$60.00**

Purr-fect Grandma, #E-3109, 1979, 5", M..................**$50.00**

Seek & Ye Shall Find, 1985 Collector's Club piece, M...**$26.00**

Sending You My Love, #109967, Bow & Arrow mark, 1989, MIB **$45.00**

Serving the Lord, #100161, Olive Branch mark, 1985, suspended 1990, 5½", M...**$35.00**

Sharing, #PM942, 1994 Members Only, MIB **$45.00**

Sharing a Gift of Love, #527114, Vessel mark, Limited Edition 1991, 5¾", M..**$35.00**

Sharing Sweet Moments Together, #526487, Butterfly mark, 1993, 5½", M...**$50.00**

Sugartown Sam's House, night light, #529605, Butterfly mark, MIB **$90.00**

Summer's Joy, #12076, 1984, limited edition 1985, 6½", M...**$75.00**

Take Time To Smell the Flowers, ornament, 1995, 3½", MIB **$8.00**

Tell It to Jesus, #521477, 1989, MIB **$38.00**

The End Is in Sight, #E-9253, Suspended 1985, MIB w/brown tag **$70.00**

This Is Your Day To Shine, #E-2822, Cross mark, 1983, retired 1988, 5½", M...**$95.00**

Thou Art Mine, E-3113, 1983, M...............................**$50.00**

Time Heals, #523739, 1990, 4¾", MIB **$45.00**

To a Special Dad, #E-5212, Dove mark, 1980, 5½", M..**$30.00**

To a Very Special Mom, E-2824, 1983, 5½", M............**$50.00**

To a Very Special Sister, #E-2825, Cross mark, 1983, 5½", M...**$65.00**

Trust in the Lord to the Finish, #PM842, Cross mark, 1984, 5½", M..**$45.00**

Waddle I Do Without You, #12459, Dove mark, 1985, retired 1989, 5½", M...**$90.00**

Walking By Faith, #E-3117, G Clef mark, 1979, 7½", M..**$65.00**

We Are God's Workmanship, #E-9258, G clef mark, 1982, 5½", M, from $40 to **$50.00**

We're Pulling For You, #106151, Cedar Tree mark, MIB w/papers..**$56.00**

Wedding Arch, #102369, Cedar Tree mark, suspended 1988, MIB **$25.00**

Wishing You a Happy Easter, #109886, 1992, M.........**$30.00**

Wishing You a Perfect Choice, #520845, Bow & Arrow mark, 1989, MIB...**$65.00**

You Are Always There for Me, #163635, 1966, M......**$45.00**

You Are My Happiness, Vessel mark, 1991 Limited Edition, MIB **$55.00**

You Are the Type I Love, #523542, Vessel mark, 1990, 6", M **$45.00**

You Have Touched So Many Hearts, #E-2821, 1983, retired, M **$56.00**

Purinton Pottery

The Purinton Pottery Company moved from Ohio to Shippenville, Pennsylvania, in 1941 and began producing several lines of dinnerware and kitchen items hand painted with fruits, ivy vines, and floral designs in bold brush strokes of color on a creamy white background. The company closed in 1959 due to economic reasons.

Purinton has a style that's popular today with collectors who like the country look. It isn't always marked, but you'll soon recognize its distinct appearance. Some of the rarer designs are Palm Tree, Peasant Garden, and Pennsylvania Dutch, and examples of these lines are considerably higher than the more common ones. You'll see more Apple and Fruit pieces than any, and in more diversified shapes.

For more information we recommend *Purinton Pottery, An Identification and Value Guide,* by Susan Morris.

Advisor: Susan Morris (See Directory, Purinton Pottery)

Apple, bowl, dessert; 4" **$8.00**
Apple, bowl, divided vegetable; 10½" **$35.00**
Apple, bowl, fruit; scalloped border, 12" **$40.00**
Apple, bowl, vegetable; 8½" **$30.00**
Apple, butter dish, 6½" L **$65.00**
Apple, canister set, wooden lids, 7½" coffee & tea, 8" flour & sugar, 4-pc **$75.00**
Apple, coffeepot, w/drip filter, 8-cup, 11" **$110.00**
Apple, cruet, oil & vinegar; 5", pr **$50.00**
Apple, cup & saucer, 2½", 5½" **$13.00**
Apple, grease jar, w/lid, 5½" **$85.00**
Apple, jug, 5¾" **$55.00**
Apple, mug, handled, 8-oz, 4" **$35.00**
Apple, pitcher, Rubel mold, 5" **$75.00**
Apple, plate, breakfast; 8½" **$20.00**
Apple, plate, chop; plain border, 12" **$35.00**
Apple, plate, dinner; 9¾" **$15.00**
Apple, plate, lap; indent for teacup, 8½" **$15.00**
Apple, plate, salad; 6¾" **$10.00**
Apple, platter, meat; 12" **$55.00**
Apple, tray, roll; 11" **$35.00**
Cactus Flower, bowl, fruit; 12" **$85.00**
Chartreuse, coffeepot, 8" **$75.00**
Chartreuse, creamer & sugar bowl, mini, 2" **$40.00**
Chartreuse, platter, grill; 12" **$30.00**
Chartreuse, relish, 3-part w/center handle, 10" **$45.00**
Chartreuse, wall pocket, 3½" **$35.00**
Crescent Flower, coaster, 3½" **$40.00**

Crescent Flower, jar, 3½" **$45.00**
Crescent Flower, salt & pepper shakers, round, 2¾", pr...**$65.00**
Daisy, canister, Tea, red trim, 9" **$60.00**
Daisy, salt & pepper shakers, cobalt trim, range style, 4", pr **$50.00**
Desert Flower, sea horse cocktail dish, 11¾" L **$75.00**
Fruit, bean pot, 5¾", +warming stand (9" overall) **$65.00**
Fruit, canister, round, wooden lid, 7½" **$65.00**

Fruit, casserole, from $75.00 to $80.00.

Fruit, coffeepot, 8-cup, 8" **$65.00**
Fruit, Kent jug, 1-pt, 4½" **$30.00**
Fruit, night bottle, 1-qt, 7½" **$45.00**
Fruit, plate, breakfast (sold in luncheon set); apple, pear, grapes or pineapple, 8½", ea **$30.00**
Fruit, plate, chop; 12" **$45.00**
Fruit, plate, dinner; 9¾" **$20.00**
Fruit, range bowl, red trim, w/lid, 5½" **$45.00**
Fruit, stacking storage jar, 8¼" **$85.00**
Fruit, teapot, 4-cup, 5" **$55.00**
Heather Plaid, cup, 2½" **$10.00**
Heather Plaid, Kent jug, 1-pt, 4½" **$30.00**
Heather Plaid, platter, meat; 12" L **$30.00**
Heather Plaid, roll tray, 11", on 14" stand **$35.00**
Heather Plaid, salt & pepper shakers, Pour 'N Shake, 4¼", pr **$60.00**
Heather Plaid, sugar bowl, w/lid, 4" **$30.00**
Heather Plaid, teapot, 6-cup, 6" **$65.00**
Heather Plaid, wall pocket, 3½" **$35.00**
Intaglio, baker, 7" **$20.00**
Intaglio, bowl, cereal; 5¼" **$10.00**
Intaglio, bowl, divided vegetable; 10½" **$30.00**
Intaglio, butter dish, 6½" L **$55.00**
Intaglio, cup, 2½" **$10.00**
Intaglio, lap plate, 8½" **$15.00**
Intaglio, pitcher, Rubel mold, 5" **$55.00**
Intaglio, plate, dinner; 9¼" **$15.00**
Intaglio, plate, salad; 6¾" **$10.00**
Intaglio, platter, meat; 12" **$30.00**
Intaglio, salt & pepper shakers, jug style, 2½", pr......**$20.00**

Intaglio, soup & sandwich, 11" plate w/2½x4" cup ...**$50.00**
Intaglio, teapot, 6-cup, 6½"..............................**$65.00**
Ivy - Red Blossom, coffeepot, 8".....................**$65.00**
Ivy - Red Blossom, pitcher, beverage, 2-pt, 6¼".........**$55.00**
Ivy - Red Blossom, teapot, 2-cup, 4"...............**$45.00**
Ivy - Yellow Blossom, teapot, 6-cup, 6" **$45.00**
Ivy - Yellow Blossom, teapot, 8-cup, 8" **$50.00**
Maywood, baker, 7"..**$15.00**
Maywood, bowl, dessert; 4" **$6.00**
Maywood, juice mug, 6-oz, 2½"......................**$15.00**
Maywood, Kent jug, 1-pt, 4½".........................**$25.00**
Maywood, plate, chop; 12" **$20.00**
Maywood, plate, dinner; 9¾"..........................**$10.00**
Maywood, platter, grill; 12"............................**$25.00**
Ming Tree, cup & saucer, 2½", 5½" **$20.00**
Ming Tree, pillow vase, 4¼".............................**$35.00**
Ming Tree, planter, 5".....................................**$35.00**
Ming Tree, platter, meat; 12"..........................**$40.00**
Mountain Rose, basket planter, 6¼"..............**$50.00**
Mountain Rose, cookie jar, oval, 9½" **$100.00**
Mountain Rose, creamer & sugar bowl, miniature, 2" **$50.00**
Mountain Rose, jar, marmalade; 4½"...............**$65.00**
Mountain Rose, Rebecca jug, 7½".....................**$45.00**
Mountain Rose, tumbler, 12-oz, 5" **$35.00**
Normandy Plaid, bowl, cereal; 5¼"..................**$10.00**
Normandy Plaid, cookie jar, oval, 9½", from $60 to...**$70.00**
Normandy Plaid, cup & saucer, 2½", 5½" **$13.00**
Normandy Plaid, grease jar, w/lid, 5½" **$60.00**
Normandy Plaid, mug, handled, 8-oz, 4"..........**$25.00**
Normandy Plaid, pitcher, beverage; 2-pt, 6¼"............**$55.00**
Normandy Plaid, plate, dinner; 9¾".................**$15.00**
Normandy Plaid, platter, meat; 12".................**$30.00**
Normandy Plaid, range bowl, w/lid, 5½" **$50.00**
Palm Tree, basket planter, 6¼"...................**$100.00**
Palm Tree, Dutch jug, 2-pt, 5¾"....................**$150.00**
Peasant Garden, bowl, vegetable; 8½"..............**$80.00**
Peasant Garden, creamer & sugar bowl, w/lid, 3½", 5"..**$125.00**
Pennsylvania Dutch, baker, 7"........................**$45.00**
Pennsylvania Dutch, bowl, cereal; 5¼"...........**$20.00**
Pennsylvania Dutch, bowl, divided vegetable; 10½"..**$50.00**
Pennsylvania Dutch, candle holders, 2x6", pr...........**$130.00**
Pennsylvania Dutch, cookie jar, square, pottery lid, 9½".**$125.00**
Pennsylvania Dutch, cup & saucer, 2½", 5½" **$28.00**
Pennsylvania Dutch, honey jug, 6¼" **$85.00**
Pennsylvania Dutch, jam bowl, 5½" **$65.00**
Pennsylvania Dutch, plate, dinner; 9¾".......**$25.00**
Pennsylvania Dutch, soup & sandwich, Rubel mold, 2½x4"
   cup, 11" plate **$75.00**
Petals, bowl, fruit; 12" **$50.00**
Petals, mug, juice; 6-oz, 2½"...........................**$15.00**
Petals, pitcher, beverage; 2-pt, 6¼" **$75.00**
Petals, vase, 5" **$35.00**
Red Feather, TV lamp, 8½".............................**$75.00**
Ribbon Flower, fruit bowl, 12"......................**$50.00**
Saraband, bowl, fruit; 12"..............................**$15.00**
Saraband, candle holder, 2x6" **$40.00**
Saraband, cookie jar, oval, 9½" **$50.00**

Saraband, cruets, oil & vinegar, square, 5", pr **$25.00**
Saraband, plate, salad; 6¾" **$4.00**
Saraband, roll tray, 11" L..............................**$12.00**
Saraband, salt & pepper shakers, miniature jug style, 2½",
   pr..**$20.00**
Saraband, tea & toast, lap plate, 8½", 2½" cup........**$13.00**
Saraband, teapot, 6-cup, 6½"...........................**$25.00**
Seaform, bowl, dessert; 4" **$20.00**
Seaform, coffee server, 9" **$125.00**
Seaform, creamer & sugar bowl, 5", pr............**$85.00**
Seaform, roll tray, 11" L..............................**$45.00**
Seaform, salt & pepper shakers, 3", pr **$55.00**
Starflower, creamer & sugar bowl, w/lid.................**$85.00**
Starflower, pitcher, 6" **$65.00**
Sunflower, plate, breakfast; 8½"....................**$45.00**
Sunflower, tumbler, 12-oz, 5".........................**$30.00**
Tea Rose, bowl, vegetable; 8½"......................**$40.00**
Tea Rose, cup & saucer, 2½", 5½" **$28.00**
Tea Rose, plate, breakfast, 8½".....................**$25.00**
Tea Rose, platter, 12" L...............................**$50.00**
Tea Rose, roll tray, 11" L.............................**$50.00**
Tea Rose, sugar bowl, w/lid, 5".....................**$45.00**
Turquoise, baker, 7".....................................**$30.00**
Turquoise, salt & pepper shakers, jug style, 2½", pr.**$30.00**
Turquoise, soup & sandwich, 11" plate, 2¼x4" cup...**$55.00**

Pennsylvania Dutch, four-piece canister set, $450.00.

Puzzles

The first children's puzzle was actually developed as a learning aid by an English map maker, trying to encourage the study of geography. Most nineteenth-century puzzles were made of wood, rather boring, and very expensive. But by the Victorian era, nursery rhymes and other light-hearted themes became popular. The industrial revolution and the inception of color lithography combined to produce a stunning variety of themes ranging from technical advancements, historical scenarios, and fairy tales. Power saws made production more cost effective, and wood was replaced with less expensive cardboard.

As early as the '20s and '30s, American manufacturers began to favor character-related puzzles, the market already influenced by radio and the movies. Some of these were advertising premiums. Die-cutters had replaced jigsaws, cardboard became thinner, and now everyone could afford puzzles. During the Depression they were a cheap form of entertainment, and no family get-together was complete without a puzzle spread out on the card table for all to enjoy.

Television and movies caused a lull in puzzle making during the '50s, but advancements in printing and improvements in quality brought them back strongly in the '60s. Unusual shapes, the use of fine art prints, and more challenging designs caused sales to increase.

If you're going to collect puzzles, you'll need to remember that unless all the pieces are there, they're not of much value, especially those from the twentieth century. The condition of the box is important as well. Right now there's a lot of interest in puzzles from the '50s through the '70s that feature popular TV shows and characters from that era. Remember, though a frame-tray puzzle still sealed in its original wrapping may be worth $10.00 or more, depending on the subject matter and its age, a well used example may well be worthless as a collectible.

To learn more about the subject, we recommend *Character Toys and Collectibles* and *Toys, Antique and Collectible*, both by David Longest; and *Schroeder's Toys, Antique to Modern*. (All are published by Collector Books.) *Toys of the Sixties, A Pictorial Guide*, by Bill Bruegman (Cap'n Penny Productions) is another good source of information.

Newsletter: *Piece by Piece*
P.O. Box 12823
Kansas City, KS 66112-9998; Subscription: $8 per year

Dick Tracy, jigsaw, Jaymar, 1961, 60-piece, NMIB, $50.00.
(Photo courtesy Bill Bruegman)

Addams Family Mystery, jigsaw, Milton Bradley, 1965, complete, EXIB **$65.00**
Alvin & the Chipmunks, jigsaw, 1984, 63 pcs, MIB **$8.00**
Archies, jigsaw, Whitman, 1970, complete, MIB **$25.00**
Augie Doggie, frame-tray, Whitman, 1960, complete, 14x11", NM **$20.00**
Baby Huey, jigsaw, Built-Rite, 1961, 70 pcs, NMIB **$20.00**
Banana Splits, jigsaw, Whitman, 1970, complete, MIB...**$50.00**
Barney Google & Snuffy Smith, frame-tray, Jaymar, 1940s-50s, complete, NM **$40.00**
Batman, jigsaw, Whitman, 1966, 150 pcs, EXIB..........**$15.00**
Beatles, jigsaw, Beatles in Pepperland, over 100 pcs, 5x7", EXIB, from $100 to...**$150.00**
Bewitched, jigsaw, Milton Bradley, 1964, complete, MIB, from $65 to...**$75.00**
Bionic Woman, jigsaw, APC, 1976, complete, EX (EX canister) **$25.00**

Buzzy the Crow, jigsaw, Built Rite, 1961, 70 pcs, MIB ..**$25.00**
Captain Marvel Rides the Engine of Doom, jigsaw, 1940s, complete, MIB, from $125 to...............................**$150.00**
Cinderella, jigsaw, 1950s, complete, EX (EX canister) ..**$30.00**
Cisco Kid, frame-tray, Saalfield, complete, 11½x10", NM...**$40.00**
Clarabelle, frame-tray, Whitman, 1954, complete, 15x11", NM...**$30.00**
David Cassidy, jigsaw, APC, 1972, 500 pcs, MIB **$45.00**
Davy Crockett, jigsaw, Davy Crocket the Indian Fighter, Jaymar, 1950s-60s, EXIB **$30.00**
Disney World, jigsaw, 1970s, features several Disney characters, EX (EX container)...**$15.00**
Donald Duck, frame-tray, Treasure, 1981, complete, 11x8", EX...**$10.00**
Donald Duck & Nephews, frame-tray, 1960s, complete, 13x10", NM..**$15.00**
Dr Seuss's Cat in the Hat, frame-tray, 1980s, complete, EX...**$20.00**
Dr Strange, jigsaw, Third Eye, 1971, 500 pcs, MIB...**$100.00**
Dukes of Hazzard, jigsaw, 1981, 200 pcs, EXIB..........**$10.00**
Family Affair, jigsaw, Whitman, 1970, 125 pcs, MIB...**$35.00**
Fantasy Island, jigsaw, HG Toys, 1977, complete, MIB ..**$20.00**
Flipper, frame-tray, 1965, complete, EX.....................**$25.00**
Gay Purr-ee, frame-tray, Whitman, 1962, complete, 14x11", NM **$15.00**
Grizzly Adams, jigsaw, House of Games, 1978, 100 pcs, MIB **$12.00**
Hoppity Hooper, frame-tray, Whitman, 1965, complete, 14x11", NM **$50.00**
Howdy Doody, frame-tray, Is That You Clarabelle?, Whitman, 1952, complete, EX...**$45.00**
Impossibles, frame-tray, Whitman, 1967, complete, 14x11", NM **$25.00**
Jetsons, frame-tray, Whitman, 1960s, complete, NM, from $35 to..**$45.00**
Jinks, frame-tray, Whitman, 1960s, complete, NM, from $20 to..**$30.00**
Jinks w/Pixie & Dixie, frame-tray, Whitman, 1960s, complete, NM, from $20 to..**$30.00**
Josie & the Pussycats, frame-tray, 1971, complete, 10x8", EX...**$15.00**
Journey to the Center of the Earth, jigsaw, Whitman, 1969, complete, NMIB..**$25.00**
Kaptain Kool & the Kongs, frame-tray, Whitman, 1978, complete, EX..**$12.00**
King Leonardo, jigsaw, Jaymar, 1962, complete, EXIB ..**$20.00**
King Leonardo & His Short Subjects, jigsaw, Jaymar, 1962, complete, MIB..**$35.00**
Kristy McNichol, jigsaw, APC, 1979, complete, MIB ...**$20.00**
Linus the Lion-Hearted, frame-tray, Whitman, 1965, complete, 14x11", NM..**$25.00**
Lone Ranger, jigsaw, Jaymar, 1940, complete, NMIB, from $100 to...**$125.00**
Mary Poppins, jigsaw, 1964, complete, MIB...............**$20.00**
Masters of the Universe, frame-tray, Golden, 1982, complete, 14x11", NM..**$20.00**

Michael Jackson, jigsaw, Colorforms, 1984, 500 pcs, MIB...**$10.00**

Mighty Heroes, frame-tray, Whitman, 1967, complete, 14x11", NM..**$50.00**

Mighty Mouse, jigsaw, Whitman, 1967, 100 pcs, NMIB..**$15.00**

Miss Piggy, frame-tray, Fisher-Price, 1981-82, complete, M..**$15.00**

Mod Squad, jigsaw, Milton Bradley, 1969, complete, MIB..**$35.00**

Monkees, jigsaw, Fairchild, 1967, complete, MIB.......**$45.00**

Mr I Magination, jigsaw, Jaymar Television Stars Series, 1951, 400 pcs, scarce, NMIB.........................**$50.00**

Peanuts, jigsaw, Charles Schulz, 1960s, complete, EX (worn box), from $50 to..............................**$75.00**

Pebbles Flintstone, frame-tray, Whitman, 1960s, complete, NM..**$20.00**

Pinky Lee, frame-tray, Gabriel, 1950s, set of 4, EX (VG box)...**$85.00**

Pinocchio, frame-tray, 1980s, complete, 13x10", EX.....**$6.00**

Pokey Little Puppy, frame-tray, 1972, complete, 14x11", EX..**$10.00**

Popeye's Comic Picture Picture Puzzle, jigsaw, Parker Bros, set of 4, EXIB.................................**$100.00**

Punky Brewster, jigsaw, 1984, complete, EXIB..........**$20.00**

Raggedy Ann & Andy, frame-tray, Milton Bradley, 1988, complete, 14½x11", M.........................**$12.00**

Raggedy Ann Picture Puzzles, frame-tray, Milton Bradley, 1944, boxed set of three, complete, 14x11", NMIB, $85.00. (Photo courtesy Martin and Carolyn Bevens)

Roger Ramjet, frame-tray, Whitman, 1966, complete, 14x11", NM..**$75.00**

Rolling Stones Schmuzzle Puzzle, jigsaw, Musidor, 1983, MIB (sealed)..**$65.00**

Rookies, jigsaw, APC, 1975, complete, EX (EX container)..**$40.00**

Rootie Kazootie, jigsaw, Fairchild, 1950s, set of 3, complete, NMIB..**$50.00**

Shazamm, jigsaw, Whitman Big Little Books series, 1960, complete, NMIB...**$50.00**

Six Million Dollar Man, jigsaw, APC, 1975, 200 pcs, EX (EX container)...**$35.00**

Sleeping Beauty, jigsaw, Jaymar, 1960s, complete, NMIB..**$20.00**

Snagglepuss, jigsaw, Whitman Jr, 1962, complete, MIB..**$25.00**

Space Kidettes, jigsaw, Whitman, 1967, 70 pcs, MIB..**$30.00**

Stingray, frame-tray, Whitman, 1966, complete, 14x11", NM..**$30.00**

Super Six, jigsaw, Whitman, 1969, complete, NMIB...**$35.00**

Superman Picture Puzzles, jigsaw, Saalfield, 1940, set of 3, complete, rare, NMIB.........................**$850.00**

Three's Company, jigsaw, APC, 1978, complete, MIB..**$30.00**

Thunderbirds, jigsaw, Whitman, 1968, complete, MIB.**$30.00**

Tom Teriffic, jigsaw, Jaymar, 1960s, complete, NMIB...**$100.00**

Tommy Tortoise & Moe Hare, jigsaw, Built-Rite, 1961, 70 pcs, MIB..**$25.00**

Twinkles the Elephant, frame-tray, Whitman, 1962, complete, rare, 14x11", NM.........................**$45.00**

Underdog, frame-tray, Whitman, 1965, complete, 11x14", NM..**$20.00**

Universal Monsters, frame-tray, Jaymar, 1963, Dracula, Mummy, or Frankenstein, complete, NM, ea.....**$150.00**

Welcome Back Kotter, frame-tray, Whitman, 1977, complete, M..**$8.00**

Woody Woodpecker, frame-tray, Whitman, 1954, complete, VG..**$25.00**

Woody Woodpecker, jigsaw, Witman Big Little Books series, 1960s, complete, NMIB.........................**$50.00**

Yogi Bear, frame-tray, Whitman, 1961, complete, 14x11", M.**$20.00**

Zorro, frame-tray, Whitman, 1965, complete, 14x11", NM..**$25.00**

Zorro, jigsaw, The Duel, Jaymar, 1950s-60s, EXIB......**$30.00**

Pyrex

Though the history of this heat-proof glassware goes back to the early years of the twentieth century, the Pyrex that we tend to remember best is more than likely those mixing bowl sets, casseroles, pie plates, and baking dishes that were so popular in kitchens all across America from the late 1940s right on through the 1960s. Patterned Pyrex became commonplace by the late 1950s; if you were a new bride, you could be assured that your bridal shower would produce at least one of the 'Cinderella' bowl sets or an 'Oven, Refrigerator, Freezer' set in whatever pattern happened to be the most popular that year. Among the most recognizable patterns you'll see today are Gooseberry, Snowflake, Daisy, and Butterprint (roosters, the farmer and his wife, and wheat sheaves). There was also a line with various solid colors on the exteriors. You'll seldom if ever find a piece that doesn't carry the familiar logo somewhere. To learn more about Pyrex, we recommend *Kitchen Glassware of the Depression Years, 5th Edition*, by Gene Florence (Collector Books).

Baking dish, Amish, red on white, rectangular, #933, 13½x9"...**$45.00**

Baking dish, Crazy Daisy/Spring Blossom, rectangular, 13½x9"...**$35.00**
Bowl, Bluebelle, square base, 12", from $25 to..........**$30.00**
Bowls, cereal; Rooster, mixed fired-on colors, set of 4...**$50.00**
Bowls, nesting; Amish, turquoise & white, 4 for.........**$45.00**

Bowls, mixing; Bluebelle, 6½", 7½", 8½", $35.00 for the three-piece set; divided relish, Bluebelle, $30.00. (Photo courtesy Gene Florence)

Bowls, nesting; Dots (blue, green, yellow & orange), set of 4 ....**$60.00**
Bowls, nesting; Friendship pattern, set of 4, from $50 to.**$70.00**
Bowls, nesting; Gooseberry, set of 4 ....**$48.00**
Bowls, nesting; mixed fired-on colors, set of 4, from $50 to..**$75.00**
Bowls, nesting; pink fired-on color, set of 4, from $55 to.**$75.00**
Bowls, nesting; red fired-on color, set of 4, from $40 to ..**$50.00**
Casserole, white 'clambroth' oval, w/lid, from $125 to...**$150.00**
Casserole set, Butterprint, pink, 1-pt, 1-qt, 1½-qt, set of 3..**$60.00**
Chip & dip set, turquoise fired-on color, 10½" & 6½" bowls w/metal frame.......................................**$30.00**
Coffeepot, percolator, range top, #7756, 6-cup, MIB..**$48.00**
Coffeepot, Vaculator Dutch Filter, General Electric, 1942, 13½"..**$50.00**
Coffeepot, w/infuser, 8-cup **$42.50**
Double boiler, blue w/clear lid, wooden handles, 1940s, rare, from $70 to...**$80.00**
Economy set, 9-pc set: measuring cup, 9½" pie plate, 6 custard cups and cup rack, MIB, from $35 to...........**$40.00**
Measuring cup, 1-spout, 1-cup, from $12 to **$15.00**
Measuring cup, 2-spout, 1-cup, from $22 to **$25.00**
Pitcher, Bluebell, 5¾", from $50 to **$60.00**
Platter, fired-on turquoise on border w/gold, 12½"....**$40.00**
Refrigerator dish, blue fired-on color, clear lid, 4¼x6¾", from $5 to...**$7.00**
Refrigerator dish, red fired-on color, clear lid, rectangular, 3½x4¾", from $4 to...................................**$5.00**
Refrigerator dish, yellow fired-on color, clear lid, rectangular, 7x9", from $8 to.......................................**$10.00**
Refrigerator dish, yellow fired-on color, clear lid, 3½x4¾", from $2.50 to..**$4.00**
Refrigerator set, mixed fired-on colors, clear lids, stacking set of 4, from $50 to.......................................**$60.00**
Refrigerator set, turquoise fired-on color, clear lids, stacking set of 4, from $50 to...............................**$60.00**
Teapot, Flameware, squat, 4-cup, w/insert & burner, from $50 to...**$75.00**

Railroadiana

It is estimated that almost two hundred different railway companies once operated in this country, so to try to collect just one item representative of each would be a challenge. Supply and demand is the rule governing all pricing, so naturally an item with a marking from a long-defunct, less prominent railroad generally carries the higher price tag.

Railroadiana is basically divided into two main categories, paper and hardware, with both having many subdivisions. Some collectors tend to specialize in only one area — locks, lanterns, ticket punches, dinnerware, or timetables, for example. Many times estate sales and garage sales are good sources for finding these items, since retired railroad employees often kept such memorabilia as keepsakes. Because many of these items are very unique, you need to get to know as much as possible about railroad artifacts in order to be able to recognize and evaluate a good piece. For more information we recommend *Railroad Collectibles, Revised 4th Edition,* by Stanley L. Baker (Collector Books).

Advisors: Fred and Lila Shrader; John White, Grandpa's Depot (See Directory Railroadiana)

Dinnerware

B&O Railroad, blue transfer on white: Butter pat, $75.00; Luncheon plate, $120.00; Cereal bowl, $90.00.

Bowl, ATSF, Mimbreno, bottom stamp, 5¼"..............**$120.00**
Bowl, berry; B&O, Centenary, back stamped, 4½".....**$82.00**
Bowl, berry; Maine Central, Bangor, top logo, 5¼"..**$300.00**
Bowl, oatmeal; ACL, Flora of the South, back stamped, 6¼"..**$165.00**
Bowl, oatmeal; NYC, Mercury, bottom stamped, 6¼" ..**$38.00**
Butter pat, ACL, Carolina, back stamped, 3½" **$11.00**
Butter pat, C&O, Silhouette, no back stamp, 3½".......**$78.00**
Butter pat, N&W, Cavalier, top mark, 4"....................**$72.00**
Butter pat, SAL, Orange Blossom, no back stamp, 3½" **$40.00**

Butter pat, SP, Prairie Mountain Wildflowers, no back stamp.**$125.00**
Compote, FH, Thistle, no back stamp, 3½x7".............**$76.00**
Creamer, FH, Encanto, w/handle, no back stamp, 2".**$36.00**
Creamer, N&W, dogwood, no handle, no back stamp, 3" ..**$18.00**
Cup, bouillon; CB&Q, Violets & Daisies, no handles, no back stamp, 4"...**$33.00**
Cup & saucer, C&O, Greenbrier, no back stamp........**$27.00**
Cup & saucer, NYC, DeWitt Clinton, no back stamp .**$95.00**
Egg cup, CP, Royal York, no back stamp, 2¼" **$35.00**
Ice cream shell, FH, Blue Chain, no back stamp, 6" including tab handle...**$37.00**
Plate, CN, Continental, BS, no TL, 5½"........................**$15.00**
Plate, CP, Blue Maple Leaf, top logo, 7½"..................**$67.00**
Plate, GN, Mountains & Flowers, back stamp, 7x6½".....**$75.00**
Plate, MP, Eagle, back stamp & top logo, 9" **$102.00**
Plate, PRR, Mountain Laurel, full back stamp, 9¾".....**$40.00**
Platter, UP, Desert Flower, back stamp, 9½x7½" **$49.00**
Soup plate, SP, Prairie Mountain Wildflowers, back stamp, 7¾"..**$135.00**

Glassware

Ashtray, Alaska RR, ARR/Mt McKinley Park Hotel, 3½"...**$49.00**
Ashtray, ATSF, Santa Fe logo, silkscreen, 5¼x3½"......**$30.00**
Champagne flute, Amtrak, Silver Star, Silver Meteor, Silver Palm, 8" **$11.00**
Cordial, UP, cut & etched Overland logo, 3½"............**$72.00**
Martini set, UP, frosted logo, pitcher, 2 roly-polys & stirrer, in original box **$49.00**
Roly-poly, PRR, diesel engine #4302, 2¾" **$9.00**
Roly-poly, SRR, Southern Serves the South, train encircles glass, 3"..**$11.00**
Shakers, SP, flowing cursive SP engraved in silver-plated tops, 3", pr..**$185.00**
Shot glass, UP, white enamel UP shield logo, 2½" **$26.00**
Tumbler, ATSF, cut Santa Fe in script & stripes, 5".....**$54.00**
Tumbler, B&O, white logo & stripes, Linking 13 Great States, 3¾"...**$33.00**
Tumbler, GM&O, white enamel logo, 4¾" **$21.00**
Tumbler, IC, white enamel diamond logo, 5" **$19.00**
Tumbler, NYC, white NYC enamel, ⅜" pedestal, 5" ...**$17.00**
Tumbler, PRR, diesel engine #4902, on-the-rocks type, 3¾" **$12.00**
Tumbler, StL&SF, blue Frisco bearskin logo, 5"...........**$11.00**
Tumbler, WP, frosted feather River logo, juice size, 3¾"...**$65.00**
Wine, IC, etched & frosted diamond logo, 3¾" **$39.00**
Wine, MKT, etched MKT logo, 5"................................**$44.00**

Lanterns

ATSF, Dressel, etched red globe, short **$75.00**
B&O, Adams & Westlake, twist-off pot, Pat 1895, VG ..**$150.00**
B&O, Dietz 999, sm marked globe, EX **$65.00**
D&SL, Adams & Westlake, embossed top, unmarked tall globe, Patent 1909 ....**$350.00**
Delaware & Hudson, Adlake, short red unmarked globe, EX...**$70.00**

Erie, Adams & Westlake, tall red globe, wire bottom, 5⅜"..**$200.00**
MOPAC, Handlan, clear unmarked globe, short **$75.00**
NP, flat vertical ribs, tall clear unmarked globe, EX .**$225.00**
Pennsylvania System (in keystone), Handlan, clear marked globe, tall...**$200.00**
PRR, Adlake Reliable, tall etched globe, wire bottom, 5⅜"...**$100.00**
ST&SF, Handlan, tall Safety First globe, twist-off pot, G ..**$150.00**
UP, Adams & Westlake, clear unmarked globe, short.**$85.00**

Linens and Uniforms

Apron, cook's, D&RGW, white w/brass grommets **$15.00**
Blanket, Pullman, pink w/woven logo, 58x90"...........**$95.00**
Coat, conductor's; NYC, silver buttons, navy wool, 1960s ...**$95.00**
Hat, Burlington Route logo, w/conductor's badge, 1940s..**$108.00**
Hat, CRI&P, Rock Island pin & separate conductor badge...**$55.00**
Head rest cover, GN in orange on white w/goat, 19x14" ...**$24.00**
Head rest cover, N&W, maroon circular logo on gray, 15x21"...**$19.00**
Head rest cover, UP, Streamliner logo in red on yellow, 18" square **$22.00**
Jacket, waiter's; D&RGW patch on collar points, white w/buttons **$39.00**
Napkin, Amtrak, stamped NRPC in black on red, cotton, 20" square **$5.00**
Napkin, Western Pacific/Feather River Route logo, white on white, 19" square **$36.00**
Pillowcase, B&O Linking 13 States w/the Nation (stamped) **$14.00**
Place mat, NP w/Yellowstone Park, Monad logo, 12x16".**$48.00**
Tablecloth, CZ logo, white on white, damask, 48x50" ..**$42.00**
Tablecloth, D&RGW, Rio Grande, white on white, damask, 34" square **$36.00**
Towel, hand; Canadian Pacific & 67 on red stripe, 16x18" **$14.00**
Towel, hand; NP, Think Safety, grommet on 1 corner, 15x18" **$8.00**

Locks

Switch lock, StPM&M RR on shackle, brass heart shape, Union Brass Co, $300.00. (Photo courtesy Stanley Baker)

Mail, US Mail Bag, stamped steel, no key **$20.00**

Master, SCL, brass, heavy duty, w/brass marked key & 8" chain **$45.00**

Signal, CRIP, brass, w/2 keys **$50.00**

Signal, Rock Island Lines, brass **$50.00**

Switch, C&A, Keen Kutter, brass **$230.00**

Switch, CRR, brass **$175.00**

Switch, UP, cast brass **$125.00**

Terminal, NY **$40.00**

Yard, Yale, mk Linen Room **$7.00**

Silverplate

Bowl, divided vegetable; PRR, Broadway, top mark & back stamp, International, 11" **$200.00**

Bowl, grapefruit; Pullman, side mark, International, 1925, 2½x6" **$85.00**

Bread tray, MP, back stamp: MOPAC, Reed & Barton, 13" L **$98.00**

Butter pat, ATSF, Santa Fe in script, rounded corners, International, 2¾" square **$58.00**

Butter pat, SP, top logo: Southern Pacific w/ball & wing, International, 3½" **$125.00**

Coffeepot, CP, side mark, pattern unknown, Marlboro, 6" to top of lid **$51.00**

Coffeepot, SRR, side mark, Reed & Barton, 16-oz **$189.00**

Compote, T&P, back stamp, Reed & Barton, 4x6¾" **$235.00**

Corn holder, UP, side mark: UP System, Reed & Barton .. **$65.00**

Creamer, NYC, mark on hinged lid, International, 4¼" ... **$120.00**

Finger bowl, SAL, side mark, Meridian, 5" **$75.00**

Fork, cocktail; NYNH&H, Modern, back stamp, International, 5½" **$25.00**

Fork, cocktail; P&LE, Kings, top mark, International, 7½" . **$48.00**

Fork, dinner; PRR, Broadway, top mark, International, 7½" **$25.00**

Ice cream dish, NP, top mark w/Monad on tab handle, International, 4½" **$75.00**

Knife, dinner; D&H, Shelburne, top mark: D&H logo, Gorham **$39.00**

Knife, dinner; DL&W, Cromwell, top marked w/logo, 9½" **$31.00**

Knife, dinner; NYC, Commonwealth, side logo: NYC Lines, Reed & Barton, 9¾" **$24.00**

Knife, dinner; SP&S, Embassy, side mark, Reed & Barton. **$20.00**

Knife, luncheon; PRR, top mark, Broadway, International **$18.00**

Sherbet, Union News logo w/4" pedestal, Reed & Barton **$72.00**

Spoon, bouillon; MStP&SStM, Windsor, top logo, Gorham, 5¾" **$29.00**

Spoon, cheese; B&O, Columbia, top mark, fluted, Reed & Barton **$29.00**

Spoon, grapefruit; MP, Devon, top mark, Wallace **$16.00**

Spoon, iced tea; ACL, Zephyr, top mark, International, 8" **$24.00**

Sugar bowl, L&N, w/lid & handles, back stamp, International, 4" **$88.00**

Sugar tongs, NYNH&H, Silhouette, side mark: NH Railroad, International **$68.00**

Teapot, SR, Queen & Crescent Route, side logo, Reed & Barton, 16-oz, 4" **$285.00**

Teaspoon, CB&Q, Windsor, Burlington Route logo, International **$23.00**

Teaspoon, Erie, Elmwood, top mark: diamond logo, Gorham **$30.00**

Tray, MP, top mark w/buzz-saw logo, MOPAC back stamp, Wallace, 11" dia **$73.00**

Miscellaneous

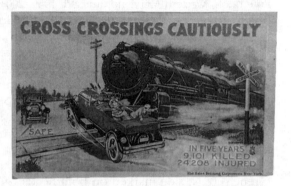

Postcard, Cross Crossings Cautiously, ca 1923, minor soiling, $40.00.

Annual report, Wabash, 1957, 21 pages, 8½x11" **$65.00**

Beverage list, D&RGW, 1950s, 5x7" **$8.00**

Blotter, GN w/goat, 3¼x6¼" **$7.00**

Book, Consolidated Code of Operating Rules, 1967 ... **$12.00**

Book, Silver San Juan, Rio Grande Southern, Ferrell, 1973 .... **$107.00**

Book, Union Pacific/Streamliners, Ranks & Kratville, 1980 .... **$47.00**

Box, first aid; NYC, embossed top mark, metal, 8½x5" .. **$19.00**

Box car seal, LVRR, unused & numbered **$4.00**

Builder's plate, NYC, Alco & GE, paint gone, 1952, 12x6" **$110.00**

Button, conductor's uniform; Wagner Palace Car Co, ⅝" **$16.00**

Button, uniform; Erie, brass color, Waterbury Button Co, ⅝" **$5.00**

Calendar, pocket; Maine Central, plastic, 1963 .... **$14.00**

Calendar, pocket; MP, plastic, 1946 .... **$12.00**

Calendar, pocket; UP, plastic, 1940-60, from $5 to **$16.00**

Calendar, wall; Amtrak, Pioneer at Olympia Station, 1993 .. **$10.00**

Catalog, Griswold Signal Co in 3-ring binder, 1966 .. **$108.00**

Dixie cup, C&O w/Chessie, from $1 to **$11.00**

Envelope, ticket; various railroads, 1940s-70s, from 50¢ to **$3.00**

Hard hat, Amtrak, complete w/inner head band **$22.00**

Insulator, PRR, aqua glass, dome style, 4" **$13.00**

Matchbook carton, B&O, containing 18 books of matches, 1960s **$26.00**

Menu, D&RGW, Rio Grande speed style, 1960s **$10.00**

Money bag, Property of CNS&M Ry Co, canvas, grommets, 5x14" **$24.00**

Oil can, SP Co embossed side logo, bail handle & side handle, 6½" dia **$21.00**

Pencil, mechanical; MP, Air Conditioned **$24.00**

Pencil, wood, no eraser, various railroads, unused, from 50¢ to **$2.00**

Pencil clip, various, metal w/plastic railroad logo, 1950-60s, from $1 to **$6.00**

Postcard, real photo of train wreck, location, railroad, etc, identified, minimum value **$5.00**

Postcard, real photo of train wreck, unidentified, minimum value **$3.00**

Rule book, BM&O, 173 pages, 1951 ....**$18.00**

Rule book, IC, unused, 1959, 141 pages **$16.00**

Rule book, Western Maryland, unused, 1959, 200+ pages ..**$16.00**

Ruler, C&NW, A Good Rule To Follow w/logos, wooden, 15" **$5.00**

Timetable, public; SP Sunset Route, Houston to Dallas, 1950 ....**$9.00**

Torch, UPRR, back stamp, 4½" dia w/9½" handle **$51.00**

Water bucket, GN Ry embossed on bottom, galvanized tin **$42.00**

Water bucket, PRR embossed on side, galvanized tin .**$45.00**

Water can, BN Inc embossed, bail handle, 14" (including lid) **$51.00**

Wrench, L&N, side marked on both heads, 24" **$22.00**

Razor Blade Banks

Razor blade banks are receptacles designed to safely store used razor blades. While the double-edged disposable razor blades date back to as early as 1904, ceramic and figural razor blade safes most likely were not produced until the early 1940s. The development of the electric razor and the later disposable razors did away with the need for these items, and their production ended in the 1960s.

Shapes include barber chairs, barbers, animals, and barber poles, which were very popular. Listerine produced a white donkey and elephant in 1936 with political overtones. They also made a white ceramic frog. These were used as promotional items for shaving cream. Suggested values are based on availability and apply to items in near-mint to excellent condition. Note that regional pricing could vary.

Advisor: Debbie Gillham (See Directory, Razor Blade Banks)

Barber, wood w/Gay Blade bottom, unscrews, Woodcraft, 1950, 6", from $65 to **$75.00**

Barber, wood w/key & metal holders for razor & brush, 9", from $85 to **$95.00**

Barber bust w/handlebar mustache, coat & tie, from $55 to **$65.00**

Barber chair, lg or sm, from $100 to **$125.00**

Barber head, different colors on collar, Cleminson, from $30 to **$40.00**

Barber pole, red & white, w/ or w/out attachments & various titles, from $20 to **$25.00**

Barber holding pole, Occupied Japan, 4", from $50.00 to $60.00.
(Photo courtesy Debbie Gillham)

Barber pole w/barber head & derby hat, white, from $35 to **$40.00**

Barber pole w/face, red & white, from $30 to **$35.00**

Barber standing in blue coat & stroking chin, from $75 to **$80.00**

Barber w/buggy eyes, pudgy full body, Gleason look-alike, from $65 to **$75.00**

Barbershop quartet, 4 singing barber heads, from $95 to ..**$125.00**

Box w/policeman holding up hand, metal, marked Used Blades, from $90 to **$125.00**

Dandy Dans, plastic w/brush holders, from $30 to **$40.00**

Frog, green, marked For Used Blades, from $65 to **$75.00**

Half barber pole, hangs on wall, may be personalized w/name, from $60 to **$70.00**

Half shaving cup, hangs on wall, marked Gay Blades w/floral design, from $65 to **$75.00**

Half shaving cup, hangs on wall, marked Gay Old Blade w/quartet, from $65 to **$75.00**

Listerine donkey, from $20 to **$30.00**

Listerine elephant, from $25 to **$35.00**

Listerine frog, from $15 to **$20.00**

Looie, right- or left-hand version, from $85 to **$100.00**

Man shaving, mushroom shape, Cleminson, from $25 to ..**$30.00**

Razor Bum, from $95 to **$125.00**

Safe, green, marked Razor on front, from $55 to **$65.00**

Shaving brush, ceramic, wide style w/decal, from $50 to **$60.00**

Tony the Barber, Ceramic Arts Studio, from $85 to **$95.00**

Reamers

Reamers were a European invention of the late 1700s, devised as a tool for extracting liquid from citrus fruits, which was often used as a medicinal remedy. Eventually the concept of freshly squeezed juice worked its way across the oceans. Many early U.S. patents (mostly for wood reamers) were filed in the mid-1880s, and thanks to the 1916 Sunkist 'Drink An Orange' advertising campaign, the reamer soon became a permanent fixture in the well-equipped American kitchen. Most of the major U.S. glass companies and pottery manufacturers included juicers as part of their kitchenware lines. However, some of the most beautiful and unique reamers are ceramic figures and hand-painted, elegant china and porcelain examples. The invention of frozen and bottled citrus juice relegated many a reamer to the kitchen shelf. However, the current trend for a healthier diet has garnered renewed interest for the manual juice squeezer.

Most of the German and English reamers listed here can be attributed to the 1920s and 1930s. Most of the Japanese imports are from the 1940s.

Advisor: Bobbie Zucker Bryson (See Directory, Reamers)

Newsletter: *National Reamer Collectors Association*
Debbie Gillham
47 Midline Ct., Gaithersburg, MD 20878, 301-977-5727
e-mail: reamers@erols.com or http://www.reamers.org

Ceramics

Clown head reamer on orange pitcher bottom, two-piece, 4½", from $85.00 to $100.00.

Baby's, 2-pc, pink w/white kitten in blue pajamas, pink, blue, green & white top, Japan, 4", from $75 to..**$85.00**
Baby's Orange, 2-pc, red & white, Japan, 4½" **$55.00**
Black face & hands, red coat & blue pants, 4¾", from $500 to..**$600.00**
Child's, 2-pc, orange lustre w/red, blue & yellow flowers, 2", from $100 to..**$125.00**
Clown, brown body & hat, blue buttons & collar, 6", from $95 to..**$125.00**
Clown, lime green & white, 4¾", from $95 to..........**$125.00**
Clown, polka dots, lustre hat, Japan, 4½", from $125 to..**$135.00**
Clown, Sourpuss, w/saucer, 4¾", from $115 to........**$135.00**
Clown, 2-pc, full body, ruffle & head in striped hat as reamer, 1940s, Mikori, Japan, 7" **$275.00**
Clown, 2-pc, sitting, head is reamer, T-T Japan, 5½"..**$225.00**
Clown, 2-pc, sitting, red & white striped suit, white head reamer, ca 1940s, 4¾" **$275.00**
Clown, 2-pc, tan & light blue w/pig head, 5", from $185 to **$225.00**

Clown, 2-pc, wearing tuxedo, 5½", from $125 to.....**$150.00**
Clown head, 2-pc, face on pitcher, reamer top, 1950s, 4¼" **$195.00**
Cottage, Carlton Ware (England), yellow w/orange & green trim, 4", from $95 to...**$125.00**
Duck, 2-pc, white w/green, red & black accents, white reamer top, lustreware, Japan, 1940s, 3½" **$185.00**
Floral w/gold, Nippon, 2-pc.....................................**$195.00**
Floral w/gold, Royal Rudolstadt, 2-pc.....................**$250.00**
Germany, Goebel, Winnie-the-Pooh, yellow w/white top, 4½"..**$300.00**
Girl's face, 2-pc, 4½x6½", EX.................................**$145.00**
Grapefruit, 2-pc, top has green reamer, bottom is grapefruit half, ca 1940s, Japan, 4", EX **$85.00**
House, 2-pc, beige w/green trees & tan branches, blue door & windmill, Japan, 4½" **$185.00**
Lemon, 2-pc, yellow w/green leaves, gold trim, Japan, 4", from $65 to..**$85.00**
Orange, 2-pc, Orange for Baby, yellow w/blue flowers, Goebel, 3½"...**$135.00**
Pear, 2-pc, top half has leaves & cherries, lustreware, Trico, Japan, 5" **$175.00**
Pear, 3-pc, leaves on top, Japan, ca 1959...................**$75.00**
Pitcher, 2-pc, beige w/multicolor flowers & black trim, Japan, 8¾"...**$50.00**
Pitcher, 2-pc, beige w/red & yellow flowers, black trim, Japan, 8½", w/6 cups, from $50 to **$65.00**
Pitcher, 2-pc, black w/gold wheat, 8"........................**$45.00**
Pitcher, 2-pc, cream w/lavender lillies & green leaves, Universal Cambridge, 9"...**$185.00**
Pitcher, 2-pc, floral decor, Japan, 5¼".....................**$110.00**
Pitcher, 2-pc, rose w/yellow & lavender flowers, green leaves, Japan, 7", +6 cups **$65.00**
Pitcher, 2-pc, rust leaves, dark blue trim, 3½" **$45.00**
Red Wing USA, cream, 6¾" **$125.00**
Rose, pink w/green leaves, Germany, 1¾" **$225.00**
Sailboat, yellow or red, 3", ea **$125.00**
Saucer, cream, tan & maroon w/blue trim, England, 3¼" dia, from $90 to..**$100.00**
Saucer, floral decor, 1940s, Japan, 2½" H.................**$110.00**
Saucer, triangular, floral decor.................................**$135.00**
Saucer, white w/pink flowers & green leaves, Germany, 4½" dia, from $85 to..**$100.00**
Saucer, 2-pc, France, Ivoire Corbelle, Henriot Quimper #1166, 4¼", from $350 to..................................**$400.00**
Sleeping Mexican, 2-pc, green shirt, red pants, gold top, Japan, 4¾", from $150 to..................................**$185.00**
Sourpuss, 4¾", from $100 to **$125.00**
Teapot, 2-pc, white w/red flowers & trim, Prussia/Germany/Royal Rudolstadt, 3¼" **$150.00**
Teapot, 2-pc, white w/yellow & maroon flowers, Nippon, 3¼"..**$90.00**
Teapot, 2-pc, yellow, tan & white, England/Shelley, 3½", from $90 to..**$100.00**
USA, Ade-O-Matic Genuine Coorsite Porcelain, green, 9"..**$150.00**
USA, Jiffy Juicer, US Pat 2,130,755, Sept 2, 1928, yellow, 5¼" **$85.00**

Glassware

Blue, Jennyware, $110.00.

Amber, spout opposite handle, Federal Glass, from $300 to **$325.00**

Chalaine Blue, embossed Sunkist, from $200 to.......**$225.00**

Cobalt, 2-cup pitcher & reamer set, Hazel Atlas, from $350 to...**$375.00**

Crystal, baby's, elephant decoration on base, Fenton, from $75 to...**$95.00**

Crystal, Crisscross, tab handle, Hazel Atlas, from $18 to .**$22.00**

Crystal, embossed ASCO, Good Morning Orange Juice, from $25 to...**$30.00**

Crystal, Glasbake, McKee on handle, from $70 to......**$75.00**

Crystal, oranges decoration, flattened loop handle, Westmoreland, from $60 to..................................**$65.00**

Crystal, square, marked Italy, from $15 to..................**$20.00**

Crystal, Valencia embossed on side, from $150 to....**$200.00**

Custard w/red trim, loop handle, embossed Sunkist, from $30 to...**$35.00**

Green, baby's, Jenkins, from $150 to.........................**$175.00**

Green, Crisscross, tab handle, Hazel Atlas, from $30 to ..**$35.00**

Green, embossed Foreign, 2-pc, from $50 to..............**$60.00**

Green, embossed Sunkist, from $50 to........................**$55.00**

Green, marked Argentina, from $125 to.....................**$150.00**

Green, Orange Juice Extractor, from $50 to **$55.00**

Green, orange reamer, loop handle, Anchor Hocking, from $25 to...**$30.00**

Green, paneled, loop handle, Federal Glass, from $30 to .**$35.00**

Green, ribbed, loop handle, Federal Glass, from $30 to..**$35.00**

Green, spout opposite handle, Indiana Glass, from $35 to **$40.00**

Green, tab handle, Hazel Atlas, sm, from $40 to........**$45.00**

Green, 2-cup pitcher reamer, Vitrock, from $30 to.....**$35.00**

Green, 4-cup, footed, Hazel Atlas, from $35 to **$40.00**

Green, 4-cup pitcher set, from $140 to......................**$150.00**

Light green, straight sides, Fry, from $25 to **$28.00**

Light pink, slick handle, US Glass, from $130 to......**$150.00**

Pink, baby's, 2-pc, Westmoreland, from $175 to.......**$195.00**

Pink, Hex Optic, bucket reamer, Jeannette, from $40 to ..**$45.00**

Pink, loop handle, Westmoreland, from $90 to **$100.00**

Pink, ribbed, loop handle, Federal, from $35 to.........**$40.00**

Rose pink, straight sides, Fry, from $55 to **$60.00**

Seville Yellow, embossed Sunkist, from $50 to...........**$55.00**

Ultramarine, Jeannette, lg, from $125 to...................**$130.00**

White, 4-cup stippled pitcher w/reamer top, Hazel Atlas, from $30 to...**$35.00**

White w/red trim, Hazel Atlas, from $22.50 to...........**$25.00**

Metal

Aluminum tilt-model, Seald Sweet Juice Extractor, attaches to counter, 13" **$60.00**

Green metal base, white porcelain bowl & cone, 3-pc, Presto Juice National Electric Appliance Corp, 7⅝", from $110 to...**$125.00**

Metal, Quam-Nicholas Co, Chicago IL, Kwicky Juicer, 5½", from $8 to..**$10.00**

Silverplate, Meriden SP Co International, S Co, 2-pc, 4⅝" dia **$95.00**

Silverplate, 2-pc, cocktail shaker, Germany, 7", from $85 to **$100.00**

Sterling silver, Black & Starr, 3¾" dia, from $300 to.**$350.00**

Records

Records are still plentiful at flea markets and some antique malls, but albums (rock, jazz, and country) from the '50s and '60s are harder to find in collectible condition (very good or better). Garage sales are sometimes a great place to buy old records, since most of what you'll find there have been stored more carefully by their original owners.

There are two schools of thought concerning what is a collectible record. While some collectors prefer the rarities — those made in limited quantities by an unknown who later became famous, or those aimed at a specific segment of music lovers — others like the vintage Top-10 recordings. Now that they're so often being replaced with CDs, we realize that even though we take them for granted, the possibility of their becoming a thing of the past may be reality tomorrow.

Whatever the slant your collection takes, learn to visually inspect records before you buy them. Condition is one of the most important factors to consider when assessing value. To be judged as mint, a record may have been played but must have no visual or audible deterioration — no loss of gloss to the finish, no stickers or writing on the label, no holes, no skips when it is played. If any of these are apparent, at best it is considered to be excellent, and its value is up to 90% lower than a mint example. Many of the records you'll find that seem to you to be in wonderful shape would be judged only very good, excellent at the most, by a knowledgeable dealer. Sleeves with no tape, stickers, tears, or obvious damage at best would be excellent; mint condition sleeves are impossible to find unless you've found old store stock.

Be on the lookout for colored vinyl or picture discs, as some of these command higher prices; in fact, older Vogue picture disks commonly sell in the $50.00 to $75.00 range, some even higher. It's not too uncommon to find old radio station discards. These records will say either 'Not for Sale' or 'Audition Copy' and may be worth more than their commercial counterparts. Our values are based on original issue — remember to cut these prices drastically when condition is less than described.

If you'd like more information, we recommend *American Premium Record Guide* by L.R. Docks.

Advisor: L.R. Docks (See Directory, Records)

45 rpm

Those 45s listed 'in picture sleeve' are of value only if the original sleeve is present and in at least excellent condition, otherwise they are nearly worthless.

Anka, Paul; Puppy Love, Paramount 10082, EX in EX picture sleeve $5.00

Baez, Joan; Be Not Too Hard, Vanguard 35055, NM in EX picture sleeve $15.00

BB King, She's Dynamite, RPM 323, EX $25.00

Beatles, I Want To Hold Your Hand, EX in EX picture sleeve $50.00

Beatniks, Blue Angel, Key-Lock 913, EX $15.00

Big Bopper, Chantilly Lace, Mercury 71343, EX..........$12.00

Boone, Pat; Ain't That a Shame, Dot 15377, M in EX picture sleeve $15.00

Buckinghams, Mercy Mercy Mercy, Columbia 44182, NM in EX picture sleeve $10.00

Cadillacs, Gloria, Capitol 765 ....$75.00

Campbell, Glenn; Turn Around Look at Me, Crest 1087, EX $10.00

Capris, The; It Was Moonglow, Gotham 7306, EX......$40.00

Channel, Bruce; Hey! Baby, Le Cam 953, EX..............$20.00

Cochran, Eddie; Pretty Girl, Liberty 55138, EX...........$12.00

Danny & the Juniors, At the Hop, ABC Paramount 9871, EX $8.00

Domino, Fats; Poor Poor Me, Imperial 5197, EX $30.00

Everly Brothers, All I Have To Do Is Dream, Cadence 1348, M in EX picture sleeve $15.00

Everly Brothers, Ebony Eyes/ Walk Right Back, Warner Bros. 5199, VG, from $10.00 to $20.00.

Fender, Freddie; Wasted Days & Wasted Nights, Duncan 1001, EX...$15.00

Five Satins, I'll Be Seeing You, Ember 1061, EX $10.00

Fleetwoods, Mr Blue, Dolton 2001, EX........................$20.00

Gerry & the Pacemakers, Don't Let the Sun Catch You Crying, Laurie 3251, M in EX picture sleeve.........$10.00

Gilley, Mickey; Susie-Q, Astro 104, EX $20.00

Gore, Lesley; It's My Party, Mercury 72119, M in EX picture sleeve $20.00

Holly, Buddy; Slippin' & Slidin', Coral 62448, EX.......$30.00

Ink Spots, Ebb Tide, King 1297, EX $15.00

John, Elton; Crocodile Rock, MCA 40000, M in EX picture sleeve $5.00

Kodaks, Teenager's Dream, Fury 1007, EX..................$20.00

Lamplighters, Tell Me You Care, Federal 12176, EX...$35.00

Lewis, Jerry Lee; Crazy Arms, Sun 259, EX.................$15.00

Little Richard, Tutti-Frutti, Specialty 561, EX.................$8.00

Majestics, Unhappy & Blue, Chex 1004, EX...............$15.00

Mamas & the Papas, California Dreamin', Dunhill 4020, M in EX picture sleeve $6.00

Moonglos, Foolish Me, Chess 1598, EX $16.00

Nelson, Ricky; Be Bop Baby, Imperial, EX in EX picture sleeve $35.00

Orbison, Roy; Only the Lonely, Monument 21, M in EX picture sleeve $20.00

Orioles, If You Believe, Jubilee 5161, EX $15.00

Presley, Elvis; Bringing It Back/Pieces of My Life, RCA R1-10401, 1975 reissue, VG, $10.00 to $12.00.

Presley, Elvis; I Got a Woman, RCA 6637, EX.............$20.00

Pretenders, Ding Dong Bells, Bethlehem 3050, EX in EX picture sleeve $15.00

Robbins, Marty; Long Tall Sally, Columbia 40679, EX ..$20.00

Sam the Sham & the Pharaohs, Wooly Bully, XL 906, EX in EX picture sleeve $20.00

Shirelles, Will You Love Me Tomorrow, Scepter 1211, EX $15.00

Teardrops, The Stars Are Out Tonight, Josie 766, EX.$75.00

Tune Weavers, Happy Happy Birthday Baby, Casa Grande 4037, EX..$30.00

Turtles, Happy Together, White Whale 244, M in EX picture sleeve $6.00

Vinton, Bobby; Roses Are Red, Epic 9509, M...............$8.00

Whitman, Slim; China Doll, Imperial 8156, EX $15.00

78 rpm

Avalon, Frankie; De De Dinah, Chancellor 1011, EX .**$20.00**

Berry, Chuck; Maybelline, Chess 1604, EX **$15.00**

Cash, Johnny; I Walk the Line, Sun 241, EX..............**$15.00**

Darin, Bobby (& the Jaybirds); Queen of the Hop, Atco 6127, EX..**$20.00**

Day, Bobby; Little Bitty Pretty One, Class 211, EX **$25.00**

Del Vikings, Come Go With Me, Dot 15538, EX.........**$40.00**

Domino, Fats; Boogie Woogie Baby, Imperial 5065, EX..**$15.00**

Eddy, Duane; Rebel-'Rouser, Jaime 1104, EX.............**$15.00**

Ellington, Duke; Birmingham Breakdown, Brunswick 3480, EX..**$13.00**

Everly Brothers, Bird Dog, Cadence 1350, EX **$30.00**

Helms, Bobby; My Special Angel, Decca 30423, EX...**$20.00**

Holiday, Billie; Time on My Hands, Okeh 5991, NM .**$10.00**

Little Richard, Long Tall Sally, Specialty 572, EX **$15.00**

Lymon, Frankie & the Teenagers; I Promise To Remember, Gee 1018, EX **$12.00**

McPhatter, Clyde & the Drifters; There You Go, Atlantic 2038, EX..**$20.00**

Nelson, Ricky; Lonesome Town, Imperial 5545, EX ...**$25.00**

Perkins, Carl; Blue Suede Shoes, Sun 234, EX............**$20.00**

Presley, Elvis; Heartbreak Hotel, RCA 6420, EX.........**$20.00**

Price, Lloyd; Stagger Lee, ABC 9972, EX **$30.00**

Rodgers, Jimmy; Honeycomb, Roulette 4015, EX **$20.00**

LP Albums

Anka, Paul; Diana, ABC Paramount 420, EX...............**$20.00**

Arnold, Eddy; All-Time Favorites, RCA Victor 1223, EX...**$20.00**

Autry, Gene; Western Classics, Columbia 9001, 10", EX ..**$20.00**

BB King, The Great BB King, Crown 5143, EX **$20.00**

Beatles, Ain't She Sweet, Atco 169, stereo, EX............**$75.00**

Berry, Chuck; Chuck Berry Is on Top, Chess 1435, EX..**$50.00**

Cadets, The; Rockin' & Rollin', Crown 5015, EX.........**$50.00**

Cash, Johnny; Greatest!, Sun 1240, EX........................**$50.00**

Chiffons, He's So Fine, Laurie 2018, EX......................**$50.00**

Cline, Patsy; Patsy Cline Showcase, Coral 4202, EX ...**$30.00**

Diddley, Bo; Have Guitar Will Travel, Chess 2974, EX...**$60.00**

Everly Brothers, 15 Everly Hits, Cadence 3062, EX **$15.00**

Fabian, Rockin' Hot, Chancellor 5019, EX...................**$40.00**

Flamingos, Sound of the Flamingos, End 316, EX **$60.00**

Gilley, Mickey; Lonely Wine, Astro 101, EX..............**$175.00**

Haley, Bill (& the Comets); Rock Around the Clock, Decca 8225, EX..**$75.00**

Holly, Buddy; The Buddy Holly Story, Coral 57279, EX..**$60.00**

Lewis, Jerry Lee; Jerry Lee's Greatest, Sun 1265, EX...**$35.00**

Muddy Waters, The Best of Muddy Waters, Chess 1427, EX..**$75.00**

Nelson, Ricky; Ricky, Imperial 9048, EX.....................**$40.00**

Perkins, Carl; Whole Lotta Shakin', Columbia 1234, EX .**$75.00**

Platters, The; The Platters, Mercury 20146, EX...........**$20.00**

Reeves, Jim; Singing Down the Lane, RCA Victor 1256, EX..**$30.00**

Robbins, Marty; The Song of Robbins, Columbia 976, EX..**$20.00**

Rydell, Bobby; Bobby's Biggest Hits, Cameo 1009, EX ..**$30.00**

Shannon, Del; Runaway, Big Top 1303, EX **$50.00**

Shirelles, Baby It's You, Scepter 504, EX....................**$50.00**

Sons of the Pioneers, Favorites, RCA Victor 1130, EX .**$15.00**

Twitty, Conway; The Rock & Roll Story, MGM 3907, EX .**$40.00**

Valens, Richie; His Greatest Hits, Del-Fi 1225, EX **$25.00**

Williams, Hank; Honky Tonkin', MGM 242, 10", EX ..**$75.00**

Red Wing

For almost a century, Red Wing, Minnesota, was the center of a great pottery industry. In the early 1900s several local companies merged to form the Red Wing Stoneware Company. Until they introduced their dinnerware lines in 1935, most of their production centered around stoneware jugs, crocks, flowerpots, and other utilitarian items. To reflect the changes made in 1935, the name was changed to Red Wing Potteries Inc. In addition to scores of lovely dinnerware lines, they also made vases, planters, flowerpots, etc., some with exceptional shapes and decorations.

Some of their more recognizable lines of dinnerware and those you'll most often find are Bob White (decorated in blue and brown brush strokes with quail), Tampico (featuring a collage of fruit including watermelon), Random Harvest (simple pink and brown leaves and flowers), and Village Green (or Brown, solid-color pieces introduced in the '50s). Often you'll find complete or nearly complete sets, and when you do, the lot price is usually a real bargain.

If you'd like to learn more about the subject, we recommend *Red Wing Stoneware, An Identification and Value Guide,* and *Red Wing Collectibles*, both by Dan and Gail DePasquale and Larry Peterson. B.L. Dollen has written a book called *Red Wing Art Pottery*. All are published by Collector Books.

Advisors: Wendy and Leo Frese, Artware (See Directory, Red Wing); and B.L. and R.L. Dollen, Dinnerware (See Directory, Red Wing)

Club/Newsletter: *Red Wing Collectors Newsletter*
Red Wing Collectors Society, Inc.
Doug Podpeskar, membership information
624 Jones St., Eveleth, MN 55734-1631; 218-744-4854
Please include SASE when requesting information.

Artware

Ash receiver, elephant, white, #875n, #420, 5"..........**$175.00**

Ash receiver, pelican, white, #880..............................**$170.00**

Bowl, console; African, brown engobe, #1329, 18"..**$300.00**

Bowl, console; luster black & white, #2310, 13".........**$75.00**

Flower frog, Fern, white, #1046 ....**$150.00**

Lamp, Grecian group, deep maroon, unmarked but molded after vase #302 ....**$125.00**

Lamp, green, elephant handles, 9"..............................**$175.00**

Lamp, yellow crackle, handles, 7x12" across, EX **$125.00**

Pitcher, Gypsy Trail, cobalt w/wood handle **$50.00**
Planter, Belle Kogin, forest green w/yellow interior, #B1401 ....**$12.00**
Planter, piano form, black (unusual color), #M-1525...**$200.00**
Planter, ram head, #739, 10" **$125.00**
Shoe, light green, #991, 5 /12", NM **$35.00**
Vase, Acorn, yellow crackle, blue circle mark, #173 ....**$100.00**
Vase, Belle 100, Dutch Blue, #792, 10" **$100.00**
Vase, cornucopia; Seafoam, #714, 8½" **$50.00**
Vase, green matt, blue circle mark, #155, 15" **$150.00**
Vase, Peacock, yellow, blue circle mk, #187 ....**$75.00**
Vase, Seafoam, #744, 7" **$75.00**
Vase, seashell form, #1066, 9" wide **$100.00**
Vase, Swan, white (scarce), #257, blue circle mark, NM..**$100.00**
Wing, maroon, Red Wing Potteries USA.....................**$50.00**

Angelfish ashtray, #933, deep green, $125.00.
(Photo courtesy Leo and Wendy Frese)

Dinnerware

Blossom Time, bowl, rim soup.....................................**$12.50**
Blossom Time, butter dish, rectangular **$22.50**
Blossom Time, celery tray...**$18.00**
Blossom Time, creamer & sugar bowl, w/lid..............**$32.50**
Blossom Time, cup, from $4 to **$8.00**
Blossom Time, plate, dinner; 10½" **$12.50**
Blossom Time, relish **$18.00**
Bob White, bowl, rim soup **$20.00**
Bob White, bowl, salad; 12" **$50.00**
Bob White, bowl, sauce **$12.00**
Bob White, butter dish, rectangular **$38.00**
Bob White, cruets, pr, w/stand....................................**$85.00**
Bob White, cup & saucer..**$10.00**
Bob White, marmite, w/lid **$22.50**
Bob White, plate, dinner; 10½" **$12.50**
Bob White, plate, 6½" **$15.00**
Bob White, platter, 13" **$75.00**
Bob White, relish, 3 compartments **$50.00**
Bob White, salt & pepper shakers, pr..........................**$40.00**
Bob White, teapot...**$95.00**
Bob White, tray, 24" **$65.00**
Brittany, bowl, cream soup; w/lid................................**$42.50**
Brittany, bowl, nappy; 9" **$32.00**
Brittany, candle holders, pr...**$75.00**

Brittany, cup & saucer...**$22.50**
Brittany, gravy boat...**$47.50**
Brittany, plate, chop; 14"..**$60.00**
Brittany, plate, dinner; 10" **$22.50**
Capistrano, bowl, cereal **$10.00**
Capistrano, bowl, fruit...**$7.50**
Capistrano, egg plate **$68.00**
Capistrano, plate, dinner; 10½" **$18.50**
Capistrano, plate, 7½"..**$10.00**
Capistrano, platter, 15" **$45.00**
Capistrano, salt & pepper shakers, pr..........................**$20.00**
Capistrano, soup tureen, w/lid.....................................**$38.00**
Capistrano, spoon rest...**$17.50**
Capistrano, teapot...**$75.00**
Iris, bowl, cereal **$10.00**
Iris, bowl, divided vegetable..**$24.00**
Iris, creamer **$14.00**
Iris, cup, coffee **$15.00**
Iris, cup & saucer..**$15.00**
Iris, plate, chop **$42.50**
Iris, plate, dinner; 10½"...**$26.00**
Iris, plate, 6½"...**$10.00**
Lexington, bowl, rim soup..**$10.00**
Lexington, casserole, w/lid, from $30 to......................**$35.00**
Lexington, creamer & sugar bowl, w/lid **$30.00**
Lexington, egg plate, w/lid...**$15.00**
Lexington, pitcher, water..**$40.00**
Lexington, plate, dinner; 10½" **$12.50**
Lexington, plate, 6½"..**$6.50**
Lexington, relish, 3-compartment **$18.00**
Lexington, salt & pepper shakers, pr **$14.00**
Lotus, bowl, cereal..**$8.00**
Lotus, creamer..**$14.00**
Lotus, cup, coffee **$12.50**
Lotus, gravy boat, w/tray...**$22.50**
Lotus, plate, dinner; 10½" **$20.00**
Lotus, plate, 3-part w/indent for cup............................**$14.50**
Lotus, spoon rest..**$18.00**
Lotus, sugar bowl, w/lid...**$17.50**
Lute Song, beverage server...**$75.00**
Lute Song, bowl, fruit...**$7.50**
Lute Song, bowl, vegetable..**$24.00**
Lute Song, bread tray..**$32.50**
Lute Song, creamer...**$14.00**
Lute Song, cup & saucer **$12.00**
Lute Song, plate, dinner; 10½"....................................**$15.00**
Lute Song, platter, sm...**$22.50**
Lute Song, relish, 6-pc..**$65.00**
Lute Song, salt & pepper shakers, pr..........................**$17.50**
Orleans, bowl, nappy; 9"..**$30.00**
Orleans, bowl, vegetable; lg...**$24.00**
Orleans, creamer & sugar bowl, w/lid..........................**$60.00**
Orleans, plate, dinner; 10" **$22.00**
Orleans, plate, 6" **$8.00**
Orleans, salt & pepper shakers, pr..............................**$38.00**
Orleans, teapot...**$115.00**
Pepe, bowl, salad; 10"..**$42.50**

Pepe, butter dish, rectangular.....................................$32.50
Pepe, casserole, w/lid, 2½-qt......................................$38.00
Pepe, celery tray..$17.50
Pepe, cup & saucer...$12.50
Pepe, cup & saucer, demitasse.....................................$17.50
Pepe, plate, dinner; 10"...$12.50
Pepe, plate, 6"..$6.00
Pepe, platter, 15"...$30.00
Random Harvest, bowl, divided vegetable.................$30.00
Random Harvest, bowl, nappy.....................................$17.00
Random Harvest, creamer...$28.00
Random Harvest, cup & saucer, from $15 to $17.50
Random Harvest, gravy boat, w/tray...........................$42.50
Random Harvest, plate, luncheon; 8½"......................$20.00
Random Harvest, plate, 6½"...$7.50
Random Harvest, platter, 15".......................................$28.00
Random Harvest, relish..$22.50
Random Harvest, salt & pepper shakers, pr...............$32.50
Round-Up, bowl, rim soup..$45.00
Round-Up, bowl, salad; 5½"..$42.50
Round-Up, bowl, salad; 12".......................................$100.00
Round-Up, creamer & sugar bowl, w/lid....................$85.00
Round-Up, cup & saucer...$75.00
Round-Up, plate, dinner; 10½"...................................$55.00
Round-Up, platter, 13"...$90.00
Round-Up, platter, 20"...$155.00
Round-Up, salt & pepper shakers, pr.........................$95.00

Round-Up, saucer, $25.00 to $30.00; Sugar bowl with lid, from $52.00 to $65.00. (Photo courtesy B.L. and R.L. Dollen)

Tampico, bowl, cereal...$16.00
Tampico, creamer...$30.00
Tampico, cup & saucer...$30.00
Tampico, mug, coffee, from $40 to............................$50.00
Tampico, pitcher, water..$90.00
Tampico, plate, dinner; 10½".....................................$35.00
Tampico, plate, 6½"...$7.50
Tampico, platter, 13"...$27.50
Tampico, relish..$22.50
Town & Country, bowl, salad; 6".................................$18.00
Town & Country, cruet, w/stopper..............................$80.00
Town & Country, plate, luncheon; 8"..........................$22.00
Town & Country, syrup jug...$50.00
Town & Country, teacup & saucer...............................$22.50

Regal China

Perhaps best known for their Beam whiskey decanters, the Regal China company (of Antioch, Illinois) also produced some exceptionally well-modeled ceramic novelties, among them their 'hugger' salt and pepper shakers, designed by artist Ruth Van Tellingen Bendel. (Of all pieces about 15% are Bendel and 85% are Van Tellingen.) Facing pairs made to 'lock' together arm-in-arm, some huggies are signed Bendel while others bear the Van Tellingen mark. Another popular design is her Peek-a-Boo Bunny line, depicting the coy little bunny in the red and white 'jammies' who's just about to pop his buttons. (The cookie jar has been reproduced.)

See also Cookie Jars; Old MacDonald's Farm.

Advisor: Rick Spencer (See Directory, Regal)

Bears, white w/pink & brown trim, pr.....................$110.00
Bunnies, white w/black & pink trim, pr, from $150 to..$200.00
Love bugs, burgundy, lg, pr, from $175 to................$225.00
Love bugs, green, sm, pr..$65.00
Pigs, kissing, gray w/pink trim, lg, pr, from $400 to....$450.00

Van Tellingen Shakers

Bears, brown, pr, from $25 to.....................................$28.00
Boy & dog, white, pr...$68.00
Bunnies, solid colors, pr, from $28 to........................$32.00
Ducks, pr..$38.00

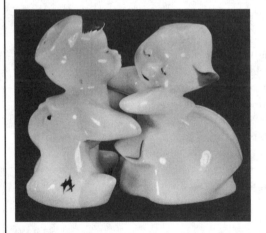

Dutch boy and girl, from $45.00 to $50.00 for the pair.

Mary & lamb, pr...$60.00
Peek-a-Boo, red dots, lg, pr (+), from $450 to.........$500.00
Peek-a-Boo, red dots, sm, pr, from $260 to..............$285.00
Peek-a-Book, white solid, sm, pr...............................$210.00
Sailor & mermaid, pr, from $225 to..........................$260.00

Miscellaneous

Salt & pepper shakers, A Nod to Abe, 3-pc nodder.$300.00
Salt & pepper shakers, cat, sitting w/eyes closed, white w/hat
   & gold bow, pr..$225.00

Salt & pepper shakers, clown, pr..............................$450.00
Salt & pepper shakers, Dutch girl, pr $275.00
Salt & pepper shakers, Fifi, pr...................................$450.00
Salt & pepper shakers, fish, mk C Miller, 1-pc...........$55.00
Salt & pepper shakers, French Chef, white w/gold trim, pr,
    from $250 to...$350.00
Salt & pepper shakers, Humpty Dumpty, pr.............$140.00
Salt & pepper shakers, pig, pink, C Miller, 1-pc.........$95.00
Salt & pepper shakers, tulip, pr..................................$50.00

Restaurant China

Restaurant china, also commonly called cafe ware, diner china, institutional china, hotelware, or commercial china, is specifically designed for use in commercial food service. In addition to restaurants, it is used on board airplanes, ships, and trains, as well as in the dining areas of hotels, railroad stations, airports, government offices, military facilities, corporations, schools, hospitals, department and drug stores, amusement and sports parks, churches, clubs, and the like. Though most hotelware produced in America before 1900 has a heavy gauge nonvitrified body, vitrified commercial china made post-1910 includes some of the finest quality ware ever produced, far surpassing that of nonvitrified household products. A break- and chip-resistant rolled or welted edge is characteristic of American ware produced from the 1920s through the 1970s and is still frequently used, though no longer a concern on the very durable high alumina content bodies introduced in the 1960s. In addition, commercial tableware is also made of porcelain, glass-ceramic, glass laminate, glass, melamine, pewter-like metal, and silverplate. Airlines use fine gauge china in first class, due to space and weight factors. And beginning in the late 1970s, fine gauge porcelain and bone china became a popular choice of upscale American restaurants, hotels, and country clubs. To reduce loss from wear, most decoration is applied to bisque, then glazed and glaze fired (i.e. underglaze) or to glaze-fired ware, then fired into the glaze (i.e. in-glaze). Until the 1970s many restaurants regularly ordered custom-decorated white-, deep tan-, blue-, or pink-bodied patterns. However, it is estimated that more than 90% of today's commercial ware is plain or embossed white. For decades collectors have searched for railroad and ship china. Interest in airline china is on the rise. Attractive standard (stock) patterns are now also sought by many. Western motifs and stencil airbrushed designs are especially treasured. The popularity of high quality American-made Oriental designs has increased. Most prefer traditional medium-heavy gauge American vitrified china, though fine china collectors no doubt favor the commercial china products of Pickard or Royal Doulton. While some find it difficult to pass up any dining concern or transportation system top-marked piece, others seek ware that is decorated with a military logo or department store, casino, or amusement park name. Some collect only creamers, other butters or teapots. Some look for ware made by a particular manufacturer (e.g. Tepco), others specific patterns such as Willow or Indian Tree, or pink, blue, or tan body colors. It is currently considered fashionable to serve home-cooked meals on mismatched top-marked hotelware. Reminiscent of days gone by, pre-1960s restaurant or railroad china brings to mind pre-freeway cross-country vacations by car or rail when dining out was an event, unlike the quick stops at today's fast-food and family-style restaurants. For a more through study of the subject, we recommend *Restaurant China, Identification & Value Guide for Restaurant, Airline, Ship & Railroad Dinnerware, Volume 1* and *Volume 2,* by Barbara Conroy (Collector Books); her website with a list of contents and details of her books along with many pages of additional restaurant china information is listed in the Directory.

In the lines below, TM indicates top-marked or side-marked. Please note: Commercial food service china is neither advertising or souvenir china, since it is not not meant to be removed from the restaurant premises.

Advisor: Barbara Conroy (See Directory, Dinnerware)

Club: RWCN Restaurant Ware Collectors
http://www.yahoo.com/clubs/rwcnrestaurantwarecollectors

Restaurant, Hotel, Department and Drug Store, Casino, and Company Cafeteria China

Fairmont Hotel (San Francisco) AD cup and saucer, Syracuse, 1951 date code, $35.00. (Photo courtesy Barbara Conroy)

Airport Marina Hotel (adjacent LA Airport) 10" plate, AM TM, Wallace, late 1950s-early 1960s..............................$22.00
American Hotel Corps cake cover, sign TMs in cobalt & white pattern, Scammell (Lamberton), 1930s.................$40.00
Andersen Pea Soup TM soup plate, Jackson, 1970s...$32.00
Antoines Restaurant (New Orleans) TM 7" plate, Syracuse, 1964 date code...$22.00
Aunt Jemima's Kitchens TM 10" plate, Wellsville, 1950s, minimum value...$150.00
Blue Willow pattern rice bowl, Hall, c 1930s.............$28.00
Blue Willow pattern 8" plate, Jackson, c 1940s..........$19.00
Branding Iron pattern brown on tan body 6" plate, Tepco...$25.00
Chicken in the Rough TM mug, Syracuse, 1950s........$80.00
Copper Penny TM mug, Shenango, 1960s.................$25.00

Denny's maroon stencil airbrush rimmed grapefruit, Denny's Coffee Shop TM, Tepco, 1950s.................**$35.00**

Desert Inn (Las Vegas NV) cream pitcher, DI & cactus TM, 1953 date code.................**$50.00**

Disneyland 6" melamine plate, D TM, Epicure mark by Plastic Mug Co, 1980s.................**$18.00**

Dunkin' Donuts tan cup w/out saucer, script letter & doughboy TM, Jackson, 1960s.................**$72.00**

Early California pattern 13" compartment plate, blue (uncommon color) on white body, Tepco.................**$200.00**

El Rancho pattern creamer, brown on tan body, Wallace, 1950s.................**$45.00**

Elias Brother's Big Boy grapefruit, mustard rim decoration & TM, Sterling, 1965 date code.................**$35.00**

Fairmont Hotel (San Francisco) 7" plate, black script TM, Shenango, 1960s.................**$12.00**

Far East Cafe (sm CA chain) 7" plate, TM in capitals, Tepco, 1950s-1960s.................**$20.00**

Ford mug, green script TM, Shenango, 1950s.................**$80.00**

Foster's 7" plate, brown transfer print border w/brown script TM, Trenton (Scammell), 1940s.................**$16.00**

General Motors 9" plate, navy blue TM, Sterling, 1968 date code.................**$60.00**

Harold's Club (casino) tan TM mug, Tepco, 1940s...**$125.00**

Hilton Hotels H TM 9" plate, Corning Pyrex, late 1960s..**$18.00**

Hobo Joe TM footed mug, Hall, 1960s.................**$26.00**

Howard Johnson's AD cup & saucer, maroon Simon & Pieman TM, Shenango, 1960s, minimum value....**$60.00**

Howard Johnson's 10" grill plate, maroon scenic border, Mayer, 1951 date code.................**$50.00**

International House of Pancakes blue Fiesta mug, IHOP TM, Homer Laughlin, 1990s.................**$100.00**

Jade-ite heavy-gauge restaurant 10-oz oatmeal (nappy), Fire-King G309, 1950s.................**$24.00**

Little Tavern Shops TM mug, Shenango, 1953 date code ..**$55.00**

Marineland (Los Angeles CA) 6" plate, script TM, Syracuse, 1962 date code.................**$32.00**

Mayer China Company advertising ashtray, Mayer China 1881 TM, 1930s.................**$50.00**

MGM Grand Casino (Las Vegas) 8" plate, Dudson, 1992-94.................**$30.00**

Mister Donut TM cup w/out saucer, chef w/heart on chest TM, Sterling, 1965 date code, minimum value.....**$65.00**

Montgomery Ward 5½" plate, stylized M above W TM, Syracuse, 1964 date code.................**$17.00**

New York Athletic Club 8½" plate, flying foot logo in wreath TM, Scammell (Lamberton), 1928.................**$35.00**

Ox Head cup & saucer, brown on tan body, Homer Laughlin, late 1960s.................**$35.00**

Peking Gourmet Inn Oriental cup, script TM, Homer Laughlin, early 1990s.................**$5.00**

Qwikee Donuts mug, brown 'Qwikee...get your daily dozen' & donut, TM, Shenango, 1969 date code.................**$110.00**

Red Lion 10" grill plate, Red Lion on tiny sign above door in overall red on white pattern, Shenango, 1960s....**$33.00**

Reddy Kilowatt 9" plate, cartoon TM, Syracuse, 1953 date code.................**$125.00**

Riviera Hotel & Casino (Las Vegas) 6½" platter, crown over R on 3 pink circles TM, Caribe, 1960s, minimum value **$25.00**

Rodeo 8" cream pitcher, multicolor on tan body, Wallace, 1950s.................**$60.00**

Roosevelt Hotel (New Orleans) AD cup & saucer, brown border & TM, Shenango, 1964 date code.................**$35.00**

Sambo's aqua stencil airbrushed 8" TM plate, Jackson, 1969 date code, minimum value.................**$60.00**

Shenango China 9" sample plate, multi-TM, c 1930s...**$120.00**

St Francis Hotel (San Francisco) 6" plate, St F TM, Syracuse, 1957 date code.................**$21.00**

Syracuse China commemorative 8" ashtray, Syracuse China 1871-1971, dated 1971.................**$35.00**

Veterans Administration 4½" TM pitcher, Shenango, 1930s.................**$25.00**

Walgreen TM tan 9½" grill plate, Syracuse Econo-Rim, 1946 date code.................**$47.00**

Walker China Company 4" tan advertising ashtray, Walker China TM, 1940s.................**$40.00**

Western Traveler 6" plate, red (less common color) on white body, Tepco, 1950s.................**$32.00**

White Castle mug, King Size black TM, Mayer, 1961 date code.................**$50.00**

White Tower mug, Good Things To Eat above script White Tower TM, Shenango, 1930s.................**$120.00**

Woolworth's mug, script TM, Syracuse, 1924 date code ..**$175.00**

Yet Wah Oriental cup, script TM, Buffalo, ca 1970s **$6.00**

20th Century Fox 10" plate, rust logo TM, Syracuse, 1993 date code.................**$35.00**

Transportation and Military China

Air Canada ivory bone china entree, no TM, Royal Doulton, 1990s.................**$5.00**

Air France 7½" plate, stylized blue & mustard dragon TM, Bernardaud & Company, 1970-1990s.................**$20.00**

Alaska Airlines 7" plate, Gold Coast TM, Rackett, 1980s..**$16.00**

American Airlines American Eagle II-IBC cup & saucer, platinum AA eagle TM on cup only, Wessco.................**$22.00**

American Airlines cobalt edge-lined 6" plate, no TM, 1980s-1990s.................**$6.00**

American European Express cup & saucer AEE TM Rego, 1997.................**$50.00**

American President Lines cup & saucer, eagle TM, Corning, 1960s-1972.................**$40.00**

Atchison, Topeka & Sante Fe California Poppy butter dish, Syracuse, to 1971, no RR mark.................**$38.00**

British Airways AD cup & saucer, gold Coat of Arms TM, by Ridgeway in 1974 only.................**$30.00**

Chesapeake & Ohio ashtray, Chessie cat TM, Syracuse, 1955-1962, minimum value.................**$85.00**

Chicago, Milwaukee, St Paul & Pacific stencil airbrushed geese & trees (Traveler) cake cover, no TM, Syracuse, 1937-69, minimum value.................**$150.00**

Chicago, Milwaukee, St Paul & Pacific stencil airbrushed geese & trees (Traveler) 7" platter, no TM, Syracuse, 1937-1969, minimum value.................**$50.00**

Delta Air Lines butter dish, name in script TM, Mayer ...**$10.00**
Delta Air Lines gold-lined 7" plate, ABCO......................**$7.00**
Department of the (US) Navy egg cup, department crest TM, Walker, 1959 date code **$12.00**

Eastern Air Lines, covered melamine casserole, 1960s, 7" long, from $8.00 to $10.00. (Photo courtesy Barbara Conroy)

Elders & Ffyes Ltd TM AD cup & saucer, Dunn Bennett, 1950s..**$85.00**
French Line 9" soup, square CGT TM, GDA, 1950s....**$90.00**
Frontier Airlines 7½" L entree, embossed logo TM, early-1980s, ABCO **$8.00**
Grace Line 6" H pitcher, name TM in script, Syracuse, 1942 date code...**$150.00**
Holland America Line 7" plate, NASM TM, Mosa, 1970 date code **$20.00**
Lickenbach Line 7" plate, pennant TM, McNicol, ca 1930s...**$35.00**
Manitou Steamship Co TM AD cup & saucer, Union Porcelain Works, ca 1890s **$265.00**
McClain Airlines cup & saucer, logo TM on cup only, Rego, 1986-88 ....**$28.00**
Midwest Express 7" L entree, name repeated inside gray line border, ABCO, 1992-96..**$12.50**
Moore-McCormack Lines 9½" plate, exclusive gray stencil airbrushed & colored decal Rio pattern, Sterling, 1950s .**$45.00**
National Airlines 7" entree, mustard Sun King logo TM, Sterling or Corning, early 1970s............................**$30.00**
Northwest Airlines salt, pepper & tray, brown & beige line on shakers, TQ Tradex, early 1990s, set....................**$18.00**
Northwest Airlines 6" plate, Regal Imperial TM, Royal Doulton, mid-1980s..**$22.00**
Norwegian American Cruises ashtray, NAC TM, Pillivuyt, 1981 date code...**$11.00**
Pan American 7½" plate, gold eagle TM (not marked Pan Am), Noritake, early 1960s....................................**$37.00**
Prudential Lines 8" platter, P in compass TM, Jackson, Paul McCobb, 1960s...**$28.00**
Royal Cruise Line mug, outlined logo TM Porsgrund, 1982 date code..**$15.00**
Singapore Airlines 6½" plate, gold logo TM & maroon & black border, 1990s...**$16.00**
Southern Pacific Daylight pattern cup & saucer, matt peach glaze, Franciscan & Southern Pacific Lines or SPCo backstamp, 1939-early '40s, minimum value **$500.00**

Southern Pacific Prairie Mountain Wild Flowers cup & saucer, no TM, Syracuse, 1930s-1950s **$110.00**
Sun Line 8" plate, navy blue logo TM, Richard-Ginori, 1980s **$30.00**
Transamerican Airlines 6" plate, gold logo TM, TQ Tradex, 1979-1986...**$12.00**
TWA cup, red & gold TWA TM, Michaud, Rego or ABCO **$6.00**
TWA Royal Ambassador cup & saucer, red & gold RA TM, Rosenthal, 1960s-1975...**$30.00**
Union Pacific Winged Streamliner cup & saucer **$85.00**
United Air Lines cup & saucer, gold logo TM, Syracuse Silhouette backstamp, 1960s **$75.00**
United Air Lines 6" L casserole, blue exterior, no TM, Coors Porcelain, dated 1951 ....**$16.00**
United Air Lines 6½" plate, platinum U TM, Wessco, ca 1977-92 ....**$12.50**
United States Army Corps of Engineers 8" plate, rust flag TM, Scammell, 1930s...**$32.00**
United States Army Medical Department 4" cream pitcher, McNicol, 1940s..**$27.00**
US Air cup (no saucer), gold logo TM, ABCO, 1990-96 ..**$5.00**
US Army Transport bouillon, USAT clover TM, Syracuse, 1942 date code..**$18.00**
US Navy Wardroom Officer's Mess cup & saucer, anchor TM, Shenango, 1950 date code **$25.00**
Western Airlines 60th year pattern 7" plate, 1926 in shield TM, ABCO, 1986......................................**$14.00**
World Airways 6" gold-lined plate, no TM, TQ Tradex, ca 1970s-1988...**$12.50**

Rock 'n Roll Memorabilia

Ticket stubs and souvenirs issued at rock concerts, posters of artists that have reached celebrity status, and merchandise such as dolls, games, clothing, etc., that was sold through retail stores during the heights of their careers are just the things that interest collectors of rock 'n roll memorabilia. Some original, one-of-a-kind examples — for instance, their instruments, concert costumes, and personal items — often sell at the large auction galleries in the east where they've realized very high-dollar prices. For more information we recommend *Rock-N-Roll Treasures* by Joe Hilton and Greg Moore (Collector Books). Greg has also written *A Price Guide to Rock and Roll Collectibles* which is distributed by L-W Book Sales. *Collector's Guide to TV Toys & Memorabilia* by Greg Davis and Bill Morgan contains additional information and photos (it is also published by Collector Books).

Note: Most posters sell in the range of $5.00 to $10.00; those listed below are the higher-end examples in excellent or better condition.

See also Beatles Collectibles; Elvis Presley Memorabilia; Magazines; Movie Posters; Pin-Back Buttons; Records.

Advisor: Bojo/Bob Gottuso (See Directory, Character and Personality Collectibles)

Alice Cooper, book, Billion Dollar Baby, Bob Green, 1974, no dust jacket, EX..............**$70.00**

Alice Cooper, CD set, Life & Crimes, Warner Archives, w/soft-cover book, EX..............**$40.00**

Alice Cooper, LP album, Pretties for You, NM **$25.00**

Alice Cooper, painting on velvet, 1970s, 24x16" **$75.00**

Alice Cooper, resin figure, Lil' Goblins, 6"...................**$35.00**

Alice Cooper, sheet music, Hello - Hooray, M...........**$20.00**

Alice Cooper, sheet music, Only Women Bleed, photo cover, 1974 ....**$20.00**

Alice Cooper, shot glass, Lace & Whiskey on clear glass .**$45.00**

Alice Cooper, toy car, Hot Rockin, diecast steel, 1/24 scale **$20.00**

Animals/Pink Floyd, concert tour program, 1977 ......**$50.00**

Animals/Pink Floyd, 2 Gold CD set, recorded in Texas May 1, 1977, NM............**$42.50**

Beatles, magazine, Official Yellow Submarine, 48 pages, VG............**$45.00**

Bee Gees, puzzle set, On Stage, sealed............**$24.00**

Big Bro, Pink Floyd, Richie Havens, poster, red & green, by Bonnie MacLean, 1967, 21x14", EX **$75.00**

Bobby Sherman, book, Bobby Sherman Still Remembering You, softcover, 234 pages, 1996, 8x11", NM.........**$22.50**

Bobby Sherman, book, The Bobby Sherman Story, many photos, George Carpozi Jr, first printing, Pyramid Books, 1972, VG............**$30.00**

Bobby Sherman, photo, pointing, color, 8x10" **$10.00**

Bobby Sherman, poster, Columbia Pictures Industries Inc, 1971, 37x24", EX............**$32.50**

Bobby Sherman, sheet music, Goin' Home, photo cover, NM **$22.50**

Bobby Vinton, poster, Surf Party, 1-sheet, 1964, NM..**$70.00**

Brenda Lee, Paper Magic Doll, cardboard 10¾" doll w/20 pcs of clothing, Weston Mdsg Corp 1964, no box or folder............**$40.00**

Dave Clark 5, lobby card, Having a Wild Weekend, 11x14", EX............**$22.00**

Dave Clark 5, music card, photo of Dave & group on 1 side, list of songs on back, 1960s, EX............**$3.00**

Dave Clark 5, tour book, color front cover, black & white photos inside, 28 pages, 1965, 10x13" **$20.00**

Dave Clark 5, video, VHS, Having a Wild Weekend, Warner Bros Home Video #11268, 1997, sealed............**$24.00**

David Cassidy, book, Fear & Loathing on the Partridge Family Bus, C'mon Get Happy, softcover, blue, M **$30.00**

David Cassidy, CD, When I'm a Rock 'n Roll Star, RCA/Razor & Tie Entertainment, 1996, M............**$20.00**

David Cassidy, Colorforms, Partridge Family, 1972, NM in EX box............**$80.00**

David Cassidy, nightshirt, Threads of Time, 100% cotton, 1995 ....**$45.00**

David Cassidy, photo badge, 1970s, 3", M, sealed......**$24.00**

David Cassidy, poster, portrait before stone wall, Artko, Columbia, 1972, 11x17", EX............**$12.50**

David Cassidy, promo photo, black & white, 5x7".....**$16.00**

David Cassidy, puzzle, portrait in front of brick wall, M in NM box............**$48.00**

David Cassidy, video, VHS, Spirit of '76, featured w/various other performers, original print, NM **$45.00**

Everly Brothers, guitar pick, photo, 5-point star cutout, M............**$20.00**

Everly Brothers, poster, Polygram Records, 1986, 36x24", EX............**$12.00**

Everly Brothers, tour book, 1985, NM **$24.00**

Frankie Avalon, pin-back button, photo portrait on pink, 3½"............**$15.00**

Grateful Dead, poster, Fox Theater, St Louis MO, 1973, 17½x23", EX............**$275.00**

Herman's Hermits, color glossy photo, 8x10" **$15.00**

Herman's Hermits, poster, Hold On!, 1966, 41x27", EX..**$32.00**

Herman's Hermits, tour book, 1967, EX **$25.00**

KISS, backstage pass, pictures band wearing make-up ...**$9.00**

KISS, belt, full-figure color picture w/leather belt, 1970s..**$30.00**

KISS, belt buckle, logo on brass, 1970s............**$28.00**

KISS, card sheet, set of 36 American Images cards, black & white, 14½x21½", uncut............**$30.00**

KISS, guitar pick, Psycho Circus, Gene, Paul or Ace, ea .**$15.00**

KISS, gum cards, Series I, complete set of 66 ....**$50.00**

KISS, lighter, Kiss Army, Zippo, w/litho sleeve...........**$22.50**

KISS, LP bag, colorful promo (given out w/LP)............**$18.00**

KISS, magazine, Rock Scene, September, 1978 ....**$12.00**

KISS, make-up kit, Official KISS Army, 1997.................**$8.00**

KISS, masks, full head, rubber w/lifelike hair, set of 4 ...**$130.00**

KISS, megaphone drinking cup, yellow, w/logo & photo, Aucoin & Pepsi, 1977, unpunched............**$75.00**

KISS, necklace, gold letters, vending machine item......**$4.00**

KISS, necklace, silver-colored lightning bolt w/chain, 1980............**$25.00**

KISS, pass, Revenge, laminated, 1992............**$15.00**

KISS, plate, bas-relief, Gartlan USA, 8" **$85.00**

KISS, program, 1984 World Tour............**$50.00**

KISS, puzzle, Gene Simmons, complete **$60.00**

KISS, puzzle, Paul Stanley, complete w/box............**$70.00**

KISS, slippers, Peter Criss, pr, w/orig Spencer Gifts tag .**$30.00**

KISS, stickers, Live II, 8x10"............**$9.00**

KISS, transistor radio, color logo and group photos on label, M, $125.00. (Photo courtesy June Moon)

Moby Grape, Country Joe & Fish, poster, by Mari Tepper, 1968, 21x14", NM..**$90.00**

Monkees, doll and record (four shown), Show Biz Babies by Remco, EX, each, $115.00. (NM on card, working, each, $200.00.) (Photo courtesy Bojo)

Partridge Family, bus, Johnny Lightening, diecast metal, 3" **$10.00**

Petula Clark, poster, Track the Man Down, 1960s, 41x28", EX...**$20.00**

Ricky Nelson, book, Ricky Nelson Story - Hollywood Hillbilly, Finnbar International, 1988.....................**$26.00**

Ricky Nelson, paperback book, More of Ricky's Exciting Adventures, Dell #998, 1959, EX+ **$20.00**

Ricky Nelson, photo, 1960s, double-matted to fit 10x12" frame...**$15.00**

Rolling Stones, backstage pass, from $5 to **$10.00**

Rolling Stones, blue jeans jacket, 98 Tour, NM **$90.00**

Rolling Stones, book, Ultimate Guide Book, 1962-65, EX..**$45.00**

Rolling Stones, concert ticket, Farewell concert at Rich Stadium, 1975, unused **$70.00**

Rolling Stones, concert tickct, New York, 1972, unused..**$165.00**

Rolling Stones, lobby card, Gimme Shelter, 13¾x22", EX, from $10 to..**$20.00**

Rolling Stones, mobile, Voodoo Lounge, poster board material, complete **$47.50**

Rolling Stones, photo book, PYX Productions, 1964, NM...**$27.50**

Rolling Stones, poster, Altamont, 14x22", M, from $10 to..**$20.00**

Rolling Stones, poster, Goats Head Soup, Atlantic Records/Rolling Stones Records, promotional, NM, from $45 to...**$75.00**

Rolling Stones, poster, Oakland Stadium, 1989, 31x23", from $20 to...**$50.00**

Rolling Stones, poster, Rock & Roll Circus, EX, from $20 to...**$40.00**

Rolling Stones, poster, Veterans Stadium, 1997, M, from $15 to...**$25.00**

Rolling Stones, poster, 1989 North American Tour, 22½x34½", NM, from $15 to............................**$25.00**

Rolling Stones, rub-off transfers, 27 lip logos, unopened..**$5.00**

Rolling Stones, slider puzzle, lips & tongue, 16 squares slide to make picture, 3x3½", EX **$22.50**

Rolling Stones, song book, Exile on Main St, 102 pages, 1972, EX..**$38.00**

Rolling Stones, T-shirt, Bridges to Babylon, Aloha Stadium, M, from $20 to **$40.00**

Rolling Stones, T-shirt, Flat Tongue tour, M, from $15 to **$30.00**

Rolling Stones, T-Shirt, Voodoo Lounge, M, from $15 to..**$25.00**

Rolling Stones, T-shirt, 1981 concert, M, from $15 to.**$25.00**

Rolling Stones, tie, Some Girls, embossed silk, by RM Style, M **$100.00**

Rolling Stones, tour book, black & white photos inside, color cover, 1965, NM..**$85.00**

Rolling Stones, tour book, 1972.............................**$22.50**

Rolling Stones, wall clock, Musidor BV Clock Works, MIB stock..**$40.00**

Rookwood

Although this company was established in 1879, it continued to produce commercial artware until it closed in 1967. Located in Cincinnati, Ohio, Rookwood is recognized today as the largest producer of high-quality art pottery ever to operate in the United States.

Most of the pieces listed here are from the later years of production, but we've included some early pieces as well. With few exceptions, all early Ohio art pottery companies produced an artist-decorated brown-glaze line — Rookwood's was called Standard. Among their other early lines were Sea Green, Iris, Jewel Porcelain, Wax Matt, and Vellum.

Virtually all of Rookwood's pieces are marked. The most familiar mark is the 'reverse R'-P monogram. It was first used in 1886, and until 1900 a flame point was added above it to represent each passing year. After the turn of the century, a Roman numeral below the monogram was used to indicate the current year. In addition to the dating mark, a die-stamped number was used to identify the shape.

The Cincinnati Art Galleries routinely hold large and important cataloged auctions. The full-color catalogs sometimes contain company history and listings of artists and designers with their monograms (as well as company codes and trademarks). Collectors now regard them as an excellent source for information and study.

Ashtray, #2602, 1934, frog, blue/green crystalline matt, 3"..**$300.00**

Bookends, #2275, 1930, rook w/berries, green crystalline, 5¼", pr...**$550.00**

Bookends, #2998, 1931, basset hounds, white matt, 4¾", minor peppering, pr...**$600.00**

Bookends, #6202, 1947, Man-O-War, yellow hi-glaze, 6¼", pr **$700.00**

Bowl, #7234, 1954, orange hi-glaze, impressed commercial information, 7½" dia................................**$60.00**

Bowl, console; #6826, 1950, celadon green hi-glaze, 4x12½" **$50.00**

Bowl, console; #7064, 1950, celadon green hi-glaze, 5½x11" **$110.00**

Figurine, #6689, carolers, beige hi-glaze, 5" **$250.00**

Flower bowl, #2923, 1948, yellow hi-glaze w/female nudes at ea end, 6⅞x12¼" **$500.00**

Paperweight, #2777, 1946, dog, cream gloss, 4¾" **$150.00**

Paperweight, #2797, 1928, elephant, blue matt, 3¼", NM..**$375.00**

Paperweight, #6030, 1956, rooster, white matt, 5" **$250.00**

Paperweight, #6461, 1934, bulldog, Nubian Black, 2⅜"....**$750.00**

Paperweight, #6488, 1946, elephant, green hi-glaze, 3⅝" **$150.00**

Paperweight, #6661, 1945, kittens, blue hi-glaze, 1⅜".......**$700.00**

Paperweight, #6992, 1948, goose, yellow mottle over green hi-glaze, 4½" **$300.00**

Pen holder, #2563A, 1951, panther, green hi-glaze, 3¾x7" .**$300.00**

Pin tray, #1084, 1939, owl figure, 4½" **$250.00**

Tile, #3077, 1930, embossed parrot, 5¾" square **$180.00**

Tray, #7149, 1949, mottled gray hi-glaze, 7½" dia **$90.00**

Tray, #7216, 1964, mottled purple hi-glaze, 7½" dia...**$300.00**

Tray, #7232, 1944, orange hi-glaze, 7" dia **$50.00**

Trivet, #3077, 1940, embossed parrot decor.............**$325.00**

Vase, #S2164, coromandel glaze, drilled for lamp, 11½" .**$600.00**

Vase, #778, 1946, cream hi-glaze, 10" **$150.00**

Vase, #778, 1951, peach hi-glaze, 9½" **$220.00**

Vase, #1632, 1922, blue-green mottle, 3-handled form w/embossed geometric decor, 5¾" dia...............**$220.00**

Vase, #2089, 1923, maroon matt w/gray mottling, 3¾"..**$200.00**

Vase, #2122, 1946, green celadon hi-glaze w/embossed berries at top...**$120.00**

Vase, #2141, 1931, yellow matt w/embossed stylized flowers, 6⅜"...**$250.00**

Vase, #2322, blue crystalline matt, embossed band of rooks below shoulder, 1924, 7¼", $850.00.

Vase, #2428, 1940, green matt, 3 handles, 5½" **$200.00**

Vase, #2587E, 1948, candy apple red hi-glaze, 5" **$130.00**

Vase, #2591, obsure date, molded floral on tan hi-glaze, 5½"..**$110.00**

Vase, #2594, 1930, pink matt w/light green highlights & embossed daisies, 6½" **$210.00**

Vase, #5550F, 1950, Bengal Brown, 3¼"....................**$140.00**

Vase, #6108, 1940, blue crystalline matt w/embossed Art Deco designs, 4¾"..**$225.00**

Vase, #6204C, 1951, turquoise hi-glaze drip over gray mottled hi-glaze, 7"...**$180.00**

Vase, #6316, 1932, blue over gray, 3⅝".........................**$375.00**

Vase, #6357, 1944, tan hi-glaze, 6½" **$100.00**

Vase, #6363, 1948, red hi-glaze w/embossed Art Deco flowers, 6"..**$225.00**

Vase, #6432, 1946, green hi-glaze w/embossed florals, 3½".**$110.00**

Vase, #6434, 1954, green hi-glaze w/embossed florals, 3½" **$120.00**

Vase, #6434, 1954, light blue hi-glaze w/embossed florals, 5½"...**$110.00**

Vase, #6474, 1958, tan hi-glaze, flattened form w/embossed florals, 4"...**$60.00**

Vase, #6503, 1936, brown drip w/blue highlights over ribbed body, 4¼"...**$160.00**

Vase, #6953, 1949, cream hi-glaze, 7" **$130.00**

Vase, #7081, 1951, celadon green hi-glaze, 3"...........**$150.00**

Vase, #7086, 1951, yellow & gray hi-glaze, unusual banded form, 7"..**$700.00**

Rooster and Roses

Back in the 1940s, newlyweds might conceivably have received some of this imported Japanese-made kitchenware as a housewarming gift. They'd no doubt be stunned to see the prices it's now bringing! Rooster and Roses (Ucagco called it Early Provincial) is one of those lines of novelty ceramics from the '40s and '50s that are among today's hottest collectibles. Ucagco was only one of several importers whose label you'll find on this pattern; among other are Py, ACSON, Norcrest, and Lefton. The design is easy to spot — there's the rooster, yellow breast with black crosshatching, brown head and, of course, the red crest and waddle, large full-blown roses with green leaves and vines, and a trimming of yellow borders punctuated by groups of brown lines. (You'll find another line having blue flowers among the roses, and one with a rooster with a green head and a green borders. These are not considered Rooster and Roses by purist collectors, though there is a market for them as well.) The line is fun to collect, since shapes are so diversified. Even though there has been relatively little networking among collectors, more than eighty items have been reported and no doubt more will surface.

Advisor: Jacki Elliott (See Directory, Rooster and Roses)

Ashtray, rectangular, 3x2"..**$9.50**

Ashtray, round or square, sm, from $15 to..................**$25.00**

Ashtray, square, lg, from $35 to **$40.00**

Basket, flared sides, 6", from $45 to **$65.00**

Bell, rooster & chicken on opposing sides, from $35 to .**$95.00**

Biscuit jar, w/wicker handle, from $65 to....................**$95.00**

Bonbon dish, pedestal base, minimum value **$55.00**

Bowl, cereal; from $14 to...**$25.00**

Bowl, rice; on saucer, from $25 to $35.00

Bowl, 8" $25.00

Bread plate, from $15 to $25.00

Butter dish, ¼-lb, from $20 to $25.00

Candle warmer (for tea & coffeepots), from $15 to ...$25.00

Candy dish, flat chicken-shaped tray w/3-dimensional chicken head, made in 3 sizes, from $75 to $100.00

Candy dish, w/3-dimensional leaf handle, from $25 to..$45.00

Canister set, round, 4-pc, from $150 to $175.00

Canister set, square, 4-pc, from $100 to $150.00

Canister set, stacking, minimum value........................$150.00

Carafe, no handle, w/stopper lid, 8", from $65 to $85.00

Carafe, w/handle & stopper lid, 8"..............................$85.00

Casserole dish, w/lid..$65.00

Castor set in revolving wire rack, 2 cruets, mustard jar & salt & pepper shakers, rare, from $75 to...................$125.00

Chamberstick, saucer base, ring handle, from $20 to.$25.00

Cheese dish, slant lid, from $40 to..............................$55.00

Cigarette box w/2 trays, hard to find, from $65 to.....$75.00

Cigarette holder w/2 ashtrays, from $65 to $75.00

Coaster, ceramic disk embedded in round wood tray, rare, minimum value..$45.00

Coffee grinder, rare, minimum value $150.00

Condiment set, 2 cruets, salt & pepper shakers w/mustard jar on tray, miniature, from $50 to....................$75.00

Condiment set, 2 cruets, salt & pepper shakers w/mustard jar atop wire & wood holder, 4 spice canisters below, minimum value $125.00

Cookie jar, ceramic handles, from $85 to $100.00

Creamer & sugar bowl, w/lid, lg..................................$25.00

Creamer & sugar bowl on rectangular tray, from $65 to ..$75.00

Cruets, cojoined w/twisted necks, sm..........................$45.00

Cruets, oil & vinegar, flared bases, pr..........................$45.00

Cruets, oil & vinegar, square, lg, pr, from $30 to........$35.00

Cruets, oil & vinegar, w/salt & pepper shakers in shadow box, from $55 to..$75.00

Cup & saucer $25.00

Demitasse pot, w/4 cups & saucer, minimum value....$150.00

Demitasse pot, w/6 cups & saucers, minimum value...$175.00

Egg cup, from $20 to $25.00

Egg cup on tray, from $35 to $45.00

Egg plate, from $55 to...$65.00

Flowerpot, buttress handles, 5", from $35 to..............$45.00

Hamburger press, wood w/embedded ceramic tray, round, minimum value..$24.00

Instant coffee jar, no attached spoon holder on side, minimum value...$35.00

Instant coffee jar, spoon-holder tube on side, rare.....$45.00

Jam & jelly containers, cojoined, w/lids & spoons, from $35 to..$45.00

Jam & jelly containers, cojoined, w/lids & spoons, w/loop handles & lids, very rare $85.00

Jam jar, attached underplate, from $35 to...................$45.00

Ketchup or mustard jar, flared cylinder w/lettered label, ea, from $25 to...$30.00

Lamp, pinup, made from either a match holder or a salt box, ea, from $75 to $100.00

Lazy Susan on wood pedestal, round covered box at center, 4 sections around outside (2 w/lids), from $150 to ..$250.00

Marmalade, round base w/tab handles, w/lid & spoon, minimum value, from $35 to....................................$55.00

Match holder, wall mount, from $65 to $85.00

Measuring cup set, 4-pc w/matching ceramic rack, from $45 to $65.00

Measuring spoons on 8" ceramic spoon-shaped rack, from $40 to $55.00

Mug, rounded bottom, med, from $20 to....................$25.00

Mug, straight upright bar handle, lg, from $20 to.......$35.00

Napkin holder, from $30 to $40.00

Pitcher, bulbous, 5", from $25 to.................................$30.00

Pitcher, lettered Milk on neck band, from $22.50 to ..$35.00

Pitcher, 3½", from $15 to $20.00

Planter, rolling pin shape, rare, minimum value.........$50.00

Plate, dinner; from $25 to $35.00

Plate, luncheon; from $15 to $25.00

Plate, side salad; crescent shape, hard to find, from $50 to $60.00

Platter, 12", from $35 to...$55.00

Recipe box, part of shadow box set, from $25 to $35.00

Relish tray, 2 round wells w/center handle, 12", from $35 to $40.00

Relish tray, 3 wells w/center handle, from $55 to $65.00

Rolling pin, minimum value $50.00

Salad fork, spoon & salt & pepper shakers w/wooden handles, on ceramic wall-mount rack, minimum value........$55.00

Salad fork & spoon w/wooden handles on ceramic wall-mount rack, from $45 to $65.00

Salt box, wooden lid, from $45 to $55.00

Slipper,   three-dimensional rose on toe, marked Ucacgo, rare, minimum value, $85.00.

(Photo courtesy Jacki Elliott)

Snack tray w/cup, oval, 2-pc, minimum value............$45.00

Snack tray w/cup, rectangular, 2-pc, from $50 to.......$60.00

Syrup pitcher, w/2 sm graduated pitchers on tray, minimum value $60.00

Toast holder, minimum value $75.00

Wall pocket, lavabo, 2-pc, mounted on board, from $85 to $125.00

Wall pocket, scalloped top, bulbous bottom, from $55 to.$65.00

Wall pocket, teapots, facing ea other, pr, minimum value..$90.00

Roselane Sparklers

Beginning as a husband and wife operation in the late 1930s, the Roselane Pottery Company of Pasadena, California, expanded their inventory from the figurines they originally sold to local florists to include a complete line of decorative items that eventually were shipped to Alaska, South America, and all parts of the United States.

One of their lines was the Roselane Sparklers. Popular in the '50s, these small animal and bird figures were air-brush decorated and had rhinestone eyes. They're fun to look for, and though prices are rising steadily, they're still not terribly expensive.

If you'd like to learn more, there's a chapter on Roselane in *The Collector's Encyclopedia of California Pottery, Second Edition,* by Jack Chipman.

Advisor: Lee Garmon (See Directory, Advertising, Reddy Kilowatt)

Angelfish, 4½", from $20 to **$25.00**
Basset hound, sitting, 4", from $15 to **$18.00**
Basset hound pup, 2", from $12 to **$15.00**
Bulldog, fierce expression, looking right, 2", from $12 to **$15.00**
Bulldog, fierce expression, looking up & right, jeweled collar, lg, from $22 to **$25.00**
Bulldog, sitting, slender body, looking right, 6".........**$25.00**
Cat, recumbent, head turned right, tail & paws tucked under body, from $20 to...**$25.00**
Cat, Siamese, sitting, looking straight ahead, jeweled collar, 7", from $25 to **$28.00**
Cat, sitting, head turned right, tail out behind, from $25 to **$28.00**
Cat, standing, head turned left, tail arched over back, jeweled collar, 5½", from $20 to...............................**$25.00**
Cat mother, looking straight ahead, 4½", w/kitten (same pose), 2-pc set, from $25 to.....................................**$30.00**
Chihuahua, sitting, left paw raised, looking straight ahead, 6½"...**$28.00**
Cocker spaniel, 4½"...**$20.00**
Deer, standing, head turned right, looking downward, 5½"...**$25.00**
Deer w/antlers, standing jeweled collar, 4½", from $22 to **$28.00**
Elephant, sitting on hind quarters, 6"..........................**$28.00**
Elephant, trunk raised, striding, jeweled headpiece, 6" ..**$28.00**
Fawn, legs folded under body, 4x3½".........................**$25.00**
Fawn, upturned head, 4x3½" **$20.00**
Fawn, 4½x1½"...**$20.00**
Kangaroo mama w/babies **$40.00**
Kitten, sitting, 1¾" **$12.00**
Owl, very stylized, lg round eyes, teardrop-shaped body, lg..**$25.00**
Owl, 3½" **$15.00**
Owl, 5¼" **$25.00**
Owl, 7"..**$30.00**

Owl baby, 2¼", from $12 to **$15.00**
Pig, lg...**$25.00**

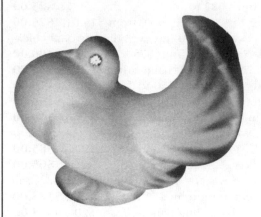

Pouter pigeon, 3½", $20.00.
(Photo courtesy Lee Garmon)

Racoon, standing, 4½", from $20 to **$25.00**
Whippet, sitting, 7½", from $25 to **$28.00**

Rosemeade

The Wahpeton Pottery Company of Wahpeton, North Dakota, chose the trade name Rosemeade for a line of bird and animal figurines, novelty salt and pepper shakers, bells, and many other items which were sold from the 1940s to the 1960s through gift stores and souvenir shops in that part of the country. They were marked with either a paper label or an ink stamp; the name Prairie Rose was also used. See *Collector's Encyclopedia of the Dakota Potteries* by Darlene Hurst Dommel (Collector Books) for more information.

Advisor: Bryce Farnsworth (See Directory, Rosemeade)

Club: North Dakota Pottery Collectors Society
Sandy Short
Box 14, Beach, ND 58621; 701-872-3236. Annual dues: $15; sponsors annual convention and includes 4 newsletters

Ashtray, fish, 6¼", from $100 to **$125.00**
Ashtray, Native American head, 4¼", from $150 to ..**$175.00**
Ashtray, pointer figurine on top, rare, 7", minimum value..**$1,000.00**
Ashtray, Roosevelt National Park Trading Post, 5", from $125 to..**$150.00**
Figurine, circus horse, solid, 4¼x4¼", from $350 to...**$400.00**
Figurine, cock pheasant, 9¼x14"...............................**$400.00**
Figurine, fighting cock, gold glaze, rare, 4⅞x5", minimum value **$400.00**
Figurine, horse, 2-color swirl, 4⅜x3", minimum value .**$500.00**
Figurine, howling coyote, 4½x3⅞", from $250 to.....**$300.00**
Pin, mallard duck, 4", minimum value **$1,000.00**
Pin, Western Meadowlark, 2½", minimum value ...**$1,000.00**
Planter, cock pheasant, 3¾x9¼", minimum value **$500.00**
Planter, lamb, recumbent, 6x6½", from $150 to........**$200.00**

Planter, rooster, flat, 7½x5", minimum value.............$300.00
Plaque, bird, flat, rare, 8x5¾", minimum value.........$300.00
Plaque, fish, many different species, 3½x6", ea, from $225
    to..$275.00
Salt & pepper shakers, bluegills, 2½x4", pr, minimum
    value $500.00
Salt & pepper shakers, mice, 1¾x1", 1¼x2", pr, from $25
    to...$50.00
Salt & pepper shakers, pigs, standing, 3¾", pr, from $125
    to...$150.00
Salt & pepper shakers, swans, 2", from $75 to $100.00
Salt & pepper shakers, wheat shock, from $125 to..$150.00
Spoon rest, tulip, 5", from $85 to..............................$100.00
Spoon rest, turkey gobbler figural, rare, 5½", minimum
    value $500.00
Tea bell, flamingo sitting on nest, 3¼", from $250 to..$300.00
Tea bell, peacock, 5½", from $250 to.......................$300.00
Tile, mallard decal, Les Kouba, square, 6", from $75 to .$125.00
Vase, 3-color swirl, 5¼", minimum value $200.00

Bank, buffalo, marked, 3½", from $200.00 to $225.00.
(Photo courtesy Beverly and Jim Mangus)

Roseville Pottery

This company took its name from the city in Ohio where they operated for a few years before moving to Zanesville in the late 1890s. They're recognized as one of the giants in the industry, having produced many lines of the finest in art pottery from the beginning to the end of their operations. Even when machinery took over many of the procedures once carefully done by hand, the pottery they produced continued to reflect the artistic merit and high standards of quality the company had always insisted upon.

Several marks were used over the years as well as some paper labels. The very early art lines often carried an applied ceramic seal with the name of the line (Royal, Egypto, Mongol, Mara, or Woodland) under a circle containing the words Rozane Ware. From 1910 until 1928 an Rv mark was used, the 'v' being contained in the upper loop of the 'R.' Paper labels were common from 1914 until 1937. From 1932 until they closed in 1952, the mark was Roseville in script, or R USA. Pieces marked RRP Co Roseville, Ohio, were not made by the Roseville Pottery but by Robinson Ransbottom of Roseville, Ohio. Don't be confused. There are many jar-

dinieres and pedestals in a brown and green blended glaze that are being sold at flea markets and antique malls as Roseville that were actually made by Robinson Ransbottom as late as the 1970s and 1980s. That isn't to say they don't have some worth of their own, but don't buy them for old Roseville.

Most of the listings here are for items produced from the 1930s on — things you'll be more likely to encounter today. If you'd like to learn more about the subject, we recommend *The Collector's Encyclopedia of Roseville Pottery, Vols 1* and *2* (2001 pricing by Mike Nickel) by Sharon and Bob Huxford (Collector Books); *A Price Guide to Roseville Pottery by the Numbers* by John Humphries (L&W Book Sales); *Roseville in All Its Splendor* by Jack and Nancy Bomm (L&W Book Sales); and *Collector's Compendium of Roseville Pottery, Vols 1* and *2*, by R.B. Monsen (Monsen & Baer).

Advisor: Mike Nickel (See the Directory, Roseville)

Newsletter: *Rosevilles of the Past*
Nancy Bomm, Editor
P.O. Box 656
Clarcona, FL 32710-0656
Subscription: $19.95 per year for 6 to 12 newsletters

Apple Blossom, bowl, #326, blue, 2½x6½", from $175 to .$250.00
Apple Blossom, jardiniere, #342, blue, 6", from $325 to.....$375.00
Apple Blossom, jardiniere, #342, pink or green, 6", from $275
    to...$325.00
Apple Blossom, vase, #388, blue, 10", from $350 to...$450.00
Apple Blossom, vase, #388, pink or green, 10", from $300
    to...$350.00
Artwood, planter, #1055, 7x9½", from $85 to..............$95.00
Baneda, bowl, #233, green, 3½x10", from $600 to...$700.00
Baneda, vase, #603, pink, 4½", from $525 to............$625.00
Bittersweet, basket, #809, 8½", from $200 to $250.00
Bittersweet, candlesticks, #851, 3", pr, from $150 to...$175.00
Bittersweet, planter, #828, 10½", from $150 to $175.00
Blackberry, basket, 8", from $1,100 to....................$1,300.00
Blackberry, jardiniere, 4", from $400 to.....................$450.00

Blackberry, vase, 5", $440.00. (Photo courtesy Jackson's Auctions)

Blackberry, vase, #571, 6", from $550 to **$600.00**
Bleeding Heart, basket, #360, blue, 10", from $500 to...**$550.00**
Bleeding Heart, basket, #360, pink or green, 10", from $425 to..**$475.00**
Bleeding Heart, hanging basket, blue, from $375 to ..**$425.00**
Bleeding Heart, hanging basket, pink or green, from $325 to **$350.00**
Bushberry, cider pitcher, #1325, blue, from $550 to.**$650.00**
Bushberry, double cornucopia, #115, green, 6", from $175 to..**$200.00**
Bushberry, double cornucopia, #155, blue, 6", from $200 to..**$225.00**
Bushberry, vase, #157, green, 8", from $225 to **$250.00**
Bushberry, vase, #157, orange, 8", from $200 to **$225.00**
Capri, leaf tray, #532, 15" L, from $65 to **$75.00**
Clemana, vase, #754, blue, w/handles, 9½", from $500 to **$550.00**
Clematis, candle holders, #1155, blue, 2½", pr, from $110 to..**$135.00**
Clematis, candle holders, #1155, green or brown, 2½", pr, from $95 to..**$110.00**
Clematis, center bowl, #458, blue, 14", from $200 to ..**$250.00**
Columbine, bookend/planter, #8, blue or tan, 5", pr, from $350 to..**$400.00**
Columbine, vase, #17, pink, 7½", from $225 to........**$275.00**
Corinthian, vase, 8½", from $150 to...........................**$175.00**
Cosmos, hanging basket, blue, from $400 to...........**$425.00**
Cosmos, vase, #950, blue, 8", from $400 to **$425.00**
Cosmos, vase, #956, green, 12½", from $600 to **$650.00**
Cremona, vase, 12", from $350 to **$400.00**
Dahrose, vase, #418, 6", from $150 to **$175.00**
Dahrose, window box, #375-10, 6x11½", from $300 to..**$350.00**
Dawn, ewer, #834, green, 16", from $650 to.............**$750.00**
Donatello, bowl, 6", from $75 to................................**$95.00**
Donatello, jardiniere, 6", from $150 to.......................**$175.00**
Donatello, vase, 9½", from $275 to............................**$325.00**
Earlam, planter, #89, w/handles, 5½x10½", from $400 to **$450.00**
Earlam, vase, #515, w/handles, 4", from $325 to **$350.00**
Falline, vase, #646, w/handles, blue, 6", from $1,200 to **$1,400.00**
Ferella, vase, #505, tan, w/handles, 6", from $700 to ..**$800.00**
Florane (late line), vase, #80, 6", from $50 to **$60.00**
Florentine, candlestick, 10½", from $150 to **$175.00**
Florentine, jardiniere, 5¾" base dia, from $200 to....**$250.00**
Foxglove, flower frog, #46, blue, from $125 to **$150.00**
Foxglove, hanging basket, blue, from $325 to..........**$375.00**
Foxglove, hanging basket, green/pink, from $200 to..**$225.00**
Foxglove, vase, #47, pink, w/handles, 8½", from $225 to...**$275.00**
Foxglove, vase, #51, blue, w/handles, 10", from $300 to...**$350.00**
Freesia, basket, #390, blue, 7", from $250 to **$275.00**
Freesia, flowerpot w/saucer, #670, green, 5½", from $225 to...**$250.00**
Freesia, vase, #124, blue, 9", from $250 to................**$275.00**
Freesia, vase, #124, green, 9", from $275 to..............**$300.00**

Freesia, vase, #124, tangerine, 9", from $225 to........**$250.00**
Fuchsia, center bowl w/frog, #351, blue, 3½x12½", from $300 to..**$350.00**
Fuchsia, vase, #893, blue, 6", from $250 to **$300.00**
Fuchsia, vase, #893, green, 6", from $200 to...........**$225.00**
Futura, vase, #382, 7", from $375 to **$450.00**
Futura, vase, #387, 7½", from $1,100 to **$1,200.00**
Futura, vase, #388, 9", from $650 to **$750.00**

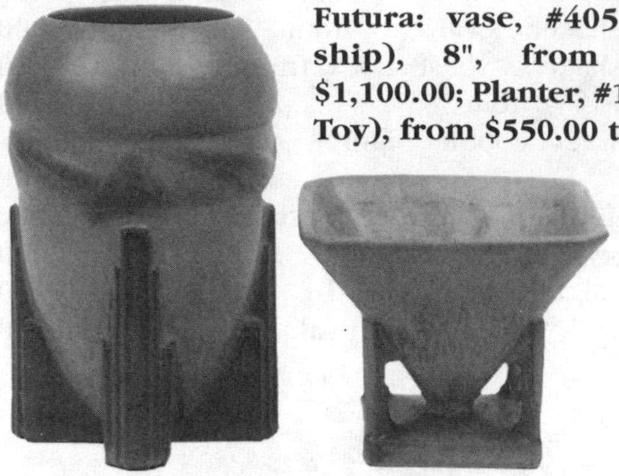

Futura: vase, #405-7½" (Space-ship), 8", from $900.00 to $1,100.00; Planter, #189-4-6" (Sand Toy), from $550.00 to $650.00.

Futura, vase, #421, 6½", from $375 to **$450.00**
Futura, vase, #429, 9", from $1,500 to **$1,750.00**
Gardenia, basket, #610, 12", from $350 to...............**$400.00**
Gardenia, bowl vase, #641, 5", from $125 to **$150.00**
Gardenia, hanging basket, 6", from $300 to............**$350.00**
Gardenia, vase, #658, 10", from $175 to...................**$225.00**
Imperial I, basket, #8, 10", from $250 to **$275.00**
Imperial II, bowl, 4½", from $400 to **$450.00**
Iris, basket, #355, blue, 9½", from $475 to..............**$550.00**
Iris, basket, #355, pink or tan, 9½", from $425 to **$475.00**
Iris, vase, #917, blue, 6½", from $175 to **$200.00**
Ivory II, candlestick, #1122, 5½", pr, from $75 to.......**$95.00**
Ivory II, hanging basket, 7", from $75 to.................**$100.00**
Ixia, vase, #857, 8½", from $125 to..........................**$150.00**
Jonquil, bowl, #523, 3", from $175 to **$225.00**
Jonquil, vase, #529, 8", from $500 to **$600.00**
La Rose, vase, 4", from $125 to **$150.00**
La Rose, wall pocket, 9", from $300 to **$350.00**
Lotus, bowl, #L6-9, 3x9", from $150 to **$175.00**
Luffa, vase, #689, 8", from $650 to **$750.00**
Mayfair, bowl, #1110, 4", from $50 to **$75.00**
Mayfair, pitcher, #1105, 8", from $150 to **$175.00**
Ming Tree, hanging basket, from $225 to................**$250.00**
Ming Tree, vase, #572, 6½", from $110 to................**$135.00**
Ming Tree, vase, #582, 12½", from $225 to **$250.00**
Mock Orange, pillow vase, #930, 7", from $150 to...**$175.00**
Mock Orange, vase, #985, 13", from $350 to **$450.00**
Mock Orange, window box, #956, 8½" L, from $100 to **$125.00**
Montacello, vase, blue, 5", from $400 to **$450.00**
Montacello, vase, tan, 5", from $350 to **$400.00**
Morning Glory, candlestick, #1102, green, 5", pr, from $750 to..**$850.00**

Morning Glory, vase, #723, green, w/handles, 5", from $475 to..**$550.00**
Moss, bowl vase, #209, pink/green, 6", from $350 to..**$400.00**
Orian, vase, #733, tan, 6", from $175 to **$200.00**
Orian, vase, #733, yellow, 6", from $200 to **$250.00**
Pasadena, planter, #526, 7" L, from $50 to **$60.00**
Pine Cone, planter, #124, blue, 5", from $250 to **$300.00**
Pine Cone, planter, #124, green, 5", from $175 to....**$225.00**
Pine Cone, tumbler, #414, blue, from $375 to **$425.00**
Pine Cone, vase, #747, blue, 10½", from $850 to.....**$950.00**
Pine Cone, vase, #747, brown, 10½", from $500 to .**$550.00**
Pine Cone, vase, #845, green, 7", from $425 to........**$475.00**
Poppy, ewer, #800, pink, 18½", from $1,000 to **$1,100.00**
Poppy, vase, #335, gray/green, 6½", from $300 to...**$350.00**
Poppy, vase, #335, pink, 6½", from $400 to **$450.00**
Primrose, vase, #760, blue or pink, 7", from $175 to..**$200.00**
Primrose, vase, #761, tan, 6½", from $150 to............**$175.00**
Raymor, butter dish, #181, 7½", from $75 to.............**$100.00**
Raymor, divided vegetable bowl, #165, 13", from $55 to...**$65.00**
Raymor, gravy boat, #190, 9½", from $30 to **$35.00**
Raymor, individual casserole, #199, 7½", from $40 to ..**$45.00**
Raymor, salad bowl, #161, 11½", from $35 to............**$40.00**
Raymor, water pitcher, #189, 10", from $100 to **$150.00**
Rosecraft Hexagon, vase, brown, 6", from $250 to...**$300.00**
Rosecraft Panel, vase, brown, 6", from $150 to **$175.00**
Rosecraft Vintage, bowl, 3", from $125 to **$150.00**
Rozane 1917, footed bowl, 5", from $175 to............**$200.00**
Rozane 1917, vase, 8", from $150 to.......................**$175.00**
Russco, vase, heavy crystals, 7", from $175 to **$200.00**
Silhouette, box, #740, 4½", from $150 to **$175.00**
Silhouette, double planter, #757, 5½", from $125 to...**$150.00**
Silhouette, ewer, #716, 6½", from $100 to................**$125.00**
Silhouette, vase, #781, 6", from $90 to......................**$110.00**

Silhouette, vase, #783, with nude, 7", from $400.00 to $450.00.

Silhouette, vase, #787, w/nude, 10", from $750 to ...**$850.00**
Snowberry, basket, #1BK, blue or pink, 12½", from $300 to...**$375.00**
Snowberry, bowl vase, #1RB, blue or pink, 6", from $200 to...**$225.00**
Snowberry, ewer, #1TK, green, 16", from $525 to....**$575.00**
Snowberry, vase, #1V1, blue or pink, 7½", from $110 to .**$130.00**

Sunflower, vase, w/handles, 5", from $600 to...........**$700.00**
Sunflower, vase, 10", from $2,000 to **$2,500.00**
Thornapple, vase, #816, 8½", from $150 to **$225.00**
Tourmaline, vase, 5½", from $100 to **$125.00**
Tuscany, vase, flaring sides w/handles, pink, 4", from $100 to..**$125.00**
Velmoss Scroll, vase, 5", from $150 to **$175.00**
Vista, basket, 12", from $1,000 to...........................**$1,200.00**
Vista, vase, 15", from $1,500 to **$1,750.00**
Water Lily, candlestick, #1155, rose w/green, 4½", pr, from $225 to...**$250.00**
Water Lily, hanging basket, blue, from $350 to **$375.00**
Water Lily, vase, #78, blue, 9", from $325 to.............**$350.00**
Water Lily, vase, #78, brown, 9", from $300 to **$325.00**
Water Lily, vase, #78, rose w/green, 9", from $350 to ..**$400.00**
White Rose, vase, #978, 4", from $80 to **$90.00**
Wincraft, bookends, #259, 6½", pr, from $175 to **$225.00**
Wincraft, cornucopia, #221, 9x5", from $150 to.......**$175.00**
Wincraft, ewer, #218, 19", from $650 to.....................**$750.00**
Wincraft, mug, 4½", from $100 to **$125.00**
Wincraft, planter, #227, 4x13½", from $150 to..........**$175.00**
Windsor, bowl, #TBD, rust w/handles, 3½x10½", from $350 to...**$400.00**
Windsor, vase, #582, blue w/handles, ferns, 7", from $1,750 to...**$2,000.00**
Wisteria, vase, #635, tan, 8½", from $650 to **$750.00**
Zephyr Lily, fan vase, #205, 6½", from $90 to **$115.00**
Zephyr Lily, hanging basket, 7½", from $150 to.......**$175.00**
Zephyr Lily, pillow vase, #206, 7", from $100 to **$125.00**
Zephyr Lily, vase, #133, 8½", from $75 to................**$100.00**
Zephyr Lily, vase, #202, 8", from $125 to.................**$150.00**

Royal China

The dinnerware and kitchenware made by Royal China of Sebring, Ohio (1934 – 1986), have become very collectible, the lines cataloged here in particular. The most sought after today have as their origins supermarket and gas station promotions; some were given away, and others distributed by stamp companies. They were also retailed through major outlet stores such as Sears Roebuck and W.T. Grant.

The Royal China Company is credited with revolutionizing the dinnerware industry through the introduction of Kenneth Doyle's stamping machine in 1948. Prior to this innovative technique, decals were laboriously applied by hand.

Veteran collectors find that the number of patterns produced by Royal seems almost endless, and many can turn up in unexpected colors. For example, Currier & Ives is not restricted to blue but can be found in pink, yellow, green, black, and even multiple colors. To simplify pattern identification, focus on the pattern's border which will be consistent (most of the time). Memory Lane features a border of oak leaves and acorns. Bucks County, an exclusive of W.T. Grant, sports a Pennsylvania Dutch tulip-motif garland. Fair Oaks has magnolia blossoms surrounded by periwinkle edging. The Willows (Blue Willow, Pink Willow, Yellow, etc.) speak for themselves. Colonial Homestead and Old Curiosity Shop are typically found in green and are often mistaken one for the other. Here's how to tell the difference: Old Curiosity Shop's border depicts metal hinges and pulls, while Colonial Homestead's features wooden boards with pegged joints. Most Currier & Ives dinnerware pieces regardless of color will have the famous scroll border designed by art director Gordon Parker.

Be on the lookout for matching accessories by a variety of manufacturers. These were done in all sorts of media including paper, plastic, glass, and metal. A wide variety of coordinating items may be found including clocks, lamps, placemats, and bakeware that match a number of Royal patterns. These items are dissapearing fast but none quicker than the matching glassware, most notably Gay Fad. From three-ounce juice tumblers to fourteen-ounce Zombie glasses, these items were produced in several treatments and styles in clear, frosted, and milk glass.

Note that our prices for Currier & Ives are for items in the blue pattern. This line was made on a very limited basis in pink as well. To evaluate that color, you'll need to double our values.

Our advisors are happy to answer any questions on American clay products from figurines to dinnerware via e-mail. For further reading on this subject with an emphasis on Currier & Ives, we highly recommend *A Collector's Guide for Currier & Ives Dinnerware by the Royal China Company* by Elden R. Aupperle (with 2001 price guide, 112 pages, soft cover) as well as the newsletter and clubs listed below.

Advisors: BA Wellman and John Canfield (See Directory, Dinnerware)

Newsletter: *Currier and Ives China by Royal*
c/o Jack and Treva Hamlin
145 Township Rd. 1088
Proctorville, OH 45669; 740-886-7644

Club: C&I Dinnerware Collectors
E.R. Aupperle, Treasurer
29470 Saxon Road
Toulon, IL 61483; 309-896-3331, fax: 309-856-6005

Blue Heaven, bowl, fruit nappy; 5½"	**$3.00**
Blue Heaven, bowl, vegetable; 10"	**$20.00**
Blue Heaven, creamer	**$5.00**
Blue Heaven, cup & saucer	**$5.00**
Blue Heaven, gravy boat	**$15.00**
Blue Heaven, plate, dinner; 10"	**$6.00**
Blue Heaven, platter, tab handles, 10½"	**$20.00**
Blue Heaven, sugar bowl	**$8.00**
Blue Willow, ashtray, 5½"	**$12.00**
Blue Willow, bowl, cereal; 6¼"	**$15.00**
Blue Willow, bowl, fruit nappy; 5½"	**$6.50**
Blue Willow, bowl, soup; 8¼"	**$15.00**
Blue Willow, bowl, vegetable; 10"	**$22.00**
Blue Willow, butter dish, ¼-lb	**$35.00**

Blue Willow, casserole, w/lid	**$95.00**
Blue Willow, creamer	**$6.00**
Blue Willow, cup & saucer	**$6.00**
Blue Willow, gravy boat	**$18.00**
Blue Willow, pie plate, 10"	**$30.00**
Blue Willow, plate, bread & butter; 6¼"	**$3.00**
Blue Willow, plate, dinner; 10"	**$6.00**
Blue Willow, plate, salad; 7¼"	**$7.00**
Blue Willow, platter, oval, 13"	**$32.00**
Blue Willow, platter, serving; tab hdls, 11"	**$20.00**
Blue Willow, salt & pepper shakers, pr	**$25.00**
Blue Willow, sugar bowl, w/lid	**$15.00**

Blue Willow, teapot, unmarked, $125.00.

Blue Willow, tray, tidbit; 2-tier	**$65.00**
Buck's County, ashtray, 5½"	**$15.00**
Buck's County, bowl, soup; 8½"	**$18.00**
Buck's County, bowl, vegetable; 10"	**$28.00**
Buck's County, casserole, w/lid	**$125.00**
Buck's County, creamer	**$8.00**
Buck's County, cup & saucer	**$8.00**
Buck's County, gravy boat	**$28.00**
Buck's County, plate, bread & butter; 6¼"	**$4.00**
Buck's County, plate, dinner; 10"	**$8.00**
Buck's County, platter, oval	**$35.00**
Buck's County, platter, serving; tab handles, 11"	**$20.00**
Buck's County, salt & pepper shakers, pr	**$25.00**
Buck's County, sugar bowl, w/lid	**$18.00**
Buck's County, teapot	**$145.00**
Colonial Homestead, bowl, cereal; 6¼"	**$15.00**
Colonial Homestead, bowl, fruit nappy; 5½"	**$4.00**
Colonial Homestead, bowl, soup; 8¼"	**$9.00**
Colonial Homestead, bowl, vegetable; 10"	**$20.00**
Colonial Homestead, casserole, angle handles, w/lid	**$75.00**
Colonial Homestead, creamer	**$5.00**
Colonial Homestead, cup & saucer	**$5.00**
Colonial Homestead, gravy boat	**$15.00**
Colonial Homestead, pie plate	**$25.00**
Colonial Homestead, plate, bread & butter; 6"	**$2.00**
Colonial Homestead, plate, chop; 12"	**$18.00**
Colonial Homestead, plate, dinner; 10"	**$4.00**
Colonial Homestead, plate, salad; rare, 7¼"	**$7.00**

Colonial Homestead, platter, oval, 13" $24.00
Colonial Homestead, platter, serving; tab handles, 11".$15.00
Colonial Homestead, salt & pepper shakers, pr..........$18.00
Colonial Homestead, sugar bowl, w/lid......................$15.00
Colonial Homestead, teapot......................................$95.00
Currier & Ives, ashtray, 5½", from $15 to $18.00
Currier & Ives, bowl, cereal; round (various sizes made)..$15.00
Currier & Ives, bowl, fruit nappy; 5½".........................$5.00
Currier & Ives, bowl, salad/cereal; tab handles, 6¼"..$48.00
Currier & Ives, bowl, soup; 8½"................................$14.00
Currier & Ives, bowl, vegetable; deep, 10"................$35.00
Currier & Ives, bowl, vegetable; 9" $25.00
Currier & Ives, butter dish, Fashionable, ¼-lb, from $40
    to $50.00
Currier & Ives, casserole, angle handles, w/lid.........$115.00
Currier & Ives, casserole, tab handles, w/lid.............$250.00
Currier & Ives, clock plate, blue numbers, 2 decals.$150.00
Currier & Ives, clock plate, non-factory.....................$50.00
Currier & Ives, creamer, angle handle.........................$8.00
Currier & Ives, creamer, round handle, tall $48.00
Currier & Ives, cup & saucer $6.00
Currier & Ives, gravy boat, pour spout, from $20 to ..$25.00
Currier & Ives, gravy boat, tab handles, w/liner (like 7"
    plate), from $100 to...$135.00
Currier & Ives, gravy ladle, 3 styles, ea, from $35 to .$50.00
Currier & Ives, lamp, candle; w/globe, from $250 to ...$300.00
Currier & Ives, pie baker, 10", (depending on picture) from
    $30 to...$90.00
Currier & Ives, plate, bread & butter; 6⅜", from $3 to.$5.00
Currier & Ives, plate, calendar; ca 1969-86, ea, from $25
    to $100.00
Currier & Ives, plate, chop; Getting Ice, 11½", from $35
    to $45.00

Currier & Ives, chop plate, Getting Ice, 12", $38.00.

Currier & Ives, plate, chop; Rocky Mountains, 11½"..$65.00
Currier & Ives, plate, dinner; 10"..................................$7.00
Currier & Ives, plate, luncheon; very rare, 9"..............$25.00
Currier & Ives, plate, salad; rare, 7"..........................$15.00
Currier & Ives, platter, oval, 13" $35.00

Currier & Ives, platter, tab handles, 10½" dia, from $20
    to $30.00
Currier & Ives, salt & pepper shakers, pr, from $30 to..$40.00
Currier & Ives, sugar bowl, angle handles $18.00
Currier & Ives, sugar bowl, no handles, flared top $48.00
Currier & Ives, sugar bowl, no handles, w/lid...........$35.00
Currier & Ives, teapot, many different styles & stampings,
    from $110 to..$150.00
Currier & Ives, tidbit tray, 2- or 3-tier, abundant, from $50
    to $100.00
Currier & Ives, tumbler, iced tea; glass, 12-oz, 5½"....$18.00
Currier & Ives, tumbler, juice; glass, 5-oz, 3½", from $8
    to $15.00
Currier & Ives, tumbler, old-fashioned; glass, 3¼", from $8
    to $15.00
Currier & Ives, tumbler, water; glass, 4¾" $15.00
Fair Oaks, bowl, divided vegetable...........................$45.00
Fair Oaks, bowl, soup $15.00
Fair Oaks, bowl, vegetable; 9".................................$30.00
Fair Oaks, butter dish..$45.00
Fair Oaks, casserole, w/lid......................................$135.00
Fair Oaks, creamer...$12.00
Fair Oaks, cup & saucer..$8.00
Fair Oaks, plate, bread & butter.................................$3.00
Fair Oaks, plate, dinner; 10" $10.00
Fair Oaks, platter, tab handles, 10½" $22.00
Fair Oaks, salt & pepper shakers, pr $22.00
Fair Oaks, sugar bowl, w/lid $18.00
Fair Oaks, teapot $125.00
Memory Lane, bowl, cereal; 6¼" $15.00
Memory Lane, bowl, fruit nappy; 5½" $3.00
Memory Lane, bowl, soup; 8½"...................................$9.00
Memory Lane, bowl, vegetable; 10" $25.00
Memory Lane, butter dish, ¼-lb $30.00
Memory Lane, creamer...$6.00
Memory Lane, gravy boat $18.00
Memory Lane, gravy boat liner, from $12 to $15.00
Memory Lane, gravy ladle, plain, white, for all sets ...$35.00
Memory Lane, plate, bread & butter; 6⅜".....................$2.00
Memory Lane, plate, chop; 12"..................................$25.00
Memory Lane, plate, chop; 13"..................................$35.00
Memory Lane, plate, dinner $6.00
Memory Lane, plate, luncheon; rare, 9¼"...................$20.00
Memory Lane, plate, salad; rare, 7"...........................$10.00
Memory Lane, platter, oval, 13" $25.00
Memory Lane, platter, tab handles, 10½"....................$15.00
Memory Lane, salt & pepper shakers, pr....................$20.00
Memory Lane, sugar bowl, w/lid................................$15.00
Memory Lane, tumbler, iced tea; glass.......................$15.00
Memory Lane, tumbler, juice; glass $8.00
Old Curiosity Shop, bowl, fruit nappy; 5½" $4.00
Old Curiosity Shop, bowl, soup/cereal; 6½" $15.00
Old Curiosity Shop, bowl, vegetable; 9".....................$22.00
Old Curiosity Shop, bowl, vegetable; 10" $25.00
Old Curiosity Shop, casserole, w/lid..........................$90.00
Old Curiosity Shop, creamer......................................$6.00
Old Curiosity Shop, cup & saucer...............................$5.00

Old Curiosity Shop, plate, bread & butter; 6⅜" **$3.00**
Old Curiosity Shop, plate, dinner; 10" **$5.00**
Old Curiosity Shop, platter, tab handles, 10½" **$15.00**
Old Curiosity Shop, salt & pepper shakers, pr............**$20.00**
Old Curiosity Shop, sugar bowl, w/lid **$12.00**
Old Curiosity Shop, teapot **$115.00**

Royal Copley

This is a line of planters, wall pockets, vases, and other novelty items, most of which are modeled as appealing animals, birds, or human figures. They were made by the Spaulding China Company of Sebring, Ohio, from 1942 until 1957. The decoration is underglazed and airbrushed, and some pieces are trimmed in gold (which can add 25% to 50% to their values). Not every piece is marked, but they all have a style that is distinctive. Some items are ink stamped; others have (or have had) labels.

Royal Copley is really not hard to find, and unmarked items may sometimes be had at bargain prices. The more common pieces seem to have stabilized, but the rare and hard-to-find examples are showing a steady increase. Your collection can go in several directions; for instance, some people choose a particular animal to collect. If you're a cat lover, they were made in an extensive assortment of styles and sizes. Teddy bears are also popular; you'll find them licking a lollipop, playing a mandolin, or modeled as a bank, and they come in various colors as well. Wildlife lovers can collect deer, pheasants, fish, and gazelles, and there's also a wide array of songbirds.

If you'd like more information, we recommend *Collector's Guide to Royal Copley Plus Royal Windsor & Spaulding, Books I* and *II,* by Joe Devine.

Advisor: Joe Devine (See Directory, Royal Copley)

Figurine, bear with mandolin, 6¾", $60.00.

Ashtray, abstract butterfly shape, 4 rests, paper label, 5x9" **$25.00**

Ashtray, heart shape w/bird, embossed letters on bottom, 5½", from $50 to **$60.00**
Bank, pig in striped shirt, blue pants, paper label or often green stamped mark, 7½", from $75 to **$85.00**
Bank, rooster, several color variations, marked Chicken Feed, Reg US Pat Office, Vic Moran, Bedford PA, 8", from $65 to **$75.00**
Bowl, sm bird perched along rim of flower form, green mark, 4", from $12 to **$14.00**
Coaster, hunting dog, from $35 to.............................**$40.00**
Figurine, Banty rooster, paper label, 6½", from $60 to **$75.00**
Figurine, cockatoo, full bodied, crest erect, paper label only, 7¼", from $30 to...**$40.00**
Figurine, hen standing in straw, paper label only, 5½", from $30 to **$35.00**
Figurine, kingfisher, colorful & scarce, 5", from $45 to...**$50.00**
Figurine, lark, full body, paper label, 6½", from $20 to .**$24.00**
Figurine, Oriental boy or girl, paper label only, 7½", ea, from $20 to...**$24.00**
Figurine, pouter pigeon, brown or gray, paper label, 5¾", from $20 to **$25.00**
Figurine, rooster & hen, stucco glazing, 7" rooster, 6½" hen, pr, from $50 to..**$60.00**
Figurine, sea gull, white w/gold trim, 8", from $50 to.**$55.00**
Figurine, swallow w/extended wings, full bodied, paper label, 7", from $80 to...**$90.00**
Figurine, warbler, bird w/head up on stump, green stamp or raised letters, 5", from $18 to...............................**$20.00**
Figurine, wren, wide variation in colors, paper label only, 6¼", from $20 to **$24.00**
Flower arranger planter, flower form, green stamp on bottom, 3½x7", from $10 to **$12.00**
Lamp base, Cocker Spaniel, 10", from $100 to **$125.00**
Pitcher, Decal, pink floral decals on ivory, gold stamp on bottom, 6", from $12 to **$16.00**
Pitcher, Floral Beauty, embossed flowers surround body, green stamp or embossed letters, colors other than cobalt, 8"..**$75.00**
Planter, Big Apple & Finch, bird perched on side of open apple planter, paper label, 6½", from $30 to **$35.00**
Planter, cat playing cello, paper label only, 7½", from $100 to **$125.00**
Planter, Cocker Spaniel, full body, paper label only, 8", from $30 to **$35.00**
Planter, dog by mailbox, black & white (black ears), 8½", from $110 to...**$125.00**
Planter, dog pulling wagon, Flyer on side of wagon, paper label, 5¾", from $40 to..**$45.00**
Planter, duck & wheelbarrow, paper label only, 3¾", from $18 to **$20.00**
Planter, Dutch boy or girl w/bucket, paper label, 6", ea, from $25 to **$30.00**
Planter, elephant w/ball, trunk up, paper label only, 7½", from $25 to...**$30.00**
Planter, gazelle (bust), gold trim, embossed letters on bottom, 9", from $40 to **$45.00**

Planter, girl w/pigtails, embossed letters on back, pastel blue or pink bonnet, 7", ea, from $50 to **$60.00**

Planter, horse (running) embossed on front, paper label only, 6", from $15 to **$20.00**

Planter, Indian boy & drum, paper label only, 6½", from $20 to...**$25.00**

Planter, kitten & birdhouse, paper label only, 8", from $100 to...**$150.00**

Planter, kitten & boot, paper label, 7½", from $50 to **$55.00**

Planter, kitten in picnic basket, paper label only, 8", from $70 to...**$75.00**

Planter, kitten on stump, gray kitten w/green eyes, paper label only, 6½", from $30 to **$35.00**

Planter, Mallard drake, sitting, 3 runners on base, paper label, 5", from $30 to **$35.00**

Planter, Mallard duck, paper label only, 8", from $15 to...**$20.00**

Planter, Oriental boy or girl w/lg basket on back, paper label only, 8", ea, from $40 to **$45.00**

Planter, palomino horse head, paper label or green stamp on bottom, 6", from $35 to **$40.00**

Planter, Peter Rabbit, bunny w/ears down beside planter, paper label only, 6½", from $55 to **$65.00**

Planter, rooster, low tail, common, 2 runners on bottom, paper label only, 7½", from $30 to **$35.00**

Planter, straw hat w/flowers at band, embossed letters on back, 7", from $40 to **$45.00**

Planter, tanager beside stump, green stamp or raised letters, 6¼", from $20 to **$25.00**

Planter, teddy bear, chocolate brown, 6¼", from $60 to..**$65.00**

**Planter, Tony, 7½",
from $70.00 to $75.00.**

Planter, woodpecker beside stump, green stamp or raised letters on bottom, 6¼", from $20 to **$25.00**

Planter/wall pocket, Cocker Spaniel head, embossed letters on the back, 5", from $28 to.................................**$34.00**

Planter/wall pocket, girl in wide-brim hat, sits on table or hangs on wall, 7½", from $40 to **$45.00**

Planter/wall pocket, salt box shape, embossed letters on the back, 5½", from $35 to...**$40.00**

Plaque/planter, Fruit Plate, embossed multicolor fruit on front, sits on table or hangs on wall, 6¾", from $35 to....**$45.00**

Razor blade receptacle, barber pole, gold top, paper label, 6¼"...**$60.00**

Vase, Carol's Corsage, cobalt, green stamp on bottom, 7", from $25 to..**$30.00**

Vase, Congratulations (baby) decal, flared top, 6x8", from $55 to...**$60.00**

Vase, Decal, pink & green floral decal on ivory, sm handles, gold stamp, 6¼", from $10 to **$14.00**

Vase, Harmony, embossed flowing leaves, various colors made, paper label, 7½", from $14 to **$16.00**

Vase, pink w/robin's egg blue specks, USA on bottom, 4½", from $8 to...**$10.00**

Vase, Trailing Leaf & Vine, stylized leaves on 2-tone vase, paper label only, 8½", from $25 to **$30.00**

Vase/planter, Oriental-style fish embossed on square body, 4 sm feet, paper label, 5½", from $12 to **$15.00**

Royal Haeger

Many generations of the Haeger family have been associated with the ceramic industry. Starting out as a brickyard in 1871, the Haeger Company (Dundee, Illinois) progressed to include artware in their production as early as 1914. That was only the beginning. In the '30s they began to make a line of commercial artware so successful that as a result a plant was built in Macomb, Illinois, devoted exclusively to its production.

Royal Haeger was their premium line. Its chief designer in the 1940s was Royal Arden Hickman, a talented artist and sculptor who also worked in mediums other than pottery. For Haeger he designed a line of wonderfully stylized animals and birds, high-style vases, and human figures and masks with extremely fine details.

Paper labels were used extensively before the mid-'30s. Royal Haeger ware has an in-mold script mark, and their Flower Ware line (1954 – 1963) is marked 'RG' (Royal Garden).

Collectors need to be aware that certain glazes can bring two to three times more than others. For those wanting to learn more about this pottery, we recommend *Haeger Potteries Through the Years* by David D. Dilley (L-W Book Sales).

Advisor: David D. Dilley (See Directory, Royal Haeger)

Club: Haeger Pottery Collectors of America
Lanette Clarke
5021 Toyon Way
Antioch, CA 94509, 925-776-7784
Monthly newsletter available

Ashtray, Brown Earth Graphic Wrap, Haeger USA #2124, 1970s, 2x7x7"...**$15.00**

Ashtray, Green Agate, free-form, Royal Haeger R-873 USA...**$15.00**

Ashtray, Lincoln, 1818-1868, brown, marked Illinois Sesquicentennial Haeger #1095 USA, 1x6¾x4⅜" ..**$30.00**

Ashtray, orange boomerang shape, Royal Haeger R-1718 USA, 1¾x13½x8" **$15.00**

Bank, dog figural, white transparent, Haeger #8034 c, 8½x7½".................................**$85.00**

Basket, owl, Bennington Brown Foam, #5015H, 7x8½" ..**$100.00**

Bells, yellow, label on outside: Sears Best, 5x3½"......**$75.00**

Bookends, water lilies, white flowers w/green leaves, R-1144, ca 1952, 7½x5x5", pr..................................**$60.00**

Bowl, Beaded, Mauve Agate, Royal Haeger R-476 USA, 4¾x14¾x7¼"...**$25.00**

Bowl, Daisy, chartreuse, Royal Haeger USA (R-224), 2x11¾"...**$45.00**

Bowl, Lilac, Royal Haeger R-333 c USA or foil label: Handcrafted, Haeger, 4½x6¼x7".................**$35.00**

Bowl, lily; Gold Tweed, Royal Haeger c #364H USA & gold stamp: Haeger Gold Tweed 22K Gold, 2½x16¼x9¼"...**$35.00**

Bowl, Open Leaf, ebony & chartreuse, Royal Haeger R-877 USA, ca 1951, 2¼x13¾x7½".................**$30.00**

Candle holder, Standing Double Fish, Mauve Agate, unmarked (R-203), 5", pr..........................**$70.00**

Candle holders, cornucopia; Mauve Agate, unmarked (R-312), 4¾x5½x3", pr...**$35.00**

Candle holders, Flower & Leaf, light blue w/light green, foil label: Royal-Haeger By Royal Hickman (R-185), 2½", pr...**$65.00**

Candle holders, swan figural, Mauve Agate, unmarked (R-516), 8x3⅝", pr...**$50.00**

Candy jar, Mandarin Orange, Royal Haeger (R-173), 10x7"..**$15.00**

Canister, Flour, blue & white w/gold trim at handle & lid, Haeger USA #8062, 9x7½".........................**$65.00**

Coffeepot, turquoise, Royal Haeger R-1585-S, ca 1957, 10½x3½"...**$45.00**

Compote, Cotton White & turquoise, Haeger c #3003 USA & foil label: Haeger in H design, 4½x12".................**$20.00**

Compote, gold with lava texture, wood finial, 10¾", **$65.00.**

Figurine, deer (running), ebony, unmarked (R-975), 5¾x11¾"...**$30.00**

Figurine, horse, Green Briar, unmarked (R-103), 8¼x5⅛x3¾"...**$35.00**

Figurine, matador, Haeger Red, gold foil crown label: Royal Haeger (#6343), 11⅜x8¼x4"...............**$125.00**

Figurine, pheasant rooster, Mauve Agate, unmarked (R-435), 12x13"...**$40.00**

Figurine, polar bear, sitting, misty gray-white, unmarked (R-375B), ca 1942, 6⅞x6½x5".........................**$75.00**

Figurine, tigress, Amber, Royal Haeger USA (R-314), 11x10¼x4¼"...**$125.00**

Figurine, Wild Goose, white matt, unmarked (F-17), ca 1941, 6½x6¼x2"...**$15.00**

Flower block, nude w/seal, Green Briar, unmarked (R-364), 13¼x5½" base...**$90.00**

Flower frog, 2 birds on base, Cloudy Blue, unmarked (R-359), 1940s, 8¾x5" dia...**$90.00**

Flower holder, colt figural, Green Briar, Royal Haeger R-235 USA, 12½x7x3¾"...**$45.00**

Lamp base, Earth Graphic Wrap, marked Green Earth Graphic Wrap, 20x10" (36" overall)...............**$110.00**

Lamp base, mermaid figural, gray on Green Agate base, #5398, 16x8½x7"...**$200.00**

Lighter, Mandarin Orange, ribbed sides, table size, #889, foil label: Haeger in H design, 1950s-60s, 5x3" dia **$15.00**

Lighter, Mandarin Orange, Royal Haeger #813-H USA (insert marked Japan), 10¾x4⅛" (at base).................**$25.00**

Pitcher vase, pearlescent tan & orange, Royal Haeger USA c (#4141), 11x3½"...**$50.00**

Planter, bird, Blue Crackle, Haeger c #8008H USA & foil label, 7¾x4¾x2¾"...**$15.00**

Planter, Brown Earth Graphic Wrap, #4185X, 5½x9½x8"...**$60.00**

Planter, cat, blue, no marks (#3311), 7x5¾x3"...........**$30.00**

Planter, Colonial girl w/flower basket, Chartreuse, unmarked (#3318), 9x6½x4¾"...**$35.00**

Planter, Comedy & Tragedy masks, Green Agate, Royal Haeger R-1170 USA, 7¼x11x4¼".................**$65.00**

Planter, Dutch boy, white matt, Royal Haeger RG-98 USA **$25.00**

Planter, elephant beside drum planter, blue, no marks (#618), 6½x5¼x3¼"...**$15.00**

Planter, goat w/planter box on back, Sable, foil crown label: Royal Haeger (R-1734), 9½x13x4¼".................**$45.00**

Planter, Madonna, white, Haeger USA (#990), 13¼x10¼x10¼"...**$55.00**

Planter, peacock, Cloudy Blue, Royal Haeger R-453 USA, 10x9x3½"...**$40.00**

Planter, Peacock, Mauve Agate, Royal Haeger R-453 USA, 10x9¾x3⅛"...**$40.00**

Planter, pilgrim hat, light brown, Haeger USA c #394, 4⅝x7¾x7½"...**$25.00**

Planter, sea shell, green, no mark (#368), 3¼x3"........**$15.00**

Planter, stallion's head, chartreuse, #4-641 (not marked), 8¾x5½x3½", pr...**$50.00**

Planter, trout, pearl carnival w/gold fins, Royal Haeger R-284 USA, 9¼x8x4"...**$100.00**

Shell bowl, chartreuse & Silver Spray, Royal Haeger R-297 USA, 2¾x14x7½"...**$30.00**

Toe Tapper, banjo player, brown textured, #8297, 12x2½".**$65.00**

TV Lamp, horse (prancing) figural, Chartreuse & Honey, gold crown foil label (R-1262), 10¼x11½x5½"..............**$40.00**

TV lamp/planter, greyhound, brown, no marks (#6202), 6¼x11½x4½"...**$75.00**

Vase, Cerulean Gold, #4034, ca 1955, 8x2½"..............**$30.00**

Vase, Cobra, Mandarin Orange, Royal Haeger c #483 USA, 16"..**$50.00**

Vase, cornucopia w/nude, chartreuse & white, no mark (R-426), 8x7½"..**$35.00**

Vase, Dancing Girl, gr, no mark (#3105), 8x5¼".........**$25.00**

Vase, Double Leaf, Antique, no mark (R-1460), 10¾x8¾x3¾"...**$35.00**

Vase, Ebony Cascade, handles, Royal Haeger USA R-1812-S, 13¼x5"..**$35.00**

Vase, Elm Leaf, Green Briar, R-320 Royal Haeger Made in USA, 12½x6"..**$35.00**

Vase, Feather Plume, blue, foil label: Genuine Haeger Pottery (#3225), 6¼x5x2⅞"..**$15.00**

Vase, Fern Agate Earth Graphic Wrap, cylindrical, Royal Haeger USA c (#4162X), 7x3½"..**$25.00**

Vase, green, ball shape w/florals in relief, no mark (#463), 6½x5⅞x4"..**$30.00**

Vase, Laurel Wreath Bow, Mauve Agate, indistinct mark (R-303), 12x7¾x4"..**$75.00**

Vase, Mandarin Orange, bottle form, Royal Haeger USA RG-68, 7¼"..**$10.00**

Vase, sunflower, green, Haeger USA (R-647), 8⅛x3¾"..**$30.00**

Vase, swan, light blue, Royal Haeger by Royal Hickman USA R-36, 15½x10"..**$50.00**

Vase, Tulip, Oxblood & white, Royal Haeger R-893 USA, 12⅛x5x3¾"..**$30.00**

Vase, Wave Style, Green Agate & chartreuse, Royal Haeger R-830 USA, 20½x7x6"..**$125.00**

Vase, wheat in relief, Green Briar, no marks (#3273), 12x7½x3⅝"..**$45.00**

Vases, Seminole Orange (squiggles): #4160X, 12", $150.00; #4171X, 14", $225.00. Other glazes will be 75% less. (Photo courtesy David Dilley)

Wall pocket, fish, Antique, crown label: Royal Haeger c (R-16275), 3¼x13¼x6½"..**$100.00**

Wall pocket, grapes, purple & green, Royal Haeger R-745 USA..**$100.00**

Wall pocket, rectangular, green, Haeger #725 USA & paper label: Royal Haeger, 5⅛x6½x2¾"..**$20.00**

Wall pocket, rocking cradle, white, label: Haeger Pottery Dundee Ill (#917A), ca 1939, 3x5x3½"..............**$15.00**

Wall shelf, Mallow, Royal Haeger R-531 USA on back, ca 1947, 4¾x7x4¼"..**$125.00**

Rozart

George and Rose Rydings (Kansas City, Missouri) were aspiring potters who in 1969 set about to produce a line of fine underglaze art pottery. They inherited some vintage American-made artware which they very much admired and set about trying to unravel the enigma of ceramic chemistry used by the old masters. Early in the 1970s, Fred Radford, grandson of Albert Radford, a well-known, remarkably talented artist who had made his presence felt in the Ohio pottery circles (ca 1890s – 1904), offered them ideas about glazing techniques, chemistry, etc., and allowed them to experiment with his grandfather's formula for Jasperware (which he had produced in his own pottery). It was then that the Ryding's pottery acquired a different look — one very reminiscent of the ware made by the turn-of-the-century American art pottery masters.

Rozart (as they named their pottery) has created many lines since its beginning; Twainware, Sylvan, Cameoware, Rozart Royal, Rusticware, Deko, Krakatoa, and Sateen to mention a few. All of their pottery is marked in some fashion. Though some items have been found with paper labels, they did not come from the Rydings. You will almost always find the initials of the artist responsible for the decorating and a date code created in one of two ways: two digits, for example '88' denoting 1988, or a month (represented by a number) separated by a slash followed by the two-digit year. The earliest mark known is 'Rozart' at the top of a circle, 'Handmade' in the center, and 'K.C.M.O.' (Kansas City, Missouri) at the bottom. In the early years, a stylized paint brush was sometimes added to the mark as well. Other marks followed over the years, including a seal which was used extensively.

The Rydings venture quickly involved several family members, some of whom developed their own lines, themes, and designs. George signs his pieces in one of three ways: 'GMR,' 'GR,' or 'RG' (with a backwards R). In the early years George worked on Twainware, Jasperware, and Cameoware. He has many wheel-thrown pieces to his credit.

Rose, who is very knowledgable about Native Americans, does scenics and portraits, using painstaking care to authenticate the exact history of a particular tribe and their culture. Her mark is either 'RR' or 'RRydings,' both written on an angle.

Four of the seven Rydings's children have worked in the pottery as well, becoming decorators in their own right. Anne Rydings White designed and executed many original pieces in addition to her work on the original Twainware line, which she signed 'AR.' Before her marriage, she used this mark or simply 'Anne.' She is still actively involved; her later creations are singed 'ARW.' Susan Rydings Ubert has specialized in design pieces (mostly Sylvan) and is an accomplished sculptor and mold maker. She signs her pieces with an 'S' over the letter R. Susan's daughter, Maureen, does female figures in the Art Deco style. Rebecca 'Becky' Rydings White, now a commercial artist, early on designed such lines as Fleamarket (depicting typical flea market scenes and merchandise), Nature's Jewels, and Animal, which she marked with the name of the line as well as her initials (B over the letter R). (When collecting Rozart, use caution if you want a particular artist's work; with two Rydings children married to two unrelated White families, it would be easy to confuse the artists and their place in history.)

Of all the children, Cynthia Rydings Cushing has always been the most prolific. Her Kittypots line depicts animated cats and kittens involved in a variety of activities on vases, jars, etc., utilizing their Rusticware glazes and shapes (usually 3" to 4" high). Her earlier work is signed with a 'C' over the 'R'; today she uses the initials 'CRC.'

The Rozart Pottery is still active today, and while prices for the older pieces have been climbing steadily for several years, they are still affordable.

Watch for the release of a book on this subject by our advisor Susan Cox. (She will welcome photos or additional information.)

Advisor: Susan Cox (See Directory, California Pottery)

Vase, Kittypots, three cat groupings in continuous sequence on sides, signed CR, 12", $300.00.

Figurine, poodle, reclining, Krakatoa line, 1970, 6" L.**$125.00**
Ginger jar, flower motif, w/lid, ca 1975, 3¾" **$75.00**
Jardiniere, Cameoware, 3 sculptured frogs, mid-1980s, 11"..**$95.00**
Jardiniere, Western theme, Cindy Cushing, w/base, 1981, 16" **$150.00**
Jug, Rusticware, Cleopatra, mid-1980s, 22"................**$350.00**
Sign, Rozart Pottery in script, base across front, 1998, 5½".**$20.00**
Sign, Rozart Pottery in script, sm vertical base, 1989, 5½".**$35.00**
Tankard, part of the Twainware series, very scarce with lid, Anne Rydings, 1974, 9½" **$325.00**
Tile, Danielle nude, Deko line, Susan Ubert, 1998, 10".**$68.00**

Tile, Two Moons Chief Joseph, Rose Rydings, 1974, 6" square..**$55.00**
Vase, Animal by Becky Rydings, 2 handles, 1988, 9¾" .**$95.00**
Vase, Deko line w/dancing nude, narrow base, mid-1980s, 12"..**$210.00**
Vase, Nature's Jewels by Becky Rydings, butterfly motif, 4"..**$24.00**
Vase, Rusticware, Indian Chief, Anne Rydings, 8" **$175.00**
Vase, stonewall w/flowers, wheel-thrown, GR, 7½"..**$95.00**
Vase, Twainware, Tom the Retired Painter, limited edition of 2,500, 6" **$155.00**
Vase, winter scene, Dove Gray glaze, GR, 1999, 9"..**$100.00**
Water set, pitcher & 4 mugs, horse motif, marked CRC .**$235.00**

Russel Wright Designs

One of the country's foremost industrial designers, Russel Wright, was also responsible for several lines of dinnerware, glassware, and spun aluminum that have become very collectible. American Modern, produced by the Steubenville Pottery Company (1939 – 1959) is his best known dinnerware and the most popular today. It had simple, sweeping lines that appealed to tastes of that period, and it was made in a variety of solid colors. Iroquois China made his Casual line, and because it was so serviceable, it's relatively easy to find today. It will be marked with both Wright's signature and 'China by Iroquois.' His spun aluminum is highly valued as well, even though it wasn't so eagerly accepted in its day, due to the fact that it was so easily damaged.

If you'd like to learn more about the subject, we recommend *The Collector's Encyclopedia of Russel Wright, Second Edition,* by Ann Kerr (Collector Books).

Note: Values are given for solid color dinnerware unless a pattern is specifically mentioned.

American Modern

The most desirable colors are Canteloupe, Glacier Blue, Bean Brown, and White; add 50% to our values for these colors. Chartreuse is represented by the low end of our range; Cedar, Black Chutney, and Seafoam by the high end; and Coral and Gray near the middle. To evaluate patterned items, deduct 25%.

Bowl, lug fruit; from $15 to **$20.00**
Cup & saucer, AD; from $25 to **$30.00**
Gravy boat, 10½", from $20 to **$30.00**
Pitcher, water; from $100 to **$135.00**
Plate, salad; 8", from $12 to..**$15.00**
Salad fork & spoon, from $125 to.............................**$150.00**
Teapot, 6x10", from $100 to **$125.00**

Iroquois Casual

To price Brick Red, Aqua, and Cantaloupe Casual, double our values; for Avocado, use the low end of the range. Oyster, White, and Charcoal are at the high end.

Bowl, cereal; 5", from $10 to.................................**$15.00**
Bowl, fruit; redesigned, 5⅜", from $12 to **$14.00**
Bowl, vegetable; open or divided (casserole), 10", from $35 to...**$40.00**
Butter dish, ½-lb, from $85 to **$100.00**
Creamer, redesigned, from $15 to **$25.00**
Cup & saucer, redesigned, from $18 to **$22.00**
Plate, dinner; 10", from $10 to...............................**$12.00**
Platter, oval, 14½", from $40 to.............................**$50.00**

Stacking creamer and sugar bowl, from $30.00 to $36.00.

Knowles

The high end of the range should be used to evaluate solid-color examples.

Bowl, soup/cereal; 6¼", from $14 to **$16.00**
Creamer, from $14 to..**$16.00**
Pitcher, 2-qt, from $150 to **$170.00**
Plate, dinner; 10¾", from $12 to.............................**$15.00**
Platter, oval, 13", from $25 to **$45.00**
Salt & pepper shakers, pr, from $30 to.....................**$40.00**
Teapot, from $175 to...**$250.00**

Plastic

These values apply to Home Decorator, Residential, and Flair (which is at the high end of the range). Copper Penny and Black Velvet items command 50% more. Meladur items are all hard to find in good condition, and values can be basically computed using the following guidelines (except for the fruit bowl, which in Meladur is valued at $7.00 to $8.00).

Bowl, lug soup; #706, from $10 to...........................**$12.00**
Bowl, onion soup; #715, w/lid, from $32 to **$36.00**
Bowl, vegetable; #713, w/lid, from $25 to **$30.00**
Bowl, vegetable; oval, deep, #709, from $15 to.........**$18.00**
Cup & saucer, #701/#702, from $8 to **$11.00**
Plate, dinner; #703, from $8 to **$10.00**
Plate, salad; #704, from $8 to **$10.00**

Spun Aluminum

Casserole, from $150 to...**$200.00**
Cheese knife, from $75 to...**$100.00**
Flower ring, from $125 to...**$150.00**
Hot relish server w/ceramic inserts, from $350 to **$400.00**
Ice bucket, from $75 to...**$100.00**
Muddler, from $75 to..**$100.00**
Pitcher, round handle, from $175 to **$200.00**
Pitcher, sherry; from $250 to **$300.00**
Vase, 12", from $150 to **$175.00**
Vase or flowerpot, sm, from $75 to **$125.00**
Wastebasket, from #125 to.......................................**$150.00**

Sterling

Values are given for undecorated examples.

Bowl, bouillon; 7-oz, from $14 to **$16.00**
Creamer, individual, 1-oz, from $10 to **$15.00**
Plate, bread & butter; 6", from $5 to.........................**$10.00**
Plate, luncheon; 9", from $9 to.................................**$14.00**
Plate, service; from $16 to..**$20.00**
Platter, oval, 7½", from $15 to **$20.00**
Sugar bowl, w/lid, 10-oz, from $22 to.......................**$25.00**

White Clover (for Harker)

Ashtray, clover decorated, from $40 to......................**$45.00**
Bowl, vegetable; open, 7½", from $25 to...................**$30.00**
Clock, General Electric, from $55 to **$60.00**
Pitcher, clover decorated, w/lid, 2-qt, from $75 to ...**$100.00**
Plate, chop; clover decorated, 11", from $25 to.........**$28.00**
Salt & pepper shakers, either size, pr, from $30 to **$35.00**
Sugar bowl, w/lid (individual ramekin), from $25 to.**$28.00**

Salt Shakers

Probably the most common type of souvenir shop merchandise from the '20 through the '60s, salt and pepper shakers can be spotted at any antique mall or flea market today by the dozens. Most were made in Japan and imported by various companies, though American manufacturers made their fair share as well. When even new shakers retail for $10.00 and up, don't be surprised to see dealers tagging the better vintage varieties with some hefty prices.

'Miniature shakers' are hard to find, and their prices have risen faster than any others'. They were all made by Arcadia Ceramics (probably an American company). They're under 1½" tall, some so small they had no space to accommodate a cork. Instead they came with instructions to 'use Scotch tape to cover the hole.'

Advertising sets and premiums are always good, since they appeal to a cross section of collectors. If you have a chance to buy them on the primary market, do so. Many of these are listed in the Advertising Character Collectibles section of this guide.

Recent sales have shown a rise in prices for some low-line shakers that are being purchased not by salt shaker collectors but people with a connection to the theme or topic they represent. (Doctors will buy doctor-related shakers, etc.) Fish-related shakers are on the rise in value and popularity. High-end shakers are getting soft. Many of the vintage rare sets are being reproduced and redesigned so collectors can own a set at a more reasonable cost.

There are several good books which we highly recommend to help you stay informed: *Salt and Pepper Shakers, Identification and Values, Vols. I, II, III,* and *IV,* by Helene Guarnaccia; and *The Collector's Encyclopedia of Salt and Pepper Shakers, Figural and Novelty, First* and *Second Series,* by Melva Davern. All are published by Collector Books.

See also Advertising Character Collectibles; Breweriana; Condiment Sets; Holt Howard; Occupied Japan; Regal China; Rosemeade; Shawnee; Vandor; and other specific companies.

Advisor: Judy Posner (See Directory, Salt and Pepper Shakers)

Club: Novelty Salt and Pepper Club
c/o Irene Thornburg, Membership Coordinator
581 Joy Rd.
Battle Creek, MI 49017
Publishes quarterly newsletter and annual roster. Annual dues: $20 in USA, Canada, and Mexico; $25 for all other countries

Advertising

Budweiser/Anheuser-Busch steins, Official Authorized set, Made in USA, 3½", pr...$29.00

Dooley and Shultz (Utica Beer), from $125.00 to $150.00 for the pair. (Photo courtesy Judy Posner)

Eveready Batteries, metal batteries w/cats jumping through 9s, metal, 2½", pr, EX...$40.00
Fingerhut truck, 2-pc truck, 1¾x3¾", EX...................$35.00
Flour Fred, hard plastic boy figural for Homepride Flour, 3½", pr, EX $55.00
Ft Pitt Beer bottles, glass, 3", pr, EX...........................$20.00
Kelloggs Snap & Pop, ceramic, Japan ink stamp, 2½", pr, EX.$60.00
Ken L Ration cat & dog, plastic, F&F Mold & Die Co, 1950s, pr...$28.00

Peerless Beer men, Hartland Plastic for La Cross Breweries in Wisconsin, 1950s, 5", pr $95.00
Prager Beer bottles, glass w/metal tops, pr................$28.00
Pure Oil Company gas pumps, plastic, red & white, blue & white, 2¾", pr..$200.00
Quaker State Motor Oil cans, heavy cardboard, 1940s-50s, 1½", pr, NM...$40.00
Safe-T Cup ice cream cones, 1 chocolate & 1 vanilla cone, 1950s, 3¾", pr...$35.00
Samovar Vodka bottles, glass w/double eagles embossed on backs, 5", pr, EX...$24.00
Schlitz Beer bottles, glass w/paper labels, metal tops, 4¼", pr $28.00
Seagrams 7, red plastic 7 on base, 1950s premium, 3¾", pr.$35.00
St Laurence Dairy cream-top bottles, glass w/metal tops, 3¼", pr, NM..$50.00
Tappan chefs, ceramic, Japan, 4¼", pr $25.00
Tee-Eff Tastee Freeze Ice Cream guys, pottery, Japan paper labels, 3¾", pr, in original wicker basket $35.00

Animals, Birds, and Fish

Ballerina bears, ceramic, PY, 3½", pr..........................$35.00
Bear artist & easel, ceramic, flat unglazed bottom, unmarked, 3¼", pr..$45.00
Bear mother holding baby, ceramic, white w/painted details, Made in Japan, 4¾", pr $26.00
Bears, dressed up, ceramic, original corks, unmarked, 3¼", pr..$20.00
Circus horses, Salty & Pepper, ceramic, vintage, 4", pr .$24.00
Dachshund dog looks at bumblebee on his tail, ceramic, 2-pc body forms shakers, 1950s, 3¼x5½", set.........$35.00
Farmer & Mrs Pig, ceramic, Enesco, 1980, 3½", pr.....$25.00
Fish (realistic Muskellunge), Relco paper label, 5¾" L, pr ..$35.00
Fish (realistic w/speckles), shiny porcelain, no mark, vintage import, 4¼", pr..$35.00
Fish (tropical), ceramic, green Japan stamp, original corks, 1950s, 2¾x4¾", pr...$34.00
Frogs w/mushrooms, bone china, Bone China Japan foil label, 2", pr...$15.00
Horse heads, ceramic, Japan paper label, 3½", pr......$15.00
Mallard ducks, ceramic, colorful, green Japan mark, 2¾", pr...$10.00
Monkey dressed up driving car (steering w/feet), Japan stamp w/cloverleaf, 1950s, 4½", pr $55.00
Monkeys, ceramic, Napco Creation Japan foil label on bottoms, 1950s, 3⅜", pr...$26.00
Owls, ceramic, black Germany stamp on bottom, 2¾", pr $32.00
Pandas (playful), ceramic, red Japan mark, 3½", pr...$12.00
Penguin Pals, glass w/plastic head & wings, 1950s, 3¼", pr, MIB $28.00
Penguins, painted wood, 1950s, 2½x2", pr $12.00
Pig head teapots, ceramic, wire bails, original paint, 1950s, 4x3½", pr...$20.00
Pig in corn car, ceramic w/cold-painted black accents, Japan mark, 3¾x4¾", pr..$32.00

Pigs, interlocking, plastic, Fitz & Floyd, 1976, 3x4", pr..**$40.00**

Pigs, smiling, pink, ceramic, marked Japan, 1950s, 2⅝", pr...**$18.50**

Purple cows, painted bisque w/gold trim, Japan paper label, 3½", pr...**$35.00**

Raccoons, ceramic, red Japan ink stamp on bottoms, 1950s, 2½", pr...**$15.00**

Scotties, chalkware, 1 black, 1 white dog, ca 1940s, 2½", pr...**$30.00**

Sea horses, ceramic, Leyden Arts, California, 4¼", pr...**$22.00**

Siamese cats, ceramic w/rhinestone eyes, Victoria Ceramics Japan paper label, 1950s, 4", pr............................**$24.00**

Skunks, ceramic, shiny, Japan, 2¾", pr.....................**$22.00**

Skunks w/flowers, ceramic, holes in eyes & nose, black Japan ink stamp, 2¾", pr.....................................**$24.00**

Squirrel & acorn, pottery (heavier), no mark, 3½", pr..**$10.00**

Woof & Poof dogs smoking pipes, ceramic, gold trim, German(?), 4¼", pr...**$50.00**

Girl pig in dress, ceramic, multicolor on white, unmarked, $25.00 to $30.00 for the pair. (Photo courtesy Helene Guarnaccia)

Black Americana

Boy & girl in turbans, dark brown skin tones, vivid shiny colors, red Japan ink stamp, 3½", pr.........................**$60.00**

Boy & girl w/bulging eyes, ceramic, hand-painted, red Japan ink stamp, 1940s-50s, 3¼", pr.............................**$60.00**

Boy on cotton bale, ceramic, Parkcraft, 3½x2½", pr..**$250.00**

Boy riding hippo & playing banjo, ceramic, hand-painted features, Japan, 1930s, 3⅞", pr.............................**$225.00**

Boy w/melon, ceramic, black Japan ink stamp, 1940s, 4", pr..**$125.00**

Chef faces, pottery, minor paint wear, Japan paper labels, 5", pr...**$50.00**

Chefs w/carving knives, ceramic, red Japan ink stamp, 3", pr...**$95.00**

Mammy & Chef, ceramic, black Japan ink stamp, older set, 2½", pr...**$55.00**

Mammy & Chef, ceramic, vintage import (unmarked), 3", pr...**$55.00**

Mammy & Mose, chalkware w/EX original paint, 1940s, 3", pr...**$65.00**

Natives in beer barrels, ceramic w/hand-painted details, pearl dangle earrings, hinged lids reveal shakers, 3", pr.**$60.00**

Turnabout man & woman, ceramic, underglaze paint, before & after images, 5¼", pr.......................................**$350.00**

Character

Babar the Elephant & girlfriend, dressed up couple, ceramic, bright colors, 3½", pr......................................**$55.00**

Bugs Bunny, shiny porcelain, Warner Bros, 1960s, pr..**$165.00**

Cereal Sisters (oats & corn anthropomorphic), Disney Copyright 1981, The Land (Epcot), 2¾", pr..........**$85.00**

Cow & moon, ceramic, unglazed bottoms, American Made, 1950s, 3", pr **$30.00**

Crows (from Dumbo), ceramic, Japan foil labels, ca 1940s-50s, 4", pr **$90.00**

Doc & Sleepy (Snow White's Dwarfs), ceramic, marked Foreign, 1930s, 2¾", pr **$125.00**

Donald Duck & Daisy shaking hands, ceramic, Japan ink stamp, 1950s, 4", pr...**$45.00**

Donald Duck & Ludwig Von Drake, ceramic, Dan Brechner Import, Walt Disney Productions, dated 1961, pr.**$155.00**

Ferdinand the Bull among flowers, ceramic, black Japan ink stamp, Disney, late 1930s, 2¾", pr.......................**$90.00**

Humpty Dumpty (Mr & Mrs), ceramic w/rhinestone eyes, red Japan labels, 3⅜", pr.......................................**$35.00**

Humpty Dumpty w/bow tie, wood, Chrissy Japan, 1950s-60s, 3⅜", pr, VG **$14.00**

Mary Had a Little Lamb, ceramic, Relco (Japan), 1950s-60s, 4", pr...**$45.00**

Mickey Mouse Chef heads, ceramic, Treasure Craft, Made in USA, 5", pr...**$55.00**

Miss Muffet & spider, ceramic, Poinsettia Studio, 2½" Miss Muffet, pr...**$95.00**

Moon Mullins, glass w/hard plastic hat, cold-painted features, Made in Japan paper label, 1930s, 3", pr.............**$95.00**

Old Mother Hubbard & dog, ceramic, bright gold trim, Poinsettia Studio paper labels, Mother: 3½", pr...**$95.00**

Oswald & Homer, ceramic, Walter Lantz Productions, Copyright 1958, Napco Japan #1c3635, 4", pr, EX.................**$175.00**

Pebbles & Bamm-Bamm, ceramic, Harry James, 4", pr..**$65.00**

Pinocchio, porcelain bisque, Made in Japan ink stamp, Disney, 5", pr...**$150.00**

Pluto, ceramic, white w/painted details, Walt Disney Productions, 1940s, 3¼", pr.....................................**$50.00**

Sad Sack, copyright George Baker, Norcrest paper label, ca 1949, 4", from $250.00 to $300.00 for the pair. (Photo courtesy Helene Guarnaccia)

Thumper, original cold paint, Walt Disney Productions, 1940s, 3½", pr, NM **$50.00**

Woody & Winnie Woodpecker, ceramic, W Lantz 1990, Universal Studios souvenir, pr **$70.00**

Yosemite Sam, ceramic, Lego paper label, 1960s, pr..**$125.00**

Ziggy & dog, ceramic, Universal Press Syndicate 1979, WWA Inc Cleveland, 3" Ziggy, pr **$40.00**

Fruit, Vegetables, and Other Food

Anthropomorphic beet man w/ruffled collar, gold trim, ceramic, unmarked (probably Japan), 2x2½", pr.**$32.00**

Anthropomorphic onion people reclining, ceramic, no mark, pr, from $18 to..............................**$22.00**

Anthropomorphic pear & orange people, 1-pc set, unmarked Japan, 2½x3¼" **$24.00**

Bacon & egg, ceramic, flat unglazed bottom, unmarked (probably American), 1950s, bacon: ¾x2½", pr...**$22.00**

Crab in clam shell, ceramic, clam: 2⅞x2⅞" w/smaller crab sitting on indentation inside clam, 1950s, pr........**$30.00**

Doughnut & cup of coffee, ceramic, no mark, pr, from $15 to..............................**$18.00**

Gingerbread man & rolling pin, ceramic, shiny, no mark, pr, from $22 to..............................**$26.00**

Ham slice in skillet, ceramic, no mark, from $18 to...**$22.00**

Ice cream soda & straws in holder, ceramic, no mark, from $12 to..............................**$20.00**

Peanuts, white hard plastic, Hong Kong, 1970s, 3½", pr..**$9.00**

Pie & ice cream, ceramic, flat unglazed bottom, unmarked (probably American), 1950s, 2x3", pr..............................**$22.00**

Pineapple slices, ceramic, no mark, from $10 to **$12.00**

Saltine crackers (realistic), ceramic, unmarked, pr, from $8 to..............................**$10.00**

Strawberries in white basket, ceramic, no mark, from $8 to..............................**$10.00**

Holidays and Special Occasions

Christmas mice atop cheese wedges, squeak when turned over, ceramic, unmarked, $15.00 for the pair. (Photo courtesy Helene Guarnaccia)

Christmas, Santa & Mrs Claus in rocking chairs, ceramic, unmarked, pr, from $10 to..............................**$20.00**

Christmas, snowman & woman, holding red S & green P, flat bisque-like finish, pr, from $8 to..............................**$10.00**

Christmas children (girl w/doll, boy w/toy rocking horse), Avon, 1983, pr..............................**$15.00**

Halloween, ghost, ceramic w/painted details, green Japan mark, 1950s, 3⅜", pr..............................**$28.00**

Halloween, skeleton-faced ghosts w/Poison on front of robes, ceramic, pr, from $10 to **$25.00**

Thanksgiving, Pilgrim boy & girl, ceramic, Hallmark, 1970, pr..............................**$15.00**

Household Items

Baseball mitt w/ball, cap w/bat, ceramic, no mark, pr, from $20 to..............................**$25.00**

Bowling ball & pin, ceramic, no mark, from $8 to.....**$10.00**

Cigar in ashtray, ceramic, unglazed bottom, no mark, 1½x2¼", pr..............................**$30.00**

Coffee grinder & coffeepot, ceramic, no mark, pr, from $18 to..............................**$22.00**

Fireplace & coal hod, ceramic, no mark, from $20 to.**$22.00**

Fried eggs, yolks are shakers, yellow & white plastic, 3-pc set, from $10 to..............................**$12.00**

Frying pan, orange plastic w/black trim, from $8 to..**$10.00**

Golf bag & ball, ceramic, flat unglazed bottoms, unmarked (probably American), bag: 3¼", pr..............................**$22.00**

Grandfather clocks, plastic, House of David, Benton Harbor MI, 4⅜", pr..............................**$26.00**

McGuffy's Reader & school bell, ceramic, flat unglazed bottom, unmarked (probably American), 1950s, 2¼", 2½", pr..............................**$30.00**

Photo album & camera, ceramic, no mark, pr, from $22 to..**$26.00**

Piano & bench, ceramic, flat unglazed bottoms, unmarked (probably American), 1950s, piano: 2½x3", pr.....**$17.50**

Pipe on pipe holder, ceramic, Trevewood, 2x3¾", pr..**$22.00**

Roller skates, multicolored plastic, pr, from $8 to **$10.00**

Stove (old-fashioned) & coal shuttle, ceramic, no mark, 3", pr..............................**$8.00**

Television, plastic, turn knob & shakers pop up, 1950s, M in 3x3½" (EX) box **$28.00**

Toaster & toast, black & white plastic (toast shakers), set, from $12 to..............................**$15.00**

Toaster & toast (stacking set), ceramic, USA Pottery, 1950s, 3⅞", pr..............................**$20.00**

Toothpaste & toothbrush, ceramic, flat unglazed bottoms, 1950s, pr..............................**$17.00**

Wood plane & square rule, ceramic, unmarked American, 1¾x3", pr..............................**$22.00**

Miniatures

Ace of Hearts & Deuce of Clubs, ceramic, Arcadia, pr .**$30.00**

Candlesticks, ceramic, Arcadia, 1½", pr **$30.00**

Diary & letters, ceramic, flat unglazed bottoms, Arcadia, pr..............................**$95.00**

Ghost & pumpkin, ceramic, Arcadia (unmarked), 1⅜", ½", pr **$125.00**

Lobster & oyster w/pearl, ceramic, unmarked, 3" L lobster, pr...**$80.00**

Oriental boy & girl, porcelain w/gold trim, Germany, 1¾", pr...**$35.00**

Parasol & high-button shoes, ceramic, unglazed bottoms w/black ink stamp: 2/67, 3", 1⅝", pr....................**$40.00**

Sewing machine & dress form, ceramic, 2", pr...........**$95.00**

Shoes (old-fashioned), ceramic, unmarked, unglazed bottoms, 1¼x2⅜", pr...**$24.00**

Stagecoach & saloon, ceramic, Arcadia, 1¼x1½", pr..**$90.00**

Teepee & Conestoga wagon, ceramic, Arcadia, pr.....**$70.00**

Telescope & planet, ceramic, gold trim, Arcadia, telescope: 2½", pr...**$95.00**

People

Alcatraz prison inmates, ceramic, Exclusive BP Japan paper labels, 4½", pr...**$35.00**

Amish couple, ceramic, black & white w/red, pr, from $8 to..**$15.00**

Barber (old-fashioned), ceramic, #1445 on bottoms, Lefton's Exclusives Japan foil label, 3¾", pr.......................**$30.00**

Baseball boy & girl, painted bisque, vintage, 2¾", pr...**$24.00**

Baseball pitcher & catcher, ceramic, Japan paper labels, 4½", pr...**$80.00**

Bellhop w/luggage, shakers are suitcases w/holes in front of 1 & in back of other, ceramic, all 1 pc, from $35 to.........**$45.00**

Boxers, 1 punching, 2nd w/black eye, ceramic, pr, from $15 to..**$35.00**

Bride & groom, 2-sided figures, back side: wife w/baby & husband questioning marriage & holding bottle, ceramic, pr..**$35.00**

Canadian soldiers, ceramic, Elmsdale Canada foil stickers, Made in Toronto, 4", pr....................................**$24.00**

Cave man & woman, ceramic, unmarked, vintage, 4", pr...**$60.00**

Chefs, 2 w/black cat & 2nd w/chicken, ceramic, Shafford mark, pr, from $20 to..**$45.00**

Child in top hat (stacking), ceramic, red Japan mark, older, 5", pr...**$45.00**

Children praying, ceramic, white w/gold trim, unmarked, 4¼", pr...**$12.00**

Clowns w/reamer heads, ceramic, colorful, black Japan ink stamps, 1940s, 2⅞", pr...**$20.00**

Colonial couple, ceramic, white w/painted details, Japan, vintage, 3½", pr..**$17.00**

Deco-style clowns, ceramic, multicolor lustres, Japan, pr, from $75 to..**$80.00**

Deep sea diver & treasure chest, ceramic, pr, from $18 to..**$22.00**

Doctor & nurse, ceramic, child-like faces, pr, from $12 to..**$25.00**

Driver tipping hat (1 shaker) sits in green car (2nd), ceramic, pr, from $45 to...**$50.00**

Dutch boy & girl kissing, ceramic, pr, from $10 to....**$12.00**

Fish w/bulging eyes, ceramic, unmarked, ca 1950s, 2¼x3½", pr...**$12.00**

Girls w/flowers on head & along hem of skirts, NAPCO, pr, from $20 to...**$22.00**

Groom carrying bride, ceramic, pr, from $10 to.........**$45.00**

Hummel-type boy & girl, ceramic, Japan, pr, from $12 to..**$15.00**

Mail man & woman, ceramic, blue & white outfits, pouches at sides, pr, from $12 to...............................**$25.00**

Mermaid & deep sea diver, ceramic, unmarked (probably American), 3½", pr...**$75.00**

Monks, comical, shiny porcelain like PY, green numbers on bottoms, 3½", pr..**$22.00**

Nudes w/pearls sitting on barrels, ceramic, crude, Japan, 1950s, 5", pr...**$35.00**

Pixie heads, shiny pottery, marked #6981 Japan, 3¼", pr..**$32.00**

Pixies, ceramic, Elbee Art, 3", pr..............................**$18.00**

Pixies w/green balls, ceramic, black Japan ink stamp, 1950s, 2¾", pr...**$14.00**

Priscilla & John Alden, names on base, ceramic, pr, from $10 to..**$12.00**

Southern Belles, ceramic, shiny, green PY Japan 'N' in circle mark, pr...**$38.00**

Uncle Sam heads, chalkware, EX original paint, 1940s, 2¼", pr...**$40.00**

Zodiac girls, ceramic, red Japan ink stamp, 4½", pr...**$55.00**

What's His Is Hers, ceramic, unmarked, from $45.00 to $55.00. (Photo courtesy Judy Posner)

Souvenir

Bahama policemen, ceramic, 1950s, 4⅜", pr...............**$38.00**

Cable car, metal, Made in Japan embossed on bottoms, Souvenir of San Francisco on tops, 1x2¼", pr.....**$24.00**

Chinese boy & girl, Chinatown NY, ceramic, Occupied Japan stamps on bottom, 3¾", pr...............................**$30.00**

Dice & cards, Reno souvenir, ceramic, Exclusive BP Japan, 3½", pr...**$26.00**

Hawaii Hula girls in relief, palm tree handles, ceramic, Japan paper label, 1950s-60s, 2⅞", pr...............**$28.00**

Hemisfair '68 Tower building, San Antonio World's Fair Tower of the Americas, original label, 5½", pr....**$50.00**

Kansas (state) & flower, ceramic, Victoria Ceramics, 1950s, pr...**$24.00**

Louisiana (state) & cotton ball, ceramic, Parkcraft, 1950s, pr..**$50.00**

Luau Tiki Restaurant, Hawaiian-style figure, ceramic, MOC Japan paper labels, 4¼", pr **$30.00**

Michigan's Mackinac Bridge, ceramic, each shaker is half of bridge, Japan label, 2x5¾", pr **$45.00**

Oriental people, Korea 67-78, carved stone, heavy, 4⅜", pr **$60.00**

Seashells, Fisherman's Wharf, San Francisco, decal on ceramic, flat unglazed bottom, 2½", pr **$15.00**

Singing Towers, silver-tone metal, Lake Wales FL, 3¼", pr **$55.00**

St Lawrence Seaway ship (smoke stacks are shakers), 1950s, 3-pc set **$50.00**

Utah (state) & covered wagon, ceramic, blue Copyright Parkcraft mark, pr **$50.00**

Washington (state) & apple, ceramic, Parkcraft ink stamp, pr...**$50.00**

Washington Monument, Bakelite, 4¼", pr **$65.00**

West Virginia (state) & coal lump, pottery, copyright Parkcraft, pr..**$50.00**

1000 Islands, Canada, plastic & metal, Made in Japan, 1950s, 4", MIB..**$15.00**

Miscellaneous

Anthropomorphic cartoon-faced train engines, ceramic, unmarked Japan, 3¼", pr **$30.00**

Anthropomorphic flower girls, ceramic, PY Japan mark, 3", pr...**$50.00**

Baseballs, pottery, realistic appearance, 1950s, 2½", pr..**$15.00**

Boxing gloves, ceramic, flat unglazed bottoms, unmarked (probably American), 1950s, 2⅞", pr **$18.00**

Cigarettes & lighter, ceramic, vintage, pr **$26.00**

Gift packages, fancy bows, pottery, unmarked (probably American), 1950s, pr..**$18.00**

Gun & bullet, ceramic, no mark, vintage, 4", pr........**$24.00**

Locomotives, metal, Mighty Locomotive 1876 Japan on bottom, 1x2½", pr **$15.00**

Racing cars, Salty & Peppy, shiny porcelain, 1¼x3½", pr **$35.00**

Scarecrow couple, ceramic, vintage American, 3", pr.**$28.00**

Schoolhouse & desk, ceramic, flat unglazed bottoms, unmarked (probably American), 1950s, desk: 4x4½", pr...**$20.00**

Teeth (2 shakers) on lower set base, My 2 Front Teeth, Arizona, 3-pc set, 2x2½" **$26.00**

Schoop, Hedi

One of the most successful California ceramic studios was founded in Hollywood by Hedi Schoop, who had been educated in the arts in Vienna and Berlin. She had studied not only painting but sculpture, architecture, and fashion design as well. Fleeing Nazi Germany with her husband, the famous composer Frederick Holander, Hedi settled in California in 1933 and only a few years later became involved in producing novelty giftware items so popular that they were soon widely copied by other California companies. She designed many animated human figures, some in matched pairs, some that doubled as flower containers. All were hand painted and many were decorated with applied ribbons, sgraffito work, and gold trim. To a lesser extent, she modeled animal figures as well. Until fire leveled the plant in 1958, the business was very productive. Nearly everything she made was marked.

If you'd like to learn more about her work, we recommend *The Collector's Encyclopedia of California Pottery, Second Edition,* by Jack Chipman (Collector Books).

Ashtray, ballerina in triangular form, 10" W..............**$175.00**

Bowl, shell form, green w/gold ruffled rim, 6"...........**$50.00**

Figurine, accordion players (boy & girl), brown, lavender, green & white, 13", NM, pr.....................................**$220.00**

Figurine, girl kneeling, brown, blue & white, 8x5".....**$85.00**

Figurine, lady w/basket on head, aqua dress w/applied cream flowers, 13" **$115.00**

Figurine, lady w/wide skirt forming bowl, green & pink w/gold, 7x13x11", NM..**$135.00**

Figurine, Oriental couple, he w/horn, she dancing, dark green w/gold, 10½", pr.......................................**$165.00**

Figurines, Oriental couple with buckets, 11½", 13", $175.00.

Flower frog, Ring Around the Rosie, 8x7½"..............**$200.00**

Flower holder, man w/top hat, 12" **$115.00**

Flower holder, Satisfied Cat, openings in pink bow...**$50.00**

Oyster plate, 6 shells form wells (3 lg & 3 sm), dark purple shaded to light blue, 12", NM...............................**$75.00**

Planter, barefoot girl beside 2 baskets, blond w/teal dress, white scarf & apron, 11½" **$135.00**

Planter, butterfly, green w/gold, pr.........................**$150.00**

Planter, girl dancer, skirt forming pocket, basket on head forming another, 12"..**$120.00**

Planter, girl w/book, 8¾x8" **$60.00**

Plaque, E Pluribus Unum Victory, 11½" dia, NM........**$60.00**

Vase, cactus shape, much color, 6x8" **$90.00**

Wall pocket, girl angel w/fingers to lips, green bow in hair **$100.00**

Scouting Collectibles

Collecting scouting memorabilia has long been a popular pastime for many. Through the years, millions of boys and girls have been a part of this worthy organization founded in England in 1907 by retired Major-General Lord Robert Baden-Powell. Scouting has served to establish goals in young people and help them to develop leadership skills, physical strength, and mental alertness. Through scouting, they learn the basic fundamentals of survival. The scouting movement came to the United States in 1910, and the first World Scout Jamboree was held in 1911 in England. If you would like to learn more, we recommend *A Guide to Scouting Collectibles With Values* by R.J. Sayers (ordering information is given in the Directory).

Advisor: R.J. Sayers (See Directory, Scouting Collectibles)

Boy Scouts

Armband, National Jamboree, 1957, Committee Staff, tan..**$100.00**
Bank, Scout w/staff, cast iron, painted, 1918 ....**$50.00**
Belt buckle, National Jamboree, 1957, double lock....**$20.00**
Belt buckle, World Jamboree, 1983, special issue, Max Solber, limited edition of 1,100 ....**$50.00**
Book, The Merit Badge Chronicle, Hubbard, 1986.......**$5.00**
Bookends, Official Boy Scout, heavy bronze, for Sea Scouts, 1930s...**$50.00**

Calendar, Boy Scout with hand raised, oath behind him, Borden's Ice Cream, 1945, 33x16", EX, $45.00.

Camera, Official Boy Scout, Kodak, bellows type, green, 1930s...**$100.00**
Canteen, plastic, w/plastic screw top, 1970...................**$4.00**
Card, membership; 3-fold, color scout scene, 1922 ......**$5.00**
Compass, black plastic, 8-point circumference, 1935 .**$10.00**
Decal, Exploring Is the Program, black **$2.00**
Decal, National Eagle Scout Association, eagle decal...**$1.50**

Decal/window sticker, Get Out & Vote..........................**$5.00**
Figurine, Boy Scout, hiker w/staff, color, hollow, Barclay .**$25.00**
Figurine, Boy Scout making fire, cast iron, full paint, Barclay..**$30.00**
First Aid Kit, Bauer & Black, rectangular, khaki case .**$22.00**
Flint & Steel Fire Starting Kit, w/flint & striker, in box.**$7.00**
Game, The Game of Boy Scouts, Parker Bros, 1912 ..**$40.00**
Handkerchief, Boy Scout, khaki w/red logo, 1920-30 ..**$8.00**
Hatchet, Tru-Temper, oak handle, 1950s **$22.00**
Lobby cards, Follow Me Boys, set of 6........................**$40.00**
Money clip, Regional Staff issue, w/Regional logo, sterling silver **$40.00**
Mugs, Regional, old regions, ceramic, boxed, set of 12 .**$25.00**
Pamphlet, Cub Scout Helps, BSA issue, 1950................**$2.00**
Pamphlet, Fun Around the Campfire, BSA, 1944 ....**$4.00**
Pamphlet, Universal Indian Sign Language, BSA **$9.00**
Pencil box, color scene of camp activities, 1930 ....**$25.00**
Pennant, National Jamboree, blue felt, lg logo, 1935 .**$100.00**
Pin, collar; BSA, brass, 1920 ....**$25.00**
Pin, Tenderfoot; safety-back clasp, 1930s **$3.00**
Plaque, Boy Scout Creed, framed, 1924......................**$20.00**
Plate, Young Doctor, Rockwell-Gorham, ceramic **$30.00**
Postcard, Hiding a Trail, color, #6, 1914 ....**$8.00**
Postcard, World Jamboree, Jesus the Scout, color, 1937 ..**$10.00**
Postcard, World Jamboree, w/logo, 1959......................**$5.00**
Record, Sousa's Boy Scout Marches, BSA approved, 78rpm.**$15.00**
Ring, full First Class, sterling.....................................**$10.00**
Ring, National Staff, logo in center, 10k gold...........**$100.00**
Ring, Sea Scout, w/anchor, sterling............................**$40.00**
Sheet music, Philmont Songs **$4.00**
Signal set, Official Triple; #1092, metal, 1950.............**$30.00**
Tie bar, Commissioners, clip-on, w/logo **$3.00**
Tie holder, laminated wood, w/logo & foldable metal loops, Cubs & Scouts variation **$10.00**
Wallet, Cub Scout, National issue, vinyl.......................**$4.00**
Watch, Official BSA, Ingersoll Pocket #1274, 1934 .....**$75.00**
Watch fob, Official BSA, Scoutmasters, green enamel center, #308 ....**$300.00**
Watch fob, scout w/crossed rifles, 1920......................**$45.00**
Woodburning kit, w/wood & cord..............................**$50.00**
Wristwatch, Official BSA, Imperial, #1547, 1941.........**$45.00**

Girl Scouts

Belt buckle, enamel w/cloverleaf, 1917........................**$25.00**
Calendar, 1920, Brown & Bigelow **$100.00**
Camera, Official GSA, Univex, 1937............................**$50.00**
Card, registration; Brownie Scout, 1921 ....**$10.00**
Catalog, uniform; Official GSA, 1930s.........................**$15.00**
Doll, uniform; Madam Hendren, 1920-22, rare **$150.00**
Emblem, Girl Scout Hospital Aide...............................**$12.00**
Flag, Official Brownie, sm, 1930s................................**$25.00**
Handbook, Official GSA, FED, 1913 ....**$200.00**
Handbook, Official GSA, tan cover, 1920 ....**$25.00**
Pin, Tenderfoot; 1918-1923 ....**$6.00**
Pin, wing; Wing Scouting, 1941...................................**$35.00**
Whistle, cylinder; Official GSA, 1920s........................**$20.00**

Handbook, 1955, VG, $15.00.

Sebastians

These tiny figures were first made in 1938 by Preston W. Baston and sold through gift stores, primarily in the New England area. When he retired in 1976, the Lance Corporation chose one hundred designs which they continued to produce under Baston's supervision. Since then, the discontinued figures have become very collectible.

Baston died in 1984, but his son, P.W. Baston, Jr., continues the tradition.

The figures are marked with an imprinted signature and a paper label. Early labels (before 1977) were green and silver foil shaped like an artist's palette; these are referred to as 'Marblehead' labels (Marblehead, Massachusetts, being the location of the factory) and figures that carry one of these are becoming hard to find and are highly valued by collectors.

Little Mother, 3½", $50.00.

Andrew Jackson	$35.00
Betsy Ross	$23.00
Candy Store	$80.00
Chiquita Banana	$300.00

Clown	$50.00
Elizabeth Monroe	$65.00
First Days of Fall	$37.50
George Washington w/cannon	$35.00
Grocery Store, Marblehead era	$65.00
Hanna Dustin, pen stand	$300.00
JF Kennedy	$60.00
Little Sister, blue label	$40.00
Mark Twain, black & silver label	$95.00
Old Salt	$75.00
Paul Revere	$45.00
Prince Philip	$200.00
Princess Elizabeth	$200.00
Sam Weller	$60.00
Sampling the Stew, Marblehead era	$55.00
Skipping Rope	$35.00
Son of the Desert	$225.00
Weaver & Loom, Marblehead era	$65.00
White House, gold	$100.00

Shawnee Pottery

In 1937 a company was formed in Zanesville, Ohio, on the suspected site of a Shawnee Indian village. They took the tribe's name to represent their company, recognizing the Indians to be the first to use the rich clay from the banks of the Muskingum River to make pottery there. Their venture was very successful, and until they closed in 1961, they produced many lines of kitchenware, planters, vases, lamps, and cookie jars that are very collectible today.

They specialized in figural items. There were 'Winnie' and 'Smiley' pig cookie jars and salt and pepper shakers; 'Bo Peep,' 'Puss 'n Boots,' 'Boy Blue,' and 'Charlie Chicken' pitchers; Dutch children; lobsters; and two lines of dinnerware modeled as ears of corn.

Values sometimes hinge on the extent of an item's decoration. Most items will increase by 100% to 200% when heavily decorated with decals and gold trimmed.

Not all of their ware was marked Shawnee; many pieces were simply marked U.S.A. (If periods are not present, it is not Shawnee) with a three- or four-digit mold number. If you'd like to learn more about this subject, we recommend *Shawnee Pottery, The Full Encyclopedia,* by Pam Curran; *The Collector's Guide to Shawnee Pottery* by Duane and Janice Vanderbilt; and *Shawnee Pottery, Identification & Value Guide,* by Jim and Bev Mangus.

See Also Cookie Jars.

Advisor: Rick Spencer (See Directory, Shawnee)

Club: Shawnee Pottery Collectors' Club
P.O. Box 713
New Smyrna Beach, FL 32170-0713
Monthly nationwide newsletter. SASE (c/o Pamela Curran) required when requesting information. Optional: $3 for sample of current newsletter

Creamer, Laurel Wreath, marked USA.........................**$22.00**
Creamer, Puss 'n Boots, no gold, marked USA 85......**$75.00**
Creamer, Sunflower, marked USA **$35.00**
Creamer, tilt; Tulip, marked USA.............................**$75.00**
Creamer, Wave, marked USA....................................**$25.00**
Jug, ball; Fruit, marked Shawnee 80, 48-oz.................**$80.00**
Jug, ball; Sunflower, marked USA, 48-oz....................**$145.00**
Jug, space-saver; embossed flower, marked USA 40, 20-oz **$26.00**
Pitcher, Chanticleer, gold & decal, marked Patented Chanticleer USA **$375.00**
Pitcher, Laurel Wreath, marked USA **$24.00**
Pitcher, Smiley, embossed clover bud, marked Pat Smiley USA...**$175.00**
Pitcher, Stars & Stripes, marked USA **$18.00**
Pitcher, utility; marked USA.......................................**$18.00**
Pitcher, Wave, marked USA **$24.00**
Planter, bird on shell, marked USA **$18.00**
Planter, birds on driftwood, marked Shawnee 502.....**$50.00**
Planter, boy & wheelbarrow, marked USA 750..........**$18.00**
Planter, Buddha, marked USA 524 ....**$24.00**
Planter, canopy bed, marked Shawnee 734................**$65.00**
Planter, cat & sax, marked USA 729..........................**$35.00**
Planter, elf shoe, gold, marked Shawnee 765 ....**$24.00**
Planter, frog & guitar, marked USA **$18.00**
Planter, globe, gold, marked Shawnee USA **$60.00**
Planter, hound dog, marked USA...............................**$8.00**
Planter, panda & cradle, marked, Shawnee USA 2031...**$30.00**
Planter, rabbit w/turnip, marked Shawnee 703..........**$30.00**
Planter, rocking horse, marked USA 526 ....**$24.00**
Planter, sitting dog, marked USA................................**$15.00**
Planter, squirrel at stump, marked USA **$10.00**
Planter, stagecoach, marked USA J545P.....................**$35.00**
Planter, swan & elf, marked Kenwood 2030 ....**$45.00**
Planter, train engine, marked USA 550 ....**$50.00**
Planter, two dogs, gold, marked USA 611 ....**$24.00**
Planter, two fawns, marked Shawnee USA 721..........**$22.00**
Planter, Valencia couple, marked USA.......................**$40.00**
Shakers, Chanticleers, sm, pr.....................................**$35.00**
Shakers, Cottage, sm, pr **$275.00**
Shakers, ducks, sm, pr...**$35.00**
Shakers, Dutch boy & girl, blue & gold, lg, pr **$85.00**
Shakers, Dutch boy & girl, brown, lg, pr **$40.00**
Shakers, ewers, 2 & 3 holes, sm, pr...........................**$30.00**
Shakers, Farmer Pigs, sm, pr **$38.00**
Shakers, flower clusters, gold, sm, pr.........................**$65.00**
Shakers, flowerpots, all white, sm, pr........................**$60.00**
Shakers, Fruit, lg, pr **$45.00**
Shakers, Jack & Jill, gold & decals, lg, pr.................**$195.00**
Shakers, Jack & Jill, lg, pr **$60.00**
Shakers, owls, gold, sm, pr..**$65.00**
Shakers, Puss 'n Boots, sm, pr....................................**$45.00**
Shakers, Smiley the Pig, green neckerchief, lg, pr....**$140.00**
Shakers, Smiley the Pig, pointed neckerchief, sm, pr.**$40.00**
Shakers, Swiss boy & girl, lg, pr................................**$35.00**
Shakers, watering cans, sm, pr...................................**$30.00**
Shakers, Wave, lg, pr...**$50.00**

Shakers, wheelbarrows, gold, sm, pr **$80.00**
Shakers, wheelbarrows, plain, sm, pr **$24.00**
Teapot, Drape, marked USA, 4-cup **$40.00**
Teapot, elephant, marked USA, 5-cup **$140.00**
Teapot, embossed rose, gold, marked USA.................**$135.00**
Teapot, Laurel Wreath, blue, yellow or green, marked USA, 6-cup **$55.00**
Teapot, Pennsylvania Dutch, marked USA 27, 27-oz..**$90.00**
Teapot, Rosette, marked USA **$40.00**
Teapot, sunflower, gold, marked USA, 7-cup............**$100.00**
Teapot, tulip flower, ribbed collar, gold, marked USA...**$65.00**

Corn Ware

Bowl, mixing; King, marked Shawnee #8, 8".............**$50.00**
Casserole, Queen, marked Shawnee #74, lg...............**$55.00**
Creamer, White Corn, marked USA, 12-oz **$35.00**
Polly Ann's popcorn set, King.....................................**$225.00**
Salt & pepper shakers, White Corn, 3¼", pr **$40.00**

Snack set, four plates and four mugs, MIB, $450.00.

Sugar bowl, King or Queen, w/lid..............................**$45.00**
Sugar shaker, White Corn, marked USA, from $55 to...**$70.00**
Tray, relish; King or Queen, marked Shawnee #79 ....**$45.00**

Lobster Ware

Bean pot, lobster finial, marked Kenwood USA 925, 40-oz **$550.00**
Bowl, mixing/open baker; #917, 7"............................**$45.00**
Bowl, salad/spaghetti; #922 ....**$80.00**
Butter dish, lobster finial, marked Kenwood USA 927 ..**$65.00**
Casserole, French; in triple-plated brass stand & warmer, 10-oz, 16-oz or 2-qt, ea **$60.00**
Casserole, French; 10-oz **$20.00**
Creamer jug, #921..**$50.00**
Mug, marked Kenwood USA 911, 8-oz.......................**$85.00**
Shakers, jug style, marked USA.................................**$110.00**
Spoon or fork, wood, #923, ea...................................**$12.00**
Utility jar, w/lid, #907 ....**$31.00**

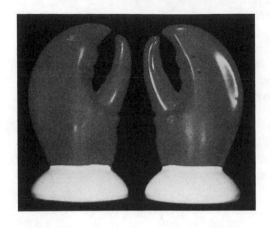

Salt and pepper shakers, marked USA, $35.00 for the pair. (Photo courtesy Jim and Bev Mangus)

Valencia

Bowl, dessert; 6"	**$17.00**
Bowl, mixing; 10"	**$35.00**
Carafe	**$75.00**
Casserole, 7½"	**$75.00**
Coffeepot, AD	**$80.00**
Cookie jar	**$140.00**
Creamer, marked Valencia	**$17.00**
Nappie, no mark, 8½"	**$25.00**
Nappie, 9½"	**$25.00**
Pie plate, 9¼"	**$85.00**
Pitcher, ice	**$30.00**
Plate, chop; 15"	**$45.00**
Plate, 9¾"	**$14.00**
Spoon, 9½"	**$65.00**
Vase, bud	**$24.00**
Vase, flower; 8"	**$28.00**

Sheet Music

Flea markets are a good source for buying old sheet music, and prices are usually very reasonable. Most examples can be bought for less than $5.00. More often than not, it is collected for reasons other than content. Some of the cover art was done by well-known illustrators like Rockwell, Christy, Barbelle, and Starmer, and some collectors like to zero in on their particular favorite, often framing some of the more attractive examples. Black Americana collectors can find many good examples with Black entertainers featured on the covers and the music reflecting an ethnic theme.

You may want to concentrate on music by a particularly renowned composer, for instance George M. Cohan or Irving Berlin. Or you may find you enjoy covers featuring famous entertainers and movie stars from the '40s through the '60s, for instance. At any rate, be critical of condition when you buy or sell sheet music. As is true with any item of paper, tears, dog ears, or soil will greatly reduce its value.

If you'd like a more thorough listing of sheet music and prices, we recommend *The Sheet Music Reference and Price Guide* by Anna Marie Guiheen and Marie-Reine A. Pafik (Collector Books), and *The Collector's Guide to Sheet Music* by Debbie Dillon.

After All the Good Is Gone, Photo cover: Conway Twitty, 1975	**$5.00**
All I Want for Christmas Is My Two Front Teeth, Don Gardner, 1946	**$3.00**
Am I That Easy To Forget?, Carl Belew & WS Stevenson, 1958	**$5.00**
Angel Face, Bowers & Saunders, Movie: Last Time I Saw Archie, Photo cover: Robert Mitchum, France Nuyen & others, 1961	**$5.00**
Are These Really Mine?, Sunny Skylar, David Saxon & Robert Cook, 1945	**$3.00**
Auf Wiederseh'n Sweetheart, John Sexton, John Turner & Eberhard Storch, Photo cover: Vera Lynn, 1951	**$5.00**
Backward, Turn Backward; Dave Colman, 1954	**$5.00**
Beau James, Baker, Movie: Beau James, Photo cover: Bob Hope & Vera Miles, 1957	**$5.00**
Beyond the Reef, Jack Pitman, Photo cover: Bing Crosby, 1949	**$3.00**
Blues, L Rosenthal, Movie: Requiem for a Heavyweight, Photo cover: Mickey Rooney, Jackie Gleason, Anthony Quinn, 1962	**$10.00**
Breakfast at Tiffany's, Henry Mancini, Movie: same title, Photo cover: Audrey Hepburn, 1961	**$5.00**
Bumming Around, Pete Graves, 1953	**$3.00**
Cara Mia, Tulio Trapani & Lee Lange, Photo cover: David Whitfield, 1954	**$3.00**
Charade, Mancini, Movie: same title, Photo cover: Cary Grant & Audrey Hepburn, 1963	**$10.00**
Coffee Time, Fred & Warren, Movie: Yolanda & the Thief, Photo cover: Fred Astaire & Lucille Bremer, 1945	**$5.00**
Consider Yourself, Lionel Bart, Musical: Oliver, Cover artist: Irene Haas, 1960	**$5.00**
Cuanto Le Gusta, Ray Gilbert & Gabriel Ruiz, Movie: A Date w/Judy: Photo cover: 6 stars from movie, 1948	**$10.00**
Darling Lili, Mercer & Mancini, Movie: same title, Photo cover: Julie Andrews, 1970	**$5.00**
Dime a Dozen, Cindy Walker, Photo cover: Sammy Kaye, 1949	**$3.00**
Don't Marry Me, Richard Rogers & Oscar Hammerstein II, Movie: Flower Drum Song, 1961	**$5.00**
Down by the River, Lorenz Hart & Richard Rogers, Movie: Mississippi: Photo cover: Bing Crosby & Joan Bennett, 1935	**$15.00**
Dreamer's Holiday, Kim Gannon & Mabel Wayne, Photo cover: Vic Damone, 1949	**$5.00**
Endless Love, Richie, Movie: same title, Photo cover: Brooke Shields & Martin Hewitt, 1981	**$3.00**
Family Sing, A Sing Along w/Mitch, Cover artist: Norman Rockwell, 1962	**$35.00**
For the Good Times, Kris Kristofferson, 1968	**$5.00**
Gee I Wish I Was Back in the Army, I Berlin, Movie: White Christmas, Photo cover: Crosby, Kay, Clooney & Ellen, 1942	**$10.00**
Girls, Cole Porter, Movie: Mexican Hayride, 1943	**$5.00**

Good-Will Movement, Cole Porter, Movie: Mexican Hayride, 1943 ....$5.00

Goodbye to Rome, Arriverderci Roma; Carl Sigman & R Rascel, Photo cover: Georgia Gibbs, 1955 ....$3.00

Guilty, Gus Kahn, Harry Akst & Richard A Whiting, Photo cover: Dinah Shore, 1931 ....$8.00

Have I Stayed Away Too Long, Frank Loesser, Cover artist: WJH, 1943 ....$5.00

Heat Wave, Irving Berlin, Musical: Easter Parade, 1933.$10.00

Here's a Hand, Lorenz Hart & Richard Rogers, Movie: All's Fair, 1942 ....$5.00

Holiday Inn, Irving Berlin, 1942 ....$5.00

House I Live In, Lewis Allen & Earl Robinson, Movie: same title, Photo cover: Frank Sinatra.............................$5.00

I Believe in Miracles, Mason & Reed, Photo cover: Engelbert Humperdinck, 1976...$3.00

I Don't Want To Be Hurt Anymore, McCarthy, Photo cover: Nat King Cole, 1962 ....$3.00

I Love the Way You Say Goodnight, Eddie Pola and George Wyle, from Lullaby of Broadway, Doris Day and Gene Nelson cover, 1951, $10.00. (Photo courtesy Guiheen & Pafik)

I Love You a Thousand Ways, Lefty Frizzell & Jim Beck, Photo cover: Lefty Frizzell, 1961......................$3.00

I Went Down to Virginia, Sammy Gallop & David Saxon, 1948...$3.00

I Wonder Who's Kissing Her Now, Hough, Adams & Howard, Movie: same title, Photo cover: June Haver, 1947 ....$5.00

I'll Be Walkin' w/My Honey, Buddy Kaye & Sam Medoff, 1945..$3.00

I'll See You in the Sunrise, Marie Calabrese, signed by composer, 1946 ....$10.00

I'm Getting Sentimental Over You, Ned Washington & George Bassman, 1940 ....$3.00

I'm Hans Christian Anderson, Frank Loesser, Movie: Hans Christian Anderson, Photo cover: Danny Kaye $5.00

I'm Old Fashioned, Mercer & Kern, Movie: You Were Never Lovelier, Photo cover: Astaire, Hayworth, Menjou & Cougat, 1942..$10.00

I've Got Plenty To Be Thankful For, Irving Berlin, 1942..$10.00

If I Were a Carpenter, Tim Hardin, Photo cover: Johnny Cash & June Carter, 1966..$3.00

In a World of My Own, Hilliard & Fain, Movie: Alice in Wonderland (Disney), 1951.................................$10.00

In the Land of Beginning Again, Clarke & Meyer, Movie: Bells of St Mary's, Photo cover: Bing Crosby, 1946........$5.00

Irish Soldier Boy, Lanyon & DeWitt, Photo cover: Connie Foley, 1950 ....$3.00

It Might as Well Be Spring, Rogers & Hammerstein, Movie: State Fair, Photo cover: Crain, Andrews, Haymes & Blaine, 1945 ....$5.00

It's Love, Love, Love; Mack David, Joan Whitney & Alex M Kramer, Cover artist: Barbelle $5.00

Ivory Tower, Jack Fulton & Louis Steele, Photo cover: Cathy Carr, 1956 ....$3.00

Judy, Hoagy Carmichael & Sammy Lerner, 1934..........$8.00

Just My Luck, Johnny Burke & James Van Heusen, 1945 ..$3.00

King's New Clothes, Frank Loesser, Movie: Hans Christian Anderson, Photo cover: Danny Kaye, 1951 ....$5.00

Lady of Liberty, John W Miller & Paul Wellbaum, 1942...$10.00

Let Freedom Ring, Shelley & Mossman, Cover artist: Starmer, 1940 ....$10.00

Let's Call the Whole Thing Off, George Gershwin, 1937 ...$5.00

Limbo Rock, William E 'Billy' Strange & Jon Sheldon, 1962 .$2.00

Little on the Lonely Side, Robertson, Cavanaugh & Weldon, Photo cover: Les Baldwin, 1944..............................$3.00

Longing for You, Bernard Jansen & Walter Dana, 1951...$3.00

Lover's Roulette, Charyl Edmonds, Jonah Thompson & Paul Raoul Arenas, Photo cover: Mel Torme, 1966 ....$5.00

Make the Man Love Me, Dorothy Fields & Arthur Schwartz, Movie: Tree Grows in Brooklyn, 1951 ....$3.00

Meet Me in Seattle, Suzie by Lassers, 1962 ....$3.00

Monsieur Baby, Hornez, Movie: Bedtime Story, Photo cover: Maurice Chevalier, 1933 ....$10.00

More & More, Kern & Harburg, Movie: Can't Help Singing, Photo cover: Deanna Durbin, 1944 ....$5.00

Muskrat Ramble, Ray Gilbert & Edward Kid Ory, Photo cover: Dennis Day, 1950 ....$5.00

My Heart Belongs to Daddy, Cole Porter, Movie: Leave It to Me, 1938..$10.00

My Melancholy Baby, Norton, Watson & Burnette, Movie: Birth of the Blues, Photo cover: Bing Crosby, 1939...........$5.00

My Ship, Kurt Weill & Ira Gershwin, Movie: Lady in the Dark, Photo cover: Gertrude Lawrence, 1941 ....$3.00

New Moon & an Old Serenade, Silver, Block & Coslow, Photo cover: Tommy Dorsey, 1939 ....$3.00

No Other One, Tot Seymour & Vee Lawnhurst, 1935...$3.00

Oh Boy, Lee Adams & Charles Strouse, Movie: Bye Bye Birdie, 1960 ....$5.00

Old Piano Roll Blues, Cy Hoben, 1949 ....$5.00

Only Forever, Johnny Burke & James V Monaco, Movie: Rhythm on the River, Photo cover: Bing Crosby & Mary Martin, 1940...$5.00

Party Down, Shelly & Brackett, Movie: Witness, Photo cover: Harrison Ford, 1985 ....$3.00

Piccolo, Irving Berlin, Movie: Top Hat, Photo cover: Fred Astaire & Ginger Rogers, 1935............................$15.00

Poor Little Rhode Island, Sammy Cahn & Jule Styne, 1944..$5.00

Put Me to the Test, Ira Gershwin & Jerome Kern, Movie: Cover Girl, 1944...$3.00

Rags to Riches, Adler and Ross, Tony Bennett photo cover, 1953, $10.00.
(Photo coutesy Guiheen & Pafik)

Red as the Rose of Maytime, Victor Leon, Leon Stein & Franz Lehar, Musical: From the Merry Widow, 1958........$5.00

Rockin' Chair, Hoagy Carmichael, 1941 ....$3.00

Rose Ann of Charing Cross, Kermit Goell & Mabel Wayne, Photo cover: Gene Krupa, 1942 ....$15.00

Sam You Made the Pants Too Long, Whitehouse, Berle, Lewis & Young, Photo cover: Barbra Striesand, 1966.......$3.00

Secretly, Marty Symes & Al Kaufman, 1943..................$3.00

Shifting Wispering Sands, VC Gilbert & Mary M Hadler, Photo cover: Billy Vaughn, 1950...$5.00

Since He Traded His Zoot Suit for a Uniform, Carmen Lombardo & Pat Innisfree, 1942 ....$10.00

Smile Away Each Rainy Day, Mercer & Mancini, Movie: Darling Lili, Photo cover: Julie Andrews, 1970.......$3.00

Some Sunday Morning, Koehler, Jerome & Heindorf, Movie: San Antonio, Photo cover: Errol Flynn & Alexis Smith, 1945...$8.00

Somethin' Stupid, C Carson Parks, Photo cover: Frank & Nancy Sinatra, 1967 ....$2.00

Spanish Eyes, Charles Singleton, Eddie Snyder & Bert Kaempfert, Photo cover: Al Martino, 1965...............$3.00

Stepping Out w/My Baby, Irving Berlin, Movie: Easter Parade, Photo cover: Garland, Lawford, Astaire & Miller, 1947 ....$10.00

Surrender, Bernie Benjamin & George Weiss, Photo cover: Perry Como, Cover artist: Barbelle, 1945 ....$5.00

Sweet Old Fashioned Girl, Bob Merrill, 1956................$3.00

Taking a Chance on Love, Latouche, Fetter & Duke, Movie: Cabin in the Sky, Cover artist: Sorokin, 1940 ....$5.00

Tender Trap, Cahn & Van Heusen, Movie: same title, Photo cover: F Sinatra, D Reynolds, D Wayne, C Holmes, 1955...$5.00

That's A-Why, Bob Merrill, Photo cover: Mindy Carson & Guy Mitchell, 1952 ....$2.00

There's Music in the Land, Styne & Cahn, Movie: Two Guys From Texas, Photo cover: D Morgan, J Carson & D Malone, 1948 ....$5.00

This Nearly Was Mine, Rodgers & Hammerstein, Movie: South Pacific, Photo cover: Mary Martin, Ezio Pinza, 1949 ....$5.00

Tico-Tico, Ervin Drake & Zequinha Abreu, Movie: Bathing Beauty, Photo cover: Red Skelton & Esther Williams, 1943..$5.00

Too Young, Sylvia Dee & Sid Lippman, Photo cover: Nat King Cole, 1951 ....$3.00

Turn on the Old Music Box, Leigh Harline & Ned Washington, Movie: Pinocchio (Disney), 1940 .....$10.00

United We Stand, Herbert Rikles, Howard Dressner & Samuel Meade, 1941 ....$10.00

Wait Till Tomorrow, Lloyd & DePaul, Movie: Ballad of Josie, Photo cover: Doris Day & Peter Graves, 1967 ....$5.00

Way Down on the Swanee River, Steven Foster, Photo cover: Ted Fioroto, 1935...$5.00

Weekend in New England, Randy Edelman, Photo cover: Barry Manilow, 1976..$3.00

What Kind of Fool Am I?, Leslie Bricusse & Anthony Newley: Movie: Stop the World I Want To Get Off, 1961 ....$5.00

When I Grow Up, Heyman & Henderson, Movie: Curly Top, Photo cover: Shirley Temple, 1935......................$10.00

When Mother Nature Sings Her Lullaby, Yoell & Brown, Photo cover: Bing Crosby, Cover artist: Leff, 1938.$5.00

When the Leaves Bid the Trees Goodbye, Tot Seymour & Vee Lawnhurst, Photo cover: Dorothy Lamour, 1935 ....$5.00

When You Hear the Time Signal, Mercer & Schertzinger, Movie: Fleet's In, Photo cover: Lamour, Dorsey & Hutton, 1942...$10.00

Where the Mountains Meet the Moon, Remus Harris & Irving Melsher, 1940...$3.00

Who Can I Turn To?, Leslie Bricusse & Anthony Newley, Musical: Roar of the Greasepaint, 1964...................$3.00

Wichita, Washington & Salter, Movie: same title, Photo cover: Joel McCrea, Lloyd Bridges & Vera Miles, 1955......$5.00

Wond'rin' When, Livingston & Evans, Movie: Isn't It Romantic, Photo cover: V Lake, M Freeman & B DeWolfe, 1948..$5.00

Years Before Us, Frank Loesser, Musical: Where's Charley, Cover: caricature of Ray Bolger, 1948....................$5.00

You Don't Have To Know the Language, Burke & Van Heusen, Movie: Rode to Rio, Photo cover: Crosby, Hope & Lamour, 1947..$10.00

You Took My Breath Away, Coslow & Whiting, Movie: Coronado, Photo cover: Duchin, Davis, Errol, Haley & Devine, 1935..$3.00

You're Breaking My Heart, Pat Genaro & Sunny Skylar, 1948...$3.00

You've Got Everything, Gus Kahn & Walter Donaldson, 1933.$3.00

Zana Zaranda, Mort Greene & Harry Revel, Movie: Call Out the Marines, 1942..$5.00

Shell Pink Glassware

Here's something relatively new to look for this year — lovely soft pink opaque glassware made by the

Jeannette Glass Company for a short time during the late 1950s. Prices, says expert Gene Florence, have been increasing by leaps and bounds! You'll find a wide variance in style from piece to piece, since the company chose shapes from several of their most popular lines to press in the satiny shell pink. Refer to *Collectible Glassware from the 40s, 50s, and 60s,* by Mr. Florence for photos and more information.

Ashtray, butterfly shape...$28.00
Base, for Lazy Susan, w/ball bearings $160.00
Bowl, Florentine, footed, 10".....................................$30.00
Bowl, Gondola, 17½"...$40.00
Bowl, Holiday, footed, 10½"......................................$45.00
Bowl, Lombardi, design in center, 4-footed, 11".........$42.00
Bowl, Napco #2250, w/berry design, footed...............$15.00
Bowl, Pheasant, footed, 8"..$37.50
Bowl, Wedding, w/lid, 6½"...$27.50
Cake plate, Anniversary $225.00
Cake stand, Harp, 10"..$45.00
Candle holders, Eagle, 3-footed, pr...........................$85.00
Candle holders, 2-light, pr $45.00
Candy dish, Floragold, 4-footed, 5¼".........................$20.00
Candy dish, square, w/lid, 6½" $30.00

Punch bowl, $60.00; stand, $35.00. (Photo courtesy Gene Florence)

Relish, Vineyard, octagonal, 4-part, 12" $42.00
Stem, sherbet; Thumbprint, 5-oz $12.50
Stem, water goblet; Thumbprint, 8-oz.........................$17.50
Sugar bowl, Baltimore Pear, footed, w/lid...................$11.00
Tray, Harp, 2-handled, 12½x9¾".................................$60.00
Tray, Lazy Susan, 5-part, 13½"...................................$55.00
Tray, snack; w/cup indent, 7¾x10"..............................$9.00
Tray, Venetian, 6-part, 16½"......................................$40.00
Tray, 5-part, 2 handles, 15¾".....................................$85.00
Tumbler, juice; Thumbprint, footed, 5-oz $8.00
Vase, cornucopia, 5" $15.00
Vase, heavy bottom, 9"...$135.00
Vase, 7" $30.00

Shirley Temple

Born April 23, 1928, Shirley Jane Temple danced and smiled her way into the hearts of America in the movie *Stand Up and Cheer.* Many successful roles followed and by the time Shirley was eight years old, she was #1 at box offices around the country. Her picture appeared in publications almost daily, and any news about her was news indeed. Mothers dressed their little daughters in clothing copied after hers and coiffed them with Shirley hairdos.

The extent of her success was mirrored in the unbelievable assortment of merchandise that saturated the retail market. Dolls, coloring books, children's clothing and jewelry, fountain pens, paper dolls, stationery, and playing cards are just a few examples of the hundreds of items that were available. Shirley's face was a common sight on the covers of magazines as well as in the advertisements they contained, and she was the focus of scores of magazine articles.

Though she had been retired from the movies for nearly a decade, she had two successful TV series in the late '50s, *The Shirley Temple Story-Book* and *The Shirley Temple Show.* Her reappearance caused new interest in some of the items that had been so popular during her childhood, and many were reissued.

Always interested in charity and community service, Shirley became actively involved in a political career in the late '60s, serving at both the state and national levels.

If you're interested in learning more about her, we rec-

Candy jar, Grapes, footed, with lid, $20.00.

Candy jar bottom, National $10.00
Celery/relish, 3-part, 12½" $45.00
Cigarette box, butterfly finial $235.00
Comport, Napco #2256, square $12.50
Compote, Windsor, 6" $20.00
Cookie jar, w/lid, 6½"..$100.00
Creamer, Baltimore Pear..$15.00
Cup, punch; 5-oz $6.00
Honey jar, beehive shape, notched lid $40.00
Pitcher, Thumbprint, footed, 24-oz...............................$27.50
Pot, Napco #2249, crosshatch design...........................$15.00
Powder jar, w/lid, 4¾"...$45.00
Punch ladle, pink plastic..$20.00

ommend *Shirley Temple Dolls and Collectibles* by Patricia R. Smith; *Toys, Antique and Collectible,* by David Longest; and *Shirley in the Magazines* by Gen Jones.

Note: The pin-back button we describe below has been reproduced, so has the cobalt glassware with Shirley's likeness. Beware!

Advisor: Gen Jones (See Directory, Character and Personality Collectibles)

Newsletter: *Lollipop News*
P.O. Box 6203
Oxnard, CA 93031; Dues: $14 per year

Newsletter: *The Shirley Temple Collectors News*
8811 Colonial Rd.
Brooklyn, NY 11209
Dues: $20 per year; checks payable to Rita Dubas

Autograph, as adult, common	$10.00
Badge, Policeman, 1937	$25.00
Book, coloring; Shirley Temple Crossing the Country, M, minimum value	$35.00
Book, Heidi, Random House, Shirley Temple edition, 1st printing, EX, from $25 to	$30.00
Book, How I Raised Shirley Temple, 1935, EX	$25.00
Book, Real Little Girl, EX	$50.00

Book, *Shirley Temple and the Spirit of Dragonwood,* Whitman #2311, Kathryn Heisenfelt, 1945, EX, $25.00. (Photo courtesy David and Virginia Brown)

Book, Shirley Temple's Favorite Poems, hardcover, EX	$45.00
Book, Shirley Temple's Favorite Tales of Long Ago, Random House, 1958, lg, VG	$12.00
Book, Shirley's Baby Book, Lorraine Burdick, #5 in series	$20.00
Book, Those Endearing Young Charms, by Marc Best, hardcover w/dust jacket, EX	$18.00
Bust, green chalkware, minimum value	$500.00
Cereal box backs, 1930s, set of 12	$150.00
Christmas card, Hallmark, 1935, M	$30.00
Cigarette card, Famous Film Stars, Shirley Temple & Cooper, Now & Forever, Gallagher Ltd #39, EX	$10.00

Creamer, portrait on cobalt glass	$40.00
Doll, celluloid, Japan, 8", M	$245.00
Doll, composition, Baby Take a Bow, 21", from $800 to	$1,000.00
Doll, composition, Bright Eyes, 25", from $900 to	$1,100.00
Doll, composition, Stand Up & Cheer, 15"	$675.00
Doll, composition, Wee Willie Winkie, 18"	$1,000.00
Doll, plastic & vinyl, 1982-83, 12", M	$35.00
Doll, vinyl, Cinderella, 1961, 15"	$300.00
Doll, vinyl, Little Bo Peep, 15"	$300.00
Doll, vinyl, Montgomery Ward, 1972, 17", M	$325.00
Doll, vinyl, 1950s, 15", M	$265.00
Doll, vinyl, 1950s, 19", M	$400.00
Drawing book, Saalfield #1725, 1935, EX, minimum value	$35.00
Embroidery set, Gabriel #311, 1960, NMIB	$20.00
Figurine, Stand Up & Cheer, Nostalgia, MIB	$80.00
Lobby card, Bachelor & Bobby Soxer, #8 in series, scene at picnic	$15.00
Magazine, Life, March 20, 1942, EX	$20.00
Magazine, Life, November 1, 1937, Shirley & stand-in cover, EX	$8.00
Magazine ad, How Shirley Temple Spends Her Vacation, Country Gentleman, August 1937, ½-pg	$4.00
Pamphlet, Story of My Life, giveaway in 1935, M	$25.00
Paper dolls, Saalfield #1739, Shirley Temple & Dresses, 1959, uncut, minimum value	$25.00
Paper dolls, Saalfield #1782, 1939, uncut, minimum value	$75.00
Pen & pencil set, 1930s, minimum value	$75.00
Pin, Shirley Temple League, portrait, England, 1930s, M	$85.00
Pin-back button, My Friend Shirley, original	$40.00

Pitcher, 4½", or mug, 3¾", white portrait on blue cobalt, original only, $40.00 each.

Plate, Baby Take a Bow	$65.00
Pocket mirror, Shirley as Heidi, 1937, NM	$40.00
Poster, Miss Annie Rooney, 27x41", reissue, G	$40.00
Program, Tournament of Roses, 1939, 38 pgs, 11½x8½"	$20.00
Ring, Club; face, sterling, 1930s, rare	$300.00
Sewing card set, Saalfield, NMIB	$30.00
Sheet music, The Good Ship Lollipop, Bright Eyes, EX	$15.00
Song album, Shirley Temple Song Album #2, EX	$30.00
Teddy bear, Bearly Temple, EX+	$50.00

Wheaties box, 1936, M...$150.00
Writing tablet, Western, 1935, M..............................$40.00

Shot Glasses

Shot glasses come in a wide variety of colors and designs. They're readily available, inexpensive, and they don't take a lot of room to display. Most sell for $5.00 and under, except cut glass, carnival glass, Depression glass, or pressed glass. Colored glass, those with etching or gold trim, or one that has an unusual shape — squared or barrel form, for instance — fall into a slightly higher range. Several advertising shot glasses, probably the most common type of all, are described in our listings. Soda advertising is unusual and may drive the value up to about $12.00 to $15.00.

Both new and older glasses alike sell for a little more in the Western part of the country. One-of-a-kind items or oddities are a bit harder to classify, especially sample glasses. Many depend on the elaborateness of their designs as opposed to basic lettering. These values are only estimates and should be used as a general guide. The club welcomes your suggestions and comments. For more information, we recommend *Shot Glasses: An American Tradition,* and *The Shot Glass Encyclopedia,* both by Mark Pickvet.

Note: Values for shot glasses in good condition are represented by the low end of our ranges, while the high end reflects estimated values for examples in mint condition.

Advisor: Mark Pickvet (See Directory, Shot Glasses)

Barrel shaped, from $5 to $7.50
Black porcelain replica, from $3.50 to $5.00
Carnival colors, plain or fluted, from $100 to $150.00
Carnival colors, w/patterns, from $125 to $175.00
Colored glass tourist, from $4 to $6.00
Culver 22 kt gold, from $6 to $8.00
Depression, colors, from $10 to $12.50
Depression, colors w/patterns or etching, from $17.50 to ..$25.00
Depression, tall, general designs, from $10 to $12.50
Depression, tall, tourist, from $5 to...............................$7.50
Frosted w/gold designs, from $6 to $8.00
General, advertising, from $4 to.....................................$6.00
General, etched designs, from $5 to $7.50
General, porcelain, from $4 to...$6.00
General, w/enameled design, from $3 to $4.00
General, w/frosted designs, from $3.50 to....................$5.00
General, w/gold designs, from $6 to $8.00
General tourist, from $3 to...$4.00
Inside eyes, from $5 to...$7.50
Iridized silver, from $5 to $7.50
Mary Gregory or Anchor Hocking Ships, from $150 to ..$200.00
Nudes, from $25 to...$35.00
Plain, w/or w/out flutes, from 75¢ to $1.00
Pop or soda advertising, from $12.50 to......................$15.00
Porcelain tourist, from $3.50 to......................................$5.00
Rounded European designs w/gold rims, from $4 to...$6.00

Ruby flashed, from $35 to..$50.00
Sayings & toasts, 1940s-50s, from $5 to $7.50
Sports, professional teams, from $5 to $7.50
Square, general, from $6 to..$8.00
Square, w/etching, from $10 to $12.50
Square, w/pewter, from $12.50 to $15.00
Square, w/2-tone bronze & pewter, from $15 to $17.50
Standard glass w/pewter, from $7.50 to.......................$10.00
Steuben crystal, from $150 to $200.00
Taiwan tourist, from $2 to...$3.00
Tiffany, Galle or fancy art, from $600 to $800.00
Turquoise & gold tourist, from $6 to $8.00
Whiskey or beer advertising, modern, from $5 to $7.50
Whiskey sample glasses, from $30 to $250.00
19th-century cut patterns, from $35 to.......................$50.00

Silhouette Pictures

These novelty pictures are familiar to everyone. Even today a good number of them are still around, and you'll often see them at flea markets and co-ops. They were very popular in their day and never expensive, and because they were made for so many years (the '20s through the '50s), many variations are available. The glass in some is flat, in others it is curved. Backgrounds may be foil, a scenic print, hand tinted, or plain. Sometimes dried flowers were added as accents. But the characteristic common to them all is that the subject matter is reverse painted on the glass. People (even complicated groups), scenes, ships, and animals were popular themes. Though quite often the silhouette was done in solid black to create a look similar to the nineteenth-century cut silhouettes, colors were sometimes used as well.

In the '20s, making tinsel art pictures became a popular pastime. Ladies would paint the outline of their subjects on the back of the glass and use crumpled tinfoil as a background. Sometimes they would tint certain areas of the glass, making the foil appear to be colored. This type is popular with with collectors of folk art.

If you'd like to learn more about this subject, we recommend *The Encyclopedia of Silhouette Collectibles on Glass; 1996 – 97 Price Guide for Encyclopedia of Silhouette Collectibles on Glass;* and *Vintage Silhouettes on Glass and Reverse Paintings* (copyright 2000, all new items pictured) by Shirley Mace. These books show examples of Benton Glass pictures with frames made of metal, wood, plaster, and plastic. The metal frames with the stripes are most favored by collectors as long as they are in good condition. Wood frames were actually considered deluxe when silhouettes were originally sold. Recently some convex glass silhouettes from Canada have been found, nearly identical to the ones made by Benton Glass except for their brown tape frames. Backgrounds seem to be slightly different as well. Among the flat glass silhouettes, the ones signed by Diefenbach are the most expensive. The wildflower pictures, especially ones with fine lines and good detail, are becoming popular with collectors.

Advisor: Shirley Mace (See Directory, Silhouette Pictures)

Convex Glass

Couple in cottage scene, BG 45-81, Benton Glass......**$35.00**

Couple in parlour, BG 68-133, Benton Glass, Copr S Colef 3-15-42 ....**$20.00**

Couple making snowman, BG 45-159, Benton Glass.**$45.00**

Couple on balcony, BG 45-19, Benton Glass..............**$32.00**

Couple w/bow & arrow, BG 45-77 ....**$30.00**

Couple w/knitting in flower garden, BG 45-59, Benton Glass **$35.00**

Courting Spanish couple, BG 45-55, Benton Glass.....**$35.00**

Fox hunt scene, MC 5½D-3, unknown.......................**$23.00**

Lady & child gardening, painted cottage in background, ER 68-6, CE Erickson, c 1941.....................................**$35.00**

Lady & child w/cat, dark blue, BG 68-7B, Benton Glass..**$60.00**

Lady at piano, plain white background, BG 45-172, Benton Glass **$30.00**

Lady equestrian jumping fence, lake scene beyond, BG 68-198 ....**$40.00**

Lady primping, maid at feet, BG 3½ 4½-27, Benton Glass.**$30.00**

Lady stands w/arms out, full skirt, ruffles, PW 57-1, Peter Watson **$30.00**

Man & boy at shore w/toy sailing ship, BG 45-121, Benton Glass **$35.00**

Man & boy in fishing boat w/rod & sm dog, BG 45-212, Benton Glass **$32.00**

Man making jump on skis, BG 45-157, Benton Glass ..**$32.00**

Man w/pipe reads newspaper in overstuffed chair, black, BG 45-15, Benton Glass...**$25.00**

Musical couple, he w/flute, she w/sheet music, black, BG 68-9, Benton Glass...**$42.00**

Sailing ship, BG 45-3, Benton Glass..........................**$25.00**

Sailing ship, PW 5D-5, Peter Watson's Studio **$20.00**

Sailing ship, white on rose, BG 68-1W, Benton Glass ..**$55.00**

Sleighing silhouette w/snow-covered cottage scene background, thermometer behind glass, ER 45 3, CE Erickson Co...**$35.00**

This Little Piggy, stuffed animal & curtains before painted (pastels) baby's portrait, C Becker, BG 68-100, Benton Glass **$38.00**

Flat Glass

At the Gate, courting couple, DE 45-26, Deltex Products Co...**$22.00**

Courting couple w/flowers, reverse-painted colors & foil, AP 710-12, Art Publishing Co......................................**$23.00**

Family scene before fireplace, NE 68-11, Newton **$28.00**

Girl chasing dog w/stolen doll, FL 44-1, Flowercraft..**$30.00**

Girl w/candle & kitten, TA 5½ 8-1, Tinsel Art **$20.00**

Hidden Pool, 2 female nudes at pool, ½" plaster, BB 68-10, Buckbee-Brehm **$20.00**

Horsemen among painted mountain scene, Jones Dairy advertising, NE 452, Made by Newton Mfg Co, Newton, Iowa **$28.00**

Howdee, mother & baby come to father in easy chair, NE 57-6, Newton...**$18.00**

Kinder Musik, nude child plays triangle, KW Diefenbach, Tallimit Art, RI 79-750, CA Richards...................**$200.00**

Lady's portrait in profile, BB 4½ 5½-6, Buckbee-Brehm...**$15.00**

Land of the Free, scout & wagon train scene, NE 57-14, Newton..**$28.00**

Nymphs dancing by water, VO 6½ 9-2, signed Ellery Friend, Volland...**$50.00**

Old Fashioned Garden, lady w/flowers, RE 711-35, Reliance Products..**$25.00**

Senorita, Spanish lady standing in archway, DE 810-7, Deltex **$30.00**

Southern Belle, lady's portrait in profile on silver background, RE 45-31, Reliance Products **$20.00**

Spinning Wheel, lady at wheel, cat w/yarn, BB 170-20, w/original metal hanger...**$35.00**

Sprite in woodland scene, FL 57-3, unmarked (Flowercraft)..**$32.00**

Swallows among flowering branch, RE 3½ 4-25, Reliance Products..**$18.00**

Swan pond, many colors, RE-711-2, Reliance Products ..**$30.00**

Terriers playing tug-of-war, RE-57-74, unmarked (Reliance Products) **$18.00**

Untitled, FL 410-1, Flowercraft, $48.00.
(Photo courtesy Shirley and Ray Mace)

When I Was Young, RI 3½D-5187, CA Richards.........**$20.00**

Winged fairy-like creature in long-stemmed glass, cut-out style, MF 7½ 12-41, unknown manufacturer........**$40.00**

Silverplated and Sterling Flatware

The secondary market is being tapped more and more as the only source for those replacement pieces needed to augment family heirloom sets, and there are many collectors who admire the vintage flatware simply because they appreciate its beauty, quality, and affordability. Several factors influence pricing. For instance, a popular pattern though plentiful may be more expensive than a scarce one that might be passed over because it very likely would be difficult to collect. When you buy silverplate, condition is very important, since replating can be expensive.

Pieces with no monograms are preferred. To evaluate monogrammed items, deduct 20% from fancy or rare examples; 30% from common, plain items; and 50% to 70% if they are worn.

Dinner knives range in size from 9⅜" to 10"; dinner forks from 7⅜" to 7¾". Luncheon knives are approximately 8½" to 8¾", while luncheon forks are about 6¾" to 7". Place knives measure 8⅞" to 9¼", and place forks 7⅛" to 7¼".

Our values are given for flatware in excellent condition. Matching services often advertise in various trade papers and can be very helpful in helping you locate the items you're looking for. One of the best sources we are aware of is *The Antique Trader*; they're listed with the trade papers in the back of this book.

If you'd like to learn more about the subject, we recommend *The Standard Encyclopedia of American Silverplate* by Frances M. Bones and Lee Roy Fisher (published by Collector Books).

Advisor: Rick Spencer (See Directory, Regal)

Silverplate

Adam, 1917, berry spoon, Oneida **$20.00**
Adam, 1917, pierced olive spoon, Oneida.....................**$8.00**
Allure, 1938, cheese server, Rogers Mfg........................**$9.00**
Allure, 1938, service for 8, 32 pcs, Rogers Mfg...........**$70.00**
Allure, 1938, sugar shell, Rogers Mfg............................**$5.00**
Allure, 1938, tablespoon, Rogers Mfg............................**$7.00**
Ambassador, 1919, bouillon spoon, 1847 Rogers..........**$9.00**
Ambassador, 1919, demitasse spoon, 1847 Rogers........**$9.00**
April, 1950, gravy ladle, International.........................**$17.00**
April, 1950, master butter dish, International **$5.00**
April, 1950, service for 12, 60 pcs, International.......**$140.00**
Berkely Square, 1935, cheese server, Oneida.................**$8.00**
Chalice, 1958, cream soup, Oneida...............................**$7.00**
Chalice, 1958, pierced tablespoon, Oneida **$14.00**
Chalice, 1958, service for 8, 40 pcs, Oneida **$95.00**
Continental, 1914, teaspoon, 1847 Rogers **$6.00**
Court, 1939, fruit spoon, Court International.................**$7.00**
Court, 1939, iced beverage spoon, Court International .**$7.00**
Court, 1939, oval soup spoon, Court International **$6.00**
Danish Queen, 1944, individual butter spreader, Harmony..**$6.00**
Danish Queen, 1944, salad fork, Harmony.....................**$6.00**
Daybreak, 1952, luncheon fork, Rogers.........................**$7.00**
Daybreak, 1952, luncheon knife, Rogers **$7.00**
Daybreak, 1952, pierced pie server, Rogers **$18.00**
Daybreak, 1952, place spoon, Rogers............................**$7.00**
Desire, 1940, iced beverage spoon, International **$7.00**
Desire, 1940, service for 8, 32 pcs, International **$70.00**
Desire, 1940, viande fork, International.........................**$6.00**

Eternally Yours, 1941, iced beverage spoon, 1847 Rogers ..**$10.00**
Eternally Yours, 1941, viande fork, 1847 Rogers...........**$7.00**
Eternally Yours, 1941, viande knife, 1847 Rogers **$7.00**
Evening Star, 1950, dinner fork, Oneida **$8.00**
Evening Star, 1950, jelly server, Oneida **$10.00**
Evening Star, 1950, teaspoon, Oneida..........................**$6.00**
First Love, 1937, bouillon spoon, 1847 Rogers............**$24.00**
First Love, 1937, roast carving set, 2-pc, 1847 Rogers....**$80.00**
First Love, 1937, service for 6, 30 pcs, 1847 Rogers .**$100.00**
Hanover, 1901, cocktail fork, Oneida..........................**$14.00**
Hanover, 1901, 3-tined pie fork, Oneida **$18.00**
Hartford, 1988, pastry server, Towle **$16.00**
Hartford, 1988, pierced tablespoon, Towle **$12.00**
Jubilee, 1953, berry spoon, International......................**$24.00**
Jubilee, 1953, cake server, International **$24.00**
Jubilee, 1953, gravy ladle, International.......................**$22.00**
Jubilee, 1953, 2-pc salad set, black plastic handles, International **$36.00**
King Edward, 1951, cocktail fork, National **$7.00**
King Edward, 1951, gumbo spoon, National.................**$7.00**
King Edward, 1951, tablespoon, National.....................**$9.00**
Lufburg, 1915, cake serving fork, Rogers....................**$18.00**
Lufburg, 1915, ice cream spoon, Rogers.....................**$10.00**
Lufburg, 1915, individual butter, Rogers **$6.00**
Lufburg, 1951, salad serving set, Rogers.....................**$32.00**
Malibu, 1934, cold meat fork, Oneida..........................**$15.00**
Malibu, 1934, oval soup, Oneida..................................**$7.00**
Malibu, 1934, tomato server, Oneida...........................**$18.00**
Meadow Brook, 1936, service for 12, 72 pcs, viande size, Oneida **$155.00**
Meadow Brook, 1936, sugar spoon, Oneida **$6.00**
Meadow Brook, 1936, tablespoon, Oneida....................**$8.00**
Morning Star, 1948, baby spoon, Oneida......................**$9.00**
Morning Star, 1948, gravy ladle, Oneida.....................**$20.00**
Morning Star, 1948, jelly server, Oneida **$8.00**
Morning Star, 1948, service for 8, 48 pcs, Oneida **$175.00**
Morning Star, 1948, 2-pc roast carving set, Oneida ..**$175.00**
Mystic, 1903, berry spoon, Rogers...............................**$30.00**
New Elegance, 1947, oval soup, Stegor........................**$7.00**
New Elegance, 1947, teaspoon, Stegor **$4.00**
Olive, 19th Century, dessert fork, various manufacturers ..**$9.00**
Olive, 19th Century, dinner fork, various manufacturers.**$8.00**
Olive, 19th Century, lunch fork, various manufacturers .**$7.00**
Olive, 19th Century, tea knife, various manufacturers.**$10.00**
Paramount, 1933, salad fork, Oneida **$7.00**
Patrician, 1914, cold meat fork, Oneida......................**$12.00**
Patrician, 1914, cream ladle, Oneida...........................**$12.00**
Patrician, 1914, pickle fork, Oneida..............................**$8.00**
Patrician, 1914, youth set, Oneida, 3-pc **$28.00**
Paul Revere, 1927, master butter, Oneida **$6.00**
Plantation, 1948, sugar spoon, 1881 Rogers **$6.00**
Plantation, 1948, tablespoon, 1881 Rogers **$10.00**
Precious Mirror, 1954, cocktail fork, International **$6.00**
Precious Mirror, 1954, pierced tablespoon, International ..**$12.00**
Precious Mirror, 1954, sm casserole spoon, International .**$15.00**
Reflection, 1959, bonbon server, 1847 Rogers............**$15.00**
Reflection, 1959, fruit spoon, 1847 Rogers...................**$8.00**

Reflection, 1959, pierced cocktail fork, 1847 Rogers **$7.00**
Rex, 1904, salad fork, Wallace **$8.00**
Rex, 1904, teaspoon, Wallace.......................................**$6.00**
Rosemary, 1919, dinner fork, International..................**$8.00**
Rosemary, 1919, dinner knife, International **$8.00**
Rosemary, 1919, iced beverage spoon, International....**$7.00**
Savoy, 1892, master butter, twisted handle, 1847 Rogers..**$25.00**
Savoy, 1892, salad fork, 1847 Rogers **$25.00**
Sierra, 1914, gravy ladle, Reed & Barton **$18.00**
Sierra, 1914, orange knife, Reed & Barton **$15.00**
Silver Tulip, 1956, pierced pie server, International......**$7.00**
Tiger Lily, 1901, berry spoon, Reed & Barton.............**$35.00**
Tiger Lily, 1901, salad fork, Reed & Barton................**$20.00**
Tiger Lily, 1901, tablespoon, Reed & Barton..............**$12.00**
Twilight, 1956, cold meat fork, Oneida **$12.00**
Twilight, 1956, fruit spoon, Oneida............................**$7.00**
Wildwood, 1908, cocktail fork, Reliance.....................**$12.00**
Wildwood, 1908, teaspoon, Reliance **$7.00**
Youth, 1940, iced beverage spoon, Holmes & Edwards..**$10.00**
Youth, 1940, master butter, Holmes & Edwards............**$6.00**

Sterling

Abbotsford, individual butter, International.................**$26.00**
Abbotsford, lunch fork, International...........................**$29.00**
Abbotsford, soup ladle, International.........................**$325.00**
Alencon Lace, teaspoon, Gorham................................**$18.00**
Apollo, ice cream spoon, Alvin **$29.00**
Belle Meade, dinner fork, Lunt..................................**$26.00**
Brandon, fruit spoon, International.............................**$23.00**
Brandon, gumbo spoon, International **$24.00**
Brandon, ice cream spoon, International.....................**$24.00**
Brandon, pastry fork, International, 6¼"......................**$26.00**
Burgundy, baby fork, Reed & Barton **$24.00**
Burgundy, berry spoon, Reed & Barton **$125.00**
Burgundy, cream soup, Reed & Barton **$29.00**
Burlington, cocktail fork, Whiting **$15.00**
Chantilly, gravy ladle, Gorham **$58.00**
Chantilly, salt spoon, Gorham **$19.00**
Chantilly, 14-pc dinner setting, Gorham **$129.00**
D'Orleans, dinner fork, Towle....................................**$30.00**
D'Orleans, iced beverage spoon, Towle **$29.00**
D'Orleans, salad fork, Towle **$28.00**
Decor, individual butter, hollow handle, Gorham.......**$28.00**
El Grande, pickle fork, Towle **$20.00**
El Grande, pie server, hollow handle, Towle..............**$35.00**
El Grande, place spoon, Towle **$30.00**
El Grande, sugar spoon, Towle **$20.00**
El Grande, 4-pc place-size setting, Towle...................**$99.00**
Essex, ice cream fork, Durgin.....................................**$24.00**
Essex, ice cream slice, all silver................................**$170.00**
Florentine, fruit spoon, Alvin.....................................**$29.00**
Florentine, tablespoon, Alvin......................................**$38.00**
Fontaine, salad fork, International...............................**$32.00**
Fontaine, tomato server, International..........................**$75.00**
George VI, master butter, Frank Smith........................**$30.00**
Grand Trianon, teaspoon, International.......................**$15.00**

Hampton, olive spoon, Tuttle.....................................**$30.00**
Hampton, place spoon, Tuttle.....................................**$30.00**
Homewood, 3-pc baby set, Steiff..............................**$110.00**
Jefferson, bonbon spoon, Lunt....................................**$32.00**
Jefferson, jelly spoon, Lunt..**$10.00**
Jefferson, relish spoon, Lunt......................................**$16.00**
King Louis, 4-pc place-size setting, International.......**$88.00**
Kings, berry spoon, Kirk, 9" **$85.00**
Kings, cocktail fork, Kirk..**$24.00**
Kings, dinner fork, Kirk..**$62.00**
La Reine, iced beverage spoon, Wallace.....................**$29.00**
Lenox, cold meat fork, Durgin **$58.00**
Lenox, teaspoon, Durgin **$9.00**
Lexington, salad fork, Dominick & Haff **$30.00**
Marlborough, sm cold meat fork, Reed & Barton.......**$62.00**
Mary Chilton, cream ladle, Towle..............................**$28.00**
Mary Chilton, demitasse spoon, Towle **$17.00**
Mary Chilton, lettuce fork, Towle...............................**$62.00**
Minuet, bouillon spoon, International..........................**$20.00**
Minuet, place fork, International **$24.00**
Plymouth, sauce ladle, International **$30.00**
Plymouth, tablespoon, International **$44.00**
Princess Mary, cheese server, hollow handle, Wallace ..**$22.00**
Princess Mary, gumbo spoon, Wallace........................**$25.00**
Princess Mary, olive spoon, Wallace..........................**$24.00**
Rondelay, gravy ladle, Lunt **$72.00**
Rondelay, teaspoon, Lunt **$29.00**
Rondo, cocktail fork, International..............................**$24.00**
Rondo, lunch fork, International **$30.00**
Rondo, lunch knife, International **$30.00**
Silver Rose, lemon fork, Heirloom..............................**$19.00**
Silver Rose, oval soup, Heirloom................................**$25.00**
Silver Rose, 1-place size setting, Heirloom..................**$65.00**
Stanton Hall, iced beverage server, Oneida................**$26.00**
Stanton Hall, individual butter spreader, Oneida **$16.00**
Stanton Hall, tablespoon, Oneida................................**$42.00**
Summer Song, buffet spoon, Flint...............................**$55.00**
Summer Song, sugar shell, Flint..................................**$16.00**
Tara, tablespoon, Reed & Barton **$60.00**
Tara, teaspoon, Reed & Barton...................................**$16.00**
Tara, 1 place-size setting, Reed & Barton..................**$100.00**
Wave Edge, fruit spoon, Tiffany **$70.00**
Wave Edge, ladle, Tiffany, 10"..................................**$575.00**
Wave Edge, tablespoon, Tiffany **$110.00**
Winchester, gumbo spoon, Shreve..............................**$78.00**
Wood Lily, bouillon, Frank Smith **$28.00**
Wood Lily, sugar shell, Frank Smith...........................**$29.00**

Skookum Indian Dolls

The Skookums Apple Packers Association of Wenatchee, Washington, had a doll made from their trademark. Skookum figures were designed and registered by a Montana woman, Mary McAboy, in 1917. Although she always made note of the Skookum's name, she also used the 'Bully Good' trademark along with other information to inform the buyer that 'Bully

Good' translated is 'Skookums.' McAboy had an article published in the March 1920 issue of *Playthings* magazine explaining the history of Skookum dolls. Anyone interested can obtain this information on microfilm from any large library.

In 1920 the Arrow Novelty Company held the contract to make the dolls, but by 1929 the H.H. Tammen Company had taken over their production. Skookums were designed with life-like facial characteristics. The dried apple heads of the earliest dolls did not last, and they were soon replaced with heads made of a composition material. Wool blankets formed the bodies that were then stuffed with dried twigs, leaves, and grass. The remainder of the body was cloth and felt.

Skookum dolls with wooden legs and felt-covered wooden feet were made between 1917 and 1949. After 1949 the legs and feet were made of plastic. The newest dolls have plastic heads. A 'Skookums Bully Good Indians' paper label was placed on one foot of each early doll. Exact dating of a Skookum is very difficult. McAboy designed many different tribes of dolls simply by using different blanket styles, beading, and backboards (for carrying the papoose).

Advisor: Jo Ann Palmieri (See Directory Skookum Dolls)

Child, plastic legs, 6" to 8", from $35 to **$50.00**
Child, plastic legs, 8" to 10", from $50 to **$75.00**
Female w/papoose, wooden legs, 8" to 10", from $75 to.....**$150.00**
Female w/papoose, wooden legs, 10" to 12", from $150 to.**$200.00**

Female with papoose, wooden legs and feet, 16", $300.00. (Photo courtesy Jo Ann Palmieri)

Male, wooden legs, 8" to 10", from $125 to **$200.00**
Male, wooden legs, 10" to 12", from $200 to **$300.00**
Male, wooden legs, 14" to 16", from $350 to **$450.00**

Smiley Face

The Smiley Face was the 1970s icon, symbolizing the 'don't worry, be happy' philosophy that was the watchword of the 'in' crowd in those days. It's enjoying renewed popularity today — you'll find many 'new' Smiley Face products in those specialty catalogs we all seem to get so many of. But if you buy the vintage examples, expect to pay several times their original retail price. Right now, these are hot!

Backpack, yellow & black plush, zipper closure, 14" dia, EX...**$26.00**
Bank, McCoy, marked USA, 6", from $40 to **$60.00**
Bank, plastic & resin, Roy Ind 1972, 5¼" **$25.00**
Basketball, white w/yellow face...................................**$18.00**
Beaded curtain, 50 strands form face..........................**$30.00**
Candy basket, ceramic, w/handle, 4x4".........................**$50.00**
Clock, neon, wall hanging, 11" dia, w/stand for table use, M **$35.00**
Cocktail set, shaker & 4 tumblers, printed faces on clear glass, metal lid, Hazelware, 6-pc set, MIB............**$55.00**

Cookie jar, $80.00; bank, from $40.00 to $60.00; mug, from $12.00 to $18.00. All items are marked McCoy.
(Photo courtesy Joyce and Fred Roerig)

Cutting board, Lucite, Don't Worry, Be Happy, 14x10" **$22.00**
Eyeglasses, plain frames, in cloth-covered case w/faces in various colors **$25.00**
Lap tray, paint metal, 17½x12½" w/6" metal legs.......**$20.00**
Mixer/measure, glass w/faces in various colors & measuring increments, 8"......................................**$28.00**
Mug, Smiley clown face, McCoy, 4", from $15 to.......**$20.00**
Mug, stars as eyes, smile lettered 'Smile America,' McCoy, 4", from $15 to......................................**$20.00**
Pencil sharpener, Berol, Made in USA, wall mount....**$50.00**
Picture frame, round opening for 3x5" photo, 'feet' on ea side are faces, 4½x4"..................................**$20.00**
Pillows, plush, w/face & daisies, 16½" dia, 3-pc set ..**$40.00**
Planter, w/attached underplate, McCoy, 1971, 4", from $15 to..**$20.00**
Plate & mug, ceramic, unmarked, 7⅛", 3¾"...............**$35.00**
Pool float, blow-up plastic, from $10 to **$12.00**
Shot glasses, Libbey, set of 4, MIB.............................**$30.00**
Thermometer, numbers around perimeter, face in center of dial, Ohio Thermometer Co, 12" dia....................**$55.00**

Thermometer, Smyly/Buick Dodge lettered on face in center, numbers around perimeter, for outdoor use **$25.00**
Timer, yellow & black, 3" dia, MIP **$32.00**
Tumbler, printed faces on clear glass, 5", 4 for...........**$40.00**

Snow Domes

Snow dome collectors buy them all, old and new. The older ones (from the thirties and forties) are made in two pieces, the round glass globe that sits on a separate base. They were made here as well as in Italy, and today this type is being imported from Austria and the Orient.

During the fifties, plastic snow domes made in West Germany were popular as souvenirs and Christmas toys. Some were half-domes with blue backs; others were made in bottle shapes or simple geometric forms.

There were two styles produced in the seventies. Both were made of plastic. The first were designed as large domes with a plastic figure of an animal, a mermaid, or some other character draped over the top. In the other style, the snow dome itself was made in an unusual shape.

Snow domes have become popular fun-type collectibles and Nancy McMichael has written an illustrated book called, of course, *Snow Domes,* which we recommend if you'd like to read more about the subject. Another great reference is *The Collector's Guide to Snow Domes* by Helene Guarnaccia.

Advisor: Nancy McMichael

Newsletter: Snow Biz
P.O. Box 53262
Washington DC 20009

Battery-operated (lights up) skull in lg glass globe on orange & black painted wood base, Silvestri...................**$22.00**
Betty Boop, black plastic base, Bully, King Features, Fleischer Studios, 1986 ....**$18.00**
Capitol Building in glass globe on ceramic base, 1940s ..**$45.00**
Christmas figure in bell-shaped dome, can be used as tree ornament **$10.00**
Dual-purpose type, bottle shape w/rings (ring toss game) **$9.00**
Dual-purpose type, Florida souvenir w/swordfish, tall dome w/opaque chamber holds salt or pepper shaker, pr..**$20.00**
Dual-purpose type, TV w/shaker chamber, souvenir of Florida, pink & blue plastic, pr..............................**$20.00**
Father Christmas holds tree & stands beside teddy bear in dome, porcelain, recent......................................**$25.00**
Mickey & Minnie Mouse in lg oval dome w/rainbow & pot of gold, WD Productions **$25.00**
Mickey Mouse, black and white, plastic, Bully/Walt Disney, 1977 ....**$18.00**
Religious scene, 3 dimensional figures, from $8 to **$10.00**
Santa in dome, pull string to activate snow, green base .**$10.00**
Santa on chimney (dome), red, white & green...........**$20.00**
Santa w/domed tummy, deer over shoulders **$18.00**

Snoopy pulling sled full of presents, Charles Schulz, Willits, 1966 ....**$20.00**
Snow White & 7 Dwarfs, Germany, green footed base..**$12.00**
Snowman w/dome in center, ceramic, red, white, green & black, Applause, 1988...**$18.00**
Souvenir of Alabama, State Capitol building & missile ...**$20.00**
Souvenir of Florida, couple on seesaw, red calendar (knobs roll up date) base **$10.00**
Souvenir of Galveston Island, dolphin atop dome **$15.00**
Souvenir of NY City, Statue of Liberty & Skyscrapers...**$12.00**
Spruce Goose, plane scene, HFB Corp, 1984.............**$15.00**
St Anthony in glass globe on Bakelite base **$45.00**

Soda-Pop Memorabilia

A specialty area of the advertising field, soft-drink memorabilia is a favorite of many collectors. Now that vintage Coca-Cola items have become rather expensive, interest is expanding to include some of the less widely known sodas — Grapette, Hires Root Beer, and Dr. Pepper, for instance. See also Coca-Cola; Pepsi-Cola.

Advisor: Craig Stifter (See Directory, Soda-Pop Memorabilia)

Newsletter: National Pop Can Collectors
5417 Midvale Dr. #4
Rockford, IL 61108-2325; Send for free information

Ashtray, Hires, glass bottle shape w/orange & white logos, EX..**$12.00**
Ashtray, Seven-Up, brown glass w/white lettering, 3 rests, 5½" dia, NM **$15.00**
Bank, Vernors, metal can shape, Original Vernors/It's Different Flavor Aged in Oak Bucket, 1960s, M ..**$15.00**
Banner for truck, Hires, canvas, 1940s, EX **$375.00**
Blotter, Royal Crown Cola, 1940s, NM.......................**$35.00**
Bottle carrier, Seven-Up, 6-pack, aluminum w/printed advertising & logo, wire handle, EX..............................**$50.00**
Bottle carrier w/bottles, Cherry Blossoms, red tin carrier w/logo, 6 6-oz green bottles w/paper labels, 11x6", EX **$500.00**
Bottle opener, Orange-Crush, metal Crushy figure, NM+ .**$25.00**
Calendar, A-Treat Beverages, 1959, complete, EX.......**$85.00**
Calendar, Cliquot Club Ginger Ale, 1942, complete, EX ..**$100.00**
Calendar, Dr Pepper's 75th Anniversary, 1960, EX **$35.00**
Calendar, NuGrape, 1957, complete, EX....................**$35.00**
Calendar, Orange-Crush, 1946, complete, EX...........**$300.00**
Calendar, Seven-Up, 1960, complete, NM...................**$25.00**
Calendar, Squirt, 1951, complete, NM.......................**$120.00**
Clock, Dad's Root Beer, Tastes Like Root Beer Should, square light-up w/cap logo, gold & white striped frame, 16", EX **$200.00**
Clock, Orange-Crush, Discover diagonally above logo on square white face, metal frame, light-up, 15½", EX.............**$150.00**
Clock, Seven-Up, light-up w/square wooden frame, You Like It...It Likes You!, EX+...**$100.00**

Clock, Sun Crest, round light-up, image of bottle surrounded by black numbers, 1950s, NM $300.00

Cooler, Whistle, metal picnic chest w/round decals on sides, wire clasp, 2 wire swing handles, Progress, 12x18x8", VG.............................$160.00

Dixie cup, Hires, waxed paper, 1960s, 4x3" dia, EX.....$2.00

Doll, Sprite's Lucky Lymon, vinyl, 1980s, MIB $35.00

Doll, Squirt Boy, squeeze vinyl, 1961, 6", rare, M $450.00

Drinking glass, Squirt, painted image of Squirt boy w/bottle, 1948, 4¼", EX.............................$70.00

Fan, Royal Crown Cola, shows all-Anerican girl, 1950s, EX.$30.00

Jug, Orange-Crush, amber glass w/name & decorative border on shoulder, screw lid, square bail handle, 11x7", G $25.00

Match holder, Dr Pepper, wall-mount, green w/black-printed logo & advertising, 6", EX.....................$80.00

Menu board, A-Treat Beverages, tin blackboard, red, white & blue, 20x18", NM+ $40.00

Menu board, Kayo, tin black board w/litho advertising showing Kayo pointing to bottle on yellow, 27x13", NM.......$90.00

Mug, A&W Root Beer, glass, lg or sm, ea $15.00

Pocket mirror, Whistle, 2 elves holding trademark sign, Golden Orange Refreshment, 1940s, 2x3", NM ..$150.00

Push bar, Nesbitt's, porcelain, 1940s, 32½" L, EX.....$195.00

Sign, cardboard, Big Boy, Ice Cold/A Real Cola/12 Fl oz/5¢, shows name on red dot & bottle on icy blue ground, 22x14", G $40.00

Sign, cardboard, Dr Pepper, Smart Lift..., girl hugging dog in winter scene & grid logo w/10-2-4 clock, 21x33", EX $300.00

Sign, cardboard, Royal Crown Cola, My Mom Knows Best, 1940s, 11x28", EX.............................$50.00

Sign, cardboard, Royal Crown Cola, Yes...Bring RC!, girl on phone holding bottle, white ground, 11x28", EX.$75.00

Sign, cardboard standup, Hire's to You!/A Toast to Good Taste!, shows party couple, she w/tray, 16x12", NM $75.00

Sign, cardboard standup, Squeeze, diecut, Drink.../ Delightfully Refreshing/Always Welcome, kids at fridge, 1940s-50s, EX $250.00

Sign, celluloid, Bubble-Up, Just Pure Pleasure! in script above logo, red & white on green oval, 9x13", NM $120.00

Sign, masonite, Orange-Crush, Rush-Rush for Orange-Crush, shows Crushy figure, 1940s, 18x48", EX.............$300.00

Sign, masonite, Squirt, Open/Closed (2-sided), Squirt boy w/bottle, black on yellow, chain hanger, 1955, 12x16", VG...................................$170.00

Sign, paper, Orange-Crush, Serve These Favorites at Home..., hand holding 6-pack, 1940s, 14x22", EX...............$20.00

Sign, porcelain, Canada Dry, Drink Canada Dry Beverages, green script & red block lettering on white, 1941, 12x35", EX $160.00

Sign, tin, Dad's Root Beer, straight-sided bottle on blue tray on yellow ground, red border, 1940s-50s, 29x13", EX+.......................................$280.00

Sign, tin, Dr Pepper, white-on-red oval logo on maroon background, self-framed, 22x35", M.....................$30.00

Sign, tin, Gold-en Girl Cola, red & white bottle-cap shape w/white embossed lettering, 33" dia, EX............$360.00

Sign, tin, Grapette Soda, embossed oval w/white & red lettering on dark blue w/white & red border, 28x48", NM.......................................$200.00

Sign, tin, Hires R-J Root Beer, w/Real Root Juices, embossed, 10x28", M.................................$125.00

Sign, tin, Royal Crown, double-sided, hanging, 1940, NM, $350.00. (Photo courtesy Craig Stifter)

Sign, tin, Royal Crown Cola, Drink.../Take Home a Carton, 25¢ 6-pack on white dot, red, yellow & black, 22x58", EX $375.00

Sign, tin, Seven-Up, colorful '60s mod design on green around white 7-Up on red, orange & yellow stripes below, 34", EX $125.00

Sign, tin, Seven-Up, diecut embossed bottle shape, logo w/bubbles, dated 7-62, NM $525.00

Sign, tin, Tru Ade, Drink a Better Beverage lettered over lg bottle on red, yellow border, 1940s-50s, 54x18", VG+ $300.00

Thermometer, Nesbitt's, 24", 1950s, NM, $275.00. (Photo courtesy Craig Stifter)

Thermometer, plastic, Dr Pepper, bottle-cap shape w/10-2-4 logo on white, 11" dia, NM..................**$100.00**

Thermometer, tin, B-1 Lemon-Lime Soda, embossed logo & lettering on striped ground, 1950s, 16x4½", EX...**$50.00**

Thermometer, tin, Dr Pepper, Hot or Cold on red curved top, bulb above V chevron logo on white, 16¼x6½", EX+ **$110.00**

Thermometer, tin, Frostie, Frostie mascot & bottle cap above bulb w/6-pack below on white, 36x8", VG........**$145.00**

Thermometer, tin, Orange-Crush, bottle shape, 1950s, 30", EX **$125.00**

Thermometer, tin, Quiky, gauge on lg green bottle on white, rounded top & bottom, 16½x8", EX **$150.00**

Tumbler, Dr Pepper, Good for Life, applied color label on glass w/tapered sides, 1940s, EX....................**$150.00**

Soda Bottles With Painted Labels

The earliest type of soda bottles were made by soda producers and sold in the immediate vicinity of the bottling company. Many had pontil scars, left by a rod that was used to manipulate the bottle as it was blown. They had a flat bottom rather than a 'kick-up,' so for transport, they were laid on their side and arranged in layers. This served to keep the cork moist, which kept it expanded, tight, and in place. Upright the cork would dry out, shrink, and expel itself with a 'pop,' hence the name 'soda pop.'

Until the '30s, the name of the product or the bottler was embossed in the glass or printed on a paper label (sometimes pasted over reused returnable bottles). Though a few paper labels were used as late as the '60s, nearly all bottles produced from the mid-'30s on had painted-on (pyro-glazed) lettering, and logos and pictures were often added. Imaginations ran rampant. Bottlers waged a fierce competition to make their soda logos eye catching and sales inspiring. Anything went! Girls, airplanes, patriotic designs, slogans proclaiming amazing health benefits, even cowboys and Indians became popular advertising ploys. This is the type you'll encounter most often today, and collector interest is on the increase. Look for interesting, multicolored labels, rare examples from small-town bottlers, and those made from glass in colors other than clear or green. If you'd like to learn more about them, we recommend *The Official Guide to Collecting Applied Color Label Soda Bottles* by Thomas E. Marsh.

Advisor: Thomas Marsh, Painted-Label Soda Bottles (See Directory, Soda-Pop Collectibles)

Ayer's, clear glass, 10-oz **$10.00**
Big Boy, clear glass, 1-qt.................................**$25.00**
California, Drink-O, clear glass, 10-oz **$25.00**
Canfield's, clear glass, 9-oz **$10.00**
Cardinal, clear glass, 12-oz..............................**$20.00**
Click, green glass, 7-oz **$25.00**
Crystal, green glass, 1-qt **$20.00**
Dodge City, amber glass/throwaway, 10-oz **$24.00**

Dybala, green glass, 1-qt................................**$15.00**
Flagship, clear glass, 10-oz **$10.00**
Glengarry, clear glass, 7½-oz............................**$15.00**
Golden Gate, clear glass, 1-qt............................**$20.00**

Hi-Q, 10-ounce, $15.00.
(Photo courtesy Thomas Marsh)

Independence, clear glass, 7-oz **$15.00**
Key City, clear glass, 12-oz...**$10.00**
Long's, clear glass, 10-oz...**$15.00**
Lulu, clear glass, Mexican, 7-oz.....................................**$65.00**
Maui, clear glass, 7-oz..**$20.00**
Mrs Lombardi's, clear glass, 12-oz.................................**$75.00**
O'Joy, clear glass, 7-oz...**$20.00**
Par-T-Pak, green glass, 1-qt **$15.00**
Playboy, green glass, 1-qt **$25.00**
Polar, clear glass, 7-oz...**$15.00**
Red Arrow, clear glass, 7-oz...**$10.00**
Royal Palm, clear glass, 6-oz..**$15.00**
Seventy-Six, green glass, 1-qt..**$15.00**
Smile, clear glass, 16-oz **$20.00**
Split Rock, green glass, 7-oz...**$15.00**
Sun Crest, clear glass, 12-oz...**$10.00**
Sunny Side, clear glass, 10-oz.......................................**$15.00**
Topflite, clear glass, 10-oz..**$15.00**
Vincent's, green glass, 7-oz...**$15.00**
Walker, green glass, 7-oz...**$10.00**
Yacht Club, green glass, 7½-oz **$15.00**
Zee, clear glass, 7-oz..**$25.00**

Sporting Goods

Catalogs and various ephemera distributed by sporting good manufacturers, ammunition boxes, and just about any other item used for hunting and fishing purposes are collectible. In fact, there are auctions devoted entirely to collectors with these interests.

One of the best known companies specializing in merchandise of this kind was the gun manufacturer, The Winchester Repeating Arms Company. After 1931, their mark was changed from Winchester Trademark USA to Winchester-Western. Remington, Ithaca, Peters, and Dupont are other manufacturers whose goods are especially sought after.

Advisor: Kevin R. Bowman (See Directory, Sports Collectibles)

Ashtray, Remington, glass, 4" dia, M **$6.00**

Book, American Bird Decoys, William Mackey Jr, hardback, 255 pages, 1987, M **$15.00**

Book, Complete Book of Rifles & Shotguns, Jack O'Conner, 477 pages, 1961 ....**$15.00**

Book, Home Taxidermy for Pleasure & Profit, 245 pages, 1944, VG..**$10.00**

Booklet, The Sport Alluring-Trap Shooting, photos & illustrations, Dupont, 1914, 40 pages, 6x9"......................**$40.00**

Bottle, Ever-Ready Machine Oil, glass, label, G **$25.00**

Bottle, Silicote Dry Fly Dressing, glass, 1946, full.........**$6.00**

Box, ammo; Dupont Remington Express, dovetailed wood, 9x9½x14½"...**$48.00**

Box, shotshell; Paragon Yellow Band Reloads, red & yellow, 12 gauge, empty, M...**$25.00**

Box, shotshell; Peters High Velocity, 2-pc bluebill, empty, EX..**$125.00**

Box, shotshell; Remington 310 Skeet, 2-pc, empty, G..**$25.00**

Box, shotshell; Western Super-X, 12 gauge, 2-pc, VG..**$45.00**

Box insert, UMC, elk pictured on cover, $30.00. (Photo courtesy Kevin Bowman)

Call, deer; Thomas Game Calls, wood, 4⅛", EX.........**$30.00**

Call, duck; Pintail PT 650, Black Duck Game Calls, wood, 3", NM (VG box) **$25.00**

Call, duck; walnut, acrylic & brass, handmade by RW Elliot, single-reed style, EX **$40.00**

Call, PS Olt Regular Goose; #L-22, M..............................**$9.00**

Call, rabbit; Herter's Rabbit Flusher #39, wood & plastic, w/original box & instructions, 6½", EX **$47.00**

Call, Weems Wildcall, for fox, wolfs, cats, Ft Worth TX, VG...**$18.00**

Can, Du Pont Pistol Powder #6, 8-oz, EX...................**$25.00**

Can, Du Pont Superfine FF Gunpowder, red, dated July 1924, EX..**$25.00**

Catalog, Winchester, 31 pages, 1975, 8½x11", NM.......**$5.00**

Catalog, Winchester, 47 pages, 1970, 8½x11", M..........**$6.00**

Catalog, Winchester Over/Under; 16 pages, 1980s, 8½x11", NM **$10.00**

Counter mat, Smith & Wesson, black rubber, 14x9"...**$10.00**

Fetch-It Duck Retriever, M (2-pc box) **$20.00**

Glasses, shooting; Winchester, G................................**$30.00**

Guide, ammunition; Winchester, 23 pages, 1985, 8½x11", M.**$3.00**

Hat, baseball; Remington, green & white **$10.00**

Mug, coffee; Federal, Time To Talk Turkey, M.............**$8.00**

Pin-back, Shoot Winchester Shells, shell shape, early, 2½" L **$80.00**

Powder flask, Dixon & Sons, brass & copper, few sm dents, 7¾"...**$170.00**

Powder flask, engraved cannon, flags & crossed flintlocks, brass & copper..**$55.00**

Powder flask, G&J Hawksley, adjustable top, copper, 7¾"...**$60.00**

Reel, Hawthorne Model #352, level wind, G **$15.00**

Reel, Hiawatha #6565, level wind, G **$14.00**

Reel, JA Coxe, Do/All Model 65C, level wind, EX.....**$35.00**

Reel, Pfluger Trump #1943, level wind, VG **$25.00**

Sign, Guns Open & Empty Beyond This Point, porcelain, 16th-inch steel, 12x24"..**$70.00**

Sign, Wright's Game Calls Bring'em In, cardboard, easel-back, 1950s, 22x14", EX **$135.00**

Squirrel call, PS Olt Perfect Call, #348205, G **$25.00**

Tape, VHS; Patterning Your Shotgun for Steel, Federal, M...**$10.00**

Tie clip, Winchester Golden Spike, M **$15.00**

Tin, Super Balistite Powder, Italy, VG..........................**$25.00**

Sports Cards

Collecting memorabilia from all kinds of sports events has been a popular hobby for years. Baseball has long been known as the 'national pastime' with literally millions of fans who avidly follow the sport at every level from 'sand lot' to the major leagues. So it only follows that many collectors find sports trading cards a worthwhile investment. Hundreds have been printed and many are worth less than 20¢ a piece, but some of the better cards bring staggering prices, as you'll see in our listings.

We've included some football cards as well, but by and large most of the interest lies in baseball. If you're totally unfamiliar with these cards, you'll need to know how to determine the various manufacturers. 1) Bowman: All are copyrighted Bowman of B.G.H.L.I. except a few from the fifties that are marked '...in the series of Baseball Picture Cards.' 2) Donruss: All are marked with the Donruss logo on the front. 3) Fleer: From 1981 to 1984, the Fleer name is on the backs of the cards; after 1985 it was also on the front. 4) Score & Sportflics: Score written on the front, Sportflics on back of each year. 5) Topps: Cards from 1951 are baseball game pieces with red or blue backs (no other identification). After that, either Topps or T.G.C. appears somewhere on the card. 6) Upper Deck: marked front and back with Upper Deck logo and hologram.

Learn to judge the condition of your card, since its condition is a very important factor when it comes to making an accurate evaluation. Superstars' and Hall of Famers' cards are most likely to appreciate, and the colored photo cards from the thirties are good investments as well. Buy modern cards by the set while they're inexpensive. Who knows what they may be worth in years to come. Any of today's rookies may be the next Babe Ruth!

Though many of these cards have cooled off considerably from their heyday of few years ago, many are holding their values well. We've listed some of the better cards and the prices they've recently realized at auction.

Art Mahaffrey, Topps, #570, 1966, VG+ **$11.50**
Bob Chance, Topps, #564, 1966, EX **$20.00**
Ernie Banks, Topps, #94, 1954, VG+ **$50.00**
Hank Aaron, Topps, #128, 1954, EX **$500.00**
Harmon Killebrew, Topps, #124, 1955, EX.................**$90.00**
Jerry Rice, Topps, #161, 1986, NM+ **$55.00**
Joe Namath, Topps, #96, 1966, VG+ **$55.00**
Joe Tinker, Topps, #205, 1911, VG............................**$50.00**
Ken Griffey Jr, Upper Deck, #1, 1989, NM+.............**$132.00**
Lew Alcindor, Topps, #25, 1969, VG+ **$110.00**

Mark McGwire, Topps, 1984, NM+, from $150.00 to $200.00.

Mark McGuire, Topps, #401, 1985, NM **$110.00**
Michael Jordan, Fleer, #57, 1986-87, NM+ **$880.00**
Mickey Mantle, Bowman, #101, 1952, VG+...............**$467.00**
Mickey Mantle, Topps, #10, 1959, VG **$80.00**
Mickey Mantle, Topps, #202, 1955, VG+ **$250.00**
Mike Cuellar, Topps, #556, 1966, VG+........................**$20.00**
Mike Schmidt, Topps, #615, 1973, VG+ **$66.00**
Roberto Clemente, Topps, #52, 1958, NM **$60.00**
Roberto Clemente, Topps, #76, 1957, NM **$90.00**
Roberto Clemente, Topps, #440, 1964, NM **$88.00**
Sandy Koufax, Topps, #79, 1956, VG..........................**$90.00**
Set, baseball, Topps, 1983, NM...................................**$77.00**
Set, football, including Marino & Elway rookie cards, Topps, 1984, NM **$100.00**
Set, football, Kelloggs, 1970, NM...............................**$66.00**
Set, football, Topps, USFL, 1984, rare, NM.................**$120.00**

Set, football, Topps, 1978, EX+..................................**$80.00**
Set, football, Topps, 1980, NM+ **$20.00**
Set, football, 1990 Rookie & Traded, M.....................**$55.00**
Ted Williams, Topps, #1, 1957, EX............................**$150.00**
Walter Payton, Topps, #148, Rookie issue, 1976, NM.**$88.00**
Willie Mays, Topps, #244, 1953, G+..........................**$190.00**
Willie Mays, Topps, #261, 1952, VG **$375.00**

Sports Collectibles

When the baseball card craze began sweeping the country a decade ago, memorabilia relating to many types of sports began to interest sports fans. Today ticket stubs, autographed baseballs, sports magazines, and game-used bats and uniforms are prized by baseball fans, and some items, depending on their age or the notoriety of the player or team they represent, may be very valuable. Baseball and golfing seem to be the two sports most collectors prefer, but hockey and auto racing are gaining ground. Game-used equipment is sought out by collectors, and where once they preferred only items used by professionals, now the sports market has expanded, and collectors have taken great interest in the youth equipment endorsed by many star players now enshrined in their respective Hall of Fame. Some youth equipment was given away as advertising premiums and bear that company's name or logo. Such items are now very desirable.

See also Autographs; Indianapolis 500 Memorabilia; Magazines; Motorcycle Memorabilia; Pin-Back Buttons; Puzzles.

Advisors: Don and Anne Kier (See Directory, Sports Collectibles)

Ashtray, 1955 Brooklyn Dodgers, pewter dish w/10-in-a-row logo w/hat under glass, EX **$230.00**
Baseball, Mike Schmidt signature, Phillies souvenir, NM...**$35.00**
Baseball, 1951 New York Giants, 24 players signatures, VG+ **$320.00**
Baseball bat, Brooks Robinson facsimile signature, Louisville Slugger store model 125, NM................................**$65.00**
Baseball bat, Mike Schmidt facsimile signature, Adirondac model 320F, NM...**$100.00**
Baseball bat, Pete Rose facsimile signature, Adirondac model 302F, NM **$100.00**
Baseball glove, Buddy Kerr model MacGregor/Goldsmith, black leather, unused, EX+ (original box).........**$135.00**
Basketball, Larry Bird facsimile signature, Spaulding Top-Flite 1000, NM **$80.00**
Cigarette case, Cleveland Indians, metal w/painted decor including Indian head, ca 1950s, NMIB.................................**$35.00**
Figurine, Don Drysdale, Salvino, signed, 1989, NMIB..**$55.00**
Figurine, Joe Montana, Gartlan, #207, signed, 1991, NM..**$50.00**
Figurine, Sandy Koufax, Salvino, signed, 1989, NMIB.**$100.00**
Football, Joe Montana facsimile signature, Wilson NFL model, NM..**$80.00**

Football, World Football League, Spaulding, brown w/2 orange stripes, VG+..............................$65.00

Game, board; baseball, Strat-O-Matic, 1962, EX+........$20.00

Game, board; International Derby, tin litho, 1933, EX .$165.00

Game, board; Sam Snead Tee Off, 1973, VG+............$30.00

Game, Talking Baseball, Kenner Starting Lineup, 1988, complete, EX (VG- box)......................................$20.00

Golf club, putter, Spaulding Pro-Flite Bobby Jones model, EX+ $65.00

Hockey stick, Mario Lemieux facsimile signature, Titan TPM 1020, from 1987-89 seasons, VG+ $145.00

Jersey, football; Princeton University, black w/orange & white trim, #21, Champion, VG+..........................$80.00

Jersey, not game-used, autographed by Pete Rose, letter of authentication, M, $350.00.

Jersey, 1984 USFL Philadelphia Stars, Howard on back, game worn, Champion label, EX....................................$115.00

Model kit, Great Moments in Sports, Dempsey vs Firpo, Aurora, 1965, EX+ (original box) $100.00

Pennant, Houston Colts, mini, ca 1960s, 12", EX........$17.00

Pennant, Philadelphia Eagles, ca 1960s, EX+ $35.00

Pennant, Pittsburg Pirates, ca 1950s, EX $40.00

Pennant, Temple University, football, red w/player graphic, ca 1920-30s, EX..$50.00

Photo, cabinet; 1914 Galveston Pirates, in street clothes in studio, players names on back, 8x10"....................$65.00

Photo, 1970-71 Milwaukee Bucks, 13 signatures, color, 16x20", NM...$110.00

Pillowcase, souvenir; Boston Red Sox, color scene of Fenway Park, ca 1950s-60s, 18" square, NM......................$30.00

Pin, New York Yankees souvenir, plastic pin bar w/glove & bat charms, ca 1940s, VG+....................................$55.00

Pin, press; Super Bowl XXVII, NM..............................$30.00

Poster, The Dream, baseball game scene w/boys, Dick Perez, signed & numbered, NM.................................$35.00

Press pass, 1957 World Series, game #4 at Milwaukee, cardboard, EX...$35.00

Print, Roger Staubach, color tri-panel of Roger in uniform, Dick Perez, NM................................$15.00

Program, 1949 World Series, Brooklyn, unscored, EX..$135.00

Program, 1956 World Series, Brooklyn, unscored, EX..$150.00

Program, 1957 Charleston Senators vs Minneapolis Millers, EX..$20.00

Program, 1966 World Series, Orioles/Dodgers, 84 pages, blank scorecard, EX......................................$35.00

Program, 1969 National League Championship Series, 30 pages, unscored, EX......................................$75.00

Program, 1977 All-Star game, Yankee Stadium, w/original ticket stub, EX......................................$20.00

Ring, 1992 National Championship, Arkansas Razorbacks, 10k gold w/3 diamond chips, NM $500.00

Scorecard, 1932 Philadelphia A's vs New York Yankees, VG...$50.00

Scorecard, 1949 Chicago Cubs vs Boston Braves, EX.$35.00

Scorecard, 1954 Brooklyn Dodgers vs St Louis Cardinals, 4-folded pages, unscored, ...$45.00

Statue, Hank Aaron, near-white w/original bat, Hartland, ca 1960-63, EX+ $165.00

Statue, Mickey Mantle, near-white w/original bat, Hartland, ca 1960-63, EX+ $165.00

Ticket, US Military Academy vs US Naval Academy, 12-13-1930, unused, NM......................................$55.00

Ticket, World Series Game #2 at St Louis, 1968, unused, NM..$80.00

Ticket stub, All-Star game at New York, 1960, EX......$45.00

Ticket stub, World Series Game #1 at Yankee Stadium, 1955, VG+...$25.00

Windbreaker, Ted Williams Hilltop Camp, white w/blue logo, adult size, unused, M $20.00

Yearbook, 1963 LA Dodgers, shows Maury Wills stealing 104th base for a 1962 record, EX $35.00

St. Clair Glass

Since 1941, the St. Clair family has operated a small glasshouse in Elwood, Indiana. They're most famous for their lamps, though they've also produced many styles of toothpick holders, paperweights, and various miniatures as well. Though the paperweights are usually stamped and dated, smaller items may not be marked at all. In addition to various colors of iridescent glass, they've also made many articles in slag glass (both caramel and pink) and custard. For more information, we recommend *St. Clair Glass Collector's Book* by Bonnie Pruitt (see Directory, St. Clair).

Ashtray, any color, 3 rests, lg, from $85 to.................$95.00

Bowl, pink slag w/clear pedestal foot, from $150 to .$175.00

Candle holder, any color, from $75 to $85.00

Covered dish, robin on nest, caramel, chocolate, mint green, cobalt, blue carnival, ea, from $100 to $125.00

Doll, any color, from $30 to $40.00

Figurine, bird, sm, from $35 to..................................$40.00

Figurine, turtle, from $150 to....................................$175.00

Goblet, Fruit Pattern, white carnival, from $45 to **$50.00**
Goblet, Wild Flower, blue carnival or Masoline, ea, from $35
   to **$40.00**
Miniature fruit, apple, from $55 to **$75.00**
Miniature fruit, strawberry, from $75 to....................**$100.00**
Paperweight, bird, cobalt or crystal, from $60 to........**$75.00**
Paperweight, butterfly, controlled bubbles, etched, from
   $250 to..**$350.00**
Paperweight, cameo, windowed **$300.00**

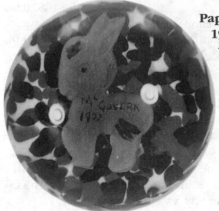

Paperweight, McGovern 1972 on donkey, clear with red, white, and blue, 3" diameter, $50.00.

Paperweight, rose, plain (not windowed), from $800 to..**$1,000.00**
Paperweight, sulfide, dove, from $140 to.................**$165.00**
Paperweight, sulfide, elephant, from $140 to...........**$165.00**
Paperweight, yellow flowers, extra-lg, from $90 to..**$125.00**
Plate, Kewpies, blue carnival or cobalt, ea, from $200 to.**$225.00**
Plate, Lyndon B Johnson, from $20 to........................**$25.00**
Plate, Reagan/Bush, any color....................................**$35.00**
Ring holder, teapot shape, any color, from $75 to **$85.00**
Ring post, from $50 to...**$55.00**
Salt cellar, swan, cobalt, blue carnival, marigold carnival or
   chocolate, ea, from $60 to **$75.00**
Salt cellar, swan, red or white carnival, ea, from $100 to .**$125.00**
Salt cellar, wheelbarrow, any color, from $25 to........**$30.00**
Toothpick holder, Fan & Feather, blue carnival, caramel,
   marigold, red, white, chocolate or green, ea, from $25
   to **$30.00**
Toothpick holder, flowers in weighted base, from $65
   to **$75.00**
Toothpick Holder, S Repeat, blue carnival, cobalt, marigold
   or chocolate, ea, from $25 to................................**$30.00**
Toothpick holder, Shriner's Hat (Fez), red or red carnival,
   from $125 to..**$150.00**
Toothpick holder, 3-Face Bicentennial, amethyst, blue cus-
   tard, cobalt or red, Bob & Maude St Clair, ea, from $27.50
   to **$35.00**
Tumbler, Grape & Cable, red, white, amethyst or chocolate,
   ea, from $30 to..**$35.00**
Tumbler, Inverted Fan & Feather, pink slag, cobalt, red,
   white carnival or blue, ea, from $30 to **$35.00**
Wine, Panel Grape, blue, marble, white carnival, ice blue
   carnival or cobalt, ea, from $50 to **$65.00**

Stanford Corn

Teapots, cookie jars, salt and pepper shakers, and other kitchen and dinnerware items modeled as ears of yellow corn with green shucks were made by the Stanford company, who marked most of their ware. The Shawnee company made two very similar corn lines; just check the marks to verify the manufacturer.

Butter dish...**$50.00**
Casserole, 8" L...**$40.00**
Cookie jar..**$85.00**
Creamer & sugar bowl **$50.00**
Cup...**$15.00**
Pitcher, 7½"...**$60.00**
Plate, 9" L..**$32.00**
Relish tray..**$40.00**

Salt and pepper shakers, large and small, $28.00 each pair.

Spoon rest **$25.00**
Teapot..**$70.00**
Tumbler..**$30.00**

Stangl Birds

The Stangl Pottery Company of Flemington and Trenton, New Jersey, made a line of ceramic birds which they introduced in 1940 to fulfill the needs of a market no longer able to access foreign imports, due to the onset of WWII. These bird figures immediately attracted a great deal of attention. At the height of their productivity, sixty decorators were employed to hand paint the birds at the plant, and the overflow was contracted out and decorated in private homes. After WWII, inexpensive imported figurines once again saturated the market, and for the most part, Stangl curtailed their own production, though the birds were made on a very limited basis until as late as 1978.

Nearly all the birds were marked. A four-digit number was used to identify the species, and most pieces were signed by the decorator. An 'F' indicates a bird that was decorated at the Flemington plant.

Advisors: Popkorn Antiques (See Directory, Stangl)

Club: Stangl/Fulper Collectors Club
P.O. Box 538
Flemington, NJ 08822
Yearly membership: $25 (includes quarterly newsletter)

Audubon Warbler, #3755, 4¼"	**$450.00**
Black Poll Warbler, #3810	**$175.00**
Blue-Headed Vireo, #3448, 4¼"	**$70.00**
Bobolink, #3595, 4¾"	**$150.00**
Brewers Blackbird, #3591	**$175.00**
Carolina Wren, #3590	**$175.00**
Chickadees, #3581, black & white	**$300.00**
Chickadees, #3581, brown & white	**$200.00**
Cockatoo, #3405, 6"	**$65.00**
Cockatoo, #3580, med, 8⅞"	**$150.00**
Feeding Duck, #3250C, Antique Gold	**$50.00**
Goldfinch, #3849	**$150.00**

Group of Goldfinches, #3635, $220.00.

Gray Cardinal, #3596, 5"	**$75.00**
Hen, #3446, yellow, 7"	**$150.00**
Hen Pheasant, #3491, 6½x11"	**$200.00**
Kentucky Warbler, #3598	**$50.00**
Magpie-Jay, #3758, 10½"	**$1,500.00**
Nuthatch, #3593	**$55.00**
Oriole, #3402, beak down, 3½"	**$125.00**
Painted Bunting, #3452, 5"	**$100.00**
Parakeets, #3582D, blue	**$275.00**
Parakeets, #3582D, green	**$225.00**
Parrot, #3449, 5½"	**$175.00**
Penguin, #3274	**$475.00**
Prothonotary Warbler, #3447	**$65.00**
Red-Breasted Nuthatch, #3851	**$85.00**
Rufous Hummingbird, #3585, 3"	**$100.00**
Scarlet Tanager, #3750D, pink, 8", pr	**$800.00**
Titmouse, #3592	**$55.00**
Turkey, #3275	**$400.00**
Western Tanager, #3749, red matt, 4¾"	**$400.00**
Wren, #3401, revised, dark brown, 3½"	**$50.00**
Yellow-Headed Verdin, #3921, minimum value	**$1,500.00**

Stangl Dinnerware

The Stangl Company of Trenton, New Jersey, grew out of the Fulper Company that had been established in Flemington early in the 1800s. Martin Stangl, president of the company, introduced a line of dinnerware in the 1920s. By 1954, 90% of their production centered around their dinnerware lines. Until 1942 the clay they used was white. Although most of the dinnerware production used solid-color glazes until WWII, they also did many hand-painted, but not carved patterns in the 1930s and early 1940s. In 1942, however, the first of the red-clay lines that have become synonymous with the Stangl name was created. Designs were hand carved into the greenware, then hand painted. More than one hundred different patterns have been cataloged. From 1974 until 1978, a few lines previously discontinued on the red clay were reintroduced with a white clay body. Soon after '78, the factory closed.

If you'd like more information on the subject, read *The Collector's Encyclopedia of Stangl Dinnerware* by Robert C. Runge, Jr. (Collector Books) and *Stangl Pottery* by Harvey Duke.

Advisors: Popkorn Antiques (See Directory, Stangl)

Amber-Glo, bowl, covered vegetable; 1954-60, 8", from $50 to	**$60.00**
Amber-Glo, bowl, salad; 1954-60, 12", from $50 to	**$55.00**
Amber-Glo, coffeepot, 1954-60, 8-cup, from $55 to	**$65.00**
Amber-Glo, egg cup, 1954-60, from $10 to	**$15.00**
Amber-Glo, plate, 1954-60, 9", from $10 to	**$12.00**
Amber-Glo, salt & pepper shakers, 1954-60, pr, from $12 to	**$16.00**
Bonita, bowl, rim soup; 1940s, from $20 to	**$25.00**
Bonita, plate, chop; 1940s, 14½", from $90 to	**$125.00**
Bonita, plate, 1940s, 9", from $25 to	**$30.00**
Bonita, teapot, 1940s, from $125 to	**$150.00**
Colonial Rose, creamer, 1970, from $20 to	**$25.00**
Colonial Rose, plate, chop; 1970, 12", from $75 to	**$85.00**
Colonial Rose, plate, 1970, 10", from $25 to	**$30.00**
Colonial Rose, salt & pepper shakers, 1970, w/tray, from $45 to	**$55.00**
Colonial Rose, tidbit, 1970, 10", from $10 to	**$15.00**
Flora, bowl, salad; 1947, 11", from $75 to	**$85.00**
Flora, coffeepot, individual, 1947, from $85 to	**$95.00**
Flora, plate, 1947, 9", from $20 to	**$25.00**
Flora, sugar bowl, 1947, from $15 to	**$20.00**
Fruit, bowl, salad; 1942+, 11", from $75 to	**$85.00**
Fruit, bowl, vegetable; 1942+, 8", from $35 to	**$50.00**
Fruit, butter dish, 1942+, from $55 to	**$65.00**
Fruit, coffeepot, 1942+, 8-cup, from $90 to	**$120.00**
Fruit, egg cup, 1942+, from $20 to	**$25.00**
Fruit, pitcher, 1942+, 1-pt, from $40 to	**$50.00**
Fruit, plate, 1942+, 9", from $20 to	**$25.00**
Fruit, relish dish, 1942+, from $35 to	**$45.00**
Fruit & Flowers, bowl, lug soup; 1958-70s, from $20 to	**$25.00**

Fruit & Flowers, cake stand, 1958-70s, from $25 to....**$30.00**

Fruit & Flowers, coffeepot, 1958-70s, 4-cup, from $120 to **$150.00**

Fruit & Flowers, cruet w/stopper, 1958-70s, from $35 to **$45.00**

Fruit & Flowers, plate, 1958-70s, 11", from $30 to......**$35.00**

Fruit & Flowers, platter, oval, 1958-70s, 11½", from $95 to **$110.00**

Fruit & Flowers, warmer, 1958-70s, from $30 to.........**$40.00**

Harvest, bowl, lug soup; 1940-45, 5", from $15 to **$22.00**

Harvest, bowl, vegetable; 1940-45, 8", from $40 to **$50.00**

Harvest, plate, 1940-45, 10", from $35 to.....................**$45.00**

Harvest, sugar bowl, w/lid, 1940-45, from $25 to.......**$30.00**

Kiddieware, bowl, cereal; Blue Carousel, 1960, from $100 to **$120.00**

Kiddieware, bowl, cereal; Little Bo Peep, 1953, from $90 to **$110.00**

Kiddieware, bowl, cereal; Peter Rabbit, 1953, from $110 to **$130.00**

Kiddieware, bowl, fruit; Bunny, 1963, from $125 to .**$150.00**

Kiddieware, bowl, soup/cereal; Circus Clown, blue or pink, 1975, from $75 to...**$90.00**

Kiddieware, cup, Ginger Boy, 1957, from $110 to ...**$135.00**

Kiddieware, cup, Woman in the Shoe, etc, 1968, from $100 to **$125.00**

Kiddieware, divided dish, ABC, 1956, from $80 to.....**$95.00**

Kiddieware, musical mug, Mary Had a Little Lamb, w/out music box, from $150 to **$225.00**

Mountain Laurel, bowl, cereal; 1944, from $18 to **$25.00**

Mountain Laurel, casserole; w/lid, 1944, 8", from $75 to..**$100.00**

Mountain Laurel, cup & saucer, 1944, from $18 to.....**$25.00**

Mountain Laurel, plate, chop; 1944, 12½", from $80 to..**$90.00**

Mountain Laurel, teapot, 1944, from $110 to **$135.00**

Orchard Song, salt and pepper shakers, $16.00 for the pair; Gravy boat, $15.00.

Sculptured Fruit, bowl, cereal; 1966-70s, from $12 to...**$15.00**

Sculptured Fruit, cup & saucer, 1966-70s, from $13 to ...**$16.00**

Sculptured Fruit, mug, 1966-70s, 13-oz, from $25 to..**$35.00**

Sculptured Fruit, plate, 1966-70s, 10", from $12 to **$15.00**

Sculptured Fruit, platter, oval, 1966-70s, 14¾", from $30 to **$35.00**

Star Flower, bowl, lug soup; 1952, from $10 to..........**$15.00**

Star Flower, bread tray, 1952, from $25 to **$35.00**

Star Flower, gravy boat, 1952, from $15 to..................**$20.00**

Star Flower, mug, coffee, 1952, from $25 to **$30.00**

Star Flower, plate, 1952, 8", from $10 to.....................**$15.00**

Star Flower, tidbit, 1952, 10", from $8 to **$10.00**

Town & Country, baking dish, blue, 1974-78, 9x14", from $75 to **$100.00**

Town & Country, bowl, porridge; straight sides, blue, 1974-78, 7½", from $35 to.......................................**$50.00**

Town & Country, bowl, salad; brown, green, honey or yellow, 1974-78, 12", ea, from $55 to **$65.00**

Town & Country, candlestick, black or crimson, chamberstick shape, 1974-78, #5299, 7½", from $45 to.....**$55.00**

Town & Country, creamer, blue, 1974-78, from $30 to...**$35.00**

Town & Country, deviled egg plate, paneled, brown, green, honey or yellow, 1974-78, 11½", from $50 to......**$80.00**

Town & Country, mug, stacking; blue, 1974-78, from $50 to..**$60.00**

Town & Country, plate, brown, green, honey or yellow, 1974-78, 10" or 10⅝", ea, from $12 to **$20.00**

Town & Country, platter, oval, blue, 1974-78, 11½", from $60 to..**$70.00**

Town & Country, tidbit, blue, 1974-78, 10⅝", from $25 to **$35.00**

Town & Country, wall pocket, blue, 1974-1978, from $75 to.**$100.00**

Town & Country, wall pocket, brown, green, honey or yellow, 1974-1978, ea, from $35 to **$50.00**

Wild Rose, bowl, oval divided vegetable; 1955-early 1960s, 8", from $30 to **$45.00**

Wild Rose, butter dish, 1955-early 1960s, from $35 to .**$45.00**

Wild Rose, egg cup, 1955-early 1960s, from $15 to....**$20.00**

Wild Rose, pepper mill, 1955-early 1960s, wood top, from $55 to..**$75.00**

Wild Rose, pitcher, 1955-early 1960s, 2-qt, from $75 to..**$85.00**

Wild Rose, plate, 1955-early 1960s, 10", from $20 to..**$25.00**

Star Trek Memorabilia

Trekkies, as fans are often referred to, number nearly 40,000 today, hold national conventions, and compete with each other for choice items of Star Trek memorabilia, some of which may go for hundreds of dollars.

The Star Trek concept was introduced to the public in the mid-1960s through a TV series which continued for many years in syndication. An animated cartoon series (1977), the release of six major motion pictures (1979 through 1989), and the success of 'Star Trek: The Next Generation' (Fox network, 1987) and two other television series, 'Deep Space 9' and 'Voyager,' all served as a bridge to join two generations of loyal fans.

Its success has resulted in the sale of vast amounts of merchandise, both licensed and unlicensed, such as clothing, promotional items of many sorts, books and comics, toys and games, records and tapes, school supplies, and party goods. Many of these are still available at flea markets around the country. An item that is 'mint in box' is worth at least twice as much as one in excellent condition but without its original packaging. For more information, refer to *Modern Toys, American Toys, 1930 – 1980,* by Linda Baker, and *Schroeder's Collectible Toys, Antique to Modern.* (Both are published by Collector Books.)

Activity set, Mix 'N Mold casting set, Captain Kirk, Mr Spock, or Dr McCoy, MIB, ea $65.00
Bank, Captain Kirk, 1973, VG..$25.00
Binoculars, Larami, MOC..$80.00

Book and record set, *Passage to Moauv/The Crier in Emptiness*, Peter Pan, 1979, MIP, $10.00.

Dish set, bowl, cup & tumbler w/images of Star Trek: The Motion Picture, plastic, Paramount, 1979, M $35.00
Doll, Captain Kirk or Mr Spock, stuffed cloth w/vinyl head, Knickerbocker, 1979, 12", MIB, ea $50.00
Figure, Applause, Deep Space 9, Kira Nerys, Odo, Quark or Sisko, 10", MIP, ea...$10.00
Figure, Applause, Next Generation, Kirk, La Forge, Picard, Riker, or Worf, 10", MIP, ea..............................$10.00
Figure, Ertl, Star Trek III, Klingon Leader or Spock, 3¾", MOC, ea..$30.00
Figure, Galoob, Next Generation, Data, 1st series, blue or spotted face, 3¾", MOC $125.00
Figure, Galoob, Next Generation, Data, 3rd series, 3¾", MOC.$20.00
Figure, Galoob, Next Generation, Tasha Yar, 3¾", MOC ..$20.00
Figure, Mego, 1974-76, Cheron or the Keeper, 2nd series, 8", MOC, ea, from $250 to................................$300.00
Figure, Mego, 1974-76, Kirk, Klingon, or Spock, 1st series, 8", MOC, ea..$55.00
Figure, Mego, 1974-76, McCoy or Uhura, 1st series, 8", MOC, ea, from $150 to $175.00
Figure, Mego, 1979, Motion Picture, Cheron, 12", NM .$85.00
Figure, Mego, 1979, Motion Picture, Decker, 3¾", MOC, from $20 to..$30.00
Figure, Mego, 1979, Motion Picture, Ilia, 12", MIB, from $75 to...$100.00
Figure, Mego, 1979, Motion Picture, Ilia, 3¾", MOC ..$20.00
Figure, Mego, 1979, Motion Picture, Kirk, McCoy, or Spock, 3¾", MOC, from $40 to $50.00
Figure, Mego, 1979, Motion Picture, Klingon, 12", MIB, from $200 to..$250.00
Figure, Next Generation, Data, 4th series, 3¾", MOC ..$8.00
Figure, Playmates, Deep Space 9, Dukat, Gil, Kira, O'Brian, or Quark, MOC, ea $15.00
Figure, Playmates, Next Generation, Admiral Kirk, 1st series, MOC...$25.00
Figure, Playmates, Next Generation, Borg, Data, La Forge, Picard, or Troi, 1st series, MOC, ea......................$20.00

Paint-by-number set, Hasbro, 1970s, MIB (sealed) $70.00
Phaser Launcher Gun, AHI, 1976, MOC $125.00
Phaser Rocket Dart Gun, plastic, Lone Star/PPC, 1974, EX (EX box) $125.00
Photograph, black & white glossy of animated series featuring Kirk, Spock, McCoy & Scotty, Nov 30, 1973, 9x7", NM+ $30.00
Playing cards, Star Trek: The Wrath of Khan, MIB $15.00
Playset, Telescreen Console, Mego, 1975, MIB $125.00
Playsets, USS Enterprise Bridge, Mego, 1975, MIB ...$125.00
Punch-Out & Play Book, Saalfield, 1975, unused, NM ...$45.00
Record, Mr Spock's Music From Outer Space, 78 rpm, Dot /Stereo, 1960s, NM (NM cover) $65.00
Rubber stamp, Motion Picture, M...............................$8.00
Silly Putty, Larami, 1979, MOC $25.00
Star Trek Tracer Gun, gold & plastic w/brown grips, fires jet disks, Rayline, 1966, 6½", MOC..........................$95.00
Sticker book, Jeopardy at Jutterdon, Whitman, 1979, unused, M $35.00
Vehicle, Klingon Warship, Dinky, MIB, from $75 to...$85.00
Vehicle, Shuttlecraft Galileo, Next Generation, Galoob, 1989, NRFB...$50.00
Vehicle, USS Enterprise, Motion Picture, Dinky #803, 1979, 4", MOC...$30.00
Wastebasket, Motion Picture, M................................$35.00
Yo-yo, Star Trek Next Generation, Lt Data photo, sculpted rim, MOC...$5.00

Star Wars

In the late '70s, the movie 'Star Wars' became a box office hit, most notably for its fantastic special effects and its ever-popular theme of space adventure. Three more movies followed, 'The Empire Strikes Back' in 1980, 'Return of the Jedi' in 1983, and 'Star Wars Episode 1' in 1998. After the first movie, an enormous amount of related merchandise was released. A large percentage of these items was action figures, made by the Kenner company who used the logo of the 20th Century Fox studios (under whom they were licensed) on everything they made until 1980. Just before the second movie, Star Wars creator, George Lucas, regained control of the merchandising rights, and items inspired by the last two films can be identified by his own Lucasfilm logo. Since 1987, Lucasfilm Ltd. has operated shops in conjunction with the Star Tours at Disneyland theme parks.

What to collect? First and foremost, buy what you yourself enjoy. But remember that condition is all-important. Look for items still mint in the box. Using that as a basis, if the box is missing, deduct at least half from its mint-in-box value. If a major accessory or part is gone, the item is basically worthless. Learn to recognize the most desirable, most valuable items. There are a lot of Star Wars bargains yet to be had!

Original packaging helps date a toy, since the package or card design was updated as each new movie was released. Naturally, items representing the older movies are more valuable than later issues. For more coverage of this subject, refer to *Schroeder's Collectible Toys, Antique to Modern* (Collector Books).

Biker Scout Laser Pistol, MIB (sealed) **$85.00**
Bop bag, R2-D2, inflatable vinyl, Kenner, 1978, 33", EX .**$40.00**
Card set, Burger King, 1980, unused, NM **$25.00**
Clock radio, Darth Vader, head figure on rectangular base, Micro Games of America, 1995, NM, from $35 to.**$50.00**
Color 'N Clean Machine, Empire Strikes Back, complete & unused, Craftmaster, 1980, NM **$25.00**
Doll, R2-D2, stuffed cloth, w/speaker, Kenner, 1978-79, 10", EX...**$25.00**
Figure, A-Wing Pilot, Power of the Force, MOC.......**$150.00**
Figure, Amanaman, Power of the Force, complete, NM..**$125.00**
Figure, Anakin Skywalker, Power of the Force, complete, NM **$30.00**
Figure, AT-AT Commander, Return of the Jedi, MOC.**$45.00**
Figure, AT-AT Driver, Return of the Jedi, M (NM+ card)...**$40.00**
Figure, Barada, Power of the Force, complete, NM....**$50.00**
Figure, Battle Droid, Episode I/Wave 1, star on chest, MOC...**$12.00**
Figure, Ben Obi-Wan Kenobi, Episode I/Wave 6, MOC ..**$15.00**
Figure, Ben Obi-Wan Kenobi, Power of the Force, M (NM card)...**$125.00**
Figure, Bib Fortuna, Return of the Jedi, complete, NM ..**$12.00**
Figure, Boba Fett, Return of the Jedi, M (EX card) ..**$300.00**

Figure, Boba Fett, Star Wars, 21-back card, MOC, $485.00.
(Photo courtesy June Moon)

Figure, Darth Vader, Star Wars, complete, NM **$15.00**
Figure, Death Squad Commander, Star Wars, complete, NM **$10.00**
Figure, Death Star Droid, Empire Strikes Back, MOC..**$100.00**
Figure, Death Star Escape, M (sealed colored box)....**$50.00**
Figure, Dengar, Empire Strikes Back, NM.....................**$8.00**
Figure, Emperor, Power of the Force, MOC...............**$90.00**
Figure, FX-7, Empire Strikes Back, MOC (unpunched) ..**$40.00**
Figure, General Madine, Return of the Jedi, MOC......**$40.00**
Figure, Greedo, Return of the Jedi, MOC...................**$75.00**
Figure, Hammerhead, Return of the Jedi, MOC..........**$50.00**

Figure, Han Solo, Empire Strikes Back, Bespin outfit, MOC .**$175.00**
Figure, Han Solo, Power of the Force, Carbonite Chamber, NM **$100.00**
Figure, IG-88, Empire Strikes Back, complete, NM.....**$10.00**
Figure, Imperial Dignitary, Power of the Force, MOC..**$100.00**
Figure, Jar Jar Binks, Episode I/Wave 1, MOC **$9.00**
Figure, Jawa, Power of the Force, MOC....................**$120.00**
Figure, Kez-Iban, Droids, complete, NM **$35.00**
Figure, Ki Adi Mundi, Episode I/Wave 3, MOC **$15.00**
Figure, Klaatu, Return of the Jedi, Skiff Guard outfit, MOC.**$25.00**
Figure, Lando Calrissian, Return of the Jedi, Skiff Guard outfit, NM..**$12.00**
Figure, Lobot, Empires Strikes Back, complete, NM...**$10.00**
Figure, Logray, Return of the Jedi, complete, NM **$10.00**
Figure, Luke Skywalker, Power of the Force, Battle Poncho, MOC...**$120.00**
Figure, Lumat, Power of the Force, MOC...................**$65.00**
Figure, Mace Windu, Episode I/Wave 3, MOC...........**$15.00**
Figure, Nikto, Return of the Jedi, MOC **$40.00**
Figure, Papaloo, Return of the Jedi, MOC.................**$55.00**
Figure, Princess Leia Organa, Empire Strikes Back, Hoth gear, MOC...**$130.00**
Figure, Princess Leia Organa, Power of the Force, Combat outfit, MOC...**$70.00**
Figure, Queen Amidala, Episode I/Wave 1, MOC.........**$9.00**
Figure, Qui-Gon Jinn, Episode I/Wave 6, MOC **$15.00**
Figure, Rancor Keeper, Return of the Jedi, complete, NM.**$12.00**
Figure, Rebel Commander, Empire Strikes Back, complete, NM..**$8.00**
Figure, Rebel Soldier, Empire Strikes Back, complete, NM **$7.00**
Figure, Romba, Power of the Force, MOC **$60.00**
Figure, Rune Haako, Episode I/Wave 5, MOC............**$15.00**
Figure, R2-D2, Episode I/Wave 5, MOC.....................**$20.00**
Figure, R2-D2, Star Wars, complete, NM....................**$10.00**
Figure, R5-D4, Return of the Jedi, MOC **$50.00**
Figure, Sand People, Star Wars, complete, NM **$12.00**
Figure, Snaggletooth, Star Wars, complete, NM...........**$10.00**
Figure, Squid Head, Return of the Jedi, MOC.............**$35.00**
Figure, Stormtrooper, Empire Strikes Back, Hoth gear, MOC **$135.00**
Figure, Teebo, Power of the Force, MOC...................**$135.00**
Figure, Thall-Joben, Droids, complete, NM+ **$40.00**
Figure, TIE Fighter Pilot, Empires Strikes Back, NMOC ..**$150.00**
Figure, Tusken Raider, Return of the Jedi, MOC.........**$80.00**
Figure, Walrus Man, Empires Strikes Back, MOC......**$100.00**
Figure, Watto, Episode I/Wave 2, MOC **$9.00**
Figure, Yak Face, Power of the Force, complete, NM ..**$200.00**
Figure, Yoda, Empire Strikes Back, brown snake, NM ..**$40.00**
Figure, Yoda, Episode I/Wave 5, MOC **$20.00**
Figure, Zuckuss, Empires Strikes Back, complete, NM ...**$12.00**
Figure, 4-LOM, Empire Strikes Back, MOC................**$125.00**
Fun Poncho, Darth Vader or C-3PO, 1977, MIB, ea ...**$30.00**
Iron-on transfer book, Ballantine, 1977, unused, M ...**$20.00**
Laser Pistol, Star Wars, plastic, Kenner, 1978-83, EX...**$40.00**
Laser Rifle, Empire Strikes Back, plastic, battery-operated, Kenner, 1980, 18½", EX.................................**$75.00**

Night light, Return of the Jedi, 6 different, MIP, ca **$10.00**
Play-Doh set, Empire Strikes Back, complete, MIB **$20.00**
Playset, Cantina Adventure Set, Sears, M (VG box)..**$225.00**
Playset, Creature Cantina, complete, M (EX box)....**$100.00**
Playset, Droid Factory, complete, M (VG box) **$80.00**
Playset, Hoth Wampa, MIB (sealed).............................**$80.00**
Playset, Hoth Wampa Cave, Micro Collection, MIB **$30.00**
Playset, Imperial Attack Base, complete, VG+ **$45.00**
Playset, Jabba the Hut Dungeon, MIB (sealed).........**$135.00**
Playset, Rebel Command Center, complete, M (VG box) ..**$135.00**
Poster art set, 3-D, complete, 1978, MIP.....................**$30.00**

Puzzle, General Mills, 1977, $12.50.

Record case & records, VG+...**$10.00**
Vehicle, A-Wing Fighter, NM.......................................**$300.00**
Vehicle, AT-AT, Empire Strikes Back, M (worn box) ..**$150.00**
Vehicle, Cloud Car, MIB **$50.00**
Vehicle, Landspeeder, MIB (sealed) **$85.00**
Vehicle, Scout Walker, M (NM sealed box)..................**$80.00**
Vehicle, Speeder Bike, MIB (sealed) **$30.00**
Vehicle, TIE Fighter, M (VG box) **$60.00**
Vehicle, X-Wing Fighter (Battle-Dammaged), MIB......**$60.00**

Stauffer, Erich

From a distance, these child-like figures closely resemble Hummel figurines. They're marked 'Designed by Erich Stauffer' in blue script, often with a pair of crossed arrows or a crown. They always carry a number, sometimes with the letter S or U before it. As an added bonus, you may find a paper label bearing the title of the featured subject. Arnart Imports Inc imported Erich Stauffer figurines from Japan from the late 1950s through the 1980s. Some of these pieces may be found with original Arnart blue and gold stickers.

Figurines range in size from 4½" up to 12½" tall. The most common is the single figure, but some may have two or three children on a single base. The most interesting are those that include accessories or animals to complete their theme. Note that Arnart Imports also made a similar line, but those pieces are smaller and not of the same quality. As a rule, figures marked Erich Stauffer and/or Arnart Imports would be valued at $3.00 to $5.00 per inch in height, sometimes a bit more if the accessories are unique and if stickers and tags are present.

Note: The majority of the listings that follow were gleaned from Internet auction sales. They reflect not only the winning bid but also include postage, insurance, and occasionally handling charges as well, those costs must be added to the winning bid to be an accurate reflection of actual cost.

Advisor: Joan Oates (See Directory, Erich Stauffer Figurines)

#U8565, Music Time, girl: 12¼", Boy: 12½", from $45.00 to $55.00 each. (Photo courtesy Ken and Joan Oates)

#S8395, By The Old Apple Tree, girl sitting playing accordion, 5" **$14.55**
#S8442, Music Frolics, girl standing playing her zither, goose at feet, 8½" **$26.00**
#S8543, Junior Nurse, girl sitting w/open bag, scissors in hand, wearing white apron on, 6¼" **$32.50**
#S8684, Little Debs, Frances, girl w/full-skirted dress carrying a drawstring purse, 4¾" **$23.00**
#2069, orange cat, sitting on its haunches, front legs straight down, marked ARNART, 5th Avenue, hand painted, 9¼"...**$12.00**
#44/121, Picnic Time, boy w/white hat on standing w/picnic basket, 6½"...**$18.00**
#44/138, boy sitting holding axe, label missing, 6".....**$18.00**
#44/138, Picnic Time, girl sitting w/basket of flowers, 5" ..**$18.00**
#44/173, Play Time, boy standing w/baseball bat in hands, 5¾"...**$12.00**
#44/63, Junior Prom, Josef look-alike, w/hang tag, 4½"..**$26.00**
#55/1581, boy standing w/watermelon in ea hand, wearing blue jacket & long pants, label missing, 5"...........**$28.00**
#55/723, Napkins, boy chef w/towel over arm, fruit by his feet, napkin holder, 5¾"......................................**$15.00**
#55/971, child's milk mug, boy standing is handle for mug, 3½"..**$29.00**

#8182, Mississippi River steamboat, plaque, 7½x10" L .**$23.00**

#8359, sailing schooner/rattlesnake, plaque, 7½x10" .**$17.00**

#8394, boy standing w/umbrella over shoulder, knapsack over umbrella, 2 geese by feet, label missing, 5".**$14.70**

Steiff Animals

These stuffed animals originated in Germany around the turn of the century. They were created by Margaret Steiff, whose company continues to operate to the present day. They are identified by the button inside the ear and the identification tag (which often carries the name of the animal) on their chest. Over the years, variations in tags and buttons help collectors determine approximate dates of manufacture.

Teddy bear collectors regard Steiff bears as some of the most valuable on the market. When assessing the worth of a bear, they use some general guidelines as a starting basis, though other features can come into play as well. For instance, bears made prior to 1912 that have long gold mohair fur start at a minimum of $75.00 per inch. If the bear has dark brown or curly white mohair fur instead, that figure may go as high as $135.00. From the 1920 to 1930 era, the rule of thumb would be about $50.00 minimum per inch. A bear (or any other animal) on cast-iron or wooden wheels starts at $75.00 per inch; but if the tires are hard rubber, the value is much lower, more like $27.00 per inch.

It's a fascinating study which is well covered in *Teddy Bears and Steiff Animals, First, Second,* and *Third Series,* by Margaret Fox Mandel. Also see Cynthia Powell's *Collector's Guide to Miniature Teddy Bears.*

Newsletter/Club: *Collector's Life*
The World's Foremost Publication for Steiff Enthusiasts
Beth Savino
P.O. Box 798
Holland, OH 43528; 1-800-862-TOYS; fax: 419-473-3947

Blackie Terrier, plush, #4184/35, ca 1980 – 90s, 12x6x12", NM, from $125.00 to $175.00. (Photo courtesy Candace Sten Davis and Patricia J. Baugh)

Basset Hound, mohair, swivel head, original green collar, chest tag, 1950s, 4½", NM.................................**$165.00**

Bear, gold mohair w/felt pads, glass eyes, all ID, 1950, 6", EX..**$225.00**

Bendy Bear, white, all ID, 1980, 3½", M.....................**$65.00**

Bengel Tiger, mohair, glass eyes, raised script button & chest tag, 1959-61, 5½", rare, M....................................**$450.00**

Bessy Cow, mohair w/felt horns & udders, glass eyes, original collar & bell, no ID, 1950s, 9", NM...............**$150.00**

Bison, mohair w/felt horns, all ID, 1950, 8", M........**$225.00**

Boar, black w/brown face, all ID, 1950s, 11", M......**$165.00**

Cat, black velvet w/mohair tail, original ribbon, US Zone tag, 1948, 3", M...**$165.00**

Collie, lying down, all ID, 1960s, 9", M.....................**$195.00**

Cosy Kamel, Dralon, all ID, 1968, 10½", M...............**$125.00**

Deer (Buck), beige mohair, black glass eyes, FF underscored button, 10", VG...**$250.00**

Deer (Doe), beige mohair, black glass eyes, FF underscored button, 9", VG...**$185.00**

Dormy Dormouse, mohair & Dralon, all ID, 1968, 7½", M..**$125.00**

Elephant, ride-on, gray mohair w/glass eyes, red & yellow felt blanket, red leather harness, steel frame, 24½", EX, A.......**$450.00**

Floppy Kitty, sleeping, tan w/black stripes, original ribbon & chest tag, 8", EX...**$95.00**

Floppy Panther, brass button & stock tag, 1972, 17", NM..**$185.00**

Foxy Dog, original ribbon & chest tag, 1950, 3", EX..**$85.00**

Froggy Frog, swimming, mohair, chest tag, 1960s, 10", NM.**$125.00**

Gogo Chinchilla, Dralon & felt, all ID, 5½", M.........**$200.00**

Hansi Parakeet, velvet w/plastic feet, all ID, 1968, 3½", EX..**$125.00**

Hide-A-Gift Cocker Spaniel, black & white, all ID, 1950, 5½", NM..**$185.00**

Hucky Raven, mohair & felt w/metal legs, all ID, 1960, 7", M...**$250.00**

Jocko Monkey, mohair & felt, glass eyes, all ID, US Zone tag, 11", M...**$225.00**

Koala Bear, fully jointed, all ID, 1955-58, 9", M........**$700.00**

Lizzy Lizzard, velvet, glass eyes, no ID, 1959-61, 12", EX...**$385.00**

Lora Parrot, mohair & felt, incised button & stock tag, 1968, 9", EX...**$150.00**

Mallard Drake, airbrushed Dralon w/black plastic eyes, yellow felt bill, 1973, 10½", EX...............................**$145.00**

Moosy Moose, mohair & felt, glass eyes, all ID, 5", rare, NM...**$425.00**

Nagy Beaver, mohair w/felt hands & feet, glass eyes, all ID, 1958, 7", M...**$165.00**

Original Camel, all ID, 1950, 11", NM.....................**$250.00**

Original Teddy, caramel mohair, fully jointed, chest tag, 3½", M...**$325.00**

Original Teddy, tan mohair, all ID, 1968, 13", M......**$225.00**

Peky Dog, mohair, glass eyes, swivel head, all ID, 1950s, 8", M...**$195.00**

Peky Dog, plush & felt, chest tag, 1950, 3", EX..........**$75.00**

Pony, mohair w/felt ears, all ID, FAO Schwarz Exclusive, 1967-68, 6½", rare..**$350.00**

Renny Reindeer, chest tag, 1950s, 4½", M................**$185.00**

Rocky Goat, all ID, 1963-67, 5", M............................**$175.00**

Scotty Dog, original collar, raised script button, 1950-57, 4", rare, NM...**$300.00**

Siamy Cat, white mohair w/brown striping, glass eyes, no ID, 1950s, 5", rare, NM...**$300.00**

Snobby Poodle, puppet, original ribbon, all ID, 1955-58, 9", NM **$100.00**

Snucki Ram, tan mohair w/black face & feet, chest tag, 1950s, 6", NM...**$125.00**

Susi Cat, mohair, plastic eyes, original pink ribbon, all ID, 1960s, 5", NM **$200.00**

Tucky Turkey, mohair w/felt wings & tail, velvet face, glass eyes, all ID, 1952, 4", M **$365.00**

Unicorn, mohair & Dralon, 1983, all ID, 7", NM.......**$165.00**

Woolie Baby Duck, metal feet, raised script button & stock tag, 1950s, 1½", M **$55.00**

Woolie Chick, plastic feet, raised script button & stock tag, 1950s, 1½", M...**$50.00**

Woolie Duck, plastic feet, no ID, 1960s, 1½", M **$40.00**

Woolie Fish, green & yellow, raised script button & stock tag, 1968, 1½", NM...**$35.00**

Woolie Mouse, gray, raised script button & stock tag, 1950, 1½", M **$45.00**

Woolie Skunk, raised script button, 1950s, 1½", NM ...**$150.00**

Yes/No Jumbo Elephant, ear button & chest tag, 1970s, 10", EX **$200.00**

Yuku Gazelle, all ID, 1962-63, 7½", rare, NM **$325.00**

Zotty Bear, caramel mohair, plastic eyes, original red ribbon chest tag, 6½", M **$245.00**

String Holders

Today we admire string holders for their decorative nature. They are much sought after by collectors. However, in the 1800s, they were strictly utilitarian, serving as dispensers of string used to wrap food and packages. The earliest were made of cast iron. Later, advertising string holders appeared in general stores. They were made of tin or cast iron and were provided by companies pedaling such products as shoes, laundry supplies, and food. These advertising string holders command the highest prices.

These days we take cellophane tape for granted. Before it was invented, string was used to tie up packages. String holders became a staple item in the home kitchen. To add a whimsical touch, in the late 1920s and 1930s, many string holders were presented as human shapes, faces, animals, and fruits. Most of these novelty string holders were made of chalkware (plaster of Paris), ceramics, or wood fiber. If you were lucky, you might have won a plaster of Paris 'Super Hero' or comic character string holder at your local carnival. These prizes were known as 'carnival chalkware.' The Indian string holder was a popular giveaway, so was Betty Boop and Superman.

Our values reflect string holders in excellent condition.

Advisor: Ellen Bercovici (See Directory, String Holders)

Apple, many variations, chalkware, from $25 to **$50.00**

Apple w/face, ceramic, Py, from $100 to **$150.00**

Babies, 1 happy, 1 crying, ceramic, Lefton, pr, from $250 to..**$300.00**

Bananas, chalkware, from $85 to **$95.00**

Bird, 'String Nest Pull,' ceramic, from $40 to.............**$60.00**

Bird on branch, scissors in head, ceramic, from $85 to..**$100.00**

Birdcage, red & white w/green leaves & yellow bird, chalkware, from $100 to **$150.00**

Bonzo (dog) w/bee on chest, ceramic, from $150 to...**$200.00**

Boy, top hat & pipe, eyes to side, chalkware, from $50 to **$60.00**

Bride, ceramic, from $100 to **$125.00**

Bride & bridesmaids, ceramic, from $100 to **$125.00**

Butler, Black man w/white lips & eyebrows, ceramic, minimum value **$300.00**

Cabbage, ceramic, Japan...**$100.00**

Chef, chalkware, from $50 to **$75.00**

Chef, Rice Crispy, chalkware, from $125 to **$150.00**

Chef w/rolling pin, full figure, chalkware, from $75 to ..**$100.00**

Cherries, chalkware, from $125 to **$200.00**

Clown w/string around tooth, chalkware, from $200 to..**$300.00**

Dog, Scottie, ceramic, from $125 to.........................**$200.00**

Dog, w/chef's hat, chalkware, from $300 to **$350.00**

Dutch girl's head, chalkware **$75.00**

Elephant, yellow, England, ceramic, from $60 to **$75.00**

Girl in bonnet, eyes to side, chalkware, from $60 to .**$75.00**

Granny in rocking chair, Py, ceramic, from $100 to.**$150.00**

Groom & bridesmaids, ceramic, from $100 to **$125.00**

Heart, puffed, Cleminson, ceramic, from $75 to......**$100.00**

House, Cleminson, ceramic, from $125 to................**$175.00**

Indian, w/headband, chalkware, from $300 to **$350.00**

Iron w/flowers, ceramic, from $200 to **$300.00**

Jester, chalkware, from $125 to **$175.00**

Kitten w/ball of yarn, ceramic....................................**$75.00**

Kitten w/ball of yarn, ceramic, homemade **$65.00**

Lady's face, Deco, ceramic, Japan, from $200 to **$225.00**

Little Red Riding Hood, chalkware, minimum value .**$250.00**

Maid, Sarsaparilla, ceramic, 1984, from $95 to **$125.00**

Mammy, full figured, plaid & polka-dot dress, ceramic, from $125 to..**$200.00**

Mammy face, many variations, chalkware, from $250 to..**$300.00**

Mammy knitting sock, ceramic, minimum value, $200.00. (Photo courtesy Ellen Bercovici)

Man in top hat w/pipe, from $65 to **$85.00**

Moon face, chalkware, from $300 to **$350.00**

Mouse, Josef Originals, ceramic, from $80 to..............**$90.00**
Penguin, ceramic, from $85 to **$100.00**
Pig, pink, ceramic, from $60 to **$75.00**
Pig w/flowers, ceramic, from $100 to **$150.00**
Pirate & gypsy, wood fiber, pr, from $100 to............**$125.00**
Prince Pineapple, chalkware, from $300 to...............**$350.00**
Rooster, Royal Bayreuth, ceramic, from $400 to **$600.00**
Rose, chalkware, from $125 to **$175.00**
Rosie the Riveter, chalkware, from $125 to **$200.00**
Sailor boy, chalkware, from $125 to **$175.00**
Senor, chalkware, from $75 to.....................................**$85.00**
Senora, chalkware, from $125 to...............................**$200.00**
Soldier, head w/cap, chalkware, from $75 to.............**$85.00**
Tomato, eyes closed, ceramic, Japan, from $150 to .**$200.00**
Witch in pumpkin, winking, ceramic, from $125 to.**$175.00**
Woman w/turban, chalkware, from $125 to.............**$150.00**

Swanky Swigs

These glasses, ranging in size from 3⅛" to 5⅝", were originally distributed by the Kraft company who filled them with their cheese spread. They were introduced in the 1930s and can still be in the supermarket today in a clear small glass with indented designs of different patterns. There are approximately 223 different variations of colors and patterns ranging from sailboats, bands, animals, dots, stars, checkers, etc.

In 1999 a few Kraft Australian Swanky Swigs started turning up. We now have the American, Canadian, and the Australian Kraft Swanky Swigs. They have been verified as Kraft Australian swigs because of the Kraft ads in magazines.

Here is a listing of some of the harder-to-find examples: In the small (Canadian) size (about 3¹⁄₁₆" to 3¼") look for Band No. 5 (two red and two black bands); Galleon (2 ships on each example, made in five colors — black, blue, green, red, and yellow); Checkers (made in four color combinations — black and red, black and yellow, black and orange, and black and white, all having a top row of black checks); and Fleur-De-Lis (black fleur-de-lis with a bright red filigree motif).

In the regular size (about 3⅜" to 3⅞") look for Dots Forming Diamonds (diamonds made up of small red dots); Lattice and Vine (white lattice with flowers in these combinations — white and blue, white and green, and white and red); Texas Centennial (a cowboy and horse in these colors — black, blue, green, and red); three special issues with dates of 1936, 1938, and 1942; and Tulip No. 2 (available in black, blue, green, and red).

In the large (Canadian) size (about 4³⁄₁₆" to 5⅝" you'll find Circles and Dot (circles with a small dot in the middle, in black, blue, green, and red); Star No. 1 (small scattered stars, made in black, blue, green, and red); Cornflower No. 2 (in dark blue, light blue, red, and yellow); Provincial Cress (made only in red/burgundy with maple leaves); and blue.

Even the lids are collectible and are valued at a minimum of $3.00, depending on condition and the advertising message they convey.

For more information we recommend *Swanky Swigs* by Ian Warner, *Collectible Glassware of the 40s, 50s, and 60s* and *The Collector's Encyclopedia of Depression Glass*, both by Gene Florence; and *Collectible Drinking Glasses* by Mark Chase and Michael Kelly.

Note: All are American issue unless noted Canadian.

Advisor: Joyce Jackson (See Directory, Swanky Swigs)

Antique #1, black, blue, brown, green, orange or red, Canadian, 3¼", ea **$8.00**
Antique #1, black, blue, brown, green, orange or red, Canadian, 1954, 4¾", ea **$20.00**
Antique #1, black, blue, brown, green, orange or red, 1954, 3¾", ea **$4.00**
Antique #2, lime green, deep red, orange, blue or black, Canadian, 1974, 4⅝", ea **$20.00**

Bachelor Button, red and white daisies with green leaves, 1955: Canadian, 4¾", $15.00; US, 3¾", $3.00; Canadian, 3¼", $6.00; Canadian, red and white flowers, no green leaves, 3¼", $20.00. (Photo courtesy Joyce Jackson)

Band #1, red & black, 1933, 3⅜"..................................**$3.00**
Band #2, black & red, Canadian, 1933, 4¾"...............**$20.00**
Band #2, black & red, 1933, 3⅜"..................................**$3.00**
Band #3, white & blue, 1933, 3⅜" **$3.00**
Band #4, blue, 1933, 3⅜" **$3.00**
Bicentennial Tulip, green, red or yellow, 1975, 3¾", ea .**$15.00**
Blue Tulips, 1937, 4¼" **$20.00**
Bustlin' Betty, blue, brown, green, orange, red or yellow, Canadian, 1953, 3¼", ea **$8.00**
Bustlin' Betty, blue, brown, green, orange, red or yellow, Canadian, 1953, 4¾", ea **$20.00**
Bustlin' Betty, blue, brown, green, orange, red or yellow, 1953, 3¾", ea **$4.00**
Carnival, blue, green, red or yellow, 1939, 3½", ea......**$6.00**
Checkerboard, white w/blue, green or red, Canadian, 1936, 4¾", ea **$20.00**
Checkerboard, white w/blue, green or red, 1936, 3½", ea .**$20.00**
Circles & Dot, any color, 1934, 3½", ea **$7.00**
Circles & Dot, black, blue, green or red, Canadian, 1934, 4¾", ea **$20.00**
Coin, clear & plain w/indented coin decor around base, Canadian, 1968, 3⅛" or 3¼", ea **$2.00**

Coin, clear & plain w/indented coin decor around base, 1968, 3¾"..**$1.00**

Colonial, clear w/indented waffle design around middle & base, 1976, 3¾", ea...**$.50**

Colonial, clear w/indented waffle design around middle & base, 1976, 4⅜", ea..**$1.00**

Cornflower #1, light blue & green, Canadian, 1941, 4⅝", ea..**$20.00**

Cornflower #1, light blue & green, Canadian, 3¼", ea.**$8.00**

Cornflower #1, light blue & green, 1941, 3½", ea.........**$4.00**

Cornflower #2, dark blue, light blue, red or yellow, Canadian, 1947, 3¼", ea..**$8.00**

Cornflower #2, dark blue, light blue, red or yellow, Canadian, 1947, 4¼", ea...**$40.00**

Cornflower #2, dark blue, light blue, red or yellow, 1947, 3½", ea..**$4.00**

Crystal Petal, clear & plain w/fluted base, 1951, 3½", ea.**$2.00**

Dots Forming Diamonds, any color, 1935, 3½", ea....**$50.00**

Ethnic Series, lime green, royal blue, burgundy, poppy red or yellow, Canadian, 1974, 4⅝", ea...........................**$20.00**

Forget-Me-Not, dark blue, light blue, red or yellow, Canadian, 3¼", ea..**$8.00**

Forget-Me-Not, dark blue, light blue, red or yellow, 1948, 3½", ea..**$4.00**

Galleon, black, blue, green, red or yellow, Canadian, 1936, 3⅛", ea...**$30.00**

Hostess, clear & plain w/indented groove base, Canadian, 1960, 3⅛" or 3¼", ea..**$2.00**

Hostess, clear & plain w/indented groove base, Canadian, 1960, 5⅝", ea..**$5.00**

Hostess, clear & plain w/indented groove base, 1960, 3¾", ea..**$1.00**

Jonquil (Posy Pattern), yellow & green, Canadian, 1941, 3¼"..**$8.00**

Jonquil (Posy Pattern), yellow & green, Canadian, 1941, 4⅝", ea..**$20.00**

Jonquil (Posy Pattern), yellow & green, 1941, 3½", ea.**$4.00**

Kiddie Kup, black, blue, brown, green, orange or red, Canadian, 1956, 3¼", ea...**$6.00**

Kiddie Kup, black, blue, brown, green, orange or red, Canadian, 1956, 4¾", ea.......................................**$20.00**

Kiddie Kup, black, blue, brown, green, orange or red, 1956, 3¾", ea...**$3.00**

Lattice & Vine, white w/blue, green or red, 1936, 3½", ea..**$50.00**

Petal Star, clear, 50th Anniversary of Kraft Cheese Spreads, 1933-1983, ca 1983, 3¾", ea.................................**$2.00**

Petal Star, clear w/indented star base, Canadian, 1978, 3¼", ea..**$2.00**

Petal Star, clear w/indented star base, 1978, 3¾", ea......**$.50**

Plain, clear, like Tulip #1 w/out design, 1940, 3½", ea.**$4.00**

Plain, clear, like Tulip #3 w/out design, 1951, 3⅞", ea...**$5.00**

Provencial Crest, red & burgundy, Canadian, 1974, 4⅝", ea..**$25.00**

Sailboat #1, blue, 1936, 3½", ea **$12.00**

Sailboat #2, blue, green, light green or red, 1936, 3½", ea..**$12.00**

Special Issue, Del Monte Violet, Greetings From Kraft, 1942, 3½", ea **$100.00**

Special Issue, Greetings From Kraft, California Retail Grocers Merchants Assn, Del Monte CA 1938, red, 1938, 3½"..**$100.00**

Special Issue, Lewis-Pacific Dairymen's Assn, Kraft Foods Co, Sept 13, 1947, Chehalis WA, 1947, 3½", ea **$100.00**

Special Issue, Pasadena blue sailboat, Greetings From Kraft, blue, 1936, 3½"..**$100.00**

Sportsmen Series, red hockey, blue skiing, red football, red baseball, or green soccer, Canadian, 1976, 4⅝", ea.**$20.00**

Stars #1, black, blue, green, red or yellow, Canadian, 1934, 4¾", ea..**$20.00**

Stars #1, black, blue, green or red, 1935, 3½", ea **$7.00**

Stars #1, yellow, 1935, 3½", ea.....................................**$25.00**

Stars #2, clear w/orange stars, Canadian, 1971, 4⅝", ea **$5.00**

Texas Centennial, black, blue, green or red, 1936, 3½", ea..**$30.00**

Tulip (Posy Pattern), red & green, Canadian, 1941, 3¼", ea..**$8.00**

Tulip (Posy Pattern), red & green, Canadian, 1941, 4⅝", ea..**$20.00**

Tulip (Posy Pattern), red & green, 1941, 3½", ea **$4.00**

Tulip #1, black, blue, green, red or yellow, Canadian, 3¼", ea..**$8.00**

Tulip #1, black, blue, green, red or yellow, 1937, 3½", ea..**$4.00**

Tulip #1, black, blue, green or red, Canadian, 1937, 4⅝", ea..**$20.00**

Tulip #2, black, blue, green or red, 1938, 3½", ea **$25.00**

Tulip #3, dark blue, light blue, red or yellow, Canadian, 1950, 4¾", ea..**$20.00**

Tulip #3, dark blue, light blue, red or yellow, Canadian, 3¼", ea..**$8.00**

Tulip #3, dark blue, light blue, red or yellow, 1950, 3⅞", ea..**$4.00**

Violet (Posy Pattern), blue & green, Canadian, 1941, 3¼", ea..**$8.00**

Violet (Posy Pattern), blue & green, Canadian, 1941, 4⅝", ea..**$20.00**

Violet (Posy Pattern), blue & green, 1941, 3½", ea.......**$4.00**

Wildlife Series, black bear, Canadian goose, moose, or red fox, Canadian, 1975, 4⅝", ea **$20.00**

Syroco

Syroco Inc. originated in New York in 1890 when a group of European wood carvers banded together to produce original hand carvings for fashionable homes of the area. Their products were also used in public buildings throughout upstate New York, including the state capitol. Demand for those products led to the development of the original Syroco reproduction process that allowed them to copy original carvings with no loss of detail. They later developed exclusive hand-applied color finishes to further enhance the product, which they continued to improve and refine over ninety years.

Syroco's master carvers use tools and skills handed down from father to son through many generations. Woods used, depending on the effect called for, include Swiss pear wood, oak, mahogany, and wormy chestnut. When a design is completed, it is transformed into a metal cast through their molding and tooling process. A compression mold system using wood fiber was employed from the early 1940s to the 1960s. Since 1962 a process has been in use in which pellets of resin are injected into a press, heated to the melting point, and then injected into the mold. Because the resin is liquid, it fills every crevice, thus producing an exact copy of the carver's art. It is then cooled, cleaned, and finished.

Other companies have produced similar items, among them are Multi Products, now of Erie, Pennsylvania. It was incorporated in Chicago in 1941 but in 1976 was purchased by John Hronas. Multi Products hired a staff of artists, made some wood originals and developed a tooling process for forms. They used a styrene-based material, heavily loaded with talc or calcium carbonate. A hydraulic press was used to remove excess material from the forms. Shapes were dried in kilns for seventy-two hours, then finished and, if the design required it, trimmed in gold. Their products included bears, memo pads, thermometers, brush holders, trays, plaques, nut bowls, napkin holders, etc., which were sold mainly as souvenirs. The large clocks and mirrors were made before the 1940s and may sell for as much as $100.00 and more, depending on condition. Syroco used gold trim, but any other painted decoration you might encounter was very likely done by an outside firm. Some collectors prefer the painted examples and tend to pay a little more to get them. You may also find similar products stamped 'Ornawood,' 'Decor-A-Wood,' and 'Swank.'

See also Motion Clocks.

Ashtray, double, glass bowls, cigarette compartment in center, from $10 to **$20.00**
Ashtray, floral at sides, rectangular receptacle, from 2 to 4 rests, Syroco, 4x6", from $6 to **$10.00**
Ashtray, florals at square sides, round receptacle, from 2 to 4 rests, Syroco, 5½x5½", from $7 to **$10.00**
Ashtray, steer & building on sides, marked Alamo TX, from $3 to..**$10.00**
Barometer, ship's captain at wheel, round mechanism at wheel's center, from $10 to....................................**$15.00**
Bookends, Diana the Huntress w/hound, pr, from $10 to **$15.00**
Bookends, End of the Trail, pr, from $10 to **$15.00**
Bookends, lg wild rose, pr, from $10 to......................**$15.00**
Bookends, Mount Rushmore, pr, from $10 to..............**$15.00**
Box, bear, waterfall & trees on lid, marked Yellowstone Nat Park, 3½x4½", from $5 to **$7.00**
Box, cowboy boots & saddle on lid, w/paper label...**$12.50**
Box, deer & trees, 4½x6", from $4 to **$6.00**
Box, floral design at sides & on lid, Syroco, 5½x5½", from $5 to **$10.00**

Box, rope design on lid, velvet lining, Syroco, 6x6", from $10 to..**$15.00**
Box, standing dog on lid, 4x6", from $5 to................**$10.00**
Box, swirl design, 5½x7", from $8 to..........................**$10.00**
Brush holder, ship w/white triple mainsails, 4½", from $7 to..**$12.00**
Brush holder, 2 drunks w/keg, 5", from $5 to **$10.00**
Brush holder, 4 puppies in basket, from $8 to **$10.00**
Figure, musician, painted, from $10 to **$15.00**
Figure, seated Indian, from $6 to **$10.00**
Figurine, Cape Cod fisherman & woman, painted, pr, from $6 to..**$15.00**
Picture frame, 3x2½" **$6.00**
Picture frame, 8x5½", from $6 to **$12.00**
Pipe holder, 2 horses at gate, 3 rests, from $12 to **$15.00**
Plate, barn & silo pastoral scene at center, fruits & vegetables at rim, 8", from $2 to....................................**$5.00**
Plate, pine cones & leaves, 4", from $2 to...................**$5.00**
Thermometer, captain at ship's wheel, painted, marked Copyright Thad Co, 4"..**$15.00**
Thermometer, Scottie dogs at sides, magnet at bottom, 4", from $5 to...**$10.00**
Tie rack, bartender behind bar w/bottles, painted, 6x9½", from $10 to..**$20.00**
Tie rack, pointer dog at top, metal hangers, 7x12", from $10 to..**$20.00**
Tray, flowers, marked Multi Products, 11" L, from $8 to .**$14.00**
Wall plaque, crucifix, white, 8", from $5 to................**$10.00**

Wall plaque, Little Things in Life, $5.00.
(Photo courtesy Doris Gibbs)

Wall plaque, Our Mother of Perpetual Help, 4x5", from $5 to..**$10.00**
Wall plaque, Scottie dog, repainted, 6", from $2 to **$8.00**
Wall shelf, floral w/acanthus leaf, bead trim at top edge, Multi Products, 9x7", pr, from $7 to....................**$12.00**

Taylor, Smith, and Taylor

Though this company is most famous for their pastel dinnerware line, Lu Ray, they made many other patterns, and some of them are very collectible in their own right. They were located in the East Liverpool area of West Virginia, the 'dinnerware capitol' of the world. Their answer to HLC's very successful Fiesta line was Vistosa. It was made in four primary colors, and though quite attractive, the line was never developed to include any more than twenty items. Other lines/shapes that collectors especially look for are Taverne (also called Silhouette — similar to a line made by Hall), Conversation (a shape designed by Walter Dorwin Teague, 1950 to 1954), and Pebbleford (a textured, pastel line on the Versatile shape, made from 1952 to 1960).

For more information we recommend *Collector's Guide to LuRay Pastels* by Bill and Kathy Meehan (Collector Books), which covers several dinnerware lines in addition to LuRay.

Note: To evaluate King O'Dell, add 15% to the values we list for Conversation. For Boutonniere, add 15% to our Ever Yours values; and for Dwarf Pine, add the same amount to the values suggested for Versatile.

See also LuRay Pastels.

Beverly, baker, vegetable; oval	$5.50
Beverly, plate, 10"	$3.00
Castle, creamer	$10.00
Castle, teacup	$5.00
Center Bouquet, nappy, vegetable; round	$15.00
Center Bouquet, plate, 6"	$6.00
Conversation, bowl, soup	$2.00
Conversation, bowl, vegetable; oval, sm	$5.00
Conversation, creamer	$3.00
Conversation, plate, dinner	$2.50
Conversation, water jug	$25.00
Delphian, creamer	$3.50
Delphian, plate, 6"	$2.25
Delphian Rose, bowl, soup	$12.50
Delphian Rose, plate, 10"	$12.50
Dogwood, plate, 9"	$10.00
Dogwood, platter, lg	$30.00
Empire, creamer	$4.00
Empire, plate, 10"	$2.50
English Abbey, cake plate	$20.00
English Abbey, tea saucer	$3.50
Ever Yours, carafe	$12.50
Ever Yours, creamer	$2.50
Ever Yours, cup	$1.50
Ever Yours, plate, dinner	$1.75
Ever Yours, platter, oval	$3.00
Ever Yours, tea tile	$20.00
Ever Yours, water jug	$15.00
Fairway, bowl, soup	$2.50
Fairway, platter, lg	$8.00
Garland, cake plate	$10.00
Garland, plate, 9"	$2.00
Laurel, bowl, '36s	$10.00
Laurel, platter, 11½"	$5.00
Laurel, teacup	$2.00
Pastoral, plate, bread & butter	$2.50
Pastoral, teacup	$3.00

Pebbleford, casserole, w/lid	$30.00
Pebbleford, coffee server	$25.00
Pebbleford, creamer	$5.00
Pebbleford, cup	$3.00
Pebbleford, egg cup, double	$10.00
Pebbleford, plate, salad	$3.00
Pebbleford, platter, 11"	$6.00
Plymouth, casserole	$27.00
Plymouth, tea saucer	$2.00
Taverne (Sihouette), platter, 7"	$20.00
Taverne (Silhouette), butter dish, w/lid	$150.00
Taverne (Silhouette), plate, 9"	$10.00
Taverne (Silhouette), sugar bowl, w/lid	$20.00
Taverne (Silhouette), tea saucer	$2.00
Taylorstone, coffee server	$10.00
Taylorstone, cup	$1.25
Taylorstone, plate, salad	$1.25
Taylorstone, platter	$6.00
Taylorstone, sugar bowl, w/lid	$2.50
Taylorton, coffee server	$21.00
Taylorton, cup	$1.75
Taylorton, plate, salad	$1.75
Taylorton, platter	$4.00
Taylorton, salt & pepper shakers, pr	$5.00
Taylorton, sugar bowl, w/lid	$3.25
Versatile, bowl, fruit	$1.50
Versatile, egg cup, double	$10.00
Versatile, plate, luncheon	$1.75
Versatile, platter, 11"	$3.00
Versatile, teapot	$20.00
Versatile, water jug	$15.00
Vistosa, bowl, salad; footed, 12"	$200.00
Vistosa, coupe soup	$25.00

Vistosa, egg cup, $25.00. (Photo courtesy Bill and Kathy Meehan)

Vistosa, plate, chop; 12"	$40.00
Vistosa, plate, 9", from $15 to	$20.00
Vistosa, salt & pepper shakers, pr	$32.00
Vistosa, sugar bowl, w/lid	$25.00
Vistosa, teacup, from $10 to	$15.00
Vogue, bowl, fruit	$2.00
Vogue, teacup	$2.50

Tiara Exclusives

Collectors are just beginning to take notice of the glassware sold through Tiara in-home parties, their Sandwich line in particular. A branch of the Lancaster Colony Corp., the Tiara Division closed in 1998. Several companies were involved in producing the lovely colored glassware they marketed over the years, among them Indiana Glass, Fenton, Dalzell Viking, and L.E. Smith.

Note: Home Interiors has just introduced Tiara Sandwich glass and the square honey box in a lovely transparent amethyst color (Plum). They are using the Tiara brand name, and pieces appear to be from Tiara molds.

Advisor: Mandi Birkinbine (See Directory, Tiara)

Crown Dinnerware

In the mid-1980s Tiara made 'Crown Dinnerware in Imperial Blue.' This is the pattern most collectors know as King's Crown Thumbprint. The color is a rich medium blue and brighter than cobalt.

Cup $3.00
Goblet, stemmed, 8-oz, from $3 to $5.00
Plate, bread; 8" $5.00
Plate, dinner; 10"..$7.00
Saucer $2.00

Honey Boxes

One of Tiara's more popular items was the honey box or honey dish. It is square with tiny tab feet and an embossed allover pattern of bees and hives. The dish measures 6" tall with the lid and was made in many different colors, ranging in value from $15.00 up to $50.00, depending on the color.

Amber, from $15 to $25.00
Black, from $25 to $35.00
Chantilly (pale) Green, from $45 to $60.00
Clear, from $35 to...$45.00
Light blue, from $25 to..$50.00
Spruce (teal) green, from $20 to $35.00

Sandwich Pattern

In the late 1960s, Tiara contracted with Indiana to produce their famous line of Sandwich dinnerware (a staple at Indiana Glass since the late 1920s). Over the years, it has been offered in many colors: ruby, teal, crystal, amber, green, pink (officially named Peach), blue, and others in limited amounts. We've listed a few pieces of Tiara's Sandwich below, and though the market is unstable and tends to vary from region to region, our estimates will serve to offer an indication of current asking prices. Because this glass is not rare and is relatively new, collectors tend to purchase only items in perfect condition. Chips or scratches will decrease value drastically.

With most items, the quickest way to tell Anchor Hocking's Sandwich from Tiara and Indiana Sandwich is by looking at the flower in the pattern. The Tiara/Indiana flower is outlined with a single line and has convex petals. Anchor Hocking's flower is made with double lines, so has a more complex appearance, and the convex area in each petal is tiny. To learn more about the two lines, we recommend *Collectible Glassware from the 40s, 50s, and 60s* by Gene Florence (Collector Books). Also available is *Collecting Tiara Amber Sandwich Glass* by our advisor, Mandi Birkinbine (see the Directory for ordering information).

Basket, amber, 10¾x4¾", from $40.00 to $50.00.
(Photo courtesy Mandi Birkinbine)

Ashtray, amber, 1¼x7½" $15.00
Bowl, salad; amber, crimped, 4¾x10", from $15 to....$18.00
Bowl, salad; Chantilly Green, 3x8⅜", from $15 to......$25.00
Butter dish, amber, domed lid, 6" H, from $20 to $25.00
Butter dish, Chantilly Green, domed lid, 6" H $35.00
Candy box, amber, w/lid, 7½", from $65 to...............$80.00
Canister, amber, 26-oz, 5⅝", from $12 to....................$20.00
Canister, amber, 38-oz, 7½", from $12 to...................$20.00
Canister, amber, 52-oz, 8⅞", from $18 to...................$26.00
Celery tray/oblong relish, Midnight Blue, 10⅜x4⅜"...$18.50
Clock, amber, wall hanging, 12" dia, from $20 to.......$25.00
Clock, amber, wall hanging, 16" dia, from $45 to.......$55.00
Compote, amber, 8"...$25.00
Creamer & sugar bowl, Midnight Blue, round, flat, pr..$15.00
Cup, coffee; amber, 9-oz...$4.00
Cup, snack/punch; & saucer, crystal, 2⅝x3⅜" $2.50
Dish, club, heart, diamond or spade shape, amber, 4", ea, from $3 to...$4.00
Egg tray, amber, 12", from $10 to...............................$15.00
Egg tray, Spruce Green, 12"...$15.00
Fairy lamp, amber, egg shape, pedestal foot, 2-pc, 5¾", from $14 to...$18.00
Goblet, table wine; amber, 8½-oz, 5⅝", from $6.50 to.$8.00

Goblet, water; amber, 8-oz, 5¼", from $6 to **$8.00**
Goblet, water; clear, 5¼", from $5 to......................**$8.00**
Goblet, water; Spruce Green, 8-oz, 5¼", from $4 to **$5.50**
Gravy boat, 3⅛x7⅜", from $45 to **$60.00**
Mug, amber, footed, 5½"......................................**$8.00**
Napkin holder, amber, footed fan shape, 4x7½", from $22 to.**$28.00**
Pitcher, amber, 8¼", from $45 to............................**$65.00**
Plate, dinner; amber, 10", from $9.50 to **$12.50**
Plate, salad; amber, 8" **$7.00**
Plate, salad; Chantilly Green, 8¼" **$9.50**
Platter, amber, sawtooth rim, 12", from $8.50 to........**$12.00**
Salt & pepper shakers, amber, 4¾", pr, from $18 to ..**$25.00**
Tray, amber, footed, 1¾x12¾"................................**$35.00**
Tumbler, amber, 8-oz, 4", from $12 to **$14.00**
Tumbler, amber, 10-oz, 6½", from $5.50 to **$7.00**
Vase, bud; amber, 3⅝", from $15 to..........................**$25.00**

Goodrich Silvertown Super 6 Ply, green embossed insert, 7" tire..**$60.00**
Goodyear All Weather 6.50-19, brass insert, 5⅜" tire w/2 different tread patterns **$100.00**
Goodyear Eagle VR50, very fat 6⅜" high performance tire, clear imprinted insert..............................**$45.00**
Goodyear Flight Eagle, 6" aircraft tire, clear imprinted insert **$50.00**
Goodyear Vector, clear insert w/manufacturer's imprint, 6" tioe..**$25.00**
Kelly-Springfield Tom Cat, solid truck tire, clear embossed insert..**$100.00**
Lee of Conshohocken Truck-Bus, clear insert, 6½" tire ..**$100.00**
Mohawk Ultissimo, 6" tire, clear imprinted insert **$35.00**
Pennsylvania Balloon 33x6.0 6 Ply Cord, 6¼" tire, green embossed insert **$100.00**

Tire Ashtrays

Manufacturers of tires issued miniature versions containing ashtray inserts that they usually embossed with advertising messages. Others were used as souvenirs from World's Fairs. The earlier styles were made of glass or glass and metal, but by the early 1920s, they were replaced by the more familiar rubber-tired variety. The inserts were often made of clear glass, but colors were also used, and once in awhile you'll find a tin one. The tires themselves were usually black; other colors are rarely found. Hundreds have been produced over the years; in fact, the larger tire companies still issue them occasionally, but you no longer see the details or colors that are evident in the pre-WWII ashtrays. Although the common ones bring modest prices, rare examples sometimes sell for up to several hundred dollars. For ladies or non-smokers, some miniature tires were called pin trays.

For more information we recommend *Tire Ashtray Collector's Guide* by Jeff McVey.

Advisor: Jeff McVey (See Directory, Tire Ashtrays)

Big O Bigfoot HP Radial 761 195/70HR14, clear imprinted insert **$40.00**
Continental Titan, clear embossed insert, 6¾" truck tire, Germany **$50.00**
Diamond Balloon 33x6.00 to fit 5" rim 21" wheel, blue embossed insert **$80.00**
Dunlop Dunlop Dunlop, clear insert w/3 rests, 5⅞" tire, Germany..**$40.00**
Firestone Champion 6.00-16 Safety Lock Cord, w/NYWF embossed insert **$125.00**
Firestone Hi-type Cushion 36x10 Non-Skid, solid truck tire, embossed metal insert..........................**$125.00**
Firestone 13.0/24.0-13 Formula 1 Super Sports GP, racing tire, mag wheel insert **$150.00**
Fisk, electric tire clock **$250.00**
General Steelex Radial, clear imprinted insert, 6½" truck tire..**$30.00**

Red River Army Depot, Our Best Nothing Less, stamped aluminum insert, $75.00. (Photo courtesy Jeff McVey)

Sava Kranj, green, blue, red or black 5⅝" tire, clear embossed insert, Yugoslavia **$40.00**
Toyo Radial Z-2, red, green or black 5⅜" tire, clear imprinted insert, Japan **$40.00**
United States Tires Are Good Tires, glass w/metal top showing 5 tread types, removable spoked wheel, ca 1915..**$300.00**
Warrior Complete Line of Tyres, blue or green 5½" tire, ceramic insert, China **$50.00**
Yokohama Super Rock Global 37/25-35 Y-S24-7¾", earthmover tire, clear imprinted insert **$50.00**

Tobacco Collectibles

Until lately, the tobacco industry spent staggering sums advertising their products, and scores of retail companies turned out many types of smoking accessories such as pipes, humidors, lighters, and ashtrays. Even though the smoking habit isn't particularly popular nowadays, collecting tobacco-related memorabilia is!

See also Advertising Character Collectibles, Joe Camel; Cigarette Lighters.

Club/Newsletter: *Tobacco Jar*
Society of Tobacco Jar Collectors
Charlotte Tarses, Treasurer
3011 Falstaff Road #307
Baltimore, MD 21209; Dues: $30 per year ($35 outside of U.S.)

Apron, Chesterfield Cigarettes, cotton canvas, Always Buy Chesterfields, shows burning cigarette, EX...........**$25.00**

Ashtray, Carter Hall Tobacco, tin, round w/embossed image of tobacco leaves, 3½" dia, NM.....................**$5.00**

Change tray, Tuxedo Havana Club Cigars, embossed leather, Berdon & Co, 6½" dia, EX+................................**$230.00**

Cigar box, Country Club, shows various sporting activities, EX+ **$85.00**

Cigar cutter, pistol shape w/Bakelite barrel, EX.........**$65.00**

Cigarette carton, Lucky Strike, image of man reading paper & smoking, It's Toasted, EX+..............................**$45.00**

Cigarette dispenser, painted wood w/storage box on 1 end & bird on other, move lever & bird picks up cigarette, EX **$75.00**

Cigarette holder, brass w/leather cover, Amity, 1950s, 3½x2½", EX...**$10.00**

Cigarette papers, Central Union Cut Plug, Price 5¢, shows head in crescent moon, white on red, EX............**$25.00**

Cigarette papers, City Club Crushed Cubes, shows man reading paper, NM **$55.00**

Cigarette papers, Culture Smoking Tobacco, shows tobacco tin on yellow, NM...**$35.00**

Clock, Kools Refresh Hour After Hour, penguins flank circle, glass w/metal frame, round, EX **$280.00**

Dispenser, Workmate Wintergreen Flavored Chewing Tobacco, vertical tube, green & white, NM+........**$75.00**

Display, Bowers New Unconditionally Guaranteed Windproof Lighter 98¢, cardboard stand-up w/6 lighters, EX...**$20.00**

Display, Old Gold Cigarettes, die-cut cardboard, Earl Christy artwork, 36x48", EX, $375.00.

Display box, Stud Choice Tobacco 5¢, cardboard, brown on yellow, complete w/12 cloth pouches, 6x10x4", EX+ .**$215.00**

Display carton, Kool Cigarettes, cardboard, w/marquee, white, light green & black, EX..............**$45.00**

Door plate, Kool Cigarettes/They're So Refreshing, shows open pack, white & green, NM+..........................**$60.00**

Door plate, L&M Cigarettes, Friendly Flavor/...Your Taste Comes Alive, open pack on blue center, 1960s, NM............**$60.00**

Fan, Kool cigarettes, diecut cardboard w/wooden handle, shows Willy w/product, premiums on back, 10x8", VG **$30.00**

Humidor, Prince Albert Tobacco, glass w/tin lid & paper labels, Humi-Seal, VG...**$20.00**

Lunch pail, Country Club, gold on blue, G.................**$68.00**

Lunch pail, Green Turtle, green, EX **$325.00**

Lunch pail, Mayo's Cut Plug, gold on dark blue, EX..**$50.00**

Match holder, Kool Cigarettes, metal, green & white, shows Willy, 8x7x4", VG+...**$30.00**

Matchbook cover, Marlboro, ...20 for 20¢, front strike, NM..**$8.00**

Pocket container, Half & Half/Burley & Bright, cardboard, 1943, EX...**$12.00**

Pocket mirror, Mascot Crushed Cut Tobacco, 2" dia, EX ..**$55.00**

Pocket tin, Chesterfield, vertical, paper label, oval portrait, EX+ **$100.00**

Pocket tin, Forest & Stream, vertical (tall), red w/oval image of duck in flight, EX+..**$100.00**

Pocket tin, Lucky Strike, flat, green, EX....................**$10.00**

Pocket tin, Lucky Strike, vertical, sample, EX+.........**$100.00**

Pocket tin, Lucky Strike, vertical, 4½", EX.................**$85.00**

Pocket tin, Maryland Club Mixture, vertical, flat top, EX+ .**$250.00**

Pocket tin, Maryland Club Mixture, vertical, flip top, EX ...**$315.00**

Pocket tin, Tortoise Shell Smoking Mixture, flat, 3x4", EX ...**$70.00**

Ruler, Philip Morris Cigarettes, thin plastic w/bellboy graphics, 6" scale, 2x6¼", NM..**$22.00**

Sign, cardboard, El Moriso Cigars, black & red lettering on yellow w/gold border, 10¼x13½", EX.................**$40.00**

Sign, cardboard stand-up, Lucky Strike, This Year Give the Best, Santa standing behind lg pack w/carton, 13", NM **$140.00**

Sign, cardboard standee, bellhop calling for Phillip Morris, 44", VG **$170.00**

Sign, cardboard standup, Chesterfield Cigarettes, Buy Your Christmas Gifts Here..., Bing Crosby on carton, 18x13", EX+ **$30.00**

Sign, cardboard standup, Kool Cigarettes, B Sharp!/Smoke... As Your Steady Smoke!, Willie playing trumpet, 13x9", NM **$115.00**

Sign, paper, Avalon Cigarettes, You'd Better Guess/They Cost You Less!, woman exposing shoulder, 1940, 15x10", NM **$25.00**

Sign, paper, Orphan Boy Smoking Tobacco, diecut pouch shape w/donkey label, 19x13", NM **$30.00**

Sign, paper, Wings King Size, Cost Less/Last Longer, shows lg open pack on yellow, 1941, 16x10", NM..........**$35.00**

Sign, tin, Black Cat Cigarettes, They Taste Better, head image of black cat on diecut circle, yellow & green, 51x48", VG...**$550.00**

Sign, tin, Camel Cigarettes, Smoke... lettered diagonally above open pack on circle, 18x12", NM..............**$60.00**

Sign, tin, Chesterfield/Best for You, 2 unopened packs on red next to yellow lettering on blue, white border, 12x30", NM **$85.00**

Sign, tin, Chesterfield/L&M Cigarettes, diecut cigarette pack, Buy...Here, 2-sided, 15x12", VG **$25.00**

Sign, tin, Imperial Club 5 cts Cigars, Smoke the.../The Best for the Money, lettering & open box on black, 10x14", EX+ **$175.00**

Store bin, Sweet Burley Light Tobacco, round canister w/square hinged lid, yellow, NM **$280.00**

Store bin, Sweet Cuba Tobacco, round canister w/square hinged lid, blue & metallic gold, G+ **$50.00**

Thermometer, Camels Sold Here, shows open pack, tin, 13½x6", EX **$40.00**

Thermometer, L&M Cigarettes, Reach for... above hand pulling cigarette from pack, tin, 13x6", G **$35.00**

Thermometer, Winston Tastes Good... Like a Cigarette Should, shows open pack at bottom, tin, 14", VG **$100.00**

Tin, Belfast Cut Plug, green, 4x6", NM **$25.00**

Tin, Dan Patch Cut Plug, black lettering & graphics on red & yellow, slip lid, 4x6", EX **$70.00**

Tin, Gallaher's Rich Dark Honeydew, parlor scene, 4x6", VG+ **$100.00**

Tin, Lucky Strike Cigarettes, flat, green w/Christmas motif, gold trim, holds 50, EX+ **$35.00**

Tin, Lucky Strike Cigarettes, round, green, holds 100, EX ..**$85.00**

Tin, Postmaster Smokers/2 for 5¢, red canister w/image of postmaster & lettering, slip lid, 5", EX+ **$125.00**

Tin, Red Man Chewing Tobacco, 1989, 6x6", EX **$10.00**

Tip card, Lucky Strike Cigarettes, Dorothy Marshall portrait, 5½x4", EX, $65.00.

Tobacco pack, Barking Dog Smoking Mixture, shows bulldog head on yellow, Never Bites, foil-lined, empty, NM **$40.00**

Tobacco pack, Honey-Bear Pipe Mixture, shows 2 bear cubs after beehive in tree on white, foil-lined, empty, NM **$35.00**

Tobacco pouch, Bull Durham, cloth w/paper label, drawstring closure, NM (sealed) **$15.00**

Tobacco pouch, Old North State Tobacco, cloth w/paper label, 1½-oz, full, NM **$10.00**

Tobacco tag, Browns Country, oval, EX **$20.00**

Tobacco tag, Old Reliable, gold-tone tobacco leaf shape, EX **$5.00**

Tobacco tag, 3 Black Crows, black crows on tree branch, yellow, diagonal, EX **$8.00**

Windup toy, tin litho penguin, Occupied Japan, 3½", EXIB (marked Kool) **$95.00**

Toothbrush Holders

Novelty toothbrush holders have been modeled as animals of all types, in human forms, and in the likenesses of many storybook personalities. Today all are very collectible, especially those representing popular Disney characters. Most of these are made of bisque and are decorated over the glaze. Condition of the paint is an important consideration when trying to arrive at an evaluation.

For more information, refer to *Pictorial Guide to Toothbrush Holders* by Marilyn Cooper.

Advisor: Marilyn Cooper (See Directory, Toothbrush Holders)

Annie Oakley, Japan, 5¾", from $100 to **$120.00**

Baby Bunting, Germany, 6¾", from $350 to **$375.00**

Baby Deer, base reads Brush Teeth Daily, Japan, 4", from $90 to **$110.00**

Bellhop w/Flowers, Japan, 5¼", from $65 to **$75.00**

Boy on Elephant, Japan, 6¼", from $85 to **$100.00**

Chef, Japan, 5¼", from $65 to **$75.00**

Children in Auto, Japan, 5", from $70 to **$85.00**

Clown, Japan, terra cotta, 5½", from $70 to **$80.00**

Clown Juggling, Japan, 5", from $85 to **$100.00**

Clown w/Mandolin, Japan, 6", from $80 to **$100.00**

Cow, Japan, 6", from $80 to **$90.00**

Cowboy Next to Cactus, Japan, 5½", from $75 to **$85.00**

Dashshund, Japan, 5¼", from $70 to **$80.00**

Donkey, Japan/Goldcastle, 5¾", from $95 to **$110.00**

Dutch Boy w/Hands on Hips, Japan, 5¼", from $65 to **$75.00**

Elephant w/Trunk Up, Japan, 5½", from $75 to **$85.00**

Genie, Japan, 5¾", from $110 to **$125.00**

Indian Chief, Japan, 4½", from $225 to **$250.00**

Kayo, Japan, 5", from $110 to **$130.00**

Lion, Japan, 6", from $75 to **$85.00**

Mexican Boy, Japan, 5½", from $80 to **$90.00**

Moon Mullins, Japan, 5¼", from $100 to **$115.00**

Old Woman in Shoe, Japan, 4½", from $70 to **$80.00**

Pluto, Japan, 4⅝", from $300 to **$325.00**

Rabbit (Norwood), Germany, 5½", from $80 to **$90.00**

Siesta, Japan, 6", from $85 to **$100.00**

The Baker, Japan/Goldcastle, 5¼", from $70 to **$80.00**

Tom Tom the Piper's Son, Japan, 5¾", from $100 to ...**$120.00**

Uncle Walt, Japan/FAS, from $85 to **$100.00**

Toys

Toy collecting has long been an area of very strong activity, but over the past decade it has literally exploded. Many of the larger auction galleries have cataloged toy auctions, and it isn't uncommon for scarce nineteenth-century toys in good condition go for $5,000.00 to $10,000.00 and up. Toy shows are popular, and there are clubs, newsletters, and magazines that cater only to the needs and wants of toy collectors. Though once buyers ignored toys less than thirty years old, in more recent years, even some toys from the '80s are sought after.

Condition has more bearing on the value of a toy than any other factor. A used toy in good condition with no major flaws will still be worth only about half (in some cases much less) as much as one in mint (like new) condition. Those mint and in their original boxes will be worth considerably more than the same toy without its box.

There are many good toy guides on the market today including: *Modern Toys, American Toys, 1930 to 1980,* by Linda Baker; *Collecting Toys* and *Collecting Toy Trains* by Richard O'Brien; *Schroeder's Collectible Toys, Antique to Modern; Elmer's Price Guide to Toys* by Elmer Duellman; *Toys of the Sixties, A Pictorial Guide,* by Bill Bruegman; *Occupied Japan Toys With Prices* by David C. Gould and Donna Crevar-Donaldson; *Toys, Antique and Collectible, Antique and Collectible Toys, 1870 – 1950, Cartoon Toys and Collectibles* and *Character Toys and Collectibles,* all by David Longest; and *Collector's Guide to Tinker Toys* by Craig Strange. More books are listed in the subcategory narratives that follow. With the exception of O'Brien's (Books Americana) and Bruegman's (Cap't Penny Productions), all the books we've referred to are published by Collector Books.

See also Advertising Character Collectibles; Breyer Horses; Bubble Bath Containers; Character Collectibles; Disney Collectibles; Dolls; Fast-Food Collectibles; Fisher-Price; Halloween; Hartland Plastics Inc.; Model Kits; Paper Dolls; Games; Puzzles; Star Trek; Star Wars; Steiff Animals; Trolls.

Action Figures and Accessories

Back in 1964, Barbie dolls were taking the feminine side of the toy market by storm. Hasbro took a risky step in an attempt to capture the interest of the male segment of the population. Their answer to the Barbie doll craze was GI Joe. Since no self-respecting boy would admit to playing with dolls, Hasbro called their boy dolls 'action figures,' and to the surprise of many, they were phenomenally successful. Today action figures generate just as much enthusiasm among toy collectors as they ever did among little boys.

Action figures are simply dolls with poseable bodies. Some — the original GI Joes, for instance, were 12" tall, while others were 6" to 9"in height. In recent years, the 3¾" figure has been favored. GI Joe was introduced in the 3¾" size in the '80s and proved to be unprecedented in action figure sales. (See also GI Joe.)

In addition to the figures themselves, each company added a full line of accessories such as clothing, vehicles, play sets, weapons, etc. — all are avidly collected. Be aware of condition! Original packaging is extremely important. In fact, when it comes to the recent issues, loose, played-with examples are seldom worth more than a few dollars.

For more information, refer to *Collectible Action Figures* by Paris and Susan Manos, *Mego Toys* by Wallace M. Crouch, and *Collector's Guide to Dolls in Uniform* by Joseph Bourgeois. (All are published by Collector Books.)

Club: The Mego Adventurers Club
Old Forest Press, Inc.
PMB 195, 223 Wall St.
Huntington, NY 11743
Membership: $18.95 per year ($30 foreign); Includes 6 issues of *Mego Head,* the official club newsletter

A-Team, figure, Cobra, Python, Rattler or Viper, Galoob, 6½", MOC, ea..**$22.00**

Action Jackson, accessory, baseball, football, hockey or karate outfit, Mego, MIB, from $10 to..................**$12.00**

Action Jackson, accessory, Fire Rescue Pack, Mego, MIB..**$15.00**

Action Jackson, figure, Action Jackson, light or dark blue jumpsuit, Mego, 8", NMIB, ea................................**$35.00**

Adventures of Indiana Jones in Raiders of the Lost Ark, accessory, Map Room Adventure Set, MIB...........**$70.00**

Adventures of Indiana Jones in Raiders of the Lost Ark, figure, Indiana Jones, Kenner, 12", MIB..................**$350.00**

Adventures of Indiana Jones in Raiders of the Lost Ark, horse, Arabian, Kenner, MOC..............................**$145.00**

Aliens, accessory, Evac Fighter or Power Loader, Kenner, MIB, ea..**$30.00**

Aliens, figures, Arachnid, King, Queen or Swarm, Kenner, MOC, ea..**$25.00**

Batman (Animated Series), accessory, Triple Attack Jet, Kenner, MOC...**$20.00**

Batman (Animated Series), figure, Bane, Bruce Wayne or Ras A Gual, Kenner, MOC, ea.....................................**$20.00**

Batman (Animated Series), figure, Clayface, Killer Kroc, Poison Ivy or Scarecrow, Kenner, MOC, ea.........**$30.00**

Batman (Animated Series), figure, Manbat, Kenner, MOC.**$25.00**

Batman (Animated Series) accessory, Joker Mobile, Kenner, MOC..**$30.00**

Battlestar Galactica, accessory, Colonial Scarab, Mattel, MIB..**$60.00**

Battlestar Galactica, figure, Commander Adama or Cylon Centurian, Mattel, 3¾", MOC, ea.........................**$25.00**

Battlestar Galactica, figure, Imperious Leader or Lieutenant Starbuck, Mattel, 3¾", MOC................................**$30.00**

Beetlejuice, figure, Shishkebab Beetlejuice, Showtime Beetlejuice or Spinhead Beetlejuice, Kenner, 1989, MOC, ea **$15.00**

Best of the West, accessory, Johnny West Adventure Jeep, Marx, VG **$40.00**

Best of the West, figure, Jaimie West, complete, Marx, MIB..**$85.00**

Best of the West, figure, Jay West, complete, Marx, NM..**$55.00**

Best of the West, figure, Princess Wildflower, complete, Marx, NMIB......................**$150.00**

Best of the West, figure & horse set, Johnny West & Thunderbolt, Marx, VG (VG box) **$100.00**

Big Jim, accessory, Motorized Dune Devil, Mattel, G (G box)..**$35.00**

Big Jim, figure, Dr Steel, Torpedo Fist, Warpath or Whip, complete, Mattel, EX, ea, from $25 to..................**$30.00**

Bonanza, figure, Ben, Hoss, Little Joe or Outlaw, American Character, 8", MIB, ea, from $200 to **$250.00**

Captain Action, accessory, Anti-Gravitational Power Pack, Ideal, complete, MIB...........................**$200.00**

Captain Action, accessory, Inter-Galactic Jet Mortar, Ideal, complete, MIB.............................**$200.00**

Captain Action, figure, Aqualad, complete, Ideal, 12", EX .**$265.00**

Captain Action, figure, Batman, complete, Ideal, 12", EX...**$200.00**

Captain Action, Superman, 1967, Ideal, MIB, $950.00.
(Photo courtesy June Moon)

Captain Power, figure, any character, Mattel, MOC, ea, from $15 to.......................................**$20.00**

Chuck Norris, figure, Kung-Fu, Battle Gear, Undercover Agent or Ninja Warrior, Kenner, 6", MOC, ea **$15.00**

Cops, figure, any character, Hasbro, 1988, MOC, ea ..**$15.00**

Dark Knight, figure, Bruce Wayne, Iron Winch Batman, Shadow-Wing Batman or Tec-Shield Batman, Kenner, MOC, ea...**$20.00**

DC Comics Super Heroes, figure, Aquaman, Green Lantern, Hawkman or Two Face, Toy Biz, 3¾", MOC, ea.**$25.00**

DC Comics Super Heroes, figure, Batman, Flash, Joker, Penguin, Riddler or Robin, Toy Biz, 3¾", MOC, ea **$20.00**

Dick Tracy, figure, any character except Flattop, Playmates, MOC, ea..**$10.00**

Dick Tracy, figure, Flattop, Playmates, MOC...............**$20.00**

Dukes of Hazzard, figure, Bo, Boss Hogg, Daisy or Luke, Mego, 8", MOC, ea **$35.00**

Dukes of Hazzard, figure, Coy, Mego, 8", MOC **$40.00**

Dukes of Hazzard, figure, Uncle Jesse, Mego, 3¾", MOC **$35.00**

Emergency, figure, John or Roy, 8", MOC, ea.............**$70.00**

Flash Gordon, figure sets, any, MIB, ea......................**$40.00**

Ghostbusters, figure, Egon Spengler, Janine or Winston Zeddmore, complete, Kenner, NM, ea **$40.00**

Happy Days, figure, any character, Mego, 8", MOC, ea, from $50 to...**$60.00**

How the West Was Won, figure, Lone Wolf or Zeb Macahan, Mattel, 9", MIB, ea, from $40 to **$50.00**

Incredible Hulk, figures, Leader, Rampaging Hulk, Savage Hulk or She-Hulk, Toy Biz, MOC, ea...................**$15.00**

James Bond 007, figure, James Bond, shorts & T-shirt w/scuba gear, Gilbert, 12", NMIB......................**$800.00**

Justice League of America, figure, Aquaman, Flash, Robin or Wonder Woman, Ideal, 3", EX, ea, from $65 to ...**$75.00**

Karate Kid, figure, Sato, Remco, MOC........................**$20.00**

Land of the Lost, accessory, Boulder Bobber Catapult Weapon, Tiger, MOC **$10.00**

Land of the Lost, figure, Annie Porter, Kevin Porter, Tom Porter, Tasha or Shung, MOC, ea **$10.00**

Land of the Lost, figure, Talking Annie, Talking Kevin or Talking Stink, MOC, ea..**$15.00**

Love Boat, figure, any character, Mego, 3½", MOC....**$25.00**

Man From UNCLE, accessory, Uncle Husky Car, Gilbert, MOC..**$225.00**

Man From UNCLE, figure, Illya Kuryakin, Gilbert, 12", VG (VG box) **$150.00**

Marvel Super Heroes, figure, Batman, complete, Mego, NM..**$75.00**

Marvel Super Heroes, figure, Catwoman, complete, Mego, EX **$125.00**

Marvel Super Heroes, figure, Green Arrow, complete, Mego, EX...**$95.00**

Marvel Super Heroes, figure, Riddler, complete, Mego, MOC (unpunched) **$225.00**

Marvel Super Heroes, figure, Spider-Man, complete, Mego, NMIB...**$50.00**

Marvel Super Heroes, figure, Toy Biz characters, any accept Invisible Woman, MOC, ea **$20.00**

Marvel Super Heroes Secret Wars, figure, Daredevil & His Secret Shield, Mattel, 3¾", MOC........................**$40.00**

Marvel Super Heroes Secret Wars, figure, Dr Doom, Kang or Magneto, Mattel, MOC, ea......................................**$15.00**

Marvel Super Heroes Secret Wars, figure, Spider-Man, Mattel, VG (VG card)..**$45.00**

Masters of the Universe, accessory, Jet Sled, Mattel, MOC..**$20.00**

Masters of the Universe, accessory, Slit Stalker, Mattel, MOC..**$10.00**

Masters of the Universe, figure, Buzz-Off, Fisto, Jitsu, Orko or Skeletor, Mattel, MOC, ea **$30.00**

Masters of the Universe, figure, Clamp Champ, Dragstor, King Hiss, Mousquitor, Rokkon or Rio Blast, MOC, ea **$15.00**

Masters of the Universe, figure, King Randor, Mattel, MOC..**$25.00**

Micronauts, figure, Acroyear, Mego, 3¾", MOC **$50.00**

Micronauts, figure, Repto, Mego, 3¾", MOC.............**$120.00**

Mortal Kombat, accessory, Dragon Wing w/Shang Tsung figure, Hasbro, 1994, MIP..................................**$30.00**

Mortal Kombat, accessory, Kombat Cycle w/Kano figure, Hasbro, 1994, MIP **$15.00**

Mortal Kombat, figure set, Goro Vs Johnny Cage, w/Battle Arena, 4", Hasbro, 1994, MIP....................**$20.00**

Official Scout High Adventure, accessory, Balloon Race or Devil's Canyon, Kenner, MIB......................**$35.00**

Official Scout High Adventure, figure, Craig Cub or Steve Scout, Kenner, NRFB, ea **$30.00**

Official World's Greatest Super Heroes, accessory, Amazing Spider Car, Mego, MIB....................**$50.00**

Official World's Greatest Super Heroes, figure, Batman, Bend 'n Flex, Mego, 5", NMOC **$50.00**

Official World's Greatest Super Heroes, figure, Batman, Mego, 12", MIB.....................**$75.00**

Official World's Greatest Super Heroes, figure, Captain America, Mego, 8", EX.....................**$50.00**

Official World's Greatest Super Heroes, figure, Green Goblin, Mego, 8", EX **$125.00**

Official World's Greatest Super Heroes, figure, Tarzan, Mego, 8", EX.....................**$45.00**

Official World's Greatest Super-Gals, figure, Catwoman, Mego, 8", EX **$95.00**

Official World's Greatest Super-Gals, figure, Invisible Girl, Mego, 8", EX **$35.00**

Our Gang, figure, Buckwheat, Mego, MOC (unpunched)..**$45.00**

Planet of the Apes, figure, Dr Zaius or Zira, bendable, Mego, 8", EX, ea.....................**$65.00**

Planet of the Apes, figure, General Urus, bendable, Mego, 8", NMOC **$200.00**

Princess of Power, accessory, Crystal Castle, Mattel, complete, MIB.....................**$120.00**

Princess of Power, figure, Angella or Bow, Mattel, MOC, ea.....................**$20.00**

Princess of Power, horse, Arrow, Mattel, MIB.............**$25.00**

Princess of Power, outfit, several different, Mattel, MOC, ea **$18.00**

Rambo, figure, Gripper, Sgt Havok or Turbo, Coleco, MOC, ea **$20.00**

Real Ghostbusters, accessory, Ghost Grab, Kenner, MOC ..**$15.00**

Real Ghostbusters, figure, any character except Stay Puft Man or Slimmer, Kenner, MOC, ea **$15.00**

Real Ghostbusters, figure, Slimer, Kenner, MOC.........**$25.00**

Real Ghostbusters, figure, Stay Puft Man, Kenner, MOC..**$30.00**

Robin Hood Prince of Thieves, figure, Friar Tuck, Kenner, MOC.....................**$30.00**

Six Million Dollar Man, accessory, Bionic Transport & Repair Station, Kenner, NMIB.....................**$60.00**

Six Million Dollar Man, accessory, Porta Communicator, Kenner, MIB.....................**$50.00**

Six Million Dollar Man, figure, Fembot, Kenner, 12", MIB.....................**$125.00**

Spawn, accessory, Spawn Alley, Todd Toys, MIB.......**$40.00**

Spawn, figure, Angela, Todd Toys, 13", MIB...............**$40.00**

Starsky & Hutch, figure, any character, Mego, 8", MOC, ea, from $40 to.....................**$50.00**

Super Powers, accessory, Justice Jogger, Kenner, MIB ...**$25.00**

Super Powers, accessory, Supermobile, Kenner, MIB.**$25.00**

Super Powers, figure, Batman, Kenner, MOC (unpunched) **$50.00**

Super Powers, figure, Brainiac, w/ID card & comic book, Kenner, NM **$30.00**

Super Powers, figure, Flash, Kenner, MOC **$15.00**

Super Powers, figure, Joker, w/ID card & comic book, Kenner, NM **$35.00**

Super Powers, figure, Lex Luther, w/ID card & comic book, Kenner, NM **$15.00**

SWAT, figure, Decon, Hondo or Luca, LJN, 8", MOC, ea..**$25.00**

Teenage Mutant Ninja Turtles, figure, any character, Playmates, MOC, ea.....................**$15.00**

Thundercats, accessory, Luna-Lasher or Mutant Skycutter, LJN, MIB, ea.....................**$35.00**

Thundercats, figure, any character, LJN, MOC, ea, from $35 to.....................**$45.00**

Universal Monsters, figure, Creature From the Black Lagoon, glow-in-the-dark, Remco, 3¾", MOC **$45.00**

Welcome Back Kotter, figure, any character, Mattel, 9", MOC, ea, from $45 to.....................**$50.00**

World Championship Wrestling, figure, Jimmy Hart, red suit & pants, San Francisco Toymakers, MOC.............**$20.00**

World Championship Wrestling, figure set, Nasty Boys, orange outfits, San Francisco Toymakers, MOC...**$25.00**

World Wrestling Federation, figure, Adam Bomb, Hasbro, MOC (green) **$28.00**

World Wrestling Federation, figure, Bart or Billy Gunn, Hasbro, MOC (green), ea.....................**$35.00**

World Wrestling Federation, figure, Hulk Hogan, Hasbro, 4", NM **$25.00**

World Wrestling Federation, figure, Ludwig Borga, Hasbro (green) **$45.00**

X-Force, figure, any except Deadpool, Domino or the Blob, MOC, ea.....................**$15.00**

X-Force, figure, Deadpool, Domino or the Blob, MOC, ea **$20.00**

X-Men (Animated Series), figure, any character, Toy Biz, MOC, ea.....................**$15.00**

X-Men (Flashback Series), figure, any character, Toy Biz, MOC, ea.....................**$15.00**

X-Men (Mutant Armor Series), figure, any character, Toy Biz, MOC, ea, from $15 to.....................**$20.00**

Battery-Operated

It is estimated that approximately 95% of the battery-operated toys that were so popular from the '40s through the '60s came from Japan. The remaining 5% were made in the United States by other companies. To market these toys in America, many distributorships were organized. Some of the largest were Cragstan, Linemar, and Rosko. But even American toy makers such as Marx, Ideal, Hubley, and Daisy sold them under their own names, so the trademarks you'll find on Japanese battery-operated toys are not necessarily that of the manufacturer, and it's sometimes just about impossible to determine the specific company that actually did make them. After peaking in the '60s, the Japanese toy industry began a decline, bowing out to competition from the cheaper diecast and plastic toy makers.

Remember that it is rare to find one of these complex toys that has survived in good, collectible condition. Batteries caused corrosion, lubricants dried out, cycles were interrupted and mechanisms ruined, rubber hoses and bellows aged and cracked, so the mortality rate was extremely high. A toy rated good, that is showing signs of wear but well taken care of, is generally worth about half as much as the same toy in mint (like new) condition. Besides condition, battery-operated toys are rated on scarcity, desirability, and the number of 'actions' they preform. A 'major' toy is one that has three or more actions, while one that has only one or two is considered 'minor.' The latter, of course, are worth much less.

In addition to the books we referenced in the beginning narrative to the toy category, you'll find more information in *Collecting Battery Toys* by Don Hultzman (Books Americana).

Alps, Balloon Blowing Monkey, 1950s, 11", MIB......**$225.00**
Alps, Bunny the Magician, 1950s, 14½", MIB............**$450.00**
Alps, Busy Housekeeper Bear, 1950s, 8½", MIB.......**$325.00**
Alps, Cappy the Happy Baggage Porter, 1960s, 12", EX..**$100.00**
Alps, Charlie the Drumming Clown, 1960s, 9½", MIB......**$325.00**
Alps, Chimpy the Jolly Drummer, 1950s, 9", EX **$75.00**
Alps, Drinking Monkey, 1950s, 10", MIB....................**$175.00**
Alps, Fido the Xylophone Player, 1950s, 9", MIB **$475.00**
Alps, Pat the Dog, 1950s, MIB...................................**$175.00**
Bandai, Champion Boat 2-J, 12", NM.........................**$250.00**
Bandai, Cycling Daddy, 1960s, 10", EX......................**$225.00**
Bandai, Excalibur Car, 1960s, 10", EX.......................**$165.00**
Bandai, Old-Fashioned Hot Rod, 1960s, 6½", NM....**$250.00**
CK, Clucking Clara, MIB **$225.00**
Cragstan, Comic Choo-Choo, 1960s, 10", EX..............**$85.00**
Cragstan, Electronic Periscope Firing Range, 1950s, 11", EX **$200.00**
DSK, Strange Explorer, 8", EXIB..............................**$250.00**
HTC, Chemical Fire Engine, 1950s, 10", EX **$200.00**
Ichida, Kissing Couple, 1950s, 10", EXIB..................**$250.00**
K, Fruit Juice Counter, 1960s, 8", NM **$250.00**
K, Mighty Mike the Barbell Lifter Bear, 1950s, 10½", EX...**$300.00**

K Co, Root Beer Counter, three actions, lithographed tin and plastic, 1960s, 8", EX, $200.00.
(Photo courtesy Don Hultzman)

KO, Airmail Helicopter, 10", EXIB.............................**$225.00**
Linemar, Ball Playing Dog, 1950s, 9", M....................**$175.00**
Linemar, Dick Tracy Police Car, 1949, remote control, 8", EXIB **$475.00**
Linemar, Walking Bambi, 1950s, 9", scarce, NM **$400.00**
Marusan, Smoking Elephant, 1950s, 9", EX **$265.00**
MT, Circus Fire Engine, 1960s, 11", EX.....................**$265.00**
MT, Clown & Lion, 1960s, 12", EX............................**$475.00**
MT, Drumming Bear, EX..**$275.00**
MT, Highway Patrol Helicopter, 1960s, 9½", MIB.....**$150.00**
MT, Rambling Ladybug, 1960s, 8", EX **$125.00**
Remco, Firebird Dashmobile, 1960s, 13", EX............**$225.00**
Rosko, Lite-O-Wheel Go Kart, NM............................**$200.00**
Rosko, Lite-O-Wheel Lincoln, 1950s, 10½", EX........**$300.00**
SAN, Shooting Bear, remote control, 10", EX............**$325.00**
SAN, Smoking Bunny, 1950s, 10½", EX.....................**$200.00**
Schuco, Alfa Romeo Magico #2010, remote control, 9½", NMIB...**$850.00**
Taiyo, Big Wheel Ice Cream Truck, 1970s, 10", EX..**$125.00**
Taiyo, M-4 Combat Tank, 11½", EX..........................**$165.00**
TN, Bingo the Clown, 1950s, 13", rare, NMIB..........**$475.00**
TN, Blushing Frankenstein, 12½", NM (EX box) **$385.00**
TN, Charley Weaver Bartender, 1962, 12", EX..........**$125.00**
TN, Drinking Licking Cat, 1950s, 10", MIB **$325.00**
TN, Firefly Bug, 1950s, 9", MIB **$150.00**
TN, John's Farm Truck, 1950s, 9", MIB....................**$325.00**
Tomiyama, Cindy the Meowing Cat, 1950s, 12", EX.**$100.00**
Tomiyama, Donny the Smiling Bulldog, 1961, 8½", EX..**$150.00**
TPS, Dune Buggy, 1960s, 11", EX **$100.00**
Y, Astro Dog (Snoopy look-alike), 1960s, 11", EX....**$200.00**
Y, Balloon Bunny, remote control, rare, MIB............**$375.00**
Y, Begging Puppy, 1960s, 9", EX...............................**$100.00**
Y, Billy the Kid Sheriff, 1950s, 10½", EX **$350.00**
Y, Blushing Gunfighter, 1960s, 11", EX (G box) **$250.00**
Y, Blushing Willie, 1960s, NMIB..............................**$150.00**
Y, Feeding Baby Bear, EX..**$175.00**
Yanoman, Tumbles the Bear, 1960, 8½", MIB...........**$165.00**

Guns

One of the bestselling kinds of toys ever made, toy guns were first patented in the late 1850s. Until WWII most were made of cast iron, though other materials were used on a lesser scale. After the war, cast iron became cost prohibitive, and steel and diecast zinc were used. By 1950 most were made of either diecast material or plastic. Hundreds of names can be found embossed on these little guns, a custom which continues to the present time. Because of their tremendous popularity and durability, today's collectors can find a diversity of models and styles, and prices are still fairly affordable.

See also Cowboy Character Collectibles.

Newsletter: *Toy Gun Collectors of America*
Jim Buskirk, Editor and Publisher
3009 Oleander Ave., San Marcos, CA 92069; 760-559-1054.
Published quarterly, covers both toy and BB guns. Dues: $17 per year

Arliss X-100 Space Gun, plastic, complete w/darts & powder, 1950, 4", EX (EX card)................$50.00

Buddy L M-99 Paper Cracker Rifle, plastic & aluminum w/purple swirl plastic stock, 1947-49, EX.............$75.00

Daisy Targeteer, black-painted pressed steel, 1955, 10", NMIB................$125.00

Elvin Space Universe Sparking Ray Gun, litho tin, 1960s, 4", NM................$35.00

Gordy Int Batman & Superman Pop-Pop Pistol, clear blue plastic, shoots ping-pong balls, 1978, 7", MIP......$50.00

Haji Atomic Products Ray Gun, litho tin w/plastic muzzle, 1969, 9", NM................$75.00

Halco Popeye Gun & Holster Set, 2 5" diecast pistols & double holster, 1961, NM (NM diecut card).............$150.00

Hubley Atomic Disintegrator Cap Pistol No 270, diecast w/zinc finish, red plastic grips, 1954, 8", NM (VG box)................$400.00

Hubley Davy Crockett Frontierland Flintlock Jr, w/fringed holster & strap, 1950s, EX................$75.00

Hubley Ric-O-Shay .45 Cap Pistol, diecast w/nickel-plated finish, black plastic grips, 13", EX................$150.00

Hubley Rifleman Flip Special, diecast w/nickel-plated finish, brown plastic stock, 1959, 32½", EX................$225.00

Hubley Scout Rifle No 202, diecast w/nickel-plated finish, black-painted barrel, brown plastic stocks, 36", EX................$125.00

Hubley Secret Agent Rifle Cap Gun, diecast, metal & plastic, 1960, EX................$100.00

Hubley Western Cap Pistol, diecast w/nickel-plated finish, purple swirl plastic longhorn grips, 1955, 9", M ..$85.00

Ja-Ru Flash Gordon Space Set, w/4½" plastic gun, laser radio & Flight Plan booklet, 1981, MOC................$30.00

Kenton Lawmaker Cap Pistol, cast iron w/silver-painted finish, white plastic grips, 1941, EX................$150.00

Kilgore Frontier Six-Shooter Cap Pistol, diecast w/nickel-plated finish, black plastic stag grips, 1960, 8½", MOC $135.00

Kilgore Wyatt Earp Cap Pistol, diecast w/nickel-plated finish, white plastic horse head grips, 1959, 9", VG $150.00

Larami Dick Tracy Automatic Repeater Water Gun, red tommy-gun shape, 1971, NMIP................$40.00

Leslie-Henry Gene Autry Cap Pistol, diecast w/nickel-plated finish, white plastic horse head grips, 1950s, 9", EX $175.00

Leslie-Henry Texas Cap Pistol, diecast w/nickel-plated finish, white plastic horse head grips, 9", EX $100.00

Leslie-Henry Texas Gold Cap Pistol, diecast w/gold finish, black plastic horse head grips, 1950s, 9", NM....$135.00

Lone Star Cowpoke Jr Cap Pistol, diecast w/silver finish, black-painted grips, 1960, 8", NM................$65.00

Lone Star Peacemaker 100 Shot Repeater Cap Gun, diecast w/silver finish, brown plastic grips, 1960s, 7", MIB $65.00

Maco 6-in-1 Invader Combination Gun, plastic tommy style, 1955, 28½", rare, NMIB................$200.00

Marx Blue & Gray Shell Shooting Civil War Cavalry Pistol, blue plastic w/brown grips, 1960-61, 10", VG......$50.00

Marx Lone Ranger Flashlight Pistol, battery-operated, 1944, NMIB................$175.00

Marx Siren Sparkling Celebration Pistol, red-painted pressed steel, friction, 1940s, 7", G $200.00

Marx Stag Special Clicker Gun, white plastic w/scroll design, 1950s, 7", NM................$50.00

Marx Thunderguns Rifle, Pistol & Holster Set, blue vinyl holster, 1960, 12½" pistol & 36" rifle, NMIB............$350.00

Marx Tom Corbett Space Cadet Clicker Gun, litho tin, 1952, 10", EX................$200.00

Marx Wanted Dead or Alive Mares Laig Cap Pistol, plastic w/diecast works, brown plastic stock, 1959, 17", EX.$175.00

Mattel Agent Zero Fanner 50 Cap Pistol, diecast w/black-painted finish, plastic woodgrain grips, 1967, 11", EX................$135.00

Mattel Agent Zero-W Rapid Fire Special Rifle, brown & black plastic, 1965, 26", M................$125.00

Mattel Colt Six-Shooter Shootin' Shell Rifle, plastic w/diecast works, 1960, 31", MIB................$250.00

Mattel Rango Fanner-50 Double Holster Set, 2 diecast guns w/silver finish, black vinyl holster, 1975, 11", MIB.$250.00

Mattel Tommy-Burst Detective Set, diecast & plastic, complete, 1961, EXIB................$225.00

Mercury Toy Mfg Planet Clicker Bubble Gun, yellow plastic w/red trim, 1950s, 8½", NM (VG box)................$100.00

Multiple/Glidrose James Bond 007 Sharpshooter Set, w/plastic pistol, ammo & villain targets, 1966, EX (EX card)................$225.00

Nasta Phantom Water Pistol w/Holster, blue plastic gun & black plastic holster, 1975, MOC................$50.00

Nichols Pasadena Stallion .38 Cap Pistol, diecast w/nickel-plated finish, black plastic grips, 1951, 9½", EX..........$100.00

Nichols Stallion .38 Six-Shooter Cap Pistol, 1955, diecast with nickel-plated finish, white plastic grips, 9½", MIB, $150.00. (Photo courtesy John Turney)

Norton-Horner Buck Rogers Sonic Ray Gun, plastic, battery-operated, 1950, 7", NMIB................$150.00

Park Plastics Sky Lab Manned Spacecraft w/Launcher, blue plastic, fires 3" saucers, 1970s, 5½", MIB.............$50.00

Randall Space Pilot Super-Sonic Gun, 1953, 9", EX..$165.00

Ray Line I Spy Gun & Holster Set, plastic, w/silencer & shoulder holster, MOC................$125.00

Redondo Galaxia Space Gun, diecast w/red plastic grips & muzzle, 1980, 4", MOC................$20.00

Redondo High Chapparal, diecast w/silver finish, brown eagle grips, 1960s, 8½", NM................................**$50.00**
Schmidt Hopalong Cassidy Cap Pistol, diecast w/gold finish, black plastic grips w/Hoppy bust, 1950, 9", EX...**$350.00**
Stevens Bang-O Cap Pistol, cast iron w/nickel-plated finish, white plastic horse head grips w/green jewels, 1940, 8", EX..**$85.00**
Topper Sixfinger, plastic finger shape, fires missiles, complete, 1965, 3½", MOC.....................................**$50.00**
Wham-O Air Blaster, black plastic, 1960, 11", NM......**$85.00**
Wyandotte Red Ranger Dummy Cap Pistol, diecast w/nickel-plated finish, white horse head & horseshoe grips, 1950s, 9", M...**$135.00**

Ramp Walkers

Though ramp-walking figures were made as early as the 1870s, ours date from about 1935 on. They were made in Czechoslovakia from the '20s through the '40s and in this country during the '50s and '60s by Marx, who made theirs of plastic. John Wilson of Watsontown, Pennsylvania, sold his worldwide. They were known as 'Wilson Walkies' and stood about 4½" high. But the majority has been imported from Hong Kong.

Advisor: Randy Welch (See Directory, Toys)

Ankylosaurus w/Clown, Marx.......................................**$40.00**
Baseball Player w/Bat & Ball, plastic.........................**$40.00**
Bear, plastic..**$20.00**
Big Bad Wolf & Three Little Pigs, Disney, Marx.......**$150.00**
Bison w/Native, Marx..**$40.00**
Black Mammy, Wilson..**$40.00**
Captain Flint, Long John Silver's, 1989......................**$15.00**
Chilly Willy, penguin on sled pulled by parent, Walter-Lantz/Marx...**$25.00**
Chinese Men w/Duck in Basket, plastic.....................**$30.00**
Circus Horse, plastic..**$20.00**
Cowboy on Horse, plastic w/metal legs, sm...............**$30.00**
Dachshund, plastic...**$20.00**
Donald Duck, Wilson...**$175.00**
Donald Duck & Goofy Riding Go-Cart, Disney/Marx....**$40.00**
Dutch Boy & Girl, plastic..**$40.00**
Elephant, plastic w/metal legs, sm..............................**$30.00**
Eskimo, Wilson..**$100.00**
Firemen, plastic...**$35.00**
Frontiersman w/Dog, plastic..**$95.00**
Goofy Riding Hippo, Disney/Marx..............................**$45.00**
Indian Chief, Wilson...**$70.00**
Jolly Ollie Orange, Funny Face Kool-Aid....................**$60.00**
Little King & Guards, King Features/Marx...................**$70.00**
Mamma Duck w/3 Ducklings, plastic..........................**$35.00**
Mickey & Pluto Hunting, Disney/Marx........................**$40.00**
Milking Cow, plastic, lg...**$40.00**
Monkey, Czechoslovakian..**$35.00**
Nurse, Wilson...**$30.00**
Olive Oyl, Wilson..**$175.00**

Pebbles on Dino, Hanna-Barbera/Marx.......................**$75.00**
Pig, Czechoslovakian..**$30.00**
Pluto, plastic w/metal legs, Disney/Marx, sm.............**$35.00**
Popeye, Wilson..**$200.00**
Popeye & Wimpy, Marx, MIB..**$85.00**
Rabbit, Wilson...**$75.00**
Reindeer, plastic...**$45.00**
Sailor, Wilson..**$30.00**
Santa, Wilson...**$90.00**
Sheriff Facing Outlaw, plastic......................................**$65.00**
Spark Plug, Marx...**$200.00**
Sydney or Sylvia Dinosaur, Long John Silver's, 1989, ea...**$15.00**
Tin Man Robot Pushing Cart, plastic...........................**$150.00**
Triceratops w/Native, Marx...**$40.00**
Wimpy, Wilson...**$175.00**
Wiz Walker Milking Cow, plastic, Charmore, lg..........**$40.00**

Wilson Walkers: Penguin $25.00; Elephant, $30.00; Pig, $30.00. (Photo courtesy Randy and Adriene Welch)

Rings

Toy rings are a fairly new interest in the collecting world. Earlier radio and TV mail-order premiums have been popular for some time but have increased in value considerably over the past few years. Now there is a growing interest in other types of rings as well — those from gumball machines, World's Fairs souvenirs, movie and TV show promotions, and any depicting celebrities. They may be metal or plastic; most have adjustable shanks. New rings are already being sought out as future collectibles.

Note: All rings listed here are considered to be in fine to very fine condition. Wear, damage, and missing parts will devaluate them considerably.

Advisors: Bruce and Jan Thalberg (See Directory, Toys)

Agent 007, seal, 1960s, from $35 to.............................**$50.00**
Bazooka Joe, initial, 1950s..**$250.00**
Beatles, plastic, w/photo inserts, 1964, set of 4, from $50 to.**$60.00**
Buck Rogers, Ring of Saturn, 1940s, from $450 to...**$475.00**
Buck Rogers, Saturn, EX+..**$650.00**
Buffalo Bill, 1950s, VG..**$45.00**
Buster Brown Club, Buster & Tige embossed on lg oval, 1940s, from $50 to..**$75.00**

Davy Crockett, profile, green or red enamel on brass, 1950s, from $75 to..**$100.00**

Dick Tracy, hat, NM **$265.00**

Dick Tracy, profile in circle, stars on sides, gold-tone, 1930s, from $200 to..**$250.00**

G-Men, adjustable w/closed sides, enamel around G-Men on ½" face, red, blue or black versions, from $125 to **$175.00**

Gene Autry, face, copper- or silver-tone, 1950s, from $100 to..**$150.00**

Gerber Baby Food, 1940s **$125.00**

Green Hornet, flicker, plastic, 1960s, 12 in set, ea from $15 to **$20.00**

Green Hornet, seal, General Mills, 1947, EX+..........**$950.00**

Have Gun Will Travel, white or black top, 1960s, from $35 to **$50.00**

Hopalong Cassidy, face, NM, from $50 to **$75.00**

Hopalong Cassidy, photo, EX+............................**$25.00**

Jack Armstrong, crocodile, 1940s **$900.00**

Jack Armstrong Siren Whistle, Egyptian design, gold-tone, 1940s, from $125 to **$150.00**

Jr G-Men, VG **$75.00**

Laugh-In Slogans, various, 1960s, ea from $25 to.......**$40.00**

Lone Ranger, filmstrip, NM **$65.00**

Lone Ranger, Flashlight ring, 1947, complete with instructions, NM (EX mailer), $200.00.

Lone Ranger, weather, EX+..**$125.00**

Man From UNCLE, flicker, silver-tone plastic w/black & white pictures, 1960s, 4 in set, ea from $50 to...............**$75.00**

Mickey Mouse Club, embossed face, plastic, 1960s, from $45 to **$75.00**

Movie Stars, black & white photos under glass, 1940s, ea from $20 to..**$35.00**

Orphan Annie, signet, 2-initial, EX+ **$150.00**

Poll Parrot/Howdy Doody, flicker, 1950s **$140.00**

Quaker, jingle bell, 1950s...**$30.00**

Roy Rogers, branding iron, 1950s, from $225 to.......**$275.00**

Roy Rogers, microscope, EX....................................**$115.00**

Roy Rogers, saddle, silver-tone, 1950s, from $250 to..**$400.00**

Shadow, secret agent, unused, MIB.........................**$125.00**

Sky King, Navajo Treasure, VG **$75.00**

Space Patrol, Hydrogen Ray Gun, M **$300.00**

Superman, airplane, Kellogg's Pep, EX+ **$250.00**

Superman, logo in center, Post Toasties, 1976, EX/NM, from $25 to **$35.00**

Tales of Texas Rangers, 1950s **$40.00**

Terry & the Pirates, Gold Ore Detector, EX+ **$115.00**

Tom Corbett, dress uniform, Kellogg's, EX..................**$20.00**

Tom Mix, magnet, EX...**$60.00**

Tom Mix, siren, NM...**$125.00**

Tom Mix, whistle, NM...**$130.00**

Zorro, logo, lg Z, 1960s..**$75.00**

Robots and Space Toys

Japanese toy manufacturers introduced their robots and space toys as early as 1948. Some of the best examples were made in the '50s, during the golden age of battery-operated toys. They became more and more complex, and today some of these in excellent condition may bring well over $1,000.00. By the '60s, more and more plastic was used in their production, and the toys became inferior.

Apollo II American Eagle Lunar Module, battery-op, litho tin, several actions, DSK, 1950s, 10", EX...................**$300.00**

Apollo Saturn Two-Stage Moon Rocket, battery-op, litho tin, several actions, TN, 1960s, 24", EX **$225.00**

Apollo Z Moon Traveler, battery-op, litho tin, several actions, TN, 1960s, 15", rare, EX **$300.00**

Astrobase, battery-op, tin & plastic, several actions, complete, Ideal, 1960s, 11", EX..**$365.00**

Atom Rocket-15 Interplanetary Spaceship, battery-op, litho tin, several actions, Y, 1960s, 13½", EX **$225.00**

Atomic Rocket X-1800, battery-op, litho tin, several actions, MT, 1960s, 9", EX..**$300.00**

Captain Robo Space Transporter, battery-op, plastic, Y, 1970s, 13½", EX..**$150.00**

Chief Robot Man, battery-op, litho tin, several actions, KO, 1950s, 12", rare, NM, minimum value **$950.00**

Cragstan Satellite, battery-op, litho tin, 1950s, 5½", VG ..**$175.00**

Cragstan's Mr Robot, battery-op, litho tin, several actions, Y, 1960s, 10½", rare, EX **$700.00**

Ding-A-Ling Super Return Space Skyway, Topper, 1971, NMIB (It is important for this to be complete) ..**$150.00**

Interplanetary Rocket, battery-op, litho tin, several actions, Y, 1960s, 15", NM...**$175.00**

Jupiter Rocket Launching Pad, battery-op, several actions, TN, 1960s, 7", EX..**$275.00**

Looping Space Tank, battery-op, several actions, Daiya, 1960s, 8", MIB **$500.00**

Lost in Space Robot, plastic, all red, Remco, 1966, 12", EXIB...**$500.00**

Lunar Loop, battery-op, litho tin, 3 actions, Daiya, 1960s, 12" dia hoop, EX...**$200.00**

Machine Robot, battery-op, tin & plastic, advances w/lights & sound, SH, 1960s, 12", EX......................................**$500.00**

Man Made Satellite, battery-op, litho tin, several actions, Hoku, 1950s, 7", scarce, NM (EX box) **$3,000.00**

Monster Robot, battery-op, 3 actions, SH, 1970s, 10", EX ..**$125.00**

Moon Crawler X-12, battery-op, M............................**$100.00**

Moon Detector, battery-op, litho tin, several actions, Y, 1960s, 10½", rare, NM...**$600.00**

Moon Patrol, battery-op, litho tin w/vinyl figure, several actions, Gakken, 1960s, 11½", NM....................**$500.00**

Moon Rocket XM-12, battery-op, litho tin, several actions, Y, 1960s, 14½", rare, NM **$650.00**

Mr Atom, battery-op, gray plastic, advances w/lights & sound, Advanced Doll & Toy, 1950s, 18", EXIB **$500.00**

NASA New Flying Saucer, battery-op, several actions, KO, 1960s, 7½", NM...**$250.00**

Radar 'N Scope Space Station, battery-op, litho tin, several actions, MT, 1960s, 6x8", MIB.....................**$425.00**

Robot, battery-operated, advances and stops as gun shoots from chest, Hong Kong, 1970s, NM, 12", $150.00. (Photo courtesy June Moon)

Robot Commando, battery-op, plastic, Ideal, MIB, from $500 to...**$600.00**

Robot R-35, remote control, litho tin, several actions, MT, 1950s, 7", NMIB...**$1,200.00**

Robotank TR-2, battery-op, several actions, TN, 1950s, 5", EX..**$275.00**

Robotank-Z, battery-op, litho tin, several actions, TN, 1960s, 10", NM...**$500.00**

Rocket Launching Pad, battery-op, litho tin, several actions, Y, 1950s, 8½", rare, EX...**$325.00**

Rocket Racer #3, friction, litho tin, Modern Toys, 1960, EXIB...**$225.00**

Rudy the Robot, battery-op, several actions, Remco, 1968, 16", EX..**$225.00**

Satellite X-107, battery-op, litho tin, several actions, MT, 1960s, 8", rare, NM **$600.00**

Smoking Engine Robot, battery-op, plastic, advances as pistons in chest spin & blow smoke, SH, 1970s, 10", MIB.**$300.00**

Space Car, battery-op, litho tin w/styrofoam ball, several actions, Y, 1950s, 9½", rare, NM, minimum value...............**$1,000.00**

Space Dog, clockwork, silver-painted tin w/red detail, advances w/jaw & ear movement, Yoshiya, 1950s, 7", EXIB...**$475.00**

Space Explorer X-7, battery-op, litho tin, several actions, MT, 1960s, 7" dia, EX...**$185.00**

Space Frontier, battery-op, litho tin, several actions, Japan, 1960s, 18", EX **$200.00**

Space Scout S-17, battery-op, litho tin & plastic, several actions, Y, 1960s, 10", rare, NM...........................**$500.00**

Space Shuttle Challenger, battery-op, MIB **$475.00**

Space Tank X-Y 101, battery-op, litho tin, bump-&-go action w/lights, Gama, 1960s, NM (EX box)................**$265.00**

Spaceship X-5, friction, litho tin, MT, 1950s, 12", NM (EX box) **$1,000.00**

Super Sonic Space Robot, battery-op, litho tin, several actions, KO, 1950s, 14", rare, EX........................**$475.00**

Television Spaceman, battery-op, litho tin, several actions, Alps, 1960s, EX (EX box), minimum value **$800.00**

Two-Stage Rocket Launching Pad, battery-op, litho tin, several actions, TN, 1950s, 8", EXIB......................**$500.00**

USA-NASA Gemini, battery-op, tin, advances w/lights & sound as astronaut circles above, 9", EX (VG box)...........**$300.00**

Slot Car Racers

Slot cars first became popular in the early 1960s. Electric raceways set up in storefront windows were commonplace. Huge commercial tracks with eight and ten lanes were located in hobby stores and raceways throughout the United States. Large corporations such as Aurora, Revell, Monogram, and Cox, many of which were already manufacturing toys and hobby items, jumped on the bandwagon to produce slot cars and race sets. By the end of the early 1970s, people were losing interest in slot racing, and its popularity diminished. Today the same baby boomers that raced slot cars in earlier days are revitalizing the sport. Vintage slot cars have made a comeback as one of the hottest automobile collectibles of the 1990s. Want ads for slot cars frequently appear in newspapers and publications geared toward the collector. As you would expect, slot cars were generally well used, so finding vintage cars and race sets in like-new or mint condition is difficult. Slot cars replicating the 'muscle' cars from the '60s and '70s are extremely sought after, and clubs and organizations devoted to these collectibles are becoming more and more commonplace. Large toy companies such as Tomy and Tyco still produce some slots today, but not in the quality, quantity, or variety of years past.

Advisor: Gary Pollastro (See Directory, Toys)

Accessory, Aurora AFX Carrying Case, black, 2-level, EX...**$15.00**

Accessory, Aurora Model Motoring Hill Track, 9", EX ..**$8.00**

Accessory, Tyco HO Scale 1973-74 Handbook, EX **$10.00**

Accessory, Tyco Trigger Controller, orange, EX............**$8.00**

Car, Aurora AFX, Chevy Nomad, #1760, blue, EX **$20.00**

Car, Aurora AFX, Corvette #7, #1827, red, white & blue, VG+ **$20.00**

Car, Aurora AFX, Datsun Baja Pickup, #1745, blue & black, EX...**$20.00**

Car, Aurora AFX, Ferrari 612, #1751, yellow & black, EX..**$10.00**

Car, Aurora AFX, Ford Baja Bronco, #1901, red, EX...**$14.00**

Car, Aurora AFX, Ford Street Van, #1943, light blue & brown, NM **$14.00**

Car, Aurora AFX, Lola T-260 Can-Am, white w/stripes, EX..**$14.00**
Car, Aurora AFX, Vega Van Gasser, #1754, yellow & red, EX..**$15.00**
Car, Aurora Cigarbox, Dino Ferrari, red, EX................**$20.00**
Car, Aurora G-Plus, Corvette, #1011, red, orange & white, EX.**$15.00**
Car, Aurora G-Plus, Corvette, #1954, red, orange & silver, EX.**$12.00**
Car, Aurora G-Plus, Ferrari F1, #1734, red & white, EX........**$25.00**
Car, Aurora Thunderjet, Chaparral 2F Tuff One, white, EX..**$25.00**
Car, Aurora Thunderjet, Cheetah, #1403, pea green, EX **$40.00**
Car, Aurora Thunderjet, Cougar, #1389, white, EX **$40.00**
Car, Aurora Thunderjet, Ford Car, #1382, white & blue, VG **$25.00**
Car, Aurora Thunderjet, Hot Rod Coupe, red, VG......**$25.00**
Car, TCR, Blazer, black, yellow w/orange flames, EX...**$15.00**
Car, TCR, Mack Truck, white & red, EX **$15.00**
Car, Tyco, Bandit Pickup, black & yellow, EX............**$12.00**
Car, Tyco, Chaparral 2G #66, #8504, VG **$14.00**
Car, Tyco, Ferrari F-40, #8967, red, VG **$12.00**
Car, Tyco, Firebird Stockcar #35, EX.........................**$10.00**
Car, Tyco, Indy Pennzoil, yellow, EX **$15.00**
Car, Tyco, Lamborghini, red, VG..............................**$12.00**
Car, Tyco, Porsche 908 #3, green & silver, EX...........**$16.00**
Car, Tyco, Superbird, #8533, red, white & blue, VG+ ..**$15.00**
Car, Tyco, Turbo Hopper #27, red, EX......................**$12.00**
Set, Aurora, Home Raceway, Sears, #79N9513C, VG..**$225.00**
Set, Aurora, Mario Andretti GP International Challenge, G (G box) **$55.00**
Set, Aurora, Stirling Moss #1313 Table Top Racing Set, 1968, NMIB...**$125.00**
Set, Eldon, Sky High Triple Road Race, w/Ferrari Lotus, Stingray & Porsche, G (G box)...........................**$75.00**
Set, Motorific, GTO Torture Track, lg, EXIB.............**$100.00**
Set, Revell, HiBank Raceway Set #49-9503, w/Cougar GTE & Pontiac Firebird, EXIB **$150.00**
Set, Strombecker, Highway Patrol, VG (VG box) **$200.00**

Set, Strombecker (Montgomery Ward), Thunderbolt Monza, VG (VG box), $150.00. (Photo courtesy Gary Pollastro)

Vehicles

These are the types of toys that are intensely dear to the heart of many a collector. Having a beautiful car is part of the American dream, and over the past eighty years, just about as many models, makes, and variations have been made as toys for children as the real vehicles for adults. Novices and advanced collectors alike are easily able to find something to suit their tastes as well as their budgets.

One area that is especially volatile includes those '50s and '60s tin scale-model autos by foreign manufacturers — Japan, U.S. Zone Germany, and English toy makers. Since these are relatively modern, you'll still be able to find some at yard sales and flea markets at reasonable prices.

There are several good references for these toys: *Collecting Toy Cars and Trucks* by Richard O'Brien; *Hot Wheels, A Collector's Guide,* by Bob Parker; *Collector's Guide to Tootsietoys* by David Richter; *Collector's Guide to Tonka Trucks, 1947 – 1963,* by Don and Barb deSalle; *Collectible Coca-Cola Toy Trucks* by Gael de Courtivron; *Matchbox Toys, 1948 to 1993,* and *Collector's Guide to Diecast Toys and Scale Models* by Dana Johnson; *The Golden Age of Automotive Toys, 1925 – 1941,* by Ken Hutchinson and Greg Johnson; and *Motorcycle Toys, Antique and Contemporary,* by Sally Gibson-Downs and Christine Gentry.

Newsletter: *The Replica*
Bridget Shine, Editor
Highways 136 and 20, Dyersville, IA 52040; 319-875-2000

Newsletter: *Matchbox USA*
Charles Mack
62 Saw Mill Rd., Durham, CT 06422; 203-349-1655

AC Williams, 1936 Roadster, cast iron, nickel trim, rubber tires, 4¼", EX **$450.00**
Ahi, Alfa Romeo Giuletta Sprint, diecast, M **$16.00**
Ahi, Dodge Military Tank Carrier, diecast, M...............**$12.00**
Arcade, 1938 Chevrolet Stake Truck, cast iron, rubber tires, 4¼", NM **$825.00**
Arcade, 1941 Ford Fire Pumper Truck, cast iron, red w/black rubber tires, 6 firemen, 13", VG **$450.00**
Arcade, 1941 Yellow Cab, cast iron, yellow & black w/silver trim, rubber tires, w/driver & passenger, 8¼", NMIB **$2,400.00**
Bandai, 1950 Cadillac, friction, white w/chrome detail, 11½", M...**$265.00**
Bandai, 1955 Ford Custom Ranch Wagon, friction, red w/black top, chrome detail, 11½", MIB..............**$375.00**
Bandai, 1963 Volkswagen Bug, friciton, blue w/chrome detail, 8", NM (EX box)......................................**$150.00**
Bandai, 1965 Chevy Corvette, friction, cream, 8", EX..**$150.00**
Bandai, 1965 Ford Mustang Coupe, friction, metallic blue w/black top, chrome detail, 8", NM....................**$200.00**
Bandai, Mazda RX7 25i, diecast, M **$5.00**
Bandai, Porsche 903, diecast, silver, M **$16.00**
BBR, 1939 Alfa Romeo 6C 2500, diecast, M **$160.00**
Corgi, #152, BRM Racer, MIB.......................................**$80.00**
Corgi, #155, Shadow FI Racer, MIB..............................**$40.00**
Corgi, #160, Hesketh Racer, MIB **$45.00**
Corgi, #164, Wild Honey Dragster, MIB.......................**$50.00**
Corgi, #200, BMC Mini 1000, MIB **$50.00**
Corgi, #201, Austin Cambridge, MIB........................**$160.00**

Corgi, #203, Detomaso Mangust, MIB.........................$40.00

Corgi, #205, Riley Pathfinder, red, MIB.....................$130.00

Corgi, #230, Mercedes Benz 222, red, MIB................$75.00

Corgi, #241, Chrysler Ghia, MIB.................................$80.00

Corgi, #258, Saint's Volvo P1800, MIB $165.00

Corgi, #264, Incredible Hulk, MIB..............................$75.00

Corgi, #292, Starsky & Hutch Ford Torino, MIB.........$85.00

Corgi, #300, Chevy Corvette, MIB $100.00

Corgi, #319, Lotus Elan, red, MIB $100.00

Corgi, #381, Renault Turbo, MIB $20.00

Corgi, #402, Ford Cortina GXL Polizei, MIB.............$150.00

Corgi, #490, VW Breakdown Truck, MIB....................$95.00

Corgi, #510, Citroen Tour De France, MIB $125.00

Corgi, #701, Intercity Minibus, MIB...........................$20.00

Corgi, #802, Mercedes Benz 300 SL, MIB $25.00

Corgi, #811, James Bond's Moon Buggy, MIB $500.00

Danbury Mint, 1959 Cadillac Series 62 Convertible, diecast, red, M $125.00

Diapet, Datsun Tow Truck #272, diecast, M...............$18.00

Diapet, Mitsubishi GTO #SV27, diecast, M $21.00

Dinky, #101 Sunbeam Alpine, MIB..........................$175.00

Dinky, #110, Aston Martin DB5................................$110.00

Dinky, #120, Happy Cab, MIB...................................$60.00

Dinky, #142, Jaguar Mark 10, MIB $100.00

Dinky, #150, Rolls Royce Silver Wraith, MIB............$100.00

Dinky, #161, Ford Mustang, MIB..............................$100.00

Dinky, #173, Nash Rambler, MIB..............................$110.00

Dinky, #184, Volvo 122S, red, MIB $130.00

Dinky, #192, DeSoto Fireflite, MIB...........................$165.00

Dinky, #202, Fiat Abarth 2000, MIB $50.00

Dinky, #265, Plymouth Taxi, MIB $170.00

Dinky, #344, Land Rover Pickup, MIB......................$50.00

Dinky, #440, Mobilgas Tanker, MIB..........................$175.00

Dinky, #518, Renault 4L, MIB $50.00

Dinky, #538, Buick Roadmaster, MIB........................$300.00

Dinky, #612, Commando Jeep, MIB..........................$50.00

Dinky, #893, UNIC Pipe-Line Transporter, MIB $275.00

Dinky, #918, Guy Van, Ever-Ready Batteries, MIB, $500.00.

Dinky, #959, Foden Dump Truck, MIB.....................$175.00

Dinky, #984, Car Carrier, MIB....................................$225.00

Ertl, 1969 Plymouth Hemi Roadrunner, diecast, yellow, M $30.00

Ertl, 1995 Dodge Ram Truck, diecast, red or black, M..$25.00

Goodee, 1953 GMC Pickup Truck, diecast, 6", M.......$25.00

Goodee, 1955 Ford Fuel Truck, diecast, 3", M............$15.00

Hot Wheels, Ambulance, red line tires, metallic brown w/cream interior, 1970, EX+..............................$15.00

Hot Wheels, Baja Bruiser, red line tires, dark blue w/plastic chrome base, yellow, white & red tampo, 1977, NM+...............$50.00

Hot Wheels, Bronco Four-Wheeler, black walls, red, NM+ .$6.00

Hot Wheels, Custom Camaro, red line tires, metallic olive, 1968, scarce, NM..$85.00

Hot Wheels, Custom VW, red line tires, metallic aqua w/cream interior, 1968, NM+ $40.00

Hot Wheels, Double Vision, red line tires, yellow w/cream interior, 1973, EX $60.00

Hot Wheels, Dune Daddy, red line tires, light green w/black interior, orange, yellow & blue tampo, 1975, NM.$32.00

Hot Wheels, Emergency Squad, black walls, red, 1977, M (EX+ card) $8.00

Hot Wheels, Fire Chief Cruiser, red line tires, red, no windshield, 1970, NM+ $20.00

Hot Wheels, Grass Hopper, red line tires, metallic green w/black interior, 1971, scarce color, NM+ $50.00

Hot Wheels, Gritty Kitty, red line tires, metallic blue, complete, 1970, EX+...$20.00

Hot Wheels, Hot Bird, black walls, blue w/orange & yellow tampo, 1980, M $30.00

Hot Wheels, Indy Eagle, red line tires, metallic green w/black interior, original decal, 1969, NM $16.00

Hot Wheels, Jack Rabbit Special, red line tires, white w/black interior, 1970, M (EX card)....................................$40.00

Hot Wheels, Khaki Kooler, red line tires, olive w/charcoal plastic base, white tampo, 1976, EX........................$8.00

Hot Wheels, Large Charge, red line tires, Super Chrome, black, yellow & orange tampo, 1976, M...............$30.00

Hot Wheels, Mercedes 540K, white walls, Super Chrome, 20th Anniversary, 1988, NM+.................................$10.00

Hot Wheels, Open Fire, red line tires, metallic magenta, 1972, NM $100.00

Hot Wheels, Prowler, black walls, Super Chrome, 1978, NM...$16.00

Hot Wheels, Rock Buster, black walls, Super Chrome, 1977, NM $20.00

Hot Wheels, Rumbler Road Hog, orange, no driver or training wheels, 1971, NM...$20.00

Hot Wheels, Rumblers High Tailer, orange, original blue driver w/white full-face helmet, training wheels, 1971, M $40.00

Hot Wheels, Rumblers Rip Snorter, orange, original tan driver w/flesh face, tan helmet, training wheels, 1971, NM+ $30.00

Hot Wheels, S'Cool Bus, red line tires, yellow, 1971, NM..$120.00

Hot Wheels, Sizzlers Anteater, metallic orange, 1971, NM.$25.00

Hot Wheels, Sizzlers Co-Motion, metallic green, 1972, EX+...$30.00

Hot Wheels, Sizzlers Hot Head, metallic green, 1970, M.$40.00

Hot Wheels, T-Bird Stocker, black walls, white w/blue back, #21 Valvoline tampo, gold wheels, 1984, M (NM+ card)..$30.00

Hot Wheels, Vega Bomb, red line tires, orange w/red, yellow & blue tampo, complete, France, 1975, NM.........$75.00

Hubley, Auto Transport, diecast, red w/silver detail, complete w/4 plastic sedans, 14", MIB......................**$250.00**

Hubley, Dump Truck, diecast, green & red w/silver detail, 14 black rubber tires, 16", MIB............................**$400.00**

Londontoy, Auto Transport, diecast, M......................**$100.00**

Londontoy, 1941 Ford Pickup, diecast, 4", M.............**$25.00**

Majorette, Sonic Flashers, Ambulance, diecast, M.......**$10.00**

Marusan, Troy Ruttman Jet Racer, litho tin w/rubber tires, friction, w/driver, 1955, 8", EXIB.........................**$500.00**

Marx, Gasoline Truck, pressed steel, red w/chrome grille, wooden tires, 7", EX...**$150.00**

Marx, Heavy Duty Dump Truck, pressed steel, w/high side extension on dump bed, MIB.............................**$300.00**

Marx, Lazy Day Farm Stake Truck, pressed steel w/litho tin bed, 18", NMIB...**$400.00**

Marx, Willy's Jeep w/Lights & Trailer, pressed steel, battery-op headlights, 22", MIB..**$300.00**

Matchbox, Daimler Bus, regular wheels, green, 1966, MIB **$20.00**

Matchbox, K-01B, Hoveringham Tipper Truck, w/labels (scarce), 1964, MIB...................................**$39.00**

Matchbox, K-07B, Refuse Truck, black wheels, 1967, MIB.**$34.00**

Matchbox, K-10B, Pipe Truck, w/4 original pipes, 1967, EX..**$24.00**

Matchbox, K-13A, Readymix Concrete Truck, silver metal wheels, 1963, NM **$29.00**

Matchbox, K-16B, Petrol Tanker, Total label, 1974, MIB .**$31.00**

Matchbox, K-67A, Dodge Monaco Fire Chief Car, yellow w/red interior, black base, amber windshield, 1978, M (VG+ box) **$12.00**

Matchbox, Y-1B, 1911 Ford Model T, cream w/maroon top, red base & seats, black plastic steering wheel, 1964, MIB.**$22.00**

Matchbox, Y-22A, 1930 Ford Model A Van, beige w/red top, brown base, white walls w/24-spoke chrome wheels, 1982, MIB **$13.00**

Matchbox, Y-29A, Walker Electric Van, green w/tan interior, red wheels, 1985, MIB..**$12.00**

Matchbox, Y-63A, 1939 Bedford Truck, Farrar tampo, red & brown w/black interior & base, chrome wheels, 1992, MIB **$25.00**

Matchbox, 1-A, Diesel Road Roller, regular black wheels, dark green, 1953, NM...**$43.00**

Matchbox, 2-B, Dumper, regular black wheels, #2 cast, metal wheels, w/driver, 1957, NM+ **$45.00**

Matchbox, 4-D, Dodge Stake Truck, regular black wheels, green stakes, 1967, MIB **$10.00**

Matchbox, 5-C, London Bus, regular black wheels, Visco Static, 1961, EX+ **$24.00**

Matchbox, 10-E, Pipe Truck, Super Fast, orange w/silver base, gray pipes, thin wheels, 1970, M.................**$24.00**

Matchbox, 14-C, Bedford Ambulance, regular black wheels, 1962, MIB **$33.00**

Matchbox, 16-D, Case Bulldozer, original treads, complete, 1969, MIB **$25.00**

Matchbox, 19-F, Road Dragster, Super Fast, red w/ivory interior, unpainted base, 8 labels, 1970, M (NM+ box).........**$15.00**

Matchbox, 21-C, Commer Milk Truck, regular black wheels, green windows, cow decals, 1961, MIB **$25.00**

Matchbox, 23-D, Volkswagen Camper, regular black wheels, turquoise, w/opening roof, 1970, M.....................**$12.00**

Matchbox, 36-F, Formula 5000, Super Fast, orange w/blue driver, labels, Maltese cross rear wheels, 1975, M......**$12.00**

Matchbox, 41-A, regular metal wheels, D-Type Jaguar, 1957, NM+...**$66.00**

Matchbox, 44-D, GMC Refrigerator Truck, Super Fast, yellow & red w/red axle covers, 1970, M (EX-box).........**$25.00**

Matchbox, 46-B, Pickford's Removal Van, regular black wheels, green, 3-line decals, 1960, MIB................**$40.00**

Matchbox, 50-A, Commer Pickup Truck, regular gray wheels, tan, 1958, NM+..**$39.00**

Matchbox, 53-A, Aston Martin, regular black wheels, med red, 1958, scarce color, NM...............................**$90.00**

Matchbox, 54-C, Cadillac Ambulance, Super Face, white w/black base, silver grille,1970, EX+.................**$18.00**

Matchbox, 59-B, Ford Thames Singer Van, regular black wheels, 1958, NM **$35.00**

Matchbox, 65-D, Saab Sonnet, Super Fast, med blue w/yellow interior, unpainted base, 1973, MIB.............**$12.00**

Matchbox, 67-D, Hot Rocker, Super Fast, med lime green w/unpainted base, 5-spoke wheels, 1973, M.......**$13.00**

Matchbox, 70-D, Dodge Dragster, Super Fast, pink w/black base, light green snake label, 4-spoke rear wheels, 1971, MIB **$18.00**

Mebetoys, Fiat 850, diecast, 1966, M...........................**$30.00**

Mebetoys, Porsche 912 Rally, diecast, 1974, M **$40.00**

Mercury, Fiat 131 Fire Chief, diecast, 1971, M............**$25.00**

Mercury, Mercedes Grand Prix, diecast, 1947, M........**$95.00**

NGS, Chevy Corvair Sedan, friction, red w/chrome detail, 8", NMIB..**$200.00**

Schuco, Construction Truck w/Extension Ladder, red w/open bed, ladder mounted on swinging platform, 10", EX.........**$850.00**

Schuco, Ford Capri RS, diecast, 1974, 2½", M.............**$10.00**

Schuco, Mercedes 220 S, wind-up, red w/white top, chrome detail, 5", EX (VG box) **$125.00**

Schuco, Packard Hawk Convertible, battery-op, 1957, 10½", EX (VG box) **$900.00**

Smith-Miller, GMC Materials Truck, pressed steel, w/4 barrels & 3 timbers, EX..**$300.00**

Smith-Miller, Mack Fire Department Aerial Ladder Truck, pressed steel, 31", G **$800.00**

Smith-Miller, Mobiloil Tanker Truck, pressed steel, red w/name & winged-horse logo, 14", VG..............**$450.00**

Solido, 1978 Jaguar XJ 12, diecast, M..........................**$10.00**

SSS, Fire Car, litho tin, friction, w/ladder & 5 fireman, 6½", NMIB..**$300.00**

Structo, DeLuxe Auto, #12, 16", EX+.........................**$800.00**

Structo, Structo Transport Tractor-Trailer, pressed steel, 1950s, 21", EX **$200.00**

Structo, US Mail Truck, #928, pressed steel, 17", NM...**$300.00**

TKK, Fire Engine, litho tin, friction, 18", EXIB..........**$125.00**

TN, Edsel Station Wagon, friction, black & red w/white trim, opening rear gate, 10½", NM............................**$500.00**

TN, 1958 Ford Skyliner, battery-op, red w/chrome detail, detachable roof, NMIB **$300.00**

Tomica, Toyota 2000-GT, #22-05, diecast, ca 1974, M ..**$10.00**

Tonka, Ace Hardware Delivery Truck, 1954, M $600.00
Tonka, Allied Van Lines Truck, 1956, NM $300.00
Tonka, Car Carrier, complete w/3 cars, 1960, NM $350.00
Tonka, Coast to Coast Utility Truck, 1952, VG..........$175.00
Tonka, Dump Truck, #180, 1949-53, NM...................$275.00
Tonka, Hi-Way Side Dump Truck, 1956, EX $250.00
Tonka, Jewel Tea Co Semi, 1954, NM........................$800.00
Tonka, True Value Box Van, 1954, EX.......................$550.00
Tootsietoy, Chevy Coupe, #231, 1940-41, med aqua, NM..$40.00
Tootsietoy, Chevy Fastback Coupe, red w/black wheels, 1947-49, NM $40.00
Tootsietoy, CJ-3 Civilian Jeep, red w/black rubber tires, 1947-54, 4", NM...$25.00
Tootsietoy, Ford Sinclair Oil Tanker, 1949-52, 6", NM ..$60.00
Tootsietoy, GMC Greyhound Bus, #3571, 1948-55, blue & silver, NM $55.00
Tootsietoy, HO Series School Bus, #2490, yellow & black, 1960s, scarce, NM $45.00
Tootsietoy, Packard 4-Door, blue & white, 1956-59, NM..$40.00
Tootsietoy, Station Wagon, #239, green & cream, 1940-41, NM $45.00
Tootsietoy, Thunderbird Coupe, 1955-60, 3", NM.......$25.00
Tootsietoy, US M-8 Armored Car, #2943, 1973-76, NM...$10.00
TT, Jaguar E-Type, friction, red w/chrome detail, 11", NM (NM box)..$475.00
Wyandotte, Auto Carrier w/Steam Shovel, pressed steel, 22½", VG...$300.00
Wyandotte, Construction & Steam Shovel Truck, pressed steel, white, blue & yellow, 1940s, NM $450.00
Wyandotte, Service & Wrecker Truck, pressed steel, red, white & green w/yellow wheels, 11½", NMIB...$500.00
Y, 1952 Oldsmobile Convertible, friction, red w/chrome detail, 10", EXIB...$500.00

Wind-Ups

Wind-up toys, especially comic character or personality related, are greatly in demand by collectors today. Though most were made through the years of the '30s through the '50s, they carry their own weight against much earlier toys and are considered very worthwhile investments. Mechanisms vary; some are key wound while others depended on lever action to tighten the mainspring and release the action of the toy. Tin and celluloid were used in their manufacture, and although it is sometimes possible to repair a tin wind-up, experts advise against putting your money into a celluloid toy whose mechanism is not working, since the material may be too fragile to tolerate the repair.

Action Toys, Cow Jumped Over the Moon, wood, pull-string action, 10", EXIB..$100.00
Alps, Balloon Santa, 1950s, 7½", MIB $200.00
Alps, Marching Drummer Bear, litho tin & plush, 6½", EXIB $150.00
Alps, Sea Wolf, litho tin, 6½", NMIB........................$200.00
American, Texas Pete on Rocking Horse, plastic, 1950s, 9", MIB $125.00

Automatic Toy, Captain Marvel Car, litho tin, 1947, 4", NM $250.00
Bandai, Old Fashioned Ice Cream Car, litho tin, friction, 6½", NMIB..$150.00
Budwill, Red Devil Racer, litho tin, w/driver, 1950, NMIB..$350.00
Buffalo Toys, Aero Speeders, litho tin, spiral action, 9½", VG+..$125.00
Chein, Big Top Tent, litho tin, 1961, 10", EXIB.........$200.00
Chein, Hand-Standing Clown, litho tin, 5", EX, from $125 to $150.00
Chein, Marine, litho tin, EX, from $200 to................$250.00
Chein, Playland Merry-Go-Round, litho tin, 10", EXIB..$650.00
Chein, Ski Ride, litho tin, 19½", EXIB, from $900 to .$1,000.00
CK, Branko Mechanical Acrobat, celluloid & tin, 13", MIB...$200.00
Cragstan, G-Men Car No 1, litho tin, friction, 4", EXIB.....$150.00
Ideal, Li'l Abner & Lonesome Polecat Canoe, plastic, 1951, 12", NMIB..$400.00
Irwin, Dancing Cinderella & Prince, plastic, 1950, 5", MIB, from $150 to..$200.00
Japan, Batman, litho tin, 1989, 8", MIB.....................$125.00
Japan, Joker, litho tin, 1989, 8", MIB $65.00
K, Western Ranger (Lone Ranger), litho tin, 5", EXIB...$250.00
Linemar, Babes in Toyland Soldier, litho tin, 1961, 6", EX..$400.00
Linemar, Disney Flivver w/Donald Duck, litho tin & celluloid, 5½", EXIB..$800.00
Linemar, Donald Duck Fire Chief Truck, litho tin, 5", NM.$500.00
Linemar, Ferdinand the Bull, tin w/rubber tail, 5½", scarce, NMIB..$900.00
Linemar, Henry Eating Candy, litho tin, 1950s, 5½", EX $400.00
Linemar, Henry Eating Ice Cream, litho tin, 6", scarce, NM..$1,000.00
Linemar, Marvel Super Heroes Tricycle, litho tin, 1960s, NMIB, from $450 to..$650.00
Linemar, Minnie Mouse Knitting in Rocking Chair, litho tin, 6½", M..$800.00
Linemar, Popeye Turnover Tank, litho tin, 4", EX $350.00
Linemar, Prehistoric Dinosaur, litho tin, 8", NMIB $350.00
Marusan, Lucky Baby Machine (Girl at Sewing Machine), litho tin & celluloid, 5½", NMIB.........................$575.00
Marx, Astro, plastic, friction, 1960s, 4", rare, EX.......$375.00
Marx, Bedrock Express Train, litho tin, 1962, 12", EX ..$250.00
Marx, Cowboy Rider, litho tin, 1941, NMIB..............$350.00
Marx, Donald Duck Duet, litho tin, 1946, 10½", MIB ..$1,200.00
Marx, Honeymoon Express, litho tin, 1940, EXIB.....$225.00
Marx, Huckleberry Hound Car, litho tin w/vinyl figure, friction, 1962, 4", NMIB..$300.00
Marx, Mickey Mouse Express, litho tin, 1950s, 9" dia, NM.$750.00
Marx, Pecos Bill Ridin' Widowmaker, plastic, 10", EX ..$600.00
Marx, Pluto Twirling Tail, plastic, 6", M.....................$150.00
Marx, Racer #12, litho tin, 1942, 16", VG..................$200.00
Marx, Sparkling Jet Plane, plastic, friction, 1950s, 12", MIB.$100.00
Marx, Spider-Man Tricycle, litho tin w/vinyl figure, 1967, 4", NMIB..$200.00
Nibo/Spain, Disneylandia, 1950s, 11x8", NMIB.........$350.00
Occupied Japan, Boy on Scooter, celluloid, M $125.00

Occupied Japan, Drunken Sailor, celluloid, 6", NM..**$300.00**
Occupied Japan, Kitty Ball Romp, celluloid, 8", EXIB ..**$100.00**
Occupied Japan, Tap Dancer (Black Man) Under Lenox Ave Sign, tin & celluloid w/cloth clothes, 8", NM **$300.00**
SAN, SSN 25 Submarine, litho tin, 10", NMIB **$200.00**
SAN, Wonder MG Car, litho tin, 12", EXIB **$350.00**
SSG, Dance Hawaiian, celluloid girl in grass skirt, 6", MIB **$165.00**
Technofix, Grand Prix Racing Set, litho tin, complete w/3 cars, 13x19" base, NMIB.....................................**$300.00**
TN, Comic Locomotive, litho tin, MIB **$150.00**
TN, Mr Dan the Hot Dog Eating Man, litho tin w/cloth coat & flocked hair, 1950s, 7", MIB **$125.00**
TPS, Animal Barber Shop, litho tin, 5", MIB.............**$500.00**
TPS, Big League Hockey Player, litho tin, 1950s, 6½", NMIB...**$650.00**

TPS/Japan, Climbing Pirate, litho tin, pull string for action, 5", NMIB, $200.00.

TPS, Gay 90s Cyclist, litho tin w/cloth clothes, 1950s, 7", EX **$350.00**
TPS, Lady Bug & Tortoise w/Babies, litho tin, 7", NMIB...**$100.00**
Unique Art, Artie the Clown, litho tin, 9½", EX........**$450.00**
Unique Art, GI Joe & His Jouncing Jeep, litho tin, 7", NMIB **$450.00**
Unique Art, Hobo Train, litho tin, 8", EX **$350.00**
Wolverine, Action Ski Jumper, litho tin, 26" ramp, MIB..**$300.00**
Wolverine, Jackie Gleason Bus, litho tin, 1955, 13", EXIB **$1,000.00**
Wyandotte, Acrobatic Monkeys, litho tin, 10" dia base, NMIB...**$600.00**
Wyandotte, Hoky & Poky on Handcar, litho tin, 6", NMIB **$400.00**
Wyandotte, Humphrey Mobile, litho tin, 1950, 8½", NMIB **$800.00**
Y, Ferry Boat, litho tin, 17", NMIB **$365.00**
Y, Vacationland Airplane Ride, litho tin, 6", EXIB.....**$125.00**

Transistor Radios

Introduced during the Christmas shopping season of 1954, transistor radios were at the cutting edge of futuristic design and miniaturization. Among the most desirable is the 1954 four-transistor Regency TR-1 which is valued at a mini-

mum of $750.00 in jade green. Black may go for as much as $300.00, other colors from $350.00 to $400.00. The TR-1 'Mike Todd' version in the 'Around the World in Eighty Days' leather book-look presentation case goes for $4,000.00 and up! Some of the early Toshiba models sell for $250.00 to $350.00, some of the Sonys even higher — their TR-33 books at a minimum of $1,000.00, their TR-55 at $1,500.00 and up! Certain pre-1960 models by Hoffman and Admiral represented the earliest practical use of solar technology and are also highly valued. Early collectible transistor radios all have civil defense triangle markings at 640 and 1240 on the frequency dial and nine or fewer transistors. Very few desirable sets were made after 1963.

Values in our listings are for radios in at least very good condition — not necessarily working, but complete and requiring very little effort to restore them to working order. Cases may show minor wear. All radios are battery-operated unless noted otherwise. For more information we recommend *Collector's Guide to Transistor Radios* (there are two editions), by Marty and Sue Bunis (Collector Books).

Advisors: Marty and Sue Bunis (See Directory, Radios)

Acme, #CH-620, Tops All, horizontal, 6 transistors, AM, battery, 1961..**$30.00**
Admiral, #4P21, horizontal, 4 transistors, AM, battery, black w/chrome swing handle, perforated grill, lg dial, 1957..**$35.00**
Admiral, #909, All World, horizontal, 9 transistors, battery, fold-down front, telescoping antenna, w/handle, 1960 ....**$75.00**
Airline, #GEN-1208A, Eldorado, horizontal, AM, shortwave/battery, telescoping antenna, 1962..............**$30.00**
Airline, #GEN-1254A, horizontal, 7 transistors, AM, battery, center Montgomery Ward logo, 1965 ....**$30.00**
Aiwa, #AR-122, horizontal, 12 transistors, AM/FM, shortwave, AC/battery, leather, telescoping antenna, 1965........**$20.00**
Aladdin, #AL65, vertical, 6 transistors, AM, battery, plastic, Aladdin's lamp logo in center of grill, 1962 ....**$30.00**
Ambassador, #A-155, horizontal, 15 transistors, AM/FM, 3 shortwave, battery, 2 telescoping antennas, 1965...**$20.00**
Americana, #ST-6X, Wayfarer, vertical, 6 transistors, AM, battery, 1962...**$40.00**
Artemis, #ST-7EL, horizontal, 7 transistors, AM, long-wave, battery, lower left logo, 1961................................**$30.00**
Arvin, #60R35, horizontal, 7 transistors, AM, battery, plastic, slate blue, A logo, 1959...**$30.00**
Arvin, #62R59, horizontal, 8 transistors, AM, battery, leather, w/handle, slide rule dial, 1962 ....**$15.00**
Arvin, #8584, horizontal, 5 transistors, AM, battery, red or blue, rotating antenna in handle, 1959 ....**$40.00**
Bulova, #892, horizontal, 7 transistors, AM, battery, slide-rule dial, lower perforated grill area, 1963....................**$35.00**
Calrad, #60A183, vertical, 6 transistors, AM, battery, perforated grill w/geometric design, 1960 ....**$40.00**
Cameo, #61N29-03, vertical, AM, battery, black plastic, lower checkered grill area, 1963 ....**$25.00**

Candle, #9TR-85C, vertical, 8 transistors, AM, battery, plastic w/lower metal perforated grill, step-down top, 1963..**$35.00**

Capehart, #T6-203, Incomparable, vertical, 6 transistors, AM, battery, crown logo on perforated grill, 1961.......**$35.00**

Channel Master, #6523, Trans-World, horizontal, 10 transistors, AM, shortwave, battery, red or black plastic, 1960 ....**$35.00**

Clairtone-Braun, #T22C, horizontal, 9 transistors, AM/FM, shortwave, battery, telescoping antenna, handled, 1963 ....**$25.00**

Continental, #TFM-1090, horizontal, 10 transistors, AM/FM, battery, 1964..**$15.00**

Continental, #160, vertical, 6 transistors, AM, battery, center front raised V, swing handle, 1959 ....**$45.00**

Corvair, #8P23, vertical, 8 transistors, AM, battery, plastic w/metal perforated grill **$25.00**

Crown, #TR-875, horizontal, 8 transistors, AM, shortwave, battery, telescoping antenna, 1960 ....**$35.00**

Dewald, #K-544, horizontal, 4 transistors, AM, battery, leather, USA, 1957.......................................**$125.00**

Dumont, #900, horizontal, 9 transistors, AM, battery, ebony or gray, swing handle, 1963.............................**$30.00**

Eico, #RA-6, horizontal, 6 transistors, AM, battery, leather, w/handle, 1961 ....**$15.00**

Elgin, #R-1900, horizontal clock/radio, 12 transistors, AM/FM, AC, telescoping antenna, footed, 1965.................**$10.00**

Emerson, #888, Vanguard, vertical, 8 transistors, AM, battery, plastic w/futuristic front, rocket logo, USA, 1958.**$75.00**

Ever-Play, PR-1266, vertical, 6 transistors, AM, battery, plastic w/metal perforated grill, Japan..............................**$35.00**

Firestone, #4C34, horizontal, 7 transistors, AM, battery, leather w/lg lattice grill area, w/handle, 1957......**$40.00**

Futura, #366, vertical, 6 transistors, AM, battery, 1963 ....**$30.00**

Gala, #TR-824, vertical, 8 transistors, AM, battery, 1965 .**$20.00**

General Electric, #P-809C, horizontal, 5 transistors, AM, battery, plastic w/woven grill area, pull-up handle, 1962 ....**$20.00**

General Electric, #P746A, horizontal, 5 transistors, AM, battery, plastic, grill area w/vertical bars, 1958 ....**$25.00**

General Electric, #P780H, Long Range, horizontal, 9 transistors, AM, battery, plastic & chrome, leather handle, 1965...**$20.00**

Grundig, Transonette, #99U, horizontal/table, 9 transistors, AM/FM, short-wave/long-wave, battery, 1964......**$20.00**

Harpers, #2TP-110, vertical, AM, battery, plastic, w/wired earphone, no volume control **$75.00**

Hitachi, #TH-862R, Marie, horizontal, 8 transistors, plastic w/lg metal perforated grill, 1960 ....**$25.00**

Hoffman, #KP706, Trans Solar, horizontal, 6 transistors, AM, battery, plastic w/perforated grill, swing handle, 1959 ....**$175.00**

Honey Tone, #FR-601, verical, 6 transistors, AM, battery, perforated grill, swing handle, 1962 ....**$30.00**

ITT, #600, vertical, 6 transistors, AM, battery, plastic w/perforated grill & metal back, 1963 ....**$20.00**

JC Penney, #620, horizontal, 12 transistors, AM/FM, battery, leather w/handle, telescoping antenna, 1963 ....**$20.00**

Jewel, #10, vertical, 9 transistors, AM, battery, plastic w/lower lattice grill, swing handle, 1965 ....**$15.00**

Kowa, #KT-63, vertical, 6 transistors, AM, battery, plastic w/metal grill, telescoping antenna, swing handle, 1961 ....**$30.00**

Lafayette, #FS-91, vertical, 9 transistors, AM, battery, plastic w/metal perforated grill, fold-out stand, Japan, 1961 ..**$40.00**

Linmark, #T-40, vertical, 4 transistors, AM, battery, perforated grill, 1960 ....**$25.00**

Magnavox, #2AM-70, vertical, 7 transistors, AM, battery, perforated grill, 1964..**$30.00**

Mascot, #RE-60, vertical, 6 transistors, AM, battery, w/strap, 1965 ....**$10.00**

Mitsubishi 6X-720, plastic, AM, battery, $35.00.
(Photo courtesy Marty and Sue Bunis)

Motorola, #6X31C, horizontal, AM, battery, metal w/plastic grill, lg swing handle, 1957................................**$50.00**

Norelco, #L0X95T/62R, horizontal, 7 transistors, AM, battery, perforated grill, Holland, 1961..............................**$30.00**

Norwood, #NT-602, horizontal, 6 transistors, AM, battery, perforated grill, 1964 ....**$20.00**

Packard Bell, #6RT1, horizontal, 5 transistors, AM, battery, leather w/checked grill cutouts, w/handle, 1958 .**$60.00**

Panasonic, #T-7, vertical, 7 transistors, AM, battery, plastic, 1963 ....**$30.00**

Raytheon, #8TP-1, horizontal, 8 transistors, AM, battery, tan leather w/metal perforated grill, w/handle, 1955.**$125.00**

RCA, #1-RG-11, vertical, 6 transistors, AM, battery, plastic w/vertical grill bars, swing handle, 1962 ....**$20.00**

Silvertone, #2208, Medalist, horizontal, 7 transistors, AM, battery, plastic w/perforated grill, swing handle, 1962..........**$25.00**

Sony, #TR-627, horizontal/table, 6 transistors, AM, battery, plastic, w/handle, footed, Japan..........................**$30.00**

Star-Lite, #FM-500, Discoverer, horizontal, 12 transistors, AM/FM, 3 shortwave, battery, antenna, w/handle, 1965 ....**$35.00**

Sylvania, #5P11R, horizontal, 5 transistors, AM, battery, 1960 ....**$35.00**

Truetone, #DC3090, vertical, 3 transistors, AM, battery, round perforated grill, swing handle, 1960....................**$50.00**

Universal, #PTR-62B, vertical, 6 transistors, AM, battery, plastic w/metal perforated grill, Japan, 1963...............**$25.00**

Valiant, #AM1400, Hi Power, vertical, AM, battery......**$30.00**

Westinghouse, #H-653P6, horizontal, 6 transistors, AM, battery, plastic, 1958 ....**$30.00**

York, #TR-103, vertical, 10 transistors, AM, battery, 1965..**$15.00**

Zenith, Royal 56, Sun Charger, horizontal, AM, battery, plastic w/metal grill, swing handle, built-in solar panel, 1966 ....**$125.00**

Trolls

The legend of the Troll originated in Scandinavia. Nordic mythology described them as short, intelligent, essentially unpleasant, supernatural creatures who were doomed to forever live underground. During the '70s, a TV cartoon special and movie based on J.R.R. Tolkien's books, *The Hobbit* and *The Lord of the Rings,* caused an increase in Trolls' popularity. As a result, books, puzzles, posters, and dolls of all types were available on the retail market. In the early '80s, Broom Hilda and Irwin Troll were featured in a series of books as well as Saturday morning cartoons. Today trolls are enjoying a strong comeback.

Troll dolls of the '60s are primarily credited to Thomas Dam of Denmark. Many, using Dam molds, were produced in America by Royalty Des. of Florida and Wishnik. In Norway A/S Nyform created a different version. Some were also made in Hong Kong, Japan, and Korea, but those were of inferior plastic and design.

The larger trolls (approximately 12") are rare and very desirable to collectors. Troll animals by Dam, such as the giraffe, horse, cow, donkey, and lion, are bringing premium prices.

For more information, refer to *Collector's Guide to Trolls* by Pat Peterson.

Advisor: Pat Peterson (See Directory, Trolls)

Ballerina, Dam, bright red mohair, green eyes, original outfit, MIP, $55.00.
(Photo courtesy Roger Inouye)

A+ Teacher, #18436, Russ/China, 4½" **$8.00**

Boy in raincoat, bank, Dam, 7½", from $40 to **$50.00**

Cave Girl, leopard-skin outfit, Dam, 3", from $20 to..**$25.00**

Caveman, leopard-skin outfit, Dam, 1964, 12", from $115 to **$155.00**

Cowboy, red hat, red print shirt & blue pants, Wishnik, 3½" **$15.00**

Cowgirl, bank, molded outfit, Creative Mfg, 1978, 8½" ..**$30.00**

Girl, bank, various outfits, hair & eye color, Dam, 7"..**$30.00**

Goo Goo Baby, Russ Trolls, 1990s, 9" **$13.00**

Here Come the Judge, Uneda (sic)/Wishnik, 6", from $45 to **$50.00**

Hunt-Nik, w/rifle, Totsy/Wishnik, from $20 to...........**$25.00**

Indian Girl, head band w/feather, felt outfit, Dam, 7", from $45 to.................**$50.00**

Koko Monkey, Norfin's Ark/Dam, 2½" **$4.00**

Lucky Shnook, nodder, Japan, 4½", from $30 to **$40.00**

Neanderthal Man, Bijou Toy Inc, 1963, 7½"...............**$35.00**

No Good-Nik, Uneeda/Wishnik, 1980s, 5" **$15.00**

Poppa-He-Nik, felt outfit, Uneeda/Wishnik, 5", from $20 to **$23.00**

Seal, Norfin Pets/Dam, 1984, 6½" **$50.00**

Shekter, smiling monkey in lacy diaper, USA, 1966, 3", from $30 to.................**$40.00**

Short Order Cook, #18582, Russ/China, 4½" **$8.00**

Viking, molded helmet & boots, felt tunic & cape, John Nissen, 7", from $50 to.................**$80.00**

TV Guides

This publication goes back to the early 1950s, and granted, those early issues are very rare. But what an interesting, very visual way to chronicle the history of TV programming!

Values in our listings are for examples in fine to mint condition; be sure to reduce them significantly when damage of any type is present. For insight into *TV Guide* collecting, we recommend *The TV Guide Catalog* by Jeff Kadet, the *TV Guide* Specialist.

Advisor: Jeff Kadet (See Directory, *TV Guides*)

1953, April 10, Jack Webb...**$88.00**

1953, December 18, Bob Hope **$71.00**

1953, June 19, Ed Sullivan **$58.00**

1954, August 14, Martin & Lewis................................**$97.00**

1955, March 5, Liberace **$37.00**

1955, May 28, Ralph Edwards.....................................**$61.00**

1956, April 21, Nanette Fabray **$21.00**

1956, February 11, Perry Como **$20.00**

1956, July 7, Lassie **$84.00**

1957, March 30, Julie Andrews **$32.00**

1957, May 18, Ester Williams **$20.00**

1957, November 30, Alfred Hitchcock **$68.00**

1958, Mar 15, James Arness & Amanda Blake..............**$75.00**

1958, May 3, Shirley Temple.......................................**$66.00**

1959, February 21, cast of Perry Mason......................**$78.00**

1959, November 21, Clint Walker as Cheyenne **$66.00**	1988, January 30, Elvis & Priscilla Presley **$24.00**
1960, April 16, Ann Sothern...............................**$45.00**	1988, June 25, Best & Worst **$15.00**
1960, June 25, cast of Bonanza **$125.00**	1988, November 19, Remembering JFK **$6.00**
1961, July 1, Flintstones **$150.00**	1989, April 15, Joan Collins.....................................**$10.00**
1961, September 9, cast of Checkmate **$30.00**	1989, February 4, Hot February................................**$14.00**
1962, April 14, cast of Route 66 ....**$125.00**	1989, March 18, Oprah/Jackee/Robin Givens.............**$8.00**
1962, January 20, Chuck Conners as Rifleman............**$99.00**	1990, January 6, Cher/Roseanne/Klingon/Rock Hudson...**$18.00**
1963, February 23, Carol Burnett.............................**$26.00**	1990, January 27, Fred Flintstone/Bugs Bunny/Peanuts....**$20.00**
1963, September 21, Richard Chamberlin **$31.00**	1990, March 24, Billy Crystal....................................**$10.00**
1964, August 29, Patty Duke & TV parents **$66.00**	1991, August 31, It's Kirk vs Picard...........................**$12.00**
1964, February 8, Petticoat Junction girls **$86.00**	1991, May 4, Larry Hagman: Adios Dallas! **$15.00**
1965, December 11, cast of F Troop..........................**$66.00**	1991, November 30, The Judds.................................**$7.00**
1965, January 2, cast of The Munsters **$234.00**	1992, December 19, Toon Boom................................**$15.00**
1966, February 5, Larry Hagman & Barbara Eden as Jeannie **$132.00**	1992, January 25, Superbowl XXVI **$15.00**
1966, June 11, cast of Gilligan's Island **$125.00**	1992, May 9, Goodby-Y-Y-Y-Y-E Johnny....................**$10.00**
1967, April 22, cast of Family Affair **$57.00**	1993, August 21, Loni Anderson................................**$6.00**
1967, January 28, Monkees **$125.00**	1993, July 3, Vanna White..**$8.00**
1968, February 10, Smothers Brothers **$20.00**	1993, November 20, Waltons Come Home Again **$25.00**
1968, July 20, cast of The Big Valley........................**$66.00**	1994, January 1, Tim Allen.......................................**$16.00**
1969, May 3, cast of Flying Nun.............................**$28.00**	1994, July 2, Reba McIntire......................................**$28.00**
1969, October 18, cast of Mission Impossible **$36.00**	1994, November 19, cast of ER.................................**$16.00**
1972, January 22, cast of Mission Impossible **$24.00**	1995, August 19, Regis..**$5.00**
1972, June 10, Doris Day **$28.00**	1995, February 25, George Clooney...........................**$15.00**
1972, March 18, Sonny & Cher...............................**$28.00**	1995, November 18, Beatles '95................................**$16.00**
1973, May 5, Peter Falk as Columbo.......................**$24.00**	1996, April 20, Cybill Shepherd **$9.00**
1973, October 20, Telly Savalas as Kojak **$58.00**	1996, August 24, William Shatner, Star Trek Turns 30 ...**$12.00**
1974, August 3, cast of Emergency...........................**$95.00**	1996, June 15, Teri Hatcher......................................**$12.00**
1974, December 7, Michael Landon **$35.00**	1997, August 16, Blue Hawaii Elvis............................**$12.00**
1975, January 11, David Janssen..............................**$43.00**	1997, March 15, Elmo **$7.00**
1975, July 19, cast of Barney Miller..........................**$19.00**	1997, November 15, cast of X-Files............................**$15.00**
1976, February 7, cast of Barney Miller **$14.00**	1998, April 11, Madonna **$15.00**
1976, September 25, Charlie's Angels.........................**$33.00**	1998, August 1, Drew Carey **$9.00**
1977, June 18, cast of Laverne & Shirley **$14.00**	1998, March 7, Patrick Stewart.................................**$15.00**
1977, November 19, Frank Sinatra **$24.00**	
1978, February 4, The Love Boat..............................**$9.00**	
1978, May 20, cast of Three's Company **$24.00**	
1979, April 14, cast of Quincy **$19.00**	
1979, November 10, Bee Gees **$19.00**	
1980, January 12, Estrada & Wilcox of CHiPs **$26.00**	
1980, June 21, cast of Hart to Hart............................**$13.00**	
1981, August 1, Miss Piggy **$19.00**	
1981, March 7, cast of Dukes of Hazzard...................**$28.00**	
1982, February 27, cast of Dynasty **$13.00**	
1982, November 20, cast of Three's Company...........**$19.00**	
1983, April 9, Elvis Presley......................................**$13.00**	
1983, July 23, cast of Knots Landing **$13.00**	
1984, April 14, cast of Knight Rider **$33.00**	
1984, January 21, TV Game Show Hosts **$17.00**	
1985, August 10, Madonna......................................**$13.00**	
1985, February 2, Cagney & Lacey............................**$9.00**	
1985, July 6, cast of Cheers.....................................**$13.00**	
1986, August 16, Suzanne Somers............................**$13.00**	
1986, October 11, cast of LA Law..............................**$13.00**	
1987, April 11, cast of Newhart **$15.00**	
1987, December 5, Connie Sellecca **$15.00**	
1987, February 7, Ann-Margret **$15.00**	

1984, April 28, cast of Happy Days 1974 – 1984, $35.00.

Twin Winton

The genius behind the designs at Twin Winton was sculptor Don Winton. He and his twin, Ross, started the company while sill in high school in the mid-1930s. In 1952 older brother Bruce Winton bought the company from his two younger brothers and directed its development nationwide. They produced animal figures, cookie jars, and matching kitchenware and household items during this time. It is important to note that Bruce was an extremely shrewd business man, and if an order came in for a nonstandard color, he would generally accommodate the buyer — for an additional charge, of course. As a result, you may find a Mopsy (Raggedy Ann) cookie jar, for instance, in a wood stain finish or some other unusual color, even though Mopsy was only offered in the Collector Series in the catalogs. This California company was active until it sold in 1976 to Roger Bowermeister, who continued to use the Twin Winton name. He experimented with different finishes. One of the most common is a light tan with a high gloss glaze. He owned the company only one year until it went bankrupt and was sold at auction. Al Levin of Treasure Craft bought the molds and used some of them in his line. Eventually, the molds were destroyed.

One of Twin Winton's most successful concepts was their Hillbilly line — mugs, pitchers, bowls, lamps, ashtrays, decanters, and novelty items molded after the mountain boys in Paul Webb's cartoon series. Don Winton was the company's only designer, though he free-lanced as well. He designed for Disney, Brush-McCoy, Revell Toys, The Grammy Awards, American Country Music Awards, Ronald Reagan Foundation, and numerous other companies and foundations.

Twin Winton has been revived by Don and Norma Winton (the original Don Winton and his wife). They are currently selling new designs as well as some of his original artwork through the Twin Winton Collector Club on the internet at twinwinton.com. Some of Don's more prominent pieces of art are currently registered with the Smithsonian in Washington, D.C.

If you would like more information, read *Collector's Guide to Don Winton Designs*, written by our advisor Mike Ellis, and published by Collector Books. Another source of information is *The Collector's Encyclopedia of Cookie Jars* (three in the series) by Joyce and Fred Roerig.

Note: Color codes in the listings below are as follows: A — avocado green; CS — Collectors Series, fully painted; G — gray; I — ivory; O — orange; P — pineapple yellow; R — red; and W — wood stain with hand-painted detail. Values are based on actual sales as well as dealers' asking prices.

See also Cookie Jars.

Advisor: Mike Ellis (See Directory, Twin Winton)

Club: Twin Winton Collector Club
Also Don Winton Designs (other than Twin Winton)
266 Rose Lane
Costa Mesa, CA 92627
714-646-7112 or fax: 7414-645-4919
Website: twinwinton.com; e-mail: ellis5@pacbell.net

Ashtray, elf, W, 8x8"	**$100.00**
Ashtray, kitten, W, 6x8"	**$100.00**
Bank, bull, W, 6x8"	**$65.00**
Bank, Dutch girl, W, I, G, A, P, O, R, 8"	**$50.00**

Bank, elf, W, I, G, A, P, O, R, 8"	**$50.00**
Bank, foo dog, W, I, G, A, P, O, R, 8"	**$125.00**
Bank, Gunfighter Rabbit, W, I, G, A, P, O, R, 8"	**$50.00**
Bank, Hotei, W, I, G, A, P, O, R, 8"	**$50.00**
Bank, kitten, W, I, G, A, P, O, R, 8"	**$50.00**
Bank, lamb, W, I, G, A, P, O, R, 8"	**$40.00**
Bank, pig, W, I, G, A, P, O, R, 8"	**$50.00**
Bank, Pirate Fox, W, I, G, A, P, O, R, 8"	**$65.00**

Bank, rabbit, wood stain with hand-painted details, $50.00. (Photo courtesy Jim and Beverly Magnus)

Bank, shoe, W, I, G, A, P, O, R, 8"	**$85.00**
Bank, squirrel w/coin on nut, W, I, G, A, P, O, R, 8"	**$50.00**
Bank, teddy bear, W, I, G, A, P, O, R, 8"	**$40.00**
Candle holder, El Greco, W, I, G, A, P, O, R, 4½x6"	**$12.00**
Candle holder, El Greco, W, I, G, A, P, O, R, 5x9½"	**$15.00**
Candle holder, Strauss, W, I, G, A, P, O, R, 4½x6"	**$12.00**
Candle holder, Verdi, W, I, G, A, P, O, R, 4x6"	**$15.00**
Candy jar, Pot O' Candy, W, I, G, A, P, O, R, 8x10"	**$65.00**
Candy jar, Ranger Bear, W, I, G, A, P, O, R, 8x10½"	**$85.00**
Candy jar, squirrel on nut, W, I, G, A, P, O, R, 8x9"	**$75.00**
Canister, Bucket Canisters, cookie bucket, W, I, G, A, P, O, R, 8x9"	**$60.00**
Canister, Bucket Canisters, sugar bucket, W, I, G, A, P, O, R, 6x7"	**$40.00**
Canister, Canister Farm, flour stable, W, I, G, A, P, O, R, 6x10"	**$65.00**
Canister, Canisterville, house, cookies, W, 8x12"	**$175.00**
Canister, Pot O' Canisters, Pot O' Coffee, W, I, G, A, P, O, R, 5x6"	**$25.00**
Canister, Pot O' Canisters, Pot O' Cookies, W, I, G, A, P, O, R, 8x10"	**$40.00**
Creamer & sugar bowl, hen & rooster, W, I, G, 5x6"	**$250.00**
Expanimals, kitten, W, 7½"	**$125.00**
Expanimals, poodle, W, 7½"	**$200.00**
Figurine, beaver, recumbent, #315, 2½x1"	**$8.00**
Figurine, Black football player, #T-10, 5½"	**$175.00**
Figurine, boy shot putting w/Yale logo on shirt, 3"	**$150.00**
Figurine, cat on hind legs, 3"	**$30.00**

Figurine, collie, W, I, G & hand painted, 7½"............**$65.00**

Figurine, elf in shoe, 6"...**$120.00**

Figurine, girl holding sucker, #T-6, 5½" **$150.00**

Figurine, girl playing dress-up, #T-19, 5½" **$200.00**

Figurine, hunting dog, W, I, G & hand painted, 7½" .**$65.00**

Figurine, mare, recumbent, #317, 1" H **$7.00**

Figurine, skunk w/head turned, #309, ¾" H (at tail)....**$7.00**

Figurine, squirrel w/mallet, 1940-43, 3x5" **$40.00**

Figurine, zebra, 5"..**$45.00**

Lamp, bear, W, 12" **$175.00**

Lamp, Hotei, W, 12" **$175.00**

Lamp, kitten, W, 13" **$175.00**

Mug, Bronco Group, #B202, cowboy on handle, 4¾"..**$50.00**

Mug, elephant head w/trunk handle, 3½x5".............**$125.00**

Mug, lamb, W, I, G, A, P, O, R, 3¼" **$85.00**

Mug, owl, W, I, G, A, P, O, R, 3¼" **$85.00**

Mug, spur & rope handle, 5"..**$30.00**

Napkin holder, butler, W, I, G, A, P, O, R, 7x5"........**$100.00**

Napkin holder, Hotei, W, I, G, A, P, O, R, 8x6" **$85.00**

Napkin holder, owl, W, I, G, A, P, O, R, 7x5"............**$65.00**

Napkin holder, poodle, W, I, G, A, P, O, R, 7x7"......**$75.00**

Napkin holder, Porky Pig, W, I, G, A, P, O, R, 8x5" ...**$75.00**

Napkin holder, potbellied stove, W, I, G, A, P, O, R, 7x5"..**$75.00**

Napkin holder, rooster, W, I, G, A, P, O, R, 7x6"........**$75.00**

Napkin holder, Sailor Elephant, W, I, G, A, P, O, R, 7x5" ..**$75.00**

Planter, Bambi, W, 8"..**$50.00**

Planter, circus elephant w/drum, W, 8" **$80.00**

Planter, fisherman basket, 6"..**$60.00**

Planter, rabbit w/cart, 7x10"...**$85.00**

Planter, squirrel by stump, W, 8".................................**$50.00**

Pouring spout, Bronco Group, #B204, 6¾" **$45.00**

Salt & pepper shakers, barrel, Artist Palette line, 3", pr..**$50.00**

Salt & pepper shakers, barrel, W, I, G, A, P, O, R, 1964-68, no mouse finial................**$50.00**

Salt & pepper shakers, bucket, W, I, G, A, P, O, R, 1963, pr.................**$30.00**

Salt & pepper shakers, butler, W, I, G, A, P, O, R, pr...**$30.00**

Salt & pepper shakers, churn, W, I, G, A, P, O, R, pr...**$40.00**

Salt & pepper shakers, cow, W, I, G, A, P, O, R, pr....**$50.00**

Salt & pepper shakers, dinosaur, W, I, G, A, P, O, R, pr..**$100.00**

Salt & pepper shakers, dobbin, W, I, G, A, P, O, R, pr.......**$45.00**

Salt & pepper shakers, dog, W, I, G, A, P, O, R, pr....**$40.00**

Salt & pepper shakers, duck, W, I, G, A, P, O, R, pr..**$75.00**

Salt & pepper shakers, duckling, W, I, G, A, P, O, R, pr..**$75.00**

Salt & pepper shakers, foo dog, W, I, G, A, P, O, R, pr..**$125.00**

Salt & pepper shakers, garlic faces, 3", pr...................**$40.00**

Salt & pepper shakers, Gunfighter Rabbit, W, I, G, A, P, O, R, pr.................**$45.00**

Salt & pepper shakers, Hotei, W, I, G, A, P, O, R, pr.**$30.00**

Salt & pepper shakers, Indian Chief, W, I, G, A, P, O, R, pr.................**$75.00**

Salt & pepper shakers, jack-in-the-box, W, I, G, A, P, O, R, pr **$125.00**

Salt & pepper shakers, kangaroo, W, I, G, A, P, O, R, pr.................**$85.00**

Salt & pepper shakers, Monk/Friar Tuck, W, I, G, A, P, O, R, pr.................**$35.00**

Salt & pepper shakers, mouse, W, I, G, A, P, O, R, pr........**$40.00**

Salt & pepper shakers, Pirate Fox, W, I, G, A, P, O, R, pr ..**$45.00**

Salt & pepper shakers, Porky Pig, W, I, G, A, P, O, R, pr...**$50.00**

Salt & pepper shakers, rooster, W, I, G, A, P, O, R, pr.......**$30.00**

Salt & pepper shakers, squirrel on nut, W, I, G, A, P, O, R, pr.................**$75.00**

Salt & pepper shakers, stove, W, I, G, A, P, O, R, pr .**$50.00**

Salt & pepper shakers, teddy bear, W, I, G, A, P, O, R, pr.................**$50.00**

Salt & pepper shakers, Tommy Turtle, W, I, G, A, P, O, R, pr.................**$40.00**

Spoon rest, cow, W, I, G, A, P, O, R, 5x10" **$40.00**

Spoon rest, elf, W, I, G, A, P, O, R, 5x10" **$40.00**

Spoon rest, Hotei, W, I, G, A, P, O, R, 5x10" **$40.00**

Spoon rest, kitten, W, I, G, A, P, O, R, 5x10" **$40.00**

Spoon rest, poodle, W, I, G, A, P, O, R, 5x10"...........**$40.00**

Spoon rest, Sailor Elephant, W, I, G, A, P, O, R, 5x10"..**$40.00**

Spoon rest, turtle, W, I, G, A, P, O, R, 5x10".............**$40.00**

Talking picture frame, Persian Cat, W, I, G, A, P, O, R, 11x7".................**$110.00**

Talking picture frame, shack, W, I, G, A, P, O, R, 10½x10½".................**$110.00**

Talking picture frame, squirrel, W, I, G, A, P, O, R, 11x7".................**$110.00**

Talking picture frame, teddy bear, W, I, G, A, P, O, R, 11x7".................**$110.00**

Toothpick dispenser, white pig w/pink florals, 5" **$60.00**

Vase, bud; Snoopy bear by tall stump, 3x4"...............**$65.00**

Wall planter, lamb, W, 5½" **$100.00**

Wall planter, puppy, W, 5½"...**$100.00**

Hillbilly Line

Ladies of the Mountains, mug, 5".................................**$50.00**

Ladies of the Mountains, stein, 8" **$70.00**

Men of the Mountains, ashtray, sm, 4½x4¼" **$20.00**

Men of the Mountains, bowl, Bathing Hillbilly, 6x6"..**$70.00**

Men of the Mountains, ice bucket, bathing, W, 7½x16" .**$450.00**

Men of the Mountains, ice bucket, bottoms up, W, 7½x14" **$250.00**

Men of the Mountains, ice bucket, suspenders, #TW-30, 7½x14".................**$250.00**

Men of the Mountains, keg, Mountain Doo, 8x12", minimum value **$350.00**

Men of the Mountains, mug, 3".....................................**$50.00**

Men of the Mountains, pretzel bowl, head on 1 end, feet on other end, 8½x6" **$60.00**

Men of the Mountains, stein, #H-103, 8" **$40.00**

Men of the Mountains, stein, w/Hillbilly handle, 7½" ..**$50.00**

Universal Dinnerware

This pottery incorporated in Cambridge, Ohio, in 1934, the outgrowth of several smaller companies in the area. They produced many lines of dinnerware and kitchenware items, most of which were marked. They're best known for their

Ballerina dinnerware (simple modern shapes in a variety of solid colors) and Cat-Tail (See Cat-Tail Dinnerware). The company closed in 1960.

Ballerina, saucer	**$2.00**
Ballerina (Green), plate, cake	**$30.00**
Ballerina (Mist), plate, bread & butter	**$6.00**
Ballerina (Mist), plate, cake	**$20.00**
Ballerina (Mist), plate, dinner	**$15.00**
Ballerina Magnolia, cup & saucer	**$5.00**
Ballerina Rose, creamer	**$15.00**
Ballerina Rose, sugar bowl, w/lid	**$25.00**
Bittersweet, casserole, w/lid	**$70.00**
Bittersweet, grease jar, w/lid	**$45.00**
Calico Fruit, bowl, oven proof, 8½"	**$45.00**
Calico Fruit, bowl, 4¼"	**$25.00**
Calico Fruit, gravy boat	**$50.00**
Calico Fruit, pitcher, 6¼"	**$50.00**
Calico Fruit, refrigerator jug, w/lid, 3-qt	**$50.00**
Cattail, plate, luncheon	**$11.00**

Fruit, refrigerator pitcher, from $20.00 to $25.00.

Harvest, bowl, fruit/dessert	**$11.00**
Harvest, cup & saucer	**$19.00**
Harvest, plate, bread & butter	**$9.00**
Harvest, plate, dinner	**$18.00**
Highland, bowl, cereal	**$15.00**
Highland, bowl, fruit/dessert	**$7.00**
Highland, creamer	**$15.00**
Highland, cup & saucer	**$12.00**
Highland, plate, bread & butter	**$5.00**
Highland, plate, salad	**$7.00**
Highland, saucer	**$3.00**
Iris, pitcher, cream; 5½x6"	**$25.00**
Iris, platter, tab handles, 11½"	**$32.00**
Iris, water server	**$35.00**
Laurella, bowl, vegetable; coral, round, open	**$19.00**
Woodvine, bowl, vegetable	**$15.00**
Woodvine, creamer	**$12.00**
Woodvine, cup & saucer	**$9.00**
Woodvine, gravy boat	**$20.00**
Woodvine, utility tray	**$22.00**

Valentines

As public awareness of Valentine collecting grows, so does the demand for more categorization (ethnic, comic character, advertising, transportation, pedigree dogs and cats, artist signed, etc.). Valentine cards tend to be ephemeral in nature, but to the Valentine elitist that carefully preserves each valuable example, this is not true. Collectors study of their subject thoroughly, from the workings of the lithography process to the history of the manufacturing companies that made these tokens of love. Valentines are slowly making their way into more and more diversified collections as extensions of each collector's original interest. For more information we recommend *Valentines for the Eclectic Collector; Valentines With Values,* and *100 Years of Valentines,* all by Katherine Kreider (available from the author).

Because space in our description lines is limited, HCPP has been used to abbreviate honeycomb paper puff.

Advisor: Katherine Kreider (See Directory, Valentines)

Newsletter: *National Valentine Collectors Bulletin*
Evalene Pulati
P.O. Box 1404
Santa Ana, CA 92702; 714-547-1355; e-mail: Kingsbry@ aol.com

Dimensional, airplane center motif, w/delivery boy, c 1940s, 8¼x5½x2¼", EX	**$25.00**
Dimensional, child in cart pulled by dog, c 1940s, MIG, 5¾x4x2", EX	**$15.00**
Dimensional, child sitting on beach under umbrella, c 1940s, 5½x4x2", EX	**$15.00**
Dimensional, cottage, 2-dimensional, c 1930s, w/HCPP, MIG, 7x10x2", EX	**$25.00**
Dimensional, dove cote w/cherubs, 2-dimensional, c 1930s, MIG, 7½x4¾x2", EX	**$45.00**
Dimensional, rocketship & child, c 1940s, 5½x3¾x2", EX	**$10.00**
Dimensional, sailor & sailboat, c 1940s, 5½x3¾x2", EX	**$10.00**
Dimensional, tugboat, filled w/children, c 1930s, MIG, 9x6x3", EX	**$25.00**
Dimensional, windmill, 3-dimensional, cherubs & blue forget-me-nots, c 1930s, MIG, 9x5½", EX	**$25.00**
Flat, African American jailbird, c 1920s, 5x4", EX	**$5.00**
Flat, Charlie Brown & Lucy, USA, c 1970s, 5x3½", EX	**$3.00**
Flat, children on sofa, possible Charles Twelvetrees, c 1940s, 5¾x5", EX	**$6.00**
Flat, cowgirl w/glitter, c 1960s, 5x3", EX	**$2.00**
Flat, For My Teacher, USA, c 1950s, 4x3½", EX	**$1.00**
Flat, girl typing, c 1940s, 7x5½", EX	**$3.00**
Flat, girl w/embossed comb, Charles Twelvetrees, c 1930s, 7½x5¾", EX	**$5.00**
Flat, little farm boy w/valentine, USA, c 1940s, 6¼x3½", EX	**$2.00**
Flat, little girl stitching heart, c 1940s, 5¾x4½", EX	**$2.00**
Flat, Lucy & Linus, USA, c 1970s, 4½x3½", EX	**$2.00**

Flat, monkey playing golf, c 1930s, 5x4½", EX.............$5.00

Flat, My Love Blossoms, w/HCPP accent, c 1950s, EX.$1.00

Flat, pickle w/glitter, c 1960s, 4¾x3", EX.....................$1.00

Flat, Scottish bagpipe player & Lassie, USA, c 1940s, 5x5½",
EX...$5.00

Flat, Snoopy, USA, c 1960s, 5½x4½", EX.............$3.00

Folded-flat, Babe Ruth caricature, c 1930s, USA, 5¾x4", EX .$20.00

Folded-flat, duck w/ducklings, c 1950s, USA, 5x3½", EX ..$1.00

Folded-flat, Olive Oyl, Popeye, olive jar, c 1930s, USA,
6x3¼", EX...$15.00

Folded-flat, Winnie the Pooh, c 1960s, 6x3½", EX........$3.00

Greeting card, Cinderella type Art Deco, accented w/lace, c
1920s, 5¾x7¼", EX......................................$5.00

Greeting card, clown w/Boston Bull, Charles Twelvetrees, c
1940s, 4x5", EX..$15.00

Greeting card, Little Red Riding Hood, c 1940s, 6x5", EX..$15.00

Greeting card, pensive child on front, Whitney, c 1940s,
3½x3½", EX...$1.00

Greeting card, To My Sister, Art Deco, c 1920s, Rust Craft,
4½x5", EX..$4.00

Honeycomb paper puff, mushroom w/cherub, c 1930s,
8½x5¾x4", EX..$15.00

Honeycomb paper puff, pedestal with children playing in snow, Made in USA, 1920s, 7½x5x3", $10.00. (Photo courtesy Katherine Kreider)

Honeycomb paper puff, pedestal, w/girl & boy watering
flowers, USA, c 1920s, 8x6x4", EX.....................$15.00

Mechanical-flat, airplane w/terrier on wing, c 1940s, 2½x5½",
EX...$3.00

Mechanical-flat, bellhop delivering heart, c 1930s, 5x3¾", EX..$3.00

Mechanical-flat, big band, c 1940s, 7¾x11", EX..........$25.00

Mechanical-flat, Boy Scout w/Native American, PIG, c 1930s,
3¾x5½", EX..$5.00

Mechanical-flat, carousel, USA, c 1940s, 6½x9", EX ...$10.00

Mechanical-flat, chimp w/boxing gloves, Charles Twelvetrees, c 1940s, 6¼x3", EX.............................$5.00

Mechanical-flat, dog playing piano, c 1940s, 5x6¾", EX..$3.00

Mechanical-flat, Gepetto, Disney, c 1930s, 4½x3", EX..$25.00

Mechanical-flat, Gideon, Disney, c 1930s, 4½x3", EX...$25.00

Mechanical-flat, girl playing cello, Germany, c 1930s, 4¾x4",
EX...$3.00

Mechanical-flat, girl washing clothes w/scrub board, USA,
6x5½", EX..$4.00

Mechanical-flat, Goofy/Jiminy Cricket, c 1930s, 5x4½", EX.$30.00

Mechanical-flat, little boy w/girl inside jar, c 1940s, USA,
9½x6½", EX..$10.00

Mechanical-flat, owl on branch, c 1940s, Canada, 6x4½",
EX...$3.00

Mechanical-flat, policeman, c 1940s, 5x3¼", EX $2.00

Mechanical-flat, Scottie dog, USA, c 1940s, 9¾x5", EX ..$15.00

Mechanical-flat, soda jerk, USA, 6x4", EX...................$10.00

Mechanical-flat, swing-go-round, Germany, c 1930s, 4x3½",
EX...$3.00

Mechanical-flat, toaster, USA, c 1950s, 5¾x3¼", EX $2.00

Mechanical-flat, young lady playing harp, c early 1900s, MIG,
4¼x3¾", EX..$3.00

Novelty, clockwork musical greeting card, Hallmark, c 1959,
9½x7½x1", EX..$15.00

Novelty, flat, finger puppet, bathing beauty, c 1950s, USA,
8x4", EX...$4.00

Novelty, greeting card, briefcase, USA, 3½x4", EX $1.00

Novelty, greeting card, Chunky coupon inside, USA, c 1980s,
8½x5½", NM..$5.00

Novelty, greeting card, Nestle Chocolate coupon inside, USA,
c 1980s, 8½x5½", NM....................................$5.00

Novelty, greeting card, sneaker, USA, c 1940s, 3½x4", EX..$1.00

Novelty, HCPP Wheel of Love, Beistle, USA, c 1920s,
9½x6½x3", EX..$20.00

Novelty, heart w/cast metal rake attached in original box,
USA, 5½x5¼", EX $15.00

Novelty, lollipop card w/minstrel playing banjo, USA, 6x5",
EX...$5.00

Novelty, Valentine paint book, Carrington Co, w/paint brush,
c 1940s, 6¾x5", EX $15.00

Vallona Starr

Triangle Studios opened in the 1930s, primarily as a gift shop that sold the work of various California potteries and artists such as Brad Keeler, Beth Barton, Cleminson, Josef Originals, and many others. As the business grew, Leona and Valeria, talented artists in their own right, began developing their own ceramic designs. In 1939 the company became known as Vallona Starr, a derivation of the three partners' names — (Val)eria Dopyera de Marsa, and Le(ona) and Everett (Starr) Frost. They made several popular ceramic lines including Winkies, Corn Design, Up Family, Flower Fairies, and the Fairy Tale Characters salt and pepper shakers. There were many others. Vallona Starr made only three cookie jars: Winkie (beware of any jars made in colors other than pink or yellow); Peter, Peter, Pumpkin Eater (used as a TV prize-show giveaway); and Squirrel on Stump (from the Woodland line). For more information we recommend *Vallona Starr Ceramics* by Bernice Stamper.

See also Cookie Jars.

Advisor: Bernice Stamper (See Directory, Vallona Starr)

Creamer & sugar bowl, pink w/hand-painted cattails all around, scalloped top......**$30.00**

Creamer & sugar bowl, stump design, squirrel finial on sugar bowl lid......**$50.00**

Cup, standing bear design, 4".....**$50.00**

Jar, corn design, w/lid, 5".....**$20.00**

Salt & pepper shakers, Aladdin & His Magic Lamp, Aladdin is green w/gold trim, gold-tone lamp, pr, from $75 to..**$100.00**

Salt & pepper shakers, woman w/rolling pin, man in doghouse, EX......**$45.00**

Salt & pepper shakers, 2 peach-colored baby birds in brown nest, birds are 1 shaker, nest is 2nd.....**$40.00**

Tumbler, corn design, 3½".....**$15.00**

Vandor

For more than thirty-five years, Vandor has operated out of Salt Lake City, Utah. They're not actually manufacturers but distributors of novelty ceramic items made overseas. Some pieces will be marked 'Made in Korea,' while others are marked 'Sri Lanka,' 'Taiwan,' or 'Japan.' Many of their best things have been made in the last few years, and already collectors are finding them appealing — anyone would. They have a line of kitchenware designed around 'Cowmen Mooranda' (an obvious take off on Carmen), another called 'Crocagator' (a darling crocodile modeled as a teapot, a bank, salt and pepper shakers, etc.), character-related items (Betty Boop and Howdy Doody, among others), and some really wonderful cookie jars reminiscent of '50s radios and jukeboxes.

For more information, we recommend *The Collector's Encyclopedia of Cookie Jars, Vol II,* by Joyce and Fred Roerig (Collector Books).

Advisor: Lois Wildman (See Directory, Vandor)

Betty Boop, bank, paper label: Vandor Made in Japan c 1986 KFS, 4", $50.00.
(Photo courtesy Beverly and Jim Mangus)

Betty Boop, ashtray, piano shape, 1984, EX **$25.00**
Betty Boop, figurine, diva in chair, musical, 1996, MIB..**$40.00**
Betty Boop, figurine, w/Pudgy in car, 1997, MIB **$110.00**
Betty Boop, figurine, wearing black 1-pc swimsuit w/white belt, 1995, w/stand, MIB **$36.00**

Betty Boop, picture frame, Puppy Love, Betty w/puppy beside heart frame, 1986.....**$20.00**

Betty Boop, salt & pepper shakers, Betty holding 2 glass shakers, 1955, 5¼", 3-pc set.....**$39.00**

Betty Boop, salt & pepper shakers, sitting w/Bimbo in wooden boat, 1993, pr.....**$35.00**

Betty Boop, teapot, 1995, 7½".....**$27.00**

Betty Boop, vase, heart shape, wearing red sexy dress, 1985, 6".....**$26.00**

Car & trailer, salt & pepper shakers, 3½" L, pr **$37.00**

Celestial Moon, mirror, round.....**$28.50**

Flintstones, salt & pepper shakers, Pebbles & Bamm-Bamm, 1990, 4¼", pr.....**$50.00**

Flintstones, salt & pepper shakers, 1989, 4½", pr, from $40 to.....**$50.00**

Harley-Davidson, salt & pepper shakers, shaped like a motor, 1998, MIB, pr **$15.00**

Howdy Doody, bank, bust, triangular sticker, 4½", from $30 to.....**$45.00**

Howdy Doody/Pink Cadillac, salt & pepper shakers, pr, from $70 to.....**$90.00**

I Love Lucy, mug, 3-D Lucy & Ethel on side, 1996, 4".**$15.00**

I Love Lucy, teapot, Lucy climbs out of TV, 1996.....**$40.00**

Jetsons, cup, Elroy, 1990 .....**$27.50**

Mona Lisa, vase, 1992, 7", MIB.....**$47.00**

Pink Flamingo, mask, emb, 1985 .....**$25.00**

Pink Flamingo, picture frame, 5½x6¾".....**$34.00**

Pink pig, plate, scalloped edge, 8¼" dia **$25.00**

Popeye & Olive, salt & pepper shakers, 7½", MIB, pr, from $70 to.....**$90.00**

Rocky & Bullwinkle, mug, Bullwinkle looking into mug w/3-D lion face in bottom, Rocky pictured on side, 4", MIB.**$27.50**

Roy Rogers, salt & pepper shakers, 1992, pr.....**$20.00**

Siamese cat, plate, cat looking into fishbowl center w/paw prints around border, 1986, 7½" dia **$28.00**

Toaster w/2 slices of bread, salt & pepper shakers, 1985, MIB (w/original sticker) **$45.00**

Vernon Kilns

Founded in Vernon, California, in 1930, this company produced many lines of dinnerware, souvenir plates, decorative pottery, and figurines. They employed several well-known artists whose designs no doubt contributed substantially to their success. Among them were Rockwell Kent, Royal Hickman, and Don Blanding, all of whom were responsible for creating several of the lines most popular with collectors today.

In 1940 they signed a contract with Walt Disney to produce a line of figurines, vases, bowls, and several dinnerware patterns that were inspired by Disney's film *Fantasia*. The Disney items were made for a short time only and are now expensive.

The company closed in 1958, but Metlox purchased some of the molds and continued to produce some of their bestselling dinnerware lines through a specially established 'Vernonware' division.

Most of the ware is marked in some form or another with the company name and in some cases the name of the dinnerware pattern.

If you'd like to learn more, we recommend *The Collector's Encyclopedia of California Pottery, Second Edition,* by Jack Chipman; and *Collectible Vernon Kilns,* (now out of print) by Maxine Feek Nelson. (Both are published by Collector Books.)

Advisor: Maxine Nelson (See Directory, Vernon Kilns)

Newsletter: *Vernon Views*
P.O. Box 24234
Tempe, AZ 85285
Published quarterly beginning with the spring issue

Anytime Shape

Patterns you will find on this shape include Tickled Pink, Heavenly Days, Anytime, Imperial, Sherwood, Frolic, Young in Heart, Rose-A-Day, and Dis 'N Dot.

Bowl, fruit; 5½", from $4 to	**$6.00**
Bowl, vegetable; divided, 9", from $15 to	**$20.00**
Butter pat, individual, 2½", from $15 to	**$18.00**
Coffeepot, w/lid, 8-cup, from $30 to	**$45.00**
Gravy boat, from $15 to	**$18.00**
Mug, 12-oz, from $12 to	**$20.00**
Plate, chop; 13", from $13 to	**$25.00**
Plate, salad; 7½", from $5 to	**$9.00**
Platter, 9½", from $9 to	**$12.00**
Relish dish, 3-section, from $20 to	**$25.00**
Sugar bowl, w/lid, from $10 to	**$18.00**
Tumbler, 14-oz, from $12 to	**$22.00**

Chatelaine Shape

This designer pattern by Sharon Merrill was made in four color combinations: Topaz, Bronze, Platinum, and Jade.

Bowl, chowder; Topaz & Bronze, 6", from $15 to	**$25.00**
Creamer, decorated Platinum & Jade, from $40 to	**$45.00**
Plate, dinner; leaf in all 4 corners, Topaz & Bronze, from $18 to	**$20.00**
Plate, dinner; leaf in 1 corner only, decorated Platinum & Jade, 10½", from $20 to	**$25.00**
Plate, salad; Topaz & Bronze, 7½", from $12 to	**$15.00**
Sugar bowl, decorated Platinum & Jade, w/lid, from $30 to	**$35.00**

Lotus and Pan American Lei Shape

Patterns on this shape include Lotus, Chinling, and Vintage. Pan American Lei was a variation with flatware from the San Marino line. To evaluate Lotus, use the low end of our range as the minimum value; the high end of values apply to Pan American Lei.

Ashtray, Pan American Lei only, 5½"	**$25.00**
Bowl, chowder; 6", from $11 to	**$18.00**
Bowl, mixing; Pan American Lei only, 6"	**$35.00**
Bowl, mixing; Pan American Lei only, 9"	**$50.00**
Bowl, salad; Lotus only, 12½", from $35 to	**$45.00**
Creamer, from $15 to	**$27.00**
Mug, 9-oz, from $15 to	**$35.00**
Pitcher, jug style, 2-qt, from $30 to	**$95.00**
Plate, chop; offset, Lotus only, 13", from $35 to	**$45.00**
Plate, coupe; Pan American Lei only, 6"	**$12.00**
Plate, offset; Lotus only, 7½", from $8 to	**$10.00**
Platter, coupe; Pan American Lei only, 13½"	**$50.00**
Salt & pepper shakers, pr, from $15 to	**$50.00**
Sugar bowl, w/lid, from $16 to	**$35.00**

Melinda Shape

Patterns found on this shape are Arcadia, Beverly, Blossom Time, Chintz, Cosmos, Dolores, Fruitdale, Hawaii (Lei Lani on Melinda is priced at two times base value), May Flower, Monterey, Native California, Philodendron. The more elaborate the pattern, the higher the value.

Bowl, fruit; 5½", from $5 to	**$8.00**
Bowl, serving; oval, 10", from $15 to	**$25.00**
Butter tray, oblong, w/lid, from $30 to	**$45.00**
Creamer, short or tall, from $10 to	**$18.00**
Egg cup, from $18 to	**$30.00**
Pitcher, 2-qt, from $40 to	**$60.00**
Plate, chop; 12", from $15 to	**$30.00**
Plate, luncheon; square, 8½", from $15 to	**$20.00**
Platter, 16", from $35 to	**$50.00**
Relish, leaf shape, 2-part, 11", from $35 to	**$45.00**
Sugar bowl, short or tall, w/lid, from $12 to	**$20.00**
Tidbit, wooden fixture, 2-tier, from $20 to	**$30.00**

Montecito Shape (and Coronado)

This was one of the company's more utilized shapes — well over two hundred patterns have been documented. Among the most popular are the solid colors, plaids, the florals, westernware, and the Bird and Turnbull series. Bird, Turnbull, and Winchester 73 (Frontier Days) are two to four times the base values. Disney hollow ware is seven to eight times the base values. Plaids (except Tweed and Calico), solid colors, Brown-eyed Susan are represented by the lower range.

Ashtray, square, 4½", from $8 to	**$12.00**
Bowl, lug chowder; tab handles, open, 6", from $12 to	**$15.00**
Bowl, mixing; 5", from $15 to	**$20.00**
Bowl, mixing; 8", from $35 to	**$45.00**
Bowl, salad; angular, 15", from $45 to	**$65.00**
Bowl, salad; 13", from $45 to	**$65.00**
Bowl, serving; oval, 10", from $18 to	**$22.00**
Bowl, serving; 8½" dia, from $15 to	**$18.00**
Butter pat, individual, 2½", from $15 to	**$25.00**
Butter tray, plain, rectangular finial, from $30 to	**$50.00**

Casserole, 2-handled, angular, w/lid, from $45 to **$50.00**
Coaster/cup warmer, 4½", from $18 to **$25.00**
Coffeepot, after dinner; 2-cup, scarce, from $60 to **$70.00**
Comport, footed, early, scarce, 9½" dia, from $45 to.**$65.00**
Creamer, angular or round, from $10 to......................**$18.00**
Egg cup, double, cupped or straight sides, from $15 to..**$20.00**
Gravy/sauce boat, angular or round, from $18 to......**$25.00**
Jam jar, notched lid, 5", from $55 to............................**$65.00**
Lemon server, center brass handle, 6", from $20 to....**$25.00**
Muffin tray, tab handles, dome cover, 9", from $50 to ..**$75.00**
Mug, straight sides, later style, 9-oz, 3½", from $16 to..**$22.00**
Pepper mill, wood encased, 4½", from $35 to............**$40.00**
Pitcher, disk; plain or decorated, 2-qt, from $35 to......**$75.00**
Pitcher, streamlined, ½-pt, 5", from $20 to..................**$30.00**
Pitcher, tankard; 1½-qt, from $50 to **$65.00**
Plate, bread & butter; 6½", from $5 to........................**$8.00**
Plate, chop; 14", from $20 to......................................**$50.00**
Plate, grill; 11", from $18 to..**$25.00**
Plate, luncheon; 9½", from $9 to................................**$14.00**
Platter, 12", from $17 to..**$25.00**
Spoon holder, from $45 to..**$65.00**
Sugar bowl, angular or round, open, from $10 to......**$15.00**
Tidbit, wooden fixture, 2-tier, from $20 to **$30.00**
Tumbler, banded rim & base, #1, 4½", from $18 to ...**$25.00**

San Fernando Shape

Known patterns for this shape are Desert Bloom, Early Days, Hibiscus, R.F.D, Vernon's 1860, and Vernon Rose.

Bowl, mixing; RFD pattern only, 7", from $22 to **$25.00**
Bowl, rim soup; 8", from $12 to..................................**$20.00**
Bowl, salad; individual, RFD pattern only, 5½", from $12 to..**$15.00**
Casserole, w/lid, 8" (inside dia), from $35 to..............**$65.00**
Coffeepot, w/lid, 8-cup, from $35 to **$65.00**
Egg cup, double, RFD pattern only, from $15 to.......**$20.00**
Olive dish, oval, 10", from $20 to **$25.00**
Plate, dinner; 10½", from $12 to..................................**$18.00**
Platter, 14", from $25 to..**$35.00**
Salt & pepper shakers, pr, from $18 to........................**$25.00**
Spoon holder, RFD pattern only, from $30 to............**$35.00**
Sugar bowl, w/lid, from $15 to **$20.00**
Tumbler, style #5, RFD pattern only, 14-oz, from $20 to..**$25.00**

San Marino Shape

Known patterns for this shape are Barkwood, Bel Air, California Originals, Casual California, Gayety, Hawaiian Coral, Heyday, Lei Lani (two times base values), Mexicana, Pan American Lei (two times base values), Raffia, Shadow Leaf, Shantung, Sun Garden, and Trade Winds.

Ashtray, 5½", from $15 to **$25.00**
Bowl, chowder; 6", from $12 to **$20.00**
Bowl, salad; 10½", from $30 to **$45.00**
Butter tray, oblong, w/lid, from $25 to......................**$35.00**
Coaster, ridged, 3¾", from $10 to...............................**$15.00**

Coffee server, w/stopper, 10-cup, from $25 to............**$30.00**
Creamer, regular, from $7 to.......................................**$12.00**
Custard, 3", from $20 to **$25.00**
Flowerpot, 4", w/saucer, from $30 to..........................**$35.00**
Pitcher, 1-qt, from $25 to **$35.00**
Plate, bread & butter; 6", from $4 to..........................**$7.00**
Platter, 9½", from $10 to..**$15.00**
Sauce boat, from $15 to..**$20.00**
Spoon holder, from $20 to..**$25.00**
Teapot, w/lid, 8-cup, 11" W, from $30 to....................**$45.00**

Ultra Shape

More than fifty patterns were issued on this shape. Nearly all the artist-designed lines (Rockwell Kent, Don Blanding, and Disney) utilized Ultra. The shape was developed by Gale Turnbull, and many of the elaborate flower and fruit patterns can be credited to him as well; use the high end of our range as a minimum value for his work. For Frederick Lunning, use the mid range. For other artist patterns, use these formulas based on the high end: Blanding — 2X (Aquarium 3X); Disney, 7 – 8X; Kent — Moby Dick and Our America, 2½X, Salamina, 5 – 7X.

Bowl, coupe soup; 7½", from $10 to............................**$18.00**
Bowl, fruit; 5½", from $6 to...**$12.00**
Bowl, mixing; 7", from $25 to **$30.00**
Bowl, salad; 11", from $40 to.......................................**$75.00**
Casserole, w/lid, 8" (inside dia), from $35 to..............**$55.00**
Creamer, open, individual, from $12 to.......................**$20.00**
Cup, jumbo, from $35 to..**$40.00**
Egg cup, from $15 to..**$20.00**
Mug, 8-oz, 3½", from $18 to..**$30.00**
Plate, bread & butter; 6½", from $5 to........................**$10.00**
Plate, chop; 14", from $35 to.......................................**$75.00**
Plate, chop; 17", from $45 to.......................................**$95.00**
Plate, luncheon; 8½", from $12 to...............................**$15.00**
Sauce boat, from $18 to..**$35.00**
Teapot, 6-cup, from $40 to **$70.00**
Tureenette, notched lid, 7", from $60 to.....................**$85.00**

Year 'Round Shape

Patterns on this shape include Country Cousin and Lollipop Tree.

Bowl, fruit; 5½", from $4 to...**$6.00**
Buffet server, trio; from $35 to **$70.00**
Butter tray, w/lid, from $25 to....................................**$35.00**
Coffeepot, w/lid, 6-cup, from $25 to **$45.00**
Cup & saucer, tea; from $8 to **$12.00**
Plate, bread & butter; 6", from $4 to..........................**$6.00**
Salt & pepper shakers, pr, from $10 to.......................**$18.00**

Fantasia

Bowl, Winged Nymph, #122, 12" base dia...............**$300.00**

Figurine, Baby Black Pegasus, #19............................$350.00
Figurine, Centaurette, #17 ....$700.00
Figurine, Donkey Unicorn, #16 ....$600.00
Figurine, Elephant, #26 ....$500.00
Salt & pepper shakers, Hop Low, #35 & #36, pr......$120.00
Vase, Cameo Goddess, #126....................................$700.00

Souvenir Plates

American Society of Civil Engineers, blue..................$25.00
Fredric Chopin, Music Masters, 8½"............................$25.00
San Jose de Guadalupe, Mission Series, 8½".............$30.00
Silverton, Oregon Centennial, 1854-1954, multicolored..$40.00

St. Augustine, maroon transfer, 10½", from $10.00 to $15.00.

Tacoma Narrows Bridge, brown..................................$35.00
US Naval Air Station, Alameda California, blue...........$65.00
Will Rogers, brown...$35.00

View-Master Reels and Packets

William Gruber was the inventor who introduced the View-Master to the public at the New York World's Fair and the Golden Gate Exposition held in California in 1939. Thousands of reels and packets have been made since that time on every aspect of animal life, places of interest, and entertainment.

Over the years the company has changed ownership five times. It was originally Sawyer's View-Master, G.A.F (in the mid-sixties), View-Master International (1981), Ideal Toy and, most recently, Tyco Toy Company. The latter three companies produced them strictly as toys and issued only cartoons, making the earlier non-cartoon reels and the three-reel packets very collectible.

Sawyer made two cameras so that the public could take their own photo reels in 3-D. They made a projector as well, so that the homemade reels could be viewed on a large screen. 'Personal' or 'Mark II' cameras with their cases usually range in value from $100.00 to $200.00; rare viewers such as the blue 'Model B' start at about $100.00, and the 'Stereo-Matic 500' projector is worth $175.00 to $200.00. Most single reels range from $1.00 to $5.00, but some early Sawyer's and G.A.F's may bring as much as $35.00 each, character-related reels sometimes even more.

Club: View-Master Reel Collector
Roger Nagely
4921 Castor Ave.
Philadelphia, PA 19124

Adventures of Tarzan, #975, M $10.00
Amazing Spider-Man, H-11, MIP (sealed)....................$25.00
Babes in Toyland, B-375, 1961, MIP $35.00
Banana Splits, 1970, MIP..$40.00
Batman Forever, #4160, MIP (sealed)..........................$10.00
Beverly Hillbillies, B-570, 1963, MIP, from $35 to.......$45.00
Blondie & Dagwood, 1960, MIP..................................$20.00
Brave Eagle, B-446, 1955, MIP...................................$30.00
Bugs Bunny in Big Top Bunny, B-549, MIP.................$20.00
Captain Kangaroo, B-560, 1957, MIP..........................$30.00
Charlotte's Web, B-321, MIP.......................................$15.00
Christmas Story, B-282, MIP (sealed) $20.00
Herbie Rides Again, B-578, MIP $15.00
Jetsons, L-27, 1981, MIP $5.00
King Kong, B-392, 1976, MIP (sealed) $25.00
Land of the Giants, B-494, 1968, MIP $60.00
Lassie & Timmy, B-474, 1959, MIP..............................$20.00
Little Drummer Boy, B-871, 1958, MIP $20.00
Mary Poppins, B-376, 1964, MIP $15.00
Million Dollar Duck, B-506, MIP (sealed)....................$30.00
Mod Squad, B-478, 1968, MIP....................................$30.00
Mork & Mindy, K-67, 1979, MIP $20.00
Nanny & the Professor, B-573, 1970, MIP, from $35 to..$45.00
Partridge Family, B-569, 1971, MIP $35.00
Pink Panther, J-12, 1978, MIP $15.00
Pluto, B-529, MIP..$15.00
Raggedy Ann & Andy, 1971, MIP $25.00
Robinson Crusoe, B-438, 1958, MIP $25.00
Shaggy DA, B-368, 1976, MIP $20.00
Snoopy & the Red Baron, B-544, MIP (sealed)...........$20.00
Waltons, B-596, 1972, MIP $20.00
Who Framed Roger Rabbit, K-37, 1979, MIP...............$35.00
Wolfman, J-30, 1978, MIP, from $15 to........................$20.00
X-Men, Captive Hearts, #1085, 1993, MIP...................$15.00
20,000 Leagues Under the Sea, B-370, 1954, MIP (sealed)..$25.00

Viking Glass

Located in the famous glass-making area of West Virginia, this company has been in business since the 1950s; they're most famous for their glass animals and birds. Their Epic Line (circa 1950s and 1960s) was innovative in design and vibrant in color. Rich tomato-red, amberina, brilliant blues, strong greens, black, amber, and deep amethyst were among the rainbow hues in production at that time. During the 1980s the company's ownership changed hands, and the firm became known as Dalzell-Viking. Viking closed their doors in 1998.

Some of the Epic Line animals were reissued in crystal,

crystal frosted, and black. If you're interested in learning more about these animals, refer to *Glass Animals of the Depression Era* by Lee Garmon and Dick Spencer (Collector Books).

Advisor: Mary Lou Bohl (See Directory, Viking)

Ashtray, alligator figural, orange, 11" L	$50.00
Ashtray, tangerine crackle, 10"	$35.00
Bell, Yesteryear, ruby, 3½"	$20.00
Bonbon, ruby, 4-scalloped bowl, footed, 1984-85, 7"	$20.00
Bookends, lion, clear, 5½", pr	$50.00

Bookends, owl figural, amber, ca 1950, 5", $25.00 for the pair. (Photo courtesy Louis Kuritzky)

Candlestick, Fleur, black satin, 1980s, 5½"	$28.00
Candlestick, Spiral, black, 1980s, 7"	$28.00
Candy dish, amber, bird finial, tail up, 12¼"	$30.00
Canoe, Daisy & Button, blue, 11½"	$38.00
Fairy lamp, Diamond Quilt, green, 6½"	$20.00
Fairy lamp, Diamond Quilt, pink, 5¼"	$20.00
Fairy lamp, Diamond Quilt, ultramarine, 7"	$20.00
Figurine, bird, dark amber, long tail, 9¾"	$35.00
Figurine, bunny, black, 1980s, 2½"	$20.00
Figurine, butterfly, blue, 5¾" wingspan	$40.00
Figurine, cat, crystal, 8"	$70.00
Figurine, duck mama, ruby, 9"	$50.00
Figurine, egret, dark med blue, 9½x12"	$50.00
Figurine, fish on base, amber, tail up, 9¾"	$60.00
Figurine, lop-eared dog, amber, 8"	$25.00
Figurine, lop-eared dog, blue, 8"	$30.00
Figurine, owl, black, 1980s, 2½"	$20.00
Figurine, pear, ruby, 8½"	$30.00
Figurine, rabbit, green, 1960s, 6½"	$25.00
Figurine, rooster, Epic; orange, 9½"	$55.00
Ice bucket, black, w/label, 1980s, 6½"	$50.00
Paperweight, lion, frosted, 5x5½"	$35.00
Paperweight, Sea Captain, clear, 6"	$35.00
Paperweight, tiger, frosted, 5¾x5½"	$35.00
Tray, black satin, Dolphin center, 1980s, 11"	$60.00

Wade Porcelain

If you've attended many flea markets, you're already very familiar with the tiny Wade figures, most of which are 2" and under. Wade made several lines of these miniatures, but the most common were made as premiums for the Red Rose Tea Company. Most of these sell for $3.50 to $7.00 or so, with a few exceptions such as the Gingerbread man. Wade also made a great number of larger figurines as well as tableware and advertising items.

The Wade Potteries began life in 1867 as Wade and Myatt when George Wade and a partner named Myatt opened a pottery in Burslem — the center for potteries in England. In 1882 George Wade bought out his partner, and the name of the pottery was changed to Wade and Sons. In 1919 the pottery underwent yet another change in name to George Wade & Son Ltd. In 1891 the world saw the establishment of another Wade Pottery — J & W Wade & Co., which in turn changed its name to A.J. Wade & Co. in 1927. At this time (1927) Wade Heath & Co. Ltd. was also formed.

These three potteries plus a new Irish pottery named Wade (Ireland) Ltd. were incorporated into one company in 1958 and given the name The Wade Group of Potteries. In 1990 the group was taken over by Beauford plc. and given the name Wade Ceramics Ltd., remaining so until the present time. In early 1999, Wade Ceramics Ltd. was bought out from Beauford plc. by the Wade management.

If you'd like to learn more, we recommend *The World of Wade, The World of Wade Book 2,* and *Wade Price Trends — First Edition* by Ian Warner and Mike Posgay.

Advisor: Ian Warner (See Directory, Wade)

Newsletters: *The Wade Watch, Ltd.*
8199 Pierson Ct.
Arvada, CO 80005
303-421-9655 or 303-424-4401 or fax: 303-421-0317

Club: Wade's World
The Official International Wade Collector's Club
Wade Ceramics Ltd.
Royal Works, Westport Rd., Burslem, Stoke-on-Trent,
Staffordshire, ST6 4AP, England, UK
e-mail: club@wade.co.uk; www.wade.co.uk/wade

Animal, Rabbit, Made in England, 4¾"	$130.00
Animal, Terrier Pup, glass eyes, 6⅜"	$150.00
Bird, Duck, Tom Smith, Wade England, 1992-93, 1⅝x1"	$12.00
Bird, Partridge, Tom Smith, Wade England, 1992-93, 1½x1¾"	$12.00
Bird, Wren, Tom Smith, marked Wade Eng, 1992-93, 1½"	$15.00
Dinosaur, Camarasaurus, Barbara Cooskey, Wade England, 1993, 2x1¾"	$9.00
Dinosaur, Protoceratops, Barbara Cooksey, Wade England, 1993, 1⅛x2⅜"	$9.00
Dinosaur, Tyrannosaurux Rex, Barbara Cooksey, Wade England, 1993, 1¾x2⅜"	$9.00
Family Pets, Fish, Tom Smith, Wade England, ca 1988-89, 1"	$10.00
Family Pets, Guinea Pig, Tom Smith, marked Wade Eng on base, 1988-89, ¾"	$10.00
Family Pets, Puppy, Tom Smith, Wade England, ca 1988-89, 1"	$10.00

Family Pets, Rabbit, Tom Smith, Wade Eng on base, 1988-89, 1⅛" **$8.00**

Giftware, Bengo Money Box, unmarked, 1960s, 6"..**$375.00**

Giftware, Exotic Fish Wall Plaque, Wade Porcelain Made in England, rare, 3¾x2½" **$350.00**

Giftware, Pig Family Cruet Set, Wade England, salt & pepper shakers (marked) on unmarked tray, complete .**$285.00**

Gothic Dish, with lid, 1950s, $90.00. (Photo courtesy Ian Warner)

Souvenir, Dish, Scottish Piper (porcelain base w/brown glaze is the only part made by Wade), 4½" **$35.00**

Souvenir, Dish, Tower Bridge, marked, 1957, 1½x4x3" **$25.00**

Souvenir, Jug, New Brunswick, marked, 3¾"..............**$35.00**

Souvenir, Shaving Mug, Victorian barber scene, marked, 3⅛x4" **$20.00**

Souvenir, Vase, Nova Scotia, Provincial flag on reverse, marked, 4½" **$15.00**

Tankard, Roosevelt & Churchill, Let's Drink to Victory, marked, 1942, 5½x7½" **$150.00**

Traufler Promotional Item, Hen & Rooster Salt & Pepper Shakers, unmarked, 1992, 3⅝", 4⅝", ea...............**$60.00**

Traufler Promotional Item, Sheep, white, unmarked, 1992, 1⅝" **$30.00**

Whimsey-in-the-Vale, Boar's Head Pub, Judith Wooten, 1993, 1½x3x1" **$12.00**

Whimsey-in-the-Vale, Florist Shop, Judith Wooten, 1993, 1½x1½x⅞" **$10.00**

Whimsey-in-the-Vale, St Lawrence Church, Judith Wooten, 1993, 2⅛x3x1⅛" **$12.00**

Whimsie - Land Series, Field Mouse, Wade England, ca 1987, 1¼x1½" **$35.00**

Whimsie - Land Series, Golden Eagle, Wade England, ca 1987, 1⅛x1¾"..**$40.00**

Whimsie - Land Series, Otter, Wade England, ca 1987, 1½x1⅝"...**$15.00**

Whimsie - Land Series, Partridge, Wade England, ca 1987, 1½x1¾"..**$30.00**

Whimsie - Land Series, Pheasant, Wade England, ca 1987, 1¼x2"..**$40.00**

Wild Life, Kangaroo, Tom Smith, Wade England, 1986-87, 1⅝"..**$10.00**

Wild Life, Koala Bear, Tom Smith, Wade England, 1986-87, 1⅜"..**$12.00**

Wild Life, Leopard, Tom Smith, Wade England, 1986-87, ⅞"..**$5.00**

Wild Life, Orang-Utan, Tom Smith, Wade England, 1986-87, 1¼"..**$5.00**

World of Dogs, Bulldog, Tom Smith, Wade England, 1990-91, 1"..**$10.00**

World of Dogs, Corgi, Tom Smith, Wade England, 1990-91, 1½"..**$10.00**

World of Dogs, Mongrel, Tom Smith, Wade England, 1990-91, 1¼"..**$8.00**

Wall Pockets

A few years ago there were only a handful of avid wall pocket collectors, but today many are finding them intriguing. They were popular well before the turn of the century. Roseville and Weller included at least one and sometimes several in many of their successful lines of art pottery, and other American potteries made them as well. Many were imported from Germany, Czechoslovakia, China, and Japan. By the 1950s, they were passè.

Some of the most popular today are the figurals. Look for the more imaginative and buy the ones you especially like. If you're buying to resell, look for those designed as animals, large exotic birds, children, luscious fruits, or those that are particularly eye catching. Appeal is everything. Examples with a potter's mark are usually more pricey (for instance Roseville, McCoy, Hull, etc.), because of the crossover interest in collecting their products. For more information refer to *Made in Japan Ceramics* (there are three in the series) by Carole Bess White; *Collector's Guide to Wall Pockets, Affordable and Others,* by Marvin and Joy Gibson; *Wall Pockets of the Past* by Fredda Perkins; and *Collector's Encyclopedia of Wall Pockets* by Betty and Bill Newbound.

Advisor: Carole Bess White (See Directory, Japan Ceramics)

Bamboo shoot form, blue, Japan, 7⅛", from $8 to.....**$10.00**

Bird, white phoenix-type w/blue trim on white vase w/vertical ribbing, glossy, Japan, 6½", from $20 to.........**$30.00**

Bird on pouch-shaped basket w/flowering dogwood branch, multicolored, semigloss & highgloss, Japan, 8", from $15 to **$20.00**

Butterflies (1 yellow embossed & 1 green applied) on green basketweave urn-shaped vase, unmarked, 6¾", from $12 to **$15.00**

Butterfly & flowers, multicolored on tan lustre vase w/2 sm loop handles, Japan, 6", from $35 to **$55.00**

Butterfly & trumpet flowers, multicolored lustre glazes, on conical form, Japan, 8½", from $40 to..................**$60.00**

Cherry blossoms, blue lustre, on conical form, Japan Mitsu-Inos, 6", from $20 to..**$35.00**

Circular form w/parrot & roses, multicolored, glossy, no mark, 7½", from $17 to **$22.00**

Cornucopia (leaf-formed), w/figural bird, various colors, unmarked, 5½", from $10 to..............**$12.00**

Cornucopia w/figural duck, unmarked, 7", from $10 to..**$15.00**

Cornucopia w/flared scalloped top & tail curled sideways, glossy, unmarked, from $8 to..............**$10.00**

Cuckoo clock w/bird in window & atop roof, porcelain w/blue, yellow & rose trim, Japan, 5⅛", from $12 to.............**$14.00**

Cuckoo clock w/strawberries, white w/red berries, green vines & brown trim, unmarked, 6¾", from $20 to...........**$25.00**

Cup & saucer, bright yellow, Camark, 7½", from $15 to .**$25.00**

Cupid holding red heart-shaped vase, semi-gloss, Japan, 5", from $12 to..............**$15.00**

Daffodils & leaves form, yellow & green, glossy, Japan, 4", from $10 to..............**$12.00**

Duck in flight on crescent vase, glossy, Japan, 6¼", from $12 to..............**$15.00**

Dutch boy or girl holding up basket, porcelain w/multicolored trim, Japan, 6½", ea from $12 to..............**$15.00**

Fish, pink, green & white, marked CermCraft, San Clemente, CA, Tropic Treasures, 9½", from $25 to..............**$35.00**

Fish mounted on wood-look plaque, glossy air-brushed colors, Japan, 2¼x3¼", from $17 to..............**$22.00**

Floral vine on tree trunk, lg red flowers, brown vine & green leaves on tan lustre trunk, Japan, 7½", from $40 to .**$60.00**

Flowers, red & white on green band, multicolor lustre glazes on conical form, Japan, 7¼", from $30 to...........**$45.00**

Girl w/basket against stone wall, porcelain, Japan, from $15 to..............**$20.00**

Give Me Time, clock form w/prayer, Norcrest, 7", from $12 to..............**$15.00**

Goat & palm trees form, glossy, Japan, 5½x7", from $15 to..............**$20.00**

Horse head & horseshoe, brown high gloss, Japan, 8½", from $20 to..............**$25.00**

Horse heads (triple) peering over fence, matt airbrushing, unmarked, 5¼x8¼", from $25 to..............**$30.00**

Iron w/floral motif, 2 openings, UCAGO China, 5½", from $12 to..............**$15.00**

Kitten in wooden bucket, pink & brown airbrushing, unmarked, 6¾", from $20 to..............**$35.00**

Lady dancing, head back holding out cape to blue flowing dress w/white flowers on skirt, semi-gloss, Japan, 9", from $45..............**$55.00**

Orange on lg leaf, from $20 to..............**$35.00**

Oriental lady figure on bamboo-form vase, Japan, 5⅜", from $12 to..............**$15.00**

Parrot on branch, rich multicolored glossy finish, Japan, 9¾", from $20 to..............**$25.00**

Peacock, moriage on tan & blue lustre, cone form, Japan, 7¼", from $35 to..............**$40.00**

Pine cone, Corteny, 4¾", from $6 to..............**$8.00**

Pitcher w/stylized bird motif, trimmed w/hash-mark design on rim, handle & base, Japan, 6¾", from $12 to .**$14.00**

Poodle seated on vase ledge, glossy, Empress, Japan, 3¾", from $8 to..............**$10.00**

Skillet w/cherries & leaves (applied), Jan's California, 7", from $18 to..............**$28.00**

Swan pr on lake, blue & tan lustre striped ground, black trim, Japan, 8¼"..............**$35.00**

Swan w/baby seated in crook of neck, lustre, marked Bradley Exclusive, Japan..............**$22.00**

Teapot w/strawberries & leaves, cold-painted colors on creamy white, from $20 to..............**$30.00**

Tokanabe-type w/butterfly & flowers, multicolored on textured vase w/dark ground, semi-gloss, 10", from $20 to..............**$35.00**

Tokanabe-type w/stemmed flower, yellow flower w/green leaves on textured tan vase, matt, Japan, 9¼", from $20..............**$30.00**

Violin, gold trim, Goldra, E Palestine OH, 8", from $12 to ..**$22.00**

Radishes, Portugal, 11½", from $28.00 to $40.00. (Photo courtesy Bill and Betty Newboud)

Wallace China

This company operated in California from 1931 until 1964, producing many lines of dinnerware, the most popular of which today are those included in their Westward Ho assortment, Boots and Saddles, Rodeo, and Pioneer Trails. All of these lines were designed by artist Till Goodan, whose signature appears in the design. All are very heavy, their backgrounds are tan, and the designs are done in dark brown with accents of rust, green, and yellow. When dinnerware with a western theme became so popular a few years ago, Rodeo was reproduced, but the new trademark includes neither 'California' nor 'Wallace China.'

Advisor: Marv Fogleman (See Directory, Dinnerware)

Ashtray, Boots & Saddle, 5½", from $45 to **$50.00**

Bowl, cereal; Boots & Saddle, from $55 to **$65.00**

Bowl, cereal; El Rancho, from $40 to **$50.00**

Bowl, El Rancho, 5"................**$45.00**

Bowl, Hibiscus, 2x5"................**$45.00**

Bowl, mixing; Boots & Saddle, 10¼"................**$650.00**

Bowl, mixing; Boots & Saddle, 7¼".........................**$215.00**
Bowl, mixing; Rodeo, 10¼"....................................**$415.00**
Bowl, mixing; Rodeo, 11¾"....................................**$460.00**
Bowl, salad; Banana Leaf..**$35.00**
Bowl, 49er, 2x4¾"...**$32.00**
Butter pat, Chuck Wagon..**$50.00**
Coffee cup, Chuck Wagon..**$72.50**
Creamer, El Rancho...**$105.00**
Creamer & sugar bowl, Rod's Steak House..............**$155.00**
Creamer & sugar bowl, Rodeo, individual **$140.00**
Cup, Magnolia, pink, heavy.....................................**$26.00**
Cup, Shadowleaf..**$30.00**
Cup & saucer, Chuck Wagon....................................**$75.00**
Cup & saucer, El Rancho **$65.00**
Cup & saucer, Rodeo, lg...**$100.00**
Gravy boat, shiny soft yellow, 3x7½x2" **$18.00**
Mug, Chuck Wagon..**$85.00**
Mug, Rodeo, 3⅝x3⅝"..**$80.00**
Pitcher, water; Boots & Saddle **$525.00**
Plate, Boots & Saddle, 7" **$50.00**
Plate, Boots & Saddle, 10½".....................................**$80.00**
Plate, Bunkhouse, W106, 7¼"...................................**$70.00**
Plate, child's, Little Buckaroo, from $100 to.............**$125.00**
Plate, chop; El Rancho, 13½"..................................**$130.00**
Plate, Chuck Wagon, 7"...**$27.50**
Plate, Chuck Wagon, 9"...**$43.00**
Plate, Dahlia, bl, 9"..**$45.00**
Plate, El Rancho, 5½"...**$30.00**
Plate, El Rancho, 7¼"...**$65.00**
Plate, Evergreen Lodge, 12½"...................................**$25.00**
Plate, grill; Magnolia, 9½", from $35 to **$45.00**
Plate, Palm Tree, 9"..**$25.00**
Plate, Poppy, Restaurantware, 7"...............................**$22.50**
Plate, Rodeo, 7", from $55 to....................................**$65.00**

Plate, Rodeo, 10½", $100.00.

Platter, El Rancho, 11½"..**$95.00**
Salt & pepper shakers, Boots & Saddle, pr **$125.00**
Salt & pepper shakers, Rodeo, pr **$125.00**
Saucer, Chuck Wagon...**$32.00**
Sugar bowl, Rodeo, w/lid...**$125.00**
Sugar bowl, Shadowleaf, w/lid..................................**$65.00**

Watt Pottery

The Watt Pottery Company operated in Crooksville, Ohio, from 1922 until sometime in 1935. It appeals to collectors of country antiques, since the body is yellow ware and its decoration rather quaint.

Several patterns were made: Apple, Autumn Foliage, Cherry, Dutch Tulip, Morning-Glory, Pansy, Rooster, Tear Drop, Starflower, and Tulip among them. All were executed in bold brush strokes of primary colors. Some items you'll find will also carry a stenciled advertising message, made for retail companies as premiums for their customers.

For further study, we recommend *Watt Pottery, An Identification and Price Guide,* by Sue and Dave Morris, published by Collector Books.

Advisor: Sue Morris (See Directory, Watt Pottery)

Club/Newsletter: *Watt's News*
Watt Collectors Association
P.O. Box 1995
Iowa City, IA 52240
Subscription: $12 per year

Apple, bean server, individual, #75...........................**$250.00**
Apple, bowl, cereal; #74 ....**$50.00**
Apple, bowl, mixing; #64...**$85.00**
Apple, bowl, mixing; ribbed, #7.................................**$50.00**
Apple, bowl, ribbed, #604 ....**$45.00**
Apple, bowl, ribbed, w/lid, #05 ....**$145.00**
Apple, bowl, ribbed, w/lid, #601 ....**$125.00**
Apple, canister, on stand, lg, #3/19.........................**$265.00**
Apple, casserole, French handled, individual, #18 ...**$225.00**
Apple, cheese crock, #80..**$1,500.00**
Apple, creamer, #62..**$100.00**
Apple, mug, #61 ....**$500.00**
Apple, pie plate, #33...**$150.00**
Apple, pitcher, ice lip, #17.......................................**$275.00**
Apple, salt & pepper shakers, barrel shape, 4", pr...**$245.00**
Apple, sugar bowl, w/lid, #98 ....**$400.00**
Apple (Double), bowl, mixing; #7 ....**$75.00**
Apple (Open), bowl, mixing; #5 ....**$85.00**
Autumn Foliage, bottle set, oil & vinegar; w/lids, #126, 7", pr..**$550.00**
Autumn Foliage, bowl, cereal; #94.............................**$30.00**
Autumn Foliage, bowl, ribbed, #8..............................**$30.00**
Autumn Foliage, fondue, 3x9"..................................**$275.00**
Autumn Foliage, pitcher, #16.....................................**$70.00**
Banded (Blue & White), pitcher, 7" **$95.00**
Banded (Brown), sugar bowl, w/lid, #98...................**$150.00**
Banded (White), casserole, w/lid, 7x9"........................**$65.00**
Basketweave (Brown), mug, #801...............................**$10.00**
Basketweave (Multicolored), bowl, from 5" to 9", ea.**$25.00**
Brown Drip Glaze, bowl, 9"...**$35.00**
Brown Glaze, electric warmer, 2x7"..........................**$125.00**
Cherry, bowl, mixing; #6...**$35.00**
Cherry, pitcher, #15 ....**$65.00**

Cut-Leaf Pansy, casserole, stick handled, individual.**$125.00**
Cut-Leaf Pansy, platter, 15" **$110.00**
Cut-Leaf Pansy (Bull's Eye w/red swirls), bowl, serving; 11"..**$60.00**
Dogwood, platter, #31, 15" dia.................................**$110.00**
Dutch Tulip, bowl, #7 ....**$70.00**
Dutch Tulip, bowl, w/lid, #5.....................................**$250.00**
Eagle, bowl, cereal; 2x5½"...**$55.00**
Eagle, bowl, mixing; #6..**$100.00**
Esmond, bowl, mixing; pear pattern.........................**$45.00**
Esmond, cookie jar, w/wooden lid, 8½x7½" dia......**$100.00**
Esmond, mug, grape pattern, #31, 3½" **$165.00**
Esmond, platter, 15" dia...**$125.00**
Goodies, jar, #59...**$225.00**
Kathy Kale, bowl, 2x5½" dia **$65.00**
Kitch-N-Queen, bowl, mixing; ribbed, #5...................**$45.00**
Kitch-N-Queen, bowl, mixing; ribbed, #9...................**$30.00**
Kitch-N-Queen, bowl, mixing; #9.................................**$30.00**
Kla Ham'rd, pie plate, #43-13....................................**$35.00**
Morning Glory, bowl, mixing; #7................................**$135.00**
Morning Glory, creamer, #97.....................................**$500.00**
Morning Glory (Yellow), casserole, w/lid, #94............**$95.00**
Old Pansy, casserole, 4½x8¾"......................................**$55.00**
Raised Pansy, casserole, French handled, individual..**$85.00**
Raised Pansy, pitcher, 7¾"...**$225.00**
Rooster, bowl, mixing; #63 ....**$50.00**
Rooster, bowl, w/lid, #67, 6½x8½" dia.....................**$200.00**
Rooster, pitcher, refrigerator; #69 ....**$500.00**
Rooster, sugar bowl, w/lid, #98.................................**$275.00**
Shaded Brown, bowl, mixing; 8" dia **$25.00**
Shaded Brown, mug, 3" **$10.00**
Shaded Brown, wall pocket, 9" dia...............................**$75.00**
Speckled Watt Ware, bowl, salad; #106 ....**$25.00**
Speckled Watt Ware, salt & pepper shakers, hourglass shape,
    4½", pr...**$55.00**
Starflower, bowl, #39...**$110.00**
Starflower, bowl, mixing; #5 ....**$45.00**
Starflower, bowl, mixing; #6 ....**$35.00**

Starflower, tumbler, slant sided, #56 ....**$225.00**
Starflower (Green on Brown), bowl, mixing; #5.........**$30.00**
Starflower (Green on Brown), casserole, w/lid, #54 .**$125.00**
Starflower (Pink on Black), bowl, 11" dia **$125.00**
Starflower (Pink on Green), bowl, berry; 5" dia.........**$35.00**
Starflower (Pink on Green), casserole, w/lid, 8½"
    dia **$125.00**
Starflower (White on Blue), bowl, spaghetti; #39.....**$175.00**
Starflower (White on Blue), mug, #121 ....**$225.00**
Tear Drop, bowl, mixing; #4..**$65.00**
Tear Drop, casserole, square, w/lid, 6x8"..................**$275.00**
Tear Drop, pitcher, #15 ....**$60.00**
Tulip, bowl, #73..**$110.00**
Tulip, bowl, mixing; #64 ....**$70.00**
Tulip, creamer, #62...**$225.00**
White Daisy, bowl, mixing; #6 ....**$55.00**
White Daisy, pitcher, 7"..**$125.00**
Woodgrain, pitcher, #613W **$75.00**

Weeping Gold

In the mid- to late 1950s, many American pottery companies produced lines of 'Weeping Gold.' Such items have a distinctive appearance; most appear to be covered with irregular droplets of lustrous gold, sometimes heavy, sometimes fine. On others the gold is in random swirls, or there may be a definite pattern developed on the surface. In fact, real gold was used; however, there is no known successful way of separating the gold from the pottery. You'll see similar pottery covered in 'Weeping Silver.' Very often, ceramic whiskey decanters made for Beam, McCormick, etc., will be trimmed in 'Weeping Gold.' Among the marks you'll find on these wares are 'McCoy,' 'Kingwood Ceramics,' and 'USA,' but most items are simply stamped '22k (or 24k) gold.'

Starflower, cookie jar, $185.00.

Planter, leaping sailfish beside swirling bowl, 11x9½", $90.00.

Starflower, pitcher, #16..**$85.00**
Starflower, salt & pepper shakers, hourglass shape, 4½",
    pr..**$175.00**

Ashtray, 3 rests in center of tray, 1¾x7¼"....................**$6.00**
Bowl, centerpc; cherub reserve in center, 4½x9" L....**$30.00**
Candlesticks, angular handles, flared wide base, Hand
    Decorated 22k Gold USA Weeping-Bright Gold, 2½x4",
    pr..**$15.00**

Creamer & sugar bowl, wide handles in the Oriental style, 3¼"...$32.50
Lamp, planter pockets ea side, original paper shade, 1950s, 10x8½x5"...$38.00
Planter, peacock, sign 24k gold, 1950s, 13½"..........$75.00
Planter, rearing horses (2), 10x9", from $80 to.........$100.00
Tea set, McCoy, 1950s, 3-pc..................................$85.00
Tidbit tray, 2-tier, 7" & 9" plates............................$30.00
Tidbit tray, 4-tier, 2-7" plates, 2-10" plates, 22k gold, 20" H.$55.00
Vase, ewer form, Hand Decorated 22k Gold USA Weeping Bright Gold, 7¾".......................................$22.00
Vase, fan; flower decor w/open-work leaf decor on sides, mk Holly Ross Decorated China 22k Gold, 7½".........$50.00
Vase, little or no embossing, footed, Hand Decorated Weeping Bright Gold 22k Gold USA, 5x7"...........$25.00

Weil Ware

Though the Weil company made dinnerware and some kitchenware, their figural pieces are attracting the most collector interest. They were in business from the 1940s until the mid-'50s, another of the small but very successful California companies whose work has become so popular today. They dressed their 'girls' in beautiful gowns of vivid rose, light dusty pink, turquoise blue, and other lovely colors enhanced with enameled 'lace work' and flowers, sgraffito, sometimes even with tiny applied blossoms. Both paper labels and ink stamps were used to mark them, but as you study their features, you'll soon learn to recognize even those that have lost their labels over the years. Four-number codes and decorators' initials are usually written on their bases.

If you want to learn more, we recommend *The Collector's Encyclopedia of California Pottery, Second Edition,* by Jack Chipman.

Ashtray, gold flecks, heavy.....................................$25.00
Bowl, berry; Birchwood, 4 for.................................$50.00
Bowl, divided vegetable; Malay Bambu....................$42.50
Bowl, divided; Malay Blossom, white flowers on soft green...$15.00
Bowl, Rose, square, w/lid, 10"................................$38.00
Bowl, serving; Rose, 8"..$20.00
Bowl, vegetable; Brentwood....................................$15.00
Bowl, vegetable; Malay Bambu, pink border, 9x7¾".$40.00
Butter dish, Malay Blossom.....................................$25.00
Casserole, Malay Bambu, w/lid, 7½" dia..................$40.00
Compote, Malay Blossom, 3½x6½"..........................$25.00
Creamer & sugar bowl, Brentwood...........................$22.00
Cup & saucer, Birchwood, 4 for...............................$20.00
Cup & saucer, Malay Blossom..................................$12.00
Cup & saucer, Rose..$18.00
Cups & saucers, Malay Bambu, 4 for........................$50.00
Figurine, flamingos, 9¾", pr...................................$70.00
Figurine, lady in yellow dress w/blue trim, 7½".........$50.00
Flower holder, girl in bright pink dress w/many hand-painted flowers stands by vase, 10"..........................$55.00

Flower holder, girl in white w/gold spaghetti-like trim at collar & on dress, opening back of waist, 12".........$50.00
Flower holder, girl in white w/hand-painted pink & blue flowers, 10"..$47.50
Flower holder, girl posed to receive kiss holds basket before her..$55.00
Flower holder, lady in white w/pink & blue trim, green & blue apron, 10"...$47.50
Flower holder, lady seated between 2 vases, #4028, 8½x7"..$55.00
Flower holder, lady w/2 baskets, #4014, 9½", NM.....$45.00
Gravy boat, Malay Blossom.....................................$20.00
Gravy bowl, Rose, attached underplate, 3¼x6½".......$38.00
Planter, lady w/push cart, #4001, 8¼x7¼x4½"..........$28.00
Plate, bread & butter; Birchwood, 4 for....................$15.00
Plate, dessert; Malay Bambu, 6 for..........................$27.50
Plate, dinner; Birchwood, 4 for...............................$25.00
Plate, dinner; Malay Blossom, 9¾", from $12 to........$15.00
Plate, dinner; Rose, 9¾"..$17.50
Plate, salad; Rose, square, 7¾", 4 for......................$28.00
Platter, Malay Bambu, pink border, 13¾x9¾", from $35 to...$45.00
Platter, Malay Blossom...$22.50
Platter, Rose, square, 13½".....................................$27.50
Shelf sitter, Oriental lady in green sits between 2 baskets, yellow straw hat, 10x6"...................................$25.00
Sugar bowl, Malay Blossom, w/lid............................$25.00
Teapot, Malay Blossom, Deco-style handle, 6¾"........$38.00
Vase, dark jade w/white interior, marked & dated 1949, 9".$18.00
Vase, 2-toned green, fan form, 7¼x8½".....................$25.00
Wall pocket, lady's head, brown hair & blue eyes, 6".$60.00
Wall pockets, Oriental girls w/straw hats & dark green clothes, #4046, pr...$55.00

Weller

Though the Weller Pottery has been closed since 1948, they were so prolific that you'll be sure to see several pieces anytime you're 'antiquing.' They were one of the largest of the art pottery giants that located in the Zanesville, Ohio, area, using locally dug clays to produce their wares. In the early years, they made hand-decorated vases, jardinieres, lamps, and other useful and decorative items for the home, many of which were signed by notable artists such as Fredrick Rhead, John Lessell, Virginia Adams, Anthony Dunlavy, Dorothy England, Albert Haubrich, Hester Pillsbury, E.L. Pickens, and Jacques Sicard, to name only a few. Some of their early lines were First and Second Dickens, Eocean, Sicardo, Etna, Louwelsa, Turada, and Aurelian. Portraits of Indians, animals of all types, lady golfers, nudes, and scenes of Dickens stories were popular themes, and some items were overlaid with silver filigree. These lines are rather hard to find at this point in time, and prices are generally high; but there's plenty of their later production still around, and some pieces are relatively inexpensive.

If you'd like to learn more, we recommend *The Collector's Encyclopedia of Weller Pottery* by Sharon and Bob Huxford.

Arcadia, bud vase, leaf-formed vessel on round base, 7½", from $25 to..**$30.00**

Arcadia, fan vase, leaves form bowl on round base, 8x15", from $90 to..**$100.00**

Arcadia, vase, allover leaf & berry design, #A-6, 8", from $75 to...**$85.00**

Atlas, candle holders, star shape, #C-12, pr, from $95 to.**$110.00**

Atlas, star dish, w/lid, #C-2, 3½", from $125 to **$175.00**

Atlas, vase, flat-sided star shape w/6 points, 7", from $95 to...**$120.00**

Barcelona, candle holder, floral medallion on ribbed ground, 2x5" dia, from $75 to................................**$100.00**

Barcelona, vase, floral medallion on ribbed bulbous form w/ruffled rim, handled, unmarked, 8", from $200 to **$250.00**

Barcelona, vase, floral medallion on ribbed tumbler shape w/lipped rim, 7", from $175 to...........................**$200.00**

Blo' Red, vase, angled pot, flat bottom, 3½", from $50 to **$60.00**

Blossom, basket, flowers & leaves, ball shape, 6", from $75 to **$85.00**

Blossom, cornucopia, flowers & leaves, ruffled rim, from $40 to **$45.00**

Blossom, planter, flowers & leaves, flared scalloped rim & footed base, 4", from $100 to **$125.00**

Bonito, bowl, painted stylized floral decor around plain rim, footed, initialed CF, 3½", from $100 to..............**$135.00**

Bonito, vase, painted stylized floral decor on handled heart shape, 5", from $100 to................................**$145.00**

Bouquet, bowl, daisy & leaves decor, #B-8, 4", from $40 to...**$45.00**

Bouquet, bowl vase, daisy & leaves decor, #B-3, 4½", from $35 to...**$40.00**

Bouquet, vase, dogwood branch decor, #B-15, 5", from $45 to **$50.00**

Cactus, cat planter, glossy tan w/brown trim, 5½", from $100 to...**$125.00**

Cactus, frog planter, glossy tan, 4", from $100 to **$125.00**

Cactus, Glouster Woman, satin turquoise, 11½", from $700 to...**$800.00**

Cameo, bowl, white flowers on solid background color, footed, unmarked, 4", from $35 to...........................**$40.00**

Cameo, hanging basket, white flowers on solid background color, unmarked, 5", from $85 to **$110.00**

Cameo, vase, white flowers on solid background color, straight-sided square w/flat bottom, 8½", from $65 to **$75.00**

Clarmont, bowl, banded grapeleaf design, handled, 3", from $50 to...**$60.00**

Clarmont, candlestick, grape design on cup & base w/ribbed shaft, 8", from $150 to................................**$175.00**

Classic, vase, cut-out scallops w/embossed flower decor from rim, footed, 6½", from $60 to.....................**$70.00**

Classic, window box, cut-out scallops w/embossed flower decor around rim, 4", from $75 to **$85.00**

Coppertone, flowerpot, textured, w/saucer, 5", from $175 to **$250.00**

Coppertone, vase, textured trumpet form w/scalloped rim, flared base, unmarked, 6½", from $150 to.........**$200.00**

Coppertone, vase, tumbler shape w/plain rim, flared bottom, unmarked, 6½", from $150 to..........................**$200.00**

Cornish, bowl, berry & leaf branch on ball form w/sm scrolled handles, footed, 4", from $55 to.............**$65.00**

Cornish, candle holder, berry & leaf branch, sm scrolled handles, 3½", from $35 to.............................**$45.00**

Cornish, jardiniere, berry & leaf branch, handled, plain rim, flat bottom, 7", from $90 to **$110.00**

Creamware, Decorated; mug, berry decal, unmarked, 5", from $50 to...**$75.00**

Creamware, Decorated; pitcher, Dutch decal, unmarked, 4", from $100 to...**$150.00**

Creamware, Decorated; vase, hand-painted grape decor, 11½", from $300 to................................**$400.00**

Creamware, fan vase, flower & lattice-look decor, 6", from $60 to...**$70.00**

Darsie, pot, tasseled rope swag decor, flared scalloped rim, 3", from $40 to...**$45.00**

Darsie, vase, tasseled rope swag on cylinder w/flared scalloped rim, 7½", from $50 to.........................**$60.00**

Darsie, vase, tasseled rope swag on tapered bowl w/flared scalloped rim, 5½", from $60 to.........................**$70.00**

Delsa, basket, multicolored pansies on dimpled ground, flared scalloped rim & base, 7", from $85 to........**$95.00**

Delsa, ewer, multicolored pansies on dimpled ground, #10, 7", from $55 to...**$65.00**

Delsa, vase, blossom branch on dimpled ground, flared scalloped rim & base, 6", from $40 to...................**$50.00**

Elberta, bowl, shaded greens & browns, 6-pointed rim, w/flower frog, 10" dia, from $150 to **$200.00**

Elberta, cornucopia, shaded browns, 8", from $85 to..**$95.00**

Elberta, nut dish, shaded green & browns on boat shape w/upturned ends, 3", from $55 to.......................**$65.00**

Flemish, tub, no mark, 4½", from $80.00 to $110.00.

Fleron, batter pitcher, ribbed w/satin finish, 11½", from $200 to...**$250.00**

Fleron, vase, ribbed w/satin finish, ruffled rim, footed, 9", from $125 to...**$175.00**

Fleron, vase, ribbed w/satin finish, flared rim, ear-shaped handles, flat bottom, 19½", from $500 to **$750.00**

Florenzo, fan vase, floral swag on vertical fluting, 5½", from $55 to...**$65.00**

Florenzo, planter, floral swag on vertical fluting, square, 4-footed, 3½", from $55 to......................................**$65.00**

Florenzo, window box, floral swag on vertical fluting, 3", from $55 to..**$70.00**

Forest, basket, woodland scene, 8½", from $250 to.**$300.00**

Forest, pitcher, woodland scene in glossy tones, 5", from $200 to...**$250.00**

Gloria, ewer, blossom branch, #G-12, 9", from $85 to .**$100.00**

Gloria, vase, blossom branch, #G-22, 8", from $55 to ..**$65.00**

Gloria, vase, flowers & butterfly, #G-13, 5", from $100 to..**$125.00**

Goldenglow, bowl, leaf design on deep gold, enclosed ribbon handles, footed, unmarked, 3½x16", from $100 to.**$125.00**

Goldenglow, bud vase, leaf design on deep gold, tubular, 3-footed, 8½", from $100 to...................................**$125.00**

Goldenglow, ginger jar, leaf design on deep gold, loop handles, w/lid, footed, 8", from $225 to **$275.00**

Goldenglow, vase, leaf design on deep gold, high/low handles, footed, 8½", from $150 to.........................**$175.00**

Greenbriar, ewer, drip glaze on horizontal ribs, double-loop handle at rim to shoulder, unmarked, 11½", from $250 to...**$300.00**

Greenbriar, jar vase, drip glaze on smooth surface, bulbous, lipped rim, unmarked, 8½", from $175 to **$225.00**

Greora, vase, mottled & shaded brown texture, plain rim, footed, 8½", from $150 to.....................................**$200.00**

Greora, vase, mottled & shaded brown texture, 3-sided & 3-footed, unmarked, 4½", from $75 to....................**$85.00**

Hobart, bowl, water waves form rounded bowl w/incurvate rim, 4-footed, matt finish, 3x9½", from $75 to **$85.00**

Ivoris, vase, embossed leaves on 3-footed conical form, 6", from $25 to..**$40.00**

Lido, ewer, swirled form, 10½", from $95 to **$115.00**

Lido, planter, leaf form w/upturned end, 2x9", from $25 to...**$30.00**

Lido, planter, leaves form 3-sided footed bowl, 4½", from $45 to...**$50.00**

Lorbeek, wall pocket, pleated conical form, 8½", from $150 to...**$200.00**

Loru, bowl, leaves on vertical panels, scalloped rim, 2½x8" dia, from $40 to **$45.00**

Loru, cornucopia, paneled w/scalloped rim, footed, 4", from $25 to...**$35.00**

Loru, vase, leaves on vertical panels, cylindrical, footed, 10", from $45 to..**$50.00**

Louella, powder jar, floral decor on pleated cloth-look ground, w/lid, 4", from $100 to.........................**$125.00**

Malverne, bud vase, bud & leaf decor entwining tall neck & bulbous base, 8½", from $95 to **$115.00**

Malverne, candle holder, bud & leaf decor forming base w/cup, 2"...**$60.00**

Malverne, circle vase, bud decor w/leaves forming handle, 8", from $150 to..**$200.00**

Malverne, wall pocket, bud & leaf decor, unmarked, 11", from $200 to...**$250.00**

Manhattan, vase, flowers & lattice work around tapered base w/flat bottom, 5½", from $35 to.........................**$40.00**

Manhattan, vase, repeated rounded leaf design around bulbous base, plain rim, flat bottom, unmarked, 8½", from $65 to...**$75.00**

Manhattan, vase, repeated vertical pointed leaf design, plain rim, footed, 9", from $85 to **$95.00**

Marvo, double bud vase, allover flowers & leaves on gate-type, unmarked, 4½", from $85 to **$95.00**

Marvo, hanging basket, allover flowers & leaves on pot w/rounded bottom, lip rim, 5", from $125 to.....**$150.00**

Melrose, basket, grapevine & floral decor, 10", from $200 to...**$250.00**

Melrose, console bowl, rose decor, ruffled rim, branch handles, 5x8½" dia, from $125 to...........................**$150.00**

Mi-Flo, bowl, band of flowers on vertical fluting, tab handles, unmarked, 4", from $50 to.................................**$60.00**

Mi-Flo, vase, flowers on horizontal ribbing, #M-8, 7", from $85 to..**$100.00**

Novelty Line, ashtray, dog howling on rim of round tray, 5", from $125 to..**$150.00**

Novelty Line, planter, kangaroo figure looking into lg pouch, orange high-gloss glaze, unmarked, 5½", from $100 to...........**$125.00**

Novelty Line, pot, gray w/gold-trimmed embossed face, 2½", unmarked, from $150 to.................................**$200.00**

Oak Leaf, basket, #G-1, 7½", from $85 to................**$110.00**

Oak Leaf, ewer, 14", from $125 to **$175.00**

Oak Leaf, planter, 6", from $90 to...........................**$100.00**

Oak Leaf, vase, in-mold script mark, 8½", from $50.00 to $60.00.

Panella, basket, pansy-like flowers on footed egg-cup shape w/pointed handle, 7", from $95 to......................**$110.00**

Panella, bowl, pansy-like flowers & leaves, footed, 3½", from $40 to...**$45.00**

Panella, ginger jar, pansy-like flowers & leaves, handled, footed, w/lid, 6½", from $100 to..........................**$125.00**

Pastel, candle holder, fan design, scalloped base, unmarked, 1½", from $20 to..**$25.00**

Pastel, circle vase, fan design, 6", from $45 to...........**$50.00**

Pastel, vase, #P-17, from $30 to.................................**$35.00**

Patra, jardiniere, floral design at scalloped rim, textured ground, footed, 6", from $225 to.......................**$250.00**

Patra, nut dish, textured, #2, 3", from $75 to **$85.00**

Patra, vase, floral design at rim on textured ground, 3-footed, 5", from $125 to..$150.00

Patricia, bowl, 3-D duck heads & embossed leaf design repeated around squatty form, 13" dia, from $125 to.....$175.00

Patricia, planter, pelican form, 5", from $95 to.........$110.00

Patricia, vase, leaf design on jar w/swan-neck handles, footed, unmarked, 8½", from $225 to.......................$275.00

Pierre, casserole, basket weave, w/lid & underplate, 3", from $20 to..$25.00

Pierre, sugar bowl, basket weave, open, 2", from $10 to ..$15.00

Pierre, teapot, basket weave, 8½", from $100 to......$150.00

Reno, bowl, brown band on tan, 3", from $25 to......$35.00

Reno, custard, brown band on tan, 2", from $15 to ...$20.00

Roba, ewer, blossom branch, twig handle, 6", from $85 to .$95.00

Roba, vase, blossom branch, shouldered w/2 twig handles, 12½", from $150 to...$225.00

Roba, wall pocket, blossom branch, 10", from $175 to .$225.00

Rosemont, jardiniere, daisies & stems on glossy black bowl w/plain rim & flat bottom, 5", from $125 to......$150.00

Rosemont, vase, bluebird & leafy branch on glossy black jar w/lipped rim, flat bottom, 10½", from $400 to ..$500.00

Rudlor, console bowl, blossom branch, beaded handles, footed, 4½x17½" L, from $100 to $125.00

Rudlor, vase, blossom branch, slightly bulbous, drooping handles, plain rim, footed, 9", from $40 to...........$50.00

Rudlor, vase, floral, slightly bulbous, high/low beaded handles, plain rim, flat bottom, 6", from $50 to.........$60.00

Sabrinian, bud vase, swirled w/ruffled rim, 7", from $90 to.$120.00

Sabrinian, window box, shell & sea horse motif, 3½x9", from, $175 to...$225.00

Senic, planter, embossed palm tree, #S-17, 5½", from $85 to $95.00

Senic, vase, embossed scene, #S-4, 5½", from $65 to..$75.00

Senic, vase, embossed scene, #S-9, 8", from $100 to.$125.00

Softone, double bud vase, 2 tubular vessels w/connecting handle, flat wavy base, 9", from $30 to $35.00

Stellar, vase, painted star design on solid background color, bulbous, plain rim, footed, 5", from $400 to......$500.00

Sydonia, console bowl, 2-tone mottled texture on fluted boat shape, 6x17", from $100 to $125.00

Sydonia, cornucopia, 2-tone mottled texture on slender form, 8", from $70 to $80.00

Sydonia, planter, 2-tone mottled texture on fluted fan shape, 4", from $40 to $50.00

Turkis, vase, drip glaze over dark plum, angular pot w/sharply angled handles from lip to shoulder, 5½", from $125 to...$150.00

Turkis, vase, drip glaze over dark plum, jar w/handles from lip to shoulder, flat bottom, 14", from $300 to...$400.00

Turkis, vase, drip glaze over dark plum, ruffled rim, footed, 8", from $150 to...$175.00

Tutone, console bowl w/frog, flowers & berries w/leaves on footed triangular form, 3½", from $100 to..........$110.00

Tutone, vase, flowers, berries & arrowhead leaves on footed bowl, 4", from $75 to $85.00

Tutone, vase/candle holder, flowers, berries & arrowhead leaves on footed comma-shaped bowl, 7", from $110.......$135.00

Tutone, wall pocket, flowers, berries & arrowhead leaves on arrowhead form, unmarked, 10½", from $250 to.$275.00

Utility Ware, bean pot, brown, w/lid, 5½", from $40 to ..$50.00

Utility Ware, flowerpot/jar, blue plaid on white, 3½", from $25 to...$30.00

Utility Ware, mustard pot, w/metal holder, 2½", from $40 to..$45.00

Utility Ware, pitcher, blue band on cream, unmarked, 7", from $50 to..$75.00

Utility Ware, teapot, Pineapple, 6½", from $150 to ..$200.00

Warwick, circle vase, bud & branch decor on bark-textured ground, 7", from $125 to.....................................$150.00

Warwick, pillow vase, bud & branch decor on bark-textured ground, footed, 4½", from $85 to.........................$95.00

Warwick, vase, bud & branch decor on bark-textured ground of tree-trunk form, 12", from $175 to.................$200.00

Wild Rose, candle holder, triple cornucopia style, 6", from $75 to..$100.00

Wild Rose, console bowl, blossom branch on footed boat shape, unmarked, 6x18", from $100 to $125.00

Wild Rose, vase, blossom branch, cylindrical w/double-loop handles, 10½", from $65 to...............................$75.00

Woodrose, bowl, rose design on wooden bucket form, handled, unmarked, 2½x8½" dia, from $75 to...........$85.00

Woodrose, vase, rose design on wooden bucket form, handled, 4", from $40 to..$50.00

Woodrose, wall pocket, roses on tapered wooden bucket form, unmarked, 6", from $100 to......................$125.00

Zona, baby plate, squirrel decor w/ABC's on rolled rim, unmarked, 7½", from $125 to.............................$150.00

Zona, mug, rabbit & bird on textured cream ground, 3", from $100 to..$125.00

Zona, pitcher, apple branch on cream, branch handle, 6", from $100 to..$125.00

West Coast Pottery

This was a small company operating in the 1940s and 1950s in Burbank, California. The founders were Lee and Bonnie Wollard; they produced decorative pottery such as is listed here. For more information on this company as well as many others, we recommend *The Collector's Encyclopedia of California Pottery* by Jack Chipman (Collector Books).

Console set, green & pink mottle w/bow decor, plus matching candle holders, 3 pcs.....................................$35.00

Flower arranger, flamingo, turquoise, 8½x9½", from $40 to..$50.00

Vase, creamy white, #100, 2⅝x5¾".....................$28.00

Vase, emerald, fan form, 8½x7".............................$25.00

Vase, floral on burgundy, 3446, 10" $40.00

Vase, mauve to green, twisted & swirled, 8½".....................$35.00

Vase, pale green leaves w/pink speckles form body, #446, 10¼"..$32.00

Wall pocket, bow, mauve & turquoise, #451, 8x6½", pr..$55.00

Wall pocket, plume-like leaf, white, 8½x6" $30.00

Vase, peacock shape, light green glaze, in-mold mark, 11", $65.00.
(Photo courtesy Jack Chipman)

Western Collectibles

Although the Wild West era ended over one hundred years ago, today cowboy gear is a hot area of collecting. These historic collectibles are not just found out west. Some of the most exceptional pieces have come from the East Coast states and the Midwest. But that should come as no surprise when you consider that the largest manufacturer of bits and spurs was the August Buemann Co. of Newark, New Jersey (1868 – 1926).

For more information refer to *Old West Cowboy Collectibles Auction Update & Price Guide*, which lists auction-realized prices of more than 650 lots, with complete descriptions and numerous photos. You can obtain a copy from our advisor, Dan Hutchins.

Advisor: Dan Hutchins (See Directory, Western Collectibles)

Branding iron, hand forged, from $50 to	**$100.00**
Bridle bit, basic port-mouth style, from $40 to	**$65.00**
Bridle bit, jointed mouth type w/twist, from $15 to	**$25.00**
Bridle bit, spade type, from $225 to	**$350.00**
Buckle, bucking bronco, marked Nickel Silver	**$30.00**
Buffalo horns, mounted on board, from $45 to	**$60.00**
Hat, black Stetson, 1930s, MIB	**$295.00**
Pendleton blanket, geometrics, fringe, 1930s, 78x74"	**$145.00**
Reins, braided leather, ornate silver ferrules, fancy, 1930s.	**$400.00**
Saddle, lady's side; leather, from $375 to	**$550.00**
Skull, cow bone, weathered, 13½x12½x7½"	**$120.00**
Spurs, Buermann, straight shank, X design, pr	**$165.00**
Spurs, Crockett, nickel-plated floral pattern, 1950s, pr.	**$275.00**
Spurs, Eureka, pr	**$150.00**
Spurs, simple brass style w/original straps, pr, from $150 to	**$275.00**
Spurs, Southwestern style w/Mexican-style rowels, pr, from $265 to	**$450.00**
Stirrups, carved wood, pr, from $45 to	**$75.00**
Tie slide, steer head w/turquoise stone eyes	**$45.00**

Westmoreland Glass

The Westmoreland Specialty Company was founded in 1889 in Grapeville, Pennsylvania. Their mainstay was a line of opalware (later called milk glass) which included such pieces as cream and sugar sets, novel tea jars (i.e., Teddy Roosevelt Bear Jar, Oriental Tea Jars, and Dutch Tea Jar), as well as a number of covered animal dishes such as hens and roosters on nests. All of these pieces were made as condiment containers and originally held baking soda and Westmoreland's own mustard recipe. By 1900 they had introduced a large variety of pressed tablewares in clear glass and opal, although their condiment containers were still very popular. By 1910 they were making a large line of opal souvenir novelties with hand-painted decorations of palm trees, Dutch scenes, etc. They also made a variety of decorative vases painted in the fashion of Rookwood Pottery, plus sprayed finishes with decorations of flowers, fruits, animals, and Indians. Westmoreland gained great popularity with their line of painted, hand-decorated wares. They also made many fancy-cut items.

These lines continued in production until 1939, when the Brainard family became full owners of the factory. The Brainards discontinued the majority of patterns made previously under the West management and introduced dinnerware lines, made primarily of milk glass, with limited production of black glass and blue milk glass. Colored glass was not put back into full production until 1964 when Westmoreland introduced Golden Sunset, Avocado, Brandywine Blue, and Ruby.

The company made only limited quantities of carnival glass in the early 1900s and then re-introduced it in 1972 when most of their carnival glass was made in limited editions for the Levay Distributing Company. J.H. Brainard, president of Westmoreland, sold the factory to Dave Grossman in 1981, and he, in turn, closed the factory in 1984. Westmoreland first used the stamped W over G logo in 1949 and continued using it until Dave Grossman bought the factory. Mr. Grossman changed the logo to a W with the word Westmoreland forming a circle around the W.

Milk glass was always Westmoreland's main line of production. In the 1950s they became famous for their milk glass tableware in the #1881 'Paneled Grape' pattern. It was designed by Jess Billups, the company's mold maker. The first piece he made was the water goblet. Items were gradually added until a complete dinner service was available. It became their most successful dinnerware line, and today it is highly collectible, primarily because of the excellence of the milk glass itself. No other company has been able to match Westmoreland's milk glass in color, texture, quality, or execution of design and pattern.

Advisor: Cheryl Schafer (See Directory, Westmoreland)

Covered Animal Dishes

Camel, emerald green or turquoise carnivals, ea......**$175.00**

Cat on rectangular lacy base, Antique Blue **$160.00**

Cat on rectangular lacy base, caramel, green or purple marbled, ea..**$250.00**

Cat on rectangular lacy base, milk glass....................**$125.00**

Cat on vertical rib base, black carnival or ruby marble, 5½", ea **$125.00**

Cat on vertical rib base, purple marble, 5½"..............**$75.00**

Chick on pile of eggs, milk glass with hand-painted details, $65.00. (Milk glass with no details, $35.00.) Beware of reproductions.
(Photo courtesy Ruth Grizel)

Dove & hand on rectangular lacy base, milk glass ..**$150.00**

Duck on wavy base, Almond, Almond Mist, Antique Blue or Antique Blue Mist, 8x6", ea................................**$85.00**

Duck on wavy base, caramel or purple marbled, 8x6", ea **$125.00**

Duck on wavy base, crystal, dark or light Blue Mist, 8x6", ea **$50.00**

Duck on wavy base, purple marbled carnival, 8x6", ea...**$150.00**

Fox on diamond or lacy base, chocolate or Electric Blue Carnival, ea **$200.00**

Fox on diamond or lacy base, milk glass w/hand-painted realistic fur, ea..**$300.00**

Fox on diamond or lacy base, purple marbled, purple marbled carnival, ruby or green marbled, ea **$275.00**

Fox on lacy base, milk glass......................................**$255.00**

Hen on basketweave base, Antique Blue, Golden Sunset or any mists, 3½", ea..**$30.00**

Hen on basketweave base, milk glass, 3½" **$20.00**

Hen on basketweave base, milk glass w/hand-painted accents, 3½", ea **$25.00**

Hen on basketweave base, Mint Green w/hand-painted accents, 3½" **$30.00**

Hen on diamond base, Antique Blue, Bermuda Blue or Brandywine Blue, 5½", ea **$60.00**

Hen on diamond base, chocolate, 7½"....................**$195.00**

Hen on diamond base, milk glass, 7½" **$40.00**

Hen on diamond base, purple, green or ruby marbled, 7½", ea **$200.00**

Hen on diamond base, ruby or purple marble (noniridized), 5½", ea...**$85.00**

Hen on diamond base, ruby or purple marble carnival, 5½", ea **$100.00**

Hen on lacy base, milk glass, 7½" **$60.00**

Lamb on picket fence base, Antique Blue, 5½"..........**$60.00**

Lamb on picket fence base, caramel or purple slag carnival, 5½"..**$125.00**

Lamb on picket fence base, milk glass, 5½" **$40.00**

Lion on diamond base, Electric Blue Carnival (500 made), turquoise or emerald green carnvial, 8", ea **$225.00**

Lion on diamond base, milk glass, 8"......................**$135.00**

Lion on diamond base, purple marbled, 8".............**$200.00**

Lion on lacy base, milk glass, 8"..............................**$150.00**

Lion on picket fence base, milk glass w/blue head, 5½"..**$125.00**

Lovebirds on base, black or pink carnival, 6½", ea .**$100.00**

Lovebirds on base, Butterscotch Carnival or vaseline (400 made), 6½", ea..**$125.00**

Lovebirds on base, Crystal Mist, Moss Green or Olive Green, 6½", ea...**$45.00**

Lovebirds on base, dark or light blue, green, pink or Yellow Mist, 6½", ea..**$55.00**

Lovebirds on base, Golden Sunset, Bermuda Blue or Brandywine Blue, 6½", ea **$55.00**

Lovebirds on base, milk glass or milk glass carnival, 6½", ea **$50.00**

Mother eagle & babies on basketweave base, Crystal Mist top on Brown Mist base, 8"...**$65.00**

Mother eagle & babies on basketweave base, purple marbled carnival (160 made), 8" **$250.00**

Mother eagle & babies on basketweave base, purple or ruby marbled, 8", ea..**$200.00**

Mother eagle & babies on basketweave base, turquoise carnival (limited edition) or chocolate, 8", ea **$225.00**

Mother eagle & babies on basketweave or lacy base, milk glass, 8", ea...**$130.00**

Rabbit (mule earred) on picket fence base, caramel or purple marbled, 5½", ea..**$100.00**

Rabbit (mule earred) on picket fence base, hand-painted milk glass or pink opaque top, on milk glass base, 5½", ea **$60.00**

Rabbit (mule earred) on picket fence base, white carnival (1,500 made) or caramel marbled carnival, 5½", ea..........**$130.00**

Rabbit w/eggs on diamond or lacy base, blue opaque, 8", ea **$175.00**

Rabbit w/eggs on diamond or lacy base, chocolate, ruby or purple marbled, 8", ea...**$200.00**

Rabbit w/eggs on diamond or lacy base, milk glass, 8", ea..**$150.00**

Rabbit w/eggs on diamond or lacy base, purple slag carnival (150 made), 8", ea **$250.00**

Rabbit w/eggs on diamond or lacy base, white carnival (1,500 made) or Electric Blue Carnival (500 made), 8", ea ..**$200.00**

Robin on twig nest base, any Mist color, 6¼".............**$60.00**

Robin on twig nest base, caramel, vaseline, purple marbled, or turquoise carnival, 6¼", ea..............................**$150.00**

Robin on twig nest base, milk glass, 6¼"...................**$50.00**

Robin on twig nest base, pink (160 made), black carnival (experimental) or ruby (2,000 made), 6¼", ea...**$150.00**

Rooster on diamond base, crystal (1,500 made), turquoise carnival (1980) or Electric Blue Carnival, 7½", ea....**$175.00**

Rooster on diamond base, milk glass, 7½"..................$70.00

Rooster on diamond base, milk glass w/Minorca decoration (hand-painted realistic feathers), 7½"..................$125.00

Rooster on diamond base, ruby, purple marbled or purple marbled carnival, 7½", ea.....................$200.00

Rooster on ribbed base, milk glass, 5½"..................$35.00

Rooster on ribbed base, purple marbled, 5½"............$85.00

Rooster on ribbed base, ruby, caramel or marbled carnival, made for Levay, 1978, limited edition, 5½", ea..$100.00

Rooster standing, Antique Blue, 8½"..........................$85.00

Rooster standing, milk glass, 8½"...............................$35.00

Rooster standing, milk glass w/Minorca decoration, hand-painted, 8½"...$75.00

Rooster standing, purple marbled or Almond w/hand-painted accents, 8½", ea............................$125.00

Swan (closed neck) on diamond base, milk glass or blue opaque, ea...$95.00

Swan (raised wing) on lacy base, black, 6x9½".$275.00

Swan (raised wing) on lacy base, emerald green, purple marbled, pink or cobalt carnival, 6x9½", ea.............$225.00

Swan (raised wing) on lacy base, Ice Blue or turquoise carnival, 6x9½", ea.............................$200.00

Swan (raised wing) on lacy base, milk glass, milk glass Mother of Pearl, light blue or Pink Mist, 6x9½", ea............$175.00

Toy chick on basketweave base, Brandywine Blue, Dark Blue Mist, Moss Green, 2", ea........................$20.00

Toy chick on basketweave base, milk glass or milk glass w/red accents, 2", ea..................................$15.00

Toy chick on basketweave base, milk glass w/any fired-on color, 2", ea..$20.00

Figurals and Novelties

Bird, ashtray or pipe holder, green marbled..............$35.00

Bulldog, Crystal Mist, painted collar, rhinestone eyes, 2½"...$35.00

Butterfly, Almond, Mint Green, Mint Green Mist or milk glass, 2½", ea..$25.00

Butterfly, Almond, Mint Green, vaseline or Antique Blue, lg, ea $40.00

Butterfly, any Mist colors, lg, ea.................................$40.00

Butterfly, Green Mist, 2½"...$25.00

Butterfly, Mist colors other than Mint Green Mist, 2½", ea..$20.00

Butterfly, pink opaque or purple carnival, 2½", ea....$30.00

Butterfly, purple, caramel or green marbled, lg, ea....$50.00

Butterfly, purple carnival, 1977 limited edition, lg, ea..$55.00

Cardinal, crystal, solid...$20.00

Cardinal, Green Mist...$20.00

Cardinal, purple marbled, solid...................................$35.00

Cardinal, ruby carnival, solid......................................$30.00

Cardinal, ruby or any Mist colors, solid, ea................$25.00

Cat in boot, green, dark blue or Yellow Mist, hollow, ea..$35.00

Duck, salt cellar, crystal carnival (1,500 made)..........$35.00

Duck, salt cellar, milk glass, Apricot, or Green Mist, ea .$25.00

Egg, trinket box, any color w/beaded bouquet, w/lid .$35.00

Egg, trinket box, any Crystal Mist w/decal, w/lid.......$25.00

Egg, trinket box, ruby w/Mary Gregory style or cameo, w/lid, ea $40.00

Egg on gold stand, Almond w/any decal or Crystal Mist w/floral spray, blown, hollow, ea.........................$50.00

Egg on gold stand, Almond w/any hand-painted decor, blown, hollow, ea.....................................$60.00

Egg on gold stand, black (plain), blown, hollow ..$40.00

Egg on gold stand, black w/Oriental Poppy, blown, hollow $60.00

Grandma's slipper, Antique Blue, Antique Blue Mist, Almond, Mint Green, dark blue or Green Mist, ea..............$30.00

Grandma's slipper, black or milk glass Mother of Pearl, ea.$35.00

Grandma's slipper, brown, crystal or Yellow Mist, ea...$25.00

Grandma's slipper, Honey, Ice Blue Carnival or Cobalt Blue Carnival, ea...$40.00

Mantel clock, candy container, Brandywine Blue, hollow, no markings $35.00

Mantel clock, candy container, milk glass w/hand-painted clock face, hollow, no markings $45.00

Mantel clock, milk glass or Moss Green, hollow, no markings, ea...$30.00

Napkin ring holder, brown, light blue or Pink Mist w/flower, 6-sided $35.00

Napkin ring holder, milk glass w/Holly decor, 6-sided ..$50.00

Napkin ring holder, milk glass w/pink flower, 6-sided...$35.00

Owl on 2 stacked books, Almond, Mint Green, Antique Blue or black, 3½", ea.......................................$30.00

Owl on 2 stacked books, any Mist colors, 3½", ea $25.00

Owl on 2 stacked books, blue, pink, yellow opaque or Brandywine Blue, 3½", ea.................................$25.00

Owl on 2 stacked books, milk glass, 3½"...................$20.00

Owl on 2 stacked books, purple marbled, 3½"..........$40.00

Owl standing on tree stump, Almond Mist, Antique Blue or Antique Blue Mist, not marked, 5½", ea..............$40.00

Owl standing on tree stump, crystal, dark blue or Yellow Mist, not marked, 5½", ea.................................$35.00

Owl standing on tree stump, crystal carnival, ruby or milk glass w/22k gold rubbed feathers, 5½", ea..........$45.00

Owl standing on tree stump, milk glass or milk glass Mother of Pearl, not marked, 5½", ea....................$30.00

Owl standing on tree stump, purple marble or ruby carnival, 5½", ea..$55.00

Owl toothpick holder, aqua, milk glass, Moss Green or pink, 3", ea..$20.00

Owl toothpick holder, crystal, 3".................................$15.00

Owl toothpick holder, green, ruby or purple marble, 3", ea $30.00

Penguin on ice floe, blue or Blue Mist, ea...............$100.00

Penguin on ice floe, Crystal Mist or milk glass, ea.....$80.00

Porky pig, cobalt carnival, 3"......................................$40.00

Porky pig, Crystal Mist w/hand-painted decor, yellow opaque, milk glass, crystal, dark Blue Mist or Mint Green, 3", ea...$30.00

Porky pig, milk glass or Mint Green w/hand-painted decor, 3", ea...$35.00

Pouter pigeon, Apricot, dark or light blue, green or Pink Mist, ea $35.00

Pouter pigeon, Lilac Mist..............................$40.00

Revolver, black milk glass or crystal w/black hand-painted grips, solid, ea...$90.00

Revolver, crystal, solid...............................$70.00

Robin, Almond, Antique Blue, Antique Blue Mist or ruby, solid, 3¼", ea..$30.00

Robin, crystal, solid, 3¼".............................$20.00

Robin, crystal, solid, 5¼".............................$20.00

Robin, dark blue, green or Pink Mist, solid, 3¼", ea..$25.00

Robin, ruby or any Mist colors, solid, 5¼", ea.........$25.00

Robin, Smoke, 5⅛"....................................$24.00

Swallow, Almond, Antique Blue or Mint Green, solid, ea..$30.00

Swallow, green or Yellow Mist, solid...................$25.00

Turtle, ashtray or pipe holder, green, Pink Mist, dark or light blue, ea...$25.00

Turtle, paperweight, dark blue, green or Lilac Mist, no holes, ea...$50.00

Turtle, paperweight, milk glass, no holes............$75.00

Wren, Almond, Almond Mist or any opaque color, solid.$35.00

Wren, milk glass or any other Mist color, solid, ea.....$30.00

Wren, pink, 2½".......................................$20.00

Wren, Smoke, 2½"......................................$20.00

Wren on square-base perch, any color combination, solid, ea...$55.00

Lamps

Fairy lamp, Irish Waterford, #1932, ruby on crystal, footed, $65.00.

Boudoir, English Hobnail/#555, milk glass, stick type w/flat base..$45.00

Candle, Almond, Mint Green or ruby w/hand-painted decor, w/shade, mini, ea.....................................$45.00

Candle, any Mist color w/out decal, w/shade, mini...$27.50

Candle, Crystal Mist w/any decal, w/shade, mini.......$30.00

Candle, Crystal Mist w/child's decal, w/shade, mini...$65.00

Candle, Crystal Mist w/Roses & Bows, w/shade, mini.$75.00

Candle, milk glass w/child's decal, w/shade, mini...$125.00

Candle, milk glass w/Roses & Bows, w/shade, mini$135.00

Electric, any child's decor, w/shade, mini..................$80.00

Electric, any color w/Mary Gregory style decor, w/shade, mini...$80.00

Electric, any color w/Roses & Bows, w/shade, mini $100.00

Electric, Brown Mist w/floral bouquet or spray, w/shade, mini, ea...$35.00

Electric, Colonial, any color or decor, brass base w/scroll work, glass shade, ea..................................$125.00

Electric, Crystal Mist w/decal, w/shade, mini...........$35.00

Electric, Dolphin, crystal...............................$125.00

Electric, Dolphin, green or pink, ea...................$175.00

Fairy, Almond w/hand-painted flowers, footed, 2-pc.$65.00

Fairy, Brandywine Blue Carnival, footed, 2-pc...........$75.00

Modern Giftware

Ashtray, Beaded Grape/#1884, Brandywine Blue, 6½x6½".$30.00

Ashtray, Colonial, purple slag.........................$30.00

Basket, English Hobnail/#555, Light Blue or Pink Mist & Blue or Pink Pastel, 9".................................$45.00

Basket, Paneled Grape/#1881, Brandywine Blue, split handle, oval..$45.00

Basket, Pansy/#757, purple or green, slag, split handle.$35.00

Basket, Rose Trellis/#1967, milk glass w/hand-painted decor, 8½"..$35.00

Bell, Cameo/#754, w/Beaded Bouquet trim, any color..$35.00

Bell, Cameo/#754, w/HP Cameo, any color...............$30.00

Bonbon, Daisy/#205, Brown Mist........................$30.00

Bonbon, Waterford/#1932, ruby on crystal, handled..$38.00

Bowl, centerpiece; Colonial/#1776, Bermuda Blue, w/2 candle holders, 3-pc set..................................$125.00

Bowl, console; Paneled Grape/#1881, milk glass, round, 12"...$125.00

Bowl, Lotus/#1821, black, round, lg....................$50.00

Bowl, Lotus/#1921, milk glass, oval....................$30.00

Bowl, Lotus/#1921, ruby or crystal, round, lg...........$75.00

Bowl, purple or green slag, leaf form, #300............$45.00

Bowl, Rose Trellis/#1967, milk glass w/hand-painted decor, 10"...$75.00

Bowl, Striped/#1814, Apricot Mist, round, footed, lg.$35.00

Bowl, wedding; ruby on crystal, #1874, 8"..............$50.00

Bowl, wedding; ruby on crystal, #1874, 10".............$65.00

Bowl (Grandfather), Sawtooth/#556, Brandywine Blue.$80.00

Box, trinket; Crystal Mist w/Roses & Bows, 4-footed, square...$35.00

Box, trinket; Purple Mist, 4-footed, square, #1902......$27.50

Candle holders, ruby on crystal, Waterford, 6", pr......$65.00

Candy dish, Beaded Bouquet/#1700, Colonial pattern, milk glass..$35.00

Candy dish, Beaded Grape/#1884, Brandywine Blue, 3½", w/lid..$35.00

Candy dish, Beaded Grape/#1884, milk glass w/Roses & Bows, low footed, w/lid, 5"..........................$47.50

Candy dish, Paneled Grape/#1881, Almond, Almond Mist or Antique Blue, open ruffled edge, 3-toed.............$30.00

Candy dish, Paneled Grape/#1881, Dark Blue Mist, crimped, 3-footed, 7½"...$35.00

Compote, Brandywine Blue Opalescent, crimped & ruffled, footed, 6½"...$45.00

Flowerpot, purple Beaded Bouquet trim, #1707........$45.00

Grandma's slipper, hand-painted Christmas decor, #1900..**$40.00**

Pin tray, Heart/#1820, Blue Mist.................................**$30.00**

Sweetmeat, ruby on crystal, 2-handled, #1700............**$35.00**

Urn, ruby on crystal, footed, #1943, w/lid..................**$95.00**

Plates

Beaded Edge/#22, milk glass w/birds, florals or poultry, 7",
  ea **$20.00**

Beaded Edge/#22, milk glass w/painted fruit & Zodiac back,
  14½"...**$80.00**

Bicentennial decoration, Paneled Grape/#1881, limited edi-
  tion, 14½"...**$225.00**

Forget-me-not/#2, black w/Mary Gregory style, 8".....**$55.00**

Forget-me-not/#2, blue or Brown Mist, w/Mary Gregory
  style, 8", ea **$60.00**

Hearts, heart shape/#HP-1, Almond or Mint Green w/dog-
  wood decal, 8", ea..**$30.00**

Hearts, heart shape/#HP-1, any color w/daisy decal, 8", ea..**$25.00**

Lattice edge/#1890, black milk glass or milk glass w/any
  hand-painted decor, 11", ea **$95.00**

Lattice edge/#1890, Dark Blue Mist, Mary Gregory style, 11".**$65.00**

Luncheon, Paneled Grape/#1881, milk glass w/hand-painted
  decor, 8½" **$40.00**

Plain, dinner/#PL-8; black milk glass w/Christmas nativity
  decor, 8½" **$80.00**

Tableware

Bowl, banana; Old Quilt/#500, milk glass, footed, 11"..**$125.00**

Bowl, banana; Paneled Grape/#1881, Electric Blue Carnival,
  footed, 12"...**$150.00**

Bowl, banana; Paneled Grape/#1881, milk glass, footed,
  12"...**$125.00**

Bowl, Paneled Grape/#1881, milk glass, belled or lipped,
  footed, oval, 11"..**$75.00**

Bowl, Paneled Grape/#1881, milk glass, cupped, 8"..**$45.00**

Bowl, Paneled Grape/#1881, milk glass, shallow, skirted foot,
  6x9"...**$60.00**

Bowl, relish; Old Quilt/#500, milk glass, round, 3-part..**$35.00**

Box, chocolate; Paneled Grape/#1881, milk glass, w/lid,
  6½" dia **$45.00**

Butter/cheese dish, Old Quilt/#500, milk glass, w/lid,
  round **$45.00**

Butter/cheese dish, Old Quilt/#500, purple marble, w/lid,
  round **$75.00**

Butter/cheese dish, Old Quilt/#500, purple marble carnival,
  w/lid, round...**$125.00**

Butter/cheese dish, Paneled Grape/#1881, milk glass, w/lid,
  round, 7"...**$50.00**

Butter/cheese dish, Paneled Grape/#1881, purple marble,
  w/lid, round, 7"...**$75.00**

Cake plate, Irish Waterford/#1932, ruby on crystal, low foot-
  ed, 12"...**$95.00**

Cake plate, Paneled Grape/#1881, milk glass, skirted, 11"..**$65.00**

Cake salver, Beaded Grape/#1884, milk glass, square, footed,
  11" **$95.00**

Cake salver, Old Quilt/#500, milk glass, skirted, bell footed,
  12" **$125.00**

Candelabra, Lotus/#1921, any Mist color, 3-light, pr...**$70.00**

Candelabra, Lotus/#1921, milk glass, 3-light, pr..........**$60.00**

Candelabra, Paneled Grape/#1881, milk glass, 3-light, pr.**$400.00**

Candle holder, Paneled Grape/#1881, milk glass, arc shape,
  2-light, 8", ea **$45.00**

Canister, Paneled Grape/#1881, green or purple marbled,
  footed, w/lid, 11½x6¾"...**$200.00**

Canister, Paneled Grape/#1881, green or purple marbled,
  footed, w/lid, 10x5¾"..**$175.00**

Canister, Paneled Grape/#1881, green or purple marbled,
  footed, w/lid, 7½x4½" **$150.00**

Canister, Paneled Grape/#1881, milk glass, footed, w/lid,
  10x5¾"..**$500.00**

Canister, Paneled Grape/#1881, milk glass, footed, w/lid,
  11½x6¾"..**$400.00**

Canister, Paneled Grape/#1881, milk glass, footed, w/lid,
  7½x4½"..**$300.00**

Cup & saucer, Paneled Grape/#1881, milk glass.........**$21.00**

Decanter, Paneled Grape/#1881, Lime Green Carnival,
  w/stopper..**$175.00**

Decanter, Paneled Grape/#1881, milk glass, w/stopper..**$150.00**

Egg tray, Paneled Grape/#1881, milk glass, w/center handle,
  10"...**$90.00**

Egg tray, Paneled Grape/#1881, milk glass, w/center handle,
  12"...**$125.00**

Epergne, Paneled Grape/#1881, Almond or Mint Green,
  flared, 3-pc set, 14", ea..**$300.00**

Epergne, Paneled Grape/#1881, milk glass, flared, 3-pc set,
  14"..**$275.00**

Epergne, Paneled Grape/#1881, milk glass, lipped, 2-pc set
  (no base), 9"..**$175.00**

Epergne, Paneled Grape/#1881, milk glass, lipped, 3-pc set,
  12"..**$275.00**

Goblet, water; Old Quilt/#500, milk glass, footed, 8-oz.**$15.00**

Goblet, water; Paneled Grape/#1881, milk glass, footed, 8-oz.**$15.00**

Goblet, wine; Paneled Grape/#1881, milk glass, footed, 2-
  oz **$22.00**

Plate, dinner; Paneled Grape/#1881, milk glass, 10½"..**$55.00**

Plate, dinner; Paneled Grape/#1881, Mint Green, 10½" .**$55.00**

Plate, Old Quilt/#500, milk glass, 10½" **$70.00**

Plate, salad; Della Robbia, crystal................................**$15.00**

Plate, salad; Old Quilt/#500, milk glass, 8½" **$35.00**

Plate, salad; Paneled Grape/#1881, milk glass, 8½"....**$22.00**

Punch bowl set, Fruits, Honey or Ice Blue Carnival, 15-pc..**$350.00**

Punch bowl set, Fruits, Lilac Opalescent, 15-pc **$350.00**

Punch bowl set, Fruits, purple or turquoise carnival, 15-pc.**$400.00**

Punch bowl set, Old Quilt/#500, milk glass,
  bowl/base/ladle/12 cups.....................................**$960.00**

Punch bowl set, Paneled Grape/#1881, milk glass,
  bowl/base/ladle/12 cups......................................**$575.00**

Tray, tidbit; Beaded Grape/#1884, milk glass, 2-tier...**$95.00**

Tray, tidbit; Paneled Grape/#1881, Light Blue Mist, 1-tier,
  8" **$35.00**

Tray, tidbit; Paneled Grape/#1881, milk glass, w/Christmas
  decor, 1-tier, 10½"...**$85.00**

Tray, tidbit; Paneled Grape/#1881, milk glass, 1-tier, 10½"...**$50.00**
Tray, tidbit; Paneled Grape/#1881, milk glass, 2-tier, 8½" & 10½" plates................**$80.00**
Tray, tidbit; Paneled Grape/#1881, milk glass, 2-tier, 8½" & 10½" plates w/Poinsettia decor............**$100.00**
Tumbler, iced tea; Paneled Grape/#1881, milk glass, 12-oz ..**$22.50**
Tumbler, juice; Old Quilt/#500, milk glass, flat, 5-oz .**$25.00**
Tumbler, old-fashioned; Paneled Grape/#1881, milk glass, flat, 6-oz................**$35.00**
Tumbler, water; Old Quilt/#500, milk glass, flat, 9-oz.**$12.00**
Water set, Old Quilt/#500, purple slag, 3-pt pitcher & 6 9-oz tumblers................**$280.00**
Water set, Paneled Grape/#1881, Lime Green Carnival, 1-qt pitcher & 6 8-oz tumblers................**$290.00**
Water set, Swirl & Ball, purple carnival, 3-pt pitcher & 6 8-oz tumblers................**$265.00**

Wheaton

The Wheaton Company of Millville, New Jersey, has produced several series of bottles and flasks which are very collectible today. One of the most popular features portraits of our country's presidents. There was also a series of twenty-one Christmas bottles produced from 1971 through 1991, and because fewer were produced during the last few years, the newer ones can be hard to find and often bring good prices. Apollo bottles, those that feature movie stars, ink bottles, and bitters bottles are among the other interesting examples. Many colors of glass have been used, including iridescents.

Apollo XIII, amber carnival, 8½"................**$15.00**
Carter's Ink, green w/8 cathedral panels, 2½" **$28.00**
Carter's Ink, red cranberry, 3"................**$60.00**
Charles Evans Hughes, blue carnival................**$13.00**
Church Ink, red w/6 cathedral panels, 3"................**$22.00**
Fisch's Bitters, fish shape, purple, 7" **$12.00**
Fisch's Bitters, green, 5"................**$17.50**
George S Patton, blue, 8¼"................**$22.00**
Humphrey Bogart, green carnival, 7¼" **$12.50**
Jean Harlow, amber, 7"................**$30.00**
Lantern, blue, 9¾" **$15.00**
McGovern/Eagleton, amber Democratic donkey, 6x7x2½"................**$16.00**
Poison, skull & crossbones on 1 side, RIP on other, green **$35.00**
Poison, skull & crossbones on 1 side, RIP on other, red **$38.00**
Robert Francis Kennedy, green, in original box, 8¼".**$15.00**
Schoolhouse, Tuckahoe Country School 1891, blue, mini................**$13.50**
Tree of Life, Straubmiller's Elixir, deep purple, 4-sided, 8" **$20.00**
Vietnam Memorial, blue, 8½"................**$13.00**
Violin flask, blue, diamond-shaped top, 9¼", from $20 to **$25.00**
WC Fields, green carnival, star shape, 7"................**$20.00**

Will-George

This is a California-based company that began operations in the 1930s. It was headed by two brothers, William and George Climes, both of whom had extensive training in pottery science. They're most famous today for their lovely figurines of animals and birds, though they produced many human figures as well. For more information on this company as well as many others, we recommend *The Collector's Encyclopedia of California Pottery* by Jack Chipman (Collector Books).

Candle holders, pink petals w/green, 6", pr................**$80.00**
Figurine, canary, bright yellow, on perch base, 3¼", NM..**$38.00**
Figurine, colt, green w/gold trim, signed in gold on belly, 9½x9½", NM **$58.50**
Figurine, crane, 9" **$170.00**
Figurine, dachshund, 8¾x6¾"................**$175.00**
Figurine, flamingo, bright colors, green base, 6½" ...**$125.00**
Figurine, flamingo, bright colors, 9¾"................**$235.00**
Figurine, macaw, bright colors, 14½"................**$365.00**

Figurine, yellow bird on branch, 2x5", $60.00.
(Photo courtesy Jack Chipman)

Winfield

The Winfield pottery first began operations in the late 1920s in Pasadena, California. In 1946 their entire line of art-ware and giftware items was licensed to the American Ceramic Products Company, who continued to mark their semiporcelain dinnerware with the Winfield name. The original Winfield company changed their trademark to 'Gabriel.' Both companies closed during the early 1960s. For more information, see *The Collector's Encyclopedia of California Pottery* by Jack Chipman (Collector Books).

Bean pot, Pussy Willow, 5¾x6½" **$37.50**
Bowl, Bamboo, 4½x10"................**$32.50**
Bowl, cereal; Bamboo **$12.50**
Bowl, fruit; Bamboo, 1¼x4¾" **$10.00**
Bowl, salad; Bamboo, square, lg **$35.00**
Cigarette box, turtle shape, 6¾" L **$40.00**
Dinnerware, Fallow, service for 4, 21 pcs **$45.00**

Gravy boat, Passion Flower, w/underplate.................$32.00
Pitcher, Bird of Paradise, 8".................................$42.00
Pitcher, Dragon Flower, 8"..................................$32.00
Pitcher, Passion, 8"...$42.50
Plate, bread & butter; Bamboo...............................$5.00
Plate, dinner; Bamboo, from $12 to.......................$14.00
Platter, Bamboo, 12x8".......................................$20.00
Platter, Bamboo, 15"..$42.50
Server, 3-tier; Pussy Willow, 16"..........................$55.00

World's Fairs and Expositions

Souvenir items have been issued since the mid-1800s for every world's fair and exposition. Few fairgoers have left the grounds without purchasing at least one. Some of the older items were often manufactured right on the fairgrounds by glass or pottery companies who erected working kilns and furnaces just for the duration of the fair. Of course, the older items are usually more valuable, but even souvenirs from the past fifty years are worth hanging on to.

Advisor: Herbert Rolfes (See Directory, World's Fairs and Expositions)

Newsletter: *Fair News*
World's Fair Collectors' Society, Inc.
Michael R. Pender, Editor
P.O. Box 20806
Sarasota, FL 34276; 941-923-2590; Dues: $12 (12 issues) per year in USA; $13 in Canada; $20 for overseas members

Chicago, 1933

Badge, pin-back; Official logo, #290, metal, EX..........$25.00
Banner, fair logo & printing in white on red w/blue fringe on gold-tipped wooden bar w/blue tassled card, 7¾x10½"......$57.00
Brochure, Travel by Train, The Milwaukee Road, photos & maps, 18 pages, VG..................................$20.00
Cane, Hall of Science 1933 Chicago Century of Progress on brass label near crook, wooden, 33¾" L, EX.......$75.00
Compact, 1833-1933 A Century of Progress, chrome w/cream paint, original felt pouch & box, M....................$70.00
Dish, lg building in center w/border of smaller buildings, Century Art Works, 4⅝" dia, EX (original box)....$23.00
Globe, Chicago World's Fair 1833-1933, metal, 3½"...$50.00
Guide to Chicago, depicts buildings & events in orange & blue, John Drury, soft cover, 203 pages, 8¼x5½", EX......$30.00
Key, Travel & Transport 1933/Hall of Science Chicago, bronze, VG...................................$27.50
Lighter, camel shape, Travel & Transportation Building, Made in Japan, VG..................................$30.00
Make-up box, 1933 A Century of Progress Chicago, metal, hinged, EX..................................$45.00
Map, Chicago Northwestern Railroad, depicts Giant Class H locomotive, folds out to 9x24", VG......................$15.00
Mug, nude handle, any color, pottery, 6½x5"............$36.00

Parasol, paper w/1933 Chicago World's Fair on wooden handle, G..................................$65.00
Pillow top, fair buildings on pink, blue fringe, floral print on back, 16" square, VG..................................$28.00
Pipe holder/figurine, Scottish Terrier w/pipe holder on side, logo on dog's warmer, bronze, 3x4"....................$50.00
Plate, sandwich; Black Forest, marked Pickard, light crazing, 7½" dia, NM..................................$55.00
Playing cards, 53 views of 1933 Century of Progress, VG (original box)..................................$40.00
Program, Official Daily Fair Rodeo; rules, regulations & conditions, VG..................................$30.00
Spoon, Official Century of Progress Chicago 1933 on handle, fairgrounds in bowl, silver-plated, Green Duck, 6"..$12.00
Thermometer, Hall of Science Building pictured in framed glass, thermometer on side, 5⅛x7¼", EX..........$27.00
Ticket book, Combination of Souvenir Tickets, 10 stubs w/1 full ticket, map inside, VG..................................$27.00
Toy wagon, Radio Flyer, metal w/original white rubber tires, souvenir, 4¾x1¾", VG..................................$150.00
Watch, pocket; Chicago & fair scenes on back, New Haven Clock & Watch Company, worn but running.....$100.00
Watch fob, FDR's head on 1 side, 'Century of Progress 1933' on other, metal, original leather strap, EX...........$38.00

New York, 1939

Ashtray, black plastic, snow globe in center w/Trylon & Perisphere, 6x4½", NM.................................$225.00
Ashtray, Theme Building, clear glass w/blue center fair logo, 4x3", EX..................................$55.00
Belt buckle & pin set, brass w/blue & orange logo, MIB..$65.00
Bookends, Christian Science Building w/landscape, L-shaped, metal, 5x4", pr..................................$60.00
Bookends, Trylon & Perisphere, Syroco w/metal base, 4½x6"..................................$75.00
Cap, blue felt soda-jerk style w/fair logo & trim in orange, 4x11", scarce, EX..................................$135.00
Child's activity set, Build-Your-Own New York World's Fair, Standard Toycraft, complete, EXIB....................$300.00
Desk calendar, New York World's Fair on brass plate, metal, 4¼x2½x1⅝", VG+..................................$40.00
Flag (lg), orange & blue w/logo on wooden stick w/gold point, 12x17", EX..................................$100.00
Flag (med), orange & blue w/logo on wooden stick w/gold point, 8x11", EX..................................$80.00
Flag (sm), orange & blue w/logo on wooden stick w/gold point, 4x5", EX..................................$40.00
Guide, Official; Trylon & Perisphere on cover, 1st edition, 256 pages, VG+..................................$37.00
Menu, Argentine Pavillion, EX..................................$58.00
Patch, fair logo in blue w/orange background, embroidered, unused, 3x3¼", EX..................................$32.00
Pennant, New York World's Fair & logo in white on blue, orange trim, felt, 3x8"..................................$27.50
Pipe, tobacco; 1939 New York World's Fair carved around bowl, walnut, 6" L..................................$100.00

Playing cards, World's Fair Souvenir..., different black & white photo on cards, Western Playing Card Co, complete, EXIB **$85.00**

Scarf, sheer silky material w/multicolored fair artwork, 20" square **$60.00**

Thermometer, key shape, shows fair scene, gold colored metal, 8½", EX **$40.00**

Tumbler, Theme Building & logo in white w/New York World's Fair 1939 in blue band at bottom, 4¾", EX **$20.00**

Seattle, 1962

Bag, Space Needle, Monorail & Seattle Center, made by Industrial Rubber Co, 18¼x14", EX **$42.00**

Model kit, Space Needle, wooden, complete w/instructions, made by Whitechester Heating, EX **$80.00**

Pendant, Century 21/Seattle WF, depicts Monorail in station, NMIB..**$16.00**

Record, Official Seattle World's Fair Band, Space Needle on cover, VG (VG cover)...**$32.00**

Tray, pictures Space Needle, US Science Building, Monorail, Coliseum, logo on blue, 11" dia, EX **$15.00**

Tumblers, single color with black and white matt finish on frosted glass, gold trim, 16-ounce, from $12.00 to $15.00 each.

New York, 1964

Belt, vinyl w/orange, blue & yellow detail, boy & girl w/balloons, Unisphere, lettering & dates, Pleasure Belt Co, NM...**$75.00**

Dime bank, Unisphere, daily register, on original cardboard holder, EX...**$125.00**

Doll, World's Fair Girl, squeeze vinyl w/molded orange & blue outfit & hair, Sun Rubber, 9", EX **$100.00**

Film, New York's World's Fair From the Air! 8mm, 5" dia, EXIB..**$30.00**

License plate, black w/gold letters, VG **$27.00**

Paperweight, Unisphere & fair buildings, metal w/silver paint, felt bottom, made in Japan for US Steel, 3¾x2" **$30.00**

Poster, for US Steel, reads Come Back to the Fair!..., shows family w/kids holding Unisphere balloons, 16x12", EX.**$45.00**

Road sign, aluminum trapezoid shape w/World's Fair above Unisphere on band above arrow pointing up, 30x24x16", EX **$200.00**

Scarf, logo & fair scenes on white w/red border, rayon, 26x28", EX **$40.00**

Sugar cube, Domino Sugar, white wrapping w/red & blue design w/logo, ½x1" **$10.00**

Tile, Souvenir of Vatican Pavillion, blue & white, 6x6"..**$26.00**

Video, World's Fair Planning by Lowell Thomas, VHS, black & white & color, 55 minutes, EX....................**$50.00**

View Master reels, General Tour, M (3 in open packet)..**$20.00**

Yona

Yona Lippin was a California ceramist who worked for Hedi Schoop in the early 1940s and later opened her own studio. Much of her work is similar to Schoop's. She signed her work with her first name. You'll also find items marked Yona that carry a 'Shafford, Made in Japan' label, suggesting a later affiliation with that importing company. For more information, see *The Collector's Encyclopedia of California Pottery* by Jack Chipman (Collector Books).

Bean pot, Country Club, red & white stripes, #87574 ...**$20.00**

Butter dish, hen & rooster, #226, 1950s **$22.50**

Canister set, barns w/rooster finials, 4-pc **$175.00**

Creamer & sugar bowl, barn w/chicken finial, #221, 4½x2½"...**$35.00**

Decanter, clown, #218, 11½" **$50.00**

Figurine, angel, Always Tell The Truth, 1956, 5¼" **$35.00**

Figurine, angel, Count Your Blessings, gold trim, 5", $35.00. (Photo courtesy Sandy Fienhold, Empty Clown Collectibles)

Figurine, angel, Love Your Country, holds flag, 1956, 5"..**$40.00**

Figurine, angel w/dog, Be Kind to Animals, 3x5".......**$40.00**

Figurine, angel w/gold wings & hat on crescent moon, 4½".**$80.00**

Figurine, clown, C 1956 in circle/Made in Japan label, 5½"..**$45.00**

Figurine, lady w/basket on her shoulder, #19, 9" **$35.00**

Figurines, Siamese dancers, green spongeware over gold, male: 12½", female: 13½", pr................................**$85.00**

Flower holder/figurine, lady in wide-brimmed hat, basket w/opening in front, 7½x5½" **$30.00**

Flower holder/figurine, lady w/muff, 7" **$25.00**

Salt & pepper shakers, clowns in acrobatic poses, 1947, 4", 3½", pr..**$35.00**

Auction Houses

Many of the auction galleries we've listed here have appraisal services. Some, though not all, are free of charge. We suggest you contact them first by phone to discuss fees and requirements.

Aston Macek Auctions
2825 Country Club Rd.
Endwell, NY 13760-3349
Phone or fax: 607-785-6598
Specializing in and appraisers of Americana, folk art, other primitives, furniture, fine glassware and china

Bill Bertoia Auctions
1881 Spring Rd.
Vineland, NJ 08361
856-692-1881 or fax: 856-692-8697
e-mail: bill@bertoiaauctions.com
www.Bertoiaauctions.com
Online Auctions: Bertoiaonline.com
Specializing in antique toys and collectibles

Cincinnati Art Gallery
225 E. Sixth St.
Cincinnati, OH 45202; 513-381-2128
www.cincinnatiartgalleries.com
Specializing in American art pottery, American and European fine paintings, watercolors

Collectors Auction Services
RD 2, Box 431
Oil City, PA 16301
814-677-6070
Specializing in advertising, oil and gas, toys, rare museum and investment-quality antiques

David Rago
Auction hall: 333 N. Main St.
Lambertville, NJ 08530
609-397-7330
Gallery: 17 S Main St.
Lambertville, NJ 08530
Specializing in American art pottery and Arts & Crafts

Dunbar Gallery
76 Haven St.
Milford, MA 01757
508-634-8697; fax: 508-634-8698
Specializing in quality advertising, Halloween, toys, coin-operated machines; holding cataloged auctions occasionally, lists available

Dynamite Auctions
Franklin Antique Mall & Auction Gallery
1280 Franklin Ave.
Franklin, PA 16323
814-432-8577 or 814-786-9211

Early Auction Co.
123 Main St.
Milford, OH 45150
www.earlyauctions.com

Flying Deuce
1224 Yellowstone
Pocatello, ID 83201
208-237-2002
fax: 208-237-4544
e-mail: flying2@nicoh.com
Specializing in vintage denim apparel; catalogs $10.00 for upcoming auctions; contact for details on consigning items

Garth's Auctions, Inc.
2690 Stratford Rd.
Box 369, Delaware, OH 43015
740-362-4771
www.garth's.com

Jackson's Auctioneers & Appraisers of
    Fine Art & Antiques
2229 Lincoln Street
Cedar Falls, IA 50613
www.jacksons@jacksonsauction.com
Specializing in: American and European art pottery and art glass, American and European paintings, decorative arts, toys and jewelry

James D. Julia
P.O. Box 830, Rt. 201
Showhegan Rd.
Fairfield, ME 04937
207-453-7125
www.juliaauctions.com

Kerry and Judy's Toys
1414 S. Twelfth St.
Murray, KY 42071
502-759-3456
e-mail: kjtoys@apex.net
Specializing in 1920s through 1960s toys; consignments always welcomed

L.R. 'Les' Docks
Box 691035
San Antonio, TX 78269-1035
Providing occasional mail-order record auctions, rarely consigned (the only consignments considered are exceptionally scarce and unusual records)

Lloyd Ralston Toys
447 Stratford Rd.
Fairfield, CT 06432

Manion's International Auction House, Inc.
P.O. Box 12214
Kansas City, KS 66112
913-299-6692; fax: 913-299-6792
e-mail: manions@qni.com
www.manions.com

Michael John Verlangieri
Verlangieri Gallery
PO Box 844, Cambria, CA 93428; 805-927-4428. Specializing in fine California pottery; cataloged auctions (video tapes available); www.calpots.com

Monson & Baer, Annual Perfume Bottle Auction
Monsen, Randall; and Baer, Rod
Box 529, Vienna, VA 22183
703-938-2129 or fax: 703-242-1357
Cataloged auctions of perfume bottles; will purchase, sell, and accept consignments; specializing in commercial, Czechoslovakian, Lalique, Baccarat, Victorian, crown top, factices, miniatures

Noel Barrett Antiques & Auctions
P.O. Box 1001
Carversville, PA 18913
215-297-5109; fax: 215-297-0457

Richard Opfer Auctioneering, Inc.
1919 Greenspring Dr.
Timonium, MD 21093; 410-252-5035

Smith House
P.O. Box 336
Eliot, ME, 03903
207-439-4614; fax: 207-439-8554
e-mail: smithtoys@aol.com
Specializing in toys

Toy Scouts Inc.
137 Casterton Ave.
Akron, OH 44303
330-836-0668; fax: 330-869-8668
e-mail: toyscouts@toyscouts.com
www.toyscouts.com
Specializing in baby-boom era collectibles

Treadway Gallery Inc.
2029 Madison Rd.
Cincinnati, OH 45208
513-321-6742; fax: 513-871-7722
www.treadwaygallery.com
Member: National Antique Dealers Association, American Art Pottery Association, International Society of Appraisers, and American Ceramic Arts Society

Clubs and Newsletters

There are hundreds of clubs and newsletters mentioned throughout this book in their respective categories. There are many more available to collectors today; some are generalized and cover the entire realm of antiques and collectibles, while others are devoted to a specific interest such as toys, coin-operated machines, character collectibles, or railroadiana. We've listed several below. You can obtain a copy of most newsletters simply by requesting one. If you'd like to try placing a 'for-sale' ad or a mail bid in one of them, see the introduction for suggestions on how your ad should be composed.

America's Most Wanted To Buy
P.O. Box 171707, CB
Little Rock, AR 72222
800-994-9268
Subscription $12.95 per year for 6 issues; up to date information about what collectors big and small are buying now

American Matchcover Collecting Club
  (AMCC)
P.O. Box 18481
Asheville, NC 28814
828-254-4487; fax: 828-254-1066
www.matchcovers.com
e-mail: bill@matchcovers.com
Dues $25 yearly + $3 registration fee for first year, includes *Front Striker Bulletin*. Also available: *Matchcover Collector's Price Guide*, 2nd edition, $25.20+$3.25 shipping and handling

Antique Advertising Association of
  America (AAAA)
P.O. Box 1121
Morton Grove, IL 60053
708-446-0904
Also *Past Times* newsletter for collectors of popular and antique advertising. Subscription: $35 per year

Antique and Collectors Reproduction News
Mark Chervenka, Circulation Dept.
P.O. Box 12130
Des Moines, IA 50312-9403
800-227-5531
Monthly newsletter showing differences between old originals and new reproductions. Subscription: $32 per year

Antique Journal
Michael F. Shores, Publisher
Jeffery Hill Editor/General Manager
2329 Santa Clara Ave. #207
Alameda, CA 94501

The Antique Trader Weekly
P.O. Box 1050 CB
Dubuque, IA 52004-1050
800-334-7165
Subscription: $37 (52 issues) per year

Antique Week
P.O. Box 90
Knightstown, IN 46148
Weekly newspaper for auctions, antique shows, antiques, collectibles, and flea markets. Write for subscription information.

The Bicycle Trader Newsletter
510 Frederick
San Francisco, CA 94117
415-876-1999 or 415-564-2304
fax: 415-876-4507
e-mail: info@bicycletrader.com
www.bicycletrader.com

Bobbing Head Doll Newsletter
Tim Hunter
4301 W. Hidden Valley Dr.
Reno, NV 89502
e-mail: thunter885@aol.com

The Carnival Pump
International Carnival Glass Assoc., Inc.
Lee Markley
Box 306
Mentone, IN 46539
Dues: $20 per family per year US and Canada payable each July 1st

Cast Iron Marketplace
P.O. Box 16466
St. Paul, MN 55116
Subscription $30 per year, includes free ads up to 200 words per issue

Coin-Op Newsletter
Ken Durham, Publisher
909 26th St., NW; Suite 502
Washington, DC 20037
www.GameRoom.antiques.com
Subscription (10 issues): $15; Sample: $5

*Dorothy Kamm's Porcelain Collector's
  Companion*
P.O. Box 7460
Port St. Lucie, FL 34985-7460; 561-465-4008

Dragonware Club, c/o Suzi Hibbard
849 Vintage Ave.
Fairfield, CA 94585
Information requires long SASE.

Early Typewriter Collectors Association
ETCetera Newsletter
Chuck Dilts/Rich Cincotta
PO Box 286
Southboro, MA 01772
etcetera@writeme.com
http://typewriter.rydia.net/etcetera.htm

Grandpa's Depot
John Grandpa White
1616 17th St., Suite 267
Denver, CO 80202
303-628-5590; fax: 303-628-5547
Publishes catalogs on railroad-related collectibles

International Golliwog Collector Club
Beth Savino
PO Box 798
Holland, OH 43528
1-800-862-TOYS; fax 419-473-3947

International Ivory Society
11109 Nicholas Dr.
Wheaton, MD 20902; 301-649-4002
Membership: $10 per year; includes 4 newsletters and roster

National Bicycle History Archive
Box 28242
Santa Ana, CA 92799; 714-647-1949
e-mail: Oldbicycle@aol.com
www.members.aol.com/oldbicycle
Resource for vintage and classic cycles from 1920 to 1970. Collection of over 1,000 classic bicycles. Over 30,000 original catalogs, books, photos. Also over 100 original old bicycle films 1930s – 70s. Restoration and purchase

Newspaper Collectors Society of America
517-887-1255
e-mail: info@historybuff.com
Publishes booklet with current values and pertinent information

Nutcracker Collectors' Club
Susan Otto, Editor
11204 Fox Run Dr.
Chesterland, OH 44026; $15.00 annual dues, quarterly newsletters sent to members, free classifieds

Old Stuff
Donna and Ron Miller, Publishers
336 N Davis
P.O. Box 1084
McMinnville, OR 97128
Published 6 times annually; Copies by mail: $3.50 each; Annual subscription: $18 ($32 in Canada)

Paper Collectors' Marketplace
470 Main St.
P.O. Box 128
Scandinavia, WI 54977-0128
715-467-2379; fax: 715-467-2243
Subscription: $19.95 (12 issues) per year in USA; Canada and Mexico add $15 per year

Paperweight Collectors Association, Inc.
P.O. Box 1263
Barker, TX 77413
Convention to be held June 2001 in Corning, NY

The Trick or Treat Trader
P.O. Box 499, Winchester, NH 03470
4 issues: $15 (USA) or $20 (International)

Paper Pile Quarterly
P.O. Box 337
San Anselmo, CA 94979-0337
415-454-5552
Subscription: $20 per year in USA and Canada

Pen Fancier's Club
1169 Overcash Dr.
Dunedin, FL 34698

Southern Oregon Antiques and Collectibles Club
P.O. Box 508
Talent, OR 97540
541-535-1231
Meets 1st Wednesday of the month; Promotes 2 shows a year in Medford, OR

Stanley Tool Collector News
c/o The Old Tool Shop
208 Front St.
Marietta, OH 45750
Features articles of interest, auction results, price trends, classified ads, etc.; Subscription: $20 per year; Sample: $6.95

Statue of Liberty Collectors' Club
Iris November
P.O. Box 535
Chautauqua, NY 14722
216-831-2646

Table Toppers
1340 West Irving Park Rd.
P.O. Box 161
Chicago, IL 60614
312-769-3184
Membership $19 (single) per year, includes *Table Topic*, a bimonthly newsletter for those interested in table-top collectibles

Thimble Collectors International
6411 Montego Rd.
Louisville, KY 40228

Three Rivers Depression Era Glass Society
Edith A. Putanko
John's Antiques & Edie's Glassware
Rte. 88 & Broughton Rd.
Bethel Park, PA 15102
412-831-2702
Meetings held 1st Monday of each month at DeMartino's Restaurant, Carnegie, PA

Tiffin Glass Collectors
P.O. Box 554
Tiffin, OH 44883
Meetings at Seneca Cty. Museum on 2nd Tuesday of each month

The Wheelmen
Magazine: *Wheelmen Magazine*
63 Stonebridge Road
Allen Park, NJ 07042-1631
609-587-6487
e-mail: hochne@aol.com
www.thewheelmen.org
A club with about 800 members dedicated to the enjoyment and preservation of our bicycle heritage

The '50s Flea
April and Larry Tvorak
P.O. Box 94
Warren Center, PA 18851
570-395-3775; e-mail: april@epix.net
Published once a year, $4 postpaid; free classified up to 30 words

Special Interests

In this section of the book we have listed hundreds of dealers/collectors who specialize in many of the fields this price guide covers. Many of them have sent information, photographs, or advised us concerning current values and trends. This is a courtesy listing, and they are under no obligation to field questions from our readers, though some may be willing to do so. If you do write to any of them, don't expect a response unless you include an SASE (stamped self-addressed envelope) with your letter. If you have items to offer them for sale or are seeking information, describe the piece in question thoroughly and mention any marks. You can sometimes do a pencil rubbing to duplicate the mark exactly. Photographs are still worth a 'thousand words,' and photocopies are especially good for paper goods, patterned dinnerware, or even smaller 3-dimensional items.

It's a good idea to include your phone number if you write, since many people would rather respond with a call than a letter. And suggesting that they call back collect might very well be the courtesy that results in a successful transaction. If you're trying to reach someone by phone, always stop to consider the local time on the other end of your call. Even the most cordial person when dragged out of bed in the middle of the night will very likely *not* be receptive to you.

With the exception of the Advertising, Books, Bottles, Character Collectibles, and Toys sections which we've alphabetized by character or type, buyers are listed alphabetically under bold topics. A line in italics indicates only the specialized interests of the particular buyer whose name immediately follows it. Recommended reference guides not available from Collector Books may be purchased directly from the authors whose addresses are given in this section.

Abingdon
Louise Dumont
318 Palo Verde Dr.
Leesburg, FL 34748
e-mail: LOUISED452@aol.com

Advertising
Aunt Jemima
Fee charged for appraisal
Judy Posner
P.O. Box 2194 SC
Englewood, FL 34295
www.judyposner.com
e-mail: judyandjef@aol.com

Big Boy
Steve Soelberg
29126 Laro Dr.
Agoura Hills, CA 91301; 818-889-9909

Campbell's Soup
Author of book
Dave Young
414 Country Ln. Ct.
Wauconda, IL 60084; 541-664-6764

Cereal boxes and premiums
Author of books; editor of magazine: Flake
Scott Bruce; Mr. Cereal Box
P.O. Box 481
Cambridge, MA 02140
617-492-5004
Buys, sells, trades, appraises; books
available from author

Gerber Baby dolls
Author of book ($44 postpaid)
Joan S. Grubaugh
2332 Brookfield Greens Circle
Sun City Center, FL 33573

Green Giant
Edits newsletter
Lil West
2343 10000 Rd.
Oswego, KS 67356
Also other related Pillsbury memorabilia

Jewel Tea products and tins
Bill and Judy Vroman
739 Eastern Ave.
Fostoria, OH 44830; 419-435-5443

Mr. Peanut
Judith and Robert Walthall
P.O. Box 4465
Huntsville, AL 35815; 256-881-9198

Old Crow
Geneva D. Addy
P.O. Box 124
Winterset, IA 50273

Poppin' Fresh (Pillsbury Doughboy)
Editor of newsletter: The Lovin' Connection
Lil West
2343 10000 Road
Oswego, KS 67356
Also other related Pillsbury memorabilia

Reddy Kilowatt and Bordon's Elsie
Lee Garmon
1529 Whittier St.
Springfield, IL 62704

Smokey Bear
Glen Brady
1134 Quines Creek Rd.
Azalea, OR 97410; 541-837-3462

Tins
Author of book
Linda McPherson
P.O. Box 381532
Germantown, TN 38183
e-mail: KPCY12A@prodigy.com

Watches
Editor of newsletter: The Premium Watch
* Watch*
Sharon Iranpour
24 San Rafel Dr.
Rochester, NY 14618-3702
716-381-9467; fax: 716-383-9248
e-mail: watcher1@rochester.rr.com

Airline Memorabilia
Richard Wallin
P.O. Box 1784
Springfield, IL 62705
217-498-9279: email: RRWALLIN@aol.com

Aluminum
Author of book
Everett Grist
P.O. Box 91375
Chattanooga, TN 37412-3955

Author of book
Dannie Woodard
P.O. Box 1346
Weatherford, TX 76086

American Bisque
Author of book
Mary Jane Giacomini
P.O. Box 404
Ferndale, CA 95536-0404

Animal Dishes
Author of book
Everett Grist
P.O. Box 91375
Chattanooga, TN 37412-3955
423-510-8052
Has authored books on aluminum,
advertising playing cards, letter openers,
and marbles

Appliances
Jim Barker
Toaster Master General
P.O. Box 746
Allentown, PA 18105

Ashtrays
Author of book
Nancy Wanvig
Nancy's Collectibles
P.O. Box 12
Thiensville, WI 53092

Autographs
Don and Anne Kier
2022 Marengo St.
Toledo, OH 43614; 419-385-8211
e-mail: d.a.k.@worldnet.att.net.

Automobilia
Leonard Needham
118 Warwick Dr. #48
Benicia, CA 94510; 707-748-4286
www.tias.com/stores/macadams

Tire ashtrays
Author of book ($12.95 postpaid)
Jeff McVey
1810 W State St., #427
Boise, ID 83702

Autumn Leaf
Gwynneth Harrison
P.O. Box 1
Mira Loma, CA 91752-0001
909-685-5434; e-mail: morgan99@pe.net

Avon Collectibles
Author of book
Bud Hastin
P.O. Box 11530
Ft. Lauderdale, FL 33339

Banks
Modern mechanical banks
Dan Iannotti
212 W Hickory Grove Rd.
Bloomfield Hills, MI 48302-1127S
248-335-5042
e-mail: modernbanks@ameritech.net

Barware
Especially cocktail shakers
Arlene Lederman Antiques
150 Main St.
Nyack, NY 10960

Specializing in vintage cocktail shakers
Author of book
Stephen Visakay
P.O. Box 1517
West Caldwell, NJ 07707-1517

Beanie Babies
Jerry and Ellen L. Harnish
110 Main St.
Bellville, OH 44813; 419-886-4782
Also character toys, dolls, GI Joe, general line; catalogs available

Amy Hopper
2161 Holt Rd.
Paducah, KY 42001

Beatnik and Hippie Collectibles
Richard M. Synchef
208 Summit Dr.
Corte Madera, CA 94925; 415-927-8844
Also Peter Max

Beatrix Potter
Nicki Budin
679 High St.
Worthington, OH 43085; 614-885-1986
Also Royal Doulton

Beer Cans
Dan Andrews
27105 Shorewood Rd.
Rancho Palos Verdes, CA 90275; 310-541-5149
e-mail: brewpub@earthlink.net

Bells
Unusual; no cow or school
Author of books
Dorothy J. Anthony
2401 S Horton St.
Ft. Scott, KS 66701-2790

Bicycles and Tricycles
Consultant, collector, dealer
Lorne Shields
Box 211
Chagrin Falls, OH 44022-0211
440-247-5632; fax: 905-886-7748
e-mail: vintage@globalserve.net
Alternate address: P.O. Box 87588
300 John St. Post Office
Thornhill, Ontario, Canada L3T 7R3

Black Americana
Buy, sell, and trade; fee charged for appraisal.
Judy Posner
R.R. 1, Box 273
Effort, PA 18330
www.tias.com/stores/jpc
e-mail: judyandjef@aol.com
Also toys, Disney, salt and pepper shakers, general line

Black Glass
Author of book
Marlena Toohey
703 S Pratt Pky.
Longmont, CO 80501; 303-678-9726

Blue Danube
Lori Simnionie
Auburn Main St. Antiques
124 E. Main St.
Auburn, WA 98002
253-927-3866 or 253-804-8041

Bobbin' Heads by Hartland
Author of guide; newsletter
Tim Hunter
4301 W. Hidden Valley Dr.
Reno, NV 89502
702-626-5029

Bookends
Author of book
Louis Kuritzky
4510 NW 17th Pl.
Gainesville, FL 32605; 352-377-3193

Books
Big Little Books
Ron and Donna Donnelly
6302 Championship Dr.
Tuscaloosa, AL 35405

Children's illustrated, Little Golden, etc.
Ilene Kayne
1308 S Charles St.
Baltimore, MD 21230
410-685-3923; e-mail: kayne@clark.net

Little Golden Books, Wonder and Elf
Author of book on Little Golden Books
Steve Santi
19626 Ricardo Ave.
Hayward, CA 94541

Bottle Openers
Charlie Reynolds
2836 Monroe St.
Falls Church, VA 22042; 703-533-1322
e-mail: reynoldstoys@erols.com

Bottles
Bitters, figurals, inks, barber, etc.
Steve Ketcham
P.O. Box 24114
Minneapolis, MN 55424; 612-920-4205
Also advertising signs, trays, calendars, etc.

Dairy and Milk
John Shaw
2201 Scenic Ridge Court
Mt. Flora, FL 32757 (Nov – May)
352-735-3831
43 Ridgecrest Dr.
Wilton, ME 04294 (June – Oct)
207-645-2442

Painted-label soda
Author of books
Thomas Marsh
914 Franklin Ave.
Youngstown, OH 44502
216-743-8600 or 800-845-7930 (book orders)

Boyd
Joyce M. Pringle
Antiques and Moore
3708 W Pioneer Pky.
Arlington, TX 76013
Website: Chipdale@flash.net
Also Summit and Mosser

Breweriana
Dan Andrews, The Brewmaster
27105 Shorewood Rd.
Rancho Palos Verdes, CA 90275
310-541-5149
e-mail: brewpub@earthlink.net

Breyer
Carol Karbowiak Gilbert
2193 14 Mile Rd. 206
Sterling Hts., MI 48310

British Royal Commemoratives
Author of book
Audrey Zeder
1320 SW 10th St
North Bend, WA 98045
Specializing in British Royalty
Commemoratives from Queen Victoria's
reign through current royal events

Brush-McCoy Pottery
Authors of book
Steve and Martha Sanford
230 Harrison Ave.
Campbell, CA 95008
408-978-8408

Bubble Bath Containers
Matt and Lisa Adams
1234 Harbor Cove
Woodstock, GA 30189-5467
770-516-6874
e-mail: mattradams@earthlink.net

Cake Toppers
Jeannie Greenfield
310 Parker Rd.
Stoneboro, PA 16153-2810
724-376-2584

Calculators
Author of book
Guy Ball
14561 Livingston St.
Tustin, CA 92780
www.mrcalc@usa.net

California Perfume Company
Not common; especially items marked
    Goetting Co.
Dick Pardini
3107 N El Dorado St., Dept. G
Stockton, CA 95204-3412
Also Savoi Et Cie, Hinze Ambrosia,
Gertrude Recordon, Marvel Electric
Silver Cleaner, and Easy Day Automatic
Clothes Washer

California Pottery
Author of several books
Susan N. Cox
800 Murray Drive
El Cajon, CA 92020
619-697-5922
email: antiqfever@aol.com
Want to buy: California pottery, especially Brayton, Catalina, Metlox, Kay Finch,
etc.; Also examples of relatively
unknown companies. Must be mint.
(Susan Cox has devoted much of the
past 15 years to California pottery
research which caught her interest when
she was the editor and publisher of the
American Clay Exchange. She would
appreciate any information collectors
might have about California pottery
companies and artists.)

Editor of newsletter: The California
    Pottery Trader
Michael John Verlangieri
Verlangieri Gallery
P.O. Box 844
Cambria, CA 93428-0844
805-927-4428
Specializing in fine California pottery; cat-
aloged auctions (video tapes available)
www.calpots.com

Cleminson
Robin Stine
P.O. Box 6202
Toledo, OH 43614
419-385-7387

Camark
Tony Freyaldenhoven
P.O. Box 1295
Conway, AR 72033
501-329-0628

Cameras
Classic, collectible, and usable
C.E. Cataldo
Gene's Cameras
2603 Artie St., S.W. Suite 16
Huntsville, Alabama 35805
205-536-6893

Wooden, detective, and stereo
John A. Hess
P.O. Box 3062
Andover, MA 01810
Also old brass lenses

Candy Containers
Glass
Jeff Bradfield
90 Main St.
Dayton, VA 22821
540-879-9961
Also advertising, cast-iron and tin toys,
postcards, and Coca-Cola

Glass
Author of book
Doug Dezso
864 Paterson Ave.
Maywood, NJ 07607
Other interests: Tonka Toys, Shafford
black cats, German bisque comic character nodders, Royal Bayreuth creamers,
and Pep pins

Cape Cod by Avon
Debbie and Randy Coe
Coes Mercantile
Lafayette School House Mall #2
748 3rd (Hwy. 99W)
Lafayette, OR 97137
Also Elegant and Depression glass, art
pottery, Golden Foliage by Libbey Glass
Company, and Liberty Blue dinnerware

Carnival Chalkware
Author of book
Thomas G. Morris
P.O. Box 8307
Medford, OR 97504-0307
e-mail: chalkman@cdsnet.net
Also Ginger Rogers memorabilia

Cast Iron
Door knockers, sprinklers, figural paper-
    weights, and marked cookware
Craig Dinner
P.O. Box 4399
Sunnyside, NY 11104; 718-729-3850

Cat Collectibles
Marilyn Dipboye
33161 Wendy Dr.
Sterling Hts., MI 48310; 810-264-0285

Karen Shanks
PO Box 150784
Nashville, TN 37215
615-297-7403 or www.catcollectors.com
e-mail: musiccitykitty@yahoo.com

Ceramic Arts Studio
BA Wellman and John Canfield
P.O. Box 673
Westminster, MA 01473
e-mail: bawellman@net1plus.com
www.dish.uni.cc

Character and Personality
    Collectibles
Author of books
Dealers, publishers, and appraisers of
    collectible memorabilia from the '50s
    through today
Bill Bruegman
Toy Scouts, Inc.
137 Casterton Ave.
Akron, OH 44303
330-836-0668; fax: 330-869-8668
e-mail: toyscouts@toyscouts.com
www.toyscouts.com

Any and all
Terri Ivers
Terri's Toys
206 E Grand
Ponca City, OK 74601
580-762-8697 or 580-762-5174
fax: 580-765-2657
e-mail: toylady@poncacity.net

Any and all
Norm Vigue
3 Timberwood Dr., #306
Goffstown, MA 03045
603-647-9951

Batman, Gumby, and Marilyn Monroe
Colleen Garmon Barnes
114 E Locust
Chatham, IL 62629

Beatles
Bojo
Bob Gottuso
P.O. Box 1403
Cranberry Twp., PA 16066-0403
Phone or fax: 724-776-0621
www.bojoonline.com; Beatles sale catalog available 4X a year, send $3 for copy

California Raisins
Ken Clee
Box 11412
Philadelphia, PA 19111; 215-722-1979

California Raisins
Larry De Angelo
516 King Arthur Dr.
Virginia Beach, VA 23464; 757-424-1691

Dick Tracy
Larry Doucet
2351 Sultana Dr.
Yorktown Hts., NY 10598
314-245-1320
e-mail: LDoucetDM@aol.com

Disney, Western heroes, Gone With the Wind, character watches ca 1930s to mid-1950s, premiums, and games
Ron and Donna Donnelly
6302 Championship Dr.
Tuscaloosa, AL 35405

Disney
Buy, sell, and trade; lists available; fee charged for appraisal
Judy Posner
R.R. 1, Box 273
Effort, PA 18330
www.tias.com/stores/jpc
e-mail: judyandjef@aol.com

Elvis Presley
Author of book
Rosalind Cranor
P.O. Box 859
Blacksburg, VA 24063

Elvis Presley
Lee Garmon
1529 Whittier St.
Springfield, IL 62704

Garfield
Adrienne Warren
1032 Feather Bed Ln.
Edison, NJ 08820
Also Smurfs and other characters, dolls, monsters, premiums; Lists available

The Lone Ranger
Terry and Kay Klepey
c/o *The Silver Bullet* newsletter
P.O. Box 553
Forks, WA 98331

Lucille Ball
Author of book
Ric Wyman
408 S Highland Ave.
Elderon, WI 54429

Peanuts and Schulz Collectibles
Freddi Margolin
P.O. Box 5124P
Bay Shore, NY 11706

Roy Rogers and Dale Evans
Author of books; biographer for Golden Boots Awards
Robert W. Phillips
1703 N Aster Pl.
Broken Arrow, OK 74012-1308
918-254-8205; fax: 918-252-9362
e-mail: rawhidebob@aol.com
One of the most widely-published writers in the field of cowboy memorabila and author of *Roy Rogers, Singing Cowboy Stars, Silver Screen Cowboys, Hollywood Cowboy Heroes*, and *Western Comics: A Comprehensive Reference*, research consultant for TV documentary *Roy Rogers, King of the Cowboys* (AMC-TV/Republic Pictures/Galen Films)

Shirley Temple
Gen Jones
294 Park St.
Medford, MA 02155

Smokey Bear
Glen Brady
1134 Quines Creek Rd.
Azalea, OR 97410; 541-837-3462

Wizard of Oz
Bill Stillman
Scarfone & Stillman Vintage Oz
P.O. Box 167
Hummelstown, PA 17036; 717-566-5538

Character and Promotional Drinking Glasses
Authors of book; editors of Collector Glass News
Mark Chase and Michael Kelly
P.O. Box 308
Slippery Rock, PA 16057
412-946-2838; fax: 724-946-9012
e-mail: cgn@glassnews.com
www.glassnews.com

Character Clocks and Watches
Author of book
Howard S. Brenner
106 Woodgate Terrace
Rochester, NY 14625

Bill Campbell
1221 Littlebrook Ln.
Birmingham, AL 35235
205-853-8227; fax: 405-658-6986
Also character collectibles, advertising premiums

Character Nodders
Matt and Lisa Adams
1234 Harbor Cove
Woodstock, GA 30189-5467
770-516-6874
e-mail: mattradams@earthlink.net

Chintz
Mary Jane Hastings
310 West 1st South
Mt. Olive, IL 62069
Phone or fax: 217-999-1222

Author of book
Joan Welsh
7015 Partridge Pl.
Hyattsville, MD 20782
301-779-6181

Christmas Collectibles
Especially from before 1920 and decorations made in Germany
J.W. 'Bill' and Treva Courter
3935 Kelley Rd.
Kevil, KY 42053
Phone: 270-488-2116; fax: 270-488-2055

Clocks
All types
Bruce A. Austin
1 Hardwood Hill Rd.
Pittsford, NY 14534
716-387-9820

Clothes Sprinkler Bottles
Ellen Bercovici
5118 Hampden Ln.
Bethesda, MD 20814
301-652-1140

Clothing and Accessories
Author of book
Sue Langley
101 Ramsey Ave.
Syracuse, NY 13224-1719
315-445-0113
e-mail: langshats@aol.com

Flying Deuce
1224 Yellowstone
Pocatello, ID 83201
208-237-2002; fax: 208-237-4544
e-mail: flying2@nicoh.com

Coca-Cola
Also Pepsi-Cola and other brands of soda
Craig Stifter
218 S. Adams St.
Hinsdale, IL 50421
630-789-5780; mobile: 847-924-7828
e-mail: cocacola@enteract.com

Coin-Operated Vending Machines
Ken and Jackie Durham
909 26th St., NW
Washington, D.C. 20037

Comic Books

Avalon Comics
Larry Curcio
P.O. Box 821
Medford, MA 02155; 617-391-5614

Compacts

Unusual shapes, also vanities and accessories
Author of book
Roselyn Gerson
P.O. Box 40
Lynbrook, NY 11563

Cookbooks

Author of book
Bob Allen
P.O. Box 56
St. James, MO 65559
Also advertising leaflets

Cookie Cutters

Author of book and newsletter
Rosemary Henry
9610 Greenview Ln.
Manassas, VA 20109-3320

Cookie Jars

Joe Devine
1411 3rd St.
Council Bluffs, IA 51503
712-323-5233 or 712-328-7305
Also Black Americana, salt and pepper shakers

Buy, sell and trade; lists available; fee charged for appraisal
Judy Posner
R.R. 1, Box 273
Effort, PA 18330
www.tias.com/stores/jpc
e-mail: judyandjef@aol.com

Corkscrews

Author of books
Donald A. Bull
PO Box 596
Wirtz, VA 24184; 540-721-1128
www.corkscrewmuseum.com
e-mail: corkscrew@bullworks.net

Cow Creamers

Shirley Green
1550 E. Kamm Ave. #116
Kingsburg, CA 93631
209-897-7125
e-mail: granas@psnw.com

Cracker Jack Items

Phil Helley
Old Kilbourn Antiques
629 Indiana Ave.
Wisconsin Dells, WI 53965
Also banks, radio premiums and wind-up toys

Wes Johnson, Sr.
106 Bauer Ave.
Louisville, KY 40207

Author of books
Larry White
108 Central St.
Rowley, MA 01969-1317; 978-948-8187
e-mail: larrydw@erols.com;

Crackle Glass

Authors of book
Stan and Arlene Weitman
101 Cypress St.
Massapequa Park, NY 11758
516-799-2619; fax: 516-797-3039
www.crackleglass.com
Also specializing in Overshot

Cuff Links

National Cuff Link Society
Eugene R. Klompus
P.O. Box 5700
Vernon Hills, IL 60061
Phone or fax: 847-816-0035
e-mail: genek@cufflink.com
Also related items

Cups and Saucers

Authors of books
Jim and Susan Harran
208 Hemlock Dr.
Neptune, NJ 07753
www.tias.com/stores/amit

Dakins

Jim Rash
135 Alder Ave.
Egg Harbor Township, NJ 08234

Decanters

Homestead Collectibles
Art and Judy Turner
R.D. 2, Rte. 150
P.O. Box 173
Mill Hall, PA 17751
570-726-3597; fax: 717-726-4488

Degenhart

Linda K. Marsh
1229 Gould Rd.
Lansing, MI 48917

deLee

Authors of book
Joanne and Ralph Schaefer
3182 Williams Rd.
Oroville, CA 95965-8300
530-893-2902 or 530-894-6263

Depression Glass

Also Elegant glassware
John and Shirley Baker
673 W Township Rd. #118
Tiffin, OH 44883
Also Tiffin glassware

Dinnerware

Blue Ridge
Author of several books; columnist for The Depression Glass Daze
Bill and Betty Newbound
2206 Nob Hill Dr.
Sanford, NC 27330
Also milk glass, wall pockets, figural planters, collectible china and glass

Cat-Tail
Ken and Barbara Brooks
4121 Gladstone Ln.
Charlotte, NC 28205

Currier & Ives Dinnerware
Author of book
Eldon R. Bud Aupperle
29470 Saxon Road
Toulon, IL 61483
309-896-3331; fax: 309-856-6005

Fiesta, Franciscan, Lu Ray, Metlox, and Homer Laughlin
Fiesta Plus
Mick and Lorna Chase
380 Hawkins Crawford Rd.
Cookeville, TN 38501; 931-372-8333
e-mail: fiestaplus@yahoo.com
www.fiestaplus.com

Homer Laughlin China
Author of book
Darlene Nossaman
5419 Lake Charles
Waco, TX 76710

Johnson Brothers
Author of book
Mary Finegan, Marfine Antiques
P.O. Box 3618
Boone, NC 28607; 828-262-3441

Liberty Blue
Gary Beegle
92 River St.
Montgomery, NY 12549; 914-457-3623
Also most lines of collectible modern American dinnerware as well as character glasses

Restaurant China
Author of books (Volume 1 and Volume 2)
Barbara J. Conroy
P.O. Box 2369
Santa Clara, CA 95055-2369
e-mail: restaurantchina@earthlink.net
www.home.earthlink.net/
~restaurantchina/homepage.htm

Royal China
BA Wellman and John Canfield
P.O. Box 673
Westminster, MA 01473-0673
e-mail: bawellman@net1plus.com
Also Ceramic Arts Studio
www.dish.uni.cc

*Russel Wright, Eva Zeisel, Homer
   Laughlin*
Charles Alexander
221 E 34th St.
Indianapolis, IN 46205
317-924-9665

Wallace China
Marv Fogleman
Marv's Memories
1814 W. Carriage Dr.
Santa Ana, CA 92704
Specializing in American, English, and
Western dinnerware

Dollhouse Furniture and Accessories
Renwal, Ideal, Marx, etc.
Judith A. Mosholder
186 Pine Springs Camp Rd.
Boswell, PA 15531
814-629-9277
e-mail: jlytwins@floodcity.net

Dolls
Annalee Mobilitee Dolls
Jane's Collectibles
Jane Holt
P.O. Box 115
Derry, NH 03038

Betsy McCall and friends
Marci Van Ausdall, Editor
P.O. Box 946
Quincy, CA 95971-0946
530-283-2770

Celebrity and character dolls
Henri Yunes
971 Main St., Apt. 2
Hackensack, NJ 07601; 201-488-2236

Chatty Cathy and Mattel talkers
Authors of books
Don and Kathy Lewis
Whirlwind Unlimited
187 N Marcello Ave.
Thousand Oaks, CA 91360; 805-499-8101
e-mail: chatty@ix.netcom.com

*Dolls from the 1960s – 70s, including Liddle
   Kiddles, Barbie, Tammy, Tressy, etc.*
*Co-author of book on Tammy, author of
   Collector's Guide to Dolls of the 1960s & 1970s*
Cindy Sabulis
P.O. Box 642
Shelton, CT 06484; 203-926-0176

*Dolls from the 1960s – 70s, including
   Liddle Kiddles, Dolly Darlings, Petal
   People, Tiny Teens, etc.*
*Author of book on Liddle Kiddles; must
   send SASE for info*
Paris Langford
415 Dodge Ave.
Jefferson, LA 70121
504-733-0667

Holly Hobbie
Helen McCale
1006 Ruby Ave.
Butler, MO 64730-2500

Holly Hobbie
*Editor of newsletter: The Holly Hobbie
   Collectors Gazette*
Donna Stultz
1455 Otterdale Mill Rd.
Taneytown, MD 21787-3032; 410-775-2570
hhgazette@netscape.net

Ideal
*Author of book; available from author or
   Collector Books*
Judith Izen
P.O. Box 623
Lexington, MA 02420
781-862-2994; e-mail: jizenres@aol.com

*Liddle Kiddles and other small dolls from
   the late '60s and early '70s*
Dawn Diaz
20460 Samual Drive
Saugus, CA 91530-3812; 661-263-TOYS

Strawberry Shortcake
Geneva D. Addy
P.O. Box 124
Winterset, IA 50273

Vogue Dolls, Inc.
*Co-author of book; available from
   author or Collector Books*
Judith Izen
P.O. Box 623
Lexington, MA 02173-5914; 781-862-2994
e-mail: jizenres@aol.com

Vogue Dolls, Inc.
*Co-author of book; available from
   author or Collector Books*
Carol J. Stover
81 E Van Buren St.
Chicago, IL 60605

Door Knockers
Craig Dinner
Box 4399
Sunnyside, NY 11104
718-729-3850

Egg Beaters
*Author of Beat This: The Egg Beater
   Chronicles*
Don Thornton
Off Beat Books
1345 Poplar Ave.
Sunnyvale, CA 94087

Egg Cups
Author of book
Brenda Blake
Box 555
York Harbor, ME 03911; 207-363-6566

Egg Timers
Ellen Bercovici
5118 Hampden Ln.
Bethesda, MD 20814
301-652-1140

Jeannie Greenfield
310 Parker Rd.
Stoneboro, PA 16153-2810
724-376-2584

Elegant Glass
Cambridge, Fostoria
Deborah Maggard Antiques
P.O. Box 211
Chagrin Falls, OH 44022
440-247-5632; e-mail:
debmaggard@worldnet.att.net
Also china and Victorian art glass

Roselle Schleifman
16 Vincent Rd.
Spring Valley, NY 10977

Erich Stauffer Figurines
Joan Oates
685 S Washington
Constantine, MI 49042
616-435-8353
e-mail: koates@remc12.k12.mi.us
Also Phoenix Bird china

Ertl Banks
Homestead Collectibles
P.O. Box 173
Mill Hall, PA 17751.
Also decanters

Eyewinker
Sophia Talbert
921 Union St.
Covington, IN 47932
765-793-3256

Fast-Food Collectibles
Author of book
Ken Clee
Box 1142
Philadelphia, PA 19111
215-722-1979

Authors of several books
Joyce and Terry Losonsky
7506 Summer Leave Lane
Columbia, MD 21046-2455
*Illustrated Collector's Guide to
McDonald's® Happy Meal® Boxes,
Premiums and Promotions ($9 plus $2
postage), McDonald's® Happy Meal® Toys
in the USA and McDonald's® Happy
Meal® Toys Around the World (both full
color, $24.95 each plus $3 postage), and
Illustrated Collector's Guide to
McDonald's® McCAPS® ($4 plus $2) are
available from the authors*

Bill and Pat Poe
220 Dominica Cir. E
Niceville, FL 32578-4085
850-897-4163; fax: 850-897-2606
e-mail: McPoes@aol.com
Also cartoon and character glasses, Pez,
Smurfs, and California Raisins

Fenton Glass
Ferill J. Rice
302 Pheasant Run
Kaukauna, WI 54130

Figural Ceramics
Especially Kitchen Prayer Lady
April and Larry Tvorak
PO Box 493401
Leesburg, FL 34749-3401
Also interested in Pyrex

Fisher-Price
Author of book
Brad Cassidy
2391 Hunters Trail
Myrtle Beach, SC 29579; 843-236-8697

Fishing Collectibles
Publishes fixed-price catalog
Dave Hoover
1023 Skyview Dr.
New Albany, IN 47150
Also miniature boats and motors

Flashlights
Editor of newsletter
Bill Utley
P.O. Box 4094
Tustin, CA 92681
714-730-1252; fax: 714-505-4067

Florence Ceramics
Author of book
Doug Foland
2014 SE Ankeny St.
Portland, OR 97214-1622

Jerry Kline
Florence Showcase
PO Box 937
Kodak, TN 37764
865-933-9060; fax: 865-933-4492

John and Peggy Scott
4640 S Leroy
Springfield, MO 65810

Flower Frogs
Bonnie Bull
Flower Frog Gazette Online
http://www.flowerfrog.com

Frankoma
Authors of book
Phyllis and Tom Bess
14535 E 13th St.
Tulsa, OK 74108

Author of books
Susan N. Cox
800 Murray Dr.
El Cajon, CA 92020
619-697-5922
e-mail: antiqfever@aol.com
Also unsharpened advertising pencils,
complete matchbooks, Horlick's advertising, women's magazines from 1900 to
1950. (Susan Cox has written 3 books
and 5 price guides on Frankoma pottery
and is currently working on an updated
price guide and a Frankoma advertising
book. She has devoted much of the past
fifteen years to California pottery
research and welcomes any information
collectors might have about California
companies and artists.)

Fruit Jars
Especially old, odd or colored jars
John Hathaway
3 Mills Rd.
Bryant Pond, ME 04219
Also old jar lids and closures

Games
Paul Fink's Fun and Games
P.O. Box 488
59 S Kent Rd.
Kent, CT 06757
203-927-4001

Paul David Morrow
1045 Rolling Point Ct.
Virginia Beach, VA 23456-6371

Gas Station Collectibles
Scott Benjamin
Oil Co. Collectibles Inc.
Petroleum Collectibles Monthly Magazine
PO Box 556
LaGrange, OH 44050-0556
440-355-6608
Specializing in gas globes, signs, and
magazines

Gay Fad Glassware
Donna S. McGrady
P.O. Box 14, 301 E. Walnut St.
Waynetown, IN 47990
765-234-2187

Geisha Girl China
Author of book
Elyce Litts
P.O. Box 394
Morris Plains, NJ 07950
e-mail: happy-memories@worldnet.att.net
Also ladies' compacts

Glass Animals
Author of book
Lee Garmon
1529 Whittier St.
Springfield, IL 62704

Glass Knives
Michele A. Rosewitz
3165 McKinley Avenue
San Bernardino, CA 92404; 909-862-8534
e-mail: rosetree@sprintmail.com

Glass Shoes
Author of book
The Shoe Lady
Libby Yalom
P.O. Box 7146
Adelphi, MD 20783

Granite Ware
Author of books
Helen Greguire
864-457-7340
Also carnival glass and toasters

Griswold
Grant Windsor
P.O. Box 72606
Richmond, VA 23235-8017
804-320-0386

Guardian Service Cookware
Dennis S. McAdams
3110 E. Lancaster Rd.
Hayden Lake, ID 83835
e-mail: HAYDENMAC4@aol.com

Guardian Service Cookware
2110 Harmony Woods Road
Owings Mills, MD 21117-1649
410-560-0777
http://members.aol.com/vettelvr93/

Hagen-Renaker
Gayle Roller
PO Box 222
San Marcos, CA 92079-0222
760-721-8239

Hallmark
The Baggage Car
3100 Justin Dr., Ste. B
Des Moines, IA 50322
515-270-9080

Halloween
Author of books; autographed copies
available from the author
Pamela E. Apkarian-Russell
Chris Russell & The Halloween Queen
Antiques
P.O. Box 499
Winchester, NH 03470
e-mail: halloweenqueen@top.cheshire.net
Also other holidays, postcards, and Joe
Camel

Hartland Plastics, Inc.
Author of book
Gail Fitch
1733 N Cambridge Ave. #109
Milwaukee, WI 53202

Specializing in Western Hartlands
Buy and sell; hold consignment auctions
specializing in vintage toys
Kerry and Judy Irvin
Kerry and Judy's Toys
1414 S. Twelfth St.
Murray, KY 42071
270-759-3456; e-mail: kjtoys@apex.net

Specializing in sports figures
James Watson
25 Gilmore St.
Whitehall, NY 12887

Holt Howard
Pat and Ann Duncan
Box 175
Cape Fair, MO 65624
417-538-2311

Homer Laughlin
Author of book
Darlene Nossaman
5419 Lake Charles
Waco, TX 76710

Horton Ceramics
Darlene Nossaman
5419 Lake Charles
Waco, TX 76710

Hull
Author of several books on Hull
Brenda Roberts
906 S. Ann Dr.
Marshall, MO 65340

Imperial Glass
Joan Cimini
67183 Stein Rd.
Belmont, OH 43718-9715
740-782-1327
e-mail: upperigladyclst.net
Also has Candlewick matching service

Imperial Porcelain
Geneva D. Addy
P.O. Box 124
Winterset, IA 50273

Indy 500 Memorabilia
Eric Jungnickel
P.O. Box 4674
Naperville, IL 60567-4674; 630-983-8339

Insulators
Mike Bruner
6980 Walnut Lake Rd.
W Bloomfield, MI 48323; 313-661-8241
Also porcelain signs, light-up advertising
clocks, exit globes, lightening rod balls,
and target balls

Jacqueline Linscott
3557 Nicklaus Dr.
Tutusville, FL 32780

Japan Ceramics
Author of books
Carole Bess White
PO Box 819
Portland, OR 97207

Jewel Tea
Products or boxes only; no dishes
Bill and Judy Vroman
739 Eastern Ave.
Fostoria, OH 44830; 419-435-5443

Jewelry
Author of book
Marcia Brown (Sparkles)
P.O. Box 2314
White City, OR 97503
541-826-3039; fax: 541-830-5385
Author of *Unsigned Beauties of Costume*
Jewelry and co-author and host of seven
Hidden Treasure book-on-tape videos

Men's accessories and cuff links only;
edits newsletter
The National Cuff Link Society
Eugene R. Klompus
PO Box 5700
Vernon Hills, IL 60061
Phone or fax: 847-816-0035

Josef Originals
Authors of books
Jim and Kaye Whitaker, Eclectic Antiques
P.O. Box 475, Dept. GS
Lynnwood, WA 98046

Kay Finch
Co-Authors of book, available from authors
Mike Nickel and Cynthia Horvath
P.O. Box 456
Portland, MI 48875; 517-647-7646

Kentucky Derby and Horse Racing
B.L. Hornback
707 Sunrise Ln.
Elizabethtown, KY 42701
e-mail: bettysantiques@KVNET.org
Inquiries require a SASE with fee expected
for appraisals and/or identification of glasses. Booklet picturing Kentucky Derby,
Preakness, Belmont, and other racing
glasses available for $15 ppd.

Kreiss; Psycho Ceramics
Authors of book
Michelle and Mike King
P.O. Box 3519
Alliance, OH 44601
330-829-5946; www.quest-for-toys.com
Exclusive source for Kreiss book.
International mail-order vintage toy com-
pany specializing in toys and memora-
bilia from the 1960s – 1980s; collect nov-
elty and character ceramics, vintage
Barbies, ad characters, Arts & Crafts
home furnishings

Kitchen Prayer Ladies
Issues price guide ($6.96 plus $1 postage
and handling)
April and Larry Tvorak
P.O. Box 493401
Leesburg, FL 34749-3401
Also interested in Enesco, Pyrex, and
figural ceramics

Lamps
Aladdin
Author of books
J.W. Courter
3935 Kelley Rd.
Kevil, KY 42053; 270-488-2116

Figural Lamps
Dee Boston
2299 N Pr. Rd. 475 W
Sullivan, IN 47882
Also dresser, pincushion, and half dolls

Motion lamps
Eclectic Antiques
Jim and Kaye Whitaker
P.O. Box 475, Dept. GS
Lynwood, WA 98046

Authors of book
Sam and Anna Samuelian
P.O. Box 504
Edgemont, PA 19028-0504; 610-566-7248
Also motion clocks, transistor and novel-
ty radios

Lefton
Author of books
Loretta DeLozier
PO Box 50201
Knoxville, TN 37950-0201

Letter Openers
Author of book
Everett Grist
P.O. Box 91375
Chattanooga, TN 37412-3955; 423-510-8052

License Plates
Richard Diehl
5965 W Colgate Pl.
Denver, CO 80227

Longaberger Baskets
The *only* reference tool for consultants, collec-
tors, and enthusiasts of Longaberger Baskets®
Jill S. Rindfuss
The Bentley Collection Guide®
5870 Zarley Street, Suite C
New Albany, OH 43054
Monday through Friday, 9:00 a.m. – 5:00
p.m. (EST) 1-800-837-4394
www.bentleyguide.com
e-mail: info@bentlyguide.com
The most accurate and reliable reference
tool available for evaluating Longaberger
Products®. Full color with individual pho-

tographs of most baskets and products produced since 1979. Published once a year in June with a free six-month update being sent in January to keep the Guide current for the entire year.

Holds exclusive auctions
Greg Michael
Craft & Michael Auction/Realty Inc.
PO Box 7
Camden, IN 46917
219-686-2615 or 219-967-4442
fax: 219-686-9100
e-mail: gpmmgtco@netusal1.net.

Lunch Boxes
Norman's Ole and New Store
Philip Norman
126 W Main St.
Washington, NC 27889-4944
252-946-3448

Terri's Toys and Nostalgia
Terri Ivers
206 E. Grand
Ponca City, OK 74601
580-762-8697 or 580-762-5174
fax: 405-765-2657
e-mail: toylady@poncacity.net

Magazines
Issues price guides to illustrators, pinups, and old magazines of all kinds
Denis C. Jackson
Illustrator Collector's News
P.O. Box 1958
Sequim, WA 98382
360-452-3810; e-mail: ticn@olypen.com

Pre-1950 movie magazines, especially with Ginger Rogers covers
Tom Morris
P.O. Box 8307
Medford, OR 97504
e-mail: chalkman@cdsnet.net

National Geographic
Author of guide
Don Smith's *National Geographic Magazines*
3930 Rankin St.
Louisville, KY 40214; 502-366-7504

Pulps
Issues catalogs on various genre of hardcover books, paperbacks, and magazines of all types
J. Grant Thiessen
Pandora's Books Ltd.
Box 54
Neche, ND 58265-0054
fax: 204-324-1628
e-mail: jgthiess@mts.net
www.pandora.ca/pandora

Marbles
Author of books
Everett Grist
P.O. Box 91375
Chattanooga, TN 37412-3955
423-510-8052

Match Safes
George Sparacio
P.O. Box 791
Malaga, NJ 08328
609-694-4167; fax: 609-694-4536
e-mail: mrvesta@aol.com

Matchcovers
Author of books
Bill Retskin
P.O. Box 18481
Asheville, NC 22814
704-254-4487; fax: 704-254-1066
e-mail: bill@matchcovers.com
www.matchcovers.com

McCoy Pottery
Authors of books
Robert and Margaret Hanson
16517 121 Ave. NE
Bothell, WA 98011

Melmac Dinnerware
Co-author of book
Alvin Daigle, Jr.
Boomerang Antiques
Gray, TN 37615
423-915-0666

Co-author of book
Gregg Zimmer
4017 16th Ave. S
Minneapolis, MN 55407

Metlox
Author of book; available from author
Carl Gibbs, Jr.
P.O. Box 131584
Houston, TX 77219-1584
713-521-9661

Milk Bottles
John Shaw
Nov. – May:
2201 Scenic Ridge Court
Mt. Flora, FL 32757
352-735-3831
June – Oct.:
43 Ridgecrest Dr.
Wilton, ME 04294
207-645-2442

Miller Studios
Paul and Heather August
7510 West Wells St.
Wauwatosa, WI 53213
414-475-0753
e-mail: packrats@execpc.com

Morton Pottery
Authors of books
Doris and Burdell Hall
B&B Antiques
210 W Sassafras Dr.
Morton, IL 61550-1245

Motion Clocks
Electric; buy, sell, trade, and restore
Sam and Anna Samuelian
P.O. Box 504
Edgemont, PA 19028-0504
610-566-7248
Also motion lamps, transistor and novelty radios

Motorcycles and Motorcycle Memorabilia
Bob 'Sprocket' Eckardt
P.O. Box 172
Saratoga Springs, NY 12866
518-584-2405
e-mail: sprocketbe@aol.com
Buying and trading

Bruce Kiper
Ancient Age Motors
2205 Sunset Ln.
Lutz, FL 33549
813-949-9660
Also related items and clothing

Movie Posters
Movie Poster Service
Cleophas and Lou Ann Wooley
Box 517
Canton, OK 73724-0517
580-886-2248; fax: 580-886-2249
e-mail: mpsposters@pldi.net
In business full time since 1972; own/operate mail-order firm with world's largest movie poster inventory

Napkin Dolls
Co-Author of book
Bobbie Zucker Bryson
1 St. Eleanoras Ln.
Tuckahoe, NY 10707
914-779-1405
e-mail: napkindoll@aol.com
www.reamers.org
To order a copy of *Collectibles for the Kitchen, Bath & Beyond* (featuring napkin dolls, egg timers, string holders, children's whistle cups and baby feeder dishes, razor blade banks, pie birds, laundry sprinkler bottles, and other unique collectibles from the same era), contact Krause Publications, 700 E. State St., Iola, WI, 54990-4612; 800-258-0929

Newspaper Collector Society
Rick Brown
517-887-1255
e-mail: info@historybuff.com

Orientalia and Dragonware
Suzi Hibbard
849 Vintage Ave.
Fairfield, CA 94585

Paden City Glassware
George and Mary Hurney
Glass Connection (mail-order only)
312 Babcock Dr.
Palatine, IL 50067; 847-359-3839

Paper Dolls
Author of books
Mary Young
P.O. Box 9244, Wright Bros. Branch
Dayton, OH 45409

Pencil Sharpeners
Phil Helley
629 Indiana Ave.
Wisconsin Dells, WI 53965; 608-254-8659

Advertising and figural
Martha Hughes
4128 Ingalls St.
San Diego, CA 92103; 619-296-1866

Pennsbury
Author of price guide
BA Wellman and John Canfield
P.O. Box 673
Westminster, MA 01473-1435
e-mail: bawellman@net1plus.com
www.dish.uni.cc

Joe Devine
1411 3rd St.
Council Bluffs, IA 51503
712-323-5322 or 712-328-7305

Shirley Graff
4515 Graff Rd.
Brunswick, OH 44212

Pepsi-Cola
Craig Stifter
218 S. Adams St.
Hinsdale, IL 60521; 630-389-5780
e-mail: cocacola@enteract.com
Other soda-pop memorablia as well

Perfume Bottles
Especially commercial, Czechoslovakian, Lalique, Baccarat, Victorian, crown top, factices, miniatures
Buy, sell, and accept consignments for auctions
Monsen and Baer
Box 529
Vienna, VA 22183; 703-938-2129

Pez
Richard Belyski
P.O. Box 124
Sea Cliff, NY 11579; 516-676-1183
e-mail: peznews@juno.com

Pie Birds
Linda Fields
158 Bagsby Hill Lane
Dover, TN 37058; 931-232-5099
e-mail: Fpiebird@compu.net.
Organizer of Piebird Collector's
Convention and author of *Four & Twenty Blackbirds;* Specializing in pie birds, pie funnels, and pie vents

Pin-Back Buttons
Michael and Polly McQuillen
McQuillen's Collectibles
P.O. Box 50022
Indianapolis, IN 46250; 317-845-1721
e-mail: mmcquillen@politicalparade.com
www.politicalparade.com

Pinup Art
Issues price guides to pinups, illustrations and old magazines
Denis C. Jackson
Illustrator Collector's News
P.O. Box 1958
Sequim, WA 98382
360-452-3810; or fax 360-683-9807
e-mail: ticn@olypen.com

Pocket Calculators
Author of book
International Assn. of Calculator Collectors
Guy D. Ball
P.O. Box 345
Tustin, CA 92781-0345
Phone or fax: 714-730-6140
e-mail: mrcalc@usa.net

Political
Michael and Polly McQuillen
McQuillen's Collectibles
P.O. Box 50022
Indianapolis, IN 46250; 317-845-1721
e-mail: mmcquillen@politicalparade.com
www.politicalparade.com

Before 1960
Michael Engel
29 Groveland St.
Easthampton, MA 01027

Pins, banners, ribbons, etc.
Paul Longo Americana
Box 5510
Magnolia, MA 01930; 978-525-2290

Poodle Collectibles
Author of book
Elaine Butler
233 S Kingston Ave.
Rockwood, TN 37854

Porcelier
Jim Barker
Toaster Master General
P.O. Box 746
Allentown, PA 10106

Author of book
Susan Grindberg
1412 Pathfinder Rd.
Henderson, NV 89014
702-898-7535
e-mail: porcelier@anv.net
or sue@porcelierconnection.com
www.porcelierconnection.com

Postcards
Pamela E. Apkarian-Russell
Chris Russell and the Halloween Queen Antiques
P.O. Box 499
Winchester, NH 03470
Also Halloween and other holidays

Powder Jars
John and Peggy Scott
4640 S Leroy
Springfield, MO 65810

Sharon Thoerner
15549 Ryon Ave.
Bellflower, CA 90706
562-866-1555
Also slag glass

Purinton Pottery
Author of book
Susan Morris
PO Box 1684
Port Orchard, WA 98366
360-871-7376
e-mail: sue@wattpottery.com
www.wattpottery.com
www.applebarrel.com

Purses
Veronica Trainer
P.O. Box 40443
Cleveland, OH 44140

Puzzles
Wooden jigsaw type from before 1950
Bob Armstrong
15 Monadnock Rd.
Worcester, MA 01609

Especially character related
Norm Vigue
3 Timberwood Dr.
Goffstown, MA 03045; 603-647-9951

Radio Premiums
Bill Campbell
1221 Littlebrook Ln.
Birmingham, AL 35235
205-853-8227; fax: 405-658-6986

Radios
Authors of several books on antique, novelty, and transistor radios
Sue and Marty Bunis
R.R. 1, Box 36
Bradford, NH 03221-9102

Author of book
Harry Poster
P.O. Box 1883
S Hackensack, NJ 07606
201-410-7525
Also televisions, related advertising
items, old tubes, cameras, 3-D viewers
and projectors, View-Master and Tru-
View reels and accessories

Railroadiana
*Also steamship and other transportation
memorabilia*
Fred and Lila Shrader
Shrader Antiques
2025 Hwy. 199
Crescent City, CA 95531; 707-458-3525
Also Buffalo, Shelley, Niloak, and
Hummels

*Any item; especially china and silver
Catalogs available*
John White, 'Grandpa'
Grandpa's Depot
1616 17th St., Ste. 267
Denver, CO 80202
303-628-5590; fax: 303-628-5547
Also related items

Razor Blade Banks
Debbie Gillham
47 Midline Ct.
Gaithersburg, MD 20878; 301-977-5727

Reamers
*Co-author of book, ordering info under
Napkin Dolls*
Bobbie Zucker Bryson
1 St. Eleanoras Ln.
Tuckahoe, NY 10707
914-779-1405
e-mail: napkindoll@aol.com
www.reamers.org

Records
45 rpm and LP's
Mason's Bookstore, Rare Books, and
Record Albums
Dave Torzillo
115 S Main St.
Chambersburg, PA 17201
717-261-0541

Picture and 78 rpm kiddie records
Peter Muldavin
173 W 78th St. Apt 5-F
New York, NY 10024
212-362-9606
e-mail:kiddie78s@aol.com

Especially 78 rpms, author of book
L.R. 'Les' Docks
Box 691035
San Antonio, TX 78269-1035
Write for want list

Red Wing
B.L. and R.L. Dollen
Dollen Books & Antiques
P.O. Box 386
Aboca, IA 51521-0386
Collector Book authors specializing in
Red Wing art pottery and dinnerware

Red Wing Artware
Hold cataloged auctions
Wendy and Leo Frese
Three Rivers Collectibles
P.O. Box 551542
Dallas, TX 75355; 214-341-5165
e-mail: rumrill@ix.netcom.com

Regal China
*Van Telligen, Bendel, Old MacDonald's
Farm*
Rick Spencer
Salt Lake City, UT; 801-973-0805
Also Coors, Shawnee, Watt, Silverplate
(especially grape patterns)

Rooster and Roses
Jacki Elliott
9790 Twin Cities Rd.
Galt, CA 95632; 209-745-3860

Rosemeade
NDSU research specialist
Bryce Farnsworth
1334 14 1/2 St. S
Fargo, ND 58103; 701-237-3597

Roseville
Mike Nickel
PO Box 456
Portland, MI, 48875
517-647-7646
Also Kay Finch; other Ohio pottery

Royal Bayreuth
Don and Anne Kier
2022 Marengo St.
Toledo, OH 43614
419-385-8211
e-mail: d.a.k.@worldnet.att.net

Royal Copley
Author of books
Joe Devine
1411 3rd St.
Council Bluffs, IA 51503
712-323-5233 or 712-328-7305
Buy, sell, or trade; Also pie birds

Royal Haeger
Author of book
David D. Dilley
D&R Antiques
P.O. Box 225
Indianapolis, IN 46206; 317-251-0575
e-mail: glazebears@aol.com
bearpots@aol.com

Co-author of book
Doris Frizzell
Doris' Dishes
5687 Oakdale Dr.
Springfield, IL 62707; 217-529-3873

RumRill
Hold cataloged auctions
Wendy and Leo Frese
Three Rivers Collectibles
P.O. Box 551542
Dallas, TX 75355; 214-341-5165
e-mail: rumrill@ix.netcom.com

Ruby Glass
Author of book
Naomi L. Over
8909 Sharon Ln.
Arvada, CO 80002; 303-424-5922

Russel Wright
Author of book
Ann Kerr
P.O. Box 437
Sidney, OH 45365

Salt and Pepper Shakers
Figural or novelty
*Buy, sell, and trade; lists available; fee
charged for appraisal*
Judy Posner
R.R. 1, Box 273
Effort, PA 18330; 717-629-6583
e-mail: judyandjef@aol.com
www.tias.com/stores/jpc

Scouting Collectibles
*Author of book: A Guide to Scouting
Collectibles With Values; available by
sending $30.95 (includes postage)*
R.J. Sayers
P.O. Box 629
Brevard, NC 28712

Sebastians
Jim Waite
112 N Main St.
Farmer City, IL 61842; 800-842-2593

Sewing Machines
Toy only
Authors of book
Darryl and Roxana Matter
P.O. Box 65
Portis, KS 67474-0065

Shawnee
Rick Spencer
Salt Lake City, UT; 801-973-0805

Shot Glasses
Author of book
Mark Pickvet
Shot Glass Club of America
5071 Watson Dr.
Flint, MI 48506

Silhouette Pictures (20th Century)
Author of books
Shirley Mace
Shadow Enterprises
P.O. Box 1602
Mesilla Park, NM 88047
505-524-6717; fax: 505-523-0940
e-mail: shadow-ent@zianet.com
www.geocities.com/MadisonAvenue/
Boardroom/1631/

Silverplated and Sterling Flatware
Rick Spencer
Salt Lake City, UT
801-973-0805
Will do appraisals

Skookum Indian Dolls
Jo Ann Palmieri
27 Pepper Rd.
Towaco, NJ 07082-1357

Snow Domes
Author of book and newsletter editor
Nancy McMichael
P.O. Box 53262
Washington, DC 20009

Soda Fountain Collectibles
Harold and Joyce Screen
2804 Munster Rd.
Baltimore, MD 21234
410-661-6765
e-mail: hscreen@home.com

Soda-Pop Memorabilia
Craig Stifter
217 S. Adams St.
Hinsdale, IL 60521
630-789-5789
e-mail: cocacola@enteract.com

Painted-label soda bottles
Author of books
Thomas Marsh
914 Franklin Ave.
Youngstown, OH 44502
216-743-8600 or 800-845-7930 (order
line)

Sports Collectibles
Sporting goods
Kevin R. Bowman
P.O. Box 471
Neosho, MO 64850-0471
417-781-6418 (Mon through Fri after 5
pm CST, Sat and Sun after 10 am CST);
e-mail: Ozrktrmnl@clandjop.com.

Equipment and player-used items
Don and Anne Kier
2022 Marengo St.
Toledo, OH 43614
419-385-8211
e-mail: d.a.k.@worldnet.att.net

Bobbin' head sports figures
Tim Hunter
4301 W Hidden Valley Dr.
Reno, NV 89502
702-856-4357; fax: 702-856-4354
e-mail: thunter885@aol.com

Golf collectibles
Pat Romano
32 Sterling Dr.
Lake Grove, NY 11202-0017

St. Clair Glass
Ted Pruitt
3350 W 700 N
Anderson, IN 46011
Book available ($15)

Stangl
Birds, dinnerware, artware
Popkorn Antiques
Bob and Nancy Perzel
P.O. Box 1057
3 Mine St.
Flemington, NJ 08822; 908-782-9631

Statue of Liberty
Mike Brooks
7335 Skyline
Oakland, CA 94611

String Holders
Ellen Bercovici
5118 Hampden Ln.
Bethesda, MD 20814; 301-652-1140

Swanky Swigs
Joyce Jackson
900 Jenkins Rd.
Aledo, TX 76008-2410; 817-441-8864
e-mail: jjpick@firstworld.net

Teapots and Tea-Related Items
Author of book
Tina Carter
882 S Mollison
El Cajon, CA 92020

Tiara Exclusives
Author of Book
Mandi Birkinbine
P.O. Box 121
Meridian, ID 83680-0121
www.shop4antiques.com
e-mail: tiara@shop4antiques.com
Collecting Tiara Amber Sandwich Glass,
available from author at above address
for $18.45 ppd. Please allow four to six
weeks for delivery.

Tire Ashtrays
Author of book ($12.95 postpaid)
Jeff McVey
1810 W State St., #427
Boise, ID 83702-3955

Toothbrush Holders
Author of book
Marilyn Cooper
P.O. Box 55174
Houston, TX 77055

Toys
Any and all
June Moon
245 N Northwest Hwy.
Park Ridge, IL 60068
847-825-1441; fax: 847-825-6090

*Aurora model kits, and especially toys from
1948 – 1972. Author of books; dealers,
publishers, and appraisers of collectible
memorabilia from the '50s through today*
Bill Bruegman
137 Casterton Dr.
Akron, OH 44303
330-836-0668; fax: 330-869-8668
e-mail: toyscout@salamander.net

Diecast vehicles
Mark Giles
P.O. Box 821
Ogallala, NE 69153-0821
308-284-4360

*Fisher-Price pull toys and playsets up to
1986*
*Author of book; available from the
author*
Brad Cassity
2391 Hunters Trail
Myrtle Beach, SC 29579; 843-236-8697

Hot Wheels
D.W. (Steve) Stephenson
11117 NE 164th Pl.
Bothell, WA 98011-4003

*Model kits other than Aurora; edits pub-
lications*
Gordy Dutt
Box 201
Sharon Center, OH 42274-0201

Puppets and marionettes
Steven Meltzer
1255 2nd St.
Santa Monica, CA 90401; 310-656-0483

Rings, character, celebrity, and souvenir
Bruce and Jan Thalberg
23 Mountain View Dr.
Weston, CT 06883-1317
203-227-8175

Sand toys
Authors of book
Carole and Richard Smyth
Carole Smyth Antiques
P.O. Box 2068
Huntington, NY 11743

Slot race cars from 1960s – 70s
Gary T. Pollastro
5047 84th Ave. SE
Mercer Island, WA 98040

Tin litho, paper on wood, comic character, penny toys, and Schoenhut
Wes Johnson, Sr.
3606 Glenview Ave.
Glenville, KY 40025

Tops and spinning toys
Bruce Middleton
5 Lloyd Rd.
Newburgh, NY 12550; 914-564-2556

Toy soldiers, figures and playsets
The Phoenix Toy Soldier Co.
Bob Wilson
16405 North 9th Place
Phoenix, AZ 85022
602-863-2891

Transformers and robots
David Kolodny-Nagy
3701 Connecticut Ave. NW #500
Washington, DC 20008
202-364-8753

Walkers, ramp-walkers, and windups
Randy Welch
Raven'tiques
27965 Peach Orchard Rd.
Easton, MD 21601-8203; 410-822-5441

Trolls
Author of book
Pat Peterson
1105 6th Ave. SE
Hampton, IA 50441-2657
SASE for information

TV Guides
Giant illustrated 1948 – 1999 TV Guide Catalog, $3.00; 2000+ catalog, $2.00
TV Guide Specialists
Jeff Kadet
P.O. Box 20
Macomb, IL 61455

Twin Winton
Author of book; available from the author or through Collector Books
Mike Ellis
266 Rose Ln.
Costa Mesa, CA 92627
949-646-7112; fax: 949-645-4919
e-mail: TwinWinton.com

Valentines
Author of books, available from author; fee charged for appraisal
Katherine Kreider
Kingsbury Antiques
P.O. Box 7957
Lancaster, PA 17604-7957
717-892-3001
email: Kingsbry@aol.com

Vallona Starr
Author of book
Bernice Stamper
7516 Eloy Ave.
Bakersfield, CA 93308-7701
805-393-2900

Van Briggle
Dated examples, author of book
Scott H. Nelson
Box 6081
Santa Fe, NM 87502
505-986-1176
Also UND (University of North Dakota), other American potteries

Vandor
Lois Wildman
175 Chick Rd.
Camano Island, WA 98282

Vernon Kilns
Author of Book
Maxine Nelson
7657 E. Hazelwood St.
Scottsdale, AZ 85251

Viking
Mary Lou Bohl
1156 Apple Blossom Dr.
Neenah, WI 54956

Wade
Author of book
Ian Warner
P.O. Box 93022
Brampton, Ontario
Canada L6Y 4V8

Watt Pottery
Author of book
Susan Morris
P.O. Box 1519
Merlin, OR 97532
541-955-8590
e-mail: sue@wattpottery.com
www.wattpottery.com
www.applebarrel.com

Western Collectibles
Author of book
Warren R. Anderson
American West Archives
P.O. Box 100
Cedar City, UT 84721; 435-586-9497
Also documents, autographs, stocks and bonds, and other ephemera

Author of books
Dan Hutchins
Hutchins Publishing Co.
P.O. Box 25040
Colorado Springs, CO 80936
719-572-1331
Also interested in cowboy collectibles, carriages, wagons, sleighs, etc.

William Manns
P.O. Box 6459
Santa Fe, NM 87502
505-995-0102

Western Heroes
Author of books, ardent researcher and guest columnist
Robert W. Phillips
Phillips Archives of Western Memorabilia
1703 N Aster Pl.
Broken Arrow, OK 74012-1308
918-254-8205; fax: 918-252-9363

Westmoreland
Cheryl Schafer
RR 2, Box 37
Lancaster, MO 63548
660-457-3510
email: cschafer@nemr.net
Winter address (November 1-May 1):
PO Box 1443
Webster, FL 33597
352-568-7383

World's Fairs and Expositions
Herbert Rolfes
Yesterday's World
P.O. Box 398
Mount Dora, FL 32756
352-735-3947
e-mail: NY1939@aol.com

Index

Schroeder's ANTIQUES Price Guide

. . . is the #1 bestselling antiques & collectibles value guide on the market today, and here's why . . .

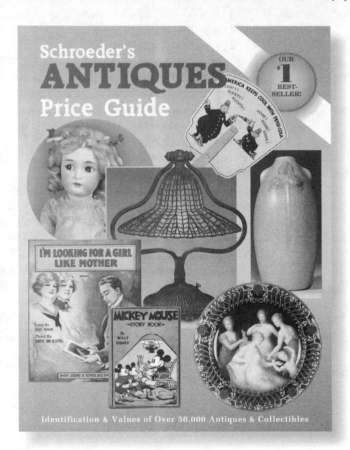

OUR #1 BEST-SELLER!

8½ x 11, 608 Pages, $14.95

- More than 450 advisors, well-known dealers, and top-notch collectors work together with our editors to bring you accurate information regarding pricing and identification.

- More than 45,000 items in almost 550 categories are listed along with hundreds of sharp original photos that illustrate not only the rare and unusual, but the common, popular collectibles as well.

- Each large close-up shot shows important details clearly. Every subject is represented with histories and background information, a feature not found in any of our competitors' publications.

- Our editors keep abreast of newly developing trends, often adding several new categories a year as the need arises.

If it merits the interest of today's collector, you'll find it in *Schroeder's*. And you can feel confident that the information we publish is up to date and accurate. Our advisors thoroughly check each category to spot inconsistencies, listings that may not be entirely reflective of market dealings, and lines too vague to be of merit. Only the best of the lot remains for publication.

Collector Books
P.O. Box 3009
Paducah, KY 42002-3009
1-800-626-5420
www.collectorbooks.com

COLLECTOR BOOKS
A Division of Schroeder Publishing Co., Inc.